Application Programming and File Processing in COBOL

Application Programming and File Processing in COBOL

Concepts, Techniques, and Applications

Yuksel Uckan
Miami University

D. C. Heath and Company
Lexington, Massachusetts   Toronto

Address editorial correspondence to:

D. C. Heath
125 Spring Street
Lexington, MA 02173

*To Emel, my best friend for thirty years. I owe her
everything that is dear to me, including this book.*

Cover: "Circular Motion Over Fractured Granite" © 1990 by Wolfgang Gersch, Meta Art Studios. Acrylic on board, 34″ × 26″.

Preface

The purpose of this book is to teach business application programming and file processing using COBOL as the programming language. Although COBOL language features are covered comprehensively, the primary emphasis is on the concepts and techniques for application program development and file processing. In designing this book, I have kept in perspective the requirements of the academic curriculum models for business application programming, and those of business and industry. Certainly a good business application programmer should be fully knowledgeable about the nature of business problems. In addition, I believe that the programmer should be

- Familiar with the syntax and semantics of some procedural programming language. Given its suitability and popularity in business applications, COBOL is an appropriate choice.
- Capable of designing algorithms for business applications and translating them into working computer programs.
- Knowledgeable in the principles and techniques of software engineering in order to develop good programs. A good program is a correct, efficient, well-documented, readable, structured, and properly modularized program that is easy to develop, debug, test, and maintain.
- Capable of designing appropriate data structures and using them to develop efficient application programs.
- Proficient in file organization and access techniques, and the principles of file design.
- Aware of the close relationship between file systems and data base systems.

Structure and Content

The book is organized into five parts and 18 chapters. Part I introduces the elementary COBOL language features necessary for writing simple COBOL programs. Chapters 1 and 2 cover the majority of the language elements in the IDENTIFICATION, ENVIRONMENT, and DATA divisions of COBOL programs. In Chapter 3, a subset of the COBOL PROCEDURE DIVISION statements is introduced. This consists of statements for simple file-oriented input-output, interactive input-output, data movement, arithmetic, the IF statement for decision making, and various forms of the PERFORM statement for internal procedure invocation and iteration. After studying the first three chapters, students will develop the ability to write programs that can handle input-output of sequential files, perform computations, and produce business reports.

Chapters 4 through 7, which make up Part II, focus on developing good application programs. In Chapter 4 we are introduced to software engineering, concepts and techniques of program logic design, structured programming, modular program design, program structure, data structure design, and top-down and bottom-up program design strategies. Chapter 5 is devoted to structured techniques for program design and includes several program logic, program structure, and data structure representation techniques. Also in this chapter we discuss programming style and style conventions as they apply to

COBOL application programs. Chapter 6 is concerned with program testing and debugging, and COBOL automated debugging tools. Chapter 7 discusses concepts, techniques, and COBOL features for modular programming.

The two chapters in Part III deal with built-in data structures in COBOL. Chapter 8, on arrays and array processing, covers one-, two-, and three-dimensional arrays as data structures, and several array operations including internal sorting and array searching. Chapter 9 is devoted to strings and string processing. It includes an extensive discussion of strings as data structures, string operations, string applications, and COBOL string processing statements.

Part IV, a systematic, in-depth study of file processing in COBOL, consists of eight chapters. In Chapter 10 we temporarily leave COBOL and concentrate on fundamental file concepts. Files and related concepts are usually quite confusing for beginning students. For this reason, I found it pedagogically useful to teach them in simple terms before introducing the complexities of related language features. This chapter also covers the principles of physical data organization.

In Chapter 11 we come back to COBOL sequential files, and discuss fixed and variable-length record sequential files and their COBOL implementations. We also explore the COBOL implementations of the traditional and in situ file update techniques for sequential files.

Chapter 12 deals with the concepts and techniques of sequential file merging, file sorting, and the COBOL SORT/MERGE feature. Chapter 13 discusses concepts and techniques of indexing, the structure of ISAM and VSAM indexed file implementations, and the COBOL language features for indexed files. Chapter 14 focuses on the relative file organization techniques. Here, we discuss a variety of hash functions, overflow handling techniques, and the COBOL language features for relative files.

Chapters 15 and 16 deal with logical file organization techniques that are not directly supported by COBOL but can be simulated using its built-in files. In Chapter 15 we discuss linear files as linked lists and inverted lists, and garbage collection as a file management technique. In Chapter 16 we concentrate on nonlinear files, that is, tree structures and tree files, and explore a variety of techniques for defining and processing them.

Chapter 17 is about the important subject of data design and data semantics. Presented in this chapter is a thorough discussion of issues pertaining to data and record structure design in computer files, including desirable properties of data, data dependencies, logical data modeling, data integrity, normalizing record structures, and a data design methodology.

Chapter 18 is Part V. Here, fundamental concepts of data base systems are introduced, the close relationship between file and data base systems is emphasized, and the role of COBOL programming in data base applications is shown. This chapter is a link between file processing and data base management, a topic that usually is covered in CIS and CS curriculum models after a course on file systems.

Guidelines for Using the Text

There is no universally accepted norm for teaching business application programming in university or college level CIS/CS programs. In designing this book, among other things, I have tried to make it comprehensive and flexible. This book is suitable for any course sequence that focuses on business application programming and/or file processing using COBOL as the vehicle. In particular, it can be used

1. As a textbook in courses based on the course sequence CIS/86-3 (Introduction to Business Application Programming) and CIS/86-4 (Intermediate Business Application Programming) in the DPMA Model Curriculum for Undergraduate CIS Education.

2. As a textbook in courses based on the course IS2 (Program, Data, and File Structures) of the ACM Information Systems Curriculum Recommendations for the 1980s.
3. As a textbook in two-year associate degree programs for a two- or three-semester course sequence aiming to teach business COBOL programming.
4. As a reference book by business application programmers, information systems analysts, and designers.

Today, the majority of college students in CIS and CS programs have some background in computer fundamentals and computer programming experience in a procedural language, usually Pascal or BASIC. For such students, the first three chapters will prove quite easy and straightforward. However, the book assumes no prerequisite exposure to any computer science subject beyond high school education. It is quite self-contained, and students will find all that is needed to understand the topics in the book, provided they are covered in the right order.

For a one-semester course stressing COBOL application programming and file processing, Chapters 1 through 4 and 7 through 14 are necessary. The instructor may also choose some topics from Chapters 5 and 6, and if time permits, cover Chapters 15 through 18. With students who have had some computer programming experience, the instructor may progress rapidly with the material in Part I. In this case, the entire book can be covered in one semester.

In a two-semester COBOL course sequence, Chapters 1 through 9 may be studied in the first course. The second course may be based on the remaining nine chapters. For a three-semester COBOL course sequence, the book may be partitioned as follows: Chapters 1 through 7, 8 through 12, and 13 through 18.

Key Features

In addition to the elementary COBOL language aspects, program design techniques, and structured programming, this book offers several other features.

COBOL Programming

- Thorough coverage of both COBOL 74 and COBOL 85 dialects of the language
- Substantial emphasis on interactive input-output
- Comprehensive treatment of modular program design techniques including subroutines and nested COBOL programs
- Thorough discussion of programming style and style conventions

Software Engineering

- Thorough discussion of program logic specification techniques such as Nassi-Shneiderman charts, action diagrams, decision tables, and decision trees
- Comprehensive discussion of program structure design and specification techniques, including structure charts, Jackson diagrams, Warnier-Orr diagrams, and action diagrams
- Discussion of modular program design factors such as coupling and cohesion
- Top-down and bottom-up program design strategies
- Program testing and debugging techniques, and COBOL automated debugging tools
- Discussion of data structure design and representation techniques, including Warnier-Orr diagrams and Jackson diagrams

Data Structures

- Discussion of the importance of data structures in application program design, types of data structures, and operations on data structures
- Thorough coverage of arrays and tables, including basic array search techniques, the COBOL SEARCH feature, array sorting, and internal sorting techniques
- Comprehensive treatment of string processing and COBOL string processing elements

Data Organization and File Processing

- Logical data organization, physical data organization, and sequential and direct-access storage devices
- Thorough coverage of fundamental file concepts and file operations
- Multiple record files and variable-length record files
- Sequential file organization and maintenance, including traditional and in situ updates of sequential disk files
- External sorting techniques, file merging, and the COBOL SORT/MERGE feature
- Thorough coverage of indexing techniques, logical organization, ISAM and VSAM implementations, and COBOL features for indexed files
- Detailed coverage of relative files including hashing and overflow handling, and the COBOL features for relative files
- Discussion of linear files: lists, inverted lists, directory files
- Fundamental file management techniques: stacks, queues, and garbage collection
- Discussion of nonlinear files: trees and networks
- Thorough treatment of issues pertaining to record structure design, including data semantics and normalization
- File design considerations such as data security and data integrity
- An introduction to data base management, and COBOL as a host language in data base processing

Pedagogical Features

The significant pedagogical features used throughout the text include the following.

- Each chapter begins with a list of chapter objectives in the section "In This Chapter You Will Learn About."
- Numerous examples for concepts, language features, data and file structures, and design techniques are provided throughout the book.
- Wherever feasible, "Review Questions" are included in the text. These questions are true-false and multiple-choice, providing students the opportunity to test their understanding of the material covered up to that point. Answers to all review questions are provided.
- Most chapters contain one or more fully machine-tested, complete COBOL programs based on the concepts and techniques studied in that chapter. Each program is explained in detail. There are 29 complete COBOL programs in the book, together with listings of accompanying input files, output files, or reports.
- Important concepts, rules, and the COBOL syntax definitions are highlighted by a color background.
- All partial COBOL examples are displayed in boxes.
- COBOL 85 features are printed in color type.

■ At the end of each chapter is an alphabetical list of key terms relating to the concepts and elements studied in that chapter.

■ Each chapter concludes with a "Study Guide" consisting of three sections: "Quick Scan," "Test Your Comprehension," and "Improve Your Problem-Solving Ability." "Quick Scan" is a comprehensive summary of the chapter that can be used by the student for preexamination review purposes. "Test Your Comprehension" includes multiple-choice questions with answers and short essay-type questions. "Improve Your Problem-Solving Ability" contains debugging and programming exercises, and programming problems.

Supplementary Material

An *Instructor's Guide* is available to the adopters of this textbook. It contains teaching notes and suggestions, solutions to debugging and programming exercises, select transparency masters, and additional material that the instructor may wish to use in the course. A printed *Test Item File* and a computerized testing program, *D. C. Heath Exam,* containing approximately 1000 questions, are also available to the instructor.

Special Thanks

This book is based on a set of notes that have been class-tested over the last 10 years in several classes that I taught at the University of Wisconsin-Milwaukee and at Miami University, Oxford, Ohio. Some of my students contributed indirectly to the quality of the material through their incisive questions and by offering constructive criticisms. I am grateful to them and also to many excellent technical reviewers provided by D. C. Heath. They read the manuscript meticulously and provided invaluable feedback. They are Ida Mae Baxter, Southwest Texas Junior College; Rick Byars, University of Texas at Austin; R. J. Daigle, University of Southern Alabama; Henry A. Etlinger, Rochester Institute of Technology; Richard Fleming, North Lake College; David W. Letcher, Trenton State College; Mark A. Mathis, East Tennessee State University; Patricia Mayer Milligan, Baylor University; Rosemary Pressly, Wharton County Junior College; James P. Robbins, Jr., University of Pittsburgh; Samuel G. Ryan, Bernard M. Baruch College, City University of New York; Harbans Sathi, University of Southern Colorado; Randy R. Snyder, University of Minnesota; Jan Vandever, South Dakota State University; Thelma F. Vaughan, Essex County College; Roger Von Holzen, Northwest Missouri State University; Michael M. Werner, Wentworth Institute of Technology; Peggy M. White, St. John's River Community College; Ronald E. Willard, Bowling Green State University, Firelands College; and Patrick K. Wong, Laredo Junior College.

In addition, Dr. Fazli Can, of Miami University, Oxford, Ohio, read some of the chapters and supplied me with extremely useful comments and suggestions. I acknowledge his contributions with gratitude.

I would like to express my special appreciation to Lee Ripley for initiating this project and encouraging it. Without her foresight and support, this book would not have been in existence. Thanks are also extended to Carter Shanklin, my acquisitions editor, for his many valuable suggestions, and to Andrea Cava and Martha Wetherill, production editors, who did a very professional and outstanding job of producing the book.

Since its conception, Emel Uckan has been the inspiration and the very soul of this project. She read every page of the manuscript I don't know how many times. She was the student, the instructor, the casual reader, the art editor, the language editor, the opponent, and the proponent. I am grateful to her for sharing this project with me. I am most grateful, however, because she herself enjoyed it.

Yuksel Uckan

Brief Contents

Contents

I

Elementary Language Features

1

An Introduction to COBOL Programming Language

CHAPTER CONTENTS

IN THIS CHAPTER YOU WILL LEARN ABOUT

- A history of COBOL
- Why COBOL is a powerful business language
- COBOL language elements
    - The character set
    - Words, constants, and level numbers
    - Clauses, statements, and sentences
    - Paragraphs and sections
    - Divisions
- Programming language syntax and semantics
- COBOL syntax description
- How to type the COBOL source code

Introduction

This chapter introduces the COBOL language. First, we will briefly discuss how COBOL has evolved into the most widely used business language and why it is so convenient for business applications. Next, we will identify the elements of the language and discuss the overall structure of COBOL programs. We will introduce the concepts of syntax and semantics for programming languages, and the available techniques for describing the COBOL syntax. Then we will study the rules for typing the COBOL source code. Finally, we will consider a simple COBOL program and identify its different language elements. We will see that we can easily read and understand it without knowing much about the language.

Evolution of COBOL

In the late 1950s only a few high-level computer languages existed, and they were specifically designed for scientific applications. Fortran is the best known of these languages. In scientific applications, input and output of large quantities of data are rare, and in-memory computational processing is predominant. Data processing applications, on the other hand, are characterized by large volumes of data and complex input and output functions. Clearly, scientific high-level languages are inadequate for these purposes, and it was recognized that a language for commercial data processing applications was needed.

In 1959 a group called the CODASYL committee (an acronym for **Conf**erence on **Data Systems Languages**) was formed. Its members were representatives from government, industry, universities, and computer manufacturers whose goal was to design a business-oriented data processing language. The committee suggested that major computer manufacturers develop compilers for the language, and the result was COBOL. The name COBOL is an acronym derived from **Common Business-Oriented Language**.

In 1960 the first COBOL compilers became available. However, COBOL programs that used a version of the language suitable for a particular manufacturer's computer system did not readily run on other computers; that is, they lacked portability due to the differences among several versions of the language. To remedy this, the American National Standards Institute (ANSI) formed a committee that over the years developed three versions of standard COBOL: COBOL 1968, COBOL 1974, and COBOL 1985. All three versions are basically similar, with variations reflecting ANSI's efforts to bring the language up to date, enhance it, and make it more versatile. In this book we stress the 1974 and 1985 versions.

COBOL as a Business Programming Language

COBOL is one of the most widely used languages in commercial application programming. Some of the characteristics that make it particularly powerful for commercial applications are as follows:

1. Existence of an extensive library of COBOL application programs
2. Wide use of COBOL in new business applications
3. High portability of COBOL programs
4. Readability of COBOL programs
5. Ease of developing structured and modular programs
6. Powerful file processing capabilities
7. Popularity as an application programming language in data base management

A large library of application programs has been developed over the last three decades using COBOL. A majority of these are still in use in business, industry, and government. In addition, it is estimated that as many as 80 percent of new business computer applications are being developed using the language.

Almost every computer manufacturer has COBOL compilers that conform to ANSI standards. Versions of the language for different computer systems show minor variations from each other, and therefore, COBOL programs have a high degree of portability. This gives businesses flexibility to use several computer systems manufactured by different vendors and still keep COBOL as the only programming language.

Of all the high-level computer languages available, COBOL is one of the most English-like. Properly coded, a COBOL program is easy to read and understand, even by people who are not familiar with the language. As a result, the programs are self-documenting and require relatively little or no additional documentation.

COBOL, especially the most recent COBOL 85, has sufficient language features to permit writing well-structured and modular programs. It also has extremely powerful file-processing capabilities. Various file organization techniques that the language supports are sufficient for most commercial data processing applications in which large volumes of data are organized into computer files. COBOL is a common application programming language for most data base management systems. Most widely used data base management systems support COBOL as the host language.

Nothing is perfect in life, however, and neither is COBOL. For example, its object codes are rather inefficient for mathematical computations. Nevertheless, the fact remains that for business applications, given the current state-of-the-art of computer technology, no other language fares better than COBOL. This is likely to remain true for quite some time. So, without further ado, we will embark on our journey to study COBOL and develop proficiency as COBOL application programmers.

REVIEW QUESTIONS

1. Data processing applications are characterized by large volumes of data and complex input and output functions. (T or F)
2. COBOL owes its existence to the need for a scientific computer language. (T or F)
3. Because the earlier versions of COBOL tended to produce programs that ran only on specific computer systems and not on others, these programs lacked _____ .
4. COBOL permits the development of well-structured and modular application program systems. (T or F)

5. Despite its powerful file-processing capabilities, COBOL is not a suitable application programming language for data base management. (T or F)
6. Which of the following is not one of COBOL's strengths?
   a. The object codes are rather inefficient for mathematical computations.
   b. If properly coded, the programs are easy to read and understand.
   c. Many business-oriented application programs are written in COBOL.
   d. Almost all COBOL compilers conform to the ANSI standards.

Answers: 1. T; 2. F; 3. portability; 4. T; 5. F; 6. a.

Elements of the COBOL Language

Like any other language, COBOL is built on some basic elements. They are as follows:

1. Characters
2. Words, constants, and level numbers
3. Clauses
4. Statements
5. Sentences
6. Paragraphs
7. Sections
8. Divisions

- **Characters** are the fundamental building blocks.
- **Words, constants,** and **level numbers** are proper combination of characters. They represent program entities, values, and hierarchies, respectively.
- **Clauses** consist of characters, constants, and words that are used to specify attributes of program entities.
- **Statements** are syntactically valid combinations of words, constants, and characters that begin with a verb. They are used in the PROCEDURE DIVISION of COBOL programs.
- **Sentences** are sequences of one or more statements, the last terminated by a period.
- **Paragraphs** are named building blocks that contain one or more sentences.
- **Sections** consist of one or more paragraphs.
- **Divisions** are made up of one or more sections.

COBOL Character Set

The basic building blocks in COBOL are characters. The COBOL character set includes 51 characters:

1. Numeric digits: 0–9
2. Letters: A–Z (some dialects also permit lower-case letters a–z)
3. Space (blank)
4. Special characters
   a. Punctuation symbols: . ; , ( ) " or '
   b. Arithmetic symbols: + − * / **
   c. Comparison symbols: = > <
   d. Dollar sign: $

Some of the special characters have specific connotations in COBOL.

1. The period denotes the end of an entry, such as a statement or a sentence. It is also used to represent numeric noninteger constant values in COBOL source programs, as in 8.5.

2. Comma and semicolon are used to delineate clauses. They improve the readability of code, and are optional in all cases.
3. Double quotation marks enclose nonnumeric constants, as in "STUDENT NAME". Single quotation marks may be alternatively used for the same purpose.
4. Left and right parentheses enclose expressions or subscripts.
5. The hyphen is used either as arithmetic minus operator or as hyphen in forming user-defined names. Here is an example:

```
COMPUTE PROFIT = SALE-PRICE - COST.
```

6. Two consecutive asterisks with no intervening blanks, **, form the exponentiation operator.

Note that the combined comparison operators "not equal to," "greater than or equal to," and "less than or equal to" (denoted in other programming languages by < >, > =, and < =, respectively) are not supported in COBOL in these forms. Instead, we write NOT =, > OR =, and < OR = to correspond to these comparison operators.

Rules Concerning Special Characters

1. Commas, semicolons, and periods, when used as punctuation symbols, should have no preceding space and must be followed by at least one space.
2. All arithmetic and comparison symbols and left and right parentheses should be preceded and followed by at least one space.
3. Special characters not included in the COBOL character set but available on the terminal keyboard may not be used in a COBOL code. There is one exception to this rule: you may use any character in a nonnumeric constant that is enclosed in double quotation marks. For example, "@#*%!" is valid as a nonnumeric constant.

Words, Constants, and Level Numbers

Characters are combined into three types of higher-level language elements in COBOL. They are words, constants, and level numbers. Their types and some examples are provided below.

Language Element and Its Types	Examples
1. Words	
a. Reserved words	`ENVIRONMENT, MOVE, PERFORM`
b. User-defined words	`STUDENT-NAME, COURSE-CODE`
2. Constants (literals)	
a. Numeric constants	`150, 23.67`
b. Nonnumeric constants	`"CLASS GRADE REPORT", "PAGE: "`
c. Figurative constants	`SPACE, ZERO, QUOTE`

Language Element and Its Types	Examples
3. Level numbers	
a. For hierarchy representation	01–49
b. For independent data items	01, 77
c. For condition names	88
d. For RENAMES clause	66

Words are classified as reserved and user-defined words. **Reserved words** are key words that identify language entities. They must appear in the correct location in a program, be typed correctly, and be used in the right context. COBOL has more than 300 reserved words. Some examples are MOVE, ADD, PICTURE, DIVISION, and DATA. A complete list is provided in Appendix A.

When writing a program, we must come up with additional words to represent and reference certain program entities. These are called **user-defined words** (also known as **identifiers**). COBOL has 17 types of program entities (data items, groups, records, files, conditions, paragraphs, sections, programs or subprograms, etc.) for which we formulate user-defined words. We need unique words to identify each entity we use in our program.

Rules for Constructing User-Defined Words

1. Maximum length is 30 characters.
2. May consist of letters, digits, and hyphens.
3. At least one character must be alphabetic. (Procedure names, i.e., names for programs, paragraphs, and sections, may be all numeric.)
4. There can be no embedded blanks.
5. First and last characters may not be hyphens.
6. Two consecutive hyphens are not permitted.
7. Reserved words cannot be used as user-defined names.

Constants (also called literals) are values that appear in the program code. There are three types of constants in COBOL: numeric, nonnumeric, and figurative.

COBOL supports **numeric literals** with or without decimal digits, such as 15, and 15.5. Note that if a decimal point is used in a numeric constant value, it must not be the last character in the field: 15.0 is acceptable, but 15. is not. Anything enclosed between quotation marks (' or ", depending on the computer system or the compiler option you choose) is a **nonnumeric literal**. A nonnumeric literal may have a maximum length of 120 characters. COBOL also supports three **figurative literals**, SPACE, ZERO, and QUOTE. These can be used in plural, as well: SPACES, ZEROS, ZEROES, and QUOTES. SPACE corresponds to one or more blanks, ZERO to one or more zeros, and QUOTE to quotation marks.

Level numbers are unsigned two-digit integers used in the DATA DIVISION of a program, with clauses that define independent data items, groups, condition names, and RENAMES clauses. For independent data items, level numbers 01 or 77 can be used interchangeably. Level number 77 is considered unnecessary in practice, and level 01 is used for independent data item definitions. For group items, the hierarchical structure can be specified by using 01 for the highest level item, and level numbers 02 through 49 for subordinate entries. The number 88 is reserved for condition name specification, and 66 for the RENAMES clause.

Clauses, Statements, and Sentences

Statements are combinations of words, symbols, and constants that make sense as a whole. In general, such combinations are our instructions to the computer. Statements in a COBOL program are located in the PROCEDURE DIVISION. They conform to particular syntax rules. With the exception of the IF statement, every statement starts with a verb. The verb in a statement is a key word, and informs the compiler about the nature of the instruction. The following are some examples of COBOL statements.

```
1. OPEN INPUT   STUDENT-TEST-SCORES-FILE
        OUTPUT TEST-SCORES-REPORT.
2. READ STUDENT-TEST-SCORES-FILE
          AT END MOVE "YES" TO END-OF-FILE-FLAG.
3. PERFORM GENERATE-AND-OUTPUT-LINES
          UNTIL END-OF-FILE.
4. CLOSE STUDENT-TEST-SCORES-FILE
         TEST-SCORES-REPORT.
5. STOP RUN.
```

In these examples, each statement terminates with a period.

Some statements in the PROCEDURE DIVISION, as well as some program entries in other divisions, have subsets that either complement the statements or specify certain attributes of the program entries. We refer to them as **clauses**. In the above set of statements, AT END MOVE "YES" TO END-OF-FILE-FLAG of statement 2 and UNTIL END-OF-FILE of statement 3 are examples of clauses. In the following DATA DIVISION entry

```
01  END-OF-FILE-FLAG       PIC XXX    VALUE "NO".
```

PIC XXX and VALUE "NO" are both clauses that define certain properties of the data item called END-OF-FILE-FLAG, in this case, type, length, and initial values.

A statement does not have to end with a period unless it is the last statement in a procedure or a sentence. A **sentence** contains one or more statements, and the last statement in it ends with a period. The following are examples of COBOL sentences.

```
1. MOVE FINAL SCORE TO OUT-FINAL-SCORE
2. COMPUTE AVERAGE-SCORE = 0.25 * TEST-1-SCORE
                         + 0.35 * TEST-2-SCORE
                         + 0.40 * FINAL-SCORE.
3. IF STUDENT-AVERAGE > 89
4.        MOVE "A" TO OUT-STUDENT-GRADE
5.        ADD 4 TO TOTAL-CREDITS.
```

Statements 1 and 2 form a sentence. Statements 4 and 5 together constitute a sentence, which is part of the IF statement in line 3. To make it possible for the compiler to parse an IF statement, COBOL considers an IF statement as a sentence and requires that it be terminated with a period. Alternatively, COBOL 85 permits use of the key word END-IF to define the scope of an IF statement. Notice that a single statement ending with a period is also a sentence.

COBOL 85

Paragraphs and Sections

In the PROCEDURE DIVISION, statements, sentences, or both are brought together in a systematic fashion to define a part of the program logic. If we want to reference this group of instructions collectively, we can assign a name to it and make sure that the last statement in it ends with a period. Such a program block is a **paragraph**. Consider the following example.

```
B3-GENERATE-PAGES.
    MOVE COURSE-CODE TO CURRENT-COURSE-CODE
    PERFORM C1-INITIALIZE-VARIABLES
    PERFORM C2-REMAINING-TERMINAL-INPUTS
    PERFORM C3-PRINT-HALF-PAGE.

    PERFORM C4-FORM-STUDENT-LINES
        UNTIL COURSE-CODE NOT EQUAL TO CURRENT-COURSE-CODE
                              OR
                          END-OF-FILE.

    PERFORM C5-PRINT-SUMMARY
    ADD 1 TO PAGE-NUMBER.
```

This paragraph contains statements that must be executed in a certain order to do a certain task. Therefore, it is a procedure. All COBOL paragraphs in the PROCEDURE DIVISION are user-defined procedures.

Certain paragraphs in other divisions of a COBOL program have reserved names and specific functions, and their contents are generally predefined by the language. For example, in the following partial code, which is found in the ENVIRONMENT DIVISION,

```
INPUT-OUTPUT SECTION.
FILE-CONTROL.
    SELECT STUDENT-TEST-SCORES-FILE ASSIGN TO INFILE.
    SELECT TEST-SCORES-REPORT       ASSIGN TO OUTFILE.
```

the paragraph named FILE-CONTROL is a required paragraph. Its purpose is to define partially the input-output files that are associated with the program. The name FILE-CONTROL is a COBOL reserved word and cannot be changed.

One or more paragraphs can be combined into what are called **sections**. Section names are followed by the key word SECTION. In the above example, the paragraph FILE-CONTROL is part of the section called INPUT-OUTPUT. Sections before the PROCEDURE DIVISION of programs are fixed sections with preassigned names. Sections may also appear in the PROCEDURE DIVISION and may consist of one or more paragraphs, or just statements and sentences. They are user-defined sections, with user-defined unique names that are again followed by the key word SECTION. Like a paragraph, a section in the PROCEDURE DIVISION is a procedure that can be invoked by its name.

The PROCEDURE DIVISION of COBOL programs can be conceived and designed as consisting of sections. In this case, the design is said to be **section oriented**. If the PROCEDURE DIVISION consists of only paragraphs, the design is **paragraph oriented**. Section-oriented procedure design is favored for large COBOL programs. The following is the structure of a section-oriented design.

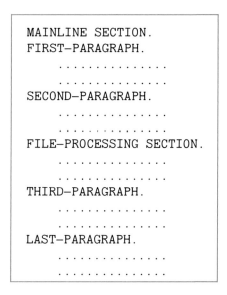

```
MAINLINE SECTION.
FIRST-PARAGRAPH.
      . . . . . . . . . . . . . .
      . . . . . . . . . . . . . .
SECOND-PARAGRAPH.
      . . . . . . . . . . . . . .
      . . . . . . . . . . . . . .
FILE-PROCESSING SECTION.
      . . . . . . . . . . . . . .
      . . . . . . . . . . . . . .
THIRD-PARAGRAPH.
      . . . . . . . . . . . . . .
      . . . . . . . . . . . . . .
LAST-PARAGRAPH.
      . . . . . . . . . . . . . .
      . . . . . . . . . . . . . .
```

Note that both paragraph names and section names end with periods.

Divisions of a COBOL Program

The highest element in the hierarchy of program elements in COBOL is a **division**. It consists of sections or paragraphs, or both. Every program has four divisions in the following order:

1. IDENTIFICATION DIVISION
2. ENVIRONMENT DIVISION
3. DATA DIVISION
4. PROCEDURE DIVISION

The IDENTIFICATION DIVISION contains documentation that enables the compiler or programmer to identify the program. The ENVIRONMENT DIVISION is used to define the computer system on which the program will be compiled and executed (CONFIGURATION SECTION). It also contains partial definitions for the files that are associated with the program (INPUT-OUTPUT SECTION).

The DATA DIVISION consists of a FILE SECTION in which the definition of program files is completed, and a WORKING-STORAGE SECTION where program variables and structures are defined that are not part of the input-output files. The PROCEDURE DIVISION contains user-defined paragraphs or sections, which together express the program logic in COBOL statements. The first three divisions have some optional sections for special language features.

Figure 1 shows the outline of a COBOL program in terms of standard divisions, sections, paragraphs, optional separators, and comment lines, which should be provided as minimal documentation. A **comment line** is a line with an asterisk in column 7. Anything that is written beyond the asterisk in column 7 is a comment, which is ignored by the compiler during compilation, and printed while a source listing is being produced. Comments are valuable as in-program documentation aids.

If you are using a text editor to type your COBOL source files, you will find it useful to create a template file of this structure and store it permanently in your account. Whenever you are ready to develop a COBOL program, you can make a copy of the template and fill in the blanks as suggested in Figure 1.

```
                              COLUMNS
     1    5   10   15   20   25   30   35   40   45   50   55   60   65   70   75
    ----|----|----|----|----|----|----|----|----|----|----|----|----|----|----|-
```

```
    *....................................................................
     IDENTIFICATION DIVISION.
     PROGRAM-ID.      name of your program


     ***********************************************************************
     ***  brief explanation of what your program does           *******
     ***********************************************************************


     AUTHOR.           your name.
     INSTALLATION.     your institution.
     DATE-WRITTEN.     date you begin working on the program.
     DATE-COMPILED.    (leave this blank, the compiler will fill it.)


    *....................................................................
     ENVIRONMENT DIVISION.
     CONFIGURATION SECTION.
     SOURCE-COMPUTER. computer system to be used for compilation.
     OBJECT-COMPUTER. computer system to be used for execution.


     INPUT-OUTPUT SECTION.
     FILE-CONTROL.


         SELECT internal file name
                ASSIGN TO external file name
                ORGANIZATION IS ----------
                ACCESS MODE  IS ----------.


         [ one SELECT for each file.]
    *....................................................................
     DATA DIVISION.
     FILE SECTION.


     FD  internal file name
         LABEL RECORDS ARE --------
         DATA RECORD   IS record name
         RECORD CONTAINS -- CHARACTERS.


     01  record name.
         --------------------
         --------------------


     [One FD block for each file.]


     WORKING-STORAGE SECTION.


    ***********> SWITCHES:
     01  --------------------
     01  --------------------
```

Figure 1 A Template for COBOL Programs

```
**********> VARIABLES:
   01 ---------------------
      ---------------------

**********> STRUCTURES:

   01 ---------------------
      ---------------------

**********> ARRAYS:

   01 ---------------------
      ---------------------
*.................................................................................
   PROCEDURE DIVISION.

   name of main module.

      [COBOL statements for the algorithm.]
```

Figure 1 (Continued)

REVIEW QUESTIONS

1. The COBOL character set includes _____ , _____ , space, and _____ .
2. Some COBOL dialects permit lower-case letters as well as capital letters. (T or F)
3. The three comparison symbols in COBOL are _____ , _____ , and _____ .
4. Which of the following characters is not in the COBOL character set?
   a. The left parenthesis, (
   b. The dollar sign, $
   c. The right bracket,]
   d. The combination ** with no intervening spaces
   e. The hyphen, -
5. Which of the following about the functions of special characters in COBOL is incorrect?
   a. ** denotes exponentiation.
   b. The hyphen is used either as the arithmetic minus operator or as a hyphen in forming user-defined words.
   c. The comma and semicolon are used to delineate clauses, and they are optional.
   d. The quotation mark is used in forming arithmetic constants.
6. The comparison operator "greater than or equal to" is represented as <= in COBOL. (T or F)
7. Any character available on the terminal keyboard can be used in a COBOL program provided it is enclosed in quotation marks. (T or F)
8. COBOL words are classified as _____ and _____ words.
9. Reserved words are key words that identify language entities. (T or F)
10. Names assigned to data items, groups, records, files, etc., are also known as identifiers. (T or F)

11. The following user-defined words are intended for use as variable names. Which ones are illegal, and why?
    a. OUT-OF-STATE-CUSTOMERS-
    b. CUSTOMER_CHECKING_ACCOUNT
    c. STUDENT-ON-DEAN'S-LIST
    d. TOTAL-NUMBER-OF-STUDENTS-ON-PROBATION
    e. ENDOFFILE MARKER
    f. 36TH-ROW-OCCUPANTS
    g. CORRESPONDING
12. Identify the following literals as legal or illegal. If illegal, state the reason.
    a. 127.78
    b. 120,000.00
    c. SPACES
    d. 147.
    e. "TOTAL COST @ $25.00 EACH: "
13. Level number 77 is used for group items. (T or F)
14. Which of the following is correct for COBOL level numbers?
    a. 88 is used for condition names.
    b. 02 through 49 are used for subordinate entries in data definition.
    c. 66 is used for the RENAMES clause.
    d. 77 and 01 can be used interchangeably for independent data items.
    e. All of the above are correct.
15. All statements in a COBOL program are located only in the DATA DIVISION. (T or F)
16. Each statement except the IF statement starts with a _____ .
17. One or more statements terminating with a period form a _____ .
18. Parts of a statement that complement it or specify certain attributes of program entries are called _____ .

Answers: 1. numeric digits, letters, special characters; 2. T; 3. =, >, <; 4. c; 5. d; 6. F; 7. T; 8. reserved, user-defined; 9. T; 10. T; 11.a. Illegal because of hyphen at the end b. Illegal because of underscores; they should be hyphens c. Illegal because of the single quotation mark d. Illegal because of its length (37 characters) e. Illegal because of the embedded blank f. Legal g. Illegal, because CORRESPONDING is a reserved word; 12.a. Legal as a numeric literal b. Illegal because of the comma c. Legal as a figurative literal d. Illegal because it ends with a period e. Legal as a nonnumeric literal; 13. F; 14. e; 15. F; 16. verb; 17. sentence; 18. clauses.

COBOL Language Syntax

Every language has its own set of rules, the correct use of which enables us to communicate with each other orally or in writing. Human languages are flexible within their boundaries. We can use many different ways to formulate the same sentence.

The rules for programming languages, on the other hand, are less complex than those for human languages, but they are also much more rigid. They require that programs using them be described precisely and clearly so that compilers can analyze and translate them into object programs. Every element of the programs we write should be correct both syntactically and semantically.

> The **syntax** of a programming language specifies the language elements that can be used and the way they can be combined to form other elements. It deals with rules that enable us to form clauses from words, statements from clauses, sentences from statements, and so on.

> On the other hand, the **semantics** tells us about the meaning and function of language elements in a program.

Let us consider a COBOL example, the following ADD statement.

```
ADD INTEREST TO ACCOUNT-BALANCE
    ON SIZE ERROR PERFORM CHECK-BALANCE.
```

In writing this statement, we have used quite a few syntax rules. They are as follows.

1. The ADD statement should begin with the key word ADD.
2. After ADD we must have at least one user-defined word representing a program variable, or a constant. In our example, it is the program variable INTEREST.
3. Next, there should be the key word TO.
4. After TO, there should be another variable name. ACCOUNT-BALANCE is the variable in the example.
5. Then, we may have the optional SIZE ERROR clause. This clause may begin with the optional key word ON, should have the key words SIZE ERROR, and should terminate with a statement. The statement that we used in this example is PERFORM CHECK-BALANCE. It is a syntactically correct form of the COBOL PERFORM statement.

This ADD statement is only one of many we can write that would conform to COBOL's syntax rules. Any syntactically correct statement is a **derivation** of the language syntax for that statement. Therefore, the above example is a derivation of the ADD statement syntax.

Clearly, writing a statement correctly is not enough. We must also know about its semantics. The semantics of the above ADD statement is expressed as follows.

> It causes the computer to add the current content of the variable INTEREST to the current value of the variable ACCOUNT-BALANCE, and to store the sum in ACCOUNT-BALANCE. While doing this addition, the computer checks to see if the result can be properly stored in the variable ACCOUNT-BALANCE. It is possible that the new value computed for ACCOUNT-BALANCE may be too large to be stored in the memory location defined for it in the program. If this is the case, a SIZE ERROR condition is raised, and the statement PERFORM CHECK-BALANCE is executed.

In describing the syntax of programming language elements, verbal descriptions such as the one given above can be rather lengthy and clumsy. Instead, it is common to use some formal notation to standardize these descriptions. The COBOL language syntax can be conveniently described using either the CBL (COBOL-like) notation or syntax diagrams.

In the following sections we will briefly discuss these equivalent notations. We will adopt the CBL notation for syntax description purposes in this book. As for semantics, no adequate formal description techniques exist. Whenever a new COBOL language element is introduced, we will describe its semantics verbally.

CBL Notation for COBOL Syntax

The CBL notation is based on a set of conventions that can be used in describing the COBOL language syntax. These conventions are given below.

> 1. Upper-case words are COBOL reserved words.
>   a. Underlined upper-case words indicate required words.
>   b. Upper-case words that are not underlined are optional and may be included in the language element to improve readability.
> 2. Lower-case words are user-defined identifiers, or constants.
> 3. Braces { } enclose two or more items, of which one must be used in obtaining a syntactically valid derivation.
> 4. Brackets [ ] enclose one or more items that are optional. None or one of them may be used.
> 5. Braces { } or brackets [ ] followed by three points . . . indicate that the last syntactical unit can be used any number of times in the derivation process.

As an example, let us consider the syntax of the COBOL ADD statement.

$$\underline{\text{ADD}} \begin{Bmatrix} \text{identifier-1} \\ \text{literal-1} \end{Bmatrix} \begin{bmatrix} \text{identifier-2} \\ \text{literal-2} \end{bmatrix} \dots \underline{\text{TO}} \text{ identifier-m } [\ \underline{\text{ROUNDED}}\ ]$$

[identifier-n [ROUNDED]] . . .
[ON SIZE ERROR imperative-statement-1]

COBOL 85

[NOT ON SIZE ERROR imperative-statement-2] [END-ADD]

This is one of the three formats available for the ADD statement. It is easy to see that this notation conveniently summarizes all the rules that apply to the statement. In view of this syntax, many ADD statement derivations are possible. Below are examples.

```
1. ADD A B C TO TOTAL.
2. ADD PROFIT 5.25 TO COST ROUNDED
        ON SIZE ERROR PERFORM CHECK-PROFIT.
3. ADD LEFT-PART MIDDLE-PART RIGHT-PART TO RAW-ADDRESS
        SIZE ERROR PERFORM TERMINATE-EXECUTION
        NOT SIZE ERROR PERFORM COMPUTE-ADJUSTED-ADDRESS
        END-ADD.
```

COBOL 85

Example 1 This ADD statement is derived by generating three identifiers after the key word ADD. None of the remaining optional elements of the syntax is used in the derivation. The ADD statement causes the computer to add the values stored in variables A, B, and C, add the sum to the value stored in TOTAL, and keep the sum thus obtained in TOTAL. After the statement is executed, the old value stored in TOTAL is replaced by its new value.

Example 2   Here we are asking the computer to add 5.25 to the content of the variable PROFIT, add the result to the value in COST, round the sum, and store it in COST. In case a SIZE ERROR condition is raised, the computer will execute the statement PERFORM CHECK-PROFIT.

Example 3   In this example the derivation has three identifiers after ADD, and a SIZE ERROR clause, a NOT SIZE ERROR clause, and the END-ADD terminator. The values stored in the variables LEFT-PART, MIDDLE-PART, and RIGHT-PART will be added to the value in RAW-ADDRESS. The sum will be stored in RAW-ADDRESS. If the result of addition gives rise to a SIZE ERROR condition, the statement PERFORM TERMINATE-EXECUTION is executed; otherwise, the statement PERFORM COMPUTE-ADJUSTED-ADDRESS is invoked.

Before we conclude our discussion, let us consider another example. The CBL description of one of the formats for the COBOL MOVE statement is given below. MOVE is used to transfer data values to a variable in COBOL.

$$\underline{\text{MOVE}} \quad \begin{Bmatrix} \text{identifier-1} \\ \text{literal} \end{Bmatrix} \quad \underline{\text{TO}} \; \{\text{identifier-2}\} \; \ldots$$

The following derivations are incorrect:

- MOVE A B TO T R.   Error: Two identifiers after MOVE.
- MOVE B TO 5.   Error: A constant after TO; it should be an identifier.
- MOVE CODE TO XCODE.   Error: CODE is a COBOL reserved word.
- MOWE 5 TO Y.   Error: The key word MOVE is misspelled as MOWE.

In this book, we will use the CBL notation to describe the COBOL language syntax. The entire language syntax in CBL notation is given in Appendix B.

Syntax Diagrams for COBOL Syntax

Another syntax notation that is becoming increasingly more popular for the COBOL syntax is based on syntax diagrams. Syntax diagrams are graphic depictions of the generation path for valid language elements. They are equivalent to the CBL notation. The conventions used in syntax diagrams are as follows.

1. A syntax diagram is read from left to right and top to bottom, following the path of the line.
2. ≫── indicates the beginning of a syntax definition.
3. ──→ indicates that the syntax diagram is continued on the next line.
4. >── indicates that the current line is the continuation of the previous line.
5. ──× indicates the end of a syntax description.
6. COBOL reserved words are written in upper-case letters.
7. User-defined identifiers or constants are written in lower-case letters.
8. Whenever a choice is possible between two or more items, such items appear vertically on and below the main path.
9. An arrow defining a cyclic path to the left above the main line indicates a syntactical element that can be repeated.

The following is a syntax diagram for the ADD statement discussed in the previous section.

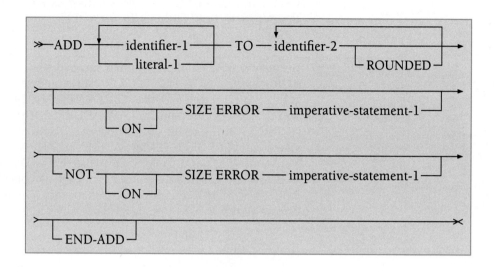

In generating valid derivations, we start at the beginning of the syntax diagram and choose a path that ultimately terminates at its end.

Typing COBOL Source Code

While developing a program, we type the COBOL source code into a text file and use a text editor for this purpose. The source file must have a record length of 80 characters. After we finish typing the code, we request the COBOL compiler to compile the source file. If the program can be compiled correctly, an object file will be created. This file will be executed under the control of the operating system, together with some standard COBOL library routines and the input-output files.

The following are rules for typing COBOL source lines.

1. Each line of the COBOL source file is divided into five zones, as shown in Figure 2. These zones are
   a. Line sequence numbers zone
   b. Column 7
   c. A margin
   d. B margin
   e. Program identification zone
2. In the older punched card systems, columns 1 through 6 could be used for line sequence numbers, and columns 73 through 80 for program identification. With modern text editors that supplement most operating systems, we do not have to use these zones. The necessary information for them is automatically inserted by the text editor.
3. The zone defined by columns 8 through 11 is known as the **A margin**. All division headers, section headers, paragraph names, FDs, and level 01s in the DATA DIVISION should be typed starting at a column in the A margin.
4. All other program entries should be typed at or beyond column 12 up to column 72. The zone from column 12 through 72 is called the **B margin**.

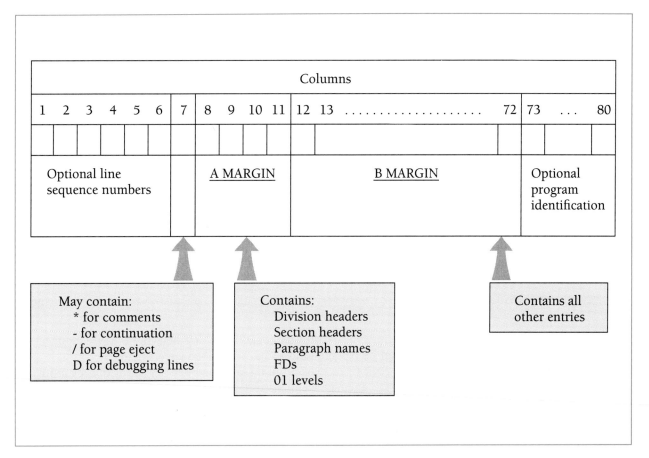

Figure 2 The Zones of COBOL Coding Line

5. Column 7 has four functions (see Figure 3).
   a. If it contains an asterisk, the rest of the line up to and including column 72 is considered to be a comment line. It will appear in the source program listing, but the compiler will not process it.
   b. If column 7 contains the letter D, the line that may contain a COBOL statement is considered as a debugging line. Debugging lines are used for program debugging purposes. They are discussed in Chapter 6.
   c. If there is a slash (/) in column 7, it will cause a page eject while the source code is being listed, and the line with a slash in column 7 and the subsequent lines will be printed on the next page. This may be used to improve the readability of program code.
   d. Column 7 may also contain a hyphen. This indicates that the line thus marked is a continuation of the preceding line. A continuation line is needed if the preceding line contains an identifier or a literal that has to be broken at column 72. In this case, in the continuation line, we should continue typing at column 12. If the element that is being split into two parts is a literal constant, the continuation line should start with a quotation mark at column 12. Figure 3 shows some examples.

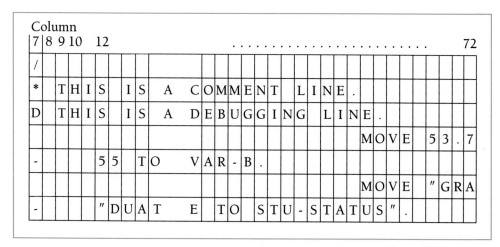

Figure 3 Uses of Column 7 on COBOL Coding Lines

REVIEW QUESTIONS

1. _____ deals with language rules that determine how language elements can be combined to form other language elements.
2. The semantics of a programming language tells us about the meaning and function of language elements in a program. (T or F)
3. Any syntactically valid MOVE statement is a _____ of the COBOL syntax for the MOVE statement.
4. The COBOL language syntax can be conveniently and formally described using either the _____ or _____ .
5. Which of the following about the CBL notation is incorrect?
   a. Underlined upper-case words indicate required key words.
   b. Lower-case words are optional key words.
   c. Braces { } enclose two or more items of which one must be used in obtaining a derivation.
   d. Brackets [ ] enclose one or more items that are optional.
6. A syntax diagram is a graphic depiction of the generation path for valid language elements. (T or F)
7. A COBOL source file must have a record length of ____ characters.
8. Columns 8–11 on each line of the COBOL source file are called the _____ .
9. All division headers, section headers, paragraph names, FDs, and level 01s should be typed in the B margin. (T or F)
10. An asterisk in column 7 of a COBOL source line indicates that the line is a debugging line. (T or F)
11. A slash in column 7 of a COBOL source line causes a page eject while the source code is being listed. (T or F)

Answers: 1. Syntax; 2. T; 3. derivation; 4. CBL notation, syntax diagrams; 5. b; 6. T; 7. 80; 8. A margin; 9. F; 10. F; 11. T.

Example Program 1: A Program to Compute Test Score Averages

To be able to relate language elements to a COBOL program and understand their relative placement and functions, we consider an example that will be our first exposure to a program written in COBOL. Program 1-Source is a compiler-produced source listing of our program. It consists of 131 lines of code, a short program in COBOL standards. The six-digit numbers at the beginning of each line are line numbers generated by the COBOL compiler.

To get such a compiler produced listing of a source program, we should go through the following activities:

1. Analyzing the given problem (we will soon see what it is)
2. Coding it in COBOL
3. Perhaps writing appropriate COBOL statements on some sheets of paper or some special forms suitable for coding COBOL statements
4. Typing the statements into a file (in the past, we used to punch them on punched cards that formed a card file)
5. Compiling the source program file by calling on the COBOL compiler through the use of appropriate job control language (JCL) statements

If we have no errors in the program, the compiler produces a source listing, such as the one in Program 1-Source. It also produces an object program. If there are errors in the program and the compiler cannot continue with compilation, it produces a source listing and a set of error diagnostic messages, telling us where the errors are and why they are errors. In case the compilation process is halted due to errors, the object code is not generated.

Before we take a closer look at the source program, let us talk about the next activity, that of executing it. In preparing for execution, we concentrate on program input data. For this program, the input data are assumed to be organized into an input data file. A **computer data file** consists of lines into which we type data values. Program 1-Input is the listing of the input data file for the example program. It consists of eight lines that are structurally identical, each containing six data values. The structure of lines in such a data file is fixed, but the file content may change. The current content of a file is called an **instance of the file**. Therefore, Program 1-Input is an instance of our data file. We can generate such an instance by typing data values into a file in the same way we typed COBOL statements into a source file.

Now we are ready for program execution. Again, we use appropriate JCLs to define the input data file and a yet nonexistent output file to the object program, and execute it. If there are no errors in the program, and ours has none, it will execute and produce an output. The output for the example program is a report, as shown in Program 1-Output.

On any computer system, to compile and execute COBOL programs we need JCLs that communicate our intentions to the operating system. The JCL statements tell the operating system to compile a program, to define files associated with it, to linkage edit the object code, and to execute it. The syntax and nature of JCLs vary for each computer and operating system. To determine the correct JCLs, the reader should consult the computer center or the computer vendor's technical manuals.

Let us return to the COBOL program of Program 1-Source. In the following examination we emphasize the main functions and omit the details. The details in the program will eventually become clear as we study the language features in Chapters 2 and 3. To understand what the program does, we concentrate on the following blocks:

1. Lines 000025 through 000040 define a file called STUDENT-TEST-SCORES-FILE and its record structure. The record structure consists of some program variables for which values will be supplied during input. These variables are STUDENT-IDNO, STUDENT-NAME, COURSE-CODE of a course taken by a student, and the student's test scores on three tests called TEST-1-SCORE, TEST-2-SCORE, and FINAL-SCORE, respectively. This file corresponds to the physical file of Program 1-Input. The lines with the key word FILLER define delimiter fields to separate data values.

2. The blocks consisting of lines 000042 through 000045 and lines 000070 through 000084 help define an output file and its record structure, which correspond to the output report of Program 1-Output. Each line of the report has values for student identification number, student name, course code, three test scores, and an average test score, represented in the program by the variables OUT-STUDENT-IDNO, OUT-STUDENT-NAME, OUT-COURSE-CODE, OUT-TEST-1-SCORE, OUT-TEST-2-SCORE, OUT-FINAL-SCORE, and OUT-AVERAGE-SCORE, respectively.

3. Lines 000054 through 000068 define a report heading called TEST-SCORES-REPORT-HEADING in line 000054. It is used to print the first line in the report of Program 1-Output.

4. The logic of the program is in the block formed by lines 000087 through 000131. The following steps are executed to produce the output report.

   a. The input data file STUDENT-TEST-SCORES-FILE is opened so that it can be read (line 000089), and the output file TEST-SCORES-REPORT is opened so that it can be loaded (line 000090).

   b. The program block consisting of lines 000105 through 000110, also known as PRODUCE-REPORT-HEADING, is executed. In it are statements that produce and write the report heading into the TEST-SCORES-REPORT file.

   c. One record is read from the STUDENT-TEST-SCORES-FILE by the READ statement at line 000094.

   d. The PERFORM statement at line 000097 causes repeated execution of the program block called GENERATE-AND-OUTPUT-LINES, consisting of lines 000112 through 000131. In this block, the input data variable values are moved to the corresponding output file record variables; an AVERAGE-SCORE is computed using the weights 0.25, 0.35, and 0.40, respectively, for the three test scores; the computed AVERAGE-SCORE value is moved to the corresponding output field called OUT-AVERAGE-SCORE; the output report line is written into the report file; and a new record is read from the input data file. The program block GENERATE-AND-OUTPUT-LINES is executed for each input record once, until the end of the input file is reached.

   e. The two files are closed by the statement at line 000100, and the statement STOP RUN at line 000103 terminates the execution of the program.

In summary, our sample program reads records from the input file of Program 1-Input, computes an average test score using three test score values for each student and course, and generates the report shown in Program 1-Output. We realize that the application here is quite simple, almost trivial, as it was intended; however, it has also been quite simple to read and understand the source code. Provided they are well written, this is true of most COBOL programs: they are indeed easy to read.

Now that we understand its function, let us reexamine the example program from another point of view and try to identify the different elements in it.

1. We see words such as IDENTIFICATION in line 000002, STUDENT-TEST-SCORES-FILE in line 000025, PERFORM in line 000092, FINAL-SCORE in line 000123, etc. These are indeed called **words**.

2. We notice **constants**, such as 0.40 in line 000123.

3. We come across numbers such as 01 in line 000049. Functionally, such numbers are not constants in COBOL. They are called **level numbers**.

4. In all words, constants, and level numbers, we observe that the basic building blocks are **characters**, which are letters, decimal digits, or some special characters.

5. We encounter at several places in the code combinations of words and numeric values; for example, "PIC 999" in line 000049, "AFTER ADVANCING 1 LINE" in line 000128, "AT END MOVE "YES" TO END-OF-FILE-FLAG" in line 000131, etc. Such combinations appear to have separate functions and are examples of **clauses**.

6. After line 000088 we have some combinations of words, constants, and clauses, which begin with a verb and end with a period. An example is the sequence beginning with the COMPUTE verb in line 000121 and ending with a period in line 000123. These combinations are **statements**.

7. In lines 000114 through 000119, six MOVE statements are combined together into what we call a **sentence**, ultimately terminating with a period.

8. Certain combinations of statements and sentences are grouped into blocks under a name, as in lines 000112 through 000131. Such groupings are **paragraphs**.

9. In lines 000014 through 000016 we notice two paragraphs called SOURCE-COMPUTER and OBJECT-COMPUTER combined together into a **section**, whose name is CONFIGURATION SECTION.

10. Finally, in lines 000013 through 000020, we notice two sections comprising a **division**, called ENVIRONMENT division.

We also have some lines in the code that start at column 7 with an asterisk. Examples are lines 000001, and 000004 through 000007. Such lines are **comments**, and are included in the code to provide clarification for the reader. They are ignored by the compiler during compilation.

Additional details for the language features found in the four divisions of a COBOL program will be studied in Chapters 2 and 3.

Key Terms

A margin	paragraph
B margin	paragraph-oriented design
CBL notation	PROCEDURE DIVISION
clause	reserved word
COBOL character set	section
constant	section-oriented design
DATA DIVISION	semantics
division	sentence
ENVIRONMENT DIVISION	statement
figurative constant	syntax
IDENTIFICATION DIVISION	syntax diagram
identifier	user-defined word
level number	

Study Guide

Quick Scan

- COBOL is the only standard language that has been developed principally for business applications. It is also the most widely used data processing language today.
- It was first proposed by the CODASYL committee in 1959, with a goal to design a business-oriented data processing language. The first COBOL compilers became available in 1960.
- Over the years, the COBOL committee of the American National Standards Institute developed three standard versions of the language. These are COBOL 1968, COBOL 1974, and COBOL 1985.

- COBOL is a particularly powerful commercial application programming language because (1) an extensive library of programs written in COBOL are still in use, (2) a majority of business application programs are still being written in COBOL, (3) COBOL programs are quite portable, (4) the language, properly used, generates a readable code, (5) it has sufficient language features to permit writing structured and modular programs, (6) it has extensive file processing capabilities, and (7) it is a common host language for many widely used data base management systems.
- COBOL is based on a character set that includes decimal digits, letters, and 15 special characters.
- The language elements are reserved and user-defined words, constants, level numbers, clauses, statements, sentences, paragraphs, sections, and divisions.
- Every COBOL program consists of four divisions: IDENTIFICATION, ENVIRONMENT, DATA, and PROCEDURE.
- Programming languages have many rules that specify their syntax and semantics. The syntax of a language indicates the language elements that can be used and the way they can be combined to form other elements. The semantics of a language specify the meanings of the elements.
- Syntax and semantics of language elements can be described in narrative form. Syntax can also be described using formal notations. For the COBOL syntax, we commonly use either the CBL notation or syntax diagrams.
- Certain rules must be obeyed in typing COBOL statements into a source program file. Division headers, section headers, paragraph names, FDs, and level 01s are all typed beginning at column 8 in the A margin, which extends to column 11. All other program entries should be typed at or beyond column 12, up to column 72. Columns 12 through 72 constitute the B margin. Column 7 has special uses: it can be used for comments, debugging lines, line continuation, or page eject during the printing of the source listing.

Test Your Comprehension

Multiple-Choice Questions

1. Which of the following is one of COBOL's strengths?
   a. There is an extensive library of COBOL application programs in business and industry.
   b. A high percentage of new business applications are being developed in COBOL.
   c. COBOL programs have a high degree of portability.
   d. COBOL is one of the most English-like high-level programming languages.
   e. All of the above are among the strengths of COBOL.
2. Which of the following statements about COBOL language elements is correct?
   a. Clauses specify certain attributes of program entities.
   b. Statements are found in the PROCEDURE DIVISION of a COBOL program and generally begin with a verb.
   c. Sentences are sequences of one or more statements, the last of which is terminated by a period.
   d. Paragraphs are named building blocks that contain one or more sentences.
   e. All of the above are correct.
3. Concerning the use of special characters, which of the following is incorrect?
   a. Periods are used to delineate clauses. They improve the readability of code and are optional in all cases.
   b. Double quotation marks enclose nonnumeric constants.

    c. The hyphen is used either as arithmetic minus operator or as a hyphen in forming literals.

    d. Two consecutive asterisks with no intervening blanks form the exponentiation operator.

4. Which of the following comparison operators is illegal in COBOL?

    a. >

    b. < >

    c. <

    d. =

5. Choose the correct statement.

    a. ENVIRONMENT is a user-defined word.

    b. ENVIRONMENT-DIVISION is a reserved word.

    c. ONE is a figurative constant.

    d. Paragraph names are user-defined words.

    e. All of the above are correct.

6. Choose the correct statement.

    a. Unless the key word END-IF is used, an IF statement should terminate with a period.

    b. The last statement in a paragraph should end with a period.

    c. Provided it is not contained within another statement, any COBOL statement may end with a period.

    d. All of the above are correct.

7. Concerning the divisions of COBOL programs, which of the following is incorrect?

    a. The ENVIRONMENT DIVISION specifies the computer system and contains partial definitions for data files used by the program.

    b. The DATA DIVISION is the last division in a program.

    c. In the PROCEDURE DIVISION, we have user-defined sections and/or paragraphs expressing the program logic in COBOL statements.

    d. The DATA DIVISION may contain a FILE SECTION and a WORKING-STORAGE SECTION.

8. Which of the following statements concerning the syntax of a programming language is correct?

    a. Syntax specifies the language elements that can be used in forming other language elements.

    b. Syntax also specifies the way language elements can be combined to form other language elements.

    c. The syntax of a programming language element can be described in narrative form.

    d. The syntax of programming languages can also be formally described using a set of simple conventions.

    e. All of the above are correct.

9. In the CBL notation for COBOL syntax:

    a. Upper-case words that are not underlined are required key words.

    b. Upper-case words that are underlined stand for user-defined identifiers.

    c. Braces or brackets followed by three points indicate that the last syntactical unit can be used any number of times in the derivation.

    d. Brackets enclose two or more items, one of which must be used in obtaining a syntactically valid derivation.

10. In a COBOL source line:

    a. Columns 1–6 are used for line sequence numbers.

    b. Columns 8–11 define the A margin, which is used for typing division headers, section headers, paragraph names, FDs, and level 01s.

    c. Columns 12–72 define the B margin, which is used for typing statements and all other program entries except those typed into the A margin.

    d. All of the above are correct.

11. If column 7 of a COBOL source line contains a hyphen, this line
    a. Is a comment line
    b. Is a continuation line
    c. Is a debugging line
    d. Will cause a page eject

Answers: 1. e; 2. e; 3. a; 4. b; 5. d; 6. d; 7. b; 8. e; 9. c; 10. d; 11. b.

Short Essay Questions

1. Explain why COBOL is a particularly powerful commercial application programming language.
2. What characters make up the COBOL character set?
3. What are the differences between reserved words and user-defined words? Give three examples of each.
4. How are constants classified in COBOL? Give two examples of each.
5. Itemize the rules for constructing user-defined words in COBOL.
6. What is a clause in COBOL? Give an example.
7. What is the difference between a COBOL statement and a sentence?
8. What is a paragraph? Why is a paragraph a significant language element?
9. What are the four program divisions in a COBOL program?
10. Explain the difference between the syntax and semantics of a programming language.
11. List the conventions used in the CBL notation for COBOL syntax.
12. Explain the significance of the A margin and B margin in COBOL source lines. What language elements are to be typed in the A and B margins?
13. Explain the uses of column 7 in COBOL source lines.

Improve Your Problem-Solving Ability

Debugging Exercises

1. For each of the following COBOL constants, state whether they are legal or not, and if illegal, why.
    a. SPACES
    b. BLANKS
    c. 12.
    d. 17,000.0
    e. "CLASS GRADE REPORT"
    f. 'HEADQUARTER'S NAME'

2. For each of the following user-defined words intended for use as variable names, specify whether they are legal or not, and if illegal, state your reason.
    a. 7890
    b. L57
    c. %-INTEREST
    d. END OF-FILE-MARKER
    e. MASTER-RECORD--POINTER
    f. MASTER-RECORD-COMING-FROM-CUSTOMER-FILE

3. The CBL notation for one format of the COBOL DIVIDE statement is given in the following syntax diagram:

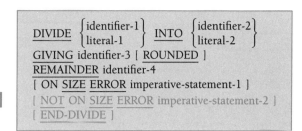

COBOL 85

In view of this syntax notation, which of the following DIVIDE statements are illegal, and why?

a. DIVIDE 67 INTO X GIVING Y REMAINDER Z ROUNDED.
b. DIVIDE A INTO B GIVING C, D.
c. DIVIDE X INTO Y REMAINDER Z.
d. DIVIDE X INTO Y GIVING W REMAINDER T END DIVIDE.
e. DIVIDE TEMP INTO XTEMP GIVING XTEMP REMAINDER TEMP.

Programming Problems

1. Type the COBOL program of Program 1-Source exactly as you see it into a source file on the computer system available for this class. Also, type the input data file of Program 1-Input. Then compile your program, and run it with the data file of Program 1-Input to obtain a report as shown in Program 1-Output.

2. Modify the program of Program 1-Source such that, in addition to generating a report such as the one in Program 1-Output, it (a) counts the number of records read and processed, and (b) prints

```
NUMBER OF RECORDS PROCESSED = XX
```

two lines after the last line on the report, where XX is the actual number of records in the input data file. Run your modified program with the data file of Program 1-Input.

```
                                    COLUMNS
    1    5    10   15   20   25   30   35   40   45   50   55   60   65   70 72
   ----|----|----|----|----|----|----|----|----|----|----|----|----|----|--

 000001    *..........................................................................
 000002    IDENTIFICATION DIVISION.
 000003    PROGRAM-ID.    STUDENT-TEST-SCORE-AVERAGES.

           comments

 000004    *****************************************************************
 000005    ***   THIS PROGRAM READS A SEQUENTIAL DISK FILE, AND GENERATES A  *
 000006    ***   LIST OF STUDENT TEST SCORE AVERAGES.                        *
 000007    *****************************************************************

 000008    AUTHOR.         UCKAN.
 000009    DATE-WRITTEN.    MARCH 30, 1991.
 000010    DATE-COMPILED. 03/30/91.
 000012    *..........................................................................
```

Program 1-Source COBOL Language Elements Shown on a Sample Program

division

```
000013    ENVIRONMENT DIVISION.

          section

000014    CONFIGURATION SECTION.
000015    SOURCE-COMPUTER.   UNIVERSITY-MAINFRAME.
000016    OBJECT-COMPUTER.   UNIVERSITY-MAINFRAME.


          section

000017    INPUT-OUTPUT SECTION.
000018    FILE-CONTROL.
000019        SELECT STUDENT-TEST-SCORES-FILE ASSIGN TO INFILE.
000020        SELECT TEST-SCORES-REPORT       ASSIGN TO OUTFILE.


000021
000022    *................................................................
000023    DATA DIVISION.
000024    FILE SECTION.
000025    FD  STUDENT-TEST-SCORES-FILE
000026        LABEL RECORDS ARE STANDARD
000027        DATA  RECORD  IS STUDENT-TEST-SCORES-RECORD.
000028    01  STUDENT-TEST-SCORES-RECORD.
000029        05   STUDENT-IDNO       PIC X(4).
000030        05   FILLER             PIC X.
000031        05   STUDENT-NAME       PIC X(25).
000032        05   FILLER             PIC X.
000033        05   COURSE-CODE        PIC X(6).
000034        05   FILLER             PIC X.
000035        05   TEST-1-SCORE       PIC 999.
000036        05   FILLER             PIC X.
000037        05   TEST-2-SCORE       PIC 999.
000038        05   FILLER             PIC X.
000039        05   FINAL-SCORE        PIC 999.
000040        05   FILLER             PIC X(31).
000041
000042    FD  TEST-SCORES-REPORT
000043        LABEL RECORDS ARE OMITTED
000044        DATA  RECORD  IS REPORT-LINE.
000045    01  REPORT-LINE            PIC X(131).
000046
000047    WORKING-STORAGE SECTION.
```

level number   clause

```
000048
000049    01  AVERAGE-SCORE            PIC 999.

000050
000051    01  END-OF-FILE-FLAG        PIC XXX   VALUE "NO".
000052        88 END-OF-FILE                    VALUE "YES".
000053
```

Program 1-Source (Continued)

```
000054    01   TEST-SCORES-REPORT-HEADING.
000055         05   FILLER               PIC X      VALUE SPACES.
000056         05   FILLER               PIC X(4)   VALUE "IDNO".
000057         05   FILLER               PIC X(2)   VALUE SPACES.
000058         05   FILLER               PIC X(25)  VALUE "STUDENT NAME".
000059         05   FILLER               PIC X(2)   VALUE SPACES.
000060         05   FILLER               PIC X(6)   VALUE "COURSE".
000061         05   FILLER               PIC X(2)   VALUE SPACES.
000062         05   FILLER               PIC X(6)   VALUE "TEST 1".
000063         05   FILLER               PIC X(2)   VALUE SPACES.
000064         05   FILLER               PIC X(6)   VALUE "TEST 2".
000065         05   FILLER               PIC X(2)   VALUE SPACES.
000066         05   FILLER               PIC X(5)   VALUE "FINAL".
000067         05   FILLER               PIC X(2)   VALUE SPACES.
000068         05   FILLER               PIC X(7)   VALUE "AVERAGE".
000069
000070    01  REPORT-DETAIL-LINE.
000071         05   FILLER               PIC X      VALUE SPACES.
000072         05   OUT-STUDENT-IDNO     PIC X(4).
000073         05   FILLER               PIC X(2)   VALUE SPACES.
000074         05   OUT-STUDENT-NAME     PIC X(25).
000075         05   FILLER               PIC X(2)   VALUE SPACES.
000076         05   OUT-COURSE-CODE      PIC X(6).
000077         05   FILLER               PIC X(4)   VALUE SPACES.
000078         05   OUT-TEST-1-SCORE     PIC ZZ9.
000079         05   FILLER               PIC X(5)   VALUE SPACES.
000080         05   OUT-TEST-2-SCORE     PIC ZZ9.
000081         05   FILLER               PIC X(4)   VALUE SPACES.
000082         05   OUT-FINAL-SCORE      PIC ZZ9.
000083         05   FILLER               PIC X(5)   VALUE SPACES.
000084         05   OUT-AVERAGE-SCORE    PIC ZZ9.
000085
000086    *....................................................................
000087    PROCEDURE DIVISION.
000088    MAIN-PROGRAM.
000089         OPEN INPUT   STUDENT-TEST-SCORES-FILE
000090              OUTPUT TEST-SCORES-REPORT.
000091
000092         PERFORM PRODUCE-REPORT-HEADING.
000093
000094         READ STUDENT-TEST-SCORES-FILE
000095              AT END MOVE "YES" TO END-OF-FILE-FLAG.
000096
000097         PERFORM GENERATE-AND-OUTPUT-LINES
000098              UNTIL END-OF-FILE.
000099
000100         CLOSE STUDENT-TEST-SCORES-FILE
000101              TEST-SCORES-REPORT.
000102
000103         STOP RUN.
000104
000105    PRODUCE-REPORT-HEADING.
000106
000107         MOVE TEST-SCORES-REPORT-HEADING TO REPORT-LINE.
```

Program 1-Source (Continued)

```
000108        WRITE REPORT-LINE AFTER ADVANCING PAGE.
000109        MOVE SPACES TO REPORT-LINE.
000110        WRITE REPORT-LINE AFTER ADVANCING 1 LINE.
000111
```

paragraph

```
000112    GENERATE-AND-OUTPUT-LINES.
000113                                                           sentence
000114        MOVE STUDENT-IDNO TO OUT-STUDENT-IDNO
000115        MOVE STUDENT-NAME TO OUT-STUDENT-NAME
000116        MOVE COURSE-CODE  TO OUT-COURSE-CODE
000117        MOVE TEST-1-SCORE TO OUT-TEST-1-SCORE
000118        MOVE TEST-2-SCORE TO OUT-TEST-2-SCORE
000119        MOVE FINAL-SCORE  TO OUT-FINAL-SCORE.
000120
000121        COMPUTE AVERAGE-SCORE = 0.25 * TEST-1-SCORE     statement
000122                             + 0.35 * TEST-2-SCORE
000123                             + 0.40 * FINAL-SCORE.
```

constant   identifier

```
000124
000125        MOVE AVERAGE-SCORE TO OUT-AVERAGE-SCORE.
000126                                                           statement
000127        WRITE REPORT-LINE FROM REPORT-DETAIL-LINE
000128              AFTER ADVANCING 1 LINE.
```

clause

```
000129                                                           statement
000130        READ STUDENT-TEST-SCORES-FILE           clause
000131            AT END MOVE "YES" TO END-OF-FILE-FLAG.
```

Program 1-Source (Continued)

```
                              COLUMNS
1   5   10   15   20   25   30   35   40   45   50   55   60   65   70   75
----|----|----|----|----|----|----|----|----|----|----|----|----|----|----|-


1120  JOHN SMITH              BUS401 067 088 099
1126  CHERYL CLARK            BUS401 098 070 067
1130  RICHARD CARLOS          BUS401 100 094 100
1145  JANE LEE                BUS401 037 055 056
0800  THOMAS CRAIG            CS 374 100 100 100    input records
1120  JOHN SMITH              CS 374 056 067 087
1120  JOHN SMITH              MTH252 078 088 095
1340  EILEEN BRADLEY          MTH252 100 100 097
```

Program 1-Input An Instance of Input File for Program 1

```
                              COLUMNS
1    5    10   15   20   25   30   35   40   45   50   55   60   65   70   75
----|----|----|----|----|----|----|----|----|----|----|----|----|----|----|-


IDNO   STUDENT NAME                 COURSE   TEST 1   TEST 2    FINAL   AVERAGE

1120   JOHN SMITH                   BUS401     67       88       99       87
1126   CHERYL CLARK                 BUS401     98       70       67       75
1130   RICHARD CARLOS               BUS401    100       94      100       97
1145   JANE LEE                     BUS401     37       55       56       50
0800   THOMAS CRAIG                 CS 374    100      100      100      100
1120   JOHN SMITH                   CS 374     56       67       87       72
1120   JOHN SMITH                   MTH252     78       88       95       88
1340   EILEEN BRADLEY               MTH252    100      100       97       98
```

Program 1-Output An Output Report Generated by Program 1

2

IDENTIFICATION, ENVIRONMENT, and DATA Divisions of a COBOL Program

IN THIS CHAPTER YOU WILL LEARN ABOUT

- IDENTIFICATION DIVISION entries
- ENVIRONMENT DIVISION entries
    The SELECT statement
    How to define files in SELECT statements
- DATA DIVISION entries
    COBOL data types and PICTURE specifications
    How to define program variables
    How to define COBOL data structures
    How to define files and records in the FILE SECTION
    WORKING-STORAGE section
    Data field editing
    Condition names
    Qualification
    Data initialization
    Sharing of memory locations
    Renaming substructures

Introduction

We will study the first three divisions of a COBOL program: IDENTIFICA-TION, ENVIRONMENT, and DATA. They should be placed in a program in this order. In these three divisions we declare program entities and properties that the compiler has to know in order to compile and execute the program's procedural component. The program logic is coded in the last division, which is the PROCEDURE DIVISION. The entities to be declared in the first three divisions are primarily program variables, data structures, and input and output files. We also declare additional information that provides clarification to the reader of the program about its function and other attributes.

IDENTIFICATION DIVISION

The first division of a COBOL program is the IDENTIFICATION DIVISION. Its main functions are to identify the program for the compiler and provide part of the necessary in-program documentation for the user. The IDENTIFICA-TION DIVISION consists of six paragraphs:

1. PROGRAM-ID
2. AUTHOR
3. INSTALLATION
4. DATE-WRITTEN
5. DATE-COMPILED
6. SECURITY

Rules About the IDENTIFICATION DIVISION

1. Of the six paragraphs, only the PROGRAM-ID paragraph is required. It should be the first paragraph in the division. All other paragraphs are optional and can be written in any order.
2. Paragraph names in the IDENTIFICATION DIVISION are supplied by the language and cannot be changed.
3. Each paragraph, except the DATE-COMPILED, can have only one comment-type entry.
4. The DATE-COMPILED paragraph should have only the paragraph header, ending with a period. The compiler will complete the paragraph during compilation by inserting the current date after the paragraph header.
5. Each entry in all other paragraphs must be terminated by a period.

An example of a full IDENTIFICATION DIVISION is given below:

```
IDENTIFICATION DIVISION.
PROGRAM-ID.    STUDENT-GRADES.
AUTHOR.        UCKAN.
DATE-WRITTEN.  AUGUST 16, 1991.
DATE-COMPILED.
INSTALLATION.  MIAMI UNIVERSITY COMPUTER CENTER.
SECURITY.      NO RESTRICTIONS.
```

ENVIRONMENT DIVISION

The second division in a COBOL program is the ENVIRONMENT DIVISION. Its two functions are to supply information about the computer system configuration that the program will be using, and to define partially the input-output files to be linked to the program. Consequently, the ENVIRONMENT DIVISION consists of two sections: CONFIGURATION SECTION and INPUT-OUTPUT SECTION.

The CONFIGURATION SECTION contains two paragraphs: SOURCE-COMPUTER and OBJECT-COMPUTER. These specify the computer system on which the program will be compiled and the system on which it will be executed, respectively. The configuration specifications are made using some comment-type entries. Most COBOL compilers are insensitive to the specified configurations. Their main purpose is in-program documentation.

The INPUT-OUTPUT SECTION contains only one paragraph, called FILE-CONTROL. The FILE-CONTROL paragraph contains a set of SELECT statements. SELECT statements are functionally significant, and require more detailed coverage.

The SELECT Statement

The principal purpose of the COBOL SELECT statement is to supply partial definition for input-output files. We will study files extensively throughout this book. For our purposes in this chapter, a few fundamental concepts will suffice.

> A **file** is a named and structured collection of similar record occurrences.

> A **record** is a named and structured collection of related data elements.

In designing data for our programs, we identify the data elements that are of interest to our application. These data elements are necessarily related to one another. For example, if we are interested in collecting and processing data about students, we may identify the relevant data elements as STUDENT-NAME, MAJOR, and YEAR to associate a student by name to the major field of study and year at the college. Clearly, these elements are related to one another in the sense that they all describe properties for a student. Next, we organize them into a structure called a **record structure**. When values are assigned to the data elements belonging in a record structure, we end up with record occurrences, or simply records.

For example, in the following conceptual schema, STUDENT-RECORD is a name we assign to a record structure. The record structure consists of three data items: STUDENT-NAME, MAJOR, and YEAR. There are several occurrences for this particular structure. All such occurrences are further structured and collected in a file, for which a proper name might be STUDENT-FILE.

STUDENT-RECORD:	⟵———————— Record structure ————————⟶		
	STUDENT-NAME	MAJOR	YEAR
Records	DICKEY, JOHN	COMPUTER SCIENCE	1
	HEILEMAN, LINDA	ACCOUNTING	2
	KRAUS, THOMAS	BIOLOGY	1
	WALTERS, JEANNE	MATHEMATICS	4

Records in a file cannot be stored in the main memory. There are two reasons for this.

1. The main memory is volatile, whereas files are permanent records of valuable information.
2. In general, large numbers of records are contained in a file and the main memory capacity is limited.

Therefore, files are normally kept in auxiliary storage, usually disks or tapes. The related records in a file can be organized in a variety of ways. The simplest is to place them in auxiliary storage one after another, which is called sequential organization.

> A file is **sequentially organized** if its records are stored and accessed one after another in the memory.

There are other, more complex and more versatile file organization techniques that we will study later.

After organization is the important issue of accessing records in a file.

> An **access technique** is the manner in which records are accessed in a file, and it depends on the way the file is organized and where it is stored.

For example, a sequentially organized file can be accessed only sequentially. In other words, records in such a file can be accessed one after another. Direct access files, as we will see later, can be accessed both sequentially and randomly.

After this brief introduction to basic file concepts, we are ready to answer the following question: how do we fully describe a file in a program for the benefit of the COBOL compiler and the operating system? Let us consider the following partial COBOL code. Using this code as an example, we will analyze the language elements needed to describe a file fully.

```
                 . . . . . . . . . . . . . . . . .
                 . . . . . . . . . . . . . . . . .
000050      ENVIRONMENT DIVISION.
                 . . . . . . . . . . . . . . . . .
                 . . . . . . . . . . . . . . . . .
000054      INPUT-OUTPUT SECTION.
000055      FILE-CONTROL.
000056          SELECT STUDENT-TEST-SCORES-FILE ASSIGN TO INFILE
000057                  ORGANIZATION IS SEQUENTIAL
000058                  ACCESS MODE  IS SEQUENTIAL.
                 . . . . . . . . . . . . . . . . .
                 . . . . . . . . . . . . . . . . .
000063      DATA DIVISION.
000064      FILE SECTION.
000065      FD  STUDENT-TEST-SCORES-FILE
000066          LABEL RECORDS ARE STANDARD
000067          DATA  RECORD  IS STUDENT-TEST-SCORES-RECORD
000068          RECORD CONTAINS 80 CHARACTERS.
000069      01  STUDENT-TEST-SCORES-RECORD.
000070          05  STUDENT-IDNO        PIC X(4).
000071          05  FILLER             PIC X.
000072          05  STUDENT-NAME        PIC X(25).
000073          05  FILLER             PIC X.
000074          05  COURSE-CODE         PIC X(8).
000075          05  FILLER             PIC X.
000076          05  FIRST-TEST-SCORE    PIC 999.
000077          05  FILLER             PIC X.
000078          05  SECOND-TEST-SCORE   PIC 999.
000079          05  FILLER             PIC X.
000080          05  FINAL-TEST-SCORE    PIC 999.
000081          05  FILLER             PIC X(29).
                 . . . . . . . . . . . . . . . . .
                 . . . . . . . . . . . . . . . . .
000186      PROCEDURE DIVISION.
000187      A-MAINLINER.
000188          OPEN INPUT  STUDENT-TEST-SCORES-FILE.
```

The complete description of a file requires the following information:

1. In the SELECT statement in the ENVIRONMENT DIVISION
   a. An internal file name
   b. An external file name
   c. File organization technique
   d. File access technique
2. In FD blocks in the DATA DIVISION
   a. Record name
   b. Record length
   c. Record structure description
   d. Optional information about the file
3. In an OPEN statement in the PROCEDURE DIVISION
   a. Open mode for the file

An **internal file name** is a name by which the programmer can reference a file in the program. Also, it is the name by which the COBOL compiler can recognize the file. Line 000056 in the example assigns the internal name STUDENT-TEST-SCORES-FILE to our file. It is by this name that any other statement in the program can reference the file.

An **external file name** is also needed for the actual file. The internal name is valid only within a program. Files, however, are entities that are external to the program. The COBOL compiler has to associate a file addressed in the program by its internal name with an actual file that has an external name. External file names (also known as implementor names) are user-defined; however, for certain computer systems they may have to be rather cryptic, such as UT-S-TRANS. In the example above, the line

```
000056          SELECT STUDENT-TEST-SCORES-FILE ASSIGN TO INFILE
```

associates the external name INFILE with the file STUDENT-TEST-SCORES-FILE. The external name INFILE is used nowhere else in the rest of the program. It is used, however, in the JCL statements required to link this file to a physical file.

The file organization technique for the file should also be specified. Certain file organization techniques are built into the COBOL language. For example, COBOL is designed to recognize the sequential organization. All we have to do is to specify "sequential" for a file. We do not have to tell the system how a sequential file is organized and how it can be accessed. Above, the organization of the STUDENT-TEST-SCORES-FILE is declared to be SEQUENTIAL in line 000057.

We must let the compiler know about the file access technique to be used in the program for a file. This information is necessary because some files can be accessed in more than one way. For sequential files, there is only one access mode, and that is sequential. Line 000058 in the example makes it explicit through the ACCESS MODE IS SEQUENTIAL clause.

Using the FD blocks in the DATA DIVISION, we must assign a record name to the records of the file. Line 000067 names the record for our file as STUDENT-TEST-SCORES-RECORD. We must also specify the record length. Line 000068 specifies this as 80 characters for the STUDENT-TEST-SCORES-RECORD.

Next, we must provide a complete record structure description. Lines 000069 through 000081 are the record structure description for the STUDENT-TEST-SCORES-RECORD. This includes declarations for the data fields in the record structure. We will discuss record structure declaration in the section devoted to the DATA DIVISION.

Some optional information about the file may also be declared. For example, line 000066 is the clause LABEL RECORDS ARE STANDARD, which requests the operating system to create and maintain label records for the file.

In an OPEN statement in the PROCEDURE DIVISION, we must state the open mode for the file. **Open mode** declares whether the file will be used as an input file, an output file, or both in the program. The OPEN statement in line 000188 defines the STUDENT-TEST-RECORDS-FILE as an input file; this open mode prepares the file for input, allowing the program to read records from it.

> ### Some Important Rules About the SELECT Statement
> 1. There must be one SELECT statement for every COBOL file that a program uses.
> 2. COBOL supports three types of file organization techniques: SEQUENTIAL, INDEXED, and RELATIVE. The default is SEQUENTIAL; in other words, if file organization is not specified, the system assumes that it is sequential.
> 3. The file ACCESS MODE for SEQUENTIAL files may be only SEQUENTIAL. For INDEXED and RELATIVE files, it may be SEQUENTIAL, RANDOM, or DYNAMIC (meaning both SEQUENTIAL and RANDOM). If an ACCESS MODE clause is not explicitly included in the SELECT statement, the COBOL compiler assumes SEQUENTIAL.

The following is a full example of an ENVIRONMENT DIVISION.

```
ENVIRONMENT DIVISION.
CONFIGURATION SECTION.
SOURCE-COMPUTER. UNIVERSITY-MAINFRAME.
OBJECT-COMPUTER. UNIVERSITY-MAINFRAME.
INPUT-OUTPUT SECTION.
FILE-CONTROL.
    SELECT STUDENT-TEST-SCORES-FILE
            ASSIGN TO INFILE
            ORGANIZATION IS SEQUENTIAL
            ACCESS MODE  IS SEQUENTIAL.

    SELECT SUMMARY-GRADES-REPORT
            ASSIGN TO OUTFILE.
```

REVIEW QUESTIONS

1. The IDENTIFICATION DIVISION identifies a program for the compiler and provides some in-program documentation. (T or F)
2. Of the six paragraphs that can be written into the IDENTIFICATION DIVISION, only _____ is required.
3. The DATE-COMPILED paragraph should be completed by the programmer by typing the date of program compilation. (T or F)
4. The ENVIRONMENT DIVISION consists of two sections: _____ and _____ .
5. If we specify the wrong computer system in the SOURCE-COMPUTER and OBJECT-COMPUTER paragraphs of the CONFIGURATION SECTION, the compiler will generate compilation error diagnostics. (T or F)
6. The SELECT statement is found in the _____ paragraph of the INPUT-OUTPUT SECTION.
7. A file is a named and _____ collection of similar _____ .
8. Data elements in a record structure are not necessarily related to one another. (T or F)
9. Files are normally stored in auxiliary storage because the main memory is volatile and its capacity is limited. (T or F)
10. If records in a file are stored one after another, such a file is _____ organized.

11. A file in a COBOL program can be described completely in a SELECT statement. (T or F)
12. Which of the following about the SELECT statement is incorrect?
    a. The SELECT statement is used to assign an internal and an external name to a file.
    b. The organization of a file is stated in its SELECT statement.
    c. The record structure description is made within a SELECT statement.
    d. There is only one SELECT statement for each file.
13. The record name, record length, and record structure descriptions for a file are provided in the _____ block of the _____ .
14. The open mode for a file tells the compiler whether or not it will be accessed sequentially, and is written as part of the SELECT statement. (T or F)

Answers: 1. T; 2. PROGRAM-ID; 3. F; 4. CONFIGURATION, INPUT-OUTPUT; 5. F; 6. FILE-CONTROL; 7. structured, records; 8. F; 9. T; 10. sequentially; 11. F; 12. c; 13. FD, DATA DIVISION; 14. F.

DATA DIVISION

The third division of a COBOL program is the DATA DIVISION. Here, all program data including input-output variables, intermediate variables, and data structures are defined. The DATA DIVISION for most COBOL programs includes two sections: FILE SECTION and WORKING-STORAGE SECTION. In the FILE SECTION all variables and data structures associated with input and output files are defined. The WORKING-STORAGE SECTION is used for the specification of all other program variables and data structures.

In addition to these two, three other special sections may be included in the DATA DIVISION. One is the LINKAGE SECTION, which is used in COBOL external subprograms to define data that are passed between a calling program and the subprogram (it is discussed in detail in Chapter 7). Another is the REPORT SECTION, used together with a special language feature, the report writer (see Appendix D). Finally, the COMMUNICATION SECTION contains messages for communicating with communication devices. Discussion of the COMMUNICATION SECTION is beyond the scope of this book.

Here, we concentrate on the two common sections of the DATA DIVISION: FILE and WORKING-STORAGE. Before we get to these, however, it is necessary to cover the fundamentals of data definition in COBOL.

Data Types and PICTURE Specifications

COBOL supports three types of data: numeric, alphabetic, and alphanumeric.

The type and field length for a data item are defined in an associated PICTURE clause. A PICTURE clause consists of the key word PICTURE (or PIC) followed by a PICTURE specification. A PICTURE specification indicates the data type, field length, and whether or not it is edited. The data type designation characters are

1. 9, denoting numeric data
2. A, for alphabetic data
3. X, denoting alphanumeric data

The field length is indicated by successive repetition of picture characters or by an unsigned nonzero integer constant enclosed in parentheses after the picture character. Some examples follow.

Picture	Field Type	Length
PIC 999	Numeric computational	3
PIC 9(6)	Numeric computational	6
PIC AAAA	Alphabetic	4
PIC X(15)	Alphanumeric	15

There are four classes of PICTURE characters for different fields:

1. Unedited field definition characters
2. Special characters for unedited numeric fields
3. Numeric field edit characters
4. Alphanumeric field edit characters

The following table shows the PICTURE character types in COBOL. We will discuss them later in detail.

PIC Character Class	Symbol	Function
Unedited Field	9	Basic numeric field specification
Definition	A	Alphabetic field specification
Characters	X	Alphanumeric field specification
Special Characters for	V	Assumed decimal point
Unedited Numeric	P	Decimal scaling
Fields	S	Arithmetic sign inclusion
Numeric Field Edit	.	Decimal point insertion
Characters	,	Comma insertion
	+	Plus sign insertion
	−	Minus sign insertion
	0	Zero insertion
	B	Blank insertion
	/	Stroke insertion
	$	Dollar sign insertion
	Z	Zero suppression
	DB, CR	Debit and credit insertion
	*	Asterisk insertion (check protection)
Alphanumeric Field	B	Blank insertion
Edit Characters	0	Zero insertion
	/	Stroke insertion

Numeric Fields. For numeric fields, the identifying picture character is 9. The fields may be computational or edited. Computational numeric fields may be used for arithmetic operations, whereas it is illegal to perform arithmetic on edited numeric fields. Edited fields, numeric or otherwise, are good only for character string processing and output.

> ## Summary of Rules for Computational Fields
>
> 1. A computational numeric field is specified with a PICTURE clause containing only suitable combinations of 9, V, P, and S PICTURE characters. If any other PICTURE character is included in the PICTURE clause, the field becomes noncomputational.
> 2. A computational numeric field may store only decimal digit values in each byte of the allocated memory location.
> 3. Numeric values are stored right-justified in a memory location. They may be padded on the left with zeros, but not with blanks.
> 4. The location of the decimal point in the value for a real number must be indicated by a single V in the PICTURE clause; V identifies an assumed decimal point location and does not add to the field length.
> 5. An input data field for a numeric computational variable may contain only decimal digit values, no special characters or blanks.
> 6. To store negative numeric value, we use the S PICTURE character.
> 7. When storing very large or very small numbers, in order to avoid typing a lot of leading or trailing zeros, we use the P PICTURE character in a PICTURE specification.

A computational numeric field may contain only decimal digit values in each byte of the allocated memory location. Each digit is stored in a single byte. Attempting to store characters such as decimal point, comma, plus, and minus sign in any byte of the field will render it an edited field, and hence it will become noncomputational.

A numeric value is right-justified in its memory location. If the length of the memory location is larger than the actual length of the numeric value, it will be padded on the left with zeros. For example,

```
01  TOTAL-POINTS    PIC 999.
```

defines an integer computational field of length 3 for TOTAL-POINTS, and the procedure division statement

```
MOVE 35 TO TOTAL-POINTS.
```

will produce the following memory location:

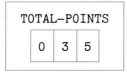

The effect of

```
MOVE -35 TO TOTAL-POINTS.
```

will be the same. TOTAL-POINTS will be assigned the value 035 and the negative sign will not be stored.

COBOL has no explicit data types for integer and real quantities. Unless the V PICTURE character is included in the PICTURE specification for the field, the value stored will be an integer. If a real number is to be stored for a variable, the location of the decimal point in the value must be indicated by a single V in the PICTURE clause; V marks an assumed decimal point location and does not add to the field length. For example:

```
01  EMP—SALARY       PIC 9(5)V99.
```

Here, EMP-SALARY is a field of length 7 for a real quantity. The statement

```
MOVE 9576.56 TO EMP-SALARY.
```

will produce the following memory cell:

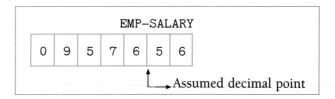

An input data field for a numeric computational variable may not contain any special characters and blanks. For example, the input field for EMP-SALARY above must be typed as 0957656. Note the absence of the decimal point and the necessity for leading zeros. COBOL will convert the data according to the governing PICTURE specification and will store it properly.

So far, we have been dealing with unsigned numeric values. What if we wish to include a sign together with the value? Enter the S PICTURE character. For example:

```
01 CUSTOMER—BALANCE      PIC S9(6)V99.
```

CUSTOMER-BALANCE is defined as a "signed" computational field of size 8. The first PICTURE character must be an S for a signed field, and there must be only one S in the specification. Like V, the S PICTURE character does not contribute to field length. Unless otherwise requested, the computer does not store the + or − sign in a separate byte. The sign is stored together with the rightmost digital value in the field. The value −25.78 for CUSTOMER-BALANCE will be stored as:

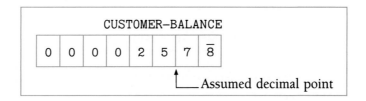

The SIGN clause enables the programmer to store the sign for a numeric field in a variety of different ways. The sign may be combined with the rightmost or the leftmost digital value in the field, or may be separately stored before the first digit or after the last. These possibilities and the use of the SIGN clause are illustrated below.

Data Definition	External Value	Internal Value
01 DATA-1 PIC S9(5)		
SIGN LEADING.	−678	0̄0678
01 DATA-2 PIC S9(5)		
SIGN LEADING SEPARATE.	−450	−00450
01 DATA-3 PIC S9(5)		
SIGN TRAILING.	+12	0001⁺2̄
01 DATA-4 PIC S9(5)		
SIGN TRAILING SEPARATE.	−67	00067−

Input of signed numeric values is awkward in COBOL. The way input data should be typed depends on the data definition for the variable. If sign is somehow to be input together with a value, the PICTURE clause must have an S character in it. Signed input values must be typed in their respective fields exactly as they would appear in their internal representations. For example, the external value of −678 for DATA-1 of the above examples must be typed as w0678, where w is the special character representing the digit 0 and a minus sign together. This special character depends on the internal character representation scheme used by a computer system; you should consult the technical manuals available at your computer installation to find out what it is.

When we are dealing with very large or very small numbers, we may have to type a lot of leading or trailing zeros. It is possible to avoid this by using the P PICTURE character in a PICTURE specification. It can be used only for numeric computational quantities if their PICTURE specification contains a V in it. Consider the following example.

```
01  LARGE-VALUES    PIC 99P(6)V.
    . . . . . . . . .
    . . . . . . . . .
    MOVE 25 TO LARGE-VALUES.
```

The MOVE statement will store the value 25000000∧ in LARGE-VALUES. The programmer does not have to type six zeros after the two-digit integer value. Here is another example.

```
01  SMALL-VALUES    PIC VP(4)9(3).
    . . . . . . . . .
    . . . . . . . . .
    MOVE 625 TO SMALL-VALUES.
```

The value assigned to SMALL-VALUES will be ∧0000625.

Nonnumeric Fields. Alphabetic fields are identified by the A picture character. They may contain only letters A through Z or blanks, no other special characters or digits.

Alphanumeric fields are symbolized by the X picture character. They are more general in that they may store character strings consisting of any characters on the terminal keyboard.

In A or X fields, values are left-justified. If the character string to be stored is shorter than the length of the field, the field is padded on the right by blanks. If the string is longer than the field, the rightmost excess characters are truncated.

For examples, consider the two variables:

```
01  A-FIELD    PIC A(6).
01  X-FIELD    PIC X(6).
```

The effect of different MOVE statements on the source fields are as follows.

	X-FIELD					
MOVE "BLACK" TO X-FIELD.	B	L	A	C	K	

	X-FIELD					
MOVE "BLACKGUARD" TO X-FIELD.	B	L	A	C	K	G

	X-FIELD					
MOVE "12*" TO X-FIELD.	1	2	*			

	A-FIELD					
MOVE "HARA" TO A-FIELD.	H	A	R	A		

MOVE "O'HARA" TO A-FIELD. Will result in an execution error because ' is not alphabetic.

MOVE "1234" TO A-FIELD. Will produce an execution error because the source string contains numeric digits.

In COBOL it is also possible to right-justify a character string in its receiving field. For this we must include a JUSTIFIED RIGHT clause in the definition of the character data. For example:

```
01  RESIDENCE-CITY  PIC X(10)  JUSTIFIED RIGHT.
    . . . . . . . . . .
    . . . . . . . . . .
    MOVE "AKRON" TO RESIDENCE-CITY.
```

The value "AKRON" will be right-justified in RESIDENCE-CITY, as shown below.

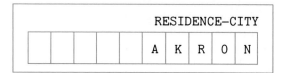

Defining Variables

Every program variable must be fully defined in the DATA DIVISION. Implicit type and length specifications are not permitted in COBOL. In other words, if an explicit definition is not provided by the programmer in the DATA DIVISION, no built-in conventions can be used to specify type and length of program variables. If variable definitions are missing, the compiler produces error messages stating that certain variables are undefined, and halts the compilation process. All input-output variables, those for which values are read, written, or both, must be defined in the FILE SECTION. All other program variables are defined in the WORKING-STORAGE SECTION.

A program variable may be a data item or a COBOL data structure.

> A **data item** is a symbolic name for which a single value is stored in the computer's memory.

For a data item, complete variable definition consists of the following minimal required specifications:

1. A variable name (also called an identifier)
2. Type of variable
3. Size of memory cell to accommodate a value for it

There are some additional optional specifications:

1. An initial value to be stored in the memory cell at compile time
2. A reference to another variable that shares the same memory cell with it
3. Internal representation to be used for the data item

As an example, consider the following.

```
01 CREDIT-RATING        PIC 9   VALUE 1.

01 CUSTOMER-RELIABILITY PIC 9   REDEFINES CREDIT-RATING.
```

The first statement allocates a one-byte memory location for the variable named CREDIT-RATING, and stores a value of 1 in it while the program is being compiled. The content of CREDIT-RATING may be changed to some other value later in the program. The second statement defines another program variable, CUSTOMER-RELIABILITY, again a one-byte numeric field. Because of the REDEFINES clause, however, both CUSTOMER-RELIABILITY and CREDIT-RATING share the same memory cell and will have the same initial value of 1. The REDEFINES feature is discussed later in this section.

The internal representation used for a data item is specified through a USAGE clause. There are five USAGE modes:

1. DISPLAY
2. COMPUTATIONAL (or COMP)
3. BINARY
4. PACKED-DECIMAL
5. INDEX

Below are some example data specifications with USAGE clauses.

```
WORKING-STORAGE SECTION.
. . . . . . . . . . . .
    01   CUSTOMER-NAME    PICTURE X(30)   USAGE IS DISPLAY.
    01   CUSTOMER-NUMBER  PICTURE 999     USAGE IS DISPLAY.
    01   CURRENT-BALANCE  PIC 9(8)V99     USAGE IS COMPUTATIONAL.
    01   INTEREST-EARNED  PIC 9(4)V99     USAGE IS BINARY.
    01   CHECKS-RETURNED  PIC 999         USAGE IS PACKED-DECIMAL.
```

In the DISPLAY mode, data are stored in character form. This mode can be specified for alphabetic, alphanumeric, or numeric data items. Each character in an alphanumeric or alphabetic field and each digit in a numeric field is stored in one byte of the main memory. In the examples above, CUSTOMER-NAME is a field of length 30 that can store a maximum of 30 characters using one byte for each character. On the other hand, CUSTOMER-NUMBER is a three-byte integer field, and it can store one digit in each byte.

DISPLAY is the default mode in COBOL for alphanumeric fields. If no usage mode is specified, DISPLAY is assumed. Therefore,

```
    01   CUSTOMER-NAME    PICTURE X(30)   USAGE IS DISPLAY.
```

is equivalent to

```
    01   CUSTOMER-NAME    PICTURE X(30).
```

The remaining usage modes, COMPUTATIONAL, BINARY, and PACKED-DECIMAL are only for numeric fields. In the COMPUTATIONAL and BINARY modes, data are stored in some binary forms; in the PACKED-DECIMAL mode they are stored in the packed-decimal form. The ways data are represented in binary and packed-decimal forms are dependent on the computer used. Therefore, we will not discuss them here. We should note, however, that these usage modes have two advantages: they speed up arithmetic operations on numeric data fields, and they cause data to require less internal storage compared to data in the DISPLAY mode.

Computational speed and internal memory capacity were important considerations for the computer systems in the 1960s. Since they are no longer major factors in today's computer systems, these usage modes have lost their significance. Their use leads to some unnecessary complications and is not recommended in business programming.

The INDEX mode is discussed later in Chapter 8, in conjunction with the COBOL SEARCH feature.

Defining Structures

In the DATA DIVISION, in addition to data items, we also define COBOL data structures.

> A **data structure** is a model that is used to represent data elements and one or more relationships existing among them.

A large number of data structures can be used in practical applications to achieve better and more efficient program design. We will concentrate on data structures and discuss them extensively throughout the remainder of the book. Here, we provide a first exposure to them within the context of the COBOL language, and introduce the simplest one that the language supports. This data structure is sometimes called, perhaps rather misleadingly, the COBOL data structure.

> The **COBOL data structure** is an extension of the concept of group items. It is a model that represents data elements (elementary data items and/or substructures) and some relationships existing among them. These relationships are the linear adjacency and superordinate and subordinate relationships.

> A **group item** consists of subordinate elementary data items. It shows not only the data items, but also the adjacency relationship existing among them.

A group item provides the programmer with the ability to address all of its contents collectively. Here is an example.

```
01   CUSTOMER-DATA.
     05   CUSTOMER-ACCOUNT-NUMBER   PIC 9(5).
     05   CUSTOMER-NAME             PIC X(10).
     05   CREDIT-RATING             PIC 9.
```

Note that this definition includes minimum specifications (i.e., name, type, length) for three data items. It defines them as subordinate to CUSTOMER-DATA. It also reflects a linear adjacency relationship among the items (i.e., the field CUSTOMER-ACCOUNT-NUMBER is next to CUSTOMER-NAME, etc.). In a program using this structure, it is possible to reference the three data items individually or all together using the common group name, CUSTOMER-DATA. The following figure shows the conceptual storage structure for CUSTOMER-DATA.

CUSTOMER-DATA		
CUSTOMER-ACCOUNT-NUMBER	CUSTOMER-NAME	CREDIT-RATING

A COBOL data structure is obtained by combining several group items and data items into a more complex structure. In it, in addition to the linear adjacency relationship, a logical superordinate or subordinate relationship is reflected. This relationship defines a hierarchy among the data elements or group items, or both. The following is an example of a COBOL data structure.

```
01  EMPLOYEE-PROFILE.
    05  EMPLOYEE-IDENTIFICATION.
        10  IDNUMBER              PIC 9(9).
        10  EMPLOYEE-NAME.
            15  LAST-NAME         PIC X(15).
            15  FIRST-NAME        PIC X(15).
    05  JOB-IDENTIFICATION.
        10  JOB-CODE             PIC X(3).
        10  JOB-DESCRIPTION      PIC X(20).
        10  COMPANY-DEPARTMENT   PIC X(10).
        10  SALARY               PIC 9(6)V99.
    05  JOB-HISTORY-1.
        10  PREVIOUS-JOB-CODE-1  PIC X(3).
        10  PREVIOUS-SALARY-1    PIC 9(6)V99.
    05  JOB-HISTORY-2.
        10  PREVIOUS-JOB-CODE-2  PIC X(3).
        10  PREVIOUS-SALARY-2    PIC 9(6)V99.
```

Notice the hierarchical structure of data. This hierarchy is achieved by level numbers. In general, line indentation is not a syntactical requirement. It merely emphasizes the hierarchy and gives the COBOL code visual impact.

We observe the following about the COBOL data structure.

1. An entry with a larger level number is subordinate to, and hence a part of, the nearest preceding entry with a smaller level number. For example, the elementary data item IDNUMBER is subordinate to the group item EMPLOYEE-IDENTIFICATION.
2. Entries with the same level numbers within a group or subgroup are independent of each other and are at the same level of hierarchy.
3. Entries that have a PICTURE clause are elementary data items.
4. Elementary data item names are used to reference individual cells, as in:

```
MOVE SALARY TO EDITED-SALARY.
```

Or, we can reference the four-item field JOB-IDENTIFICATION as in:

```
MOVE JOB-IDENTIFICATION TO OUT-JOB-IDENTIFICATION.
```

Syntax Rules for the COBOL Data Structure

1. The major structure name must have a level number of 01. All other subordinate items may be assigned any appropriate level number in the range 02–49.
2. Level numbers for subordinate entries do not have to be consecutive.
3. For a given subentry, the identifier used to name the entry may be followed by any number of permissible clauses, such as PICTURE, VALUE, REDEFINES, etc. Only one of each may be used for an identifier. The order in which these clauses are written is immaterial.
4. Only elementary data items may have PICTURE clauses.
5. The major structure name (level 01 entry) cannot have any clauses after it.
6. An entry may extend over any number of COBOL lines, but each one must be concluded with a period.

REVIEW QUESTIONS

1. In the DATA DIVISION, all program variables and data structures are defined. (T or F)
2. The DATA DIVISION may contain up to _____ sections. The most commonly used sections are _____ and _____ .
3. The only data types COBOL supports are decimal numeric, alphabetic, and alphanumeric. (T or F)
4. A PICTURE specification for a field indicates its data type, field length, and whether or not it is edited. (T or F)
5. Which of the following statements about the COBOL PICTURE characters is correct?
   a. 9 PICTURE character is used for numeric fields.
   b. X is used for alphanumeric fields.
   c. S is used for arithmetic sign inclusion.
   d. V is used to denote an assumed decimal point.
   e. All of the above are correct.
6. COBOL has special data type codes that can be used to differentiate between integer and real quantities. (T or F)
7. Alphabetic and alphanumeric data are left-justified in their allocated field, and the clause JUSTIFIED RIGHT can be used to change this. (T or F)
8. A data item is a _____ name for which _____ value can be stored in the computer's memory.
9. Models that are used to represent data elements and relationships that exist among them are called _____ .
10. The COBOL data structure is an extension of the concept of group items. (T or F)

11. Which of the following statements about the COBOL data structure is incorrect?
    a. Level numbers for subordinate entries do not have to be consecutive.
    b. Only elementary data items in a COBOL data structure may have associated PICTURE clauses.
    c. The major structure name may have a PICTURE clause associated with it.
    d. Each entry may extend over any number of COBOL lines, but each must be concluded with a period.

Answers: 1. T; 2. 5, FILE, WORKING-STORAGE; 3. T; 4. T; 5. e; 6. F; 7. T; 8. symbolic, a single; 9. data structures; 10. T; 11. c.

The FILE SECTION

The FILE SECTION is the first section of the DATA DIVISION in a COBOL program. Its purpose is to define input and output files used by the program. Each file requires an FD (file description) block in the FILE SECTION. An FD block contains

1. An internal name for the file, which must be the same as the one in the corresponding SELECT statement
2. Label record specification for the file
3. A unique name for the record of the file
4. Block length, if the file is blocked
5. Record length in characters
6. A COBOL data structure for the record of the file

As far as the contents of FD blocks are concerned, we know about all but label records and block lengths.

A **label record** is a special record that the operating system generates and maintains for a file, if requested by the user. The file must be a tape or a disk file to have label records. Label records contain information that is useful in identifying and maintaining files, such as the number of records stored, until what date they are protected, and so on. In storing records in auxiliary storage, computers insert markers between any two consecutive records. The amount of storage enclosed by two such markers is known as a **physical record**, or a **block**. If for a file the record size and content are the same as those of the corresponding physical records, such a file is called **unblocked**. If, on the other hand, two or more records are brought together and stored as a single physical record, the file is said to be **blocked**. More can be found on label records and blocking in Chapter 10.

Let us take a look at an example of a complete COBOL file definition.

```
. . . . . . . . . . . . . . . . . . . .
ENVIRONMENT DIVISION.
. . . . . . . . . . . . . . . . . . . .
INPUT-OUTPUT SECTION.
FILE-CONTROL.
     SELECT EMPLOYEE-FILE ASSIGN TO INFILE
         ORGANIZATION IS SEQUENTIAL
         ACCESS MODE IS SEQUENTIAL.
```

```
. . . . . . . . . . . . . . . . . .
DATA DIVISION.
FILE SECTION.
FD    EMPLOYEE-FILE
      LABEL RECORDS ARE STANDARD
      BLOCK CONTAINS 3 RECORDS
      RECORD CONTAINS 102 CHARACTERS
      DATA RECORD IS EMPLOYEE-PROFILE.

01    EMPLOYEE-PROFILE.
      05   EMPLOYEE-IDENTIFICATION.
           10   IDNUMBER                PIC 9(9).
           10   EMPLOYEE-NAME.
                15   LAST-NAME          PIC X(15).
                15   FIRST-NAME         PIC X(15).
      05   JOB-IDENTIFICATION.
           10   JOB-CODE                PIC X(3).
           10   JOB-DESCRIPTION         PIC X(20).
           10   COMPANY-DEPARTMENT      PIC X(10).
           10   SALARY                  PIC 9(6)V99.
      05   JOB-HISTORY-1.
           10   PREVIOUS-JOB-CODE-1     PIC X(3).
           10   PREVIOUS-SALARY-1       PIC 9(6)V99.
      05   JOB-HISTORY-2.
           10   PREVIOUS-JOB-CODE-2     PIC X(3).
           10   PREVIOUS-SALARY-2       PIC 9(6)V99.
. . . . . . . . . . . . . . . . . .
```

In this example the SELECT statement identifies this file as a sequentially organized and hence sequentially accessible file. Its internal name is EMPLOYEE-FILE. Whenever we refer to this file in the program, we must use its internal name. The external name, INFILE, is for the operating system's use.

The corresponding FD block for EMPLOYEE-FILE specifies the following.

1. LABEL RECORDS ARE STANDARD indicates that the file should include label records that are automatically created and maintained by the operating system. This implies that the file is either a tape or disk file.
2. The clause BLOCK CONTAINS 3 RECORDS specifies that the records are to be blocked and that each block will contain three records. This also means that the file is either a tape or a disk file.
3. RECORD CONTAINS 102 CHARACTERS shows that the record length is 102 characters.
4. DATA RECORD IS EMPLOYEE-PROFILE assigns the name EMPLOYEE-PROFILE to the record of this file.
5. The COBOL data structure called EMPLOYEE-PROFILE defines the file's record structure. It also determines the record length as the sum of field lengths for all elementary data items in the structure EMPLOYEE-PROFILE. This length is 102 characters. The result must match what is declared to be the record length in the RECORD CONTAINS clause.

Multiple Record Files. So far we have seen that a COBOL file, regardless of its organization, must be assigned a name and must have a named and structured record. COBOL also permits more than one record structure specified for a given file. As an example, consider the following multiple-record file.

```
FD     STUDENT-FILE
       LABEL RECORDS ARE OMITTED
       DATA RECORDS ARE STUDENT-IDENTIFICATION, ENROLLMENT.

01     STUDENT-IDENTIFICATION.
       05     STUDENT-NUMBER      PIC 9(4).
       05     FILLER              PIC XX.
       05     RECORD-TYPE         PIC X.
       05     FILLER              PIC XX.
       05     STUDENT-NAME        PIC X(15).
       05     FILLER              PIC XX.
       05     STUDENT-MAJOR       PIC X(10).
       05     FILLER              PIC XX.
       05     STUDENT-YEAR        PIC 9.
       05     FILLER              PIC X(41).

01     ENROLLMENT.
       05     STUDENT-NUMBER      PIC 9(4).
       05     FILLER              PIC XX.
       05     RECORD-TYPE         PIC X.
       05     FILLER              PIC XX.
       05     ACADEMIC-YEAR       PIC 99.
       05     FILLER              PIC XX.
       05     SEMESTER            PIC 9.
       05     FILLER              PIC XX.
       05     COURSE-CODE         PIC X(7).
       05     FILLER              PIC XX.
       05     GRADE               PIC X.
       05     FILLER              PIC X(54).
```

An instance of this file (i.e., records in the file at a given time) may be

```
1000   I   JOHN BLACKWELL     COMP. SCI.   2
1000   E   84   1   CS  221   A
1000   E   84   1   CS  238   B
1000   E   84   1   MTH 255   A
2000   I   MARY ROBINS        ACCOUNTING   3
2000   E   84   1   ACT 320   A
2000   E   84   1   MGT 216   C
```

The file contains two record structures, called STUDENT-IDENTIFICATION and ENROLLMENT, respectively. They have some common elements; in this case, STUDENT-NUMBER and RECORD-TYPE. RECORD-TYPE is a variable used to differentiate between the two record types. If RECORD-TYPE contains "I", the record is a STUDENT-IDENTIFICATION record; if it contains "E", it is an ENROLLMENT record.

Output of multiple-record files does not pose a special problem in COBOL because the WRITE verb, which is used for file output, references the file using its record name. While reading a multiple-record file, however, we have to be more careful. The COBOL READ verb for file input uses file name and not a record name to reference a file record. Let us assume that STUDENT-FILE is sequentially organized. An input statement such as

```
READ STUDENT-FILE
     AT END MOVE "DONE" TO FILE-INPUT.
```

may fill either the STUDENT-IDENTIFICATION or the ENROLLMENT record structure. In this case, a field such as RECORD-TYPE is necessary to determine what type of record has just been input. The code given below is proper and correct.

```
. . . . . . . . . . . . . . . . . . .
READ STUDENT-FILE
     AT END MOVE "DONE" TO FILE-INPUT.

IF RECORD-TYPE OF STUDENT-IDENTIFICATION = "I"
     PERFORM PROCESS-MAIN-STU-INFORMATION
ELSE
     PERFORM ENROLLMENT-INFORMATION.
. . . . . . . . . . . . . . . . . . .
```

On the other hand, the following code, based on the same multiple-record file, may result in an execution error, in case the record just read is not an enrollment record.

```
. . . . . . . . . . . . . . . . . . . . . . . .
 READ STUDENT-FILE
      AT END MOVE "DONE" TO FILE-INPUT.

ADD 1 TO SEMESTER.
. . . . . . . . . . . . . . . . . . . . . . . .
```

Programs using single record files are usually simpler and easier to understand. As a multiple-record file can easily be replaced by two or more single-record files, it is a better practice to use the latter whenever possible.

The WORKING-STORAGE SECTION

The second section in the DATA DIVISION of a COBOL program is WORKING-STORAGE SECTION. This is where all program variables that do not directly participate in file input or output are defined.

Data definition conventions for WORKING-STORAGE variables are exactly the same as those discussed for the FILE SECTION entities. The only exception is that the FDs required for files in the FILE SECTION do not have counterparts in the WORKING-STORAGE SECTION.

Additional Rules for the WORKING-STORAGE SECTION

1. The section header, WORKING-STORAGE SECTION, followed by a period, is required.
2. Independent elementary data items may be defined in two different ways: either as level 01 entries or as level 77 entries, with PICTURE clauses.

For example, the following definitions are equivalent.

```
01    DEPENDENT-VAR   PIC 999.

77    DEPENDENT-VAR   PIC 999.
```

Level 77 specifications for independent data items are generally considered confusing. Level 01 is preferred.

Field Editing

Data as stored in the computer's memory, even after they are converted to an external and readable form, may still not be appropriate for a business report. For example, if we want a printout for one record of a file with the following record structure

```
. . . . . . . . . .
  01  EMPLOYEE-REPORT.
        05    EMPLOYEE-NAME        PIC X(16).
        05    EMPLOYEE-JOB-TITLE   PIC X(10).
        05    HOURS-WORKED         PIC 999.
        05    NET-PAY              PIC 9(6)V99.
```

we may get a line such as

```
WILLIAM BLACKMANSUPERVISOR04500045675
```

whereas, it would be definitely more desirable to obtain something like:

EMPLOYEE NAME	JOB TITLE	HOURS	NET PAY
WILLIAM BLACKMAN	SUPERVISOR	45	$ 456.75

For the time being, let us forget about the column headers. We still would want to do two types of editing before we could have such a line printed.

1. Output record editing: insert blanks between fields to separate values from each other and thus enhance readability.
2. Field editing: suppress leading zeros in the numeric fields HOURS-WORKED and NET-PAY, and insert a leading dollar sign and a decimal point into the NET-PAY field value.

Output record editing can be accomplished in two different ways: by using blank FILLER separator fields between data fields, or by editing data fields to accomplish the same result.

First, let us use blank FILLER separator fields between data fields. We rewrite the above record structure for EMPLOYEE-REPORT as:

```
. . . . . . . . . .
   01  EMPLOYEE-REPORT.
       05  EMPLOYEE-NAME        PIC X(16).
       05  FILLER               PIC X(3)    VALUE SPACES.
       05  EMPLOYEE-JOB-TITLE   PIC X(10).
       05  FILLER               PIC X(4)    VALUE SPACES.
       05  HOURS-WORKED         PIC 999.
       05  FILLER               PIC X(5)    VALUE SPACES.
       05  NET-PAY              PIC 9(6)V99.
```

FILLER is a COBOL reserved word that is used to specify a field without a symbolic address, or a name. The VALUE clause can be used to initialize this field to an appropriate value. The FILLER field between EMPLOYEE-NAME and EMPLOYEE-JOB-TITLE above defines an unaddressable blank field of three bytes, thereby effectively inserting three blanks between them.

COBOL 85   As FILLER is a field with no name, the ANS COBOL 85 version allows such a field to be defined without using this reserved word. The above example can be written in COBOL 85 as:

```
. . . . . . . . . .
01  EMPLOYEE-REPORT.
    05  EMPLOYEE-NAME        PIC X(16).
    05                       PIC X(3)    VALUE SPACES.
    05  EMPLOYEE-JOB-TITLE   PIC X(10).
    05                       PIC X(4)    VALUE SPACES.
    05  HOURS-WORKED         PIC 999.
    05                       PIC X(5)    VALUE SPACES.
    05  NET-PAY              PIC 9(6)V99.
```

Now let us edit data fields to do the same as what we have done above. We can rewrite the record structure as:

```
. . . . . . . . . .
01  EMPLOYEE-REPORT.
    05  EMPLOYEE-NAME        PIC X(16)B(3).
    05  EMPLOYEE-JOB-TITLE   PIC X(10)B(4).
    05  HOURS-WORKED         PIC 999B(5).
    05  NET-PAY              PIC 9(6)V99.
```

Here, B is a special PICTURE character that inserts blanks in a data field. Either method will produce the following line:

EMPLOYEE NAME	JOB TITLE	HOURS	NET PAY
WILLIAM BLACKMAN	SUPERVISOR	045	00045675

Our editing task, however, is not finished. We must also properly edit the two numeric fields, HOURS-WORKED and NET-PAY. Let us write these two fields in the EMPLOYEE-REPORT as:

```
 . . . . . . . . . .
 01   EMPLOYEE-REPORT.
        05   EMPLOYEE-NAME        PIC X(16)B(3).
        05   EMPLOYEE-JOB-TITLE   PIC X(10)B(4).
        05   HOURS-WORKED         PIC ZZ9B(5).
        05   NET-PAY              PIC $ZZZ999.99.
```

Now we get a more acceptable record printout.

EMPLOYEE NAME	JOB TITLE	HOURS	NET PAY
WILLIAM BLACKMAN	SUPERVISOR	45	$ 456.75

In a program, for most edited fields, there probably are corresponding unedited source fields, whose contents are moved into the edited fields prior to printing. Arithmetic operations cannot be performed on an edited numeric field. After editing, it should be used either for output, or as a character string field.

The characters Z, $, and . in the PICTURE specifications for HOURS-WORKED and NET-PAY are special **edit** characters. COBOL has many field edit characters. From a functional point of view, they can be classified as zero suppression PICTURE characters or insertion PICTURE characters.

Zero Suppression. The zero suppression PICTURE character is Z. It applies to numeric fields and its purpose is to suppress the first or all leading zeros, replacing them by blanks in the field. One or more consecutive Zs may be included in a PICTURE specification, starting with the leftmost 9 and replacing one or more 9s from left to right.

If only one Z is used in the PICTURE clause in place of the leftmost 9 in the specification, only one digit in that field will be suppressed, provided it is zero. Two or more Zs in lieu of leftmost 9s (called floated Z) will suppress all leading zeros until the first nonzero digit or the decimal point is encountered. If Zs have been designated for all positions of the field and the value in the field is zero, the entire field is replaced by blanks. For example:

Field Definition	Value	Storage Representation
01 NUM-VALUE PIC Z999.	6500	6500
01 NUM-VALUE PIC Z999.	0850	b850
01 NUM-VALUE PIC Z999.	0095	b095
01 NUM-VALUE PIC ZZ99.	0095	bb95
01 NUM-VALUE PIC ZZZZ.	0095	bb95
01 NUM-VALUE PIC ZZZZ.	0000	bbbb

Note: b represents a blank.

Character Insertion. The symbols, functions and rules concerning the PIC-TURE insertion characters are summarized in the following table.

Function	Symbol	Where/How Many Inserted?	Type of Source Field	Can Be Floated?
Decimal Point Insertion	.	Between whole and fraction/only one	9	No
Comma Insertion	,	Anywhere/one or more	9	No
Plus Sign Insertion	+	Leftmost or rightmost/one or more	9	Yes
Minus Sign Insertion	–	Leftmost or rightmost/one or more	9	Yes
Zero Insertion	0	Anywhere/one or more	9, A, X	No
Blank Insertion	B	Anywhere/one or more	9, A, X	No
Stroke Insertion	/	Anywhere/one or more	9, A, X	No
Dollar Sign Insertion	$	Left of first significant digit or leftmost/one or more	9	Yes
Debit and Credit Insertion	DB, CR	Rightmost/only one	9	No
Asterisk Insertion	*	Leftmost after $ insertion/one or more	9	Yes

As a general rule, the insertion characters may appear in combinations among themselves or with other picture characters discussed previously (P, V, Z, and S).

Rules for Decimal Point and Comma Insertion Characters

1. These characters are only for numeric edited fields.
2. There can be only one decimal point insertion character in a PICTURE clause; however, a field may contain more than one comma insertion character.
3. After data conversion, the V of the unedited field will be aligned with the period of the edited field.
4. A field cannot contain both a period and a V PICTURE character.
5. These characters, unlike V, contribute to the length of the edited field.

Examples of decimal point and comma insertion characters are as follows.

Source Picture	Source Value	Target Picture	Target Value
PIC 9(6)V99	05575025	ZZZ,999.99	b55,750.25
PIC 9(6)V99	00002550	ZZZ,999.99	bbbbb25.50
PIC 9(6)V99	00000000	ZZZ,999.99	bbbbbbbbbb

Rules for Plus and Minus Sign Insertion Characters

1. These insertion characters are used for numeric fields only.
2. Both + and − signs may be inserted in the rightmost or the leftmost position of the PICTURE specification. Then the sign will appear to the right or the left of the numeric value.
3. The plus sign insertion character produces a + if the source field is unsigned or positively signed. It produces a − if the source value is negative.
4. The minus sign insertion character produces a blank if the source field is unsigned or contains a positive value. It produces a − if the source value is negative.
5. Plus and minus insertion characters may not exist together in the same PICTURE specification.
6. These characters may be floated to the right in a field starting with the leftmost position. In this case, if the field contains leading zeros, floated + or − will zero-suppress the field. It will place the sign immediately before the first nonzero significant digit in the field (see the second example below). If the field contains a zero value, floated + or − will result in a blank edited field (see the fourth and fifth examples below).
7. If + or − is used together with a floated dollar insertion character, + or − cannot be floated and must be used for insertion into the rightmost position of the field.

Examples of plus and minus sign insertion characters are as follows.

Source Picture	Source Value	Target Picture	Target Value
PIC 9(6)V99	00050000	+9(6).99	+000500.00
PIC 9(6)V99	00050000	++99999.99	bbb+500.00
PIC 9(6)V99	00050000	ZZZ,ZZZ.99+	bbbb500.00+
PIC 9(6)V99	00000000	++++,+++.++	bbbbbbbbbb
PIC 9(6)V99	00000000	----,---.--	bbbbbbbbbb
PIC S9999	+0700	+9999	+0700
PIC S9999	0700+	+9999	+0700
PIC S9999	0700−	+9999	−0700
PIC S9999	−0700	+9999	−0700
PIC S9999	+0700	−9999	b0700
PIC S9999	0700+	−9999	b0700
PIC S9999	0700−	−9999	−0700
PIC S9999	−0700	−9999	−0700
PIC S9999	−1700	9999−	1700−

Rules for Zero, Blank, and Stroke Insertion Characters

1. These insertion characters may be used for all field types.
2. They may be used alone, or in combination with other edit characters, for insertion at any point in the field, any number of times.

Examples of zero, blank, and stroke insertion characters are shown below.

Source Picture	Source Value	Target Picture	Target Value
PIC X(5)	ABCDE	X0XB(2)X/X(2)	A0BbbC/DE

Rules for Debit (DB) and Credit (CR) Insertion Characters

1. They are used only for numeric fields containing monetary values.
2. DB or CR should appear only to the right of the field.
3. If the numeric value in the field is positive, DB or CR will produce two blank positions at the right of the field. If the value is negative, DB or CR will follow the numeric value.

Both DB and CR are especially useful in accounting and related applications. Examples follow.

Source Picture	Source Value	Target Picture	Target Value
PIC S9(3)V99	+10075	9(3).99DB	100.75bb
PIC S9(3)V99	+10075	9(3).99CR	100.75bb
PIC S9(3)V99	−10075	9(3).99DB	100.75DB
PIC S9(3)V99	−10075	9(3).99CR	100.75CR

Rules for the Dollar Sign Insertion Character

1. The $ insertion character is for numeric edited fields.
2. It can be inserted once as the leftmost character in the field. If it appears more than once (i.e., floated $), it functions as a zero-suppression character. In this case, all leading zeros are replaced by blanks, and a dollar sign is inserted before the first significant digit.
3. If the dollar sign floats over the entire field and the field contains a zero value, only blanks will be stored in the edited field.

Examples of dollar sign insertion characters are shown here.

Source Picture	Source Value	Target Picture	Target Value
PIC 9(6)V99	00530000	$ZZZ,999.99	$bb5,300.00
PIC 9(6)V99	00035000	$$$9,999.99	bbbb$350.00
PIC 9(6)V99	00000000	$$$$,$$$.$$	bbbbbbbbbb

The asterisk insertion character is also known as a check-protect character. It is used to protect dollar amounts written on checks or other documents. It is essentially similar to the Z or $. Usually, it is floated after a single $ character until a . insertion character. All the leading zeros in the field after the dollar sign will then be replaced by asterisks. Examples of the asterisk insertion (check-protect) character are as follows.

Source Picture	Source Value	Target Picture	Target Value
PIC 9(3)V99	50050	$*****.99	$**500.50
PIC 9(5)V99	1500000	$**,***.99	$15,000.00

REVIEW QUESTIONS

1. The purpose of the FILE section is to define files and independent data items used in a program. (T or F)
2. In addition to an internal file name, record name, record length, and record description, an FD block for a file may contain a specification of _____ records and _____ .
3. The clause LABEL RECORDS ARE STANDARD implies that the file is either a tape or a disk file. (T or F)
4. In a multiple record file, all record structures should contain a common field that can be used to differentiate between different record types during processing. (T or F)
5. Output of multiple record files in COBOL does not present a special problem because the WRITE statement references a file using its _____ name.
6. In the WORKING-STORAGE section of the DATA division, all program variables and structures that do not participate in file input or output are defined. (T or F)
7. Output record editing to improve readability of output can be accomplished by inserting _____ separator fields between data fields, or by _____ data fields.
8. Which of the following statements concerning COBOL field edit characters is correct?
   a. 0 is used for zero suppression.
   b. Z is used for zero insertion.
   c. B is used for blank insertion.
   d. − is used for arithmetic manipulation of negative quantities.
9. If the period insertion character is used in a PICTURE clause, after data conversion, the V of the unedited field will be aligned with the . of the edited field. (T or F)
10. Zero, blank, and stroke insertion characters can be used for numeric, alphabetic, and alphanumeric fields. (T or F)

Answers: 1. F; 2. label, block length; 3. T; 4. T; 5. record; 6. T; 7. blank, editing; 8. c; 9. T; 10. T.

Condition Names

COBOL does not support an important data type that is available in many other programming languages: Boolean or logical data type. The language element that comes closest to a Boolean quantity in COBOL is a condition name.

> A **Boolean quantity** is one that may assume only a logical value of **true** or **false**.

Boolean quantities are used for decision making in computer programming. A computer language that supports the Boolean data type (some examples are Fortran, PL/I, and Pascal) permits the programmer to define variables as

Boolean and use them. In this case, the compiler allocates memory locations for them. Memory locations for Boolean variables may contain only true or false as values, and are, of course, individually addressable.

> A **condition name** in COBOL is a name assigned to a simple comparison condition (or predicate) that associates two numeric or nonnumeric quantities using the "equals" comparison operator.

A condition name is one of the many available condition types in COBOL. In general, conditions are used for decision-making or for iteration-control purposes in a program. An example of the equal-comparison condition is

```
STUDENT-YEAR IS EQUAL TO 1
```

Depending on the current value of the variable STUDENT-YEAR, the above condition may produce a value of true or false. If the value contained in STUDENT-YEAR is 1, the logical value computed for the condition is true; otherwise, it is false. Note, however, that this logical value is not stored in a memory location that is accessible by its symbolic name. It is used by the computer for decision-making purposes.

A properly defined condition name may be associated with an equal-comparison condition to improve the readability of a program. The DATA DIVISION entry for STUDENT-YEAR

```
01  STUDENT-YEAR    PIC 9.
```

may be expanded to include condition names as follows:

```
01    STUDENT-YEAR    PIC 9.
      88   FRESHMAN         VALUE 1.
      88   SOPHOMORE        VALUE 2.
      88   JUNIOR           VALUE 3.
      88   SENIOR           VALUE 4.
      88   GRADUATE         VALUE 5.
      88   ERROR-YEAR       VALUES 0, 6 THRU 9.
```

These definitions may be placed either in the FILE SECTION or the WORKING-STORAGE SECTION of the DATA DIVISION, depending on whether or not STUDENT-YEAR is part of a record structure. They define STUDENT-YEAR as a numeric one-byte field, and the identifiers FRESHMAN, SOPHOMORE, JUNIOR, SENIOR, GRADUATE, and ERROR-YEAR as condition names for the variable STUDENT-YEAR. Values of condition names for a given identifier are determined by the current value of that identifier. In this case, the value of STUDENT-YEAR is yet undefined, and so are the values of the associated condition names. If STUDENT-YEAR is set to, say 1, the condition name FRESHMAN becomes true, and all other condition names become false.

With these condition names associated with STUDENT-YEAR, the equal-comparison condition STUDENT-YEAR IS EQUAL TO 1 becomes the same as FRESHMAN, and STUDENT-YEAR IS EQUAL TO 4 will be equivalent to SENIOR. Therefore, an IF statement in the procedure division of the program, such as

```
IF STUDENT-YEAR IS EQUAL TO 1 ........
```

may be replaced by the more readable and self-documenting equivalent IF:

```
IF FRESHMAN .........
```

Note that the VALUE clause does not have the same implication in an 88 level entry as when it is used with the definition of an elementary data item. For example, in the definition

```
01   STUDENT-STATUS      PIC XX   VALUE "GR".
     88    GRADUATE               VALUE "GR".
     88    UNDERGRADUATE          VALUE "UG".
```

the clause VALUE "GR" belonging to STUDENT-STATUS initializes this variable to the value "GR" during program compilation. The clause VALUE "GR" corresponding to the condition name GRADUATE means that GRADUATE will assume a value of true if STUDENT-STATUS ever becomes "GR", otherwise it will be false. In this case, after the program is compiled and until STUDENT-STATUS is assigned another value, GRADUATE will be true and the other condition name, UNDERGRADUATE, will remain false.

Rules Governing the Use of Condition Names

1. Condition names must be defined as level 88 entries.
2. Condition names must be associated with elementary data items. They may not belong to a group item, or structure.
3. A condition name entry requires a VALUE clause and should end with a period.
4. Any FILE SECTION or WORKING-STORAGE SECTION elementary data item variable may be associated with condition names.

Multiple Data Names and Qualification

In general, all identifiers in a COBOL program must be unique. To avoid ambiguity, a program entity (i.e., paragraph, data structure, group item, variable, etc.) is not permitted to have more than one name. Similarly, each name is taken to represent only one entity.

Sometimes, however, it is desirable to make exceptions to this general rule.

1. We may want to assign two or more names to the same storage location. In other words, we may want to use the same storage location for two or more

program variables or structures. This enables us to keep storage overhead down. COBOL permits that through the use of the REDEFINES clause.

2. To avoid the need for extraneous identifiers for program entities of similar nature, we may want to use the same name for two or more program entities. In COBOL this is possible with the use of the RENAMES feature. We will discuss this later in the chapter.

If a COBOL entity is part of a hierarchical structure and is subordinate to another entity in the structure, it may be assigned a nonunique name provided it is qualified by the superordinate entity. That superordinate entity is a qualifier.

> A **qualifier** is defined as an entity name of a higher hierarchical level than the name of the entity it qualifies.

Two hierarchical structures are of interest to us here:

1. A sequence of paragraphs that make up a section
2. Elementary data items or substructures that make up a COBOL data structure

If the section-oriented approach is used in designing the PROCEDURE DIVISION, paragraphs are grouped within sections with unique names. This defines a hierarchical structure in which section names are superordinate. Suppose SUMMATION is the name of a paragraph included in a section called FINAL-PROCESSING. SUMMATION may be qualified as follows:

```
SUMMATION OF FINAL-PROCESSING
or
SUMMATION IN FINAL-PROCESSING
```

Provided the reference to the paragraph SUMMATION is qualified as shown, the paragraph name SUMMATION need not be unique. There may be another paragraph with the same name within the same program, but not within the same section.

As discussed before, substructures within a COBOL data structure together define a hierarchy. Consider the following two structures.

```
. . . . . . . . . . . . . . . . . . . . . . . . . .
01   SALES-DEPARTMENT.
     05   MANAGER              PIC X(20).
     05   NO-OF-EMPLOYEES      PIC 99.
. . . . . . . . . . . . . . . . . . . . . . . . . .
01   ACCOUNTING-DEPARTMENT.
     05   MANAGER              PIC X(20).
     05   NO-OF-EMPLOYEES      PIC 99.
. . . . . . . . . . . . . . . . . . . . . . . . . .
```

Both of these COBOL structures have two data items with the same names. As far as data definition is concerned, this is acceptable, but references to such items must use qualification to avoid ambiguity. Proper references in this case would be like:

```
MANAGER OF SALES DEPARTMENT

NO-OF-EMPLOYEES IN ACCOUNTING-DEPARTMENT
```

It should be noted that, with the right choice of descriptive identifier names, qualification adds to the readability of the code.

Summary of Rules for Qualification

1. If the same name is used for subordinate program entities, qualification is required.
2. Only subordinate program entities, such as paragraph names, subgroup names, and elementary data item names, may be qualified. The qualifiers are the superordinate entities (i.e., section names and superordinate structure names).

Unless it is deemed necessary to use qualifications in a program, we suggest that they be avoided, as they may lead to a code that is difficult to read.

Compile-Time Data Initialization

When we define a variable in the DATA DIVISION of our program, we know that the computer will allocate a memory location to it. Will it also assign an initial value to our program variable?

The answer depends on the design of the COBOL compiler that is being used. Some versions of the COBOL compiler may initialize all numeric variables to zero and all nonnumeric variables to blanks. Others will not do this and leave the values undefined. It is always safer to assume that data initialization is not handled by the compiler and to assign initial values to program variables. Data may be initialized in two ways in a program, at run time and at compile time.

We can initialize variables at run time using MOVE or COMPUTE statements. For example:

```
MOVE 1 TO FIRST-SUBSCRIPT.
or
COMPUTE FIRST-SUBSCRIPT = 1.
```

Here, the MOVE statement duplicates the value 1 in the target field FIRST-SUBSCRIPT. The COMPUTE statement takes the constant value of 1 to the right of the equal sign and stores it in the identifier FIRST-SUBSCRIPT. The MOVE and COMPUTE statements are studied in detail in Chapter 3.

To initialize a variable at compile time, we must use the VALUE clause while defining the data item. For example:

```
01  FIRST-SUBSCRIPT      PIC 99     VALUE 1.
```

Compile-time data initialization is useful when large numbers of variables (e.g., arrays) are to be initialized according to some pattern. The method is useful for two reasons.

1. The PROCEDURE DIVISION becomes more code efficient because we do not need MOVEs or COMPUTEs and perhaps some other statements actually to do the job.
2. The program will run in less time, and hence will be more execution efficient.

A common programming error stems from the incorrect assumption that once a variable is initialized at compile time, this value remains associated with the variable throughout the execution of the program. This is true if you do not change the value of the variable. If you do, and you need the same initial value, say in the next cycle of iteration, you should reset the variable to the initial value, this time actively in the PROCEDURE DIVISION.

Additional Data Division Features

Sometimes the segment of the main computer memory allocated to an application program may be limited in size, requiring the programmer to be prudent in using the available memory. COBOL has a feature that makes it possible to have two or more identifiers sharing the same memory location, and another feature that enables the programmer to assign a new name to a portion of a COBOL data structure.

Redefining Data. Let us consider an example COBOL code in which we define a structure called CUSTOMER-DATA, consisting of CUSTOMER-NAME and CUSTOMER-ADDRESS.

```
      . . . . . . . . . . . . . . . . . .
   01   CUSTOMER-DATA.
        05   CUSTOMER-NAME          PIC X(25).
        05   CUSTOMER-ADDRESS       PIC X(30).
```

Say we also define a working storage structure, called DETAILED-ADDRESS, in which the components of a full address are separated.

```
   01   DETAILED-ADDRESS.
        05   STREET-ADDRESS PIC X(13).
        05   CITY           PIC X(10).
        05   STATE          PIC XX.
        05   ZIP-CODE       PIC 9(5).
```

In the machine's memory, a memory location of length 30 will be allocated to CUSTOMER-ADDRESS and another location of the same length will be used for DETAILED-ADDRESS. The two fields are compatible, and data may be moved back and forth in between them.

If we know that throughout the execution of our program CUSTOMER-ADDRESS and DETAILED-ADDRESS will always store the same values, and we wish to use two different names and structures to address the same storage location, we may force the machine to do just that: assign two different names and structures to one memory location. This requires the use of the REDE-FINES clause, which is exemplified below.

```
WORKING-STORAGE SECTION.
.....................
01   CUSTOMER-DATA.
     05    CUSTOMER-NAME        PIC X(25).
     05    CUSTOMER-ADDRESS     PIC X(30).

01   DETAILED-ADDRESS     REDEFINES CUSTOMER-ADDRESS.
     05    STREET-ADDRESS       PIC X(13).
     05    CITY                 PIC X(10).
     05    STATE                PIC XX.
     05    ZIP-CODE             PIC 9(5).
```

The storage structure for CUSTOMER-ADDRESS (or DETAILED-ADDRESS) is shown in the following figure.

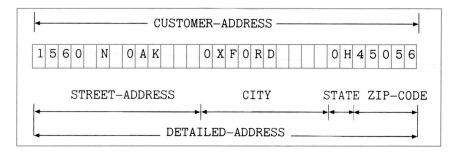

Any change in the content of CUSTOMER-ADDRESS will be reflected in the content of DETAILED-ADDRESS, and vice versa, because they both refer to the same memory location. Thus, the statement

```
MOVE "1560 N OAK    OXFORD    OH45056" TO CUSTOMER-ADDRESS.
```

will store the value "OH" in STATE, and the value "45056" in ZIP-CODE. Here is another example.

```
01   ITEM-CODE           PIC X(5).
01   INVENTORY-NUMBER REDEFINES ITEM-CODE.
     05    ALPHA-PART      PIC XX.
     05    NUMERIC-PART    PIC 999.
```

Now consider the following sequence of PROCEDURE DIVISION statements.

```
MOVE "AX 45" TO ITEM-CODE.

ADD 1 TO NUMERIC-PART.
```

The MOVE statement will store in ITEM-CODE the character string value "AX 45". As INVENTORY-NUMBER is sharing the same memory location with ITEM-CODE, the value that will be stored in NUMERIC-PART will be "45". Despite the fact that NUMERIC-PART has been defined as a numeric computational field, the machine will not object to this value until we attempt to perform arithmetic on NUMERIC-PART. The ADD statement will force the machine to treat the content of NUMERIC-PART as a computational value. This will result in an execution error.

Rules for the REDEFINES Clause

1. The entry for which a REDEFINES clause is used must have a level number. It can be any level number except 66 or 88.
2. The identifier names before and after the key word REDEFINES are data items or structure names, defined in the WORKING-STORAGE SECTION.
3. The REDEFINES clause may not be used for level 01 entries in the FILE SECTION, but may be used in association with lower-level entries.
4. The REDEFINES clause must be at the same level number as the field being redefined.
5. The identifier with REDEFINES clause must immediately follow the definition of the field being redefined.

Renaming Substructures. COBOL has a feature that enables the programmer to regroup elementary data items in a data structure and assign a new name to the group. This can be done by using the RENAMES clause. As an example, consider again the structure EMPLOYEE-PROFILE.

```
01   EMPLOYEE-PROFILE.
     05   EMPLOYEE-IDENTIFICATION.
          10   IDNUMBER                PIC 9(9).
          10   EMPLOYEE-NAME.
               15   LAST-NAME          PIC X(15).
               15   FIRST-NAME         PIC X(15).
     05   JOB-IDENTIFICATION.
          10   JOB-CODE                PIC X(3).
          10   JOB-DESCRIPTION         PIC X(20).
          10   COMPANY-DEPARTMENT      PIC X(10).
          10   SALARY                  PIC 9(6)V99.
     05   JOB-HISTORY-1.
          10   PREVIOUS-JOB-CODE-1     PIC X(3).
          10   PREVIOUS-SALARY-1       PIC 9(6)V99.
     05   JOB-HISTORY-2.
          10   PREVIOUS-JOB-CODE-2     PIC X(3).
          10   PREVIOUS-SALARY-2       PIC 9(6)V99.
```

Let us say that we find it convenient to regroup the data items LAST-NAME, FIRST-NAME, JOB-CODE, and JOB-DESCRIPTION under another structure called EMPLOYEE-BRIEF. We can do that without explicitly defining EMPLOYEE-BRIEF as a COBOL data structure, provided the four elementary data items are included in EMPLOYEE-PROFILE in the desired order. The code that does this is given in the next example.

```
01   EMPLOYEE-PROFILE.
     05   EMPLOYEE-IDENTIFICATION.
          10   IDNUMBER                 PIC 9(9).
          10   EMPLOYEE-NAME.
               15   LAST-NAME           PIC X(15).
               15   FIRST-NAME          PIC X(15).
     05   JOB-IDENTIFICATION.
          10   JOB-CODE                 PIC X(3).
          10   JOB-DESCRIPTION          PIC X(20).
          10   COMPANY-DEPARTMENT       PIC X(10).
          10   SALARY                   PIC 9(6)V99.
     05   JOB-HISTORY-1.
          10   PREVIOUS-JOB-CODE-1      PIC X(3).
          10   PREVIOUS-SALARY-1        PIC 9(6)V99.
     05   JOB-HISTORY-2.
          10   PREVIOUS-JOB-CODE-2      PIC X(3).
          10   PREVIOUS-SALARY-2        PIC 9(6)V99.

     66   EMPLOYEE-BRIEF   RENAMES      LAST-NAME
                                        THROUGH JOB-DESCRIPTION.
```

The result of this definition is equivalent to the following data structure.

```
01   EMPLOYEE-BRIEF.
     05   LAST-NAME               PIC X(15).
     05   FIRST-NAME              PIC X(15).
     05   JOB-CODE                PIC X(3).
     05   JOB-DESCRIPTION         PIC X(20).
```

By using RENAMES instead of explicitly defining the structure EMPLOYEE-BRIEF, we will be forcing the computer to use a portion of another defined data structure for EMPLOYEE-BRIEF. Thus, it becomes possible to reference the structure EMPLOYEE-BRIEF by this name.

Rules for the RENAMES Feature
1. RENAMES should be defined in a level 66 entry.
2. The identifier for which RENAMES is used should be a user-defined structure name.
3. The identifiers that follow the key word RENAMES are elementary data items in the data structure. If the THRU option is used, the identifiers should be such that the one before THRU should precede the one after it in the original structure.
4. If the THRU option is not used, the range of RENAMES is specified by the last data item in the structure.

1. A condition name is a name assigned to a simple comparison condition that uses the equality operator. (T or F)
2. Which of the following rules about condition names is incorrect?
    a. Condition names must be defined as level 88 entries.
    b. Condition names must be associated with elementary data items.
    c. A condition name entry requires a VALUE clause.
    d. Only WORKING-STORAGE SECTION elementary data items may be associated with condition names.
3. An independent data item may be assigned a nonunique name provided it is properly qualified. (T or F)
4. In COBOL, data may be initialized either actively at _____ or passively at _____ .
5. To initialize variables at compile time, we use the VALUE clause. (T or F)
6. The REDEFINES clause may be used with any entry in the FILE section, including the level 01 entries. (T or F)
7. The RENAMES clause is defined in a level ____ entry.
8. The RENAMES clause permits the programmer to regroup elementary data items within a COBOL data structure, and assign a new name to the group. (T or F)

Answers: 1. T; 2. d; 3. F; 4. run time, compile time; 5. T; 6. F; 7. 66; 8. T.

Key Terms

access technique	INSTALLATION
AUTHOR	internal file name
character insertion	multiple record file
COBOL data structure	open mode
condition name	PICTURE specification
CONFIGURATION SECTION	PROGRAM-ID
DATA DIVISION	qualification
data item	record
DATE-COMPILED	record length
DATE-WRITTEN	record name
DISPLAY usage mode	record structure
ENVIRONMENT DIVISION	REDEFINES clause
external file name	RENAMES clause
FD block	SECURITY
file	SELECT
file organization	sequential organization
FILE SECTION	USAGE clause
FILLER	VALUE clause
group item	WORKING-STORAGE SECTION
IDENTIFICATION DIVISION	zero suppression
INPUT-OUTPUT SECTION	

Study Guide

Quick Scan

- IDENTIFICATION DIVISION provides the user and the compiler with some documentation, including the name assigned to the program.
- ENVIRONMENT DIVISION specifies the computer system on which the program is compiled and executed, and partially defines the input and output files that are associated with the program.

- DATA DIVISION is where all program data are fully defined. It can consist of up to five sections: (1) FILE SECTION, (2) WORKING-STORAGE SECTION, (3) LINKAGE SECTION, (4) REPORT SECTION, and (5) COMMUNICATION SECTION. In this chapter we explored the FILE and WORKING-STORAGE SECTIONs.
- In the FILE SECTION, the definitions of input and output files that the program uses and generates are completed. (These definitions start in the ENVIRONMENT DIVISION.) Each file has a file definition (FD) block in which the record structures for the file are described for the compiler.
- In the WORKING-STORAGE SECTION, all program variables and structures that do not participate in file-oriented input-output are defined.
- The simplest form of data in COBOL is an elementary data item. An elementary data item definition requires an associated PICTURE clause in which its type, size, and edit characteristics are specified.
- COBOL supports three types of data: (1) numeric, (2) alphabetic, and (3) alphanumeric. Numeric fields may contain integer or noninteger values. Only unedited numeric fields can be used for arithmetic.
- Data fields are edited before output to put them in more readable forms. Many edit characters are included in PICTURE specifications for the fields.
- Field edit characters either suppress zeros in numeric fields or insert special characters into numeric or nonnumeric fields. The characters that are inserted into data fields are blank, dollar sign, minus or plus, decimal point, comma, debit or credit, and asterisk.
- Data items are brought together to reflect the adjacency relationship among them, and are assigned a common name. The resulting data structure is called a group item. Group items and data items can be combined in a hierarchical fashion into more complex structures. Such structures are known as COBOL data structures. COBOL data structures, arrays, and files are the only data structures directly supported by the language.
- In addition to the type and size of data, in the DATA DIVISION the programmer can also assign initial values to data items using the VALUE clause.
- In a COBOL program, data and structure names must be unique. For data or group items included in COBOL data structures, however, several data names may be used. In this case, proper reference to such identifiers requires qualification. A qualified variable has a qualifier that is the unique name assigned to its superordinate structure.
- Variables in a COBOL program may be initialized at compile time using the VALUE clause. Compile-time initialization, compared to initializing data using statements such as MOVE or COMPUTE in the PROCEDURE division, improves the program's execution and code efficiency.
- The REDEFINES clause can be used to allow two or more identifiers to share the same memory location.
- The RENAMES clause permits the programmer to regroup elementary data items within a COBOL data structure, and assign a new name to the group.

Test Your Comprehension

Multiple-Choice Questions

1. Which of the following about the IDENTIFICATION DIVISION is correct?
   a. It is the second division in a COBOL program.
   b. It consists of up to six sections.
   c. The AUTHOR paragraph is completed by the compiler; it inserts the name of the programmer after the paragraph header.
   d. All paragraphs except the PROGRAM-ID are optional.

2. Which of the following about the ENVIRONMENT DIVISION is incorrect?
   a. In this division, we supply information about the computer system configuration used by the program.
   b. Partial definitions of input-output files are provided in the INPUT-OUTPUT SECTION of the ENVIRONMENT DIVISION.
   c. The SELECT statement is written in the CONFIGURATION SECTION.
   d. The ENVIRONMENT DIVISION is the second division in a COBOL program.

3. Choose the correct statement.
   a. If the file organization technique is not explicitly specified in a SELECT statement, COBOL assumes INDEXED organization.
   b. The file access mode for sequential files may only be sequential.
   c. If an access mode is not explicitly specified in a SELECT statement, the COBOL default for it is RANDOM.
   d. COBOL supports only sequentially organized files.

4. Which of the following about the COBOL PICTURE characters is incorrect?
   a. A is used for alphabetic field specification.
   b. P permits arithmetic sign inclusion.
   c. V is used to denote an assumed decimal point.
   d. 9 is used for numeric fields.

5. Which of the following statements about the placement of data values in their fields is correct?
   a. Numeric values are right-justified in their fields.
   b. Alphanumeric values are left-justified in their fields.
   c. If a character string is longer than its allocated field, the rightmost excess characters are truncated.
   d. The clause JUSTIFIED RIGHT can be used to right-justify character strings in their field.
   e. All of the above are correct.

6. Which of the following statements about group items and the COBOL data structure is incorrect?
   a. A group item consists of subordinate elementary data items and the adjacency relationship that exists among them.
   b. A group item is the building block for the COBOL data structure.
   c. A COBOL data structure may include elementary data items or group items as its subordinate elements.
   d. The level number for the major structure name in a COBOL data structure can be any level number in the range 02 through 49.

7. Which of the following statements concerning COBOL field edit characters is incorrect?
   a. $ is used for dollar sign insertion.
   b. / is used for stroke insertion.
   c. * is used for zero suppression.
   d. B is used for blank insertion.

8. Which of the following rules about condition names is correct?
   a. Condition names must be defined as level 66 entries.
   b. Only WORKING-STORAGE SECTION elementary data items may be associated with condition names.
   c. Condition names must be associated with elementary data items, and may not belong to group items or structures.
   d. A condition name evaluates to the value of the variable it replaces.

Answers: 1. d; 2. c; 3. b; 4. b; 5. e; 6. d; 7. c; 8. c.

Short Essay Questions

1. What are the paragraphs that may be included in the IDENTIFICATION DIVISION?
2. What are the main functions of the ENVIRONMENT DIVISION?
3. Briefly define the following related concepts:
   a. File
   b. Record
   c. File organization
   d. File access technique
4. What information is necessary to define completely a COBOL file? Which of these items are included in the SELECT statement?
5. What are the file organization techniques that are built into the COBOL language?
6. What is the main function of the DATA DIVISION? What are the sections that may be included in it?
7. Briefly explain the functions of the FILE SECTION and WORKING-STORAGE SECTION.
8. What are the data types supported by the COBOL language? What PICTURE characters are used for each type?
9. What can be the contents of a numeric field if it is going to be used in arithmetic operations?
10. Explain the functions of the PICTURE characters V, P, and S.
11. How do we define an integer numeric field in COBOL?
12. What are the uses of the SIGN clause?
13. Is there a convenient way of handling very large and very small numeric data in COBOL?
14. What are the differences between alphabetic fields and alphanumeric fields?
15. Explain the following terms:
    a. Data item
    b. Group item
    c. COBOL data structure
16. What level numbers can be used to define structures?
17. What are specified in an FD block in the FILE SECTION?
18. Explain the significance of the clause LABEL RECORDS ARE STANDARD.
19. How do we define multiple record files in an FD block?
20. Why is input of a multiple record file more critical than its output?
21. Why do we have to edit fields in a COBOL program?
22. What are the insertion type PICTURE characters? Discuss decimal point insertion in detail.
23. What is a condition name? How do we define condition names in COBOL?
24. What is the difference between a VALUE clause associated with a data item and one associated with a condition name?
25. Explain the concept and need for qualification in a COBOL program.
26. Explain the functional difference between the REDEFINES and the RENAMES clauses.

Improve Your Problem-Solving Ability

Debugging Exercises

1. Find and correct the errors in the following partial program consisting of an IDENTIFICATION DIVISION and an ENVIRONMENT DIVISION.

```
IDENTIFICATION-DIVISION.
PROGRAM-ID. PROGRAM-15
AUTHOR: JOHN SMITH.
ENVIRONMENT DIVISION.
    CONFIGURATION SECTION.
    SOURCE-COMPUTER. MY-OWN-MICRO.
    OBJECT-COMPUTER. DITTO.
INPUT-OUTPUT SECTION.
FILE-CONTROL PARAGRAPH.
    SELECT STUDENT-MASTER-FILE ASSIGN TO STUFILE
        ORGANIZATION IS SEQ
        ACCESS MODE IS SEQ.
```

2. In each of the following DATA DIVISION entries, find, explain, and correct the syntax errors, if any.

```
a.  01  PERSONNEL-RANK  PIC 9.
        66  MANAGER          VALUE 1.
        66  ASST-MANAGER     VALUE 2.
        66  EMPLOYEE         VALUE 3.


b.  01  EMPLOYEE-NAME           PIC X(30).
    01  SUPERVISOR-DATA.
        05  EMPLOYEE-NAME       PIC X(30).
        05  EMPLOYEE-ADDRESS    PIC X(40).


c.  01  EMPLOYEE-AGE    PICTURE 999    VALUE "OLD".


d.  88  EMPLOYEE-NUMBER      PIC 9(6).
    01  ID-NUMBER REDEFINES EMPLOYEE-NUMBER.
        05  FIRST-PART          PIC 999.
        05  LAST-PART           PIC 999.
```

Programming Exercises

1. For each of the following PICTURE specifications, identify the field type as numeric, alphabetic, or alphanumeric, state whether or not it is edited, and specify the field length.

PICTURE	Field Type	Edited? (Y or N)	Field Length
PIC 9(6)			
PIC S999			
PIC 99V999			
PIC 9(6)V9(4)			
PIC 9(4)P(4)V			
PIC VP(3)P(3)			
PIC XXXX			
PIC AAAAAA			

PICTURE	Field Type	Edited? (Y or N)	Field Length
PIC X(10)B(2)			
PIC ZZZZZ			
PIC $$$$$9.99			
PIC Z(4)9(2)B(5)			
PIC ZZZ,ZZZ.99			
PIC +++.++			
PIC -9(5).99			
PIC 9999-			
PIC X(2)OX(3)/XX			

2. Suppose we are executing the following MOVE statement: MOVE X–SOURCE TO X–TARGET. Each line of the following table gives the PICTURE specifications for X-SOURCE and X-TARGET, and the value stored in the memory for X-SOURCE. Indicate in the table the value that will be stored in X-TARGET after this MOVE statement is executed.

X-SOURCE		X-TARGET	
PICTURE	Value	PICTURE	Value
PIC 9999	3255	PIC 99999999	
PIC 9(3)	123	PIC 9(5)P(5)V99	
PIC X(10)	JOHN BLACK	PIC X(12)	
PIC X(10)	JOHN BLACK	PIC X(8)	
PIC 99999	00050	PIC Z99999	
PIC 99999	00050	PIC ZZ9999	
PIC 99999	00050	PIC ZZZZZZ	
PIC 9(4)V99	001250	PIC 9,999.99	
PIC 9(4)V99	001250	PIC Z,999.99	
PIC 9(4)V99	001250	PIC Z,Z99.99	
PIC X(5)	ABCDE	PIC XBBXOX/XX	
PIC 9(5)V999	00055689	PIC ZZ,ZZZ.999	
PIC 9(8)	00244455	PIC 999,999.99	
PIC 9(6)V99	00044000	PIC ++99999.99	
PIC X(7)	JOHNSON	PIC XXXXB(2)/BXXX	
PIC 9(7)V99	000100000	PIC $Z,ZZZ,ZZZ.99	

3. Write all the necessary ENVIRONMENT DIVISION entries to define a disk file called EMPLOYEE-SKILLS-FILE. Assume that the file is sequentially organized and sequentially accessed.

4. For the EMPLOYEE-SKILLS-FILE of problem 3, the following additional information is given. Write a complete FD block to reflect them properly. Do not use any defaults.

   a. The name of the record is EMPLOYEE-SKILLS-RECORD.

   b. We would like the computer system to create label records for it.

   c. The record should have the following fields:

   A nine-digit employee Social Security number
   A 25-byte employee name
   A four-byte employee skill code
   A 20-byte skill description
   A two-digit years of employee experience using this skill

5. Draw a figure depicting the conceptual storage structure corresponding to the following COBOL data structure.

```
01   ACCOUNTS-RECORD.
     05   AF-ACCOUNT-NUMBER            PIC X(4).
     05   FILLER                       PIC X.
     05   AF-CUSTOMER-NAME             PIC X(20).
     05   FILLER                       PIC X.
     05   AF-CUSTOMER-ADDRESS.
          10   AF-STREET-ADDRESS       PIC X(20).
          10   AF-CITY-STATE-ZIP       PIC X(20).
     05   FILLER                       PIC X.
     05   AF-BALANCE-FROM-LAST-MONTH   PIC 9(6)V99.
     05   FILLER                       PIC X(5).
```

6. Rewrite the code of the COBOL data structure of problem 5 such that it contains no FILLER fields. Instead, assume that the FILLER fields imply blanks, and use appropriate field edit characters in the PICTURE clauses for the data fields.

7. Suppose we have a WORKING-STORAGE field called TRANSACTION-TYPE defined with the PICTURE XX specification. TRANSACTION-TYPE will use the encoding scheme:

Field Value	*Meaning*
WD	Withdrawal
DE	Deposit
CH	Checking account debit
WA	Withdrawal using automated teller
DA	Deposit using automated teller

Write a complete description for the data item and the associated condition names to reflect the above data encoding scheme.

PROCEDURE DIVISION of a COBOL Program

77

Example Program 1: Class Grade Reports Generator

Key Terms

Study Guide
Quick Scan
Test Your Comprehension
Improve Your Problem-Solving Ability

IN THIS CHAPTER YOU WILL LEARN ABOUT

- COBOL statement types
- File input and output
- Interactive input and output
- In-memory data transfer
- Arithmetic manipulation of numeric data
- Two-way and multiway decision making
- Internal procedures and how to invoke them
- Repetitive execution of program blocks

Introduction

The last division of a COBOL program is the PROCEDURE DIVISION, in which we use COBOL statements to define the program logic. The PROCEDURE DIVISION can be designed in two different ways: section-oriented or paragraph-oriented. In the section-oriented approach, the PROCEDURE DIVISION consists of user-defined sections. In the paragraph-oriented approach, it contains user-defined paragraphs and no sections. In this chapter we will emphasize paragraph-oriented design. Section-oriented design is discussed in Chapter 7.

In contrast to the language elements that we can include in the IDENTIFICATION, ENVIRONMENT, and DATA divisions, statements in the PROCEDURE DIVISION are active. They cause the compiler to take some action. There are about 50 different COBOL statements that we can use to describe algorithms. Some of them are quite advanced and are designed for specialized tasks; we will discuss them later in the book. In this chapter, we will introduce the essential statements, about 17 of them, to enable us to develop reasonably sophisticated application programs. After we study their syntax, functions, variations, and options, we will demonstrate their use in an application program.

COBOL Statement Types

Before we review the more commonly used COBOL statements, let us classify them according to their functions:

1. File input-output statements: OPEN, CLOSE, READ, WRITE
2. Interactive input-output statements: ACCEPT, DISPLAY
3. Data movement statement: MOVE
4. Arithmetic statements: ADD, SUBTRACT, MULTIPLY, DIVIDE, COMPUTE
`COBOL 85` 5. Decision making statements: IF, EVALUATE
6. Statements affecting program flow of control: PERFORM, EXIT, STOP, GO TO

It is useful to note that COBOL language syntax rules given in Appendix B refer to all statements except the decision-making statements as **imperative statements**. The decision-making statements are also known as **conditionals**.

An imperative statement starts with a verb indicating action. It has operands that are affected by the action, and some required or optional clauses. In this chapter we will study the basic COBOL statements given in the classification.

File Input and Output

Majority of input and output in COBOL programs are file oriented. In **file-oriented I-O**, values for data elements are read from or written into files. Input and output of variables defined in the FILE SECTION of the DATA DIVISION can be accomplished through file-oriented I-O. Occasionally, we may wish to read or write values for variables defined in the WORKING-STORAGE SECTION. This happens in interactive programming, which is discussed after file-oriented I-O.

For file-oriented I-O, there are four COBOL statements:

1. OPEN
2. READ
3. WRITE
4. CLOSE

The OPEN statement readies a file for input-output. A file must be opened before it can be accessed for I-O purposes.

The READ statement reads a record from a file. It causes a record to be copied from the external file storage medium into the record structure of the file in the memory. The record structure is also called the input-output buffer.

The WRITE statement writes a record into a file. It takes the record already formed by the program in the I-O buffer for a file and copies it into a file on an external storage medium. The syntax and optional and required clauses of the READ and WRITE statements depend on the organization and access mode of the file.

After input or output for a file is completed, the file has to be closed. This is done by issuing a CLOSE statement. CLOSE dissociates the file from the program. If a file that is in output mode is closed, the CLOSE statement causes an end-of-file marker to be placed into the file.

Opening and Closing Files

To open a file we use an OPEN statement. A simplified syntax of the OPEN statement is given below.

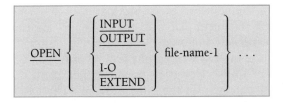

Functionally, the OPEN statement prepares the system to execute I-O instructions for the file. It also causes the system to point to the first physical record in the file. In other words, after a file is opened, the first execution of a READ or WRITE instruction will affect the first record in a sequentially organized or sequentially accessed file.

While opening a file, we also specify the **open mode** for the file. There are four open modes for COBOL files: INPUT, OUTPUT, I-O, and EXTEND. If a file is to be used only for input purposes, it should be opened in INPUT mode. In other words, the only I-O statement we can use for a file that has been opened in input mode is READ.

OUTPUT open mode is specified for files that will be used only in WRITE statements in the program. The first execution of a WRITE statement for a file opened in OUTPUT mode writes the content of the I-O buffer as the first physical record in a sequential file.

The I-O open mode is required for files if we are planning to read from and write into that file in the same program segment. Only disk files can be opened in I-O mode.

The EXTEND open mode is used for sequential files for the purpose of adding new records to them. This mode enables the system to point to the location immediately after the last physical record in the file. A WRITE statement will then add a record to the end of the existing file. Only some COBOL compilers support this open mode. The following are examples of the OPEN statement.

```
1. OPEN INPUT   STUDENT-MASTER-FILE.
2. OPEN OUTPUT  NEW-STUDENT-MASTER-FILE.
3. OPEN INPUT   STUDENT-TEST-SCORES-FILE
        OUTPUT  SUMMARY-GRADES-REPORT.
```

Example 1 opens the file called STUDENT-MASTER-FILE in input mode, and 2 readies the NEW-STUDENT-MASTER-FILE as an output file. As in example 3, it is possible to open more than one file in a single OPEN statement. In fact, it is good programming practice to open all your files early in the program using only one OPEN statement.

Closing files is done using the CLOSE statement. A simplified syntax of the CLOSE statement is

```
CLOSE   {   file-name   }   . . .
```

An example derivation of this syntax is given here.

```
CLOSE STUDENT-TEST-SCORES-FILE
      SUMMARY-GRADES-REPORT.
```

We should close every file that we open when we are done with it. The CLOSE statement places an end-of-file marker in an output file. In this respect, it is especially important to ensure that output files are closed, otherwise, we may lose the last written physical record.

After a file is closed, its previous open mode may be redefined using another OPEN statement in the same program. The OPEN statement permits the program to jump to the first record at the beginning of the file. Consider the following example.

```
1. OPEN OUTPUT NEW-STUDENT-MASTER-FILE.
   . . . . . . . . . . . . . . .
2. CLOSE NEW-STUDENT-MASTER-FILE.
   . . . . . . . . . . . . . . .
3. OPEN INPUT  NEW-STUDENT-MASTER-FILE.
   . . . . . . . . . . . . . . .
4. CLOSE NEW-STUDENT-MASTER-FILE.
```

In this sequence of statements, the first OPEN statement opens a new file, called NEW-STUDENT-MASTER-FILE, in output mode so that records can be written into it. Before closing it at 2, the system will be pointing to a location immediately after the last record that has been written into it. Statement 2 closes the file and places an end-of-file marker in it. Statement 3 reopens it, this time in input mode, enabling the programmer to read records from it, starting with the first record in the file.

Reading Files

Input from files opened in input mode can be done using the READ statement. The syntax and options of the READ statement are determined by the organization and access mode of the file. For sequential files, the syntax is

COBOL 85

```
READ   file-name   RECORD   [ INTO identifier ]
       [ AT END  imperative-statement-1 ]
         [ NOT AT END  imperative-statement-2 ]   [ END-READ ]
```

Semantically, the READ statement causes the computer system to transfer the current record into the main memory and store it in the record structure that belongs to the file being read.

The AT END clause in the READ statement is optional, provided the FILE STATUS option is used in the SELECT statement that corresponds to the file being read. Otherwise, it is required, and it checks whether an end-of-file condition has occurred during input.

The imperative sentence specifies one or more actions to be performed if the end-of-file marker is encountered. When a record is read and no end-of-file marker is found, the program control passes to the sentence that follows the READ statement. Therefore, as a rule, the READ statement should end with a period.

The INTO clause is also optional. If used, the READ statement becomes equivalent to a READ followed by a MOVE statement. It causes the record brought into the input-output area by the READ statement to be duplicated in a WORKING-STORAGE structure. Of course, for this to be possible, a structure definition that is compatible with the record structure of the file must exist in the WORKING-STORAGE section of the program.

COBOL 85
COBOL 85 provides two new options with the READ statement:

1. NOT AT END clause
2. END-READ bracket keyword

The NOT AT END clause is similar to AT END, except it contains instructions to be performed if an end-of-file condition does not occur during input. The END-READ bracket key word can be used in lieu of the concluding period.

The following are examples of READ.

```
1. READ NEW-STUDENT-MASTER-FILE
       AT END MOVE 1 TO END-REACHED-FLAG.

2. READ NEW-STUDENT-MASTER-FILE RECORD
       INTO WS-RECORD-IMAGE
       AT END MOVE 1 TO END-REACHED-FLAG
              ADD 1 TO NO-OF-TIMES-END-REACHED.
```

COBOL 85   In statement 2, when the end-of-file marker is met by the computer, it executes the MOVE and ADD statements within the READ sentence. Using the COBOL 85 options, statement 2 can be coded as follows.

```
READ NEW-STUDENT-MASTER-FILE RECORD
     INTO WS-RECORD-IMAGE
     AT END MOVE 1 TO END-REACHED-FLAG
             ADD 1 TO NO-OF-TIMES-END-REACHED
     NOT AT END
             PERFORM INITIAL-TASKS
END-READ
```

Writing Files

To write records into files, we use the COBOL WRITE statement. For sequential files, the syntax of the WRITE statement is

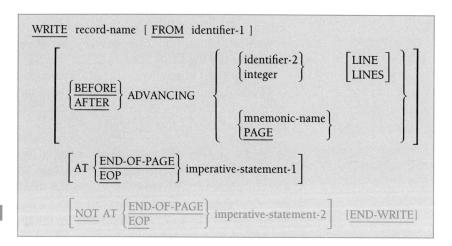

Before the WRITE statement can be used for output, the file should be opened in OUTPUT, I-O, or EXTEND mode. In the program, first, the record structure for the file should be loaded with values, and then a WRITE statement should be issued.

In case the WORKING-STORAGE SECTION contains a structure definition that is compatible with the record structure of the file, a FROM clause can be used to fill the record structure with a record. A WRITE statement with FROM is equivalent to a MOVE followed by a WRITE statement.

Examples of WRITE are

```
WRITE PAYROLL-RECORD.
WRITE PAYROLL-RECORD FROM WS-RECORD-IMAGE.
```

The WRITE statement for printer files involves additional options. A **printer file** is ordinarily a sequential tape or disk file that contains line printer carriage control characters in addition to records that are to be printed. Stored carriage control characters are used while such files are being printed.

In the syntax of the WRITE statement, every element after the FROM clause is related to printer files. These include the BEFORE ADVANCING, AFTER ADVANCING, AT END-OF-PAGE, and NOT AT END-OF-PAGE clauses.

COBOL 85

The BEFORE ADVANCING LINES clause specifies the number of lines to be skipped after the current line is printed. On the other hand, the AFTER ADVANCING LINES clause tells the computer first to skip the specified number of lines and then print the current line. BEFORE and AFTER ADVANCING PAGE options cause a page eject after and before printing the current line, respectively.

AT END-OF-PAGE refers to a sentence containing statements that are to be executed when an end-of-page condition is met during printing.

COBOL 85

NOT AT END-OF-PAGE is a COBOL 85 option. It is used to define statements to be performed if no end-of-page condition is met. END-WRITE is also a COBOL 85 option. It concludes the write statement. Some examples of the WRITE statement for printer files follow.

COBOL 74 version

```
WRITE REPORT-LINE FROM WS-PRINT-LINE
        AFTER ADVANCING PAGE.

WRITE REPORT-LINE
        AFTER ADVANCING NO-OF-LINES LINES.

WRITE REPORT-LINE
        BEFORE ADVANCING 5 LINES.

WRITE REPORT-LINE
        AFTER ADVANCING 1 LINE
        AT END-OF-PAGE
            ADD 1 TO PAGE-COUNTER.
```

COBOL 85 version

COBOL 85

```
WRITE REPORT-LINE
        AFTER ADVANCING 1 LINE
        AT END-OF-PAGE
            ADD 1 TO PAGE-COUNTER
            MOVE PAGE-COUNTER TO OUT-PAGE-COUNTER
        NOT AT END-OF-PAGE
            ADD 1 TO LINE-COUNTER
END-WRITE
```

Interactive Input and Output

Sometimes in a program it becomes desirable and even necessary to input values for variables using the terminal keyboard, or to display values on the cathode ray tube (CRT) terminal screen. In such cases the user participates in executing the program by providing input values for variables, or by inspecting intermediate values for problem parameters and accordingly interacting with the program. In essence, the user and the computer system are in a continual dialogue. Such a setup is referred to as **interactive processing**.

The COBOL language provides a limited interactive processing capability through the ACCEPT and DISPLAY statements.

Interactive Input

The ACCEPT statement is used for reading a value into a program variable. This can be either from a designated device or from some system parameter. The ACCEPT statement syntax is shown below.

COBOL 85

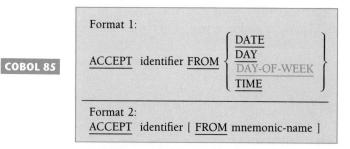

Format 1:

ACCEPT identifier FROM { DATE / DAY / DAY-OF-WEEK / TIME }

Format 2:
ACCEPT identifier [FROM mnemonic-name]

The identifier in this syntax stands for a variable name that becomes the symbolic address of the memory location to store the input value. The FROM clause specifies the source of input. There are five possible source designators for the FROM clause:

1. DATE
2. DAY
3. TIME

COBOL 85
4. DAY-OF-WEEK (only in COBOL 85)
5. An input device

DATE supplies a six-digit integer value according to the year-month-day format (e.g., 870825 for Aug. 25, 1987). DAY stores in the ACCEPT variable a five-digit integer value, which consists of the last two digits of the current year followed by the day of the year counting from January 1. For example, on January 5, 1988, the value returned is 88005. TIME is an eight-digit field consisting of hours, minutes, seconds, and hundredths of a second. It gives the current time based on a 24-hour clock.

COBOL 85
DAY-OF-WEEK is a COBOL 85 feature. It returns a single-digit field that is 1 if the day is Monday, 2 if Tuesday, and so on.

The first four source designators, DATE, DAY, TIME, and DAY-OF-WEEK, are predefined fields for which values are maintained by the computer system. The last source designator for the FROM clause in the ACCEPT statement in format 2 is either a mnemonic name that stands for an input device previously defined in the SPECIAL-NAMES paragraph of the ENVIRONMENT DIVISION, or a default device name for an input device, such as CONSOLE. Two examples are as follows.

```
ACCEPT TODAYS-DATE FROM DATE.
ACCEPT CURRENT-TIME FROM TIME.
```

Provided TODAYS-DATE and CURRENT-TIME are properly defined program variables or structures, the above ACCEPT statements will store in them date and time values corresponding to the time of execution of the statements in the program. On the other hand, the statement

```
ACCEPT ACADEMIC-SEMESTER FROM CONSOLE.
```

when executed will freeze the terminal screen after a prompt supplied by the system is displayed on it, and will wait for the user to type a value to be stored as ACADEMIC-SEMESTER. As soon as the user types a value and hits the return key on the keyboard, program execution resumes.

Interactive Output

In addition to file-oriented output, COBOL offers limited interactive output capability. Values of one or more program variables and constants can be written on an output medium, such as a CRT screen. For this purpose, we must use the DISPLAY statement. The DISPLAY statement has the following syntax.

COBOL 85

$$\underline{\text{DISPLAY}} \left\{ \begin{array}{l} \text{identifier} \\ \text{literal} \end{array} \right\} \dots [\ \underline{\text{UPON}} \quad \text{mnemonic-name}\ ]\ [\ \text{WITH}\ \underline{\text{NO}}\ \underline{\text{ADVANCING}}\ ]$$

The UPON clause contains a mnemonic name that denotes an output device. This name should be defined in the SPECIAL-NAMES paragraph of the ENVIRONMENT DIVISION. For some computer systems, if the optional UPON clause is not used, the output device default is the CRT screen.

COBOL 85

The COBOL 85 optional feature WITH NO ADVANCING is useful when writing on a video monitor. It prevents the cursor from moving down. If this feature is not used, after the DISPLAY list is printed on the screen, the cursor moves to the beginning of the next line.

The DISPLAY statement is used primarily for two reasons:

1. To enable the programmer to monitor program execution
2. To provide prompts for interactive data input

It performs the first function by allowing the programmer to see some crucial intermediate results. Consider the following example.

```
    . . . . . . . . . . . . . . . . . . . . . . . .
    DISPLAY "SALARY AFTER TAXES IS "  OUT-NET-SALARY.
    DISPLAY "DO YOU WANT TO CONTINUE?  ENTER Y/N. ".
    ACCEPT USER-RESPONSE FROM CONSOLE.
    IF USER-RESPONSE = "Y"
        PERFORM REST-OF-PAYROLL-COMPUTATIONS
    ELSE
        PERFORM TERMINATE-PROGRAM.
    . . . . . . . . . . . . . . . . . . . . . . .
```

These statements will produce a screen such as the following after execution.

```
SALARY AFTER TAXES IS 34,555.78
DO YOUR WANT TO CONTINUE?  ENTER Y/N.
Y
  . . . . . . . .
  . . . . . . . .
```

In interactive data input, prompt messages can be generated using DISPLAY, as in the following example.

```
. . . . . . . . . . . . . "——> . . . . . . . . . . . . . .
DISPLAY "——> CURRENT COURSE CODE IS " CURRENT-COURSE-CODE.
DISPLAY "    ENTER COURSE NAME: ".
ACCEPT COURSE-NAME     FROM CONSOLE.
. . . . . . . . . . . . . . . . . . . . . . . .
```

REVIEW QUESTIONS

1. The COBOL file input-output statements are _____, _____ , _____ , and _____ .
2. For interactive input and output, we use the ACCEPT and DISPLAY statements. (T or F)
3. Which of the following statements is not correct for file-oriented I-O in COBOL?
   a. A file must be opened before it can be accessed for I-O purposes.
   b. The optional and required clauses of the READ statement depend on the organization and access mode of the file.
   c. A READ statement causes all records in a file to be accessed simultaneously.
   d. A WRITE statement writes the record in the I-O buffer into a file.
4. The open mode for a file is indicated in its OPEN statement in the PROCEDURE DIVISION. (T or F)
5. Which of the following statements about file open modes is correct?
   a. If we are planning to read a file, we should open it in INPUT mode.
   b. A file that has been opened in I-O mode can be used for reading records from it.
   c. The EXTEND open mode is used for sequential files to add records after the last physical record in them.
   d. All of the above are correct.
6. If we close a file and then open it in the same program in INPUT mode, we will effectively be jumping back to its beginning. (T or F)
7. If we close a file and then open it in the same program in OUTPUT mode, we will lose all the records stored in it. (T or F)
8. In a sequential WRITE statement, the key word WRITE should be followed by a _____ name.
9. A WRITE statement with the optional FROM clause is equivalent to a _____ statement followed by a WRITE statement.
10. Which of the following statements is not correct for a WRITE statement used for printer files?
    a. BEFORE or AFTER ADVANCING PAGE causes a page eject before or after printing.
    b. AT END-OF-PAGE refers to a block of statements to be executed when an end-of-page condition is met during printing.
    c. AFTER ADVANCING LINES specifies the number of lines to be skipped after printing the current line.
    d. The NOT AT END-OF-PAGE clause is a COBOL 85 feature.
11. The source designators in an ACCEPT statement are a device name, _____ , _____ , _____ , and _____ .
12. The DISPLAY statement enables the programmer to monitor the execution of the program and provide prompts for interactive data input. (T or F)

Data Movement

Transferring a constant value or the content of a memory location to another memory location is a common programming task. In COBOL, data transfer is made possible with the MOVE statement. The three character string processing statements INSPECT, STRING, and UNSTRING can also be used for this purpose. We will study character string processing in Chapter 9.

Syntactically, the MOVE statement is defined as follows.

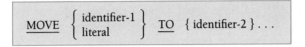

$$\underline{\text{MOVE}} \left\{ \begin{array}{l} \text{identifier-1} \\ \text{literal} \end{array} \right\} \underline{\text{TO}} \ \{ \text{identifier-2} \} \dots$$

The constant value or identifier after the key word MOVE is called the **sending field**, and the identifiers after the key word TO are called the **receiving fields**. Examples of the MOVE statements are given below.

```
MOVE TODAYS-YEAR   TO PROCESSING-YEAR.
MOVE TODAYS-MONTH  TO PROCESSING-MONTH.
MOVE TODAYS-DAY    TO PROCESSING-DAY.
MOVE 1             TO PAGE-NUMBER  LINE-NUMBER.
```

Note that the MOVE statement takes the content of the sending field and duplicates it in one or more receiving fields by overwriting them. As a result of data transfer, values previously stored in the receiving fields are lost; however, the value existing in the sending field is kept intact. Consider the following example.

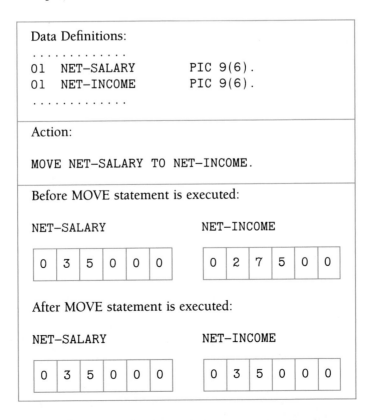

Data Definitions:
```
. . . . . . . . . . . .
01  NET-SALARY       PIC 9(6).
01  NET-INCOME       PIC 9(6).
. . . . . . . . . . . .
```

Action:
```
MOVE NET-SALARY TO NET-INCOME.
```

Before MOVE statement is executed:

NET-SALARY

| 0 | 3 | 5 | 0 | 0 | 0 |

NET-INCOME

| 0 | 2 | 7 | 5 | 0 | 0 |

After MOVE statement is executed:

NET-SALARY

| 0 | 3 | 5 | 0 | 0 | 0 |

NET-INCOME

| 0 | 3 | 5 | 0 | 0 | 0 |

Whether data transfer with a MOVE statement is done correctly and satisfactorily depends on the types and sizes of sending and receiving fields as determined by their respective PICTURE specifications.

Rules for Valid Data Transfer Using the MOVE Statement

1. An alphabetic field can be moved to an alphabetic or alphanumeric receiving field. If field sizes are incompatible, the value in the receiving field will be either truncated or padded by blanks on the right.
2. An alphanumeric sending field can be moved to an alphanumeric field. If the content of an alphanumeric sending field is purely alphabetic (i.e., contains only letters and blanks), the field can be moved to an alphabetic field as well. In case the receiving field is smaller or larger than the sending field, the value in it will be either truncated or padded by blanks on the right.
3. Numeric integer values can be moved to alphanumeric fields. They can also be moved to numeric fields of any kind (integer, noninteger, or edited).
4. A noninteger numeric field can be moved to numeric fields of any kind.
5. A numeric edited field can be moved to a receiving field that is alphanumeric in type. In COBOL 85, a numeric edited field can also be moved to numeric fields of any kind. This way, data in an edited field would be de-edited and become computational.

COBOL 85

The following examples illustrate moving alphabetic fields to alphabetic or alphanumeric fields.

Data definitions:

```
. . . . . . . . . . . .
01 SENDING-FIELD        PIC A(4).
01 RECEIVING-FIELD-1    PIC A(6).
01 RECEIVING-FIELD-2    PIC X(2).
. . . . . . . . . . . .
```

Actions:

```
MOVE SENDING-FIELD TO RECEIVING-FIELD-1.
MOVE SENDING-FIELD TO RECEIVING-FIELD-2.
```

Effects:

SENDING-FIELD	RECEIVING-FIELD-1	RECEIVING-FIELD-2
A D A M	A D A M _ _	A D

In these MOVE statements, RECEIVING-FIELD-1 is a field larger than SENDING-FIELD. Consequently, the value ADAM will be placed in it left-justified, and it will be padded on the right. Since RECEIVING-FIELD-2 is smaller than SENDING-FIELD, the value ADAM will be truncated on the right to AD, and this will then be placed in the RECEIVING-FIELD. The examples below illustrate moving an alphanumeric field to an alphanumeric or alphabetic receiving field.

```
Data definitions:
. . . . . . . . . . . .
01 SENDING-FIELD        PIC X(4).
01 RECEIVING-FIELD-1    PIC X(6).
01 RECEIVING-FIELD-2    PIC A(2).
. . . . . . . . . . . .
```

```
Actions:

MOVE SENDING-FIELD TO RECEIVING-FIELD-1.
MOVE SENDING-FIELD TO RECEIVING-FIELD-2.
```

Effects:

SENDING-FIELD	RECEIVING-FIELD-1	RECEIVING-FIELD-2
J A N	J A N _ _ _	J A

Some compilers consider all characters in the COBOL character set as legitimate alphabetic characters. For them, moving a literal such as "A+12*" to an alphabetic field would be legal. On the other hand, as # and % are not in the COBOL character set, a literal such as "#123%" would cause a program error.

In the following examples, integer values are moved to numeric or nonnumeric receiving fields.

```
Data definitions:
. . . . . . . . . . . .
01  SENDING-FIELD        PIC 9(4).
01  RECEIVING-FIELD-1    PIC X(6).
01  RECEIVING-FIELD-2    PIC X(2).
01  RECEIVING-FIELD-3    PIC 9(6).
01  RECEIVING-FIELD-4    PIC 9(5)V99.
01  RECEIVING-FIELD-5    PIC 9(5).99.
. . . . . . . . . . . .
```

```
Actions:

MOVE SENDING-FIELD TO RECEIVING-FIELD-1.
MOVE SENDING-FIELD TO RECEIVING-FIELD-2.
MOVE SENDING-FIELD TO RECEIVING-FIELD-3.
MOVE SENDING-FIELD TO RECEIVING-FIELD-4.
MOVE SENDING-FIELD TO RECEIVING-FIELD-5.
```

Effects:

SENDING-FIELD	RECEIVING-FIELD-1	RECEIVING-FIELD-2
0 1 9 5	0 1 9 5 _ _	0 1

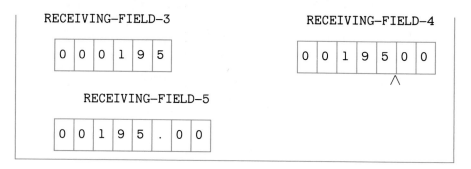

Next we consider examples of moving numeric real values to numeric or edited numeric receiving fields.

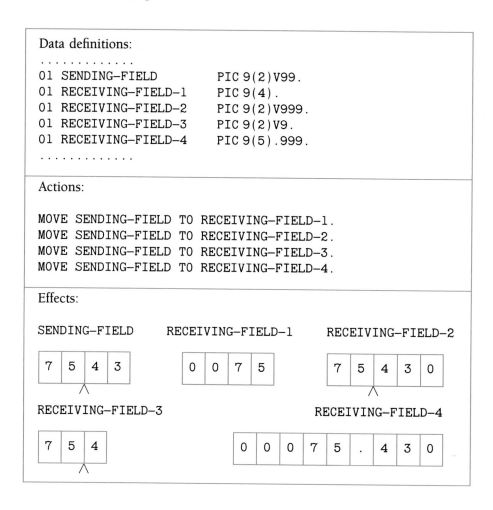

The following examples show how to move edited numeric fields to other types of receiving fields.

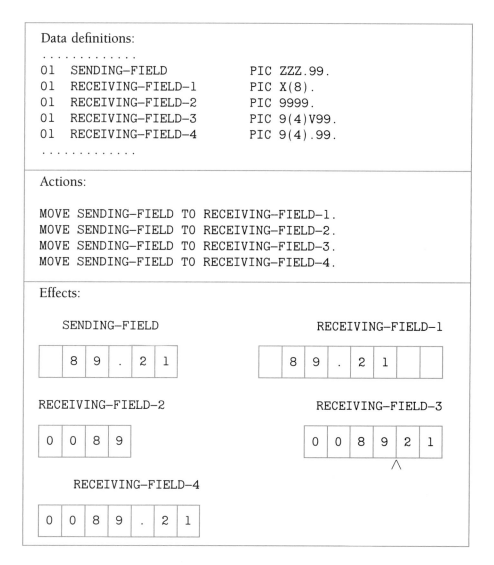

```
Data definitions:
. . . . . . . . . . . .
01   SENDING-FIELD             PIC ZZZ.99.
01   RECEIVING-FIELD-1         PIC X(8).
01   RECEIVING-FIELD-2         PIC 9999.
01   RECEIVING-FIELD-3         PIC 9(4)V99.
01   RECEIVING-FIELD-4         PIC 9(4).99.

. . . . . . . . . . . .
```

Actions:

```
MOVE SENDING-FIELD TO RECEIVING-FIELD-1.
MOVE SENDING-FIELD TO RECEIVING-FIELD-2.
MOVE SENDING-FIELD TO RECEIVING-FIELD-3.
MOVE SENDING-FIELD TO RECEIVING-FIELD-4.
```

Effects:

SENDING-FIELD

| | 8 | 9 | . | 2 | 1 |

RECEIVING-FIELD-1

| | 8 | 9 | . | 2 | 1 | |

RECEIVING-FIELD-2

| 0 | 0 | 8 | 9 |

RECEIVING-FIELD-3

| 0 | 0 | 8 | 9 | 2 | 1 |

RECEIVING-FIELD-4

| 0 | 0 | 8 | 9 | . | 2 | 1 |

The following table summarizes the valid combinations of field types for the MOVE statement.

Sending Field Type	Receiving Field Type
Alphabetic	Alphabetic
	Alphanumeric
Alphanumeric	Alphanumeric
	Alphabetic (depends on the sending field content)
Numeric integer	Alphanumeric
	Numeric (any kind)
Numeric noninteger	Numeric (any kind)
Numeric edited	Alphanumeric
	Numeric (any kind) (only in COBOL 85)

Moving Structures

The MOVE statement can be used to transfer contents of COBOL data structures to other fields or data structures. Consider the following WORKING-STORAGE SECTION entries.

```
. . . . . . . . . . . .
01    STUDENT-DESCRIPTION.
      05   LAST-NAME              PIC X(10).
      05   FIRST-NAME            PIC X(10).
      05   AGE                   PIC 99.

01    OUT-STUDENT-DESCRIPTION.
      05   OUT-LAST-NAME         PIC X(10).
      05   OUT-FIRST-NAME        PIC X(10).
      05   OUT-AGE               PIC 99.

01    ADDRESS-LINE-1.
      05   ADDRESS-FIRST-NAME    PIC X(10).
      05   FILLER                PIC XX        VALUE SPACES.
      05   ADDRESS-LAST-NAME     PIC X(10).

01    REPORT-STUDENT-DATA.
      05   FIRST-NAME            PIC X(10).
      05   FILLER                PIC XXX       VALUE SPACES.
      05   LAST-NAME             PIC X(10).
      05   FILLER                PIC XXX       VALUE SPACES.
      05   AGE                   PIC ZZ.

01    REPORT-LINE                PIC X(28).
. . . . . . . . . . . .
```

Suppose at some point in the program, the structure STUDENT-DESCRIPTION contains the value

```
JONES      WILLIAM    23
```

Because this structure is completely compatible with OUT-STUDENT DESCRIPTION, the following MOVE statement is legal, and is equivalent to three consecutive moves for the three elementary data items in the structures.

```
MOVE STUDENT-DESCRIPTION TO OUT-STUDENT-DESCRIPTION.
```

We can also move a structure to an elementary data item, or vice versa, as in:

```
MOVE OUT-STUDENT-DESCRIPTION TO REPORT-LINE.
```

On the other hand, if we want to transfer the values for LAST-NAME and FIRST-NAME to the corresponding locations in the structure ADDRESS-LINE-1, because the structures are incompatible, we should use two moves, one for each data item.

```
MOVE LAST-NAME  OF STUDENT-DESCRIPTION TO ADDRESS-LAST-NAME.
MOVE FIRST-NAME OF STUDENT-DESCRIPTION TO ADDRESS-FIRST-NAME.
```

As LAST-NAME, FIRST-NAME, and AGE are nonunique data names in this example code, they have to be qualified in the statements above.

Now consider the structures STUDENT-DESCRIPTION and REPORT-STUDENT-DATA. These two structures are incompatible, and a statement such as

```
MOVE STUDENT-DESCRIPTION TO REPORT-STUDENT-DATA.
```

will result in storing a wrong value in the receiving structure. For example, if the content of STUDENT-DESCRIPTION is

| J | O | N | E | S | | | | W | I | L | L | I | A | M | | | 2 | 3 |

the above MOVE statement will cause the value

| J | O | N | E | S | | | | | | L | I | A | M | | | 2 | 3 | | | | |

to be stored in REPORT-STUDENT-DATA.

Data items can be placed properly in the receiving structure in two ways:

1. By using several separate MOVE statements, one for each data item
2. By using the MOVE CORRESPONDING statement if the two structures contain data items with the same names

The MOVE CORRESPONDING statement is a variation of the MOVE statement in COBOL. Its syntax is

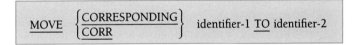

Both identifiers in a MOVE CORRESPONDING statement must be structure names with some data items that have nonunique names. An example is given below.

```
MOVE CORRESPONDING STUDENT-DESCRIPTION TO REPORT-STUDENT-DATA.
```

This statement is equivalent to three MOVE statements for the elementary data items in the structure STUDENT-DESCRIPTION, as discussed above.

REVIEW QUESTIONS

1. A MOVE statement may have one sending field and one or more receiving fields. (T or F)
2. The receiving fields in a MOVE statement may be either constants or variables. (T or F)

3. Suppose we have the MOVE statement

      MOVE A TO B.

Which of the following is an incorrect end to the following statement? This data movement operation is always legal if
a. A and B are both alphanumeric
b. A is alphanumeric and B is alphabetic
c. A is a numeric edited field and B is alphanumeric
d. A is a numeric integer field and B is alphanumeric

4. The content of a COBOL data structure can be transferred to the content of another COBOL data structure using a MOVE statement if, and only if, both structures have the same overall length. (T of F)

5. The MOVE CORRESPONDING statement requires that both the sending field and the receiving field be COBOL data structures containing items with identical names. (T or F)

Answers: 1. T; 2. F; 3. b; 4. F; 5. T.

Arithmetic Manipulation of Data

COBOL supports arithmetic manipulation of data through five statements: ADD, SUBTRACT, MULTIPLY, DIVIDE, and COMPUTE. Earlier versions of the language had only the first four statements for simple operations and provided limited arithmetic capability. Later versions incorporated the more powerful and versatile COMPUTE statement, which we discuss first.

The COMPUTE statement has the following syntax.

COBOL 85

> COMPUTE { identifier [ROUNDED] } . . . = arithmetic-expression
>   [ON SIZE ERROR imperative-statement-1]
>   [NOT ON SIZE ERROR imperative-statement-2] [END-COMPUTE]

The identifiers after the key word COMPUTE must be computational elementary data item names. There can be any number of identifiers, and each can be optionally followed by the ROUNDED clause. The ROUNDED clause indicates that the computed result is to be rounded before it is stored in the identifier. The computer evaluates the arithmetic expression to the right of the equals sign, and stores the computed value in the memory locations assigned to the variable names.

The ON SIZE ERROR clause is optional. It contains an imperative sentence. If any of the variables to the left of the equals sign does not have a field definition to store the computed value adequately, a size error condition is raised. In this case, the imperative sentence in the ON SIZE ERROR clause will be executed.

COBOL 85

The NOT ON SIZE ERROR clause is also optional, and is a COBOL 85 feature. The imperative sentence it contains is executed if a SIZE ERROR condition is not raised after computations.

The optional END-COMPUTE bracket is also a COBOL 85 feature. It can be used instead of a terminating period if an ON SIZE ERROR or a NOT ON SIZE ERROR clause has been used in the COMPUTE statement.

The equal operator in the COMPUTE statement is equivalent to the MOVE statement. It is known as the **assignment operator**, and causes the value computed for the expression to its right to be stored in the identifiers on its left. Some examples follow.

COBOL 74 version

```
COMPUTE DISCRIMINANT SAVE-DISCRIMINANT ROUNDED =
        ( B ** 2 - 4 * A * C ) / ( 2 * A )
        ON SIZE ERROR
                PERFORM DISPLAY-CAUSE-OF-ERROR
                PERFORM CONCLUDE-PROCESSING.
```

COBOL 85 version

COBOL 85

```
COMPUTE  MONTHLY-NET-SALARY ROUNDED =
        MONTHLY-EARNINGS - TOTAL-DEDUCTIONS
        ON SIZE ERROR
                PERFORM DISPLAY-ERROR-MESSAGE
                PERFORM PROCESS-NEXT-EMPLOYEE
        NOT ON SIZE ERROR
                PERFORM GENERATE-PAY-CHECK
END-COMPUTE.
```

Let us briefly explain the second example, which is more general than the first. With this COMPUTE statement, we are asking the computer to do the following for us.

1. Using the values stored in MONTHLY-EARNINGS and TOTAL-DEDUC-TIONS, compute a value for the expression (MONTHLY-EARNINGS − TOTAL-DEDUCTIONS) by subtracting the value in the second memory location from the first.
2. Store this value in the memory location MONTHLY-NET-SALARY after rounding the result. As an example let us say that the picture specification for MONTHLY-NET-SALARY is PIC 9999V99, and the computed value is 1250.873. In this case the value will be rounded down to 1250.87. For the same variable, a value of 1250.876 will be rounded up to 1250.88. If we had not used the ROUNDED attribute, a simple truncation would have occurred, and in either case the computer would have stored 1250.87 in MONTHLY-NET-SALARY.
3. If the computed value for the expression would cause an overflow in the memory location called MONTHLY-NET-SALARY (i.e., for PIC 9999V99, the value to be stored turns out to be, say, 12567.22, which cannot be accommodated in the memory without losing the most significant digit), do not store the result, but execute the procedures DISPLAY-ERROR-MES-SAGE and PROCESS-NEXT-EMPLOYEE, and pass control to the statement that follows COMPUTE.
4. If, on the other hand, the value computed for the expression does not cause an overflow in the field in which it is to be stored, store the value and execute the procedure called GENERATE-PAY-CHECK, and on return, pass control to the statement that follows the COMPUTE statement.

All features of the compute statement are explained above except the arithmetic expression. It is the central feature of the COMPUTE statement.

An **arithmetic expression** is an appropriate combination of numeric variables, constants, and arithmetic operators. The rules for constructing arithmetic expressions in COBOL are quite the same as in almost all other high-level languages (e.g., Fortran, Basic, Pascal, PL/I, etc.). It is likely that the reader is already familiar with it.

COBOL supports five arithmetic operators:

1. $+$ for addition
2. $-$ for subtraction
3. $*$ for multiplication
4. $/$ for division
5. $**$ for exponentiation

In addition, the unary $-$ is used for changing the sign of an arithmetic quantity.

Rules for Constructing Arithmetic Expressions

1. If the arithmetic expression contains different types of operators, the computer uses the following precedence scheme to compute for the expression.
   a. First, the unary minus $-$ operators will be executed.
   b. Next, the exponentiation operations will be handled.
   c. After this, multiplication and/or division will be given priority.
   d. Finally, addition and/or subtraction will be performed.
2. At all levels of this precedence scheme, for operations of the same hierarchy, the order of computation is always from left to right.
3. To change the order of computations, portions of an expression can be enclosed in parentheses, and these subexpressions can be nested. In such cases, the parenthesized expressions will be given higher priority, starting from the innermost subexpressions.
4. While coding an arithmetic expression, all arithmetic operators and left and right parentheses should be preceded and followed by at least one blank.

The following examples illustrate the way a complex arithmetic expression is computed in COBOL.

Example 1   Consider the expression

$$-A + D - 5 * C / 4 ** 2$$

Let us assume that the initial values stored for the variables A, C, and D are 10, 8, and 3, respectively. If we substitute these values for the variables, the expression becomes

$$-(10) + 3 - 5 * 8 / 4 ** 2$$

When the computations start the highest priority in the expression is given to the unary minus. The expression becomes

$$-10 + 3 - 5 * 8 / 4 ** 2$$

Next, the exponentiation in $(4 ** 2)$ is performed, to yield

$$-10 + 3 - 5 * 8 / 16$$

Then the multiplication in the subexpression $(5 * 8)$ is done.

$$-10 + 3 - 40 / 16$$

Among the remaining operations, division has the highest priority.

$$-10 + 3 - 2.5$$

Now, using the left-to-right ordering for the two operations, $(-10 + 3)$ is evaluated.

$$-7 - 2.5$$

Finally, subtraction gives the result of -9.5.

The next example illustrates the use of parentheses to specify the order of computations in an arithmetic expression.

Example 2   In the expression

$$(B ** 2 - 4) * ((A + C) / (2 * A))$$

the computation will follow the sequence shown below.

$$(B ** 2 - 4) * ((A + C) / (2 * A))$$
$$ 3 4 6 1 5 2$$

Here, the integers in the bottom line indicate the order in which each operation is performed in computing the expression. If parentheses were not used, the order of computations would have been

$$B ** 2 - 4 * A + C / 2 * A$$
$$ 1 5 2 6 3 4$$

The tasks that require the four basic arithmetic statements can easily be handled using COMPUTE. In a program, one can always use COMPUTE instead of ADD, SUBTRACT, MULTIPLY, and DIVIDE; however, these are alternatives to COMPUTE. The following table covers the syntactical possibilities for these statements, and also provides the COMPUTE equivalent for each example. For the full syntax of these statements, the reader is referred to Appendix B.

Example of Arithmetic Statement	*The COMPUTE Equivalent*
ADD 1 TO X	COMPUTE X = X + 1
ADD 1, Y TO X W	COMPUTE X, W = X + Y + 1
ADD 1, Y, Z GIVING X, W	COMPUTE X, W = 1 + Y + Z
SUBTRACT 2 FROM X	COMPUTE X = X - 2
SUBTRACT 2, X FROM Y, W	COMPUTE Y = Y - 2 - X COMPUTE W = W - 2 - X
SUBTRACT 2, X FROM Y GIVING V, W	COMPUTE V, W = Y - 2 - X
MULTIPLY 3 BY Y	COMPUTE Y = 3 * Y
MULTIPLY X BY Y, Z ROUNDED	COMPUTE Y = X * Y COMPUTE Z ROUNDED = X * Z
MULTIPLY 3 BY X GIVING Y	COMPUTE Y = 3 * X
MULTIPLY 3 BY X GIVING Y ROUNDED, Z	COMPUTE Y ROUNDED, Z = 3 * X
DIVIDE 3 INTO X	COMPUTE X = X / 3
DIVIDE 3 INTO X ROUNDED, Y	COMPUTE X ROUNDED = X / 3 COMPUTE Y = Y / 3
DIVIDE 3 INTO X GIVING Y, Z	COMPUTE Y, Z = X / 3
DIVIDE X BY 3 GIVING X, Y	COMPUTE X, Y = X / 3
DIVIDE 3 INTO X GIVING Y REMAINDER Z	COMPUTE Y = X / 3 *COMPUTE Z = X - (X / 3) * 3
DIVIDE X BY 3 GIVING Y REMAINDER Z	COMPUTE Y = X / 3 *COMPUTE Z = X - (X / 3) * 3

*This is correct if all variables have been defined as numeric integers.

COBOL 85   COBOL arithmetic statements also support the optional ROUNDED and ON SIZE ERROR clauses. The COBOL 85 version of the language additionally permits the use of the NOT ON SIZE ERROR clause and the brackets END-ADD, END-SUBTRACT, END-MULTIPLY, and END-DIVIDE. Their use is similar to the features associated with the COMPUTE statement.

It should be stressed that in COBOL, arithmetic operations can be performed only on numeric unedited fields. Nor does the language support other mathematical functions (e g., logarithms, trigonometric functions, square root, ceiling, floor, etc.) usually included as library functions in other programming languages. We should remember that COBOL was designed as a business-oriented language, and that is what it remains. It is not suitable for scientific computing. It has limited arithmetic capabilities, as was originally intended, but its arithmetic manipulation functions are generally sufficient for business applications.

REVIEW QUESTIONS

1. In COBOL, arithmetic computations are done using the _____ , _____ , _____ , _____ , and _____ statements.
2. In the COMPUTE statement, the equals sign has the same meaning as the equality operator in a simple relation condition. (T or F)
3. Using a single COMPUTE statement, we can assign a computed value to more than one program variable. (T or F)
4. Which of the following statements concerning the precedence of arithmetic operators in COBOL is incorrect?
   a. Unary minus has a higher priority than exponentiation.
   b. The addition operation has a higher priority than subtraction.
   c. Multiplication and division have the same priority.
   d. Equal-priority operations are done from left to right.
5. Any COBOL COMPUTE statement can be equivalently expressed using a single ADD, SUBTRACT, MULTIPLY, or DIVIDE statement. (T or F)

Answers: 1. ADD, SUBTRACT, MULTIPLY, DIVIDE, COMPUTE; 2. F; 3. T; 4. b; 5. F.

Decision Making

Occasionally we may wish to execute a particular program segment in a program provided a certain condition is dynamically satisfied at that point. For example, in a banking application, we may want to add the dollar amount to a customer's current balance if it is part of a transaction of deposit type; otherwise, we want to subtract it from the current balance. Every high-level language has constructs that enable us to do that, and almost always it is an IF statement. COBOL also supports an IF statement for two-way decision making. In COBOL, we could code this problem as follows.

```
IF TRANSACTION-TYPE = "DEPOSIT" THEN
    ADD TRANSACTION-AMOUNT TO CURRENT-BALANCE
ELSE
    SUBTRACT TRANSACTION-AMOUNT FROM CURRENT-BALANCE.
```

The COBOL IF statement has the following syntax.

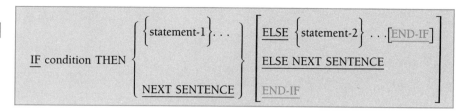

From a functional point of view, the IF statement does several things.

1. The computer evaluates the condition after the key word IF. A condition is a test based on some program variables, and it produces a value of either **true** or **false**. Quantities that compute to true or false are known as **Boolean** (or logical) quantities. COBOL does not explicitly support Boolean quantities, but it does incorporate conditions. A value computed for a condition is not stored in the computer's memory. It is used as follows.
2. If the condition value is true, the then-part of the IF statement is executed. The then-part consists of the statements after the IF condition up to either the key word ELSE or, in case the ELSE is missing, up to the end of the IF statement.
3. If the condition turns out to be false, the statements following the ELSE key word (known as the else-part) until the end of IF are executed.
4. NEXT SENTENCE in an IF statement is treated as an empty statement.
5. After the execution of the contents of either the then-part or else-part, control passes to the statement that follows the IF statement.

In COBOL 74, an IF statement is terminated with a period. COBOL 85, in addition to the period, allows the use of END-IF as an IF statement terminator. Statements that make up the then-part or the else-part of an IF statement should not end with a period.

In an IF statement, the then-part or else-part, but not both, may be empty. Either part may, on the other hand, contain additional IF statements. Such IF statements are said to be **nested**. They can be used in implementing multiway decision-making program structures in which more than two conditional branches may be specified. As an alternative approach, multiway decision structures can be implemented using GO TO . . . DEPENDING ON in COBOL 1974, or EVALUATE in COBOL 85. Nested IFs and multiway decision making are discussed in detail in Chapter 4. In this section we continue exploring the elements of the basic selection structure, the IF statement. Examples of the COBOL IF statement follow.

COBOL 74 version

```
IF STUDENT-AVERAGE > 89
        MOVE "A" TO OUT-STUDENT-GRADE
        ADD 4    TO TOTAL-CREDITS.
. . . . . . . . . . . . . .
IF STUDENT-AVERAGE > 89
        MOVE "A" TO OUT-STUDENT-GRADE
        ADD 4    TO TOTAL-CREDITS
```

```
    ELSE
            IF STUDENT-AVERAGE > 79
                    MOVE "B" TO OUT-STUDENT-GRADE
                    ADD 3    TO TOTAL-CREDITS
            ELSE

                    NEXT SENTENCE.
. . . . . . . . . . . . . .
```

COBOL 85 version

```
IF STUDENT-AVERAGE > 89
        MOVE "A" TO OUT-STUDENT-GRADE
        ADD 4    TO TOTAL-CREDITS
END-IF
. . . . . . . . . . . . . .
IF STUDENT-AVERAGE > 89
        MOVE "A" TO OUT-STUDENT-GRADE
        ADD 4    TO TOTAL-CREDITS
ELSE
        IF STUDENT-AVERAGE > 79
                MOVE "B" TO OUT-STUDENT-GRADE
                ADD 3    TO TOTAL-CREDITS
        ELSE

                NEXT SENTENCE
        END-IF
END-IF
. . . . . . . . . . . . . .
```

The main component of the COBOL IF statement is the condition on which the decision is based. COBOL has eight types of conditions:

1. Relation
2. Negated
3. Combined
4. Abbreviated
5. Condition-name
6. Sign
7. Class
8. Switch

The first seven are most commonly used in application programming.

Relation Conditions

A relation condition compares two arithmetic quantities (constants, variables, or arithmetic expressions) using comparison operators. The comparison operators supported by COBOL and some examples of relation conditions are given in the following table.

Comparisons Operator	COBOL Expression	Example Condition	Value of Condition (Assume A = 5, B = 10)
Equal	IS EQUAL TO IS =	A IS EQUAL TO B	False
Not equal	IS NOT EQUAL TO IS NOT =	(A + B) NOT = 15	False
Less than	IS LESS THAN IS <	(A − B) IS < 0	True
Not less than	IS NOT LESS THAN IS NOT <	(A * B) NOT < 100	False
Less than or equal to (COBOL 85 only)	IS LESS THAN OR EQUAL TO IS < =	B IS < = A	False
Greater than	IS GREATER THAN IS >	B IS GREATER THAN A	True
Not greater than	IS NOT GREATER THAN IS NOT >	A IS NOT > B	True
Greater than or equal to (COBOL 85 only)	IS GREATER THAN OR EQUAL TO IS > =	(B − A) > = 5	True

In the acceptable COBOL expressions for comparison operators, the key words IS, TO, and THAN are optional and are used to improve code readability.

Negated Conditions

As is seen above, the key word NOT can be used within a comparison operator to negate the basic operator. The Boolean operator NOT for negation can also be used to negate a condition. In other words, we could write the condition

```
NOT ( A IS EQUAL TO B )
```

and this would be equivalent to the relation condition

```
A IS NOT EQUAL TO B
```

In the first condition, NOT is the unary Boolean negation. In the second, it is part of the comparison operator "not equal to". In this case, the two are functionally equivalent. The Boolean NOT can be used with more complex conditions, however, and is therefore more versatile. It has the effect of negating a logical value: NOT false is true, and NOT true is false.

Combined Conditions

More complex decision-making problems may require the use of the Boolean operators AND, OR, and NOT. Operands for these are other conditions. Possible computed values for conditions are either true or false. Conditions in which other conditions are combined using AND, OR, or both are called **combined conditions**. The syntax of the COBOL combined condition is

$$\text{condition-1}\left\{\left\{\frac{\text{AND}}{\text{OR}}\right\}\text{condition-2}\right\}\ldots$$

Before we give examples of combined conditions, here are the truth tables that can be used to determine the value of the result in combined conditions.

AND	true	false		OR	true	false		NOT	
true	true	false		true	true	true		true	false
false	false	false		false	true	false		false	true

The truth table for AND shows that the result of two conditions combined with AND is true if, and only if, the conditions themselves are true. Otherwise, the result is false. For OR, the final result for the condition is false if, and only if, both operands are false.

In a combined condition, unless parentheses are used to change the order of computations, the sequence of logical expression is as follows.

1. First, the arithmetic expressions are evaluated using the rules for arithmetic operator precedence.
2. Next, the relation conditions are computed.
3. Finally, the Boolean operators are applied in the following order:
   a. NOT
   b. AND
   c. OR

Consider the following combined condition within an If statement.

```
IF STUDENT-MAJOR = "COMPUTER SCIENCE"
            AND
    NOT STUDENT-AGE IS LESS THAN 19
            OR
    STUDENT-YEAR + 1 IS NOT LESS THAN 3
        PERFORM OTHER-STUDENTS.
```

This is equivalent to the following statement in which the condition is fully parenthesized.

```
IF ( ( ( STUDENT-MAJOR = "COMPUTER SCIENCE" )
                AND
     ( NOT ( STUDENT-AGE IS LESS THAN 19 ) ) )
                OR
     ( ( STUDENT-YEAR + 1 ) IS NOT LESS THAN 3 ) )

        PERFORM OTHER-STUDENTS.
```

Let us assume that the current values for STUDENT-MAJOR, STUDENT-AGE, and STUDENT-YEAR are "COMPUTER SCIENCE", 22, and 3, respectively. The execution order for the combined condition is as follows.

Sequence No	Subexpression No	Subexpression Evaluated	Result of Evaluation
1	[1]	STUDENT-YEAR + 1	4
2	[2]	STUDENT-MAJOR = "COMPUTER SCIENCE"	True
3	[3]	STUDENT-AGE IS LESS THAN 19	False
4	[4]	[1] IS NOT LESS THAN 3	True
5	[5]	NOT [3]	True
6	[6]	[2] AND [5]	True
7		[6] OR [4]	True

The combined condition has computed to true, and hence the paragraph OTHER-STUDENTS will be executed.

Abbreviated Combined Conditions

In some cases, the relation conditions in a combined condition may have a common identifier, or a common comparison operator, as in:

```
STUDENT-AGE = 19 OR STUDENT-AGE = 20 OR STUDENT-AGE > 25
```

It is possible to abbreviate such conditions, and write them as:

```
STUDENT-AGE = 10 OR 20 OR > 25
```

The syntax of abbreviated combined condition is

$$\text{relation-condition} \left\{ \left\{ \begin{matrix} \underline{AND} \\ \underline{OR} \end{matrix} \right\} [\ \underline{NOT}\ ]\ [\ \text{relation-operator}\ ]\ \text{object} \right\} \ldots$$

Additional examples are as follows.

Expanded Form for Combined Condition	Equivalent Abbreviated Form
(X > Y) OR (X NOT < Z) AND (X = 5)	X > Y OR NOT < Z AND = 5
(X NOT = Y) OR (X NOT = Z)	X NOT = Y OR Z

Condition-Name Conditions

We introduced the concept of condition-names in Chapter 2 and discussed its use. Just to summarize, we can define in the DATA DIVISION a level 88 condition-name for an elementary data item and use it in lieu of an equal-relational condition in the PROCEDURE DIVISION. For example, in the partial code

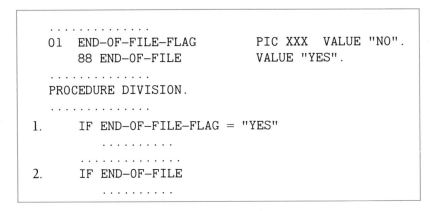

```
          . . . . . . . . . . . .
     01  END-OF-FILE-FLAG        PIC XXX   VALUE "NO".
         88 END-OF-FILE          VALUE "YES".
          . . . . . . . . . . . .
     PROCEDURE DIVISION.
          . . . . . . . . . . . .
   1.    IF END-OF-FILE-FLAG = "YES"
          . . . . . . . . . .
          . . . . . . . . . . . . .
   2.    IF END-OF-FILE
          . . . . . . . . . .
```

the IF statements 1 and 2 are equivalent, and 2 uses a condition-name condition instead of the equal-relation condition.

The value of a condition-name can be changed in two ways.

1. Change the field value for which the condition name is defined.
2. Use the SET statement in COBOL 85.

We can change the field value for which a condition name is specified by moving a value to that field. In the above partial code, the PROCEDURE DIVISION statement

```
    MOVE "YES" TO END-OF-FILE-FLAG
```

will change the value of the condition-name END-OF-FILE to true in the program.

COBOL 85   COBOL 85 provides a new feature to do the same thing. We can use the SET statement as follows.

```
    SET END-OF-FILE TO TRUE.
```

This SET statement at the same time causes the computer to change the value of the associated data item to the value defined for the condition-name. In the example, the variable END-OF-FILE-FLAG becomes "YES".

Sign Conditions

A special COBOL condition is available to test the sign of an arithmetic quantity (either an arithmetic variable or an arithmetic expression) in the form of a sign condition. The syntax for sign condition is as follows.

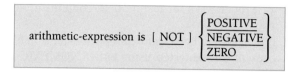

The same test can also be done by using simple relation conditions. Some examples follow.

Sign Condition	Equivalent Relation Condition
DISCRIMINANT IS NOT POSITIVE	DISCRIMINANT IS GREATER THAN ZERO
TEMPERATURE IS NOT ZERO	TEMPERATURE IS NOT = 0
DISCRIMINANT IS NOT NEGATIVE	DISCRIMINANT IS NOT < 0

Class Conditions

A COBOL condition, known as class condition, enables the programmer to determine whether the contents of a field are numeric or alphabetic. The class condition has the following syntax.

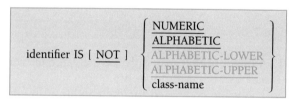

Variations in the syntax are illustrated in the following examples.

```
IF TEST-FIELD IS NUMERIC .................
IF TEST-FIELD IS NOT NUMERIC .............
IF TEST-FIELD IS ALPHABETIC ..............
IF TEST-FIELD IS NOT ALPHABETIC ..........
```

COBOL 85   COBOL 85 distinguishes between lower-case and upper-case letters. As a result, the following tests are also valid.

```
IF TEST-FIELD IS ALPHABETIC-LOWER ........
IF TEST-FIELD IS NOT ALPHABETIC-LOWER .....
IF TEST-FIELD IS ALPHABETIC-UPPER ........
IF TEST-FIELD IS NOT ALPHABETIC-UPPER .....
```

Defining a data item in the DATA DIVISION as a numeric or alphabetic field does not guarantee that during the program execution its content will be numeric or alphabetic. A field defined as numeric may be loaded with a nonnumeric value during input. An attempt to perform arithmetic on this field will result in a program error. Class conditions make it possible to check current contents of data fields and thus avoid errors that may cause the program to abort. Proper ways for testing field contents are described below.

1. If a field has been defined as a numeric field in the DATA DIVISION, its content can be tested using either NUMERIC or NOT NUMERIC class conditions. Other class tests are invalid for numeric fields.
2. For an alphabetic field, the class tests that can be used are ALPHABETIC and NOT ALPHABETIC. COBOL 85 class conditions can also be used with alphabetic fields.
3. There are no special tests for alphanumeric fields. We recall that alphanumeric fields can contain any combination of characters. However, the two basic class tests can be combined in the following manner to ensure alphanumeric content for an alphanumeric field.

```
IF TEST-FIELD IS NOT NUMERIC
    IF TEST-FIELD IS NOT ALPHABETIC
        DISPLAY "TEST-FIELD CONTENT IS ALPHANUMERIC"
    ELSE
        DISPLAY "TEST-FIELD CONTENT IS ALPHABETIC"
ELSE
    DISPLAY "TEST-FIELD CONTENT IS NUMERIC".
```

REVIEW QUESTIONS

1. A quantity that may only have a value of true or a value of false is known as a _____ quantity.
2. The value computed for the condition in an IF statement is stored in the computer's memory as that condition's value. (T or F)
3. Which of the following about the COBOL IF statement is correct?
   a. The then-part of an IF statement consists of all statements after the IF condition up to either the key word ELSE or, in case the ELSE is missing, the end of the IF statement.
   b. The end of an IF statement is marked by either a period or END-IF (in COBOL 85).
   c. NEXT SENTENCE in an IF statement is treated as an empty statement.
   d. In case an IF statement's condition evaluates to true, the then-part of the statement will be executed and the else-part will be skipped.
   e. All of the above are correct.
4. A condition in which two arithmetic quantities are compared using a comparison operator is known as a _____ condition.
5. In the condition
     A NOT EQUAL TO 5
   the operator NOT is a Boolean operator. (T or F)
6. In the condition
     NOT A EQUAL TO 5
   the operator NOT is a Boolean operator. (T or F)
7. The logical operator that produces true if, and only if, both of its operands are true is the operator _____ .

8. The Boolean operator that produces true as long as one or both of its operands are true is the operator _____ .
9. In a combined COBOL condition, the expressions involving the AND operator are evaluated before the expressions involving the OR operator. (T or F)
10. The value of a COBOL condition-name can be changed by changing the value of the identifier for which the condition-name has been defined. (T or F)
11. In COBOL 85 we can change the value of a condition-name by using the _____ statement.
12. Whenever a sign condition is indicated in a program, we can instead use an appropriate simple relation condition. (T or F)
13. To test field contents for identifiers, we use _____ conditions in COBOL.

Answers: 1. Boolean (or logical); 2. F; 3. e; 4. relation; 5. F; 6. T; 7. AND; 8. OR; 9. T; 10. T; 11. SET; 12. T; 13. class.

Flow of Control

In our study of the PROCEDURE DIVISION statements so far, only the IF statement has emerged as one that can alter the sequential execution of instructions in a program. We can use it to bypass a group of statements and, depending on the condition associated with it, execute another group. Additional control statements are needed to direct the flow of execution according to a pattern dictated by an algorithm. They are classified as follows:

1. PERFORM statement for internal procedure invocation
2. PERFORM UNTIL, PERFORM TIMES, and PERFORM VARYING statements for repetitive internal procedure execution (iteration)
3. GO TO statement for unconditional transfer of control
4. STOP RUN statement to terminate program execution

COBOL 85 5. The no-operation EXIT and CONTINUE statements

Internal Procedure Invocation

The PROCEDURE DIVISION paragraphs and sections defined by the programmer are, in fact, modules designed to execute specific tasks in a program. They are parts of a program, and thus can be regarded as internal procedures. Program modularization and related COBOL considerations are discussed in detail in Chapters 4, 5, and 7 of this book. Here we will study the COBOL PERFORM statement, which is used for paragraph or section invocation.

Syntactically, the PERFORM statement looks like this:

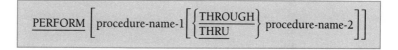

$$\underline{\text{PERFORM}} \left[\text{procedure-name-1} \left[\left\{ \begin{array}{l} \underline{\text{THROUGH}} \\ \underline{\text{THRU}} \end{array} \right\} \text{procedure-name-2} \right] \right]$$

Functionally, the PERFORM statement transfers control to the first statement in a paragraph or section. The invoked paragraph or section is executed. After this, control is returned to the first statement immediately after the PERFORM statement that called on the procedure. Some examples of PERFORM are shown here.

```
      . . . . . . . . . . . . . . .
      PERFORM B1-PREPARATIONS.
      PERFORM B2-INITIAL-TERMINAL-INPUTS.
      . . . . . . . . . . . . . . .
      . . . . . . . . . . . . . . .
  B1-PREPARATIONS.
      ACCEPT TODAYS-DATE FROM DATE.
      MOVE TODAYS-YEAR  TO PROCESSING-YEAR.
      MOVE TODAYS-MONTH TO PROCESSING-MONTH.
      MOVE TODAYS-DAY   TO PROCESSING-DAY.
      MOVE 1            TO PAGE-NUMBER.

  B2-INITIAL-TERMINAL-INPUTS.
      DISPLAY "--> ENTER ACADEMIC YEAR, LIKE 1953-54: "
      ACCEPT ACADEMIC-YEAR     FROM CONSOLE.
      DISPLAY "--> ENTER SEMESTER AS FALL, SPRING, OR SUMMER: "
      ACCEPT ACADEMIC-SEMESTER FROM CONSOLE.

  B3-GENERATE-PAGES.
      . . . . . . . . . . . . . . .
```

Note that the two consecutive PERFORMs above could have been coded as:

```
PERFORM B1-PREPARATIONS THROUGH B2-INITIAL-TERMINAL-INPUTS.
```

This statement uses the optional THROUGH clause. In this case, the program control passes to the procedure whose name comes before the key word THROUGH. Its instructions are executed. Next, the instructions of the paragraphs or sections physically following it are executed. This continues until the procedure whose name appears after THROUGH is done. Then the program control returns to the statement that follows PERFORM.

The range of the PERFORM statement when the THROUGH option is used is a sequence of physically contiguous procedures. Although this option provides a shortcut, its use is not recommended because it can create difficulties in future program maintenance efforts. For example, the programmer charged with making additions to an existing application program may inadvertently insert a new paragraph in between two paragraphs that may be in the range of a PERFORM . . . THROUGH statement used elsewhere in the program. Such an insertion may result in programming errors that are hard to debug.

Repeated Execution of Internal Procedures

Iteration on one or more paragraphs or sections in COBOL can be defined using three versions of the PERFORM statement: PERFORM UNTIL, PERFORM TIMES, and PERFORM VARYING.

PERFORM UNTIL Statement. The following CBL notation partially describes the syntax of the PERFORM UNTIL statement. In order not to cause unnecessary confusion, some of the features of this statement are intentionally omitted and are discussed later in the book.

COBOL 85

$$\text{PERFORM} \left[\text{procedure-name-1} \left[\left\{ \begin{array}{l} \underline{\text{THROUGH}} \\ \underline{\text{THRU}} \end{array} \right\} \text{procedure-name-2} \right] \right]$$

$$\underline{\text{UNTIL}} \text{ condition } [\text{ imperative-statement } \underline{\text{END-PERFORM}}]$$

Previously, we discussed all elements of this syntax except the UNTIL clause. This clause contains a condition that is used in controlling the iteration. Semantically, the PERFORM UNTIL statement executes the range of the PER-FORM statement as long as the condition that follows the key word UNTIL computes to false. The condition can be any type of condition as in the IF state-ment. If it becomes true, the program control passes to the statement that fol-lows PERFORM. The programmer should ensure that the condition after UN-TIL will eventually compute to true to avoid a perpetual loop. For example:

```
PERFORM B3-GENERATE-PAGES
        UNTIL END-OF-FILE.
```

This statement executes the paragraph named B3-GENERATE-PAGES as long as the condition-name END-OF-FILE is false. In each cycle of iteration, it first checks the condition. If it is false, it calls on the procedure. This is known as a pretest iteration structure.

> **A pretest iteration structure** is one in which a test is done before the loop body (i.e., the code that is repetitively executed) is referenced.

Chapter 4 discusses iteration structures and their implementation in COBOL in greater detail.

PERFORM TIMES Statement. PERFORM TIMES can be used to iterate on the range of the PERFORM statement a prescribed number of times. Its syntax is as follows.

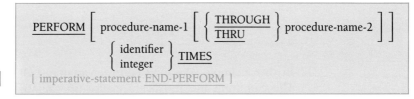

The TIMES clause contains a positive nonzero integer constant or variable. For example:

```
PERFORM B3-GENERATE-PAGES 10 TIMES.
PERFORM B3-GENERATE-PAGES HOW-MANY TIMES.
```

The first statement executes the paragraph 10 times; the second does it for the value contained in the variable HOW-MANY. If the second form is used, the programmer must ensure that the variable preceding TIMES is an integer by its definition in the DATA DIVISION, and that it contains a positive nonzero value at the time the PERFORM TIMES statement is executed.

PERFORM VARYING Statement. PERFORM VARYING in COBOL is more powerful and also more complex than the other forms. Its partial syntax is given here.

PERFORM $\left[\text{procedure-name-1} \left[\left\{ \begin{array}{l} \underline{\text{THROUGH}} \\ \underline{\text{THRU}} \end{array} \right\} \text{procedure-name-2} \right] \right]$

$\underline{\text{VARYING}} \left\{ \begin{array}{l} \text{identifier-1} \\ \text{index-name-1} \end{array} \right\} \underline{\text{FROM}} \left\{ \begin{array}{l} \text{identifier-2} \\ \text{index-name-2} \\ \text{literal-1} \end{array} \right\} \underline{\text{BY}} \left\{ \begin{array}{l} \text{identifier-3} \\ \text{literal-2} \end{array} \right\}$

$\underline{\text{UNTIL}}$ condition-1

$\left[\underline{\text{AFTER}} \left\{ \begin{array}{l} \text{identifier-4} \\ \text{index-name-3} \end{array} \right\} \underline{\text{FROM}} \left\{ \begin{array}{l} \text{identifier-5} \\ \text{index-name-4} \\ \text{literal-3} \end{array} \right\} \underline{\text{BY}} \left\{ \begin{array}{l} \text{identifier-6} \\ \text{literal-4} \end{array} \right\} \right.$

$\left. \underline{\text{UNTIL}} \text{ condition-2} \right] \ldots$

COBOL 85

[imperative-statement $\underline{\text{END-PERFORM}}$]

The clause VARYING contains an integer variable name called the **loop control variable**. The clause FROM contains an integer constant or variable called the **initial value**. The clause BY consists of another integer constant or variable, the **increment value**. The UNTIL clause has the same function as that in the PERFORM UNTIL statement; it involves a condition that is used to control the iteration. An example is given below.

```
PERFORM SUM-ALL
    VARYING LOOP-INDEX
    FROM 1
    BY 2
UNTIL LOOP-INDEX > 100
        OR
    END-OF-FILE.
```

In this example, the loop control variable, LOOP-INDEX, is initialized to 1. The condition in the UNTIL clause is evaluated. If it is false, the procedure SUM-ALL is executed. On return, LOOP-INDEX is incremented by 2 and becomes 3. Again the test is performed, and depending on the outcome, the iteration continues or is terminated. Note that the values LOOP-INDEX in successive cycles of iteration will assume are 1, 3, 5, 7, and so on.

PERFORM VARYING is especially well suited for array handling. For this reason, we will explore it further in Chapter 8.

Execution of Program Blocks

COBOL 74 does not permit blocking statements for single or repeated execution unless they are collected in a paragraph or a section with a name. In other words, the language is not block structured. This occasionally leads to unjustified program modularization.

COBOL 85   COBOL 85 introduces block structuring into the language. This is accomplished using "in-line" forms for PERFORM. In such forms, instead of the procedure names in the PERFORM statement, we specify an imperative sentence and terminate the block by the END-PERFORM bracket. The syntax of the in-line PERFORM statement is as follows.

```
PERFORM  imperative-statement   END-PERFORM
```

Some examples are provided in the following table.

COBOL 74 Version	COBOL 85 Version

``
    PERFORM B1-PREPARATIONS.
....
B1-PREPARATIONS.
   ACCEPT TODAY-DATE FROM DATE.
   MOVE TODAY-YEAR TO PROC-YEAR.
   MOVE TODAY-MONTH TO PROC-MONTH.
   MOVE TODAY-DAY   TO PROC-DAY.
   MOVE 1   TO PAGE-NUMBER.
``
	``
	PERFORM
	   ACCEPT TODAY-DATE FROM DATE
	   MOVE TODAY-YEAR TO PROC-YEAR
	   MOVE TODAY-MONTH TO PROC-MONTH
	   MOVE TODAY-DAY TO PROC-DAY
	   MOVE 1 TO PAGE-NUMBER
	END-PERFORM.
	``

``
    PERFORM SUM-ALL
         UNTIL INT-VALUE > 100.
....
SUM-ALL.
   ADD 1 TO INT-VALUE.
   ADD INT-VALUE TO SUM-OF-INTEGERS.
``
	``
	PERFORM UNTIL INT-VALUE > 100
	   ADD 1 TO INT-VALUE
	   ADD INT-VALUE TO SUM-OF-INTEGERS
	END-PERFORM.
	``

``
    PERFORM SUM-ALL 100 TIMES.
....
SUM-ALL.
   ADD 1 TO INT-VALUE.
   ADD INT-VALUE TO SUM-OF-INTEGERS.
``
	``
	PERFORM 100 TIMES
	   ADD 1 TO INT-VALUE
	   ADD INT-VALUE TO SUM-OF-INTEGERS
	END-PERFORM.
	``

Unconditional Transfer of Control

It is possible to direct program flow unconditionally to a paragraph or a section using the GO TO statement, as in:

```
GO TO SUM-ALL.
```

If this is done, unlike in PERFORM, it is the programmer's responsibility to keep track of the program branch and ensure logical correctness. Use of too many GO TOs in a program makes reading the code difficult for debugging, repair, or maintenance. In view of the structured features of the language (see Chapter 4), the use of GO TO is definitely not recommended.

Terminating Program Execution

Every algorithm must have an end, and so must every program. COBOL requires the STOP RUN statement to mark the termination of program execution. Each program must have at least one STOP RUN statement. It is a good programming practice to have a single termination point, preferably in a paragraph or section of a high hierarchy.

No-Operation Statements

COBOL 85   The COBOL 1974 EXIT and COBOL 1985 CONTINUE statements are null statements that simply pass control to whatever physically or logically follows. EXIT may be used to define null paragraphs that may be needed in programs whose PROCEDURE DIVISIONs are designed in terms of sections rather than paragraphs. The following is an example of an empty paragraph that does nothing.

```
END-OF-SECTION-ONE.
    EXIT.
```

COBOL 85   COBOL 85 CONTINUE may be used in lieu of the NEXT SENTENCE clause in an IF statement.

```
IF SEX-CODE = "MALE" OR "FEMALE"
    CONTINUE
ELSE
    PERFORM ERROR-IN-SEX-CODE
END-IF
```

REVIEW QUESTIONS

1. An internal procedure in COBOL is either a _____ or a _____ .

2. To invoke an internal procedure in COBOL, we use the _____ statement.

3. Which of the following statements concerning the iteration statements in COBOL is correct?
   a. PERFORM UNTIL executes a paragraph or a section a prescribed number of times.
   b. Any PERFORM UNTIL statement can be expressed in terms of an equivalent PERFORM TIMES statement.
   c. In a PERFORM VARYING statement, no loop control variable is needed.
   d. All of the above are incorrect.

4. An iteration structure in which a test is done before the loop body is executed is called a _____ iteration structure.

5. In the PERFORM VARYING statement, the constant or variable after the key word FROM is called the _____ , and the constant or variable after the key word BY is called the _____ .

6. In the COBOL 85 in-line PERFORM statement, the block to be executed must be terminated by a period. (T or F)

7. In COBOL, the EXIT and CONTINUE statements are _____ statements.

Answers: 1. paragraph, section; 2. PERFORM; 3. d; 4. pretest; 5. initial value, increment value; 6. F; 7. no-operation.

Example Program 1: Class Grade Reports Generator

This sample program illustrates most of the language features we covered in this chapter. The program, which is an elaboration of the sample COBOL program of Chapter 1 (see Program 1-Source) is based on the following problem description.

Problem   We have a disk file storing student test scores according to the following format:

- A four-digit student identification number starting at column 1
- A 25-byte student name field starting at column 6
- An 8-byte course name field, beginning at column 32
- Three student test scores, two for midsemester tests and one for the final examination, each a three-digit integer, beginning at columns 41, 45, and 49, respectively

In this file the records are ordered first by course code, and then for each course code, by student identification number.

We would like to write a COBOL program that processes this file and produces class grade reports. Each class grade report begins on a new page. In the input disk file, the records are arranged in blocks for each course (see Program 1-Input). During input, when a new block begins the program is expected to generate the totals for the current course and print them. Then it should eject to a new page for the next course. In traditional data processing terminology, we say that a **control break** occurs from one course to the next. The template for the reports is shown below.

```
                  CLASS GRADE REPORT          DATE: XX-XX-XX
                                              PAGE:  9


              1987-88 SPRING

XXXXXXX   XXXXXXXXXXXXXXXXXXXXXXXXX


          STUDENT NAME                SEMESTER AVERAGE      GRADE
          ---------------------       ----------------      -----
          XXXXXXXXXXXXXXXXXXXXXXXXX          999               X
          XXXXXXXXXXXXXXXXXXXXXXXXX          999               X
          XXXXXXXXXXXXXXXXXXXXXXXXX          999               X

                        INSTRUCTOR        : XXXXXXXXXXXXXXXXXXX
                        NUMBER OF STUDENTS: 999
                        CLASS AVERAGE     : 9.99
```

The following problem parameters are to be typed interactively by the users:

- Current academic year
- Current semester
- Course name for a course defined by the course code field in the input file
- Instructor name for the course

The average score for each student should be computed using the formula

$$(0.25 * first\text{-}test\text{-}score + 0.35 * second\text{-}test\text{-}score + 0.40 * final\text{-}exam\text{-}score)$$

The class grade reports contain a class average field, which should be computed as

$$[4 * (number\ of\ A\ grades) + 3 * (number\ of\ B\ grades) + 2 * (number\ of\ C$$
$$grades) + 1 * (number\ of\ D\ grades)] / (number\ of\ students\ in\ class)$$

Solution   Program 1-Input shows a set of sample records in the STUDENT-TEST-SCORES-FILE. We use this instance of the file to test the program. The compiler-generated listing of the program is provided in Program 1-Source. Program 1-Output(a) is a sample output created by the program, and Program 1-Output(b) is the terminal session that has occurred during the test run of the program.

Let us take a closer look at the source code of this program.

1. Line 000003 names the program STUDENT-GRADES. Some compilers may find this too long as a program name and generate a warning diagnostic message, informing the programmer that the name will be truncated during compilation. For a source program that is not invoked by another program, this truncation is not important. The descriptive character of the name may be retained despite the compiler's warning.

2. Note the abundant use of comments in lines 000004 through 000043, explaining the purpose of the program, its input and output, and certain operational and algorithmic details. We will use such comments liberally in programs to be developed in this book. In general, they are very useful in describing a program to readers of the code.

3. In lines 000056 through 000058 in the FILE-CONTROL paragraph of the INPUT-OUTPUT SECTION of the ENVIRONMENT DIVISION, we begin the definition of the STUDENT-TEST-SCORES-FILE in a SELECT statement. This file is our input file. Here we associate this file with an external data set named INFILE, specify its organization as sequential, and tell the compiler that we are planning to access it sequentially.

4. In the SELECT statement of line 000060, we do the same for the output file whose in-program name is SUMMARY-GRADES-REPORT. This time we use defaults to define it as a sequentially organized file with sequential access mode.

5. Under the DATA DIVISION, FILE SECTION, the first FD block extending from line 000065 to 000081 completes the definition of the STUDENT-TEST-SCORES-FILE. Here we specify its label records as being standard and request the operating system to process the file accordingly. Because label records have been created for this file, it is either a disk or a tape file.

Then we assign the identifier STUDENT-TEST-SCORES-RECORD as the name of its record structure. Next we declare its record length as 80 characters. Finally, in a COBOL data structure, we describe its record structure such that it is consistent with the format of its records, as shown in Program 1-Input. Note that the record length as determined by adding the field lengths in this record structure is 80 characters, the same as that of the physical data file itself, and also the previously declared record length in the RECORD CONTAINS clause.

6. The next FD block in lines 000083 through 000087 belongs to the output file SUMMARY-GRADES-REPORT. Here, since this is a printer file, we ask the compiler to omit label records, assign the name REPORT-LINE to the file's record structure, and specify its length as 131 characters. A printer line can contain 132 characters; however, on some systems the first print position is reserved for carriage control characters. This reduces the usable print positions to 131. Note that in this case REPORT-LINE is a field name, not a structure.

7. In the WORKING-STORAGE SECTION we include the definitions of program variables and structures that cannot be declared in the FILE SECTION. They are the file control switch called END-OF-FILE-FLAG and the associated condition name END-OF-FILE, the program variables for which the user is expected to supply values interactively (ACADEMIC-YEAR, ACADEMIC-SEMESTER, COURSE-NAME, and INSTRUCTOR-NAME), and variables that are needed to store results of computations (PAGE-NUMBER, NUMBER-OF-STUDENTS, TOTAL-CREDITS, CLASS-AVERAGE, STUDENT-AVERAGE, and CURRENT-COURSE-CODE). We also have some structures that are declared in lines 000111 through 000183 to facilitate printing the report heading lines.

8. In the PROCEDURE DIVISION the monitor procedure is a paragraph. It is the first paragraph in that division, called A-MAINLINER. In it, we first open the two files STUDENT-TEST-SCORES-FILE and SUMMARY-GRADES-REPORT in INPUT and OUTPUT modes, respectively.

9. Next we call on the paragraph B1-PREPARATIONS using a PERFORM statement. In this paragraph we have an ACCEPT statement to get today's date and store it in the structure called TODAYS-DATE. We also have three MOVE statements to move the content of TODAYS-DATE to the structure PROCESSING-DATE. The structure PROCESSING-DATE helps separate month, day, and year from each other by hyphens. Also, in this paragraph we initialize PAGE-NUMBER to 1.

10. After the control is back into the monitor paragraph, the PERFORM statement on line 000191 is executed. This statement invokes the paragraph called B2-INITIAL-TERMINAL-INPUTS, in which there are DISPLAY and ACCEPT statements needed for interactive input of ACADEMIC-YEAR and ACADEMIC-SEMESTER values. The DISPLAY statements prompt the user for input.

11. The program control is now at line 000192. We have a READ statement to read a record from the STUDENT-TEST-SCORES-FILE.

12. The PERFORM UNTIL statement that follows triggers repetitive execution of the paragraph B3-GENERATE-PAGES. In this paragraph we first save the COURSE-CODE value coming from the record just read in CURRENT-COURSE-CODE. Then we sequentially execute three paragraphs: C1-INITIALIZE-VARIABLES, C2-REMAINING-TERMINAL-INPUTS to read

values for the variables COURSE-NAME and INSTRUCTOR-NAME corresponding to the CURRENT-COURSE-CODE, and C3-PRINT-HALF-PAGE to print the report heading lines on the first page of the report.

13. Now we are at the PERFORM UNTIL statement of line 000222, which executes the paragraph C4-FORM-STUDENT-LINES until either the end of the input file is encountered, or the COURSE-CODE value read is no longer the same as that in the CURRENT-COURSE-CODE. So far, we have defined a doubly nested loop in the program.

14. In the paragraph C4-FORM-STUDENT-LINES, we do the following:
    a. Increment NUMBER-OF-STUDENTS by 1 (line 000279).
    b. Compute the STUDENT-AVERAGE (lines 000280–000283).
    c. Execute the paragraph D1-DETERMINE-GRADE, which finds and stores in OUT-STUDENT-GRADE a letter grade for the student and course combination being processed (line 000284).
    d. Move values into output fields defined for them (lines 000285–000288) and print a detail line (line 000289).
    e. Read the next record from the input file (line 000291).

15. In the paragraph D1-DETERMINE-GRADE we have a series of IF statements to determine a value for OUT-STUDENT-GRADE corresponding to the STUDENT-AVERAGE, and to add 1, 2, 3, or 4 to TOTAL-CREDITS depending on whether the OUT-STUDENT-GRADE value is D, C, B, or A.

16. After the PERFORM UNTIL statement of line 000222 is fully executed, the detail lines on a report page will have been printed. The next statement is the PERFORM statement of line 000227, which triggers the paragraph C5-PRINT-SUMMARY. In this paragraph we compute the CLASS-AVERAGE by dividing TOTAL-CREDITS by NUMBER-OF-STUDENTS for that class, and prepare and print the last three lines on a report page [see Program 1-Output(a)].

17. The program control gets back to line 000228, which is an ADD statement to keep track of the PAGE-NUMBER. After this, the paragraph B3-GENERATE-PAGES has completed execution. We are now at the PERFORM UNTIL of line 000195 of the monitor paragraph. If the last attempt to read from the input file encountered a record, the paragraph B3-GENERATE-PAGES will be executed once again to generate a new report page. Otherwise, we are done with the iteration structure.

18. At lines 000198 through 000199 we close the input and output files and, with the STOP RUN statement on line 000200, terminate program execution.

It should be noted that the following statement in the code is the implementation of the single level control break concept for this problem.

```
000222          PERFORM C4-FORM-STUDENT-LINES
000223              UNTIL COURSE-CODE NOT EQUAL TO CURRENT-COURSE-CODE
000224                          OR
000225                      END-OF-FILE.
000226
000227          PERFORM C5-PRINT-SUMMARY.
000228          ADD 1 TO PAGE-NUMBER.
```

Key Terms

abbreviated combined condition
ACCEPT
ADD
arithmetic expression
assignment operator
Boolean operator
class condition
CLOSE
combined condition
COMPUTE
conditionals
condition-name condition
control break
decision making
DISPLAY
DIVIDE
EXIT
file-oriented I-O
GO TO
IF
imperative statements
interactive I-O

internal procedures
in-line PERFORM•
MOVE
MOVE CORRESPONDING
MULTIPLY
negated condition
no-operation statement
OPEN
open mode
PERFORM
PERFORM TIMES
PERFORM UNTIL
PERFORM VARYING
printer file
READ
relation condition
sign condition
STOP
SUBTRACT
unconditional transfer
WRITE

Study Guide

Quick Scan

- The PROCEDURE DIVISION is the last division in a COBOL program. Here the logic of the program is specified in terms of executable statements. These statements are classified into five categories: input-output, data movement, arithmetic, decision making, and control.
- File-oriented input-output requires the use of OPEN, CLOSE, READ, and WRITE statements for COBOL sequential files.
- Interactive input-output statements are the ACCEPT and DISPLAY statements.
- MOVE is the main statement for data movement in COBOL.
- Arithmetic operations can be handled by the versatile COMPUTE statement. In addition, COBOL supports the statements ADD, SUBTRACT, MULTIPLY, and DIVIDE for the four basic arithmetic operations.
- The IF statement is used for two-way decision making based on a condition. Many types of conditions in the language enable the programmer to formulate simple or complex predicates.
- IF statements can be used in a nested fashion for multiway decision making. COBOL also provides special language constructs, EVALUATE, and GO TO . . . DEPENDING ON, for the same purpose.
- Internal procedure (i.e., paragraph or section) invocation can be accomplished using the PERFORM statement. Different forms of PERFORM can be used for iterative invocation of internal procedures.
- Every COBOL program should include at least one STOP RUN statement to terminate the program execution.

Test Your Comprehension

Multiple-Choice Questions

1. Choose the correct statement about file open modes.
   a. The I-O file open mode readies a file for input purposes only.
   b. If a file has been opened in OUTPUT mode, we can write records into it.
   c. More than one file with different open modes cannot be opened using a single OPEN statement.
   d. The EXTEND file open mode is used for initial loading of files.
2. Concerning the sequential READ statement in COBOL,
   a. The key word READ is followed by a record name.
   b. The AT END clause may contain an IF statement.
   c. The optional INTO clause renders the READ statement equivalent to a READ followed by a MOVE statement.
   d. The NOT AT END clause is a COBOL 74 feature that is used to indicate the action to be taken if the current record in the file is the first record in it.
3. Concerning the source designators in the ACCEPT statement,
   a. DATE supplies a single-digit field that contains 1 if it is Monday, 2 if it is Tuesday, etc.
   b. DAY-OF-WEEK supplies a character string such as "MON" for Monday, "TUE" for Tuesday, etc.
   c. TIME returns the current time in the usual am/pm format.
   d. DAY returns a five-digit integer value such as 89003 for January 3, 1989.
4. Suppose we have the MOVE statement
   ```
   MOVE 12.5 TO B.
   ```
   Choose the correct answer. This data movement operation is not legal if
   a. B is a numeric integer field.
   b. B is numeric edited.
   c. B is alphabetic.
   d. B is a numeric noninteger field.
5. Which of the options about arithmetic expressions in COBOL completes the following statement correctly? In computing arithmetic expressions,
   a. Parenthesized expressions are given higher priority.
   b. Parenthesized expressions are evaluated starting with the innermost subexpressions in parentheses.
   c. Of all arithmetic operators, the unary minus has the highest priority.
   d. Of all arithmetic operators, addition and subtraction have the lowest priority.
   e. All of the above are correct.
6. Choose the correct IF statement semantics element.
   a. In case the IF statement's condition evaluates to true, the else-part of the statement is executed.
   b. If the condition evaluates to false, the IF statement's then-part is executed.
   c. After either the else-part or the then-part is executed, the program control passes to the IF statement's condition.
   d. None of the above is correct.
7. Which of the options incorrectly completes the following statement? In computing the value for a COBOL combined condition,
   a. First, the arithmetic expressions are evaluated.
   b. Next, the relational conditions are computed.
   c. Then the Boolean operator NOT is applied to its operand.
   d. Then the expressions involving OR or AND are evaluated in the order they are encountered from left to right.
8. Which of the following about the iteration statements in COBOL is correct?
   a. A PERFORM TIMES statement needs an UNTIL clause.

b. The UNTIL clause in a PERFORM VARYING statement must have a condition based on the loop control variable for the PERFORM VARYING statement.

c. In the UNTIL clause of the PERFORM UNTIL statement, only simple relation conditions can be used.

d. The PERFORM TIMES statement executes an internal procedure a prescribed number of times.

Answers: 1. b; 2. c; 3. d; 4. c; 5. e; 6. d; 7. d; 8. d.

Short Essay Questions

1. Give a classification of COBOL PROCEDURE DIVISION statements.
2. Explain the functions of the following statements:
    a. OPEN
    b. CLOSE
    c. READ
    d. WRITE
3. What are the file open modes that can be defined in an OPEN statement? What open mode is used for what circumstances?
4. Explain why it is important to close all files at the end of processing.
5. Briefly discuss the COBOL 85 options for the READ statement.
6. How do we specify the printer carriage control characters for print files?
7. What values will be supplied by the system when the words
    a. DATE
    b. DAY
    c. DAY-OF-WEEK
    are used in an ACCEPT statement?
8. What are the functions of the DISPLAY statement?
9. Briefly explain the rules for moving alphabetic fields using the MOVE statement.
10. Discuss the COBOL rules for moving numeric data fields.
11. When do we need to use the CORRESPONDING option of the MOVE statement?
12. Discuss the rules for forming arithmetic expressions in the COMPUTE statement.
13. What is the function of the ON SIZE ERROR clause in arithmetic statements?
14. What does ROUNDED accomplish in arithmetic computations?
15. What is the order of computations used by the COBOL compiler in evaluating arithmetic expressions in the absence of parentheses?
16. Explain the syntactical elements of the COBOL IF statement.
17. Explain why the IF statement in COBOL 74 requires a terminating period.
18. What is a Boolean quantity? Does COBOL support Boolean quantities?
19. List at least six types of COBOL conditions.
20. What are the truth tables for the logical operators AND and OR?
21. What is the order of precedence for logical operators in a combined condition in COBOL?
22. Explain the functions of class conditions. How do we determine that a field contains alphanumeric data in COBOL using class conditions?
23. Briefly explain the functions of the following COBOL statements:
    a. PERFORM
    b. PERFORM UNTIL
    c. PERFORM VARYING
    d. CONTINUE
    e. STOP RUN

Improve Your Problem-Solving Ability

Debugging Exercises

In view of the ENVIRONMENT and DATA DIVISIONs of Program 1-Source, specify whether or not the following COBOL statements are valid. In case you find any errors, explain them and suggest ways to correct them.

```
 1.  OPEN INPUT  STUDENT-TEST-SCORES-RECORD
         OUTPUT SUMMARY-GRADES-REPORT.
 2.  READ STUDENT-TEST-SCORES-RECORD
         AT END MOVE "YES" TO END-OF-FILE-FLAG.
 3.  PERFORM B3-GENERATE-PAGES
         UNTIL END-OF-FILE-FLAG.
 4.  CLOSE INPUT STUDENT-TEST-SCORES-FILE.
 5.  ACCEPT TODAYS-DATE FROM CURRENT-DATE.
 6.  MOVE 1 TO DATE.
 7.  DISPLAY --> ENTER ACADEMIC YEAR, LIKE 1953-54: "
 8.  PERFORM C4-FORM-STUDENT-LINES
         UNTIL COURSE-CODE NOT EQUAL TO CURRENT-COURSE-CODE
                            OR
                    END-OF-FILE-FLAG.
 9.  WRITE REPORT-LINE
         AFTER ADVANCING 2 PAGES.
10.  COMPUTE STUDENT-AVERAGE, AVERAGE =
         0.25 * FIRST-TEST-SCORE +
         0.35 * SECOND-TEST-SCORE +
         0.40 * FINAL-TEST-SCORE.
11.  IF STUDENT-AVERAGE > 79
         AND
     STUDENT-AVERAGE < 90
         MOVE "B" TO OUT-STUDENT-GRADE.
         ADD 3   TO TOTAL-CREDITS.
```

Programming Exercises

1. Write an OPEN statement to ready for input an existing disk file called ACCOUNTS-RECEIVABLE-FILE, and to ready for output a yet nonexistent disk file called TODAYS-SUMMARY.

2. Write a READ statement to read a record from a sequential file called ACCOUNTS-RECEIVABLE-FILE and store the record in a WORKING-STORAGE SECTION structure called WS-RECEIVABLES-RECORD. If no records are available for reading at the time your READ statement executes, the program control should pass to a paragraph called TERMINAL-PROCESSING.

3. Write an ACCEPT statement to get the current date and store it in a WORKING-STORAGE SECTION structure called WS-DATE.

4. Suppose we are executing the MOVE statement
   ```
   MOVE X-SOURCE TO X-TARGET.
   ```
   The picture specifications for X-SOURCE and X-TARGET, as well as the current content of X-SOURCE, are as shown in the following table. For each case, determine what the value of X-TARGET will be after the MOVE statement is executed.

X-SOURCE PICTURE	X-SOURCE Value	X-TARGET PICTURE	X-TARGET Value
PIC X(12)	"STUDENT NAME"	PIC X(8)	
PIC X(12)	"STUDENT IDNO"	PIC X(15)	
PIC X(12)	"CLASS "	PIC A(8)	
PIC 9(4)	0120	PIC 9(6)	
PIC 9(4)	0120	PIC 9(4)V99	
PIC 9(4)	0120	PIC X(6)	
PIC 9(4)	0120	PIC 9(6).999	
PIC 9(4)V99	012030	PIC 9(6)	
PIC 9(4)V99	012030	PIC 9(6)V9	
PIC 9(4)V99	012030	PIC Z(6).9	
PIC Z(4).999	120.123	PIC X(8)	
PIC Z(4).999	120.123	PIC 9999	
PIC Z(4).999	120.123	PIC 9(4)V99	
PIC Z(4).999	120.123	PIC 9(5).99	

5. Suppose in a program we have the following WORKING-STORAGE SEC-
   TION structures.

   ```
   01   CUSTOMER-INFO.
        05   CUSTOMER-NAME.
             10   LAST-NAME        PIC X(10).
             10   FIRST-NAME       PIC X(10).
        05   TRANS-TYPE            PIC X.
        05   TRANS-AMOUNT          PIC 9(6)V99.


   01   REPORT-LINE.
        05   CUSTOMER-NAME         PIC X(20).
        05   FILLER                PIC XX    VALUE SPACES.
        05   TRANS-TYPE            PIC X.
        05   FILLER                PIC XXXX.
        05   TRANS-AMOUNT          PIC $Z(6).99.
   ```

   a. What values will be stored in LAST-NAME, FIRST-NAME, TRANS-
      TYPE, and TRANS-AMOUNT after the following statement is executed?
      ```
      MOVE "SMITH-JACKSON THOMASD00034556" TO CUSTOMER-INFO.
      ```
   b. What will be the content of the structure REPORT-LINE after the fol-
      lowing MOVE statement is executed?
      ```
      MOVE CORRESPONDING CUSTOMER-INFO TO REPORT-LINE.
      ```
6. Given is the COMPUTE statement
   ```
   COMPUTE X ROUNDED, Y = A ** 2 + B * B / 5 - C / D / 2
            + 2.75
   ```
   a. Rewrite the statement using parentheses to clarify the meaning.
   b. Suppose at the time the statement is executing the variables A, B, C, and
      D store the values 3, 6, 9, and 2, respectively. Also, suppose the fields X
      and Y both have been defined by the same PICTURE specification, PIC-
      TURE 9(4)V9. What will be stored in X and Y as the result of this state-
      ment? Explain your answer.

7. For each of the following arithmetic expressions, write a COMPUTE statement to compute and store the result in a variable called RESULT.

   a. $x + y^2 + \dfrac{t}{z}$

   b. $\dfrac{a^3 + b^3}{c^2 - d^2}$

   c. $\dfrac{1}{m} + \dfrac{1 - j}{1 - k}$

8. For each arithmetic expression given in programming exercise 7, write all necessary COBOL ADD, SUBTRACT, MULTIPLY, and DIVIDE statements in their proper sequence to accomplish the same results.

9. Write an IF statement that directs control to a paragraph called PROCESS-NON-DEPOSIT in case TRANSACTION-TYPE is neither withdrawal nor withdrawal using automated teller. Otherwise, the IF statement should pass control to whatever follows it in the program. Use the data definition for TRANSACTION-TYPE as in programming exercise 7 of Chapter 2, and the appropriate condition names in the condition for IF.

10. Given is the following partial COBOL code.

```
      . . . . . . . . . . . . . .
            MOVE 5 TO VAR-A.
            IF VAR-B = VAR-C
                NEXT SENTENCE
            ELSE
                MOVE VAR-B TO VAR-C
                IF VAR-C NOT = VAR-B
                    MOVE VAR-C TO VAR-B
                ELSE
                    NEXT SENTENCE
                PERFORM PART-TWO
                    UNTIL VAR-C = VAR-B
                IF VAR-B = 1
                    PERFORM PART-TWO
                        UNTIL ALL-DONE  "YES"
                ELSE
                    PERFORM PART-TWO.
 (30)       . . . . . . . . . . . . . .

            . . . . . . . . . . . . . .
        PART-TWO.
            ADD 7 TO VAR-A.
            . . . . . . . . . . . . . .
```

   a. Rewrite the IF statement as a sequence of unnested IF statements such that the function of the code does not change.

   b. What will be the value of the variable VAR-A at line 30? Explain your answer.

11. Consider the following COBOL combined condition.
    ```
    0.2 * QTY NOT GREATER THAN 50 AND NOT ICODE LESS THAN
    JCODE OR WEIGHT = 15 AND GIRTH < 23
    ```
    a. Rewrite the condition using parentheses.

    b. Assume that the current values of the variables in the expression are
    ```
    QTY = 80, ICODE = "A23X", JCODE = "823X"
    WEIGHT = 15, and GIRTH = 45.
    ```
    What value will be computed for the above condition? Explain why.

12. How many times will the paragraph named SUM-ALL be executed in the following statement?

```
PERFORM SUM-ALL
      VARYING LOOP-VAR
      FROM 7
      BY 4
      UNTIL LOOP-VAR = 27.
```

Programming Problems

1. Rewrite and run the sample program for this chapter (Program 1-Source) such that, in addition, it generates a summary page for which the following is the template.

```
          CLASS GRADE REPORT SUMMARY      DATE: XX-XX-XX
                                          PAGE:  9


                      1991-92 SPRING

TOTAL NUMBER OF COURSES      : 999
TOTAL NUMBER OF STUDENTS     : 999
CLASS AVERAGE FOR ALL COURSES: 9.99

MINIMUM CLASS AVERAGE
      COURSE CODE    : XXXXXXXX
      COURSE NAME    : XXXXXXXXXXXXXXXXXXXXXXXXX
      INSTRUCTOR NAME: XXXXXXXXXXXXXXXXXXX
      CLASS AVERAGE  : 9.99

MAXIMUM CLASS AVERAGE
      COURSE CODE    : XXXXXXXX
      COURSE NAME    : XXXXXXXXXXXXXXXXXXXXXXXXX
      INSTRUCTOR NAME: XXXXXXXXXXXXXXXXXXX
      CLASS AVERAGE  : 9.99
```

2. We have a disk file of student test scores with the following record format.

```
01   STUDENT-RECORD.
     05   STUDENT-IDNO    PIC X(4).
     05   TEST-SCORE-1    PIC 999.
     05   TEST-SCORE-2    PIC 999.
     05   TEST-SCORE-3    PIC 999.
```

Test scores are integers in the range 40 through 100 for each student.

a. Prepare a sequential student test scores file in which you have 20 records conforming to the above format.

b. Write a full COBOL program that reads one record at a time from the student test scores file, and computes and outputs on the terminal the following:

Minimum average test score and the corresponding student identification number

Maximum average test score and the corresponding student identification number

Average of all student test score averages

3. Write an interactive COBOL program that accepts values for loan amount, yearly interest rate, and monthly payment amount from the terminal, and computes and displays on the terminal screen a loan repayment table. Your program execution session should have the same layout as the following sample terminal run.

```
ENTER LOAN AMOUNT: 1000000
ENTER YEARLY INTEREST RATE: 1790
ENTER MONTHLY PAYMENT: 5000
***> MONTHLY PAYMENT TOO SMALL.
ENTER MONTHLY PAYMENT: 100000

  BEGINNING     PAYMENT      INTEREST    PRINCIPAL      ENDING
  BALANCE                                               BALANCE
  ----------    ----------   ----------  ----------    ----------

   10000.00      1000.00      149.17      850.83        9149.16
    9149.16      1000.00      136.47      863.52        8285.64
    8285.64      1000.00      123.59      876.41        7409.23
    7409.23      1000.00      110.52      889.48        6519.75
   ......................................

   ......................................

    1869.33      1000.00       27.88      972.12         897.21
     897.21       897.21        0.00      897.21           0.00
```

You should note the following.
a. Monthly interest is computed on the beginning balance as (beginning balance) * (interest rate) / 12.
b. Principal is obtained by subtracting monthly interest from monthly payment.
c. Ending balance is beginning balance minus principal paid.
d. The beginning balance for a month is the same as the ending balance for the previous month.
e. When the beginning balance for a month becomes less than or equal to the monthly payment amount, no interest is charged, and the monthly payment is considered as the principal amount. In this case, the monthly payment would be considered the final payment on the loan.

4. We have a sequential disk file called FACULTY-SALARIES. The records in this file have the following format.

```
01  FACULTY-SALARIES-RECORD.
    05  FACULTY-IDNO            PIC X(9).
    05  FACULTY-NAME            PIC X(25).
    05  CURRENT-SALARY          PIC 9(6)V99.
    05  PERFORMANCE-LEVEL       PIC X.
```

The data field PERFORMANCE-LEVEL can have the values S, G, and A for superior, good, and average, respectively. Develop a COBOL program that reads the FACULTY-SALARIES file, and computes and displays on the terminal screen the cost of a proposed pay increase scheme. The pay increase scheme assumes a 3.5% across-the-board increase for all faculty plus a merit raise. Merit raise percentages depend on the PERFORMANCE-LEVEL; for superior performance it is 2.5%, for good performance it is 1.5%, and for average performance no merit raise is considered. Test your program on the following data set.

```
                                              COLUMN
       1    5    10   15   20   25   30   35   40   45
      ----|----|----|----|----|----|----|----|----|---

       111111111THOMAS  SMITH              04000000S
       111222222ANNE  BLACK                04250000S
       111333333JANE  ROMAN                03350000A
       111444444WILLIAM  TURNER            03670000G
       111555555MARGARET  ALISON           05500000S
       111666666JAMES  KIRKLAND            03100000A
```

```
                                COLUMNS
        5    10   15   20   25   30   35   40   45   50   55   60   65   70   75
      ----|----|----|----|----|----|----|----|----|----|----|----|----|----|-

      1120  JOHN  SMITH              BUS401-A 067 088 099
      1126  CHERYL  CLARK            BUS401-A 098 070 067
      1130  RICHARD  CARLOS          BUS401-A 100 094 100
      1145  JANE  LEE                BUS401-A 037 055 056
      0800  THOMAS  CRAIG            CS 374-C 100 100 100
      1120  JOHN  SMITH              CS 374-C 056 067 087
      1120  JOHN  SMITH              MTH252-A 078 088 095
      1340  EILEEN  BRADLEY          MTH252-A 100 100 097
```

Program 1-Input Input Data (STUDENT-TEST-SCORES-FILE) for Program 1

```
000001     *.................................................................
000002       IDENTIFICATION DIVISION.
000003       PROGRAM-ID.  STUDENT-GRADES.
000004       ******************************************************************
000005     ***   THIS PROGRAM READS A SEQUENTIAL DISK FILE, CALLED "STUDENT  *
000006     ***   TEST SCORES", AND GENERATES A LIST OF STUDENT SEMESTER      *
000007     ***   AVERAGES AND FINAL LETTER GRADES.                           *
000008     ***        THE RECORDS OF STUDENT-TEST-SCORES FILE CONSIST OF:    *
000009     ***            1. STUDENT ID-NO,                                  *
000010     ***            2. STUDENT-NAME,                                   *
000011     ***            3. CLASS-CODE,                                     *
000012     ***            4. FIRST-TEST-SCORE,                               *
000013     ***            5. SECOND-TEST-SCORE,                              *
000014     ***            6. FINAL-TEST-SCORE.                               *
000015     ***                                                              *
000016     ***   THE LIST TO BE GENERATED SHOULD INCLUDE:                    *
000017     ***            1. A REPORT HEADER CONSISTING OF:                  *
000018     ***               (A) REPORT TITLE,                              *
000019     ***               (B) COURSE CODE AND COURSE NAME,               *
000020     ***               (C) PROCESSING DATE,                           *
000021     ***               (D) PAGE NUMBER.                               *
000022     ***                                                              *
000023     ***            2. ONE SUMMARY LINE FOR EACH STUDENT CONSISTING OF: *
000024     ***               (A) STUDENT NAME,                              *
000025     ***               (B) SEMESTER AVERAGE,                          *
000026     ***               (C) END-OF-SEMESTER LETTER GRADE.              *
```

Program 1-Source Program to Generate Class Grade Reports

```
000027   ***                                                              *
000028   ***           3. A SUMMARY SECTION CONSISTING OF:                *
000029   ***              (A) INSTRUCTOR NAME,                            *
000030   ***              (B) NUMBER OF STUDENTS IN CLASS,                *
000031   ***              (C) GRADE POINT AVERAGE FOR CLASS.             *
000032   ***                                                              *
000033   ***   VALUES FOR "COURSE NAME" AND "INSTRUCTOR NAME" ARE TO BE   *
000034   ***   INPUT INTERACTIVELY AT THE TERMINAL.                      *
000035   ***                                                              *
000036   ***   AVERAGE SCORE FOR STUDENTS WILL BE COMPUTED USING THE     *
000037   ***   FOLLOWING FORMULA:                                        *
000038   ***      0.25 * FIRST-TEST-SCORE + 0.35 * SECOND-TEST-SCORE     *
000039   ***        + 0.40 * FINAL-EXAM-SCORE.                           *
000040   ***                                                              *
000041   ***   THE RECORDS IN STUDENT-TEST-SCORES FILE ARE PRESORTED BY  *
000042   ***   STUDENT-IDNO AND COURSE-CODE.                             *
000043   ********************************************************************
000044
000045   AUTHOR.         UCKAN.
000046   DATE-WRITTEN.   APRIL 4, 1991.
000047   DATE-COMPILED. 04/04/91.
000048
000049   *...............................................................
000050   ENVIRONMENT DIVISION.
000051   CONFIGURATION SECTION.
000052   SOURCE-COMPUTER. UNIVERSITY-MAINFRAME.
000053   OBJECT-COMPUTER. UNIVERSITY-MAINFRAME.
000054   INPUT-OUTPUT SECTION.
000055   FILE-CONTROL.
000056       SELECT STUDENT-TEST-SCORES-FILE ASSIGN TO INFILE
000057               ORGANIZATION IS SEQUENTIAL
000058               ACCESS MODE  IS SEQUENTIAL.
000059
000060       SELECT SUMMARY-GRADES-REPORT    ASSIGN TO OUTFILE.
000061
000062   *...............................................................
000063   DATA DIVISION.
000064   FILE SECTION.
000065   FD  STUDENT-TEST-SCORES-FILE
000066       LABEL RECORDS ARE STANDARD
000067       DATA  RECORD  IS STUDENT-TEST-SCORES-RECORD
000068       RECORD CONTAINS 80 CHARACTERS.
000069   01  STUDENT-TEST-SCORES-RECORD.
000070       05  STUDENT-IDNO       PIC X(4).
000071       05  FILLER             PIC X.
000072       05  STUDENT-NAME       PIC X(25).
000073       05  FILLER             PIC X.
000074       05  COURSE-CODE        PIC X(8).
000075       05  FILLER             PIC X.
000076       05  FIRST-TEST-SCORE   PIC 999.
000077       05  FILLER             PIC X.
000078       05  SECOND-TEST-SCORE  PIC 999.
000079       05  FILLER             PIC X.
000080       05  FINAL-TEST-SCORE   PIC 999.
```

Program 1-Source (Continued)

```
000081          05  FILLER               PIC X(29).
000082
000083     FD   SUMMARY-GRADES-REPORT
000084          LABEL RECORDS ARE OMITTED
000085          DATA  RECORD  IS REPORT-LINE
000086          RECORD CONTAINS 131 CHARACTERS.
000087     01   REPORT-LINE               PIC X(131).
000088
000089     WORKING-STORAGE SECTION.
000090
000091     **********> SWITCHES:
000092
000093     01   END-OF-FILE-FLAG     PIC XXX   VALUE "NO".
000094          88 END-OF-FILE                 VALUE "YES".
000095
000096     **********> VARIABLES:
000097
000098     01   PAGE-NUMBER          PIC 99.
000099     01   ACADEMIC-YEAR        PIC X(7).
000100     01   ACADEMIC-SEMESTER    PIC X(6).
000101     01   COURSE-NAME          PIC X(25).
000102     01   INSTRUCTOR-NAME      PIC X(21).
000103     01   NUMBER-OF-STUDENTS   PIC 999.
000104     01   TOTAL-CREDITS        PIC 9999.
000105     01   CLASS-AVERAGE        PIC 9V99.
000106     01   CURRENT-COURSE-CODE  PIC X(8).
000107     01   STUDENT-AVERAGE      PIC 999.
000108
000109     **********> STRUCTURES:
000110
000111     01   PROCESSING-DATE.
000112          05  PROCESSING-MONTH  PIC XX.
000113          05  FILLER            PIC X     VALUE "-".
000114          05  PROCESSING-DAY    PIC XX.
000115          05  FILLER            PIC X     VALUE "-".
000116          05  PROCESSING-YEAR   PIC XX.
000117
000118     01   TODAYS-DATE.
000119          05  TODAYS-YEAR       PIC XX.
000120          05  TODAYS-MONTH      PIC XX.
000121          05  TODAYS-DAY        PIC XX.
000122
000123     01   REPORT-TITLE-1.
000124          05  FILLER            PIC X(30)  VALUE SPACES.
000125          05  FILLER            PIC X(18)  VALUE "CLASS GRADE REPORT".
000126          05  FILLER            PIC X(10)  VALUE SPACES.
000127          05  FILLER            PIC X(6)   VALUE "DATE: ".
000128          05  OUT-DATE          PIC X(8).
000129
000130     01   REPORT-LINE-2.
000131          05  FILLER            PIC X(58)  VALUE SPACES.
000132          05  FILLER            PIC X(6)   VALUE "PAGE: ".
000133          05  OUT-PAGE-NUMBER   PIC ZZ.
000134
```

Program 1-Source (Continued)

```
000135        01    YEAR-SEMESTER-LINE.
000136              05    FILLER                 PIC X(27)   VALUE SPACES.
000137              05    OUT-ACADEMIC-YEAR      PIC X(8).
000138              05    OUT-ACADEMIC-SEMESTER  PIC X(7).
000139              05    FILLER                 PIC X(8)    VALUE SPACES.
000140
000141        01    COURSE-DESCRIPTION-LINE.
000142              05    FILLER                 PIC X(3)    VALUE SPACES.
000143              05    OUT-COURSE-CODE        PIC X(10).
000144              05    OUT-COURSE-NAME        PIC X(25).
000145
000146        01    STUDENT-INFO-HEADER.
000147              05    FILLER                 PIC X(13)   VALUE SPACES.
000148              05    FILLER                 PIC X(12)   VALUE "STUDENT NAME".
000149              05    FILLER                 PIC X(14)   VALUE SPACES.
000150              05    FILLER                 PIC X(16)   VALUE "SEMESTER AVERAGE".
000151              05    FILLER                 PIC X(5)    VALUE SPACES.
000152              05    FILLER                 PIC X(5)    VALUE "GRADE".
000153
000154        01    STUDENT-INFO-UNDERLINE.
000155              05    FILLER                 PIC X(13)   VALUE SPACES.
000156              05    FILLER                 PIC X(21)   VALUE ALL "-".
000157              05    FILLER                 PIC X(5)    VALUE SPACES.
000158              05    FILLER                 PIC X(16)   VALUE ALL "-".
000159              05    FILLER                 PIC X(5)    VALUE SPACES.
000160              05    FILLER                 PIC X(5)    VALUE ALL "-".
000161
000162        01    STUDENT-LISTING-LINE.
000163              05    FILLER                 PIC X(13)   VALUE SPACES.
000164              05    OUT-STUDENT-NAME       PIC X(21).
000165              05    FILLER                 PIC X(11)   VALUE SPACES.
000166              05    OUT-STUDENT-AVERAGE    PIC ZZZ.
000167              05    FILLER                 PIC X(14)   VALUE SPACES.
000168              05    OUT-STUDENT-GRADE      PIC X.
000169
000170        01    INSTRUCTOR-NAME-LINE.
000171              05    FILLER            PIC X(30)   VALUE SPACES.
000172              05    FILLER            PIC X(20)   VALUE "INSTRUCTOR         : ".
000173              05    OUT-INSTR-NAME PIC X(21).
000174
000175        01    NUMBER-OF-STUDENTS-LINE.
000176              05    FILLER            PIC X(30)   VALUE SPACES.
000177              05    FILLER            PIC X(20)   VALUE "NUMBER OF STUDENTS: ".
000178              05    OUT-NO-STUDENTS PIC ZZZ.
000179
000180        01    CLASS-AVERAGE-LINE.
000181              05    FILLER            PIC X(30)   VALUE SPACES.
000182              05    FILLER            PIC X(20)   VALUE "CLASS AVERAGE      : ".
000183              05    OUT-CLASS-AVG     PIC Z.ZZ.
000184
```

Program 1-Source (Continued)

```
000185    *...................................................................
000186      PROCEDURE DIVISION.
000187      A—MAINLINER.
000188          OPEN INPUT  STUDENT—TEST—SCORES—FILE
000189               OUTPUT SUMMARY—GRADES—REPORT.
000190          PERFORM B1—PREPARATIONS.
000191          PERFORM B2—INITIAL—TERMINAL—INPUTS.
000192          READ STUDENT—TEST—SCORES—FILE
000193                  AT END MOVE "YES" TO END—OF—FILE—FLAG.
000194
000195          PERFORM B3—GENERATE—PAGES
000196                  UNTIL END—OF—FILE.
000197
000198          CLOSE STUDENT—TEST—SCORES—FILE
000199                SUMMARY—GRADES—REPORT.
000200          STOP RUN.
000201
000202      B1—PREPARATIONS.
000203          ACCEPT TODAYS—DATE FROM DATE.
000204          MOVE TODAYS—YEAR  TO PROCESSING—YEAR.
000205          MOVE TODAYS—MONTH TO PROCESSING—MONTH.
000206          MOVE TODAYS—DAY   TO PROCESSING—DAY.
000207          MOVE 1           TO PAGE—NUMBER.
000208
000209      B2—INITIAL—TERMINAL—INPUTS.
000210          DISPLAY "—> ENTER ACADEMIC YEAR, LIKE 1953—54: "
000211          ACCEPT ACADEMIC—YEAR      FROM CONSOLE.
000212          DISPLAY "—> ENTER SEMESTER AS FALL, SPRING, OR SUMMER: "
000213          ACCEPT ACADEMIC—SEMESTER FROM CONSOLE.
000214
000215
000216      B3—GENERATE—PAGES.
000217          MOVE COURSE—CODE TO CURRENT—COURSE—CODE.
000218          PERFORM C1—INITIALIZE—VARIABLES.
000219          PERFORM C2—REMAINING—TERMINAL—INPUTS.
000220          PERFORM C3—PRINT—HALF—PAGE.
000221
000222          PERFORM C4—FORM—STUDENT—LINES
000223                  UNTIL COURSE—CODE NOT EQUAL TO CURRENT—COURSE—CODE
000224                                    OR
000225                             END—OF—FILE.
000226
000227          PERFORM C5—PRINT—SUMMARY.
000228          ADD 1 TO PAGE—NUMBER.
000229
000230      C1—INITIALIZE—VARIABLES.
000231          MOVE 0    TO NUMBER—OF—STUDENTS.
000232          MOVE ZERO TO TOTAL—CREDITS.
000233
000234      C2—REMAINING—TERMINAL—INPUTS.
000235          DISPLAY "—> CURRENT COURSE CODE IS " CURRENT—COURSE—CODE.
000236          DISPLAY "   ENTER COURSE NAME: ".
000237          ACCEPT COURSE—NAME     FROM CONSOLE.
```

Program 1-Source (Continued)

```
000238            DISPLAY "—> ENTER INSTRUCTOR NAME FOR THIS COURSE: ".
000239            ACCEPT INSTRUCTOR-NAME FROM CONSOLE.
000240
000241     C3-PRINT-HALF-PAGE.
000242            MOVE SPACES          TO REPORT-LINE.
000243            MOVE PROCESSING-DATE TO OUT-DATE.
000244            MOVE REPORT-TITLE-1  TO REPORT-LINE
000245            WRITE REPORT-LINE
000246                    AFTER ADVANCING PAGE.
000247
000248            MOVE SPACES         TO REPORT-LINE.
000249            MOVE PAGE-NUMBER    TO OUT-PAGE-NUMBER.
000250            MOVE REPORT-LINE-2 TO REPORT-LINE.
000251            WRITE REPORT-LINE
000252                    AFTER ADVANCING 1 LINE.
000253
000254            MOVE SPACES             TO REPORT-LINE.
000255            MOVE ACADEMIC-YEAR      TO OUT-ACADEMIC-YEAR.
000256            MOVE ACADEMIC-SEMESTER  TO OUT-ACADEMIC-SEMESTER.
000257            MOVE YEAR-SEMESTER-LINE TO REPORT-LINE.
000258            WRITE REPORT-LINE
000259                    AFTER ADVANCING 3 LINES.
000260
000261            MOVE SPACES                TO REPORT-LINE.
000262            MOVE CURRENT-COURSE-CODE   TO OUT-COURSE-CODE.
000263            MOVE COURSE-NAME           TO OUT-COURSE-NAME.
000264            MOVE COURSE-DESCRIPTION-LINE TO REPORT-LINE.
000265            WRITE REPORT-LINE
000266                    AFTER ADVANCING 2 LINES.
000267
000268            MOVE SPACES                TO REPORT-LINE.
000269            MOVE STUDENT-INFO-HEADER TO REPORT-LINE.
000270            WRITE REPORT-LINE
000271                    AFTER ADVANCING 2 LINES.
000272
000273            MOVE SPACES                TO REPORT-LINE.
000274            MOVE STUDENT-INFO-UNDERLINE TO REPORT-LINE.
000275            WRITE REPORT-LINE
000276                    AFTER ADVANCING 1 LINE.
000277
000278     C4-FORM-STUDENT-LINES.
000279            ADD 1 TO NUMBER-OF-STUDENTS.
000280            COMPUTE STUDENT-AVERAGE =
000281                    0.25 * FIRST-TEST-SCORE +
000282                    0.35 * SECOND-TEST-SCORE +
000283                    0.40 * FINAL-TEST-SCORE.
000284            PERFORM D1-DETERMINE-GRADE.
000285            MOVE STUDENT-NAME        TO OUT-STUDENT-NAME.
000286            MOVE STUDENT-AVERAGE     TO OUT-STUDENT-AVERAGE.
000287            MOVE SPACES              TO REPORT-LINE.
000288            MOVE STUDENT-LISTING-LINE TO REPORT-LINE.
```

Program 1-Source (Continued)

```
000289          WRITE REPORT-LINE
000290                  AFTER ADVANCING 1 LINE.
000291          READ STUDENT-TEST-SCORES-FILE
000292                  AT END MOVE "YES" TO END-OF-FILE-FLAG.
000293
000294     C5-PRINT-SUMMARY.
000295          COMPUTE CLASS-AVERAGE = TOTAL-CREDITS / NUMBER-OF-STUDENTS.
000296
000297          MOVE SPACES              TO REPORT-LINE.
000298          MOVE INSTRUCTOR-NAME     TO OUT-INSTR-NAME.
000299          MOVE INSTRUCTOR-NAME-LINE TO REPORT-LINE.
000300          WRITE REPORT-LINE
000301                  AFTER ADVANCING 3 LINES.
000302
000303          MOVE SPACES                TO REPORT-LINE.
000304          MOVE NUMBER-OF-STUDENTS       TO OUT-NO-STUDENTS.
000305          MOVE NUMBER-OF-STUDENTS-LINE TO REPORT-LINE.
000306          WRITE REPORT-LINE
000307                  AFTER ADVANCING 1 LINE.
000308
000309          MOVE SPACES            TO REPORT-LINE.
000310          MOVE CLASS-AVERAGE     TO OUT-CLASS-AVG.
000311          MOVE CLASS-AVERAGE-LINE TO REPORT-LINE.
000312          WRITE REPORT-LINE
000313                  AFTER ADVANCING 1 LINE.
000314
000315     D1-DETERMINE-GRADE.
000316        IF STUDENT-AVERAGE > 89
000317                  MOVE "A" TO OUT-STUDENT-GRADE
000318                  ADD 4    TO TOTAL-CREDITS.
000319
000320        IF STUDENT-AVERAGE > 79
000321                  AND
000322           STUDENT-AVERAGE < 90
000323                  MOVE "B" TO OUT-STUDENT-GRADE
000324                  ADD 3    TO TOTAL-CREDITS.
000325
000326        IF STUDENT-AVERAGE > 69
000327                  AND
000328           STUDENT-AVERAGE < 80
000329                  MOVE "C" TO OUT-STUDENT-GRADE
000330                  ADD 2    TO TOTAL-CREDITS.
000331
000332        IF STUDENT-AVERAGE > 59
000333                  AND
000334           STUDENT-AVERAGE < 70
000335                  MOVE "D" TO OUT-STUDENT-GRADE
000336                  ADD 1    TO TOTAL-CREDITS.
000337
000338        IF STUDENT-AVERAGE < 60
000339                  MOVE "F" TO OUT-STUDENT-GRADE.
```

Program 1-Source (Continued)

```
                  CLASS GRADE REPORT              DATE: 04-04-91
                                                  PAGE:   1


              1990-91 SPRING


BUS401-A   ACCOUNTING

           STUDENT NAME                SEMESTER AVERAGE        GRADE
           --------------------        ----------------        -----
           JOHN SMITH                        87                  B
           CHERYL CLARK                      75                  C
           RICHARD CARLOS                    97                  A
           JANE LEE                          50                  F



                      INSTRUCTOR         : PROF. SMITH
                      NUMBER OF STUDENTS:   4
                      CLASS AVERAGE     : 2.25
```

```
                  CLASS GRADE REPORT              DATE: 04-04-91
                                                  PAGE:   2


              1990-91 SPRING


CS 374-C   DATA STRUCTURES

           STUDENT NAME                SEMESTER AVERAGE        GRADE
           --------------------        ----------------        -----
           THOMAS CRAIG                     100                  A
           JOHN SMITH                        72                  C


                      INSTRUCTOR          : PROF. LEE
                      NUMBER OF STUDENTS:   2
                      CLASS AVERAGE     : 3.00
```

```
                  CLASS GRADE REPORT              DATE: 04-04-91
                                                  PAGE:   3


              1990-91 SPRING


MTH252-A   CALCULUS

           STUDENT NAME                SEMESTER AVERAGE        GRADE
           --------------------        ----------------        -----
           JOHN SMITH                        88                  B
           EILEEN BRADLEY                    98                  A

                      INSTRUCTOR        : PROF. BLACK
                      NUMBER OF STUDENTS:   2
                      CLASS AVERAGE     : 3.50
```

Program 1-Output(a) Output of Sample Program 1

```
 --> ENTER ACADEMIC YEAR, LIKE 1953-54:
IGZOOOI, AWAITING REPLY.
 1988-89
 --> ENTER SEMESTER AS FALL, SPRING, OR SUMMER:
IGZOOOI, AWAITING REPLY.
 SPRING
 --> CURRENT COURSE CODE IS BUS401-A
      ENTER COURSE NAME:
IGZOOOI, AWAITING REPLY.
 ACCOUNTING
 --> ENTER INSTRUCTOR NAME FOR THIS COURSE:
IGZOOOI, AWAITING REPLY.
 PROF. SMITH
 --> CURRENT COURSE CODE IS CS 374-C
      ENTER COURSE NAME:
IGZOOOI, AWAITING REPLY.
 DATA STRUCTURES
 --> ENTER INSTRUCTOR NAME FOR THIS COURSE:
IGZOOOI, AWAITING REPLY.
 PROF. LEE
 --> CURRENT COURSE CODE IS MTH252-A
      ENTER COURSE NAME:
IGZOOOI, AWAITING REPLY.
 CALCULUS
 --> ENTER INSTRUCTOR NAME FOR THIS COURSE:
IGZOOOI, AWAITING REPLY.
 PROF. BLACK
```

Program 1-Output(b) A Terminal Session for Sample Program 1

II

Developing Good Application Programs

Software Engineering with COBOL: Program Design Principles

137

Study Guide
Quick Scan
Test Your Comprehension
Improve Your Problem-Solving Ability

I N   T H I S   C H A P T E R   Y O U   W I L L   L E A R N   A B O U T

- What a good program is
- Systems, systems analysis, and systems design
- Software engineering
- Structured programming in COBOL
    Sequence structure
    Selection structures
    Iteration structures
- Modular program design
    Program structures
    Module size
    Coupling
    Cohesion
- Data structure design
    Primitive data structures
    Composite data structures
    Implementation of data structures
- Top-down and bottom-up program design strategies

Introduction

The primary purpose of this chapter is to introduce concepts and principles that enable us to design and develop good computer programs. For this we rely on a relatively new discipline: software engineering. Although the principles of software engineering are especially well suited for application programs written in some recent high-level programming languages such as Pascal, Modula-2, and Ada, they also can be used with COBOL. The second purpose of this chapter is to associate these principles with application program development in COBOL.

Writing Good Programs

As a beginner in the field of computing, and during your previous exposure to computer programming languages, you probably concentrated on writing programs that produced correct results. You were trying to master the syntactical and logical intricacies of the language in which you developed programs. You did not really have time or perhaps even any reason to worry about other factors that make a program good. It was quite satisfying to write programs that ran correctly.

As you are reading this book, you have apparently decided to further your skills in computer programming. Maybe you are planning to work as an application programmer in the future, or maybe you just want to create elegant programs. In this section, we will briefly review a few concepts and then concentrate on the properties of good programs. Later, we will study the principles and techniques that will enable you to achieve your goal of becoming a better programmer.

Programs and Software

To solve problems in a corporate setting, an application programmer is routinely faced with the task of developing a program that is to be used either alone or, more frequently, together with other computer programs. Such problems are related to one or more **corporate functions** and generally make use of **corporate data**. As application programmers, we begin the process of program development by analyzing a problem in view of the relevant corporate functions and corporate data. Then we develop a set of general solutions that can be used to solve the problem. For most problems, unless they are simple, it is usually possible to formulate more than one method of solution. We pick the best and express it in the form of an algorithm.

> An **algorithm** is a finite collection of logically related steps that can be used to solve a problem correctly and efficiently in a finite amount of time.

The next step is to translate the algorithm into a computer program using a language such as COBOL.

> A **computer program** is a series of instructions or statements expressed in a computer language that can be interpreted and executed by a computer system to produce the desired solution for the problem.

Frequently, the terms computer program and software are used interchangeably. What then is software? We loosely define it as follows.

> **Software** is a set of related programs that interact with each other to produce the solution for a relatively complex problem.

In other words, relatively speaking, a program is small and software is large. In business and industry, most programs that application programmers write are components of application software systems. We should note that the above definition of software is restrictive in scope. A better definition is given below.

> **Software** is a collection of **computer programs, data structures, and documentation**. The computer programs properly manipulate data that are embedded in appropriately chosen data structures, to produce with efficiency the desired solution for the problem. The third component, documentation, describes the operation and use of the software system for users of the software and the systems personnel.

This means that as a contributor to the development of application software packages, an application programmer should be able to

1. Design and develop good programs
2. Make intelligent use of data structures relevant to the programs being developed
3. Produce good documentation

Properties of Good Programs

The properties of a good program are

1. Reliability and correctness
2. Understandability, readability, simplicity and architectural unity
3. Ease of modification and maintainability
4. Developmental efficiency and simplicity
5. Resource utilization efficiency

Reliability and correctness: A computer program should be able to solve the problem it is designed to solve, and do it correctly for all possible logical paths in its algorithm. Errors in a computer program may be due to a variety of factors:

1. Ambiguity in problem specification concerning the problem functions, inputs, and outputs
2. Use of incorrect algorithms
3. Mistakes in logic on the part of the programmer

Clearly, the most important characteristic of a program is correctness. In practice, program testing can be used successfully to find and correct errors. In general, however, testing cannot be used to formally prove program correctness. Although certain techniques have been developed to demonstrate correctness of small programs, no general-purpose technique is yet available for large software systems. During the 1980s some automated approaches to proof of correctness for computer programs have been developed. Proof of correctness and programs called *automated correctness provers* are still subjects of research and development.

Understandability, readability, simplicity, and architectural unity: A computer program should be simple in design with clean interfaces between simple modules. It should also have a clear and unified architectural design. In other words, similar design principles and constructs should be used for the entire system.

Application program maintenance is an important activity in the life cycle of software systems. The maintainer may be the original author of the program, or programmers who are not familiar with its conception. Whoever are the maintainers, they must be able to understand and modify the code. Therefore, the code should be written in an understandable and readable manner, should contain sufficient in-program documentation, and should be supplemented with additional documentation as needed.

Readability is achieved through standardization of program style. Understandability and simplicity are achieved through the use of appropriate program and data structures, and correct modularization. These all boil down to the use of proper design techniques.

Ease of modification and maintainability: All software systems must be modified occasionally to satisfy changing requirements of the corporate environment. Ease of maintainability depends on simplicity of design, architectural unity, and readability of code. In addition, maintainability is achieved through consistent use of well-established design techniques and conventions in a data processing shop.

Developmental efficiency and simplicity: The amount of time spent in developing a software system should be controllable. Developmental efficiency can be achieved through good project management techniques, sound principles of system design, appropriate program modularization, and use of automated design tools and automatic code generators. Although developmental efficiency is important, it is secondary to the first three characteristics.

Resource utilization efficiency: A good program should execute efficiently; that is, it should not take up excessive computer processing time and storage. This is achieved through the use of efficient algorithms, correct data structures, and optimally written and generated computer codes. Since computer hardware cost is continuously decreasing relative to software development cost, efficiency of resource utilization is less important than the first four characteristics. Furthermore, in some instances, it may be difficult to reconcile this factor with our more important objectives of understandability and developmental efficiency. We should try to find and use better algorithms and data structures without sacrificing from our main objectives, however.

In summary, writing a good computer program is largely a matter of using good design principles and techniques. In the remainder of this chapter, we study design and documentation techniques that may, when correctly used, enable us to

1. Develop programs with good structure
2. Describe the overall structure
3. Describe the detailed logic of the program
4. Describe the data structures used
5. Produce readable and understandable code
6. Simplify software development efforts

Software Development Process

Before we proceed with our discussion of software, a proper perspective of the software development process will be useful. Software is not an isolated element. Invariably, it is part of a system, complex or otherwise, that has something to do with computers. It may be a business system, an information system, a data base system, a communication system, a control system, an engineering system, a decision support system, and so on.

What Is a System?

> Whatever its nature, a **system** is a collection of interrelated components that perform some function to satisfy a set of goals. A system interacts with its environment, and is self-regulating and self-correcting.

Everything we see around us is either a system or a component of one. The planet earth is a part of the solar system and is also a system in itself. On a smaller scale, the human body is a system. These two are natural systems. There are also systems that are conceived and developed by humans, called **artificial systems**. Business systems are examples of artificial systems. In modern civilization, we are interested in the development, operation, and maintenance of artificial systems.

Let us consider a business system. One of its purposes may be to make a profit. To accomplish this, its components dynamically interact with one another and with their environment. This is self-regulation. The system should be designed to check for unusual conditions and possible errors, and when found, correct them. This is self-correction.

A system may consist of components that are themselves systems, called **subsystems**. For example, a business system for a corporation may consist of purchasing, manufacturing, sales, advertising, and accounting subsystems. If it uses computers to achieve its goals, we refer to it as a **computer-based system** (computer-supported system). On the other hand, a system whose main goal is processing information to facilitate corporate functions is an **information system**. Most information systems heavily depend on computers for information storage and information processing. Therefore, in addition to other subsystems, they contain a special subsystem called **software system**. In this book, we are interested in the development of software systems. The systems development life cycle for a software system consists of the following activities:

1. Analysis
2. Design
3. Coding
4. Testing

Systems Analysis

Within the context of software systems development, analysis is the process of defining the problem requirements in light of the corporate functions. During analysis, we determine needs of the future users of the software system, define the system constraints and requirements, and propose a solution. The output of the analysis phase is the **functional specification**.

A functional specification describes in detail how the software system will meet the requirements in terms of the following:

1. Functions to be performed
2. Corporate data resources and data structures to be used
3. Outputs to be produced
4. Interfaces to be maintained with other subsystems

A functional specification should be precise, formal, and understandable to systems analysts, programmers, and users, including management. During analysis, we also try to find alternative solutions to the problem and determine the feasibility of each one. On the basis of the functional specifications for these alternatives and their feasibility analyses, we make our choice and proceed to the design phase.

The computer systems analyst is generally dependent on others in the corporation for information. To collect information, the analyst uses a variety of techniques and information sources, including

1. Interviews
2. Questionnaires
3. Written procedures and other available documentation

After studying and verifying the collected information, the analyst proposes one or more methods of solution and prepares the functional specification.

A functional specification has two components: corporate functions or processes, and corporate data. Ultimately, corporate processes will evolve into computer algorithms, and corporate data will become appropriate data structures within the software system. The functional specification should include an overview of corporate functions, and detailed logical process and data specifications. Since the 1970s some structured techniques have been developed to specify logical processes and data. They are shown in the following table.

Structured Techniques for Specification of Corporate Functions	Structured Techniques for Specification of Logical Processes	Structured Techniques for Specification of Corporate Data	Structured Techniques for Specification of Logical Data
Organization charts Action diagrams Warnier-Orr diagrams	Data flow diagrams Action diagrams Warnier-Orr diagrams HIPO (hierarchical inputs, process output) diagrams	Data models	Data flow diagrams Logical data modeling techniques Entity-relationship diagrams Relational data modeling Other data modeling techniques

Systems Design

Systems design is the process of generating a blueprint for implementation. The output of the analysis phase, functional specification, is the input for the design process. The systems analyst chooses a design philosophy and methodology to generate the specifications.

The systems design phase is usually carried out in two steps: logical design and physical design. During **logical design**, the systems analyst (or designer) develops general specifications for the system. These should be independent of the technical specifications and constraints of the computer hardware and software system to be used for implementation. Logical design specifications consist of descriptions of system functions, data structures, system inputs, and outputs. Processes and data are described in logical terms. For processes, the descriptions include what is to be done and how it will be performed in non-machine-specific terms. For data, input, and output, the descriptions are in terms of what they contain and how they will be accessed, again in nonmachine-specific terms.

Physical design associates the logical design specifications with the computer system to be used for implementation. During this step the designer takes into consideration the programming language, available file management and base data management software, characteristics of input and output devices, operating system, and data communication system. The result is a detailed, technical blueprint that will eventually become the input for the program development phase.

A table of structured techniques that can be used by the systems designer to describe the design specifications is given below. The majority of these techniques are discussed in detail in Chapter 5.

Structured Techniques for Specification of Overall Program Structure	Structured Techniques for Specification of Detailed Program Logic	Structured Techniques for Specification of Program Data
Structure charts Action diagrams Warnier-Orr diagrams Jackson diagrams HIPO (hierarchical input, process output) diagrams HOS (higher-order software) charts	Flow-charting Pseudocoding and structured English Action diagrams Nassi-Schneiderman charts Decision tables, decision trees	Physical data modeling techniques Relational data modeling Other data modeling techniques Warnier-Orr diagrams Michael Jackson diagrams Data navigation diagrams

Each structured analysis or design technique has its own merits and short-comings. The choice depends partly on the nature of the problem and partly on the conventions adopted by the department responsible for software development. In this book we will stress design and program development. This is not because the analysis phase is unimportant. It most definitely is a crucial phase of the system life cycle, and errors made during analysis are expensive to remedy. The subject is outside the scope of this book, however. Our focus is on good program design and development. Therefore, in the rest of this chapter we will discuss techniques and conventions for specifying program logic and structure, data structures, and coding. Testing, which is the last phase of the system development life cycle, is discussed in Chapter 6.

REVIEW QUESTIONS

1. A finite collection of logically related steps that is performed to solve a problem correctly and efficiently in a finite amount of time is called an _____ .

2. A computer program is a translation of an algorithm into a series of statements expressed in a computer language. (T or F)

3. Software is a word that is used to connote relatively large programming systems, and is a collection of _____ , _____ , and _____ .

4. If a software system consists of programs that are easy to understand, easy to read, and simple, it is generally easy to maintain. (T or F)

5. A good program should be
   a. Reliable and correct
   b. Understandable, readable, and simple
   c. Easy to modify and maintain
   d. Simple and efficient to develop
   e. All of the above

6. Which of the following statements concerning systems is correct?
   a. A system is a collection of interrelated components that perform some function to satisfy a set of goals.
   b. A system interacts with its environment.
   c. A system is self-regulated.
   d. A system is self-correcting.
   e. All of the above.

7. Information systems and software systems are examples of natural systems. (T or F)

8. The development life cycle for a software system consists of _____ , _____ , _____ , and _____ .

9. The output of the systems analysis phase is known as _____ .

10. During _____ , the designer develops general design specifications for the system independent of the properties of the computer system to be used for implementation. The computer system is taken into consideration during _____ .

Answers: 1. algorithm; 2. T; 3. computer programs, data structures, documentation; 4. T; 5. e; 6. e; 7. F; 8. analysis, design, coding, testing; 9. functional specification; 10. logical design, physical design.

An Engineering Approach to Program Development: Software Engineering

In the early days of computing, computer hardware was expensive. As a consequence, computer-based systems were developed using hardware-oriented management techniques. Most of the programs were custom designed for individual applications. Programming was considered an art rather than science or engineering, and almost no formal methods existed. Programmers learned their craft through training, and by trial and error.

In the words of R. M. Graham,* programs were built ". . . like the Wright brothers built airplanes —build the whole thing, push it off a cliff, let it crash, and start over again."

Beginning in the mid-1970s and especially in the 1980s, the picture changed dramatically. Advances in science and technology resulted in powerful and relatively inexpensive computer hardware. The computing power and sophistication of many mainframes of yesterday are easily surpassed even by microcomputers of today. The ever-growing need for computer-based systems emphasized what is commonly termed the software crisis. Developing programs that can measure up to the computing potentials offered by new generations of hardware and at the same time satisfy the demand for more sophisticated computer-based systems is becoming increasingly difficult. Software development has become very complex, expensive, and time consuming. Most software development projects are unacceptably behind schedule; large-scale software systems are almost never error free; testing is a major problem. Old software developed using inadequate resources and poor design techniques are very difficult to maintain.

Clearly, the informal and individualistic attitude toward developing software had to change. A more disciplined and formal approach—an engineering-style approach—was essential. It was found in a new discipline called software engineering.

> **Software engineering** consists of methods, tools, and procedures that enable the programmer to develop high-quality software in a productive and efficient manner, and enable the manager of software development to control the project effectively.

Software engineering is concerned with the following:

1. Software development project planning and estimation
2. System and software requirements analysis
3. Design of data structures
4. Design of program structure and algorithms
5. Program coding
6. Software quality assurance
7. Program testing and verification
8. Software maintenance and configuration management

Of these, we are interested in design of program structure and algorithms, design of data structures, program coding, and program testing. The other issues are covered in courses on systems analysis and design and software engineering, and are outside the scope of this book. While exploring the principles and techniques for program structure, algorithm, and data structure design, program coding, and program testing, we will emphasize the relatively recent techniques that are considered to be within the realm of software engineering.

*R. M. Graham, panel discussion in *Software Engineering,* ed. P. Naur and B. Randall. Brussels: NATO Scientific Affairs Division, 1969.

Program Logic Design: Structured Programming

We know that, unless otherwise told, a computer will execute instructions in a program consecutively, one after another. We also know that most algorithms require repeated or conditional execution of blocks of code at some point in a program. While converting such algorithms into programs, we therefore must intentionally alter the tendency of computers to execute instructions consecutively. We do this by specifying branches to other instructions in our program.

There are two types of branches in a program structure: unconditional and conditional. Unconditional branches take program control to another point in the program without providing a return to the point of branching. A conditional branch defines a jump to a block of code, and then returns control back either to the point of branching or to a predetermined point in the program. Most programming languages implement unconditional branching through one form or another of GO TO instruction.

Older high-level programming languages such as FORTRAN, PL/I, and COBOL have statements for unconditional branching that were used liberally in application programming. This tendency produced programs that are colloquially referred to as "spaghetti codes"; codes into which a large number of long, one-way, logical paths are incorporated. Such programs are usually difficult to debug, read, and maintain.

At the same time, a number of computer scientists became increasingly concerned with the fact that programming languages, while growing naturally, borrowed too many features from one another and evolved into unnecessarily crowded and hard-to-learn tools. Clearly, leaner languages were needed. Computer scientists such as Dijkstra, Wirth, Hoare, Bohm, and Jacopini pioneered a new discipline called structured programming. They advocated and proved the following principles.

1. Any program can be written using only three structures: sequence, selection, and iteration.
2. Unconditional branching, or GO TO statement, is not an essential control structure in programming.
3. The three basic control structures of structured programming are easy to comprehend and modify. Also, from a practical standpoint, they result in programs that are easier to write, read, debug, and maintain compared to those that use GO TOs liberally.

These principles constitute the foundations of a discipline of programming, known as structured programming. Structured programming as a formal programming methodology is proven both sufficient and necessary for software development. A definition of structured programming follows.

> **Structured programming** is the discipline of making a program's logic easy to follow by using three primitive program structures: sequence, selection, and iteration. Use of structured programming primitives in the program development process ensures well-designed programs.

The objectives of structured programming are to

1. Simplify the program design process
2. Minimize program complexity
3. Increase program readability
4. Simplify program maintenance
5. Define a disciplined programming methodology

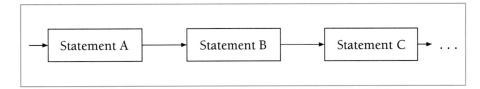

Figure 1 The Sequence Structure

The three primitive constructs of structured programming are shown in Figures 1, 2, and 3. They are

1. The sequence structure
2. The selection structure
3. The iteration structure

A **sequence structure** (Figure 1) consists of any number of program statements, sentences, or predefined processes (modules) that are executed one after another. An example of COBOL implementation of the sequence structure is as follows.

```
OPEN INPUT  STUDENT-FILE,
     OUTPUT STUDENT-REPORT.
DISPLAY "--> ENTER STUDENT ID NUMBER: ".
ACCEPT SEARCH-ID FROM CONSOLE.
MOVE SEARCH-ID TO OUT-SEARCH-ID.
PERFORM B1-PRODUCE-REPORT-HEADINGS.
READ STUDENT-FILE RECORD
        AT END MOVE "YES" TO END-OF-FILE-REACHED.
```

The **selection structure** (Figure 2) first tests a condition (predicate) and executes the then-part if the condition evaluates to true. If the condition evaluates to false, the selection structure executes the else-part. Both the then-part and the else-part are well-formed program segments. Again, they can be a single

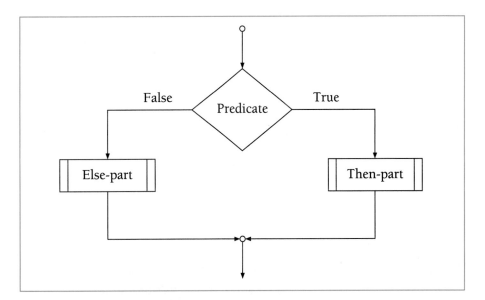

Figure 2 The Selection Structure

statement, a block of statements, or a sequence of predefined processes. In a well-written program, a selection structure may contain an empty then-part or an empty else-part, but both should not be empty. A selection structure, as the flow chart of Figure 2 depicts, is for two-way decision making. Some COBOL examples follow.

COBOL 74 version

```
IF RECORD-TYPE OF STUDENT-IDENTIFICATION = "I"
    PERFORM C1-PRINT-MAIN-INFORMATION
ELSE
    PERFORM C2-PRINT-ENROLLMENT-INFO.
```

COBOL 85 version

COBOL 85

```
IF RECORD-TYPE OF STUDENT-IDENTIFICATION = "I"
    THEN
        PERFORM C1-PRINT-MAIN-INFORMATION
    ELSE
        PERFORM C2-PRINT-ENROLLMENT-INFO
END-IF.
```

The **iteration structure** is used for controlled repetition (looping). It executes a well-formed program segment, called the loop body, a finite number of times. The repeated execution is controlled by a predicate associated with the iteration structure.

There are two basic variations of the iteration structure: pretest and posttest. The **pretest iteration structure** (Figure 3) tests a predicate before entering the loop body. If the predicate computes to false, the loop body is executed; otherwise, the program control drops out of the iteration structure to the next structure in the code. To control the iteration, the programmer should provide for a mechanism within the loop body that renders the predicate true after a finite number of repetitions. This iteration structure is also referred to as DO WHILE

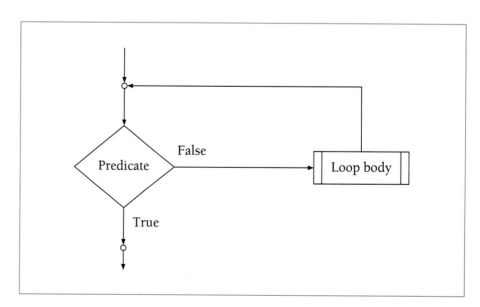

Figure 3 The Pretest Iteration Structure

structure ("Do while predicate is false"). Following are examples of COBOL implementation of the pretest iteration structure.

COBOL 74 version

```
PERFORM B2-PROCESS-RECORDS
        UNTIL END-OF-FILE.
```

COBOL 85 version

```
PERFORM B2-PROCESS-RECORDS
        WITH TEST BEFORE
        UNTIL END-OF-FILE.
```

The **posttest iteration structure** (Figure 4) first executes the loop body. Then a predicate, also called a termination condition, is tested. If the predicate produces a value of false, the loop body is executed again. Otherwise, control drops out of the iteration structure. Another name for this basic structure is DO UNTIL ("Do until predicate is true").

COBOL 74 version

```
PERFORM B2-PROCESS-RECORDS.
PERFORM B2-PROCESS-RECORDS
        UNTIL END-OF-FILE.
```

COBOL 85 version

```
PERFORM B2-PROCESS-RECORDS
        WITH TEST AFTER
        UNTIL END-OF-FILE.
```

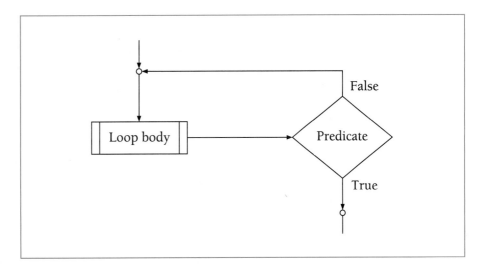

Figure 4 The Posttest Iteration Structure

Occasionally in a program the programmer has to define multiway (N-way) decision making structures. This task can be accomplished in three basic manners.

1. Define a series of consecutive two-way selection structures.
2. Use a composite selection structure consisting of two or more primitive selection structures (nested IFs).
3. Use special language constructs (known as the **CASE structure**) that specify multiple branches at a decision point.

The following COBOL codes exemplify three-way selection using consecutive unnested IFs.

COBOL 74 version

```
IF SEX-CODE = 1
    PERFORM MALE-STUDENTS.

IF SEX-CODE = 2
    PERFORM FEMALE-STUDENTS.

IF SEX-CODE NOT = 1 OR NOT = 2
    PERFORM ERROR-IN-SEX-CODE.
```

COBOL 85 version

COBOL 85

```
IF SEX-CODE = 1
    PERFORM MALE-STUDENTS
END-IF
IF SEX-CODE = 2
    PERFORM FEMALE-STUDENTS
END-IF
IF SEX-CODE NOT = 1 OR NOT = 2
    PERFORM ERROR-IN-SEX-CODE
END-IF
```

An IF statement that includes other IF statements in its then-part and/or else-part is known as a **nested IF**. The logic of a two-level nested IF is shown in the flow chart of Figure 5.

For the example considered above, two COBOL implementations of three-way decision making, this time using nested IFs, are given below.

COBOL 74 version

```
IF SEX-CODE = 1
    PERFORM MALE-STUDENTS
ELSE
    IF SEX-CODE = 2
        PERFORM FEMALE-STUDENTS
    ELSE
        PERFORM ERROR-IN-SEX-CODE.
```

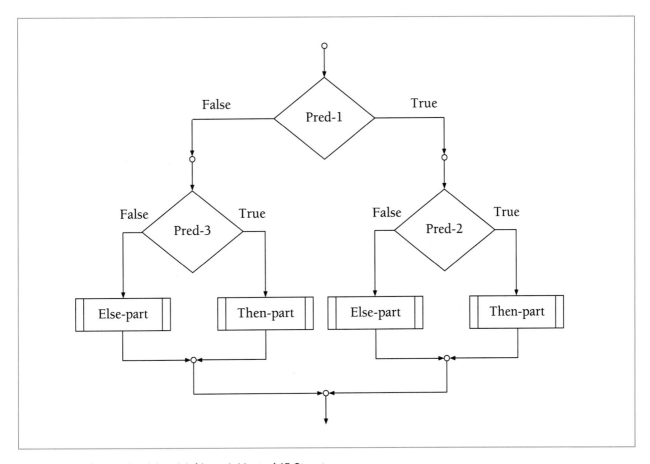

Figure 5 Multiway Decision Making: A Nested IF Structure

COBOL 85 version

COBOL 85

```
IF SEX-CODE = 1
  THEN
     PERFORM MALE-STUDENTS
  ELSE
     IF SEX-CODE = 2
       THEN
          PERFORM FEMALE-STUDENTS
       ELSE
          PERFORM ERROR-IN-SEX-CODE
     END-IF
END-IF
```

As you can see, two techniques of multiway decision making studied so far are logically equivalent but not identical. The nested IF composite selection structure is more efficient from the point of view of program execution. We should exercise restraint in use of multiply nested selection structures, however. Nesting in excess of three levels makes the code difficult to understand for most programmers and therefore is not recommended.

Figure 6 is a flow chart depicting the logic of the CASE structure. At the entry point to the structure, an expression is evaluated. If the value of that expression is 1, the first path is taken and the program block Case-1 is executed; if the expression is evaluated as 2, the program block Case-2 is executed, COBOL 85 and so on. The CASE structure is implemented in COBOL 85 through the EVALUATE statement. The syntax of the EVALUATE statement is as follows.

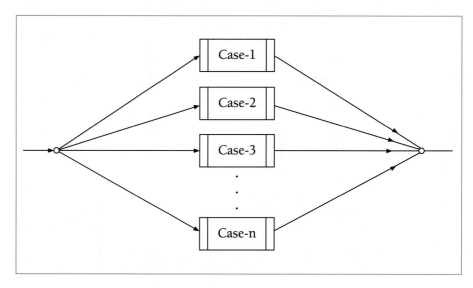

Figure 6 Multiway Decision Making: The CASE Structure

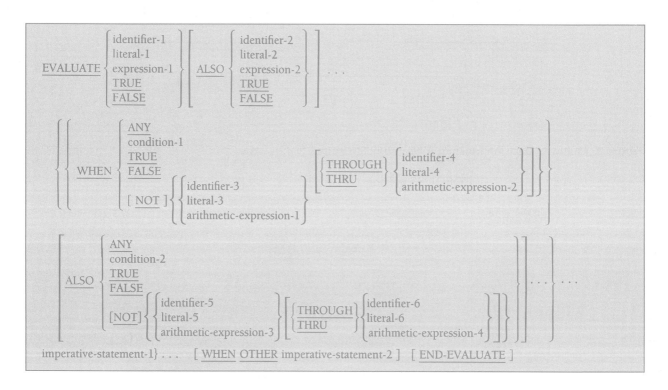

COBOL 85   An example of its use for multiway decision making is as follows.

```
EVALUATE SEX-CODE
     WHEN 1       PERFORM MALE-STUDENTS
     WHEN 2       PERFORM FEMALE-STUDENTS
     WHEN OTHER   PERFORM ERROR-IN-SEX-CODE.
```

If the current value of the variable SEX-CODE is 1, the internal procedure MALE-STUDENTS is executed. If it is 2, FEMALE-STUDENTS is invoked. For any other value of SEX-CODE, the procedure ERROR-IN-SEX-CODE is called on.

In COBOL 74 a special language feature, the GO TO . . . DEPENDING ON statement, can be used for the same purpose. The syntax of GO TO . . . DEPENDING ON is given here.

<u>GO</u> <u>TO</u> { procedure-name } . . . <u>DEPENDING</u> ON identifier

Consider the following example.

```
DECISION-POINT.
      GO TO MALE-STUDENTS
            FEMALE-STUDENTS
      DEPENDING ON SEX-CODE.
      GO TO ERROR-IN-SEX-CODE.

MALE-STUDENTS.
      . . . . . . . . . .
      . . . . . . . . . .
      GO TO END-DECISION-POINT.

FEMALE-STUDENTS.
      . . . . . . . . . .
      . . . . . . . . . .
      GO TO END-DECISION-POINT.

ERROR-IN-SEX-CODE.
      . . . . . . . . . .
      . . . . . . . . . .
END-DECISION-POINT.

NEXT-PARAGRAPH.
      . . . . . . . . . .
      . . . . . . . . . .
```

Note that in this example we had to use GO TO statements and we had to define an empty paragraph (END-DECISION-POINT) to ensure proper exit out of the multiway decision structure. In other words, we had to be more careful to specify the necessary program control structures. We also ended up with a highly vulnerable code, in that a careless insertion of another paragraph between ERROR-IN-SEX-CODE and END-DECISION-POINT in the future will certainly result in a program with logic errors.

In general, use of the GO TO . . . DEPENDING ON statement in COBOL necessitates GO TO statements. Therefore, the resulting code is inevitably unstructured. We do not recommend the use of GO TO . . . DEPENDING ON statements in program development in COBOL. If the EVALUATE of COBOL 85 is not available in your compiler, you can always use nested IFs for multiway decision making.

Earlier in this section we mentioned that any given algorithm can be expressed in terms of the three primitive structures of structured programming. We will not attempt to prove this assertion. We will, however, demonstrate this fact using the procedure division of the sample program of this chapter (see Program 1-Source). Let us number the statements of the procedure division to reference individual statements or groups of statements (Figure 7). The logic of the program is shown in the abbreviated flow chart of Figure 8. Such a flow chart, also known as a **flow graph**, can be used effectively for program debugging purposes. A more detailed discussion of flow graphs appears in Chapter 6. Figure 9 shows, for the same program, the detailed program logic in terms of the three primitive structures. Both of these figures indicate that the algorithm of the program of Figure 7 is expressible in terms of sequence, selection, and iteration structures, and that no other primitive is necessary to specify the algorithm. This is true of any structured program.

As our discussion shows, COBOL has language constructs for all primitives of structured programming. Consequently, in this sense, it is a structured language.

In summary, a program that uses the three primitives of structured programming and the CASE construct is a structured program. In its purest form, structured programming can be considered to be synonymous to "GOTO-less programming". Throughout this book we will write and study structured programs, and avoid the use of GO TO and GO TO . . . DEPENDING ON statements.

```
          PROCEDURE DIVISION.

          A—MAIN—PARAGRAPH.
    1         OPEN INPUT   STUDENT-FILE,
    2              OUTPUT STUDENT-REPORT.
    3         DISPLAY "--> ENTER STUDENT ID NUMBER: ".
    4         ACCEPT SEARCH-ID FROM CONSOLE.
    5         MOVE SEARCH-ID TO OUT-SEARCH-ID.
    6         PERFORM B1-PRODUCE-REPORT-HEADINGS.
    7         READ STUDENT-FILE RECORD
                    AT END MOVE "YES" TO END-OF-FILE-REACHED.

    8         PERFORM B2-PROCESS-RECORDS
                    UNTIL END-OF-FILE.

    9         CLOSE STUDENT-FILE,
   10              STUDENT-REPORT.
   11         STOP RUN.

          B1-PRODUCE-REPORT-HEADINGS.
   61         MOVE SPACES           TO REPORT-LINE.
   62         MOVE MAIN-TITLE       TO REPORT-LINE.
   63         WRITE REPORT-LINE
                    AFTER ADVANCING PAGE.
   64         MOVE TITLE-1          TO REPORT-LINE.
   65         WRITE REPORT-LINE
                    AFTER ADVANCING 4 LINES.
   66         MOVE COLUMN-HEADING-1 TO REPORT-LINE.
   67         WRITE REPORT-LINE
                    AFTER ADVANCING 2 LINES.
   68         MOVE DASHED-LINE-1    TO REPORT-LINE.
   69         WRITE REPORT-LINE
                    AFTER ADVANCING 1 LINE.
```

Figure 7 Procedure Division of a Sample COBOL Structured Program

```
          B2-PROCESS-RECORDS.
81            IF STUDENT-NUMBER OF STUDENT-IDENTIFICATION-REC = SEARCH-ID
82                IF RECORD-TYPE OF STUDENT-IDENTIFICATION-REC = "I"
83                    PERFORM C1-PRINT-MAIN-INFORMATION
                  ELSE
84                    PERFORM C2-PRINT-ENROLLMENT-INFO.

85            READ STUDENT-FILE RECORD
                  AT END MOVE "YES" TO END-OF-FILE-REACHED.


          C1-PRINT-MAIN-INFORMATION.
831           MOVE STUDENT-NUMBER OF STUDENT-IDENTIFICATION-REC
                          TO OUT-STUDENT-NUMBER.
832           MOVE STUDENT-NAME    TO OUT-STUDENT-NAME.
833           MOVE STUDENT-MAJOR   TO OUT-STUDENT-MAJOR.
834           MOVE STUDENT-YEAR    TO OUT-STUDENT-YEAR.
835           MOVE OUT-MAIN        TO REPORT-LINE.
836           WRITE REPORT-LINE
                  AFTER ADVANCING 1 LINE.


          C2-PRINT-ENROLLMENT-INFO.
841           IF FIRST-ENROLLMENT-RECORD = "YES"
842             PERFORM D1-PRODUCE-OTHER-HEADINGS
843             MOVE "NO" TO FIRST-ENROLLMENT-RECORD.


844           PERFORM D2-PRINT-ENROLLMENT.


          D1-PRODUCE-OTHER-HEADINGS.
8421          MOVE SPACES          TO REPORT-LINE.
8422          MOVE TITLE-2         TO REPORT-LINE.
8423          WRITE REPORT-LINE
                  AFTER ADVANCING 4 LINES.
8424          MOVE COLUMN-HEADINGS-2 TO REPORT-LINES.
8425          WRITE REPORT-LINE
                  AFTER ADVANCING 2 LINES.
8426          MOVE DASHED-LINE-2     TO REPORT-LINE.
8427          WRITE REPORT-LINE
                  AFTER ADVANCING 1 LINE.


          D1-PRINT-ENROLLMENT.
8441          MOVE ACADEMIC-YEAR  TO OUT-ACADEMIC-YEAR.
8442          MOVE SEMESTER       TO OUT-SEMESTER.
8443          MOVE COURSE-CODE    TO OUT-COURSE-CODE.
8444          MOVE GRADE          TO OUT-GRADE.
8445          MOVE OUT-ENROLLMENT TO REPORT-LINE.
8446          WRITE REPORT-LINE
                  AFTER ADVANCING 1 LINE.
```

Figure 7 (Continued)

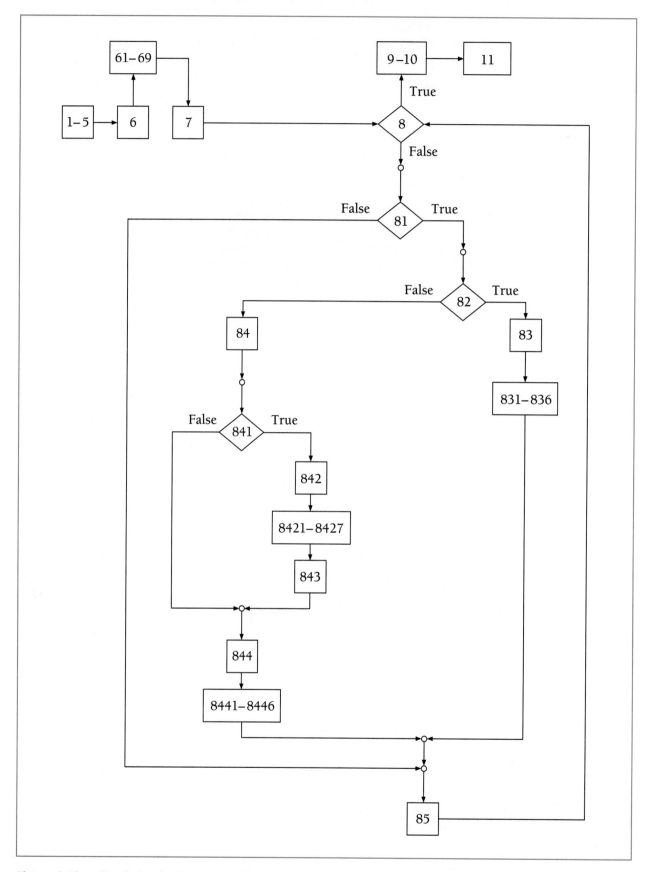

Figure 8 Flow Graph for the Program of Figure 7

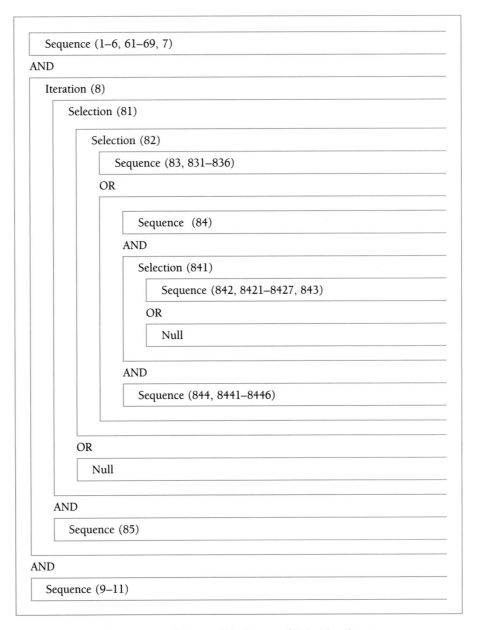

Figure 9 Logic of Program of Figure 7 in Terms of Primitive Structures

REVIEW QUESTIONS

1. Which of the following statements about software engineering is correct?
   a. Software engineering consists of methods, tools, and procedures that enable the programmer to develop high-quality software in a productive and efficient manner.
   b. Software engineering is not concerned with design of data structures.
   c. Program testing and verification are done by the users after the software engineer develops the software systems.
   d. Design of program structures and algorithms is completed before the software engineer starts working on a software development project.
2. The three primitive structures of structured programming are _____, _____, and _____.
3. Minimizing program complexity is not one of the objectives of structured programming. (T or F)

4. The iteration structure that tests a predicate before entering the loop body is called the _____ iteration structure.

5. In COBOL 85, the posttest PERFORM UNTIL statement requires the use of the _____ clause.

6. Multiway decision making can be accomplished in a program using
   a. A series of consecutive two-way selection structures
   b. Nested IF structures
   c. CASE structures
   d. All of the above

7. Which of the following about the nested IF structure in COBOL is correct?
   a. The else-part of an IF statement cannot contain another IF statement.
   b. In COBOL 85, a nested IF cannot have more than one END-IF bracket.
   c. A nested IF is more execution efficient that an equivalent series of consecutive unnested IF statements.
   d. In a nested IF structure, an inner IF statement may not have an ELSE clause.

8. The CASE structure is implemented in COBOL 85 through the _____ statement.

9. The use of the GO TO . . . DEPENDING ON statement in COBOL for multiway decision making necessitates the use of unconditional transfer of control statements (GO TO statements) in the code. (T or F)

Answers: 1. a; 2. sequence, selection, iteration; 3. F; 4. pretest; 5. WITH TEST AFTER; 6. d; 7. c; 8. EVALUATE; 9. T.

Modular Program Design and Program Structure

In almost every software development project we write thousands of lines of code. If we squeeze all the statements in our system into one program, we end up with a huge and complex program. Such a monolithic program would be extremely difficult to develop, test, and debug. To expedite the software development process, we work in teams. If we write one large program, how do we divide the programming tasks among the team members? Even if we can do that, it would be extremely hard to integrate the different segments of code developed by the members into one program.

In addition, there is the problem of software maintenance. Assuming we could develop a software system in the form of a single and colossal program, it would be difficult for the software maintenance personnel to understand the intricacies of the product and to repair or expand it when needed.

The problem facing us is common to the development of all large-scale artificial systems. For instance, a car is not manufactured as a single task. The process is divided into smaller, more manageable tasks of manufacturing individual engine and chassis components. These are assembled into larger components, such as the distributor, battery, transmission, and so on. The parts are separately tested and eventually are integrated into the final product, the car.

A software system in general is a complex artificial system. In developing it, we use a similar strategy, namely the divide-and-conquer approach. While designing a program, we divide it into smaller functional units, called modules, that are easier to develop than the full program. Each module is expected to perform a specific and relatively simple function that can be expressed in one or two sentences, and can be described in the form of an algorithm. Each one is developed as an initially independent program, and tested and debugged. Then they are integrated in view of the relationships that must exist between them, and are combined to work under the supervision of a driver module. Thus, a software system is obtained that is capable of performing its assigned task because each module does its function correctly at the right time. This design and development strategy is referred to as modular programming.

> **Modular programming** is defined as organizing a program into small, independent modules that are separately named and addressable elements. These are integrated to become a software system that satisfies the problem requirements.

In modular programming, each module must have the following properties.

1. It represents a single logical function.
2. It has a name and can be invoked by any other module.
3. It has a single entry point and a single exit point.
4. It is separately testable.
5. It has well-defined control, data, and functional interfaces.

Modular programming has some advantages.

1. Because module size is manageably small and module function is simple, it is easier to understand a modular program than a monolithic one.
2. As a result, program debugging and testing, expansion, repair, and maintenance are facilitated.
3. Program development time is substantially reduced, as teamwork is enhanced and it becomes easier to manage the program-development project.
4. In modular programs, machine-dependent functions are easy to separate. This improves program portability in that a program that is developed for a computer system can run with minimal or no changes on another computer system.
5. Some general purpose modules of a software system can be used without any change in other software development projects. This greatly improves the efficiency of program development.

Program Structure

During the implementation of a modular program, each module emerges as a procedure or a subprogram. Integration of separate procedures requires definition and implementation of a higher-level module, usually referred to as the main program (monitor or driver). The main program calls on the procedures in a specified order for execution. When it terminates execution, the problem is solved. The procedures in a modular program are related to one another and they define a relationship, the "invoked by" relationship. The logical modules together with the "invoked by" relationship define a structure, the program structure.

> A **program structure** is a collection of logical program modules and the "invoked by" relationship existing among the modules.

We can represent the structure of any modular program in the form of a graph. Figure 10 shows the program structure for Program 1 in which the modules are paragraphs. Each module is shown as a labeled node. Node labels

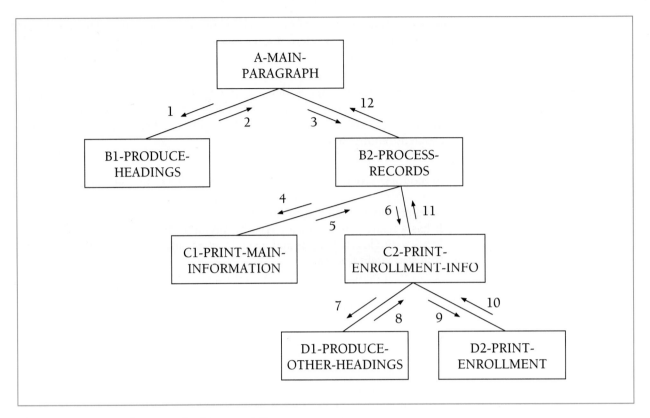

Figure 10 Program Structure for Program 1-Source

are the paragraph names. Nodes are connected to other nodes by arcs. The arcs together stand for the "invoked by" relationship. The arc from A-MAIN-PARA-GRAPH to B1-PRODUCE-HEADINGS, for example, implies that the module B1-PRODUCE-HEADINGS is invoked by the procedure A-MAIN-PARAGRAPH sometime during program execution. Procedure invocations bring control into the invoked modules. After invoked modules are executed, control should be returned to the calling module. Invocations that do not guarantee a proper return to the invoking module are undesirable. The numbered arrows in Figure 10 indicate transfers of control among the modules and the sequence in which they take place.

Proper procedure invocations in COBOL can be accomplished using a form of the PERFORM verb for paragraphs or sections, or the CALL verb for external subroutines. Invocations with no return use GO TO statements. We will avoid GO TOs in this book.

In general there are three types of program structures: tree, hierarchical, and network. Figure 11 shows a **tree program structure**. Nodes A, B, and C represent procedures whose executions require a single invocation, each within the node M. We refer to them as level 1 nodes. Nodes D, E, and F require two invocations each for execution. They constitute level 2 of the tree structure. The root node M is said to be at level 0. This classification of nodes by their level numbers reflects a hierarchical structure inherent in a tree structure. Consequently, a tree structure is also a hierarchical structure. A more detailed discussion of tree structures can be found in Chapter 5.

Figure 12 illustrates a structure that resembles the tree structure of Figure 11. The only difference is that the node G has two parents, nodes B and F. This means the procedure G is called twice during the program execution, once by B and once by F. This situation is not compatible with the characteristics of tree structures, as in a tree all nodes may have at most one parent. Hence, the

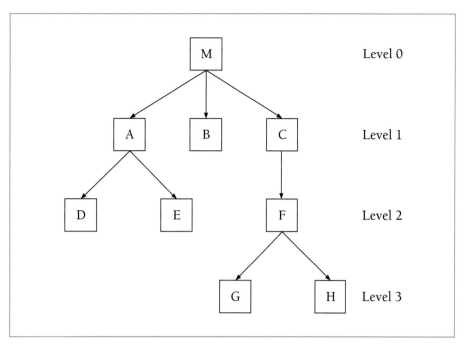

Figure 11 A Tree Program Structure

structure of Figure 12 is no longer a tree. As a hierarchical relationship is still reflected, however, we call it a **hierarchical structure**.

Finally, Figure 13 exemplifies a **network structure**. A network has no distinguishable root node or leaves. Any node can have any number of arcs originating from it and terminating at it. A network is the most general graph structure. Usually, networks are more difficult to process than tree structures because they may have more arcs than a tree of the same number of nodes.

Network structures do not reflect a particular module hierarchy and thus it is generally more difficult to understand programs with network structures. More important, computer implementations of network program structures are much more complex than those of tree or hierarchical structures, and require the use of GO TO statements. Hence, network structures are undesirable as program structures. As a general design rule, we should avoid them and aim for tree or hierarchical structures.

Design Considerations for Modular Programs

So far we have concentrated on structural considerations for modular programs. Other factors also influence the design. One of these is the matter of how large a module should be. In our previous discussion, as far as we were concerned, modules were black boxes. We regarded each one as a process for which we knew what was needed (input), what was expected (output), and the function to be performed, but we neither knew nor cared about contents or size.

On the other hand, there are issues that pertain to module relationships. We concluded that, structurally speaking, tree or hierarchical structures are to be favored, but we did not spend any time on their desirable properties. In what follows, we explore these issues.

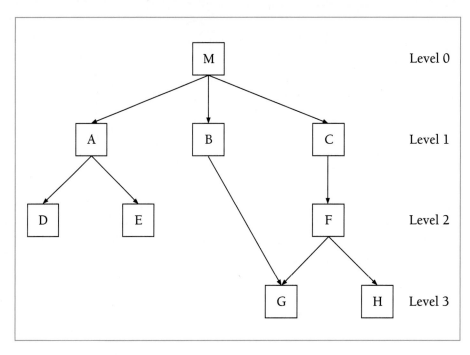

Figure 12 A Hierarchical Program Structure

Module Size. In modular programming, module size is an important factor. Given the functional specification for a module, the number of statements in the final code depends on the algorithm designed for it, how the algorithm is coded, and the programming language used for implementation. A poor and inefficient algorithm will result in a lengthy code. A good algorithm inexpertly transformed into program code will produce a long program. Certain programming languages, by their nature, result in longer source programs compared to other languages. COBOL is one such language. In general, a COBOL program written for an algorithm will be longer than, say, a Pascal program written for the same algorithm. Regardless of how the algorithm is designed and coded, and the programming language, the software designer or programmer can control module size. A module that is too long can always be split into two or more modules, each corresponding to a subfunction of the given function. On the other hand, modules that are too short can be combined into a larger module in a serial manner. Consider the COBOL module on the next page, which is somewhat hard to follow and also is quite long (50 lines).

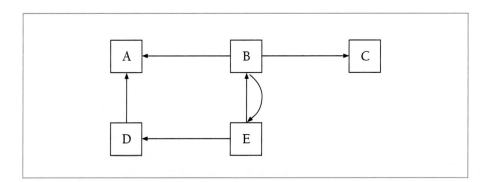

Figure 13 A Network Program Structure

```
B2-PROCESS-RECORDS.
    IF STUDENT-NUMBER OF STUDENT-IDENTIFICATION-REC = SEARCH-ID
        IF RECORD-TYPE OF STUDENT-IDENTIFICATION-REC = "I"

            MOVE STUDENT-NUMBER OF STUDENT-IDENTIFICATION-REC
                                 TO OUT-STUDENT-NUMBER
            MOVE STUDENT-NAME    TO OUT-STUDENT-NAME
            MOVE STUDENT-MAJOR   TO OUT-STUDENT-MAJOR
            MOVE STUDENT-YEAR    TO OUT-STUDENT-YEAR
            MOVE OUT-MAIN        TO REPORT-LINE
            WRITE REPORT-LINE
                AFTER ADVANCING 1 LINE


        ELSE
            IF FIRST-ENROLLMENT-RECORD = "YES"

            MOVE SPACES            TO REPORT-LINE
            MOVE TITLE-2           TO REPORT-LINE
            WRITE REPORT-LINE
                AFTER ADVANCING 4 LINES
            MOVE COLUMN-HEADINGS-2 TO REPORT-LINE
            WRITE REPORT-LINE
                AFTER ADVANCING 2 LINES
            MOVE DASHED-LINE-2      TO REPORT-LINE
            WRITE REPORT-LINE
                AFTER ADVANCING 1 LINE

            MOVE "NO" TO FIRST-ENROLLMENT-RECORD
            MOVE ACADEMIC-YEAR  TO OUT-ACADEMIC-YEAR
            MOVE SEMESTER       TO OUT-SEMESTER
            MOVE COURSE-CODE    TO OUT-COURSE-CODE
            MOVE GRADE          TO OUT-GRADE
            MOVE OUT-ENROLLMENT TO REPORT-LINE
            WRITE REPORT-LINE
                AFTER ADVANCING 1 LINE

        ELSE
            MOVE ACADEMIC-YEAR  TO OUT-ACADEMIC-YEAR
            MOVE SEMESTER       TO OUT-SEMESTER
            MOVE COURSE-CODE    TO OUT-COURSE-CODE
            MOVE GRADE          TO OUT-GRADE
            MOVE OUT-ENROLLMENT TO REPORT-LINE
            WRITE REPORT-LINE
                AFTER ADVANCING 1 LINE.

READ STUDENT-FILE RECORD
        AT END MOVE "YES" TO END-OF-FILE-REACHED.
```

We can easily recode this module by splitting it into shorter modules such that each is short, functionally more cohesive, and definitely easier to read. One possible modularization scheme is exemplified in the following equivalent program segment.

```
B2-PROCESS-RECORDS.
    IF STUDENT-NUMBER OF STUDENT-IDENTIFICATION-REC = SEARCH-ID
            IF RECORD-TYPE OF STUDENT-IDENTIFICATION-REC = "I"
                PERFORM C1-PRINT-MAIN-INFORMATION
            ELSE
                PERFORM C2-PRINT-ENROLLMENT-INFO.

    READ STUDENT-FILE RECORD
            AT END MOVE "YES" TO END-OF-FILE-REACHED.

C1-PRINT-MAIN-INFORMATION.
    MOVE STUDENT-NUMBER OF STUDENT-IDENTIFICATION-REC
                        TO OUT-STUDENT-NUMBER.
    MOVE STUDENT-NAME    TO OUT-STUDENT-NAME.
    MOVE STUDENT-MAJOR   TO OUT-STUDENT-MAJOR.
    MOVE STUDENT-YEAR    TO OUT-STUDENT-YEAR.
    MOVE OUT-MAIN        TO REPORT-LINE.
    WRITE REPORT-LINE
            AFTER ADVANCING 1 LINE.

C2-PRINT-ENROLLMENT-INFO.
    IF FIRST-ENROLLMENT-RECORD = "YES"
        PERFORM D1-PRODUCE-OTHER-HEADINGS
        MOVE "NO" TO FIRST-ENROLLMENT-RECORD.

    PERFORM D2-PRINT-ENROLLMENT.

D1-PRODUCE-OTHER-HEADINGS.
    MOVE SPACES            TO REPORT-LINE.
    MOVE TITLE-2           TO REPORT-LINE.
    WRITE REPORT-LINE
            AFTER ADVANCING 4 LINES.
    MOVE COLUMN-HEADINGS-2 TO REPORT-LINE.
    WRITE REPORT-LINE
            AFTER ADVANCING 2 LINES.
    MOVE DASHED-LINE-2     TO REPORT-LINE.
    WRITE REPORT-LINE
            AFTER ADVANCING 1 LINE.

D2-PRINT-ENROLLMENT.
    MOVE ACADEMIC-YEAR   TO OUT-ACADEMIC-YEAR.
    MOVE SEMESTER        TO OUT-SEMESTER.
    MOVE COURSE-CODE     TO OUT-COURSE-CODE.
    MOVE GRADE           TO OUT-GRADE.
    MOVE OUT-ENROLLMENT TO REPORT-LINE.
    WRITE REPORT-LINE
            AFTER ADVANCING 1 LINE.
```

We are concerned with module size in modular program design for some very good reasons. A long module is generally difficult to understand, debug, test, and maintain. Conversely, modules containing small number of statements produce a program structure with too many nodes (procedures) and increase structural complexity. There is no rule about the optimum module size, but there are some guidelines. We will adopt and use the following guideline.

> In modular program design, module size should be kept in the range of 10 to 50 statements.

This should be taken only as a rough rule-of-thumb. The number 50 is an IBM guideline. It is the number of lines that can be comfortably printed on a page of source listing, making it possible for the reader to see the contents of a module at a glance. A maximum size of 24 can also be used for on-line program development and testing using CRT terminals.

Coupling. Another important issue in modular program design pertains to the effects of the relationships in the overall program structure on modules. We already know that the relationships among modules are components of the "invoked by" relationship. Several additional things may happen during module invocation, thereby defining varying degrees of module interface complexity.

1. Data items or structures may be transferred among modules.
2. Data transferred during invocation may affect execution of the invoked module.
3. The point of entry into a module may not be the first statement in that module.
4. The contents of a module may specify additional interfaces with external media or modules that are not explicitly part of the program structure under consideration.

> **Coupling** is a measure of module interface complexity in modular programming.

Coupling can be thought of as defining a spectrum from loose to tight. Loose coupling means simple module interfaces, and tight coupling connotes complex interfaces. In software design, it is advisable to aim for loose coupling as it results in modules that are easy to understand. It also yields highly independent modules that are easier to develop, test, and debug.

Seven types of couplings can be defined:

1. No direct coupling
2. Data coupling
3. Stamp coupling
4. Control coupling
5. External coupling
6. Common coupling
7. Content coupling

We will use the program structure of Figure 14 to illustrate types of couplings.

No direct coupling: Modules that have no direct or indirect interfaces have no direct coupling occurring among them. For example, in Figure 14, modules

B and C are on different branches of the tree structure. Therefore they are uncoupled. In addition, modules B and H have no direct coupling either.

Data coupling: During interaction, if a module transfers simple data items to a subordinate module through a conventional argument list, the two modules are said to have data coupling. In the figure, modules B and E are data coupled.

Stamp coupling is a variation of data coupling. If a module passes a data structure or a portion of it to another module, between the two modules stamp coupling occurs. In modules written in COBOL, we may transfer a COBOL data structure or an array through argument lists from one module to the other, as between modules E and J.

Control coupling: Information that may affect the execution of a subordinate module may be passed from one module to another. Such an interaction is called control coupling. For example, in module C, we may set a flag to a specific value (MOVE 0 TO FLAG) and pass the variable FLAG to module G. If

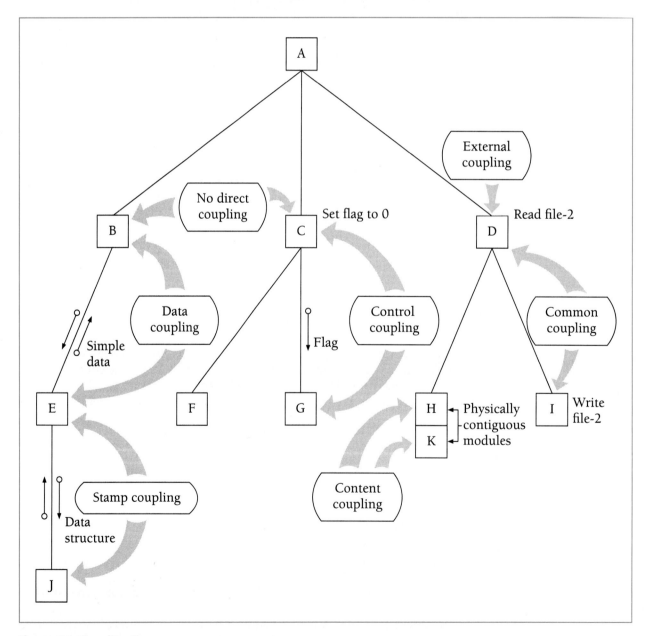

Figure 14 Coupling Types

module G contains a selection structure based on the variable FLAG, control in module G partially depends on a variable that has been assigned a value in the superordinate module C. While developing module G, the designer has to keep in mind the contents of module C. Control coupling among modules is a common occurrence in software design. To minimize the ripple effect due to errors in a module propagating to other modules, it should be avoided or minimized.

External coupling: Inevitably, there are statements in programs that tie a module to external storage devices, or to standard programs such as protocols, libraries, or utilities. Such interactions are not normally shown in structure charts. They are known as external couplings. For example, suppose module D has an input statement ("read file-2") that couples it to a specific I-O device, say, a disk drive. Then module D is externally coupled to this particular disk drive. External coupling is certainly necessary in program development; however, it is a good idea to restrict it to as few modules as possible.

Common coupling occurs when two or more modules reference a global data area, such as a file. In Figure 14, if module D reads file-2 and module I subsequently writes into the same file, they are common coupled to file-2. Common coupling among modules should be carefully controlled.

Content coupling occurs between two modules if one module contains a one-way reference to another. When this happens, the second module will be using data or control information that should normally be confined to the domain of the first module.

In COBOL, content coupling is possible under two circumstances.

1. GO TO statements in one module direct control to another module without a guaranteed return.
2. A paragraph or a section executes fully without encountering a transfer statement, and control passes to another paragraph or section that physically follows the first. This is known as **control due to physical contiguity**.

In Figure 14, content coupling is illustrated between modules H and K. This is the tightest form of coupling and should be avoided in program design.

Certain forms of coupling in software design are necessary and even desirable; however, the designer should aim for a minimum amount. In general, module interactions should be as loose as possible. The process of achieving this is referred to as **decoupling**.

Guidelines for Decoupling

1. Minimize data coupling by passing only necessary data among modules. Avoid passing data through intermediate modules to a target module.
2. Reduce stamp coupling by passing only the required parts of a composite data structure. Group these parts into another data structure in the calling module, and pass it through the parameter list.
3. Minimize control coupling by eliminating as many flag variables as possible.
4. Minimize external and common coupling by limiting the number of modules that access common data areas or external software components.
5. Eliminate content coupling entirely. Do not define one-way transfers between modules. Do not permit control due to physical continuity.

Cohesion. Simplifying module interfaces through the decoupling concept described above is one way of achieving what we call **functional independence** of modules. Functional independence is also achieved by designing modules with single-minded functions. This leads us to another measure of "goodness" in software design, namely cohesion.

> **Cohesion** is a measure of a module's capability to represent a single function. If elements within a module are strongly related to each other for a specific purpose, this module is said to be **highly cohesive**.

Cohesion is important because it is easy to understand and develop modules for single-minded functions. Like coupling, cohesion can range from low to high. Several types of cohesion have been identified:

1. Coincidental
2. Logical
3. Temporal
4. Procedural
5. Communicational
6. Sequential
7. Functional

In the following discussion, we will explain and exemplify different levels of cohesion.

Coincidental cohesion: A module that performs a set of tasks that are either loosely related or not related at all to each other is said to have coincidental cohesion or no cohesion. The following is an example of a COBOL procedure with coincidental cohesion.

```
MAIN-PARAGRAPH.
    OPEN STUDENT-FILE INPUT.
    READ STUDENT-FILE
        AT END MOVE "YES" TO END-OF-FILE.
    MOVE ZERO TO TOTAL-STUDENTS.
    READ FACULTY-FILE
        AT END MOVE "YES" TO END-OF-FAC-FILE.
    PERFORM MAIN-PROCESSING.
```

The statements in this paragraph are somewhat loosely related to each other in that they are all necessary to process records in the STUDENT-FILE and FACULTY-FILE. However, statements of different type and function (OPEN, READ, MOVE, PERFORM) are collected together in the module. This has a very low level of cohesion.

Logical cohesion: If all statements in a module perform a certain class of tasks, the module is said to possess logical cohesion. The statements in the following example are all of the data movement type. Hence, the module is logically cohesive.

```
PREPARE-MAIN-INFORMATION.
    MOVE STUDENT-NUMBER OF STUDENT-IDENTIFICATION
                        TO OUT-STUDENT-NUMBER.
    MOVE STUDENT-NAME    TO OUT-STUDENT-NAME.
    MOVE STUDENT-MAJOR   TO OUT-STUDENT-MAJOR.
    MOVE STUDENT-YEAR    TO OUT-STUDENT-YEAR.
    MOVE OUT-MAIN        TO REPORT-LINE.
```

Temporal cohesion: If all statements in a module define tasks that take place within the same time span, the module has temporal cohesion. The following paragraph opens two files and sets a flag variable to zero before anything else is undertaken.

```
OPEN-FILES.
    OPEN INPUT  STUDENT-FILE.
    OPEN OUTPUT STUDENT-REPORT.
    MOVE ZERO TO FILE-READY-FLAG.
```

Procedural cohesion: When a module defines a decision or an iteration process as the sole basis for procedure, it is procedurally cohesive.

```
PROCESS-RECORDS.
 IF STUDENT-NUMBER OF STUDENT-IDENTIFICATION = SEARCH-ID
         IF RECORD-TYPE OF STUDENT-IDENTIFICATION = "I"
             PERFORM C1-PRINT-MAIN-INFORMATION
         ELSE
             PERFORM C2-PRINT-ENROLLMENT-INFO.
```

Communicational cohesion: If the statements in a module are all such that they make use of the same data structure or the same portion of a data structure, the level of cohesion is communicational. Another term for this is **data-related cohesion**. The following example is communicationally cohesive, as all three statements work with the record structure STUDENT-RECORD.

```
UPDATE-STUDENT-RECORDS.
    ADD 1 TO STUDENT-CLASS.
    REWRITE STUDENT-RECORD.
    READ STUDENT-FILE NEXT RECORD
        AT END MOVE "YES" TO END-OF-FILE.
```

Sequential cohesion: If the elements of a module perform a series of tasks where the output of one is input for the next, the module is said to have sequential cohesion. An example follows.

```
GENERATE-STUDENT-REPORT.
    PERFORM READ-STUDENT-RECORD.
    PERFORM PROCESS-STUDENT-RECORD.
    PERFORM OUTPUT-STUDENT-SUMMARY.
```

Functional cohesion is the highest level of cohesion. It occurs when each element of a module is essential to perform only one well-defined function. Consider this example.

```
PROCESS-STUDENT-INFORMATION.
    PERFORM COMPUTE-TOTAL-HOURS.
    PERFORM COMPUTE-TOTAL-CREDITS.
    PERFORM COMPUTE-GRADE-POINT-AVERAGE.
```

The three statements in this module are all needed for the module's function, which is to compute a student's grade point average.

It is usually difficult to differentiate levels of cohesion clearly. A module that has apparent procedural cohesiveness may also be temporally cohesive. It should be emphasized that cohesion is a qualitative measure of how good a module is. It appears as if the most desirable level is functional and the least desirable is coincidental. This is not strictly true. Obviously, we should try to avoid low levels of cohesion; however, the middle range of the spectrum (i.e., temporal, procedural, communicational, and sequential) is perhaps as good as the high end. It is not necessary for the software designer to pinpoint the level precisely. An understanding of the concept and the guidelines that enable the designer to determine the level approximately is sufficient. The following table contains some guidelines that can be used to determine level of cohesion.

Full Functional Description for Module	*Probable Level of Cohesion*
Requires a simple imperative sentence	Functional
Requires a compound sentence, or contains a comma, or contains more than one statement	Sequential Communicational Logical
Contains time-related words, such as when, first, next, after, before, etc.	Sequential Temporal
Contains more than one object after the statement	Logical
Contains words such as initialize, clean-up, etc.	Temporal

Structural Properties of Modular Programs. In addition to coupling and cohesion, other structural properties of modular programs have some bearing on how good the design is. These are fan-out, fan-in, and scope of effect for modules.

> **Fan-out** (also called **span of control** or **out-degree**) is the number of modules that are invoked by the module under consideration. Using graph-theoretic terms, it can also be defined as the total number of arcs in the structure chart originating from a module and terminating elsewhere.

In Figure 15, module D has a fan-out of 5, as it invokes modules H through L that are subordinate to it.

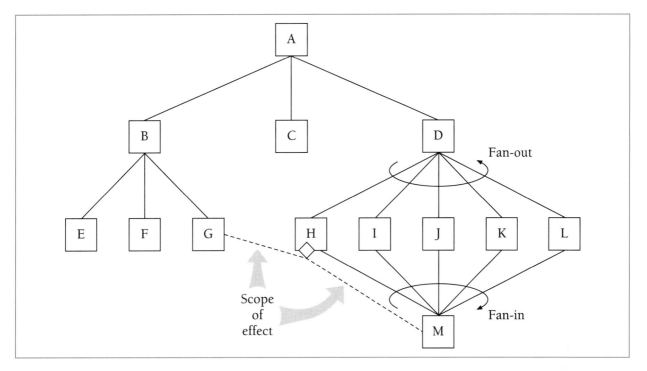

Figure 15 Some Structural Properties of Modular Programs

If fan-out for certain modules is excessive, the structure of the program becomes difficult to understand. Very low fan-out may also be taken as a possible indicator of a poor modularization scheme. It has been demonstrated that the capacity of human short-term memory is about five to nine items of information. This implies that an average designer can handle, for a given module, about seven submodules in its span of control without confusion and possible error. For this reason, we should remember the following design rule.

> The fan-out for modules in any modularization scheme should be restricted to approximately seven.

For a modular program with a hierarchical structure that is not a tree, certain modules can have more than one parent modules.

> The number of superordinate modules for a given module is known as the **fan-in** (also called **in-degree**) for the module under consideration.

Module M in Figure 15 has five modules (H through L) that call on it. Therefore, it has a fan-in of 5.

An examination of the content of a module immediately reveals its fan-out. For example, in a COBOL procedure, the number of CALL and PERFORM statements is that module's fan-out. To determine a module's fan-in, we have to look into other modules to see how many of them invoke it. Stated somewhat differently, while repairing a module, we can tell what modules will be affected on the basis of the module's fan-out, but we have to examine at least a cross-reference table to determine what parent modules may be affected by the changes. If more than one module needs the same procedure in a program, fan-ins greater than 1 should be preferred. Otherwise, unnecessary duplication of code is inevitable. We should certainly try to keep fan-in to a minimum, however, thus achieving loose coupling and content independence of modules. Here is a related design rule.

> In modularization schemes, try to minimize module fan-ins.

Our final concern has to do with what is called scope of effect.

> **Scope of effect** for a module is defined as the set of all other modules that are affected by a decision in the one under consideration.

In Figure 15, the decision structure in module H affects modules B and M. Therefore, the scope of effect of module H includes modules B and M. A design rule to be remembered is.

> The scope of effect of a module should be kept within its scope of control i.e., those modules that are subordinate to it.

REVIEW QUESTIONS

1. In modular programming, we organize a program into small and independent modules, and later integrate them into a software system satisfying the problem requirements. (T or F)
2. Which of the following is a property that should be satisfied in modular programming?
   a. Each module represents a single logical function.
   b. Each module has a name and can be invoked by any other module.
   c. Each module is separately testable.
   d. Each module has well-defined control, data, and functional interfaces.
   e. All of the above are properties that modules should satisfy in modular programming.
3. Program debugging, testing, expansion, repair, and maintenance are facilitated in a modular software system. (T or F)
4. As a strategy, modular programming has no positive effect on the efficiency of program development. (T or F)
5. A program structure is a collection of logical program modules and the _____ relationship existing among them.
6. Of the three program structures, tree, hierarchical, and network, networks are most complex and should be avoided. (T or F)
7. Ideal module size is between _____ and _____ statements.
8. Which of the following statements concerning coupling is correct?
   a. Coupling is a measure of module interface complexity in modular programming.

b. If a module transfers data to a subordinate module through an argument list at the time of invocation, the two modules are said to have data coupling.

c. If information that may affect the execution of an invoked module is passed from a calling module to the subordinate module, the two modules have control coupling.

d. Common coupling occurs when two or more modules reference a global data area.

e. All of the above are correct.

9. Cohesion is a measure of a module's capability to represent a single function. (T or F)

10. Which of the following statements about cohesion is incorrect?

a. If all statements in a module perform a certain class of tasks, the module is said to have coincidental cohesion.

b. If all statements in a module define tasks that take place within the same time span, the module has temporal cohesion.

c. If all statements in a module make use of the same data structure, the module has communicational cohesion.

d. If each element of a module is essential to perform only one well-defined task, the module has functional cohesion.

11. The number of modules that is invoked by a module is that module's _____ , and the number of modules that invoke a module is that module's _____ .

Answers: 1. T; 2. e; 3. T; 4. F; 5. invoked by; 6. T; 7. 10, 50; 8. e; 9. T; 10. a; 11. fan-out, fan-in.

Data Structure Design

We stressed previously in this chapter that software design encompasses three major phases: procedure, program structure, and data structure design. So far, we have considered the first two in detail. The third design phase is just as important. Data structures in software are abstract representations of corporate data. They have an enormous impact on the program structure and procedural logic of the software system. This section is the formal introduction to data structures. We will explore the topic in greater detail later in the book.

Data Structures

The concept of data structures is not new to anybody who has written computer programs in a high-level computer language. All such languages support some simple data structures, such as arrays or records. In computer programming, if we use data structures it is because we must represent real-world data in our program. In software design, we resort to data structuring techniques because we have to represent and make appropriate use of the corporate data.

> A **data structure** is a named set of related data and one or more logical relationships existing among them.

Conceptually, a data structure is much like a program structure, but with two principal differences.

1. A data structure is concerned with data, whereas a program structure deals with procedures.

2. A data structure includes one or more relationships, and a program structure represents only the "invoked by" relationship.

There are large numbers of data structures. Their organization and level of sophistication are limited only by the ingenuity of the designer. In this section, and later in this book, we will cover those that are most useful in COBOL programming and information system software development. Before we do that, however, we should note that in all data structures the basic building block is a data item, also called a scalar item.

> **A data item** represents an element of information that cannot be split into ingredients, and can be addressed and accessed by an identifier.

For example, the user-defined variable EMPLOYEE-AGE is a data item. The variable EMPLOYEE-ADDRESS may be considered as consisting of STREET-ADDRESS, CITY, STATE, and ZIP-CODE, and therefore, is not a data item.

As abstractions, data structures are classified as primitive and composite data structures.

Primitive Data Structures

We can start with data items, and we can define some primitive data structures. Such data structures depend on the relationships that we would like to represent, and the manner in which we would like to access data. These primitives are shown in Figures 16 through 20. **Primitive data structures** are based on data items. Using them we can define more complex data structures, called **composite data structures**.

Primitive data structures can be classified as lists, networks, or trees.

> **A list** is a set of data and a relationship among data items. The relationship in a list is the "preceded by" relationship.

The two types of lists are sequential and linked.

Figure 16 is a list in which data consist of a set of names, and the relationship is "physically preceded by". Each data item value is in a different location of the computer's memory, called a **cell**. A cell is an individually addressable memory location that can store a word of information, in this case a name such as "John". In Figure 16, "John" is the value stored in the cell whose address is 101. In this data structure, we know what value is stored and where it is stored. We also know the positions of data values relative to each other. For example, we know that "Amy" is stored in cell 102, and is preceded by "John" in cell 101. Such a list is known as a **sequentially allocated list**.

A list can also be based on **linked allocation**. Suppose, as in Figure 17, we store "John" in cell 121, and the next element of the list, which is "Amy", cannot be stored physically next to "John" but can be stored in cell 105. Assuming

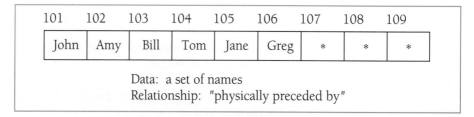

Data: a set of names
Relationship: "physically preceded by"

Figure 16 A Linear List: Sequential Allocation

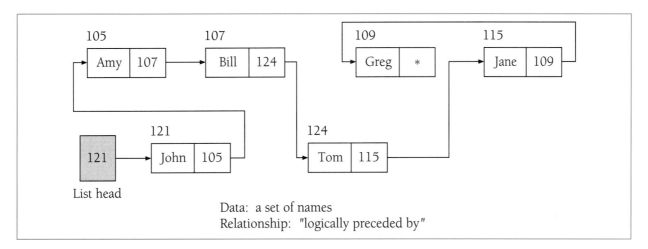

Figure 17 A Linear List: Linked Allocation

that we wish to preserve the relative order of names as in Figure 17, we can define a **link** from "John" to "Amy", another one from "Amy" to "Bill", and so on. A link is actually a pointer that is associated with each data value, telling us the location of the **logical successor** of that particular data value. For Figure 17 we use a modified cell structure for the data items in which both the data item value and the address of the logical successor are stored. For example, the cell for "John" will contain:

```
DATA    LINK (or POINTER)
```

John	105

This way, on accessing the cell containing data for "John", if we wish to access its successor, we use the pointer address 105. The pointers are shown as arcs in the graph representation used in Figure 17. Such a list is known as a **linked list**. We note that the relationship in this data structure is "logically preceded by".

A list can be made to reflect more interesting and useful relationships. Suppose we wish to store a set of names in alphabetical order. Figure 18 shows the same set of names of Figure 17 with different pointers, such that when we traverse the linked list we end up with an ordered sequence of names. Thus, this

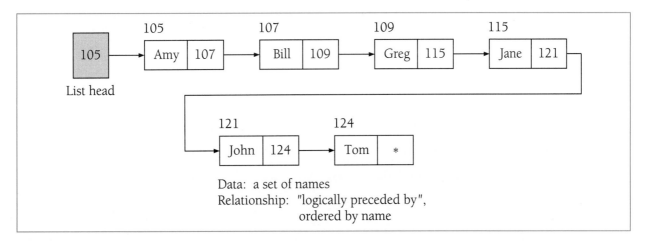

Figure 18 An Ordered Linked List

is an **ordered linked list**. A sequential list can also be ordered. We already know that an unordered sequential list, such as that in Figure 16, can be transformed into an equivalent ordered list through **sorting**. Sorting for sequential lists requires data movement (**physical sorting**), whereas linked lists can be sorted by changing the cell pointers, without moving data items (**logical sorting**).

It is necessary to identify the beginning and end of list structures. The way this is done depends on the host storage structure containing the list. A list can be stored in a fixed-size storage structure, which may be a one-dimensional array in the main memory. It may also be a direct access file in the secondary storage whose elements can be accessed consecutively or directly by an index. The beginning of a list is known as the **list head**. A separate memory location must be allocated to store the list head address for a list.

The end of a sequential list is the last element before an empty location. For a linked list, it is the element that has an empty pointer field. An empty cell in a list contains "garbage", that is, a representation that is of no value or concern to us. We use the asterisk (*) to denote an empty cell; in actual implementations, other conventions may be used. Once again, let us stress that in general, a storage structure used to contain a list has a fixed number of memory locations, whereas a list may change in size due to additions or deletions. For example, the sequential list in Figure 16 is of size 6 and is stored in an array of size 9.

It should be noted that a list is a simple form of what we call a **graph structure**. More elaborate graph structures can be used for complex data structures. Figure 19 is a general data structure, which is a graph structure, also known as a **network**. It represents a set of names, and the relationship "is child of" among the members of the population. Existence of an arc from "Bill" to "Greg" implies that "Greg is a child of Bill". Such a network structure is a generalized version of lists, and can be implemented in a manner analogous to lists: store the data values in addressable locations, and use one or more pointers associated with

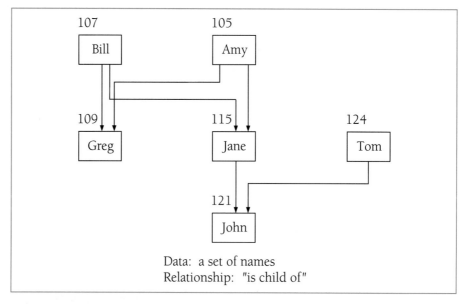

Figure 19 A Network Data Structure

each data cell to correspond to the arcs. For example, in Figure 19 the cell for "Bill" may have the following conceptual structure.

```
DATA   LINK-1   LINK-2
```

Bill	109	115

Figure 20 shows a **tree data structure** corresponding to a set of names and the "is subordinate to" relationship among the names as in an organization chart. We will learn more about tree structures in Chapter 5, while studying program structures. They are also widely used as data structures.

Composite Data Structures

Using primitive data structures as building blocks, we can define and use a variety of composite data structures. Some examples are shown in Figure 21. Many other types can be designed and used in application program development.

Figure 21a shows a composite data structure known as a **group item**. It contains any number of different data items arranged in a particular order relative to each other. This structure has the following COBOL representation.

```
01   EMPLOYEE.
     05   NAME        PIC X(6).
     05   SEX         PIC X(6).
     05   AGE         PIC 99.
     05   TITLE       PIC X(20).
```

The data item SEX is preceded by NAME, is followed by AGE, and so on. Group items are directly supported in COBOL. The entire structure has a name, in this case EMPLOYEE. You can combine several occurrences of a group item into an array, as in Figure 21b; combine one-dimensional arrays into two-dimensional arrays (Figure 21c); have group items combined into a

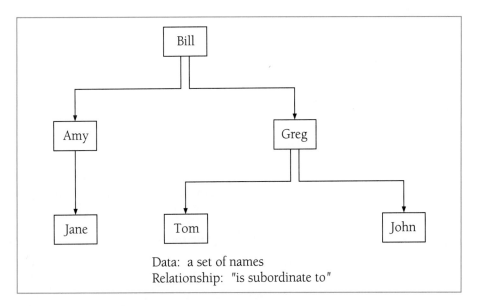

Data: a set of names
Relationship: "is subordinate to"

Figure 20 A Tree Data Structure

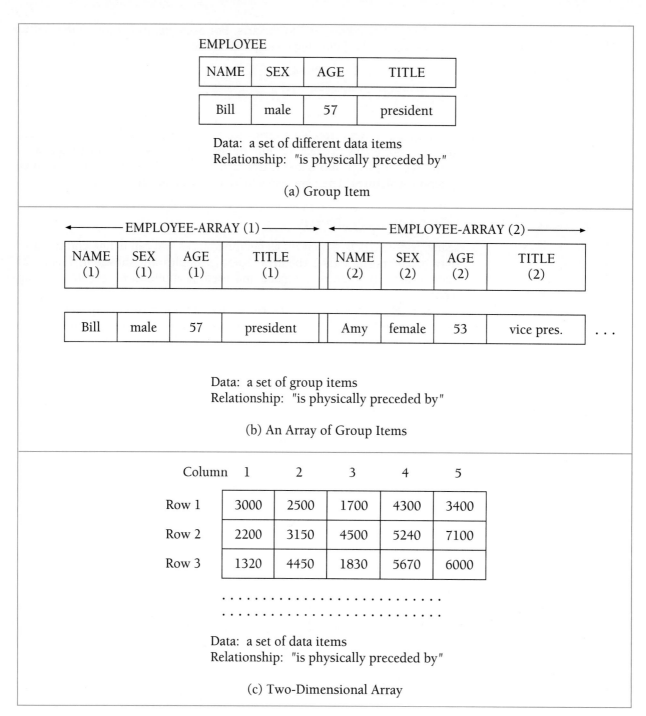

Figure 21 Some Composite Data Structures

linked list (Figure 21d); or have a tree structure in which each node is a group item (Figure 21e). In practice, such a structure, if implemented as a file, would be the basis for what we call a tree file.

Clearly, any data structure has a template that depicts its structural properties. The template for the group item of Figure 21a is

EMPLOYEE

NAME	SEX	AGE	TITLE

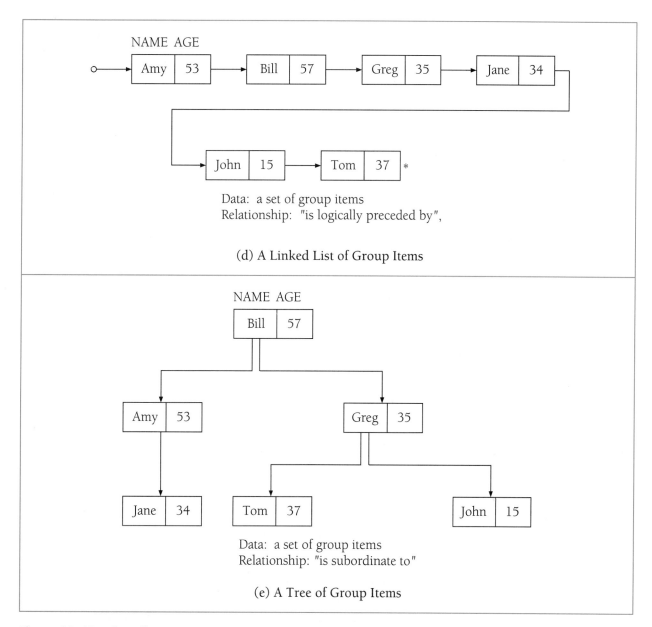

(d) A Linked List of Group Items

(e) A Tree of Group Items

Figure 21 (Continued)

A data structure also has **occurrences** (sometimes called **instances**) that show appropriate combination of data values and relationships according to the template for the structure. The following is an occurrence of the EMPLOYEE data structure of Figure 21a.

bill	male	57	president

Implementation of Data Structures

Not all data structures that may be required in application software development are supported by programming languages. Each high-level language has a few basic ones built into it. We call them **built-in data structures**; they are also known as **data types**. If a data structure is supported by a language compiler, the programmer has only to specify its type while writing a program. The compiler will recognize it and will permit the programmer to define and access it. Data structures that are not built-in for a language are not directly accepted by a program written in that language. The programmer has to write special programs to define and access a new data structure in terms of the existing built-in ones. Stated differently, the programmer has to simulate a data structure that is not supported by a language using those that are built into it. The built-in data structures in COBOL are

1. Basic COBOL data structure
2. Arrays
3. Files (sequential, indexed, and relative)

We used the basic COBOL data structure previously to define group items, structures, and record structures for files. For example,

```
01   FULL-NAME.
     02 LAST-NAME              PIC X(15).
     02 MIDDLE-INITIAL         PIC X.
     02 FIRST-NAME             PIC X(15).
```

defines a composite data structure, which is a group item. The COBOL compiler recognizes this definition, creates a storage structure corresponding to it, and permits the programmer to access the structure or its constituents at will. All a programmer has to do to define and use a basic COBOL data structure is to include its definition correctly in the DATA DIVISION of the program. As this data structure is built into COBOL, no special routines to control definition and access are necessary. If we wish to implement a linked list such as in Figure 17 or a tree structure as in Figure 20, however, we have to write programs to simulate it. We will devote some time to this subject in future chapters.

Data structures are also classified according to the type of memory used to implement them as internal or external. An **internal data structure** is stored in the computer's main memory while being processed. An **external data structure** resides in auxiliary memory (tape or disk storage) during and after processing. In COBOL, the basic COBOL data structure and arrays are internal data structures. While a program is running, their definitions and instances are kept in the main memory and are accessed there directly. Files of all types, however, are external data structures. The structure and instance of a disk file are partially stored in the disk storage, and each record is accessed using a particular technique that is compatible with the organization of the file.

Top-Down and Bottom-Up Design Strategies

Before we conclude our discussion of program design, let us briefly examine two strategies that can be used for program design and development: top-down and bottom-up. These are quite general, and are used in engineering design problems as well.

If we want to manufacture a car we have two extreme design possibilities. In one, we start from scratch, think about the problem of designing a car in general, and realize that it is a complex process. Then we partition the problem into subproblems, and further partition the subproblems until each becomes a task that we can handle without difficulty. The major problem of building a car is reduced to that of designing and developing a set of components, such as the engine block, distributor, alternator, braking system, body, and so on. We design and manufacture the components, test them individually, and integrate them into a car. This is the **top-down** approach.

The second extreme assumes that we have some automotive components conceived and developed either by ourselves or by someone else. We choose the ones that appear suitable, test them, and integrate them into a car. This approach is called **bottom-up**. In most real-life design problems, a combination of these two approaches turns out to be viable.

Top-Down Design

In modular program development, **top-down design** calls for progressive partitioning of a function into subfunctions until a good modular program structure is achieved and each module can be developed easily. Progressive partitioning (also called stepwise refinement) includes not only procedures but also data structures necessary for the program. Once the designer is satisfied with the structure thus obtained, work on individual modules begins. Modules are each logically designed, coded, and tested, starting from the top of the hierarchy and going down to lower levels. This pattern is carried out until all modules are finished. Then several modules are integrated and tested to ensure correctness. This way, the program grows gradually, a few modules at a time, until a complete software system emerges. Top-down program development involves several steps.

Step 1: Partition the problem into subproblems ultimately to define a hierarchical structure. For example, in Figure 11 a structure is defined in terms of functional modules M and A through H. So far, each module is a black box. We know what each one should do, how it interacts with other modules, and what the inputs and outputs are; but we have not yet defined how the functions are to be performed. We have an intuitive feel, however, that each module can be easily coded and tested.

Step 2: We start program development from the top of the hierarchy. We temporarily consider the second-level modules A, B, and C as empty, and concentrate on M. We design and code M such that it invokes A, B, and C in that order. Then we test M.

Step 3: Next, we take the second-level modules A, B, and C and similarly design their procedures. At the end of this step, M, A, B, and C are fully developed. The third-level modules D, E, and F are still black boxes, however. We test A, B, and C individually. Then, we test the modules developed so far (i.e., the first two levels of the structure) together.

We continue in this way until the entire program structure is developed, integrated, coded, and tested. The pattern for each module in this approach conforms to the "design-code-test" template.

Bottom-Up Design

In the bottom-up approach, as in top-down, we develop a structure for the program by progressively decomposing upper-level functions into subfunctions. Once the program structure is decided, we start program development at the bottom. For example, in the structure of Figure 11,

1. We first design, code, and test module G.
2. Then we do the same for H.
3. Now that we have the low-level modules, we develop F as a "driver" and test F, G, and H together.

We continue this way, from bottom to top, until the entire program structure is developed.

The bottom-up program development strategy is useful in that it produces modular programs and offers a systematic approach to program design and development. It is progressive concatenation, whereas top-down design is essentially stepwise refinement. In both approaches, design, coding, and testing are done in a stepwise manner. Therefore, both are viable and better alternatives than the traditional all-in-one program development approach in which the entire program is designed, then coded, and finally tested.

Advantages of the top-down and bottom-up approaches are

1. During program development, each step of design, coding, and testing is simple, as each module is conceived to represent a simple task.
2. As the program structure becomes available before actual procedural design and coding begin, these approaches enable project managers to determine accurately the computer and personnel resources required for program development.
3. In both top-down and bottom-up development we test programs in progressive steps. This makes it possible to discover and prevent serious problems in the program that would otherwise emerge during final testing.

Depending on the nature of the problem and available resources, one strategy may be preferable to the other. In practice, however, a combination may be more practical than a pure top-down or bottom-up approach.

REVIEW QUESTIONS

1. The three major design activities in software design are _____ , _____ , and _____ .
2. A data structure is a named set of related _____ and one or more _____ existing among the data.
3. Primitive data structures can be classified as lists, trees, and networks. (T or F)
4. In a _____ list, list elements are stored in memory locations that are next to each other.
5. Concerning linked lists, which of the following statements is incorrect?
    a. A link is a pointer that specifies the location of the logical successor of a data element.
    b. A linked list based on a data element must have a list head.
    c. Linked lists cannot be ordered.
    d. The end of a linked list is the element that has an empty pointer field.
6. The COBOL group item is a composite data structure. (T or F)
7. Data structures supported by programming languages are called _____ .
8. As built-in data structures, COBOL has _____ , _____ , and _____ .
9. Data structures that can be stored in the computer's main memory are called _____ ; those that are stored in the auxiliary storage are called _____ .
10. Progressive partitioning of a function into subfunctions until a good modular structure is achieved and each module can be develop easily is the basis of the _____ design approach.

Answers: 1. procedure design, program structure design, data structure design; 2. data, relationships; 3. T; 4. sequentially allocated; 5. c; 6. T; 7. built-in; 8. the COBOL data structure, arrays, files; 9. internal, external; 10. top-down.

Example Program 1:   Student Report Generator

The sample program example for this chapter is based on the following problem description.

Problem   Suppose a student file has two types of records to describe each student. The first record type identifies students in terms of

- Unique identification number
- Student name
- Student major
- Student year

The second record type contains enrollment information for each student. Structurally, enrollment records consist of

- Student identification number
- Academic year
- Semester
- Course code
- End-of-semester grade a student has earned from this specific course

There is only one identification record for each student, followed by any number of enrollment records. An instance of the student file is given in Program 1-Input.

We want to write a COBOL program to process the student file and generate a report that conforms to the following format specifications.

```
STUDENT INFORMATION FOR STUDENT: XXXX

              GENERAL INFORMATION

  STUDENT ID      STUDENT NAME      MAJOR      YEAR
  ----------      ------------      -----      ----

    XXXX        XXXXXXXXXXXX    XXXXXXXXXX      9



              ENROLLMENT INFORMATION

  ACADEMIC YEAR      SEMESTER      COURSE CODE      GRADE
  -------------      --------      -----------      -----
       99               9           XXXXXXX          9
       99               9           XXXXXXX          9
       99               9           XXXXXXX          9
       99               9           XXXXXXX          9
```

The report for each student should begin on the first line of a new page. Also, the user should be able to specify interactively the student for whom a report is to be generated by that student's identification number.

Solution	The compiler-produced listing of the COBOL program for this problem is given in Program 1-Source. In this chapter, we referred to this program on several occasions; hence, you are familiar with it. It was written using the majority of the design concepts and conventions discussed in this chapter. Program 1-Output is a sample output file generated by this program.

Key Terms

algorithm	linked list
bottom-up design	list
built-in data structure	logical cohesion
cohesion	logical design
coincidental cohesion	modular programming
common coupling	module size
communicational cohesion	nested IFs
computer program	network
content coupling	out-degree
control coupling	physical design
coupling	posttest iteration structure
data coupling	pretest iteration structure
data structure	procedural cohesion
data type	program structure
EVALUATE	selection structure
external coupling	sequence structure
external data structure	sequential allocation
fan-in	sequential cohesion
fan-out	software
functional cohesion	software engineering
functional specification	software system
GO TO . . . DEPENDING ON	stamp coupling
graph	structured programming
hierarchical structure	system
in-degree	systems analysis
information system	systems design
internal data structure	temporal cohesion
iteration structure	top-down design
linked allocation	tree

Study Guide

Quick Scan

- A computer program is an expression of an algorithm in a computer language. It can be interpreted and executed by a computer system, and it produces the desired solution for a problem.
- Software, on the other hand, is a set of related computer programs. Compared to a computer program, software is larger and corresponds to a relatively more complex problem.
- Software includes computer programs, data structures, and associated documentation. An application programmer should be able to design and develop good computer programs and data structures, and produce sufficient documentation for them.
- A good computer program or software system should be reliable, correct, simple, and maintainable. It should also have developmental and resource utilization efficiency.

- Software is a system. It may be a subsystem of an information system or a computer-based system. An information system, on the other hand, may be a subsystem of a business system. A business system is an example of man-made (artificial) systems.
- All systems, regardless of their nature, are collections of interrelated components that perform some functions to satisfy a set of goals. They interact with their environments, and are self-regulating and self-correcting.
- The systems development life cycle for software has four phases: analysis, design, coding, and testing. Our principal interest in this chapter is the design phase.
- Good design for computer programs requires formal methodologies, tools, and techniques. We find them within the realm of a relatively new discipline, called software engineering.
- Software engineering is concerned with the entire life cycle of software systems development, from project conception and planning to maintenance and management.
- From a program design perspective, software engineering emphasizes structured program logic and modular program structure.
- Structured programming is the discipline of making a program's logic easy to follow by using three primitive programming constructs: sequence, selection, and iteration. Every program is expressible in terms of the three primitives without requiring any other control structure.
- Structured programming simplifies a program's design and maintenance, minimizes its complexity, and increases its readability. Equally important, it defines a disciplined programming methodology.
- Another technique that helps us achieve good software design is modular programming. This is the process of organizing a monolithic program into small, manageable modules that are appropriately integrated into a system.
- Modular programming produces programs that are easy to understand, develop, test, debug, and maintain. It improves program development time and efficiency. It also tends to improve software portability.
- A modular program has a structure: the program modules and the "invoked by" relationship existing among these modules.
- The three types of program structures are tree, hierarchical, and network. Network structures are complex, hard to understand, and usually require unstructured program code. They should be avoided in program structure design.
- There are additional design considerations for modular programs. The first pertains to module size. We should avoid designing modules that are excessively small or large. A good rule limits size to 10 to 50 program instructions.
- Another design consideration is concerned with the complexity of module interfaces in a modular program structure. A measure of this is known as coupling. Several types of coupling have been defined, from loose to tight. Loosely coupled modules have simple interfaces. In modular program design, the designer should aim for loose coupling.
- In modular programming, simplicity of design dictates the existence of functionally independent modules in the structure. A measure of functional independence is cohesion, which is a module's capability of representing a single function. There are several types of cohesion, ranging from low to high. The more single-minded a module, the higher is its level of cohesion. A good design rule is to aim for reasonably cohesive modules.
- The software designer is also concerned with data structures and their design. A data structure is a set of related data and one or more relationships existing among them. Corporate data can be described in terms of data structure models.

- There are large numbers of data structure types. Their types and complexity depend on the properties of the actual corporate data and the designer's ability to conceptualize them. All, however, are combinations of three types of primitive data structures: lists, networks, and trees.
- Programming languages support a limited number of data structures. These are called built-in data structures. COBOL has the basic COBOL data structure, arrays, and files as its built-in data structures.
- Another factor that influences the design process is the design strategy. The traditional all-in-one strategy has many shortcomings. Instead, two relatively recent strategies are suggested: top-down and bottom-up.
- Top-down design strategy calls for progressive partitioning of a module into submodules until a good program structure is achieved. Design, coding, and testing of modules start from the top and proceed to the bottom of the structure.
- In the bottom-up strategy, after a good program structure is obtained, development starts at the bottom of the structure and progresses upward.
- In most real-life cases, appropriate combinations of the top-down and bottom-up strategies turn out to be practical.

Test Your Comprehension

Multiple-Choice Questions

1. Which of the following is not a property of a good program?
   a. Reliability and correctness
   b. Understandability, readability, simplicity, and architectural unity
   c. Ease of modification and maintainability
   d. Ease of compilation
   e. Developmental efficiency and simplicity
2. Which of the following is not one of the concerns of software engineering?
   a. Software development project planning and estimation
   b. Systems and software requirements analysis
   c. Design of data structures
   d. Design of structured programming techniques
   e. Design of program structures and algorithms
3. Which of the following statements concerning structured programming constructs is incorrect?
   a. Two-way selection can be used as the basis for multiway decision making.
   b. In COBOL 85, the PERFORM UNTIL statement with the WITH TEST BEFORE clause is used for posttest iteration.
   c. GO TO . . . DEPENDING ON is an unstructured version of multiway decision making.
   d. The COBOL 85 EVALUATE statement is a structured multiway decision-making construct.
4. Which of the following statements about modules in a modular software system is correct?
   a. A module may have multiple entry points and multiple exit points.
   b. We do not have to assign names to modules.
   c. A module should represent a single logical function.
   d. Modules need not be separately testable.
5. Which of the following statements about coupling is incorrect?
   a. A GO TO statement in a module referencing another module causes content coupling between the two modules.
   b. The design process that aims to achieve a low degree of coupling in a modular software system is called decoupling.

c. If two or more modules reference a global data area, such as a file, stamp coupling exists between them.

d. If a module transfers simple data items to a subordinate module during invocation through an argument list, the two modules are said to be data coupled.

6. Which of the following statements about cohesion is correct?
   a. If the elements of a module perform a series of tasks such that the output of one is input for the next task, the module is said to have sequential cohesion.
   b. Functional cohesion is the highest level of cohesion.
   c. Coincidental cohesion is the lowest level of cohesion.
   d. All of the above are correct.
   e. None of a, b, or c is correct.

7. Concerning data structures and COBOL, which of the following statements is correct?
   a. Linked lists are built-in data structures in COBOL.
   b. Files are built-in external data structures in COBOL.
   c. A network is a data structure that cannot be simulated in COBOL.
   d. COBOL does not support arrays as an internal data structure type.

Answers: 1. d; 2. d; 3. b; 4. c; 5. c; 6. d; 7. b.

Short Essay Questions

1. Define algorithm and computer program.
2. What is software? What is the difference between a computer program and software?
3. What are the properties of a good program?
4. Briefly explain what is meant by reliability and correctness of a computer program.
5. What do you understand by the term "architectural unity" of computer software?
6. How do we achieve ease of modification and maintainability of computer programs?
7. Briefly define the following related terminology:
   a. System
   b. Artificial system
   c. Computer-based system
   d. Information system
   e. Software system
8. What are the activities that make up the software system development life cycle?
9. What are described in the functional specification, which is the output of the systems analysis phase?
10. Briefly describe the systems analysis and systems design phases in the system life cycle.
11. How can you differentiate between logical design and physical design?
12. Define software engineering.
13. What are the main concerns of software engineering as a discipline?
14. Explain what structured programming is.
15. What are the objectives of structured programming?
16. Draw a flow chart for a two-way selection structure. Give a COBOL example.
17. Draw a flow chart for pretest iteration structure. Explain how pretest iteration structure is implemented in COBOL.
18. Draw a flow chart for posttest iteration structure. Explain how it is implemented in COBOL.

19. In how many different ways can one define a multiway decision-making structure in a program? Demonstrate different ways of doing that in COBOL.
20. Discuss the reasons why the COBOL GO TO . . . DEPENDING ON statement is detrimental to good program design.
21. Define modular programming.
22. What are the desirable properties of modules in modular programming?
23. Discuss the advantages of program modularization.
24. What is meant by program structure?
25. What are the types of program structures?
26. Why should networks be avoided as program structures?
27. Explain why uniformity in module size is important in program development. How do we achieve such uniformity?
28. Define the concept of coupling.
29. What are the types of coupling? What is the most desirable form?
30. Briefly explain control coupling.
31. What is meant by content coupling?
32. Define cohesion.
33. What are the types of cohesion?
34. Explain why functional cohesion is the most desirable form.
35. What is meant by procedural cohesion? Give an example of a COBOL module that exhibits procedural cohesion.
36. Explain why it is usually difficult to differentiate clearly levels of cohesion on the cohesion spectrum. Try to come up with a COBOL example that demonstrates this difficulty.
37. Define the following related terms:
    a. Fan-out
    b. Fan-in
    c. Scope of effect
38. What is a data structure?
39. What is a primitive data structure? How can we classify primitive data structures?
40. Define a list as a data structure.
41. What are the differences between sequentially allocated lists and linked lists?
42. What are the COBOL built-in data structures? Which of them are external data structures and why?
43. Briefly explain the top-down design strategy.
44. Briefly explain the bottom-up design strategy.
45. What are the advantages of top-down and bottom-up design strategies compared to the traditional program development strategy?

Improve Your Problem-Solving Ability

Debugging Exercises

In each of the following statements, find and correct any errors that you can detect.

```
1. IF TRANSACTION-TYPE = "D"
       NEXT SENTENCE
   ELSE
       NEXT SENTENCE.
2. IF STUDENT-YEAR > 2
       IF STUDENT-MAJOR = "MIS"
           PERFORM MIS-JUNIORS-AND-SENIORS.
   ELSE
       PERFORM MIS-FRESHMEN-AND-SOPHOMORES.
```

```
3. IF EMPLOYEE-SEX = "FEMALE"
        IF RETIREMENT-DECISION = "YES"
            PERFORM PROCESS-FEMALE-RETIREMENT
        ELSE
            PERFORM PROCESS-FEMALE-REGULAR
            PERFORM GENERATE-EMPLOYEE-SUMMARY
    ELSE
        IF RETIREMENT-DECISION = "YES"
            PERFORM PROCESS-MALE-RETIREMENT
        ELSE
            PERFORM PROCESS-MALE-REGULAR.
            PERFORM GENERATE-EMPLOYEE-SUMMARY.
4. EVALUATE STUDENT-YEAR ALSO STUDENT-SEX
        WHEN 1 THROUGH 4 ALSO "FEMALE"
            ADD 1 TO NO-OF-FEMALE-UNDERGRADS
        WHEN 1 THROUGH 4 ALSO "MALE"
            ADD 1 TO NO-OF-MALE-UNDERGRADS
        IF NOT
            ADD 1 TO NO-OF-GRADS
    END-EVALUATE
5. IF STUDENT-YEAR < 0 OR STUDENT-YEAR > 5
        PERFORM ERROR-IN-STUDENT-YEAR
    ELSE
        EVALUATE STUDENT-YEAR
            WHEN 1 THROUGH 4
                ADD 1 TO NO-OF-UNDERGRADS
            WHEN 5
                ADD 1 TO NO-OF-GRADS
            ELSE
                NEXT SENTENCE
        END-EVALUATE
    END-IF
```

Programming Exercises

1. Consider the procedure division of the sample COBOL program in Chapter 3 (Program 1-Source).
   a. Explain why the program is a structured program.
   b. Draw a flow graph for the program, and highlight and identify the three basic constructs of structured programming on it.
   c. For the same program, draw a diagram similar to Figure 9 showing the program logic in terms of the three primitive constructs of structured programming.
2. Given is the following partial COBOL code. You can see that it is not properly structured.

```
00042   PROCEDURE DIVISION.
00043   MAINLINE.
00044       OPEN OUTPUT NEW-FILE.
00045       GO TO TERMINAL-INPUT.
00046
00047   TERMINAL-INPUT.
00048       DISPLAY "***** TYPE ID IN COLS. 1-4.".
00049       DISPLAY "           TO TERMINATE INPUT, TYPE END."
00050       ACCEPT VARIAB FROM CONSOLE.
00051       MOVE VARIAB TO NEW-ID.
```

```
00052        DISPLAY "***** NOW TYPE NAME IN COLS. 1-25.".
00053        ACCEPT VARIAB FROM CONSOLE.
00054        MOVE VARIAB TO NEW-NAME.
00055        DISPLAY "***** NOW TYPE AGE IN COLS. 1-2.".
00056        ACCEPT VARIAB FROM CONSOLE.
00057        MOVE VARIAB TO NEW-AGE.
00058
00059  ITER-CONTROL.
00060      IF VARIAB NOT = "END"
00061         GO TO WRITE-THEN-READ.
00062      CLOSE NEW-FILE.
00063      STOP RUN.
00064
00065  WRITE-THEN-READ.
00066      WRITE NEW-RECORD.
00067      DISPLAY "***** TYPE ID IN COLS. 1-4.".
00068      DISPLAY "           TO TERMINATE INPUT, TYPE END."
00069      ACCEPT VARIAB FROM CONSOLE.
00070      IF VARIAB NOT = "END"
00071              PERFORM ENTER-THE-REST.
00072      GO TO ITER-CONTROL.
00073
00074  ENTER-THE-REST.
00075      MOVE VARIAB TO NEW-ID.
00076      DISPLAY "***** NOW TYPE NAME IN COLS. 1-25.".
00077      ACCEPT VARIAB FROM CONSOLE.
00078      MOVE VARIAB TO NEW-NAME.
00079      DISPLAY "***** NOW TYPE AGE IN COLS. 1-2.".
00080      ACCEPT VARIAB FROM CONSOLE.
00081      MOVE VARIAB TO NEW-AGE.
```

    a. Explain why it is not a structured program.

    b. Revise and rewrite the code such that it becomes a structured program. Explain how you did it.

3. Study the sample COBOL program of Chapter 5 (Program 1-Source). It is a modular program in which the modules are COBOL paragraphs.

    a. In your opinion, are there modules in the program that require further modularization? Explain why.

    b. Rewrite the PROCEDURE DIVISION such that a better modularization is obtained, and run the program on your computer system.

4. Study the sample COBOL program of this chapter (Program 1-Source) and answer the following questions.

    a. In view of the structure of this program as given in Figure 9 and the contents of each paragraph, try to determine the types of coupling inherent in all module interfaces. In each case, explain your reasoning.

    b. For each paragraph of the given program, determine the level of cohesion and defend your conclusions.

    c. Consider the paragraph labeled B2-PROCESS-RECORDS in isolation. Can you determine the fan-out and fan-in of this module without looking at the structure chart or the other modules in the program? Explain your answer.

Programming Problems

1. Our department has the policy of evaluating all courses and instructors at the end of each academic semester. For this purpose we use a standard form with five questions that aim to measure students' evaluation of the instructor's knowledge of subject matter, organization, effectiveness, helpfulness, etc. Response to each question may be excellent (E), good (G), average (A), poor (P), or unsatisfactory (U).

   Student responses are coded and stored in a sequentially organized disk file. The record of this file consists of the following fields:

   1. Instructor number: 3-digit integer
   2. Course number: 3-digit integer
   3. Section number: 1-digit integer
   4. Year: 2-digit integer
   5. Semester: 1-digit integer (1 for Fall, 2 for Spring, and 3 for Summer)
   6. Question 1: E, G, A, P, or U
   7. Question 2: E, G, A, P, or U
   8. Question 3: E, G, A, P, or U
   9. Question 4: E, G, A, P, or U
   10. Question 5: E, G, A, P, or U

   The following is a sample instance of the course evaluation file.

```
       COLUMN
 1    5    10   15    20
----|----|----|----|--

 5002001881EEGEE
 5002001881EGGGE
 5002001881GGGEE
 5002001881GGAGA
 5002001881AGGAE
 5002001881GGGAE
 5002001881GGGAA
 5502301881EEEEE
 5502301881EEEGE
 5502301881GEEEE
 . . . . . . . . . . . .
```

   The records in this file are kept in increasing order of the instructor number and course number. Each record corresponds to one evaluation form completed by a student for a class. Write a structured and modular COBOL program to read the course evaluation file and produce summary evaluation reports to be returned to the instructors. The format and content of the report are as shown below. Each page of the report should correspond to one instructor and one course. The report should conform precisely to the format shown.

```
                                                PAGE:  1
                                                DATE: JUNE 1, 1991


                  COURSE/INSTRUCTOR EVALUATION SUMMARY


   YEAR             : 1991
   SEMESTER         : FALL
   INSTRUCTOR NUMBER: 500
   COURSE NUMBER    : 200
   SECTION          : 1


       NUMBER OF PARTICIPANTS: 19
       AVERAGES:
             QUESTION 1        3.69
             QUESTION 1        3.60
             QUESTION 1        3.85
             QUESTION 1        3.70
             QUESTION 1        3.90

       INSTRUCTOR AVERAGE    : 3.75
```

In computing averages for the questions, use a numeric weight of 4 for E, 3 for G, 2 for A, 1 for P, and 0 for U. The final instructor average should be computed using the formula:

$$
\begin{aligned}
\text{INSTRUCTOR-AVERAGE} = \ & 0.15 * \text{QUESTION-1-AVERAGE} + \\
& 0.23 * \text{QUESTION-2-AVERAGE} + \\
& 0.08 * \text{QUESTION-3-AVERAGE} + \\
& 0.32 * \text{QUESTION-4-AVERAGE} + \\
& 0.22 * \text{QUESTION-5-AVERAGE}
\end{aligned}
$$

2. In Chapter 3, programming example 3, we developed a COBOL program to compute and display a loan repayment table. In this project, revise your program to ensure that it is properly modular and well structured. Then enhance it so that it computes and displays on the terminal screen, in addition to the loan repayment table, total interest amount paid on the loan.

3. Suppose a bank has a LOANS-FILE with the following record structure.

```
   01   LOANS-RECORD.
        05   CUSTOMER-IDNO          PIC X(5).
        05   LOAN-AMOUNT            PIC 9(8)V99.
        05   YEARLY-INTEREST-RATE   PIC 99V99.
        05   MONTHLY-PAYMENT        PIC 9(4)V99.
```

The bank president wants to know in how many months all loans in this file will be fully repaid, and the amount of total interest that will be earned on them. Write a modular COBOL program to compute and display this information on the terminal screen. You can use the program developed for problem 2 above as your starting point. To test run your program, create a sequential disk file of at least 10 records conforming to the format given above for the LOANS-FILE record.

4. The payroll office in a company has to withhold state income tax on the gross income of each employee. The amount to be withheld on an annual basis is computed using the following schedule.

Annual Gross Income	State Tax
$ 0–5,000	0.715 % of gross income
$ 5,000–10,000	$ 35.75 plus 1.430 % of excess over 5,000
$ 10,000–15,000	$ 107.25 plus 2.915 % of excess over 10,000
$ 15,000–20,000	$ 253.00 plus 3.830 % of excess over 15,000
$ 20,000–40,000	$ 444.50 plus 4.670 % of excess over 20,000
$ 40,000–80,000	$ 1,378.50 plus 5.302 % of excess over 40,000
$ 80,000–100,000	$ 3,499.30 plus 6.025 % of excess over 80,000
Over $100,000	$ 4,704.30 plus 7.115 % of excess over 100,000

Write a modular and well-structured COBOL program to compute and report the monthly state income tax withholding for employees of the company using an EMPLOYEE-FILE as the input file. The EMPLOYEE-FILE has a record structure that is similar to that of the FACULTY-SALARIES file of programming problem 3 in Chapter 3. The report should show employee identification number and monthly withholding for each employee in the file. Design your test data critically to ensure testing of all logical branches in your program.

```
COLUMN
1    5    10   15   20   25   30   35   40   45
----|----|----|----|----|----|----|----|----|----

1000  I   JOHN SMITH          COMP. SCI.  2
1000  E   84  1  CS  210  A
1000  E   84  1  CS  226  B
1000  E   84  1  MTH 200  B
1000  E   84  1  ACT 155  C
2000  I   MARY BROWN           MATH.       2
2000  E   84  1  CS  210  A
2000  E   84  1  MTH 200  A
2000  E   84  1  MTH 261  A
```

Program 1-Input Input Data (STUDENT-FILE) for Program 1

```
000001    *................................................................
000002     IDENTIFICATION DIVISION.
000003     PROGRAM-ID.     STUDENT-REPORT.
000004
000005     ****************************************************************
000006     ***   THIS PROGRAM READS A MULTIPLE-RECORD SEQUENTIAL FILE, CALLED*
000007     ***   "STUDENT-FILE", AND GENERATES A REPORT FOR A STUDENT IN THE *
000008     ***   FILE. ID NUMBER OF THE STUDENT IS INTERACTIVELY INPUT AT    *
000009     ***   THE TERMINAL.                                               *
000010     ****************************************************************
000011
000012     AUTHOR.         UCKAN.
000013     INSTALLATION.   MIAMI UNIVERSITY.
000014     DATE-WRITTEN.   APRIL 7, 1991.
000015     DATE-COMPILED.  04/07/91.
```

Program 1-Source Sample COBOL Program to Generate Student Reports

```
000016     *.................................................................
000017      ENVIRONMENT DIVISION.
000018      CONFIGURATION SECTION.
000019      SOURCE-COMPUTER. UNIVERSITY-MAINFRAME.
000020      OBJECT-COMPUTER. UNIVERSITY-MAINFRAME.
000021
000022      INPUT-OUTPUT SECTION.
000023
000024      FILE-CONTROL.
000025
000026          SELECT STUDENT-FILE   ASSIGN TO INFILE
000027                  ORGANIZATION IS SEQUENTIAL
000028                  ACCESS MODE  IS SEQUENTIAL.
000029
000030          SELECT STUDENT-REPORT ASSIGN TO OUTFILE.
000031     *.................................................................
000032      DATA DIVISION.
000033      FILE SECTION.
000034
000035      ********************************************************************
000036      *** "STUDENT-FILE" IS A MULTIPLE RECORD SEQUENTIAL FILE,          *
000037      *** CONTAINING STUDENT IDENTIFICATION RECORDS AND ENROLLMENT      *
000038      *** RECORDS.                                                      *
000039      ********************************************************************
000040
000041      FD  STUDENT-FILE
000042          LABEL RECORDS ARE OMITTED
000043          DATA  RECORDS ARE STUDENT-IDENTIFICATION-REC
000044                             ENROLLMENT-REC
000045          RECORD CONTAINS 80 CHARACTERS.
000046
000047      01  STUDENT-IDENTIFICATION-REC.
000048          05  STUDENT-NUMBER       PIC X(4).
000049          05  FILLER               PIC XX.
000050          05  RECORD-TYPE          PIC X.
000051          05  FILLER               PIC XX.
000052          05  STUDENT-NAME         PIC X(15).
000053          05  FILLER               PIC XX.
000054          05  STUDENT-MAJOR        PIC X(10).
000055          05  FILLER               PIC XX.
000056          05  STUDENT-YEAR         PIC 9.
000057          05  FILLER               PIC X(41).
000058
000059      01  ENROLLMENT-REC.
000060          05  STUDENT-NUMBER       PIC X(4).
000061          05  FILLER               PIC XX.
000062          05  RECORD-TYPE          PIC X.
000063          05  FILLER               PIC XX.
000064          05  ACADEMIC-YEAR        PIC 99.
000065          05  FILLER               PIC XX.
000066          05  SEMESTER             PIC 9.
000067          05  FILLER               PIC XX.
000068          05  COURSE-CODE          PIC X(7).
000069          05  FILLER               PIC XX.
000070          05  GRADE                PIC X.
```

Program 1-Source (Continued)

```
000071              05   FILLER                PIC X(54).
000072
000073   FD   STUDENT-REPORT
000074        LABEL RECORDS ARE OMITTED
000075        RECORD CONTAINS 131 CHARACTERS
000076        DATA RECORD IS REPORT-LINE.
000077   01   REPORT-LINE               PIC X(131).
000078
000079   WORKING-STORAGE SECTION.
000080
000081   ***********> SWITCHES:
000082
000083   01   END-OF-FILE-REACHED   PIC XXX      VALUE "NO".
000084        88 END-OF-FILE                     VALUE "YES".
000085   01   FIRST-ENROLLMENT-RECORD PIC XXX    VALUE "YES".
000086
000087   ***********> VARIABLES:
000088
000089   01   SEARCH-ID                PIC X(4).
000090
000091   ***********> STRUCTURES:
000092
000093   01   MAIN-TITLE.
000094        05   FILLER                PIC X(10)   VALUE SPACES.
000095        05   FILLER                PIC X(19)
000096                                   VALUE "STUDENT INFORMATION".
000097        05   FILLER                PIC X(14)
000098                                   VALUE " FOR STUDENT: ".
000099        05   OUT-SEARCH-ID         PIC 9(4).
000100        05   FILLER                PIC X(33)   VALUE SPACES.
000101
000102   01   COLUMN-HEADINGS-1.
000103        05   FILLER    VALUE SPACES          PIC X(5).
000104        05   FILLER    VALUE "STUDENT ID"    PIC X(10).
000105        05   FILLER    VALUE SPACES          PIC X(5).
000106        05   FILLER    VALUE "STUDENT NAME"  PIC X(12).
000107        05   FILLER    VALUE SPACES          PIC X(5).
000108        05   FILLER    VALUE "MAJOR"         PIC X(5).
000109        05   FILLER    VALUE SPACES          PIC X(5).
000110        05   FILLER    VALUE "YEAR"          PIC X(4).
000111        05   FILLER    VALUE SPACES          PIC X(29).
000112
000113   01   DASHED-LINE-1.
000114        05   FILLER    VALUE SPACES          PIC X(5).
000115        05   FILLER    VALUE "----------"    PIC X(10).
000116        05   FILLER    VALUE SPACES          PIC X(5).
000117        05   FILLER    VALUE "------------"  PIC X(12).
000118        05   FILLER    VALUE SPACES          PIC X(5).
000119        05   FILLER    VALUE "-----"         PIC X(5).
000120        05   FILLER    VALUE SPACES          PIC X(5).
000121        05   FILLER    VALUE "----"          PIC X(4).
000122        05   FILLER    VALUE SPACES          PIC X(29).
000123
000124   01   OUT-MAIN.
000125        05   FILLER                VALUE SPACES   PIC X(5).
```

Program 1-Source (Continued)

```
000126          05  OUT-STUDENT-NUMBER                       PIC B(3)9(4).
000127          05  FILLER               VALUE SPACES        PIC X(7).
000128          05  OUT-STUDENT-NAME                         PIC X(15).
000129          05  FILLER               VALUE SPACES        PIC X.
000130          05  OUT-STUDENT-MAJOR                        PIC X(10).
000131          05  FILLER               VALUE SPACES        PIC X(4).
000132          05  OUT-STUDENT-YEAR                         PIC 9.
000133          05  FILLER               VALUE SPACES        PIC X(31).
000134
000135      01  TITLE-1.
000136          05  FILLER               VALUE SPACES        PIC X(20).
000137          05  FILLER               VALUE "GENERAL INFORMATION"
000138                                                       PIC X(19).
000139          05  FILLER               VALUE SPACES        PIC X(41).
000140
000141      01  TITLE-2.
000142          05  FILLER               VALUE SPACES        PIC X(20).
000143          05  FILLER               VALUE "ENROLLMENT INFORMATION"
000144                                                       PIC X(22).
000145          05  FILLER               VALUE SPACES        PIC X(38).
000146
000147      01  COLUMN-HEADINGS-2.
000148          05  FILLER     VALUE SPACES             PIC X(5).
000149          05  FILLER     VALUE "ACADEMIC YEAR"    PIC X(13)B(5).
000150          05  FILLER     VALUE "SEMESTER"         PIC X(8)B(5).
000151          05  FILLER     VALUE "COURSE CODE"      PIC X(11)B(5).
000152          05  FILLER     VALUE "GRADE"            PIC X(5).
000153          05  FILLER     VALUE SPACES             PIC X(23).
000154
000155      01  DASHED-LINE-2.
000156          05  FILLER     VALUE SPACES             PIC X(5).
000157          05  FILLER     VALUE "-------------"    PIC X(13)B(5).
000158          05  FILLER     VALUE "--------"         PIC X(8)B(5).
000159          05  FILLER     VALUE "-----------"      PIC X(11)B(5).
000160          05  FILLER     VALUE "-----"            PIC X(5).
000161          05  FILLER     VALUE SPACES             PIC X(23).
000162
000163      01  OUT-ENROLLMENT.
000164          05  OUT-ACADEMIC-YEAR                        PIC B(10)9(2).
000165          05  OUT-SEMESTER                             PIC B(15)9.
000166          05  OUT-COURSE-CODE                          PIC B(10)X(7).
000167          05  OUT-GRADE                                PIC B(9)X.
000168          05  FILLER     VALUE SPACES             PIC X(25).
000169  *.............................................................................
000170  PROCEDURE DIVISION.
000171
000172  A-MAIN-PARAGRAPH.
000173      OPEN INPUT  STUDENT-FILE,
000174           OUTPUT STUDENT-REPORT.
000175      DISPLAY "--> ENTER STUDENT ID NUMBER: ".
000176      ACCEPT SEARCH-ID FROM CONSOLE.
000177      MOVE SEARCH-ID TO OUT-SEARCH-ID.
000178      PERFORM B1-PRODUCE-REPORT-HEADINGS.
000179      READ STUDENT-FILE RECORD
000180          AT END MOVE "YES" TO END-OF-FILE-REACHED.
```

Program 1-Source (Continued)

```
000181
000182          PERFORM B2-PROCESS-RECORDS
000183                UNTIL END-OF-FILE.
000184
000185        CLOSE STUDENT-FILE,
000186              STUDENT-REPORT.
000187        STOP RUN.
000188
000189    B1-PRODUCE-REPORT-HEADINGS.
000190        MOVE SPACES              TO REPORT-LINE.
000191        MOVE MAIN-TITLE          TO REPORT-LINE.
000192        WRITE REPORT-LINE
000193                AFTER ADVANCING PAGE.
000194        MOVE TITLE-1             TO REPORT-LINE.
000195        WRITE REPORT-LINE
000196                AFTER ADVANCING 4 LINES.
000197        MOVE COLUMN-HEADINGS-1 TO REPORT-LINE.
000198        WRITE REPORT-LINE
000199                AFTER ADVANCING 2 LINES.
000200        MOVE DASHED-LINE-1      TO REPORT-LINE.
000201        WRITE REPORT-LINE
000202                AFTER ADVANCING 1 LINE.
000203
000204    B2-PROCESS-RECORDS.
000205        IF STUDENT-NUMBER OF STUDENT-IDENTIFICATION-REC = SEARCH-ID
000206            IF RECORD-TYPE OF STUDENT-IDENTIFICATION-REC = "I"
000207                PERFORM C1-PRINT-MAIN-INFORMATION
000208            ELSE
000209                PERFORM C2-PRINT-ENROLLMENT-INFO.
000210
000211        READ STUDENT-FILE RECORD
000212                AT END MOVE "YES" TO END-OF-FILE-REACHED.
000213
000214    C1-PRINT-MAIN-INFORMATION.
000215        MOVE STUDENT-NUMBER OF STUDENT-IDENTIFICATION-REC
000216                            TO OUT-STUDENT-NUMBER.
000217        MOVE STUDENT-NAME    TO OUT-STUDENT-NAME.
000218        MOVE STUDENT-MAJOR   TO OUT-STUDENT-MAJOR.
000219        MOVE STUDENT-YEAR    TO OUT-STUDENT-YEAR.
000220        MOVE OUT-MAIN        TO REPORT-LINE.
000221        WRITE REPORT-LINE
000222                AFTER ADVANCING 1 LINE.
000223
000224    C2-PRINT-ENROLLMENT-INFO.
000225        IF FIRST-ENROLLMENT-RECORD = "YES"
000226            PERFORM D1-PRODUCE-OTHER-HEADINGS
000227            MOVE "NO" TO FIRST-ENROLLMENT-RECORD.
000228
000229        PERFORM D2-PRINT-ENROLLMENT.
000230
000231    D1-PRODUCE-OTHER-HEADINGS.
000232        MOVE SPACES              TO REPORT-LINE.
000233        MOVE TITLE-2             TO REPORT-LINE.
000234        WRITE REPORT-LINE
000235                AFTER ADVANCING 4 LINES.
```

Program 1-Source (Continued)

```
000236          MOVE COLUMN-HEADINGS-2 TO REPORT-LINE.
000237          WRITE REPORT-LINE
000238              AFTER ADVANCING 2 LINES.
000239          MOVE DASHED-LINE-2    TO REPORT-LINE.
000240          WRITE REPORT-LINE
000241              AFTER ADVANCING 1 LINE.
000242
000243      D2-PRINT-ENROLLMENT.
000244          MOVE ACADEMIC-YEAR   TO OUT-ACADEMIC-YEAR.
000245          MOVE SEMESTER        TO OUT-SEMESTER.
000246          MOVE COURSE-CODE     TO OUT-COURSE-CODE.
000247          MOVE GRADE           TO OUT-GRADE.
000248          MOVE OUT-ENROLLMENT TO REPORT-LINE.
000249          WRITE REPORT-LINE
000250              AFTER ADVANCING 1 LINE.
```

Program 1-Source (Continued)

```
        STUDENT INFORMATION FOR STUDENT: 1000




                GENERAL INFORMATION

   STUDENT ID      STUDENT NAME      MAJOR      YEAR
   ----------      ------------      -----      ----
      1000         JOHN SMITH      COMP. SCI.    2




                ENROLLMENT INFORMATION

 ACADEMIC YEAR      SEMESTER      COURSE CODE      GRADE
 -------------      --------      -----------      -----
      84               1          CS  210           A
      84               1          CS  226           B
      84               1          MTH 200           B
      84               1          ACT 155           C
```

Program 1-Output Output (STUDENT-REPORT) of Program 1

CHAPTER 5

Software Engineering with COBOL: Structured Techniques for Program Design

IN THIS CHAPTER YOU WILL LEARN ABOUT

- Structured techniques for program and data structure design
- Why structured techniques are important
- Program logic representation techniques
    - Flow charting
    - Structured English and pseudocoding
    - Nassi-Shneiderman charts
    - Action diagrams
    - Decision tables and decision trees
- Program structure representation techniques
    - Structure charts
    - Jackson diagrams
    - Warnier-Orr diagrams
    - Action diagrams
- Data structure representation techniques
    - Warnier-Orr diagrams
    - Jackson diagrams
- COBOL programming style and conventions

Introduction

Until the 1970s, designing software systems was a highly subjective and informal activity. There were almost no rules and techniques other than those suggested by the programming language, and the designer's experience and common sense. It is not surprising that most programs written at that time were inefficient. It took too much time and effort to develop, test, and debug them. Most were poorly designed and documented. As a result, it was extremely difficult to maintain large-scale software systems.

Computer hardware, on the other hand, was becoming more and more powerful, and computerization was more and more widespread. Almost every aspect of our daily life was coming to be dependent on computers. Software systems had to be developed for a greater variety of applications, and they had to be more complex and larger. It was unacceptable to spend too much time and money developing poor-quality programs. Something had to be done to expedite the software development process.

The first significant developments came in the early 1970s with the introduction of structured programming as a coding methodology, and the concepts of stepwise refinement and top-down design strategies. They were followed by analysis and design techniques, referred to as **structured techniques**, that are meant to formalize analysis and design. They simplify program development, making teamwork possible and easy, and the entire development process economically feasible.

Structured techniques for program design are classified into three categories:

1. Detailed program logic specification techniques
2. Overall program structure specification techniques
3. Program data specification techniques

They are meant to be used as design aids as well as for software documentation. In this chapter, we will study the more significant structured techniques from a COBOL programming perspective. We will also explore some programming conventions to enable us to write programs that are visually appealing, and easy to read and understand. This way, a program itself becomes part of the program documentation package.

Importance of Structured Techniques

Processes identified during systems analysis ultimately translate into algorithms in the design phase. Each algorithm is converted into one or more program modules during program implementation. Algorithms are part of the output of the design phase, and part of the input of the program implementation phase. It is likely that the programmer in a software development team is not the same person as the systems designer who specified the algorithm, program structure, and data structures to be used. The designer must properly communicate these to the programmer, and therefore this individual should be proficient in structured techniques.

In large-scale software development projects, more than one programmer is employed for program implementation. As all programs are part of a well-defined system, each one is logically related to many other program modules. Programmers have to interact and communicate with one another. The communication elements are program logic, and program and data structures. Therefore, a thorough knowledge of structured techniques is important for programmers.

Programmers are bound to commit programming errors during program development. To find these errors and correct them, programmers employ debugging techniques. Sometimes, errors in a program may turn out to be evasive to find and fix. A useful debugging technique under such circumstances is to consult other programmers and ask for their help. This is known as group debugging. In group debugging, structured design techniques provide indispensable system documentation.

Programmers should be familiar with structured techniques so they can maintain programs. Systems are dynamic entities; so are programs, and they have to be modified occasionally to serve the changing needs of a business. Finally, it is likely that the programmer responsible for software maintenance will not be the same person who developed the system. Clearly, proper and adequate software documentation is important, and structured techniques form the core of system documentation.

To summarize, structured design techniques are important because they

1. Enable the systems designers to communicate with programmers
2. Enable the programmers working as a team to communicate with one another
3. Provide programmer with invaluable debugging tools
4. Constitute the major portion of program documentation that is essential for software maintenance

Program Logic Representation Techniques

Many formal techniques have been developed for program logic specification. Some of the most effective are flow charting, pseudocoding, structured English, Nassi-Shneiderman charts, action diagrams, decision tables, and decision trees.

Flow Charting

Flow charting is one of the earliest methods used for specifying the logical structure of an algorithm or a program. A flow chart is basically a graph consisting of nodes that are connected by flow lines. The nodes represent types and functions of steps in a program. The type of step is represented by the shape of the node symbol, and its details are written inside each symbol. Examples of flow charts were given in Figures 1 through 6 in Chapter 4. Additional examples, together with a more detailed coverage of flow charting symbols and techniques, can be found in Appendix C.

The value of flow charts as a program design and documentation technique is highly debatable. Flow charts can certainly represent the logic of a program module. They have certain disadvantages, however.

1. For large programs, flow charts tend to become much larger than the program they are drawn for. This severely limits their usefulness as a program documentation technique.
2. Detailed flow charts are generally less useful than other structured techniques in facilitating program understanding, debugging, or maintenance.
3. Drawing detailed flow charts for large programs is tedious and time consuming.

As flow charting is easy to learn and the charts are easy to read, programmers or analysts should certainly become familiar with them. They can be useful for small programs or program segments. We do not recommend their use as a structured design or documentation technique, however. In this book, they are used mainly to explain semantics of the COBOL language elements.

Structured English and Pseudocode

Another useful tool for describing program logic is structured English. This is a semiformal way of algorithm specification that uses a subset of the English language. Its main objective is to provide the reader with an easy-to-understand narrative notation that defines the procedural logic of an algorithm or a program.

Unless a user is proficient in a particular programming language and the program code is well written, the logic of an algorithm is usually difficult to understand. A program code may be excessively cryptic depending on the nature of the programming language used. It also necessarily includes the syntactical constraints and idiosyncrasies of the language. In general, this makes the code hard to read. Because we are after a technique that can be used for design and documentation, we should stress clarity, ease, and simplicity.

It appears that the most natural way to express program logic is to describe it in plain English. Unfortunately, English, like all natural languages, easily lends itself to ambiguities. As an example, consider the following process description in English.

> Execute the module called EXCEPTIONS for all students who are majoring in computer science and whose grade point average is below 3.00 or whose current status is GRADUATE.

We could translate this into a COBOL IF sentence in two different ways.

```
IF ( STUDENT-MAJOR = "COMPUTER SCIENCE" AND GPA LESS THAN 3.00 )
      OR STATUS = "GRADUATE"
   PERFORM EXCEPTIONS.
```

```
IF STUDENT-MAJOR = "COMPUTER SCIENCE"
        AND ( GPA LESS THAN 3.00 OR STATUS = "GRADUATE" )
   PERFORM EXCEPTIONS.
```

For a student who is not majoring in computer science and who has graduate standing, these predicates will produce different results. On the basis of this example, we can easily see that the use of everyday English for program logic definition is inappropriate. We compromise and turn to a subset of English that not only produces readable descriptions and adequately reflects the structure of a program, but also prevents ambiguities. For this purpose, we formulate a set of conventions. It should be emphasized at this point that no universal set of conventions exists for structured English, and that the version adopted in a data processing installation somewhat resembles the programming language that is being used there as the implementation tool. Naturally, since we are studying COBOL, our version of the structured English resembles the COBOL language. The conventions are listed below, with examples to illustrate the rules.

> **Rule 1.** A structured English text consists of key words, block titles, bracket clauses, user-defined words, constant values, and punctuation symbols. The punctuation symbols are colon, semicolon, comma, and period.

A **key word** is a word that we use consistently to define a structure template, or certain operators. A **block title** is a user-defined name assigned to a block of structured English sentences. A **bracket clause** is used to mark the end of a block or a basic program structure. Consider the following structured English text. We have numbered the lines for reference purposes.

```
1       PRODUCE-REPORT-HEADINGS:
2           move spaces to REPORT-LINE;
3           IF TITLE-INDICATOR is EQUAL TO 1 THEN
4               move MAIN-TITLE to REPORT-LINE;
5               add 1 to TITLE-INDICATOR, LINE-NUMBER;
6           ELSE
7               move SECONDARY-TITLE to REPORT-LINE;
8           ENDIF;
9           write REPORT-LINE
                after advancing one line;
10      EXIT PRODUCE-REPORT-HEADINGS;
```

Here, IF, THEN, ELSE, and EQUAL TO are key words. PRODUCE-REPORT-HEADINGS of line 1 is an example of a block title. ENDIF and EXIT PRODUCE-REPORT-HEADINGS are examples of bracket clauses.

> **Rule 2.** All key words, block titles, bracket clauses, and user-defined names should be written in upper-case letters. All other entries should be lower-case.

> **Rule 3.** A colon is used after a block title. A semicolon terminates a sentence of a block. Commas separate elements of a list of constants or user-defined words. The entire structured English text is terminated by a period.

Rules 2 and 3 are illustrated in the previous example.

> **Rule 4.** Each sentence of a structured English text should be placed on a separate line. In case a sentence requires more than one line, the continuation lines should be indented.

Use of this rule is shown in line 9.

The next four rules are concerned with the basic constructs of structured programming.

> **Rule 5.** No special key words are necessary for sequence structures. Unambiguous lower-case words should be used to reflect the meaning of the action in a sentence, such as read, write, move, and so on.
>
> Instructions that together make up a sequence structure and help define a single function may be grouped into a block. Such a block structure may be preceded by a unique title to facilitate reference and may be terminated by the bracket clause EXIT ⟨sequence-title⟩.

Lines 4 and 5 give an example of a sequence structure.

> **Rule 6.** We use the key words IF, THEN, and ELSE, and the bracket ENDIF for selection structures.

Lines 3 through 8 define a selection structure. Another example follows.

```
IF SEX-CODE is EQUAL TO 1 THEN
     perform MALE-EMPLOYEES;
ELSE
     perform FEMALE-EMPLOYEES;
ENDIF;
```

> **Rule 7.** To clarify the case structures, the key words EVALUATE and WHEN are used within the EVALUATE ... WHEN ... WHEN ... template. (This template is consistent with the COBOL ANS 1985 EVALUATE statement.) The bracket ENDEVALUATE terminates the case structure.

The following is an example of the CASE structure.

```
EVALUATE SEX-CODE
     WHEN 1 perform MALE-EMPLOYEES;
     WHEN 2 perform FEMALE-EMPLOYEES;
     WHEN OTHER perform ERROR-IN-SEX-CODE;
ENDEVALUATE;
```

In this template, EVALUATE, WHEN, and OTHER are key words, and ENDEVALUATE is a bracket clause.

> Rule 8. The key word REPEAT UNTIL and the bracket ENDREPEAT will be used for iteration. (Note that DO UNTIL, ENDDO, and LOOP UNTIL, ENDLOOP could have been chosen for iteration structures; however, it is important to choose a set of key words and use them consistently in a data processing department.)

Iteration is illustrated in the following example.

```
1       set EVENS to 0;
2       set ODDS to 0;
3       set COUNT to 0;
4       REPEAT UNTIL (COUNT EQUAL to 100) OR (INTEGER LESS THAN 0)
5           read INTEGER;
6     * Test to see if INTEGER is odd or even.  We use the function
7     * MOD for this purpose.
8           IF mod (INTEGER, 2) = 0 THEN
9               add 1 to EVENS;
10          ELSE
11              add 1 to ODDS;
12          ENDIF;
13          add 1 to COUNT;
14      ENDREPEAT;
15      print EVENS, ODDS.
```

> Rule 9. The contents of blocks and structures should be indented to emphasize the logical hierarchy.

> Rule 10. The following key words will be adopted for comparison operators: EQUAL TO, GREATER THAN, LESS THAN, GREATER THAN OR EQUAL TO, LESS THAN OR EQUAL TO, and NOT EQUAL TO. For logical operators, we use the key words, AND, OR, and NOT.

> Rule 11. Parentheses are used to avoid ambiguities in arithmetic or logical expressions.

Note the use of parentheses in line 4 of the last example.

> Rule 12. All other wording should be chosen to be unambiguous, and as easy as possible for nonprogrammers to understand.

Certain words that are key words in COBOL can be freely used in a structured English text provided they are unambiguous. For example, we can use "perform" or "execute" to connote the same meaning as that of the PERFORM verb in COBOL. It is advisable to be consistent in the use of verbs or other clauses in structured English.

> Rule 13.   Comment lines begin with an asterisk.

Lines 6 and 7 in the example are comment lines.

     Figure 1 shows the structured English description of the sample COBOL program of Program 1 in Chapter 4. As you can see, the representation is easily readable and understandable. Also, it closely resembles a well-written COBOL

```
MAIN-PARAGRAPH:

    open STUDENT-FILE in input mode;
    open STUDENT-REPORT file in output mode;
    display "---> ENTER STUDENT ID NUMBER: " on terminal screen;
    input SEARCH-ID from terminal;
    move SEARCH-ID to OUT-SEARCH-ID;

    PRODUCE-REPORT-HEADINGS:
        move spaces to REPORT-LINE;
        move MAIN-TITLE to REPORT-LINE;
        write REPORT-LINE after advancing page;
        move TITLE-1 to REPORT-LINE;
        write REPORT-LINE after advancing 4 lines;
        move COLUMN-HEADINGS-1 to REPORT-LINE;
        write REPORT-LINE after advancing 2 lines;
        move DASHED-LINE-1 to REPORT-LINE;
        write REPORT-LINE after advancing 1 line;
    EXIT PRODUCE-REPORT-HEADINGS;

    read STUDENT-FILE record;

    IF end-of-file is reached THEN
        move "YES" to END-OF-FILE-REACHED;
    ENDIF;

    REPEAT UNTIL END-OF-FILE is true

        IF STUDENT-NUMBER of STUDENT-IDENTIFICATION = SEARCH-ID THEN

            IF RECORD-TYPE OF STUDENT-IDENTIFICATION = "I" THEN
                move STUDENT-NUMBER of STUDENT-IDENTIFICATION
                    to OUT-STUDENT-NUMBER;
                move STUDENT-NAME  to OUT-STUDENT-NAME;
                move STUDENT-MAJOR to OUT-STUDENT-MAJOR;
                move STUDENT-YEAR    to OUT-STUDENT-YEAR;
                move OUT-MAIN  to REPORT-LINE;
                write REPORT-LINE after advancing 1 line;
            ELSE
                IF FIRST-ENROLLMENT-RECORD = "YES" THEN
                    move SPACES to REPORT-LINE;
                    move TITLE-2 to REPORT LINE;
                    write REPORT-LINE after advancing 4 lines;
                    move COLUMN-HEADINGS-2 to REPORT-LINE;
                    write REPORT-LINE after advancing 2 lines;
                    move DASHED-LINE-2 to REPORT-LINE;
                    write REPORT-LINE after advancing 1 line;
                    move "NO" to FIRST-ENROLLMENT-RECORD;
```

Figure 1 Structured English Description for Program 1 in Chapter 4

```
                    ENDIF;
                    move ACADEMIC-YEAR    to OUT-ACADEMIC-YEAR;
                    move SEMESTER         to OUT-SEMESTER;
                    move COURSE-CODE      to OUT-COURSE-CODE;
                    move GRADE            to OUT-GRADE;
                    move OUT-ENROLLMENT to REPORT-LINE;
                    write REPORT-LINE after advancing 1 line;
                ENDIF;
            ENDIF;

            read STUDENT-FILE record;

            IF end-of-file is reached THEN
                move "YES" to END-OF-FILE-REACHED;
            ENDIF;

        ENDREPEAT;

        close STUDENT-FILE;
        close STUDENT-REPORT;

    EXIT MAIN-PARAGRAPH.
```

Figure 1 (Continued)

program. In fact, if you write a good and clearly documented COBOL program, you will end up with something that is close to structured English. The major differences will be due to COBOL syntax rules. (This is not true for some other, more cryptic programming languages such as FORTRAN.) We will keep this observation in mind throughout this book, and try to write COBOL programs as if we are writing in structured English. This is one measure of how good and readable our program is.

Pseudocode and structured English are sometimes used interchangeably. The main difference is that pseudocode is a more formal, more cryptic, and hence generally more concise representation of the program logic. It is suitable for communication between computer scientists and professionals. In this book, we recommend the use of structured English as a technique of specifying program logic. As far as we are concerned, pseudocode is synonymous with structured English.

Nassi-Shneiderman Charts

Nassi-Shneiderman (N-S) charts provide a structured and hierarchical view of program logic in a pictorial fashion. This technique is similar to flow charting in that both are graphic representations for algorithms. Nassi-Shneiderman charts use only symbols for the fundamental constructs of structured programming, however, and thus they discourage unstructured programs with GO TOs. They can be used as a program design aid and as program documentation. Figure 2 shows the graphic symbols used in constructing N-S charts for the sequence, selection, case, and iteration constructs of structured programming.

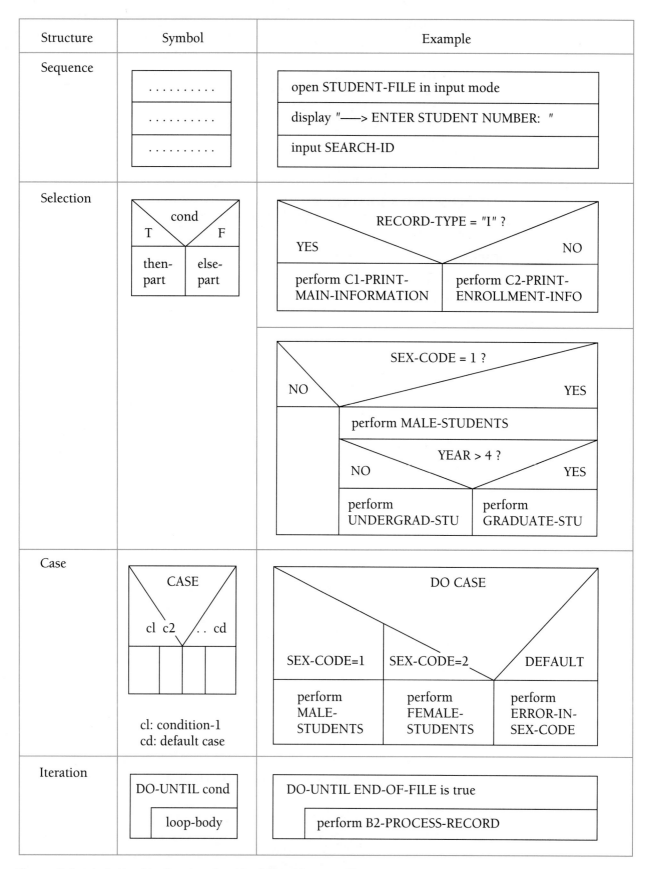

Figure 2 Symbols Used in Constructing Nassi-Shneiderman Charts

> ## Conventions Used in Nassi-Shneiderman Charts
>
> 1. Sequence is represented by a vertical stack of process boxes.
> 2. Selection is shown by dividing a box into five parts. The middle triangular box at the top is used to indicate the predicate on which the decision is based. The left and the right triangles contain the symbols T for true and F for false, respectively. Immediately below the T and F triangles are the boxes that contain the true and false parts of the two-way decision-making construct.
> 3. The box used for the case structure is an extension of the selection box, as shown in Figure 2.
> 4. The DO-UNTIL version of the iteration construct contains the key word DO-UNTIL, followed by the termination condition. The loop body is a subdivision of the DO-UNTIL box.

Nesting of selection and iteration structures can easily be shown in an N-S chart.

An example of an N-S chart for a partial COBOL code is given in Figure 3. Note that the chart is a box that consists of layers of boxes and/or subdivisions, and it reflects the program logic in a hierarchical manner. An N-S chart is most useful if it is drawn on one page. When it becomes too large, the program should be divided into modules, and the logical details of the modules should be shown on separate charts.

Nassi-Shneiderman charts are used primarily for detail program design in a top-down fashion. They should be supplemented with additional documentation to show the high-level program structure and the relevant data structures. Basically, the technique provides the designer with an alternative to flow charting, pseudocoding, and action diagrams. Its main power is in that it is a visual tool, and therefore easy to read and convert to program code. Compared to pseudocoding, however, N-S charts take more time to draw.

Action Diagrams

The three techniques we have studied so far in this section, flow charting, pseudocoding, and N-S charting, are all used exclusively for defining the procedural program logic. As we will see in the next section, we are also interested in depicting the high-level structural overview of programs. For this purpose, we resort to a number of different structured techniques.

As it is, none of the structured techniques available for representing high-level structure of a program is compatible with the three for program logic specification. It certainly is desirable to have similar techniques for the two purposes for program design and documentation. Action diagrams provide this. They can be used for defining program logic as well as for structure specification. In this section we study how action diagrams can be used to show program logic. In the next section, we will study them as a technique for overall structure specification.

The notation used in drawing action diagrams is shown in Figure 4 for the four basic structures of structured programming. As is seen, left brackets are the main symbols used.

```
. . . . . . . . . . . . . .
    PERFORM B2-PROCESS-RECORDS
            UNTIL END-OF-FILE.

    . . . . . . . . . . . . . .

B2-PROCESS-RECORDS.
    IF STUDENT-NUMBER OF STUDENT-IDENTIFICATION = SEARCH-ID
            IF RECORD-TYPE OF STUDENT-IDENTIFICATION = "I"
                PERFORM C1-PRINT-MAIN-INFORMATION
            ELSE
                PERFORM C2-PRINT-ENROLLMENT-INFO.

    READ STUDENT-FILE RECORD
            AT END MOVE "YES" TO END-OF-FILE-REACHED.
    . . . . . . . . . . . . . .
```

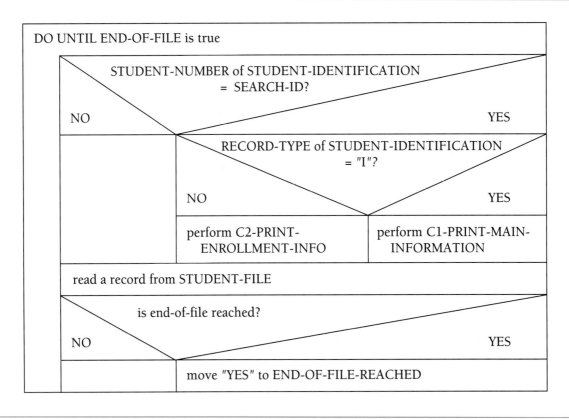

Figure 3 Nassi-Shneiderman Chart for a Partial COBOL Code

Conventions Used in Drawing Action Diagrams

1. A simple bracket isolates a sequence structure. It is also used to show a program block. Brackets can be nested with respect to each other, as can program blocks.
2. The selection structure is represented with a bracket of two divisions.
3. The case structure is a natural extension of selection structure, and requires a bracket with multiple divisions.
4. Iteration is shown using a bold bracket with a double line at its top.

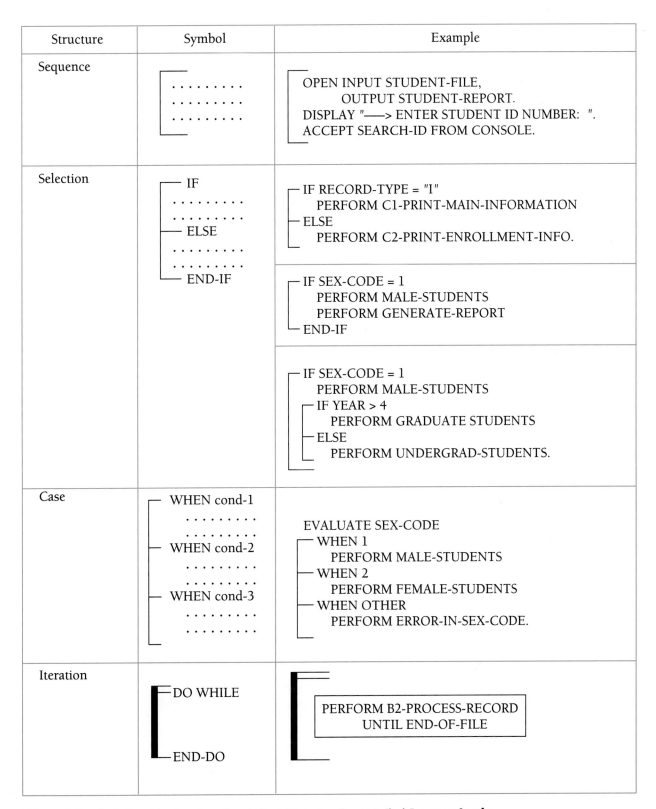

Structure	Symbol	Example
Sequence	. . . .	OPEN INPUT STUDENT-FILE, OUTPUT STUDENT-REPORT. DISPLAY "——> ENTER STUDENT ID NUMBER: ". ACCEPT SEARCH-ID FROM CONSOLE.
Selection	— IF . . . . — ELSE . . . . — END-IF	IF RECORD-TYPE = "I" PERFORM C1-PRINT-MAIN-INFORMATION ELSE PERFORM C2-PRINT-ENROLLMENT-INFO. IF SEX-CODE = 1 PERFORM MALE-STUDENTS PERFORM GENERATE-REPORT END-IF IF SEX-CODE = 1 PERFORM MALE-STUDENTS IF YEAR > 4 PERFORM GRADUATE STUDENTS ELSE PERFORM UNDERGRAD-STUDENTS.
Case	— WHEN cond-1 . . . . — WHEN cond-2 . . . . — WHEN cond-3	EVALUATE SEX-CODE WHEN 1 PERFORM MALE-STUDENTS WHEN 2 PERFORM FEMALE-STUDENTS WHEN OTHER PERFORM ERROR-IN-SEX-CODE.
Iteration	DO WHILE END-DO	PERFORM B2-PROCESS-RECORD UNTIL END-OF-FILE

Figure 4 Symbols Used in Constructing Action Diagrams for Detailed Program **Logic**

To highlight subprocedures, their names or statements invoking them are placed in rectangular boxes. Instead of using brackets, one can use rectangular boxes to show the fundamental program structures.

Figure 5 shows the action diagram for the procedure division of the sample COBOL program of Chapter 4, Program 1. In this diagram, we are using the bracket notation. In Figure 6 we have the second half of the procedure division, this time using the rectangular box format.

The advantages of action diagrams are that

1. They are easy to learn.
2. They are graphic, and thus easy to comprehend.
3. They are easy to draw.
4. They are appropriate for both manual sketching and computerized editing.
5. They can be used not only for program logic specification, but also, as described in the next section, for high-level overall structure specification.

For complete program logic specification, however, action diagrams must be drawn on either a listing of program code or, better yet, a structured English description of a program logic. In other words, they become a valuable design and documentation tool when used together with other structured tools.

Decision Tables and Decision Trees

The program logic specification techniques discussed so far are all capable of representing selection and case structures for two-way or multiway decision processes. For complex decision processes, decision tables and decision trees provide clearer representations. For design and documentation purposes, the systems designer may occasionally find it useful to supplement the design package with one or both of them. We briefly discuss them here.

Introduction to Tree Structures.
It is appropriate to introduce at this point a useful representation technique known as a tree. Trees are widely used in computer information systems. We touched on them briefly in previous discussions. Here, we provide more details.

Figure 7 includes some terminology for trees. A **tree** is a special form of a **graph** that consists of a set of nodes and a set of directional lines (**arcs**) connecting the nodes. The nodes represent discrete entities comprising a finite set. The arcs together stand for the relationship among the nodes. A tree defines a hierarchical structure, as shown in Figure 7.

> A node at a higher level of hierarchy is termed a **parent** node, and nodes that are subordinate to a parent node are called **child** nodes.

Node A in Figure 7 is the parent for the child nodes B, C, and D.

In a graph or a tree structure, each node may have some arcs originating from it and some terminating at it.

> The **in-degree** of a node is the number of arcs originating from other nodes and terminating at that node.

> The **out-degree** of a node is the number of arcs originating from that node and terminating elsewhere.

```
    PROCEDURE DIVISION.

    A-MAIN-PARAGRAPH.

        OPEN INPUT STUDENT-FILE,
             OUTPUT STUDENT-REPORT.
        DISPLAY "---> ENTER STUDENT ID NUMBER: ".
        ACCEPT SEARCH-ID FROM CONSOLE.
        MOVE SEARCH-ID TO OUT-SEARCH-ID.
        PERFORM B1-PRODUCE-REPORT-HEADINGS.
        READ STUDENT-FILE RECORD
                AT END MOVE "YES" TO END-OF-FILE-REACHED.

          ┌──────────────────────────────────┐
          │  PERFORM B2-PROCESS-RECORDS       │
          │          UNTIL END-OF-FILE.       │
          └──────────────────────────────────┘

        CLOSE STUDENT-FILE,
              STUDENT-REPORT.
        STOP RUN.

    B1-PRODUCE-REPORT-HEADINGS.

        MOVE SPACES              TO REPORT-LINE.
        MOVE MAIN-TITLE          TO REPORT-LINE.
        WRITE REPORT-LINE
                AFTER ADVANCING PAGE.
        MOVE TITLE-1             TO REPORT-LINE.
        WRITE REPORT-LINE
                AFTER ADVANCING 4 LINES.
        MOVE COLUMN-HEADINGS-1 TO REPORT-LINE.
        WRITE REPORT-LINE
                AFTER ADVANCING 2 LINES.
        MOVE DASHED-LINE-1      TO REPORT-LINE.
        WRITE REPORT-LINE
                AFTER ADVANCING 1 LINE.

    B2-PROCESS-RECORDS.

        IF STUDENT-NUMBER OF STUDENT-IDENTIFICATION-REC = SEARCH-ID
                IF RECORD-TYPE OF STUDENT-IDENTIFICATION-REC = "I"

                  ┌──────────────────────────────────────────┐
                  │  PERFORM C1-PRINT-MAIN-INFORMATION        │
                  └──────────────────────────────────────────┘
                ELSE

                  ┌──────────────────────────────────────────┐
                  │  PERFORM C2-PRINT-ENROLLMENT-INFO.        │
                  └──────────────────────────────────────────┘

        READ STUDENT-FILE RECORD
                AT END MOVE "YES" TO END-OF-FILE-REACHED.
```

Figure 5 Action Diagram for a COBOL Program (use of brackets)

```
C1—PRINT—MAIN—INFORMATION.

        MOVE STUDENT—NUMBER OF STUDENT—IDENTIFICATION—REC
                             TO OUT—STUDENT—NUMBER.
        MOVE STUDENT—NAME    TO OUT—STUDENT—NAME.
        MOVE STUDENT—MAJOR   TO OUT—STUDENT—MAJOR.
        MOVE STUDENT—YEAR    TO OUT—STUDENT—YEAR.
        MOVE OUT—MAIN        TO REPORT—LINE.
        WRITE REPORT—LINE
                AFTER ADVANCING 1 LINE.

C2—PRINT—ENROLLMENT—INFO.

    ┌── IF FIRST—ENROLLMENT—RECORD = "YES" ───────────
    │
    │       ┌─────────────────────────────────────────┐
    │       │ PERFORM D1—PRODUCE—OTHER—HEADINGS        │
    │       └─────────────────────────────────────────┘
    │       MOVE "NO" TO FIRST—ENROLLMENT—RECORD.
    │

        ┌─────────────────────────────────┐
        │ PERFORM D2—PRINT—ENROLLMENT.     │
        └─────────────────────────────────┘

D1—PRODUCE—OTHER—HEADINGS.

        MOVE SPACES           TO REPORT—LINE.
        MOVE TITLE—2          TO REPORT—LINE.
        WRITE REPORT—LINE
                AFTER ADVANCING 4 LINES.
        MOVE COLUMN—HEADINGS—2 TO REPORT—LINE.
        WRITE REPORT—LINE
                AFTER ADVANCING 2 LINES.
        MOVE DASHED—LINE—2    TO REPORT—LINE.
        WRITE REPORT—LINE
                AFTER ADVANCING 1 LINE.

D2—PRINT—ENROLLMENT.

        MOVE ACADEMIC—YEAR   TO OUT—ACADEMIC—YEAR.
        MOVE SEMESTER        TO OUT—SEMESTER.
        MOVE COURSE—CODE     TO OUT—COURSE—CODE.
        MOVE GRADE           TO OUT—GRADE.
        MOVE OUT—ENROLLMENT TO REPORT—LINE.
        WRITE REPORT—LINE
                AFTER ADVANCING 1 LINE.
```

Figure 6 Action Diagram for a COBOL Program (use of rectangular boxes)

In a tree there is a single node called the **root** of the tree, whose in-degree is zero.

Certain nodes in a tree have out-degrees of zero; they are referred to as **terminal nodes (leaves)**.

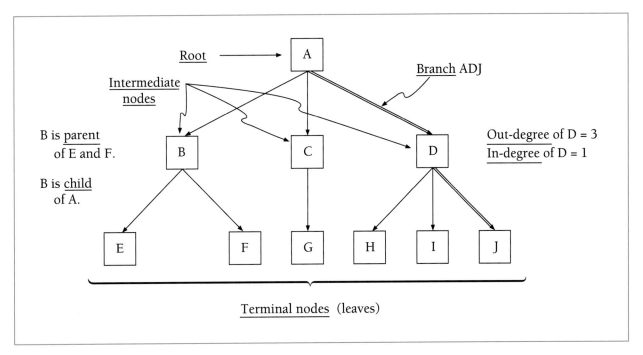

Figure 7 Tree Terminology

The node labeled A in the tree of Figure 7 is the root node. Every other node in a tree has an in-degree of 1. Nodes E through J are the leaves of the tree. All nodes except the root and the leaves are called **intermediate nodes**.

In a tree, a path that originates from the root and terminates at a leaf is called a **branch**.

The path A-D-J is a branch.

In a tree with a single root, every node but the root has an in-degree of 1. This implies that no branch in a tree can contain cycles. Therefore, we can define a tree as follows.

A tree is a graph with no cycles. Such graphs are called **acyclic**.

A special kind of tree in which all nodes have out-degrees of zero, 1 or 2 is called a **binary tree**.

Because they are relatively easy to manipulate, binary trees are common representations in computer applications. Figure 8 is an example of a binary tree in which the nodes represent nonrepeating integers, and the arcs stand for the greater than or less than relationships among the integers. Every node except the leaves has at most two arcs originating from it. The left arc leads to a child node that contains a number that is less than the content of the parent node. The right arc points to a node with a value that is greater than that of the parent node. Incidentally, this binary tree is an example of what is called a **binary search tree**, and is a basis for a useful search technique (see Chapter 8).

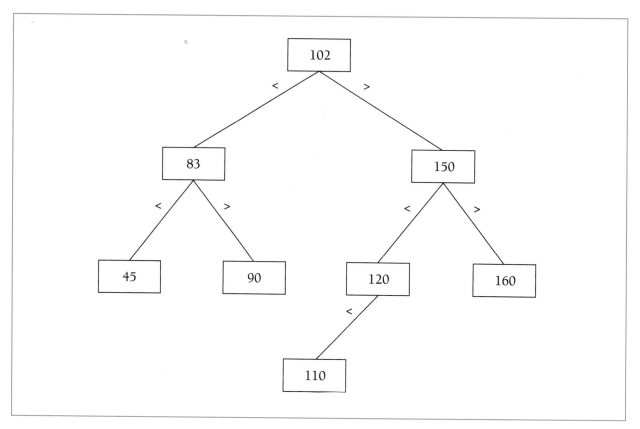

Figure 8 A Binary Tree

Decision Trees. Now we can focus on decision trees.

> A **decision tree** is a tree structure in which intermediate nodes represent conditions or variables, and terminal nodes represent actions to be performed depending on the outcome of conditions or variable values.

Arcs originating from an intermediate node are assigned weights that are the values of the condition or the variable associated with the node. These arcs lead down either to another intermediate node representing another condition or variable, or to a terminal node representing the action to be performed.

Suppose we wish to trigger the procedures FRESHMEN, SOPHOMORES, JUNIORS, or SENIORS, depending on the value of the variable YEAR, which may be any integer from 1 to 4. This decision process can be depicted graphically as in Figure 9a. The tree in this figure has one root node whose label is the variable YEAR. Four arcs originate from this node, with respective weights of 1, 2, 3, and 4. The four terminal nodes (e.g., "execute FRESHMEN") represent the actions that are mutually exclusive of one another. The decision process is equivalent to the COBOL code on the next page.

The tree of Figure 9a can be rotated by 90 degrees counterclockwise and represented as in Figure 9b. This produces the traditional representation for decision trees. We will use this graphic form in our discussion.

Additional examples of decision trees are shown in Figures 10 and 11. The one in Figure 10 is constructed to represent a doubly nested COBOL IF statement in which there are two different simple conditions. The decision tree of

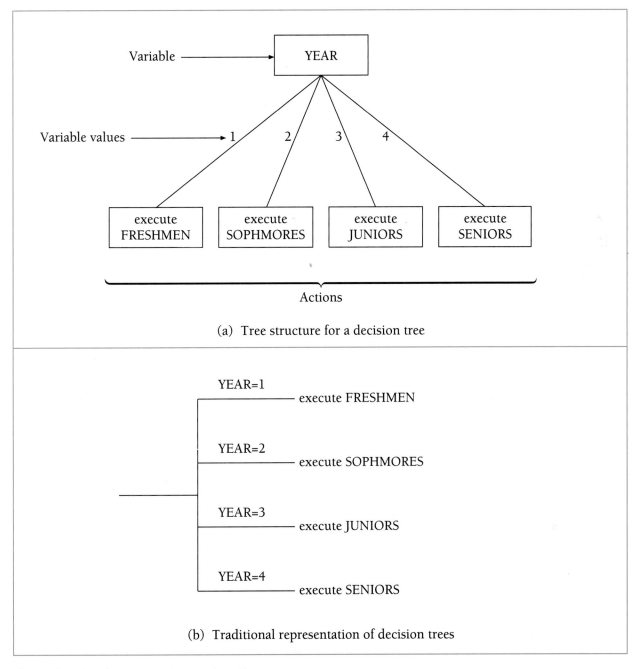

(a) Tree structure for a decision tree

(b) Traditional representation of decision trees

Figure 9 A Simple Decision Tree and Its Elements

```
IF YEAR = 1
     PERFORM FRESHMEN
ELSE
     IF YEAR = 2
     PERFORM SOPHOMORES
ELSE
     IF YEAR = 3
          PERFORM JUNIORS
     ELSE
          PERFORM SENIORS.
```

Figure 11 corresponds to the narrative description of a complex decision process.

The following points should be noted about decision trees.

1. If all intermediate nodes are used to represent conditions, the decision tree is binary.
2. A variable or a condition appears only once in a path originating from the root of the tree and ending at a terminal node. This property makes it possible to avoid redundant testing. The root of a decision tree is the first variable or condition considered in the decision process. The terminal nodes are those from which no branches originate.
3. Decision trees can easily show nested decision processes.

Decision Tables. An equivalent tabular representation for decision processes is provided by decision tables. A **decision table** consists of two portions. The upper portion is used to tabulate variables and/or conditions to be evaluated or tested, and their respective values. The first column of the upper portion lists variables or conditions. The remaining columns define all possible combinations of values for variables and conditions. The lower portion, on the other hand, lists in its first column all actions relevant to the decision process, and in the remaining columns, the specific action to be taken, shown with an X. The

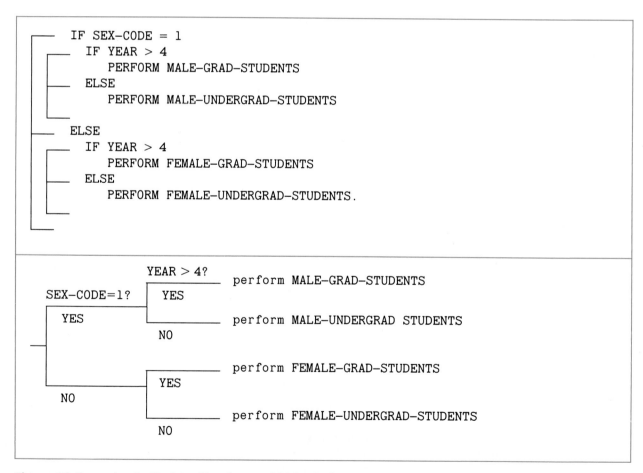

```
      IF SEX-CODE = 1
         IF YEAR > 4
            PERFORM MALE-GRAD-STUDENTS
         ELSE
            PERFORM MALE-UNDERGRAD-STUDENTS

      ELSE
         IF YEAR > 4
            PERFORM FEMALE-GRAD-STUDENTS
         ELSE
            PERFORM FEMALE-UNDERGRAD-STUDENTS.
```

Figure 10 Example of a Decision Tree from a COBOL Code

The Registrar's Office will process student records to generate end-of-semester grade report sheets. If the DIVISION field is invalid, an appropiate error message will be generated and the student record will be rejected. If the DIVISION field designates the School of Business (BS), a special set of procedures will be used to generate the grade report sheets. For all other divisions (AS, EG, ED for Arts and Sciences, Engineering, and Education, respectively) another set of procedures exists. In all cases, the grade report sheet generation procedures for graduate and undergraduate students are different. In addition, for graduating students (field GR containing 1) complete transcript printouts are required.

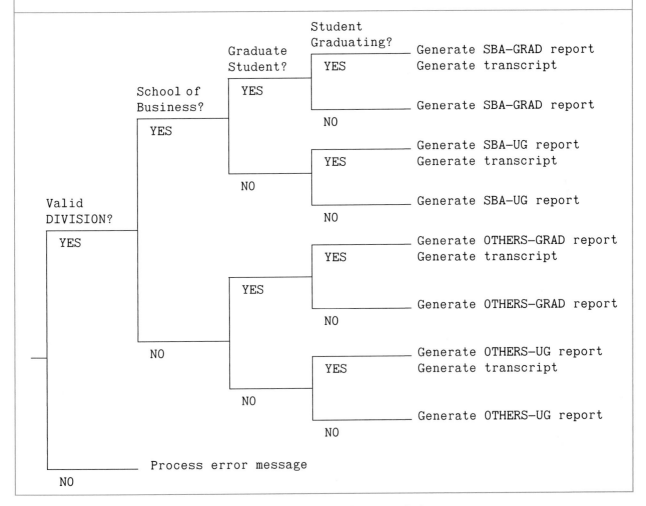

Figure 11 Example of a Decision Tree from a Narrative Problem Description

columns indicating a combination of values and what action is to be taken when this combination arises are referred to as **rules**.

Here is an example of a simple decision table for the problem of Figure 9.

Conditions/Variables	Rules			
Year	1	2	3	4
Actions				
execute FRESHMEN	X			
execute SOPHOMORES		X		
execute JUNIORS			X	
execute SENIORS				X

Conditions				
Is sex-code = 1?	YES	YES	NO	NO
Is year > 4?	YES	NO	YES	NO
Actions				
Perform MALE-GRAD-STUDENTS	X			
Perform MALE-UNDERGRAD-STUDENTS		X		
Perform FEMALE-GRAD-STUDENTS			X	
Perform FEMALE-UNDERGRAD-STUDENTS				X

Figure 12 Example of a Decision Table for the Decision Tree of Figure 10

Figures 12 and 13 contain other examples of more complex decision tables. It should be noted that in certain rule columns, some of the variables or conditions may be irrelevant to the action to be taken; we use dashes to represent this.

In summary,

1. Decision trees and decision tables are equivalent representations that can be used as design and documentation aids for complex decision processes.
2. Both decision trees and decision tables can represent decision processes comprehensively and in an unambiguous manner.
3. As they can only represent decision processes, they are not stand-alone design tools. They should be supplemented with other program logic specification techniques such as pseudocoding, N-S charting, and action diagrams.
4. If in a decision process the number of conditions and/or variables is relatively small, decision trees are preferred to decision tables because they are easier to read and understand.
5. When the decision process is complex, involving a large number of rules, a decision table provides a clearer representation than a decision tree.
6. If software that automatically converts them to program code is available, decision tables may be preferred.

Conditions									
Valid DIVISION?	NO	YES	YES	YES	YES	YES	YES	YES	YES
School of Business?		YES	YES	YES	YES	NO	NO	NO	NO
Graduate Student?		YES	YES	NO	NO	YES	YES	NO	NO
Student Graduating?		YES	NO	YES	NO	YES	NO	YES	
Actions									
Process error message	X								
Generate SBA-GRAD report		X	X						
Generate SBA-UG report				X	X				
Generate OTHERS-GRAD report						X	X		
Generate OTHERS-UG report								X	X
Generate transcript		X		X		X		X	

Figure 13 Example of a Decision Table for the Decision Tree of Figure 11

1. Structured techniques for program design can be used to specify _____ , _____ , and _____ .
2. Structured techniques are meant to be used as design aids as well as for software documentation. (T or F)
3. Flow charting, pseudocoding, structured English, N-S charting, action diagrams, decision tables, and decision trees are formal techniques for _____ .
4. Which of the following about flow charting conventions is incorrect?
   a. Rectangular boxes represent processes.
   b. Diamond-shaped boxes are used for iteration structures.
   c. Oval boxes stand for the beginning and end of an algorithm.
   d. A parallelogram denotes an input or output process.
5. One of the disadvantages of flow charts is that drawing them for large programs may be tedious and time consuming. (T or F)
6. A well-written, clearly documented COBOL program is close to a structured English representation of the program logic. (T or F)
7. Which of the following statements about Nassi-Shneiderman charts is correct?
   a. N-S charts are boxes that consist of layers of subdivisions.
   b. They show the program logic in a hierarchical manner.
   c. They are most useful if drawn on a single page.
   d. They are used primarily for detail program design in a top-down fashion.
   e. All of the above are correct.
8. In an action diagram, a bracket of two divisions represents the _____ structure.
9. One of the drawbacks of action diagrams is that they can be used only for detailed program logic specification. (T or F)
10. Which of the following concepts about a tree structure is incorrect?
    a. A tree is a graph with no cycles.
    b. The number of arcs originating from a node in a tree is that node's in-degree.
    c. The node whose in-degree is zero is the root node in a tree.
    d. Nodes whose out-degrees are zero are called leaf nodes.
11. A tree in which all nodes have out-degrees of zero, 1, or 2 is called a _____ tree.
12. In a decision tree, intermediate nodes represent actions and terminal nodes represent conditions. (T or F)
13. A decision table can be used to represent all basic structures of structured programming. (T or F)

Answers: 1. program logic, program structure, program data; 2. T; 3. program logic specification; 4. b; 5. T; 6. T; 7. e; 8. selection; 9. F; 10. b; 11. binary; 12. F; 13. F.

Program Structure Representation Techniques

We have seen that a modular program has a structure in terms of its modules, and the modules are related to one another by the invocation relationship. We have also seen that this structure should ideally be either a tree or a hierarchical structure. A graph such as that in Figure 10 provides us with an overall view of program structure. Such graphic depictions of program structure for modular programs serve two purposes: they can be used as design tools and they constitute part of program documentation.

A variety of graphic techniques can be used to describe structure of a modular software system. In the following sections, we will discuss the common ones, including structure charts, Jackson diagrams, Warnier-Orr diagrams, and action diagrams.

Structure Charts

A structure chart is similar to the graph of Figure 10. However, a complete structure chart shows the following elements:

1. Program modules
2. Module invocations
3. Data transfers, if any, between modules
4. Order of module invocations
5. Nature of module invocations (simple, conditional, and repetitive)

Figure 14 shows a structure chart for Program 1 of Chapter 4.

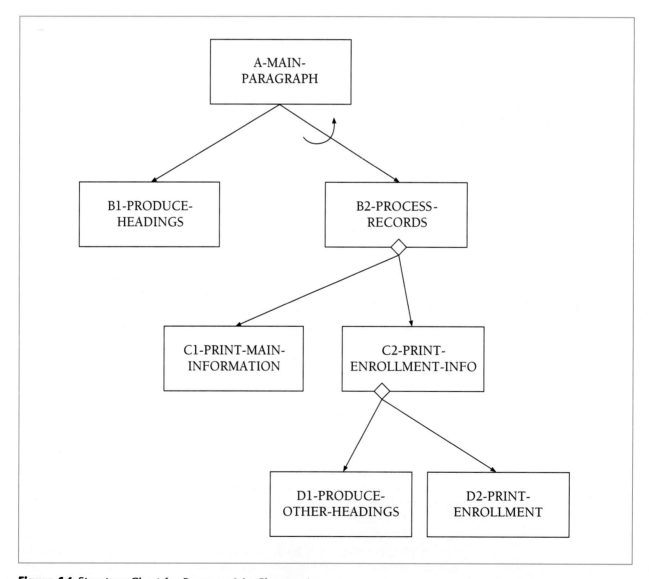

Figure 14 Structure Chart for Program 1 in Chapter 4

Conventions Used in Drawing Structure Charts

1. The basic building blocks for structure charts are rectangular boxes, each representing a program module. Write the names assigned to program modules inside the boxes.
2. Assign descriptive names to program modules. Also, use prefixes with module names to reflect their locations in the hierarchy and their order of invocation at a given level.
3. If a module invokes another module, place the box for the invoking module above that of the subordinate module to reflect the hierarchy, and connect them with a directional line.
4. For unconditional or simple invocations (for which you would use the PERFORM verb in COBOL), use a simple connecting line.
5. For conditional invocations (requiring one or two PERFORM verbs within an IF sentence in COBOL), draw a small diamond-shaped block on the bottom edge of the box for the calling module, and connect the diamond to one or two lower-level modules.
6. For repetitive module invocations (corresponding to PERFORM UNTIL or PERFORM TIMES verbs in COBOL), draw a counterclockwise arc over the line connecting the modules.
7. When control passes from one module to another during invocation, sometimes data are also transferred in either direction. If data transfers are to be shown on the structure chart, use a small arrow (○——▶) drawn parallel to the line connecting the modules, and write the data names next to the arrow to identify the data that are passed.
8. In the program structures of hierarchical type, certain modules may have more than one parent module. Under such circumstances, drawing the arcs to represent all invocations may produce a cluttered and confusing diagram. As a matter of convention, replicate the common module so that the resulting structure is a simple tree. The replicated common module boxes are highlighted by drawing wedges at some corner. In such cases, the prefixing system uses the level designation of the first appearance of the replicated boxes.

In this book we use a two-character prefixing system such as in B2-PROCESS-RECORDS (see Figure 14). In this example, PROCESS-RECORDS is the name assigned to the module in the program, B denotes that this module is a level 1 module (A corresponding to level zero, or the root of the tree; C to level 2, etc.), and 2 implies that it is the second module from left in the structure chart, and hence the second module called by the parent A-MAIN-PARAGRAPH. Intermodule data transfers are exemplified in Figure 15, and module replication is shown in Figure 16a.

Jackson Diagrams

Another diagramming technique used for program structure representation is proposed by Michael Jackson. In general, Jackson diagrams can be used to represent both program structures and data structures. For program structures, they are essentially similar to structure charts, with a few convention differences. The conventions for Jackson diagrams are shown in Figure 17.

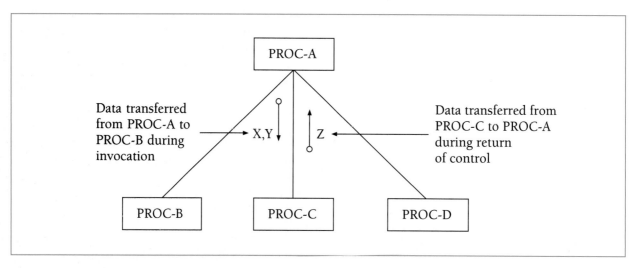

Figure 15 Showing Data Transfers Between Modules in Structure Charts

Conventions Used in Drawing Jackson Diagrams for Program Structures

1. Sequence structures are shown by a two-level tree. The root represents the program module that invokes the subordinate modules in a specified order. The order of invocation is shown by reading the diagram from left to right.
2. Conditional invocation of modules is shown by placing a small circle in the upper right-hand corner of the conditionally invoked modules.
3. Repetitive invocation is shown by placing an asterisk in the upper right-hand corner of the boxes for repetitively invoked modules.
4. All other conventions used for drawing structure charts can also be used for drawing Jackson diagrams.

Figure 18 is an example of a Jackson diagram drawn for the structure of Program 1 in Chapter 4.

Warnier-Orr Diagrams

Another alternative to structure charts and Jackson diagrams is proposed by Jean-Dominique Warnier and Ken Orr. Warnier-Orr diagrams are essentially variants of structure diagrams. They can be obtained by rotating a tree counterclockwise by 90 degrees, and replacing the set of arcs from a module by a left bracket.

Like Jackson diagrams, Warnier-Orr diagrams can be used to represent both program and data structures, provided they conform to tree structures. For program structures, the basic building block consists of a superordinate module name, followed by a left bracket, followed by names of subordinate modules written from top to bottom in the bracket. The representations for fundamental program structures in Warnier-Orr diagrams are given in Figure 19.

Conventions of Warnier-Orr Diagrams

1. Each bracket starts with BEGIN at the top and concludes with END at the bottom.
2. Sequence structures are shown by grouping subordinate modules inside the bracket. The subordinate modules are executed beginning at the top and going down to the bottom of the group. (*continued*)

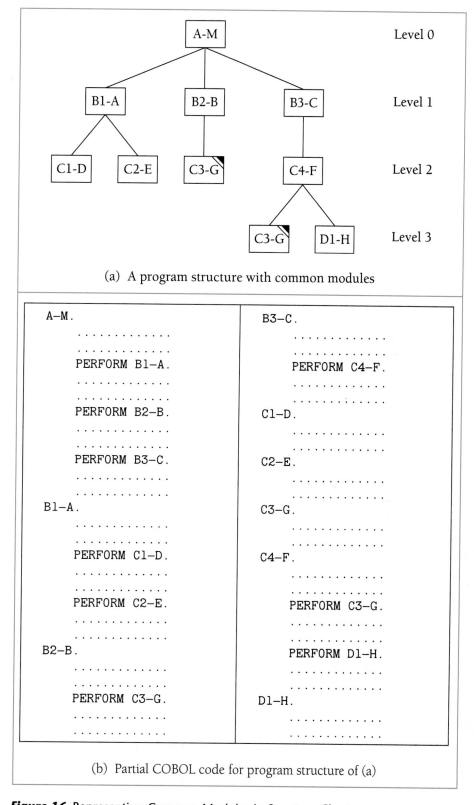

(a) A program structure with common modules

(b) Partial COBOL code for program structure of (a)

Figure 16 Representing Common Modules in Structure Charts

3. Conditional invocations are indicated by inserting a + sign in a circle in between the same level module names.
4. Repetitive invocations are shown by writing underneath the superordinate module n in parentheses, where n may be a constant value or a variable. In case further explanations are needed, a special notation of the form ? m, where m is a number, is used. This is understood as a reference to a footnote, which is included as part of the documentation to clarify any ambiguities. For example,

A
 (n) ?1

may mean that the module A will execute its bracket content repetitively, and footnote number 1 may further state that the loop will terminate when the end of the input file is encountered.

Figure 20 is the Warnier-Orr representation of Program 1 in Chapter 4.

Structure	Representation	Meaning
Sequence		Module A executes module B, followed by C and by D.
Selection		Module A conditionally executes B, C, or D.
Iteration		Module A repetitively executes module B.

Figure 17 Representation of Program Structures in Jackson Diagrams

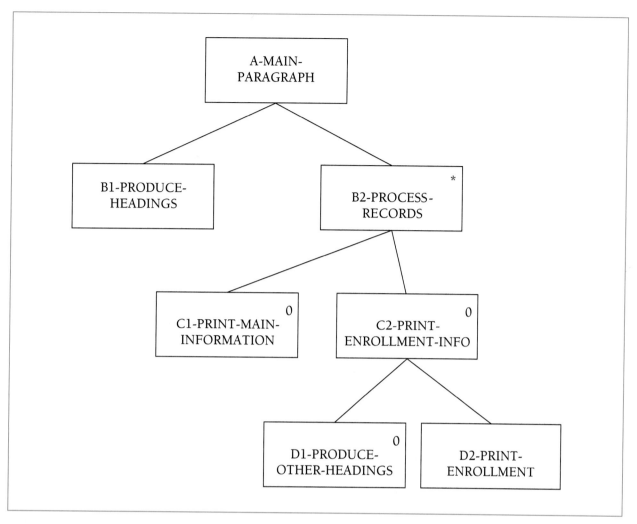

Figure 18 Jackson Diagram for Program 1 in Chapter 4

Structure	Representation	Meaning
Sequence	A { BEGIN / B / C / D / END	Module A executes module B, followed by C and by D.
Selection	A { BEGIN / B / + / C / + / D / END	Module A conditionally executes B, C, or D.
Iteration	A (n) { BEGIN / B / END	Module A executes module B n times.

Figure 19 Representation of Program Structures in Warnier-Orr Diagrams

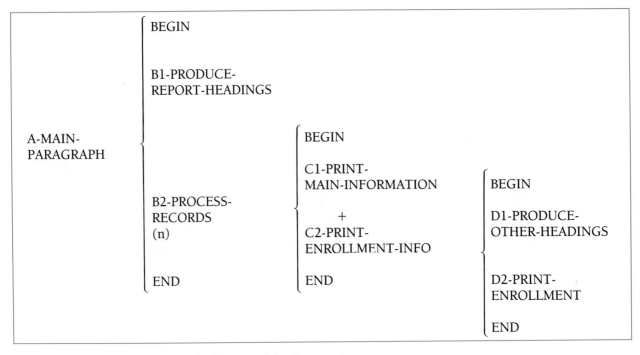

Figure 20 Warnier-Orr Diagram for Program 1 in Chapter 4

Action Diagrams

The last diagramming technique is action diagrams. We used them in the previous section as a tool for program logic specification. Note that the symbols used in constructing action diagrams given in Figure 4 contain symbols for the three basic program structures, namely, sequence, selection, and iteration. We can use these symbols in a nested fashion to represent simple, conditional, and repetitive module invocations in a program structure of a modular program. In fact, action diagrams for program structure representation closely resemble Warnier-Orr diagrams. An example is provided in Figure 21.

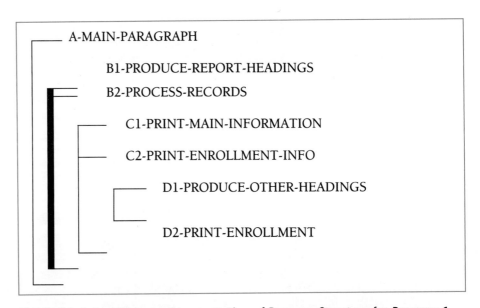

Figure 21 Action Diagram Representation of Program Structure for Program 1 in Chapter 4

**Data Structure
Representation
Techniques**

A data structure is a representation of **data** and **relationships** among them. The relationships can be linear, as in lists; hierarchical, as in trees; or complex, as in networks.

During the design process, the designer should have available some specification techniques to define the proposed data structures. Such specifications need not be machine-specific during design. All we wish to show are data and their relationships. Data specification of this type is known as **logical data organization**.

During program development, detailed knowledge of exactly where and how each data item is stored in the machine's memory may become important. The actual storage structure specifications are called **physical data organization**.

At this point we are interested in logical data organization. A variety of techniques can be used to specify the logical organization of data structures. Among them are special data modeling techniques that have been developed for data base structures, and some data representation techniques that have been proposed primarily as software engineering design tools. The latter include Warnier-Orr and Jackson diagrams.

A few words about data bases would be timely. The discipline of data base management deals with design, development, and maintenance of data bases. A **data base** contains functionally related computer files that are structured according to a particular data organization technique. It is the informational component of a computer information system. Therefore, its design should go hand in hand with that of an information system. Corporate data bases have a strong impact on application software design and development.

As data base systems are concerned with organization, storage, and dissemination of corporate data, one of the principal problems in this field is data structure design. Many data structure design and representation techniques have been devised for data base systems. They depend on the level at which we wish to represent data structures as well as on the way we want to model our data. The manner in which data are organized and represented is determined by the data model chosen for a data base system. A large number of data modeling approaches have been proposed, among which a few have evolved into prominence. They are the relational, hierarchical, and network data models for which implementations are widely available. The entity-relationship data model is also considered important as a design technique. Each of these data models has different techniques that are used for logical data structure representation.

In the remainder of this section we discuss two data structure representation techniques that have their roots in software engineering: Warnier-Orr diagrams and Jackson diagrams.

Warnier-Orr Diagrams

The Warnier-Orr diagrams that we studied for program structure representation can also be used for logical data structure representation. They can conveniently show hierarchical and linear structures of data as long as a data structure is linear, hierarchical, or a combination of both.

Warnier-Orr diagrams can be employed to represent hierarchical data structures as well. The same graphic symbol of left bracket is used to define different levels of hierarchy. Linear structures at a specific level of hierarchy are shown by listing data elements from top to bottom.

> ### Conventions of Warnier-Orr Diagrams for Data Structure Representation
> 1. Linear data relationships are shown by grouping data elements inside a bracket in a top-to-bottom order.
> 2. Conditional data element existence is indicated by inserting a + alone or in a circle in between data element subgroups. The + implies OR (one or the other or both) and a circled + means EXCLUSIVE OR (one or the other but *not* both).
> 3. The number of occurrences of data element groups is shown using the notation (m, n), where m and n indicate, respectively, the minimum and maximum number of occurrences of the data group in the structure.

An example of Warnier-Orr representation for a hierarchical data structure is shown in Figure 22. The data structure considered is the STUDENT-FILE record structure of Program 1 in Chapter 4. The Warnier-Orr representation states that STUDENT-FILE consists of what we call a file header, followed by the file body, together comprising the highest level of structural hierarchy. File header for a COBOL file is the file label records. File body contains data records. We have two types of data records in this file: STUDENT-IDENTIFICATION and ENROLLMENT. The structures of the two record types are logically described within left brackets at the lowest level of hierarchy. The notation (1, m) for STUDENT IDENTIFICATION record means that the file contains at least one occurrence of this record type, and at most m occurrences (i.e., any number of record occurrences, but at least one). On the other hand (0, n) for the ENROLLMENT record type means there may be no occurrences of this record type in the file.

Jackson Diagrams

Another diagramming technique that is useful for representing program structures is Jackson diagrams. Like Warnier-Orr diagrams, they are suitable for representing combinations of linear and hierarchical structures. Therefore, if a data structure is linear, hierarchical, or both, Jackson diagrams can be a favorable structured representation technique.

> ### Conventions for Jackson Data Diagrams
> 1. A sequence of same-level data elements is shown as a series of boxes connected to a parent box at a higher level of hierarchy. The parent box is assigned the name of the group item as its label. The linear order among data elements is the left-to-right order among the boxes.
> 2. That a certain substructure occurrence is multiple in the data structure is indicated by placing an asterisk in the upper right-hand corner of the box for the substructure in the diagram. Asterisk means that the indicated data element of substructure can occur zero, one, or more times in the data structure.
> 3. Conditional existence of a data element or substructure is shown by placing a small circle in the upper right-hand corner of the box. The small circle is equivalent to EXCLUSIVE OR of the Warnier-Orr diagrams.

Figure 23 shows a Jackson diagram representation for the STUDENT-FILE structure of Program 1 in Chapter 4.

```
FD STUDENT-FILE
     LABEL RECORDS ARE OMITTED
     DATA  RECORDS ARE STUDENT-IDENTIFICATION-REC
                        ENROLLMENT-REC
     RECORD CONTAINS 80 CHARACTERS.

01  STUDENT-IDENTIFICATION-REC.
     05  STUDENT-NUMBER      PIC X(4).
     05  FILLER              PIC XX.
     05  RECORD-TYPE         PIC X.
     05  FILLER              PIC XX.
     05  STUDENT-NAME        PIC X(15).
     05  FILLER              PIC XX.
     05  STUDENT-MAJOR       PIC X(10).
     05  FILLER              PIC XX.
     05  STUDENT-YEAR        PIC 9.
     05  FILLER              PIC X(41).

01  ENROLLMENT-REC.
     05  STUDENT-NUMBER      PIC X(4).
     05  FILLER              PIC XX.
     05  RECORD-TYPE         PIC X.
     05  FILLER              PIC XX.
     05  ACADEMIC-YEAR       PIC 99.
     05  FILLER              PIC XX.
     05  SEMESTER            PIC 9.
     05  FILLER              PIC XX.
     05  COURSE-CODE         PIC X(7).
     05  FILLER              PIC XX.
     05  GRADE               PIC X.
     05  FILLER              PIC X(54).
```

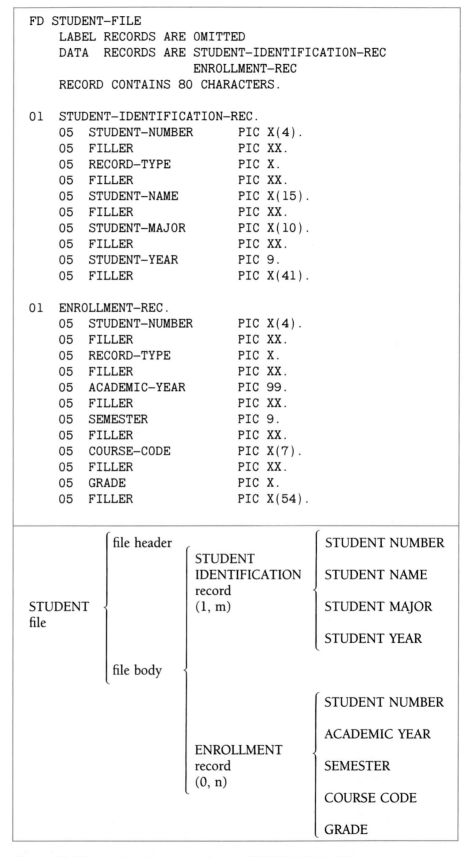

Figure 22 Warnier-Orr Representation for STUDENT-FILE of Program 1 in Chapter 4

```
FD STUDENT-FILE
    LABEL RECORDS ARE OMITTED
    DATA  RECORDS ARE STUDENT-IDENTIFICATION-REC
                      ENROLLMENT-REC
    RECORD CONTAINS 80 CHARACTERS.

01   STUDENT-IDENTIFICATION-REC.
     05   STUDENT-NUMBER      PIC X(4).
     05   FILLER              PIC XX.
     05   RECORD-TYPE         PIC X.
     05   FILLER              PIC XX.
     05   STUDENT-NAME        PIC X(15).
     05   FILLER              PIC XX.
     05   STUDENT-MAJOR       PIC X(10).
     05   FILLER              PIC XX.
     05   STUDENT-YEAR        PIC 9.
     05   FILLER              PIC X(41).

01   ENROLLMENT-REC.
     05   STUDENT-NUMBER      PIC X(4).
     05   FILLER              PIC XX.
     05   RECORD-TYPE         PIC X.
     05   FILLER              PIC XX.
     05   ACADEMIC-YEAR       PIC 99.
     05   FILLER              PIC XX.
     05   SEMESTER            PIC 9.
     05   FILLER              PIC XX.
     05   COURSE-CODE         PIC X(7).
     05   FILLER              PIC XX.
     05   GRADE               PIC X.
     05   FILLER              PIC X(54).
```

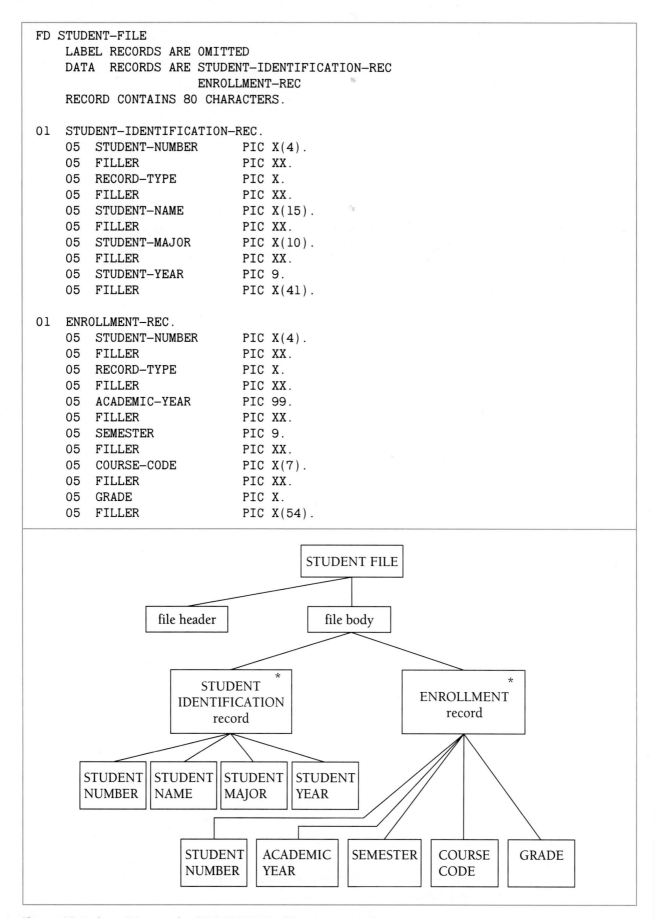

Figure 23 Jackson Diagram for STUDENT-FILE of Program 1 in Chapter 4

1. A structure chart shows the overall program structure only in terms of modules and module invocations. (T or F)
2. Which of the following concerning the conventions used in drawing structure charts is incorrect?
   a. Rectangular boxes represent program modules.
   b. A simple connecting line stands for an unconditional module invocation.
   c. For repetitive module invocations, we write the number of repetitions on lines connecting modules.
   d. If data are transferred during module invocations, we show the variables or data structures transferred together with their direction.
3. Jackson diagrams can be used to represent both program structures and data structures. (T or F)
4. The relationship involved in a data structure can be _____, _____, or _____ .
5. The actual storage structure representation for data structures is called logical data organization. (T or F)
6. In a Jackson data diagram, an asterisk in the upper right-hand corner of a box indicates that this data element can occur any number of times in the superordinate data structure. (T or F)

Answers: 1. F; 2. c; 3. T; 4. linear, hierarchical, complex; 5. F; 6. T.

Programming Style and Style Conventions

When we are first learning a computer language, all we want is to write programs that run correctly. But at the level of this book, we will try to write good programs that are easy to develop, correct, test, understand, and repair. All the principles, concepts, and techniques that we have studied in this chapter have one purpose: to help us achieve this goal. We may create a program that exhibits almost every desirable characteristic we usually associate with good programs. Our program may be modular, well structured, correct, reasonably well documented, and even efficient, but it may still be somewhat less than optimal, somewhat short of "perfect."

What is lacking? The answer is **style**, in other words, a collection of techniques that one develops over time and through experience, enabling one to write programs in an elegant yet simple and efficient manner. Techniques of style are highly personal and subjective, and are mostly a matter of common sense. A program with style has aesthetic worth; it is a pleasure to read. Hence, it may be easy to understand and maintain by someone other than the original developer.

Undoubtedly, as you write more and more programs you will develop your own techniques that will become part of your style as a programmer. Thousands of COBOL programmers have, over time, formulated and used some rules of style or programming conventions. Such conventions have evolved into coding standards in commercial data processing installations. The majority of data processing departments require their employees to make use of a set of coding standards. You may not agree with some of them—in this context, there are no absolute rights or wrongs—however, you may agree with the main objective of coding standards: if they are used in an installation by every programmer, program development and maintenance over a relatively long period of time, and by a continuously changing crew, become easier and more efficient.

COBOL is a reasonably free form language. There are some restrictions about where and how we should type our statements, but we also have many choices. If we choose wisely, we will end up with stylish programs. The following coding conventions are among the standards of many installations, and they will help us write better programs. It should be stressed that they are not universally accepted, but I have found them useful for COBOL programming. Their uses are illustrated in the sample program of Chapter 4, Program 1. Whenever necessary, additional examples are provided.

IDENTIFICATION DIVISION

1. For most COBOL compilers, only the PROGRAM-ID paragraph is required, and the remaining paragraphs are optional; however, the IDENTIFICATION DIVISION is an important part of in-program documentation and should be used fully. We suggest that, in addition to PROGRAM-ID, you should include

   AUTHOR.
   INSTALLATION.
   DATE-WRITTEN.
   DATE-COMPILED.

   paragraphs, and either the REMARKS paragraph or a few lines of comments. The comments should briefly describe the purpose of the program, other program modules it interacts with, and major external data files the program uses.

ENVIRONMENT DIVISION

2. List SELECT statements in the same sequence as FDs in the DATA DIVISION. This improves the clarity of the program as far as files are concerned.
3. Choose descriptive file names for files and follow the names by the suffix -FILE, -REPORT, etc.

```
STUDENT-FILE, END-OF-MONTH-REPORT.
```

4. Certain COBOL compilers and operating systems allow a choice of assigning a file in the SELECT statement to either a specific device or a mnemonic that is the external file name. If it is allowed, we suggest that you choose a descriptive mnemonic as the external file name. This clearly produces a more flexible and portable program. For example, instead of

```
SELECT STUDENT-FILE ASSIGN TO UT-S-SYSIN.
```

it is better to write

```
SELECT STUDENT-FILE ASSIGN TO INFILE.
```

5. The subordinate clauses of the SELECT statement (ORGANIZATION IS, ACCESS MODE IS, etc.) should be typed on separate lines and should be indented to improve readability.

```
SELECT STUDENT-FILE ASSIGN TO INFILE
   ORGANIZATION IS SEQUENTIAL
   ACCESS MODE  IS SEQUENTIAL.
```

DATA DIVISION

6. Arrange FD blocks in the FILE SECTION such that the files most frequently used in that program are coded first.
7. Type FD and file name on one line. Type each of the FD block clauses (e.g., LABEL RECORDS, DATA RECORDS, RECORD CONTAINS, etc.) on a separate line, indented by the same number of columns.

```
***************************************************************
*** TRANSACTION-FILE IS A DISK FILE CONTAINING STUDENT TRANS-  *
*** ACTION RECORDS. EACH RECORD HAS A TRANSACTION-TYPE FIELD   *
*** (A, ADD NEW RECORD; D, DELETE RECORD; U, UPDATE RECORD) AND *
*** RELEVANT RECORD UPDATE INFORMATION.                         *
***************************************************************

FD  TRANSACTION-FILE
    LABEL RECORDS ARE STANDARD
    DATA RECORD IS TRANSACTION-RECORD
    BLOCK CONTAINS 3 RECORDS
    RECORD CONTAINS 80 CHARACTERS.
01  TRANSACTION-RECORD.
    05 .......
    .........
    .........
```

8. Use comment lines before FD blocks of significant files to describe the file briefly.
9. In FD blocks, although not required, include the clause RECORD CONTAINS nn CHARACTERS. This not only makes record length explicit, it also enables the compiler to verify the record length as determined by the record structure specification in the FD block.
10. If a file is a single record file, use the file name as the record name with a suffix of -RECORD or -REC instead of -FILE.
11. In the WORKING-STORAGE SECTION, group entities of similar characteristics (i.e., structures, switches, counters, etc.) together, and use comments to clarify such groupings and their purpose.

```
***********> SWITCHES:

01  END-OF-FILE-REACHED     PIC XXX    VALUE "NO".
    88 END-OF-FILE                     VALUE "YES".
01  FIRST-ENROLLMENT-RECORD PIC XXX    VALUE "YES".
```

12. Use alphanumeric designation (PICTURE X) for data items unless numeric type is necessary because of arithmetic operations. PICTURE 9 is generally less efficient than X, and may cause data exception errors.

13. In the WORKING-STORAGE SECTION, do not use level 77 data entries. They are unnecessary and confusing. Instead, use level 01 for independent data items. For example, instead of

```
**********> VARIABLES:

77   SEARCH-ID              PIC X(4).
     . . . . . . . . . . . .
```

use

```
**********> VARIABLES:

01   SEARCH-ID              PIC X(4).
     . . . . . . . . . . . .
```

14. Start structure specifications with level 01, and use 05, 10, 15, etc., as level numbers for lower-level entities. This approach facilitates adding intermediate-level entries in the future. Consider the following example.

```
01   FULL-TIME-FACULTY-DATA.
     05   SOCIAL-SECURITY NUMBER        PIC X(9).
     05   FACULTY-NAME.
          10   LAST-NAME                PIC X(15).
          10   MIDDLE-INITIAL           PIC X.
          10   FIRST-NAME               PIC X(15).
     05   YEARS-OF-SERVICE              PIC 99.
     05   RANK                          PIC X.
```

15. For PICTURE clauses, choose one variation of four that COBOL syntax allows (i.e., PICTURE, PICTURE IS, PIC, PIC IS) and use that form consistently.
16. In a structure or group of data item specifications, align all similar clauses (e.g., PICTURE, VALUE, etc.) on the same columns.
17. Use readable, descriptive names for data items and structures, and if necessary, hyphenate them for readability.
18. Do not use too many on-off switches to control the logic of a program. Excessive switches make a program difficult to understand and debug.
19. Initialize all of your switches to the off condition (e.g., zero for numeric switches, no for alphanumeric switches, etc.) even if your compiler would automatically do this.
20. Assign appropriate initial values to variables in the WORKING-STORAGE DIVISION. Some compilers may automatically initialize variables; however, doing that increases the portability of the program.

PROCEDURE DIVISION

21. The first module in the PROCEDURE DIVISION should be the main module (driver). It should be concise, ideally fit on one page of program listing, and reflect the major functions of the program.

22. Avoid typing more than one statement on a line.
23. Indent the statements in the then-part and the else-part of IF statements to emphasize the structure.

```
IF POSITION = "ACADEMIC"
    IF YEARS-OF-SERVICE IS GREATER THAN 10
        PERFORM SENIOR-FACULTY
    ELSE
        PERFORM JUNIOR-FACULTY
ELSE
    IF YEARS-OF-SERVICE IS GREATER THAN 10
        PERFORM SENIOR-STAFF
    ELSE
        PERFORM JUNIOR-STAFF.
```

24. Further indent each level and its conditional statements in nested IFs to clarify the structure.
25. Type the ELSE key word of IF statements on a separate line and align each ELSE with its respective IF.
26. Code AND/OR conditions on separate lines and align the condition tests.

```
IF POSITION = "ACADEMIC"
        AND
    (YEARS-OF-SERVICE IS GREATER THAN 10
        OR
    RANK = "PROFESSOR" )
..........
..........
```

27. In compound conditional statements, avoid the NOT condition test. Positive condition tests are easier to understand than tests containing NOTs.
28. Use parentheses to clarify complex conditions in IF statements.
29. Restrict nested IF structures to three levels. Any nesting greater than this generally produces code that is difficult to understand.
30. Highlight the decision and iteration structures in the PROCEDURE DIVISION by inserting blank lines before and after such structures.
31. Vertically align similar clauses of a particular type of statement if they appear consecutively.

```
MOVE SPACES              TO REPORT-LINE.
MOVE MAIN-TITLE          TO REPORT-LINE.
MOVE-COLUMN-HEADINGS-1 TO REPORT-LINE.
.............
.............
```

32. Code the clauses of verbs (e.g., AT END of READ) on separate lines and indent them from the main verb.

```
READ STUDENT-FILE RECORD
    AT END MOVE "YES" TO END-OF-FILE-REACHED.
```

```
PERFORM B2-PRODUCE-REPORT-LINES
    VARYING LOOP-CONTROL-VAR
    FROM 1
    BY 1
    UNTIL LOOP-CONTROL-VAR > 55.
```

33. Open all files in a single statement, if possible. As OPEN is an expensive statement, this will cause the machine to link the open routines only once.

```
OPEN INPUT   OLD-MASTER-FILE
     INPUT   TRANSACTION-FILE
     OUTPUT  NEW-MASTER-FILE.
```

General Style Conventions

34. Do not use continuation lines in COBOL. If a statement is too long to type on one line, simply continue typing on the next line. While doing that, however, you should
   a. Avoid splitting a clause over two lines
   b. Indent successive lines of the same entry for visual clarity
   For example, instead of

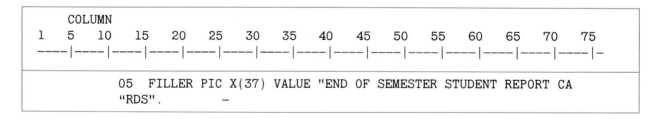

type your code as

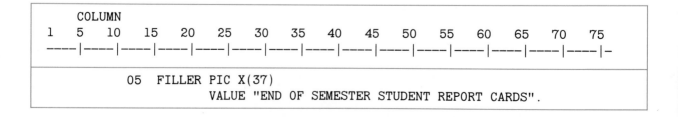

35. Type division, section, and paragraph headers alone on individual lines.
36. Make liberal use of page ejects and blank lines in your program. This way you can improve the readability of the program. For page ejects, depending on the available compiler, you can use EJECT statement, or / in column 7 of the line that you want to be printed starting on a new page.
37. Use a period to close out every COBOL statement even if it is not required.
38. Avoid using commas, as they can be confused with periods during coding or reading a program. Instead, whenever a comma can be used, write the items on separate lines or use blanks as separators.
39. As COBOL can produce readable codes, avoid unnecessary comments. The following comment is redundant.

```
****** THIS PARAGRAPH GENERATES STUDENT REPORT.

PRODUCE-STUDENT-REPORT.
    . . . . . . . . . . . . . . . . .
    . . . . . . . . . . . . . . . . .
```

40. Highlight comment lines by using blank lines before and after, or by enclosing them in rows of asterisks.
41. Choose and use descriptive user-defined names for every element in your program, including variables, paragraph, section, and subroutine names, and so on.

REVIEW QUESTIONS

1. Style in program design is a collection of techniques that enable us to write programs in an elegant, simple, and efficient manner. (T or F)
2. Style conventions in COBOL programming are verified by the compiler before compilation is attempted. (T or F)
3. In a COBOL program, the purpose of the program can be briefly described in either a _____ or a _____ .
4. Using a descriptive mnemonic as the external file name for a SELECT statement, if allowed by the compiler, may produce a more flexible and portable program. (T or F)
5. Using indentation while typing COBOL source code improves program _____ .
6. As the RECORD CONTAINS clause is not required for FD blocks, we should avoid using it in COBOL programming. (T or F)
7. PICTURE 9 is generally less efficient than PICTURE X and may cause _____ errors. (T or F)
8. In structure descriptions, we should start with level 01, and use levels 02, 03, and so on, for subordinate entries. (T or F)
9. Since positive condition tests are easier to understand than tests containing NOTs, we should avoid the NOT condition test in compound conditional statements. (T or F)
10. We should open all files in a single OPEN statement because _____ .
11. Using commas and semicolons in COBOL as delimiters is a good practice, since they tend to improve program readability. (T or F)

Answers: 1. T; 2. F; 3. comment line, REMARKS paragraph; 4. T; 5. readability; 6. F; 7. data exception; 8. F; 9. T; 10. OPEN is an expensive statement; 11. F.

Example Program 1: *Checking Account Statement Generator*

We have the following problem specification for our sample program in this chapter.

Problem   The New National Bank wants to generate end-of-month checking account statements for its customers. The format of the statement report is given below.

```
                         NEW NATIONAL BANK
                           OXFORD, OHIO

        C H E C K I N G   A C C O U N T   S T A T E M E N T

      Customer name                        DATE      XX/XX/XX
      Street address                       STATEMENT PERIOD
      City, State ZIP                      FROM      XX/XX/XX
                                           THROUGH   XX/XX/XX


 DATE      TRANSACTIONS                           AMOUNT     BALANCE
 ____      _____                           _____     _____
 XX/XX     XXXXXXXXXXXXXXXXXXXXXXXXX          999,999.99  999,999.99
 XX/XX     XXXXXXXXXXXXXXXXXXXXXXXXX          999,999.99  999,999.99
 XX/XX     XXXXXXXXXXXXXXXXXXXXXXXXX          999,999.99+ 999,999.99
 XX/XX     XXXXXXXXXXXXXXXXXXXXXXXXX          999,999.99  999,999.99
 XX/XX     XXXXXXXXXXXXXXXXXXXXXXXXX          999,999.99+ 999,999.99


              S U M M A R Y   O F   A C C O U N T

 ACCOUNT    BEGINNING    TOTAL      TOTAL      MISC     TOTAL     CURRENT
 NUMBER     BALANCE      CREDITS    DEBITS     CHARGES  INTEREST  BALANCE

  XXXX     999,999.99   999,999.99 999,999.99  999.99   999.99  999,999.99

                                               ITEMS ENCLOSED   999


                    First line of message
                    Second line of message
```

As is seen, the checking account statement has four parts.

1. Part 1 contains fixed headers, customer name and address, date of processing, and the statement period in terms of from and through dates.
2. Part 2 lists all transactions that have occurred for this account during the statement period. Transaction lines in this part include date, transaction description, amount (followed by a + if deposit), and balance after the transaction is recorded.
3. Part 3 is an account summary. It has a single line of summary information that includes account number, beginning balance, total credits and debits that have occurred for this account during the month, miscellaneous charges, total interest earned, and current balance.

Miscellaneous charges for this problem is a fixed service charge of $5.00 if the minimum balance in the account falls below $300.00.

Interest is earned at the rate of 5.5% on the minimum balance, provided the minimum balance is greater than or equal to $1000.00.

This part also contains an ITEMS ENCLOSED line indicating the number of cashed checks, which will be mailed back to the customer together with the statement.

4. Part 4 contains two lines of a message to the customers.

As input, there are two disk files and interactive input for a few problem parameters. The disk files are ACCOUNTS-FILE and CHECKING-TRANSAC-TIONS-FILE. ACCOUNTS-FILE record structure consists of

- Account number: a 4-digit customer identifier
- Customer name: alphanumeric, 20 bytes
- Customer address: consisting of street address: alphanumeric, 20 bytes; and city, state, and ZIP: combined field, alphanumeric, 20 bytes
- Balance from last month: 8-digit, numeric computational field, with 2 decimal places

CHECKING-TRANSACTIONS-FILE has the following record structure:

- Account number: 4 digits
- Transaction date: in terms of month (2 bytes) and day (2 bytes)
- Transaction type: alphanumeric, 1 byte [assume that there can be only three transaction types: D (deposit), W (withdrawal), and C (check written against customer's account)]
- Transaction description: alphanumeric, 25 bytes
- Transaction amount: numeric computational, 8 bytes, 2 decimal places

Program 1-Input(a) and (b) shows example instances for the two input files. The following problem variables are to be interactively input at the terminal once for all accounts:

- Statement-from date, a 6-digit field for month-day-year
- Statement-through-date, also a 6-digit fields for month-day-year
- Two message lines, each 50 bytes long

Solution The compiler listing of a COBOL program written to produce the desired report is given in Program 1-Source. We will refer back to this program occasionally in the end-of-chapter problems.

Program 1-Output(a) is a sample output produced by the program.

Finally, Program 1-Output(b) shows an example terminal session for interactive data input required by the program.

Key Terms

action diagram	Nassi-Shneiderman chart
binary tree	parent node
branch	programming style
child node	pseudocode
decision table	root
decision tree	structure chart
flow chart	structured English
Jackson diagram	tree
leaf	Warnier-Orr diagram

Study Guide

Quick Scan

- Structured techniques that have evolved since the early 1970s are important tools for application program development. They facilitate the program design process; enable designers, programmers, and system maintenance personnel to communicate with one another; and make up a major part of the program documentation.
- The logic of a program can be represented using a variety of methods. The oldest diagramming technique is flow charting. Flow charting is not a structured technique. Since it has some disadvantages as a design tool, its use should be limited.
- Among the available structured techniques for program logic description are structured English, Nassi-Shneiderman charts, action diagrams, decision trees, and decision tables.
- Structured English, Nassi-Shneiderman charts, and action diagrams provide the designer and programmer with general purpose design and documentation techniques. They can handle all basic constructs of structured programming, including sequence, selection, and iteration.
- Decision trees and decision tables are limited-scope program logic design techniques. They can be used only to represent complex decision processes. Therefore, they are not stand-alone and should be used to supplement the other design techniques.
- Several structured techniques are available for program structure design and representation. The most commonly used is structure charting; Jackson diagrams and Warnier-Orr diagrams are variations of structure charts. These techniques can graphically show hierarchical and sequential relations among a set of objects. Therefore, they can be used to advantage for program structure representation.
- Action diagramming is a versatile design technique. It can be used for program logic representation and is also suitable for program structure design.
- Some of the techniques that are appropriate for program structure design are also usable as hierarchical data structure design techniques; for example, Warnier-Orr diagrams and Jackson diagrams.
- A program may be correct, logically structured, and even exhibit a good modularization scheme. Still, it may be difficult to understand by people other than the writer. To make programs more readable and understandable, many style conventions have been developed.
- Style conventions are dependent on the programming language used for implementation. For COBOL programs, the use of good style conventions helps produce better programs with greater appeal and higher documentation value.

Test Your Comprehension

Multiple-Choice Questions

1. Structured techniques for program design are important, because
   a. They enable designers to communicate with programmers.
   b. They enable programmers working as a team to communicate with one another.
   c. They provide programmers with an invaluable debugging tool.
   d. They constitute the major portion of program documentation.
   e. All of the above are correct.
2. Which of the following is not a structured technique that is suitable for the specification of detailed program logic?
   a. Nassi-Shneiderman charts
   b. Action diagrams

     c. Jackson diagrams

     d. Decision tables

3. Which of the following statements about decision trees and decision tables is incorrect?

     a. They are equivalent representations.

     b. They can be used to represent decision and iteration processes.

     c. They are not stand-alone tools and should be supplemented with other structured techniques.

     d. If in a decision process there are a large number of rules, a decision table representation may provide a clearer picture than a decision tree.

4. Choose the correct statement.

     a. A Jackson diagram cannot be used to represent data structures.

     b. A Warnier-Orr diagram is suitable only for program logic representation.

     c. An action diagram can be used both for detail program logic and program structure representations.

     d. All of the above are correct.

5. Which of the following is a style convention in COBOL?

     a. In the PROCEDURE DIVISION, each sentence should terminate with a period.

     b. Parentheses should be used to clarify complex conditions in IF statements.

     c. A condition should follow the key word UNTIL in a PERFORM UNTIL statement.

     d. The target fields in a MOVE statement should be identifiers.

Answers: 1. e; 2. c; 3. b; 4. c; 5. b.

Short Essay Questions

1. Explain why structured techniques for program design and documentation are important.

2. Name at least four techniques that can be used for program logic specification.

3. What are the disadvantages of flow charts as a program logic design and documentation technique compared to other structured techniques? Under what circumstances is a flow chart useful?

4. Why is English not a good tool for expressing program logic?

5. Discuss the validity of the following statement: the more cryptic a programming language is, the more necessary it becomes to use structured English to describe the logic of programs written in that language.

6. Explain why the version of structured English presented in this chapter is sufficient to describe the logic of any algorithm, no matter how complex it may be.

7. Consider our version of structured English. Explain what is "structured" about it.

8. What is a pseudocode? What makes a pseudocode different from a structured English text for the same algorithm?

9. How do we represent selection in N-S charts? Give an example.

10. How do we represent iteration in N-S charts? Give an example.

11. Briefly discuss the advantages and disadvantages of N-S charts compared to other structured techniques.

12. What is the convention for representing selection and case structures in an action diagram? Give an example for each structure.

13. How do we represent iteration in an action diagram? Give an example.

14. What is a tree structure? Why is a tree also a hierarchical structure?

15. Briefly define the following terms for trees:

     a. Parent node

     b. Child node

    c. In-degree and out-degree

    d. Root node

    e. Leaf nodes

    f. Branch

16. Define binary tree. Give an example of a binary tree from everyday life.

17. What is a decision tree? Can we use decision trees as a general program logic representation technique? Explain your answer.

18. Explain why decision trees and decision tables are equivalent representations.

19. Under what circumstances should we prefer decision trees to decision tables?

20. Under what circumstances should decision tables be preferred to decision trees? Explain your answer.

21. Name at least three graphic techniques that can be used to represent the structure of a modular program.

22. What are depicted in a structure chart?

23. What do the interconnecting lines stand for in a structure chart?

24. How do we represent selection and iteration in a structure chart?

25. How do we represent data transfers between two modules in a structure chart?

26. Under what circumstances and how should common modules in a structure chart be replicated?

27. Explain the similarities and differences between Jackson diagrams and structure charts.

28. How do we represent conditional and iterative invocations in a Jackson diagram?

29. What are the differences and similarities between Warnier-Orr and Jackson diagrams?

30. How do we represent conditional and iterative invocations in a Warnier-Orr diagram?

31. In general, what are the types of relationships that can be represented in a data structure?

32. What is meant by logical data organization? How does it differ from physical data organization?

33. Can we use the Warnier-Orr diagramming technique for the representation of complex (i.e., network) data structures? Explain your answer.

34. Why are Warnier-Orr and Jackson diagrams suitable for specification of certain data structures as well as program structures? Explain your answer.

35. Explain the difference between OR and EXCLUSIVE OR. How are they represented in Warnier-Orr diagrams?

36. How do we represent multiple occurrences of data groups in Warnier-Orr diagrams?

37. How do we represent multiple occurrences of data groups in Jackson diagrams?

38. How can the conditional existence of a data element be shown on a Jackson diagram?

39. Look for the definition of the word "style" in several dictionaries. Then discuss style as it applies to any fine art form that you especially find appealing.

40. Briefly explain what is meant by a program of style.

41. Explain why programming style conventions are important.

42. In COBOL, the clause RECORD CONTAINS nn CHARACTERS for FD blocks is optional. Explain why it is a good idea to use this clause consistently in your programs.

43. Explain why it is not a good practice in COBOL to use continuation lines (i.e., hyphens in column 7).

Improve Your Problem-Solving Ability

Programming Exercises

1. Using the conventions for structured English that we have adopted in this chapter, write a structured English description of the paragraph B4-MATCH-RECORDS of Program 1-Source.
2. The following is a structured English description for an algorithm.

```
 1  set EVENS to 0;
 2  set ODDS to 0;
 3  set COUNT to 0;
 4  REPEAT UNTIL (COUNT EQUAL to 100) OR (INTEGER LESS THAN 0)
 5          read INTEGER;
 6  * Test to see if INTEGER is odd or even. We use the function
 7  * MOD for this purpose.
 8          IF mod (INTEGER, 2) = 0 THEN
 9                  add 1 to EVENS;
10      ELSE
11                  add 1 to ODDS;
12      ENDIF;
13      add 1 to COUNT;
14  ENDREPEAT;
15  print EVENS, ODDS.
```

Express the logic of this algorithm with an N-S chart.

3. Make a photocopy of the procedure division of the sample program in Program 1-Source, and on the program listing draw an action diagram to clarify the program logic.
4. Given is the decision tree of Figure 11. Draw an N-S chart to correspond to this nested decision structure.
5. Given is the following decision table. Draw a decision tree that is equivalent to it.

Conditions									
Is employee full-time?	No	Yes	Yes	Yes	Yes	Yes	Yes	Yes	Yes
Is employee male?	—	Yes	Yes	Yes	Yes	No	No	No	No
Is employee managerial?	—	Yes	Yes	No	No	Yes	Yes	No	No
More than 10 years of service in present position?	—	Yes	No	Yes	No	Yes	No	Yes	No
Actions									
Execute PART-TIME-EMPLOYEE	X								
Execute MALE-SENIOR-MANAGERS		X							
Execute MALE-JUNIOR-MANAGERS			X						
Execute MALE-SENIOR-STAFF				X					
Execute MALE-JUNIOR-STAFF					X				
Execute FEMALE-SENIOR-MANAGERS						X			
Execute FEMALE-JUNIOR-MANAGERS							X		
Execute FEMALE-SENIOR-STAFF								X	
Execute FEMALE-JUNIOR-STAFF									X
Execute FEDERAL-STATISTICS						X	X	X	X
Execute SENIOR-EMPLOYEE-PROFILE		X		X		X		X	

6. For the decision table of problem 5, write an equivalent, well-structured partial COBOL code, once using a nested IF statement and once using unnested IF statements.

7. Draw a structure chart for the procedure division of Program 1. Replicate the common modules in the structure chart. Do not show data transfers between modules.

8. For the procedure division of Program 1, draw a Jackson diagram depicting the program structure.

9. For the procedure division of Program 1, draw a Warnier-Orr diagram for the program structure.

10. Represent the program structure of the procedure division of Program 1 as an action diagram.

11. Given is the following COBOL FD block for the EMPLOYEE-PROFILE-FILE. Draw a Warnier-Orr diagram to represent this data structure. Assume that this is a disk file and is never empty.

```
FD   EMPLOYEE-PROFILE-FILE
     LABEL RECORDS ARE STANDARD
     DATA   RECORD   IS   EMPLOYEE-PROFILE-RECORD
     RECORD CONTAINS 102 CHARACTERS.
01   EMPLOYEE-PROFILE-RECORD.
     05   EMPLOYEE--IDENTIFICATION.
          10   IDNUMBER              PIC X(9).
          10   EMPLOYEE-NAME.
               15   LAST-NAME        PIC X(15).
               15   FIRST-NAME       PIC X(15).
     05   JOB-IDENTIFICATION.
          10   JOB-CODE              PIC X(3).
          10   JOB-DESCRIPTION       PIC X(20).
          10   COMPANY-DEPARTMENT    PIC X(10).
          10   SALARY                PIC 9(6)V99.
     05   JOB-HISTORY-1.
          10   PREVIOUS-JOB-CODE-1   PIC X(3).
          10   PREVIOUS-SALARY-1     PIC 9(6)V99.
     05   JOB-HISTORY-2.
          10   PREVIOUS-JOB-CODE-2   PIC X(3).
          10   PREVIOUS-SALARY-2     PIC 9(6)V99.
```

12. For the file of problem 11, draw a Jackson diagram representation.

13. Examine the following COBOL program from a style point of view. Then rewrite it as a program of good style without changing the basic logic and structure.

```
00001    *************************************************************
00002    * THIS PROGRAM CREATES A SEQUENTIAL DISK FILE FROM TERMINAL.    *
00003    *************************************************************
00004    IDENTIFICATION DIVISION.
00005    PROGRAM-ID. SFFT.
00006    ENVIRONMENT DIVISION.
00007    CONFIGURATION SECTION.
00008    SOURCE-COMPUTER. IBM-370.
00009    OBJECT-COMPUTER. IBM-370.
00010    INPUT-OUTPUT SECTION.
```

```
00011      FILE-CONTROL.
00012          SELECT NF ASSIGN TO XF.
00013      DATA DIVISION.
00014      FILE SECTION.
00015      FD  NF
00016          LABEL RECORDS STANDARD
00017          DATA RECORD NR.
00018      01  NR.
00019          02 IDN PIC XXXX.
00020          02 NAME PIC X(25).
00021          02 AGE PIC XX.
00022      WORKING-STORAGE SECTION.
00023      01  V PIC X(25).
00024      PROCEDURE DIVISION.
00025      MAINLINE.
00026          OPEN OUTPUT NF.
00027          DISPLAY "***** TYPE ID IN COLS. 1-4.".
00028          DISPLAY "          TO TERMINATE INPUT, TYPE END."
00029          ACCEPT V FROM CONSOLE. MOVE V TO IDN
00030          DISPLAY "***** NOW TYPE NAME IN COLS. 1-25.".
00031          ACCEPT V FROM CONSOLE.
00032          MOVE V TO NAME.
00033          DISPLAY "***** NOW TYPE AGE IN COLS. 1-2."
00034          ACCEPT V FROM CONSOLE
00035          MOVE V TO AGE
00036          PERFORM WR-RD UNTIL V = "END".
00037          CLOSE NF. STOP RUN.
00038      WR-RD.
00039          WRITE NR
00040          DISPLAY "***** TYPE ID IN COLS. 1-4."
00041          DISPLAY "          TO TERMINATE INPUT, TYPE END."
00042          ACCEPT V FROM CONSOLE
00043          IF NOT V = "END" PERFORM ENT-RST.
00044      ENT-RST.
00045          MOVE V TO IDN
00046          DISPLAY "***** NOW TYPE NAME IN COLS. 1-25.".
00047          ACCEPT V FROM CONSOLE.
00048          MOVE V TO NAME.
00049          DISPLAY "***** NOW TYPE AGE IN COLS. 1-2.".
00050          ACCEPT V FROM CONSOLE.
00051          MOVE V TO AGE.
```

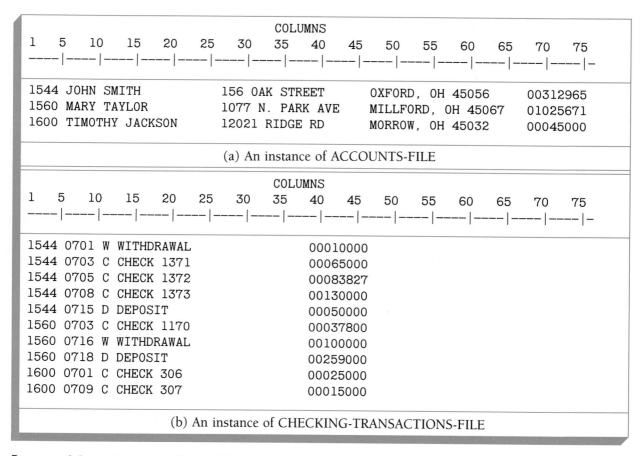

Program 1-Input Instances of Input Files for Checking Account Statement Generator

```
000001   *..........................................................................
000002      IDENTIFICATION DIVISION.
000003      PROGRAM-ID.      CHECKING-STATEMENT.
000004
000005   **********************************************************************
000006   ***   THIS PROGRAM READS A SEQUENTIAL CHECKING ACCOUNTS FILE, AND *
000007   ***   ANOTHER SEQUENTIAL MONTHLY CHECKING ACCOUNT TRANSACTIONS    *
000008   ***   FILE, AND GENERATES END-OF-MONTH CHECKING ACCOUNT STATEMENTS*
000009   ***   FOR THE CUSTOMERS OF THE NEW NATIONAL BANK, OXFORD, OHIO.   *
000010   ***   IMPORTANT PROBLEM REQUIREMENTS FOLLOW:                      *
000011   ***      1) IF A CUSTOMER'S MINIMUM BALANCE ANY TIME DURING THE   *
000012   ***         MONTH FALLS BELOW $300.00, A SERVICE FEE OF $5.00 WILL*
000013   ***         BE CHARGED.                                          *
000014   ***      2) IF THE MINIMUM BALANCE IS ABOVE $1000.00, THE ACCOUNT *
000015   ***         EARNS INTEREST AT THE RATE OF 5.5 %.                  *
000016   ***      3) THE STATEMENTS CONSIST OF FOUR PARTS:                 *
000017   ***            . A HEADER BLOCK CONTAINING CUSTOMER ADDRESS, ETC.,*
000018   ***            . A LIST OF TRANSACTIONS,                          *
000019   ***            . A SUMMARY OF ACCOUNT,                            *
000020   ***            . A TWO-LINE MESSAGE BY THE BANK TO CUSTOMERS.     *
000021   **********************************************************************
000022
000023      AUTHOR.          UCKAN.
000024      INSTALLATION.    MIAMI UNIVERSITY.
```

Program 1-Source Program to Generate Monthly Checking Account Statement

```
000025     DATE-WRITTEN.     APRIL 7, 1991.
000026     DATE-COMPILED.  04/07/91.
000028     *...............................................................
000029     ENVIRONMENT DIVISION.
000030     CONFIGURATION SECTION.
000031     SOURCE-COMPUTER. UNIVERSITY-MAINFRAME.
000032     OBJECT-COMPUTER. UNIVERSITY-MAINFRAME.
000033
000034     INPUT-OUTPUT SECTION.
000035
000036     FILE-CONTROL.
000037
000038         SELECT ACCOUNTS-FILE
000039                ASSIGN TO ACCOUNTS
000040                ORGANIZATION IS SEQUENTIAL
000041                ACCESS MODE  IS SEQUENTIAL.
000042
000043         SELECT CHECKING-TRANSACTIONS-FILE
000044                ASSIGN TO TRANS
000045                ORGANIZATION IS SEQUENTIAL
000046                ACCESS MODE  IS SEQUENTIAL.
000047
000048         SELECT TRANSACTIONS-REPORT
000049                ASSIGN TO EOMSTAT.
000050
000051     *...............................................................
000052     DATA DIVISION.
000053     FILE SECTION.
000054
000055     FD  ACCOUNTS-FILE
000056         LABEL RECORDS ARE STANDARD
000057         DATA RECORD   IS ACCOUNTS-RECORD
000058         RECORD CONTAINS 80 CHARACTERS.
000059
000060     01  ACCOUNTS-RECORD.
000061         05   AF-ACCOUNT-NUMBER         PIC X(4).
000062         05   FILLER                    PIC X.
000063         05   AF-CUSTOMER-NAME          PIC X(20).
000064         05   FILLER                    PIC X.
000065         05   AF-CUSTOMER-ADDRESS.
000066             10   AF-STREET-ADDRESS     PIC X(20).
000067             10   AF-CITY-STATE-ZIP     PIC X(20).
000068         05   FILLER                    PIC X.
000069         05   AF-BALANCE-FROM-LAST-MONTH PIC 9(6)V99.
000070         05   FILLER                    PIC X(5).
000071
000072     FD  CHECKING-TRANSACTIONS-FILE
000073         LABEL RECORDS ARE STANDARD
000074         DATA RECORD   IS CHECKING-TRANSACTIONS-RECORD
000075         RECORD CONTAINS 80 CHARACTERS.
000076     01  CHECKING-TRANSACTIONS-RECORD.
000077         05   CF-ACCOUNT-NUMBER         PIC X(4).
000078         05   FILLER                    PIC X.
000079         05   CF-TRANSACTION-DATE.
000080             10   CF-TRANSACTION-MONTH   PIC XX.
```

Program 1-Source (Continued)

```
000081              10  CF-TRANSACTION-DAY        PIC XX.
000082          05  FILLER                        PIC X.
000083          05  CF-TRANSACTION-TYPE           PIC X.
000084          05  FILLER                        PIC X.
000085          05  CF-TRANSACTION-DESCRIPTION    PIC X(25).
000086          05  FILLER                        PIC X.
000087          05  CF-TRANSACTION-AMOUNT         PIC 9(6)V99.
000088          05  FILLER                        PIC X(34).
000089
000090      FD  TRANSACTIONS-REPORT
000091          LABEL RECORDS ARE OMITTED
000092          DATA RECORD   IS TRANSACTION-LINE
000093          RECORD CONTAINS 131 CHARACTERS.
000094      01  TRANSACTION-LINE        PIC X(131).
000095
000096      WORKING-STORAGE SECTION.
000097
000098      ***********> SWITCHES:
000099
000100      01  END-OF-ACCOUNTS-FILE-REACHED      PIC XXX    VALUE "NO".
000101          88  END-OF-ACCOUNTS-FILE                     VALUE "YES".
000102      01  END-OF-TRANS-FILE-REACHED         PIC XXX    VALUE "NO".
000103          88  END-OF-TRANSACTIONS-FILE                 VALUE "YES".
000104
000105      ***********> VARIABLES:
000106
000107      01  WS-ACCOUNT-REC-NUMBER     PIC X(4).
000108      01  WS-TRANS-REC-NUMBER       PIC X(4).
000109      01  WS-MINIMUM-BALANCE        PIC 9(6)V99.
000110      01  WS-CURRENT-BALANCE        PIC 9(6)V99.
000111      01  WS-INTEREST-EARNED        PIC 999V99.
000112      01  WS-TOTAL-CREDITS          PIC 9(6)V99.
000113      01  WS-TOTAL-DEBITS           PIC 9(6)V99.
000114      01  WS-ITEM-COUNT             PIC 999.
000115      01  WS-FIRST-MESSAGE-LINE     PIC X(50).
000116      01  WS-SECOND-MESSAGE-LINE    PIC X(50).
000117
000118      ***********> STRUCTURES:
000119
000120      01  TODAYS-DATE.
000121          05  TODAYS-YEAR           PIC XX.
000122          05  TODAYS-MONTH          PIC XX.
000123          05  TODAYS-DAY            PIC XX.
000124
000125      01  FROM-DATE.
000126          05  FROM-MONTH            PIC XX.
000127          05  FROM-DAY             PIC XX.
000128          05  FROM-YEAR            PIC XX.
000129
000130      01  THROUGH-DATE.
000131          05  THROUGH-MONTH         PIC XX.
000132          05  THROUGH-DAY          PIC XX.
000133          05  THROUGH-YEAR         PIC XX.
000134
```

Program 1-Source (Continued)

```
000135     01   PART-1-LINE-1.
000136          05   FILLER          PIC X(30)  VALUE SPACES.
000137          05   FILLER          PIC X(17)  VALUE "NEW NATIONAL BANK".
000138
000139     01   PART-1-LINE-2.
000140          05   FILLER          PIC X(33)  VALUE SPACES.
000141          05   FILLER          PIC X(12)  VALUE "OXFORD, OHIO".
000142
000143     01   PART-1-LINE-3.
000144          05   FILLER          PIC X(13)  VALUE SPACES.
000145          05   FILLER          PIC X(34)
000146                             VALUE "C H E C K I N G   A C C O U N T   ".
000147          05   FILLER          PIC X(17)  VALUE "S T A T E M E N T".
000148
000149     01   PART-1-LINE-4.
000150          05   FILLER              PIC X(5)   VALUE SPACES.
000151          05   OUT-CUSTOMER-NAME   PIC X(20).
000152          05   FILLER              PIC X(28)  VALUE SPACES.
000153          05   FILLER              PIC X(9)   VALUE "DATE     ".
000154          05   OUT-TODAYS-DATE.
000155               10   OUT-MONTH      PIC XX.
000156               10   FILLER         PIC X      VALUE "/".
000157               10   OUT-DAY        PIC XX.
000158               10   FILLER         PIC X      VALUE "/".
000159               10   OUT-YEAR       PIC XX.
000160
000161     01   PART-1-LINE-5.
000162          05   FILLER              PIC X(5)   VALUE SPACES.
000163          05   OUT-STREET-ADDRESS  PIC X(20).
000164          05   FILLER              PIC X(28)  VALUE SPACES.
000165          05   FILLER              PIC X(16)  VALUE "STATEMENT PERIOD".
000166
000167     01   PART-1-LINE-6.
000168          05   FILLER              PIC X(5)   VALUE SPACES.
000169          05   OUT-CITY-STATE-ZIP  PIC X(20).
000170          05   FILLER              PIC X(28)  VALUE SPACES.
000171          05   FILLER              PIC X(9)   VALUE "FROM     ".
000172          05   OUT-FROM-DATE.
000173               10   OUT-FROM-MONTH PIC XX.
000174               10   FILLER         PIC X      VALUE "/".
000175               10   OUT-FROM-DAY   PIC XX.
000176               10   FILLER         PIC X      VALUE "/".
000177               10   OUT-FROM-YEAR  PIC XX.
000178
000179     01   PART-1-LINE-7.
000180          05   FILLER               PIC X(53)  VALUE SPACES.
000181          05   FILLER               PIC X(9)   VALUE "THROUGH  ".
000182          05   OUT-THROUGH-DATE.
000183               10   OUT-THROUGH-MONTH  PIC XX.
000184               10   FILLER            PIC X       VALUE "/".
000185               10   OUT-THROUGH-DAY   PIC XX.
000186               10   FILLER            PIC X       VALUE "/".
000187               10   OUT-THROUGH-YEAR  PIC XX.
000188
```

Program 1-Source (Continued)

```
000189     01   PART-2-LINE-1.
000190          05   FILLER            PIC X(11)   VALUE " DATE       ".
000191          05   FILLER            PIC X(12)   VALUE "TRANSACTIONS".
000192          05   FILLER            PIC X(36)   VALUE SPACES.
000193          05   FILLER            PIC X(17)   VALUE "AMOUNT    BALANCE".
000194
000195     01   PART-2-LINE-2.
000196          05   FILLER            PIC X(11)   VALUE " -----      ".
000197          05   FILLER            PIC X(13)   VALUE "-------------".
000198          05   FILLER            PIC X(35)   VALUE SPACES.
000199          05   FILLER            PIC X(18)   VALUE "------    --------".
000200
000201     01   PART-2-MAIN-LINE.
000202          05   FILLER                PIC X      VALUE SPACES.
000203          05   OUT-TRANSACTION-MONTH PIC XX.
000204          05   FILLER                PIC X      VALUE "/".
000205          05   OUT-TRANSACTION-DAY   PIC XX.
000206          05   FILLER                PIC X(5)   VALUE SPACES.
000207          05   OUT-TRANSACTION-DESCR PIC X(25).
000208          05   FILLER                PIC X(19)  VALUE SPACES.
000209          05   OUT-TRANSACTION-AMOUNT PIC ZZZ,ZZZ.ZZ.
000210          05   OUT-TRANSACTION-SIGN  PIC XX.
000211          05   OUT-BALANCE           PIC ZZZ,ZZZ.ZZ.
000212
000213     01   PART-SEPARATOR.
000214          05   FILLER                PIC X      VALUE SPACE.
000215          05   FILLER                PIC X(76)  VALUE ALL "-".
000216
000217     01   PART-3-LINE-1.
000218          05   FILLER            PIC X(21) VALUE SPACES.
000219          05   FILLER            PIC X(16) VALUE "S U M M A R Y  ".
000220          05   FILLER            PIC X(19) VALUE "O F   A C C O U N T".
000221
000222     01   PART-3-LINE-2.
000223          05   FILLER            PIC X(12) VALUE " ACCOUNT    ".
000224          05   FILLER            PIC X(15) VALUE "BEGINNING      ".
000225          05   FILLER            PIC X(11) VALUE "TOTAL      ".
000226          05   FILLER            PIC X(11) VALUE "TOTAL      ".
000227          05   FILLER            PIC X(10) VALUE "MISC      ".
000228          05   FILLER            PIC X(10) VALUE "TOTAL     ".
000229          05   FILLER            PIC X(7)  VALUE "CURRENT".
000230
000231     01   PART-3-LINE-3.
000232          05   FILLER            PIC X(12) VALUE " NUMBER     ".
000233          05   FILLER            PIC X(15) VALUE "BALANCE        ".
000234          05   FILLER            PIC X(11) VALUE "CREDITS    ".
000235          05   FILLER            PIC X(11) VALUE "DEBITS     ".
000236          05   FILLER            PIC X(10) VALUE "CHARGES   ".
000237          05   FILLER            PIC X(10) VALUE "INTEREST  ".
000238          05   FILLER            PIC X(7)  VALUE "BALANCE".
000239
000240     01   PART-3-MAIN-LINE.
000241          05   FILLER                PIC XX     VALUE SPACES.
000242          05   OUT-ACCOUNT-NUMBER    PIC X(4).
```

Program 1-Source (Continued)

```
000243          05   FILLER                    PIC X(4)  VALUE SPACES.
000244          05   OUT-BEGINNING-BALANCE      PIC ZZZ,ZZZ.ZZ.
000245          05   FILLER                    PIC X(5)  VALUE SPACES.
000246          05   OUT-TOTAL-CREDITS          PIC ZZZ,ZZZ.ZZ.
000247          05   FILLER                    PIC X     VALUE SPACE.
000248          05   OUT-TOTAL-DEBITS           PIC ZZZ,ZZZ.ZZ.
000249          05   FILLER                    PIC X(4)  VALUE SPACES.
000250          05   OUT-MISC-CHARGES           PIC ZZZ.ZZ.
000251          05   FILLER                    PIC X(3)  VALUE SPACES.
000252          05   OUT-TOTAL-INTEREST         PIC ZZZ.ZZ.
000253          05   FILLER                    PIC X(2)  VALUE SPACES.
000254          05   OUT-CURRENT-BALANCE        PIC ZZZ,ZZZ.ZZ.
000255
000256     01   PART-3-LINE-4.
000257          05   FILLER                    PIC X(53) VALUE SPACES.
000258          05   FILLER                    PIC X(14) VALUE "ITEMS ENCLOSED".
000259          05   FILLER                    PIC XX    VALUE SPACES.
000260          05   OUT-ITEMS-ENCLOSED         PIC ZZZ.
000261
000262     *......................................................................
000263     PROCEDURE DIVISION.
000264
000265     A-MAIN-PARAGRAPH.
000266          OPEN INPUT   ACCOUNTS-FILE
000267               INPUT   CHECKING-TRANSACTIONS-FILE
000268               OUTPUT  TRANSACTIONS-REPORT.
000269          PERFORM B1-COMMON-TASKS.
000270          PERFORM B2-READ-ACCOUNTS-FILE.
000271          PERFORM B3-READ-TRANSACTIONS-FILE.
000272
000273          PERFORM B4-MATCH-RECORDS
000274               UNTIL END-OF-ACCOUNTS-FILE.
000275
000276          CLOSE ACCOUNTS-FILE
000277                CHECKING-TRANSACTIONS-FILE
000278                TRANSACTIONS-REPORT.
000279          STOP RUN.
000280
000281     B1-COMMON-TASKS.
000282          PERFORM C1-TERMINAL-INPUTS.
000283          PERFORM C2-MOVE-DATES.
000284
000285     B2-READ-ACCOUNTS-FILE.
000286          MOVE ZERO TO WS-TOTAL-CREDITS
000287                       WS-TOTAL-DEBITS
000288                       WS-ITEM-COUNT
000289                       WS-INTEREST-EARNED
000290                       WS-CURRENT-BALANCE
000291                       WS-MINIMUM-BALANCE.
000292
000293          READ ACCOUNTS-FILE
000294               AT END MOVE "YES" TO END-OF-ACCOUNTS-FILE-REACHED.
000295
000296          IF NOT END-OF-ACCOUNTS-FILE
000297               MOVE AF-ACCOUNT-NUMBER TO WS-ACCOUNT-REC-NUMBER.
```

Program 1-Source (Continued)

```
000298
000299      B3-READ-TRANSACTIONS-FILE.
000300          READ CHECKING-TRANSACTIONS-FILE
000301              AT END MOVE "YES" TO END-OF-TRANS-FILE-REACHED.
000302
000303          IF NOT END-OF-TRANSACTIONS-FILE
000304              MOVE CF-ACCOUNT-NUMBER TO WS-TRANS-REC-NUMBER
000305          ELSE
000306              MOVE "XXXX" TO WS-TRANS-REC-NUMBER.
000307
000308      B4-MATCH-RECORDS.
000309          IF WS-ACCOUNT-REC-NUMBER = WS-TRANS-REC-NUMBER
000310              PERFORM C3-MOVE-ADDRESS
000311              PERFORM C4-PRINT-PART-1
000312              PERFORM C5-PRINT-PART-2-TITLE
000313              MOVE AF-BALANCE-FROM-LAST-MONTH TO WS-MINIMUM-BALANCE
000314              MOVE AF-BALANCE-FROM-LAST-MONTH TO WS-CURRENT-BALANCE
000315
000316              PERFORM C6-PROCESS-TRANSACTIONS
000317                  UNTIL WS-ACCOUNT-REC-NUMBER NOT = WS-TRANS-REC-NUMBER
000318
000319              PERFORM C7-COMPLETE-STATEMENT.
000320
000321          PERFORM B2-READ-ACCOUNTS-FILE.
000322
000323      C1-TERMINAL-INPUTS.
000324          ACCEPT TODAYS-DATE FROM DATE.
000325
000326          DISPLAY "===> ENTER FROM-DATE FOR STATEMENT PERIOD.".
000327          DISPLAY "       TYPE XXYYZZ, WHERE XX IS MONTH, YY IS DAY,".
000328          DISPLAY "       AND ZZ IS YEAR: ".
000329          ACCEPT FROM-DATE FROM CONSOLE.
000330
000331          DISPLAY "===> ENTER THROUGH-DATE FOR STATEMENT PERIOD.".
000332          DISPLAY "       TYPE XXYYZZ, WHERE XX IS MONTH, YY IS DAY,".
000333          DISPLAY "       AND ZZ IS YEAR: ".
000334          ACCEPT THROUGH-DATE FROM CONSOLE.
000335
000336          DISPLAY "===> NOW, ENTER FIRST LINE OF MONTHLY MESSAGE: ".
000337          ACCEPT WS-FIRST-MESSAGE-LINE FROM CONSOLE.
000338
000339          DISPLAY "===> ENTER SECOND LINE OF MONTHLY MESSAGE: ".
000340          ACCEPT WS-SECOND-MESSAGE-LINE FROM CONSOLE.
000341
000342      C2-MOVE-DATES.
000343          MOVE TODAYS-MONTH     TO OUT-MONTH.
000344          MOVE TODAYS-DAY       TO OUT-DAY.
000345          MOVE TODAYS-YEAR      TO OUT-YEAR.
000346
000347          MOVE FROM-MONTH       TO OUT-FROM-MONTH.
000348          MOVE FROM-DAY         TO OUT-FROM-DAY.
000349          MOVE FROM-YEAR        TO OUT-FROM-YEAR.
000350
000351          MOVE THROUGH-MONTH    TO OUT-THROUGH-MONTH.
```

Program 1-Source (Continued)

```
000352              MOVE THROUGH-DAY       TO OUT-THROUGH-DAY.
000353              MOVE THROUGH-YEAR      TO OUT-THROUGH-YEAR.
000354
000355          C3-MOVE-ADDRESS.
000356              MOVE AF-CUSTOMER-NAME    TO OUT-CUSTOMER-NAME.
000357              MOVE AF-STREET-ADDRESS   TO OUT-STREET-ADDRESS.
000358              MOVE AF-CITY-STATE-ZIP   TO OUT-CITY-STATE-ZIP.
000359
000360          C4-PRINT-PART-1.
000361              MOVE SPACES            TO TRANSACTION-LINE.
000362              WRITE TRANSACTION-LINE
000363                      AFTER ADVANCING PAGE.
000364              MOVE PART-SEPARATOR TO TRANSACTION-LINE.
000365              WRITE TRANSACTION-LINE
000366                      AFTER ADVANCING 1 LINE.
000367              MOVE SPACES            TO TRANSACTION-LINE.
000368              MOVE PART-1-LINE-1  TO TRANSACTION-LINE.
000369              WRITE TRANSACTION-LINE
000370                      AFTER ADVANCING 2 LINES.
000371              MOVE SPACES            TO TRANSACTION-LINE.
000372              MOVE PART-1-LINE-2  TO TRANSACTION-LINE.
000373              WRITE TRANSACTION-LINE
000374                      AFTER ADVANCING 1 LINE.
000375              MOVE SPACES            TO TRANSACTION-LINE.
000376              MOVE PART-1-LINE-3  TO TRANSACTION-LINE.
000377              WRITE TRANSACTION-LINE
000378                      AFTER ADVANCING 3 LINES.
000379              MOVE SPACES            TO TRANSACTION-LINE.
000380              MOVE PART-1-LINE-4  TO TRANSACTION-LINE.
000381              WRITE TRANSACTION-LINE
000382                      AFTER ADVANCING 4 LINES.
000383              MOVE SPACES            TO TRANSACTION-LINE.
000384              MOVE PART-1-LINE-5  TO TRANSACTION-LINE.
000385              WRITE TRANSACTION-LINE
000386                      AFTER ADVANCING 1 LINE.
000387              MOVE SPACES TO TRANSACTION-LINE.
000388              MOVE PART-1-LINE-6  TO TRANSACTION-LINE.
000389              WRITE TRANSACTION-LINE
000390                      AFTER ADVANCING 1 LINE.
000391              MOVE SPACES TO TRANSACTION-LINE.
000392              MOVE PART-1-LINE-7  TO TRANSACTION-LINE.
000393              WRITE TRANSACTION-LINE
000394                      AFTER ADVANCING 1 LINE.
000395
000396          C5-PRINT-PART-2-TITLE.
000397              MOVE SPACES            TO TRANSACTION-LINE.
000398              MOVE PART-SEPARATOR TO TRANSACTION-LINE.
000399              WRITE TRANSACTION-LINE
000400                      AFTER ADVANCING 2 LINES.
000401              MOVE SPACES TO TRANSACTION-LINE.
000402              MOVE PART-2-LINE-1  TO TRANSACTION-LINE.
000403              WRITE TRANSACTION-LINE
000404                      AFTER ADVANCING 1 LINE.
000405              MOVE SPACES            TO TRANSACTION-LINE.
000406              MOVE PART-2-LINE-2  TO TRANSACTION-LINE.
```

Program 1-Source (Continued)

```
000407          WRITE TRANSACTION-LINE
000408              AFTER ADVANCING 1 LINE.
000409
000410     C6-PROCESS-TRANSACTIONS.
000411         IF CF-TRANSACTION-TYPE = "D"
000412            ADD CF-TRANSACTION-AMOUNT TO WS-CURRENT-BALANCE
000413            MOVE "  " TO OUT-TRANSACTION-SIGN
000414            ADD CF-TRANSACTION-AMOUNT TO WS-TOTAL-CREDITS
000415         ELSE
000416            SUBTRACT CF-TRANSACTION-AMOUNT FROM WS-CURRENT-BALANCE
000417            MOVE "+ " TO OUT-TRANSACTION-SIGN
000418            ADD CF-TRANSACTION-AMOUNT TO WS-TOTAL-DEBITS.
000419
000420         IF CF-TRANSACTION-TYPE = "C"
000421            ADD 1 TO WS-ITEM-COUNT.
000422
000423         PERFORM D1-PRINT-REST-OF-PART-2.
000424
000425         IF WS-CURRENT-BALANCE IS LESS THAN WS-MINIMUM-BALANCE
000426             MOVE WS-CURRENT-BALANCE TO WS-MINIMUM-BALANCE.
000427
000428         PERFORM B3-READ-TRANSACTIONS-FILE.
000429
000430     C7-COMPLETE-STATEMENT.
000431         IF WS-MINIMUM-BALANCE IS LESS THAN 300
000432            MOVE 5.00 TO OUT-MISC-CHARGES
000433            SUBTRACT 5 FROM WS-CURRENT-BALANCE
000434         ELSE
000435            MOVE ZERO TO OUT-MISC-CHARGES.
000436
000437         IF WS-MINIMUM-BALANCE IS NOT LESS THAN 1000.00
000438            COMPUTE WS-INTEREST-EARNED = 0.055 * WS-MINIMUM-BALANCE
000439            MOVE WS-INTEREST-EARNED TO OUT-TOTAL-INTEREST
000440            ADD WS-INTEREST-EARNED TO WS-CURRENT-BALANCE
000441         ELSE
000442            MOVE ZERO TO OUT-TOTAL-INTEREST.
000443
000444         PERFORM D2-PRINT-PART-3.
000445         PERFORM D3-PRINT-PART-4.
000446
000447     D1-PRINT-REST-OF-PART-2.
000448         MOVE CF-TRANSACTION-MONTH       TO OUT-TRANSACTION-MONTH.
000449         MOVE CF-TRANSACTION-DAY         TO OUT-TRANSACTION-DAY.
000450         MOVE CF-TRANSACTION-DESCRIPTION TO OUT-TRANSACTION-DESCR.
000451         MOVE CF-TRANSACTION-AMOUNT      TO OUT-TRANSACTION-AMOUNT.
000452         MOVE WS-CURRENT-BALANCE         TO OUT-BALANCE.
000453         MOVE SPACES                     TO TRANSACTION-LINE.
000454         MOVE PART-2-MAIN-LINE           TO TRANSACTION-LINE.
000455         WRITE TRANSACTION-LINE
000456             AFTER ADVANCING 1 LINE.
000457
000458     D2-PRINT-PART-3.
000459         MOVE SPACES                     TO TRANSACTION-LINE.
000460         MOVE PART-SEPARATOR             TO TRANSACTION-LINE.
```

Program 1-Source (Continued)

```
000461          WRITE TRANSACTION-LINE
000462              AFTER ADVANCING 2 LINES.
000463          MOVE SPACES                      TO TRANSACTION-LINE.
000464          MOVE PART-3-LINE-1               TO TRANSACTION-LINE.
000465          WRITE TRANSACTION-LINE
000466              AFTER ADVANCING 2 LINES.
000467          MOVE SPACES                      TO TRANSACTION-LINE.
000468          MOVE PART-3-LINE-2               TO TRANSACTION-LINE.
000469          WRITE TRANSACTION-LINE
000470              AFTER ADVANCING 2 LINES.
000471          MOVE SPACES                      TO TRANSACTION-LINE.
000472          MOVE PART-3-LINE-3               TO TRANSACTION-LINE.
000473          WRITE TRANSACTION-LINE
000474              AFTER ADVANCING 1 LINE.
000475          MOVE SPACES                      TO TRANSACTION-LINE.
000476          MOVE AF-ACCOUNT-NUMBER           TO OUT-ACCOUNT-NUMBER.
000477          MOVE AF-BALANCE-FROM-LAST-MONTH TO OUT-BEGINNING-BALANCE.
000478          MOVE WS-TOTAL-CREDITS            TO OUT-TOTAL-CREDITS.
000479          MOVE WS-TOTAL-DEBITS             TO OUT-TOTAL-DEBITS.
000480          MOVE WS-CURRENT-BALANCE          TO OUT-CURRENT-BALANCE.
000481          MOVE PART-3-MAIN-LINE            TO TRANSACTION-LINE.
000482          WRITE TRANSACTION-LINE
000483              AFTER ADVANCING 2 LINES.
000484          MOVE SPACES                      TO TRANSACTION-LINE.
000485          MOVE WS-ITEM-COUNT               TO OUT-ITEMS-ENCLOSED.
000486          MOVE PART-3-LINE-4               TO TRANSACTION-LINE.
000487          WRITE TRANSACTION-LINE
000488              AFTER ADVANCING 2 LINES.
000489
000490      D3-PRINT-PART-4.
000491          MOVE SPACES               TO TRANSACTION-LINE.
000492          MOVE PART-SEPARATOR       TO TRANSACTION-LINE.
000493          WRITE TRANSACTION-LINE
000494              AFTER ADVANCING 2 LINES.
000495          MOVE SPACES               TO TRANSACTION-LINE.
000496          MOVE WS-FIRST-MESSAGE-LINE  TO TRANSACTION-LINE.
000497          WRITE TRANSACTION-LINE
000498              AFTER ADVANCING 2 LINES.
000499          MOVE SPACES               TO TRANSACTION-LINE.
000500          MOVE WS-SECOND-MESSAGE-LINE TO TRANSACTION-LINE.
000501          WRITE TRANSACTION-LINE
000502              AFTER ADVANCING 1 LINE.
000503          MOVE SPACES               TO TRANSACTION-LINE.
000504          MOVE PART-SEPARATOR       TO TRANSACTION-LINE.
000505          WRITE TRANSACTION-LINE
000506              AFTER ADVANCING 2 LINES.
```

Program 1-Source (Continued)

```
                    NEW NATIONAL BANK
                    OXFORD, OHIO

        C H E C K I N G   A C C O U N T   S T A T E M E N T


    JOHN SMITH                          DATE      04/07/91
    156 OAK STREET                      STATEMENT PERIOD
    OXFORD, OH 45056                    FROM      07/01/89
                                        THROUGH   07/31/89
    _____

    DATE      TRANSACTIONS                         AMOUNT     BALANCE
    ____      _____                         _____     _____

    07/01     WITHDRAWAL                           100.00    3,029.65
    07/03     CHECK 1371                           650.00    2,379.65
    07/05     CHECK 1372                           838.27    1,541.38
    07/08     CHECK 1373                         1,300.00      241.38
    07/15     DEPOSIT                              500.00+     741.38
    _____

            S U M M A R Y   O F   A C C O U N T

    ACCOUNT   BEGINNING    TOTAL      TOTAL     MISC      TOTAL      CURRENT
    NUMBER    BALANCE      CREDITS    DEBITS    CHARGES   INTEREST   BALANCE

     1544     3,129.65      500.00   2,888.27    5.00                736.38


                                            ITEMS ENCLOSED    3
    _____

        AT NEW NATIONAL, WE ARE ALWAYS READY TO HELP !!
             CALL TOLL FREE 1-800-565-7766
```

Program 1-Output(a) Sample Output for Program 1

```
            EXECUTION BEGINS...
 ===> ENTER FROM-DATE FOR STATEMENT PERIOD.
      TYPE XXYYZZ, WHERE XX IS MONTH, YY IS DAY,
      AND ZZ IS YEAR:
IGZ000I, AWAITING REPLY.
 070187
 ===> ENTER THROUGH-DATE FOR STATEMENT PERIOD.
      TYPE XXYYZZ, WHERE XX IS MONTH, YY IS DAY,
      AND ZZ IS YEAR:
IGZ000I, AWAITING REPLY.
 073187
 ===> NOW, ENTER FIRST LINE OF MONTHLY MESSAGE:
IGZ000I, AWAITING REPLY.
    AT NEW NATIONAL, WE ARE ALWAYS READY TO HELP!!
 ===> ENTER SECOND LINE OF MONTHLY MESSAGE:
IGZ000I, AWAITING REPLY.
        CALL TOLL FREE 1-800-565-7766
```

Program 1-Output(b) Sample Terminal Session for Program 1

Software Engineering with COBOL: Program Testing and Debugging

259

Key Terms

Study Guide
Quick Scan
Test Your Comprehension
Improve Your Problem-Solving Ability

IN THIS CHAPTER YOU WILL LEARN ABOUT

- Program verification and validation
- Program testing
    - Program testing techniques
    - Steps involved in program testing
- Program debugging
    - Software errors
    - Programming errors
    - Debugging compilation errors
    - Debugging execution errors
    - Common execution errors in COBOL programming
    - Debugging tools and techniques
- COBOL automated debugging tools
    - Use of DISPLAY statement for debugging
    - EXHIBIT statement
    - TRACE statement
    - USE FOR DEBUGGING declaratives
    - USE EXCEPTION/ERROR declaratives
    - Debugging lines
    - COBOL compiler debugging facilities
    - Special COBOL on-line debugging tools

Introduction

In Chapter 4 we noted that the system development life cycle for a software system consists of four activities: analysis, design, coding, and testing. We also noted that one of the properties of a good program is reliability and correctness. As software is developed, it must be tested to ascertain program correctness, since errors may lead to expensive, embarrassing, and dangerous consequences in practice. An unreliable program controlling credit card transactions over a nationwide computer network, for example, may wreak havoc in the underlying financial system, and may even facilitate the criminal intents of a defrauder. An erroneous software that monitors a military weapons system may cause truly tragic results. It is easy to think of many other examples of what might happen because of unreliable software. In fact, the computer and data processing industry has had its share of embarrassments in the past due to errors in programs. Clearly, reliability is one of the most important properties of a program.

In this chapter, we will take a software engineering look at program reliability. We will study the concepts and techniques of program verification, testing, and debugging, which are closely related activities. We will emphasize debugging techniques and discuss them within the context of COBOL programming. We will also discuss COBOL debugging features.

Fundamentals of Program Verification and Validation

Program verification and validation are related concepts in software engineering.

> **Program verification** is concerned with a program's correctness at different phases of its life cycle, during and after analysis, design, and coding. **Program validation** is concerned with the finished program, and aims to ensure that it correctly meets user requirements.

To verify and validate a program, many different techniques can be applied. During the analysis phase, we may prove the correctness of the requirements specification through inspections, peer reviews, or by using some automated tools (e.g., data flow analyzers). The design specifications may be verified by applying algorithm analysis, formal verification techniques, and so on. The program code may be verified manually (desk-checking, inspections, etc.) or by using automated tools such as debugging compilers, data flow analyzers, and cross-reference maps. We also establish the correctness of a program code by actually executing it; that is, by testing it.

> **Program testing** is the process of executing a program to demonstrate its correctness or otherwise find errors in it.

A program must be tested using a sufficiently large sample of carefully designed test data sets. If we find errors during or after execution, we try to correct them by identifying and removing their sources. This process is known as debugging.

> **Program debugging** is the activity of identifying the source of errors in a program, and modifying the program to eliminate these errors.

Debugging may follow testing if errors are uncovered. The process also includes correcting errors before running a program, and during program development and compilation.

In summary, program testing is a process of verification and validation, and debugging may take place after testing. In this chapter we concentrate on these two activities. That does not mean that we belittle the significance of the other aspects of verification and validation. The restriction is due to the fact that the central theme of this book is application programming.

Program Testing

The fundamental motivation behind program testing is to demonstrate the program's correctness. At this point, it is logical to ask why we bother with testing, which is clearly a tedious process. Why not instead strive for a formal proof of correctness for a program? In fact, proof of correctness is one of the fields of research and development in software engineering.

Proving that a program is correct is similar to proving that a theorem is correct. Except for some small and simple programs, however, it is generally extremely difficult to prove program correctness formally, as few techniques have been developed for this purpose. To facilitate it, automated correctness provers have been designed, but they are still in the research stage of development. The few available ones work only on small programs; we do not have general purpose tools for large-scale software systems. Therefore, the current state of the art in this field is far from being of practical significance. In the future, if automated correctness provers become available for large software systems, it is safe to say that testing will no longer be required.

Until that time, we must demonstrate that a program conforms to its specification requirements and works correctly by testing. Conceivably, a program could be exhaustively tested, that is, it could be run with all possible sets of input data, thus uncovering and correcting errors or demonstrating that it is correct. The major problem is that for nontrivial programs exhaustive testing is impractical, because for most programs the number of test data is either infinite or very large.

Program Testing Techniques

The so-called exact testing techniques such as formal proof of correctness and exhaustive testing are either difficult to apply or impractical. Consequently, we employ some approximate methods. These fall into one of the following categories:

1. Structural
2. Functional
3. Automated
4. Informal

Structural Testing. In this testing technique we are interested in verifying the structure of the procedural design of a given program. For this, we design test cases to guarantee that all logical paths within the program are traversed at least once, and that the internal data structures incorporated into the program are correct. Structural testing is also known as **white box testing**.

To design test data that guarantee the execution of all independent logical paths in a program, it is useful to draw a flow graph for it. A **flow graph** is quite similar to a flow chart, except that it concentrates on the flow of control in the program, and disregards details of operations. Figure 1 shows the conventions that we can use in constructing flow graphs for various program structures, including sequence, decision, and iteration. A flow graph can be constructed from any description of the program logic, such as a source program listing, a pseudocode, or a flow chart. For program testing purposes, we start with the actual source code, number each statement in it, and use these numbers as nodes in the flow graph. The arcs connecting the nodes indicate the flow of control between statements.

As an example of flow graph construction, consider Program 1 in Chapter 5, which generates periodic checking account statements for the customers of a bank. Figure 2 is the PROCEDURE DIVISION of this program in which each statement is sequentially numbered. In view of the conventions summarized in Figure 1, the flow graph for this program can be drawn as in Figure 3. The starting point is node 1, and the terminal point is node 7. In between these nodes we can identify 556 distinct and independent paths. For example, one of the paths is

(1, 2, 8, 27–39, 9, 40–48, 3, 10–11, 12, 13, 4, 14, 15, 16, 5, 18, 19, 49–51, 20, 52–76, 21, 77–85, 22–23, 24, 86, 87–89, 93, 95, 110–117, 96, 98, 14, 15, 16, 24, 25, 99, 102, 103, 107, 108, 118–141, 109, 142–153, 26, 10–11, 12, 13, 5, 6, 7).

This path is highlighted in Figure 4.

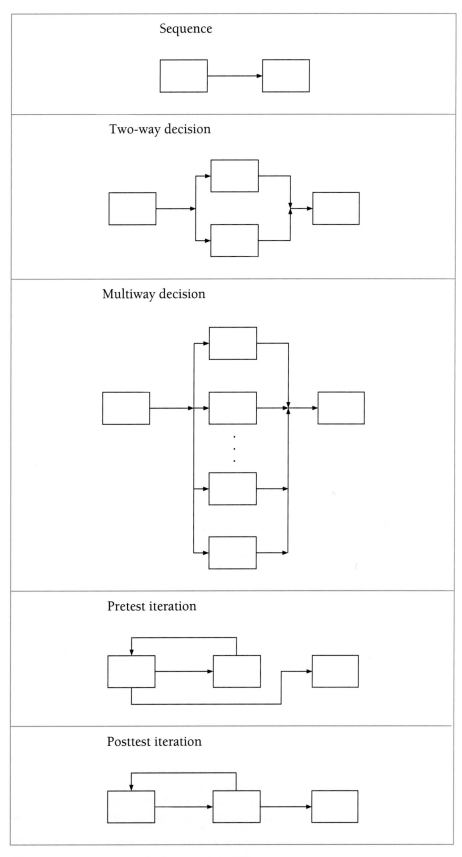

Figure 1 Conventions Used in Flow Graphs

```
        PROCEDURE DIVISION.

        A-MAIN-PARAGRAPH.
1           OPEN INPUT   ACCOUNTS-FILE
                 INPUT   CHECKING-TRANSACTIONS-FILE
                 OUTPUT TRANSACTIONS-REPORT.
2           PERFORM B1-COMMON-TASKS.
3           PERFORM B2-READ-ACCOUNTS-FILE.
4           PERFORM B3-READ-TRANSACTIONS-FILE.

5           PERFORM B4-MATCH-RECORDS
                    UNTIL END-OF-ACCOUNTS-FILE.

6           CLOSE ACCOUNTS-FILE
                  CHECKING-TRANSACTIONS-FILE
                  TRANSACTIONS-REPORT.
7           STOP RUN.


        B1-COMMON-TASKS.
8           PERFORM C1-TERMINAL-INPUTS.
9           PERFORM C2-MOVE-DATES.


        B2-READ-ACCOUNTS-FILE.
10          MOVE ZERO TO WS-TOTAL-CREDITS
                         WS-TOTAL-DEBITS
                         WS-ITEM-COUNT
                         WS-INTEREST-EARNED
                         WS-CURRENT-BALANCE
                         WS-MINIMUM-BALANCE.

11          READ ACCOUNTS-FILE
                    AT END MOVE "YES" TO END-OF-ACCOUNTS-FILE-REACHED.

12          IF NOT END-OF-ACCOUNTS-FILE
13              MOVE AF-ACCOUNT-NUMBER TO WS-ACCOUNT-REC-NUMBER.


        B3-READ-TRANSACTIONS-FILE.
14          READ CHECKING-TRANSACTIONS-FILE
                    AT END MOVE "YES" TO END-OF-TRANS-FILE-REACHED.

15          IF NOT END-OF-TRANSACTIONS-FILE
16              MOVE CF-ACCOUNT-NUMBER TO WS-TRANS-REC-NUMBER
            ELSE
17              MOVE "XXXX" TO WS-TRANS-REC-NUMBER.


        B4-MATCH-RECORDS.
18          IF WS-ACCOUNT-REC-NUMBER = WS-TRANS-REC-NUMBER
19              PERFORM C3-MOVE-ADDRESS
20              PERFORM C4-PRINT-PART-1
21              PERFORM C5-PRINT-PART-2-TITLE
22              MOVE AF-BALANCE-FROM-LAST-MONTH TO WS-MINIMUM-BALANCE
```

Figure 2 A COBOL PROCEDURE DIVISION for Generating Monthly Checking Account Statements

```
23              MOVE AF-BALANCE-FROM-LAST-MONTH TO WS-CURRENT-BALANCE

24            PERFORM C6-PROCESS-TRANSACTIONS
                 UNTIL WS-ACCOUNT-REC-NUMBER NOT = WS-TRANS-REC-NUMBER

25            PERFORM C7-COMPLETE-STATEMENT.

26         PERFORM B2-READ-ACCOUNTS-FILE.

        C1-TERMINAL-INPUTS.
27          ACCEPT TODAYS-DATE FROM DATE.

28          DISPLAY "===> ENTER FROM-DATE FOR STATEMENT PERIOD.".
29          DISPLAY "        TYPE XXYYZZ, WHERE XX IS MONTH, YY IS DAY,".
30          DISPLAY "        AND ZZ IS YEAR: ".
31          ACCEPT FROM-DATE FROM CONSOLE.

32          DISPLAY "===> ENTER THROUGH-DATE FOR STATEMENT PERIOD.".
33          DISPLAY "        TYPE XXYYZZ, WHERE XX IS MONTH, YY IS DAY,".
34          DISPLAY "        AND ZZ IS YEAR: ".
35          ACCEPT THROUGH-DATE FROM CONSOLE.

36          DISPLAY "===> NOW, ENTER FIRST LINE OF MONTHLY MESSAGE: ".
37          ACCEPT WS-FIRST-MESSAGE-LINE FROM CONSOLE.

38          DISPLAY "===> ENTER SECOND LINE OF MONTHLY MESSAGE: ".
39          ACCEPT WS-SECOND-MESSAGE-LINE FROM CONSOLE.

        C2-MOVE-DATES.
40          MOVE TODAYS-MONTH    TO OUT-MONTH.
41          MOVE TODAYS-DAY      TO OUT-DAY.
42          MOVE TODAYS-YEAR     TO OUT-YEAR.

43          MOVE FROM-MONTH      TO OUT-FROM-MONTH.
44          MOVE FROM-DAY        TO OUT-FROM-DAY.
45          MOVE FROM-YEAR       TO OUT-FROM-YEAR.

46          MOVE THROUGH-MONTH   TO OUT-THROUGH-MONTH.
47          MOVE THROUGH-DAY     TO OUT-THROUGH-DAY.
48          MOVE THROUGH-YEAR    TO OUT-THROUGH-YEAR.

        C3-MOVE-ADDRESS.
49          MOVE AF-CUSTOMER-NAME    TO OUT-CUSTOMER-NAME.
50          MOVE AF-STREET-ADDRESS   TO OUT-STREET-ADDRESS.
51          MOVE AF-CITY-STATE-ZIP   TO OUT-CITY-STATE-ZIP.

        C4-PRINT-PART-1.
52          MOVE SPACES          TO TRANSACTION-LINE.
53          WRITE TRANSACTION-LINE
                 AFTER ADVANCING PAGE.
54          MOVE PART-SEPARATOR TO TRANSACTION-LINE.
55          WRITE TRANSACTION-LINE
                 AFTER ADVANCING 1 LINE.
56          MOVE SPACES          TO TRANSACTION-LINE.
```

Figure 2 (Continued)

```
57        MOVE PART-1-LINE-1  TO TRANSACTION-LINE.
58        WRITE TRANSACTION-LINE
                  AFTER ADVANCING 2 LINES.
59        MOVE SPACES          TO TRANSACTION-LINE.
60        MOVE PART-1-LINE-2  TO TRANSACTION-LINE.
61        WRITE TRANSACTION-LINE
                  AFTER ADVANCING 1 LINE.
62        MOVE SPACES          TO TRANSACTION-LINE.
63        MOVE PART-1-LINE-3  TO TRANSACTION-LINE.
64        WRITE TRANSACTION-LINE
                  AFTER ADVANCING 3 LINES.
65        MOVE SPACES          TO TRANSACTION-LINE.
66        MOVE PART-1-LINE-4  TO TRANSACTION-LINE.
67        WRITE TRANSACTION-LINE
                  AFTER ADVANCING 4 LINES.
68        MOVE SPACES          TO TRANSACTION-LINE.
69        MOVE PART-1-LINE-5  TO TRANSACTION-LINE.
70        WRITE TRANSACTION-LINE
                  AFTER ADVANCING 1 LINE.
71        MOVE SPACES TO TRANSACTION-LINE.
72        MOVE PART-1-LINE-6  TO TRANSACTION-LINE.
73        WRITE TRANSACTION-LINE
                  AFTER ADVANCING 1 LINE.
74        MOVE SPACES TO TRANSACTION-LINE.
75        MOVE PART-1-LINE-7  TO TRANSACTION-LINE.
76        WRITE TRANSACTION-LINE
                  AFTER ADVANCING 1 LINE.


      C5-PRINT-PART-2-TITLE.
77        MOVE SPACES          TO TRANSACTION-LINE.
78        MOVE PART-SEPARATOR TO TRANSACTION-LINE.
79        WRITE TRANSACTION-LINE
                  AFTER ADVANCING 2 LINES.
80        MOVE SPACES TO TRANSACTION-LINE.
81        MOVE PART-2-LINE-1  TO TRANSACTION-LINE.
82        WRITE TRANSACTION-LINE
                  AFTER ADVANCING 1 LINE.
83        MOVE SPACES          TO TRANSACTION-LINE.
84        MOVE PART-2-LINE-2  TO TRANSACTION-LINE.
85        WRITE TRANSACTION-LINE
                  AFTER ADVANCING 1 LINE.


      C6-PROCESS-TRANSACTIONS.
86        IF CF-TRANSACTION-TYPE = "D"
87           ADD CF-TRANSACTION-AMOUNT TO WS-CURRENT-BALANCE
88           MOVE "+ " TO OUT-TRANSACTION-SIGN
89           ADD CF-TRANSACTION-AMOUNT TO WS-TOTAL-CREDITS
          ELSE
90           SUBTRACT CF-TRANSACTION-AMOUNT FROM WS-CURRENT-BALANCE
91           MOVE "  " TO OUT-TRANSACTION-SIGN
92           ADD CF-TRANSACTION-AMOUNT TO WS-TOTAL-DEBITS.

93        IF CF-TRANSACTION-TYPE = "C"
```

Figure 2 (Continued)

```
 94            ADD 1 TO WS-ITEM-COUNT.

 95         PERFORM D1-PRINT-REST-OF-PART-2.

 96         IF WS-CURRENT-BALANCE IS LESS THAN WS-MINIMUM-BALANCE
 97             MOVE WS-CURRENT-BALANCE TO WS-MINIMUM-BALANCE.

 98         PERFORM B3-READ-TRANSACTIONS-FILE.

     C7-COMPLETE-STATEMENT.
 99         IF WS-MINIMUM-BALANCE IS LESS THAN 300
100             MOVE 5.00 TO OUT-MISC-CHARGES
101             SUBTRACT 5 FROM WS-CURRENT-BALANCE
            ELSE
102             MOVE ZERO TO OUT-MISC-CHARGES.

103         IF WS-MINIMUM-BALANCE IS NOT LESS THAN 1000.00
104             COMPUTE WS-INTEREST-EARNED = 0.055 * WS-MINIMUM-BALANCE
105             MOVE WS-INTEREST-EARNED TO OUT-TOTAL-INTEREST
106             ADD WS-INTEREST-EARNED TO WS-CURRENT-BALANCE
            ELSE
107             MOVE ZERO TO OUT-TOTAL-INTEREST.

108         PERFORM D2-PRINT-PART-3.
109         PERFORM D3-PRINT-PART-4.

     D1-PRINT-REST-OF-PART-2.
110         MOVE CF-TRANSACTION-MONTH       TO OUT-TRANSACTION-MONTH.
111         MOVE CF-TRANSACTION-DAY         TO OUT-TRANSACTION-DAY.
112         MOVE CF-TRANSACTION-DESCRIPTION TO OUT-TRANSACTION-DESCR.
113         MOVE CF-TRANSACTION-AMOUNT      TO OUT-TRANSACTION-AMOUNT.
114         MOVE WS-CURRENT-BALANCE         TO OUT-BALANCE.
115         MOVE SPACES                     TO TRANSACTION-LINE.
116         MOVE PART-2-MAIN-LINE           TO TRANSACTION-LINE.
117         WRITE TRANSACTION-LINE
                    AFTER ADVANCING 1 LINE.

     D2-PRINT-PART-3.
118         MOVE SPACES                     TO TRANSACTION-LINE.
119         MOVE PART-SEPARATOR             TO TRANSACTION-LINE.
120         WRITE TRANSACTION-LINE
                    AFTER ADVANCING 2 LINES.
121         MOVE SPACES                     TO TRANSACTION-LINE.
122         MOVE PART-3-LINE-1              TO TRANSACTION-LINE.
123         WRITE TRANSACTION-LINE
                    AFTER ADVANCING 2 LINES.
124         MOVE SPACES                     TO TRANSACTION-LINE.
125         MOVE PART-3-LINE-2              TO TRANSACTION-LINE.
126         WRITE TRANSACTION-LINE
                    AFTER ADVANCING 2 LINES.
127         MOVE SPACES                     TO TRANSACTION-LINE.
128         MOVE PART-3-LINE-3              TO TRANSACTION-LINE.
129         WRITE TRANSACTION-LINE
                    AFTER ADVANCING 1 LINE.
130         MOVE SPACES                     TO TRANSACTION-LINE.
```

Figure 2 (Continued)

```
131        MOVE AF-ACCOUNT-NUMBER             TO OUT-ACCOUNT-NUMBER.
132        MOVE AF-BALANCE-FROM-LAST-MONTH TO OUT-BEGINNING-BALANCE.
133        MOVE WS-TOTAL-CREDITS             TO OUT-TOTAL-CREDITS.
134        MOVE WS-TOTAL-DEBITS              TO OUT-TOTAL-DEBITS.
135        MOVE WS-CURRENT-BALANCE           TO OUT-CURRENT-BALANCE.
136        MOVE PART-3-MAIN-LINE             TO TRANSACTION-LINE.
137        WRITE TRANSACTION-LINE
                    AFTER ADVANCING 2 LINES.
138        MOVE SPACES                       TO TRANSACTION-LINE.
139        MOVE WS-ITEM-COUNT                TO OUT-ITEMS-ENCLOSED.
140        MOVE PART-3-LINE-4                TO TRANSACTION-LINE.
141        WRITE TRANSACTION-LINE
                    AFTER ADVANCING 2 LINES.


       D3-PRINT-PART-4.
142        MOVE SPACES               TO TRANSACTION-LINE.
143        MOVE PART-SEPARATOR       TO TRANSACTION-LINE.
144        WRITE TRANSACTION-LINE
                    AFTER ADVANCING 2 LINES.
145        MOVE SPACES               TO TRANSACTION-LINE.
146        MOVE WS-FIRST-MESSAGE-LINE  TO TRANSACTION-LINE.
147        WRITE TRANSACTION-LINE
                    AFTER ADVANCING 2 LINES.
148        MOVE SPACES               TO TRANSACTION-LINE.
149        MOVE WS-SECOND-MESSAGE-LINE TO TRANSACTION-LINE.
150        WRITE TRANSACTION-LINE
                    AFTER ADVANCING 1 LINE.
151        MOVE SPACES               TO TRANSACTION-LINE.
152        MOVE PART-SEPARATOR       TO TRANSACTION-LINE.
153        WRITE TRANSACTION-LINE
                    AFTER ADVANCING 2 LINES.
```

Figure 2 (Continued)

In structural testing, the test cases should be chosen such that each of these 556 paths is traversed at least once. A single test data set may cause the program to traverse quite a few logical paths in its flow graph. Still, in general, a large number of data sets may be required to test a complex software system fully.

Some software engineering techniques have been developed to reduce the number of necessary test cases to a reasonable minimum by defining a **basis set** of execution paths for a program. These techniques are studied in advanced courses in software engineering, and are outside the scope of this book.

Functional Testing. In functional testing, we disregard the program control structure and concentrate on the functions the program is expected to perform. Because the details of the program logic are intentionally ignored and the program is considered as a black box, this technique is also known as **black box testing**. We try to devise test data to answer the question of whether or not the program does what it is expected to do. There are different functional testing techniques, but they are also outside the scope of our coverage.

Automated Testing. Some automated tools have been developed that are invaluable in reducing the time it takes to test a software system. As of now, however, most of them are still in the research phase and are not in wide use.

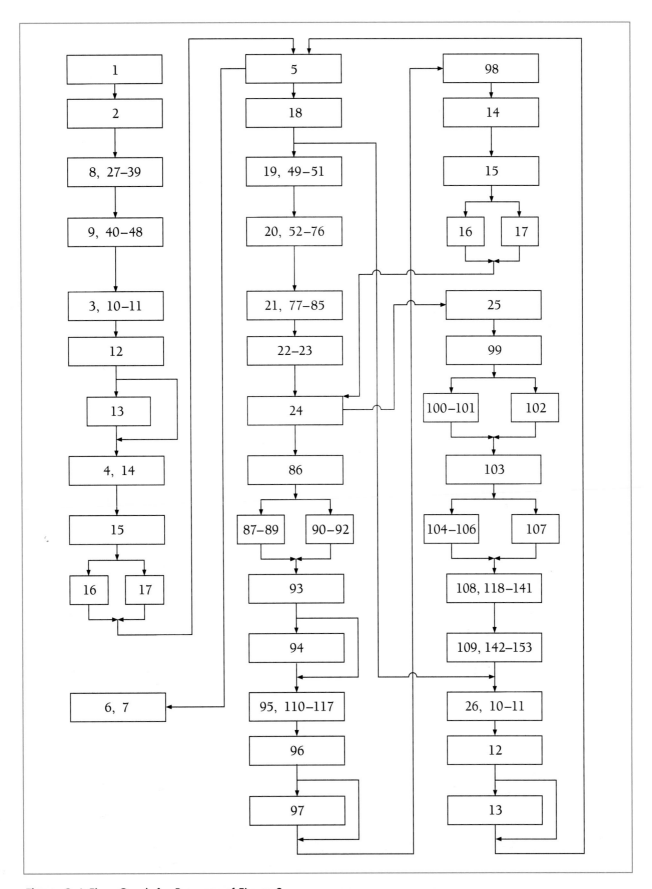

Figure 3 A Flow Graph for Program of Figure 2

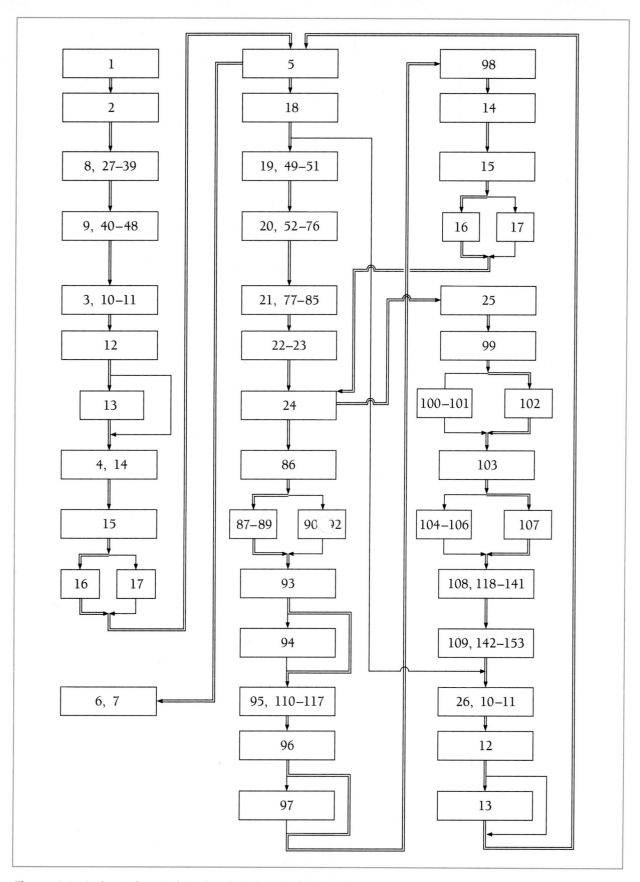

Figure 4 An Independent Path in the Flow Graph of Figure 3

Among them are data flow analyzers, output comparators, test data generators, and code auditors.

Data flow analyzers track the flow of data through a program and look for data-related errors such as undefined data references. Output comparators facilitate comparing one set of output from a program with other sets from the same program to determine differences. Test data generators help to select appropriate test data for program testing. Code auditors check the program to ensure that it meets minimum coding standards.

Informal Testing. The traditional software testing technique, known as informal testing, is based on some rules of thumb and the programmer's instinct. Desk-checking a program for correctness and running it with a limited number of test cases constitute the basis of informal testing. It is usually sufficient to test every program statement and every logical path once, provided the number of paths is not excessive.

Steps in Program Testing

An application program is usually a complex system consisting of a number of modules. To ensure its correctness, not only should the entire system be properly tested, but also all of its components and the interactions among them should be validated. The structured program development approach discussed in Chapter 4 shows its influence here, as its methodologies are taken into account in program testing.

Four steps involved in program testing are as follows:

1. Unit testing
2. Integration testing
   a. Top-down
   b. Bottom-up
3. System testing
4. Acceptance testing

Unit Testing. Each program module is subjected to unit testing before it is integrated with the other modules. Given that a program module may be designed to be reasonably small, the programmer may unit-test it during coding without much difficulty. Unit testing is structural testing. It entails executing each statement in the module and traversing every logical path in it. The module should be tested using all possible variations of the input data.

Top-Down Integration Testing. Integration testing is also structural testing performed on groups of modules comprising subsystems. A subsystem, in this sense, is two or more modules that interact to perform a specific function. For example, in the structure chart of Figure 14 in Chapter 5, the superordinate module C2-PRINT-ENROLLMENT-INFO, together with the two subordinates D1-PRODUCE-OTHER-HEADINGS and D2-PRINT-ENROLLMENT, make up a subsystem. As each module has already been unit-tested, in integration testing we regard them as black boxes, and concentrate on verifying that the modules function correctly within the subsystem and that module interfaces are correct.

In each step of integration testing we add one module to the subsystem that has already been tested, and test the new subsystem. We continue until all modules are included, and the final system is demonstrated to function properly.

Just as there are two program design strategies (i.e., top-down and bottom-up), there are two program testing strategies. In the first one, top-down testing, we start with high-level modules and go down in the structure chart. This strategy necessitates creation of dummy subordinate modules called stubs. A stub is a module that does nothing but return control back to the calling program. For example, in the structure chart of Figure 14 in Chapter 5, after unit-testing the modules A-MAIN-PARAGRAPH, B1-PRODUCE-HEADINGS, and B2-PROCESS-RECORDS, we integrate them and apply top-down integration tests. To do that, we consider the two modules C1-PRINT-MAIN-INFORMATION and C2-PRINT-ENROLLMENT-INFO, which are subordinate to B2-PROCESS-RECORDS, as two stubs. After integration testing on the subsystem consisting of three modules, we expand the subsystem by adding C1-PRINT-MAIN-INFORMATION to it, and proceed with integration testing from top to bottom until the full structure is tested.

Bottom-Up Integration Testing. In this approach, we start with lowest-level modules in the program structure and move up one module at a time until the full system is tested. To do this, we have to create temporary test programs that invoke the subsystem being tested. These programs are called drivers.

Let us demonstrate bottom-up testing on the structure chart of Figure 14 in Chapter 5. Suppose the lower level modules D1-PRODUCE-OTHER-HEADINGS, D2-PRINT-ENROLLMENT, and C2-PRINT-ENROLLMENT-INFO have been unit tested. We combine these modules into a subsystem and write a temporary program, a driver, to invoke C2-PRINT-ENROLLMENT-INFO. After this subsystem is validated, we add C1-PRINT-MAIN-INFORMATION and B2-PROCESS-RECORDS to it, and write another driver to call upon B2-PROCESS-RECORDS during testing, and so on.

In bottom-up testing, construction of drivers may be time consuming compared to the creation of stubs in top-down testing. Both strategies are widely used, separately or together, in testing software systems.

System Testing. In system testing we try to demonstrate that the entire software system performs according to its requirements specification. This is functional testing for normal input data, for extremes in input data values and volume, and for exceptions using data values outside their acceptable range.

Acceptance Testing. Acceptance testing is also functional testing of the entire program. Here, we assume no knowledge of the program's logic and structure, and use live data to validate that the software system performs according to the requirements.

REVIEW QUESTIONS

1. Program correctness at different phases of the program life cycle is the primary concern of _____ , whereas the purpose of _____ is to ensure that the finished program correctly meets user requirements.
2. Program testing is the activity of identifying the source of errors in a program, and modifying the program to eliminate these errors. (T or F)
3. Proving that a program is correct is similar to proving that a theorem is correct. (T or F)
4. Which of the following statements about program testing is correct?
    a. Exhaustive testing is generally impractical and unfeasible.
    b. Structural testing is concerned with verifying the structure of a program's procedural design.
    c. Structural testing is also known as white box testing.
    d. In functional testing, we concentrate on the functions a program is expected to perform.
    e. All of the above are correct.

5. In _____ testing we use desk-checking, and run the program with a limited number of test cases.
6. The steps involved in program testing are _____ , _____ , _____ , and _____ .
7. System testing is functional testing of a program. (T or F)

Answers: 1. program verification, program validation; 2. F; 3. T; 4. e; 5. informal; 6. unit testing, integration testing, system testing, acceptance testing; 7. T.

Program Debugging

Because software is developed by people, all phases of its development life cycle are prone to mistakes. No matter how careful we are, it is probable that the end product of our efforts may not function as expected because of errors introduced into it at some point. Before we can produce a reliable program, we should discover such errors and eliminate their causes. This process is called debugging. The four types of software errors are

1. Design errors
2. Programming errors
3. Testing errors
4. External errors

Design errors occur during the analysis and design phases, and they may arise for several reasons. We may pick an incorrect method of solution for the problem at hand, we may make mistakes in translating a correct method of solution to algorithmic form, or we may design erroneous data for the program. Then again, the method of solution, its algorithmic counterpart, and the data may all be correct, but we may inadvertently incorporate errors into the software during programming. Such errors are called **programming errors**, and they may become obvious when the program is compiled and executed.

The fact that a program may compile and execute without any error diagnostics does not necessarily mean that it is correct. To guarantee correctness, we test. Even then, however, it is conceivable that we may make errors due to the use of invalid test procedures and test data, or we may misinterpret the test results. These are **testing errors**.

Finally, the program may not execute properly because of errors in the hardware or in the interfacing software. Errors of this type are **external errors**.

Design, testing, and external errors are outside the scope of our discussion. Because we are primarily concerned with application program development, we will concentrate on programming errors and the available tools and techniques for debugging them.

Types of Programming Errors

During the process of translating a correct algorithm to a computer program, several errors may be committed by a programmer. Depending on when programming errors are diagnosed, they can be classified as compilation or execution errors.

Compilation errors are due to violations of the syntax and certain semantic rules of the programming language used. Every language compiler has the capability of determining rule violations during compilation and producing error diagnostics to inform the programmer what went wrong. In a language as rich as COBOL, the number of possible violations of its rules is large. They include misspelling reserved words, using an improper sequence of words or literals, referencing previously undefined variables, specifying improper operations on data fields, and so on. Some COBOL examples follow.

```
* MISSPELLED KEY WORD "SUBSTRACT":
    SUBSTRACT 5 FROM UNIT-COST.

* INCORRECT SEQUENCE OF WORDS FOR SUBTRACT STATEMENT:
    SUBTRACT FROM UNIT-COST 5.

* IMPROPER OPERATION (SUBTRACT) ON NONNUMERIC DATA:
    SUBTRACT "5" FROM UNIT-COST.

* INCORRECTLY CONSTRUCTED USER-DEFINED WORD "UNIT COST":
    SUBTRACT 5 FROM UNIT COST.
```

Additional examples are shown later in this chapter. Since the compiler produces a listing of error diagnostics to help the programmer pinpoint the sources of errors, compilation errors are usually easy to detect and correct.

Execution errors surface at the time the program is executed. They may cause the program to **abend** (a contraction of the term **abnormal end**, meaning termination of program execution without completing its function). They may also be errors that result in no program abend or error diagnostics, but produce unexpected or incorrect results. Execution errors are, in fact, logic errors. They are due to instructions in the program that require the computer system to do something that it cannot do, such as divide a quantity by a variable whose value is zero at the time of division, or something that it should not be doing in view of the problem requirements, such as addition instead of subtraction. In general, execution errors are more difficult to debug than compilation errors.

Minimizing Debugging Effort

Debugging is tedious and difficult. Unfortunately, in most program development projects, errors are committed and debugging cannot be avoided. Because it is always better to have fewer "bugs" in a program than to resort to debugging to eliminate them, programmers should take steps to minimize errors during program development. Three basic techniques can be used to minimize errors: program structure description techniques, manual review of code (desk-checking), and structured walk-throughs.

During program development and coding, using an appropriate algorithm and program structure description technique such as pseudocoding, flow charting, or flow graphs may help reveal potential errors and thus may substantially reduce future debugging efforts.

After coding the program and before compiling, it is a good idea to desk-check it. For this, either a printer listing of the source code can be used, or the content of the source program file can be examined through a terminal. By desk-checking a program, many typographical errors, omissions, and even logic errors can be detected and corrected.

A **structured walk-through** is a manual process in which the programmer examines the source code in view of a carefully selected sample data set to ensure that it does what it is supposed to do correctly. This requires a step-by-step trace of the program statements, and may be time consuming. Especially for relatively small programs or program modules, however, a walk-through may help eliminate many programming errors.

Debugging Compilation Errors

Even if we are careful in coding a program, errors may still exist. Some are detected by the compiler during the compilation process. While translating the source statements into machine language, the compiler checks the correctness of each source program element from the point of view of applicable syntactical and semantic rules. These elements in COBOL are identifiers, constant values, clauses, statements, sentences, program structure elements, paragraphs, sections, and divisions. Whenever a rule violation is detected, the compiler produces a diagnostic message informing the programmer of the location of the violation and the reason for it.

A list of such diagnostic messages is included in the source program listing produced by the compiler. Depending on the way a compiler is designed, the messages may be immediately before or after each source statement in which one or more errors are found, or they may follow the source listing. Typically, an error diagnostic message consists of the following three components:

1. A source program line identification number
2. An error message code
3. An error message text

Source program line numbers are sequence numbers assigned to each line by the compiler and can be used to identify the line containing an error. Each compilation error type has an associated error message code and a brief explanatory text. Usually an error message text is sufficient to describe the violation that has caused a diagnostic message. Further clarification and explanation can be found by consulting the programmer's manual for the language.

Figure 5 is a partial listing of Program 1 in Chapter 5, which has been intentionally altered to include some rule violations. The places in the program where these occur are indicated by arrows in Figure 5. After this program is compiled by a COBOL compiler, some error diagnostic messages are produced. These are shown in Figure 6, together with some compiler-generated statistics. Figure 7 lists the COBOL statements that contained errors after the errors have been corrected; the statements for which informational and warning messages have been generated during compilation are not shown.

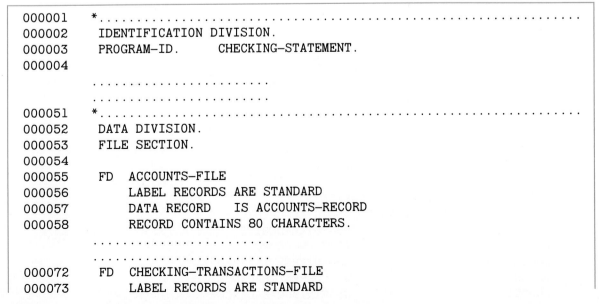

```
000001     *...........................................................
000002     IDENTIFICATION DIVISION.
000003     PROGRAM-ID.     CHECKING-STATEMENT.
000004

           ......................
           ......................
000051     *...........................................................
000052     DATA DIVISION.
000053     FILE SECTION.
000054
000055     FD  ACCOUNTS-FILE
000056         LABEL RECORDS ARE STANDARD
000057         DATA RECORD    IS ACCOUNTS-RECORD
000058         RECORD CONTAINS 80 CHARACTERS.
           ......................
           ......................
000072     FD  CHECKING-TRANSACTIONS-FILE
000073         LABEL RECORDS ARE STANDARD
```

Figure 5 Partial Listing of Program 1 in Chapter 5 with Compilation Errors

```
000074          DATA RECORD   IS CHECKING-TRANSACTIONS-RECORD
000075          RECORD CONTAINS 80 CHARACTERS.
                . . . . . . . . . . . . . . . . . . . . . .
                . . . . . . . . . . . . . . . . . . . . . .
000090     FD   TRANSACTIONS-REPORT
000091          LABEL RECORDS ARE OMITTED
000092          DATA RECORD   IS TRANSACTION-LINE
000093          RECORD CONTAINS 131 CHARACTERS.
                . . . . . . . . . . . . . . . . . . . . .
                . . . . . . . . . . . . . . . . . . . . .
000104
000105     ***********> VARIABLES:
000106
000107     01   WS-ACCOUNT-REC-NUMBER        PIC X(4).
000108     01   WS-TRANS-REC-NUMBER          PIC X(4).
000109     01   WS-MINIMUM-BALANCE           PIC 9(6)V99.
000110     01   WS-CURRENT-BALANCE           PIC 9(6)V99.
000111     01   WS-INTEREST-EARNED           PIC 999V99.
000112     01   WS-TOTAL-CREDITS             PIC 9(6)V99.
000113     01   WS-TOTAL-DEBITS              PIC 9(6)V99.
000114     01   WS-ITEM-COUNT                PIC 999.
000115     01   WS-FIRST-MESSAGE-LINE        PIC X(50).
000116     01   WS-SECOND-MESSAGE-LINE       PIC X(50).
                . . . . . . . . . . . . . . . . . . . . . .
                . . . . . . . . . . . . . . . . . . . . . .
000262     *. . . . . . . . . . . . . . . . . . . . . . . . . . . . . . . . . . . . . . . . . . . . . . . . . . . . . . . . . . . . . . . . .
000263     PROCEDURE DIVISION.
000264
000265     A-MAIN-PARAGRAPH.
000266         OPEN INPUT   ACCOUNTS-FILE
000267              INPUT   CHECKING-TRANSACTIONS-FILE
000268              OUTPUT  TRANSACTIONS-REPORT.
000269         PERFORM B1-COMMON-TASKS.
000270         PERFORM B2-READ-ACCOUNTS-FILE.
000271         PERFORM B3-READ-TRANSACTIONS-FILE.
000272
000273         PERFORM B4-MATCH-RECORDS
000274                 UNTIL END-OF-ACCOUNTS-FILE.
000275
000276         CLOSE ACCOUNTS-FILE
000277               CHECKING-TRANSACTIONS-FILE
000278               TRANSACTIONS-REPORT.
000279         STOP RUN.
000280
000281     B1-COMMON-TASKS.
000282         PERFORM C1-TERMINAL-INPUTS.
000283         PERFORM C2-MOVE-DATES.
000284
000285     B2-READ-ACCOUNTS-FILE.
000286         MOVE ZERO TO WS-TOTAL-CREDITS
000287                      WS-TOTAL-DEBITS.      ◄———— Extraneous period
000288                      WS-ITEM-COUNT
000289                      WS-INTEREST-EARNED
000290                      WS-CURRENT-BALANCE
000291                      WS-MINIMUM-BALANCE.
```

Figure 5 (Continued)

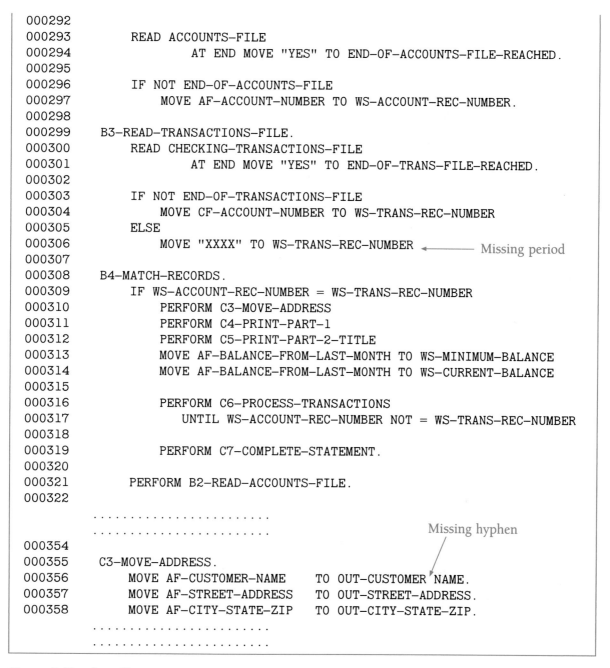

```
000292
000293         READ ACCOUNTS-FILE
000294             AT END MOVE "YES" TO END-OF-ACCOUNTS-FILE-REACHED.
000295
000296         IF NOT END-OF-ACCOUNTS-FILE
000297             MOVE AF-ACCOUNT-NUMBER TO WS-ACCOUNT-REC-NUMBER.
000298
000299     B3-READ-TRANSACTIONS-FILE.
000300         READ CHECKING-TRANSACTIONS-FILE
000301             AT END MOVE "YES" TO END-OF-TRANS-FILE-REACHED.
000302
000303         IF NOT END-OF-TRANSACTIONS-FILE
000304             MOVE CF-ACCOUNT-NUMBER TO WS-TRANS-REC-NUMBER
000305         ELSE
000306             MOVE "XXXX" TO WS-TRANS-REC-NUMBER  ←——————— Missing period
000307
000308     B4-MATCH-RECORDS.
000309         IF WS-ACCOUNT-REC-NUMBER = WS-TRANS-REC-NUMBER
000310             PERFORM C3-MOVE-ADDRESS
000311             PERFORM C4-PRINT-PART-1
000312             PERFORM C5-PRINT-PART-2-TITLE
000313             MOVE AF-BALANCE-FROM-LAST-MONTH TO WS-MINIMUM-BALANCE
000314             MOVE AF-BALANCE-FROM-LAST-MONTH TO WS-CURRENT-BALANCE
000315
000316             PERFORM C6-PROCESS-TRANSACTIONS
000317                 UNTIL WS-ACCOUNT-REC-NUMBER NOT = WS-TRANS-REC-NUMBER
000318
000319             PERFORM C7-COMPLETE-STATEMENT.
000320
000321         PERFORM B2-READ-ACCOUNTS-FILE.
000322
           . . . . . . . . . . . . . . . . . . . . . .
           . . . . . . . . . . . . . . . . . . . . . .                     Missing hyphen
000354
000355     C3-MOVE-ADDRESS.
000356         MOVE AF-CUSTOMER-NAME    TO OUT-CUSTOMER NAME.
000357         MOVE AF-STREET-ADDRESS   TO OUT-STREET-ADDRESS.
000358         MOVE AF-CITY-STATE-ZIP   TO OUT-CITY-STATE-ZIP.
           . . . . . . . . . . . . . . . . . . . . . .
           . . . . . . . . . . . . . . . . . . . . . .
```

Figure 5 (Continued)

As is seen in Figure 6, each diagnostic message code has a suffix that can be I (for informational, which obviously is not an error condition, but is a situation about which the compiler informs the programmer), W (warning), E (error), S (severe), or T (terminating). These suffix values make up a classification scheme for compilation errors.

A COBOL compilation error diagnostic message may be one of the following four types:

1. Warning
2. Error
3. Severe
4. Terminating

```
LINEID  MESSAGE CODE  MESSAGE TEXT ( IMBEDDED MESSAGES MAY BE IDENTIFIED
                                  BY THE <*> PRECEDING THE MESSAGE CODE )

    3   IGYDS0020-W   PROGRAM NAME < CHECKING-STATEMENT > WAS PROCESSED AS
                      < CHECKING >.

   55   IGYGR1216-I   A "RECORDING MODE" OF < F > WAS ASSUMED FOR
                      FILE < ACCOUNTS-FILE > .

   72   IGYGR1216-I   A "RECORDING MODE" OF < F > WAS ASSUMED FOR
                      FILE < CHECKING-TRANSACTIONS-FILE > .

   90   IGYGR1216-I   A "RECORDING MODE" OF < F > WAS ASSUMED FOR
                      FILE < TRANSACTIONS-REPORT > .

  288   IGYPS2072-S   < WS-ITEM-COUNT > WAS INVALID. SKIPPED TO
                      NEXT VERB, PERIOD OR PROCEDURE-NAME DEFINITION.

  308   IGYPS2008-E   A PERIOD WAS REQUIRED BEFORE PROCEDURE-NAME
                      < B4-MATCH-RECORDS >. A PERIOD WAS ASSUMED
                      BEFORE < B4-MATCH-RECORDS >.

  356   IGYPS2121-S   < OUT-CUSTOMER > WAS NOT DEFINED AS A DATA-NAME.
                      THE STATEMENT WAS DISCARDED.

  356   IGYPS2121-S   < NAME > WAS NOT DEFINED AS A DATA-NAME.
                      THE STATEMENT WAS DISCARDED.


TOTAL MESSAGES  INFORMATIONAL  WARNING  ERROR  SEVERE  TERMINATING
       8              3           1       1       3


* STATISTICS FOR COBOL PROGRAM CHECKING:
*    SOURCE RECORDS  =  506
*    DATA DIVISION STATEMENTS  =  87
*    PROCEDURE DIVISION STATEMENTS  =  155
```

Figure 6 Compiler Generated Error Diagnostics for Program of Figure 5

The names used to designate compilation errors differ from one software vendor to the next. For example, warning diagnostics are also known as W-level or level-0 messages. Error diagnostics may be called C-level or level-1 messages. Severe error diagnostics have the names E-level, level-2, and fatal error diagnostics. Despite the different names, they imply more or less the same things.

A **warning diagnostic message** pinpoints a minor error that may cause a problem during program execution. These errors do not result in termination of the compilation process; they may not be at all important, as exemplified in Figure 6, line 3 diagnostic. This warns the programmer that the program name CHECKING-STATEMENT is unacceptably long and is reduced to CHECKING. If uncorrected, however, some warning diagnostics may also lead to an execution error. In general, it is a good practice to take warning diagnostics seriously, and eliminate their causes in the code.

An **error diagnostic message** is produced if the compiler decides that a default adjustment can be made for the error. In other words, after detecting an

```
             . . . . . . . . . . . . . . . . . . . .
             . . . . . . . . . . . . . . . . . . . .
   000285    B2-READ-ACCOUNTS-FILE.
   000286        MOVE ZERO TO WS-TOTAL-CREDITS
   000287                    WS-TOTAL-DEBITS
   000288                    WS-ITEM-COUNT
   000289                    WS-INTEREST-EARNED
   000290                    WS-CURRENT-BALANCE
   000291                    WS-MINIMUM-BALANCE.
   000292
             . . . . . . . . . . . . . . . . . .
             . . . . . . . . . . . . . . . . . .
   000303        IF NOT END-OF-TRANSACTIONS-FILE
   000304            MOVE CF-ACCOUNT-NUMBER TO WS-TRANS-REC-NUMBER
   000305        ELSE
   000306            MOVE "XXXX" TO WS-TRANS-REC-NUMBER.
   000307
             . . . . . . . . . . . . . . . . . . .
             . . . . . . . . . . . . . . . . . . .
   000354
   000355    C3-MOVE-ADDRESS.
   000356        MOVE AF-CUSTOMER-NAME    TO OUT-CUSTOMER-NAME.
   000357        MOVE AF-STREET-ADDRESS   TO OUT-STREET-ADDRESS.
   000358        MOVE AF-CITY-STATE-ZIP   TO OUT-CITY-STATE-ZIP.
             . . . . . . . . . . . . . . . . . . .
             . . . . . . . . . . . . . . . . . . .
```

Figure 7 Code of Program of Figure 5 After Compilation Errors Have Been Corrected

error of this type, the compiler uses a default assumption for the incorrect entry and continues with compilation. An example is in line 308 diagnostic of Figure 6. The compiler has detected that a period is missing before the paragraph named B4-MATCH-RECORDS and has corrected the code by assuming a period concluding the previous paragraph. This automatic correction is quite proper. Certain corrections suggested and made for E-type errors by the compiler may be inappropriate, however, and may result in an execution error. Again, it is recommended that the programmer carefully analyze and eliminate such errors before proceeding with the program.

A **severe error diagnostic** is generated if the compiler comes across a rule violation for which no automatic correction can be made, and therefore the compilation process cannot continue. Some examples are shown in Figure 6. Finally, a **terminating error diagnostic** is an indication of a major error that baffles the compiler as to what to do. In such a case, program compilation may not even start, and if already in progress, it is immediately aborted. Terminating errors are rare, and usually happen if the program cannot be recognized as a regular COBOL program (e.g., when the first source line does not contain the reserved words IDENTIFICATION DIVISION).

In connection with compilation errors, the following should also be noted.

1. Sometimes a single error may result in more than one error diagnostic, and when the error source is removed, all such diagnostics also vanish.
2. If a statement contains more than one rule violation, the diagnostic message generated by the compiler may identify only the first error. The remaining errors may be caught only after eliminating the first error and recompiling the program.

```
                        NEW NATIONAL BANK
                         OXFORD, OHIO


               CHECKING  ACCOUNT  STATEMENT


    JOHN SMITH                           DATE       03/06/91
    156 OAK STREET                       STATEMENT PERIOD
    OXFORD, OH 45056                     FROM       07/01/90
                                         THROUGH    07/31/90


    DATE    TRANSACTIONS                          AMOUNT    BALANCE


    07/01   WITHDRAWAL                            100.00   3,029.65
    07/03   CHECK 1371                            650.00   2,379.65
    07/05   CHECK 1372                            838.27   1,541.38
    07/08   CHECK 1373                          1,300.00     241.38
    07/15   DEPOSIT                               500.00+    741.38


                   SUMMARY  OF  ACCOUNT


    ACCOUNT    BEGINNING    TOTAL    TOTAL    MISC      TOTAL      CURRENT
    NUMBER     BALANCE      CREDITS  DEBITS   CHARGES   INTEREST   BALANCE


     1544      3,129.65     500.00  2,888.27   5.00                 736.38


                                         ITEMS ENCLOSED     3


         AT NEW NATIONAL, WE ARE ALWAYS READY TO HELP ! !
              CALL TOLL FREE 1-800-565-7766
```

Figure 8 An Incorrect Checking Account Statement

Debugging Execution Errors

Even after all compilation errors have been eliminated in a COBOL program, there is no guarantee that it will execute correctly. To verify a program, we must test it thoroughly using carefully designed sets of test data. During or after execution the program may reveal different types of errors that could not be detected earlier in its life cycle. Errors that are uncovered during execution or on examining the output are known as execution errors.

For a reasonably complicated application program, one can conceive of a large number of circumstances that may lead to execution errors. It is therefore not possible to devise a thorough classification scheme for these errors. We can only classify them according to whether or not they cause an abnormal termination during execution, and whether they are due to errors in the data or the program itself.

Depending on the computer system's reaction, execution errors are classified as those that result in an abnormal termination or produce incorrect output. Depending on their source, they can also be classified as being due to incorrect input data or to errors in the program code. To exemplify different types of execution errors, we consider three examples based on the application program developed in Program 1 in Chapter 5.

```
                        NEW NATIONAL BANK
                         OXFORD, OHIO


              CHECKING ACCOUNT STATEMENT


  MARY TAYLOR                         DATE      03/06/91
  1077 N. PARK AVE                    STATEMENT PERIOD
  MILLFORD, OH 45067                  FROM      07/01/90
                                      THROUGH   07/31/90
  _____

  DATE     TRANSACTIONS                   AMOUNT    BALANCE
  ____     _____                   _____    _____

  07/03    CHECK 1170                      378.00   9,878.71
  07/16    WITHDRAWAL                    1,000.00   8,878.71
  07/18    DEPOSIT                       2,590.00+ 11,468.71
  _____

                  SUMMARY OF ACCOUNT
```

ACCOUNT NUMBER	BEGINNING BALANCE	TOTAL CREDITS	TOTAL DEBITS	MISC CHARGES	TOTAL INTEREST	CURRENT BALANCE
1560	10,256.71	2,590.00	1,378.00		488.32	11,468.71
				ITEMS ENCLOSED		1

```
        AT NEW NATIONAL, WE ARE ALWAYS READY TO HELP !!
              CALL TOLL FREE 1-800-565-7766
```

Figure 8 (Continued)

> **Example 1**   Program 1 in Chapter 5, as given, is correct and produces correct results if there are no errors in the input data. Suppose, however, that we have typed the statement 00440 in Program 1-Source in Chapter 5 as

```
ADD WS-INTEREST-EARNED TO WS-MINIMUM-BALANCE
```

instead of the correct form, which is

```
ADD WS-INTEREST-EARNED TO WS-CURRENT-BALANCE.
```

When we run the program on the input data shown in Program 1-Input in Chapter 5, we get the checking account statements of Figure 8. The checking account statements for JOHN SMITH and TIMOTHY JACKSON are both correct; however, the one for MARY TAYLOR is incorrect. During the statement period, there has been a total debit of $1378.00 and a total credit of $2590.00, plus an earned interest of $488.32. Given that the beginning balance was $10,256.71, the current balance should have been $11,957.03, whereas it is

```
┌─────────────────────────────────────────────────────────────────────────┐
│                                                                           │
│   ──────────────────────────────────────────────────────────────────     │
│                         NEW NATIONAL BANK                                  │
│                          OXFORD, OHIO                                      │
│                                                                           │
│                                                                           │
│            C H E C K I N G   A C C O U N T   S T A T E M E N T            │
│                                                                           │
│                                                                           │
│   TIMOTHY JACKSON                          DATE           03/06/91        │
│   12021 RIDGE RD                           STATEMENT PERIOD               │
│   MORROW, OH 45032                         FROM           07/01/90        │
│                                            THROUGH        07/31/90        │
│   ──────────────────────────────────────────────────────────────────     │
│   DATE     TRANSACTIONS                           AMOUNT     BALANCE      │
│   ────     ────────────                           ──────     ───────      │
│   07/01    CHECK 306                              250.00      200.00      │
│   07/09    CHECK 307                              150.00       50.00      │
│   ──────────────────────────────────────────────────────────────────     │
│                                                                           │
│                    S U M M A R Y   O F   A C C O U N T                     │
│                                                                           │
│   ACCOUNT     BEGINNING    TOTAL     TOTAL    MISC      TOTAL     CURRENT  │
│   NUMBER      BALANCE      CREDITS   DEBITS   CHARGES   INTEREST  BALANCE  │
│                                                                           │
│    1600        450.00                400.00    5.00                45.00  │
│                                                                           │
│                                            ITEMS ENCLOSED          2      │
│   ──────────────────────────────────────────────────────────────────     │
│                                                                           │
│          AT NEW NATIONAL, WE ARE ALWAYS READY TO HELP ! !                 │
│               CALL TOLL FREE 1-800-565-7766                               │
│                                                                           │
└─────────────────────────────────────────────────────────────────────────┘
```

Figure 8 (Continued)

shown to be $11,468.71. The difference between the correct and incorrect values of the current balance is $488.32, exactly the amount of total interest earned. A moment's reflection leads us to suspect that the computed interest is not being added to the current balance. This error points to the program statement 00440, shown in its incorrect form in the partial listing of Figure 9. Clearly, the reason the other two checking statements were correct is that none earned any interest in the statement period.

This program error did not result in an abnormal program termination, and was detected on examining the output. Such errors can be quite difficult to debug. In real-world applications, as would have been in the above application, they can also be quite embarrassing.

Example 2   Let us now assume that we correct the program error discussed above, and run the program on the input data shown in Figure 10. This input data set is somewhat different than that given in Program 1-Input in Chapter 5, and we will soon see why. The execution of Program 1 in Chapter 5 on this input data set produces the checking account statement shown in Figure 11 for JOHN SMITH. Examination of this statement against the input data set reveals that something is wrong: the beginning balance appears as $663,129.65 on the statement, whereas according to the instance of the ACCOUNTS-FILE in Fig-

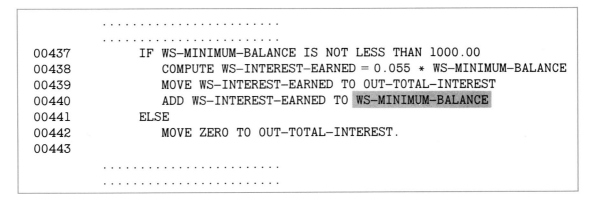

```
                  . . . . . . . . . . . . . . . . . . . . .
                  . . . . . . . . . . . . . . . . . . . . .
00437             IF WS-MINIMUM-BALANCE IS NOT LESS THAN 1000.00
00438                COMPUTE WS-INTEREST-EARNED = 0.055 * WS-MINIMUM-BALANCE
00439                MOVE WS-INTEREST-EARNED TO OUT-TOTAL-INTEREST
00440                ADD WS-INTEREST-EARNED TO WS-MINIMUM-BALANCE
00441             ELSE
00442                MOVE ZERO TO OUT-TOTAL-INTEREST.
00443
                  . . . . . . . . . . . . . . . . . . . . .
                  . . . . . . . . . . . . . . . . . . . . .
```

Figure 9 The Logical Error That Produced the Incorrect Output of Figure 8

```
     5    10    15    20    25    30    35    40    45    50    55    60    65    70    75
----|----|----|----|----|----|----|----|----|----|----|----|----|----|----|-

1544 JOHN SMITH            156 OAK STREET        OXFORD, OH 45056      00312965
1560 MARY TAYLOR           1077 N. PARK AVE      MILLFORD, OH 45067    01025671
1600 TIMOTHY JACKSON       12021 RIDGE RD        MORROW, OH 45032      00045000
```

(a) An instance of ACCOUNTS-FILE

```
     5    10    15    20    25    30    35    40    45    50    55    60    65    70    75
----|----|----|----|----|-- --|----|----|----|----|----|----|----|----|-

1544 0701 W WITHDRAWAL                  00010000
1544 0703 C CHECK 1371                  00065000
1544 0705 C CHECK 1372                  00083827
1544 0708 C CHECK 1373                  00130000
1544 0715 D DEPOSIT                     00050000
1560 0703 C CHECK 1170                  00037800
1560 0716 W WITHDRAWAL                  00100000
1560 0718 D DEPOSIT                     00259000
1600 0701 C CHECK 306                   00025000
1600 0709 C CHECK 307                   00015000
```

(b) An instance of CHECKING-TRANSACTIONS-FILE

Figure 10 Input Data Error That Caused the Incorrect Output of Figure 11

ure 10, it should have been $3,129.65. This is a difference of $660,000, certainly a large sum even for our bank! Why did this happen?

We realize that the data value in the ACCOUNTS-FILE for JOHN SMITH corresponding to the field AF-BALANCE-FROM-LAST-MONTH (see line 00069 in Program 1-Source in Chapter 5) has been incorrectly typed as OO312965 instead of the correct value 00312965, with two preceding letter Os instead of zeroes. Some compilers could have abended the program on encountering a nonnumeric value in a numeric field; our compiler did not. It merely converted the letters to some digits and continued with the processing. Had we specified a COMPUTATIONAL mode for the field AF-BALANCE-FROM-LAST-MONTH instead of the default DISPLAY mode, this would not have happened. This execution error had its source in the input data.

```
                        NEW NATIONAL BANK
                          OXFORD, OHIO

            CHECKING  ACCOUNT  STATEMENT

   JOHN SMITH                          DATE       03/06/91
   156 OAK STREET                      STATEMENT PERIOD
   OXFORD, OH 45056                    FROM       07/01/90
                                       THROUGH    07/31/90

   DATE      TRANSACTIONS                       AMOUNT      BALANCE

   07/01     WITHDRAWAL                         100.00    663,029.65
   07/03     CHECK 1371                         650.00    662,379.65
   07/05     CHECK 1372                         838.27    661,541.38
   07/08     CHECK 1373                       1,300.00    660,241.38
   07/15     DEPOSIT                            500.00+   660,741.38


                     SUMMARY  OF  ACCOUNT

   ACCOUNT    BEGINNING    TOTAL     TOTAL    MISC      TOTAL      CURRENT
   NUMBER     BALANCE      CREDITS   DEBITS   CHARGES   INTEREST   BALANCE

    1544     663,129.65    500.00   2,888.27            313.27   661,054.65


                                           ITEMS ENCLOSED        3


          AT NEW NATIONAL, WE ARE ALWAYS READY TO HELP !!
               CALL TOLL FREE 1-800-565-7766
```

Figure 11 An Incorrect Checking Account Statement

Example 3 Now we attempt to run our program on the input data of Figure 12 and find that this causes an abend at run time. The CF-TRANSACTION-AMOUNT field of the CHECKING-TRANSACTION-FILE for the first transaction record belonging to the customer 1544 has been typed as 000100.0, with a decimal point in the numeric field. This time our compiler has reacted by terminating the program execution and giving us a clue as to the source of error.

Common Execution Errors in COBOL Programming. If we examine a sufficiently large sample of programs written in a specific programming language we encounter some common error types that are almost particular to that language. The following are common to COBOL programming:

1. Failure to initialize or reset numeric identifiers
2. Allowing nonnumeric values in numeric fields
3. Specifying inadequate data fields for numeric identifiers
4. Specifying inadequate alphabetic or alphanumeric fields
5. Failure to reset end-of-file flags in repeated processing of files
6. Using one end-of-file flag for more than one file without resetting it
7. Dividing a numeric expression by zero
8. Failure to properly delimit conditional clauses containing imperative statements

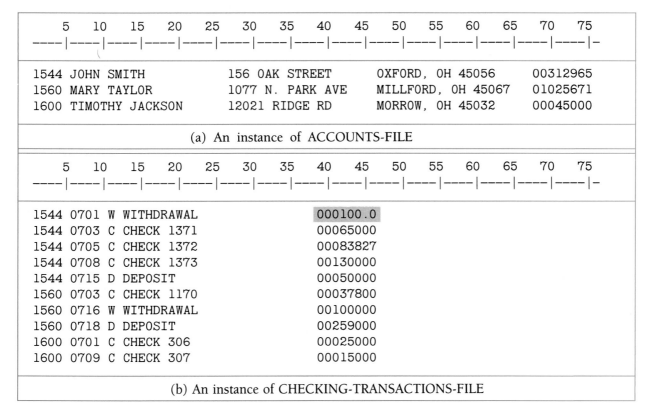

	5	10	15	20	25	30	35	40	45	50	55	60	65	70	75
----		----		----		----		----		----		----		----		----		----		----		----		----		----		----	|-

```
1544 JOHN SMITH          156 OAK STREET      OXFORD, OH 45056      00312965
1560 MARY TAYLOR         1077 N. PARK AVE    MILLFORD, OH 45067    01025671
1600 TIMOTHY JACKSON     12021 RIDGE RD      MORROW, OH 45032      00045000
```

(a) An instance of ACCOUNTS-FILE

	5	10	15	20	25	30	35	40	45	50	55	60	65	70	75

```
1544 0701 W WITHDRAWAL                000100.0
1544 0703 C CHECK 1371                00065000
1544 0705 C CHECK 1372                00083827
1544 0708 C CHECK 1373                00130000
1544 0715 D DEPOSIT                   00050000
1560 0703 C CHECK 1170                00037800
1560 0716 W WITHDRAWAL                00100000
1560 0718 D DEPOSIT                   00259000
1600 0701 C CHECK 306                 00025000
1600 0709 C CHECK 307                 00015000
```

(b) An instance of CHECKING-TRANSACTIONS-FILE

Figure 12 Input Data Error That Causes an Abend at Run-Time

Failure to initialize or reset numeric identifiers: Numeric identifiers that appear as operands in arithmetic computations in a program must be initialized to their proper initial values. An example is as follows.

```
                . . . . . . . . . . . . . . . . . . . .
                . . . . . . . . . . . . . . . . . . . .
000285     B2-READ-ACCOUNTS-FILE.
000286         MOVE ZERO TO WS-TOTAL-CREDITS
000287                     WS-TOTAL-DEBITS
000288   *                 WS-ITEM-COUNT
000289                     WS-INTEREST-EARNED
000290                     WS-CURRENT-BALANCE
000291                     WS-MINIMUM-BALANCE.
000292
000293         READ ACCOUNTS-FILE
000294             AT END MOVE "YES" TO END-OF-ACCOUNTS-FILE-REACHED.
000295
000296     IF NOT END-OF-ACCOUNTS-FILE
000297         MOVE AF-ACCOUNT-NUMBER TO WS-ACCOUNT-REC-NUMBER.
000298

                . . . . . . . . . . . . . . . . . . . .
                . . . . . . . . . . . . . . . . . . . .
000410     C6-PROCESS-TRANSACTIONS.
                . . . . . . . . . . . . . . . . . . . .
                . . . . . . . . . . . . . . . . . . . .
000420         IF CF-TRANSACTION-TYPE = "C"
000421             ADD 1 TO WS-ITEM-COUNT.
                . . . . . . . . . . . . . . . . . . . .
                . . . . . . . . . . . . . . . . . . . .
```

This is a partial COBOL code extracted from Program 1-Source in Chapter 5. Here we intentionally altered the code by suppressing line 000288 in which the identifier WS-ITEM-COUNT is being set to zero. In the PROCEDURE DIVISION, line 000421 has an ADD statement that increments WS-ITEM-COUNT by 1 by adding to its previous content. The first time this statement is executed, the COBOL compiler will find no value for WS-ITEM-COUNT. What happens at this point depends on the design characteristics of the COBOL compiler.

1. Some compilers require that a proper value be stored in such identifiers, and failure to do that will result in an execution error.
2. Other COBOL compilers will automatically initialize all numeric identifiers to zero or spaces, and all alphanumeric identifiers to spaces. In this case, the initial value for numeric identifiers will be taken as zero whether intended or not. If zero is not the proper initial value, the program will compute incorrect values without generating error diagnostics. This may lead to execution errors that are quite difficult to debug.

Therefore, it is highly advisable that the programmer initialize all identifiers properly, and not rely on the compiler for initialization or resetting.

Allowing nonnumeric values in numeric fields usually occurs due to errors in input data. The different possible reactions of the computer system to such errors were discussed in the previous section and illustrated in examples 2 and 3. Whether or not a run-time error diagnostic is generated depends on the design of the compiler.

Specifying inadequate data fields for numeric identifiers: We should try to estimate the length of numeric value that will be computed for an identifier in our program, and accordingly specify adequate field lengths. Failure to do so may result in numeric value truncation, as is illustrated in the following extract from Program 1-Source in Chapter 5.

```
            . . . . . . . . . . . . . . . . . .
000096      WORKING-STORAGE SECTION.
            . . . . . . . . . . . . . . . . . .
            . . . . . . . . . . . . . . . . . .
000111      01  WS-INTEREST-EARNED              PIC 9V99.
            . . . . . . . . . . . . . . . . . .
            . . . . . . . . . . . . . . . . . .
000263      PROCEDURE DIVISION.
            . . . . . . . . . . . . . . . . . .
000438          COMPUTE WS-INTEREST-EARNED = 0.055 * WS-MINIMUM-BALANCE
000439          MOVE WS-INTEREST-EARNED TO OUT-TOTAL-INTEREST
000440          ADD WS-INTEREST-EARNED TO WS-CURRENT-BALANCE
            . . . . . . . . . . . . . . . . . .
```

Here, the identifier WS-INTEREST-EARNED in line 000111 is defined using the PICTURE specification of 9V99. For example, for a WS-MINIMUM-BALANCE value of $10,000, the arithmetic expression in line 000438 will compute a value of $550.00, which clearly requires a PICTURE specification of at least 999V99. The inadequate field definition will cause a left truncation, and an incorrect value of $0.00 will be stored in WS-INTEREST-EARNED.

Specifying inadequate alphabetic or alphanumeric fields for identifiers that appear as target identifiers in MOVE statements results in string truncation. Consider the following partial code.

```
                . . . . . . . . . . . . . . . . . . . .
                . . . . . . . . . . . . . . . . . . . .
     000055      FD   ACCOUNTS-FILE
                . . . . . . . . . . . . . . . . . .
                . . . . . . . . . . . . . . . . . .
     000060      01   ACCOUNTS-RECORD.
                . . . . . . . . . . . . . . . . . . .
                . . . . . . . . . . . . . . . . . . .
     000063          05   AF-CUSTOMER-NAME            PIC X(20).
                . . . . . . . . . . . . . . . . . . .
                . . . . . . . . . . . . . . . . . . .
     000149      01   PART-1-LINE-4.
     000150          05   FILLER              PIC X(5)   VALUE SPACES.
     000151          05   OUT-CUSTOMER-NAME   PIC X(8).
                . . . . . . . . . . . . . . . . . . .
                . . . . . . . . . . . . . . . . . . .
     000355      C3-MOVE-ADDRESS.
     000356          MOVE AF-CUSTOMER-NAME    TO OUT-CUSTOMER-NAME.
                . . . . . . . . . . . . . . . . . . .
                . . . . . . . . . . . . . . . . . . .
```

Suppose the value stored in AF-CUSTOMER-NAME is JOHN SMITH. Since the field length for OUT-CUSTOMER-NAME is 8, as defined by PIC X(8) in line 000150, the MOVE statement of line 000356 will truncate the character string JOHN SMITH to JOHN SMI and will store this truncated value in OUT-CUSTOMER-NAME.

To demonstrate **failure to reset end-of-file flags in repeated processing of files**, we consider the following partial code, which is a variation of Program 1 in Chapter 5.

```
                . . . . . . . . . . . . . . . . . . .
                . . . . . . . . . . . . . . . . . . .
     000096      WORKING-STORAGE SECTION.
     000097
     000098      ***********> SWITCHES:
     000099
     000100      01   END-OF-ACCOUNTS-FILE-REACHED   PIC XXX    VALUE "NO".
     000101          88   END-OF-ACCOUNTS-FILE                  VALUE "YES".
     000102      01   END-OF-TRANS-FILE-REACHED      PIC XXX    VALUE "NO".
     000103          88   END-OF-TRANSACTIONS-FILE              VALUE "YES".
                . . . . . . . . . . . . . . . . . .
                . . . . . . . . . . . . . . . . . .
     000263      PROCEDURE DIVISION.
     000264
     000265      A-MAIN-PARAGRAPH.
     000266          OPEN INPUT   ACCOUNTS-FILE
     000267               INPUT   CHECKING-TRANSACTIONS-FILE
     000268               OUTPUT  TRANSACTIONS-REPORT.
     000269          PERFORM B1-COMMON-TASKS.
     000270          PERFORM B2-READ-ACCOUNTS-FILE.
     000271          PERFORM B3-READ-TRANSACTIONS-FILE.
     000272
```

```
000273              PERFORM B4-MATCH-RECORDS
000274                  UNTIL END-OF-ACCOUNTS-FILE.
000275
000276              CLOSE ACCOUNTS-FILE
000277                  CHECKING-TRANSACTIONS-FILE
000278                  TRANSACTIONS-REPORT.
000279
000280              OPEN INPUT ACCOUNTS-FILE.
000281              PERFORM B2-READ-ACCOUNTS-FILE.
000282
000283              PERFORM B5-LIST-ACCOUNTS-FILE
000284                  UNTIL END-OF-ACCOUNTS-FILE.
000285
000286              CLOSE ACCOUNTS-FILE.
000287              STOP RUN.
                    . . . . . . . . . . . . . . . . . . .
                    . . . . . . . . . . . . . . . . . . .
```

In addition to the tasks carried out by the original program, suppose we want to produce a listing of the ACCOUNTS-FILE after we complete processing the account statements. Line 000276 closes the ACCOUNTS-FILE. Then we open it in INPUT mode, read a record, and get into a controlled loop on the procedure B5-LIST-ACCOUNTS-FILE. This code will not work, however, simply because the procedures before line 000280 have caused a value of "YES" stored in END-OF-ACCOUNTS-FILE-REACHED, thus making END-OF-ACCOUNTS-FILE true. For this code to work we should have reset the file switch END-OF-ACCOUNTS-FILE-REACHED to "NO" before the loop of line 000283.

As an example of **using one end-of-file flag for more than one file without resetting it,** consider the partial code given below.

```
                    . . . . . . . . . . . . . . . . . . .
                    . . . . . . . . . . . . . . . . . . .
000096         WORKING-STORAGE SECTION.
000097
000098         ***********> SWITCHES:
000099
000100         01  END-OF-FILE-REACHED          PIC XXX      VALUE "NO".
000101             88  END-OF-FILE                           VALUE "YES".
                    . . . . . . . . . . . . . . . . . . .
                    . . . . . . . . . . . . . . . . . . .
000263         PROCEDURE DIVISION.
000264
000265         A-MAIN-PARAGRAPH.
                    . . . . . . . . . . . . . . . . . . .
                    . . . . . . . . . . . . . . . . . . .
000280             OPEN INPUT ACCOUNTS-FILE.
000281             READ ACCOUNTS-FILE
000282                 AT END MOVE "YES" TO END-OF-FILE-REACHED.
000283
000284             PERFORM B5-LIST-ACCOUNTS-FILE
000285                 UNTIL END-OF-FILE.
000286
000287             CLOSE ACCOUNTS-FILE.
000288
000289             OPEN INPUT CHECKING-TRANSACTIONS-FILE.
```

```
000290          READ CHECKING-TRANSACTIONS-FILE
000291              AT END MOVE "YES" TO END-OF-FILE-REACHED.
000292
000293          PERFORM B6-LIST-TRANSACTIONS-FILE
000294              UNTIL END-OF-FILE.
000295
000296          CLOSE CHECKING-TRANSACTIONS-FILE.
000297
000298          STOP RUN.
                . . . . . . . . . . . . . . . . . . . .
                . . . . . . . . . . . . . . . . . . . .
```

Starting at line 000280 we want to produce a sequential listing of the ACCOUNTS-FILE, and after this, a sequential listing of the CHECKING-TRANSACTIONS-FILE. We are using a single file switch called END-OF-FILE-REACHED for both files. After the listing for ACCOUNTS-FILE is generated, the file switch END-OF-FILE-REACHED will become "YES". Unless it is reset to "NO", the iterative PERFORM in line 000293 will not execute, since it is based on the same file switch. Therefore, before line 000293, END-OF-FILE-REACHED should be reset to "NO".

As an example of **dividing a numeric expression by zero**, consider the following COBOL code.

```
    . . . . . . . . . . . . . . . . . . . .
    . . . . . . . . . . . . . . . . . . .
    WORKING-STORAGE SECTION.
    . . . . . . . . . . . . . . . . . . .
    . . . . . . . . . . . . . . . . . . .
    01  TOTAL-TRANSACTIONS      PIC 9999   VALUE ZERO.
    01  NUMBER-OF-CUSTOMERS     PIC 9999   VALUE ZERO.
    01  AVG-TRANS-PER-CUSTOMERS PIC 999V99.
    . . . . . . . . . . . . . . . . . . .
    . . . . . . . . . . . . . . . . . . . .
    PROCEDURE DIVISION.
    A-MAIN-PARAGRAPH.
        OPEN INPUT   ACCOUNTS-FILE
             INPUT   CHECKING-TRANSACTIONS-FILE
             OUTPUT  TRANSACTIONS-REPORT.
        PERFORM B1-COMMON-TASKS.
        PERFORM B2-READ-ACCOUNTS-FILE.
        PERFORM B3-READ-TRANSACTIONS-FILE.

        PERFORM B4-MATCH-RECORDS
             UNTIL END-OF-ACCOUNTS-FILE.

        CLOSE ACCOUNTS-FILE
              CHECKING-TRANSACTIONS-FILE
              TRANSACTIONS-REPORT.

        COMPUTE AVG-TRANS-PER-CUSTOMER =
             TOTAL-TRANSACTIONS / NUMBER-OF-CUSTOMERS.

        STOP RUN.
    . . . . . . . . . . . . . . . . . . .
    . . . . . . . . . . . . . . . . . . .
```

In this variation of Program 1 in Chapter 5, we want to compute the average number of transactions per customer. To do this, the program can be designed such that every time a transaction record is read from the CHECKING-TRANSACTIONS-FILE, the identifier TOTAL-TRANSACTIONS is incremented by 1, and every time a record is accessed in the ACCOUNTS-FILE, 1 is added to the identifier NUMBER-OF-CUSTOMERS. The COMPUTE statement just before STOP RUN will compute a value for AVG-TRANS-PER-CUSTOMER, provided the ACCOUNTS-FILE is not empty. If this file is empty in a run, the COMPUTE statement will cause an abend due to division by zero.

Failure to properly delimit conditional clauses containing imperative statements: In some COBOL compilers, the imperative statements included in the AT END and INVALID KEY clauses of the READ statement and in the ON SIZE ERROR clause of the arithmetic statements are, in fact, imperative sentences. They may consist of one or more nonconditional statements, and hence must be properly delimited. For example, consider the following code.

```
. . . . . . . . . . . . . . . . . . .
   COMPUTE AVG-TRANS-PER-CUSTOMER =
         TOTAL-TRANSACTIONS / NUMBER-OF-CUSTOMERS
         ON SIZE ERROR
   DISPLAY "AVG-TRANS-PER-CUSTOMER INCORRECTLY COMPUTED."

   STOP RUN.
. . . . . . . . . . . . . . . . . .
. . . . . . . . . . . . . . . . . .
```

Here, the imperative sentence in the ON SIZE ERROR clause of the COMPUTE statement is interpreted by the compiler as consisting of the DISPLAY and STOP RUN statements. This may not be the programmer's intent, and thus may cause an error. The above code is written using the COBOL 74 conventions, which require that the imperative sentence be terminated by a period. In COBOL 85, the END-COMPUTE terminator could have been used for this purpose, as shown below.

```
. . . . . . . . . . . . . . . . . . .
. . . . . . . . . . . . . . . . . . .
   COMPUTE AVG-TRANS-PER-CUSTOMER =
         TOTAL-TRANSACTIONS / NUMBER-OF-CUSTOMERS
         ON SIZE ERROR
   DISPLAY "AVG-TRANS-PER-CUSTOMER INCORRECTLY COMPUTED."
   END-COMPUTE.

   STOP RUN.
. . . . . . . . . . . . . . . . . .
. . . . . . . . . . . . . . . . . .
```

Debugging Techniques and Tools for Execution Errors. Execution errors can be substantially more difficult to debug than compilation errors. Certain debugging tools exist, and based on them, we can specify debugging methodologies. Despite this, and the fact that debugging is a logical, systematic process, finding and correcting errors in a computer program is still more of an art than a science. An error may be indicated during program execution by the computer system, usually in the form of an abend and an accompanying diagnostic message. In such cases, it may be easy to determine the cause of the error. More often than not, however, an error is detected by its external manifestation in the output, and it may be difficult indeed to tie it to its cause in the program. In fact, the process may take hours and even days of frustrating hard work. In this respect, debugging is the mental process that associates the symptom of an error to its cause. It is much like solving a mystery, and people who enjoy reading and solving mystery stories make excellent program debuggers.

The purpose of debugging is to eliminate the error sources so that a program functions according to specifications. The best thing that can be done in this respect is to avoid, or at least minimize, errors during program design and development. That is one of the main reasons for modular program design and structured programming.

Earlier in this chapter we emphasized the importance of minimizing the debugging effort. Some of the techniques that were discussed there are also applicable to our discussion of program debugging for execution errors. To debug execution errors in a program, the following techniques and tools may be used:

1. Manual review of code
2. Program structure description techniques
3. Structured walk-throughs
4. DISPLAY/WRITE in the program
5. Automated debugging tools
   a. Debugging compilers
   b. Automatic debug features
   c. Storage dumps
   d. Automatic flow charters
   e. On-line debuggers
6. Group debugging
7. Recoding the program

Manual review of code: Usually, the first thing to do in debugging a program is review the source code manually. In desk-checking a program, we produce and use a listing of the input data and an output listing in addition to the source code listing. Also, in desk-checking, we examine the code from the point of view of common errors, such as those discussed in the previous section, and verify that they do not exist in our program.

Use of program structure description techniques: To uncover execution errors it is useful to generate flow charts, flow graphs, or pseudocodes corresponding to the source listing of the program in error. For example, while drawing a flow graph from a source listing, many errors of logic may become obvious and may be easily corrected.

Structured walk-throughs: A step-by-step tracing of the program code, especially when confined to a relatively small module of a program, may be extremely useful in revealing errors. Manual tracing of the execution starting at the point an error has occurred and going back in the program logic until one or more errors are diagnosed (called **backtracking**) can also be effective.

Use of DISPLAY/WRITE in the program: Another good debugging technique entails inserting some output statements (e.g., DISPLAY in COBOL) into the program at some critical points and executing the program with these statements. The inserted output statements may be used to produce a listing of values of some carefully chosen program variables at different stages in the program execution. This way, we are in fact tracing the execution of the program from the point of view of some preselected program variables. This technique provides valuable insight into the behavior of the code. The section that follows gives an example of program debugging using DISPLAY statements.

Use of automated debugging tools: Many different types of automated debugging tools may be used in program debugging, including

1. Debugging compilers
2. Automatic debug features
3. Storage dumps
4. Automatic flow charters
5. On-line debuggers

Debugging compilers are language compilers that check a program more thoroughly for errors than a regular compiler. In addition to verifying the correctness of each statement from a syntactical point of view, they check for syntax and semantic errors by examining statements in relation to other statements in the program, and may help uncover many different types of errors.

Automatic debug features are available in some languages in the form of special statements that facilitate debugging. The ANS COBOL has some standard debugging features. In addition, certain vendors enhance their versions of the COBOL compiler with a few nonstandard statements. The more common COBOL debugging features are discussed later in this chapter.

All COBOL compilers can produce storage dumps if requested by the programmer. Storage dumps are listings of the contents of a computer's internal memory that provide valuable information concerning the contents of program variables, how they are organized internally, and so on. They are in machine language format, however, usually expressed in hexadecimal notation. Ability to read storage dumps requires familiarity with the machine language of a particular computer system. Because of this difficulty, storage dumps are probably the last resort in debugging.

Automatic flow charters are software tools that generate flow charts from a source listing, thus freeing the programmer from the tedious task of manually constructing a flow chart. Careful examination of a flow chart may reveal the source of logical errors in the program.

Some software manufacturers supplement their COBOL compilers with on-line debugging tools that can be effective in program debugging. More is written on the capabilities of on-line debuggers for COBOL compilers later in this chapter.

Group debugging: Sometimes it is useful to ask the help of other programmers in program debugging. An error source that may have escaped you for a long time may be immediately obvious to somebody else. It has been found that when two or more programmers work to debug a program developed by one of them, the effort is substantially more effective than when the owner of the program works alone. This effectiveness is in terms of both programmer time and computer time.

Recoding the program: If debugging cannot be completed within a reasonably short time and with a reasonable amount of effort, it may be logical and feasible to drop that portion of the code that contains the elusive source of the error and recode it completely. If an equally efficient but somewhat different algorithm can be found for the procedure containing the error, on coding and incorporating it into the program, the original debugging problem may be eliminated.

An Example of Program Debugging for Execution Errors. Before we conclude our discussion of execution errors, let us consider an example and illustrate the use of the COBOL DISPLAY statement to debug execution errors. The example is again Program 1 in Chapter 5. Let us suppose that the programmer has omitted line 000288 in Program 1-Source in Chapter 5, which initializes the identifier WS-ITEM-COUNT to zero for each checking account customer. If we run the program with line 000288 missing, we get erroneous checking account statements with respect to the ITEMS ENCLOSED field on the statements (see Figure 8).

To debug the program, we identify some critical points in the code and insert DISPLAY statements at these points to allow us to trace the variation of WS-ITEM-COUNT. These critical points are

1. Immediately after line 000271 where the first ACCOUNTS-FILE and the first CHECKING-TRANSACTIONS-FILE records have been read for the first customer
2. After line 000321 where a customer's checking statement is fully completed
3. After line 000328 where a new customer's account record has just been read

The modified code is shown below.

```
                . . . . . . . . . . . . . . . . . . . .
                . . . . . . . . . . . . . . . . . . . .
000263     PROCEDURE DIVISION.
000264
000265     A-MAIN-PARAGRAPH.
                . . . . . . . . . . . . . . . . . . . .
                . . . . . . . . . . . . . . . . . . . .
000270         PERFORM B2-READ-ACCOUNTS-FILE.
000271         PERFORM B3-READ-TRANSACTIONS-FILE.
000272
000273         DISPLAY "TOTAL-ITEMS FOR ACCOUNT " WS-ACCOUNT-REC-NUMBER
000274                 " IS " WS-ITEM-COUNT " BEFORE PROCESSING.".
000275
000276         PERFORM B4-MATCH-RECORDS
000277             UNTIL END-OF-ACCOUNTS-FILE.
                . . . . . . . . . . . . . . . . . . . .
                . . . . . . . . . . . . . . . . . . . .
000288     B2-READ-ACCOUNTS-FILE.
000289         MOVE ZERO TO WS-TOTAL-CREDITS
000290                      WS-TOTAL-DEBITS
000291                      WS-INTEREST-EARNED
000292                      WS-CURRENT-BALANCE
000293                      WS-MINIMUM-BALANCE.
                . . . . . . . . . . . . . . . . . . . .
                . . . . . . . . . . . . . . . . . . . .
000310     B4-MATCH-RECORDS.
000311         IF WS-ACCOUNT-REC-NUMBER = WS-TRANS-REC-NUMBER
000312             PERFORM C3-MOVE-ADDRESS
000313             PERFORM C4-PRINT-PART-1
000314             PERFORM C5-PRINT-PART-2-TITLE
000315             MOVE AF-BALANCE-FROM-LAST-MONTH TO WS-MINIMUM-BALANCE
000316             MOVE AF-BALANCE-FROM-LAST-MONTH TO WS-CURRENT-BALANCE
000317
000318             PERFORM C6-PROCESS-TRANSACTIONS
000319                 UNTIL WS-ACCOUNT-REC-NUMBER NOT = WS-TRANS-REC-NUMBER
000320
000321             PERFORM C7-COMPLETE-STATEMENT.
```

```
000322
000323          DISPLAY "TOTAL-ITEMS FOR ACCOUNT " WS-ACCOUNT-REC-NUMBER
000324              " IS " WS-ITEM-COUNT " AFTER PROCESSING.".
000325
000326          PERFORM B2-READ-ACCOUNTS-FILE.
000327
000328          IF NOT END-OF-ACCOUNTS-FILE
000329              DISPLAY "TOTAL-ITEMS FOR ACCOUNT " WS-ACCOUNT-REC-NUMBER
000330                  " IS " WS-ITEM-COUNT " BEFORE PROCESSING.".
000331
                .....................
                .....................
```

If we run the program with these DISPLAY insertions, we get the following output on the terminal screen.

```
TOTAL-ITEMS FOR ACCOUNT 1544 IS     BEFORE PROCESSING.
TOTAL-ITEMS FOR ACCOUNT 1544 IS 003 AFTER PROCESSING.
TOTAL-ITEMS FOR ACCOUNT 1560 IS 003 BEFORE PROCESSING.
TOTAL-ITEMS FOR ACCOUNT 1560 IS 004 AFTER PROCESSING.
TOTAL-ITEMS FOR ACCOUNT 1600 IS 004 BEFORE PROCESSING.
TOTAL-ITEMS FOR ACCOUNT 1600 IS 006 AFTER PROCESSING.
```

This leads us to several observations.

1. The identifier WS-ITEM-COUNT has an initial value of spaces for the first customer.
2. Its computed value is correct for the first customer.
3. It is not reset to zero for the second and third customers.

We can easily conclude that this error is due to our failure to initialize and reset WS-ITEM-COUNT to zero. If we do that, the code becomes the same as that given in Program 1-Source in Chapter 5. Now we can get rid of the unneeded DISPLAY statements in the program.

REVIEW QUESTIONS

1. Which of the following error types is not a software error?
   a. Design
   b. Programming
   c. External
   d. Communication
2. Compilation errors are due to violations of the syntax and certain semantic rules of the programming language used in writing a program. (T or F)
3. To minimize program debugging efforts, we may use program structure description techniques. (T or F)
4. Examining a program source code in view of a carefully selected sample data set to ensure that it does what it is supposed to do correctly is known as _____ .
5. An error diagnostic message consists of a source program line identification number, an error message code, and an error message text. (T or F)

6. Which of the following is not a COBOL compilation error message type?
   a. Warning
   b. Division by zero
   c. Severe
   d. Terminating
7. If the compiler decides that a default adjustment can be made for an error during compilation, it will produce an _____ diagnostic message.
8. If the compiler comes across a rule violation for which no automatic correction can be made during compilation, it produces a terminating error diagnostic. (T or F)
9. In general, if a statement contains more than one rule violation, the COBOL compiler may correctly identify them all and produce appropriate error diagnostics. (T or F)
10. All execution errors result in a program abend. (T or F)
11. Which of the following is not a technique or a tool that can be used to debug execution errors in a program?
    a. Structured walk-throughs
    b. Optimizing compilers
    c. Flow graphs
    d. Memory dumps

Answers: 1. d; 2. T; 3. T; 4. structured walk-through; 5. T; 6. b; 7. error; 8. F; 9. F; 10. F; 11. b.

COBOL Automated Debugging Tools

In general, several debugging tools are supported by COBOL compilers, and their variety and nature depend on a specific vendor's product. Only a few of them are standard. In this section we attempt to provide the reader with an overview of these tools. In practical situations, they depend on their availability and the programmer's preference. For further detail on each automated tool, the reader is referred to the manufacturer's manuals.

The COBOL automated debugging tools can be classified as follows:

1. Language features designed to facilitate debugging, including
   a. DISPLAY statement
   b. EXHIBIT statement
   c. TRACE statement
   d. USE FOR DEBUGGING declaratives
   e. USE EXCEPTION/ERROR declaratives
   f. Debugging lines
2. Compiler debugging facilities
3. Special on-line debugging tools

In our previous discussion we demonstrated how the DISPLAY statement can be used to debug execution errors. In the following sections we discuss the others.

EXHIBIT Statement

The EXHIBIT statement is not an ANS standard COBOL feature but is supported by some COBOL compilers. From a functional point of view, the EXHIBIT statement is similar to the DISPLAY statement. It is used to print values stored in some program identifiers. It is placed at critical points in a program to trace the variation of selected program identifiers. The syntax of the EXHIBIT statement is shown here.

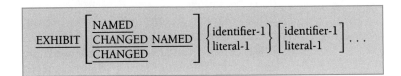

The following are some examples.

```
EXHIBIT WS-ITEM-COUNT WS-CURRENT-BALANCE.
```

This statement will print the values currently available in the memory location allocated to the variables WS-ITEM-COUNT and WS-CURRENT-BALANCE. These will become part of a printed output file generated by the program. As the printed lines produced by the EXHIBIT statement are included in a regular printed output, it may be desirable to identify them. The following variation is useful for this purpose.

```
EXHIBIT NAMED WS-ITEM-COUNT.
```

This statement will produce a printed line such as

```
WS-ITEM-COUNT = 006
```

that associates the value printed with the name of the identifier.

Sometimes we may want the EXHIBIT statement to be executed only if the identifier value it references actually is altered by the program. This conditional printing of identifier values is achieved by including the key word CHANGED in its syntax.

```
EXHIBIT CHANGED WS-ITEM-COUNT.
```

```
EXHIBIT CHANGED NAMED WS-ITEM-COUNT.
```

TRACE Statement

This nonstandard debugging feature is useful if we want to trace the actual path of a COBOL program in terms of the paragraph names encountered during its execution. To start a path trace, we include in the PROCEDURE DIVISION of our program the statement

```
READY TRACE
```

This statement will cause the compiler to produce a listing of the paragraph names encountered during execution until one of the following takes place.

1. A STOP RUN statement is encountered.
2. A RESET TRACE statement is encountered.
3. A program abend occurs before the trace is terminated.

As an example, consider the A-MAIN-PARAGRAPH procedure of Program 1 in Chapter 5. Suppose we insert a READY TRACE statement after line 000268 and a RESET TRACE statement after line 000315.

```
          . . . . . . . . . . . . . . . . . . . . . .
000265    A-MAIN-PARAGRAPH.
000266        OPEN INPUT  ACCOUNTS-FILE
000267            INPUT  CHECKING-TRANSACTIONS-FILE
000268            OUTPUT TRANSACTIONS-REPORT.
          READY TRACE.
000269        PERFORM B1-COMMON-TASKS.
000270        PERFORM B2-READ-ACCOUNTS-FILE.
000271        PERFORM B3-READ-TRANSACTIONS-FILE.
000272
000273        PERFORM B4-MATCH-RECORDS
000274            UNTIL END-OF-ACCOUNTS-FILE.
000275
000276        CLOSE ACCOUNTS-FILE
000277            CHECKING-TRANSACTIONS-FILE
000278            TRANSACTIONS-REPORT.
000279        STOP RUN.
000280
          . . . . . . . . . . . . . . . . . . . . . .
          . . . . . . . . . . . . . . . . . . . . . .
000308    B4-MATCH-RECORDS.
000309        IF WS-ACCOUNT-REC-NUMBER = WS-TRANS-REC-NUMBER
000310            PERFORM C3-MOVE-ADDRESS
000311            PERFORM C4-PRINT-PART-1
000312            PERFORM C5-PRINT-PART-2-TITLE
000313            MOVE AF-BALANCE-FROM-LAST-MONTH TO WS-MINIMUM-BALANCE
000314            MOVE AF-BALANCE-FROM-LAST-MONTH TO WS-CURRENT-BALANCE
000315
          RESET TRACE
000316            PERFORM C6-PROCESS-TRANSACTIONS
000317                UNTIL WS-ACCOUNT-REC-NUMBER NOT = WS-TRANS-REC-NUMBER
000318
000319            PERFORM C7-COMPLETE-STATEMENT.
000320
000321        PERFORM B2-READ-ACCOUNTS-FILE.
          . . . . . . . . . . . . . . . . . . . . . .
```

If there is no error in the program to cause program termination, the compiler will generate a printout of paragraph names.

```
B1-COMMON-TASKS
C1-TERMINAL-INPUTS
C2-MOVE-DATES
B2-READ-ACCOUNTS-FILE
B3-READ-TRANSACTIONS-FILE
B4-MATCH-RECORDS
C3-MOVE-ADDRESS
C4-PRINT-PART-1
C5-PRINT-PART-2-TITLE
```

As can be seen, the TRACE feature can be useful in pinpointing the paragraph where a statement causes an abnormal termination of program execution.

USE FOR DEBUGGING Declaratives

USE FOR DEBUGGING is a special COBOL statement that can be used in conjunction with DECLARATIVES, the compile-time switch, and the object-time switch. These constitute an automated debugging tool that was a standard for COBOL 74, but is marked obsolete in COBOL 85. This means that it will be discontinued and deleted from the language in its next revision. As it still exists, however, we discuss it briefly here.

To debug a program using this feature, we must

1. Include in the source program a compile-time switch
2. Include in the PROCEDURE DIVISION of the program a DECLARATIVES block
3. Include in the DECLARATIVES block a USE FOR DEBUGGING statement and some appropriate paragraphs to be executed for debugging purposes
4. Activate the object-time switch so that the debugging feature can be executed

Compile-Time Switch. The statements included in a program for debugging purposes are needed until the errors are detected and corrected. After that, they should be removed from the program, and the program should be recompiled. To avoid this, a compile-time switch is activated by the SOURCE-COMPUTER paragraph of the CONFIGURATION SECTION in the ENVIRONMENT DIVISION, and this is done through the use of the WITH DEBUGGING MODE clause. An example is given below.

```
SOURCE-COMPUTER. UNIVERSITY-MAINFRAME WITH DEBUGGING MODE.
```

With this compile-time switch activated, all program statements, including those that are specifically for debugging purposes, are compiled.

DECLARATIVES Section. After activating the compile-time switch, we should include in the PROCEDURE DIVISION a DECLARATIVES block. The purpose of the DECLARATIVES block in a COBOL program is to specify procedures that are to be executed under special circumstances. Three special circumstances require the use of a DECLARATIVES block: debugging, input-output errors, and use of the COBOL Report Writer feature. DECLARATIVES for debugging and input-output errors are discussed in this chapter. The use of DECLARATIVES for COBOL Report Writer can be found in Appendix D. In general, the DECLARATIVES block has the following structure.

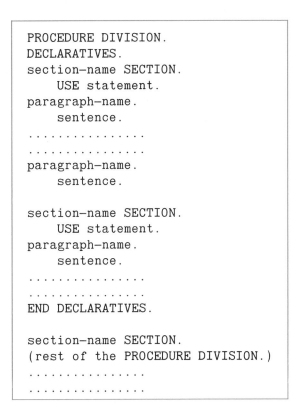

```
PROCEDURE DIVISION.
DECLARATIVES.
section-name SECTION.
    USE statement.
paragraph-name.
    sentence.
. . . . . . . . . . . . . . .
. . . . . . . . . . . . . . .
paragraph-name.
    sentence.

section-name SECTION.
    USE statement.
paragraph-name.
    sentence.
. . . . . . . . . . . . . . .
. . . . . . . . . . . . . . .
END DECLARATIVES.

section-name SECTION.
(rest of the PROCEDURE DIVISION.)
. . . . . . . . . . . . . . .
. . . . . . . . . . . . . . .
```

Applicable Rules for the DECLARATIVES Block

1. Immediately after the PROCEDURE DIVISION header, starting at the A margin, we must write the key word DECLARATIVES.
2. This should be followed by a section header containing a user-defined section name.
3. The first statement after the section header is an appropriate USE statement that specifies the special conditions under which the DECLARATIVES block is to be executed. The USE statement must be terminated by a period.
4. The rest of the block may have any number of paragraphs that are to be executed if the condition implied by the USE statement arises during program execution.
5. There may be any number of such declaratives within a DECLARATIVES block.
6. The DECLARATIVES block is terminated with the key words END DECLARATIVES, followed by a period.
7. After the DECLARATIVES block, the rest of the PROCEDURE DIVISION is written. Some compilers require that the remaining code in the PROCEDURE DIVISION be defined as a section.
8. A declarative procedure may call on other declarative procedures using the PERFORM statement. However, it is illegal to invoke a procedure that is outside a declarative procedure from a point inside it, or to call on a declarative procedure from a point that is outside the DECLARATIVES block.

As mentioned, the condition under which a declarative procedure is executed is defined by the USE statement in it. In the following discussion we examine the USE FOR DEBUGGING form of the USE statement.

USE FOR DEBUGGING Statement. This statement defines the declarative block in which it is placed as the one to be executed for debugging purposes. It has the following syntax.

$$
\underline{\text{USE}} \text{ FOR } \underline{\text{DEBUGGING}} \text{ ON}
\begin{Bmatrix}
\text{cd-name} \\
[\ \underline{\text{ALL REFERENCES OF}}\ ]\ \text{identifier} \\
\text{file-name} \\
\text{procedure-name} \\
\underline{\text{ALL}}\ \underline{\text{PROCEDURES}}
\end{Bmatrix} \dots
$$

To understand how the USE statement interacts with the COBOL debugging feature, we should note that a special record description, called DEBUG-ITEM, is automatically inserted into the object code by the COBOL compiler when it detects the USE FOR DEBUGGING statement. The structure of the DEBUG-ITEM, which should not be defined by the programmer, is given below.

```
01   DEBUG-ITEM.
     05   DEBUG-LINE              PIC X(6).
     05   FILLER                  PIC X(1)    VALUE SPACES.
     05   DEBUG-NAME              PIC X(30).
     05   FILLER                  PIC X(1)    VALUE SPACES.
     05   DEBUG-SUB-1             PIC 9(4).
     05   FILLER                  PIC X(1)    VALUE SPACES.
     05   DEBUG-SUB-2             PIC 9(4).
     05   FILLER                  PIC X(1)    VALUE SPACES.
     05   DEBUG-SUB-3             PIC 9(4).
     05   FILLER                  PIC X(1)    VALUE SPACES.
     05   DEBUG-CONTENTS          PIC X(nn).
```

The fields DEBUG-SUB-1, DEBUG-SUB-2, and DEBUG-SUB-3 are used to store the subscript value of an identifier, if the identifier is an array name. This identifier is specified in the USE FOR DEBUGGING statement. If the statement does not contain an identifier, or if it is not an array name, these fields contain blanks.

On the other hand, the contents of the fields DEBUG-LINE, DEBUG-NAME, and DEBUG-CONTENTS depend on what follows the key word ON in the USE FOR DEBUGGING statement. As is seen from its syntax, this may be an identifier, a file name, or a procedure. In this regard, the following rules apply.

1. If the USE FOR DEBUGGING statement references an identifier,
   a. DEBUG-LINE stores the source statement line number containing the identifier.
   b. DEBUG-NAME contains the data name of the identifier.
   c. DEBUG-CONTENTS contains the value of the identifier after the statement in which it appears is executed.
2. If the USE FOR DEBUGGING statement references a file name,
   a. DEBUG-LINE contains the source statement line number referencing the file name.
   b. DEBUG-NAME contains the name of the file.
   c. DEBUG-CONTENTS stores spaces for OPEN and CLOSE statements, and the contents of the input record occurrence for READ statements.

3. If the USE FOR DEBUGGING statement references a procedure,
   a. DEBUG-LINE stores the source statement line number before the procedure name if the procedure name is encountered sequentially. If the procedure name is encountered by branching, this field contains the line number of the source statement that causes the branching.
   b. DEBUG-NAME contains the name of the procedure.
   c. DEBUG-CONTENTS stores spaces if the procedure name is encountered by branching, or the literal FALL THROUGH if it is encountered sequentially.

Now we can give some examples to demonstrate the function of the USE FOR DEBUGGING statement.

Example 1   We again consider Program 1 in Chapter 5. Suppose we observe that the variable WS-ITEM-COUNT is being computed incorrectly and we want to trace its variation. We add the following DECLARATIVES block to the PROCEDURE DIVISION.

```
...............
...............
PROCEDURE DIVISION.
DECLARATIVES.

ERROR-DEBUG SECTION.

    USE FOR DEBUGGING ON ALL REFERENCES OF WS-ITEM-COUNT.

PRINT-DEBUG-INFO.

    DISPLAY DEBUG-ITEM.

END DECLARATIVES.

MAIN-PROGRAM SECTION.
A-MAIN-PARAGRAPH.
...............
...............
```

The USE FOR DEBUGGING statement is the first statement in the section called ERROR-DEBUG. After it is a paragraph, PRINT-DEBUG-INFO, which is the procedure to be executed for debugging purposes. It merely displays the content of DEBUG-ITEM that is described above. In general, the procedure after the USE FOR DEBUGGING statement may consist of any number of paragraphs written by the programmer to facilitate debugging. In this example, during program execution, every time a statement containing the variable WS-ITEM-COUNT is encountered, the USE FOR DEBUGGING statement invokes the procedure after it (i.e., the paragraph PRINT-DEBUG-INFO). After this, the program control returns to the point immediately after the statement at which the debug feature took over. For Program 1 in Chapter 5 and the input data of Program 1-Input in Chapter 5, this example will produce the following sequence of DEBUG-ITEM occurrences.

```
000286 WS-ITEM-COUNT    000
000421 WS-ITEM-COUNT    001
000421 WS-ITEM-COUNT    002
000421 WS-ITEM-COUNT    003
000286 WS-ITEM-COUNT    000
000421 WS-ITEM-COUNT    001
000286 WS-ITEM-COUNT    000
000421 WS-ITEM-COUNT    001
000421 WS-ITEM-COUNT    002
```

Once again, we stress the fact that the USE FOR DEBUGGING statement specifies the user-defined procedures to be performed when a debugging-related condition is satisfied during program execution. The USE FOR DEBUGGING statement itself is not an executable statement; it is part of the declaratives in the DECLARATIVES block.

Example 2 The following partial code has a USE FOR DEBUGGING statement that specifies the debugging condition in relation to one of the files in the program (i.e., ACCOUNTS-FILE). During program execution, whenever a statement referencing the ACCOUNTS-FILE is encountered, the execution is temporarily interrupted until the procedure in the DECLARATIVES block defined by the USE FOR DEBUGGING statement is performed. In general, the statements in which a file is referenced by its name are OPEN, READ, DELETE, START, and CLOSE.

```
   . . . . . . . . . . . . . . .
   . . . . . . . . . . . . . . .
   DECLARATIVES.

   ERROR-DEBUG SECTION.

       USE FOR DEBUGGING ON ACCOUNTS-FILE.
   . . . . . . . . . . . . . . .
   . . . . . . . . . . . . . . .
```

Example 3 If we want to monitor the execution of a particular procedure in the program, say, the paragraph B4-MATCH-RECORDS, the USE FOR DEBUGGING statement is written as

```
   . . . . . . . . . . . . . . .
   . . . . . . . . . . . . . . .
   DECLARATIVES.

   ERROR-DEBUG SECTION.

       USE FOR DEBUGGING ON PROCEDURE B4-MATCH-RECORDS.
   . . . . . . . . . . . . . . .
   . . . . . . . . . . . . . . .
```

Example 4   In case we would like to see the sequence in which all of the procedures in our program are executed, we use the ALL PROCEDURES option with the USE FOR DEBUGGING statement.

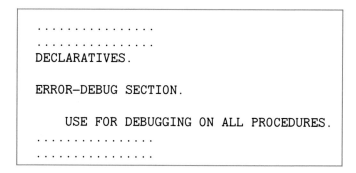

```
          . . . . . . . . . . . . . . .
          . . . . . . . . . . . . . . .
     DECLARATIVES.

     ERROR—DEBUG SECTION.

          USE FOR DEBUGGING ON ALL PROCEDURES.
          . . . . . . . . . . . . . . .
          . . . . . . . . . . . . . . .
```

Object-Time Switch. Even when we compile a program with some debugging-oriented procedures using the USE FOR DEBUGGING statement, we may wish to suppress their execution at run time. To enable dynamic control of the execution of debugging procedures, we make use of an object-time switch. The switch is set on or off by job control language statements. As JCLs are system-specific, the reader is advised to consult the manufacturer's manuals for correct syntax and usage. When the object-time switch is on, the debug procedures defined in a DECLARATIVES block are executed; otherwise, their execution is suppressed.

USE EXCEPTION/ERROR Declaratives

During program debugging for execution errors we may conclude that the error is due to an input-output procedure in the program. In such a case the USE EXCEPTION/ERROR declarative may be effective.

The DECLARATIVES block to be specified for I-O error debugging resembles that used for USE FOR DEBUGGING statement, with two differences.

1. The USE statement should be a USE EXCEPTION/ERROR statement.
2. The user-defined procedures in the DECLARATIVES block after the USE EXCEPTION/ERROR statement should be appropriate to the present situation.

The syntax of the USE EXCEPTION/ERROR statement is given below.

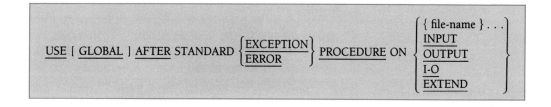

USE [GLOBAL] AFTER STANDARD { EXCEPTION / ERROR } PROCEDURE ON { { file-name } . . . / INPUT / OUTPUT / I-O / EXTEND }

Some examples of the USE EXCEPTION/ERROR statement follow.

```
* EXAMPLE 1:
     USE AFTER STANDARD ERROR PROCEDURE ON ACCOUNTS-FILE.

* EXAMPLE 2:
     USE AFTER ERROR PROCEDURE ON INPUT.

* EXAMPLE 3:
     USE AFTER STANDARD EXCEPTION PROCEDURE ON OUTPUT.
```

The USE statement in example 1 causes the subsequent user-defined procedures to be executed if an input-output error occurs during the processing of the ACCOUNTS-FILE. The USE statements in examples 2 and 3 trigger the execution of the user-defined procedures in the DECLARATIVES block if input and output errors, respectively, occur in I-O operations on any one of the files in the program.

Important Rules for the USE ERROR/EXCEPTION Statement

1. The USE EXCEPTION/ERROR declaratives are activated when an I-O error occurs during the execution of the READ, WRITE, DELETE, REWRITE, or START statement.
2. Attempts to reopen a file that is already open will cause activation of the USE EXCEPTION/ERROR declaratives. If the file has not been opened in the program, however, the declarative will not be activated.
3. If a file is currently closed and a CLOSE statement is issued, the EXCEPTION/ERROR declarative will not be executed. For an open file, if the execution of an input-output statement, including a CLOSE statement, is unsuccessful, this declarative will be activated.
4. The key words ERROR and EXCEPTION are synonymous, and either one may be chosen to the same effect.
5. If an I-O error occurs due to an input-output statement in which an AT END or an INVALID KEY clause has been specified, upon an error, control is transferred to the statement after the AT END or INVALID KEY phrase. In such a situation, the USE EXCEPTION/ERROR declarative is not executed.

Debugging Lines

As an alternative to the USE FOR DEBUGGING declaratives, some COBOL compilers offer a nonstandard feature called debugging lines. A **debugging line** is a statement included in the source program by the programmer to be used exclusively for debugging purposes, and is thus identified in the source code. It is identified by a D in column 7 of a COBOL source line. An example follows.

```
        ........................
        ........................
000410     C6-PROCESS-TRANSACTIONS.

        D     DISPLAY "PARAGRAPH C6-PROCESS-TRANSACTIONS ENTERED.".

000411        IF CF-TRANSACTION-TYPE = "D"
000412           ADD CF-TRANSACTION-AMOUNT TO WS-CURRENT-BALANCE
000413           MOVE "+ " TO OUT-TRANSACTION-SIGN
000414           ADD CF-TRANSACTION-AMOUNT TO WS-TOTAL-CREDITS
000415        ELSE
000416           SUBTRACT CF-TRANSACTION-AMOUNT FROM WS-CURRENT-BALANCE
000417           MOVE "  " TO OUT-TRANSACTION-SIGN
000418           ADD CF-TRANSACTION-AMOUNT TO WS-TOTAL-DEBITS.
000419
000420        IF CF-TRANSACTION-TYPE = "C"
000421           ADD 1 TO WS-ITEM-COUNT.

        D     IF CF-TRANSACTION-TYPE = "C"
        D        DISPLAY "VALUE OF WS-ITEM-COUNT IS: " WS-ITEM-COUNT.
        ........................
        ........................
```

If the debugging lines marked by Ds in column 7 are included in the object code, it is possible to trace the execution of the procedure C6-PROCESS-TRANSACTIONS and the variation of the identifier WS-ITEM-COUNT.

Rules for Debugging Lines

1. Debugging lines are compiled together with the rest of the code if the compile-time switch is on. Otherwise, they are considered as program comments.
2. Debugging lines, once compiled, are executed at run-time together with the rest of the code, and their execution cannot be controlled by an object-time switch.
3. Debugging lines can be used to trace the variation of program identifiers or procedures in a program.
4. Debugging lines can be included anywhere below the compile-time switch (i.e., the SOURCE-COMPUTER paragraph of the ENVIRONMENT DIVISION) in the ENVIRONMENT, DATA, and PROCEDURE DIVISIONs of a program.

Special Compiler Debugging Facilities

Some COBOL compilers offer several options that may be specified during program compilation to help debug compilation and execution errors. These options depend on the individual compilers, and for details the reader should consult technical manuals provided by the vendor. Typically, such options can be used to

1. Specify where the syntax error messages will appear in the source listing (either at the end of the source listing or embedded in it)
2. Determine whether or not the source statements are out of sequence

3. Tell the compiler to generate a cross-reference listing of variable names and procedure names
4. Instruct the compiler to produce a listing of items defined in the DATA DIVISION
5. Request a storage dump, and so on

On-Line Debug Tools

As mentioned earlier in this chapter, the only ANS standard COBOL language debugging tool, USE FOR DEBUGGING declaratives, has been declared obsolete and will be eventually deleted from the language. This is an indication of a trend to externalize automated debugging tools from the language. As a logical outcome of this trend, some manufacturers have introduced on-line debugging tools for their COBOL compilers. The interactive debugging tool by IBM, called COBTEST, is one such product.

Although their use entails additional study on the part of the user to become familiar with their features, on-line debugging tools are quite versatile and useful. A detailed discussion of a particular tool is outside the scope of this text; however, this is a partial listing of their capabilities.

1. Display contents of program variables and arrays.
2. Establish break points at COBOL statements in the program, and suspend program execution at such points.
3. Resume program execution after suspensions at break points.
4. Follow the execution progress in a step-by-step fashion.
5. Trace control transfers during execution.
6. Determine how far the program has gone before an abend occurs.
7. Count the number of times a statement has been executed in the program.
8. Test subroutines individually by simulating the behavior of the main program and blocking transfers to the subordinate modules.

REVIEW QUESTIONS

1. The COBOL automated debugging tools are used to debug compilation errors. (T or F)
2. USE FOR DEBUGGING declaratives are one of the COBOL compiler debugging facilities. (T or F)
3. Functionally, the EXHIBIT statement is similar to the COBOL _____ statement.
4. The CHANGED version of the EXHIBIT statement is executed only if the identifier value in it is actually altered by the program. (T or F)
5. To debug a program using the USE FOR DEBUGGING declaratives, we must include in the program an object-time switch. (T or F)
6. The WITH DEBUGGING MODE clause in the SOURCE-COMPUTER paragraph activates a _____ .
7. A DECLARATIVES block is needed for
   a. Debugging
   b. Input-output errors
   c. The COBOL Report Writer feature
   d. All of the above
8. Debugging lines can be used to trace the variation of program variables or procedures in a program. (T or F)

Answers: 1. F; 2. F; 3. DISPLAY; 4. T; 5. F; 6. compile-time switch; 7. d; 8. T.

Key Terms

acceptance testing
automated debugging
automated testing
compilation error
compile-time switch
debugging
debugging line
DECLARATIVES
design error
DISPLAY
error diagnostics
execution error
EXHIBIT
external error
flow graph
functional testing
group debugging

informal testing
integration testing
object-time switch
program testing
program validation
program verification
programming error
severe error diagnostics
structural testing
system testing
terminating error diagnostics
testing error
TRACE
unit testing
USE EXCEPTION/ERROR
USE FOR DEBUGGING
warning diagnostics

Study Guide

Quick Scan

- Two of the most important characteristics of a computer program are reliability and correctness.
- Software testing is an activity that aims to ascertain software reliability.
- Verification is concerned with program correctness at all phases of its life cycle. Validation is concerned with the correctness of the end product, i.e., the completed program.
- Testing is the process of executing a program for the purpose of demonstrating its correctness.
- Debugging is the activity of identifying the source of errors in a program and modifying the program to eliminate these errors.
- Verification, validation, testing, and debugging are closely related activities. They share the common objective of ensuring software reliability.
- Instead of testing, one may try to prove program correctness formally. This is difficult, however, and few techniques have been developed for this purpose. Therefore, we use approximate testing techniques.
- There are four program testing categories: structural, functional, automated, and informal.
- In structural testing (also known as white box testing) the structure of the procedural design of the program is verified. For this, test cases are designed to guarantee traversal of all logical paths within the program at least once.
- To determine all independent logical paths in a program, it is useful to draw a flow graph. This is similar to a flow chart, except in a flow graph we disregard details of operations in the program and emphasize its flow of control.
- In functional testing (also known as black box testing) we concentrate on the functions a program is expected to perform, and disregard its logical structure.
- In automated testing, we use automated software testing tools that substantially reduce the time it takes to test programs. Data flow analyzers, output comparators, test data generators, and code auditors are examples of automated testing tools.

- Informal testing is based on some heuristics and the programmer's instincts. Desk-checking a program for correctness and running it with a limited number of test cases constitute the basis of informal testing.
- Four steps are involved in software testing: unit testing, integration testing, system testing, and acceptance testing.
- In unit testing, we apply structural testing to every program module that makes up the software system.
- Integration testing is also structural testing, but it is performed on groups of modules to verify that they function correctly as a group and that module interfaces are correct. Integration testing can be top-down or bottom-up, or both approaches can be mixed for large software systems.
- In system testing, we try to verify that the entire software system is functionally correct. Therefore, it is black box testing on the full program. Acceptance testing is system testing with live data.
- After software testing, if errors are uncovered, we debug a program. There are several types of software errors: design, programming, testing, and external. We are mainly concerned with programming errors in this book.
- Programming errors can be diagnosed during program compilation and during or after program execution. Accordingly, they are called compilation and execution errors.
- Compilation errors occur due to violations of the syntax and semantic rules of the programming language. They are detected by the compiler at compile-time. Execution errors occur due to logic mistakes or errors in input data. They may cause abnormal program termination at run-time, or be manifested as unexpected or incorrect program output.
- Examination of program structure represented in the form of flow charts, flow graphs, pseudocodes, manual review of program code, and structured walk-throughs are some techniques that can be used to detect and correct potential programming errors, or at least to minimize them.
- Compilation errors are easily debugged using the compiler-generated error diagnostics. Compilation error diagnostic messages may be one of the following types: warning, error, severe, and terminating. It is a good programming habit to correct and eliminate all types.
- Execution errors are generally more difficult to debug than compilation errors. Several techniques and tools can be used to debug them: manual review of code, program structure description techniques, structured walk-throughs, DISPLAY statements in the program, automated debugging tools, group debugging, and recoding the program.
- Some automated debugging tools can be used in COBOL programming. These emerge in the form of COBOL language features, compiler debugging facilities, and special on-line debug tools.
- The COBOL language features that can be used for debugging execution errors are the DISPLAY statement, the nonstandard EXHIBIT and TRACE statements, USE FOR DEBUGGING and USE EXCEPTION/ERROR declaratives, and debugging lines.
- Some special compiler options can be used to obtain storage dumps, cross-reference tables and DATA DIVISION item lists, and so on. They may be useful for debugging evasive execution errors.
- The current trend in automated debugging tools for COBOL programming is to externalize such tools from the language. Some on-line debugging tools exist for COBOL. These may be used to trace the variation of program identifiers, to follow the program execution in a step-by-step fashion, to trace control transfers during execution, and so on.

Test Your Comprehension

Multiple-Choice Questions

1. Which of the following statements concerning program testing is incorrect?
   a. Functional testing is concerned with the functions a program is expected to perform.
   b. Functional testing is also known as black box testing.
   c. In informal testing we concentrate on verifying the structure of the procedural design of a program.
   d. A flow graph is a useful tool in structural testing.
2. Which of the following statements about software errors is correct?
   a. A compilation error is a type of design error.
   b. Errors caused by erroneous data for a program constitute a form of programming error.
   c. Constructing an improper algorithm for a method of solution is a form of design error.
   d. Errors in hardware are a form of external error.
3. Which of the following errors is a COBOL compilation error message type?
   a. Failure to initialize numeric variables
   b. Error
   c. Allowing nonnumeric values in numeric fields
   d. Division by zero
4. Which of the following is not an automated debugging tool for debugging execution errors?
   a. Flow graphs
   b. Automatic flow charters
   c. On-line debuggers
   d. Debugging compilers
5. Which of the following incorrectly completes this statement? The READY TRACE statement will cause the compiler to produce a listing of the executed paragraphs until
   a. An EXIT statement is encountered
   b. A STOP RUN statement is encountered
   c. A RESET TRACE statement is encountered
   d. A program abend occurs
6. To debug a program using the USE FOR DEBUGGING declaratives, we must include in the program
   a. A compile-time switch
   b. A DECLARATIVES section
   c. A USE FOR DEBUGGING statement and some paragraphs to be executed for debugging purposes in the DECLARATIVES section
   d. All of the above
7. If the USE FOR DEBUGGING statement references an identifier, the DEBUG-NAME field contains
   a. The name of that identifier
   b. The file name in which the identifier is an element
   c. The procedure name in which the identifier is used
   d. None of the above
8. Which of the following rules about debugging lines is correct?
   a. They are compiled with the rest of the program if the compile-time switch is on. Otherwise, they are considered program comments.
   b. Their execution cannot be controlled by an object-time switch.
   c. They can be used to trace the variation of program identifiers or procedures in a program.
   d. All of the above are correct.

Answers: 1. c; 2. c; 3. b; 4. a; 5. a; 6. d; 7. a; 8. d.

Short Essay Questions

1. Briefly explain why reliability is one of the most important properties of software.
2. Define the concepts of program verification and program validation, and explain their difference.
3. What is meant by program testing? How does testing relate to program debugging?
4. Explain why formal proofs of program correctness cannot be used in lieu of program testing.
5. How do we classify program testing techniques?
6. Explain the differences between structural and functional testing.
7. What is a flow graph? Why is it useful in program testing?
8. Give at least two examples of automated testing tools and describe their functions.
9. What is meant by informal program testing?
10. Explain the differences between unit testing and integration testing.
11. Briefly explain top-down and bottom-up integration testing strategies.
12. How do we classify software errors?
13. Explain the differences between design errors and programming errors.
14. Explain the techniques commonly used to minimize debugging efforts.
15. What are the components of a typical compiler-generated diagnostic message?
16. Explain the difference between an error diagnostic message and a severe error diagnostic message.
17. Briefly discuss some of the common execution errors in COBOL programming.
18. What are the techniques and tools that may be used to debug execution errors?
19. Briefly explain the functions of the following automated debugging tools:
    a. Debugging compilers
    b. Storage dumps
    c. On-line debuggers
20. Explain why group debugging can be an effective debugging technique.
21. Briefly explain how you would use the COBOL DISPLAY or EXHIBIT statements to debug execution errors.
22. What are the programming requirements for using the USE FOR DEBUGGING declaratives in a COBOL program?
23. Differentiate between the compile-time switch and the object-time switch.
24. Explain when the USE EXCEPTION/ERROR declaratives in COBOL can be used as a debugging tool.
25. What is a debugging line in COBOL? How do we use these lines?
26. Explain the difference between special compiler debugging features and on-line debug tools.

Improve Your Problem-Solving Ability

Debugging Exercises

Examine the COBOL program segments given below in problems 1–6, and for each case identify the compilation errors, if any. Explain your reasoning.

1. ```
   B1-PRINT-TITLE-AND-DATE-LINES.
       MOVE REPORT-TITLE-LINE TO REPORT-LINE.
       WRITE REPORT-LINE AFTER PAGE.
       ACCEPT TODAYS-DATE FROM DATE.
       COMPUTE YEAR = TODAYS - YEAR + 1900
       MOVE YEAR TO REPORT-YEAR.
       MOVE TODAYS-DAY TO REPORT-DAY.
   ```
   ```

```
2. 01   SEARCH-FLAG                      PIC 9.
        88   SEARCH-BY-IDNO                          VALUE 1.
        88   SEARCH-BY-NAME                          VALUE 2.
        88   SEARCH-BY-DEPARTMENT                    VALUE 3.
        88   WRONG-INPUT                             VALUE 0,
                                                     4 THROUGH 10.
3. IF SEARCH-BY-NAME
           ACCEPT SEARCH-KEY-NAME FROM CONSOLE
           PERFORM D2-SEQUENTIAL-SEARCH-BY-NAME
                    UNTIL FOUND OR NOT-IN-FILE
   IF SEARCH-BY-DEPARTMENT
           ACCEPT SEARCH-KEY-DEPT FROM CONSOLE
           MOVE "YES" TO DISPLAY-FLAG
           PERFORM D3-SEQUENTIAL-SEARCH-BY-DEPT
                    UNTIL SEARCH-ENDS.
4. B1-READ-MASTER-FILE.
       READ MASTER-FILE
               AT END MOVE "YES" TO END-OF-MASTER-FILE-FLAG
       IF TRANSACTION-FILE-ENDS
               PERFORM C1-COPY-MASTER-FILE
                       UNTIL MASTER-FILE-ENDS.
5. 01   ERROR-RECORD-IDNO-LINE.
        05   FILLER                      PIC X(20)   VALUE SPACES.
        05   FILLER                      PIC X(28)   VALUE
                                    "TRANSACTION RECORD ID NUMBER: ".
        05   ERROR-TRANS-IDNO            PIC XXX.
6. B3-UPDATE-MASTER-FILE.
       IF   EMPLOYEE-IDNO-MS = EMPLOYEE-IDNO-TR
               PERFORM C1-CHECK-FOR-ADD-ERROR
       ELSE
               IF EMPLOYEE-IDNO-MS < EMPLOYEE-IDNO-TR
                       PERFORM B1-READ-MASTER-FILE.
               ELSE
                       PERFORM C2-CHECK-FOR-ADDITION.
```

7. The following is a partial COBOL code.

```
    . . . . . . . . . . . . . . . . . .
 A-DETERMINE-GRADE.
    IF ST-AVERAGE > 89
            MOVE "A" TO ST-GRADE
            ADD 4    TO CREDIT-TOTALS.

    IF ST-AVERAGE > 79
            AND
       ST-AVERAGE < 90
            MOVE "B" TO ST-GRADE
            ADD 3    TO CREDIT-TOTALS.

    IF ST-AVERAGE > 69
            AND
       ST-AVERAGE < 80
            MOVE "C" TO ST-GRADE
            ADD 2    TO CREDIT-TOTALS.
```

```
IF  ST-AVERAGE > 59
        AND
    ST-AVERAGE < 70
        MOVE "D" TO ST-GRADE
        ADD 1    TO CREDIT-TOTALS.
ELSE
        MOVE "F" TO ST-GRADE.
. . . . . . . . . . . . . . . . . .
```

Examine this code carefully and identify an execution error in it. Explain the reason for the error. How will this error manifest itself during execution?

Exercises

1. Draw a flow graph for Program 1 of Chapter 1. Then carefully count the number of independent distinct paths in this flow graph.

7

Modular Programming and Subprograms

313

Introduction

Modular programming as a program design methodology was discussed in Chapter 4. As we saw there, it has several advantages over monolithic (single-module) programming.

1. Modular program design is more amenable to teamwork. Therefore, it may substantially improve program development time and efficiency.
2. Compared to a lengthy monolithic program, a modular program is easier to understand, test, debug, repair, and maintain.
3. Program portability is generally much greater for modular software systems.

In this chapter we will take a closer look at modular programs. We will classify them, and for each type, we will explore the manner in which modules work together and communicate data with one another. Our objective is to acquire a better understanding of how modules are specified in a software system, and the way they interact. We will also examine the COBOL implementations of program modules as internal and external procedures.

Modular Programs and Subprograms

A modular program is defined as follows.

> A **modular program** is a system of program modules that consists of a main program and any number of subprograms. Subprograms are also known as procedures. The main program and its subprograms cooperate to perform a set of tasks for which the system is designed.

The COBOL programs we have studied so far are all modular in that their PROCEDURE DIVISIONs consist of some user-defined paragraphs. A PROCEDURE DIVISION paragraph is a subprogram because it is a functional module, capable of performing an individual task. All modular program systems have a main program. In COBOL, this is always the first paragraph or the first section of the PROCEDURE DIVISION.

Paragraph-oriented program design is not the only way to achieve modularization. In this chapter we study several different approaches. In view of what we know about paragraph-oriented program design in COBOL, however, we can easily identify certain characteristics of a modular program system.

1. There is only one main program.
2. The main program monitors the other program modules and, therefore, is capable of invoking other subprograms.
3. The execution of a modular program system begins and ends in the main program.

4. Subprograms may call on other subprograms; however, no subprogram is permitted to call on the main program.
5. Subprograms are called using their names. To permit this, each must have a unique name. Depending on the type of modularization, the main program also may require a name.
6. The invocation of a subprogram entails a transfer of control from the calling module to the invoked subprogram.
7. After the invoked subprogram is completed, program control passes to the calling module.
8. A module invocation may also result in data communication between the calling and called modules.

Most of these characteristics are straightforward, and we have studied them before. However, intermodule transfer of control and data communication are two aspects that require additional consideration. These depend on the type of subprograms. Therefore, before we discuss them, let us give a classification of subprograms.

Types of Subprograms

Depending on whether or not subprograms are coded as part of the main program, they are classified as internal or external.

> An **internal subprogram** is designed and coded as a part of the main program, and is compiled and executed with it.

> An **external subprogram** is coded and compiled independent of the main program or subprogram that invokes it; however, it is executed with the main program.

COBOL has three types of subprograms:

1. Internal subprograms as paragraphs or sections
2. Internal subprograms as nested programs (a COBOL 85 feature)
3. External subprograms as subroutines

Internal Procedures as Paragraphs and Sections

The simplest way that we can define a module in COBOL is by using paragraphs or sections in the PROCEDURE DIVISION. The first paragraph or first few paragraphs in the PROCEDURE DIVISION may be designed to serve as the main program. The remaining paragraphs or sections are invoked in a hierarchical manner, starting at the main program. Program execution always begins in the main program and should preferably terminate in it. We can call on other paragraphs from within any paragraph or section.

Intermodule Transfer of Control

In internal procedure invocation there are four critical points for intermodule transfer of control: point of invocation, point of entry, point of exit, and point of return. The **point of invocation** is in the calling program. This is the point at which a suitable language feature calls on a subprogram. The **point of entry** is in the invoked program. Usually, this is the first executable statement in a subprogram. The **point of exit** is also in the subprogram. It corresponds to a statement that returns control back to the calling module. Finally, the **point of return** is a point in the calling program. Program execution continues in the calling program after this point.

As an example, let us consider the partial COBOL code in Figure 1, in which paragraph B1-PREPARATIONS is a subprogram. It is invoked by the PERFORM B1-PREPARATIONS statement in the calling program A-MAIN-LINER. Therefore, this statement is the point of invocation. The first statement that will be executed in B1-PREPARATIONS is ACCEPT TODAYS-DATE FROM DATE. This is the point of entry. The last statement executed in this subprogram is MOVE 1 TO PAGE-NUMBER; it is the point of exit. After this, program control returns to the calling program at statement PERFORM B2-INITIAL-TERMINAL-INPUTS, which is the point of return.

An internal procedure designed as a paragraph or a section has only a single point of entry, and it is the first statement in its body. There is also a single exit point, which is the last statement that is executed in it. In COBOL, such internal procedures can be invoked by any form of the versatile PERFORM statement.

Internal procedures may also be implemented as sections in the PROCEDURE DIVISION of a COBOL program. All program sections that exist in the other divisions have reserved names, such as FILE SECTION. Sections in the PROCEDURE DIVISION are identified by user-defined names. If the PROCEDURE DIVISION of a program contains sections, it is said to have **section-oriented design**. The following partial code is an example of section-oriented design in COBOL.

```
B1-INITIAL-TASKS SECTION.
B11-PREPARATIONS.
    ACCEPT TODAYS-DATE FROM DATE.
    MOVE TODAYS-YEAR  TO PROCESSING-YEAR.
    MOVE TODAYS-MONTH TO PROCESSING-MONTH.
    MOVE TODAYS-DAY   TO PROCESSING-DAY.
    MOVE 1            TO PAGE-NUMBER.

B12-INITIAL-TERMINAL-INPUTS.
    DISPLAY "---> ENTER ACADEMIC YEAR, LIKE 1953-54: "
    ACCEPT ACADEMIC-YEAR     FROM CONSOLE.
    DISPLAY "---> ENTER SEMESTER AS FALL, SPRING, OR SUMMER: "
    ACCEPT ACADEMIC-SEMESTER FROM CONSOLE.

B2-GENERATE-PAGES SECTION.
    MOVE COURSE-CODE TO CURRENT-COURSE-CODE.
    PERFORM C1-REPORT-PREPARATION.
    PERFORM C2-REPORT-PRINTING.
    ADD 1 TO PAGE-NUMBER.
    . . . . . . . . . . . . . . . .
```

In section-oriented design, each section consists of either paragraphs or just any number of sentences. In the example, the section called B1-INITIAL-TASKS contains two paragraphs: B11-PREPARATIONS, and B12-INITIAL-TERMINAL-INPUTS. The section B2-GENERATE-PAGES contains four sentences.

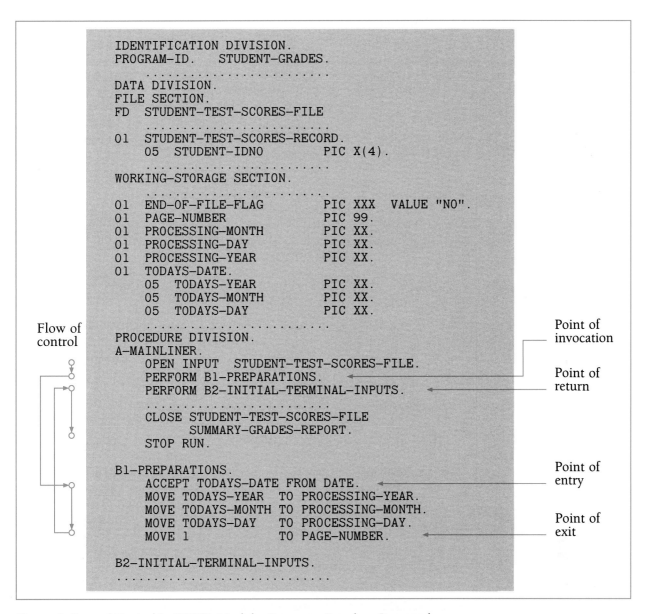

Figure 1 Flow of Control in COBOL Modular Programs Based on Paragraphs

Program control passes to a section in three ways:

1. By means of a PERFORM statement, which treats the section as a procedure
2. By means of a GO TO statement, which considers the section a program block
3. Because of the contiguity of sections in the program

In all of these cases, the content of the section is executed sequentially until its end. The end of a section is marked by the beginning of another section, or by the end of the source program. If the section is treated as a procedure and invoked by a PERFORM statement, control is returned back to the statement after PERFORM in the section or paragraph containing the PERFORM statement. If a section is triggered by a GO TO statement, after the content of the section is executed, the program control drops down to the next section. This is passing control to a section due to physical contiguity.

It should be noted that section-oriented design is similar to paragraph-oriented design with one basic difference: the building block for sections is a paragraph, whereas for paragraphs it is a sentence. This fact leads to some undesirable structural properties in section-oriented programs. If we wish to bypass the next paragraph in a section or jump to its end, we must use the notorious GO TO statement. We do not have to do that at all in a paragraph-oriented design. Also, in case we want to jump to the end of a section from a point in it, we must define a final paragraph at the end containing a no-operation statement (EXIT or CONTINUE) as in:

```
B1-INITIAL-TASKS SECTION.
B11-PREPARATIONS.
    ................
    GO TO B13-END-INITIAL-TASKS-SECTION.
    ................

B12-INITIAL-TERMINAL-INPUTS.
    ................

    ................

B13-END-INITIAL-TASKS-SECTION.
    EXIT.

B2-GENERATE-PAGES SECTION.
    ................
```

Section-oriented program design may be preferred in large-scale software development projects. Because paragraphs in a section are executed consecutively, however, maintenance, expansion, and repair of an application software system developed using this approach are rather critical. We should exercise special care in inserting new modules in the form of paragraphs into such programs. We may easily insert a module at an inappropriate point in the program, causing severe errors in its execution.

Intermodule Data Communication

In paragraph- and section-oriented designs, all procedures, that is, PROCEDURE DIVISION paragraphs and sections, including the main program, are parts of the same program. Data definitions in the DATA DIVISION are recognized by all modules. Therefore, data communication between modules does not present a special problem. As we will see, for other types of subprograms, intermodule communication requires special consideration.

Example Program 1:   *Class Grade Reports Generator (Section-Oriented Design)*

As an example of the section-oriented program design and implementation, we can use Program 1-Source in Chapter 3. All problem specifications are the same in this application, but this time, we will design the PROCEDURE DIVISION to consist of sections instead of paragraphs.

Program 1-Source is the compiler-generated listing of the PROCEDURE DIVISION of the COBOL program. The other program divisions are the same as in Program 1-Source in Chapter 3. The structure of this section-oriented design is shown in Figure 2. It should be noted that this structure chart uses somewhat different conventions than those explained in Chapter 5, because it is for a program designed using the section-oriented approach. The conventions used in Figure 2 are presented below.

Additional Conventions for Structure Charts of Section-Oriented Programs

1. A section is represented as a rectangle containing smaller rectangular boxes, each corresponding to the paragraphs of that section, as in:

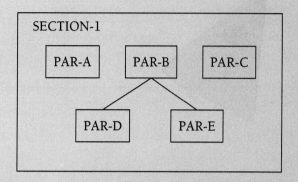

2. Inside a box for a section, the sequence of paragraph boxes from left to right indicates the sequence of invocations of these paragraphs. If the paragraphs in a section invoke one another, the box for the section depicts a structure subchart.

3. Occasionally, a section may be designed to consist of an unnamed block of statements only. Or, it may begin with some statements that are not gathered in a paragraph, although the rest of the section may have been blocked into paragraphs. Such unnamed sequences of statements that are not blocked into paragraphs are considered to form **phantom paragraphs**. In a structure chart, a phantom paragraph is represented as a rectangular box with dashed boundary lines and is assigned the name of the section, as below.

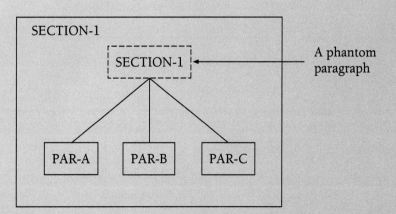

4. Unidirectional transfers of control between modules by GO TO statements are shown using lines with a single arrowhead.

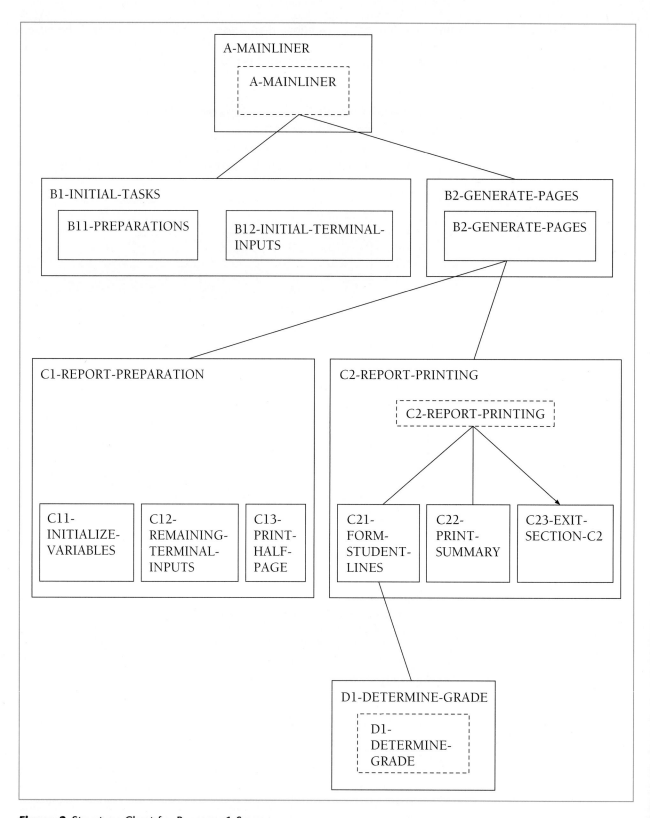

Figure 2 Structure Chart for Program 1-Source

1. A modular program system can be more easily adapted to teamwork than a monolithic program. (T or F)
2. A modular program is a system of program modules that consists of a _____ program and any number of _____ .
3. A COBOL PROCEDURE DIVISION paragraph is a subprogram. (T or F)
4. Which of the following is not a characteristic of a modular program system?
   a. A modular program system may have more than one main program.
   b. The main program can call on all other subprograms.
   c. The execution of a modular program begins and ends in the main program.
   d. A subprogram can invoke other subprograms, but is not permitted to call on the main program.
5. A subprogram that is designed, coded, compiled, and executed with its main program is called an _____ subprogram.
6. An external subprogram is coded with its main program, but can be executed separately. (T or F)
7. Which of the following statements concerning intermodule transfer of control is correct?
   a. The point of invocation is a statement in a calling program.
   b. The point of exit is a statement in a calling program.
   c. The point of return is a statement in a calling program that is immediately after the point of invocation.
   d. The point of entry is the first executable statement in a calling program.
8. Internal procedures communicate data to other procedures using _____ and _____ .
9. Global program variables can be specified only in modular program systems where subprograms are _____ to the calling program.
10. In _____ the PROCEDURE DIVISION consists of user-defined sections.
11. In section-oriented design, program control passes to a section by means of a _____ or a _____ , or because of _____ .
12. Sections in the PROCEDURE DIVISION are internal subprograms and can be invoked by any form of the PERFORM statement. (T or F)
13. In drawing structure charts for a COBOL program designed using the section-oriented approach, a sequence of statements in a PROCEDURE DIVISION that are not grouped within a paragraph is considered as a _____ .

Answers: 1. T; 2. main, subprograms; 3. T; 4. a; 5. internal; 6. F; 7. a; 8. global program variables, external variables; 9. internal; 10. section-oriented design; 11. PERFORM statement, GO TO statement, contiguity of sections; 12. T; 13. phantom paragraph.

Internal Procedures as Nested Programs

COBOL 85

COBOL 85 has introduced a way of defining internal procedures that is similar to more recent and structured programming languages such as Pascal. In this section we study this interesting feature, called nested COBOL programs, that can be used to design and develop modular software systems.

A **nested COBOL program** is a program that contains other functionally related, full COBOL programs.

A nested COBOL program is considered to be a block that starts with the IDENTIFICATION DIVISION header and concludes with the statement END PROGRAM. It can contain any number of programs, each defined as a block. A program contained in another program may, in turn, contain programs, thus producing a nested structure.

Structure of Nested Programs

The basic structural principles underlying nested COBOL programs are as follows.

1. The outer block is the main program, and all contained programs are subprograms.
2. Either the main program or the subprograms may call on any program that is directly or indirectly contained in it.
3. A subprogram cannot invoke itself or any other subprogram in which it is contained.
4. A subprogram cannot call on another subprogram that it does not contain, unless such a subprogram is a common program. A subprogram may be declared to be common.

```
PROGRAM—ID.   PROCEDURE—B IS COMMON PROGRAM.
```

A common subprogram may be invoked by any subprogram contained within a nested program, except by the subprograms that it contains.
5. The main program or a subprogram may invoke another subprogram using the CALL statement. A simplified syntax of the CALL statement is given below.

$$\underline{\text{CALL}} \begin{Bmatrix} \text{identifier-1} \\ \text{literal-1} \end{Bmatrix}$$
$$[\,\text{ON } \underline{\text{OVERFLOW}} \text{ imperative-statement-1 } [\,\underline{\text{END-CALL}}\,]\,]$$

The CALL statement is studied in detail later in this chapter.
6. Each subprogram contains at least one EXIT PROGRAM statement to return control to the calling program.

Figure 3 shows the structure of a typical nested program. Here, the MAIN-PROGRAM contains PROCEDURE-A and PROCEDURE-C. The subprogram PROCEDURE-A, in turn, contains another subprogram, PROCEDURE-B. Because of this structure, MAIN-PROGRAM may invoke all three subprograms, and PROCEDURE-A may call on PROCEDURE-B. In addition, because PROCEDURE-A has been declared to be COMMON, it may be called by PROCEDURE-C as well.

> If a program can be called by another program, it is said to be in the latter's scope.

Accordingly, the scope of the MAIN-PROGRAM in Figure 3 includes all three subprograms, and the scope of PROCEDURE-C is limited to PROCEDURE-A.

```
IDENTIFICATION DIVISION.
PROGRAM-ID.  MAIN-PROGRAM.
. . . . . . . . . . . . . .
ENVIRONMENT DIVISION.
. . . . . . . . . . . . . .
DATA DIVISION.
. . . . . . . . . . . . . .
PROCEDURE DIVISION.
. . . . . . . . . . . . . .

    IDENTIFICATION DIVISION.
    PROGRAM-ID.  PROCEDURE-A IS COMMON.
    . . . . . . . . . . . . . .
    ENVIRONMENT DIVISION.
    . . . . . . . . . . . . . .
    DATA DIVISION.
    . . . . . . . . . . . . . .
    PROCEDURE DIVISION.
    . . . . . . . . . . . . . .

        IDENTIFICATION DIVISION.
        PROGRAM-ID.  PROCEDURE-B.
        . . . . . . . . . . . . . .
        ENVIRONMENT DIVISION.
        . . . . . . . . . . . . . .
        DATA DIVISION.
        . . . . . . . . . . . . . .
        PROCEDURE DIVISION.
        . . . . . . . . . . . . . .
        END PROGRAM PROCEDURE-B.

    END PROGRAM PROCEDURE-A.

    IDENTIFICATION DIVISION.
    PROGRAM-ID.  PROCEDURE-C.
    . . . . . . . . . . . . . .
    ENVIRONMENT DIVISION.
    . . . . . . . . . . . . . .
    DATA DIVISION.
    . . . . . . . . . . . . . .
    PROCEDURE DIVISION.
    . . . . . . . . . . . . . .
    END PROGRAM PROCEDURE-C.

END PROGRAM MAIN-PROGRAM.
```

Figure 3 Structure of Nested COBOL Programs

Intermodule Transfer of Control

The subprogram invocation logic in COBOL nested programs is similar to that for modular programs based on paragraphs or sections. The four critical points prominent in the flow of control are shown on a nested program example in Figure 4. Here we have a main program called STUDENT-GRADES containing B1-PREPARATIONS as a nested program. The statement CALL B1-PREPARATION is the point of invocation in the main program. The statement ACCEPT TODAYS-DATE FROM YEAR in the contained program is the point of entry. The statement EXIT PROGRAM is the point of exit. Finally, the statement PERFORM B2-INITIAL-TERMINAL-INPUTS in the main program is the point of return.

Intermodule Data Communication

In general, each procedure in a modular program must have access to data elements in order to carry out its assigned function. Also, to execute the program properly, the procedures should communicate data values with one another. Before we can understand the intermodule data communication logic in nested programs, we must study how COBOL 85 classifies program variables according to their accessibility by nested program modules. From this point of view, the variables are classified as local, global, or external.

> **Local variables** are program variables that are defined in a module exclusively for its use.

A data element defined in the DATA DIVISION of a program is accessible to every statement in its PROCEDURE DIVISION, and is local with respect to that program. Local data elements are not recognized by the containing or contained programs for that program. Therefore, they cannot be used for data communication purposes.

> **Global variables** are variables that are specified in the calling program in a modular program system where subprograms are internal to the calling program. Global variables are generally accessible to the subprograms contained in the calling program.

A data element may be specified to be global in the DATA DIVISION. In this case, it is accessible to not only the program in which it is defined, but also to subprograms that are contained in the program. Therefore, global variables can be used as a means of intermodule data communication. In COBOL, the definition of a data element as a global element requires the use of the IS GLOBAL clause in the WORKING-STORAGE SECTION.

Example definitions for global data elements in COBOL 85 follow.

```
01   TOTAL-CREDITS      IS GLOBAL.
     05                            PIC 9999.
01   STUDENT-AVERAGE    IS GLOBAL.
     05                            PIC 999.
01   TERMINAL-FLAG      IS GLOBAL.
     05                            PIC XXX   VALUE "NO".
        88 INITIAL-INPUTS                    VALUE "YES".
```

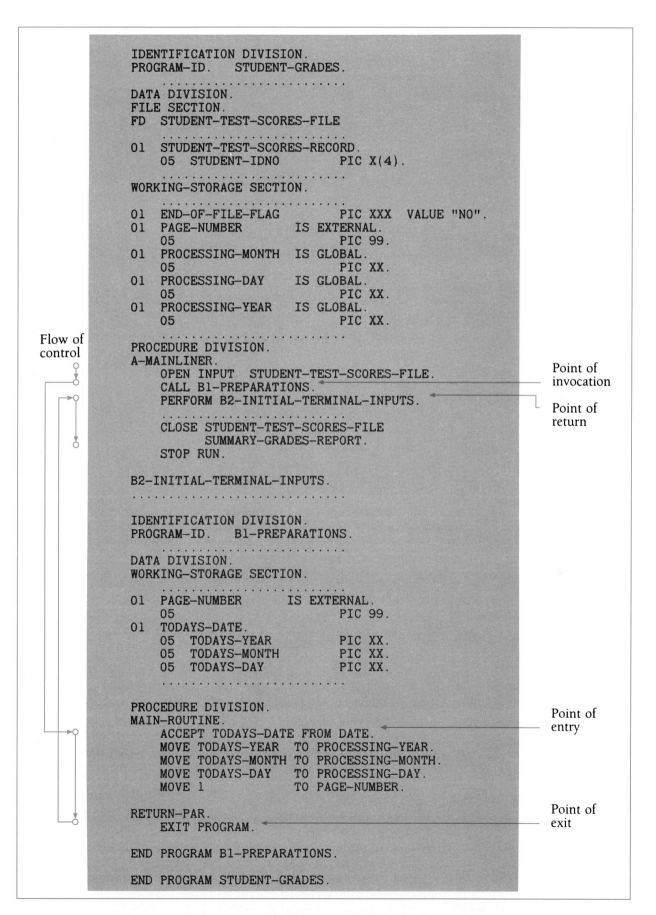

```
            IDENTIFICATION DIVISION.
            PROGRAM-ID.   STUDENT-GRADES.
            . . . . . . . . . . . . . . . . . . . . . . . . . . .
            DATA DIVISION.
            FILE SECTION.
            FD  STUDENT-TEST-SCORES-FILE
                . . . . . . . . . . . . . . . . . . . . . . . . .
            01  STUDENT-TEST-SCORES-RECORD.
                05  STUDENT-IDNO          PIC X(4).
                . . . . . . . . . . . . . . . . . . . . . . . .
            WORKING-STORAGE SECTION.
                . . . . . . . . . . . . . . . . . . . . . .
            01  END-OF-FILE-FLAG          PIC XXX   VALUE "NO".
            01  PAGE-NUMBER       IS EXTERNAL.
                05                        PIC 99.
            01  PROCESSING-MONTH  IS GLOBAL.
                05                        PIC XX.
            01  PROCESSING-DAY    IS GLOBAL.
                05                        PIC XX.
            01  PROCESSING-YEAR   IS GLOBAL.
                05                        PIC XX.
                . . . . . . . . . . . . . . . . . . . . . . . .
            PROCEDURE DIVISION.
            A-MAINLINER.
                OPEN INPUT  STUDENT-TEST-SCORES-FILE.
                CALL B1-PREPARATIONS.
                PERFORM B2-INITIAL-TERMINAL-INPUTS.

                CLOSE STUDENT-TEST-SCORES-FILE
                      SUMMARY-GRADES-REPORT.
                STOP RUN.

            B2-INITIAL-TERMINAL-INPUTS.

                . . . . . . . . . . . . . . . . . . . . . . . . .

            IDENTIFICATION DIVISION.
            PROGRAM-ID.   B1-PREPARATIONS.
                . . . . . . . . . . . . . . . . . . . . . .
            DATA DIVISION.
            WORKING-STORAGE SECTION.
                . . . . . . . . . . . . . . . . . . . . . .
            01  PAGE-NUMBER       IS EXTERNAL.
                05                        PIC 99.
            01  TODAYS-DATE.
                05  TODAYS-YEAR       PIC XX.
                05  TODAYS-MONTH      PIC XX.
                05  TODAYS-DAY        PIC XX.
                . . . . . . . . . . . . . . . . . . . . . .

            PROCEDURE DIVISION.
            MAIN-ROUTINE.
                ACCEPT TODAYS-DATE FROM DATE.
                MOVE TODAYS-YEAR  TO PROCESSING-YEAR.
                MOVE TODAYS-MONTH TO PROCESSING-MONTH.
                MOVE TODAYS-DAY   TO PROCESSING-DAY.
                MOVE 1            TO PAGE-NUMBER.

            RETURN-PAR.
                EXIT PROGRAM.

            END PROGRAM B1-PREPARATIONS.

            END PROGRAM STUDENT-GRADES.
```

Flow of
control

Point of
invocation

Point of
return

Point of
entry

Point of
exit

Figure 4 Flow of Control in COBOL Nested Programs

Both local and global data elements are stored in the memory in a partition that is allocated by the compiler to the program in which they are defined. COBOL 85 also allows specification of data elements in a program for which a separate partition is provided. These are called external data elements.

> External variables are program variables that are stored in a segment of the main memory that is public. That is, all program modules containing such variables declared as external are permitted access to this segment of the memory.

Consequently, external variables may be used for transferring data between program modules. External data elements defined in a subprogram are not stored in the memory partition for that subprogram. They are stored in a separate memory partition that is associated with the entire nested program. This memory partition is called a **run unit**. External data elements may be referenced by any subprogram in the run unit provided they are declared identically in the subprogram.

In COBOL 85, an external data element is specified using the IS EXTERNAL clause in the WORKING-STORAGE SECTION.

```
01  PAGE-NUMBER IS EXTERNAL.
    05                      PIC 99.
```

Let us examine these concepts for the example of Figure 5. In this figure, PROGRAM-1 is the main program, containing two nested subprograms, PROGRAM-2 and PROGRAM-4. PROGRAM-2, in turn, contains PROGRAM-3. Data element declarations for the programs of the run unit are as follows.

Data Element Type	PROGRAM-1	PROGRAM-2	PROGRAM-3	PROGRAM-4
Local	A1	A2	A3	A4, B4
Global	B1	B2	—	—
External	C1	C1	B3	B3

Consequently, these data elements will be stored in the memory as shown below.

```
┌──────────────────────────────────────────┐
│  ┌────────────────────────────────────┐  │
│  │ PARTITION FOR PROGRAM-1            │  │
│  │    Data elements A1, B1           │  │
│  ├────────────────────────────────────┤  │
│  │ PARTITION FOR PROGRAM-2           │  │
│  │    Data elements A2, B2           │  │
│  ├────────────────────────────────────┤  │
│  │ PARTITION FOR PROGRAM-3           │  │
│  │    Data element A3                │  │
│  ├────────────────────────────────────┤  │
│  │ PARTITION FOR PROGRAM-4           │  │
│  │    Data elements A4, B4           │  │
│  ├────────────────────────────────────┤  │
│  │ PARTITION FOR EXTERNAL DATA       │  │
│  │    Data elements C1, B3           │  │
│  └────────────────────────────────────┘  │
└──────────────────────────────────────────┘
```

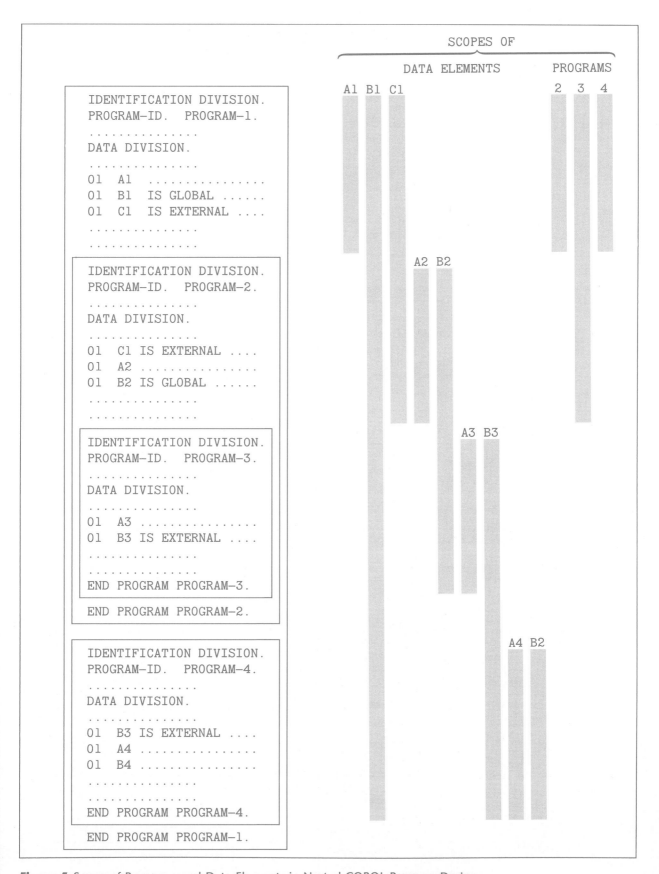

Figure 5 Scope of Programs and Data Elements in Nested COBOL Program Design

PROGRAM-1 and PROGRAM-2 can communicate with each other by way of the data element C1, and PROGRAM-3 and PROGRAM-4 can do so using the external data element B3.

Scopes of programs and data elements depend on the structure of a nested program and data declarations in it. The scope for a subprogram includes subprograms that may invoke it. The scope for a data element is the subprograms in which it may be accessed. For example, the scope of PROGRAM-3 includes PROGRAM-2 because it is contained in PROGRAM-2. The scope for A2 is restricted to PROGRAM-2 because A2 is locally defined in it. The scope of B2 includes PROGRAM-2 and PROGRAM-3 as it is global in PROGRAM-2, and PROGRAM-2 contains PROGRAM-3. Finally, the scope of C1 includes PROGRAM-1 and PROGRAM-2 because C1 is external to both. The scopes of the subprograms and data elements of Figure 5 are shown graphically to the right of the program. They are also shown in the scope table of Figure 6.

In summary, subprograms in a nested program communicate with each other through either global data elements or external data elements. A data ele-

Program or Data Element	PROGRAM			
	PROGRAM-1	PROGRAM-2	PROGRAM-3	PROGRAM-4
PROGRAM-1	—	—	—	—
A1	yes	—	—	—
B1	yes	yes	yes	yes
C1	yes	yes	—	—
PROGRAM-2	yes	—	—	—
A2	—	yes	—	—
B2	—	yes	yes	—
C1	yes	yes	—	—
PROGRAM-3	yes	yes	—	—
A3	—	—	yes	—
B3	—	—	yes	yes
PROGRAM-4	yes	—	—	—
A4	—	—	—	yes
B4	—	—	—	yes
B3	—	—	yes	yes

Figure 6 Table of Scopes for Programs in the Nested Structure of Figure 5

ment that is globally defined in a containing subprogram may be accessed and altered by both the subprogram itself and all other subprograms that are contained in it. Similarly, an external data element may be accessed and altered by all subprograms sharing it.

Summary of Scope Rules for COBOL 85 Nested Programs

1. The scope of a subprogram includes all subprograms that contain it.
2. The scope of a COMMON subprogram is defined by all subprograms in the nested program except those that it contains.
3. The scope of a local data element is limited to the subprogram in which it is defined.
4. The scope of a global data element includes the subprogram in which it is declared, and all subprograms that are nested within this subprogram.
5. The scope of an external data element includes all subprograms in which the data element is identically declared as external.

Finally, COBOL 85 permits a subprogram in a nested program to be declared with the INITIAL option.

```
PROGRAM-ID.  PROGRAM-2 IS INITIAL PROGRAM.
```

All data elements that are local to an INITIAL program are automatically initialized to their intended initial values every time such a program is invoked.

REVIEW QUESTIONS

1. A nested COBOL program starts with _____ and ends with _____ .
2. In a nested program, the main program is the innermost block that contains no other programs. (T or F)
3. Choose the correct ending for the following statement. In a nested COBOL program
   a. A main program may call on any other program including itself.
   b. A subprogram may call on any other subprogram except the main program.
   c. A common subprogram may be invoked by any subprogram contained within a nested program, except the subprograms that it contains.
   d. All of the above are correct.
4. In nested programs, subprogram invocation requires the COBOL CALL statement with the USING clause. (T or F)
5. To return control to the calling program, each program in a nested COBOL program contains at least one _____ statement.
6. The scope of a program consists of all subprograms that it can legally invoke. (T or F)
7. A global data element is accessible to the program in which it is defined, and also to programs contained in that program. (T or F)
8. The scope of an external data element includes all subprograms in which the data element is identically declared as external. (T or F)

Answers: 1. IDENTIFICATION DIVISION header, END PROGRAM statement; 2. F; 3. c; 4. F; 5. EXIT PROGRAM; 6. T; 7. T; 8. T.

Example Program 2:   *Class Grade Reports Generator (Use of Nested Programs)*

To illustrate the use of the principles and rules for nested programs, we code our sample software system that generates class grade reports as a nested COBOL program. The code is given in Program 2-Source. This time, our modularization scheme calls for three program modules:

1. A main program named STUDENT-GRADES
2. A nested subprogram named C1-TERMINAL-INPUTS
3. Another nested subprogram named D1-DETERMINE-GRADES

The main program STUDENT-GRADES monitors all necessary functions, including invoking the two nested programs.

The program C1-TERMINAL-INPUTS handles interactive data input operations that we have performed in two locations in the previous version of the program (Program 1-Source in Chapter 3), once before the STUDENT-TEST-SCORES-FILE records are input, and once more for each block of records for different courses. These are lines 000191 and 000219, respectively, in Program 1-Source in Chapter 3.

The program D1-DETERMINE-GRADES does the same thing as the paragraph of the same name in Program 1-Source in Chapter 3.

In C1-TERMINAL-INPUTS, the data element INPUT-FLAG has been defined in the WORKING-STORAGE SECTION of the subprogram. Hence, this data element is local to the subprogram and cannot be accessed in the main program. However, all data definitions for data elements in the containing program STUDENT-GRADES are valid for the contained subprograms as well. Therefore, data communication is by global data elements defined in the calling program.

Similarly, the subprogram D1-DETERMINE-GRADES communicates with the calling main program through global data elements, which are STUDENT-AVERAGE, OUT-STUDENT-GRADE, and TOTAL-CREDITS. Only ST-GRADE is locally needed by the subprogram, and thus it is defined in its WORKING-STORAGE SECTION.

External Procedures as Subroutines

External procedures are independently developed and compiled program modules. They are integrated during execution under the control of a single main module.

In modular program design, it may be preferable to implement certain modules as external procedures rather than internal ones. The reasons for this are

1. Ease of subdividing tasks in group projects
2. Ease of top-down and bottom-up software development
3. Ease of testing and debugging software

In top-down design of application software systems, after the conceptual modularization phase, modules are usually assigned to individual team members for implementation. Ideally, each team member should develop his or her modules independent of other modules in the system. If modules are implemented as external procedures, task assignment becomes simple. This way, a high degree of developmental independence can be achieved, because the programmers have to interact with other team members only to resolve the problem of intermodule communication. They are free to choose their own algorithms, program variables, and data structures. In other words, implementation of modules as external procedures facilitates subdivision of labor in large-scale software system development projects.

Also, external procedures are helpful in bottom-up design and development. If modules with well-defined functions are implemented as general purpose external procedures, they can be adopted for use in the development of new software systems. On the other hand, existence of standard external procedures in a company's library of programs facilitates bottom-up design and development of application software systems. Finally, external procedures can be debugged and tested independent of other modules. Testing a procedure in isolation is generally easier and more efficient than testing an entire system of modules.

Intermodule Transfer of Control

COBOL supports external procedures as subroutines. A subroutine is a program that performs a specific task and interacts with the program that calls it. Otherwise, it is a regular program consisting of the four program divisions, IDENTIFICATION, ENVIRONMENT, DATA, and PROCEDURE.

Figure 7 shows the flow of control in COBOL modular programs based on subroutines. The principles that determine the flow of control and procedure interactions are the same as those for internal procedures, with two exceptions.

1. There are no global variables in this architecture. Therefore, input-output through global variables is not possible.
2. After a procedure has completed execution, there is no automatic return of control to the calling procedure. At this point, a special statement is required to accomplish a return.

In Figure 7, the main program is STUDENT-GRADES and the procedure B1-PREPARATIONS is a subroutine. Program execution begins with the first statement in the PROCEDURE DIVISION of the main program. The statement CALL B1-PREPARATIONS in the main program transfers control to the subroutine. This statement corresponds to the point of invocation. The first statement that is executed in the subroutine is ACCEPT TODAYS-DATE FROM DATE, and this is the point of entry into the subroutine. After all the statements in the subroutine are executed, the computer comes across the statement EXIT PROGRAM, which corresponds to the point of exit. At this point, the main program takes over at the statement that is immediately after the CALL statement. It is the statement PERFORM B2-INITIAL-TERMINAL-INPUTS, and it defines the point of return.

In a program, the CALL statement is used to invoke a subroutine. A simplified syntax definition for the CALL statement is given below. The full syntax will be studied later in this chapter.

$$\underline{\text{CALL}} \begin{Bmatrix} \text{identifier-1} \\ \text{literal-1} \end{Bmatrix} [\ \underline{\text{USING}}\ \{\text{identifier-2}\}\ldots]$$
$$[\ \text{ON}\ \underline{\text{OVERFLOW}}\ \text{imperative-statement-1}\ ]$$

The name of the subroutine following the key word CALL may be either an identifier or a literal. If it is a literal, as in CALL "GRADES", the CALL statement is a direct reference to a specific subroutine known by that name that must be present at run-time in the main memory. If it is an identifier, as in

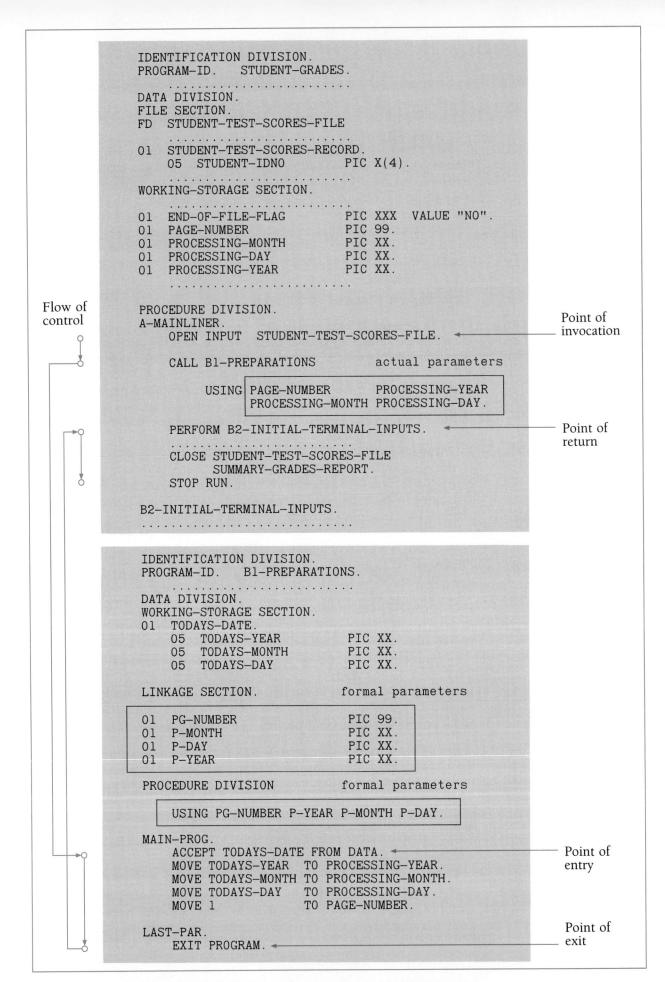

Flow of control

```
IDENTIFICATION DIVISION.
PROGRAM-ID.  STUDENT-GRADES.
.........................
DATA DIVISION.
FILE SECTION.
FD  STUDENT-TEST-SCORES-FILE
    .......................
01  STUDENT-TEST-SCORES-RECORD.
    05  STUDENT-IDNO        PIC X(4).
    .......................
WORKING-STORAGE SECTION.
    .......................
01  END-OF-FILE-FLAG        PIC XXX  VALUE "NO".
01  PAGE-NUMBER            PIC 99.
01  PROCESSING-MONTH       PIC XX.
01  PROCESSING-DAY         PIC XX.
01  PROCESSING-YEAR        PIC XX.

    .......................
PROCEDURE DIVISION.
A-MAINLINER.
    OPEN INPUT  STUDENT-TEST-SCORES-FILE.      ◄──── Point of invocation

    CALL B1-PREPARATIONS         actual parameters

       USING│PAGE-NUMBER        PROCESSING-YEAR
            │PROCESSING-MONTH   PROCESSING-DAY.

    PERFORM B2-INITIAL-TERMINAL-INPUTS.         ◄──── Point of return
    ...........................
    CLOSE STUDENT-TEST-SCORES-FILE
          SUMMARY-GRADES-REPORT.
    STOP RUN.

B2-INITIAL-TERMINAL-INPUTS.
    ...........................
```

```
IDENTIFICATION DIVISION.
PROGRAM-ID.  B1-PREPARATIONS.
.........................
DATA DIVISION.
WORKING-STORAGE SECTION.
01  TODAYS-DATE.
    05  TODAYS-YEAR         PIC XX.
    05  TODAYS-MONTH        PIC XX.
    05  TODAYS-DAY          PIC XX.

LINKAGE SECTION.            formal parameters

01  PG-NUMBER              PIC 99.
01  P-MONTH               PIC XX.
01  P-DAY                 PIC XX.
01  P-YEAR                PIC XX.

PROCEDURE DIVISION         formal parameters

    USING PG-NUMBER P-YEAR P-MONTH P-DAY.

MAIN-PROG.
    ACCEPT TODAYS-DATE FROM DATA.              ◄──── Point of entry
    MOVE TODAYS-YEAR  TO PROCESSING-YEAR.
    MOVE TODAYS-MONTH TO PROCESSING-MONTH.
    MOVE TODAYS-DAY   TO PROCESSING-DAY.
    MOVE 1            TO PAGE-NUMBER.

LAST-PAR.                                       Point of exit
    EXIT PROGRAM.                              ◄────
```

Figure 7 Flow of Control in COBOL Modular Programs Based on Subroutines

CALL SUB-A, it is the programmer's responsibility to store a literal value in that variable. After that, a CALL command may be issued. For example,

```
MOVE "GRADES" TO SUB-A.
CALL SUB-A.
```

is equivalent to

```
CALL "GRADES".
```

The ability to have the name of a subroutine stored in an identifier makes it possible to use one CALL statement to invoke different subroutines conditionally.

In the above syntax, the list of identifiers after the key word USING is a list of actual parameters. Actual parameters are one of the two elements of the intermodule data transfer mechanism for subroutines. The other element is formal parameters. Actual and formal parameters are discussed in detail later in this chapter. Here we should mention that the USING clause is optional. It may be missing if the called subroutine does not require any parameters.

The imperative statements in the ON OVERFLOW clause are executed if the CALL statement fails due to insufficient storage or unavailability of the called subroutine in the memory. An example of CALL is as follows.

```
CALL "GRADES" USING
        STUDENT-AVERAGE OUT-STUDENT-GRADE TOTAL-CREDITS
    ON OVERFLOW PERFORM SUBROUTINE-CALL-FAILED.
```

This statement passes control to the subprogram called GRADES whose object module must be resident in the main memory.

In external procedures, program control does not automatically return to the calling program after the last statement is executed. External procedures require a special statement, that is, the EXIT PROGRAM in COBOL, to define their exit points and to return control to the calling program.

After the statements in the PROCEDURE DIVISION are executed, control should be returned to the calling program. Execution is never terminated inside a subroutine. Therefore, instead of the STOP RUN statement, the EXIT PROGRAM statement should be used in the PROCEDURE DIVISION of a subprogram in at least one point, to define the point of exit. It is possible to have more than one EXIT PROGRAM statement in a subroutine; however, we recommend a single exit point specification to comply with the one-entry-point–one-exit-point rule of structured programming. The EXIT PROGRAM statement should be the last executable statement in the subprogram. In some versions of COBOL compilers, the EXIT PROGRAM statement should be included in a paragraph, and it should be the only statement in that paragraph.

Intermodule Data Communication

External subprograms communicate data through their parameter lists. A parameter list in a subroutine is called a formal parameter list. A formal parameter list must have a counterpart in a calling program in the form of an actual parameter list.

Formal Parameters. For data communication, we should specify a list of formal parameters in a subroutine.

> A **formal parameter list** is a list of variables that provide input and/or output for a subprogram.

Formal parameters of subroutines are specified at two locations: in the LINKAGE SECTION of the DATA DIVISION and in the USING clause of the PROCEDURE DIVISION header. They are program variables, and like all program variables, must be defined in the DATA DIVISION. COBOL requires that formal parameters be defined in the LINKAGE SECTION of the DATA DIVISION. The LINKAGE SECTION follows the FILE SECTION, and the WORKING-STORAGE SECTION, if any. Syntactically, the content of the LINKAGE SECTION is similar to that of the WORKING-STORAGE SECTION. An example of the LINKAGE SECTION is given below.

```
DATA DIVISION.
LINKAGE SECTION.
01   INPUT-VALUES.
      05   ACADEMIC-YEAR       PIC X(7).
      05   ACADEMIC-SEMESTER   PIC X(6).
      05   COURSE-NAME         PIC X(25).
      05   INSTRUCTOR-NAME     PIC X(21).
      05   CURRENT-COURSE-CODE PIC X(8).

01   INPUT-FLAG               PIC XXX.
      88   START-INPUT                    VALUE "YES".
```

Formal parameters are also listed in the USING clause of the PROCEDURE DIVISION header, as in

```
PROCEDURE DIVISION USING
                   ST-AVERAGE ST-GRADE CREDIT-TOTALS.
```

Syntactically, they are separated from each other by commas or blanks in the USING clause. Their order in the list should be consistent with the order of the corresponding actual parameters of the CALL statement in the calling program. Formal parameters may be

1. Program variables that transfer values from a subroutine to a calling program
2. Variables that transfer values from a calling program to a subroutine
3. Variables that are used to transfer values in both directions

In the above example, the parameter ST-AVERAGE transfers values from the calling program to the subroutine. The other two parameters, ST-GRADE and CREDIT-TOTALS, send values computed in the subroutine to the calling program. Together, the logic of the subroutine and the calling program determine the direction of data transfer in the subroutine-calling program interaction.

Sometimes a subroutine may correspond to a task for which no data values are needed and none are generated. For example, it may be designed simply to print a template with a fixed content. In this case, no formal parameters are required.

Actual Parameters. If the calling program is to transfer data to a subroutine, it should contain a list of actual parameters.

> The proper invocation of a subprogram with a formal parameter list requires its name and a list of parameters corresponding to the formal parameter list. This is known as the **actual parameter list**.

Actual parameters are specified in the USING clause of a CALL statement in the calling program.

```
CALL "GRADES" USING
        STUDENT-AVERAGE OUT-STUDENT-GRADE TOTAL-CREDITS
```

In COBOL, actual parameters may be program variables or constant values. Syntactically, they are separated from each other either by commas or by one or more spaces. At run-time, one-to-one correspondence is established between the elements of an actual parameter list in CALL and those of the corresponding formal parameter list in the subroutine. Assuming the above CALL is for a subroutine whose formal parameters are defined as

```
PROCEDURE DIVISION USING
                ST-AVERAGE ST-GRADE CREDIT-TOTALS.
```

the correspondence of parameters is

- STUDENT-AVERAGE   corresponds to ST-AVERAGE.
- OUT-STUDENT-GRADE corresponds to ST-GRADE.
- TOTAL-CREDITS   corresponds to CREDIT-TOTALS.

We should make sure that the number of parameters in the actual parameter list of CALL is the same as that in the formal parameter list of the subroutine, and that the same order of parameters is reflected in both lists to achieve correct correspondence.

After this parameter linkage process, the addresses and therefore values of the parameters STUDENT-AVERAGE, OUT-STUDENT-GRADE, and TOTAL-CREDITS will be carried into the parameters ST-AVERAGE, ST-GRADE, and CREDIT-TOTALS in the subroutine. Also, any changes made in the values of the parameters in the subroutine will be reflected in the values of the actual parameters in the calling program upon return. If an actual parameter is not a variable but a constant, the parameter linkage process is one-way. In this case, the constant value will be assigned as the value of the corresponding formal parameter in the subroutine.

The Parameter Association Process. Let us take a closer look at the parameter linkage. Suppose in the calling program the subroutine reference is

```
CALL "SUBPROGRAM-A" USING X Y Z.
```

and in the subroutine called SUBPROGRAM-A, the formal parameter definition is

```
PROCEDURE DIVISION USING A B C.
```

During the compilation of the calling program, the compiler assigns memory locations and addresses to all program variables, including X, Y, and Z, which are the actual parameters in the subroutine call. However, while the subroutine is being compiled, the formal parameters are not assigned addresses. Instead, the link-editor associates the parameters by letting A share the memory location of X, B that of Y, and C that of Z. In other words, at run-time, the address of A will be the same as that of X. The subprogram may then access the memory locations for its parameters and use their contents. Clearly, data definitions for respective parameters in the calling program and the subprogram must be compatible, or at least convertible. For example, if parameter X is defined in the calling program as an alphanumeric field, the formal parameter A corresponding to it should be defined in the LINKAGE SECTION of the subprogram as either alphanumeric or numeric.

Field width compatibility is also important. For example,

```
01   X   PIC X(3).
```

in the calling program, corresponding to

```
01   A   PIC X(4).
```

in the subroutine, may result in garbage in the last position of the variable A in the subroutine, coming from the field that is immediately adjacent to X in the main program. Therefore, it is advisable to use fully compatible parameter associations, in terms of both type and field width, in subroutine references.

A subroutine may always access contents of its formal parameters; however, it may or may not be allowed to change them. Depending on whether or not a subroutine may alter the contents of its formal parameters, parameter association in COBOL can be done in two ways: by REFERENCE and by CONTENT.

> **Parameter association by REFERENCE** allows a subroutine to change the contents of its formal parameters. Therefore, in this mode of linkage, the actual parameters are not write-protected.

In COBOL 74, parameter association is always by reference, and the programmer does not have the option of protecting parameters in the subroutine. **COBOL 85** COBOL 85, however, offers the option of parameter association by CONTENT.

Parameter association by CONTENT write-protects formal parameters in a subroutine. In this mode, a parameter can be accessed by the called program, but its content cannot be altered.

This is a useful feature in case the programmer wishes to protect some of the actual parameters against inadvertent contamination in the subprogram.

Summary of Important Rules About Subroutine Design in COBOL

1. If a subroutine has formal parameters, these should be defined in the LINKAGE SECTION of the DATA DIVISION.
2. In the LINKAGE SECTION, formal parameters should be defined as level 01 or 77 entries. They may be independent data items or group items.
3. In the LINKAGE SECTION, no variable should be initialized using the VALUE clause.
4. Formal parameters should also be listed in a USING clause in the PROCEDURE DIVISION header.
5. A subroutine may be invoked by a main program or by any other subroutine. A subroutine may not call on the main program, however, and it may not, directly or indirectly, call on itself.
6. To invoke a subroutine, a CALL statement is needed. If a subroutine has formal parameters in its definition, the USING clause of the CALL statement should list the corresponding actual parameters.
7. Actual parameters should be variables or constant values.
8. Actual parameters should be fully compatible with the formal parameters in number, order, field type, and field length.
9. To return control to the main program, the PROCEDURE DIVISION of a subroutine should contain at least one EXIT PROGRAM statement.
10. To write-protect parameters in a subroutine, parameter association by CONTENT should be used. This is a COBOL 85 feature.
11. In COBOL 74, only parameter association by REFERENCE is implicitly allowed. In this case, a subroutine may alter the contents of its parameters.

Dynamic Storage Management for Load Modules

Large-scale software systems may require large numbers of subroutines running under the supervision of a main program. As mentioned before, we must compile each subroutine separately, as well as the main program, to produce object modules. The link-editor, a systems software, combines the object programs into an executable module called the **load module**. The process of building the load module is defined using job control language statements and is consequently system dependent.

It is also possible to compile subroutines and save the corresponding object modules in secondary storage for future use. Such a collection is called a **load library**. When a load module is being executed, the object modules for the main program and all subroutines explicitly referenced in the CALL statements are brought together by the link-editor, and a load module is formed. The load module resides in the memory during execution. Therefore, copies of the object modules for the main program and subroutines are available in the main memory.

An explicit subroutine reference is provided by the CALL literal form of the CALL statement, specifying a particular subroutine by its name. We have seen that the CALL identifier form of the CALL statement enables the programmer to reference a subroutine dynamically, when needed. During the execution of the load module, when an implicit subroutine call becomes explicit, the link-editor loads the object module for that subroutine into the main memory. Hence, the number of object modules for subroutines that are memory resident at a given time during execution depends on the previous references.

At a particular instance during execution, many subroutine object modules may be in the main memory despite the fact that they are not required at that time. COBOL provides a feature in the form of the CANCEL statement that can be used to remove object modules from the memory when they are no longer needed. The CANCEL statement releases the storage occupied by a subroutine. Here are examples of the CANCEL statement.

```
CANCEL "GRADES" "TERMIN".

CANCEL SUB-A.
```

As can be seen, CANCEL, like CALL, allows both explicit and implicit subroutine references. After a subroutine has been canceled, it is possible to call it again through a subsequent CALL. This causes the object module for the subroutine to be reloaded and link-edited with the load module. The programmer should remember that a subroutine CALL after a CANCEL results in the execution of the subroutine as if it were its first execution in the job.

COBOL 85   *COBOL 85 Features for Subroutines*

COBOL 85 fully supports the features in the previous versions of the language for subroutine definition and invocation. In addition, it introduces some features that make the EXIT PROGRAM and CALL statements more flexible.

The EXIT PROGRAM statement that defines the logical end of a subroutine has to be present by itself within a paragraph in the previous versions of the language. In COBOL 85, the EXIT PROGRAM statement may be included in a paragraph with other statements.

The CALL statement has been enhanced to support the following:

1. Parameter association BY CONTENT in addition to BY REFERENCE
2. The optional ON EXCEPTION and NOT ON EXCEPTION clauses
3. The END-CALL statement terminator

There are two formats for the CALL statement in COBOL 85.

```
Format 1.
CALL  {identifier-1}  [USING  {[ BY REFERENCE ] {identifier-2} . . . }  ] . . . ]
      {literal-1   }          {BY CONTENT {identifier-3} . . .        }
        [ ON OVERFLOW imperative-statement-1 [ END-CALL ] ]
Format 2.
CALL  {identifier-1}  [USING  {[ BY REFERENCE ] {identifier-2} . . . }  ] . . . ]
      {literal-1   }          {BY CONTENT {identifier-3} . . .        }
        [ ON EXCEPTION imperative-statement-1 ]
        [ NOT ON EXCEPTION imperative-statement-2 ]    [ END-CALL ]
```

Consider the following example.

```
CALL "GRADES" USING
        BY CONTENT STUDENT-AVERAGE
        BY REFERENCE OUT-STUDENT-GRADE TOTAL-CREDITS
    ON EXCEPTION PERFORM SUBROUTINE-CALL-FAILED
    NOT ON EXCEPTION PERFORM SUBROUTINE-CALL-OK
END-CALL
```

This subroutine call has three actual parameters: STUDENT-AVERAGE, OUT-STUDENT-GRADE, and TOTAL-CREDITS. BY CONTENT for STUDENT-AVERAGE protects this field against alterations in the subroutine. GRADES can only read the content of the memory location for STUDENT-AVERAGE, and use it to compute OUT-STUDENT-GRADE and TOTAL-CREDITS. The parameters OUT-STUDENT-GRADE and TOTAL-CREDITS are associated with their counterparts in the subroutine BY REFERENCE. This means that they are not write-protected in the subroutine.

The ON EXCEPTION clause is analogous to the COBOL 74 feature of ON OVERFLOW. It indicates an error condition and specifies one or more imperative statements that are to be executed in case an error (e.g., insufficient storage, nonexistent subroutine, etc.) occurs. The NOT ON EXCEPTION clause triggers a set of imperative statements if the subroutine can be invoked normally.

Example Program 3: *Class Grade Reports Generator (Use of Subroutines)*

This time we code the same application of Program 1 or 2 using a main program with two subroutines. The compiler-generated source listing of the main program is given in Program 3-Source(a). The main program, named STUDENT-GRADES, makes use of two subroutines: C1-TERMINAL-INPUTS [Program 3-Source(b)] and D1-DETERMINE-GRADES [Program 3-Source(c)]. The tasks assigned to these subroutines are the same as their nested program counterparts in Program 2-Source. The differences are due to data communication channels between the calling and called programs.

In this case, since we have subroutines, we must distinguish the data elements each subroutine needs to fulfill its assigned functions, and data elements that it uses to return values to the calling program. These data elements make up the formal parameter list for each subroutine.

The subroutine C1-TERMINAL-INPUTS, by its logical design, has to differentiate between the initial and the remaining interactive input phases. This can be accomplished by sending it a value of YES stored in the variable location called INPUT-FLAG to force it to do the initial phase, and NO to take care of the remaining input. The subroutine will then acquire values for the variables ACADEMIC-YEAR, ACADEMIC-SEMESTER, COURSE-NAME, INSTRUCTOR-NAME, and CURRENT-COURSE-CODE, and return them to the calling program. Therefore, its formal parameter list includes the variable INPUT-FLAG, providing input for the subroutine, and the group item INPUT-VALUES, containing all other variables that are outputs from the subroutine. The formal parameters are defined in the LINKAGE SECTION and indicated in the PROCEDURE DIVISION header as follows.

```
     ...................
     LINKAGE SECTION.

     01   INPUT-VALUES.
          05   ACADEMIC-YEAR       PIC X(7).
          05   ACADEMIC-SEMESTER   PIC X(6).
          05   COURSE-NAME         PIC X(25).
          05   INSTRUCTOR-NAME     PIC X(21).
          05   CURRENT-COURSE-CODE PIC X(8).

     01   INPUT-FLAG              PIC XXX.
          88   START-INPUT                    VALUE "YES".

     PROCEDURE DIVISION USING
                    INPUT-FLAG INPUT-VALUES.
     ...................
```

From a functional point of view, the subroutine D1-DETERMINE-GRADES must have the student average to determine the letter grade and update the total credits field. Consequently, the parameters that provide input for the subroutine are ST-AVERAGE and CREDIT-TOTALS. Using the value brought by ST-AVERAGE, the subroutine computes a letter grade value, stores it in ST-GRADE, updates the contents of CREDIT-TOTALS, and sends them back. The LINKAGE SECTION and the PROCEDURE DIVISION headers for the subroutine are

```
     ...................
     LINKAGE SECTION.

     01   ST-AVERAGE    PIC 999.
     01   ST-GRADE      PIC X.
     01   CREDIT-TOTALS PIC 9999.

     PROCEDURE DIVISION USING
                    ST-AVERAGE ST-GRADE CREDIT-TOTALS.
     ...................
```

The main program STUDENT-GRADES invokes the subroutine C1-TERMINAL-INPUTS twice: once with the value of YES for TERMINAL-FLAG at line 000220 in Program 3-Source(a) and once with the value of NO at line 000227. The second invocation is repetitive. After this, the main program calls the subroutine D1-DETERMINE-GRADES for every student record at line 00286.

The structure chart for the main program of the sample application software system is given in Figure 8. This shows all paragraph invocations as well as the subroutine calls. The subroutines are distinguished from paragraphs by using rectangular boxes with two parallel lines for their vertical sides. Data transfers between the main program and the subroutines through parameter lists are clearly indicated on the chart. Data transfers between the calling and called paragraphs need not be shown, as every paragraph can access every data element defined within the main program. Of course, each subroutine should have its own structure chart for complete documentation of the design.

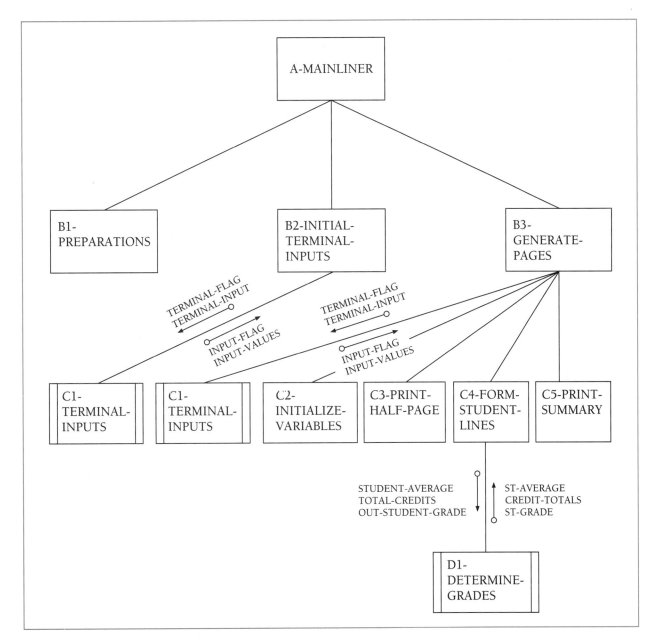

Figure 8 Structure Chart for Program 3

Functions and Recursive Procedures

Functions and recursive procedures are other subprogram types that can be useful in modular program design. Although they are not supported by COBOL, we discuss them briefly.

Functions

Depending on whether or not they return a value under their names, subprograms are classified as functions or procedures.

> A **function** subprogram returns a single value under its name when it transfers control back to the calling program.

> Subprograms that do not transfer values under their names are more general, and are known as **procedures**.

All types of subprograms that we have studied in this chapter are procedures.

In a function, the name of the subprogram serves two purposes. It references the subprogram and it transfers a value to the calling program on return. Similar to procedures, functions can also be designed as either internal and external subprograms. Function subprograms are suitable mostly for mathematical computations. As COBOL is a business-oriented language with little mathematical emphasis, it does not support functions. This is not a serious shortcoming, however, because any function may be coded instead as a procedure.

Recursive Procedures and Accidental Recursion

An internal or external procedure may call on other procedures as long as it does not violate this important rule.

> The logical paths defined by the flow of control during procedure invocations should not contain cycles. In other words, a procedure should not directly or indirectly, through other procedure calls, invoke a parent procedure.

Recursive procedure invocations are the only exception to this rule.

> A **recursive procedure** is a procedure that calls on itself.

Recursive procedures are useful if the problem itself is recursive. Clearly, recursive procedure invocations involve some sort of repetition. For them to be meaningful, the repetitions should be on a dynamic loop body that changes in each cycle of iteration. Also, the loop should ultimately end. When programming recursive procedure calls, the programmer must define terminating cases that control repetitive invocations.

Some programming languages, PL/I, Pascal, and LISP among them, have recursive procedure invocation capabilities. COBOL does not, but this is not a big loss. First, in application areas in which COBOL is the predominant language, recursion is rarely if ever needed. Second, any recursive specification can be equivalently expressed using iteration.

In software systems developed in COBOL, the main program does not have an internal name by which it can be invoked by another procedure. Accidental recursion is still possible among external or internal lower-level procedures, however. COBOL compilers do not diagnose accidental recursive calls. Therefore, inadvertently defined cyclic procedure invocations result in indefinite loops during program execution. This is one of the common programming errors. An effective way to prevent or eliminate such errors is to represent the program using a structured diagramming technique, such as structure charting, Jackson, Warnier-Orr, or action diagram (see Chapter 5).

1. Formal parameters in a COBOL subroutine should be defined in the _____ of DATA DIVISION.
2. Formal parameters in a subroutine should be listed in the USING clause of the PROCEDURE DIVISION header. (T or F)
3. Which of the following statements concerning formal parameters in COBOL subroutines is incorrect?
   a. Formal parameters may be elementary data items or COBOL data structures.
   b. Formal parameters may also be parts of COBOL data structures.
   c. They should be defined in the LINKAGE SECTION of the DATA DIVISION.
   d. They should not be initialized using the VALUE clause in the LINKAGE SECTION.
4. Subroutines are invoked using the CALL statement, whereas internal procedures in the form of paragraphs or sections are invoked using the PERFORM statement. (T or F)
5. The USING clause in a CALL statement contains _____ .
6. Formal and actual parameters in COBOL subroutine definitions and invocations should match in _____ , _____ , _____ , and _____ .
7. Parameter association by REFERENCE allows a subroutine to change the contents of its formal parameters. (T or F)
8. Parameter association by CONTENT is a COBOL 85 feature. It write-protects formal parameters in a subroutine. (T or F)
9. Object programs are converted by the _____ into executable modules that are called _____ .
10. The CANCEL statement cancels out the effects of a COBOL subroutine after it is executed. (T or F)
11. A formal parameter list is associated with an invocation statement, whereas an actual parameter list is associated with a procedure definition. (T or F)
12. To return control to a calling module, an external procedure needs a special statement. (T or F)
13. The main difference between a function and a procedure is that, a function returns _____ under its name, whereas a procedure does not.
14. A procedure that calls on itself is called _____ .

Answers: 1. LINKAGE SECTION; 2. T; 3. b; 4. T; 5. a list of actual parameters; 6. number, order, field type, field length; 7. T; 8. T; 9. link-editor, load module; 10. F; 11. F; 12. T; 13. a single value; 14. recursive.

Key Terms

actual parameter list
CALL statement
CANCEL statement
COMMON subprogram
EXIT PROGRAM statement
external data element
external subprogram
external variable
formal parameter list
function
global variable
INITIAL program
internal subprogram
LINKAGE SECTION
load library
load module
local data element
local variable
modular program design
nested program
ON OVERFLOW clause

paragraph-oriented design
parameter association BY CONTENT
parameter association BY
    REFERENCE
parameter linkage
parameter list
PERFORM statement
phantom paragraph
point of entry
point of exit
point of invocation
point of return
procedure
program scope
recursion
recursive procedure
run unit
section-oriented design
subprogram
subroutine
USING clause

Study Guide

Quick Scan

- Medium- to large-scale software systems should have modular structures. Modular program design facilitates teamwork and improves program development efficiency and portability. Furthermore, it is generally easier to understand, debug, test, repair, and maintain these programs.
- In a modular software system, one of the modules serves as the monitor. It is the main program. The other modules are subprograms, designed to carry out specific tasks.
- A subprogram may be designed together with other modules, and may be included in the main program in a nested fashion. Such a subprogram is compiled and executed together with all other related modules and the main program that contains it. Subprograms of this type are called internal subprograms.
- On the other hand, it is generally possible to design, code, and compile subprograms independently of invoking programs. These are called external subprograms. After compilation, object modules of the related subprograms are executed together with that of the monitor program.
- When a program calls on a subprogram, the flow of program control is transferred to the called subprogram, and execution continues in it until its task is completed. When the logical end of the subprogram is reached, control passes to the main program. This architecture defines four critical points, two in the calling programs, called points of invocation and return, and two in the invoked subprogram, called points of entry and exit. The point of invocation and point of exit are represented by appropriate program statements in COBOL.
- Modules in a modular program may have to communicate data with one another at the time control is transferred to and from the called subprograms. Data communication between modules may be accomplished using global variables, external variables, and parameter lists.

- Intermodule data communication between internal procedures may be handled using global and external variables. A containing program may define global variables and use them to communicate data to a contained subprogram. Two or more subprograms may define external variables for which the compiler allocates storage in a separate part of the main memory, and communicate by such variables.
- In general, external subprograms communicate with other modules only through parameter lists.
- Paragraph-oriented program design in COBOL is one way of defining internal procedures. Each paragraph may be considered as a procedure and is invoked by a form of the PERFORM statement. Using GO TO statements to pass control to paragraphs, and permitting transfer of control because of physical contiguity of paragraphs are programming practices that are not recommended. All variables defined in the DATA DIVISION may be seen as global variables that can be used to communicate data to and from individual paragraphs.
- Section-oriented design in COBOL is another way of modularizing a program, and is similar to paragraph-oriented design. In this case, the PROCEDURE DIVISION is specified in terms of user-defined sections. Each section may consist of a phantom paragraph and any number of ordinary paragraphs. A phantom paragraph is a set of sentences written immediately after a section header.
- Paragraphs in a PROCEDURE DIVISION section are executed consecutively unless otherwise directed. Due to this property, section-oriented design may necessitate use of unconditional transfer statements. Repairing and maintaining software systems that use this strategy may require special care.
- COBOL 85 supports another way of defining internal procedures as nested programs. In this approach, a COBOL program may be designed to contain any number of other COBOL programs in a nested fashion.
- In a nested program, a main or contained program may invoke any other program that it contains. Also, a program may call on any other program provided it is declared to be common.
- Nested programs are invoked by CALL statements. As such programs do not use formal parameter lists, the CALL statement does not require an actual parameter list. The EXIT PROGRAM statement defines the logical end of a subprogram, and is used to return control to the calling program.
- Data communication between nested programs is possible using global variables and external variables.
- Each nested program may also contain definitions for local variables that are exclusively for its own use.
- The scope of a program in a nested program is the set of programs in which it may be invoked. The scope of a variable is the set of programs in which it is recognized and can be accessed.
- In a nested program, the scope of a subprogram includes all programs that contain it, and excludes those that it contains. The scope of a common program includes all programs in the nested program except those that it contains.
- The scope of a local data element in a nested program is limited to the program in which it is defined. The scope of a global data element includes the program in which it is defined and all programs that are nested in it.
- The scope of an external data element includes all programs in which the data element is declared as external.

- Both COBOL 74 and 85 support external procedures as subroutines. A subroutine is an independently designed COBOL program. Subroutines communicate with other programs through formal parameter lists. Formal parameters should be included in the USING clause of the PROCEDURE DIVISION header.
- If a subroutine has a formal parameter list, the data elements in the list should be defined in the LINKAGE SECTION of the DATA DIVISION in the subroutine.
- Subroutine invocation requires the CALL statement together with an actual parameter list. An actual parameter list should match the formal parameter list of the subroutine in number and order of parameters, and in type and size of the corresponding parameters.
- The formal parameters in a subroutine are not assigned addresses during program compilation. At link-edit time, however, the link-editor passes addresses of actual parameters to the subroutine. This kind of actual-formal parameter association is called by REFERENCE.
- In COBOL 85 the programmer also has the option of associating parameters by CONTENT. This way, an actual parameter may be accessed by the corresponding formal parameter and its value may be used in the subroutine; however, the subroutine may not change the content of such a parameter.
- At execution time, the object modules of subroutines may be dynamically loaded into the memory whenever such subroutines are invoked by the CALL statement. COBOL also provides the CANCEL statement that can be used to remove object modules of unneeded subprograms from the main memory.
- A subprogram may be designed to return a single value under its name. Such a subprogram is called a function. COBOL does not support function subprograms.
- Subprograms that do not transfer values under their names are more general, and are known as procedures.
- Certain programming languages permit procedures to invoke themselves either directly or indirectly. Such invocations are called recursive. COBOL does not support recursive procedure invocations.

Test Your Comprehension

Multiple-Choice Questions

1. Which of the following statements about modular programs is correct?
   a. Compared to a monolithic program, a modular program system is more easily adaptable to teamwork.
   b. A modular program system is easier to understand, test, debug, repair, and maintain.
   c. Program portability is generally much greater for modular software systems.
   d. All of the above are correct.
2. Which of the following statements is incorrect?
   a. A global variable is specified in the calling program in a modular program system where subprograms are internal.
   b. Local variables are program variables defined in a module exclusively for its own use.
   c. Global variables can also be defined in modular systems consisting of external subprograms.
   d. An external variable is a program variable that is stored in a segment of the main memory accessible to all program modules.

3. Which of the following is a subprogram type that COBOL does not support?
   a. Internal
   b. Recursive
   c. External
   d. Procedure
4. Choose the phrase that incorrectly completes the following statement. Compared to internal procedures, external procedures
   a. Facilitate subdivision of tasks in group projects
   b. Speed up program execution
   c. Facilitate software testing and debugging
   d. Facilitate top-down and bottom-up software development
5. Concerning formal and actual parameter association in COBOL subroutines, choose the phrase that incorrectly completes the following statement. Formal and actual parameters should match in their
   a. Numbers
   b. Orders
   c. Names
   d. Field types and lengths
6. Choose the phrase that incorrectly completes the following statement. In a nested COBOL program
   a. The main program may call on any program contained in it.
   b. A subprogram may invoke any other subprogram provided that subprogram is contained in it.
   c. A subprogram may also invoke other subprograms in which it is contained.
   d. A subprogram cannot call on another subprogram that it does not contain, unless that subprogram is a common program.
7. In a nested COBOL program
   a. Local data elements defined in a program are not recognized by containing or contained programs for that program.
   b. Global data elements are accessible to the program in which they are defined, as well as all subprograms contained in the program.
   c. External data elements are stored in a separate memory partition and are accessible to all subprograms in which they are specified as external.
   d. All of the above are correct.

Answers: 1. d; 2. c; 3. b; 4. b; 5. c; 6. c; 7. d.

Short Essay Questions

1. What are the advantages of program modularization?
2. Explain the differences between internal and external subprograms.
3. What are the four critical points in the process of intermodule transfer of control? Where are they located?
4. In general, how do procedures communicate data to one another?
5. Distinguish between global and local variables.
6. What is an external variable? How do we communicate data using external variables?
7. What is meant by a formal parameter list? An actual parameter list?
8. Explain the processes of control and data transfers for internal procedures.
9. Explain the processes of control and data transfers for external procedures.
10. Explain the section-oriented program design strategy. Discuss its advantages and disadvantages relative to paragraph-oriented design.
11. What is a phantom paragraph? In a structure chart of a program designed using the paragraph-oriented strategy, we do not have any phantom paragraphs. Why? Explain your answer.
12. Briefly explain the structural properties of nested programs in COBOL 85.

13. What is a COMMON subprogram in a COBOL 85 nested program? How do we declare a subprogram to be COMMON?
14. What is meant by the scope of a program? Explain the scope rules for programs in nested programs.
15. How is intermodule data communication accomplished in COBOL nested programs?
16. Distinguish between global and external data elements, and explain how each type is defined in COBOL nested programs.
17. What is meant by the scope of a variable? Explain the scope rules for variables in nested COBOL programs.
18. How do we specify formal parameters in a COBOL subroutine?
19. Explain why we cannot initialize variables in the LINKAGE SECTION of a program using the VALUE clause.
20. Explain the syntax and semantics of the COBOL CALL statement.
21. Explain the process of associating formal and actual parameters for a calling program-subroutine interaction in COBOL 74.
22. What is the difference between parameter association BY REFERENCE and parameter association BY CONTENT in COBOL 85?
23. Explain the terms load module and load library.
24. Explain the use of the CANCEL statement in COBOL.
25. Define recursion. How do we handle recursive problems in COBOL, given that COBOL does not allow recursion?

Improve Your Problem-Solving Ability

Debugging Exercises

Suppose in a COBOL main program we have the following data definitions.

```
 . . . . . . . . . . . . . . . .
 . . . . . . . . . . . . . . . .
 WORKING-STORAGE SECTION.

 01   TOTAL-CREDITS          PIC 9999.
 01   STUDENT-GRADE          PIC X.
 01   STUDENT-AVERAGE        PIC 999.
 . . . . . . . . . . . . . . . .
 . . . . . . . . . . . . . . . .
```

The LINKAGE SECTION of a subroutine named DETERMINE-GRADES and its PROCEDURE DIVISION header are as follows.

```
 . . . . . . . . . . . . . . . .
 . . . . . . . . . . . . . . . .
 LINKAGE SECTION.

 01   ST-AVERAGE     PIC 999.
 01   ST-GRADE       PIC X.
 01   CREDIT-TOTALS  PIC 9999.
 . . . . . . . . . . . . . . . .
 . . . . . . . . . . . . . . . .
 PROCEDURE DIVISION USING
                    ST-AVERAGE ST-GRADE CREDIT-TOTALS.
 . . . . . . . . . . . . . . . .
 . . . . . . . . . . . . . . . .
```

In each of the following CALL statements to be used in the main program, point out the errors, if any.

1. CALL DETERMINE-GRADES USING STUDENT-AVERAGE STUDENT-GRADE TOTAL CREDITS.
2. CALL "DETERMINE-GRADES" USING ST-AVERAGE ST-GRADE CREDIT-TOTALS.
3. CALL "DETERMINE-GRADES" USING STUDENT-AVERAGE STUDENT-GRADE.
4. CALL "DETERMINE-GRADES" USING STUDENT-AVERAGE TOTAL-CREDITS STUDENT-GRADE.

Programming Exercises

1. Consider the sample Program 1 in Chapter 5 developed to generate monthly checking account statements. Examine the PROCEDURE DIVISION of this program and redesign it in terms of sections. Try to produce as good a design as possible, minimizing the use of GO TO statements. After running your program and verifying that it does the same task as the original, offer an in-depth discussion of both versions, and defend the section-oriented design.
2. For the section-oriented program developed in programming exercise 1, draw a structure chart using the conventions introduced in this chapter.
3. Consider the sample Program 1 in Chapter 4, which generates student reports. Redesign the program as a main program and six subroutines. The main program should do what the paragraph called A-MAIN-PARAGRAPH does in Program 1-Source in Chapter 4. The other paragraphs of the PROCEDURE DIVISION should each become a separate COBOL subroutine.
4. Draw a detailed structure chart for the modular software system developed in programming exercise 3.
5. Compare the program developed for programming exercise 3 to its original version and discuss the relative merits and shortcomings of both. How would you react to this task if it were a real-world application in a data processing center? Explain your reaction.
6. Design and develop a COBOL subroutine which returns a program flag with the value "TRUE" if an external sequential disk file for the STUDENT-TEST-SCORES-FILE of Program 3-Source(a) is presorted in ascending sequence by COURSE-CODE and STUDENT-IDNO. Otherwise, it should return "FALSE". An instance of the schema for such a file can be found in Program 1-Output in Chapter 3.
7. Figure 9 shows the structure of a COBOL nested program. Draw a scope table for it and explain your reasoning.
8. Again, consider the sample Program 1 in Chapter 4 and redesign the program as a main program and six properly nested subprograms. The main program should do what the paragraph called A-MAIN-PARAGRAPH does in Program 1-Source in Chapter 4. The other paragraphs of the PROCEDURE DIVISION should each be coded as a nested internal procedure.

Programming Problems

We have a sequential disk file called ACADEMIC-PERSONNEL with the following record structure.

```
01   ACADEMIC-PERS-RECORD.
     05   IDNO              PIC XXX.
     05   NAME              PIC X(12).
     05   SEX-CODE          PIC X.
     05   DEPARTMENT        PIC XXX.
     05   RANK              PIC X(5).
     05   YEARS-OF-SERVICE  PIC 99.
     05   TENURE-STATUS     PIC XXX.
```

```
          IDENTIFICATION DIVISION.
          PROGRAM-ID.  PROGRAM-X.
          ..............
          DATA DIVISION.
          01  AX   ..............
          01  BX   IS GLOBAL ......
          ..............

               IDENTIFICATION DIVISION.
               PROGRAM-ID.  PROGRAM-Y.
               ..............
               DATA DIVISION.
               01  AY IS ............
               01  BY IS GLOBAL.......
               01  CY IS EXTERNAL ....
               ..............

                    IDENTIFICATION DIVISION.
                    PROGRAM-ID.  PROGRAM-Z.
                    ..............
                    DATA DIVISION.
                    01  AZ IS GLOBAL ......
                    ..............

                         IDENTIFICATION DIVISION.
                         PROGRAM-ID   PROGRAM-U.
                         ..............
                         DATA DIVISION.
                         01  AU ..............
                         01  BU ..............
                         ..............
                         END PROGRAM PROGRAM-U.

                    END PROGRAM PROGRAM-Z.

               END PROGRAM PROGRAM-Y.


               IDENTIFICATION DIVISION.
               PROGRAM-ID.  PROGRAM-V.
               ..............
               DATA DIVISION.
               01  CY IS EXTERNAL ....
               01  AV IS GLOBAL ......
               01  BV ..............
               ..............

                    IDENTIFICATION DIVISION.
                    PROGRAM-ID.  PROGRAM-W.
                    ..............
                    DATA DIVISION.
                    01  AW ..............
                    01  BW ..............
                    ..............
                    END PROGRAM PROGRAM-W.

               END PROGRAM PROGRAM-V.

          END PROGRAM PROGRAM-X.
```

Figure 9 Structure of Nested COBOL Programs

The data item SEX-CODE is either M or F. DEPARTMENT values can be CS for computer science, MTH for mathematics, PHY for physics, MAN for management, ACC for accounting, and OR for operations research. RANK is PROF for full professor, ASSOC for associate professor, and ASST for assistant professor. Finally, TENURE-STATUS may be YES or NO. The following is an instance of the ACADEMIC-PERSONNEL file.

```
                    COLUMNS
         5    10   15   20   25   30
     ----|----|----|----|----|----|---

     800SMITH        MCS PROF 14YES
     810BROWN        FMTHASSOC08YES
     820JOHNSON      FCS ASSOC11NO
     8300'CONNOR     MCS ASST 04NO
     840ULLMAN       MPHYASST 03NO
     850FRY          MMANPROF 16YES
     860MARTIN       FACCASSOC09YES
     870MAIER        MCS PROF 08YES
     880YANG         FOR ASSOC03NO
     890RICH         MACCPROF 09YES
```

First, create this file as a sequential disk file in your computer account. Then do the following.

1. Design a COBOL subroutine that processes the ACADEMIC-PERSONNEL file, and determines and outputs to the screen the number of tenured professors as well as their names.
2. Design a COBOL subroutine that computes the average years of service for professors at each rank and at all ranks. That is, we want to see on the screen the average years of service for full, associate, and assistant professors, and the average years of service for all professors according to the format 99.99.
3. Design another subroutine that determines and prints on the screen the names and departments of professors who are female and tenured.
4. Now write a main program that calls upon the three subroutines of problems 1, 2, and 3 to execute them all on the ACADEMIC-PERSONNEL file.
5. Solve Problems 1–4 above using nested programs instead of subroutines.
6. An automotive service center maintains a sequential disk file for its spare parts inventory. The inventory file consists of two types of records. The first record has a four-character inventory item category code, a four-digit value representing the maximum desired inventory level, a two-digit value for the critical percentage for the item, and some additional information. The second record contains a five-character code for different makes of an inventory item, a four-digit value for amount in stock, and other information that is irrelevant to this application. A representative instance of the file is given in the following example.

```
P100    0100   80   . . . . . . . . . .      ← An occurrence of first record type
P1001   0030        . . . . . . . . . . . . . )
P1002   0045        . . . . . . . . . . . . . }   ← Occurrences of second record type
P1003   0010        . . . . . . . . . . . . . )
P102    0075   85   . . . . . . . . . .
P1022   0025        . . . . . . . . . . . . .
P1024   0050        . . . . . . . . . . . . .
        . . . . . . . . . . . . . . . . . . . . . .
```

The file is periodically updated to reflect the current stock levels, and its records are presorted by inventory number, as shown.

Write a COBOL subroutine that processes the file and produces a listing of inventory item categories if they are below the critical level; that is, if the sum of the available items of the inventory category drops below the critical inventory level obtained by multiplying the maximum desired inventory level by the critical percentage. Then write a main program to test this subroutine.

```
000185    *. . . . . . . . . . . . . . . . . . . . . . . . . . . . . . . . . . . . . . . . . . . . . . . . . . . . . . . . . . . .
000186    PROCEDURE DIVISION.
000187    A-MAINLINER SECTION.
000188        OPEN INPUT STUDENT-TEST-SCORES-FILE
000189            OUTPUT SUMMARY-GRADES-REPORT.
000190        PERFORM B1-INITIAL-TASKS.
000191        READ STUDENT-TEST-SCORES-FILE
000192            AT END MOVE "YES" TO END-OF-FILE-FLAG.
000193
000194        PERFORM B2-GENERATE-PAGES
000195            UNTIL END-OF-FILE.
000196
000197        CLOSE STUDENT-TEST-SCORES-FILE
000198            SUMMARY-GRADES-REPORT.
000199        STOP RUN.
000200
000201    B1-INITIAL-TASKS SECTION.
000202    B11-PREPARATIONS.
000203        ACCEPT TODAYS-DATE FROM DATE.
000204        MOVE TODAYS-YEAR  TO PROCESSING-YEAR.
000205        MOVE TODAYS-MONTH TO PROCESSING-MONTH.
000206        MOVE TODAYS-DAY   TO PROCESSING-DAY.
000207        MOVE 1            TO PAGE-NUMBER.
000208
000209    B12-INITIAL-TERMINAL-INPUTS.
000210        DISPLAY "---> ENTER ACADEMIC YEAR, LIKE 1953-54: "
000211        ACCEPT ACADEMIC-YEAR     FROM CONSOLE.
000212        DISPLAY "---> ENTER SEMESTER AS FALL, SPRING, OR SUMMER: "
000213        ACCEPT ACADEMIC-SEMESTER FROM CONSOLE.
000214
000215    B2-GENERATE-PAGES SECTION.
000216        MOVE COURSE-CODE TO CURRENT-COURSE-CODE.
000217        PERFORM C1-REPORT-PREPARATION.
000218        PERFORM C2-REPORT-PRINTING.
000219        ADD 1 TO PAGE-NUMBER.
```

Program 1-Source Section-Oriented Design for Program 1 in Chapter 3

```
000220
000221     C1-REPORT-PREPARATION SECTION.
000222     C11-INITIALIZE-VARIABLES.
000223          MOVE 0    TO NUMBER-OF-STUDENTS.
000224          MOVE ZERO TO TOTAL-CREDITS.
000225
000226     C12-REMAINING-TERMINAL-INPUTS.
000227          DISPLAY "---> CURRENT COURSE CODE IS " CURRENT-COURSE-CODE.
000228          DISPLAY "    ENTER COURSE NAME: ".
000229          ACCEPT COURSE-NAME    FROM CONSOLE.
000230          DISPLAY "---> ENTER INSTRUCTOR NAME FOR THIS COURSE: "
000231          ACCEPT INSTRUCTOR-NAME FROM CONSOLE.
000232
000233     C13-PRINT-HALF-PAGE.
000234          MOVE SPACES           TO REPORT-LINE.
000235          MOVE PROCESSING-DATE TO OUT-DATE.
000236          MOVE REPORT-TITLE-1  TO REPORT-LINE.
000237          WRITE REPORT-LINE
000238                 AFTER ADVANCING PAGE.
000239
000240          MOVE SPACES          TO REPORT-LINE.
000241          MOVE PAGE-NUMBER    TO OUT-PAGE-NUMBER.
000242          MOVE REPORT-LINE-2 TO REPORT-LINE.
000243          WRITE REPORT-LINE
000244                 AFTER ADVANCING 1 LINE.
000245
000246          MOVE SPACES           TO REPORT-LINE.
000247          MOVE ACADEMIC-YEAR      TO OUT-ACADEMIC-YEAR.
000248          MOVE ACADEMIC-SEMESTER  TO OUT-ACADEMIC-SEMESTER.
000249          MOVE YEAR-SEMESTER-LINE TO REPORT-LINE.
000250          WRITE REPORT-LINE
000251                 AFTER ADVANCING 3 LINES.
000252
000253          MOVE SPACES                 TO REPORT-LINE.
000254          MOVE CURRENT-COURSE-CODE    TO OUT-COURSE-CODE.
000255          MOVE COURSE-NAME            TO OUT-COURSE-NAME.
000256          MOVE COURSE-DESCRIPTION-LINE TO REPORT-LINE.
000257          WRITE REPORT-LINE
000258                 AFTER ADVANCING 2 LINES.
000259
000260          MOVE SPACES               TO REPORT-LINE.
000261          MOVE STUDENT-INFO-HEADER TO REPORT-LINE.
000262          WRITE REPORT-LINE
000263                 AFTER ADVANCING 2 LINES.
000264
000265          MOVE SPACES                TO REPORT-LINE.
000266          MOVE STUDENT-INFO-UNDERLINE TO REPORT-LINE.
000267          WRITE REPORT-LINE
000268                 AFTER ADVANCING 1 LINE.
000269
000270     C2-REPORT-PRINTING SECTION.
000271          PERFORM C21-FORM-STUDENT-LINES
000272                 UNTIL COURSE-CODE NOT EQUAL TO CURRENT-COURSE-CODE
000273                                        OR
000274                                END-OF-FILE.
```

Program 1-Source (Continued)

```
000275          PERFORM C22-PRINT-SUMMARY.
000276          GO TO C23-EXIT-SECTION-C2.
000277
000278     C21-FORM-STUDENT-LINES.
000279          ADD 1 TO NUMBER-OF-STUDENTS.
000280          COMPUTE STUDENT-AVERAGE =
000281               0.25 * FIRST-TEST-SCORE +
000282               0.35 * SECOND-TEST-SCORE +
000283               0.40 * FINAL-TEST-SCORE.
000284          PERFORM D1-DETERMINE-GRADE.
000285          MOVE STUDENT-NAME        TO OUT-STUDENT-NAME.
000286          MOVE STUDENT-AVERAGE     TO OUT-STUDENT-AVERAGE.
000287          MOVE SPACES              TO REPORT-LINE.
000288          MOVE STUDENT-LISTING-LINE TO REPORT-LINE.
000289          WRITE REPORT-LINE
000290               AFTER ADVANCING 1 LINE.
000291          READ STUDENT-TEST-SCORES-FILE
000292               AT END MOVE "YES" TO END-OF-FILE-FLAG.
000293
000294     C22-PRINT-SUMMARY.
000295          COMPUTE CLASS-AVERAGE = TOTAL-CREDITS / NUMBER-OF-STUDENTS.
000296
000297          MOVE SPACES              TO REPORT-LINE.
000298          MOVE INSTRUCTOR-NAME     TO OUT-INSTR-NAME.
000299          MOVE INSTRUCTOR-NAME-LINE TO REPORT-LINE.
000300          WRITE REPORT-LINE
000301               AFTER ADVANCING 3 LINES.
000302
000303          MOVE SPACES                TO REPORT-LINE.
000304          MOVE NUMBER-OF-STUDENTS    TO OUT-NO-STUDENTS
000305          MOVE NUMBER-OF-STUDENTS-LINE TO REPORT-LINE.
000306          WRITE REPORT-LINE
000307               AFTER ADVANCING 1 LINE.
000308
000309          MOVE SPACES              TO REPORT-LINE.
000310          MOVE CLASS-AVERAGE       TO OUT-CLASS-AVG.
000311          MOVE CLASS-AVERAGE-LINE TO REPORT-LINE.
000312          WRITE REPORT-LINE
000313               AFTER ADVANCING 1 LINE.
000314
000315
000316     C23-EXIT-SECTION-C2.
000317          EXIT.
000318
000319     D1-DETERMINE-GRADE SECTION.
000320          IF STUDENT-AVERAGE > 89
000321               MOVE "A" TO OUT-STUDENT-GRADE
000322               ADD 4    TO TOTAL-CREDITS.
000323
000324          IF STUDENT-AVERAGE > 79
000325               AND
000326            STUDENT-AVERAGE < 90
000327               MOVE "B" TO OUT-STUDENT-GRADE
000328               ADD 3    TO TOTAL-CREDITS.
000329
```

Program 1-Source (Continued)

```
000330            IF STUDENT-AVERAGE > 69
000331                    AND
000332               STUDENT-AVERAGE < 80
000333                    MOVE "C" TO OUT-STUDENT-GRADE
000334                    ADD 2    TO TOTAL-CREDITS.
000335
000336            IF STUDENT-AVERAGE > 59
000337                    AND
000338               STUDENT-AVERAGE < 70
000339                    MOVE "D" TO OUT-STUDENT-GRADE
000340                    ADD 1    TO TOTAL-CREDITS.
000341
000342            IF STUDENT-AVERAGE < 60
000343                    MOVE "F" TO OUT-STUDENT-GRADE.
```

Program 1-Source (Continued)

```
*.................................................................
 IDENTIFICATION DIVISION.
 PROGRAM-ID.    STUDENT-GRADES.
*****************************************************************
***    THIS PROGRAM READS A SEQUENTIAL DISK FILE, CALLED "STUDENT  *
***    TEST SCORES", AND GENERATES A LIST OF STUDENT SEMESTER      *
***    AVERAGES AND FINAL LETTER GRADES.                           *
***         THE RECORDS OF STUDENT-TEST-SCORES FILE CONSIST OF:    *
***            1. STUDENT ID-NO,                                   *
***            2. STUDENT-NAME,                                    *
***            3. CLASS-CODE,                                      *
***            4. FIRST-TEST-SCORE,                                *
***            5. SECOND-TEST-SCORE,                               *
***            6. FINAL-TEST-SCORE.                                *
***                                                                *
***    THE LIST TO BE GENERATED SHOULD INCLUDE:                    *
***            1. A REPORT HEADER CONSISTING OF                    *
***                (A) REPORT TITLE,                               *
***                (B) COURSE CODE AND COURSE NAME,                *
***                (C) PROCESSING DATE,                            *
***                (D) PAGE NUMBER,                                *
***                                                                *
***            2. ONE SUMMARY LINE FOR EACH STUDENT CONSISTING OF: *
***                (A) STUDENT NAME,                               *
***                (B) SEMESTER AVERAGE,                           *
***                (C) END-OF-SEMESTER LETTER GRADE.               *
***                                                                *
***            3. A SUMMARY SECTION CONSISTING OF:                 *
***                (A) INSTRUCTOR NAME,                            *
***                (B) NUMBER OF STUDENTS IN CLASS,                *
***                (C) GRADE POINT AVERAGE FOR CLASS.              *
***                                                                *
***    VALUES FOR "COURSE NAME" AND "INSTRUCTOR NAME" ARE TO BE    *
***    INPUT INTERACTIVELY AT THE TERMINAL.                        *
***                                                                *
```

Program 2-Source Sample COBOL Nested Program

```
***    AVERAGE SCORE FOR STUDENTS WILL BE COMPUTED USING THE        *
***    FOLLOWING FORMULA:                                           *
***       0.25 * FIRST-TEST-SCORE + 0.35 * SECOND-TEST-SCORE        *
***        + 0.40 * FINAL-EXAM-SCORE.                               *
***                                                                 *
***    THE RECORDS IN STUDENT-TEST-SCORES FILE ARE PRESORTED BY     *
***    STUDENT-IDNO AND COURSE-CODE.                                *
***    THE PROGRAM USES TWO NESTED PROGRAMS CALLED:                 *
***         C1-TERMINAL-INPUTS, AND                                 *
***         D1-DETERMINE-GRADES, RESPECTIVELY.                      *
*********************************************************************

   AUTHOR.         UCKAN.
   INSTALLATION. MIAMI UNIVERSITY.
   DATE-WRITTEN. OCTOBER 7, 1990.
   DATE-COMPILED.
*..................................................................
   ENVIRONMENT DIVISION.
   CONFIGURATION SECTION.
   SOURCE-COMPUTER. UNIVERSITY-MAINFRAME.
   OBJECT-COMPUTER. UNIVERSITY-MAINFRAME.
   INPUT-OUTPUT SECTION.
   FILE-CONTROL.
       SELECT STUDENT-TEST-SCORES-FILE ASSIGN TO INFILE
              ORGANIZATION IS SEQUENTIAL
              ACCESS MODE  IS SEQUENTIAL.

       SELECT SUMMARY-GRADES-REPORT    ASSIGN TO OUTFILE.
*..................................................................
   DATA DIVISION.
   FILE SECTION.

   FD STUDENT-TEST-SCORES-FILE
       LABEL RECORDS ARE STANDARD
       DATA  RECORD  IS STUDENT-TEST-SCORES-RECORD
       RECORD CONTAINS 80 CHARACTERS.
   01  STUDENT-TEST-SCORES-RECORD.
       05  STUDENT-IDNO        PIC X(4).
       05  FILLER              PIC X.
       05  STUDENT-NAME        PIC X(25).
       05  FILLER              PIC X.
       05  COURSE-CODE         PIC X(8).
       05  FILLER              PIC X.
       05  FIRST-TEST-SCORE    PIC 999.
       05  FILLER              PIC X.
       05  SECOND-TEST-SCORE   PIC 999.
       05  FILLER              PIC X.
       05  FINAL-TEST-SCORE    PIC 999.
       05  FILLER              PIC X(29).

   FD  SUMMARY-GRADES-REPORT
       LABEL RECORDS ARE OMITTED
       DATA  RECORD  IS REPORT-LINE
       RECORD CONTAINS 131 CHARACTERS.
   01  REPORT-LINE             PIC X(131).
```

Program 2-Source (Continued)

```
WORKING-STORAGE SECTION.

**********> SWITCHES:

01  END-OF-FILE-FLAG         PIC XXX   VALUE "NO".
    88 END-OF-FILE                     VALUE "YES".

**********> VARIABLES:

 01  PAGE-NUMBER             PIC 99.
 01  NUMBER-OF-STUDENTS      PIC 999.
 01  CLASS-AVERAGE           PIC 9V99.

***********> GLOBAL PROGRAM VARIABLES.

 01  TOTAL-CREDITS     IS GLOBAL.
     05                      PIC 9999.
 01  STUDENT-AVERAGE   IS GLOBAL.
     05                      PIC 999.
 01  TERMINAL-FLAG     IS GLOBAL.
     05                      PIC XXX   VALUE "NO".
         88 INITIAL-INPUTS             VALUE "YES".

**********> STRUCTURES:

 01  TERMINAL-INPUT.
     05  ACADEMIC-YEAR      PIC X(7).
     05  ACADEMIC-SEMESTER  PIC X(6).
     05  COURSE-NAME        PIC X(25).
     05  INSTRUCTOR-NAME    PIC X(21).
     05  CURRENT-COURSE-CODE PIC X(8).

 01  PROCESSING-DATE.
     05  PROCESSING-MONTH   PIC XX.
     05  FILLER             PIC X     VALUE "-".
     05  PROCESSING-DAY     PIC XX.
     05  FILLER             PIC X     VALUE "-".
     05  PROCESSING-YEAR    PIC XX.

 01  TODAYS-DATE.
     05  TODAYS-YEAR        PIC XX.
     05  TODAYS-MONTH       PIC XX.
     05  TODAYS-DAY         PIC XX.

 01  REPORT-TITLE-1.
     05  FILLER             PIC X(30)  VALUE SPACES.
     05  FILLER             PIC X(18)  VALUE "CLASS GRADE REPORT".
     05  FILLER             PIC X(10)  VALUE SPACES.
     05  FILLER             PIC X(6)   VALUE "DATE: ".
     05  OUT-DATE           PIC X(8).

 01  REPORT-LINE-2.
     05  FILLER             PIC X(58)  VALUE SPACES.
     05  FILLER             PIC X(6)   VALUE "PAGE: ".
     05  OUT-PAGE-NUMBER    PIC ZZ.
```

Program 2-Source (Continued)

```
01  YEAR-SEMESTER-LINE.
    05  FILLER                 PIC X(27)  VALUE SPACES.
    05  OUT-ACADEMIC-YEAR      PIC X(8).
    05  OUT-ACADEMIC-SEMESTER  PIC X(7).
    05  FILLER                 PIC X(8)   VALUE SPACES.

 01  COURSE-DESCRIPTION-LINE.
    05  FILLER                 PIC X(3)   VALUE SPACES.
    05  OUT-COURSE-CODE        PIC X(10).
    05  OUT-COURSE-NAME        PIC X(25).

01  STUDENT-INFO-HEADER.
    05  FILLER                 PIC X(13)  VALUE SPACES.
    05  FILLER                 PIC X(12)  VALUE "STUDENT NAME".
    05  FILLER                 PIC X(14)  VALUE SPACES.
    05  FILLER                 PIC X(16)  VALUE "SEMESTER AVERAGE".
    05  FILLER                 PIC X(5)   VALUE SPACES.
    05  FILLER                 PIC X(5)   VALUE "GRADE".

01  STUDENT-INFO-UNDERLINE.
    05  FILLER                 PIC X(13)  VALUE SPACES.
    05  FILLER                 PIC X(21)  VALUE ALL "-".
    05  FILLER                 PIC X(5)   VALUE SPACES.
    05  FILLER                 PIC X(16)  VALUE ALL "-".
    05  FILLER                 PIC X(5)   VALUE SPACES.
    05  FILLER                 PIC X(5)   VALUE ALL "-".

01  STUDENT-LISTING-LINE.
    05  FILLER                 PIC X(13)  VALUE SPACES.
    05  OUT-STUDENT-NAME       PIC X(21).
    05  FILLER                 PIC X(11)  VALUE SPACES.
    05  OUT-STUDENT-AVERAGE    PIC ZZZ.
    05  FILLER                 PIC X(14)  VALUE SPACES.

* ANOTHER GLOBAL VARIABLE:
    05  OUT-STUDENT-GRADE IS GLOBAL.
        10                     PIC X.

01  INSTRUCTOR-NAME-LINE.
    05  FILLER           PIC X(30)  VALUE SPACES.
    05  FILLER           PIC X(20)  VALUE "INSTRUCTOR        : ".
    05  OUT-INSTR-NAME PIC X(21).

01  NUMBER-OF-STUDENTS-LINE.
    05  FILLER           PIC X(30)  VALUE SPACES.
    05  FILLER           PIC X(20)  VALUE "NUMBER OF STUDENTS: ".
    05  OUT-NO-STUDENTS PIC ZZZ.

01  CLASS-AVERAGE-LINE.
    05  FILLER           PIC X(30)  VALUE SPACES.
    05  FILLER           PIC X(20)  VALUE "CLASS AVERAGE     : ".
    05  OUT-CLASS-AVG    PIC Z.ZZ.
```

Program 2-Source (Continued)

```
*.............................................................
   PROCEDURE DIVISION.
   A-MAINLINER.
        OPEN INPUT STUDENT-TEST-SCORES-FILE
             OUTPUT SUMMARY-GRADES-REPORT.
        PERFORM B1-PREPARATIONS.
        PERFORM B2-INITIAL-TERMINAL-INPUTS.
        READ STUDENT-TEST-SCORES-FILE
             AT END MOVE "YES" TO END-OF-FILE-FLAG.

        PERFORM B3-GENERATE-PAGES
             UNTIL END-OF-FILE.

        CLOSE STUDENT-TEST-SCORES-FILE
             SUMMARY-GRADES-REPORT.
        STOP RUN.

   B1-PREPARATIONS.
        ACCEPT TODAYS-DATE FROM DATE.
        MOVE TODAYS-YEAR  TO PROCESSING-YEAR.
        MOVE TODAYS-MONTH TO PROCESSING-MONTH.
        MOVE TODAYS-DAY   TO PROCESSING-DAY.
        MOVE 1            TO PAGE-NUMBER.

   B2-INITIAL-TERMINAL-INPUTS.
        MOVE SPACES TO TERMINAL-INPUT.
        MOVE "YES" TO TERMINAL-FLAG.
        CALL "C1-TERMINAL-INPUTS".

   B3-GENERATE-PAGES.
        MOVE COURSE-CODE TO CURRENT-COURSE-CODE.
        PERFORM C2-INITIALIZE-VARIABLES.
        MOVE "NO" TO TERMINAL-FLAG.
        CALL "C1-TERMINAL-INPUTS".
        PERFORM C3-PRINT-HALF-PAGE.

        PERFORM C4-FORM-STUDENT-LINES
             UNTIL COURSE-CODE NOT EQUAL TO CURRENT-COURSE-CODE
                              OR
                          END-OF-FILE.

        PERFORM C5-PRINT-SUMMARY.
        ADD 1 TO PAGE-NUMBER.

   C2-INITIALIZE-VARIABLES.
        MOVE 0    TO NUMBER-OF-STUDENTS.
        MOVE ZERO TO TOTAL-CREDITS.

   C3-PRINT-HALF-PAGE.
        MOVE SPACES           TO REPORT-LINE.
        MOVE PROCESSING-DATE TO OUT-DATE.
        MOVE REPORT-TITLE-1  TO REPORT-LINE.
```

Program 2-Source (Continued)

```
        WRITE REPORT-LINE
                AFTER ADVANCING PAGE.

        MOVE SPACES          TO REPORT-LINE.
        MOVE PAGE-NUMBER     TO OUT-PAGE-NUMBER.
        MOVE REPORT-LINE-2 TO REPORT-LINE.
        WRITE REPORT-LINE
                AFTER ADVANCING 1 LINE.
        MOVE SPACES              TO REPORT-LINE.
        MOVE ACADEMIC-YEAR       TO OUT-ACADEMIC-YEAR.
        MOVE ACADEMIC-SEMESTER   TO OUT-ACADEMIC-SEMESTER.
        MOVE YEAR-SEMESTER-LINE TO REPORT-LINE.
        WRITE REPORT-LINE
                AFTER ADVANCING 3 LINES.

        MOVE SPACES                  TO REPORT-LINE.
        MOVE CURRENT-COURSE-CODE     TO OUT-COURSE-CODE.
        MOVE COURSE-NAME             TO OUT-COURSE-NAME.
        MOVE COURSE-DESCRIPTION-LINE TO REPORT-LINE.
        WRITE REPORT-LINE
                AFTER ADVANCING 2 LINES.

        MOVE SPACES              TO REPORT-LINE.
        MOVE STUDENT-INFO-HEADER TO REPORT-LINE.
        WRITE REPORT-LINE
                AFTER ADVANCING 2 LINES.

        MOVE SPACES                 TO REPORT-LINE.
        MOVE STUDENT-INFO-UNDERLINE TO REPORT-LINE.
        WRITE REPORT-LINE
                AFTER ADVANCING 1 LINE.

C4-FORM-STUDENT-LINES.
        ADD 1 TO NUMBER-OF-STUDENTS.
        COMPUTE STUDENT-AVERAGE =
                0.25 * FIRST-TEST-SCORE +
                0.35 * SECOND-TEST-SCORE +
                0.40 * FINAL-TEST-SCORE.
        CALL "D1-DETERMINE-GRADES".

        MOVE STUDENT-NAME       TO OUT-STUDENT-NAME.
        MOVE STUDENT-AVERAGE    TO OUT-STUDENT-AVERAGE.
        MOVE SPACES             TO REPORT-LINE.
        MOVE STUDENT-LISTING-LINE TO REPORT-LINE.
        WRITE REPORT-LINE
                AFTER ADVANCING 1 LINE.
        READ STUDENT-TEST-SCORES-FILE
                AT END MOVE "YES" TO END-OF-FILE-FLAG.

C5-PRINT-SUMMARY.
        COMPUTE CLASS-AVERAGE = TOTAL-CREDITS / NUMBER-OF-STUDENTS.

        MOVE SPACES              TO REPORT-LINE.
        MOVE INSTRUCTOR-NAME     TO OUT-INSTR-NAME.
        MOVE INSTRUCTOR-NAME-LINE TO REPORT-LINE.
```

Program 2-Source (Continued)

```
          WRITE REPORT-LINE
                  AFTER ADVANCING 3 LINES.

          MOVE SPACES                   TO REPORT-LINE.
          MOVE NUMBER-OF-STUDENTS       TO OUT-NO-STUDENTS
          MOVE NUMBER-OF-STUDENTS-LINE TO REPORT-LINE.
          WRITE REPORT-LINE
                  AFTER ADVANCING 1 LINE.

          MOVE SPACES               TO REPORT-LINE.
          MOVE CLASS-AVERAGE        TO OUT-CLASS-AVG.
          MOVE CLASS-AVERAGE-LINE TO REPORT-LINE.
          WRITE REPORT-LINE
                  AFTER ADVANCING 1 LINE.
 *.............................................................
  IDENTIFICATION DIVISION.
  PROGRAM-ID.     C1-TERMINAL-INPUTS.
 ***************************************************************
 ***   THIS SUBPROGRAM PROVIDES FOR INTERACTIVE INPUT FOR THE    *
 ***   PROBLEM VARIABLES.  IT IS INVOKED BY THE MAIN PROGRAM CALLED*
 ***   "STUDENT-GRADES".                                         *
 ***************************************************************

  AUTHOR.         UCKAN.
  DATE-WRITTEN.   OCTOBER 7, 1990.
 *.............................................................
  DATA DIVISION.
  WORKING-STORAGE SECTION.
  01  INPUT-FLAG            PIC XXX.
      88  START-INPUT                     VALUE "YES".
 *.............................................................
  PROCEDURE DIVISION.
  A-MAINLINE.
      MOVE TERMINAL-FLAG TO INPUT-FLAG.
      IF START-INPUT
              PERFORM B2-INITIAL-INPUTS
      ELSE
              PERFORM B3-REMAINING-INPUTS.

  B1-RETURN-TO-MAIN-PROGRAM.
      EXIT PROGRAM.

  B2-INITIAL-INPUTS.
      DISPLAY "---> ENTER ACADEMIC YEAR, LIKE 1953-54: "
      ACCEPT ACADEMIC-YEAR      FROM CONSOLE.
      DISPLAY "---> ENTER SEMESTER AS FALL, SPRING OR SUMMER: "
      ACCEPT ACADEMIC-SEMESTER FROM CONSOLE.

  B3-REMAINING-INPUTS.
      DISPLAY "---> CURRENT COURSE CODE IS " CURRENT-COURSE-CODE.
      DISPLAY "     ENTER COURSE NAME: ".
      ACCEPT COURSE-NAME      FROM CONSOLE.
      DISPLAY "---> ENTER INSTRUCTOR NAME FOR THIS COURSE: ".
      ACCEPT INSTRUCTOR-NAME FROM CONSOLE.
  END PROGRAM C1-TERMINAL-INPUTS.
```

Program 2-Source (Continued)

```
*...............................................................
  IDENTIFICATION DIVISION.
  PROGRAM-ID. D1-DETERMINE-GRADES.
  **************************************************************
  ***   THIS SUBPROGRAM DETERMINES THE LETTER GRADE FOR A STUDENT,   *
  ***   GIVEN THE AVERAGE SCORE FOR THE STUDENT.   THE LETTER GRADE   *
  ***   IS DETERMINED USING THE FOLLOWING TABLE:                      *
  ***        AVERAGE SCORE        LETTER GRADE                        *
  ***        _____        _____                       *
  ***         90 - 100                 A                              *
  ***         80 - 89                  B                              *
  ***         70 - 79                  C                              *
  ***         60 - 69                  D                              *
  ***          0 - 59                  F                              *
  ***                                                                 *
  ***   THE SUBPROGRAM IS INVOKED BY THE MAIN PROGRAM, CALLED         *
  ***   "STUDENT-GRADES".                                             *
  **************************************************************

  AUTHOR.         UCKAN.
  DATE-WRITTEN.   OCTOBER 7, 1990

*...............................................................
  DATA DIVISION.
  WORKING-STORAGE SECTION.

  01  ST-GRADE        PIC X.
*...............................................................
  PROCEDURE DIVISION.
  A-DETERMINE-GRADE.
      IF STUDENT-AVERAGE > 89
            MOVE "A" TO ST-GRADE
            ADD 4    TO TOTAL-CREDITS.

      IF STUDENT-AVERAGE > 79
            AND
         STUDENT-AVERAGE < 90
            MOVE "B" TO ST-GRADE
            ADD 3    TO TOTAL-CREDITS.

      IF STUDENT-AVERAGE > 69
            AND
         STUDENT-AVERAGE < 80
            MOVE "C" TO ST-GRADE
            ADD 2    TO TOTAL-CREDITS.

      IF STUDENT-AVERAGE > 59
            AND
         STUDENT-AVERAGE < 70
            MOVE "D" TO ST-GRADE
            ADD 1    TO TOTAL-CREDITS.

      IF STUDENT-AVERAGE < 60
            MOVE "F" TO ST-GRADE.

      MOVE ST-GRADE TO OUT-STUDENT-GRADE.
```

Program 2-Source (Continued)

```
      B-RETURN-TO-MAIN-PROGRAM.
         EXIT PROGRAM.

      END PROGRAM D1-DETERMINE-GRADES.
     *..............................................................

      END PROGRAM STUDENT-GRADES.
```

Program 2-Source (Continued)

```
000001     *..............................................................
000002      IDENTIFICATION DIVISION.
000003      PROGRAM-ID.    STUDENT-GRADES.
000004     ****************************************************************
000005     ***   THIS PROGRAM READS A SEQUENTIAL DISK FILE, CALLED "STUDENT  *
000006     ***   TEST SCORES", AND GENERATES A LIST OF STUDENT SEMESTER      *
000007     ***   AVERAGES AND FINAL LETTER GRADES.                           *
000008     ***        THE RECORDS OF STUDENT-TEST-SCORES FILE CONSIST OF:    *
000009     ***           1. STUDENT ID-NO,                                   *
000010     ***           2. STUDENT-NAME,                                    *
000011     ***           3. CLASS-CODE,                                      *
000012     ***           4. FIRST-TEST-SCORE,                                *
000013     ***           5. SECOND-TEST-SCORE,                               *
000014     ***           6. FINAL-TEST-SCORE.                                *
000015     ***                                                               *
000016     ***   THE LIST TO BE GENERATED SHOULD INCLUDE:                    *
000017     ***           1. A REPORT HEADER CONSISTING OF                    *
000018     ***              (A) REPORT TITLE,                                *
000019     ***              (B) COURSE CODE AND COURSE NAME,                 *
000020     ***              (C) PROCESSING DATE,                             *
000021     ***              (D) PAGE NUMBER                                  *
000022     ***                                                               *
000023     ***           2. ONE SUMMARY LINE FOR EACH STUDENT CONSISTING OF: *
000024     ***              (A) STUDENT NAME,                                *
000025     ***              (B) SEMESTER AVERAGE,                            *
000026     ***              (C) END-OF-SEMESTER LETTER GRADE.                *
000027     ***                                                               *
000028     ***           3. A SUMMARY SECTION CONSISTING OF:                 *
000029     ***              (A) INSTRUCTOR NAME,                             *
000030     ***              (B) NUMBER OF STUDENTS IN CLASS,                 *
000031     ***              (C) GRADE POINT AVERAGE FOR CLASS.               *
000032     ***                                                               *
000033     ***   VALUES FOR "COURSE NAME" AND "INSTRUCTOR NAME" ARE TO BE    *
000034     ***   INPUT INTERACTIVELY AT THE TERMINAL.                        *
000035     ***                                                               *
000036     ***   AVERAGE SCORE FOR STUDENTS WILL BE COMPUTED USING THE       *
000037     ***   FOLLOWING FORMULA:                                          *
000038     ***      0.25 * FIRST-TEST-SCORE + 0.35 * SECOND-TEST-SCORE       *
000039     ***       + 0.40 * FINAL-EXAM-SCORE.                              *
000040     ***                                                               *
000041     ***   THE RECORDS IN STUDENT-TEST-SCORES FILE ARE PRESORTED BY    *
000042     ***   STUDENT-IDNO AND COURSE-CODE.                               *
```

Program 3-Source(a) Main Program for Sample Application Software to Generate Class Grade Reports

```
000043    ***   THE PROGRAM USES TWO SUBROUTINES CALLED:              *
000044    ***        C1-TERMINAL-INPUTS, AND                          *
000045    ***        D1-DETERMINE-GRADES, RESPECTIVELY.               *
000046    *******************************************************************
000047
000048     AUTHOR.        UCKAN.
000049     INSTALLATION. MIAMI UNIVERSITY.
000050     DATE-WRITTEN. OCTOBER 7, 1990.
000051     DATE-COMPILED. OCT  7,1990.
000052     *...............................................................
000053     ENVIRONMENT DIVISION.
000054     CONFIGURATION SECTION.
000055     SOURCE-COMPUTER. UNIVERSITY-MAINFRAME.
000056     OBJECT-COMPUTER. UNIVERSITY-MAINFRAME.
000057     INPUT-OUTPUT SECTION.
000058     FILE-CONTROL.
000059         SELECT STUDENT-TEST-SCORES-FILE ASSIGN TO INFILE
000060                 ORGANIZATION IS SEQUENTIAL
000061                 ACCESS MODE  IS SEQUENTIAL.
000062
000063         SELECT SUMMARY-GRADES-REPORT    ASSIGN TO OUTFILE.
000064     *...............................................................
000065     DATA DIVISION.
000066     FILE SECTION.
000067
000068     FD STUDENT-TEST-SCORES-FILE
000069         LABEL RECORDS ARE STANDARD
000070         DATA  RECORD  IS STUDENT-TEST-SCORES-RECORD
000071         RECORD CONTAINS 80 CHARACTERS.
000072     01  STUDENT-TEST-SCORES-RECORD.
000073         05   STUDENT-IDNO      PIC X(4).
000074         05   FILLER            PIC X.
000075         05   STUDENT-NAME      PIC X(25).
000076         05   FILLER            PIC X.
000077         05   COURSE-CODE       PIC X(8).
000078         05   FILLER            PIC X.
000079         05   FIRST-TEST-SCORE  PIC 999.
000080         05   FILLER            PIC X.
000081         05   SECOND-TEST-SCORE PIC 999.
000082         05   FILLER            PIC X.
000083         05   FINAL-TEST-SCORE  PIC 999.
000084         05   FILLER            PIC X(29).
000085
000086     FD  SUMMARY-GRADES-REPORT
000087         LABEL RECORDS ARE OMITTED
000088         DATA  RECORD  IS REPORT-LINE
000089         RECORD CONTAINS 131 CHARACTERS.
000090     01  REPORT-LINE            PIC X(131).
000091
000092     WORKING-STORAGE SECTION.
000093
000094     **********> SWITCHES:
000095
000096     01  END-OF-FILE-FLAG       PIC XXX  VALUE "NO".
000097         88 END-OF-FILE                  VALUE "YES".
```

Program 3-Source(a) (Continued)

```
000098
000099     01   TERMINAL-FLAG              PIC XXX   VALUE "NO".
000100          88 INITIAL-INPUTS                    VALUE "YES".
000101
000102     **********> VARIABLES:
000103
000104     01   PAGE-NUMBER               PIC 99.
000105     01   NUMBER-OF-STUDENTS        PIC 999.
000106     01   TOTAL-CREDITS             PIC 9999.
000107     01   CLASS-AVERAGE             PIC 9V99.
000108     01   STUDENT-AVERAGE           PIC 999.
000109
000110     **********> STRUCTURES:
000111
000112     01   TERMINAL-INPUT.
000113          05   ACADEMIC-YEAR        PIC X(7).
000114          05   ACADEMIC-SEMESTER    PIC X(6).
000115          05   COURSE-NAME          PIC X(25).
000116          05   INSTRUCTOR-NAME      PIC X(21).
000117          05   CURRENT-COURSE-CODE  PIC X(8).
000118
000119     01   PROCESSING-DATE.
000120          05   PROCESSING-MONTH     PIC XX.
000121          05   FILLER               PIC X     VALUE "-".
000122          05   PROCESSING-DAY       PIC XX.
000123          05   FILLER               PIC X     VALUE "-".
000124          05   PROCESSING-YEAR      PIC XX.
000125
000126     01   TODAYS-DATE.
000127          05   TODAYS-YEAR          PIC XX.
000128          05   TODAYS-MONTH         PIC XX.
000129          05   TODAYS-DAY           PIC XX.
000130
000131     01   REPORT-TITLE-1.
000132          05   FILLER               PIC X(30)  VALUE SPACES.
000133          05   FILLER               PIC X(18)  VALUE "CLASS GRADE REPORT".
000134          05   FILLER               PIC X(10)  VALUE SPACES.
000135          05   FILLER               PIC X(6)   VALUE "DATE: ".
000136          05   OUT-DATE             PIC X(8).
000137
000138     01   REPORT-LINE-2.
000139          05   FILLER               PIC X(58)  VALUE SPACES.
000140          05   FILLER               PIC X(6)   VALUE "PAGE: ".
000141          05   OUT-PAGE-NUMBER      PIC ZZ.
000142
000143     01   YEAR-SEMESTER-LINE.
000144          05   FILLER                   PIC X(27)  VALUE SPACES.
000145          05   OUT-ACADEMIC-YEAR        PIC X(8).
000146          05   OUT-ACADEMIC-SEMESTER    PIC X(7).
000147          05   FILLER                   PIC X(8)   VALUE SPACES.
000148
000149     01   COURSE-DESCRIPTION-LINE.
000150          05   FILLER                   PIC X(3)   VALUE SPACES.
000151          05   OUT-COURSE-CODE          PIC X(10).
000152          05   OUT-COURSE-NAME          PIC X(25).
```

Program 3-Source(a) (Continued)

```
000153
000154     01   STUDENT-INFO-HEADER.
000155          05   FILLER              PIC X(13)   VALUE SPACES.
000156          05   FILLER              PIC X(12)   VALUE "STUDENT NAME".
000157          05   FILLER              PIC X(14)   VALUE SPACES.
000158          05   FILLER              PIC X(16)   VALUE "SEMESTER AVERAGE".
000159          05   FILLER              PIC X(5)    VALUE SPACES.
000160          05   FILLER              PIC X(5)    VALUE "GRADE".
000161
000162     01   STUDENT-INFO-UNDERLINE.
000163          05   FILLER              PIC X(13)   VALUE SPACES.
000164          05   FILLER              PIC X(21)   VALUE ALL "-".
000165          05   FILLER              PIC X(5)    VALUE SPACES.
000166          05   FILLER              PIC X(16)   VALUE ALL "-".
000167          05   FILLER              PIC X(5)    VALUE SPACES.
000168          05   FILLER              PIC X(5)    VALUE ALL "-".
000169
000170     01   STUDENT-LISTING-LINE.
000171          05   FILLER              PIC X(13)   VALUE SPACES.
000172          05   OUT-STUDENT-NAME    PIC X(21).
000173          05   FILLER              PIC X(11)   VALUE SPACES.
000174          05   OUT-STUDENT-AVERAGE PIC ZZZ.
000175          05   FILLER              PIC X(14)   VALUE SPACES.
000176          05   OUT-STUDENT-GRADE   PIC X.
000177
000178     01   INSTRUCTOR-NAME-LINE.
000179          05   FILLER         PIC X(30)  VALUE SPACES.
000180          05   FILLER         PIC X(20)  VALUE "INSTRUCTOR      : ".
000181          05   OUT-INSTR-NAME PIC X(21).
000182
000183     01   NUMBER-OF-STUDENTS-LINE.
000184          05   FILLER         PIC X(30)  VALUE SPACES.
000185          05   FILLER         PIC X(20)  VALUE "NUMBER OF STUDENTS: ".
000186          05   OUT-NO-STUDENTS PIC ZZZ.
000187
000188     01   CLASS-AVERAGE-LINE.
000189          05   FILLER         PIC X(30)  VALUE SPACES.
000190          05   FILLER         PIC X(20)  VALUE "CLASS AVERAGE   : ".
000191          05   OUT-CLASS-AVG  PIC ZZZ.
000192
000193 *............................................................
000194  PROCEDURE DIVISION.
000195  A-MAINLINER.
000196      OPEN INPUT STUDENT-TEST-SCORES-FILE
000197           OUTPUT SUMMARY-GRADES-REPORT.
000198      PERFORM B1-PREPARATIONS.
000199      PERFORM B2-INITIAL-TERMINAL-INPUTS.
000200      READ STUDENT-TEST-SCORES-FILE
000201           AT END MOVE "YES" TO END-OF-FILE-FLAG.
000202
000203      PERFORM B3-GENERATE-PAGES
000204           UNTIL END-OF-FILE.
000205
000206      CLOSE STUDENT-TEST-SCORES-FILE
000207           SUMMARY-GRADES-REPORT.
```

Program 3-Source(a) (Continued)

```
000208        STOP RUN.
000209
000210    B1-PREPARATIONS.
000211        ACCEPT TODAYS-DATE FROM DATE.
000212        MOVE TODAYS-YEAR  TO PROCESSING-YEAR.
000213        MOVE TODAYS-MONTH TO PROCESSING-MONTH.
000214        MOVE TODAYS-DAY   TO PROCESSING-DAY.
000215        MOVE 1            TO PAGE-NUMBER.
000216
000217    B2-INITIAL-TERMINAL-INPUTS.
000218        MOVE SPACES TO TERMINAL-INPUT.
000219        MOVE "YES" TO TERMINAL-FLAG.
000220        CALL "C1-TERMINAL-INPUTS" USING
000221             TERMINAL-FLAG TERMINAL-INPUT.
000222
000223    B3-GENERATE-PAGES.
000224        MOVE COURSE-CODE TO CURRENT-COURSE-CODE.
000225        PERFORM C2-INITIALIZE-VARIABLES.
000226        MOVE "NO" TO TERMINAL-FLAG.
000227        CALL "C1-TERMINAL-INPUTS" USING
000228             TERMINAL-FLAG TERMINAL-INPUT.
000229        PERFORM C3-PRINT-HALF-PAGE.
000230
000231        PERFORM C4-FORM-STUDENT-LINES
000232             UNTIL COURSE-CODE NOT EQUAL TO CURRENT-COURSE-CODE
000233                              OR
000234                           END-OF-FILE.
000235
000236        PERFORM C5-PRINT-SUMMARY.
000237        ADD 1 TO PAGE-NUMBER.
000238
000239    C2-INITIALIZE-VARIABLES.
000240        MOVE 0    TO NUMBER-OF-STUDENTS.
000241        MOVE ZERO TO TOTAL-CREDITS.
000242
000243    C3-PRINT-HALF-PAGE.
000244        MOVE SPACES          TO REPORT-LINE.
000245        MOVE PROCESSING-DATE TO OUT-DATE.
000246        MOVE REPORT-TITLE-1  TO REPORT-LINE.
000247        WRITE REPORT-LINE
000248             AFTER ADVANCING PAGE.
000249
000250        MOVE SPACES       TO REPORT-LINE.
000251        MOVE PAGE-NUMBER  TO OUT-PAGE-NUMBER.
000252        MOVE REPORT-LINE-2 TO REPORT-LINE.
000253        WRITE REPORT-LINE
000254             AFTER ADVANCING 1 LINE.
000255
000256        MOVE SPACES           TO REPORT-LINE.
000257        MOVE ACADEMIC-YEAR     TO OUT-ACADEMIC-YEAR.
000258        MOVE ACADEMIC-SEMESTER TO OUT-ACADEMIC-SEMESTER.
000259        MOVE YEAR-SEMESTER-LINE TO REPORT-LINE.
000260        WRITE REPORT-LINE
000261             AFTER ADVANCING 3 LINES.
000262
```

Program 3-Source(a) (Continued)

```
000263          MOVE SPACES                     TO REPORT-LINE.
000264          MOVE CURRENT-COURSE-CODE    TO OUT-COURSE-CODE.
000265          MOVE COURSE-NAME              TO OUT-COURSE-NAME.
000266          MOVE COURSE-DESCRIPTION-LINE TO REPORT-LINE.
000267          WRITE REPORT-LINE
000268                  AFTER ADVANCING 2 LINES.
000269
000270          MOVE SPACES                   TO REPORT-LINE.
000271          MOVE STUDENT-INFO-HEADER TO REPORT-LINE.
000272          WRITE REPORT-LINE
000273                  AFTER ADVANCING 2 LINES.
000274
000275          MOVE SPACES                     TO REPORT-LINE.
000276          MOVE STUDENT-INFO-UNDERLINE TO REPORT-LINE.
000277          WRITE REPORT-LINE
000278                  AFTER ADVANCING 1 LINE.
000279
000280      C4-FORM-STUDENT-LINES.
000281          ADD 1 TO NUMBER-OF-STUDENTS.
000282          COMPUTE STUDENT-AVERAGE =
000283                  0.25 * FIRST-TEST-SCORE
000284                  0.35 * SECOND-TEST-SCORE +
000285                  0.40 * FINAL-TEST-SCORE. +
000286          CALL "D1-DETERMINE-GRADES" USING
000287                  STUDENT-AVERAGE OUT-STUDENT-GRADE TOTAL-CREDITS.
000288          MOVE STUDENT-NAME           TO OUT-STUDENT-NAME.
000289          MOVE STUDENT-AVERAGE      TO OUT-STUDENT-AVERAGE.
000290          MOVE SPACES                 TO REPORT-LINE.
000291          MOVE STUDENT-LISTING-LINE TO REPORT-LINE.
000292          WRITE REPORT-LINE
000293                  AFTER ADVANCING 1 LINE.
000294          READ STUDENT-TEST-SCORES-FILE
000295                  AT END MOVE "YES" TO END-OF-FILE-FLAG.
000296
000297      C5-PRINT-SUMMARY.
000298          COMPUTE CLASS-AVERAGE = TOTAL-CREDITS / NUMBER-OF-STUDENTS.
000299
000300          MOVE SPACES                 TO REPORT-LINE.
000301          MOVE INSTRUCTOR-NAME      TO OUT-INSTR-NAME.
000302          MOVE INSTRUCTOR-NAME-LINE TO REPORT-LINE.
000303          WRITE REPORT-LINE
000304                  AFTER ADVANCING 3 LINES.
000305
000306          MOVE SPACES                     TO REPORT-LINE.
000307          MOVE NUMBER-OF-STUDENTS       TO OUT-NO-STUDENTS
000308          MOVE NUMBER-OF-STUDENTS-LINE TO REPORT-LINE.
000309          WRITE REPORT-LINE
000310                  AFTER ADVANCING 1 LINE.
000311
000312          MOVE SPACES               TO REPORT-LINE.
000313          MOVE CLASS-AVERAGE      TO OUT-CLASS-AVG.
000314          MOVE CLASS-AVERAGE-LINE TO REPORT-LINE.
000315          WRITE REPORT-LINE
000316                  AFTER ADVANCING 1 LINE.
```

Program 3-Source(a) (Continued)

```
000001     *.................................................................
000002      IDENTIFICATION DIVISION.
000003      PROGRAM-ID.    C1-TERMINAL-INPUTS.
000004      ***********************************************************************
000005      ***   THIS SUBROUTINE PROVIDES FOR INTERACTIVE INPUT FOR THE      *
000006      ***   PROBLEM VARIABLES.  IT HAS TWO FORMAL PARAMETERS:           *
000007      ***       1. INPUT-FLAG: THE CALLING PROGRAM SENDS A VALUE FOR    *
000008      ***          THIS PARAMETER.  IF THE VALUE IS "YES", THEN VALUES  *
000009      ***          FOR THE VARIABLES ACADEMIC-YEAR AND ACADEMIC-SEMESTER*
000010      ***          ARE INTERACTIVELY READ AND RETURNED TO THE CALLING   *
000011      ***          PROGRAM.  OTHERWISE, VALUES FOR THE REMAINING        *
000012      ***          VARIABLES ARE INPUT AND RETURNED.                    *
000013      ***       2. INPUT-VALUES: IS A GROUP ITEM, CONTAINING ALL PROBLEM*
000014      ***          VARIABLES FOR WHICH VALUES ARE INPUT AND RETURNED.   *
000015      ***   THIS SUBROUTINE IS INVOKED BY THE MAIN PROGRAM CALLED       *
000016      ***   "STUDENT-GRADES".                                          *
000017      ***********************************************************************
000018
000019      AUTHOR.         UCKAN.
000020      INSTALLATION.  MIAMI UNIVERSITY.
000021      DATE-WRITTEN.  OCTOBER 7, 1990.
000022      DATE-COMPILED. OCT  7,1990.
000023     *.................................................................
000024      ENVIRONMENT DIVISION.
000025      CONFIGURATION SECTION.
000026      SOURCE-COMPUTER. UNIVERSITY-MAINFRAME.
000027      OBJECT-COMPUTER. UNIVERSITY-MAINFRAME.
000028     *.................................................................
000029      DATA DIVISION.
000030      LINKAGE SECTION.
000031
000032      01   INPUT-VALUES.
000033           05   ACADEMIC-YEAR       PIC X(7).
000034           05   ACADEMIC-SEMESTER   PIC X(6).
000035           05   COURSE-NAME         PIC X(25).
000036           05   INSTRUCTOR-NAME     PIC X(21).
000037           05   CURRENT-COURSE-CODE PIC X(8).
000038
000039      01   INPUT-FLAG              PIC XXX.
000040           88   START-INPUT                     VALUE "YES".
000041
000042     *.................................................................
000043      PROCEDURE DIVISION USING
000044                      INPUT-FLAG INPUT-VALUES.
000045
000046      A-MAINLINE.
000047          IF START-INPUT
000048                  PERFORM B2-INITIAL-INPUTS
000049          ELSE
000050                  PERFORM B3-REMAINING-INPUTS.
000051
000052      B1-RETURN-TO-MAIN-PROGRAM.
000053          EXIT PROGRAM.
000054
```

Program 3-Source(b) Subprogram C1-TERMINAL-INPUTS for Sample Application Software to Generate Class Grade Reports

```
000055      B2-INITIAL-INPUTS.
000056          DISPLAY "---> ENTER ACADEMIC YEAR, LIKE 1953-54: "
000057          ACCEPT ACADEMIC-YEAR      FROM CONSOLE.
000058          DISPLAY "---> ENTER SEMESTER AS FALL, SPRING OR SUMMER: "
000059          ACCEPT ACADEMIC-SEMESTER FROM CONSOLE.
000060
000061      B3-REMAINING-INPUTS.
000062          DISPLAY "---> CURRENT COURSE CODE IS " CURRENT-COURSE-CODE.
000063          DISPLAY "     ENTER COURSE NAME: ".
000064          ACCEPT COURSE-NAME      FROM CONSOLE.
000065          DISPLAY "---> ENTER INSTRUCTOR NAME FOR THIS COURSE: ".
000066          ACCEPT INSTRUCTOR-NAME FROM CONSOLE.
```

Program 3-Source(b) (Continued)

```
000001      *...........................................................
000002      IDENTIFICATION DIVISION.
000003      PROGRAM-ID. D1-DETERMINE-GRADES.
000004      *****************************************************************
000005      ***   THIS SUBROUTINE DETERMINES THE LETTER GRADE FOR A STUDENT, *
000006      ***   GIVEN THE AVERAGE SCORE FOR THE STUDENT.  THE LETTER GRADE  *
000007      ***   IS DETERMINED USING THE FOLLOWING TABLE:                    *
000008      ***        AVERAGE SCORE        LETTER GRADE                      *
000009      ***        -------------        ------------                      *
000010      ***          90 - 100               A                            *
000011      ***          80 - 89                B                            *
000012      ***          70 - 79                C                            *
000013      ***          60 - 69                D                            *
000014      ***           0 - 59                F                            *
000015      ***                                                              *
000016      ***   THE SUBROUTINE IS INVOKED BY THE MAIN PROGRAM, CALLED      *
000017      ***   "STUDENT-GRADES".  IT HAS THREE FORMAL PARAMETERS:         *
000018      ***      1. ST-AVERAGE: REPRESENTS AVERAGE TEST SCORE.  THE      *
000019      ***         CALLING PROGRAM SENDS A VALUE FOR THIS PARAMETER.    *
000020      ***      2. ST-GRADE: REPRESENTS THE LETTER GRADE, COMPUTED AND  *
000021      ***         RETURNED TO THE CALLING PROGRAM BY THIS SUBROUTINE.  *
000022      ***      3. CREDIT-TOTALS: REPRESENTS THE TOTAL CREDITS FOR THE  *
000023      ***         STUDENT.  THE CALLING PROGRAM SENDS A VALUE FOR IT,  *
000024      ***         AND THIS SUBROUTINE UPDATES IT BY ADDING 4 TO IT IF  *
000025      ***         THE GRADE IS "A", 3 IF IT IS "B", 2 IF IT IS "C",    *
000026      ***         1 IF "D", AND 0 IF "F".                              *
000027      *****************************************************************
000028
000029      AUTHOR.         UCKAN.
000030      INSTALLATION.   MIAMI UNIVERSITY.
000031      DATE-WRITTEN.   OCTOBER 7, 1990
000032      DATE-COMPILED. OCT  7,1990.
000033      *...........................................................
000034      ENVIRONMENT DIVISION.
000035      CONFIGURATION SECTION.
000036      SOURCE-COMPUTER.  UNIVERSITY-MAINFRAME.
000037      OBJECT-COMPUTER.  UNIVERSITY-MAINFRAME.
000038      *...........................................................
```

Program 3-Source(c) Subprogram D1-DETERMINE-GRADES for Sample Application Software to Generate Class Grade Reports

```
000039     DATA DIVISION.
000040     LINKAGE SECTION.
000041
000042     01  ST-AVERAGE      PIC 999.
000043     01  ST-GRADE        PIC X.
000044     01  CREDIT-TOTALS   PIC 9999.
000045
000046     *..............................................................
000047     PROCEDURE DIVISION USING
000048                         ST-AVERAGE ST-GRADE CREDIT-TOTALS.
000049     A-DETERMINE-GRADE.
000050         IF ST-AVERAGE > 89
000051                 MOVE "A" TO ST-GRADE
000052                 ADD 4    TO CREDIT-TOTALS.
000053
000054         IF ST-AVERAGE > 79
000055                 AND
000056           ST-AVERAGE < 90
000057                 MOVE "B" TO ST-GRADE
000058                 ADD 3    TO CREDIT-TOTALS.
000059
000060         IF ST-AVERAGE > 69
000061                 AND
000062           ST-AVERAGE < 80
000063                 MOVE "C" TO ST-GRADE
000064                 ADD 2    TO CREDIT-TOTALS.
000065
000066         IF ST-AVERAGE > 59
000067                 AND
000068           ST-AVERAGE < 70
000069                 MOVE "D" TO ST-GRADE
000070                 ADD 1    TO CREDIT-TOTALS.
000071
000072          IF ST-AVERAGE < 60
000073                 MOVE "F" TO ST-GRADE.
000074
000075     B-RETURN-TO-MAIN-PROGRAM.
000076         EXIT PROGRAM.
```

Program 3-Source(c) (Continued)

III

Data Structures in COBOL

8

Tables, Arrays, and Array Processing

Introduction

In many programming applications we find it necessary to define and use identifiers with multiple values. An example of this is when we have to store the salaries of 1000 employees at the same time in the computer's memory. It is extremely awkward to invent 1000 different identifiers such as EMPLOYEE-SALARY-1, EMPLOYEE-SALARY-2, and so on, and keep track of them while designing the program. Instead, we look for a data type that can accept all of these values and store them under a single identifier. An array is such a data type.

Arrays are common data structures and are supported by all computer programming languages. In COBOL it is one of the important built-in data structures. Conceptually, an array is an index set and an associated value set. An index, in this context, is not a hardware address; it is a relative address, indicating the location of a memory cell within a predefined segment of the memory, namely the array. The principal advantage of an array lies in the fact that given an index, we can directly access and retrieve the associated value. The second advantage is that we do not have to invent separate names to address individual elements. Instead, the array name, together with an index, is enough for memory access.

In data processing we ordinarily structure related data elements and store them together. In external storage we accomplish this by structuring data into files. As we have seen for sequential files, accessing a record enables us to retrieve all data elements defined in the record structure. In the main memory, if we want to store more than one record in a structured fashion, an array is indicated. In other words, arrays are the internal data structure counterpart of sequential files. For this reason, they are frequently used in data processing.

An array contains similarly structured occurrences of data elements, each one of which can be accessed directly by a relative address. There are two common operations on data that are stored in arrays.

1. It may be desirable to order an array by its content. The technique devised for this purpose is called **sorting**.
2. We may want to find and access an array element by its content. This is array **searching**, also known as table look-up.

In this chapter we will study arrays, array processing, and COBOL implementation of arrays. We will also discuss array sorting and searching, and the COBOL features for array searching.

Arrays

This section introduces the basic concepts of and operations for arrays. Following the discussion of the fundamentals, we will study how arrays are implemented and handled in COBOL.

Arrays and Lists

Arrays are used in many computer applications as an internal data structure because they are convenient for defining and storing a list, which is a related collection of data elements under a common name.

> A **list** (also called a **linear list**) is a variable-size set of ordered data elements.

For example, if our application requires that we store and process a group of student names, instead of using separate program variables for each name (e.g., STUDENT-NAME-1, STUDENT-NAME-2, etc.) and assigning values to them, we can collect them into a list, as in

        STUDENT—NAME = [WILLIAM, JOHN, JANE, MARY].

Such a grouping is convenient because we use only one program variable to represent the entire collection, and we may refer to each value of the group using a relative address or an index. Hence, STUDENT-NAME (1) would be a reference to the first value in the group, namely WILLIAM. Also, if necessary, we may define an order between the elements of the collection. If ordered alphabetically, the above list becomes

        STUDENT—NAME = [JANE, JOHN, MARY, WILLIAM].

We may add new values to a list or delete existing values from it. For example, we may add ANNE and ROBERT to the STUDENT-NAME list, and delete MARY. These operations will change the list to

        STUDENT—NAME = [ANNE, JANE, JOHN, ROBERT, WILLIAM].

Such operations not only change the content of a list, they may also change its size. Hence, a list is a variable-size data structure.

We must have a storage structure to store a list in the computer's memory. If this storage structure is to exist in external storage, the list is stored in a file. If we want to store and process the list in the main memory, we need an array.

> An **array** is an ordered set of a fixed number of consecutive memory locations each accessed by a relative address. The number of memory locations in an array is its **size**. The individually addressable memory locations in an array are its **elements**.

Thus, an array is a fixed-size storage structure hosting a variable-size list. Figure 1 shows a list of size 4 in an array of size 7. A list is a dynamic entity in that its size may grow by the addition of new elements, or may decrease by the deletion of existing elements. On the other hand, once defined, the size of an array does not change.

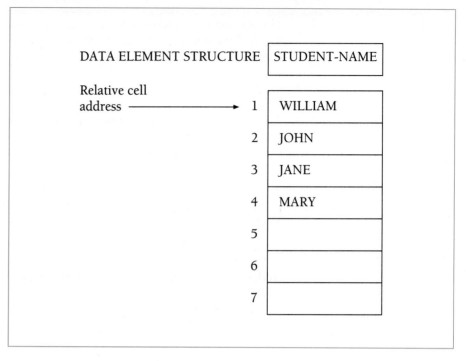

Figure 1 An Unordered List in an Array

The elements of a list contained in an array may be composite data elements. In Figure 2 each array element consists of STUDENT-NAME, STUDENT-MAJOR, and STUDENT-AGE fields. The array is called STUDENT-INFORMATION. The array reference STUDENT-INFORMATION (1) retrieves WILLIAM, MATHEMATICS, and 22 for the three fields, respectively. Depending on how the array is implemented, it may also be possible to reference its individual elements, as in STUDENT-MAJOR (1). For the structure of Figure 2, this retrieves MATHEMATICS.

Array elements are accessed using relative addresses, which are integer values. Relative addresses are also known as **subscripts**. In most systems, including COBOL, the smallest value a subscript may assume for an array is 1. The largest value is determined by the size of an array.

In Figures 1 and 2, a list element contained in an element of the host array has its **successor** in the next element of the array. In most implementations of arrays, the elements are physically contiguous in the memory.

Storing the list elements in consecutive array elements is known as **sequential allocation**. In sequentially allocated lists, the successor of a list element is found in the next element of the array.

Another type of allocation for lists is **linked allocation**, in which the logical successor of a list element is not necessarily stored in the next element of the containing array.

In a sequentially allocated list, if the successors of list elements define an ascending or descending ordering by the values of the list elements, the list is called an **ordered list**.

STUDENT-INFORMATION		
STUDENT-NAME	STUDENT-MAJOR	STUDENT-AGE

DATA ELEMENT STRUCTURE

Relative cell address ⟶ 1

WILLIAM	MATHEMATICS	22
JOHN	COMPUTER SCI.	21
JANE	COMPUTER SCI.	23
MARY	MATHEMATICS	21

Figure 2 An Unordered List of Structured Elements in an Array

Figure 3 shows an ordered list of size 4 hosted by an array of size 7. The values of STUDENT-NAME in the array increase as the relative addresses of array elements increase. The lists of Figures 1 and 2 are unordered lists.

All arrays we have considered so far require a single subscript to specify relative location of an element. These are **one-dimensional arrays**. Each element of a one-dimensional array can be made to contain another one-dimensional

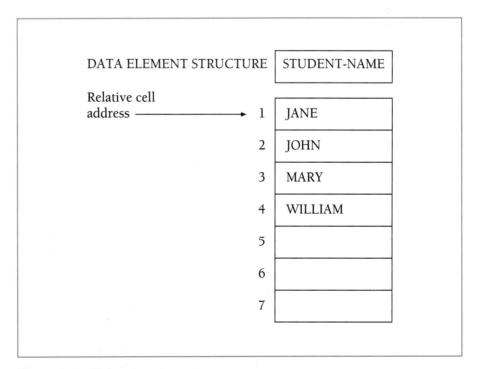

Figure 3 An Ordered List in an Array

array. Such a data structure is a two-dimensional array. We can define higher-dimensional arrays in this manner.

> A **two-dimensional array** is an array of one-dimensional arrays. Similarly, a **three-dimensional array** is an array of two-dimensional arrays, and so on.

Figure 4 is an example of a two-dimensional array called CLASS-ENROLLMENT. It shows student enrollments in four courses offered by three disciplines as major fields of study. This two-dimensional array can be thought of as an array of four elements, such that each element contains an array of three elements. Viewed as a two-dimensional table, this array has four **rows** and three **columns**. A specific element of the array is accessed by means of two subscript values. For instance, CLASS-ENROLLMENT (2,1) is a reference to the first element in the second row, containing a value of 23. A two-dimensional array is also known as a **matrix**.

Figure 5 is an example of a three-dimensional array, also called CLASS-ENROLLMENT. It contains three two-dimensional arrays, like the one in Figure 4, each for a different college. The structure here may be visualized as a succession of two-dimensional arrays, or as a one-dimensional array with each element containing a two-dimensional array of similar structure. Accessing an element of a three-dimensional array requires three subscripts. CLASS-ENROLLMENT (1,2,2) is the enrollment figure for COURSE 1, in MAJOR 2 of COLLEGE 2, which is 15 in the figure.

Although arrays of more than three dimensions are certainly conceivable, in most data processing applications up to three-dimensional arrays are usually sufficient.

Defining Arrays in COBOL

The definition of an array in COBOL requires three elements:

1. A name
2. Specification of its dimensions
3. Specification of its size for each dimension

An array should be defined in the DATA DIVISION of a program at a level other than 01. Each definition should be included in a superordinate structure at level 01. The superordinate structure may include other arrays, as well as

CLASS-ENROLLMENT	MAJOR 1	MAJOR 2	MAJOR 3
COURSE 1	32	27	23
COURSE 2	23	11	19
COURSE 3	11	15	16
COURSE 4	29	34	28

Figure 4 A Two-Dimensional Array

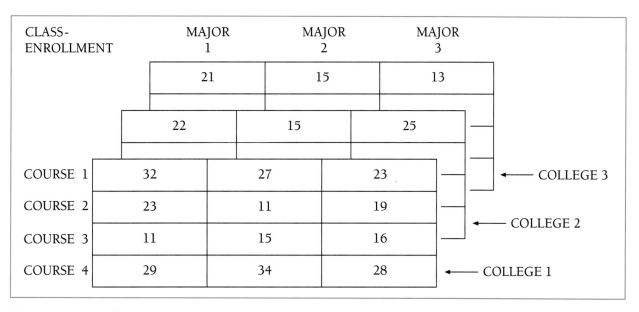

Figure 5 A Three-Dimensional Array

group items and elementary data items. Such a superordinate structure containing arrays is viewed as a table. For this reason, **table** is taken as synonymous with array.

Here is an example:

```
01   STUDENT-TABLE.
     05  ST-NAME   PIC X(10)        OCCURS 3 TIMES.
```

STUDENT-TABLE is a table containing an array called ST-NAME. The size of the array is indicated by the OCCURS clause. OCCURS 3 TIMES establishes ST-NAME as a one-dimensional array of size 3. Each element of the array is alphanumeric and of length 10, as defined by the PICTURE clause. This definition is converted by the compiler during compilation to a storage structure in which there are three consecutive memory cells for the elements of the array ST-NAME. Array elements may be accessed using a proper subscript value that shows its relative location in the structure. Also, the entire array can be referenced using the table name STUDENT-TABLE. The conceptual storage structure for STUDENT-TABLE is as follows.

STUDENT-TABLE			← Table name
ST-NAME 1	ST-NAME 2	ST-NAME 3	← Array element references
JOHN	MARY	JEAN	← Array element values

In COBOL, array elements may be composite or atomic. An array with atomic element values consists of an elementary data item value in each element. It must have a PICTURE clause associated with its name, before or after the OCCURS clause, as in the previous example. On the other hand, an array with composite elements must have an OCCURS clause together with the array name, followed by a substructure specification for the array elements. An example of a one-dimensional COBOL array with composite elements is given below.

```
01   STUDENT-TABLE.
     05   ST-NAME                        OCCURS 3 TIMES.
          10   LAST-NAME     PIC X(10).
          10   FIRST-NAME    PIC X(10).
```

STUDENT-TABLE contains a one-dimensional array called ST-NAME. ST-NAME is an array of size 3. Each of its elements consists of a LAST-NAME and a FIRST-NAME.

COBOL considers higher-dimensional arrays as arrays of one-dimensional arrays. In other words, a two-dimensional array is an array of fixed-size one-dimensional arrays. A three-dimensional array is an array of fixed-size two-dimensional arrays, and so on. The following are examples of two- and three-dimensional COBOL array definitions.

```
01 ENROLLMENT-TABLE.

   05 MAJORS         OCCURS 3 TIMES.
      10 COURSES     OCCURS 4 TIMES PIC 999.

   05 COLLEGES                    OCCURS 3 TIMES.
      10 MAJORS-IN-COLLEGES       OCCURS 3 TIMES.
         15 COURSES-IN-MAJORS   OCCURS 4 TIMES PIC 999.
```

The arrays MAJORS and COLLEGES are one-dimensional. COURSES and MAJORS-IN-COLLEGES are two-dimensional because they are associated with OCCURS clauses, and are contained in the one-dimensional arrays MAJORS and COLLEGES, respectively. COURSES-IN-MAJORS is a three-dimensional array. In both COURSES and COURSES-IN-MAJORS, the array elements are three-digit numeric fields.

COBOL 85   In COBOL 74, up to three-dimensional arrays can be specified. In COBOL 85, the maximum number of dimensions has been extended to seven.

COBOL permits a variety of ways in which arrays may be defined within structures. In an application program, the way an array is defined is primarily determined by how the programmer intends to reference and use the components of the structure. Several examples of array definitions are provided in Figures 6 through 9. With each example the corresponding conceptual storage structure is also given. Let us examine them more closely.

In Figure 6, structure A contains a one-dimensional array named B. Array B has three elements, each of which consists of a group item named C and two elementary data items, F and G. Finally, the group item C contains two elementary data items, D and E.

In Figure 7, the structure A contains three one-dimensional arrays, B, E, and F, each of size 3. E and F are arrays with atomic data values. B has composite elements consisting of C and D.

Structure A in Figure 8 contains a group item B and two one-dimensional arrays named E and F. B, on the other hand, has two one-dimensional arrays, C and D. Arrays E, F, C, and D are all size 3.

COBOL structure specification

```
01  A.
    05  B                OCCURS 3 TIMES
        10  C.
            15  D  PIC X(5).
            15  E  PIC X(5).
        10  F        PIC X(3).
        10  G        PIC X.
```

Conceptual storage structure

A											
B 1				B 2				B 3			
C 1		F 1	G 1	C 2		F 2	G 2	C 3		F 3	G 3
D 1	E 1			D 2	E 2			D 3	E 3		
. . . . .	. . . . .	. . .	.	. . . . .	. . . . .	. . .	.	. . . . .	. . . . .	. . .	.

Examples of legal references

```
A, B (1), C (1), D (1), E (1), F (1), G (1)
```

Figure 6 Example of a One-Dimensional Array Definition in COBOL

Finally, Figure 9 shows a structure called A, containing three one-dimensional arrays, B, E, and G. B contains a two-dimensional array named C, which, in turn, contains a three-dimensional array, D. The one-dimensional array E includes the definition for a two-dimensional array D.

Summary of Rules for Array Definition in COBOL

1. Arrays should be defined within a superordinate structure at levels other than 01.
2. Array size should be specified by the OCCURS clause. The OCCURS clause must have an unsigned nonzero integer constant value, followed by the key word TIMES.
3. If the element of an array is an elementary data item, it should have a PICTURE clause associated with its name before or after the OCCURS clause.
4. If the array element is a composite data item, an OCCURS clause should follow the array name, with a substructure specification for the array elements.
5. COBOL 74 supports one-, two-, and three-dimensional arrays. In COBOL 85, arrays up to seven dimensions can be defined.

COBOL 85

COBOL structure specification

```
01   A.
     05   B                    OCCURS 3 TIMES.
          10   C   PIC X(5).
          10   D   PIC X(5).
     05   E        PIC X(3)    OCCURS 3 TIMES.
     05   F        PIC X       OCCURS 3 TIMES.
```

Conceptual storage structure

A											
B 1		B 2		B 3		E 1	E 2	E 3	F 1	F 2	F 3
C 1	D 1	C 2	D 2	C 3	D 3						
. . . . .	. . . . .	. . . . .	. . . . . .	. . . . .	. . . . . .	. . .	. . .	. . .	.	.	.

Examples of legal references

```
A, B (1), C (1), D (1), E (1), F (1)
```

Figure 7 Example of One-Dimensional Array Definitions in COBOL

COBOL structure specification

```
01   A.
     05   B.
          10   C   PIC X(5)    OCCURS 3 TIMES.
          10   D   PIC X(5)    OCCURS 3 TIMES.
     05   E        PIC X(3)    OCCURS 3 TIMES.
     05   F        PIC X       OCCURS 3 TIMES.
```

Conceptual storage structure

A											
B						E 1	E 2	E 3	F 1	F 2	F 3
C 1	C 2	C 3	D 1	D 2	D 3						
. . . . .	. . . . .	. . . . .	. . . . .	. . . . .	. . . . .	. . .	. . .	. . .	.	.	.

Examples of legal references

```
A, B, C (1), D (1), E (1), F (1)
```

Figure 8 Example of One-Dimensional Array Definitions in COBOL

COBOL structure specification

```
01   A.
     05   B              OCCURS 2 TIMES.
          10   C         OCCURS 3 TIMES.
               15   D    OCCURS 2 TIMES    PIC X(2).
     05   E              OCCURS 2 TIMES.
          10   F         OCCURS 3 TIMES    PIC X(2).
     05   G              OCCURS 4 TIMES    PIC X(3).
```

Conceptual storage structure

A																	
B 1			B 2			E 1			E 2			G 1	G 2	G 3	G 4		
C 1, 1	C 1, 2	C 1, 3	C 2, 1	C 2, 2	C 2, 3	F 1, 1	F 1, 2	F 1, 3	F 2, 1	F 2, 2	F 2, 3					
D 1, 1, 1	D 1, 1, 2	D 1, 2, 1	D 1, 2, 2	D 1, 3, 1	D 1, 3, 2	D 2, 1, 1	D 2, 1, 2	D 2, 2, 1	D 2, 2, 2	D 2, 3, 1	D 2, 3, 2				
. .	. .	. .	. .	. .	. .	. .	. .	. .	. .	. .	. .	. .	. .	. . .	. . .	. . .	. . .

Examples of legal references

```
A, B (1), C (1, 2), D (1, 1, 2), E (1), F (1, 2), G (1)
```

Figure 9 Example of One-, Two-, and Three-Dimensional Array Definitions in COBOL

Referencing Array Elements

Array elements are referenced by name and subscript. Subscripts indicate the relative locations of the elements. In COBOL, a subscript can be a nonzero, positive integer constant, or an integer variable that can assume such a constant value. Arithmetic expressions cannot be used as subscripts.

A variable name and associated subscripts form a subscripted variable.

> A **subscripted variable** is an identifier followed by one or more subscripts, all enclosed in parentheses and separated by commas.

A subscripted variable is used to reference array elements in COBOL. One-dimensional array references require a single subscript and multidimensional array references use multiple subscripts.

Consider the following example:

```
01 ENROLLMENT-TABLE.
   05 COLLEGES                OCCURS 3 TIMES.
      10 MAJORS-IN-COLLEGES   OCCURS 3 TIMES.
         15 COURSES-IN-MAJORS OCCURS 4 TIMES PIC 999.
```

Here, COLLEGES (1) is a subscripted variable. It is a reference to the first element of the one-dimensional array called COLLEGES. MAJORS-IN-COLLEGES (1,2) is another subscripted variable. It permits access to the second major of the first college in the two-dimensional array MAJORS-IN-COLLEGES. Any identifier that is associated with an OCCURS clause at the level where it is defined, or at a subordinate level, requires subscripts.

COBOL does not permit global references to arrays. For example, the identifier COLLEGES used in a PROCEDURE DIVISION statement is illegal. The entire content of a structure containing arrays can be referenced by the table name, however. MOVE ENROLLMENT-TABLE TO OUT-TABLE transfers the arrays contained in the table ENROLLMENT-TABLE to a compatible structure, which is OUT-TABLE in this case.

In a subscripted variable, a subscript value that is less than 1 or greater than the size of the array results in an error. For the above table, COLLEGES (K) is illegal if the integer variable K assumes, say, a value of 4 sometime during the program execution.

If an array contains a composite structure in its elements, the constituents of the structure are treated as subscripted variables. An individual field of an array element can be accessed using its name and a single subscript. For example, in Figure 6, the one-dimensional array B contains a structure made up of C, F, and G. C consists of D and E. E (1), for instance, accesses the E-component of the first element of the array. Legal references in a structure containing arrays depend on the way the structure is defined. Figures 6 through 9 are examples of legal references for the structures indicated.

We mentioned earlier that a structure containing arrays is defined according to the programmer's plans for its use. Let us reexamine the structures in Figures 7 and 8. The structure of Figure 7 is suitable if we want to transfer the elements of the array B, one at a time, as in

```
MOVE B (1) TO ...
```

If our plan is to move all elements of B to a compatible structure somewhere in the program, the structure of Figure 8 is better. Based on it, we can write

```
MOVE B TO ...
```

This will move all three elements of the arrays C and D.

Summary of Rules for COBOL Subscripted Variables and Array References

1. One-dimensional array references require a single subscript. Multidimensional array references use multiple subscripts.
2. The name of an array cannot be used without a subscript. The only exception is the SEARCH statement. However, to reference the full content of an array, it may be included in a table, and the name of the table can be used.

3. A subscript value in a subscripted variable should not be less than 1 or greater than the size of the array.
4. If an array contains composite structures in its elements, the constituents of these structures are treated as subscripted variables. An individual field of an array element can be accessed using its name and a single subscript.
5. In some COBOL compilers the name of the subscripted variable should be followed by at least one space before the left parenthesis.

Processing Arrays

There are some operations commonly performed on arrays, ranging from simple functions such as loading arrays with values, to more complex ones like ordering or searching them. These operations are assigning values to array elements, reading and writing arrays, moving whole arrays or array elements, performing arithmetic on array elements, ordering lists in arrays, and searching lists stored in arrays.

Assigning Values to Array Elements. There are four ways to assign values to array elements:

1. Run-time individual element value assignment using MOVE statements
2. Run-time global value assignment using MOVE statements
3. Compile-time value assignment using VALUE clauses
4. Compile-time value assignment using REDEFINES clauses

Individual elements of an array can be assigned values at run-time by means of the MOVE statement, as in

```
MOVE ZERO TO COURSES-IN-MAJORS (1,1,2).
```

All elements can be initialized to a value at run-time by using the table name as target variable in a MOVE statement.

```
MOVE ZEROS TO ENROLLMENT-TABLE.
```

Initialization can also be accomplished at compile-time using the VALUE clause.

```
01 ENROLLMENT-TABLE.
   05 COLLEGES                OCCURS 3 TIMES.
      10 MAJORS-IN-COLLEGES   OCCURS 3 TIMES.
         15 COURSES-IN-MAJORS OCCURS 4 TIMES PIC 999
                                          VALUE ZERO.
```

If elements are to be initialized to different values at compile-time, we must make use of a template structure and the REDEFINES clause.

```
01 DAYS-OF-WEEK.
   05 FILLER            VALUE "MONTUEWEDTHUFRISATSUN" PIC X(21).

01 DAYS-TABLE REDEFINES DAYS-OF-WEEK.
   05 WEEK-DAY          OCCURS 7 TIMES                PIC XXX.
```

The code accomplishes the compile-time initialization of WEEK-DAYS (1) to MON, WEEK-DAYS (2) to TUE, and so on.

Reading and Writing Arrays. We can use the interactive input statement ACCEPT to read a value into an array element.

```
ACCEPT COURSES-IN-MAJORS (1,1,2) FROM CONSOLE.
```

At the time we are prompted to provide a value, if we enter 5, the element COURSES-IN-MAJORS (1,1,2) will be set to 5.

The DISPLAY statement can be used interactively to output values contained in array elements.

```
DISPLAY COURSES-IN-MAJORS (1,1,2).
```

Provided they are defined within the record structure of a file, arrays may be input or output using file-oriented I-O statements. Suppose we have the following FILE SECTION.

```
. . . . . . . . . . . . . . . . . . . . . . . . . . . .
DATA DIVISION.
FILE SECTION.
FD STUDENT-INFORMATION-FILE
   LABEL RECORDS ARE STANDARD
   DATA RECORD IS STUDENT-INFORMATION
   RECORD CONTAINS 60 CHARACTERS.
01 STUDENT-INFORMATION.
   05 STU-NO-NAME      OCCURS 3 TIMES.
      10  STUDENT-IDNO               PIC X(4).
      10  STUDENT-NAME               PIC X(16).
. . . . . . . . . . . . . . . . . . . . . . . . . . . .
```

Furthermore, suppose we have the following instance for the STUDENT-IN-FORMATION-FILE.

```
                            COLUMNS
        5    10   15   20   25   30   35   40   45   50   55   60
    ----|----|----|----|----|----|----|----|----|----|----|----|--

    1000JOHN SMITH        2000JEAN COLLINS    3000WILLIAM BLACK
        . . . . . . . . . . . . . . . . . . . . . . . . . .
```

The READ statement

```
READ STUDENT-INFORMATION-FILE
     AT END PERFORM TERMINATION-PARAGRAPH.
```

will assign 1000 to STUDENT-IDNO (1), JOHN SMITH to STUDENT-NAME
(1), 2000 to STUDENT-IDNO (2), and so on.

We can also use WRITE statements to output the contents of an array, as in

```
WRITE STUDENT-INFORMATION.
```

Moving Arrays. As we can move elementary data items or structures in a
COBOL program, we can also move individual array elements or tables containing arrays. Consider these WORKING-STORAGE SECTION entries.

```
    . . . . . . . . . . . . . . . . . . . . . . . .
    WORKING-STORAGE SECTION.
    01  CITY-DATA.
        05  CITY-ATTRIBUTES    OCCURS 5 TIMES.
            10  CITY-NAME           PIC X(10).
            10  POPULATION          PIC 9(8).
        05  TOTAL-CITIES        PIC 99.
    . . . . . . . . . . . . . . . . . . . .
    01  OUTPUT-LINE                 PIC X(92).
    01  CITY-DESCRIPTION            PIC X(18).
    01  NAME-OF-CITY                PIC X(10).
    . . . . . . . . . . . . . . . . . . . . . . . .
```

The following MOVE statements are all legal.

```
MOVE CITY-DATA            TO OUTPUT-LINE.
MOVE CITY-ATTRIBUTES (1)  TO CITY-DESCRIPTION.
MOVE CITY-NAME (1)        TO NAME-OF-CITY.
```

However, the statement

```
MOVE CITY-ATTRIBUTES TO OUTPUT-LINE.
```

is illegal, because CITY-ATTRIBUTE is an array and needs a subscript.

Performing Arithmetic on Arrays. If an array contains numeric elements, we can use arithmetic operations to compute and assign values to its elements. For the array CITY-ATTRIBUTES used in the example above, the following ADD statement is valid:

```
ADD 1 TO POPULATION (2).
```

whereas

```
ADD 1 TO POPULATION.
```

is illegal.

Ordering Lists in Arrays: Internal Sorting. A common operation performed on lists is to order their elements, known as sorting. Sorting transforms an unordered list to an equivalent ordered list of the same size. Many different techniques can be used to sort lists. They are classified as internal or external.

> An **internal sorting** technique is one that requires list elements to be kept in the computer's main memory throughout the sorting process. In **external sorting**, list elements are stored in external storage during and after the sorting process.

We resort to external sorting techniques if a list is excessively large and all of its elements cannot be accommodated in the computer's main memory at one time. In general, lists are stored in arrays for internal sorting and in files for external sorting. COBOL has a built-in feature that can be used to sort lists stored as sequential files, and therefore makes use of some external sorting techniques. In Chapter 12 we will examine the COBOL sort feature and some important external sorting techniques. This section deals with internal sorting.

Many internal sorting algorithms have been developed for ordering lists within arrays, although no one of them can be said to be the best. Each method has its own merits and shortcomings, depending on the characteristics of data elements in the list, allocation of the list elements within the host array, purpose in ordering the list, and the machine used to sort it. For sequentially allocated linear lists, the available techniques perform what is called **physical sorting**, because the list elements are physically moved within the array during the process. Techniques that establish an order of elements in a list without actually moving the list elements are said to do **logical sorting**. In logical sorting, the list must have linked allocation, and the relative location of an element in the ordered list is determined by pointers associated with each list element.

An application programmer should know different sorting techniques, and should understand how they work so that he or she can make an intelligent choice for a particular application. Readers who are interested in learning more on sorting can find some excellent books available on the subject. Here we study two physical internal sorting techniques, insertion and bubble sort. Both are used in the COBOL sample program that follows this discussion.

The insertion sort algorithm is described in Figure 10. The steps of the algorithm are demonstrated on a sample list, and a pseudocode for the algorithm is given.

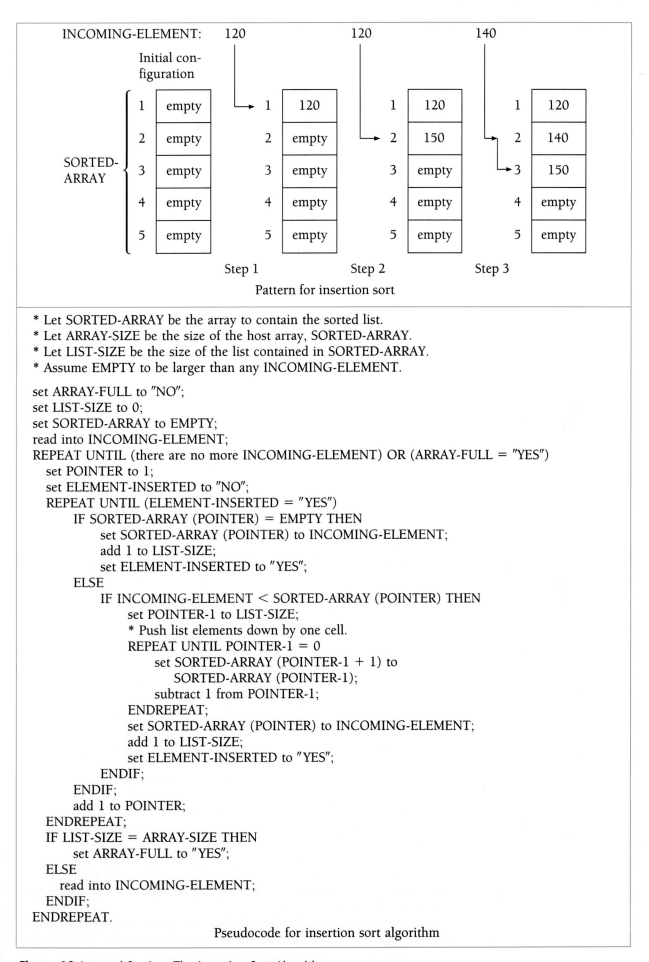

Pattern for insertion sort

* Let SORTED-ARRAY be the array to contain the sorted list.
* Let ARRAY-SIZE be the size of the host array, SORTED-ARRAY.
* Let LIST-SIZE be the size of the list contained in SORTED-ARRAY.
* Assume EMPTY to be larger than any INCOMING-ELEMENT.

```
set ARRAY-FULL to "NO";
set LIST-SIZE to 0;
set SORTED-ARRAY to EMPTY;
read into INCOMING-ELEMENT;
REPEAT UNTIL (there are no more INCOMING-ELEMENT) OR (ARRAY-FULL = "YES")
   set POINTER to 1;
   set ELEMENT-INSERTED to "NO";
   REPEAT UNTIL (ELEMENT-INSERTED = "YES")
       IF SORTED-ARRAY (POINTER) = EMPTY THEN
           set SORTED-ARRAY (POINTER) to INCOMING-ELEMENT;
           add 1 to LIST-SIZE;
           set ELEMENT-INSERTED to "YES";
       ELSE
           IF INCOMING-ELEMENT < SORTED-ARRAY (POINTER) THEN
               set POINTER-1 to LIST-SIZE;
               * Push list elements down by one cell.
               REPEAT UNTIL POINTER-1 = 0
                   set SORTED-ARRAY (POINTER-1 + 1) to
                       SORTED-ARRAY (POINTER-1);
                   subtract 1 from POINTER-1;
               ENDREPEAT;
               set SORTED-ARRAY (POINTER) to INCOMING-ELEMENT;
               add 1 to LIST-SIZE;
               set ELEMENT-INSERTED to "YES";
           ENDIF;
       ENDIF;
       add 1 to POINTER;
   ENDREPEAT;
   IF LIST-SIZE = ARRAY-SIZE THEN
       set ARRAY-FULL to "YES";
   ELSE
       read into INCOMING-ELEMENT;
   ENDIF;
ENDREPEAT.
```

Pseudocode for insertion sort algorithm

Figure 10 Internal Sorting: The Insertion Sort Algorithm

In insertion sort, we assume that we have an unordered list contained in an array. Let us define another array of the same size and call it SORTED-ARRAY; this will contain the ordered list. Elements of the unordered list are introduced one at a time in a variable called INCOMING-ELEMENT. Initially, SORTED-ARRAY is empty. Depending on the nature of the data elements in the list, "empty" can be represented using a value that is outside the range of the set of values for the list elements. For example, if the list contains three-digit positive integers, empty can be any negative integer.

In the first step, INCOMING-ELEMENT contains the first element of the unordered list, and is directly stored as the first element of the SORTED-ARRAY. SORTED-ARRAY contains a list of size 1 and is ordered as such. In subsequent steps we consider the next element of the unordered list introduced in the INCOMING-ELEMENT one by one, and search the ordered list in SORTED-ARRAY sequentially to determine the point of insertion. In case the point of insertion for an INCOMING-ELEMENT is an empty array element, we simply store the new list element there. Otherwise, we push all list elements down by one array element to accommodate the INCOMING-ELEMENT. In Figure 10, step 3 involves 140 as the INCOMING-ELEMENT, and the SORTED-ARRAY contains 120, followed by 150. The point of insertion for 140 is the second array element. Therefore, 150 is pushed down to array element 3, and 140 is stored as the second array element. This technique ensures that the list contained in the SORTED-ARRAY will be an ordered list at each step. The algorithm terminates after all INCOMING-ELEMENT values are properly inserted.

Program 3-Source(b) shows a COBOL subroutine that implements the insertion sort algorithm for the Example Program 3.

Bubble sort is a technique that can be used to order a list by repetitively comparing two consecutive list elements, selecting the smallest (or the largest, as the case may be), and exchanging the two if necessary. It is also known as an exchange selection sort. Figure 11 describes the phases and steps in bubble sort on a sample pattern, and gives the pseudocode for the algorithm.

In bubble sort, we start with an unordered list in an array. Suppose we have five elements in the list, as in Figure 11, and we want to order the list in ascending order. In the first step of the first phase we compare the last two elements, that is, the fourth and fifth. If the fifth element is less than the fourth, we exchange them so that the smaller element "bubbles up." In the second step we consider the third and fourth elements and exchange them, if necessary. At the end of the fourth step of the first phase we will have moved the smallest list element to the top of the array. Now we may say that the array consists of an ordered list of size 1 followed by an unordered list of size 4.

In the next phase we do the exchange selection three times to pick the next smallest element and bubble it up to the array element 2. In this phase we do not process the list element contained in the first cell of the array, as the first list element is already in the right cell.

If the unordered list contains N elements, the bubble sort technique requires $(N - 1)$ phases. The first phase involves $(N - 1)$ steps, the second involves $(N - 2)$ steps, and the $(N - 1)$th phase involves a single step. Program 1-Source(c) is a COBOL implementation of the bubble sort algorithm in the form of a subroutine.

Searching Lists in Arrays: Internal Search. Another commonly executed task in data processing is searching a list for an element. The problem of searching can be stated as follows.

Suppose we have a list of N elements. We are also given a specified search key. A **search key** is a data element that is compatible with the data elements stored in the list. The problem is to find one or more list elements that match the given search key. If matching elements are found, we say the search is successful, otherwise, it is unsuccessful.

As in sorting, list searching can also be classified as internal or external.

> In **internal searching**, the list is stored in an array and kept in the memory during the entire process. In **external searching**, the list is contained in a file, and only part of it is brought into the main memory for processing.

Searching is the most important application in data and information retrieval and in data base processing. This is understandable. After all, we store data at substantial cost to retrieve them eventually, and before we can retrieve them we must perform a search.

The searching technique in an application depends on the structure used to store data. Each data structure, therefore, has some search techniques that are best suited for retrieval. We are concerned with linear lists here; later we will occasionally return to searching. For each data structure or file structure that we study, we will also consider some appropriate searching techniques.

The three fundamental searching techniques for linear lists contained in arrays depend on whether or not the list is ordered. These techniques are sequential search of unordered lists, sequential search of ordered lists, and binary search of ordered lists. COBOL has a built-in SEARCH facility that can be used to search arrays by applying sequential or binary search techniques. This feature is discussed later in this chapter. Here we discuss the fundamental algorithms for these techniques, which are important not only for linear lists, but also for other, more complex data structures.

Sequential Search of Unordered Lists: We can do only one thing to search an unordered list: access each element of the host array sequentially, starting with the first, and compare it to the search key. If a match is found, we announce success and terminate the algorithm. If no match is found and the list has already been fully processed, we say that the search has failed.

Figure 12 describes this technique in the form of a pseudocode and shows the steps involved on a simple array. It should be noted that, in the event that no match is found for the search key, the number of comparisons required for this technique is the same as the list size. If the search is successful, however, the number of comparisons may be anywhere between 1 and a maximum of N, where N is the list size. The expected number of comparisons in this case is N/2.

Sequential Search of Ordered Lists: We can apply the same sequential search technique to ordered lists. In case the search is successful, as the list element matching the search key may be anywhere in the list, the expected number of comparisons is N/2. Thus, if a match exists in the list, we do not gain anything by sorting the list. On the other hand, if there is no match, by successive comparisons we may determine where in the list the match should have been, and terminate the search without exhaustively processing the list. So we gain something: the expected number of comparisons will become N/2, instead of N, if the result is failure. Figure 13 describes this search technique.

Binary Search of Ordered Lists: Ordering a list before searching it is advantageous if the number of looks can be substantially reduced in case of either success or failure. The binary search technique achieves this advantage. Let us

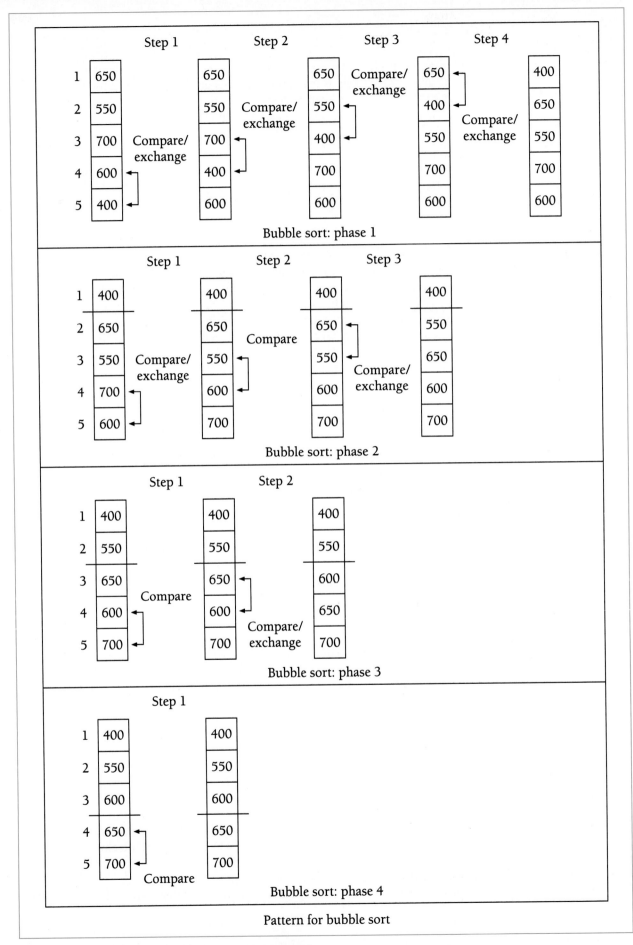

Figure 11 Internal Sorting: The Bubble Sort Algorithm

```
* Let SORT-ARRAY be the array containing an unordered list to be sorted.
* SORT-ARRAY will also be used to store the ordered list after sorting.
* Let LIST-SIZE be the size of the list contained in SORT-ARRAY.

set SORTED-LIST-SIZE to 0;
set LIST-SORTED to "NO";
set OUTER-LOOP-COUNT to 1;

REPEAT UNTIL (LIST-SORTED = "YES") OR (OUTER-LOOP-COUNT = LIST-SIZE)

  set NUMBER-OF-SWITCHES to 0;
 set POINTER to LIST-SIZE;

 REPEAT UNTIL (POINTER = SORTED-LIST-SIZE + 1)

    IF SORT-ARRAY (POINTER) < SORT-ARRAY (POINTER − 1) THEN
       set TEMP to SORT-ARRAY (POINTER);
       set SORT-ARRAY (POINTER) to SORT-ARRAY (POINTER − 1);
       set SORT-ARRAY (POINTER − 1) to TEMP;
       add 1 to NUMBER-OF-SWITCHES;
    ENDIF;

    subtract 1 from POINTER;
 ENDREPEAT;

 IF NUMBER-OF-SWITCHES = 0 THEN
    set LIST-SORTED to "YES";
 ENDIF;

 add 1 to SORTED-LIST-SIZE;
 add 1 to OUTER-LOOP-COUNT;
ENDREPEAT.
```

Pseudocode for bubble sort algorithm

Figure 11 (Continued)

explain how binary search works on the example list of Figure 14. In the first step we consider the entire list of 10 elements and determine the midpoint, which is the fifth element. Next, we access the fifth element to compare it with the search key. At this point, there are three possibilities.

1. We may hit a match, in which case, the search is terminated.
2. The search key value may be less than the value of the middle list element, so we know that the match can be found only among the first four elements.
3. The search key may be larger than the value of the middle element, and we should consider only the second half of the list, or the last five elements.

In the next step, we have roughly half the original list to search, either the top or the bottom half. To search the list systematically, we must define which half is to be considered at each step. For this we use two variables, a low index and a high index. In the first step of Figure 14, the low and high index values are 1 and 10, respectively. In the second step, 6 is the low index, 10 is the high index, and so on. Therefore, the list of Figure 14 can be searched in a maximum of four comparisons. It is possible to prove that, for a list of size N, the maximum number of comparisons in case of success or failure is k, where k satisfies the condition

$$2 k - 1 <= N < 2 k$$

The following table compares binary search to sequential search of an ordered table for different values of list size N.

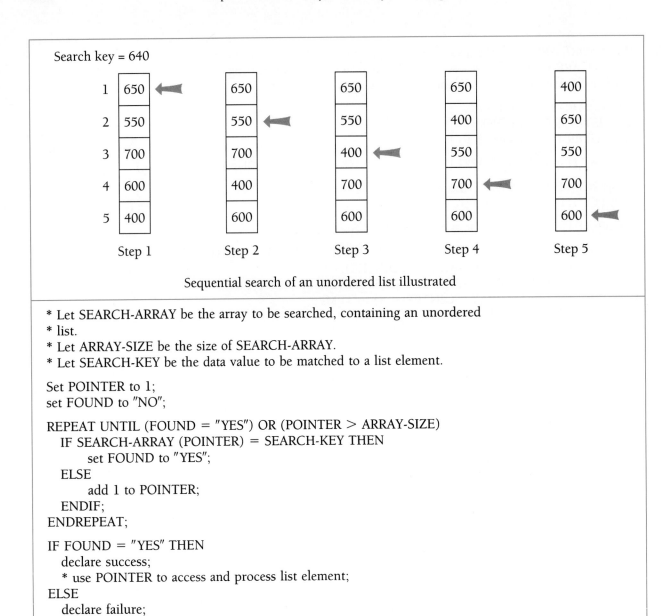

Search key = 640

Step 1 Step 2 Step 3 Step 4 Step 5

Sequential search of an unordered list illustrated

```
* Let SEARCH-ARRAY be the array to be searched, containing an unordered
* list.
* Let ARRAY-SIZE be the size of SEARCH-ARRAY.
* Let SEARCH-KEY be the data value to be matched to a list element.

Set POINTER to 1;
set FOUND to "NO";

REPEAT UNTIL (FOUND = "YES") OR (POINTER > ARRAY-SIZE)
  IF SEARCH-ARRAY (POINTER) = SEARCH-KEY THEN
      set FOUND to "YES";
  ELSE
      add 1 to POINTER;
  ENDIF;
ENDREPEAT;

IF FOUND = "YES" THEN
  declare success;
  * use POINTER to access and process list element;
ELSE
  declare failure;
ENDIF.
```

Pseudocode for sequential search of an unordered list

Figure 12 Array Searching: Sequential Search of an Unordered List

	Sequential Search	Binary Search
List Size (N)	Expected Number of Comparisons (N/2)	Maximum Number of Comparisons (k)
10	5	4
50	25	6
100	50	7
500	250	9
10,000	5,000	14

As seen, especially for large lists, the binary search algorithm is substantially more efficient than the sequential search. Figure 14 also gives the pseudocode for the binary search algorithm.

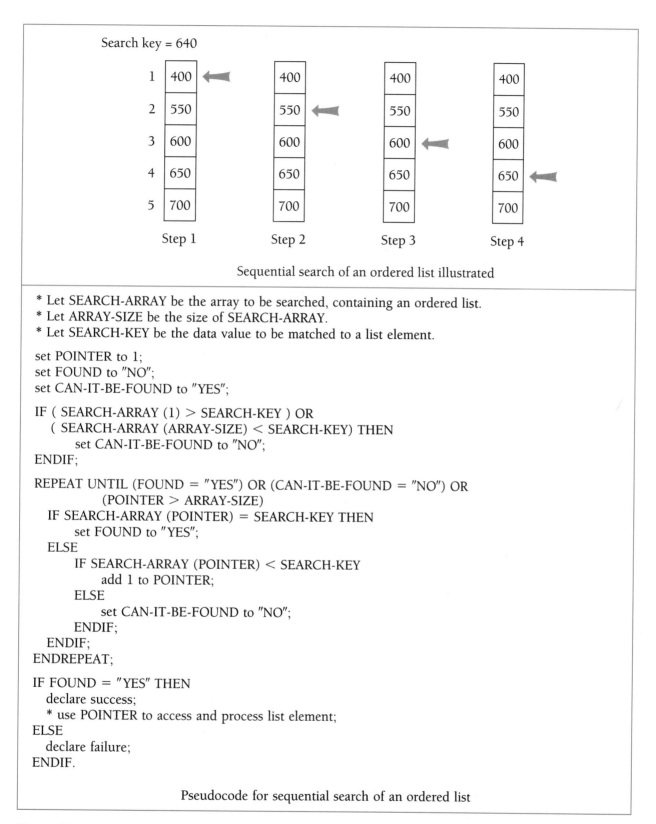

Sequential search of an ordered list illustrated

* Let SEARCH-ARRAY be the array to be searched, containing an ordered list.
* Let ARRAY-SIZE be the size of SEARCH-ARRAY.
* Let SEARCH-KEY be the data value to be matched to a list element.

set POINTER to 1;
set FOUND to "NO";
set CAN-IT-BE-FOUND to "YES";

IF (SEARCH-ARRAY (1) > SEARCH-KEY) OR
    (SEARCH-ARRAY (ARRAY-SIZE) < SEARCH-KEY) THEN
        set CAN-IT-BE-FOUND to "NO";
ENDIF;

REPEAT UNTIL (FOUND = "YES") OR (CAN-IT-BE-FOUND = "NO") OR
            (POINTER > ARRAY-SIZE)
    IF SEARCH-ARRAY (POINTER) = SEARCH-KEY THEN
        set FOUND to "YES";
    ELSE
        IF SEARCH-ARRAY (POINTER) < SEARCH-KEY
            add 1 to POINTER;
        ELSE
            set CAN-IT-BE-FOUND to "NO";
        ENDIF;
    ENDIF;
ENDREPEAT;

IF FOUND = "YES" THEN
    declare success;
    * use POINTER to access and process list element;
ELSE
    declare failure;
ENDIF.

Pseudocode for sequential search of an ordered list

Figure 13 Array Searching: Sequential Search of an Ordered List

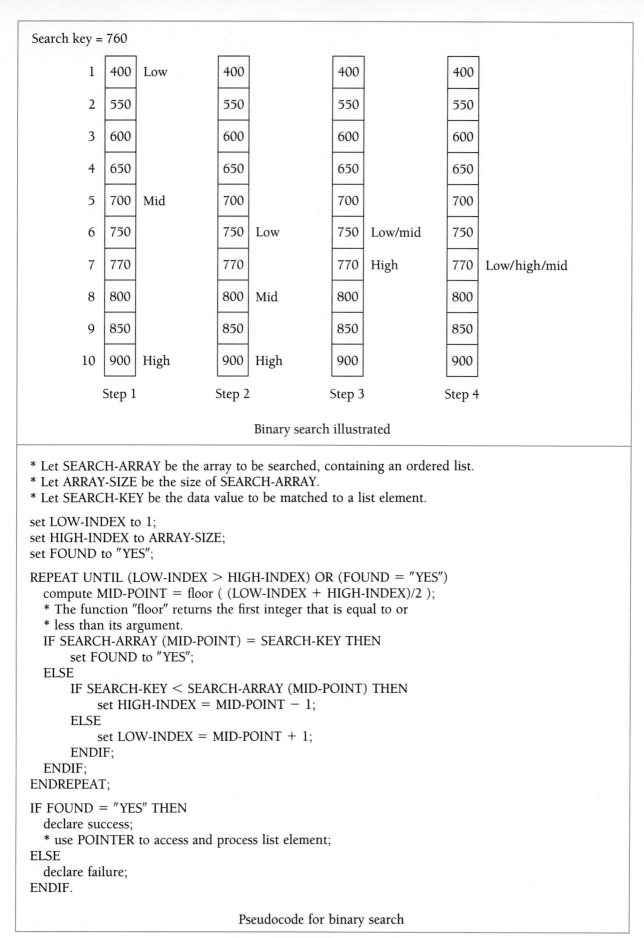

Search key = 760

	Step 1			Step 2			Step 3			Step 4	
1	400	Low	1	400		1	400		1	400	
2	550		2	550		2	550		2	550	
3	600		3	600		3	600		3	600	
4	650		4	650		4	650		4	650	
5	700	Mid	5	700		5	700		5	700	
6	750		6	750	Low	6	750	Low/mid	6	750	
7	770		7	770		7	770	High	7	770	Low/high/mid
8	800		8	800	Mid	8	800		8	800	
9	850		9	850		9	850		9	850	
10	900	High	10	900	High	10	900		10	900	

Binary search illustrated

* Let SEARCH-ARRAY be the array to be searched, containing an ordered list.
* Let ARRAY-SIZE be the size of SEARCH-ARRAY.
* Let SEARCH-KEY be the data value to be matched to a list element.

set LOW-INDEX to 1;
set HIGH-INDEX to ARRAY-SIZE;
set FOUND to "YES";

REPEAT UNTIL (LOW-INDEX > HIGH-INDEX) OR (FOUND = "YES")
  compute MID-POINT = floor ((LOW-INDEX + HIGH-INDEX)/2);
  * The function "floor" returns the first integer that is equal to or
  * less than its argument.
  IF SEARCH-ARRAY (MID-POINT) = SEARCH-KEY THEN
     set FOUND to "YES";
  ELSE
     IF SEARCH-KEY < SEARCH-ARRAY (MID-POINT) THEN
       set HIGH-INDEX = MID-POINT − 1;
     ELSE
       set LOW-INDEX = MID-POINT + 1;
     ENDIF;
  ENDIF;
ENDREPEAT;

IF FOUND = "YES" THEN
  declare success;
  * use POINTER to access and process list element;
ELSE
  declare failure;
ENDIF.

Pseudocode for binary search

Figure 14 Array Searching: Binary Search of an Ordered List

REVIEW QUESTIONS

1. In contrast to a single-value program variable, an array can store _____ values.
2. A list is a _____ -size set of ordered data elements, whereas an array has a _____ size.
3. Array elements are referenced using their relative addresses together with the array name. (T or F)
4. If a list is stored such that its elements are in consecutive array elements, the allocation is known as _____ .
5. If the successors of list elements in a sequentially allocated list define an order by element values, such a list is called an ordered list. (T or F)
6. Which of the following statements about arrays is correct?
   a. An array requiring a single subscript for element access is a one-dimensional array.
   b. A two-dimensional array is an array of one-dimensional arrays.
   c. A two-dimensional array is also known as a matrix.
   d. In a two-dimensional array, the first subscript references rows, and the second subscript references columns.
   e. All of the above are correct.
7. In COBOL, the size of an array is specified in an _____ .
8. In COBOL 74, a maximum of three dimensions is allowed for arrays, whereas in COBOL 85 this has been extended to seven dimensions. (T or F)
9. The entire content of an array cannot be referenced using the array name; however, by using the table name in which the array is defined, the full array content can be addressed. (T or F)
10. Which of the following is illegal for subscripts in COBOL?
    a. Assigning negative values
    b. Assigning zero values
    c. Using an arithmetic expression
    d. Using a structure name
    e. All of the above
11. It is not possible to change the value of an array element at run-time using an arithmetic statement. (T or F)
12. At compile-time we can assign values to array elements using either the _____ or the _____ clause.
13. Which of the following about sorting is correct?
    a. In internal sorting of a list, if the list elements are moved around in the memory, the technique is called logical sorting.
    b. A sorting technique is external if it requires all list elements to be stored in the main memory at all times.
    c. Insertion sorting is an internal sorting technique.
    d. Bubble sorting is an external sorting technique.
14. Binary search is more efficient than sequential search for ordered lists. (T or F)

Answers: 1. multiple; 2. variable, fixed; 3. T; 4. sequential; 5. T; 6. e; 7. OCCURS clause; 8. T; 9. T; 10. e; 11. F; 12. VALUE, REDEFINES; 13. c; 14. T.

Example Program 1:   Distribution of Students by Majors

In this section we develop a COBOL application program that makes use of one-dimensional arrays as data structures. In the next section we expand this program to illustrate the use of two-dimensional arrays.

Problem   The academic data base for a college contains a student file with the following record structure:

- A four-digit student identification number, uniquely assigned to each student enrolled in the college, in columns 1–4
- A 20-character student name field in columns 6–25
- A three-character major code in columns 27–29 describing the discipline in which the student is majoring
- Entrance year for the student in columns 31–32
- Student classification in column 34 (1, freshman; 2, sophomore; 3, junior; 4, senior)
- Cumulative grade point average (on a scale of 4.00) in columns 36–38

We assume that the college has academic programs in the following disciplines, shown with the corresponding major codes.

Major Code	Academic Program
ACC	Accounting
BOT	Botany
CSC	Computer science
ENG	English
MAN	Management
MTH	Mathematics
PHY	Physics
ZOO	Zoology

The student file is a sequentially organized disk file and its records are ordered by the student identification number field. Program 1-Input is an instance of the student file for this application.

We will develop a COBOL program that reads records from such a student file and computes the number of students majoring in each academic discipline. The distribution table to be generated will be displayed on the terminal screen.

Solution   The compiler generated listing of the COBOL program developed for this application is given in Program 1-Source. The following should be noted about this program.

1. The arrays are defined as follows.

```
000064    01  DISTRIBUTION-BY-MAJORS-TABLE.
000065        05  MAJORS.
000066            10  MAJOR          OCCURS 20 TIMES   PIC XXX.
000067        05  DISTRIBUTIONS.
000068            10  NO-OF-STUDENTS OCCURS 20 TIMES   PIC 999.
```

These are regarded as parallel arrays. In other words, NO-OF-STUDENTS (3), for example, will contain the number of students majoring in the discipline whose major code is stored in MAJOR (3).

2. Initially, the arrays are empty. We indicate this by initializing the variable ARRAY-EMPTY to YES in line 000106. To keep track of the first available space in the arrays, we use the variable EMPTY-POINTER. We initialize EMPTY-POINTER to 1 in line 000103.

3. After we read the first record we execute the paragraph B3-GENERATE-DISTRIBUTIONS. For the first record, as the arrays are empty, the IF statement in this paragraph will trigger the paragraph C1-ADD-NEW-ELEMENT. C1-ADD-NEW-ELEMENT inserts the first MAJOR-CODE value into the array MAJOR, adds 1 to the corresponding element of the array NO-OF-ELEMENTS, and increments ARRAY-POINTER by 1. After this, in the then-part of the IF statement in B3-GENERATE-DISTRIBUTIONS we change the value of ARRAY-EMPTY to NO so that the subsequent MAJOR-CODE values are not considered as the initial element to be stored in the array MAJOR.

4. After the initial record, every new record will bring in a MAJOR-CODE value that is either in the array MAJOR or has not yet been included in it. We determine what to do by executing a sequential search. The PERFORM statement of line 000120 corresponds to the sequential search of the MAJOR array. If the new MAJOR-CODE value is in one of the elements of the array MAJOR, all we have to do is to increment the corresponding NO-OF-STUDENTS array element by 1 (see line 000143). If not, we have to treat it as a new element, and insert it into the array MAJOR (lines 000126–000127).

Program 1-Output shows the result of the execution of this program on the sequential student file of Program 1-Input.

Example Program 2: *Distribution of Students by Major and Academic Standing*

Problem Here we enhance the previous application so that, in addition to generating a distribution table by majors, we can also have a distribution by academic standing for each major. Student academic standing is determined on the basis of the grade point average as follows.

- If the grade point average is less than 2.00, academic standing is probationary.
- If the grade point average is greater than 1.99 and less than 3.00, academic standing is satisfactory.
- If the grade point average is greater than 2.99, academic standing is honors.

Solution The COBOL source program for this problem is given in Program 2-Source. In addition to the two one-dimensional arrays, MAJOR and NO-OF-STUDENTS of Program 1-Source, we make use of a two-dimensional array called ACADEMIC-STATUS, defined as follows.

```
000066     01  DISTRIBUTION-BY-MAJORS-TABLE.
000067         05  MAJORS.
000068             10  MAJOR              OCCURS 20 TIMES   PIC XXX.
000069         05  DISTRIBUTIONS.
000070             10  NO-OF-STUDENTS     OCCURS 20 TIMES   PIC 999.

000071             10  MAJOR-STATUS       OCCURS 20 TIMES.
000072                 15  ACADEMIC-STATUS  OCCURS 3 TIMES   PIC 999.
```

In this two-dimensional array, the element ACADEMIC-STATUS (1,1), ACADEMIC-STATUS (1,2), and ACADEMIC-STATUS (1,3) will store the number of students majoring in the first academic discipline with probationary, satisfactory, and honor status, respectively.

Otherwise, the logic of Program 2-Source is quite similar to that of the previous application. The major addition is the paragraph D1-GENERATE-STAT-DISTR. Here we have a nested IF statement that generates the academic standing distribution in the array ACADEMIC-STATUS using GRADE-POINT-AVR.

Program 2-Output shows the output generated by this application program on the student file of Program 1-Input.

Example Program 3:   Student Status Report Generator

We will develop a COBOL application program that makes use of a majority of the concepts and techniques we have covered so far. It will use one- and two-dimensional arrays as data structures, and will have a modularization scheme based on three subroutines.

Problem We have the same STUDENT-INFORMATION-FILE of the previous two example programs. An instance of this file is as shown in Program 1-Input. We suppose that college departments occasionally request academic status reports for their students. We wish to develop a program that permits the user to enter the following information interactively:

- Department code for department requesting the report
- Type of academic status report requested
- Identification numbers of the students for whom information is sought

The application program to be developed is expected to produce two types of academic status reports and an exception report if needed. The first lists the students in alphabetical order by name. The format of this report is given in the template at the top of the next page. The COMMENTS column indicates whether the student's classification is consistent with his or her time spent in the college. For example, a student entered in 1990 is expected to be a junior in 1992. If that is so, the COMMENTS entry will be NORMAL. If the same student is currently a sophomore, it is indicated by the message BEHIND 1 YEAR. If he or she is a senior, the entry is AHEAD 1 YEAR.

```
                    ACADEMIC STATUS REPORT


DATE PROCESSED   : XXXXXXX   XX, XXXX
REQUESTED BY     : DEPARTMENT OF XXXXXXXXXX


LIST ORDERED BY : |X|   STUDENT NAME
                  | |   ACADEMIC STATUS AND STUDENT NAME


STUDENT NAME             STUDENT ID   ACADEMIC STANDING   COMMENTS
_____   _____   _____   _____
XXXXXXXXXXXXXXXXXXXXX       XXXX       HONOR               NORMAL
XXXXXXXXXXXXXXXXXXXXX       XXXX       HONOR               BEHIND  1 YEAR
XXXXXXXXXXXXXXXXXXXXX       XXXX       PROBATION           AHEAD   1 YEAR
```

The second type of academic status report provides the user with an alphabetical listing of students by name in each academic status category. Four status categories are used:

- Probation, if the student grade point average (GPA) is less than 2.00
- Satisfactory, if GPA is between 2.00 and 2.99
- Honors, if GPA is between 3.00 and 3.49
- High honors, if GPA is 3.50 or above

The format of this type of academic status report is as shown below.

```
                    ACADEMIC STATUS REPORT


DATE PROCESSED   : XXXXXXXX   XX, XXXX
REQUESTED BY     : DEPARTMENT OF XXXXXXXXXX


LIST ORDERED BY : | | STUDENT NAME
                  |X| ACADEMIC STATUS AND STUDENT NAME

ACADEMIC STATUS      STUDENT NAME               STUDENT ID    COMMENTS
_____      _____     _____    _____
HIGH HONOR           XXXXXXXXXXXXXXXXXXXXXXX       XXXX        AHEAD    1 YRS
                     XXXXXXXXXXXXXXXXXXXXXXX       XXXX        NORMAL
                     XXXXXXXXXXXXXXXXXXXXXXX       XXXX        AHEAD    1 YRS

HONOR                XXXXXXXXXXXXXXXXXXXXXXX       XXXX        NORMAL
                     XXXXXXXXXXXXXXXXXXXXXXX       XXXX        NORMAL

SATISFACTORY         XXXXXXXXXXXXXXXXXXXXXXX       XXXX        BEHIND   1 YRS
                     XXXXXXXXXXXXXXXXXXXXXXX       XXXX        NORMAL

PROBATION            XXXXXXXXXX                    XXXX        NORMAL
                     XXXXXXXXXXXXXXXXXXXXXXX       XXXX        NORMAL
```

The exception report should indicate the identification numbers of students for whom there are no records in the student file, and/or the identification numbers of students for whom the major does not match the academic department requesting the report. A template for the exception report is

```
                        EXCEPTIONS REPORT


    REQUESTED BY    : DEPARTMENT OF XXXXXXXXXX


    THE FOLLOWING STUDENTS ARE NOT MAJORING IN THE DEPARTMENT:

                      XXXX
                      XXXX

    THE FOLLOWING STUDENT ID NUMBERS ARE NOT IN THE FILE:

                      XXXX
```

Solution   The application program package to generate the desired reports consists of a main program and three subprograms. Their compiler-generated listings are shown in Program 3-Source(a) through (d). The functions of the four modules are explained below.

1. The subroutine B2-INPUT-AND-SORT-IDNO [Program 3-Source(b)] handles interactive terminal inputs consisting of department code, type of list requested, and student identification numbers. Student identification numbers are entered in an arbitrary order by the user. This subroutine implements insertion sort, and orders the entered identification numbers in a one-dimensional array called STUDENT-IDNO, defined in lines 00041 and 00042. The subroutine returns the input parameters and the ordered array to the main program through its parameter list.
2. The subroutine C2-BUBBLE-SORT [Program 1-Source(c)] is designed to sort a one-dimensional array using the bubble sort algorithm. It requires an array containing the unordered list (TABLE-TO-BE-SORTED) and the list size (ARRAY-LENGTH). After sorting is completed, it returns the ordered list in the table called TABLE-TO-BE-SORTED to the main program. The main program uses this subroutine to sort the student records by student name before generating the requested report.
3. The subroutine D4-REPORT-PRINTER [Program 3-Source(d)] formats and generates the desired academic status report, and an exception report, if needed.
4. The main program, called STUDENT-STATUS-REPORT [Program 3-Source(a)], makes use of the above subroutines. After the list containing the sorted student identification numbers is returned by B2-INPUT-AND-SORT-IDNO, the main program reads records from STUDENT-INFORMATION-FILE sequentially and searches this file for the corresponding student records. The main program uses four structures of one-dimensional arrays, and one of a two-dimensional array. See lines 000089 through 000120 in Program 3-Source(a).

Program 3-Output(a) is an example of the academic status report and an exceptions report generated by the sample program. Program 3-Output(b) is the interactive terminal session corresponding to this run.

Table Searching in COBOL

Earlier in this chapter we introduced the concept of list searching, emphasized its importance in data processing, and discussed three basic internal search algorithms. In practice, external searching is more frequently performed. In other words, searching is decidedly a significant application for files. Although specialized techniques exist for searching files, they are dependent on the underlying file organization method. The simplest external search technique does not take into account a file's organizational aspects. It entails breaking down a file into fixed-size blocks of records (called pages), loading each page into an array, and searching the array in the main memory. The search in this strategy is internal.

COBOL supports a built-in SEARCH feature that enables the application programmer to search a table without having to write a procedure such as those in Figures 12, 13, and 14. To understand the COBOL SEARCH feature, we must study

1. The concept of indexed arrays
2. Using indexes to access array elements
3. Specifying ordered arrays in COBOL
4. The SEARCH statement, which searches a table for the occurrence of a particular array element

Table Processing with Indexes and Indexed Tables

An alternative way to access array elements in COBOL is to use an index instead of a subscript. A subscript defines the relative location of an array element within an array. Therefore, a legitimate subscript value for an array is an integer ranging in value between 1 and the size of the array. On the other hand, an index works differently.

> An **index** is a compiler-controlled variable that can be used to access array elements by their relative displacements from the beginning of the array.

> The **displacement** of an array element is the relative address of its first byte within the segment of the storage allocated to the array.

The first element of an array has a displacement of 0. Displacements of other array elements depend on the size of element values.

As an example, consider the table:

```
01   SEARCH-TABLE.
     05   EMPLOYEE-RECORD          OCCURS 3 TIMES.
          10   EMP-IDNO            PIC 9(4).
          10   EMP-NAME            PIC X(10).
```

The following figure shows the conceptual storage structure for this table.

SEARCH–TABLE					
EMPLOYEE–RECORD (1)		EMPLOYEE–RECORD (2)		EMPLOYEE–RECORD (3)	
EMP– IDNO (1)	EMP–NAME (1)	EMP– IDNO (2)	EMP–NAME (2)	EMP– IDNO (3)	EMP–NAME (3)
. . . .	. . . .	. . . .	. . . .	. . . .	. . . .

Subscript → (row 2)
Subscript → (row 3)
Displacement → 0   14   28

The first element of the array, EMPLOYEE-RECORD (1), has a displacement of zero. The second element has a displacement of 14 because the size of the composite data element EMPLOYEE-RECORD (1) is 14 bytes. Similarly, the third element has a displacement of 28. Let us assume that we have the following partial COBOL code.

```
WORKING–STORAGE SECTION.
01  SUBSCR     PIC 99.
. . . . . . . . . . . .
PROCEDURE DIVISION.
. . . . . . . . . . . .
MOVE 2 TO SUBSCR.
MOVE EMPLOYEE–RECORD (SUBSCR) TO . . . . .
```

The user-defined variable SUBSCR is being used as a subscript for the array EMPLOYEE-RECORD. The computer will access the array element EMPLOYEE-RECORD (SUBSCR) after the following steps.

1. A value of 2 is first stored in SUBSCR.
2. The subscript value 2 is converted to the correct displacement value of 14.
3. This displacement is added to the absolute address of the first byte of the array to get the absolute address of the first byte of the second array element. The computer then uses this absolute hardware address to access the array element.

If we use an index rather than a subscript to access the array element, the second step above, that is, converting the relative location 2 to the correct displacement, will not be necessary, as an index always contains displacements, not relative addresses. This is why accessing arrays using indexes instead of subscripts is more efficient.

We can define indexes in COBOL for array processing in two ways.

1. We can define an index variable in the WORKING-STORAGE section of the program using the USAGE IS INDEX clause without a PICTURE clause.
2. We can associate an index with an array while defining the array, using the INDEXED BY clause.

The following is an example of index definition through the use of the USAGE IS INDEX clause.

```
01  T–INDEX USAGE IS INDEX.
```

An example of index specification at the time an array is being defined is given below.

```
01  SEARCH-TABLE.
    05  EMPLOYEE-RECORD            OCCURS 3 TIMES
        INDEXED BY TABLE-INDEX.
        10  EMP-IDNO               PIC 9(4).
        10  EMP-NAME               PIC X(10).
```

In these examples the variables T-INDEX and TABLE-INDEX will be automatically defined by the compiler as full-word pure binary integer fields. Index variables may be used as subscripts in array element references. An index that is defined in the WORKING-STORAGE SECTION may be used as a subscript for any array in the program. One that is specifically associated with an array, however, may be used only with that array and all subscripted variables defined within that array. EMPLOYEE-RECORD (TABLE-INDEX) and EMP-NAME (TABLE-INDEX) are legitimate references for the example above.

Under certain circumstances, the programmer may have to assign values to index variables, or may have to change their values. The COBOL arithmetic statements and the MOVE statement cannot be used with index variables, because index variables store displacements, not values.

To assign a value to an index we use the SET statement, which is a variation of the MOVE statement. The SET statement has several formats. The one describing the version that can be used to assign values to an index is given below.

$$\underline{SET} \left\{ \begin{array}{l} \text{index-name-1} \\ \text{identifier-1} \end{array} \right\} \ldots \underline{TO} \left\{ \begin{array}{l} \text{index-name-2} \\ \text{identifier-2} \\ \text{integer} \end{array} \right\}$$

If the index is associated with an array, we may assign a relative location value to it.

```
SET TABLE-INDEX TO 1.
```

This statement causes a displacement assignment of zero to TABLE-INDEX. The statement

```
SET TABLE-INDEX TO 2.
```

on the other hand, assigns a displacement of 14 to the index variable, and not the integer value 2. If, however, the index is a general index variable partially defined in the WORKING-STORAGE SECTION, the SET statement may be used to assign only displacement values to it. For the general index T-INDEX, the assignment

```
SET T-INDEX TO TABLE-INDEX.
```

is valid, but SET T-INDEX TO 1, for example, is not.

The SET statement may be used with the clauses UP BY or DOWN BY to increment or decrement index variables. The relevant format is

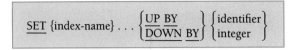

$$\underline{\text{SET}}\ \{\text{index-name}\}\ \dots\ \begin{Bmatrix} \underline{\text{UP}}\ \underline{\text{BY}} \\ \underline{\text{DOWN}}\ \underline{\text{BY}} \end{Bmatrix} \begin{Bmatrix} \text{identifier} \\ \text{integer} \end{Bmatrix}$$

Some examples follow.

```
SET TABLE-INDEX UP BY 2.
SET TABLE-INDEX DOWN BY K.
```

The clause UP BY corresponds to arithmetic ADD, and DOWN BY to SUB-TRACT. Let us assume that TABLE-INDEX currently contains a displacement value of zero. The first SET statement above increments it by a displacement of 28. The second statement causes a number of bytes representing K occurrences to be subtracted from the current value of TABLE-INDEX. The variable K above must be an integer variable storing a nonzero positive value.

As is seen, an index is a compromise between the user and the machine. If the user wants to assign or change an index value, he or she specifies a relative location that is legitimate for the array for which the index is defined. The compiler automatically translates this relative location to a displacement using the storage properties of the associated array.

Besides the SET statement, the only other statement that may change the value of an index is the PERFORM VARYING statement.

```
PERFORM SET-TO-ZERO
    VARYING TABLE-INDEX
        FROM 1 BY 1
        UNTIL END-OF-ARRAY-REACHED.
```

Let us summarize our discussion for index variables and indexed tables.

1. An index may be associated with an array. Such an array is called an indexed array.
2. An index may be partially defined in the WORKING-STORAGE SECTION of a program without being associated with an array. This is a general index.
3. Indexes do not store relative array element addresses, they store displacements.
4. An index associated with an array by definition may be used as a subscript only with that array, whereas a general index may be used as a subscript with any array.
5. Indexes associated with arrays may be assigned values using the SET statement. The assigned values are relative address values for the array. The compiler converts such values to displacements.
6. General indexes may be assigned only displacement values.
7. Variation of index values may be controlled only by the SET statement with the UP BY or DOWN BY options, and the PERFORM VARYING statement.

Specifying Ordered Arrays

Indexes are especially useful with the COBOL SEARCH statement. The SEARCH statement has two variations for table searching that work on ordered arrays. They correspond to the sequential search and the binary search of an ordered array. In both variations the programmer assumes the responsibility of ascertaining that the table to be searched is properly ordered and that the compiler is informed of this fact. This is done using the ASCENDING KEY or DESCENDING KEY optional clause in the array definition. Here is an example:

```
01   SEARCH-TABLE.
     05   EMPLOYEE-RECORD               OCCURS 6 TIMES
     ASCENDING KEY IS EMP-IDNO.
     10   EMP-IDNO                      PIC 9(4).
     10   EMP-NAME                      PIC X(20).
     10   EMP-DEPARTMENT                PIC X(10).
```

The ASCENDING KEY clause instructs the COBOL compiler that the array is ordered in ascending sequence by the element mentioned. In this example, the array elements are expected to be in increasing order by EMP-IDNO. The DESCENDING KEY clause does the opposite.

The COBOL SEARCH Feature

The COBOL built-in search feature is based on the SEARCH statement. The SEARCH statement causes the compiler to generate the code necessary to carry out either sequential or binary search, depending on its format. The array to be searched must be an indexed array. The SEARCH statement has two forms: the SEARCH form, which conducts a sequential search, and the SEARCH ALL form, which is used to perform a binary search.

Sequential Search Using the SEARCH Statement. The SEARCH form tells the compiler to generate and execute a code that performs sequential search of an indexed table. The algorithm inherent in the generated code is for sequential search of an unordered table. Syntactically, the SEARCH statement for sequential search is as follows.

COBOL 85

$$\text{SEARCH identifier-1} \left[\underline{\text{VARYING}} \left\{ \begin{matrix} \text{identifier-2} \\ \text{index-name} \end{matrix} \right\} \right]$$
$$[\text{ AT } \underline{\text{END}} \text{ imperative-statement-1 }]$$
$$\left\{ \underline{\text{WHEN}} \text{ condition} \left\{ \begin{matrix} \text{imperative-statement-2} \\ \underline{\text{NEXT}} \ \underline{\text{SENTENCE}} \end{matrix} \right\} \right\} \dots [\text{END-SEARCH}]$$

The name of the indexed array should be defined at the same level as the OCCURS clause, and should be written without a subscript. The optional VARYING clause specifies either an index or a subscript. The AT END clause is also optional, and includes a set of imperative statements. At least one WHEN clause should exist in the SEARCH statement. It contains a condition followed by a set of imperative statements or the clause NEXT SENTENCE. The semantics of the SEARCH statement are as follows.

1. The index or subscript in the VARYING clause should belong to an array other than the one being searched. If specified in the VARYING clause, it is varied in parallel to the index for the array being searched.
2. If none of the search conditions in the WHEN clause is satisfied by the time the end of the array is reached, the search is unsuccessful. In this case, the imperative statements in the AT END clause is executed, and control drops down to the statement that follows SEARCH. If the search terminates successfully, the contents of the AT END clause is ignored.
3. Ordinarily, the conditions in the WHEN clauses should be one or more search conditions that will return true if the search proves successful. In this case, the indicated set of imperative statements is executed and control is transferred to the statement after SEARCH. If NEXT SENTENCE is used instead of an imperative sentence, the statement after SEARCH is executed next. The imperative statements are actions to be taken if the search conditions are met.
4. The SEARCH statement initiates a sequential search starting with the array element defined by the current value of the index for the array. The programmer should indicate the array element with which the search is to begin by assigning an initial value to the array index before SEARCH.
5. The search continues until the search conditions are met, or until the end of the array is reached. If, for a particular array element, none of the WHEN conditions is satisfied, the index is automatically incremented by one so that the next element in the array is considered. If the array contains a list whose size is less than the size of the host array, the programmer should provide for the termination of the search in a WHEN clause.

The following are examples of the use of the SEARCH statement.

Example 1   Sequential search of an array using SEARCH with VARYING.

```
. . . . . . . . . . . . . . . . . . . . . . . . .
01   SEARCH-TABLE.
     05   EMP-IDNO          PIC 9(4)
                            OCCURS 90 TIMES
                            INDEXED BY NUMBER-INDEX.
     05   OTHER-EMP-INFO    OCCURS 90 TIMES
                            INDEXED BY INFO-INDEX.
          10   EMP-NAME              PIC X(20).
          10   EMP-DEPARTMENT        PIC X(10).
. . . . . . . . . . . . . . . . . . . . . . .

. . . . . . . . . . . . . . . . . . . . . . .
SET NUMBER-INDEX TO 1.
SET INFO-INDEX   TO 1.

SEARCH EMP-IDNO
       VARYING INFO-INDEX
       AT END
             PERFORM SEARCH-FAILED
       WHEN EMP-IDNO (NUMBER-INDEX) = GIVEN-EMP-IDNO
             MOVE "YES"                     TO RECORD-FOUND
             MOVE OTHER-EMP-INFO (INFO-INDEX) TO
                  OUTPUT-TEMPLATE.
```

In this program segment the structure SEARCH-TABLE has two one-dimensional arrays in it: EMP-IDNO and OTHER-EMP-INFO. Both are of the same size, 90 elements. The structure SEARCH-TABLE defines separate indexes for the two arrays: NUMBER-INDEX and INFO-INDEX, respectively. The search array is EMP-IDNO, and a search key stored in GIVEN-EMP-IDNO is to be matched with a value in EMP-IDNO. If the search proves successful, we want to access the corresponding element of the array OTHER-EMP-INFO. As the two arrays have individual index variables, these variables must be varied together. This accounts for the two SET statements initializing both indexes to 1, so that they can be varied in parallel and the entire array starting from the first element can be searched. It also accounts for the VARYING clause in the SEARCH statement.

Example 2   Sequential search of an unordered array (no VARYING clause).

```
. . . . . . . . . . . . . . . . . . . . . . . . . . . .
01  SEARCH-TABLE.
    05  EMPLOYEE-RECORD OCCURS 90 TIMES
                        INDEXED BY NUMBER-INDEX.
        10  EMP-IDNO               PIC 9(4).
        10  EMP-NAME               PIC X(20).
        10  EMP-DEPARTMENT         PIC X(10).
    . . . . . . . . . . . . . . . . . . . . . .
    . . . . . . . . . . . . . . . . . . . . . .
    SET NUMBER-INDEX TO 5.

    SEARCH EMPLOYEE-RECORD
           AT END
                 PERFORM SEARCH-FAILED
           WHEN EMP-IDNO (NUMBER-INDEX) = GIVEN-EMP-IDNO
                 AND
                EMP-DEPARTMENT = "ACCOUNTING"
                  MOVE "YES"                  TO RECORD-FOUND
                  MOVE EMP-NAME (NUMBER-INDEX) TO OUT-NAME.
```

This code is based on a slightly different table. Here SEARCH-TABLE consists of a single one-dimensional array, EMPLOYEE-RECORD. Each element of the array is a composite data structure including EMP-IDNO, EMP-NAME, and EMP-DEPARTMENT. The array is unordered, and one index, NUMBER-INDEX, is defined for it. All data fields in each array element are controlled by this index. Therefore, we do not need the VARYING clause in the SEARCH statement. Setting NUMBER-INDEX to 5 causes the sequential search to commence with the fifth array element. Also note that a combined condition is used as the search condition.

Binary Search Using the SEARCH Statement.   The second format generates and runs a code corresponding to the binary search of an ordered array. It is also referred to as the SEARCH ALL format. Syntactically, it has the following elements.

SEARCH ALL identifier-1 [AT END imperative-statement-1]

$$\text{WHEN} \left\{ \begin{array}{l} \text{data-name-1} \left\{ \begin{array}{l} \text{IS } \underline{\text{EQUAL}} \text{ TO} \\ \text{IS } = \end{array} \right\} \left\{ \begin{array}{l} \text{identifier-2} \\ \text{literal-1} \\ \text{arithmetic-expression-1} \end{array} \right\} \\ \text{condition-name-1} \end{array} \right\}$$

$$\left[\underline{\text{AND}} \left\{ \begin{array}{l} \text{data-name-2} \left\{ \begin{array}{l} \text{IS } \underline{\text{EQUAL}} \text{ TO} \\ \text{IS } = \end{array} \right\} \left\{ \begin{array}{l} \text{identifier-3} \\ \text{literal-2} \\ \text{arithmetic-expression-2} \end{array} \right\} \\ \text{condition-name-2} \end{array} \right\} \right] \cdots$$

COBOL 85

$$\left\{ \begin{array}{l} \text{imperative-statement-2} \\ \underline{\text{NEXT}} \ \underline{\text{SENTENCE}} \end{array} \right\} \quad [\ \underline{\text{END-SEARCH}} \ ]$$

As in the SEARCH statement for sequential search, the AT END clause indicates actions to be taken if the search proves unsuccessful. The predicate in the WHEN clause describes the search conditions; however, its form is somewhat different. The WHEN predicate may be

1. A simple relation condition involving an ASCENDING or DESCENDING KEY data item and the equal-to comparison operator
2. A condition name that has only a single value and is associated with an ASCENDING or DESCENDING KEY data item
3. A complex predicate combining any number of such simple conditions or condition names using the AND Boolean operator

When using the SEARCH ALL statement, the array index need not be set to an initial value. The search code automatically initializes and varies the array index, at all times keeping its values within the boundaries of the array.

Example 3   Binary search of an ordered array.

```
. . . . . . . . . . . . . . . . . . . . . . . . .
01   SEARCH-TABLE.
     05   EMPLOYEE-RECORD OCCURS 90 TIMES
                          ASCENDING KEY IS EMP-IDNO
                          INDEXED BY NUMBER-INDEX.
          10   EMP-IDNO              PIC 9(4).
          10   EMP-NAME              PIC X(20).
          10   EMP-DEPARTMENT        PIC X(10).
     . . . . . . . . . . . . . . . . . . . . . . .
     . . . . . . . . . . . . . . . . . . . . . . .
     SEARCH ALL EMPLOYEE-RECORD
          AT END PERFORM SEARCH-FAILED
          WHEN EMP-IDNO (NUMBER-INDEX) = GIVEN-EMP-IDNO
               MOVE "YES"                    TO RECORD-FOUND
               MOVE EMP-NAME (NUMBER-INDEX)       TO OUT-NAME
               MOVE EMP-DEPARTMENT (NUMBER-INDEX) TO OUT-DEPT.
```

The array EMPLOYEE-TABLE is presorted in ascending order by EMP-IDNO. Thus, the binary search algorithm is applicable provided the search domain is EMP-IDNO. Note the form of the WHEN condition and the absence of the SET statement.

COBOL 85   *COBOL 85 Features for the SEARCH Statement.* In the new version of the language, the SEARCH statement essentially remains unchanged, except for the inclusion of the scope terminator END-SEARCH. Example 3 written in COBOL 85 becomes

```
SEARCH ALL EMPLOYEE-RECORD
        AT END PERFORM SEARCH-FAILED
        WHEN EMP-IDNO (NUMBER-INDEX) = GIVEN-EMP-IDNO
            MOVE "YES"                          TO RECORD-FOUND
            MOVE EMP-NAME (NUMBER-INDEX)        TO OUT-NAME
            MOVE EMP-DEPARTMENT (NUMBER-INDEX) TO OUT-DEPT
END-SEARCH.
```

REVIEW QUESTIONS

1. In COBOL, the SEARCH statement is used for external searching of sequential files. (T or F)
2. An index is a compiler-controlled variable that can be used to access array elements by their relative _____ from the beginning of the array.
3. The USAGE IS INDEX clause defines an index variable that can be used for only the array for which it is defined. (T or F)
4. Which of the statements about index variables is correct?
   a. The statement SET TABLE-INDEX TO 1 assigns a value of zero to TABLE-INDEX, if TABLE-INDEX is an index variable.
   b. The value of an index variable may be changed using only the SET statement.
   c. To increment the value of an index variable, we must use the SET UP BY form of the SET statement.
   d. All of the above are correct.
   e. None of a, b, or c is correct.
5. To tell the compiler that an array is presorted in increasing order, we use the _____ clause.
6. The SEARCH statement searches an array using _____, whereas SEARCH ALL uses _____.
7. Which of the following about the COBOL SEARCH statement is correct?
   a. In sequentially searching an array, before the SEARCH statement is executed, the array index should be initialized to some appropriate value.
   b. In the SEARCH ALL form of the SEARCH statement, the array index need not be set to an initial value.
   c. A complex condition in the WHEN clause of a SEARCH statement may have only the AND Boolean operator.
   d. All of the above are correct.

Answers: 1. F; 2. displacements; 3. F; 4. d; 5. ASCENDING KEY; 6. sequential search, binary search; 7. d.

Example Program 4: Data Retrieval from a Sequential File

As we have stressed, searching is frequently used to retrieve data from files. A simple way to search a file is to read a fixed number of records (i.e., a page) from the file into an array, and search the array until a match is found or all pages of the file are processed. In this section, we develop a sample program to implement this technique, thereby using the COBOL SEARCH feature in a practical application.

Problem Let us suppose we have a sequential employee information file consisting of records with the following structure:

- A four-digit employee identification number, unique for each employee, in columns 1–4
- A 20-byte employee name, again uniquely defining each record, in columns 6–25.
- A 10-byte department name for departments where the employees work in columns 28–37

Program 4-Input shows an instance of the employee information file. This file is frequently searched using any of the three fields as the search domain. We will develop a program to do the following.

1. Ask the user to input the search column and a search key that is compatible with the search column. The search column may be employee identification number, employee name, or department name.
2. Read a fixed number of records from the file into a one-dimensional array. In our program, the page size is taken as six records.
3. If the search column is employee identification number, search the array for each page using binary search (i.e., the SEARCH ALL statement).
4. If the search column is employee name, search the array using sequential search (SEARCH statement) for each page.
5. If the search column is department name, first sort the page array in ascending order by department, for which we use the bubble sort technique, and apply sequential search to find all records satisfying the search condition. In this case, after the first record for the given department name is found using the SEARCH statement, the remaining records in each page for the same department are sequentially retrieved from the page array without using the SEARCH statement again. This is possible because sorting the page array before searching causes the records to be grouped together for different department name values.
6. Consider all pages in the file similarly until data retrieval is complete, successful or otherwise.
7. Display the retrieved records on the screen.

Solution The compiler listing of the developed program is given in Program 4-Source. To find the number of pages in the EMPLOYEE-INFORMATION-FILE, the program first determines the number of records in the file by reading it until its end and counting the number of records. The file that has been opened in input mode is then closed and reopened in input mode for subsequent processing. Closing and reopening the file brings the current record pointer back to the first record in the file. Then, records are read and stored in the page array called EMPLOYEE-RECORD, six records at a time, and the same search technique is applied to retrieve the qualifying records.

Program 4-Output is a sample interactive session obtained by running the program to test it thoroughly.

Key Terms

array
array column
array element
array row
ASCENDING KEY clause
binary search
bubble sort
DESCENDING KEY clause
dimension
DOWN BY clause
external search
external sorting
index
indexed array
INDEXED BY clause
insertion sort
internal search
internal sorting
list
logical sorting
matrix
OCCURS clause
one-dimensional array

ordered list
PERFORM VARYING statement
physical sorting
relative address
relative displacement
SEARCH ALL statement
search key
SEARCH statement
searching
sequential search
SET statement
sorting
subscript
subscripted variable
table
table look-up
three-dimensional array
two-dimensional array
unordered list
UP BY clause
USAGE IS INDEX clause
WHEN clause

Study Guide

Quick Scan

- Arrays are useful internal data structures commonly supported by high-level programming languages, including COBOL.
- A list is a variable-size set of data elements of the same type. An array, on the other hand, is an ordered set of a fixed number of consecutive memory locations, each accessed by a relative address. Thus, a list is a data structure, and an array is a storage structure.
- Arrays are used to store lists in the computer's main memory. In the external storage, lists are stored in files. Therefore, both arrays and files are storage structures that can host lists.
- Elements in an array are referenced using the array name together with a subscript. Subscripts are relative addresses for array elements.
- A list may be hosted in an array by storing list elements in consecutive array elements. Such an allocation is sequential. In sequential allocation, the successor of a list element is in the next element of the array.
- In linked allocation, the successor of a list element may be stored anywhere in the host array, and the location of the successor may be indicated by a link that is stored together with the value of the list element.
- In a sequentially allocated list, list elements may define an ascending or descending ordering by element values. Such a list is called an ordered list.
- The process of transforming an unordered list into an equivalent ordered list is called sorting.

- Higher-dimensional arrays may be defined using one-dimensional arrays. For example, a two-dimensional array is an array of a fixed number of similar one-dimensional arrays, and so on.
- In a two-dimensional array (also called a matrix) relative locations of array elements are indicated by two subscripts, specifying the row and column of the array element in the corresponding conceptual tabular structure.
- In COBOL, arrays are defined in the DATA DIVISION within a superordinate structure. The size of an array is indicated by the OCCURS clause.
- COBOL array elements may be atomic or composite. An array with atomic element values has a PICTURE clause associated with its name at the same level as the OCCURS clause.
- An array with composite elements has an OCCURS clause with the array name and a substructure specification for the array elements.
- Higher-dimensional arrays in COBOL are defined as extensions of one-dimensional arrays. A two-dimensional array includes a one-dimensional array whose elements are themselves one-dimensional arrays, and so on. COBOL 74 supports up to three-dimensional arrays; however, in COBOL 85 the maximum number of dimensions has been extended to seven.
- COBOL offers a great deal of flexibility in defining arrays in a program. The way arrays are defined depends on how the programmer plans to use them.
- Subscripted variables are used to reference array elements. One-dimensional arrays require one subscript after the array name; two-dimensional arrays need two subscripts separated by a comma, and so on. If an array element is a composite structure, its constituents are treated as subscripted variables.
- In addition to simple operations for arrays and array elements (e.g., initializing, reading, writing, processing array elements), two commonly performed operations on arrays are sorting the lists contained in them, and searching the lists for occurrences of a specific value.
- If the list to be sorted is hosted in an array and the entire list remains in the main memory during processing, the corresponding sorting method is internal sorting. If the list cannot be accommodated in its entirety in the main memory and should be stored in secondary storage during sorting, such a technique is external sorting.
- There are many internal sorting techniques, and a good programmer should be familiar with a variety of them. In this chapter, the insertion and bubble sort algorithms are described.
- Similarly, searching can be classified as external or internal depending on whether the list to be searched is kept in the memory during the search or not. Three fundamental internal search techniques are described: sequential search of unordered lists, sequential search of ordered lists, and binary search of ordered lists.
- COBOL has a built-in search feature that requires the array to be indexed. Indexing is a technique of accessing elements of an array, like subscripting. Unlike a subscript, however, an index variable stores relative displacements of array elements.
- In COBOL, an index may be defined to belong to an array. It is also possible to define general index variables without associating them with particular arrays.
- Value initialization and change for index variables require the use of the SET, SET UP BY, and SET DOWN BY statements. COBOL MOVE and arithmetic statements may not be used with index variables.
- If an array contains an ordered list and the programmer plans to take advantage of this fact, the compiler should be informed of this. While defining an array, we can use the ASCENDING KEY or DESCENDING KEY clause to declare that that array is ordered.

- We can use the SEARCH statement to search an array in a COBOL program. The SEARCH statement causes the compiler to generate a procedural code that implements the search.
- The SEARCH statement has two forms. One form is suitable for sequential search. The other, SEARCH ALL, can be used to apply binary search to an ordered array.

Test Your Comprehension

Multiple-Choice Questions

1. Which of the following statements about arrays is correct?
   a. An array has a fixed number of consecutive memory locations.
   b. The size of an array is the number of memory locations in it.
   c. Array elements are referenced using their relative addresses together with the array name.
   d. The relative addresses specifying array elements are also known as subscripts.
   e. All of the above are correct.
2. Which of the following statements about COBOL arrays is incorrect?
   a. An array can be defined as a level 01 entry.
   b. The size of an array is indicated in an accompanying OCCURS clause.
   c. The OCCURS clause should have an unsigned nonzero integer constant value, followed by the key word TIMES.
   d. A two-dimensional COBOL array is defined as a one-dimensional array whose elements are themselves one-dimensional arrays.
3. In COBOL, an array element may be assigned values
   a. Using a MOVE, an arithmetic statement, or an ACCEPT statement at run-time
   b. Moving a value to the table name containing the array at run-time
   c. Using a VALUE clause at compile-time
   d. Using the REDEFINES clause at compile-time
   e. By all four methods
4. In internal list searching,
   a. Sequential search becomes more efficient under all circumstances if the list is sorted.
   b. Binary search may be applied to any list, ordered or not.
   c. Binary search is more efficient than sequential search because it halves the list to be searched after each unsuccessful comparison.
   d. All of the above are correct.
5. Which of the following statements concerning indexes and indexed arrays in COBOL is correct?
   a. An index is another name for a subscript.
   b. An index can be used as if it were a subscript.
   c. The value of an index variable can be changed using a MOVE statement.
   d. To increment the value stored in an index variable, we may use the ADD statement.
6. Which of the following statements concerning the COBOL SEARCH statement is correct?
   a. SEARCH ALL executes a binary search of an unordered array.
   b. The SEARCH form of the SEARCH statement is used for sequential searching of an ordered or unordered array.
   c. If the condition in the WHEN clause is complex, we may have all kinds of Boolean operators in it.
   d. All of the above are correct.

Answers: 1. e; 2. a; 3. e; 4. c; 5. b; 6. b.

Short Essay Questions

1. Define a list and an array. What is the difference between a list and an array?
2. What is meant by sequential and linked allocation of lists?
3. Explain how a one-dimensional array can be defined in COBOL.
4. How do we define two-dimensional arrays in COBOL?
5. Distinguish between internal and external sorting.
6. Discuss the following related issues. COBOL has a file sort feature, which is discussed in Chapter 12, so why should a programmer be familiar with a variety of sorting techniques? Also, COBOL supports an array SEARCH feature that we can use even if we do not know the fundamental search algorithms. Is studying search techniques a waste of time?
7. What is an index? What is the difference between an index and a subscript?
8. How do we define an index associated with an array in COBOL? Give a simple example.
9. What are the differences between a general index variable and an index associated with an array?
10. Explain why a special statement, SET, is needed to manipulate index variables in COBOL.
11. How do we specify an ordered array in the DATA DIVISION? Why and when do we have to inform the COBOL compiler that an array contains an ordered list?
12. Explain the full semantics of the COBOL SEARCH statement for sequential search.
13. Explain the full semantics of the COBOL SEARCH ALL statement for binary search.
14. Under what conditions do we have to use the VARYING clause in the SEARCH statement? Explain your answer.
15. Suppose we want to search the first half of an array using the SEARCH statement for sequential search. How do we go about it?
16. How can we write the SEARCH statement so that only the second half of an array can be searched sequentially using the SEARCH statement?
17. The content of the WHEN clause in the SEARCH ALL version of the SEARCH statement is different from the one in the version for sequential search. Why?

Improve Your Problem-Solving Ability

Debugging Exercises

In each of the following COBOL constructs or statements, identify any errors that you can find, and explain why they are errors.

```
1. 01  COURSES-TAUGHT-BY OCCURS 3 TIMES.
       05  FACULTY-NUMBER    PIC X(5).
       05  NUMBER-OF-COURSES PIC 9.
       05  COURSE-CODES      PIC X(6)
       OCCURS 6 TIMES.
2. 01  FACULTY-TABLE.
       05  FACULTY-DATA      OCCURS 50 TIMES
           ASCENDING KEY IS FACULTY-NUMBER
           INDEX IS F-INX.
           10  FACULTY-NUMBER     PIC X(5).
           10  FACULTY-NAME       PIC X(20).
           10  FACULTY-DEPT       PIC X(10).
           10  FACULTY-RANK       PIC X.
           10  YEARS-OF-SERVICE   PIC 99.
```

```
3. SET 5 TO NUMBER-INDEX.
4. SET TABLE-INDEX UP TO 2.
5. SEARCH EMPLOYEE-RECORD
        AT END
                PERFORM SEARCH-FAILED
        WHEN EMP-IDNO (NUMBER-INDEX) = GIVEN-EMP-IDNO
                OR
        EMP-DEPARTMENT = "ACCOUNTING"
                MOVE "YES"                       TO RECORD-FOUND
                MOVE EMP-NAME (NUMBER-INDEX) TO OUT-NAME.
```

Programming Exercises

1. For the following COBOL structures containing arrays, draw figures showing the conceptual storage structures that will be generated by the compiler.

   a.
   ```
   01  EXERCISE-1A.
       05  A1      OCCURS 2 TIMES.
           10  A2  OCCURS 3 TIMES.
               15  A3   PIC XX.
               15  A4   PIC 9.
           10  A5       PIC 99.
   ```

   b.
   ```
   01  EXERCISE-1B.
       05  B1.
           10  B2    OCCURS 3 TIMES  PIC 9.
           10  B3    OCCURS 2 TIMES.
               15  B4   PIC X.
               15  B5   PIC 9    OCCURS 2 TIMES.
       05  B6        PIC X    OCCURS 4 TIMES.
   ```

2. Write a COBOL structure named STUDENT-TABLE, containing three one-dimensional arrays, STUDENT-NAME, STUDENT-MAJOR, and STUDENT-YEAR, such that

   a. Each array is of size 200.

   b. The array STUDENT-NAME contains a list presorted in descending order.

   c. An index variable, STU-INDEX, controls all three arrays.

   d. STUDENT-NAME is alphanumeric and of length 20; STUDENT-MAJOR is alphanumeric and of length 10; and STUDENT-YEAR is unedited numeric of length 2.

3. Given is the COBOL structure:

   ```
   01  FACULTY-TABLE.
       05  FACULTY-DATA      OCCURS 50 TIMES
           INDEXED BY F-INX.
           10  FACULTY-NUMBER        PIC X(5).
           10  FACULTY-NAME          PIC X(20).
           10  FACULTY-DEPT          PIC X(10).
           10  FACULTY-RANK          PIC X.
           10  YEARS-OF-SERVICE      PIC 99.
   ```

   Write the SEARCH statement and the other necessary statements to do the following search tasks. In all cases, if search fails, display an appropriate message on the terminal screen.

   a. Find and display the name of the faculty whose identification number is 20200.

   b. Find and display the name of the first faculty in the department of ACCOUNTING whose rank is professor (FACULTY-RANK value P).

   c. Find and display names and years of service of all professors (FACULTY-RANK value P) in the department of FINANCE.

Programming Problems

1. Given is the two-dimensional COBOL array definition:

```
01  INPUT-MATRIX.
    05  ROWS OCCURS 10 TIMES.
        10  ELEMS OCCURS 10 TIMES PIC 9(6)V99.
```

Write a COBOL subroutine that accepts the structure INPUT-MATRIX as one of its formal parameters, determines if the two-dimensional array is a symmetric matrix or not, and returns a variable that contains YES if the array is a symmetric matrix, and NO if not.

(Note: A square matrix is a two-dimensional array of equal numbers of rows and columns. A square matrix is said to be **symmetric** if all off-diagonal elements are equal to their symmetric counterparts with respect to the main diagonal. In other words, the matrix A is symmetric if $A(I,J) = A(J,I)$ for all $I <> J$.)

2. For the same array of programming problem 1, develop a COBOL subroutine that accepts the structure INPUT-MATRIX as one of its formal parameters, and computes and returns two one-dimensional arrays that are the sums of rows and columns of the two-dimensional array in the structure.

3. Assume the structure of programming exercise 3 has been modified as follows.

```
01  FACULTY-TABLE.
    05  FACULTY-DATA    OCCURS 50 TIMES
        ASCENDING KEY IS FACULTY-NUMBER
        INDEXED BY F-INX.
        10  FACULTY-NUMBER      PIC X(5).
        10  FACULTY-NAME        PIC X(20).
        10  FACULTY-DEPT        PIC X(10).
        10  FACULTY-RANK        PIC X.
        10  YEARS-OF-SERVICE    PIC 99.
```

We also have the structure:

```
01  TEACHING-ASSIGNMENTS.
    05  COURSES-TAUGHT OCCURS 200 TIMES.
    10  FAC-IDNO           PIC X(5).
    10  COURSE-CODE        PIC X(6).
    10  MEET-TIME          PIC X(8).
    10  MEET-ROOM          PIC X(10).
```

Write a COBOL subroutine that accepts the structures FACULTY-TABLE and TEACHING-ASSIGNMENTS and a faculty identification number as its formal parameters, and computes and returns the following structure.

```
01  COURSES-TAUGHT-BY.
    05  FACULTY-NUMBER    PIC X(5).
    05  NUMBER-OF-COURSES PIC 9.
    05  COURSE-CODES      PIC X(6)
            OCCURS 6 TIMES.
```

In this structure, COURSE-CODES is an array containing a list whose size is determined by NUMBER-OF-COURSES. The number of courses taught by a faculty member may vary between 0 and 6. Your program should verify the existence of the faculty number in the FACULTY-TABLE before it searches the structure TEACHING-ASSIGNMENTS. Make use of the COBOL SEARCH statement and its binary search version whenever possible.

4. In Example Program 1 we developed a program that read records from the STUDENT-INFORMATION-FILE, and created two parallel one-dimensional arrays. The array called MAJOR (see Program 1-Source) had different major codes in it, and the other array, NO-OF-STUDENTS, told us about the number of students majoring in a corresponding discipline. The array MAJOR was not ordered.

Redesign this program such that the final content of MAJOR reflects an increasing order of major codes. For this, define two other one-dimensional arrays compatible with MAJOR and NO-OF-STUDENTS arrays. Let us call them ORDERED-MAJOR and ORDERED-NUMBER. Then have your program choose the smallest major code out of MAJOR, and insert it into ORDERED-MAJOR, one smallest major code, at a time. (What you are doing here is the insertion sort algorithm of Figure 10.)

```
                          Column
1   5   10   15   20   25   30   35   40   45   50
----|----|----|----|----|----|----|----|----|----|----

0800 MORRISON WILLIAM F    ACC 85 4 375
0890 EASTMAN THOMAS        ACC 85 3 230
0980 WAYNE WILLIS          ACC 84 4 320
1000 JEFFERSON JOHN D      ACC 85 2 298
1123 KILDARE WAYNE         ACC 84 3 290
1200 CROSETTE CARLOS J     ACC 84 4 325
1210 DOWSON DAVID          ENG 83 3 220
1300 PEAR JANE             BOT 84 2 301
1350 JASON TERRY           PHY 85 1 355
1400 DIONNE WILLIAM        ZOO 83 4 380
1500 KAYSER TOM            ACC 85 3 185
3000 BRAUN ALLISON S       ACC 84 4 340
3500 GORDON AARON          ACC 84 4 340
```

Program 1-Input An Instance of STUDENT-INFORMATION-FILE for Program 1

```
000001    *.........................................................
000002     IDENTIFICATION DIVISION.
000003     PROGRAM-ID.      MAJOR-DISTRIBUTION.
000004     ***********************************************************
000005     ***   THIS PROGRAM PROCESSES STUDENT RECORDS STORED IN THE    *
000006     ***   "STUDENT-INFORMATION-FILE", WHICH IS A SEQUENTIALLY ORGA-  *
000007     ***   NIZED DISK FILE, AND COMPUTES THE NUMBER OF STUDENTS MAJOR-  *
000008     ***   ING IN EACH DEPARTMENT.                                 *
000009     ***********************************************************
000010
000011     AUTHOR.          UCKAN.
000012     INSTALLATION.    UNIVERSITY.
000013     DATE-WRITTEN.    APRIL 22, 1991.
000014     DATE-COMPILED. 04/22/91.
000015
000016    *.........................................................
000017     ENVIRONMENT DIVISION.
000018     CONFIGURATION SECTION.
000019     SOURCE-COMPUTER.  UNIVERSITY-MAINFRAME.
000020     OBJECT-COMPUTER.  UNIVERSITY-MAINFRAME.
000021     INPUT-OUTPUT SECTION.
```

Program 1-Source Program to Generate Distribution of Students by Major

```
000022      FILE-CONTROL.
000023          SELECT STUDENT-INFORMATION-FILE ASSIGN TO INFILE
000024                  ORGANIZATION IS SEQUENTIAL
000025                  ACCESS MODE  IS SEQUENTIAL.
000026
000027      *..........................................................
000028      DATA DIVISION.
000029      FILE SECTION.
000030      FD STUDENT-INFORMATION-FILE
000031          LABEL RECORDS ARE STANDARD
000032          DATA RECORD IS STUDENT-INFORMATION
000033          RECORD CONTAINS 80 CHARACTERS.
000034      01  STUDENT-INFORMATION.
000035          05   STUDENT-IDNO-IN          PIC X(4).
000036          05   FILLER                   PIC X.
000037          05   STUDENT-NAME-IN          PIC X(20).
000038          05   FILLER                   PIC X.
000039          05   MAJOR-CODE               PIC X(3).
000040          05   FILLER                   PIC X.
000041          05   ENTRANCE-YEAR            PIC 99.
000042          05   FILLER                   PIC X.
000043          05   CLASS-IN                 PIC 9.
000044          05   FILLER                   PIC X.
000045          05   GRADE-POINT-AVR          PIC 9V99.
000046          05   FILLER                   PIC X(42).
000047
000048      WORKING-STORAGE SECTION.
000049
000050      *********> SWITCHES:
000051
000052      01  END-OF-FILE-FLAG             PIC XXX    VALUE "NO".
000053          88  END-OF-FILE                         VALUE "YES".
000054      01  ARRAY-EMPTY                  PIC XXX.
000055      01  UPDATE-DONE                  PIC XXX.
000056
000057      *********> SUBSCRIPTS:
000058
000059      01  ARRAY-INDEX                          PIC 99.
000060      01  EMPTY-POINTER                        PIC 99.
000061
000062      *********> ARRAYS:
000063
000064      01  DISTRIBUTION-BY-MAJORS-TABLE.
000065          05  MAJORS.
000066              10  MAJOR        OCCURS 20 TIMES   PIC XXX.
000067          05  DISTRIBUTIONS.
000068              10  NO-OF-STUDENTS OCCURS 20 TIMES  PIC 999.
000069
000070      *********> STRUCTURES:
000071
000072      01  REPORT-HEADER.
000073          05  FILLER    VALUE "MAJOR  NO-OF-STUDENTS"  PIC X(21).
000074
```

Program 1-Source (Continued)

```
000075    01  REPORT-LINE.
000076        05  FILLER        VALUE SPACE               PIC X.
000077        05  OUT-MAJOR                               PIC XXX.
000078        05  FILLER        VALUE SPACES              PIC X(9).
000079        05  OUT-NUMBER                              PIC ZZ9.
000080
000081    *...................................................................
000082    PROCEDURE DIVISION.
000083    A-MAINLINE.
000084        OPEN INPUT STUDENT-INFORMATION-FILE.
000085
000086        PERFORM B1-PREPARATIONS.
000087
000088        PERFORM B2-READ-STUDENT-FILE.
000089
000090        PERFORM B3-GENERATE-DISTRIBUTIONS
000091              UNTIL END-OF-FILE.
000092
000093        DISPLAY REPORT-HEADER.
000094
000095        PERFORM B4-DISPLAY-DISTRIBUTIONS
000096              VARYING ARRAY-INDEX FROM 1 BY 1
000097              UNTIL ARRAY-INDEX = EMPTY-POINTER.
000098
000099        CLOSE STUDENT-INFORMATION-FILE.
000100        STOP RUN.
000101
000102    B1-PREPARATIONS.
000103        MOVE 1      TO EMPTY-POINTER.
000104        MOVE SPACES TO MAJORS.
000105        MOVE ZEROS  TO DISTRIBUTIONS.
000106        MOVE "YES"  TO ARRAY-EMPTY.
000107
000108    B2-READ-STUDENT-FILE.
000109        READ STUDENT-INFORMATION-FILE
000110              AT END MOVE "YES" TO END-OF-FILE-FLAG.
000111
000112    B3-GENERATE-DISTRIBUTIONS.
000113
000114        IF ARRAY-EMPTY = "YES"
000115              PERFORM C1-ADD-NEW-ELEMENT
000116              MOVE "NO" TO ARRAY-EMPTY
000117        ELSE
000118              MOVE "NO" TO UPDATE-DONE
000119
000120              PERFORM C2-UPDATE-DISTRIBUTION
000121                  VARYING ARRAY-INDEX FROM 1 BY 1
000122                  UNTIL ARRAY-INDEX = EMPTY-POINTER
000123                                    OR
000124                  UPDATE-DONE = "YES".
000125
000126        IF UPDATE-DONE = "NO"
000127              PERFORM C1-ADD-NEW-ELEMENT.
000128
```

Program 1-Source (Continued)

```
000129          PERFORM B2-READ-STUDENT-FILE.
000130
000131     B4-DISPLAY-DISTRIBUTIONS.
000132          MOVE MAJOR (ARRAY-INDEX)          TO OUT-MAJOR.
000133          MOVE NO-OF-STUDENTS (ARRAY-INDEX) TO OUT-NUMBER.
000134          DISPLAY REPORT-LINE.
000135
000136     C1-ADD-NEW-ELEMENT.
000137          MOVE MAJOR-CODE TO MAJOR (EMPTY-POINTER).
000138          ADD 1 TO NO-OF-STUDENTS (EMPTY-POINTER).
000139          ADD 1 TO EMPTY-POINTER.
000140
000141     C2-UPDATE-DISTRIBUTION.
000142          IF MAJOR (ARRAY-INDEX) = MAJOR-CODE
000143               ADD 1 TO NO-OF-STUDENTS (ARRAY-INDEX)
000144               MOVE "YES" TO UPDATE-DONE.
```

Program 1-Source (Continued)

```
MAJOR   NO-OF-STUDENTS
  ACC          9
  ENG          1
  BOT          1
  PHY          1
  ZOO          1
```

Program 1-Output A Sample Output of Program 1

```
000001    *..................................................................
000002      IDENTIFICATION DIVISION.
000003      PROGRAM-ID.     MAJOR-STATUS-DISTRIBUTION.
000004      *****************************************************************
000005      ***   THIS PROGRAM PROCESSES STUDENT RECORDS STORED IN THE       *
000006      ***   "STUDENT-INFORMATION-FILE", WHICH IS A SEQUENTIALLY ORGA-  *
000007      ***   NIZED DISK FILE, AND COMPUTES THE NUMBER OF STUDENTS MAJOR- *
000008      ***   ING IN EACH DEPARTMENT.  ALSO, IT COMPUTES THE NUMBER OF   *
000009      ***   STUDENTS IN PROBATIONARY, SATISFACTORY, AND HONOR STATUS   *
000010      ***   ON THE BASIS OF EACH STUDENT'S GRADE POINT AVERAGE.        *
000011      *****************************************************************
000012
000013      AUTHOR.        UCKAN.
000014      INSTALLATION.  UNIVERSITY.
000015      DATE-WRITTEN.  APRIL 23, 1991.
000016      DATE-COMPILED. 04/23/91.
000017
000018    *..................................................................
000019      ENVIRONMENT DIVISION.
000020      CONFIGURATION SECTION.
000021      SOURCE-COMPUTER.  UNIVERSITY-MAINFRAME.
000022      OBJECT-COMPUTER.  UNIVERSITY-MAINFRAME.
000023      INPUT-OUTPUT SECTION.
```

Program 2-Source Program to Generate Distributions by Major and Academic Standing

```
000024      FILE-CONTROL.
000025          SELECT STUDENT-INFORMATION-FILE ASSIGN TO INFILE
000026              ORGANIZATION IS SEQUENTIAL
000027              ACCESS MODE  IS SEQUENTIAL.
000028
000029     *..........................................................
000030      DATA DIVISION.
000031      FILE SECTION.
000032      FD STUDENT-INFORMATION-FILE
000033          LABEL RECORDS ARE STANDARD
000034          DATA RECORD IS STUDENT-INFORMATION
000035          RECORD CONTAINS 80 CHARACTERS.
000036      01   STUDENT-INFORMATION.
000037           05   STUDENT-IDNO-IN        PIC X(4).
000038           05   FILLER                 PIC X.
000039           05   STUDENT-NAME-IN        PIC X(20).
000040           05   FILLER                 PIC X.
000041           05   MAJOR-CODE             PIC X(3).
000042           05   FILLER                 PIC X.
000043           05   ENTRANCE-YEAR          PIC 99.
000044           05   FILLER                 PIC X.
000045           05   CLASS-IN               PIC 9.
000046           05   FILLER                 PIC X.
000047           05   GRADE-POINT-AVR        PIC 9V99.
000048           05   FILLER                 PIC X(42).
000049
000050      WORKING-STORAGE SECTION.
000051
000052      **********> SWITCHES:
000053
000054      01  END-OF-FILE-FLAG             PIC XXX    VALUE "NO".
000055          88  END-OF-FILE                         VALUE "YES".
000056      01  ARRAY-EMPTY                  PIC XXX.
000057      01  UPDATE-DONE                  PIC XXX.
000058
000059      **********> SUBSCRIPTS:
000060
000061      01  ARRAY-INDEX                  PIC 99.
000062      01  EMPTY-POINTER                PIC 99.
000063
000064      **********> ARRAYS:
000065
000066      01  DISTRIBUTION-BY-MAJORS-TABLE.
000067          05  MAJORS.
000068              10  MAJOR             OCCURS 20 TIMES   PIC XXX.
000069          05  DISTRIBUTIONS.
000070              10  NO-OF-STUDENTS    OCCURS 20 TIMES   PIC 999.
000071              10  MAJOR-STATUS      OCCURS 20 TIMES.
000072                  15  ACADEMIC-STATUS  OCCURS 3 TIMES   PIC 999.
000073
000074      **********> STRUCTURES:
000075
000076      01  REPORT-HEADER.
000077          05  FILLER                              PIC X(44)
000078              VALUE "MAJOR  PROBATION  SATISFACTORY  HONOR   TOTAL".
```

Program 2-Source (Continued)

```
000079
000080     01   REPORT-LINE.
000081          05   FILLER        VALUE SPACE                PIC X.
000082          05   OUT-MAJOR                                PIC XXX.
000083          05   FILLER        VALUE SPACES               PIC X(6).
000084          05   OUT-PROBATION                            PIC ZZ9.
000085          05   FILLER        VALUE SPACES               PIC X(10).
000086          05   OUT-SATISFACTORY                         PIC ZZ9.
000087          05   FILLER        VALUE SPACES               PIC X(7).
000088          05   OUT-HONOR                                PIC ZZ9.
000089          05   FILLER        VALUE SPACES               PIC X(4).
000090          05   OUT-TOTAL                                PIC ZZ9.
000091
000092     *.........................................................................
000093     PROCEDURE DIVISION.
000094     A-MAINLINE.
000095         OPEN INPUT STUDENT-INFORMATION-FILE.
000096
000097         PERFORM B1-PREPARATIONS.
000098
000099         PERFORM B2-READ-STUDENT-FILE.
000100
000101         PERFORM B3-GENERATE-DISTRIBUTIONS
000102              UNTIL END-OF-FILE.
000103
000104         DISPLAY REPORT-HEADER.
000105
000106         PERFORM B4-DISPLAY-DISTRIBUTIONS
000107              VARYING ARRAY-INDEX FROM 1 BY 1
000108              UNTIL ARRAY-INDEX = EMPTY-POINTER.
000109
000110         CLOSE STUDENT-INFORMATION-FILE.
000111         STOP RUN.
000112
000113     B1-PREPARATIONS.
000114         MOVE 1      TO EMPTY-POINTER.
000115         MOVE SPACES TO MAJORS.
000116         MOVE ZEROS  TO DISTRIBUTIONS.
000117         MOVE "YES"  TO ARRAY-EMPTY.
000118
000119     B2-READ-STUDENT-FILE.
000120         READ STUDENT-INFORMATION-FILE
000121              AT END MOVE "YES" TO END-OF-FILE-FLAG.
000122
000123     B3-GENERATE-DISTRIBUTIONS.
000124
000125         IF ARRAY-EMPTY = "YES"
000126              PERFORM C1-ADD-NEW-ELEMENT
000127              MOVE "NO" TO ARRAY-EMPTY
000128         ELSE
000129              MOVE "NO" TO UPDATE-DONE
000130
```

Program 2-Source (Continued)

```
000131                    PERFORM C2-UPDATE-DISTRIBUTION
000132                         VARYING ARRAY-INDEX FROM 1 BY 1
000133                         UNTIL ARRAY-INDEX = EMPTY-POINTER
000134                                        OR
000135                         UPDATE-DONE = "YES".
000136
000137        IF UPDATE-DONE = "NO"
000138                 PERFORM C1-ADD-NEW-ELEMENT.
000139
000140        PERFORM B2-READ-STUDENT-FILE.
000141
000142    B4-DISPLAY-DISTRIBUTIONS.
000143        MOVE MAJOR (ARRAY-INDEX)              TO OUT-MAJOR.
000144        MOVE NO-OF-STUDENTS (ARRAY-INDEX)     TO OUT-TOTAL.
000145        MOVE ACADEMIC-STATUS (ARRAY-INDEX, 1) TO OUT-PROBATION.
000146        MOVE ACADEMIC-STATUS (ARRAY-INDEX, 2) TO OUT-SATISFACTORY.
000147        MOVE ACADEMIC-STATUS (ARRAY-INDEX, 3) TO OUT-HONOR.
000148
000149        DISPLAY REPORT-LINE.
000150
000151    C1-ADD-NEW-ELEMENT.
000152        MOVE MAJOR-CODE TO MAJOR (EMPTY-POINTER).
000153        ADD 1 TO NO-OF-STUDENTS (EMPTY-POINTER).
000154
000155        IF GRADE-POINT-AVR < 2.00
000156             ADD 1 TO ACADEMIC-STATUS (EMPTY-POINTER, 1)
000157        ELSE
000158             IF GRADE-POINT-AVR < 3.00
000159                  ADD 1 TO ACADEMIC-STATUS (EMPTY-POINTER, 2)
000160             ELSE
000161                  ADD 1 TO ACADEMIC-STATUS (EMPTY-POINTER, 3).
000162
000163        ADD 1 TO EMPTY-POINTER.
000164
000165    C2-UPDATE-DISTRIBUTION.
000166        IF MAJOR (ARRAY-INDEX) = MAJOR-CODE
000167             ADD 1 TO NO-OF-STUDENTS (ARRAY-INDEX)
000168             PERFORM D1-GENERATE-STAT-DISTR
000169             MOVE "YES" TO UPDATE-DONE.
000170
000171    D1-GENERATE-STAT-DISTR.
000172        IF GRADE-POINT-AVR < 2.00
000173             ADD 1 TO ACADEMIC-STATUS (ARRAY-INDEX, 1)
000174        ELSE
000175             IF GRADE-POINT-AVR < 3.00
000176                  ADD 1 TO ACADEMIC-STATUS (ARRAY-INDEX, 2)
000177             ELSE
000178                  ADD 1 TO ACADEMIC-STATUS (ARRAY-INDEX, 3).
```

Program 2-Source (Continued)

MAJOR	PROBATION	SATISFACTORY	HONOR	TOTAL
ACC	1	3	5	9
ENG	0	1	0	1
BOT	0	0	1	1
PHY	0	0	1	1
ZOO	0	0	1	1

Program 2-Output Sample Output of Program 2

```
00001     *.................................................................
00002      IDENTIFICATION DIVISION.
00003      PROGRAM-ID.      STUDENT-STATUS-REPORT.
00004     *****************************************************************
00005     ***    THIS PROGRAM PROCESSES STUDENT RECORDS STORED IN THE        *
00006     ***    "STUDENT-INFORMATION-FILE", WHICH IS A SEQUENTIALLY ORGA-    *
00007     ***    NIZED DISK FILE, AND GENERATES A STUDENT STATUS REPORT.      *
00008     ***                                                                *
00009     ***    THE USER IS PROMPTED TO ENTER THE DEPARTMENT CODE FOR WHICH  *
00010     ***    THE REPORT IS TO BE GENERATED, THE TYPE OF REPORT, AND THE   *
00011     ***    STUDENT ID NUMBERS FOR STUDENTS TO BE INCLUDED IN THE        *
00012     ***    REPORT.                                                      *
00013     ***                                                                *
00014     ***    THIS PROGRAM CALLS THREE SUBROUTINES:                        *
00015     ***        1. B2-INPUT-AND-SORT-IDNO,                               *
00016     ***        2. C2-BUBBLE-SORT,                                       *
00017     ***        3. D4-REPORT-PRINTER.                                    *
00018     *****************************************************************
00019
00020      AUTHOR.         UCKAN.
00021      INSTALLATION.   MIAMI UNIVERSITY.
00022      DATE-WRITTEN.   SEPTEMBER 23, 1990.
00023      DATE-COMPILED. OCT 27,1990.
00025     *.................................................................
00026      ENVIRONMENT DIVISION.
00027      CONFIGURATION SECTION.
00028      SOURCE-COMPUTER.  IBM-370.
00029      OBJECT-COMPUTER.  IBM-370.
00030      INPUT-OUTPUT SECTION.
00031      FILE-CONTROL.
00032          SELECT STUDENT-INFORMATION-FILE ASSIGN TO INFILE
00033                  ORGANIZATION IS SEQUENTIAL
00034                  ACCESS MODE  IS SEQUENTIAL.
00035
00036     *.................................................................
00037      DATA DIVISION.
00038      FILE SECTION.
00039      FD STUDENT-INFORMATION-FILE
00040          LABEL RECORDS ARE STANDARD
00041          DATA RECORD IS STUDENT-INFORMATION
00042          RECORD CONTAINS 80 CHARACTERS.
00043      01  STUDENT-INFORMATION.
00044          05  STUDENT-IDNO-IN              PIC X(4).
```

Program 3-Source(a) Main Program for Sample Application Software to Generate Academic Status Reports

```
00045          05   FILLER                       PIC X.
00046          05   STUDENT-NAME-IN              PIC X(20).
00047          05   FILLER                       PIC X.
00048          05   MAJOR-CODE                   PIC X(3).
00049          05   FILLER                       PIC X.
00050          05   ENTRANCE-YEAR                PIC 99.
00051          05   FILLER                       PIC X.
00052          05   CLASS-IN                     PIC 9.
00053          05   FILLER                       PIC X.
00054          05   GRADE-POINT-AVR              PIC 9V99.
00055          05   FILLER                       PIC X(42).
00056
00057     WORKING-STORAGE SECTION.
00058
00059     **********> SWITCHES:
00060
00061     01  END-OF-FILE-FLAG                   PIC XXX     VALUE "NO".
00062          88  END-OF-FILE                               VALUE "YES".
00063
00064     01  REPORT-FLAG                        PIC 9       VALUE 2.
00065          88  ORDERED-BY-NAME                           VALUE 1.
00066
00067     01  RECORD-FOUND                       PIC XXX     VALUE "NO".
00068          88  FOUND                                     VALUE "YES".
00069
00070     01  RECORD-NOT-IN-FILE                 PIC XXX     VALUE "NO".
00071          88  NOT-IN-FILE                               VALUE "YES".
00072
00073     01  EXCEPTION-FLAG                     PIC XXX     VALUE "NO".
00074          88  EXCEPTION-REPORT                          VALUE "YES".
00075
00076
00077     **********> SUBSCRIPTS:
00078
00079     01  TABLE-SUBSC                             PIC 99.
00080     01  NUMBER-TABLE-SUBSC                      PIC 99.
00081
00082     **********> VARIABLES:
00083
00084     01  NORMAL-STATE                            PIC 9.
00085     01  DIFFERENCE-IN-YEARS                     PIC 9.
00086     01  FLAG                                    PIC 99.
00087     01  DEPARTMENT-CODE                         PIC XXX.
00088
00089     **********> ARRAYS:
00090
00091     01  STUDENT-NUMBER-TABLE.
00092          05   STUDENT-NUMBER                PIC X(4)   OCCURS 20 TIMES.
00093
00094     01  TABLE-BY-STUDENT-NAME.
00095          05   STUDENT-INFORMATION-1         OCCURS 20 TIMES.
00096               10   STUDENT-NAME-1                PIC X(20).
00097               10   STUDENT-IDNO-1                PIC X(4).
00098               10   ACADEMIC-STANDING-1           PIC X(12).
```

Program 3-Source(a) (Continued)

```
00099                10    COMMENTS-1.
00100                      15    COMMENT-DESCRIPTION-1         PIC X(7).
00101                      15    COMMENT-NO-OF-YEARS-1         PIC XX.
00102                      15    COMMENT-YEAR-1                PIC XXX.
00103
00104        01    TABLE-BY-STANDING-AND-NAME.
00105              05    ACADEMIC-STANDING-GROUPS      OCCURS 4 TIMES.
00106                10    ACADEMIC-STANDING-TYPE            PIC X(12).
00107                10    STUDENT-INFORMATION-2      OCCURS 20 TIMES.
00108                      15    STUDENT-NAME-2               PIC X(20).
00109                      15    STUDENT-IDNO-2               PIC X(4).
00110                      15    COMMENTS-2.
00111                            20    COMMENT-DESCRIPTION-2  PIC X(7).
00112                            20    COMMENT-NO-OF-YEARS-2  PIC XX.
00113                            20    COMMENT-YEAR-2         PIC XXX.
00114
00115        01    EXCEPTIONS-TABLE.
00116              05    NUMBERS-NOT-IN-DEPARTMENT    PIC X(4)    OCCURS 20 TIMES.
00117              05    NUMBERS-NOT-IN-FILE          PIC X(4)    OCCURS 20 TIMES.
00118
00119        01    ACADEMIC-STD-LENGTH-TABLE.
00120              05    ACD-STD-ARRAY-LENGTH         PIC 99      OCCURS 4 TIMES.
00121
00122        **********> STRUCTURES:
00123
00124        01    TODAYS-DATE.
00125              05    TODAYS-YEAR                  PIC 99.
00126              05    TODAYS-MONTH                 PIC 99.
00127              05    TODAYS-DAY                   PIC 99.
00128
00129        01    EXCEPTION-TABLE-SUBSCRIPTS.
00130              05    EXCEPTION-TABLE-SUBSC1       PIC 99.
00131              05    EXCEPTION-TABLE-SUBSC2       PIC 99.
00132
00133        01    ACADEMIC-STANDING-SUBSCRIPTS.
00134              05    ACD-STD-GROUP-SUBSC          PIC 99.
00135              05    ST-INFO-SUBSC                PIC 99.
00136              05    HIGH-HONOR-SUBSC             PIC 99.
00137              05    HONOR-SUBSC                  PIC 99.
00138              05    SATISFACTORY-SUBSC           PIC 99.
00139              05    PROBATION-SUBSC              PIC 99.
00140
00141        01    ARRAY-LENGTHS.
00142              05    EXCEPTION-TABLE-LENGTH-1     PIC 99.
00143              05    EXCEPTION-TABLE-LENGTH-2     PIC 99.
00144              05    NUMBER-TABLE-LENGTH          PIC 99.
00145              05    TABLE-LENGTH                 PIC 99.
00146
00147        *...........................................................
00148        PROCEDURE DIVISION.
00149        A-MAINLINE.
00150            OPEN INPUT STUDENT-INFORMATION-FILE.
00151
00152            PERFORM B1-PREPARATIONS.
```

Program 3-Source(a) (Continued)

```
00153
00154          CALL "B2-INPUT-AND-SORT-IDNO"
00155              USING
00156                  DEPARTMENT-CODE
00157                  STUDENT-NUMBER-TABLE
00158                  NUMBER-TABLE-LENGTH
00159                  REPORT-FLAG.
00160
00161          READ STUDENT-INFORMATION-FILE
00162                  AT END MOVE "YES" TO END-OF-FILE-FLAG.
00163
00164          PERFORM B3-SEARCH-ROUTINE
00165                  VARYING NUMBER-TABLE-SUBSC
00166                      FROM 1 BY 1
00167                      UNTIL NUMBER-TABLE-SUBSC > NUMBER-TABLE-LENGTH.
00168
00169          PERFORM B4-GENERATE-REPORTS.
00170
00171          CLOSE STUDENT-INFORMATION-FILE.
00172          STOP RUN.
00173
00174      B1-PREPARATIONS.
00175          ACCEPT TODAYS-DATE FROM DATE.
00176
00177          MOVE ZEROS TO EXCEPTION-TABLE-SUBSC1
00178                        EXCEPTION-TABLE-SUBSC2
00179                        TABLE-SUBSC
00180                        HIGH-HONOR-SUBSC
00181                        HONOR-SUBSC
00182                        SATISFACTORY-SUBSC
00183                        PROBATION-SUBSC
00184                        ACADEMIC-STD-LENGTH-TABLE.
00185
00186          MOVE "HIGH HONOR"    TO ACADEMIC-STANDING-TYPE(1).
00187          MOVE "HONOR"         TO ACADEMIC-STANDING-TYPE(2).
00188          MOVE "SATISFACTORY"  TO ACADEMIC-STANDING-TYPE(3).
00189          MOVE "PROBATION"     TO ACADEMIC-STANDING-TYPE(4).
00190
00191      B3-SEARCH-ROUTINE.
00192          MOVE "NO" TO RECORD-FOUND
00193                       RECORD-NOT-IN-FILE.
00194
00195          PERFORM C1-SEARCH-IDNO-IN-FILE
00196                  UNTIL FOUND OR NOT-IN-FILE.
00197
00198      B4-GENERATE-REPORTS.
00199          CALL "C2-BUBBLE-SORT"
00200              USING
00201                  TABLE-BY-STUDENT-NAME
00202                  TABLE-LENGTH.
00203
```

Program 3-Source(a) (Continued)

```
00204          IF ORDERED-BY-NAME
00205                  PERFORM C3-CALL-PRINT-SUBROUTINE
00206          ELSE
00207                  PERFORM C4-GROUP-BY-ACADEMIC-STANDING
00208                          VARYING TABLE-SUBSC FROM 1 BY 1
00209                          UNTIL TABLE-SUBSC > TABLE-LENGTH
00210                  PERFORM C3-CALL-PRINT-SUBROUTINE.
00211
00212
00213      C1-SEARCH-IDNO-IN-FILE.
00214
00215          IF STUDENT-IDNO-IN = STUDENT-NUMBER(NUMBER-TABLE-SUBSC)
00216                  PERFORM D1-PROCESS-STUDENT-INFO
00217                  PERFORM D2-READ-FROM-FILE
00218          ELSE
00219              IF STUDENT-IDNO-IN < STUDENT-NUMBER(NUMBER-TABLE-SUBSC)
00220                      PERFORM D2-READ-FROM-FILE
00221              ELSE
00222                  IF STUDENT-IDNO-IN >
00223                      STUDENT-NUMBER(NUMBER-TABLE-SUBSC)
00224                          OR
00225                      END-OF-FILE
00226                          PERFORM D3-PROCESS-NUMBERS-NOT-IN-FILE.
00227
00228      C3-CALL-PRINT-SUBROUTINE.
00229          CALL "D4-REPORT-PRINTER"
00230              USING
00231                  TABLE-BY-STUDENT-NAME
00232                  TABLE-BY-STANDING-AND-NAME
00233                  ACADEMIC-STD-LENGTH-TABLE
00234                  EXCEPTIONS-TABLE
00235                  DEPARTMENT-CODE
00236                  REPORT-FLAG
00237                  EXCEPTION-FLAG
00238                  TABLE-LENGTH
00239                  EXCEPTION-TABLE-LENGTH-1
00240                  EXCEPTION-TABLE-LENGTH-2.
00241
00242          IF EXCEPTION-REPORT
00243                  CALL "D4-REPORT-PRINTER"
00244                      USING
00245                          TABLE-BY-STUDENT-NAME
00246                          TABLE-BY-STANDING-AND-NAME
00247                          ACADEMIC-STD-LENGTH-TABLE
00248                          EXCEPTIONS-TABLE
00249                          DEPARTMENT-CODE
00250                          REPORT-FLAG
00251                          EXCEPTION-FLAG
00252                          TABLE-LENGTH
00253                          EXCEPTION-TABLE-LENGTH-1
00254                          EXCEPTION-TABLE-LENGTH-2.
00255
```

Program 3-Source(a) (Continued)

```
00256     C4-GROUP-BY-ACADEMIC-STANDING.
00257         IF ACADEMIC-STANDING-1(TABLE-SUBSC) = "HIGH HONOR"
00258                 ADD 1                      TO HIGH-HONOR-SUBSC
00259                 MOVE HIGH-HONOR-SUBSC TO
00260                                          ST-INFO-SUBSC
00261                                          ACD-STD-ARRAY-LENGTH(1)
00262                 MOVE 1               TO ACD-STD-GROUP-SUBSC
00263
00264                 PERFORM D5-LOAD-ACADEMIC-STD-TABLE.
00265
00266         IF ACADEMIC-STANDING-1(TABLE-SUBSC) = "HONOR"
00267                 ADD 1         TO HONOR-SUBSC
00268                 MOVE HONOR-SUBSC TO
00269                                     ST-INFO-SUBSC
00270                                     ACD-STD-ARRAY-LENGTH(2)
00271                 MOVE 2           TO ACD-STD-GROUP-SUBSC
00272
00273                 PERFORM D5-LOAD-ACADEMIC-STD-TABLE.
00274
00275         IF ACADEMIC-STANDING-1(TABLE-SUBSC) = "SATISFACTORY"
00276                 ADD 1                  TO SATISFACTORY-SUBSC
00277                 MOVE SATISFACTORY-SUBSC TO
00278                                          ST-INFO-SUBSC
00279                                          ACD-STD-ARRAY-LENGTH(3)
00280                 MOVE 3               TO ACD-STD-GROUP-SUBSC
00281
00282                 PERFORM D5-LOAD-ACADEMIC-STD-TABLE.
00283
00284         IF ACADEMIC-STANDING-1(TABLE-SUBSC) = "PROBATION"
00285                 ADD 1                  TO PROBATION-SUBSC
00286                 MOVE PROBATION-SUBSC TO
00287                                         ST-INFO-SUBSC
00288                                         ACD-STD-ARRAY-LENGTH(4)
00289                 MOVE 4               TO ACD-STD-GROUP-SUBSC
00290
00291                 PERFORM D5-LOAD-ACADEMIC-STD-TABLE.
00292
00293
00294     D1-PROCESS-STUDENT-INFO.
00295         MOVE "YES" TO RECORD-FOUND.
00296
00297         IF MAJOR-CODE NOT = DEPARTMENT-CODE
00298                 PERFORM E1-PROCESS-NUMBERS-NOT-IN-DEPT
00299         ELSE
00300                 PERFORM E2-LOAD-TABLE-BY-NAME.
00301
00302     D2-READ-FROM-FILE.
00303         READ STUDENT-INFORMATION-FILE
00304                 AT END MOVE "YES" TO END-OF-FILE-FLAG.
00305
00306     D3-PROCESS-NUMBERS-NOT-IN-FILE.
00307         MOVE "YES" TO RECORD-NOT-IN-FILE.
00308         MOVE "YES" TO EXCEPTION-FLAG.
00309         ADD 1      TO EXCEPTION-TABLE-SUBSC1.
```

Program 3-Source(a) (Continued)

```
00310            MOVE STUDENT-NUMBER(NUMBER-TABLE-SUBSC) TO
00311                 NUMBERS-NOT-IN-FILE(EXCEPTION-TABLE-SUBSC1).
00312            MOVE EXCEPTION-TABLE-SUBSC1 TO EXCEPTION-TABLE-LENGTH-1.
00313
00314        D5-LOAD-ACADEMIC-STD-TABLE.
00315            MOVE STUDENT-NAME-1(TABLE-SUBSC) TO
00316                 STUDENT-NAME-2(ACD-STD-GROUP-SUBSC, ST-INFO-SUBSC).
00317            MOVE STUDENT-IDNO-1(TABLE-SUBSC) TO
00318                 STUDENT-IDNO-2(ACD-STD-GROUP-SUBSC, ST-INFO-SUBSC).
00319            MOVE COMMENTS-1(TABLE-SUBSC)      TO
00320                 COMMENTS-2(ACD-STD-GROUP-SUBSC, ST-INFO-SUBSC).
00321
00322        E1-PROCESS-NUMBERS-NOT-IN-DEPT.
00323            MOVE "YES" TO EXCEPTION-FLAG.
00324            ADD 1      TO EXCEPTION-TABLE-SUBSC2.
00325            MOVE STUDENT-NUMBER(NUMBER-TABLE-SUBSC) TO
00326                 NUMBERS-NOT-IN-DEPARTMENT(EXCEPTION-TABLE-SUBSC2).
00327            MOVE EXCEPTION-TABLE-SUBSC2 TO EXCEPTION-TABLE-LENGTH-2.
00328
00329        E2-LOAD-TABLE-BY-NAME.
00330            ADD 1                 TO TABLE-SUBSC.
00331            MOVE STUDENT-NAME-IN TO STUDENT-NAME-1(TABLE-SUBSC).
00332            MOVE STUDENT-IDNO-IN TO STUDENT-IDNO-1(TABLE-SUBSC).
00333            PERFORM F1-COMPUTE-ACADEMIC-STANDING.
00334            PERFORM F2-COMPUTE-COMMENTS.
00335            MOVE TABLE-SUBSC TO TABLE-LENGTH.
00336
00337        F1-COMPUTE-ACADEMIC-STANDING.
00338            IF GRADE-POINT-AVR < 2.00
00339                MOVE "PROBATION" TO ACADEMIC-STANDING-1(TABLE-SUBSC).
00340
00341            IF GRADE-POINT-AVR > 1.99
00342                    AND
00343                GRADE-POINT-AVR < 3.00
00344                MOVE "SATISFACTORY" TO
00345                                    ACADEMIC-STANDING-1(TABLE-SUBSC).
00346
00347            IF GRADE-POINT-AVR > 2.99
00348                    AND
00349                GRADE-POINT-AVR < 3.50
00350                MOVE "HONOR" TO ACADEMIC-STANDING-1(TABLE-SUBSC).
00351
00352            IF GRADE-POINT-AVR > 3.49
00353                MOVE "HIGH HONOR" TO
00354                                    ACADEMIC-STANDING-1(TABLE-SUBSC).
00355
00356        F2-COMPUTE-COMMENTS.
00357            COMPUTE NORMAL-STATE = TODAYS-YEAR - ENTRANCE-YEAR + 1.
00358
00359            IF CLASS-IN = NORMAL-STATE
00360                    MOVE "NORMAL" TO COMMENT-DESCRIPTION-1(TABLE-SUBSC)
00361                    MOVE SPACES   TO COMMENT-NO-OF-YEARS-1(TABLE-SUBSC)
00362                    MOVE SPACES   TO COMMENT-YEAR-1(TABLE-SUBSC).
00363
```

Program 3-Source(a) (Continued)

```
00364            IF CLASS-IN < NORMAL-STATE
00365                    MOVE "BEHIND" TO COMMENT-DESCRIPTION-1(TABLE-SUBSC)
00366                    COMPUTE DIFFERENCE-IN-YEARS = NORMAL-STATE -
00367                                              CLASS-IN
00368                    MOVE DIFFERENCE-IN-YEARS TO
00369                                  COMMENT-NO-OF-YEARS-1(TABLE-SUBSC)
00370                    MOVE "YRS" TO COMMENT-YEAR-1(TABLE-SUBSC).
00371
00372            IF CLASS-IN > NORMAL-STATE
00373                    MOVE "AHEAD" TO COMMENT-DESCRIPTION-1(TABLE-SUBSC)
00374                    COMPUTE DIFFERENCE-IN-YEARS = CLASS-IN -
00375                                              NORMAL-STATE
00376                    MOVE DIFFERENCE-IN-YEARS TO
00377                                  COMMENT-NO-OF-YEARS-1(TABLE-SUBSC)
00378                    MOVE "YRS" TO COMMENT-YEAR-1(TABLE-SUBSC).
```

Program 3-Source(a) (Continued)

```
00001    *..........................................................
00002       IDENTIFICATION DIVISION.
00003       PROGRAM-ID.    B2-INPUT-AND-SORT-IDNO.

00004    ****************************************************************
00005    ***   THIS SUBROUTINE IS CALLED BY THE PROGRAM "STUDENT-STATUS-  *
00006    ***   REPORT".                                                   *
00007    ***                                                             *
00008    ***   THIS SUBROUTINE HANDLES INTERACTIVE INPUT, AND USES        *
00009    ***   INSERTION SORT TO ORDER THE STUDENT ID NUMBERS.            *
00010    ****************************************************************
00011
00012       AUTHOR.        UCKAN.
00013       INSTALLATION.  MIAMI UNIVERSITY.
00014       DATE-WRITEN.   SEPTEMBER 10, 1990.
00015       DATE-COMPILED. OCT 27,1990.
00017    *..........................................................
00018       ENVIRONMENT DIVISION.
00019       CONFIGURATION SECTION.
00020       SOURCE-COMPUTER.  IBM-370.
00021       OBJECT-COMPUTER.  IBM-370.
00022
00023    *..........................................................
00024       DATA DIVISION.
00025
00026       WORKING-STORAGE SECTION.
00027
00028       01  STUDENT-IDNO-IN        PIC X(4).
00029       01  OUTER-SUBSC            PIC 99.
00030       01  INNER-SUBSC            PIC 99.
00031       01  SUBSC                  PIC 99.
00032       01  SUBSC-MINUS            PIC 99.
00033       01  SMALLEST               PIC X(4).
00034
00035       LINKAGE SECTION.
```

Program 3-Source(b) Subprogram B2-INPUT-AND-SORT-IDNO for Sample Application Software to Generate Academic Status Reports

```
00036
00037     01   DEPT-CODE              PIC XXX.
00038     01   ARRAY-LENGTH           PIC 99.
00039     01   LIST-ORDER-FLAG        PIC 9.
00040
00041     01   STUDENT-IDNO-TABLE.
00042          05   STUDENT-IDNO      PIC X(4)     OCCURS 20 TIMES.
00043
00044   *.....................................................................
00045     PROCEDURE DIVISION
00046          USING
00047                    DEPT-CODE
00048                    STUDENT-IDNO-TABLE
00049                    ARRAY-LENGTH
00050                    LIST-ORDER-FLAG.
00051
00052     A-MAINLINE.
00053         PERFORM B1-INPUT-FROM-TERMINAL.
00054         SUBTRACT 1 FROM ARRAY-LENGTH.
00055
00056         PERFORM B2-REMOVE-SMALLEST
00057                 VARYING SUBSC FROM 2 BY 1
00058                 UNTIL SUBSC > ARRAY-LENGTH.
00059
00060         SUBTRACT 1 FROM ARRAY-LENGTH.
00061
00062         PERFORM B3-RETURN-TO-MAIN-PROGRAM.
00063
00064     B1-INPUT-FROM-TERMINAL.
00065         DISPLAY "---> ENTER THE DEPARTMENT CODE: ".
00066         ACCEPT DEPT-CODE FROM CONSOLE.
00067
00068         DISPLAY "---> HOW DO YOU WANT THE LIST TO BE ORDERED?".
00069         DISPLAY "---> IF BY NAME, ENTER 1: ".
00070         DISPLAY "---> IF BY ACADEMIC STATUS, ENTER 2: ".
00071         ACCEPT LIST-ORDER-FLAG FROM CONSOLE.
00072
00073         MOVE "0000" TO STUDENT-IDNO(1).
00074         DISPLAY "START ENTERING STUDENT ID NUMBERS".
00075         DISPLAY "WHEN FINISHED ENTER DONE: ".
00076         ACCEPT STUDENT-IDNO-IN FROM CONSOLE.
00077
00078         MOVE STUDENT-IDNO-IN TO STUDENT-IDNO(2).
00079         MOVE 2                TO SUBSC.
00080         MOVE 2                TO ARRAY-LENGTH.
00081
00082         PERFORM C1-INPUT-STUDENT-ID-NUMBERS
00083                 UNTIL STUDENT-IDNO-IN = "DONE".
00084
00085     B2-REMOVE-SMALLEST.
00086         COMPUTE SUBSC-MINUS = SUBSC - 1.
00087         MOVE STUDENT-IDNO(SUBSC) TO STUDENT-IDNO(SUBSC-MINUS).
00088
00089     B3-RETURN-TO-MAIN-PROGRAM.
00090         EXIT PROGRAM.
```

Program 3-Source(b) (Continued)

```
00091
00092    C1-INPUT-STUDENT-ID-NUMBERS.
00093        ACCEPT STUDENT-IDNO-IN FROM CONSOLE.
00094        ADD 1 TO SUBSC.
00095        ADD 1 TO ARRAY-LENGTH.
00096        MOVE STUDENT-IDNO-IN TO STUDENT-IDNO(SUBSC).
00097
00098        PERFORM D1-SORT-STUDENT-ID-NUMBERS
00099                VARYING OUTER-SUBSC FROM 2 BY 1
00100                UNTIL OUTER-SUBSC > ARRAY-LENGTH
00101                         OR
00102                STUDENT-IDNO-IN = "DONE".
00103
00104    D1-SORT-STUDENT-ID-NUMBERS.
00105        MOVE STUDENT-IDNO(OUTER-SUBSC) TO SMALLEST.
00106        MOVE OUTER-SUBSC                TO INNER-SUBSC.
00107        COMPUTE SUBSC-MINUS = INNER-SUBSC - 1.
00108
00109        PERFORM E1-INSERTION-SORT
00110                UNTIL STUDENT-IDNO(SUBSC-MINUS) < SMALLEST.
00111
00112        MOVE SMALLEST TO STUDENT-IDNO(INNER-SUBSC).
00113
00114    E1-INSERTION-SORT.
00115        MOVE STUDENT-IDNO(SUBSC-MINUS) TO
00116                STUDENT-IDNO(INNER-SUBSC).
00117        COMPUTE INNER-SUBSC = INNER-SUBSC - 1.
00118        COMPUTE SUBSC-MINUS = INNER-SUBSC - 1.
```

Program 3-Source(b) (Continued)

```
00001    *..................................................................
00002    IDENTIFICATION DIVISION.
00003    PROGRAM-ID.    C2-BUBBLE-SORT.
00004    *********************************************************************
00005    ***   THIS SUBROUTINE IS CALLED BY THE PROGRAM "STUDENT-STATUS-   *
00006    ***   REPORT".                                                    *
00007    ***                                                               *
00008    ***   ITS MAIN FUNCTION IS TO ORDER ARRAYS USING THE BUBBLE SORT  *
00009    ***   TECHNIQUES.                                                 *
00010    *********************************************************************
00011
00012    AUTHOR.        UCKAN.
00013    INSTALLATION.  MIAMI UNIVERSITY.
00014    DATE-WRITTEN.    SEPTEMBER 10, 1990.
00015    DATE-COMPILED. OCT 27,1990.
00017    *..................................................................
00018    ENVIRONMENT DIVISION.
00019    CONFIGURATION SECTION.
00020    SOURCE-COMPUTER.   IBM-370.
00021    OBJECT-COMPUTER.   IBM-370.
00022
```

Program 3-Source(c) Subprogram C2-BUBBLE-SORT for Sample Application Software to Generate Academic Status Reports

```
00023   *..............................................................
00024   DATA DIVISION.
00025   WORKING-STORAGE SECTION.
00026
00027   01   OUTER-SUBSC          PIC 99.
00028   01   SUBSC               PIC 99.
00029   01   SUBSC-PLUS          PIC 99.
00030
00031   01   END-OF-FILE-FLAG    PIC XXX          VALUE "YES".
00032        88   END-OF-FILE                     VALUE "NO".
00033
00034   01   TEMPORARY-STORAGE.
00035        05   DUMMY-SORT-KEY     PIC X(20).
00036        05   DUMMY-OTHER-DATA   PIC X(28).
00037
00038   LINKAGE SECTION.
00039
00040   01   TABLE-TO-BE-SORTED.
00041        05   ARRAY-ELEMENT    OCCURS 20 TIMES.
00042            10   SORT-KEY      PIC X(20).
00043            10   OTHER-DATA    PIC X(28).
00044
00045   01   ARRAY-LENGTH         PIC 99.
00046
00047   *..............................................................
00048   PROCEDURE DIVISION
00049        USING
00050                TABLE-TO-BE-SORTED
00051                ARRAY-LENGTH.
00052
00053   A-MAINLINE.
00054       PERFORM B1-BUBBLE-SORT
00055               VARYING OUTER-SUBSC FROM ARRAY-LENGTH BY -1
00056               UNTIL OUTER-SUBSC < 2.
00057
00058       PERFORM B2-RETURN-TO-MAIN-PROGRAM.
00059
00060   B1-BUBBLE-SORT.
00061       PERFORM C1-COMPARE-SORT-KEYS
00062               VARYING SUBSC FROM 1 BY 1
00063               UNTIL SUBSC > ARRAY-LENGTH - 1.
00064
00065   C1-COMPARE-SORT-KEYS.
00066       COMPUTE SUBSC-PLUS = SUBSC + 1.
00067       IF SORT-KEY(SUBSC) > SORT-KEY(SUBSC-PLUS)
00068               MOVE ARRAY-ELEMENT(SUBSC)        TO TEMPORARY-STORAGE
00069               MOVE ARRAY-ELEMENT(SUBSC-PLUS) TO
00070                   ARRAY-ELEMENT(SUBSC)
00071               MOVE TEMPORARY-STORAGE           TO
00072                   ARRAY-ELEMENT(SUBSC-PLUS).
00073
00074   B2-RETURN-TO-MAIN-PROGRAM.
00075       EXIT PROGRAM.
```

Program 3-Source(c) (Continued)

```
00001    *...............................................................
00002     IDENTIFICATION DIVISION.
00003     PROGRAM-ID.     D4-REPORT-PRINTER.
00004     ********************************************************************
00005     ***   THIS SUBROUTINE IS CALLED BY THE PROGRAM "STUDENT-STATUS-    *
00006     ***   REPORT".                                                     *
00007     ***                                                                *
00008     ***   ITS FUNCTION IS TO FORMAT AND PRINT THE REQUIRED REPORT.     *
00009     ********************************************************************
00010
00011     AUTHOR.          UCKAN.
00012     INSTALLATION.    MIAMI UNIVERSITY.
00013     DATE-WRITTEN.    SEPTEMBER 10, 1990.
00014     DATE-COMPILED. OCT 27,1990.
00015    *...............................................................
00016     ENVIRONMENT DIVISION.
00017     CONFIGURATION SECTION.
00018     SOURCE-COMPUTER. IBM-370.
00019     OBJECT-COMPUTER. IBM-370.
00020     INPUT-OUTPUT SECTION.
00021     FILE-CONTROL.
00022         SELECT STUDENT-STATUS-REPORT ASSIGN TO OUTFILE.
00023
00024    *...............................................................
00025     DATA DIVISION.
00026     FILE SECTION.
00027     FD   STUDENT-STATUS-REPORT
00028          LABEL RECORDS ARE OMITTED
00029          DATA RECORD IS REPORT-LINE
00030          RECORD CONTAINS 131 CHARACTERS.
00031     01   REPORT-LINE              PIC X(131).
00032
00033     WORKING-STORAGE SECTION.
00034
00035    **********>  VARIABLES:
00036
00037     01   MONTH-TABLE-SUBSC        PIC 99.
00038     01   TABLE-SUBSC              PIC 99.
00039     01   DEPT-CODE-TB-SUBSC       PIC 99.
00040     01   ACD-STD-SUBSC            PIC 99.
00041     01   ST-INFO-SUBSC            PIC 99.
00042     01   EXCEPTION-TB-1-SUBSC     PIC 99.
00043     01   EXCEPTION-TB-2-SUBSC     PIC 99.
00044     01   ITERATION-SUBSC          PIC 99.
00045
00046     01   YEAR                     PIC 9(4).
00047
00048    **********>  STRUCTURES:
00049
00050     01   TODAYS-DATE.
00051          05   TODAYS-YEAR         PIC 99.
00052          05   TODAYS-MONTH        PIC 99.
00053          05   TODAYS-DAY          PIC 99.
```

Program 3-Source(d) Subprogram D4-REPORT-PRINTER for Sample Application Software to Generate Academic Status Reports

```
00054
00055     01   REPORT-DATE.
00056          05   REPORT-MONTH       PIC X(9).
00057          05   FILLER            PIC X          VALUE SPACES.
00058          05   REPORT-DAY        PIC 99.
00059          05   FILLER            PIC XX         VALUE ", ".
00060          05   REPORT-YEAR       PIC 9(4).
00061
00062     01   REPORT-TITLE-LINE.
00063          05   FILLER            PIC X(28)      VALUE SPACES.
00064          05   FILLER            PIC X(22)      VALUE
00065                                               "ACADEMIC STATUS REPORT".
00066
00067     01   REPORT-DATE-LINE.
00068          05   FILLER            PIC X(5)       VALUE SPACES.
00069          05   FILLER            PIC X(18)      VALUE
00070                                               "DATE PROCESSED  : ".
00071          05   OUT-REPORT-DATE   PIC X(18).
00072
00073     01   REPORT-REQUEST-LINE.
00074          05   FILLER            PIC X(5)       VALUE SPACES.
00075          05   FILLER            PIC X(18)      VALUE
00076                                               "REQUESTED BY    : ".
00077          05   FILLER            PIC X(14)      VALUE
00078                                               "DEPARTMENT OF ".
00079          05   OUT-DEPT-NAME     PIC X(16).
00080
00081     01   REPORT-SORT-ORDER-LINE-1.
00082          05   FILLER            PIC X(5)       VALUE SPACES.
00083          05   FILLER            PIC X(19)      VALUE
00084                                               "LIST ORDERED BY : |".
00085          05   OUT-SORT-ORDER-1  PIC X.
00086          05   FILLER            PIC X(15)      VALUE
00087                                               "|   STUDENT NAME".
00088
00089     01   REPORT-SORT-ORDER-LINE-2.
00090          05   FILLER            PIC X(23)      VALUE SPACES.
00091          05   FILLER            PIC X          VALUE "|".
00092          05   OUT-SORT-ORDER-2  PIC X.
00093          05   FILLER            PIC X(35)      VALUE
00094                                "|   ACADEMIC STATUS AND STUDENT NAME".
00095
00096     01   STUDENT-INFO-HEADER-1.
00097          05   FILLER            PIC X(5)       VALUE SPACES.
00098          05   FILLER            PIC X(12)      VALUE "STUDENT NAME".
00099          05   FILLER            PIC X(10)      VALUE SPACES.
00100          05   FILLER            PIC X(10)      VALUE "STUDENT ID".
00101          05   FILLER            PIC X(3)       VALUE SPACES.
00102          05   FILLER            PIC X(17)      VALUE
00103                                               "ACADEMIC STANDING".
00104          05   FILLER            PIC X(3)       VALUE SPACES.
00105          05   FILLER            PIC X(8)       VALUE "COMMENTS".
00106
```

Program 3-Source(d) (Continued)

```
00107     01   STUDENT-INFO-UNDERLINE-1.
00108          05   FILLER                PIC X(5)      VALUE SPACES.
00109          05   FILLER                PIC X(20)     VALUE ALL "-".
00110          05   FILLER                PIC X(2)      VALUE SPACES.
00111          05   FILLER                PIC X(10)     VALUE ALL "-".
00112          05   FILLER                PIC X(3)      VALUE SPACES.
00113          05   FILLER                PIC X(17)     VALUE ALL "-".
00114          05   FILLER                PIC X(3)      VALUE SPACES.
00115          05   FILLER                PIC X(16)     VALUE ALL "-".
00116
00117     01   STUDENT-LISTING-LINE-1.
00118          05   FILLER                       PIC X(5)    VALUE SPACES.
00119          05   OUT-STUDENT-NAME-1           PIC X(20).
00120          05   FILLER                       PIC X(5)    VALUE SPACES.
00121          05   OUT-STUDENT-ID-1             PIC X(4).
00122          05   FILLER                       PIC X(6)    VALUE SPACES.
00123          05   OUT-ACADEMIC-ST-1            PIC X(12).
00124          05   FILLER                       PIC X(8)    VALUE SPACES.
00125          05   OUT-COMMENT-DESC-1           PIC X(7).
00126          05   FILLER                       PIC X       VALUE SPACES.
00127          05   OUT-COMMENT-NO-OF-YEARS-1    PIC XX.
00128          05   OUT-COMMENT-YEAR-1           PIC X(5).
00129
00130
00131     01   STUDENT-INFO-HEADER-2.
00132          05   FILLER                PIC X(5)      VALUE SPACES.
00133          05   FILLER                PIC X(15)     VALUE
00134                                                   "ACADEMIC STATUS".
00135          05   FILLER                PIC X(5)      VALUE SPACES.
00136          05   FILLER                PIC X(12)     VALUE "STUDENT NAME".
00137          05   FILLER                PIC X(13)     VALUE SPACES.
00138          05   FILLER                PIC X(10)     VALUE "STUDENT ID".
00139          05   FILLER                PIC X(5)      VALUE SPACES.
00140          05   FILLER                PIC X(8)      VALUE "COMMENTS".
00141
00142     01   STUDENT-INFO-UNDERLINE-2.
00143          05   FILLER                PIC X(5)      VALUE SPACES.
00144          05   FILLER                PIC X(15)     VALUE ALL "-".
00145          05   FILLER                PIC X(5)      VALUE SPACES.
00146          05   FILLER                PIC X(22)     VALUE ALL "-".
00147          05   FILLER                PIC X(3)      VALUE SPACES.
00148          05   FILLER                PIC X(10)     VALUE ALL "-".
00149          05   FILLER                PIC X(3)      VALUE SPACES.
00150          05   FILLER                PIC X(16)     VALUE ALL "-".
00151
00152     01   STUDENT-LISTING-LINE-2.
00153          05   FILLER                       PIC X(5)    VALUE SPACES.
00154          05   OUT-ACADEMIC-ST-2            PIC X(12).
00155          05   FILLER                       PIC X(8)    VALUE SPACES.
00156          05   OUT-STUDENT-NAME-2           PIC X(20).
00157          05   FILLER                       PIC X(5)    VALUE SPACES.
00158          05   OUT-STUDENT-ID-2             PIC X(4).
00159          05   FILLER                       PIC X(9)    VALUE SPACES.
00160          05   OUT-COMMENT-DESC-2           PIC X(7).
```

Program 3-Source(d) (Continued)

```
00161           05   FILLER                    PIC X       VALUE SPACES.
00162           05   OUT-COMMENT-NO-OF-YEARS-2 PIC XX.
00163           05   OUT-COMMENT-YEAR-2        PIC X(5).
00164
00165      01   EXCEPTIONS-TITLE-LINE.
00166           05   FILLER            PIC X(31)      VALUE SPACES.
00167           05   FILLER            PIC X(17)      VALUE
00168                                             "EXCEPTIONS REPORT".
00169      01   IDNO-NOT-IN-DEPT-LINE.
00170           05   FILLER            PIC X(5)       VALUE SPACES.
00171           05   FILLER            PIC X(59)      VALUE
00172      "THE FOLLOWING STUDENTS ARE NOT MAJORING IN THE DEPARTMENT: ".
00173
00174      01   IDNO-NOT-IN-FILE-LINE.
00175           05   FILLER            PIC X(5)       VALUE SPACES.
00176           05   FILLER            PIC X(53)      VALUE
00177           "THE FOLLOWING STUDENT ID NUMBERS ARE NOT IN THE FILE:".
00178
00179      01   EXCEPTION-INFO-LINE.
00180           05   FILLER            PIC X(20)      VALUE SPACES.
00181           05   EXC-STUDENT-ID-NO PIC X(4).
00182
00183      **********>  ARRAYS:
00184
00185      01   MONTH-NAMES.
00186           05   FILLER            PIC X(9)       VALUE "JANUARY  ".
00187           05   FILLER            PIC X(9)       VALUE "FEBRUARY ".
00188           05   FILLER            PIC X(9)       VALUE "MARCH    ".
00189           05   FILLER            PIC X(9)       VALUE "APRIL    ".
00190           05   FILLER            PIC X(9)       VALUE "MAY      ".
00191           05   FILLER            PIC X(9)       VALUE "JUNE     ".
00192           05   FILLER            PIC X(9)       VALUE "JULY     ".
00193           05   FILLER            PIC X(9)       VALUE "AUGUST   ".
00194           05   FILLER            PIC X(9)       VALUE "SEPTEMBER".
00195           05   FILLER            PIC X(9)       VALUE "OCTOBER  ".
00196           05   FILLER            PIC X(9)       VALUE "NOVEMBER ".
00197           05   FILLER            PIC X(9)       VALUE "DECEMBER ".
00198
00199      01   MONTH-TABLE       REDEFINES  MONTH-NAMES.
00200           05   MONTH             PIC X(9)       OCCURS 12 TIMES.
00201
00202      01   DEPARTMENT-CODES-AND-NAMES.
00203           05   FILLER     PIC X(20)   VALUE "ACC ACCOUNTING      ".
00204           05   FILLER     PIC X(20)   VALUE "BOT BOTANY          ".
00205           05   FILLER     PIC X(20)   VALUE "CSC COMPUTER SCIENCE".
00206           05   FILLER     PIC X(20)   VALUE "ENG ENGLISH         ".
00207           05   FILLER     PIC X(20)   VALUE "MAN MANAGEMENT      ".
00208           05   FILLER     PIC X(20)   VALUE "MTH MATHEMATICS     ".
00209           05   FILLER     PIC X(20)   VALUE "PHY PHYSICS         ".
00210           05   FILLER     PIC X(20)   VALUE "ZOO ZOOLOGY         ".
00211
00212      01   DEPARTMENT-CODE-NAME-TABLE REDEFINES
00213                           DEPARTMENT-CODES-AND-NAMES.
```

Program 3-Source(d) (Continued)

```
00214            05 DEPARTMENT-CODE-NAME    OCCURS 8 TIMES.
00215                 10   DEPARTMENT-CODE   PIC XXX.
00216                 10   FILLER            PIC X.
00217                 10   DEPARTMENT-NAME   PIC X(17).
00218
00219    LINKAGE SECTION.
00220
00221    01  DEPT-CODE                       PIC XXX.
00222    01  LENGTH-IN                       PIC 99.
00223    01  EXC-LENGTH1                     PIC 99.
00224    01  EXC-LENGTH2                     PIC 99.
00225    01  EXCEPTION-FLAG                  PIC XXX.
00226    01  SORT-FLAG                       PIC 9.
00227
00228    01  STUDENT-NAME-INPUT-TABLE.
00229        05   ST-INFORMATION-1           OCCURS 20 TIMES.
00230             10   ST-NAME-1             PIC X(20).
00231             10   ST-IDNO-1             PIC X(4).
00232             10   ACADEMIC-STAND-1      PIC X(12).
00233             10   COMMENTS-1.
00234                  15   COMMENT-DESC-1      PIC X(7).
00235                  15   COMMENT-NO-YEARS-1  PIC XX.
00236                  15   COMMENT-YEAR-1      PIC XXX.
00237
00238    01  STANDING-AND-NAME-INPUT-TABLE.
00239        05   ACADEMIC-STANDING-GROUPS   OCCURS 4 TIMES.
00240             10   ACADEMIC-ST-TYPE          PIC X(12).
00241             10   STUDENT-INFORMATION-2     OCCURS 20 TIMES.
00242                  15   ST-NAME-2             PIC X(20).
00243                  15   ST-IDNO-2             PIC X(4).
00244                  15   COMMENTS-2.
00245                       20   COMMENT-DESC-2     PIC X(7).
00246                       20   COMMENT-NO-YEARS-2 PIC XX.
00247                       20   COMMENT-YEAR-2     PIC XXX.
00248
00249    01  EXCEPTIONS-INPUT-TABLE.
00250        05   ID-NOT-IN-DEPT   PIC X(4)   OCCURS 20 TIMES.
00251        05   ID-NOT-IN-FILE   PIC X(4)   OCCURS 20 TIMES.
00252
00253    01  ACADEMIC-STD-LENGTH-TABLE.
00254        05   ACD-STD-GROUP-LENGTH      PIC 99 OCCURS 4 TIMES.
00255    *.....................................................................
00256    PROCEDURE DIVISION
00257         USING
00258              STUDENT-NAME-INPUT-TABLE
00259              STANDING-AND-NAME-INPUT-TABLE
00260              ACADEMIC-STD-LENGTH-TABLE
00261              EXCEPTIONS-INPUT-TABLE
00262              DEPT-CODE
00263              SORT-FLAG
00264              EXCEPTION-FLAG
00265              LENGTH-IN
00266              EXC-LENGTH1
00267              EXC-LENGTH2.
```

Program 3-Source(d) (Continued)

```
00268
00269    A-MAINLINE.
00270
00271        OPEN OUTPUT STUDENT-STATUS-REPORT.
00272        PERFORM B1-PRINT-TITLE-AND-DATE-LINES.
00273
00274        PERFORM B2-PRINT-REQUESTING-DEPT-LINE.
00275
00276        PERFORM B3-CHECK-FOR-LISTING-ORDER.
00277
00278        CLOSE STUDENT-STATUS-REPORT.
00279
00280        PERFORM B4-RETURN-TO-MAIN-PROGRAM.
00281
00282    B1-PRINT-TITLE-AND-DATE-LINES.
00283        MOVE REPORT-TITLE-LINE        TO REPORT-LINE.
00284        WRITE REPORT-LINE
00285                 AFTER PAGE.
00286
00287        ACCEPT TODAYS-DATE FROM DATE.
00288        COMPUTE YEAR = TODAYS-YEAR + 1900.
00289        MOVE YEAR                      TO REPORT-YEAR.
00290        MOVE TODAYS-DAY                TO REPORT-DAY.
00291        MOVE TODAYS-MONTH              TO MONTH-TABLE-SUBSC.
00292        MOVE MONTH(MONTH-TABLE-SUBSC) TO REPORT-MONTH.
00293        MOVE REPORT-DATE              TO OUT-REPORT-DATE.
00294
00295        MOVE SPACES                   TO REPORT-LINE.
00296        MOVE REPORT-DATE-LINE         TO REPORT-LINE.
00297        WRITE REPORT-LINE
00298                 AFTER ADVANCING 2 LINES.
00299
00300    B2-PRINT-REQUESTING-DEPT-LINE.
00301        MOVE 1 TO DEPT-CODE-TB-SUBSC.
00302
00303        PERFORM C1-SEARCH-DEPARTMENT-NAME
00304              VARYING ITERATION-SUBSC FROM 1 BY 1
00305              UNTIL DEPT-CODE =
00306                   DEPARTMENT-CODE(ITERATION-SUBSC).
00307
00308        MOVE DEPARTMENT-NAME(DEPT-CODE-TB-SUBSC) TO OUT-DEPT-NAME.
00309
00310        MOVE SPACES                            TO REPORT-LINE.
00311        MOVE REPORT-REQUEST-LINE               TO REPORT-LINE.
00312        WRITE REPORT-LINE
00313                 AFTER ADVANCING 1 LINE.
00314
00315    B3-CHECK-FOR-LISTING-ORDER.
00316        IF SORT-FLAG = 1
00317              PERFORM C2-PRINT-REPORT-BY-NAME
00318        ELSE
00319              PERFORM C3-PRINT-REPORT-BY-STANDING.
00320
00321        IF EXCEPTION-FLAG = "YES"
00322              PERFORM C4-PRINT-EXCEPTION-REPORT.
```

Program 3-Source(d) (Continued)

```
00323
00324     B4-RETURN-TO-MAIN-PROGRAM.
00325         EXIT PROGRAM.
00326
00327     C1-SEARCH-DEPARTMENT-NAME.
00328         IF DEPARTMENT-CODE(ITERATION-SUBSC) = DEPT-CODE
00329                 MOVE ITERATION-SUBSC TO DEPT-CODE-TB-SUBSC.
00330
00331     C2-PRINT-REPORT-BY-NAME.
00332         MOVE "X"                      TO OUT-SORT-ORDER-1.
00333         MOVE SPACES                   TO REPORT-LINE.
00334         MOVE REPORT-SORT-ORDER-LINE-1 TO REPORT-LINE.
00335         WRITE REPORT-LINE
00336                 AFTER ADVANCING 2 LINES.
00337
00338         MOVE " "                      TO OUT-SORT-ORDER-2.
00339         MOVE SPACES                   TO REPORT-LINE.
00340         MOVE REPORT-SORT-ORDER-LINE-2 TO REPORT-LINE.
00341         WRITE REPORT-LINE
00342                 AFTER ADVANCING 1 LINE.
00343
00344         MOVE SPACES                   TO REPORT-LINE.
00345         MOVE STUDENT-INFO-HEADER-1    TO REPORT-LINE.
00346         WRITE REPORT-LINE
00347                 AFTER ADVANCING 2 LINES.
00348
00349         MOVE SPACES                   TO REPORT-LINE.
00350         MOVE STUDENT-INFO-UNDERLINE-1 TO REPORT-LINE.
00351         WRITE REPORT-LINE
00352                 AFTER ADVANCING 1 LINE.
00353
00354         PERFORM D1-PRINT-STUDENT-INFO-1
00355                 VARYING TABLE-SUBSC FROM 1 BY 1
00356                 UNTIL TABLE-SUBSC > LENGTH-IN.
00357
00358     C3-PRINT-REPORT-BY-STANDING.
00359         MOVE " "                      TO OUT-SORT-ORDER-1.
00360         MOVE SPACES                   TO REPORT-LINE.
00361         MOVE REPORT-SORT-ORDER-LINE-1 TO REPORT-LINE.
00362         WRITE REPORT-LINE
00363                 AFTER ADVANCING 2 LINES.
00364
00365         MOVE "X"                      TO OUT-SORT-ORDER-2.
00366         MOVE SPACES                   TO REPORT-LINE.
00367         MOVE REPORT-SORT-ORDER-LINE-2 TO REPORT-LINE.
00368         WRITE REPORT-LINE
00369                 AFTER ADVANCING 1 LINE.
00370
00371         MOVE SPACES                 TO REPORT-LINE.
00372         MOVE STUDENT-INFO-HEADER-2 TO REPORT-LINE.
00373         WRITE REPORT-LINE
00374                 AFTER ADVANCING 2 LINES.
00375
00376         MOVE SPACES                   TO REPORT-LINE.
```

Program 3-Source(d) (Continued)

```
00377            MOVE STUDENT-INFO-UNDERLINE-2 TO REPORT-LINE.
00378            WRITE REPORT-LINE
00379                    AFTER ADVANCING 1 LINE.
00380
00381            PERFORM D2-CHECK-ACADEMIC-STD-GROUPS
00382                    VARYING ACD-STD-SUBSC FROM 1 BY 1
00383                    UNTIL ACD-STD-SUBSC > 4.
00384
00385        C4-PRINT-EXCEPTION-REPORT.
00386            MOVE SPACES                    TO REPORT-LINE.
00387            MOVE EXCEPTIONS-TITLE-LINE TO REPORT-LINE.
00388            WRITE REPORT-LINE
00389                    AFTER ADVANCING PAGE.
00390
00391            IF EXC-LENGTH1 > 0
00392                    PERFORM D3-PRINT-NUMBERS-NOT-IN-DEPT.
00393
00394            IF EXC-LENGTH2 > 0
00395                    PERFORM D4-PRINT-NUMBERS-NOT-IN-FILE.
00396
00397        D1-PRINT-STUDENT-INFO-1.
00398            MOVE SPACES                    TO REPORT-LINE.
00399            MOVE ST-NAME-1(TABLE-SUBSC)          TO OUT-STUDENT-NAME-1.
00400            MOVE ST-IDNO-1(TABLE-SUBSC)          TO OUT-STUDENT-ID-1.
00401            MOVE ACADEMIC-STAND-1(TABLE-SUBSC)  TO OUT-ACADEMIC-ST-1.
00402            MOVE COMMENT-DESC-1(TABLE-SUBSC)    TO OUT-COMMENT-DESC-1.
00403            MOVE COMMENT-NO-YEARS-1(TABLE-SUBSC) TO
00404                                    OUT-COMMENT-NO-OF-YEARS-1.
00405            MOVE COMMENT-YEAR-1(TABLE-SUBSC)    TO OUT-COMMENT-YEAR-1.
00406
00407            MOVE SPACES                         TO REPORT-LINE.
00408            MOVE STUDENT-LISTING-LINE-1         TO REPORT-LINE.
00409            WRITE REPORT-LINE
00410                    AFTER ADVANCING 1 LINE.
00411
00412        D2-CHECK-ACADEMIC-STD-GROUPS.
00413
00414            IF ACD-STD-GROUP-LENGTH(ACD-STD-SUBSC) > 0
00415                    PERFORM E1-PRINT-ACADEMIC-STD-LINES
00416                            VARYING ST-INFO-SUBSC FROM 1 BY 1
00417                            UNTIL ST-INFO-SUBSC >
00418                                    ACD-STD-GROUP-LENGTH(ACD-STD-SUBSC)
00419
00420                            MOVE SPACES TO REPORT-LINE
00421                            WRITE REPORT-LINE
00422                                    AFTER ADVANCING 1 LINE.
00423
00424        D3-PRINT-NUMBERS-NOT-IN-DEPT.
00425            MOVE SPACES                    TO REPORT-LINE.
00426            MOVE REPORT-REQUEST-LINE TO REPORT-LINE.
00427            WRITE REPORT-LINE
00428                    AFTER ADVANCING 2 LINES.
00429
00430            MOVE SPACES                    TO REPORT-LINE.
```

Program 3-Source(d) (Continued)

```
00431          MOVE IDNO-NOT-IN-DEPT-LINE TO REPORT-LINE.
00432          WRITE REPORT-LINE
00433                  AFTER ADVANCING 2 LINES.
00434
00435          MOVE SPACES                    TO REPORT-LINE.
00436          WRITE REPORT-LINE
00437                  AFTER ADVANCING 1 LINE.
00438
00439      PERFORM E2-PRINT-NUMBERS-NOT-IN-DEPT
00440              VARYING EXCEPTION-TB-1-SUBSC FROM 1 BY 1
00441              UNTIL EXCEPTION-TB-1-SUBSC > EXC-LENGTH2.
00442
00443  D4-PRINT-NUMBERS-NOT-IN-FILE.
00444          MOVE SPACES                    TO REPORT-LINE.
00445          MOVE IDNO-NOT-IN-FILE-LINE TO REPORT-LINE.
00446          WRITE REPORT-LINE
00447                  AFTER ADVANCING 2 LINES.
00448
00449          MOVE SPACES                    TO REPORT-LINE.
00450          WRITE REPORT-LINE
00451                  AFTER ADVANCING 1 LINE.
00452
00453      PERFORM E3-PRINT-NUMBERS-NOT-IN-FILE
00454              VARYING EXCEPTION-TB-2-SUBSC FROM 1 BY 1
00455              UNTIL EXCEPTION-TB-2-SUBSC > EXC-LENGTH1.
00456
00457  E1-PRINT-ACADEMIC-STD-LINES.
00458      IF ST-INFO-SUBSC = 1
00459              MOVE ACADEMIC-ST-TYPE(ACD-STD-SUBSC)          TO
00460                      OUT-ACADEMIC-ST-2
00461      ELSE
00462              MOVE SPACES TO OUT-ACADEMIC-ST-2.
00463
00464          MOVE ST-NAME-2(ACD-STD-SUBSC, ST-INFO-SUBSC)     TO
00465                              OUT-STUDENT-NAME-2.
00466          MOVE ST-IDNO-2(ACD-STD-SUBSC, ST-INFO-SUBSC)     TO
00467                              OUT-STUDENT-ID-2.
00468          MOVE COMMENT-DESC-2(ACD-STD-SUBSC, ST-INFO-SUBSC)    TO
00469                              OUT-COMMENT-DESC-2.
00470          MOVE COMMENT-NO-YEARS-2(ACD-STD-SUBSC, ST-INFO-SUBSC) TO
00471                              OUT-COMMENT-NO-OF-YEARS-2.
00472          MOVE COMMENT-YEAR-2(ACD-STD-SUBSC, ST-INFO-SUBSC)    TO
00473                              OUT-COMMENT-YEAR-2.
00474
00475          MOVE SPACES                    TO REPORT-LINE.
00476          MOVE STUDENT-LISTING-LINE-2 TO REPORT-LINE.
00477          WRITE REPORT-LINE
00478                  AFTER ADVANCING 1 LINE.
00479
00480  E2-PRINT-NUMBERS-NOT-IN-DEPT.
00481      MOVE ID-NOT-IN-DEPT(EXCEPTION-TB-1-SUBSC) TO
00482                          EXC-STUDENT-ID-NO.
00483
00484      MOVE SPACES                              TO REPORT-LINE.
```

Program 3-Source(d) (Continued)

```
00485            MOVE EXCEPTION-INFO-LINE              TO REPORT-LINE.
00486            WRITE REPORT-LINE
00487                 AFTER ADVANCING 1 LINE.
00488
00489      E3-PRINT-NUMBERS-NOT-IN-FILE.
00490            MOVE ID-NOT-IN-FILE(EXCEPTION-TB-2-SUBSC) TO
00491                          EXC-STUDENT-ID-NO.
00492
00493            MOVE SPACES                           TO REPORT-LINE.
00494            MOVE EXCEPTION-INFO-LINE              TO REPORT-LINE.
00495            WRITE REPORT-LINE
00496                 AFTER ADVANCING 1 LINE.
00497
```

Program 3-Source(d) (Continued)

```
                         ACADEMIC STATUS REPORT

DATE PROCESSED   : OCTOBER   27, 1990
REQUESTED BY     : DEPARTMENT OF ACCOUNTING


LIST ORDERED BY : |X|   STUDENT NAME
                  | |   ACADEMIC STATUS AND STUDENT NAME


STUDENT NAME           STUDENT ID   ACADEMIC STANDING   COMMENTS
_____    _____   _____   _____

BRAUN ALLISON S           3000      HONOR               NORMAL
GORDON AARON              3500      HONOR               NORMAL
KAYSER TOM               1500      PROBATION            NORMAL
                          EXCEPTIONS REPORT


REQUESTED BY      : DEPARTMENT OF ACCOUNTING


THE FOLLOWING STUDENTS ARE NOT MAJORING IN THE DEPARTMENT:

            1210


THE FOLLOWING STUDENT ID NUMBERS ARE NOT IN THE FILE:

            0870
```

Program 3-Output(a) A Sample Output for Academic Status Reports Generator

```
 ---> ENTER THE DEPARTMENT CODE:
IKF990D, AWAITING REPLY.
 ACC
 ---> HOW DO YOU WANT THE LIST TO BE ORDERED?
 ---> IF BY NAME, ENTER 1:
 ---> IF BY ACADEMIC STATUS, ENTER 2:
IKF990D, AWAITING REPLY.
 1
 START ENTERING STUDENT ID NUMBERS
 WHEN FINISHED ENTER DONE:
IKF990D, AWAITING REPLY.
 3500
IKF990D, AWAITING REPLY.
 3000
IKF990D, AWAITING REPLY.
 1210
IKF990D, AWAITING REPLY.
 1500
IKF990D, AWAITING REPLY.
 0870
IKF990D, AWAITING REPLY.
 DONE
```

Program 3-Output(b) A Sample Interactive Session for Program 3

```
                                            Column
        5     10    15    20    25    30    35    40
----|----|----|----|----|----|----|----|----

1000  CARLSON JANET        ACCOUNTING
2000  EVANS RICHARD        ACCOUNTING
3000  BLACK THOMAS         PURCHASING
4000  STEELE MARY          ACCOUNTING
5000  THOMPSON KAREN       DATA PROC.
6000  WARNERS KIM          DATA PROC.
7000  ADDAMS DALE          ACCOUNTING
7500  MARTIN ROBERT        PURCHASING
7700  VETTERS JENIFER      ACCOUNTING
7800  FRY ALBERT           PURCHASING
8000  HUGHES JAMES         DATA PROC.
8300  JOHNSON PATRICIA     DATA PROC.
8400  KRUSE ERMA           ACCOUNTING
8500  CARVER JACQUELINE    PURCHASING
8600  LONDON DOROTHY       DATA PROC.
```

Program 4-Input An Instance of EMPLOYEE-INFORMATION-FILE for Program 4

```
00001    *............................................................
00002      IDENTIFICATION DIVISION.
00003      PROGRAM-ID.    SEARCH-EMPLOYEE-FILE.
00004      ****************************************************************
00005      ***    THIS PROGRAM PROCESSES A SEQUENTIAL DISK FILE NAMED      *
00006      ***    "EMPLOYEE-INFORMATION-FILE".  EACH RECORD OF THIS FILE   *
00007      ***    CONSISTS OF THREE FIELDS:                                *
00008      ***        1. EMPLOYEE-IDNO,                                    *
00009      ***        2. EMPLOYEE-NAME,                                    *
00010      ***        3. EMPLOYEE-DEPARTMENT.                              *
00011      ***    THE FILE IS ORDERED UP BY EMPLOYEE-IDNO.                 *
00012      ***                                                            *
00013      ***    THE PROGRAM ALLOWS THE USER TO SEARCH THE FILE BY ANY    *
00014      ***    FIELD.  SEARCH IS DONE BY LOADING A FIXED NUMBER OF RECORDS*
00015      ***    INTO AN ARRAY.  THE SIZE OF THE ARRAY (I.E., PAGE SIZE) IS *
00016      ***    6 RECORDS.  ALL THREE VARIATIONS OF THE COBOL SEARCH VERB  *
00017      ***    ARE EXEMPLIFIED IN THE PROGRAM.                          *
00018      ****************************************************************
00019
00020      AUTHOR.        UCKAN.
00021      INSTALLATION. MIAMI UNIVERSITY.
00022      DATE-WRITTEN. OCTOBER 13, 1990.
00023      DATE-COMPILED. OCT 29,1990.
00025      *............................................................
00026      ENVIRONMENT DIVISION.
00027      CONFIGURATION SECTION.
00028      SOURCE-COMPUTER.   IBM-370.
00029      OBJECT-COMPUTER.   IBM-370.
00030      INPUT-OUTPUT SECTION.
00031      FILE-CONTROL.
00032          SELECT EMPLOYEE-INFORMATION-FILE ASSIGN TO INFILE
00033                 ORGANIZATION IS SEQUENTIAL
00034                 ACCESS MODE  IS SEQUENTIAL.
00035
00036      *............................................................
00037      DATA DIVISION.
00038      FILE SECTION.
00039      FD  EMPLOYEE-INFORMATION-FILE
00040          LABEL RECORDS ARE STANDARD
00041          DATA RECORD IS EMPLOYEE-INFORMATION
00042          RECORD CONTAINS 80 CHARACTERS.
00043      01  EMPLOYEE-INFORMATION.
00044          05   EMPLOYEE-IDNO            PIC 9(4).
00045          05   FILLER                   PIC X.
00046          05   EMPLOYEE-NAME            PIC X(20).
00047          05   FILLER                   PIC XX.
00048          05   EMPLOYEE-DEPARTMENT      PIC X(10).
00049          05   FILLER                   PIC X(43).
00050
00051      WORKING-STORAGE SECTION.
```

Program 4-Source Program for Data Retrieval from a Sequential File

```
00052
00053     **********> SWITCHES:
00054
00055     01   END-OF-FILE-FLAG              PIC XXX      VALUE "NO".
00056          88   END-OF-FILE                            VALUE "YES".
00057
00058     01   END-OF-INPUT-FLAG            PIC XXX      VALUE "YES".
00059          88   END-OF-INPUT                           VALUE "NO".
00060
00061     01   END-OF-PAGES-FLAG           PIC XXX      VALUE "NO".
00062          88   LAST-PAGE                              VALUE "YES".
00063
00064     01   END-OF-SEARCH-FLAG          PIC XXX      VALUE "NO".
00065          88   SEARCH-ENDS                            VALUE "YES".
00066
00067     01   DISPLAY-FLAG                 PIC XXX      VALUE "NO".
00068          88   DISPLAY-BEGINS                         VALUE "YES".
00069
00070     01   RECORD-FOUND                 PIC XXX      VALUE "NO".
00071          88   FOUND                                  VALUE "YES".
00072
00073     01   RECORD-NOT-IN-FILE          PIC XXX      VALUE "NO".
00074          88   NOT-IN-FILE                            VALUE "YES".
00075
00076     01   SEARCH-FLAG                  PIC 9.
00077          88   SEARCH-BY-IDNO                         VALUE 1.
00078          88   SEARCH-BY-NAME                         VALUE 2.
00079          88   SEARCH-BY-DEPARTMENT                   VALUE 3.
00080          88   WRONG-INPUT                            VALUE 0,
00081                                                        4 THROUGH 9.
00082     **********> SUBSCRIPTS:
00083
00084     01   ITERATION-SUBSC              PIC 9.
00085     01   OUTER-SUBSC                  PIC 9.
00086     01   INNER-SUBSC                  PIC 9.
00087     01   SUBSC-PLUS                   PIC 9.
00088     01   DISPLAY-SUBSC                PIC 9.
00089
00090     **********> VARIABLES:
00091
00092     01   PAGE-SIZE                    PIC 9.
00093     01   FILE-SIZE                    PIC 99.
00094     01   PAGE-COUNT                   PIC 99.
00095     01   RECORDS-REMAINING-IN-FILE    PIC 99.
00096
00097     **********> ARRAYS:
00098
00099     01   SEARCH-TABLE.
00100          05   EMPLOYEE-RECORD         OCCURS 6 TIMES
00101               ASCENDING KEY IS EMP-IDNO
00102               INDEXED BY TABLE-INDEX.
00103               10   EMP-IDNO           PIC 9(4).
00104               10   EMP-NAME           PIC X(20).
00105               10   EMP-DEPARTMENT     PIC X(10).
```

Program 4-Source (Continued)

```
00106
00107      **********> STRUCTURES:
00108
00109      01  SEARCH-KEYS.
00110          05  SEARCH-KEY-IDNO          PIC 9(4).
00111          05  SEARCH-KEY-NAME          PIC X(20).
00112          05  SEARCH-KEY-DEPT          PIC X(10).
00113
00114      01  TEMPORARY-STORAGE.
00115          05  DUMMY-IDNO               PIC 9(4).
00116          05  DUMMY-NAME               PIC X(20).
00117          05  DUMMY-DEPT               PIC X(10).
00118
00119      *....................................................................
00120      PROCEDURE DIVISION.
00121      A-MAINLINE.
00122          OPEN INPUT  EMPLOYEE-INFORMATION-FILE.
00123
00124          MOVE ZEROS TO FILE-SIZE
00125                        PAGE-COUNT.
00126          MOVE 6     TO PAGE-SIZE.
00127
00128          READ EMPLOYEE-INFORMATION-FILE
00129                  AT END MOVE "YES" TO END-OF-FILE-FLAG.
00130
00131          PERFORM B1-DETERMINE-FILE-SIZE
00132                  UNTIL END-OF-FILE.
00133
00134          CLOSE EMPLOYEE-INFORMATION-FILE.
00135
00136          PERFORM B2-INPUT-SEARCH-INFORMATION
00137                  UNTIL END-OF-INPUT.
00138
00139          STOP RUN.
00140
00141      B1-DETERMINE-FILE-SIZE.
00142          ADD 1 TO FILE-SIZE.
00143          READ EMPLOYEE-INFORMATION-FILE
00144                  AT END MOVE "YES" TO END-OF-FILE-FLAG.
00145
00146      B2-INPUT-SEARCH-INFORMATION.
00147          PERFORM C1-INPUT-SEARCH-COLUMN.
00148
00149          IF WRONG-INPUT
00150          DISPLAY " "
00151                  DISPLAY "ILLEGAL NUMBER: "  SEARCH-FLAG
00152                  PERFORM C1-INPUT-SEARCH-COLUMN.
00153
00154          OPEN INPUT  EMPLOYEE-INFORMATION-FILE.
00155
00156          READ EMPLOYEE-INFORMATION-FILE
00157                  AT END MOVE "YES" TO END-OF-FILE-FLAG.
00158
00159          PERFORM C2-SEARCH-FOR-EMPLOYEE-RECORD.
```

Program 4-Source (Continued)

```
00160
00161     C1-INPUT-SEARCH-COLUMN.
00162         DISPLAY " ".
00163         DISPLAY "INPUT SEARCH COLUMN.  TYPE".
00164         DISPLAY " ".
00165         DISPLAY "1 FOR EMPLOYEE ID NUMBER,".
00166         DISPLAY "2 FOR EMPLOYEE NAME,".
00167         DISPLAY "3 FOR EMPLOYEE DEPARTMENT.".
00168         DISPLAY " ".
00169         ACCEPT SEARCH-FLAG FROM CONSOLE.
00170
00171     C2-SEARCH-FOR-EMPLOYEE-RECORD.
00172         DISPLAY "INPUT SEARCH KEY: ".
00173
00174         IF SEARCH-BY-IDNO
00175                 ACCEPT SEARCH-KEY-IDNO FROM CONSOLE
00176                 PERFORM D1-BINARY-SEARCH-BY-IDNO
00177                     UNTIL FOUND
00178                         OR
00179                     NOT-IN-FILE.
00180
00181         IF SEARCH-BY-NAME
00182                 ACCEPT SEARCH-KEY-NAME FROM CONSOLE
00183                 PERFORM D2-SEQUENTIAL-SEARCH-BY-NAME
00184                     UNTIL FOUND
00185                         OR
00186                     NOT-IN-FILE.
00187
00188         IF SEARCH-BY-DEPARTMENT
00189                 ACCEPT SEARCH-KEY-DEPT FROM CONSOLE
00190                 MOVE "YES" TO DISPLAY-FLAG
00191                 PERFORM D3-SEQUENTIAL-SEARCH-BY-DEPT
00192                     UNTIL SEARCH-ENDS.
00193
00194         CLOSE EMPLOYEE-INFORMATION-FILE.
00195
00196         PERFORM D4-CONTINUE-INPUT.
00197
00198     D1-BINARY-SEARCH-BY-IDNO.
00199         PERFORM E1-LOAD-A-PAGE.
00200
00201         IF EMP-IDNO(1) > SEARCH-KEY-IDNO
00202                 MOVE "YES" TO RECORD-NOT-IN-FILE
00203
00204         ELSE
00205                 SEARCH ALL EMPLOYEE-RECORD
00206                     WHEN EMP-IDNO(TABLE-INDEX) = SEARCH-KEY-IDNO
00207                         MOVE "YES" TO RECORD-FOUND
00208                         DISPLAY " "
00209                         DISPLAY
00210                             "EMPLOYEE RECORD FOR EMPLOYEE ID-NUMBER "
00211                                 SEARCH-KEY-IDNO
00212                         SET DISPLAY-SUBSC TO TABLE-INDEX
00213                         PERFORM E2-DISPLAY-EMPLOYEE-RECORD.
```

Program 4-Source (Continued)

```
00214
00215        IF LAST-PAGE AND NOT FOUND
00216               MOVE "YES" TO RECORD-NOT-IN-FILE
00217               DISPLAY " "
00218               DISPLAY "EMPLOYEE ID NUMBER " SEARCH-KEY-IDNO
00219               DISPLAY "IS NOT IN EMPLOYEE FILE".
00220
00221    D2-SEQUENTIAL-SEARCH-BY-NAME.
00222        PERFORM E1-LOAD-A-PAGE.
00223
00224        SET TABLE-INDEX TO 1.
00225        SEARCH EMPLOYEE-RECORD
00226               WHEN EMP-NAME(TABLE-INDEX) = SEARCH-KEY-NAME
00227                     MOVE "YES" TO RECORD-FOUND
00228                     DISPLAY " "
00229                     DISPLAY
00230                        "EMPLOYEE RECORD FOR EMPLOYEE NAME "
00231                          SEARCH-KEY-NAME
00232                     SET DISPLAY-SUBSC TO TABLE-INDEX
00233                     PERFORM E2-DISPLAY-EMPLOYEE-RECORD.
00234
00235
00236        IF LAST-PAGE AND NOT FOUND
00237               MOVE "YES" TO RECORD-NOT-IN-FILE
00238               DISPLAY " "
00239               DISPLAY "EMPLOYEE NAME " SEARCH-KEY-NAME
00240               DISPLAY "IS NOT IN EMPLOYEE FILE".
00241
00242    D3-SEQUENTIAL-SEARCH-BY-DEPT.
00243        PERFORM E1-LOAD-A-PAGE.
00244
00245        PERFORM E3-SORT-WITH-BUBBLE-SORT.
00246
00247        SET TABLE-INDEX TO 1.
00248        SEARCH EMPLOYEE-RECORD
00249               WHEN EMP-DEPARTMENT(TABLE-INDEX) = SEARCH-KEY-DEPT
00250                     MOVE "YES" TO RECORD-FOUND
00251                     PERFORM E4-DISPLAY-DEPARTMENT-RECORDS.
00252
00253        IF LAST-PAGE AND NOT FOUND
00254               MOVE "YES" TO RECORD-NOT-IN-FILE
00255               MOVE "YES" TO END-OF-SEARCH-FLAG
00256               DISPLAY " "
00257               DISPLAY "THERE IS NOT ANY EMPLOYEE RECORDS"
00258               DISPLAY "BELONGING TO THE " SEARCH-KEY-DEPT
00259                     " DEPARTMENT EMPLOYEES"
00260               DISPLAY "IN THE EMPLOYEE FILE".
00261
00262        IF LAST-PAGE
00263               MOVE "YES" TO END-OF-SEARCH-FLAG.
00264
00265    D4-CONTINUE-INPUT.
00266        MOVE ZEROS TO PAGE-COUNT.
00267        MOVE 6     TO PAGE-SIZE.
```

Program 4-Source (Continued)

```
00268          MOVE "YES" TO DISPLAY-FLAG.
00269          MOVE "NO" TO
00270                      RECORD-NOT-IN-FILE
00271                      RECORD-FOUND
00272                      END-OF-PAGES-FLAG
00273                      END-OF-SEARCH-FLAG.
00274
00275          DISPLAY " ".
00276          DISPLAY "*******************************************".
00277          DISPLAY "DO YOU WANT TO SEARCH FOR ANOTHER RECORD?"
00278          DISPLAY "TYPE YES OR NO: ".
00279          DISPLAY "*******************************************".
00280          ACCEPT END-OF-INPUT-FLAG FROM CONSOLE.
00281
00282      E1-LOAD-A-PAGE.
00283          COMPUTE RECORDS-REMAINING-IN-FILE =
00284                  FILE-SIZE - PAGE-SIZE * PAGE-COUNT.
00285
00286          IF RECORDS-REMAINING-IN-FILE < PAGE-SIZE
00287                  MOVE RECORDS-REMAINING-IN-FILE TO PAGE-SIZE
00288                  MOVE "YES"                     TO END-OF-PAGES-FLAG.
00289
00290          ADD 1 TO PAGE-COUNT.
00291          PERFORM F1-LOAD-WITH-EMPLOYEE-RECORD
00292                  VARYING ITERATION-SUBSC FROM 1 BY 1
00293                  UNTIL   ITERATION-SUBSC > PAGE-SIZE.
00294
00295      E2-DISPLAY-EMPLOYEE-RECORD.
00296          DISPLAY " ".
00297          DISPLAY "EMPLOYEE-ID: "  EMP-IDNO(DISPLAY-SUBSC).
00298          DISPLAY "EMLOYEE-NAME: "  EMP-NAME(DISPLAY-SUBSC).
00299          DISPLAY "DEPARTMENT: "    EMP-DEPARTMENT(DISPLAY-SUBSC).
00300
00301      E3-SORT-WITH-BUBBLE-SORT.
00302          PERFORM F2-BUBBLE-SORT-OUTER-CYCLE
00303                  VARYING OUTER-SUBSC FROM PAGE-SIZE BY -1
00304                  UNTIL   OUTER-SUBSC < 2.
00305
00306      E4-DISPLAY-DEPARTMENT-RECORDS.
00307
00308          IF DISPLAY-BEGINS
00309                      DISPLAY " "
00310                      DISPLAY
00311                        "EMPLOYEE RECORDS FOR "
00312                         SEARCH-KEY-DEPT  " DEPARTMENT"
00313                        MOVE "NO" TO DISPLAY-FLAG.
00314          PERFORM E2-DISPLAY-EMPLOYEE-RECORD
00315                  VARYING DISPLAY-SUBSC FROM TABLE-INDEX BY 1
00316                  UNTIL EMP-DEPARTMENT(DISPLAY-SUBSC) NOT =
00317                                              SEARCH-KEY-DEPT
00318                          OR
00319                      DISPLAY-SUBSC > PAGE-SIZE.
00320
```

Program 4-Source (Continued)

```
00321     F1-LOAD-WITH-EMPLOYEE-RECORD.
00322         MOVE EMPLOYEE-IDNO TO EMP-IDNO(ITERATION-SUBSC).
00323         MOVE EMPLOYEE-NAME TO EMP-NAME(ITERATION-SUBSC).
00324         MOVE EMPLOYEE-DEPARTMENT TO EMP-DEPARTMENT(ITERATION-SUBSC).
00325         READ EMPLOYEE-INFORMATION-FILE
00326             AT END MOVE "YES" TO END-OF-FILE-FLAG.
00327
00328     F2-BUBBLE-SORT-OUTER-CYCLE.
00329         PERFORM G-BUBBLE-SORT-INNER-CYCLE
00330             VARYING INNER-SUBSC FROM 1 BY 1
00331             UNTIL   INNER-SUBSC > PAGE-SIZE - 1.
00332
00333     G-BUBBLE-SORT-INNER-CYCLE.
00334         COMPUTE SUBSC-PLUS = INNER-SUBSC + 1.
00335
00336         IF EMP-DEPARTMENT(INNER-SUBSC) > EMP-DEPARTMENT(SUBSC-PLUS)
00337             MOVE EMPLOYEE-RECORD(INNER-SUBSC) TO
00338                                     TEMPORARY-STORAGE
00339             MOVE EMPLOYEE-RECORD(SUBSC-PLUS)  TO
00340                                     EMPLOYEE-RECORD(INNER-SUBSC)
00341             MOVE TEMPORARY-STORAGE            TO
00342                                     EMPLOYEE-RECORD(SUBSC-PLUS).
```

Program 4-Source (Continued)

```
 INPUT SEARCH COLUMN.   TYPE

 1 FOR EMPLOYEE ID NUMBER,
 2 FOR EMPLOYEE NAME,
 3 FOR EMPLOYEE DEPARTMENT.

IKF990D, AWAITING REPLY.
 1
 INPUT SEARCH KEY:
IKF990D, AWAITING REPLY.
 8500

 EMPLOYEE RECORD FOR EMPLOYEE ID-NUMBER 8500

 EMPLOYEE-ID: 8500
 EMPLOYEE-NAME: CARVER JACQUELINE
 DEPARTMENT: PURCHASING


 ********************************************
 DO YOU WANT TO SEARCH FOR ANOTHER RECORD?
 TYPE YES OR NO:
 ********************************************
IKF990D, AWAITING REPLY.
 YES

 INPUT SEARCH COLUMN.   TYPE

 1 FOR EMPLOYEE ID NUMBER,
```

Program 4-Output A Sample Interactive Session for Program 4

```
2 FOR EMPLOYEE NAME,
3 FOR EMPLOYEE DEPARTMENT.

IKF990D, AWAITING REPLY.
 1
 INPUT SEARCH KEY:
IKF990D, AWAITING REPLY.
 7750
 EMPLOYEE ID NUMBER 7750
 IS NOT IN EMPLOYEE FILE


 *****************************************
 DO YOU WANT TO SEARCH FOR ANOTHER RECORD?
 TYPE YES OR NO:
 *****************************************
IKF990D, AWAITING REPLY.
 YES

 INPUT SEARCH COLUMN.  TYPE

 1 FOR EMPLOYEE ID NUMBER,
 2 FOR EMPLOYEE NAME,
 3 FOR EMPLOYEE DEPARTMENT.

IKF990D, AWAITING REPLY.
 2
 INPUT SEARCH KEY:
IKF990D, AWAITING REPLY.
 KRUSE ERMA

 EMPLOYEE RECORD FOR EMPLOYEE NAME KRUSE ERMA

 EMPLOYEE-ID:8400
 EMPLOYEE-NAME: KRUSE ERMA
 DEPARTMENT: ACCOUNTING

 *****************************************
 DO YOU WANT TO SEARCH FOR ANOTHER RECORD?
 TYPE YES OR NO:
 *****************************************
IKF990D, AWAITING REPLY.
 YES

 INPUT SEARCH COLUMN.  TYPE

 1 FOR EMPLOYEE ID NUMBER,
 2 FOR EMPLOYEE NAME,
 3 FOR EMPLOYEE DEPARTMENT.

IKF990D, AWAITING REPLY.
 2
 INPUT SEARCH KEY:
IKF990D, AWAITING REPLY.
 FRY JIM
```

Program 4-Output (Continued)

```
      EMPLOYEE NAME FRY JIM
      IS NOT IN EMPLOYEE FILE


      *******************************************
      DO YOU WANT TO SEARCH FOR ANOTHER RECORD?
      TYPE YES OR NO:
      *******************************************
   IKF990D, AWAITING REPLY.
    YES


      INPUT SEARCH COLUMN.  TYPE


      1 FOR EMPLOYEE ID NUMBER,
      2 FOR EMPLOYEE NAME,
      3 FOR EMPLOYEE DEPARTMENT.


   IKF990D, AWAITING REPLY.
    3


      INPUT SEARCH KEY:
   IKF990D, AWAITING REPLY.
    DATA PROC.


      EMPLOYEE RECORDS FOR DATA PROC. DEPARTMENT


      EMPLOYEE-ID: 5000
      EMPLOYEE-NAME: THOMPSON KAREN
      DEPARTMENT: DATA PROC.


      EMPLOYEE-ID: 6000
      EMPLOYEE-NAME: WARNERS KIM
      DEPARTMENT: DATA PROC.



      EMPLOYEE-ID: 8000
      EMPLOYEE-NAME: HUGHES JAMES
      DEPARTMENT: DATA PROC.



      EMPLOYEE-ID: 8300
      EMPLOYEE-NAME: JOHNSON PATRICIA
      DEPARTMENT: DATA PROC.



      EMPLOYEE-ID: 8600
      EMPLOYEE-NAME: LONDON DOROTHY
      DEPARTMENT: DATA PROC.


      *******************************************
      DO YOU WANT TO SEARCH FOR ANOTHER RECORD?
      TYPE YES OR NO:
      *******************************************
   IKF990D, AWAITING REPLY.
    YES
```

Program 4-Output (Continued)

```
 INPUT SEARCH COLUMN.   TYPE

 1 FOR EMPLOYEE ID NUMBER,
 2 FOR EMPLOYEE NAME,
 3 FOR EMPLOYEE DEPARTMENT.

IKF990D, AWAITING REPLY.
 3
 INPUT SEARCH KEY:
IKF990D, AWAITING REPLY.
 SALES

 THERE IS NOT ANY EMPLOYEE RECORD
 BELONGING TO THE SALES      DEPARTMENT EMPLOYEES
 IN THE EMPLOYEE FILE

 ********************************************
 DO YOU WANT TO SEARCH FOR ANOTHER RECORD?
 TYPE YES OR NO:
 ********************************************
IKF990D, AWAITING REPLY.
 NO
```

Program 4-Output (Continued)

String Processing

Introduction

In scientific computing the emphasis is on numeric data and its processing. In business applications, although numeric data processing is occasionally needed, its extent is rather limited. The primary emphasis is on the manipulation of nonnumeric data. Both conceptually and in practice, nonnumeric data emerge as a special data type, called string.

Simply defined, a string is a sequence of characters represented one after another. Strings are used commonly in computer system operations. For example, data are stored as strings in external storage media. Records in a file are strings. So is the memory representation for a document stored in a text file, or whatever we enter at the terminal keyboard in interactive programming. Processing of data takes place in the computer's main memory. To make it possible for the computer to process data fields, records that are stored as strings in an external storage medium have to be decomposed into its constituent fields once they are brought into the main memory. This process is string oriented and requires string processing functions. It is usually handled by the computer during input-output and data conversion.

Occasionally, however, the programmer must extract appropriate ingredients from a string, or combine strings into longer ones. For example, if the record structure for a file is included in our program, the computer will decompose a record, stored as a string on external storage, into its fields. Unless we write specific programs, however, the computer will not fully validate our input data. Neither will it, by itself, translate legible data first into an indecipherable form to ensure its security, and then back into its original form. Also, it will not index and retrieve business documents stored in a computerized environment without a program written for this purpose. These processes are all string based and require a good understanding of strings.

In this chapter we will study strings as a data structure. We will first formalize the concepts relevant to strings and string processing, and discuss fundamental operations. Then we will examine the string representation and processing features of the COBOL language. Finally, we will devote part of the chapter to some important applications of string processing functions in business data processing. These include input data validation, data encryption and decryption, text processing, and key-word-in-context indexing.

Fundamental String Processing Operations

Strings are defined over an alphabet. In most business applications, the concept of an alphabet is equivalent to that of the character set of the computer. It includes letters, decimal digits, and all special characters that a terminal keyboard supports.

> A **string** over an alphabet is a finite sequence of characters of that alphabet.

For example, GO is a string obtained by bringing together the characters G and O, in that order. This string is a result of an operation known as concatenation.

> The **concatenation** of two characters yields a sequence of characters consisting of the first character followed by the second. Thus, we obtain a string of size 2.

The concatenation of the characters P and I produces the string PI. Any number of characters can be concatenated into a string of arbitrary length. The concatenation of P, I, L, and L yields the string PILL. Note that the concatenation operation is not commutative; that is, A concatenated with B is not the same as B concatenated with A.

A string processing system should support the following fundamental string operations:

1. Creation
2. Concatenation
3. String comparison
4. Length computation
5. Searching for a substring in a string and subsequently
   Copying the substring
   Deleting the substring
   Replacing the substring

Creation of Strings

A string processing system should be able to construct a data structure for a string and store the string in that structure, thus creating it. A variety of data structures can be used to store strings in the computer's memory. We discuss four: fixed-length words, arrays, linked lists, and workspace/index tables.

Storing Strings in Fixed-Length Words. Most string processing languages can store a string in a word whose length is large enough to accommodate it. The length of the word is fixed and cannot be changed without recompiling the program. If the string constant that we wish to store in such a variable is longer than the word, the string is truncated on the right. If the length of the string constant is shorter than the string variable, the string is usually left-justified in the word and padded with blanks on the right. In COBOL, we can use this technique without difficulty.

```
WORKING-STORAGE SECTION.
. . . . . . . . . . . .
01   STRING-1                    PIC X(30).
. . . . . . . . . . . .
PROCEDURE DIVISION.
. . . . . . . . . . . .
MOVE "ADVANCED" COBOL TO STRING-1.
. . . . . . . . . . . .
```

Figure 1 Data Structures for Strings: Fixed-Length Word

The content of the variable STRING-1 after the MOVE statement is executed is shown in Figure 1.

The primary advantage of the fixed-length word method is the ease with which string values are stored in the memory and manipulated in a string processing program. It has two serious disadvantages, however.

1. Whenever a string value is padded on the right with blanks and stored in a fixed-length memory location, we waste memory due to blank padding. In the above example we have wasted 16 bytes in STRING-1. The amount of wasted storage may become substantial.
2. This method may result in inefficient processing for other fundamental string processing functions, such as concatenation.

Storing Strings in Arrays. We can use an array to hold a string, such that each character of the string is stored in a one-byte array element. Of course, the size of the array is fixed. The string stored in it occupies precisely the amount of storage that it needs, however, and no storage is wasted due to blank padding. An example is shown in Figure 2, which is reflected in the following partial COBOL code.

```
WORKING-STORAGE SECTION.
. . . . . . . . . . . . .
01   STRING-ARRAY.
     05  STRING-1    PIC X   OCCURS 30 TIMES.
. . . . . . . . . . . . .
PROCEDURE DIVISION.
     . . . . . . . . . . . . .
     MOVE "ADVANCED COBOL" TO STRING-ARRAY.
     . . . . . . . . . . . . .
```

The first 14 elements of the array STRING-1 contain the string "ADVANCED COBOL". The remaining 16 bytes in the word STRING-ARRAY are not wasted and are usable. They can be accessed as elements of the array STRING-1, and may be used to store other strings.

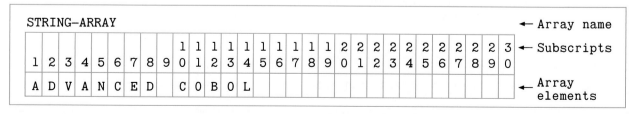

Figure 2 Data Structures for Strings: Array

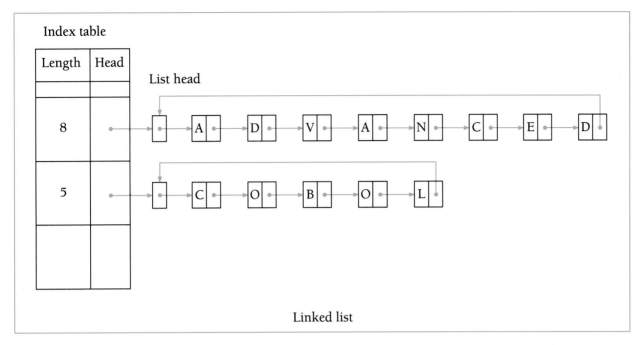

Figure 3 Data Structures for Strings: Linked List

Storing Strings in Linked Lists. Another data structure that is suitable for storing a text of strings is a linked list. We were introduced to linked lists in Chapter 4.

Figure 3 shows a data structure that is suitable for storing a text of strings. Each string is represented in a linked list; in addition, we have an index table. For each string in the text, this index table contains the length of the string, and an address that takes us directly to the head of the list that is reserved for that string. The strings are stored in separate, circularly linked lists in which the last list elements point to the first.

Linked lists are especially useful as data structures for strings when an application program is written in a language that supports them through dynamic variables (e.g., Pascal). The main advantages of dynamic variables are that only the necessary amount of storage is automatically allocated by the system to store data, and there is no storage overhead due to padding. Unlike Pascal, COBOL has no dynamic data structures; therefore, the only option is to simulate linked lists in fixed-size arrays.

The Workspace/Index Table Method for String Representation. A more useful data structuring technique based on the idea of storing strings in arrays is the **workspace/index table**. We define a workspace as a one-dimensional array of a sufficiently large number of elements, each of size 1. We also define an index table to store the start address and length of each string value kept in the workspace. Figure 4a illustrates this technique. The following partial COBOL code defines the necessary data structures for the workspace/index table.

```
WORKING-STORAGE SECTION.
. . . . . . . . . . . . .
01  WORK-SPACE.
    05  STRING-1       PIC X    OCCURS 20000 TIMES.
    05  START-ADDRESS  PIC 999  OCCURS    40 TIMES.
    05  STRING-LENGTH  PIC 999  OCCURS    40 TIMES.
. . . . . . . . . . . . .
```

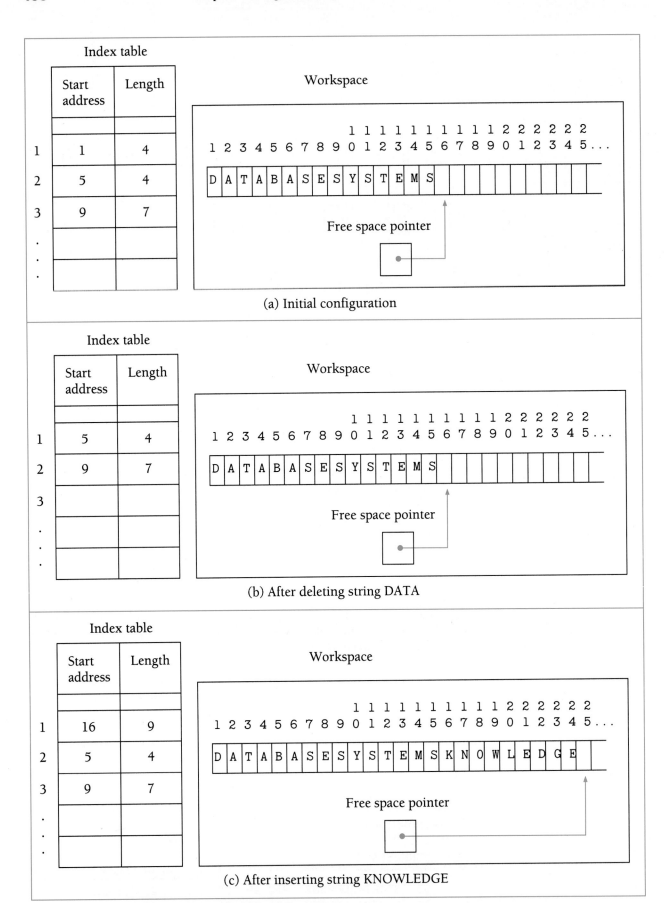

Figure 4 Workspace/Index Table Method of String Processing

A memory location, called free space pointer, is reserved for storing the beginning address of the free space. In Figure 4a, three strings are stored in the first 15 elements of the workspace. The start address and length of each string are recorded in the index table in the order in which they appear in the text. Suppose the string DATA is to be deleted. A logical delete can be accomplished by eliminating the first index entry in the index table, as in Figure 4b. Physically, the deleted string still exists in the workspace, and unless a garbage-collection technique is used, the memory locations occupied by the logically deleted string are not available for use.

Now let us assume we wish to insert the string KNOWLEDGE so that the text stored in the workspace reads KNOWLEDGE BASE SYSTEMS. We store the new string in the workspace beginning with the first available location in the free space. Then we include an index entry in the index table for the new string and update the free space pointer. The final configuration is shown in Figure 4c.

The workspace/index table has the following advantages.

1. No storage is wasted while storing strings in the workspace.
2. Inserting or deleting a string into or from the text kept in the workspace is easy. Such operations require updates in the index table, and no data movement in the workspace.

The main disadvantage of the workspace/index table is with respect to the insertion and concatenation operations. In both cases, the text in the workspace grows in length, and a garbage-collection technique is necessary to reclaim the unused space. Nevertheless, it is generally more efficient than the fixed-length word technique.

Concatenation

At the beginning of this section, while providing a definition for strings, we introduced the concatenation operation for two characters. This operation can be generalized to apply to two strings.

> Let A and B be two strings of sizes m and n, respectively. Concatenation produces a new string of size (m + n) by tagging after string A the characters that make up string B.

For example, the concatenation of DATA and BASE results in a new string DATABASE.

This primitive operation is extremely important in that it is our main tool for generating new strings. Many programming languages (e.g., Snobol, Basic, PL/I) directly provide for concatenation. As we will see, COBOL supports concatenation in the form of the STRING statement.

In string processing systems based on the fixed-length word, concatenation requires

1. A mechanism that extracts the strings to be concatenated from the fixed-length storage locations by specifying appropriate delimiters
2. Specification of a fixed-length target word that stores the result
3. A mechanism that copies source strings into the target

In both the workspace/index table and linked-list methods, strings to be concatenated are easily accessed and extracted by their relative locations and lengths. In the workspace/index table the result is stored in the workspace without any storage waste. In the linked-list technique the result is stored in a dynamically created linked list, again with no storage waste.

String Comparison

In computer programming we occasionally have to compare two strings using comparison operators. The result of such a comparison is either true or false, and it depends on the collating sequence used by the computer.

A **collating sequence** is the ordering of characters in a given character coding system. The two commonly used character coding systems are EBCDIC (Extended Binary Coded Decimal Interchange Code) and ASCII (American Standard Code for Information Interchange). The collating sequence for EBCDIC for letters, decimal digits, and the special character blank is the ordering:

$$" " < "a" < "b" < \ldots < "z" < "A" < "B" < \ldots < "Z" < "0" < "1" < \ldots < "9"$$

where $<$ represents "precedes," or the internal machine code for the left-hand character is less than that for the right-hand one. The collating sequence for ASCII is different.

$$" " < "0" < "1" < \ldots < "9" < "A" < "B" < \ldots < "Z" < "a" < "b" < \ldots < "z"$$

> For two strings to be **equal**, they must have equal lengths, and every character in the first string must match the corresponding character in the second string at the same relative location.

The following are some examples of string comparison operations and the results produced in the EBCDIC and ASCII character coding systems.

Comparison Expression	Result in EBCDIC	Result in ASCII
"DATA" = "DATA"	TRUE	TRUE
"DATE" = "DATA"	FALSE	FALSE
"DATE" > "DATA"	TRUE	TRUE
"DATE8" > "8DATE"	FALSE	TRUE

Computing Length of a String

We need a function that computes and returns length of a string stored in a string variable. In the workspace/index table and linked-list methods, string length is kept in index tables and can be easily returned. In systems based on fixed-length word representation, additional character-by-character processing of the memory word is required to compute string length. In COBOL, the INSPECT TALLYING statement can be used for this purpose.

Substring Search

Given a string, we may want to search it for the existence of a substring. The substring to be searched can be specified either implicitly or explicitly. An implicit specification requires either some appropriate delimiters that may exist in the source string, or the start address and length of the substring to be searched. An explicit specification requires the value for the substring to be searched.

For example, suppose we have the following source string:

"DATABASE MANAGEMENT SYSTEMS"

"Search for the substring delimited by the substrings 'TA' on the left and a blank on the right" is an example of implicit substring specification by delimiters, and will return the substring BASE. "Search for the substring starting at relative location 4 and of length 4" is an example of implicit substring specification by start address and size. It returns the same substring, BASE. Finally, "Search for the substring 'BASE'" exemplifies explicit specification (also called **pattern matching**). As the substring exists in the given string, in this case, it will return true.

String search using implicit substring specification by start address and length can be handled efficiently in the workspace/index table method. Substring specification by delimiters, or explicitly by its value, generally requires character-by-character inspection of the source string in all of the techniques.

In general, after searching and locating a substring in a source string, we may want to do one or more of the following operations.

1. Copy it into another memory location.
2. Delete its occurrence(s) in the source string.
3. Replace its occurrence(s) in the string.
4. Count the number of its occurrence(s) in the string.

These suboperations can also be defined and implemented as primitive operations in a string processing system. The ease of implementation and efficiency of the resulting system are largely dependent on the data structures chosen for representing strings.

REVIEW QUESTIONS

1. A record in a computer file is stored as a string on external storage. (T or F)
2. Strings are defined over an _____ .
3. The generative operation for strings is _____ .
4. Which of the following is not a fundamental string processing operation?
   a. Concatenation
   b. String comparison
   c. String input
   d. Computing length of a string
5. The data structures that are commonly used for representing strings are _____ , _____ , _____ , and _____ .
6. One of the disadvantages of the fixed-length word method for string representation is that the amount of wasted storage may become substantial. (T or F)
7. One of the advantages of the workspace/index table technique is that it facilitates string insertion and deletion operations.
8. The ordering of characters in a character coding system is known as _____ .

Answers: 1. T; 2. alphabet; 3. concatenation; 4. c; 5. fixed-length words, arrays, linked lists, workspace/index table; 6. T; 7. T; 8. collating sequence.

String Processing Features in COBOL

COBOL is a powerful string processing language with built-in features that consist of three statements: STRING, UNSTRING, and INSPECT. The statement EXAMINE is the older version of INSPECT, and is not covered in this book.

COBOL uses the fixed-length word method for string representation, on which the three statements described below are based. As COBOL also supports arrays, it is certainly possible to design a string processing system that is analogous to the workspace/index table method. In this case, however, the programmer has to write procedures for the necessary string processing primitives.

Both COBOL 74 and COBOL 85 support the STRING, UNSTRING, and INSPECT statements. The INSPECT statement has four forms:

1. INSPECT TALLYING
2. INSPECT REPLACING
3. INSPECT TALLYING/REPLACING

COBOL 85 4. COBOL 85 INSPECT CONVERTING

The following table summarizes the functions of the COBOL string processing statements in terms of their fundamental operations.

COBOL String Processing Statement	Operation
STRING	Extract a substring from a string
	Concatenate two or more substrings
	Compute length of concatenated strings
UNSTRING	Extract one or more substrings from a string
	Compute length of extracted substrings
INSPECT TALLYING	Verify existence of a substring in a string
	Count number of occurrences of a substring in a string
INSPECT REPLACING	Replace an existing substring in a string with another substring
INSPECT TALLYING/REPLACING	Verify existence of a substring in a string
	Count number of occurrences of a substring in a string
	Replace an existing substring in a string with another substring
COBOL 85 INSPECT CONVERTING	Replace one or more substrings in a string with other substrings

These statements correspond to complex procedures that are built into the COBOL compiler and are invoked automatically whenever they are encountered in a program. They provide certain flexibilities for character string processing.

The STRING Statement

The main functions of the STRING statement are to

1. Extract a substring from a given string and copy it into a target field.
2. Concatenate two or more strings into another string.
3. Compute the length of the resulting string after extraction or concatenation.

Syntactically, the STRING statement is defined as follows.

```
STRING  { identifier-1 }  ... DELIMITED BY  { identifier-2 }  ...
        { literal-1    }                    { literal-2    }
                                            { SIZE         }

        INTO identifier-3 [ WITH POINTER identifier-4 ]
        [ ON OVERFLOW imperative-statement-1 ]
        [ NOT ON OVERFLOW imperative-statement-2 ] [ END-STRING ]
```

COBOL 85

The elements of this syntax are

1. One or more source string constants or variables after the key word STRING
2. For each source string, a DELIMITED BY clause that specifies a delimiter
3. An INTO clause that defines the target string to contain the result
4. An optional WITH POINTER clause that defines an integer identifier pointing to the next character in the target string to be processed
5. An optional ON OVERFLOW clause that contains an imperative sentence to be executed in case of overflow

COBOL 85

6. A COBOL 85 optional NOT ON OVERFLOW clause that contains an imperative sentence to be executed in case no overflow condition is raised during processing
7. A COBOL 85 optional statement terminator, END-STRING

The delimiter in the DELIMITED BY clause may be a string constant or a variable. In that case, the source string is transferred into the target string beginning at its left and proceeding until that delimiter is encountered. If SIZE is used as the delimiter, the entire source string is transferred. For example, let us assume that the variables STRING-ONE and STRING-TWO contain "DATABASE " and "AS", respectively. Then,

```
STRING-ONE DELIMITED BY STRING-TWO ...   transfers "DATAB".
STRING-ONE DELIMITED BY "E" ...          transfers "DATABAS".
STRING-ONE DELIMITED BY SIZE ...         transfers "DATABASE  ".
STRING-ONE DELIMITED BY SPACE ...        transfers "DATABASE".
STRING-TWO DELIMITED BY STRING-ONE ...   transfers "AS".
```

The WITH POINTER clause gives the programmer the option of specifying an explicit pointer variable. This variable should be written in the WITH POINTER clause. Also, it should be defined in the WORKING-STORAGE SECTION as an elementary integer data item, large enough to contain a value that is equal to the length of the target string plus 1. The pointer variable points to the location in the target string into which a single character will be written during processing. Therefore, if the programmer wishes to begin data transfer into the target string at its first position, he or she should initialize the pointer variable to 1. In this case, the length of the target string can be computed by subtracting 1 from the value of this pointer variable.

If the WITH POINTER clause is not included in the STRING statement, the system will define an implicit pointer variable, set it to 1, and use it to control the transfer of characters for concatenation. In this case, the implicit pointer variable cannot be accessed by the programmer.

The ON OVERFLOW clause contains an imperative sentence to be executed in case an overflow condition is raised. The permissible range for a pointer variable is 1 through the size of the target field. At any time during the execution of the STRING statement, if the pointer variable assumes a value that is outside this range, the data transfer process ceases and an overflow condition is raised. If an ON OVERFLOW clause exists in the STRING statement, its content is executed and control passes to the next executable statement. Otherwise, the next statement is simply executed.

COBOL 85   The NOT ON OVERFLOW clause is a COBOL 85 feature. If used, it should contain an imperative sentence. If no overflow occurs during processing, this sentence is executed after the STRING statement is fully processed.

The semantics of the STRING statements consist of the following procedure.

1. The first source string is transferred, one character at a time, into the target string until the specified delimiter for the first string is met. The delimiter is not carried into the target string. Every time a character is written into the target string, the explicit or implicit pointer variable is incremented by 1. The delimiter should be a substring of the source string. If it is not, it will be discarded, and as the default in this case is SIZE, the entire string will be transferred.

2. After this, the remaining source strings are processed similarly. At the end of processing the explicit pointer variable points to the location that is next to the most recently written character in the target string variable. Therefore, the size of the string in the target field is 1 less the value of the pointer variable.

The source and target strings should be elementary data items. They may be alphanumeric, numeric, or integer fields that must have the USAGE DISPLAY clause, either explicitly or implicitly. If integer fields are used in concatenation, they should not contain the symbol P in their PICTURE clauses. This same rule also applies to the pointer variable.

Examples of the STRING statement follow.

Example 1   Suppose we have the WORKING-STORAGE SECTION definitions below.

```
WORKING-STORAGE SECTION.
. . . . . . . . . . . .
01   STRING-ONE                    PIC X(10).
01   STRING-TWO                    PIC X(5).
01   STRING-THREE                  PIC X(10).
01   STRING-FOUR                   PIC X(10).
01   RESULT-STRING                 PIC X(40).
01   PTR-X                         PIC 99.
```

We consider the STRING statement:

```
STRING STRING-ONE       DELIMITED BY STRING-TWO
       STRING-THREE     DELIMITED BY SIZE
       " "              DELIMITED BY SIZE
       STRING-FOUR      DELIMITED BY SPACE
  INTO RESULT-STRING
  WITH POINTER PTR-X
  ON OVERFLOW
            DISPLAY "OVERFLOW!".
```

Assuming the values of PTR-X, STRING-ONE, STRING-TWO, STRING-THREE, and STRING-FOUR are 1, "DATA BASE ", "BASE ", "MANAGEMENT", and "SYSTEMS   ", respectively, after processing the value of RESULT-STRING will be

"DATA MANAGEMENT SYSTEMSbbbbbbbbbbbbbbbbb"

where b represents a blank. The variable PTR-X will contain 24. The length of the string after concatenation in RESULT-STRING is therefore 23.

Example 2   Now consider the following WORKING-STORAGE SECTION variables.

```
WORKING-STORAGE SECTION.
. . . . . . . . . . . .
01   STRING-ONE                  PIC X(5).
01   STRING-TWO                  PIC X(5).
01   STRING-THREE                PIC X(5).
01   STRING-FOUR                 PIC X(5).
01   RESULT-STRING               PIC X(15).
01   PTR-X                       PIC 99.
```

This time, suppose we execute the STRING statement:

```
STRING STRING-ONE
       STRING-THREE     DELIMITED BY SPACE
       STRING-FOUR      DELIMITED BY SIZE
  INTO RESULT-STRING
  WITH POINTER PTR-X.
```

The following figure shows the values stored in the source strings STRING-ONE, STRING-THREE, and STRING-FOUR before processing. The pointer variable PTR-X is assumed to be initialized to 1. After processing, the STRING statement generates a string in the target string RESULT-STRING and changes the value stored in the pointer variable PTR-X to 13.

Before processing:

STRING—ONE   STRING—THREE   STRING—FOUR   PTR—X

| A | B | C | b | b |

| D | E | F | G | b |

| H | I | b | b | b |

| 0 | 1 |

After processing:

RESULT—STRING   PTR—X

| A | B | C | D | E | F | G | H | I | b | b | b | | | |

| 1 | 3 |

For STRING-ONE and STRING-THREE, the delimiter is the first space from the left. Thus, the substrings ABC and DEFG are extracted. The source string, STRING-FOUR, has SIZE as its delimiter. This means that it will be extracted fully as HIbbb. These three strings are concatenated and placed in the target string, RESULT-STRING.

Example 3 Here we use the same WORKING-STORAGE SECTION variables as in example 2. The STRING statement is as follows.

```
STRING STRING—ONE      DELIMITED BY STRING—TWO
       STRING—THREE    DELIMITED BY SIZE
       STRING—FOUR     DELIMITED BY ","
  INTO RESULT—STRING
  WITH POINTER PTR—X.
```

This statement specifies STRING-TWO as the delimiter for the source string STRING-ONE. As shown in the following figure, STRING-ONE has ABCDE stored in it. The current value of STRING-TWO is Bbbbb, and it is not a substring that exists in STRING-ONE. Hence, STRING-TWO is ignored as the delimiter, and, by default, SIZE becomes the delimiter for STRING-ONE. The before and after processing pictures for the variables involved are shown below.

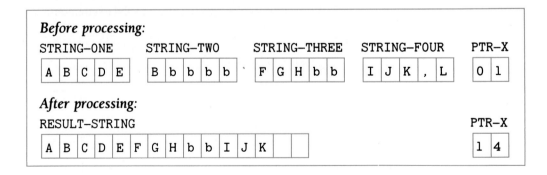

Before processing:

STRING—ONE   STRING—TWO   STRING—THREE   STRING—FOUR   PTR—X

| A | B | C | D | E |

| B | b | b | b | b |

| F | G | H | b | b |

| I | J | K | , | L |

| 0 | 1 |

After processing:

RESULT—STRING   PTR—X

| A | B | C | D | E | F | G | H | b | b | I | J | K | | |

| 1 | 4 |

Example 4 Consider the following WORKING-STORAGE SECTION variables.

```
WORKING-STORAGE SECTION.
............
01    STRING-ONE                PIC X(5).
01    STRING-TWO                PIC X(2).
01    STRING-THREE              PIC X(5).
01    STRING-FOUR               PIC X(5).
01    RESULT-STRING             PIC X(15).
01    PTR-X                     PIC 99   .
```

The STRING statement is

```
STRING STRING-ONE       DELIMITED BY STRING-TWO
       ", "             DELIMITED BY SIZE
       STRING-THREE     DELIMITED BY SPACE
       ", "             DELIMITED BY SIZE
       STRING-FOUR      DELIMITED BY SPACE
INTO RESULT-STRING
WITH POINTER PTR-X.
```

The before and after processing pictures for the variables involved are

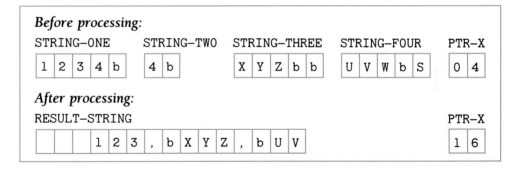

While the character W in STRING-FOUR was being processed, the size of the target string RESULT-STRING was exceeded and an overflow condition was raised.

Example 5 Finally, for the same WORKING-STORAGE SECTION variables as those in example 4, we have the following STRING statement.

```
STRING STRING-ONE     DELIMITED BY STRING-TWO
   INTO RESULT-STRING
   WITH POINTER PTR-X.
```

This statement extracts a substring from STRING-ONE and copies it into RESULT-STRING.

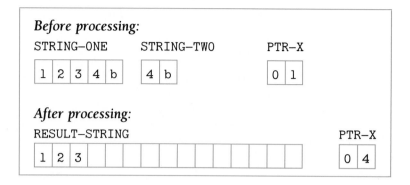

The UNSTRING Statement

The UNSTRING statement does the opposite of STRING. It splits a given string into one or more substrings and stores them in specified fields. It can also compute and store the lengths of the extracted substrings in program variables. The syntax of the UNSTRING statement is given below.

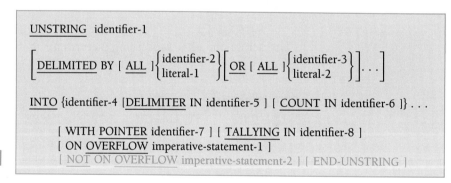

The UNSTRING statement is a powerful, albeit complex, statement in COBOL. Before we describe its semantics, let us clarify several features associated with it.

1. After the key word UNSTRING, there is a source string variable.
2. Optionally, we may have any number of DELIMITED BY clauses after the source string variable.
3. The INTO clause is required, and it specifies one or more target identifiers that will contain the extracted substrings.
4. For each target identifier we may optionally specify a DELIMITER IN clause. This clause references a character string variable that holds the delimiter used in extracting the substring in the target identifier.
5. Also, for each target identifier we may specify a COUNT IN clause. This clause contains an integer variable that stores the length of the extracted substring in that target field.
6. The optional WITH POINTER clause defines a pointer variable indicating the character that is being processed in the source string.
7. The TALLYING IN clause is also optional. If used, it should contain an integer variable. This stores the number of extracted substrings after UNSTRING is fully executed.
8. The ON OVERFLOW clause is similar to that available for STRING.

9. The NOT ON OVERFLOW clause is a COBOL 85 option. It contains an imperative sentence to be executed if no overflow condition is raised during execution.
10. Finally, END-UNSTRING is an optional COBOL 85 statement terminator.

The DELIMITED BY clause is used to specify the delimiters for substring extraction. The delimiters may be character string constants or variables. More than one delimiter may be specified using the OR connector. Some examples of legal delimiter specifiers found in the DELIMITED BY clause are

```
DELIMITED BY ALL SPACES OR "." OR ","
DELIMITED BY "*" OR DEL-STRING OR ALL "$"
DELIMITED BY "/"
```

The optional DELIMITER IN clause can be used only if the DELIMITED BY clause is specified in the statement. It contains a string variable that stores the delimiter actually used for the current step of string decomposition. If this clause is not specified, the delimiter string cannot be accessed.

The COUNT IN clause is also optional and also requires the DELIMITED BY clause. It contains an integer variable that stores the number of characters transferred from the source string to the substring for which COUNT IN has been specified. The integer variables in the COUNT IN clause are automatically initialized to zero by the system, and are incremented by 1 every time a character is moved into the target strings.

An example for both the DELIMITER IN and COUNT IN clauses is given below.

```
INTO STRING-2  DELIMITER IN DELIMITER-2  COUNT IN COUNT-2
```

As in the STRING statement, the WITH POINTER clause permits the programmer to specify a pointer variable explicitly. This pointer variable should be defined in the WORKING-STORAGE SECTION as an integer variable large enough to contain a value that is equal to the length of the source string variable plus 1. In the case of the UNSTRING statement, the pointer variable stores the relative address of the character being processed in the source string. To point to the relative location in the source string where the string decomposition is to begin, the programmer should initialize the pointer variable before the UNSTRING statement is executed.

If the programmer does not define an explicit pointer variable, the system uses an implicit one. This is initialized to 1, and the string decomposition starts at the first location in the source string.

The TALLYING IN clause enables the programmer to specify an integer variable to keep track of the number of substrings extracted from the source string. The variable in the TALLYING clause is user-defined in the WORKING-STORAGE SECTION as an integer variable, and should be initialized to a positive integer value. If it is initialized to zero, after UNSTRING is executed, it contains a count of the number of target string fields that have received substrings from the source string.

The ON OVERFLOW clause contains one or more imperative statements that are executed if the variable in the WITH POINTER clause contains a value that is less than 1, or if all the target strings have received data and the source string field still contains characters that are not yet processed. If either of these two conditions arises, the execution of the UNSTRING statement ceases and the imperative statements are executed. Control then passes to the statement after UNSTRING.

The semantics of the UNSTRING statement follows.

1. Starting at the relative location of the source string specified by an explicit or implicit pointer variable, characters are transferred one at a time from the source string into the first target string. This continues until one of the delimiters included in the DELIMITED BY clause is encountered. If the DELIMITER IN clause is specified, the current delimiter is saved in the DELIMITER IN variable. If the COUNT IN clause exists in the statement, the variable in COUNT IN is incremented ultimately to contain the number of characters transferred to the first target field. The delimiter is not transferred and is not represented in the value stored in the count variable. After the first substring transfer is completed, the variable in the TALLYING IN clause, if specified, is incremented by 1. The pointer variable will now point to the beginning of the next substring.
2. If more than one target string has been specified in the SUBSTRING statement, the processing continues in a similar fashion.

Some examples of the UNSTRING statement are given below.

Example 1   Consider the following WORKING-STORAGE SECTION variables.

```
WORKING-STORAGE SECTION.
. . . . . . . . . . . . . . . .
01  STRING-1        PIC X(40).
01  STRING-2        PIC X(12).
01  STRING-3        PIC X(12).
01  STRING-4        PIC X(12).
01  STRING-5        PIC X(12).
01  DELIMITER-2     PIC X(3).
01  DELIMITER-3     PIC X(3).
01  DELIMITER-4     PIC X(3).
01  DELIMITER-5     PIC X(3).
01  COUNT-2         PIC 99.
01  COUNT-3         PIC 99.
01  COUNT-4         PIC 99.
01  COUNT-5         PIC 99.
01  POINTER-VAR     PIC 99.
01  TALLY-VAR       PIC 99.
. . . . . . . . . . . . . . . . . .
```

Suppose in the PROCEDURE DIVISION we have

```
. . . . . . . . . . . . . . . . .
    MOVE 1 TO POINTER-VAR.
    MOVE 0 TO TALLY-VAR.
. . . . . . . . . . . . . . . . .
    UNSTRING STRING-1
        DELIMITED BY ALL SPACES OR ":" OR "."
        INTO STRING-2  DELIMITER IN DELIMITER-2   COUNT IN COUNT-2
             STRING-3  DELIMITER IN DELIMITER-3   COUNT IN COUNT-3
             STRING-4  DELIMITER IN DELIMITER-4   COUNT IN COUNT-4
             STRING-5  DELIMITER IN DELIMITER-5   COUNT IN COUNT-5
        WITH POINTER POINTER-VAR
        TALLYING IN TALLY-VAR
        ON OVERFLOW
            MOVE "OVERFLOW" TO OVERFLOW-FLAG.
```

Let us assume that the variable STRING-1 initially contains

"PROGRAMMING LANGUAGES:A PERSPECTIVEbbbbb"

The UNSTRING statement above makes use of most of the available options. The explicitly defined pointer variable POINTER-VAR has been initialized to 1. Therefore, processing of the source string STRING-1 begins with the first character, P. Three delimiters have been specified: a field containing one or more blanks, and the characters colon and period. A tally variable, TALLY-VAR, has also been defined and set to zero.

After the UNSTRING statement is executed, the contents of the associated variables will be

STRING-2 : "PROGRAMMINGb"	DELIMITER-2 : "bbb"	COUNT-2 : 11
STRING-3 : "LANGUAGESbbb"	DELIMITER-3 : ":bb"	COUNT-2 : 09
STRING-4 : "Abbbbbbbbbbb"	DELIMITER-4 : "bbb"	COUNT-4 : 01
STRING-5 : "PERSPECTIVEb"	DELIMITER-5 : "bbb"	COUNT-2 : 11
POINTER-VAR : 41	TALLY-VAR : 04	

Again, "b" stands for a blank.

It should be noted that because one of the delimiters is ALL SPACES, the delimiter associated with STRING-5 is all the right padding blanks in the field STRING-1, and hence all characters in the source field are processed. If the delimiter ALL SPACES were replaced by SPACE, the execution of the UNSTRING statement would have yielded essentially the same results, except for POINTER-VAR, which would have become 37, and we would have an overflow condition because not all characters in the source field would have been processed.

Example 2   Consider the following variable definitions.

```
    WORKING-STORAGE SECTION.
    . . . . . . . . . . . . . .
    01  STRING-1                    PIC X(20).
    01  STRING-2                    PIC X(8).
```

```
01   STRING-3                        PIC X(8).
01   STRING-4                        PIC X(8).
01   DEL-2                           PIC X(3).
01   DEL-3                           PIC X(3).
01   DEL-4                           PIC X(3).
01   COUNT-2                         PIC 99.
01   COUNT-3                         PIC 99.
01   COUNT-4                         PIC 99.
01   PTR-X                           PIC 99.
01   TALL-X                          PIC 99.
```

Suppose we execute the UNSTRING statement:

```
UNSTRING STRING-1
            DELIMITED BY SPACE OR ","
      INTO STRING-2  DELIMITER IN DEL-2  COUNT IN COUNT-2
           STRING-3  DELIMITER IN DEL-3  COUNT IN COUNT-3
           STRING-4  DELIMITER IN DEL-4  COUNT IN COUNT-4
      WITH POINTER PTR-X      TALLYING IN TALL-X
      ON OVERFLOW DISPLAY "OVERFLOW!".
```

The before and after processing contents of the variables involved are shown below.

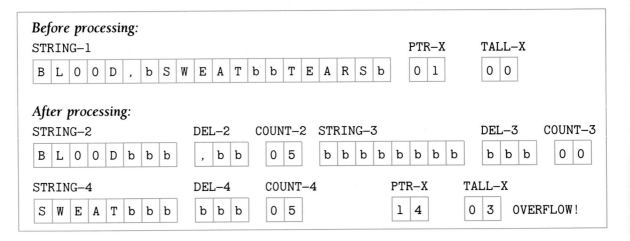

Let us trace the execution of this UNSTRING statement.

1. The first delimiter, the comma (,), is used to extract the first substring, BLOOD, and store it in STRING-2. The corresponding COUNT variable, COUNT-2, will contain 5, the length of the extracted substring.
2. The next delimiter encountered in STRING-1 is the blank in the seventh position. This time, no substring is extracted and STRING-3 will be left blank. The delimiter, SPACE, is transferred to DEL-3. As no substring has been transferred into STRING-3 the corresponding COUNT variable COUNT-3 will be set to zero.

3. The third extracted substring will be SWEAT. It will be stored in STRING-4, with blanks in DEL-4 and 5 in COUNT-4. At this point, we have run out of target variables in the UNSTRING statement to hold the substrings to be extracted. We still have some substrings that can be transferred from the source string, however. Consequently, an overflow condition will be raised.

Example 3   The following UNSTRING statement is based on the same set of WORKING-STORAGE SECTION variables as those used in example 3.

```
UNSTRING STRING-1
          DELIMITED BY ALL SPACE
     INTO STRING-2  DELIMITER IN DEL-2  COUNT IN COUNT-2
          STRING-3  DELIMITER IN DEL-3  COUNT IN COUNT-3
          STRING-4  DELIMITER IN DEL-4  COUNT IN COUNT-4
     WITH POINTER PTR-X       TALLYING IN TALL-X
     ON OVERFLOW DISPLAY "OVERFLOW!".
```

The before and after processing pictures are shown below.

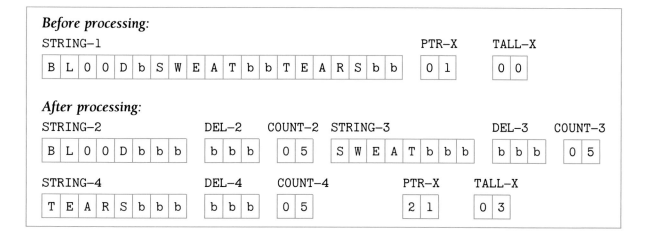

Example 4   Finally, consider the UNSTRING statement that uses the same set of variables as in the previous two examples.

```
UNSTRING STRING-1
          DELIMITED BY ALL SPACE
     INTO STRING-2  DELIMITER IN DEL-2  COUNT IN COUNT-2
          STRING-3  DELIMITER IN DEL-3  COUNT IN COUNT-3
          STRING-4  DELIMITER IN DEL-4  COUNT IN COUNT-4
     WITH POINTER PTR-X       TALLYING IN TALL-X
     ON OVERFLOW DISPLAY "OVERFLOW!".
```

The result of processing is depicted as follows.

Before processing:

STRING-1   PTR-X   TALL-X

| B | L | O | O | D | b | S | W | E | A | T | b | b | T | E | A | R | S | b | b | | 0 | 4 | | 0 | 0 |

After processing:

STRING-2   DEL-2   COUNT-2 STRING-3   DEL-3   COUNT-3

| O | D | b | b | b | b | b | | b | b | b | | 0 | 2 | | S | W | E | A | T | b | b | b | | b | b | b | | 0 | 5 |

STRING-4   DEL-4   COUNT-4   PTR-X   TALL-X

| T | E | A | R | S | b | b | b | | b | b | b | | 0 | 5 | | 2 | 1 | | 0 | 3 |

The INSPECT Statement

COBOL 85

The INSPECT statement has four forms: INSPECT TALLYING, INSPECT RE-PLACING, INSPECT TALLYING/REPLACING, and INSPECT CONVERTING. The INSPECT TALLYING form can be used to examine a character string and count the number of occurrences of a specified substring in it. The INSPECT REPLACING form is used to examine a given string and replace occurrences of a given substring in it with other substrings. These two functions can be combined if we make use of the INSPECT TALLYING/REPLACING form.

```
INSPECT STRING-1
    TALLYING NO-OF-COMMAS FOR ALL ","
    REPLACING ALL "," BY SPACE AFTER INITIAL "*".
```

COBOL 85   The COBOL 85 statement INSPECT CONVERTING is used to replace one or more substrings in a string with other substrings.

INSPECT TALLYING Form.   This form has the following syntax.

```
INSPECT identifier-1 TALLYING

     ⎧                ⎧ CHARACTERS [⎧BEFORE⎫ INITIAL ⎧identifier-3⎫]...        ⎫
     ⎨ identifier-2 FOR⎨            ⎩AFTER ⎭         ⎩literal-1   ⎭              ⎬ ... ...
     ⎩                ⎩ ⎧ALL    ⎫ ⎧identifier-4⎫ [⎧BEFORE⎫INITIAL⎧identifier-5⎫]... ⎭
                        ⎩LEADING⎭ ⎩literal-2   ⎭  ⎩AFTER ⎭       ⎩literal-3   ⎭
```

The identifier after the key word INSPECT should be a character string variable that contains the string to be examined. The identifiers after the key word TALLYING should be integer variables. Each stores the number of occurrences of a substring that is specified after the key word FOR. These integer variables should be initialized to zero by the programmer.

The ALL choice enables the programmer to count all occurrences of the specified substring in the given string. The LEADING choice does the same thing, except that only the leading occurrences of the substring are counted.

The CHARACTERS choice counts the number of characters in the specified string. This, in fact, is the size of the string variable.

The BEFORE INITIAL and AFTER INITIAL options are useful in that they enable the programmer to indicate the position in the source string at which the inspection is to begin. The CHARACTERS choice is useful when used together with one of these options. Then we would be counting the size of specified substrings in the given string. Otherwise, if we use CHARACTERS without BEFORE or AFTER INITIAL, the tally function computes the length of the source string field.

Let us consider some examples based on the following WORKING-STORAGE SECTION variables.

```
WORKING-STORAGE SECTION.
. . . . . . . . . . . . . . . . .
01   STRING-ONE       PIC X(13)  VALUE SPACES.
01   TALL-X           PIC 99     VALUE ZERO.
. . . . . . . . . . . . . . . . .
```

The following table shows several examples of the INSPECT TALLYING statement, and in each case, the effect of the statement on the associated program variables.

INSPECT Statement	Effect	

INSPECT STRING-ONE
  TALLYING
    TALL-X FOR ALL "A"
    BEFORE INITIAL "C".
	STRING-ONE
	`S A N b F R A N C I S C O`
		TALL-X
		`0 2`

INSPECT STRING-ONE
  TALLYING
    TALL-X FOR ALL "NG"
    AFTER INITIAL "K".
	STRING-ONE
	`K I N G b K O N G b b b b`
		TALL-X
		`0 2`

INSPECT STRING-ONE
  TALLYING
    TALL-X FOR CHARACTERS
    BEFORE INITIAL " ".
	STRING-ONE
	`O L D b K I N G b C O L E`
		TALL-X
		`0 3`

INSPECT STRING-ONE
  TALLYING
    TALL-X FOR CHARACTERS.
	STRING-ONE
	`A R I Z O N A b b b b b b`
		TALL-X
		`1 3`

INSPECT STRING-ONE
  TALLYING
    TALL-X FOR LEADING "0"
    BEFORE INITIAL "2".
	STRING-ONE
	`0 0 0 0 0 1 1 2 4 5 2 8 b`
		TALL-X
		`0 5`

(continued)

INSPECT Statement	Effect	

INSPECT STRING—ONE
  TALLYING
    TALL—X FOR LEADING "U"
    AFTER INITIAL "R".
	STRING—ONE
	
	`S T R U C T U R E b b b b`
		TALL—X
		
		`0 1`

INSPECT STRING—ONE
  TALLYING
    TALL—X FOR LEADING "U"
    AFTER INITIAL "T".
	STRING—ONE
	
	`S T R U C T U R E b b b b`
		TALL—X
		
		`0 0`

INSPECT STRING—ONE
  TALLYING
    TALL—X FOR ALL "TH"
	STRING—ONE
	
	`T H A T ' S b T H A T b b`
		TALL—X
		
		`0 2`

INSPECT REPLACING Form. The syntax of this form is shown below.

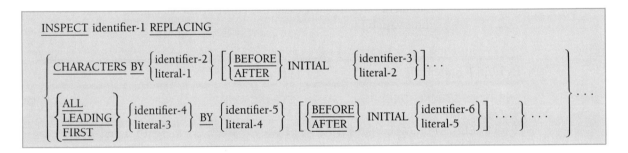

```
INSPECT identifier-1 REPLACING

⎧                     ⎧identifier-2⎫ ⎡⎧BEFORE⎫          ⎧identifier-3⎫⎤    ⎫
⎢ CHARACTERS BY       ⎨           ⎬ ⎢⎨      ⎬ INITIAL ⎨           ⎬⎥...  ⎢
⎢                     ⎩literal-1  ⎭ ⎣⎩AFTER ⎭          ⎩literal-2  ⎭⎦    ⎢
⎨                                                                        ⎬...
⎢ ⎧ALL    ⎫ ⎧identifier-4⎫    ⎧identifier-5⎫ ⎡⎧BEFORE⎫         ⎧identifier-6⎫⎤   ⎫
⎢ ⎨LEADING⎬ ⎨           ⎬ BY ⎨           ⎬ ⎢⎨      ⎬ INITIAL ⎨           ⎬⎥...⎬...
⎩ ⎩FIRST  ⎭ ⎩literal-3  ⎭    ⎩literal-4  ⎭ ⎣⎩AFTER ⎭         ⎩literal-5  ⎭⎦   ⎭
```

As in the INSPECT TALLYING form, the identifier after the key word IN-SPECT should be a character string variable that contains the string to be examined. The key word REPLACING is followed by one or more replacement specifiers. Each replacement specifier consists of the key words CHARACTERS, ALL, LEADING, or FIRST, followed by a string constant or variable that indicates the substring to be replaced.

The key word BY is followed by a string constant or variable that specifies the substring to replace the previously defined substring. The BEFORE INITIAL and AFTER INITIAL clauses are optional, and contain a string constant or identifier.

The CHARACTERS BY option enables the programmer to replace every character in a given string, or a specified portion of it, with a substring of size 1. The ALL, LEADING, and FIRST options can be used to replace all, or leading, or just the first occurrence of a substring with another substring of equal size.

Let us study some examples of the INSPECT REPLACING statement. They are based on the identifier STRING-1 defined as follows.

```
WORKING—STORAGE SECTION.
............
01  STRING—1                          PIC X(15).
............
```

This table shows some examples.

INSPECT Statement	Effect		

INSPECT STRING-1
   REPLACING
      CHARACTERS BY "*"
      AFTER INITIAL " ".
	STRING-1
	Before:
	
	After:
		`N E W b Y O R K b b b b b`
		
		`N E W b * * * * * * * * *`	

INSPECT STRING-1
   REPLACING
      CHARACTERS BY "*"
      BEFORE INITIAL " ".
	STRING-1
	Before:
	
	After:
		`N E W b Y O R K b b b b b`
		
		`* * * b Y O R K b b b b b`	

INSPECT STRING-1
   REPLACING
      ALL "ENC" BY "ING"
      AFTER INITIAL "A".
	STRING-1
	Before:
	
	After:
		`F L A M E N C O b b b b b`
		
		`F L A M I N G O b b b b b`	

INSPECT STRING-1
   REPLACING
      ALL "0" BY " "
      BEFORE INITIAL "D".
	STRING-1
	Before:
	
	After:
		`5 0 0 b D O L L A R S b b`
		
		`5 b b b D O L L A R S b b`	

INSPECT STRING-1
   REPLACING
      LEADING "E" BY "A".
	STRING-1
	Before:
	
	After:
		`E E R O N b W H I T E b b`
		
		`A A R O N b W H I T E b b`	

INSPECT STRING-1
   REPLACING
      FIRST "N" BY "M".
	STRING-1
	Before:
	
	After:
		`A L I C E b N O R T O N b`
		
		`A L I C E b M O R T O N b`	

INSPECT STRING-1
   REPLACING
      ALL "OO" BY "EE".
	STRING-1
	Before:
	
	After:
		`G O O S E b & b M O O S E`
		
		`G E E S E b & b M E E S E`	

INSPECT TALLYING/REPLACING Form. This form is simply a combination of the previous two forms for the INSPECT statement. The syntax of the combination requires the TALLYING elements to be written first, followed by the REPLACING elements. With this form, the programmer can determine the number of occurrences of specified substrings in a string and subsequently replace them with other substrings in the original string. The syntax definition of the INSPECT TALLYING/REPLACING statement follows.

INSPECT identifier-1 TALLYING

$$\left\{ \text{identifier-2 } \underline{\text{FOR}} \left\{ \begin{array}{l} \underline{\text{CHARACTERS}} \left[\left\{ \begin{array}{l} \underline{\text{BEFORE}} \\ \underline{\text{AFTER}} \end{array} \right\} \text{INITIAL} \left\{ \begin{array}{l} \text{identifier-3} \\ \text{literal-1} \end{array} \right\} \right] \dots \\ \left\{ \begin{array}{l} \underline{\text{ALL}} \\ \underline{\text{LEADING}} \end{array} \right\} \left\{ \left\{ \begin{array}{l} \text{identifier-4} \\ \text{literal-2} \end{array} \right\} \left[\left\{ \begin{array}{l} \underline{\text{BEFORE}} \\ \underline{\text{AFTER}} \end{array} \right\} \text{INITIAL} \left\{ \begin{array}{l} \text{identifier-5} \\ \text{literal-3} \end{array} \right\} \right] \dots \right\} \dots \end{array} \right\} \dots \right\} \dots$$

REPLACING

$$\left\{ \begin{array}{l} \underline{\text{CHARACTERS}} \ \underline{\text{BY}} \left\{ \begin{array}{l} \text{identifier-6} \\ \text{literal-4} \end{array} \right\} \left[\left\{ \begin{array}{l} \underline{\text{BEFORE}} \\ \underline{\text{AFTER}} \end{array} \right\} \text{INITIAL} \left\{ \begin{array}{l} \text{identifier-7} \\ \text{literal-5} \end{array} \right\} \right] \dots \\ \left\{ \begin{array}{l} \underline{\text{ALL}} \\ \underline{\text{LEADING}} \\ \underline{\text{FIRST}} \end{array} \right\} \left\{ \begin{array}{l} \text{identifier-8} \\ \text{literal-6} \end{array} \right\} \underline{\text{BY}} \left\{ \begin{array}{l} \text{identifier-9} \\ \text{literal-7} \end{array} \right\} \left[\left\{ \begin{array}{l} \underline{\text{BEFORE}} \\ \underline{\text{AFTER}} \end{array} \right\} \text{INITIAL} \left\{ \begin{array}{l} \text{identifier-10} \\ \text{literal-8} \end{array} \right\} \right] \dots \right\} \dots \end{array} \right\} \dots$$

An example of the INSPECT TALLYING/REPLACING follows.

```
WORKING-STORAGE SECTION.
..................
01  STRING-1                          PIC X(40).
01  TALL-X      VALUE ZERO            PIC 99.
PROCEDURE DIVISION.

    ................
    MOVE "DATA BASE ANALYSIS AND DESIGN" TO STRING-1.
    ................
    INSPECT STRING-1
        TALLYING
            TALL-X FOR ALL " "
                BEFORE INITIAL "DESIGN"
        REPLACING
            ALL " " BY "*"
                BEFORE INITIAL "SIGN".
```

In this example, after the INSPECT statement is executed, the tally variable TALL-X will contain 04, and STRING-1 will have "DATA*BASE*ANALYSIS* AND*DESIGN" in it.

COBOL 85 *INSPECT CONVERTING Form.* In addition to these three forms, a variation is available for the INSPECT statement in COBOL 85, the INSPECT CONVERT-ING statement. It can be used to replace a set of distinct characters in a string with other characters. The syntax of INSPECT CONVERTING is as follows.

$$\text{INSPECT identifier-1 } \underline{\text{CONVERTING}} \left\{ \begin{array}{l} \text{identifier-2} \\ \text{literal-1} \end{array} \right\} \underline{\text{TO}} \left\{ \begin{array}{l} \text{identifier-3} \\ \text{literal-2} \end{array} \right\}$$

$$\left[\left\{ \begin{array}{l} \underline{\text{BEFORE}} \\ \underline{\text{AFTER}} \end{array} \right\} \text{INITIAL} \left\{ \begin{array}{l} \text{identifier-4} \\ \text{literal-3} \end{array} \right\} \right] \dots$$

Here is an example of the INSPECT CONVERTING statement.

```
INSPECT STRING-1
    CONVERTING "ABCDEF" TO "123456"
        AFTER INITIAL STRING-2.
```

This statement is, in fact, equivalent to the following INSPECT/REPLACING.

```
INSPECT STRING-1 REPLACING
        ALL "A" BY "1"
        ALL "B" BY "2"
        ALL "C" BY "3"
        ALL "D" BY "4"
        ALL "E" BY "5"
        ALL "F" BY "6"
    AFTER INITIAL STRING-2.
```

Assuming STRING-1 and STRING-2 contain THE BEST EXAMPLE and H, respectively, the value stored in STRING-1 after processing will be TH5 25ST 5X1MPL5. A conversion such as this is meaningful as a data encryption technique in which the legible text is scrambled using an encryption key before transmission.

String Processing Using Arrays

The fixed-length string representation inherent in the design of COBOL and the string processing features based on this representation provide the COBOL programmer with a powerful string processing environment. Many essential primitives are incorporated into the three statements, STRING, UNSTRING, and INSPECT, that we just studied. Certain operations are difficult if not impossible to program using these COBOL features, however. Some examples of such operations are

1. Determining length of a left-justified string with embedded blanks in a string variable, as in "IT IS SUNNY   OUTSIDE   TODAY ".
2. Counting occurrences of a substring in a string, if the string contains overlapping occurrences of the substring. For example, the substring "ABA" occurs twice in the string "ADDIS ABABA". However, the COBOL statement

```
INSPECT "ADDIS ABABA" TALLYING TALL-X FOR ALL "ABA".
```

will result in a value of 1 in TALL-X.
3. Replacing a substring in a string with another substring of unequal length, as in replacing DATA with KNOWLEDGE in the string DATA BASE SYSTEMS.
4. Compressing a string by eliminating all embedded blanks.
5. Deleting a substring occurrence from a given string, or inserting a substring into a string, and so on.

In applications where implementation of such primitives becomes necessary, the programmer may complement the COBOL string processing features with procedures that use array representations for strings. Any string field can be defined as a one-dimensional array such that each element is a string of size 1. Using this representation, the programmer is able to access individual characters in the string. For example, the data definition

```
01  STRING-1.
    05  STRING-ARRAY  PIC X  OCCURS 50 TIMES.
```

permits character-by-character processing of the data item STRING-1, whereas the definition

```
01 STRING-1 PIC X(50).
```

does not.

Taking advantage of the characteristics of arrays, many useful supplementary program modules can be developed and incorporated into a string processing software system. We give two examples below.

Example 1   The following COBOL subroutine can be used to compute the length of a string in a fixed-length field.

```
00001    *...............................................................
00002     IDENTIFICATION DIVISION.
00003     PROGRAM-ID. STRING-LENGTH.
00004    *...............................................................
00005     ENVIRONMENT DIVISION.
00006    *...............................................................
00007     DATA DIVISION.
00008     WORKING-STORAGE SECTION.
00009     01  LENGTH-COMPUTED         PIC XXX.
00010
00011     LINKAGE SECTION.
00012     01  SOURCE-STRING.
00013         05  STRING-ARRAY        PIC X  OCCURS 80 TIMES.
00014     01  LENGTH-OF-SOURCE-STRING  PIC 99.
00015    *...............................................................
00016     PROCEDURE DIVISION
00017            USING SOURCE-STRING
00018                    LENGTH-OF-SOURCE-STRING.
00019        MOVE 80   TO LENGTH-OF-SOURCE-STRING.
00020        MOVE "NO" TO LENGTH-COMPUTED.
00021
00022        PERFORM COMPUTE-STRING-LENGTH
00023              UNTIL LENGTH-COMPUTED  "YES".
00024
00025        PERFORM RETURN-TO-MAIN.
00026
```

```
00027    RETURN-TO-MAIN.
00028       EXIT PROGRAM.
00029
00030    COMPUTE-STRING-LENGTH.
00031       IF STRING-ARRAY (LENGTH-OF-SOURCE-STRING) = " "
00032             SUBTRACT 1 FROM LENGTH-OF-SOURCE-STRING
00033       ELSE
00034             MOVE "YES" TO LENGTH-COMPUTED.
```

Example 2   The following subroutine eliminates embedded blanks in a text of strings.

```
00001    *...........................................................
00002    IDENTIFICATION DIVISION.
00003    PROGRAM-ID.  COMPRESS-STRING.
00004    *...........................................................

00005    ENVIRONMENT DIVISION.
00006    *...........................................................
00007    DATA DIVISION.
00008    WORKING-STORAGE SECTION.
00009    01  WORKING-STRING.
00010        05  WORKING-ARRAY       PIC X  OCCURS 80 TIMES.
00011    01  SOURCE-INDEX            PIC 99.
00012    01  WORKING-INDEX           PIC 99.
00013    01  SOURCE-STRING-LENGTH    PIC 99.
00014
00015    LINKAGE SECTION.
00016    01  SOURCE-STRING.
00017        05  STRING-ARRAY        PIC X  OCCURS 80 TIMES.
00018    *...........................................................
00019    PROCEDURE DIVISION
00020            USING SOURCE-STRING.
00021
00022       CALL "STRING-LENGTH" USING SOURCE-STRING
00023                                  SOURCE-STRING-LENGTH.
00024
00025       MOVE SOURCE-STRING TO WORKING-STRING.
00026       MOVE SPACES        TO SOURCE-STRING.
00027       MOVE 1             TO SOURCE-INDEX.
00028
00029       PERFORM COMPRESS-STRING
00030            VARYING WORKING-INDEX FROM 1 BY 1
00031                UNTIL WORKING-INDEX > SOURCE-STRING-LENGTH.
00032
00033       PERFORM RETURN-TO-MAIN.
00034
00035    RETURN-TO-MAIN.
00036       EXIT PROGRAM.
00037
00038    COMPRESS-STRING.
```

```
00039          IF WORKING-ARRAY (WORKING-INDEX) = " "
00040              NEXT SENTENCE
00041      ELSE
00042              MOVE WORKING-ARRAY (WORKING-INDEX) TO
00043                  STRING-ARRAY (SOURCE-INDEX)
00044              ADD 1 TO SOURCE-INDEX.
```

Both subroutines use one-dimensional arrays as data structures for string variables.

REVIEW QUESTIONS

1. The STRING, UNSTRING, and INSPECT statements in COBOL are based on the linked-list method for string representation. (T or F)
2. The STRING statement can be used to _____ strings, _____ , and _____ of the resulting string.
3. In the STRING statement, the portion of the source string to participate in concatenation is specified by the _____ clause.
4. In the DELIMITED BY clause of the STRING statement, SIZE implies that the source string is considered in its entirety. (T or F)
5. After a STRING statement is executed, the size of the resulting string is the value stored in the pointer variable defined in its WITH POINTER clause. (T or F)
6. The UNSTRING statement can be used to extract one or more substrings from a string, and to compute the length of the extracted substrings. (T or F)
7. Which of the following statements concerning the clauses in the UNSTRING statement is correct?
   a. The DELIMITED BY clause specifies the delimiters for substring extraction.
   b. The COUNT IN clause contains an integer variable that stores the number of characters transferred from the source string to the substring being extracted.
   c. The WITH POINTER clause specifies a pointer variable to hold the relative address of the character in the source string at which string decomposition is to begin.
   d. All of the above are correct.
   e. None of a, b, or c is correct.
8. In the UNSTRING statement, the variable in the TALLYING IN clause stores the number of substrings extracted from the source string after the statement is executed. (T or F)
9. The _____ form of the INSPECT statement can be used to count the number of occurrences of a specified substring in a string.
10. The INSPECT TALLYING/REPLACING statement can be used to
    a. Count the number of occurrences of a substring in a string.
    b. Replace a substring in a string with another substring.
    c. Compute the length of a substring or the length of the source string.
    d. Do all of the above.
11. In general, the COBOL 85 INSPECT CONVERTING statement can be equivalently expressed using the _____ form of the INSPECT statement.

Answers: 1. F; 2. concatenate, extract substrings, compute length; 3. DELIMITED BY; 4. T; 5. F; 6. T; 7. d; 8. T; 9. INSPECT/TALLYING; 10. d; 11. REPLACING.

Example Program 1: Key Word Analyzer

Problem   To illustrate the use of string processing concepts and related COBOL language features, we develop a limited-scope key word analyzer. We have a text file consisting of records of length 80, as shown in Program 1-Input. This is a sequential disk file into which a text of words is freely typed. We would like to develop a COBOL program that reads records from this text file, extracts its words, and produces a table of words and the number of times each one occurs in the text.

Solution   Program 1-Source is the compiler-generated listing of the program developed for this problem. In this program, we are using some COBOL 85 features, such as in-line PERFORM, and terminator key words END-READ, END-PERFORM, and so on. Obviously, to run this program with COBOL 74 compilers, certain modifications are necessary.

The following features are noteworthy in Program 1-Source.

1. The PERFORM VARYING statement in lines 000074–000080 is used to initialize the arrays KEYWORD and OCCURRENCE, which will contain key words to be extracted from the text and the number of times they occur in the text. These arrays are defined in lines 000056–000059 in the WORKING-STORAGE SECTION.
2. For each record coming from TEXT-FILE, we first extract the words. The paragraph B1-EXTRACT-TOKENS is designed for this purpose. It uses the UNSTRING statement of lines 000115–000120 to extract and store words in the elements of the array called TOKEN. The words in TOKEN may contain punctuation symbols.
3. Our next task is to get rid of the punctuation symbols. The paragraph B2-GET-RID-OF-PUNCTUATIONS uses the INSPECT REPLACING statement of lines 000133–000137 to eliminate the period, comma, semicolon, and colon by replacing each with a space.
4. Next, we process the array TOKEN to extract distinct key words and store them in the array KEYWORD. Also, we count the occurrences of each key word and store them in the parallel array OCCURRENCE. These are done in the paragraph B3-CREATE-KEYWORD-OCCURRENCES. The logic used here is similar to that of Program 1 in Chapter 8.

Applications of String Processing Functions

String processing concepts and functions play a fundamental role in many important application areas. Three of them are text processing, key-word-in-context indexing, and input data validation.

Text Processing

Text processing is one of the most common application areas of string processing concepts and functions. Given the advances in personal computing in the 1980s, the likelihood that you have used a text processor or a word processor on a microcomputer system is very high indeed. Text processors are extensively used for newspaper, magazine, and book editing and typesetting. Mainframe, minicomputers and microcomputer systems offer on-line text editors that can be used to prepare programs and data. After we prepare our text, be it a document, a computer program, or a data file, we store it on an external storage medium such as a disk or a diskette. If the stored text is a program, it can be compiled and executed. Also, it can be printed in a desired format.

In all text or word processors, the main data structure is the string. Different storage structures may be used to store strings, as discussed previously. Of course, we do not develop word processing programs in COBOL; however, it is useful to understand the major functions embedded in a word processing system, as they are relevant to string manipulation, and as we occasionally use string processing in business applications.

Text processing functions can be classified into two categories: text editing and text formatting. **Text editing** encompasses the necessary functions to create and restructure a text. **Text formatting** handles those functions that are required to produce output in a desired layout.

A text processor may be designed to be **command driven**, supporting a set of commands through which the user communicates with the text processing program. Alternatively, it may be **menu driven**. In a menu-driven system the user activates menu items that trigger certain commands to execute basic text handling functions. In command-driven systems, a simple command language is embedded into the text processor. The commands have to be distinguishable from the possible elements of an ordinary text string. Different systems use different command markers and/or keystroke combinations to enter commands into a text or to execute commands on a portion of text. Most text processors are hybrids in the sense that they are partially menu and partially command driven.

On-line text processors make use of the screen cursor to mark a position in the text string. Characters are entered at the location of the cursor. In general, the cursor points to the beginning of a substring in the text. In other words, depending on where it is relative to a substring, it serves as left or right delimiter for it. On-line text processors should possess the following general capabilities:

1. Moving the cursor to specified locations on the screen and within a text
2. Scrolling up and down within a text file.
3. File operations, including making copies, deleting, printing, and merging files

In light of this background information, the following are the functions of the text editing component of a typical word processing system.

1. Create and store in a text file strings of arbitrary length using all printable keyboard characters.
2. Insert substrings into the existing text. These may be single characters, words, or blocks of words.
3. Delete substrings (i.e., characters, words, or blocks of words) from the existing text.
4. Mark blocks of text in the text file.
5. Move marked blocks of text in the text file.
6. Make copies of a marked block.
7. Search for occurrences of a substring in the text and, if asked, replace them with another substring.

The capabilities of the text formatter should include the following:

1. Splitting the text file into lines, paragraphs, and pages of specified sizes
2. Right-justifying paragraphs, if needed

3. Changing left, right, top, and bottom page margins, and accordingly reformatting blocks of text
4. Centering strings in a line
5. Setting line spacing
6. Numbering pages in the text and lines in a page
7. Printing texts according to specified print options

Most modern text processors support all of these functions, as well as many
other miscellaneous capabilities, such as spell checking, incorporating graphics
into text, performing on-screen mathematics, generating indexes and tables of
contents, and so on. With the exception of graphics, these capabilities depend
on appropriate storage structures for strings.

Key-Word-in-Context Indexing

Searching for something in a wealth of recorded information is an activity that
we do routinely in everyday life. We look up a topic in an encyclopedia. We
search for articles of interest in the periodicals section of the library to write a
term paper. We try to find the pages in a book describing a concept. In all such
endeavors, we deal with the essence of an important discipline in information
processing. It is called **information retrieval**.

Information retrieval from computer data bases consists of searching for existence and subsequent retrieval of data, information, or documents stored in
direct-access mass storage devices. If the data base is large, an exhaustive
search would take too much time, so in such cases we use indexes. An index in
this sense is a table that associates a key entry with a location indicator. The location indicator may be page numbers in a book, volume numbers in an encyclopedia, volume and issue numbers for a periodical publication, or hardware
address of the relevant data in a computer data base.

To make effective use of indexes for searching unstructured data, we must
have a good indexing scheme. One such scheme is **key-word-in-context**
(KWIC) indexing that relies heavily on string processing concepts and techniques. It is commonly used in library systems and can also be used in business
applications.

Suppose in our business we store documents, reports of all kinds, operational guidelines, job specifications, position descriptions, and so on, electroni-
cally in an integrated text-processing/document-storage/data base environment.
Assume that each document is stored as a document file and can be accessed by
its file name. Furthermore, assume that each document is assigned a title that is
reasonably descriptive of its content. For example, a document entitled
"JOB DESCRIPTION FOR COMPUTER PROGRAMMERS" is stored in
FILE-27. Another document, "1987 LOCAL METROPOLITAN COMPUTER
PROGRAMMERS SALARY SURVEY", is kept in FILE-35. Yet another report
entitled "FUTURE FOR COMPUTER PROGRAMMERS: JOB SATISFACTION
AND SALARY" is in FILE-54.

To facilitate retrieval of the relevant documents, we analyze each title, extract key words, and build an index. Key words in such an index are indicative
of the context for each of their occurrences. For example, we decompose the title "JOB DESCRIPTION FOR COMPUTER PROGRAMMERS" into its tokens,
which are the substrings JOB, DESCRIPTION, FOR, COMPUTER, and PRO-
GRAMMERS. We eliminate the ordinary words such as A, FOR, TO, and so on
because they do not have much to offer in describing the subject of the document. In general, prepositions, conjunctions, adverbs, adjectives, pronouns,

and even verbs are eliminated. We end up with a set of key words, each pointing to one or more document files whose titles, and therefore contexts, have some relevance. The three example documents,

```
"JOB DESCRIPTION FOR COMPUTER PROGRAMMERS"
"1987 LOCAL METROPOLITAN COMPUTER PROGRAMMERS SALARY SURVEY"
"FUTURE FOR COMPUTER PROGRAMMERS: JOB SATISFACTION AND SALARY"
```

produce the following index table.

Key Word	File
COMPUTER	FILE-27, FILE-35, FILE-54
DESCRIPTION	FILE-27
FUTURE	FILE-54
JOB	FILE-27, FILE-54
METROPOLITAN	FILE-35
PROGRAMMERS	FILE-27, FILE-35, FILE-54
SALARY	FILE-35, FILE-54
SATISFACTION	FILE-54

This index table can now be used to retrieve the required documents. This is the gist of the KWIC indexing technique. In summary, a KWIC generator essentially

1. Considers each title as a string and extracts its tokens.
2. Eliminates the common words. The remaining tokens are the key words.
3. Constructs an index entry for each key word associating it with the document identifiers, and stores the index entry in the index table.

It is easy to see that all of these steps are string processing oriented. In the sample program for this chapter we have an application for input data validation. However, the paragraph C1-PARSE-RECORD (lines 00196–00213) contains a partial code that extracts tokens from a given string using the COBOL UNSTRING statement. This is the first step of the KWIC indexing technique.

Input Data Validation

In data processing applications that involve large volumes of data, the correctness of input data is of extreme importance. Before we attempt to process data, it is necessary to verify them and correct any errors in them. It is reasonable to expect that data entry operators will make occasional errors no matter how skillful they are. Validation routines can be incorporated into special purpose interactive or batch application systems. Such routines may help cut the errors due to initial data entry by a significant amount.

It should be understood that software systems developed to validate data cannot possibly catch all kinds of errors. Furthermore, it is not feasible, or even possible, to write comprehensive general purpose validation routines, as there are too many data fields in practical applications with different characteristics. Given a set of input data, many validation tests are possible.

1. Field validation tests
   a. Value length test
   b. Value characteristics test
   c. Value presence/absence test

 d. Value range test
 e. Value limits test
 f. Self-checking value validation
2. Field integrity validation tests
3. Record structure validation tests
4. File structure validation tests

Field validation is verifying correctness of data values in isolation on the basis of the properties of data value. For different data value properties, we have separate tests.

Value length test verifies the actual length of field value or those of its substrings. For a social security number such as 599-99-9999, field length should be 11, and the lengths of the three substrings that are delimited by - should be 3, 2, and 4, respectively.

Value characteristics test is for verifying the type of data field or that of its substrings. The first three, fifth and sixth, and the last four characters of a social security number should be numeric, and the fourth and seventh characters should be the special character -.

Value presence/absence test is to ensure that certain substrings such as blanks are not present in a given field or its specified substrings, or that the field contains only some specified characters, such as blanks.

Value range test verifies that a field value is in the expected range. Employee sex field may contain M for male and F for female, and no other value is acceptable.

Value limits test is used to verify that a field value or a specific substring value is within known limits. For example, employee salary for a company is known to be above $15,000 and below $90,000.

Self-checking value validation ensures that a self-checking number is correctly entered. Self-checking numbers are used in financial applications, for example, as account numbers. A self-checking number is a numeric code with a check digit, calculated using an arithmetic method. One such method, called the modulus-11 method, is illustrated below.

Steps	*Example*
Assign weights to each digit of the code number such that the weight for the units position is 2, for the tens position is 3, for the hundreds position is 4, etc.	Code: 1 2 4 4 5 Weights: 6 5 4 3 2
Multiply each digit with its assigned weight.	Products: 6 10 16 12 10
Sum the products.	Sum of products: 54
Divide the sum by 11 and compute the remainder.	Remainder on division by 11: 10
If the remainder is zero, the check digit is zero; otherwise, the check digit is obtained by subtracting the remainder from 11.	Check digit: $11 - 10 = 1$ Code with check digit: 124451

A data validation routine may be designed to recalculate the check digit using the basic code, and thus verify the field value.

Field integrity validation aims to validate a data field value in view of what is contained in another field, either within the same record or in another file. Let an employee master file contain employee numbers. Suppose our file system or data base system includes another file, the employee job history file, and its record structure also contains the employee number field. While validating records of the employee job history file, we should ensure that the employee number field value matches the employee number field value of a record in the employee master file.

Record structure validation establishes that the number of data fields in a given record of a file matches the number of data fields in its record structure.

File structure validation is used to verify that the records of a file are in correct order with respect to the values contained in one or more record sequence fields.

REVIEW QUESTIONS

1. Text processing functions can be classified as _____ and _____ .
2. Text editing includes the necessary functions to produce output in a desired layout. (T or F)
3. Which of the following is a capability of an on-line text processor?
   a. Copying files
   b. Moving the cursor on the screen
   c. Scrolling within a text
   d. All of the above
4. Setting line spacing in a text file is one of the capabilities of the text formatting component. (T or F)
5. Which of the following is a function of a KWIC generator?
   a. Extracting words from a document title
   b. Eliminating the common words from a title
   c. Constructing an index for each key word in a title
   d. All of the above
6. The value presence/absence test is a form of _____ tests.
7. The aim of self-checking value validation tests is to ensure that a self-checking number is correctly entered. (T or F)
8. The _____ test aims to validate a data field value in view of what is contained in another field, either within the same record or in another file.

Answers: 1. text editing, text formatting; 2. F; 3. d; 4. T; 5. d; 6. field validation; 7. T; 8. field integrity validation.

Example Program 2:   *Data Validation*

In this section we develop a limited-scope input data validation program. We use this opportunity to exemplify a practical application of the COBOL string processing features including STRING, UNSTRING, and INSPECT statements. The program includes a routine that is the basis of the key-word-in-context problem.

Problem Assume that an employee file has been created interactively using either an application program for file input or a screen panel interface. The records of the file contain the following fields:

1. An 11-character employee social security number.
2. A 6-digit numeric, company-assigned employee identification number, with the units digit being a check digit computed using the modulus-11 method.
3. Employee last name and first name.
4. Code for the department in which the employee works. This is a 3-character alphabetic field, and there are only four admissible values for it: ACC, DPR, FIN, and SLS, for Accounting, Data Processing, Finance, and Sales Departments, respectively.
5. Yearly employee salary, entered with a comma, as in 45,700.
6. Employee start date in the company, typed using the month/year form, as in 01/91.

Each field value is separated from the next by one or more blanks. The input file record length is 80 characters. Program 2-Input shows an instance of the employee input file that is sequentially organized. We would like to validate the data records automatically. The program will test for the following requirements.

1. Each record contains 7 fields delimited by spaces.
2. The employee social security field value
   a. Has a length of 11.
   b. Consists of three parts of lengths 3, 2, and 4, respectively.
   c. All three parts are numeric substrings.
   d. The first part, also called the area indicator, is less than 600.
3. The employee identification number field value
   a. Is of length 6.
   b. Is numeric.
   c. Has the correct check digit value in the units position.
4. The last and first employee names are both alphabetic.
5. The department code field value
   a. Has a length of 3.
   b. Is in the set of values ACC, DPR, FIN, or SLS.
6. The employee salary field value
   a. Is of length 6.
   b. Contains a comma separating the thousands portion from the hundreds portion.
   c. Has both the thousands and hundreds portions numeric.
   d. Is not less than 20,000 or greater than 80,000.
7. The employee start date field value
   a. Has a length of 5 characters.
   b. Consists of a month value, a /, and a year value.
   c. Has both the month and year values numeric.
   d. Shows the month value in the correct range, that is, 01–12.
   e. Gives the year value not less than 60 or greater than 87.

The program will validate the data records, and if an error is found, an entry will be included in a printer output file called ERROR-FILE. Such an entry will consist of a message explaining the nature of the error and an echo-print of the record involving the error. All data records that are not in error will be reformatted and written into a sequential disk file, which will then be used for processing. This file is called OUTPUT-FILE in the program, and its records will consist of the following fields:

1. A 9-digit employee social security number in columns 1–9
2. A 6-digit employee identification number in columns 12–17
3. A 25-character employee last name and first name in columns 20–44
4. A 3-character department code in columns 47–49
5. A 5-digit computational salary value in columns 52–56
6. A 4-digit computational year/month value, for start date, in columns 59–62

Solution Program 2-Source is the compiler listing of the COBOL program developed to solve the problem. The program first inputs a data record from the INPUT-FILE containing the input data to be validated, into an 80-byte, fixed-length memory word. The input string is then decomposed into its tokens. For this we use the UNSTRING statement (see lines 00196–00214 of the code). Each token is a substring delimited by blanks and is stored in an element of a one-dimensional array. At the same time we store the length of each extracted string and also compute the number of tokens extracted from the record. This procedure is the essential logic of the key-word-in-context.

The extracted substrings are then validated according to the stipulated requirements. In the modules designed for data validation we make use of the UNSTRING and INSPECT REPLACING statements. As the result of this processing, two files are generated: the ERROR-FILE that contains error messages, and the OUTPUT-FILE that includes the error-free reformatted records. Program 2-Output(a) and (b) are instances of the ERROR-FILE and OUTPUT-FILE generated by running the sample program.

Key Terms

AFTER INITIAL clause	INTO clause
ASCII	key-word-in-context indexing
BEFORE INITIAL clause	linked list
collating sequence	menu-driven
command-driven	NOT ON OVERFLOW clause
concatenation	ON OVERFLOW clause
COUNT IN clause	pattern matching
data encryption	pointer
DELIMITED BY clause	REPLACING clause
DELIMITER IN clause	string
EBCDIC	STRING statement
information retrieval	TALLYING clause
input data validation	TALLYING IN clause
INSPECT CONVERTING statement	test editing
INSPECT REPLACING statement	text formatting
INSPECT statement	text processing
INSPECT TALLYING statement	UNSTRING statement
INSPECT TALLYING/REPLACING	WITH POINTER clause
statement	workspace/index table technique

Study Guide

Quick Scan

- Strings are data structures commonly used by businesses in such areas as input data validation, text processing, data security, and key-word-in-context indexing.
- A string is a finite sequence of characters of an alphabet. The generative operation for strings is concatenation.
- In addition to concatenation, a string processing system should support appropriate data structures to store strings, and be able to compute string length, compare strings, and search strings for a substring.
- After a string is searched for a substring, if found, it may be copied, deleted, or replaced by another substring. These abilities are also among the primitive string processing functions.
- The four useful data structures for storing strings in the computer's memory are fixed-length words, arrays, linked lists, and workspace/index tables.
- The advantage of the fixed-length word method is its ease in storing strings in the memory. It tends to cause storage waste and inefficient processing, however.
- Arrays can also be used as storage structures for strings. Each string character can be stored in an individual array element.
- A valuable data structure uses an array as the workspace in which the string is stored, and an index table in which the start address and length of each token in the workspace are kept. This is referred to as the workspace/index table technique. A free space pointer is used to indicate the beginning address of the free space.
- In the workspace/index table method, there is no storage overhead due to right padding, and insert and delete operations are relatively easily handled. This method should be complemented with a garbage-collection technique to reclaim unused space.
- A text of strings can also be stored in a linked list. As COBOL has no pointer variables and dynamic memory variables among its data types, it cannot support linked lists based on pointer variables. The programmer can simulate a linked list using arrays.
- The concatenation operation can be used to generate a new string by copying two strings one after another.
- Another fundamental string operation is comparison of two strings. The result is a logical value (true or false) and depends on the character coding system used by the computer.
- Searching a string for existence of a substring is also known as pattern matching. After the substring occurrences are found, it is possible to copy them, delete or replace their occurrences with other substrings, or count the number of their occurrences in the given string.
- COBOL has powerful string processing features made up of three statements: STRING, UNSTRING, and INSPECT.
- The storage structure used in COBOL for a string is a fixed-length word. The three string processing statements are based on this representation.
- The STRING statement concatenates two or more strings into a single string variable. The source strings may be literals or strings stored in variables. Strings that are stored in variables may be considered in full during concatenation, or substrings may be extracted using delimiters. This is achieved through the use of the DELIMITED BY clause in the STRING statement.
- The STRING statement performs concatenation by transferring one character at a time from the source strings into the target string. The WITH POINTER

clause can be used to specify a pointer variable in order to control the character transfer process. If at any time during concatenation a pointer variable assumes a value that is outside the range defined by the target string, an overflow condition is raised.

- The UNSTRING statement splits a given string into one or more substrings and stores them in specified variables. It has features that enable the programmer to extract a substring of the source string, save the delimiters in string variables, count the number of characters transferred from the source string to a target string, and count the number of extracted substrings from the source string.
- The INSPECT statement has three forms: INSPECT TALLYING, INSPECT REPLACING, and the combination INSPECT TALLYING/REPLACING.
- INSPECT TALLYING can be used to examine a character string and count the number of times a specified substring occurs in it.
- INSPECT REPLACING locates the occurrences of a substring in a given string and replaces them with another string.
- The INSPECT TALLYING/REPLACING does the TALLYING function first, and then the REPLACING function.
- COBOL 85 also supports the INSPECT/CONVERTING form for the INSPECT statement. This form can be used to replace a set of distinct characters in a string with other characters.
- In COBOL it is possible to use arrays as storage structures for strings, and write programs that process strings stored in arrays.
- Three important applications of string processing are text processing, key-word-in-context indexing, and input data validation.
- Text processing is a common application area of string processing concepts and functions. Text processors have been written for mainframe and microcomputer systems. They are extensively used for newspaper, magazine, and book editing and typesetting, and for preparing computer programs and data files.
- Basic text processing functions are editing and formatting. The text editing component is used to create and restructure a text. The text formatter helps produce the output in a desired layout.
- A text processor may be command driven, menu driven, or a combination of both.
- On-line text processors should be capable of moving the cursor on the screen and within the text, scrolling up and down in the text file, and some file operations such as copying, deleting, printing, and merging.
- The functions of the text editor are creating and storing a text file, inserting substrings into the text, deleting substrings from the text, marking blocks of text in it, moving and/or copying marked blocks of text, and searching for occurrences of a substring in the text.
- The functions of the text formatter are splitting the text file into lines, paragraphs, and pages; right-justifying paragraphs; changing page margins; reformatting blocks of text; centering lines; setting line spacing; numbering pages and lines; and printing texts.
- Another application area of string processing is key-word-in-context indexing in information retrieval. Unstructured information such as documents, reports, and so on may be stored as text files together with their titles. A key-word-in-context generator is a string processing system capable of extracting from text titles descriptive key words and storing them in an index table. A document retrieval request can then be processed efficiently by using the index table to match the key words and directly accessing the texts indicated by the key words.
- A third application of string processing emerges in input data validation. Programs can be developed to detect and help correct errors that may occur during data entry.

- The many possible input data validation tests include field, field integrity, record structure, and file structure validation. Input data validation programs rely on string processing concepts and features.

Test Your Comprehension

Multiple-Choice Questions

1. Which of the following is a fundamental string processing operation?
   a. Searching a string for a substring
   b. Deleting a substring in a string
   c. Computing length of a string
   d. Comparing two strings
   e. All of the above
2. Which of the following about the STRING statement is incorrect?
   a. It can be used to concatenate strings.
   b. It can be used to compute the length of the resulting string.
   c. The WITH POINTER clause specifies a pointer variable that should be initialized before the STRING statement.
   d. The ON OVERFLOW clause contains an imperative sentence to be executed if the pointer variable assumes a value of 1.
3. Which of the following is a string operation that cannot be done using the UNSTRING statement?
   a. Extracting substrings from a string
   b. Concatenating two or more strings
   c. Computing length of substrings in a string
   d. Saving substring delimiters in variables
4. Which of the following about the clauses of the UNSTRING statement is incorrect?
   a. The INTO clause specifies one or more target identifiers that contain the extracted substrings.
   b. The DELIMITER IN clause specifies the delimiters to be used in substring extraction.
   c. The COUNT IN clause contains an integer variable that stores the length of an extracted substring.
   d. The TALLYING IN clause has an integer variable that stores the number of extracted substrings.
5. Concerning the INSPECT statement,
   a. The INSPECT TALLYING form is used to count the number of occurrences of a substring in a string.
   b. The INSPECT REPLACING statement can be used to count the number of occurrences of a substring in a string.
   c. In the INSPECT TALLYING/REPLACING form, the replacement function precedes the tally function.
   d. The INSPECT CONVERTING statement is equivalent to the INSPECT TALLYING form.
6. Which of the following is not a function of the text editor?
   a. Inserting substrings into an existing text
   b. Making copies of a marked block of text
   c. Centering strings in a line
   d. Searching for substring occurrences in a string
7. Which of the following is not a form of field validation test?
   a. Value length test
   b. Record structure validation
   c. Value range test
   d. Value limits test

Answers: 1. e; 2. d; 3. d; 4. b; 5. a; 6. c; 7. b.

Short Essay Questions

1. Briefly explain the importance of string processing in business applications.
2. Define a string. Explain the role of concatenation in string generation.
3. What are the fundamental string processing operations?
4. Explain the fixed-length word method as a storage representation technique for strings, and discuss its relative merits and shortcomings.
5. Briefly describe the workspace/index table technique. Discuss its advantages and disadvantages.
6. Describe how we can use a linked list as a data structure for a string processing system.
7. Explain why the result of comparing two strings depends on the computer's collating system.
8. Explain what is meant by pattern matching.
9. What are the functions of the STRING statement in COBOL?
10. Explain the syntax and semantics of the STRING statement.
11. Briefly discuss the functions of the UNSTRING statement.
12. Explain the options of the UNSTRING statement and their uses.
13. Explain the syntax and semantics of the UNSTRING statement.
14. What are the three forms of the COBOL INSPECT statement, and what are their functions?
15. Make a listing of the fundamental string processing functions and for each, indicate which COBOL language feature can be used.
16. What is the function of the COBOL 85 INSPECT/CONVERTING statement?
17. How do you classify the basic text-processing functions?
18. What are the general capabilities of on-line text processors?
19. What are the basic functions of a text editor?
20. Give a listing of the basic capabilities of a text formatter.
21. Explain the key-word-in-context indexing scheme. What string processing capabilities does it involve?
22. Explain why input data validation software systems are basically string processing systems.
23. Give a classification of data validation tests.
24. Briefly explain field validation.
25. What do you understand by self-checking value validation?
26. Explain field integrity validation.
27. What are meant by record structure and file structure validation?

Improve Your Problem-Solving Ability

Debugging Exercises

In each of the following string processing statements, identify and explain any errors that you find.

```
1. STRING STRING-ONE     DELIMITED BY STRING-TWO
          STRING-THREE
          STRING-FOUR     DELIMITED BY SPACE
       INTO RESULT-STRING STRING-TWO
          WITH POINTER PTR-X.
2. UNSTRING STRING-1 STRING-3 STRING-4
          DELIMITED BY ALL SPACE
                INTO STRING-2  DELIMITER IN DEL-2   COUNT IN COUNT-2
                    WITH POINTER PTR-X     TALLYING IN TALL-X
          ON OVERFLOW DISPLAY "OVERFLOW!".
```

```
3. INSPECT STRING-ONE
        TALLYING
                TALL-X FOR ALL LEADING "0"
                BEFORE INITIAL "2".
4. INSPECT STRING-1
        REPLACING
                ALL "ENC" BY "ING"
                        AFTER INITIAL "A".
5. INSPECT STRING-1
        REPLACING
                ALL " " BY "*"
                        BEFORE INITIAL "SIGN"
        TALLYING
                TALL-X FOR ALL " "
                        BEFORE INITIAL "DESIGN".
```

Programming Exercises

1. Given is the following program segment.

```
. . . . . . . . . . . .
WORKING-STORAGE SECTION.
01   FIELD-1                          PIC X(30).
01   FIELD-2                          PIC X(7).
01   FIELD-3                          PIC X(7).
01   FIELD-4                          PIC X(10).
01   FINAL-FIELD                      PIC X(40).
01   POINTER-VARIABLE                 PIC 99.
. . . . . . . . . . . .
        STRING FIELD-1        DELIMITED BY FIELD-2
               FIELD-3        DELIMITED BY SIZE
               FIELD-4        DELIMITED BY SPACE
           INTO FINAL-FIELD
           WITH POINTER POINTER-VARIABLE
           ON OVERFLOW
                        DISPLAY "OVERFLOW!".
```

Let us assume that the variables FIELD-1, FIELD-2, FIELD-3, and FIELD-4 contain, respectively, the values ROUND NUMBERS ARE PRECISE, PRECISE, ALWAYS, and FALSE. Further assume that POINTER-VARIABLE is initialized to 1. What values will be stored in FINAL-FIELD and POINTER-VARIABLE after the STRING statement is executed?

2. Consider the following partial code.

```
. . . . . . . . . . . . . . . .
01   STRING-1        PIC X(40).
01   STRING-2        PIC X(12).
01   STRING-3        PIC X(12).
01   STRING-4        PIC X(12).
01   STRING-5        PIC X(12).
01   COUNT-2         PIC 99.
01   COUNT-3         PIC 99.
01   COUNT-4         PIC 99.
```

```
01   COUNT-5          PIC 99.
01   POINTER-VAR      PIC 99.
01   TALLY-VAR        PIC 99.
. . . . . . . . . . . . . . . . . .
     MOVE 1 TO POINTER-VAR.
     MOVE 0 TO TALLY-VAR.

     UNSTRING STRING-1
         DELIMITED BY ALL SPACES
         INTO STRING-2   COUNT IN COUNT-2
              STRING-3   COUNT IN COUNT-3
              STRING-4   COUNT IN COUNT-4
              STRING-5   COUNT IN COUNT-5
         WITH POINTER POINTER-VAR
         TALLYING IN TALLY-VAR
         ON OVERFLOW
             MOVE "OVERFLOW" TO OVERFLOW-FLAG.
```

The source string STRING-1 contains the text WIPE AWAY ALL TRIVIAL FOND RECORDS. What will be the values of the above variables after execution of the UNSTRING statement?

3. In the following code, what will be the values stored in TALL-X and STRING-1 after execution of the INSPECT verb?

```
WORKING-STORAGE SECTION.
. . . . . . . . . . . . . . . . . .
01   STRING-1                        PIC X(40).
01   TALL-X      VALUE ZERO          PIC 99.

PROCEDURE DIVISION.
     . . . . . . . . . . . . . . . .
     MOVE "RELATIONAL INFORMATION SYSTEMS" TO STRING-1.
     . . . . . . . . . . . . . . .
     INSPECT STRING-1
         TALLYING
             TALL-X FOR ALL "A"
         REPLACING
             ALL " " BY "*"
                 BEFORE INITIAL "S".
```

Programming Problems

1. Suppose we have a pile file; that is, an unstructured file in which data are recorded in the order in which they arrive. Records in a pile file contain attribute name and value pairs, separated from each other by a delimiter, say a comma. The records may be of variable length, and not all have the same set of elements.

The pile file contains the following data about students: STUDENT-IDNO, STUDENT-NAME, STUDENT-MAJOR, and STUDENT-AGE. To simplify the problem, assume that the record length is fixed at 80 bytes. Some sample records for the pile file are given below.

```
STUDENT-IDNO = 100, STUDENT-AGE = 22, STUDENT-NAME = BILL HARRIS
STUDENT-NAME = LINDA BLACK, STUDENT-MAJOR = CS, STUDENT-AGE = 25
```

Write a COBOL program that reads the pile file and creates a sequentially organized structured student file with the following record structure.

```
01  STUDENT-RECORD.
    05  STUDENT-IDNO          PIC XXX.
    05  STUDENT-NAME          PIC X(25).
    05  STUDENT-MAJOR         PIC XXX.
    05  STUDENT-AGE           PIC 99.
```

2. We are about to print and authorize some checks with face values not to exceed $4000. Assume that each check has only dollar amounts and no fractions. We wish to convert the numerical value for each check to a corresponding written expression, as in THREE THOUSAND FIVE HUNDRED SIXTY SEVEN for $3567.

   Write a COBOL program that interactively accepts a check number and a dollar amount, and converts the dollar amount to its corresponding written expression.

3. Write a COBOL program that reads a text of characters and eliminates the following commonly recurring English words: A, AN, THE, TO, FROM, THAT, THIS.

4. Write a COBOL subroutine that accepts a string and replaces all occurrences of a specified substring in it with another string of an arbitrary length. The parameter list of the subroutine should include the source string, substring to be replaced, and the replacing substring. Your program should, for example, return

   ```
   "COBOL RULES FOR PROFESSIONAL COBOL PROGRAMMERS"
   ```

   if the input string contains

   ```
   "PASCAL RULES FOR PROFESSIONAL PASCAL PROGRAMMERS"
   ```

   and the substrings to be replaced are PASCAL and COBOL, respectively. Use arrays as the storage structure for strings.

```
                              COLUMNS
     5    10    15    20    25    30    35    40    45    50    55    60    65    70
----|----|----|----|----|----|----|----|----|----|----|----|----|----|----

AS IN THE STRING STATEMENT, THE WITH POINTER CLAUSE PERMITS THE
PROGRAMMER TO EXPLICITLY SPECIFY A POINTER VARIABLE.  THIS POINTER
VARIABLE SHOULD BE DEFINED IN THE WORKING-STORAGE SECTION AS AN INTEGER
VARIABLE, LARGE ENOUGH TO CONTAIN A VALUE THAT IS EQUAL TO THE LENGTH OF
THE SOURCE STRING VARIABLE PLUS ONE.
```

Program 1-Input An Instance of TEXT-FILE for Program 1

```
000001    *.............................................................
000002    IDENTIFICATION DIVISION.
000003    PROGRAM-ID.       KEYWORD-ANALYZER.
000004    AUTHOR.           UCKAN.
000005    **************************************************************
000006    ***   THIS PROGRAM READS A TEXT FROM A SEQUENTIAL DISK FILE, AND  *
000007    ***   DETERMINES THE NUMBER OF OCCURRENCES OF EACH WORD IN THE    *
000008    ***   TEXT.                                                       *
000009    **************************************************************
000010    DATE-WRITTEN.    APRIL 24, 1991.
000011    DATE-COMPILED. 04/24/91.
000012
000013    *.............................................................
000014    ENVIRONMENT DIVISION.
000015    CONFIGURATION SECTION.
000016    SOURCE-COMPUTER. UNIVERSITY-MAINFRAME.
000017    OBJECT-COMPUTER. UNIVERSITY-MAINFRAME.
000018    INPUT-OUTPUT SECTION.
000019    FILE-CONTROL.
000020        SELECT TEXT-FILE ASSIGN TO TEXTIN
000021                ORGANIZATION IS SEQUENTIAL
000022                ACCESS MODE  IS SEQUENTIAL.
000023    *.............................................................
000024    DATA DIVISION.
000025    FILE SECTION.
000026
000027    FD  TEXT-FILE
000028        LABEL RECORDS ARE STANDARD
000029        RECORD CONTAINS 80 CHARACTERS
000030        DATA RECORD IS TEXT-RECORD.
000031    01  TEXT-RECORD                   PIC X(80).
000032
000033    WORKING-STORAGE SECTION.
000034
000035    **********> VARIABLES:
000036
000037    01  ARRAY-INDEX                   PIC 999.
000038    01  ARR-INDEX                     PIC 999.
000039    01  LOCATION-POINTER              PIC 99.
000040    01  NO-OF-WORDS                   PIC 999.
000041    01  NO-OF-TOKENS                  PIC 999.
000042    01  OUT-INDEX                     PIC ZZ9.
000043    01  OUT-NUMBER                    PIC ZZ9.
000044    01  TOKEN-EXISTS                  PIC XXX.
000045
000046    **********> SWITCHES:
000047
000048    01  END-OF-FILE            PIC X(3)      VALUE "NO".
000049        88  INPUT-COMPLETED                  VALUE "YES".
000050
000051    01  END-OF-TOKEN-EXTRACTION  PIC X(3)    VALUE "NO".
000052        88  EXTRACTION-COMPLETED             VALUE "YES".
000053
```

Program 1-Source Source Program for Key Word Analyzer

```
000054     **********> ARRAYS:
000055
000056     01  KEYWORD-OCCURRENCE-TABLE.
000057         05  KEYWORD-OCCURRENCE  OCCURS 50 TIMES.
000058             10  KEYWORD          PIC X(25).
000059             10  OCCURRENCE       PIC 999.
000060
000061     01  TOKEN-TABLE.
000062         05 TOKEN  OCCURS 50 TIMES    PIC X(25).
000063
000064     *...............................................................
000065     PROCEDURE DIVISION.
000066
000067     A-MAINLINE.
000068         OPEN INPUT TEXT-FILE.
000069
000070         READ TEXT-FILE
000071             AT END MOVE "YES" TO END-OF-FILE
000072         END-READ.
000073
000074         PERFORM VARYING ARRAY-INDEX FROM 1 BY 1
000075             UNTIL ARRAY-INDEX > 50
000076
000077             MOVE SPACES TO KEYWORD (ARRAY-INDEX)
000078             MOVE ZERO   TO OCCURRENCE (ARRAY-INDEX)
000079
000080         END-PERFORM.
000081
000082         MOVE 1    TO ARRAY-INDEX.
000083         MOVE ZERO TO NO-OF-TOKENS.
000084
000085         PERFORM UNTIL INPUT-COMPLETED
000086
000087             PERFORM B1-EXTRACT-TOKENS
000088             READ TEXT-FILE
000089                 AT END MOVE "YES" TO END-OF-FILE
000090             END-READ
000091         END-PERFORM.
000092
000093         PERFORM B2-GET-RID-OF-PUNCTUATIONS.
000094
000095         PERFORM B3-CREATE-KEYWORD-OCCURRENCES.
000096
000097         PERFORM VARYING ARRAY-INDEX FROM 1 BY 1
000098             UNTIL ARRAY-INDEX > NO-OF-WORDS
000099
000100             MOVE ARRAY-INDEX              TO OUT-INDEX
000101             MOVE OCCURRENCE (ARRAY-INDEX) TO OUT-NUMBER
000102             DISPLAY OUT-INDEX, " ", KEYWORD (ARRAY-INDEX), " ",
000103                 OUT-NUMBER
000104         END-PERFORM.
000105
000106         CLOSE TEXT-FILE.
000107         STOP RUN.
000108
```

Program 1-Source (Continued)

```
000109      B1-EXTRACT-TOKENS.
000110          MOVE "NO" TO END-OF-TOKEN-EXTRACTION.
000111          MOVE 1    TO LOCATION-POINTER.
000112
000113          PERFORM UNTIL EXTRACTION-COMPLETED
000114
000115                  UNSTRING TEXT-RECORD
000116                        DELIMITED BY ALL SPACES
000117                        INTO TOKEN (ARRAY-INDEX)
000118                        WITH POINTER LOCATION-POINTER
000119                        TALLYING IN NO-OF-TOKENS
000120                  END-UNSTRING
000121
000122                  IF LOCATION-POINTER > 80
000123                        MOVE "YES" TO END-OF-TOKEN-EXTRACTION
000124                  END-IF
000125
000126                  ADD 1 TO ARRAY-INDEX
000127          END-PERFORM.
000128
000129      B2-GET-RID-OF-PUNCTUATIONS.
000130          PERFORM VARYING ARRAY-INDEX FROM 1 BY 1
000131                  UNTIL ARRAY-INDEX > NO-OF-TOKENS
000132
000133                  INSPECT TOKEN (ARRAY-INDEX)
000134                        REPLACING ALL "." BY SPACE
000135                                  ALL "," BY SPACE
000136                                  ALL ";" BY SPACE
000137                                  ALL ":" BY SPACE
000138          END-PERFORM.
000139
000140      B3-CREATE-KEYWORD-OCCURRENCES.
000141          MOVE          1 TO NO-OF-WORDS.
000142          MOVE TOKEN (1) TO KEYWORD (1).
000143          MOVE          1 TO OCCURRENCE (1).
000144
000145          PERFORM VARYING ARRAY-INDEX FROM 2 BY 1
000146                  UNTIL ARRAY-INDEX > NO-OF-TOKENS
000147                  MOVE "NO" TO TOKEN-EXISTS
000148
000149                  PERFORM VARYING ARR-INDEX FROM 1 BY 1
000150                        UNTIL ARR-INDEX > NO-OF-WORDS
000151
000152                        IF TOKEN (ARRAY-INDEX) = KEYWORD (ARR-INDEX)
000153                              ADD 1 TO OCCURRENCE (ARR-INDEX)
000154                              MOVE "YES" TO TOKEN-EXISTS
000155                        END-IF
000156                  END-PERFORM
000157                  IF TOKEN-EXISTS = "NO"
000158                        ADD 1 TO NO-OF-WORDS
000159                        MOVE TOKEN (ARRAY-INDEX) TO
000160                              KEYWORD (NO-OF-WORDS)
000161                        MOVE 1 TO OCCURRENCE (NO-OF-WORDS)
000162                  END-IF
000163          END-PERFORM.
```

Program 1-Source (Continued)

```
                                    COLUMNS
  1    5    10   15   20   25   30   35   40   45   50   55   60   65   70
----|----|----|----|----|----|----|----|----|----|----|----|----|----|--

  514 67-4542   123218   MORRISON WILLIAM        ACC  43,265  02/72
  334-12-1126   124451   EASTMAN THOMAS          ACC  50,000  10/80
  338-67-878A   234559   WAYNE WILLIS            DPR  34,700  11/79
  411-22-7127   245003   JEFFERSON JOHN          DPR  27,900  10/85
  412-45-4566   246771   KILDARE WAYNE           SLS  37,890  03/79
  213-23-3342   248908   CROSETTE CARLOS         SLS  47,000  07/78
  303-77-9832   249009   6OWSON DAVID            DPR  75,790  08/68
  452-67-8989   267902   PEAR JANE               ACC  66,800  12/80
  511-56-4341   268003   JASON TERRY             FIC  32,500  04/86
  443-60-0900   280097   DIONNE WILLIAM          DPR  37,780  01/81
  277-56-5678   300330   PETERS DAVID            FIN  86,000  03/83
  444-55-1232   350885   TEAL JASON              ACC  43,900  10/77
  511-44-8899   370789   MASON ELLEN             DPR  40,000  01/40
  512-78-8787   390879   PAULSON TERENCE         FIN  55,000  01/80
```

Program 2-Input Input Data for Program 2

```
00001    *..............................................................
00002      IDENTIFICATION DIVISION.
00003      PROGRAM-ID.      DATA-VALIDATION.
00004      AUTHOR.          UCKAN.
00005      ****************************************************************
00006      ***   THIS PROGRAM USES STRING PROCESSING OPERATIONS TO VALIDATE  *
00007      ***   DATA FIELDS IN THE RECORDS OF A SEQUENTIAL FILE CALLED       *
00008      ***   "INPUT-FILE".    THE FIELDS TO BE VALIDATED ARE:             *
00009      ***     . EMPLOYEE SOCIAL SECURITY NUMBER, FORMAT: 999-99-9999     *
00010      ***     . EMPLOYEE ID NUMBER,              FORMAT: 999999          *
00011      ***     . EMPLOYEE LAST NAME AND FIRST NAME                        *
00012      ***     . EMPLOYEE DEPARTMENT,             FORMAT: XXX             *
00013      ***     . EMPLOYEE SALARY,                 FORMAT: 99,999          *
00014      ***     . EMPLOYEE START DATE,             FORMAT 99/99.           *
00015      ***                                                               *
00016      ***   CHECKS ON SOCIAL SECURITY NUMBER:                           *
00017      ***       1. ALL THREE PARTS SHOULD BE NUMERIC,                    *
00018      ***       2. FIRST PART (AREA INDICATOR) SHOULD BE LESS THAN 600. *
00019      ***   CHECKS ON EMPLOYEE ID NUMBER:                               *
00020      ***       1. SHOULD BE NUMERIC,                                   *
00021      ***       2. THE SIXTH DIGIT IS A CHECK DIGIT COMPUTED USING THE  *
00022      ***          MODULUS-11 TECHNIQUE.                                *
00023      ***   CHECKS ON LAST NAME AND FIRST NAME:                         *
00024      ***       1. BOTH SHOULD BE ALPHABETIC.                           *
00025      ***   CHECKS ON DEPARTMENT CODE:                                  *
00026      ***       1. ACCEPTABLE VALUES ARE "ACC", "SLS", "DPR" AND "FIN". *
00027      ***                                                               *
00028      ***   CHECKS ON SALARY:                                           *
00029      ***       1. SHOULD BE NUMERIC,                                   *
00030      ***       2. MAXIMUM VALUE IS 80,000 AND MINIMUM IS 20,000.       *
```

Program 2-Source Program to Validate Input Data

```
00031   ***    CHECKS ON START DATE:                                          *
00032   ***        1. BOTH MONTH AND YEAR SHOULD BE NUMERIC,                   *
00033   ***        2. RANGE FOR MONTH IS 01-12,                               *
00034   ***        3. RANGE FOR YEAR IS 60-87.                                *
00035   ***                                                                    *
00036   ***    RECORDS FOUND IN ERROR WILL BE STORED IN AN ERROR FILE WITH *
00037   ***    APPROPRIATE ERROR MESSAGES.                                    *
00038   ***                                                                    *
00039   ***    RECORDS THAT ARE ERROR-FREE WILL BE STORED IN AN OUTPUT       *
00040   ***    FILE ACCORDING TO THE FOLLOWING FORMAT:                        *
00041   ***            . EMPLOYEE-SSNO    PIC 9(9).                           *
00042   ***            . SPACES           PIC XX.                             *
00043   ***            . EMPLOYEE-IDNO    PIC 9(6).                           *
00044   ***            . SPACES           PIC XX.                             *
00045   ***            . EMPLOYEE-NAME    PIC X(25).                          *
00046   ***            . SPACES           PIC XX.                             *
00047   ***            . DEPARTMENT-CODE PIC XXX.                             *
00048   ***            . SPACES           PIC XX.                             *
00049   ***            . SALARY           PIC 9(5).                           *
00050   ***            . SPACES           PIC XX.                             *
00051   ***            . START YEAR/MONTH PIC 9999.                           *
00052   **********************************************************************
00053    DATE-WRITTEN.    JAN  4, 1991.
00054    DATE-COMPILED. JAN  8, 1991.
00055
00056   *..................................................................
00057    ENVIRONMENT DIVISION.
00058    CONFIGURATION SECTION.
00059    SOURCE-COMPUTER. IBM-370.
00060    OBJECT-COMPUTER. IBM-370.
00061    INPUT-OUTPUT SECTION.
00062    FILE-CONTROL.
00063        SELECT INPUT-FILE     ASSIGN TO   INFILE.
00064        SELECT OUTPUT-FILE    ASSIGN TO   OUTFILE.
00065        SELECT ERROR-FILE     ASSIGN TO   ERRFILE.
00066   *..................................................................
00067    DATA DIVISION.
00068    FILE SECTION.
00069
00070    FD  INPUT-FILE
00071        LABEL RECORDS ARE OMITTED
00072        RECORD CONTAINS 80 CHARACTERS
00073        DATA RECORD IS INPUT-RECORD.
00074    01  INPUT-RECORD                  PIC X(80).
00075
00076    FD  OUTPUT-FILE
00077        LABEL RECORDS ARE STANDARD
00078        RECORD CONTAINS 62 CHARACTERS
00079        DATA RECORD IS MASTER-RECORD.
00080    01  MASTER-RECORD                 PIC X(62).
00081
00082    FD  ERROR-FILE
00083        LABEL RECORDS ARE STANDARD
00084        RECORD CONTAINS 131 CHARACTERS
```

Program 2-Source (Continued)

```
00085            DATA RECORD IS ERROR-RECORD.
00086     01   ERROR-RECORD                    PIC X(131).
00087
00088   WORKING-STORAGE SECTION.
00089     01   SOURCE-STRING                   PIC X(80).
00090     01   POSITION-MARKER                 PIC 99.
00091     01   FIELD-COUNT                     PIC 99.
00092     01   TOKEN-NUMBER                    PIC 99.
00093     01   FULL-NAME                       PIC X(25).
00094
00095     01   VARIABLES-FOR-SSNO.
00096          05   NONNUM-SSNO-PART1           PIC X(4).
00097          05   NONNUM-SSNO-PART2           PIC X(3).
00098          05   NONNUM-SSNO-PART3           PIC X(5).
00099          05   ABBR-NONNUM-SSNO-PART1      PIC X(3).
00100          05   ABBR-NONNUM-SSNO-PART2      PIC X(2).
00101          05   ABBR-NONNUM-SSNO-PART3      PIC X(4).
00102          05   SSNO-PART1                  PIC 9(4).
00103          05   SSNO-PART2                  PIC 9(3).
00104          05   SSNO-PART3                  PIC 9(5).
00105          05   AREA-INDICATOR              PIC 999.
00106          05   NONNUM-AREA-INDICATOR       PIC XXX.
00107
00108     01   VARIABLES-FOR-EMPLOYEE-NUMBER.
00109          05   EMPNO                       PIC 9(10).
00110          05   NONNUM-EMPNO                PIC X(10).
00111          05   WEIGHTED-SUM-OF-DIGITS      PIC 999.
00112          05   QUOTIENT                    PIC 99.
00113          05   REMAINDER-UPON-DIVISION     PIC 99.
00114          05   CHECK-DIGIT                 PIC 9.
00115
00116     01   VARIABLES-FOR-START-DATE.
00117          05   NONNUM-START-MONTH          PIC XXX.
00118          05   NONNUM-START-YEAR           PIC XXX.
00119          05   START-MONTH                 PIC 999.
00120          05   START-YEAR                  PIC 999.
00121          05   ABBR-START-MONTH            PIC 99.
00122          05   ABBR-START-YEAR             PIC 99.
00123          05   ABBR-NONNUM-START-MONTH     PIC XX.
00124          05   ABBR-NONNUM-START-YEAR      PIC XX.
00125
00126     01   VARIABLES-FOR-SALARY.
00127          05   NONNUM-SALARY-PART1         PIC XXX.
00128          05   NONNUM-SALARY-PART2         PIC XXXX.
00129          05   ABBR-NONNUM-SALARY-PART1    PIC XX.
00130          05   ABBR-NONNUM-SALARY-PART2    PIC XXX.
00131          05   SALARY-PART1                PIC 999.
00132          05   SALARY-PART2                PIC 9999.
00133          05   ABBR-SALARY-PART1           PIC 99.
00134          05   ABBR-SALARY-PART2           PIC 999.
00135          05   SALARY                      PIC 9(5).
00136
00137   **********> ARRAYS:
00138
```

Program 2-Source (Continued)

```
00139     01  FIELD-ATTRIBUTE-ARRAYS.
00140         05  FIELD-ATTRIBUTES   OCCURS 10 TIMES.
00141             10  TOKEN            PIC X(25).
00142             10  FIELD-DELIMITER  PIC X(20).
00143             10  FIELD-LENGTH     PIC 99.
00144
00145     01  EMPLOYEE-NUMBER-DIGITS.
00146         05  EMPNO-DIGITS  OCCURS 6 TIMES  PIC 9.
00147
00148
00149
00150     **********> SWITCHES:
00151
00152     01  END-OF-INPUT-FILE          PIC X(3)    VALUE "NO".
00153         88  INPUT-COMPLETED                    VALUE "YES".
00154
00155     01  END-OF-PARSING             PIC X(3).
00156         88  PARSING-COMPLETED                  VALUE "YES".
00157
00158     01  THERE-ARE-ERRORS           PIC X(3).
00159         88  NO-ERRORS                          VALUE "NO".
00160
00161     *..........................................................
00162     PROCEDURE DIVISION.
00163
00164     A-MAINLINE.
00165         OPEN INPUT  INPUT-FILE
00166              OUTPUT OUTPUT-FILE
00167              OUTPUT ERROR-FILE.
00168         READ INPUT-FILE
00169              AT END MOVE "YES" TO END-OF-INPUT-FILE.
00170
00171         PERFORM B1-VALIDATE-RECORD
00172              UNTIL INPUT-COMPLETED.
00173
00174         CLOSE INPUT-FILE
00175              OUTPUT-FILE
00176              ERROR-FILE.
00177         STOP RUN.
00178
00179     B1-VALIDATE-RECORD.
00180
00181         MOVE "NO"        TO END-OF-PARSING.
00182         MOVE INPUT-RECORD TO SOURCE-STRING.
00183         MOVE 1           TO TOKEN-NUMBER.
00184         MOVE 1           TO POSITION-MARKER.
00185         MOVE ZERO        TO FIELD-COUNT.
00186         MOVE "NO"        TO THERE-ARE-ERRORS.
00187
00188         PERFORM C1-PARSE-RECORD
00189              UNTIL PARSING-COMPLETED.
00190
00191         PERFORM C2-DATA-VALIDATIONS.
00192
```

Program 2-Source (Continued)

```
00193          READ INPUT-FILE
00194               AT END MOVE "YES" TO END-OF-INPUT-FILE.
00195
00196   C1-PARSE-RECORD.
00197   ********************************************************************
00198   ***   THIS PROCEDURE EXTRACTS FIELD VALUES FROM THE INPUT RECORD, *
00199   ***   AND STORES THEM IN THE ELEMENTS OF A 1-D ARRAY.             *
00200   ********************************************************************
00201
00202          UNSTRING SOURCE-STRING
00203               DELIMITED BY ALL SPACES
00204             INTO TOKEN (TOKEN-NUMBER)
00205               DELIMITER IN FIELD-DELIMITER (TOKEN-NUMBER)
00206               COUNT     IN FIELD-LENGTH (TOKEN-NUMBER)
00207             WITH POINTER     POSITION-MARKER
00208             TALLYING       IN FIELD-COUNT.
00209
00210          IF POSITION-MARKER > 80
00211               MOVE "YES" TO END-OF-PARSING.
00212
00213          ADD 1 TO TOKEN-NUMBER.
00214
00215   C2-DATA-VALIDATIONS.
00216
00217          PERFORM D1-CHECK-NUMBER-OF-FIELDS.
00218
00219          IF NO-ERRORS
00220               PERFORM D2-CHECK-SSNUMBER.
00221
00222          IF NO-ERRORS
00223               PERFORM D3-CHECK-EMPLOYEE-IDNO.
00224
00225          IF NO-ERRORS
00226               PERFORM D4-CHECK-START-DATE.
00227
00228          IF NO-ERRORS
00229               PERFORM D5-CHECK-SALARY.
00230
00231          IF NO-ERRORS
00232               PERFORM D6-CHECK-DEPARTMENT.
00233
00234          IF NO-ERRORS
00235               PERFORM D7-CHECK-NAMES.
00236
00237          IF NO-ERRORS
00238               PERFORM D8-FORM-OUTPUT-RECORD.
00239
00240   D1-CHECK-NUMBER-OF-FIELDS.
00241   ********************************************************************
00242   ***   IS THE TOTAL NUMBER OF DATA FIELDS EQUAL TO 7?             *
00243   ********************************************************************
00244
```

Program 2-Source (Continued)

```
00245          IF FIELD-COUNT NOT EQUAL TO 7
00246                  MOVE "YES" TO THERE-ARE-ERRORS
00247                  MOVE "INCORRECT NUMBER OF FIELDS IN RECORD: "
00248                      TO ERROR-RECORD
00249                  PERFORM E1-PRINT-RECORD-IN-ERROR.
00250
00251   D2-CHECK-SSNUMBER.
00252   ********************************************************************
00253   ***   IS THE LENGTH OF SSNO FIELD EQUAL TO 11?                    *
00254   ********************************************************************
00255
00256          IF FIELD-LENGTH (1) NOT EQUAL TO 11
00257                  MOVE "YES" TO THERE-ARE-ERRORS
00258                  MOVE "ERROR IN LENGTH OF SSNO IN RECORD: "
00259                      TO ERROR-RECORD
00260                  PERFORM E1-PRINT-RECORD-IN-ERROR.
00261
00262          IF NO-ERRORS
00263                  PERFORM E2-FURTHER-CHECKS-OF-SSNO.
00264
00265   D3-CHECK-EMPLOYEE-IDNO.
00266   ********************************************************************
00267   ***   IS THE LENGTH OF EMPNO FIELD EQUAL TO 6?  IS THE EMPNO FIELD*
00268   ***   VALUE NUMERIC?                                             *
00269   ********************************************************************
00270
00271          MOVE TOKEN (2) TO NONNUM-EMPNO.
00272
00273          INSPECT NONNUM-EMPNO
00274                  REPLACING ALL " " BY "0".
00275
00276          MOVE NONNUM-EMPNO TO EMPNO.
00277
00278          IF FIELD-LENGTH (2) IS NOT EQUAL TO 6
00279                  MOVE "YES" TO THERE-ARE-ERRORS
00280          ELSE
00281                  IF EMPNO NOT NUMERIC
00282                          MOVE "YES" TO THERE-ARE-ERRORS.
00283
00284          IF NO-ERRORS
00285                  PERFORM E3-VERIFY-CHECK-DIGIT.
00286
00287          IF NOT NO-ERRORS
00288                  MOVE "ERROR IN EMPLOYEE NUMBER IN RECORD:"
00289                      TO ERROR-RECORD
00290                  PERFORM E1-PRINT-RECORD-IN-ERROR.
00291
00292   D4-CHECK-START-DATE.
00293   ********************************************************************
00294   ***   IS THE LENGTH OF START-DATE FIELD EQUAL TO 5?               *
00295   ********************************************************************
00296
```

Program 2-Source (Continued)

```
00297          IF FIELD-LENGTH (7) NOT EQUAL TO 5
00298               MOVE "YES" TO THERE-ARE-ERRORS
00299               MOVE "ERROR IN FIELD LENGTH OF START DATE IN RECORD:"
00300                    TO ERROR-RECORD
00301               PERFORM E1-PRINT-RECORD-IN-ERROR.
00302
00303        IF NO-ERRORS
00304               PERFORM E4-FURTHER-CHECKS-OF-START-DT.
00305
00306     D5-CHECK-SALARY.
00307     **********************************************************************
00308     ***   IS THE LENGTH OF SALARY FIELD EQUAL TO 6?                     *
00309     **********************************************************************
00310
00311          IF FIELD-LENGTH (6) NOT EQUAL TO 6
00312               MOVE "YES" TO THERE-ARE-ERRORS
00313               MOVE "ERROR IN FIELD LENGTH OF SALARY IN RECORD:"
00314                    TO ERROR-RECORD
00315               PERFORM E1-PRINT-RECORD-IN-ERROR.
00316
00317        IF NO-ERRORS
00318               PERFORM E5-FURTHER-CHECKS-OF-SALARY.
00319
00320     D6-CHECK-DEPARTMENT.
00321     **********************************************************************
00322     ***   IS THE LENGTH OF DEPARTMENT FIELD EQUAL TO 3?  IS THE         *
00323     ***   DEPARTMENT FIELD VALUE ONE OF THE LEGITIMATE VALUES, I.E.,    *
00324     ***   "ACC", "DPR", "SLS" OR "FIN" ?                                *
00325     **********************************************************************
00326
00327          IF FIELD-LENGTH (5) IS NOT EQUAL TO 3
00328               MOVE "YES" TO THERE-ARE-ERRORS.
00329
00330        IF NO-ERRORS
00331               IF NOT ( TOKEN (5) EQUAL TO "ACC" OR "DPR"
00332                                      OR "SLS" OR "FIN" )
00333                    MOVE "YES" TO THERE-ARE-ERRORS.
00334
00335        IF NOT NO-ERRORS
00336               MOVE "ERROR IN DEPARTMENT CODE OF RECORD:"
00337                    TO ERROR-RECORD
00338               PERFORM E1-PRINT-RECORD-IN-ERROR.
00339
00340     D7-CHECK-NAMES.
00341     **********************************************************************
00342     ***   ARE BOTH THE EMPLOYEE LAST NAME AND FIRST NAME ALPHABETIC?    *
00343     **********************************************************************
00344
00345          IF TOKEN (3) IS NOT ALPHABETIC
00346                  OR
00347            TOKEN (4) IS NOT ALPHABETIC
00348               MOVE "YES" TO THERE-ARE-ERRORS
00349               MOVE "ERROR IN EMPLOYEE NAME OF RECORD:"
00350                    TO ERROR-RECORD
00351               PERFORM E1-PRINT-RECORD-IN-ERROR.
```

Program 2-Source (Continued)

```
00352
00353    D8-FORM-OUTPUT-RECORD.
00354    ********************************************************************
00355    ***   FOR CORRECT INPUT RECORDS, FORM THE OUTPUT RECORD USING THE *
00356    ***   STRING VERB.                                                *
00357    ********************************************************************
00358
00359        MOVE SPACES TO FULL-NAME.
00360
00361        STRING
00362               TOKEN (3)  DELIMITED BY SPACE
00363               " "        DELIMITED BY SIZE
00364               TOKEN (4)  DELIMITED BY SPACE
00365           INTO FULL-NAME.
00366
00367        STRING
00368               ABBR-NONNUM-SSNO-PART1  DELIMITED BY SIZE
00369               ABBR-NONNUM-SSNO-PART2  DELIMITED BY SIZE
00370               ABBR-NONNUM-SSNO-PART3  DELIMITED BY SIZE
00371               " "                     DELIMITED BY SIZE
00372               TOKEN (2)               DELIMITED BY SPACE
00373               " "                     DELIMITED BY SIZE
00374               FULL-NAME               DELIMITED BY SIZE
00375               " "                     DELIMITED BY SIZE
00376               TOKEN (5)               DELIMITED BY SPACE
00377               " "                     DELIMITED BY SIZE
00378               SALARY                  DELIMITED BY SIZE
00379               " "                     DELIMITED BY SIZE
00380               ABBR-START-YEAR         DELIMITED BY SIZE
00381               ABBR-START-MONTH        DELIMITED BY SIZE
00382           INTO MASTER-RECORD.
00383
00384        WRITE MASTER-RECORD.
00385
00386    E1-PRINT-RECORD-IN-ERROR.
00387        WRITE ERROR-RECORD
00388               AFTER ADVANCING 2 LINES.
00389        MOVE INPUT-RECORD TO ERROR-RECORD.
00390        WRITE ERROR-RECORD
00391               AFTER ADVANCING 1 LINE.
00392
00393    E2-FURTHER-CHECKS-OF-SSNO.
00394    ********************************************************************
00395    ***   ARE ALL THREE PARTS OF THE SSNO NUMERIC?  IS THE FIRST PART,*
00396    ***   AREA INDICATOR, LESS THAN 600?                              *
00397    ********************************************************************
00398
00399        UNSTRING TOKEN (1)
00400               DELIMITED BY "-" OR " "
00401           INTO NONNUM-SSNO-PART1
00402               NONNUM-SSNO-PART2
00403               NONNUM-SSNO-PART3.
00404
```

Program 2-Source (Continued)

```
00405           MOVE NONNUM-SSNO-PART1      TO ABBR-NONNUM-SSNO-PART1.
00406           MOVE NONNUM-SSNO-PART2      TO ABBR-NONNUM-SSNO-PART2.
00407           MOVE NONNUM-SSNO-PART3      TO ABBR-NONNUM-SSNO-PART3.
00408

00409           MOVE NONNUM-SSNO-PART1       TO NONNUM-AREA-INDICATOR.
00410           MOVE NONNUM-AREA-INDICATOR TO AREA-INDICATOR.
00411

00412           INSPECT NONNUM-SSNO-PART1
00413               REPLACING ALL " " BY "0".
00414           INSPECT NONNUM-SSNO-PART2
00415               REPLACING ALL " " BY "0".
00416           INSPECT NONNUM-SSNO-PART3
00417               REPLACING ALL " " BY "0".
00418

00419           MOVE NONNUM-SSNO-PART1 TO SSNO-PART1.
00420           MOVE NONNUM-SSNO-PART2 TO SSNO-PART2.
00421           MOVE NONNUM-SSNO-PART3 TO SSNO-PART3.
00422

00423           IF SSNO-PART1 NOT NUMERIC
00424               MOVE "YES" TO THERE-ARE-ERRORS
00425               MOVE "ERROR IN PART ONE OF SSNO IN RECORD:"
00426                     TO ERROR-RECORD
00427               PERFORM E1-PRINT-RECORD-IN-ERROR
00428           ELSE
00429               IF AREA-INDICATOR GREATER THAN 600
00430               MOVE "YES" TO THERE-ARE-ERRORS
00431               MOVE "AREA INDICATOR OF SSNO GREATER THAN 600 IN RECO
00432       -          "RD:" TO ERROR-RECORD
00433               PERFORM E1-PRINT-RECORD-IN-ERROR.
00434

00435           IF SSNO-PART2 NOT NUMERIC
00436               MOVE "YES" TO THERE-ARE-ERRORS
00437               MOVE "ERROR IN PART TWO OF SSNO IN RECORD:"
00438                     TO ERROR-RECORD
00439               PERFORM E1-PRINT-RECORD-IN-ERROR.
00440

00441           IF SSNO-PART3 NOT NUMERIC
00442               MOVE "YES" TO THERE-ARE-ERRORS
00443               MOVE "ERROR IN PART THREE OF SSNO IN RECORD:"
00444                     TO ERROR-RECORD
00445               PERFORM E1-PRINT-RECORD-IN-ERROR.
00446

00447        E3-VERIFY-CHECK-DIGIT.
00448        ********************************************************************
00449        ***   IS THE CHECK DIGIT FOR THE EMPNO FIELD VALUE CORRECT?   THE   *
00450        ***   CHECK DIGIT IS CALCULATED USING THE MODULUS-11 TECHNIQUE.     *
00451        ********************************************************************
00452

00453           MOVE TOKEN (2) TO EMPLOYEE-NUMBER-DIGITS.
```

Program 2-Source (Continued)

```
00454              COMPUTE WEIGHTED-SUM-OF-DIGITS
00455                              EMPNO-DIGITS (5) * 2 +
00456                              EMPNO-DIGITS (4) * 3 +
00457                              EMPNO-DIGITS (3) * 4 +
00458                              EMPNO-DIGITS (2) * 5 +
00459                              EMPNO-DIGITS (1) * 6.
00460
00461         COMPUTE QUOTIENT = WEIGHTED-SUM-OF-DIGITS / 11.
00462
00463         COMPUTE REMAINDER-UPON-DIVISION =
00464                      WEIGHTED-SUM-OF-DIGITS - 11 * QUOTIENT.
00465
00466         IF REMAINDER-UPON-DIVISION IS EQUAL TO 0
00467              MOVE REMAINDER-UPON-DIVISION TO CHECK-DIGIT
00468         ELSE
00469              COMPUTE CHECK-DIGIT = 11 - REMAINDER-UPON-DIVISION.
00470
00471         IF CHECK-DIGIT NOT EQUAL TO EMPNO-DIGITS (6)
00472              MOVE "YES" TO THERE-ARE-ERRORS.
00473
00474      E4-FURTHER-CHECKS-OF-START-DT.
00475     ***************************************************************
00476     ***   ARE BOTH START MONTH AND START YEAR FIELD VALUES NUMERIC?   *
00477     ***   IS START MONTH IN THE RANGE OF 01 - 12?  IS START YEAR IN   *
00478     ***   THE RANGE OF 60 - 87?                                       *
00479     ***************************************************************
00480
00481         UNSTRING TOKEN (7)
00482              DELIMITED BY "/" OR " "
00483           INTO NONNUM-START-MONTH
00484              NONNUM-START-YEAR.
00485
00486         INSPECT NONNUM-START-MONTH
00487              REPLACING ALL " " BY "0".
00488         INSPECT NONNUM-START-YEAR
00489              REPLACING ALL " " BY "0".
00490
00491     MOVE NONNUM-START-MONTH TO ABBR-NONNUM-START-MONTH.
00492     MOVE NONNUM-START-YEAR  TO ABBR-NONNUM-START-YEAR.
00493
00494     MOVE NONNUM-START-MONTH TO START-MONTH.
00495     MOVE NONNUM-START-YEAR  TO START-YEAR.
00496
00497     IF START-MONTH IS NOT NUMERIC OR START-YEAR IS NOT NUMERIC
00498              MOVE "YES" TO THERE-ARE-ERRORS.
00499
00500     IF NO-ERRORS
00501              MOVE ABBR-NONNUM-START-MONTH TO ABBR-START-MONTH
00502              MOVE ABBR-NONNUM-START-YEAR  TO ABBR-START-YEAR
00503              IF ABBR-START-MONTH LESS THAN 1 OR GREATER THAN 12
00504                   OR
00505                 ABBR-START-YEAR LESS THAN 60 OR GREATER THAN 87
00506                      MOVE "YES" TO THERE-ARE-ERRORS.
00507
```

Program 2-Source (Continued)

```
00508          IF NOT NO-ERRORS
00509                MOVE "ERROR IN START DATE OF RECORD:"
00510                     TO ERROR-RECORD
00511                PERFORM E1-PRINT-RECORD-IN-ERROR.
00512
00513    E5-FURTHER-CHECKS-OF-SALARY.
00514    ********************************************************************
00515    ***   ARE BOTH PARTS OF THE SALARY FIELD VALUE NUMERIC?  IS SALARY*
00516    ***   IN THE CORRECT RANGE, I.E., 20,000 - 80,000?               *
00517    ********************************************************************
00518
00519          UNSTRING TOKEN (6)
00520                DELIMITED BY "," OR " "
00521             INTO NONNUM-SALARY-PART1
00522                NONNUM-SALARY-PART2.
00523
00524          MOVE NONNUM-SALARY-PART1 TO ABBR-NONNUM-SALARY-PART1.
00525          MOVE NONNUM-SALARY-PART2 TO ABBR-NONNUM-SALARY-PART2.
00526
00527          INSPECT NONNUM-SALARY-PART1
00528                REPLACING ALL " " BY "0".
00529          INSPECT NONNUM-SALARY-PART2
00530                REPLACING ALL " " BY "0".
00531
00532          MOVE NONNUM-SALARY-PART1 TO SALARY-PART1.
00533          MOVE NONNUM-SALARY-PART2 TO SALARY-PART2.
00534
00535          IF SALARY-PART1 IS NOT NUMERIC
00536                     OR
00537             SALARY-PART2 IS NOT NUMERIC
00538                MOVE "YES" TO THERE-ARE-ERRORS
00539                MOVE "ERROR IN SALARY FIELD OF RECORD:"
00540                     TO ERROR-RECORD
00541                PERFORM E1-PRINT-RECORD-IN-ERROR.
00542
00543          IF NO-ERRORS
00544                MOVE ABBR-NONNUM-SALARY-PART1 TO SALARY-PART1
00545                MOVE ABBR-NONNUM-SALARY-PART2 TO SALARY-PART2
00546                COMPUTE SALARY = SALARY-PART1 * 1000 + SALARY-PART2
00547                IF SALARY LESS THAN 20000 OR GREATER THAN 80000
00548                     MOVE "YES" TO THERE-ARE-ERRORS
00549                     MOVE "ERROR IN SALARY VALUE IN RECORD:"
00550                          TO ERROR-RECORD
00551                     PERFORM E1-PRINT-RECORD-IN-ERROR.
```

Program 2-Source (Continued)

```
                                  COLUMNS
    1    5    10   15   20   25   30   35   40   45   50   55   60   65   70
    ----|----|----|----|----|----|----|----|----|----|----|----|----|----|--
```

```
INCORRECT NUMBER OF FIELDS IN RECORD:
514 67-4542   123218   MORRISON WILLIAM        ACC  43,265  02/72

ERROR IN PART THREE OF SSNO IN RECORD:
338-67-878A   234559   WAYNE WILLIS            DPR  34,700  11/79

ERROR IN EMPLOYEE NUMBER IN RECORD:
412-45-4566   246771   KILDARE WAYNE           SLS  37,890  03/79

ERROR IN EMPLOYEE NAME OF RECORD:
303-77-9832   249009   6OWSON DAVID            DPR  75,790  08/68

ERROR IN DEPARTMENT CODE OF RECORD:
511-56-4341   268003   JASON TERRY             FIC  32,500  04/86

ERROR IN SALARY VALUE IN RECORD:
277-56-5678   300330   PETERS DAVID            FIN  86,000  03/83

ERROR IN START DATE OF RECORD:
511-44-8899   370789   MASON ELLEN             DPR  40,000  01/40
```

Program 2-Output(a) Error File Produced by Program 2

```
                                  COLUMNS
    1    5    10   15   20   25   30   35   40   45   50   55   60   65   70
    ----|----|----|----|----|----|----|----|----|----|----|----|----|----|--
```

```
334121126   124451   EASTMAN THOMAS            ACC  50000  8010
411227127   245003   JEFFERSON JOHN            DPR  27900  8510
213233342   248908   CROSETTE CARLOS           SLS  47000  7807
452678989   267902   PEAR JANE                 ACC  66800  8012
443600900   280097   DIONNE WILLIAM            DPR  37780  8101
444551232   350885   TEAL JASON                ACC  43900  7710
512788787   390879   PAULSON TERENCE           FIN  55000  8001
```

Program 2-Output(b) Output File Produced by Program 2

P A R T

IV

File Processing in COBOL

10

Fundamental File Concepts

Introduction

So far we have concentrated on the elements of the COBOL language and programming, the principles and techniques of developing high-quality application software, and the essentials of data structure design. We have acquired an impressive COBOL background. We are capable of writing sophisticated application programs using software engineering techniques and data structures; however, we have more to learn. At this point, we will begin a study of file processing, one of COBOL's main strengths.

Since the beginning of our study we have been exposed to some elementary concepts of files and their applications because a majority of input and output in COBOL is file oriented. We have used one particular file organization technique, sequential files, throughout the programs developed in this book. But there are much more to files than these elementary applications. In this chapter we will formalize and advance our knowledge of files and file storage devices. We will study the fundamental terminology of file processing, logical and physical files, file storage devices, and operations on files. We will not do any COBOL programming, but we will more than compensate for it in the rest of the book. In Chapter 11 we will add to our knowledge of sequential files, and study them within the context of some advanced applications. In subsequent chapters we will take up file sorting and merging, indexed sequential files, direct-access files, and other file organization and access techniques. The last two chapters concentrate on file design techniques and a brief introduction to data base management systems, a natural follow-up for this course of study. In summary, files will be with us for the rest of the book.

The file concepts and file processing techniques that we have studied so far are generally simple and easy to understand. This simplicity is reflected in the corresponding COBOL language elements. The file processing techniques that are presented after this point are more advanced and can be confusing, and even students who are quite comfortable with the previous material often have substantial difficulty understanding them. This is why we will temporarily depart from COBOL in this chapter and focus our attention on the fundamental file concepts and operations.

We have seen that a **file** is a collection of structured and permanently recorded data. Computer files that are stored on mass storage devices are extremely important in data processing and data base applications. There are several reasons for this.

1. Computer files store data permanently.
2. They are inexpensive storage facilities.
3. They facilitate sharing of data by many applications.
4. They can be used to represent data relationships as well as data values.

In data processing we deal with large volumes of data that make up the computerized corporate data resource. Data resource should be recorded and maintained in permanent storage. This requirement suggests a tape or disk storage device, rather than the computer's main memory, which is a volatile storage medium. As permanence is one of their main characteristics, files are ideal for storing the corporate data resource.

The data resource is large, so it is imperative that the storage medium for it be of high capacity and inexpensive. These considerations also indicate files that are kept on tape or disk storage devices.

Data defined and created in the computer's main memory by a program belong to that program and can be accessed only by that program. Data stored on external storage in files, however, can be shared by several programs simultaneously.

Finally, the corporate data should reflect not only data values, but also data relationships. This can be achieved by organizing data into files.

The permanence of data in files is a function of the storage medium and therefore is physical. Structuring data in a file is a matter of design, and thus is abstract or logical. To understand files, we must be familiar with their physical aspects, including properties of storage media and devices. We must also be acquainted with the principles of data structuring. In this chapter we will study both logical and physical aspects of files.

Logical Data Organization

In an information system we store and maintain data. To facilitate storage, maintenance, and processing, we should structure data before storing them. From a user's point of view, data structuring and management are abstractions. This point of view is called **logical data organization**. In logical data organization, the user need not be, in fact should not be, concerned with issues related to the actual storage of data; that is, issues that pertain to **physical data organization**.

There are three phases in logical data organization:

1. Record organization
2. File organization
3. Data base organization

In this section we will discuss the first two phases and related concepts. The discussion of data base organization is deferred to Chapter 18.

Record Organization

We know that a record consists of data items and group items. For example, the record structure description in COBOL for EMPLOYEE-RECORD

```
01   EMPLOYEE-RECORD.
     05   EMPLOYEE-IDNO        PICTURE 999.
     05   EMPLOYEE-NAME        PICTURE X(30).
     05   DATE-OF-BIRTH        PICTURE X(8).
```

contains the data items EMPLOYEE-IDNO, EMPLOYEE-NAME, and DATE-OF-BIRTH. These are some of the properties of employees. An employee is an entity. Properties of employees such as these data items are attributes.

> An **entity** is an element of a set of similar but distinguishable beings, objects, or things.

Our universe is full of entities about which we wish to collect and store data in information systems. For example, each employee working for the same company is an entity, as is each inventory item in a warehouse. These are physical entities. Human emotions and schools of thought in philosophy are abstract entities.

Entities of the same type form **entity sets**. All employees working for a company form an employee entity set. All human emotions constitute the entity set of human emotions.

> All entities have properties that can be used to describe them or distinguish them from similar entities. These properties are known as **attributes**. Values for attributes are obtained through either measurement or observation.

For the EMPLOYEES entity set, EMPLOYEE-IDNO, EMPLOYEE-NAME, and DATE-OF-BIRTH are attributes. An entity set may have many attributes. We select only those that are relevant to our applications and store them in our information system.

In addition to entities, we are interested in recording and processing information about relationships that exist among them. Let us consider the following COBOL description for EMPLOYEE-JOB-DESCRIPTION-RECORD.

```
01   EMPLOYEE-JOB-DESCRIPTION-RECORD.
     05   EMPLOYEE-IDNO        PICTURE 999.
     05   DEPARTMENT-CODE      PICTURE XXX.
     05   SALARY               PICTURE 9(6)V99.
```

Here we have three attributes. EMPLOYEE-IDNO is an attribute of the employee entity set. DEPARTMENT-CODE is an attribute of another entity set, the departments in a company. The attribute SALARY does not belong to either one of these two entity sets. It is a property of a relationship defined between the entity sets of employees and departments. In other words, SALARY does not exist unless a person is employed in a department of the company. Therefore, it is an attribute that qualifies this relationship between an employee and a department.

A **relationship** is a specification that associates two or more entity sets.

A collection of similar relationships constitutes a **relationship set**. All specifications describing employees, the departments in which they work, and their salaries form a relationship set.

We assign unique names to entity and relationship sets to distinguish them from others. We use the name EMPLOYEE for the set of people working for our company. We use the name EMPLOYEE-JOB-DESCRIPTION for the set describing employees by their EMPLOYEE-IDNO, the department in which they work, and their salaries. For both EMPLOYEE and EMPLOYEE-JOB-DESCRIPTION we have already defined a structure. This is a record structure.

A **record** is a named and structured collection of attributes all belonging to a specific entity or relationship set.

A record structure represents relative locations of attributes within the set of attributes for an entity or relationship set. It can be represented in a variety of ways. We have already seen how it can be defined in COBOL. We can also use diagrams to represent it. For example, the EMPLOYEE-RECORD can be represented pictorially.

```
EMPLOYEE-RECORD

  EMPLOYEE-IDNO    EMPLOYEE-NAME    DATE-OF-BIRTH
```

Record structure organization is the first phase in data organization. Once we determine what attributes are needed for an entity or relationship, we can easily combine them into what is basically a linear structure. It really does not matter in what order we combine them. We could have defined the EMPLOYEE-RECORD as

```
EMPLOYEE-RECORD

  EMPLOYEE-NAME    DATE-OF-BIRTH    EMPLOYEE-IDNO
```

without losing anything.

From this point of view, record structure organization appears to be an easy problem. However, combining attributes into record structures without considering data semantics leads to files that are quite difficult to maintain. We will study the effect of data semantics on record structure design in Chapter 17.

File Organization

Now that we have a record structure for the entity set EMPLOYEE, we can use it as a template. We fill this template with appropriate data values to specify one of its members. For employee William F. Morrison, with an identification number of 100 and a date of birth of 10/03/54, we get:

```
EMPLOYEE—RECORD

  EMPLOYEE—IDNO      EMPLOYEE—NAME        DATE—OF—BIRTH


         100       MORRISON WILLIAM F     10/03/54
```

For each member of an entity or relationship set for which a record structure is defined, there is one occurrence of that structure.

> A **record occurrence** is an ordered collection of attribute values that conforms to a record structure and describes a member of an entity or a relationship set.

A record occurrence can also be referred to as a record. Our company has many employees, for each of whom we must create and store a record. If we consider them all, we end up with a file. Figure 1 shows an EMPLOYEE-FILE with six records. The question is how to structure several occurrences of a record in a file so that we can access them efficiently. At that point we come to the second phase of data organization, file organization. First, let us give a definition for files in terms of some concepts we have introduced so far.

> A **file** is a named and structured collection of records, each representing a member of an entity or a relationship set.

The EMPLOYEE-FILE of Figure 1 corresponds to an entity set. Its records describe the members of the entity set EMPLOYEE. Figure 2 shows another example file called EMPLOYEE-JOB-DESCRIPTION-FILE. It describes the attributes of a relationship set between employees and the departments in which they work.

In Figure 1, several occurrences of the EMPLOYEE-RECORD are collected in the EMPLOYEE-FILE. They are not put into the file in a haphazard fashion, but must be organized to reflect a relationship existing among the records. The relationship may be physical or logical, depending on the needs of our application. For example, it may suit our application to use a physical relationship in which we place the record for employee 150 immediately next to the record for employee 100. On the other hand, it may be more convenient to use a logical relationship. The relative location of a record in the file may tell us something about a real-world relationship among the entity members, such as one employee being superordinate to another within the organizational hierarchy.

EMPLOYEE-RECORD

EMPLOYEE IDNO	EMPLOYEE NAME	DATE-OF-BIRTH

Record structure

Attributes

EMPLOYEE-FILE

100	MORRISON WILLIAM F	10/03/54
150	EASTMAN THOMAS	12/23/55
170	WAYNE WILLIS	03/21/60
180	JEFFERSON JOHN D	11/20/50
186	KILDARE WAYNE	08/08/40
189	CROSETTE CARLOS J	04/18/57

Records

Attribute values

Figure 1 An Example File for an Entity Set

Organizing records in a file to describe relationships between records is known as **file organization**.

To organize records in a file, we should have a means of identifying each record in it. This can be done in physical or logical terms. Physical record identification is possible by the address of the memory location where a record is stored. Logical record identification is based on some attribute values that are

EMPLOYEE-JOB-DESCRIPTION-RECORD

EMPLOYEE IDNO	DEPARTMENT-CODE	SALARY

EMPLOYEE-JOB-DESCRIPTION-FILE

100	ACC	03277000
150	ACC	04530000
170	DP	02760000
180	DP	03530000
186	SLS	03600000
189	SLS	04470000

Figure 2 An Example File for a Relationship Set

part of a record. Attributes that can be used to identify records are called entity identifiers. Another term for them is keys.

> An **entity identifier** (or **key**) for a record structure is the set of one or more attributes that uniquely identifies a record.

For the EMPLOYEE-FILE, the attribute EMPLOYEE-IDNO serves as the entity identifier for the record structure. As we will see later, entity identifiers play an important role in file organization.

Many business applications depend on more than one file as their data resource. Although a file may appear as an independent abstraction, several relationships among separate ones may exist. Figure 3 shows a relationship between the EMPLOYEE-FILE and EMPLOYEE-JOB-DESCRIPTION-FILE. Here, the relationship consists of the fact that for each record in the EMPLOYEE-FILE, there is a corresponding record in the EMPLOYEE-JOB-DESCRIPTION-FILE. One may also say that the EMPLOYEE-JOB-DESCRIPTION-FILE

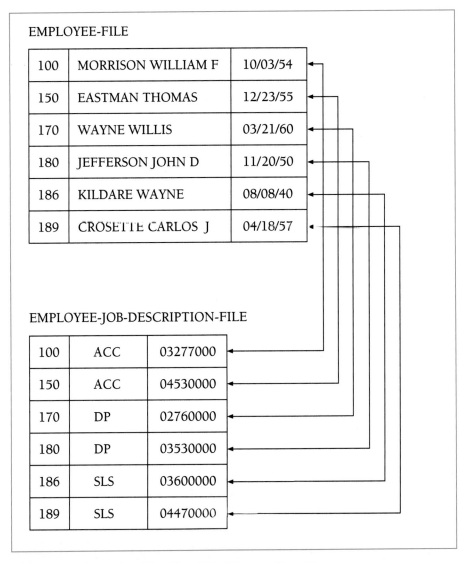

Figure 3 An Example of Relationships Between Two Files

itself constitutes a relationship set between the EMPLOYEE-FILE and a DEPARTMENT-FILE, as shown in Figure 4. We previously mentioned that the EMPLOYEE-JOB-DESCRIPTION-FILE is a representation for the relationship between the employee and department entity sets. Figure 4 indicates that every department in the DEPARTMENT-FILE has one or more employees working for it. In fact, this is the real-world relationship "works-for." Implicit in such relationships is some valuable information that we would like to store in our data resource. To do this, we must structure data files into an integrated collection called a data base.

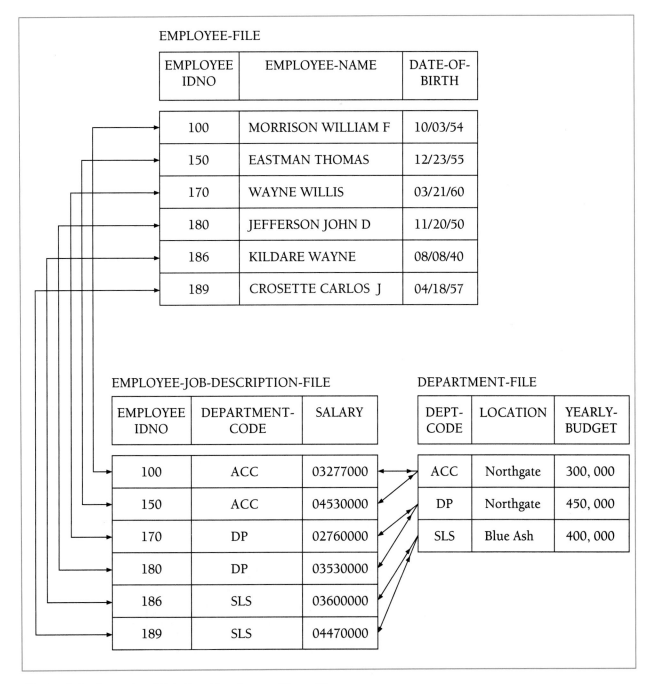

Figure 4 An Example of Relationships Among Three Files

> A **data base** is a named and structured collection of files representing all files pertinent to one or more applications, and all relationships that exist among them.

Organizing related files into a data base is the third and last phase of the process of data organization. Data base organization is outside the scope of this book; however, we will make an introduction to data base management in Chapter 18.

Let us give another and somewhat different definition for file organization.

> **File organization** is the manner in which records are arranged relative to one another to define one or more relationships existing among them.

Notice how close this definition is to that of a data structure, as given in Chapter 4. In fact, a file structure is a type of data structure. In files, however, data elements are records, and in physical files they are stored in a mass storage device rather than in the main memory. As a result of this consideration, we can conclude that there are as many different file organization techniques as there are different data structures. We refer to the collection of all possible file structures as **logical file organization techniques**. Logically, a file can be described as a sequentially allocated list, a linked list, a tree structure, or any one of the many possible data structures mentioned in Chapter 4. Therefore, representing a particular interrecord relationship in a logical file is a matter of selecting the right data structure for it.

Figures 5 through 7 show the logical file EMPLOYEE of Figure 1 structured in a variety of ways. In Figure 5 it is organized as a linked list based on EMPLOYEE-IDNO. In Figure 6 it is a linked list based on EMPLOYEE-NAME.

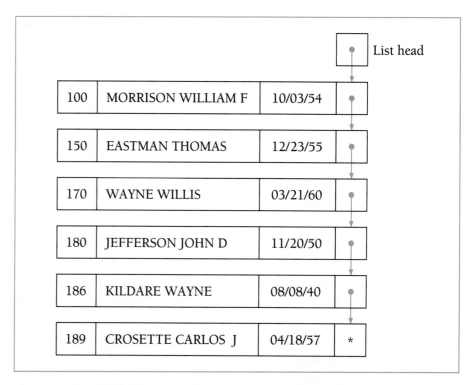

Figure 5 EMPLOYEE-FILE as a Linked List Based on EMPLOYEE-IDNO

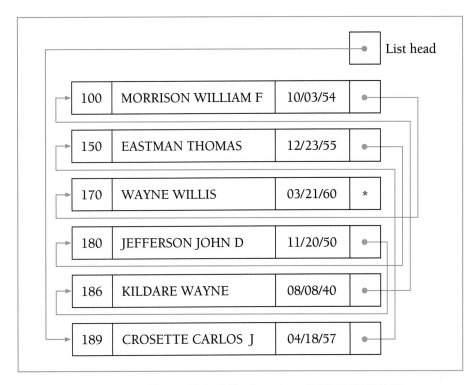

Figure 6 EMPLOYEE-FILE as a Linked List Based on EMPLOYEE-NAME

Finally, in Figure 7 it is a tree structure reflecting a partial organization chart. Figures 5 and 6 are file structures depicting linear order relationships among EMPLOYEE file records based on EMPLOYEE-IDNO and EMPLOYEE-NAME, respectively. Figure 7 represents the elements of the superordinate relationship among the employees. We should note that many other logical file organization techniques exist.

Each logical file structure has its own strong points in practical applications. There are so many possibilities that each computer language supports only a few of the organizations. The ones that are readily recognized by computer languages are known as **built-in file organization techniques**. Sequential and direct file organization techniques are supported by many computer languages. COBOL is richer than most other programming languages because it supports three built-in file organization techniques: sequential, direct (also known as random or relative organization), and indexed sequential.

An issue that is closely related to file organization is file access.

File access is the manner in which records in a file can be accessed and retrieved.

File access depends on two factors: file organization and characteristics of storage device used. In general, records are stored consecutively. In Figure 1, the record for employee 150 is stored immediately after the record for employee 100, and so on. Hence, the records can be accessed one after another. For the EMPLOYEE-FILE in Figure 1, after we access the record for employee 100 using a READ statement, the next READ statement execution will access the record for employee 150. This is known as **sequential-access mode**. It is used

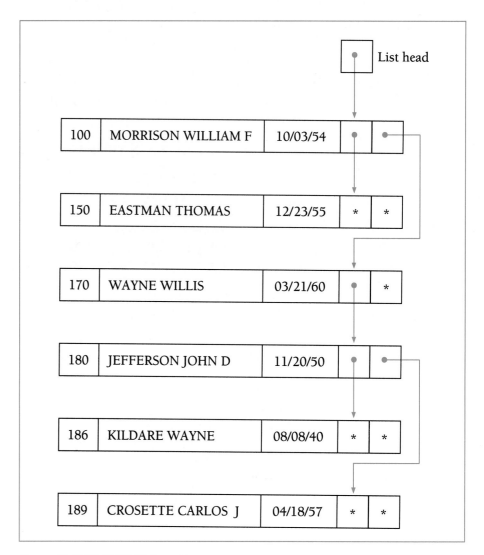

Figure 7 EMPLOYEE-FILE as a Tree

for files stored on sequential-access devices such as tapes, as well as those stored on direct-access devices, such as disks. The EMPLOYEE-FILE of Figure 6 is organized as a linked list based on EMPLOYEE-NAME. As before, its records are arranged consecutively. Therefore, sequential access to records is possible.

In addition, for the EMPLOYEE-FILE of Figure 6, provided we use the pointers in the linked list and the file storage device permits direct access, direct access from one record to another in increasing order of EMPLOYEE-NAME is also possible. This is called **direct access** or **random access**. While processing the EMPLOYEE-FILE of Figure 6, if we execute a READ statement to access the record for employee 100, the next direct-access READ statement will access the record for employee 170.

In conclusion, any file, no matter how it is organized and where it is stored, can be accessed sequentially. Only properly organized files stored on direct access devices can be accessed directly, however.

COBOL permits sequential access for sequential, relative, and indexed sequential files. Random access is allowed only for relative and indexed COBOL files.

1. The user's viewpoint of data organization is _____ data organization, whereas issues related to the actual storage of data pertain to _____ data organization.
2. The three phases of data organization are _____ , _____ , and _____ .
3. An _____ is an element of a set of similar but distinguishable beings, objects, or things.
4. A relationship set is a set of specifications that associate two or more entity sets. (T or F)
5. A record may describe attributes belonging to an entity or a relationship set. (T or F)
6. Which of the following statements about files is incorrect?
   a. A file is a form of data structure.
   b. Organizing records in a file to describe relationships among records is known as file organization.
   c. A file may correspond to an entity set.
   d. Files do not describe relationship sets existing between entity sets.
7. File organization techniques recognized by computer languages are called _____ .
8. File access is the manner in which records in a file can be accessed and retrieved. (T or F)

Answers: 1. logical, physical; 2. record, file, data base; 3. entity; 4. T; 5. T; 6. d; 7. built-in; 8. T.

Fundamental Operations on Files

In its lifetime, a file is subjected to a number of operations. For a single file considered in isolation, these operations range from its initial definition and creation to those required to maintain it in a usable form. All of these fundamental operations can be done either by writing and running application programs, or by using special programs, called utility programs, that are supplied by computer software vendors.

For a single file, the fundamental operations can be categorized as follows:

1. Definition and creation
2. Access and retrieval
3. Maintenance
4. Copying
5. Sorting
6. Indexing

Also, two operations are performed on files in a file system: merging and joining. A file system is two or more logically related files, as in a data base.

File Definition and Creation

The first operation that we have to do for a file is to define and create it. The former requires defining record structures, a file organization method, and the access modes in an application program. The latter entails loading the file with records.

To define a file completely, we should do the following.

1. Define record structure.
   a. Assign a name to the record.
   b. Specify record structure in terms of fields by field name, type, and length for each field.
   c. Specify information pertaining to physical record formatting.
   d. Specify one or more attributes in the record structure as the organization key, if the file organization and access require them.
2. Define file characteristics.
   a. Assign a name to it.
   b. Specify an organization technique.
   c. Specify access modes consistent with the organization.
3. Associate the file with a mass storage device, or a physical file on a mass storage device.
4. Specify additional options such as file directory parameters.

In Chapter 2 we saw how we could do most of these in COBOL. If a file is defined in an application program, the complete definition is compiled together with the rest of the code in the program and stored in the computer's memory for use at run-time. If we use the same file in more than one application program, we must repeat its definition in each program.

In data base management, a file is defined using a special data base language. This definition is compiled and the object code corresponding to it is stored in a system catalog. Whenever this file is referenced, the existing object code for it will be executed, thus ensuring that a consistent definition for the file is always available for the system, and that physical and logical files can be associated correctly.

Once we have defined a file, we may load records into it. This is an operation. Any file operation requires input or output, or both. Before we can read or write into a file, we must open it. This readies it for input or output. Therefore, while opening a file we must specify a file open mode. In general, the file open mode can be input, output, or input-output. The file open mode of input means that the file will be used for reading. Output implies that it will be used for writing records into it. If input-output mode is used, the programmer may read the file or write into it as desired.

In file loading we write records into the file. To write into a file, it should be opened in output mode. If the load operation is carried out by a program, for each record the record structure template for the file should be properly filled with values. After this an output statement should be issued to write the current content of the record structure into the file.

Data base systems have special instructions for loading files that implicitly open the files in output mode. The file definition is fetched automatically from the system catalogs and used while loading the file with user-supplied records.

Record Access and Retrieval

Once a file is created, in every application program that uses it we are concerned with accessing and retrieving its records. The words access and retrieval are closely related, but they are not synonymous.

> **Record access** is the operation of locating the storage segment in which a desired record resides. **Record retrieval** is the operation of bringing a copy of the located record into the main memory for processing.

Earlier we saw that access is closely related to organization and the type of mass storage device used for the file. Retrieval, on the other hand, is a matter of data transfer rate of the storage device. Data transfer rate is the number of bytes that can be transferred from a mass storage device to a location in the computer's main memory in one second.

Accessing and subsequently retrieving a record are referred to as **fetching a record**. Three kinds of fetch operations are generally considered significant in determining the efficiency of a file system: fetching a specified record, fetching the next record, and fetching all records in a file.

Fetching a specified record is the most general access and retrieval operation. To do this, we must supply the file management system with either an address or an attribute value pointing to a particular record. For direct-access files, if an attribute value is supplied, an index table or a computational procedure is required to obtain the address of the storage location that contains the record. The index table is searched to get the address; it may be an absolute or a relative address. If it is a relative address, the computer system goes through another conversion process to transform the relative address to its corresponding absolute address. Ultimately, it is the absolute address that is necessary to access a storage location.

If the file is sequentially organized, an index table or a transformation function cannot be used. In this case, the entire file should be searched to locate and retrieve the desired record.

In Figure 8 we have an instance of the EMPLOYEE-JOB-DESCRIPTION-FILE. Its records are stored in memory locations with relative addresses 1 through 6. Figure 9a illustrates the result of fetching a record by its relative location in this file. Here, the fourth record is located and retrieved by making a copy in a main memory location.

After a specified record is located, fetching the next record is generally an efficient operation. Of course, this depends on what is meant by "next." If the next or successor record is physically close to the current record location, fetching it can be accomplished rapidly. All it takes is a sequential read statement. If the successor record is linked to the current record by a pointer in the latter, fetching it takes roughly the same amount of time as fetching an arbitrary record in a direct-access file. Therefore, in addition to device characteristics, file organization technique, and the file access mode, the efficiency of fetching the next record is a function of the location of the related records in

EMPLOYEE-JOB-DESCRIPTION-FILE			
	EMPLOYEE IDNO	DEPARTMENT-CODE	SALARY
1	100	ACC	32,770
2	150	ACC	45,300
3	170	DP	27,600
4	180	DP	35,300
5	186	SLS	36,000
6	189	SLS	44,700

Figure 8 An Instance of EMPLOYEE-JOB-DESCRIPTION-FILE

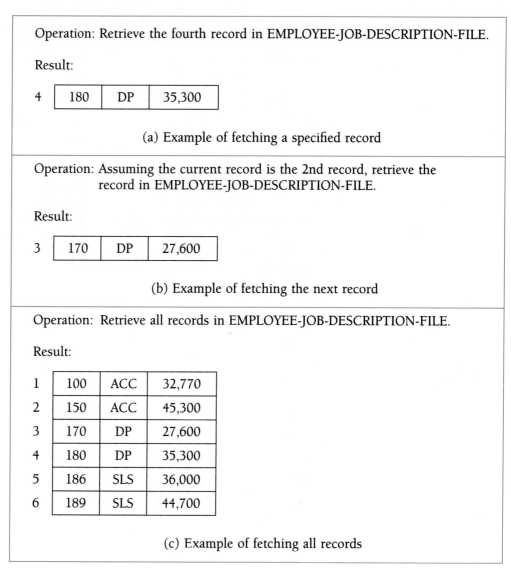

Figure 9 Record Access and Retrieval

the storage. Figure 9b illustrates fetching next record on the EMPLOYEE-JOB-DESCRIPTION-FILE.

Certain applications require fetching all records in a file. The order in which successive records are fetched may parallel the physical placement of the records in the memory. In this case, a sequentially organized file is no worse than a direct-access file, and the overall performance is largely dependent on the storage device characteristics. If the order of retrieval necessitates random jumps to different segments of the mass storage, direct-access capability is needed, and the performance of the system is affected by the manner in which the file is structured. Fetching all records is also known as exhaustive retrieval. Figure 9c exemplifies this operation.

File Maintenance

Files correspond to entities or relationships in the real world. The contents of entity and relationship sets change over time. New employees may be hired, some old employees may leave the company, an employee in the Sales Department may be transferred to the Data Processing Department. Such changes affect the contents of corresponding files in our information system. Operations that modify the contents of files are known as file maintenance operations, or **file update operations**. The three types of file maintenance operations are record update, record insertion, and record deletion.

Record Update. When one or more field values in a specific record have to be altered, we go through three basic steps.

1. Access and retrieve a specified record, bringing it into the main memory and storing it in the file record structure.
2. Make necessary changes in the contents of the fields to be updated.
3. Write the modified record into the same record location in the file.

Obviously, record access and retrieval play an important role in this operation. For record update, to permit reading and writing in a program without the necessity of closing and opening a file, the file must be opened in input-output mode.

Record Insertion. In record insertion our purpose is to insert a new record into an existing file. The logic for this operation is essentially similar to that for initial file loading, except that the file that we are about to expand is not empty. First, there is the question of where to insert the new record in the file. Insertions that are to be made after the last record in the file are known as **appending**. Some versions of the COBOL compiler allow expansion of sequential disk files through a file open mode called EXTEND. In general, however, the number of records that can be stored in a file is determined during file creation and cannot be changed later on.

If a new record is to be inserted after a certain record in a file, it becomes necessary to locate the latter before insertion can be made. This requires record access and retrieval. The file is searched until the point of insertion is found. A storage location is secured for the new record and it is inserted. For example, suppose we wish to insert a record for employee 175 into the EMPLOYEE-JOB-DESCRIPTION-FILE of Figure 8 after the record for employee 170. Employee 175 will be working in the Sales Department with a salary of $30,000. First, we prepare a record for the new employee in the main memory according to the record structure of the file.

EMPLOYEE IDNO	DEPARTMENT-CODE	SALARY
175	SLS	30,000

Now we initiate a search of the file. We read one record at a time until we encounter the record for employee 170. Since it is the third record, the new record is written into the file as the fourth. This insertion process forces all records after the third record in the original file to be moved down by one record length.

Record Deletion. To delete a record we must first locate it. It may be specified by its relative sequence number in the file, as in "delete the fifth record." Alternatively, it may be identified by the content of some of its fields. In Figure 8 we may want to delete the record for employee 180. As in record update, the first step is to access and retrieve the record to be deleted. After the record has been retrieved, how it is deleted depends on the storage device characteristics. We discuss them below.

File Maintenance Strategies

The two commonly used strategies for file update are traditional update through copying and in situ update. Both strategies contain three functional files: old master, transaction, and new master files.

The **old master file** is the one to be updated before updates take place. The **transaction file** contains the new records to be inserted and updated, and identifies the records to be deleted. After the file update, a new file is created. This is the **new master file**. It stores all records in the old master file and reflects all changes included in the transaction file.

Traditional File Update. In this strategy, the records in the old master file are sorted with respect to the key attributes. The transaction file contains records that are structurally similar to those in the old master file, with one difference. We should include in its structure a data field that can be used to differentiate among transactions of delete, insert, and update type. If the record structure of the old master file is

EMPLOYEE IDNO	DEPARTMENT– CODE	SALARY

the record structure of the transaction file would be:

EMPLOYEE IDNO	TRANS– CODE	DEPARTMENT– CODE	SALARY

Here, the field TRANS-CODE is used to specify records to be updated, inserted, and deleted. We collect all transactions in the transaction file and sort its records in the same order and with respect to the same attribute as in the old master file.

The logic of the traditional file update strategy differs slightly depending on the nature of the transaction. We will consider record update, insertion, and deletion separately.

For record update, the logic of the strategy consists of the following steps.

Step 1:　Open the old master file and the transaction file in input mode, and the new master file in output mode.
Step 2:　Read a transaction record.
Step 3:　Read an old master record.

Step 4: Compare the key of the master record with that of the transaction record.

    Step 4.1: If the key of the master record is less than that of the transaction record, write the master record in the main memory into the new master file. Then go to step 3 to read the next record from the old master file.

    Step 4.2: If the key of the master record is greater than that of the transaction record, conclude that the transaction is for a master record that does not exist in the file. Produce a message stating that the transaction is in error. Read the next transaction record and go to step 4.

    Step 4.3: If the key of the master record matches that of the transaction record, move the fields in the transaction record to the corresponding fields in the master record. Write the master record into the new master file and go to step 2.

Step 5: If at any time during processing no more records remain in the transaction file, copy the rest of the records in the old master file into the new master file, reading and writing them one at a time.

If the transaction type is delete, steps 1, 2, 3, and 5 remain unchanged. The fourth step in the traditional file update algorithm becomes

Step 4: Compare the key of the transaction record with that of the old master record.

    Step 4.1: If the key of the old master record is less than that of the transaction record, write the master record in the main memory into the new master file. Then go to step 3 to read the next record from the old master file.

    Step 4.2: If the key of master record is greater than that of the transaction record, conclude that the transaction is for a master record that does not exist in the file. Produce a message stating that the transaction is in error. Read the next transaction record and go to step 4.

    Step 4.3: If the key of the master record matches that of the transaction record, read another old master record and go to step 4.

For record insertion, the first three steps of the algorithm are the same as above. To find the point of insertion, however, we have to keep in the main memory two old master records at the same time. One of them can be kept in the old master file record structure. For the other, we must specify a buffer area. A **buffer**, in this context, is a part of the main memory reserved for a record. In COBOL programming it is a WORKING-STORAGE SECTION structure, compatible with the record structure for a file.

The record insertion logic after step 3 is as follows.

Step 4: Move the old master record in the memory into the old master record buffer and read the next master record. Now the main memory contains two master records. If there are no more records in the old master file, store a dummy record in the old master record. The key value of the dummy record should be larger than the key value of any transaction record in the transaction file.

Step 5:   Compare the key of the transaction record with the keys of the two old master records in the memory.

    Step 5.1:   If the key of the old master record in the buffer is greater than that of the transaction record, move the transaction record into the new master record and write it. Read the next transaction record. Go to step 4.

    Step 5.2:   If the key of the transaction record is greater than that of the master record in the buffer and less than the key of the old master record, write the master record in the buffer into the new master file, provided it is not a dummy record. Then transfer the elements of the transaction record into the respective fields in the record structure of the new master file, and write this new record into the new master file. Read another transaction record. Go to step 4.

    Step 5.3:   If the key of the transaction record is greater than the keys of both the master record in the buffer and the master record in the I-O area, write the master record in the buffer into the new master file and go to step 4.

    Step 5.4:   If the key of the master record in the buffer matches that of the transaction record, generate an error message informing the user that the transaction record cannot be inserted. Read a new transaction record. Go to step 5.

Step 6:   If there are no more records in the transaction file, copy the rest of the records in the old master file into the new master file.

The algorithms for record update, deletion, and insertion can be combined into a single application program, as shown in Figure 10. Here, both the old master file and the transaction file are sorted in increasing order of EMPLOYEE-IDNO. The new master file is similarly ordered. The steps involved in applying the strategy to the master and transaction files of Figure 10 are shown in the trace table of Figure 11.

For the traditional file update strategy, we should note the following.

1. Three files are involved in this strategy: an old master file, a transaction file, and a new master file.
2. The old master file and the transaction file are the inputs for the algorithm. The new master file is its output.
3. All files are sequentially organized and sequentially accessed. They may be either tape or disk files. Even if they are disk files, the algorithm does not take advantage of the medium's direct-access capability.
4. The old master and transaction files are sorted in increasing or decreasing order by a key.
5. If record update operations are restricted to updating values of attributes other than the key attribute, the new master file will also be sorted in the same order as the old master file. Otherwise, the records in it will no longer be in order, and it will have to be sorted before the next file update operation.

In Situ File Update. In the previous strategy, the execution efficiency is negatively affected due to the necessity of copying. Even the records that are not updated are copied from the old master file into the new one. Provided the master file is a disk file, it is possible to avoid unnecessary copying.

For this, we should open the disk master file in input-output mode and read it to retrieve the record to be updated. The record is modified in the main memory and then written into the same storage location as before. This type of

Operation: Change salary value for employee 150 to 50,000.
Change department code for employee 180 to SLS.
Delete employee record for employee 170.
Add a new employee record for employee 175, who will be
working for the Sales Department with a salary of $30,000.

EMPLOYEE-JOB-DESCRIPTION-FILE
(OLD-MASTER-FILE)

	EMPLOYEE IDNO	DEPARTMENT-CODE	SALARY
1	100	ACC	32,770
2	150	ACC	45,300
3	170	DP	27,600
4	180	DP	35,300
5	186	SLS	36,000
6	189	SLS	44,700

TRANSACTION-FILE

	EMPLOYEE IDNO	TRANS-CODE	DEPARTMENT-CODE	SALARY
1	150	UPDATE	ACC	50,000
2	170	DELETE		
3	175	INSERT	SLS	30,000
4	180	UPDATE	SLS	35,300

EMPLOYEE-JOB-DESCRIPTION-FILE
(NEW-MASTER-FILE)

	EMPLOYEE IDNO	DEPARTMENT-CODE	SALARY
1	100	ACC	32,770
2	150	ACC	50,000
3	175	SLS	30,000
4	180	SLS	35,300
5	186	SLS	36,000
6	189	SLS	44,700

Figure 10 An Example of Traditional File Update Through Copying

file output requires a REWRITE statement instead of a WRITE. It writes a modified record into its previous location in the file. Therefore, this record update strategy is known as **in situ update**. As we will see, the REWRITE statement in COBOL can be used for all kinds of built-in file organization techniques.

In addition to record update, it is possible to use in situ update for record deletion. For this we must modify the record structure of the master file and include in it a special delete-flag field. For example, we may create the EMPLOYEE-JOB-DESCRIPTION-FILE with the following record structure.

EMPLOYEE IDNO	DELETE–FLAG	DEPARTMENT–CODE	SALARY

STEP	OPERATION	OLD-MASTER RECORD			OLD-MASTER-BUFFER			TRANSACTION RECORD				NEW-MASTER RECORD		
1	READ TRANSACTION							150	UPDATE	ACC	50,000			
2	READ OLD-MASTER	100	ACC	32,770				150	UPDATE	ACC	50,000			
3	MOVE OLD-MASTER TO NEW-MASTER	100	ACC	32,770				150	UPDATE	ACC	50,000	100	ACC	32,770
4	WRITE NEW-MASTER	100	ACC	32,770				150	UPDATE	ACC	50,000	100	ACC	32,770
5	READ NEW-MASTER	150	ACC	45,300				150	UPDATE	ACC	50,000			
6	MOVE TRANSACTION TO NEW-MASTER	150	ACC	45,300				150	UPDATE	ACC	50,000	150	ACC	50,000
7	WRITE NEW-MASTER	150	ACC	45,300				150	UPDATE	ACC	50,000	150	ACC	50,000
8	READ TRANSACTION	150	ACC	45,300				170	DELETE					
9	READ OLD-MASTER	170	DP	27,600				170	DELETE					
10	READ TRANSACTION	170	DP	27,600				175	INSERT	SLS	30,000			
11	MOVE OLD-MASTER TO OLD-MASTER-BUFFER	170	DP	27,600	170	DP	27,600	175	INSERT	SLS	30,000			
12	READ OLD-MASTER	180	DP	35,300	170	DP	27,600	175	INSERT	SLS	30,000			
13	MOVE TRANSACTION TO NEW-MASTER	180	DP	35,300	170	DP	27,600	175	INSERT	SLS	30,000	175	SLS	30,000
14	WRITE NEW-MASTER	180	DP	35,300	170	DP	27,600	175	INSERT	SLS	30,000	175	SLS	30,000
15	READ TRANSACTION	180	DP	35,300				180	UPDATE	SLS	35,300			
16	MOVE TRANSACTION TO NEW-MASTER	180	DP	35,300				180	UPDATE	SLS	35,300	180	SLS	35,300
17	WRITE NEW-MASTER	180	DP	35,300				180	UPDATE	SLS	35,300	180	SLS	35,300
18	READ TRANSACTION	180	DP	35,300										
19	READ OLD-MASTER	186	SLS	36,000										
20	MOVE OLD-MASTER TO NEW-MASTER	186	SLS	36,000								186	SLS	36,000
21	WRITE NEW-MASTER	186	SLS	36,000								186	SLS	36,000
22	READ OLD-MASTER	189	SLS	44,700										
23	MOVE OLD-MASTER TO NEW-MASTER	189	SLS	44,700								189	SLS	44,700
24	WRITE NEW-MASTER	189	SLS	44,700								189	SLS	44,700

Figure 11 Trace of Traditional File Update Strategy for Files of Figure 10

During file loading we may leave the DELETE-FLAG field empty in every record. Later, to delete a record all we have to do is to locate it and modify the DELETE-FLAG field value by changing it to, say, D. Records with a D in their DELETE-FLAG field are considered to be logically deleted. Physically, they will exist in the file. They may be removed later, during file reorganization.

In situ update can be applied to sequential- or direct-access files. For sequential files, however, this strategy does not readily permit record insertion.

Figure 12 shows an example of in situ file update for the EMPLOYEE-JOB-DESCRIPTION-FILE. Figure 13 is a trace table of the steps involved for the files of Figure 12.

File Copying

In data processing installations, making backup copies of files for data security and recovery purposes is a common operation. A system failure (e.g., disk crash) may result in an irrevocable loss of valuable files.

Operation: Change salary value for employee 150 to 50,000.
Change department code for employee 180 to SLS.
Delete employee record for employee 170.

EMPLOYEE-JOB-DESCRIPTION-FILE

	EMPLOYEE IDNO	DELETE-FLAG	DEPARTMENT-CODE	SALARY
1	100		ACC	32,770
2	150		ACC	45,300
3	170		DP	27,600
4	180		DP	35,300
5	186		SLS	36,000
6	189		SLS	44,700

TRANSACTION-FILE

	EMPLOYEE IDNO	TRANS-CODE	DEPARTMENT-CODE	SALARY
1	150	UPDATE	ACC	50,000
2	170	DELETE		
3	180	UPDATE	SLS	35,300

EMPLOYEE-JOB-DESCRIPTION-FILE

	EMPLOYEE IDNO	DELETE-FLAG	DEPARTMENT-CODE	SALARY
1	100		ACC	32,770
2	150		ACC	50,000
3	170	D	DP	27,600
4	180		SLS	35,300
5	186		SLS	36,000
6	189		SLS	44,700

Figure 12 An Example of In Situ File Update

The file copy operation requires definition of a target file with a similar record structure as the source file to be copied. The organizations of source and target files need not be the same. Usually, on-line files are disk files, whereas backup files are sequentially organized tape files. File copying can be done using vendor-supplied utility programs. For full file copying, we rarely write application programs.

Occasionally, we may want to produce partial copies of files because not every record or every field value may be relevant to an application. This way, we obtain a smaller file and may speed up the execution of our application program. A file can be partially copied in three ways: by projection, selection, and projection and selection.

We may visualize a file as a two-dimensional table in which the rows are records and the columns are attribute values. In an application we may be interested in only some designated attribute values for all records. Given the EMPLOYEE-JOB-DESCRIPTION-FILE of Figure 8, we may want to make a

STEP	OPERATION	MASTER-RECORD				TRANSACTION RECORD			
1	READ TRANSACTION					150	UPDATE	ACC	50,000
2	READ MASTER-RECORD	100		ACC	32,770	150	UPDATE	ACC	50,000
3	READ MASTER-RECORD	150		ACC	45,300	150	UPDATE	ACC	50,000
4	MOVE TRANSACTION TO MASTER-RECORD	150		ACC	50,000	150	UPDATE	ACC	50,000
5	REWRITE MASTER-RECORD	150		ACC	50,000	150	UPDATE	ACC	50,000
6	READ TRANSACTION					170	DELETE		
7	READ MASTER-RECORD	170		DP	27,600	170	DELETE		
8	MOVE "D" TO DELETE-FLAG	170	D	DP	27,600	170	DELETE		
9	REWRITE MASTER-RECORD	170	D	DP	27,600	170	DELETE		
10	READ TRANSACTION-RECORD					180	UPDATE	SLS	35,300
11	READ MASTER-RECORD	180		DP	35,300	180	UPDATE	SLS	35,300
12	MOVE TRANSACTION TO MASTER-RECORD	180		SLS	35,300	180	UPDATE	SLS	35,300
13	REWRITE MASTER-RECORD	180		SLS	35,300	180	UPDATE	SLS	35,300
14	READ TRANSACTION-RECORD								

Figure 13 Trace of In Situ File Update Strategy for Files of Figure 12

copy of all records with only EMPLOYEE-IDNO and SALARY values, thus suppressing the DEPARTMENT-CODE field. This operation is equivalent to extracting a vertical subset of the file content, and is known as **projection**. Projection is illustrated in Figure 14.

In other applications we may wish to retain the record structure of the source file in the copy file, but include only some qualifying records in the result. Copying the records for employees whose salary is higher than $40,000 in the EMPLOYEE-JOB-DESCRIPTION-FILE is an example. The operation of extracting a horizontal subset of a file's content is called **selection** (Figure 15).

Projection and selection operations may be combined, as shown in Figure 16. Here, we make a partial copy of the EMPLOYEE-JOB-DESCRIPTION-FILE containing only the EMPLOYEE-IDNO and SALARY fields for employees of the Data Processing Department.

File Sorting

Another frequently performed file operation in data processing is sorting. Especially in sequential exhaustive file processing, it may be critical to have records in files ordered by some specified field values. File sorting requires specification of sort keys. Sort keys are the attributes whose values determine the physical or logical order in which records appear in a file. For example, for the sorted file in Figure 17, the sort key consists of DEPARTMENT-CODE defining an increasing order, followed by SALARY, which defines a decreasing order. File sorting merits more extensive consideration. We will return to it in Chapter 12.

Operation: Copy employee numbers and salary of employees in the EMPLOYEE-JOB-DESCRIPTION-FILE to EMPLOYEE-SALARIES-FILE.

Result:

EMPLOYEE-SALARIES-FILE

	EMPLOYEE IDNO	SALARY
1	100	32,770
2	150	45,300
3	170	27,600
4	180	35,300
5	186	36,000
6	189	44,700

Figure 14 Partial File Copying (Projection)

File Indexing

For files stored on direct-access storage devices (DASDs), the ability to access records directly depends on the file organization technique. Sequentially organized files, even if stored on DASDs, allow sequential access and retrieval only. Fortunately, most file management systems and language compilers also support direct-access files, in which records generally are accessed by their relative locations. For example, the EMPLOYEE-JOB-DESCRIPTION-FILE of Figure 8, if stored as a direct-access file, allows users to access directly, say, the fourth record without having to access consecutively the records that are before it. This capability is known as **access-by-address**.

Although useful, access-by-address is not sufficiently user oriented. It is definitely more desirable for a user to be able to request access to the record for the employee whose identification number is 180. This kind of access is known

Operation: Copy EMPLOYEE-JOB-DESCRIPTION-FILE records for employees whose salary is higher than $40,000 into HIGH-SALARY-EMPLOYEES-FILE.

Result:

HIGH-SALARY-EMPLOYEES-FILE

	EMPLOYEE IDNO	DEPARTMENT-CODE	SALARY
1	150	ACC	45,300
2	189	SLS	44,700

Figure 15 Partial File Copying (Selection)

Operation: Copy employee numbers and salary of employees in the DP department to DP-EMPLOYEE-SALARIES-FILE.

Result:

DP-EMPLOYEE-SALARIES-FILE

	EMPLOYEE IDNO	SALARY
1	170	27,600
2	180	35,300

Figure 16 Partial File Copying (Projection and Selection)

as **access-by-content**. It is ideal from a user's point of view, whereas access-by-address is a reality for the present-day computer systems.

To compromise, we resort to a technique known as indexing.

> An **index** is a table whose entries associate values with memory addresses.

To simulate access-by-content for a direct file, we construct an index table for it. We select a set of attributes on which the index table is based, and examine records in the file. For each record we create an index entry consisting of the value of the attribute set for the record and the address of the storage segment that contains the record. The index table in Figure 18 is generated for the EMPLOYEE-JOB-DESCRIPTION-FILE and is based on the attribute DEPARTMENT-CODE. Each entry of this index table consists of a value for

Operation: Sort the EMPLOYEE-JOB-DESCRIPTION-FILE in ascending order of department code and descending order of salary.

Result:

1	150	ACC	45,300
2	100	ACC	32,770
3	180	DP	35,300
4	170	DP	27,600
5	189	SLS	44,700
6	186	SLS	36,000

Figure 17 File Sorting

Operation: Generate an index for EMPLOYEE-JOB-DESCRIPTION-FILE based on
DEPARTMENT-CODE field.

Result:

DEPT-INDEX

DEPT-CODE	RELATIVE-ADDRESS
ACC	1
ACC	2
DP	3
DP	4
SLS	5
SLS	6

Figure 18 File Indexing

DEPARTMENT-CODE and a relative record address pointing to a record with
this DEPARTMENT-CODE value. The index entry

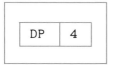

implies that the fourth record in the direct-access file has a DEPARTMENT-
CODE value of DP.

Once an index table is constructed it can be stored permanently as a file. Of
course, certain updates made in the file for which the index file is constructed
will also affect the content of the index file. A file management system should
be capable of updating an index file whenever the base file is updated.

To access directly records of a direct file by content of an attribute in it, we
first search its index file for the relevant index entries. Then, making use of the
addresses in the index file, we directly access the records in the base file. Indexing has many variations. It is widely used in file processing, but has
significance only for direct-access files. We will return to the subject in Chapter 13.

Operations on File Systems

The two kinds of operations that combine two or more files to generate a single
file are merging and joining.

File Merging. Two or more files can be combined by merging their contents,
provided they have identical record structures. **Merging** creates a new file that
has the same record structure as those of the source files and contains all
records existing in them. In a sense, merging is equivalent to the operation of

EMPLOYEE-JOB-DESCRIPTION-FILE

	EMPLOYEE IDNO	DEPARTMENT-CODE	SALARY
1	100	ACC	32,770
2	150	ACC	45,300
3	170	DP	27,600
4	180	DP	35,300
5	186	SLS	36,000
6	189	SLS	44,700

NEW-EMPLOYEE-JOB-DESCR-FILE

	EMPLOYEE IDNO	DEPARTMENT-CODE	SALARY
1	145	DP	38,000
2	185	ACC	25,000

(a) Instances of EMPLOYEE-JOB-DESCRIPTION-FILE
and NEW-EMPLOYEE-JOB-DESCR-FILE

Operation: Merge EMPLOYEE-JOB-DESCRIPTION-FILE and NEW-EMPLOYEE-JOB-DESCR-FILE into COMBINED-JOB-DESCR-FILE.

Result:

COMBINED-JOB-DESCR-FILE

	EMPLOYEE IDNO	DEPARTMENT-CODE	SALARY
1	100	ACC	32,770
2	145	DP	38,000
3	150	ACC	45,300
4	170	DP	27,600
5	180	DP	35,300
6	185	ACC	25,000
7	186	SLS	36,000
8	189	SLS	44,700

(b) Instance of merged file

Figure 19 File Merging

union in traditional set theory. In fact, a file can be perceived as a set of records, provided no two are identical. If we preserve this requirement that every record in a file be distinct, merging becomes the same operation as union.

If two files are merged, the process is known as **2-way merge**. It is possible to generalize the basic algorithm to apply to any number, say, P, of source files. The technique is then called **P-way merge**. To merge files conveniently, in practice we require them to be similarly ordered. If so, the resulting file will also be ordered the same way. The EMPLOYEE-JOB-DESCRIPTION-FILE and NEW-EMPLOYEE-JOB-DESCR-FILE of Figure 19a are combined under merging into the file of Figure 19b.

EMPLOYEE-JOB-DESCRIPTION-FILE

	EMPLOYEE IDNO	DEPARTMENT-CODE	SALARY
1	100	ACC	32,770
2	150	ACC	45,300
3	170	DP	27,600
4	180	DP	35,300
5	186	SLS	36,000
6	189	SLS	44,700

DEPARTMENT-FILE

DEPT-CODE	LOCATION	YEARLY-BUDGET
ACC	Northgate	300,000
DP	Northgate	450,000
SLS	Blue Ash	400,000

(a) Instances of EMPLOYEE-JOB-DESCRIPTION-FILE and DEPARTMENT-FILE

Operation: Join EMPLOYEE-JOB-DESCRIPTION-FILE and DEPARTMENT-FILE over DEPARTMENT-CODE into EXTENDED-JOB-DESCR-FILE.

Result:

EXTENDED-JOB-DESCR-FILE

	EMPLOYEE IDNO	DEPARTMENT-CODE	SALARY	LOCATION	YEARLY-BUDGET
1	100	ACC	32,770	Northgate	300,000
2	150	ACC	45,300	Northgate	300,000
3	170	DP	27,600	Northgate	450,000
4	180	DP	35,300	Northgate	450,000
5	186	SLS	36,000	Blue Ash	400,000
6	189	SLS	44,700	Blue Ash	400,000

(b) Instance of join file

Figure 20 Joining Files

Many available file sorting algorithms rely on the concept of merging. In this sense, merging is closely related to file sorting. These topics will be discussed in greater detail in Chapter 12.

Joining Files. **Join** is a special operation that requires two files. At least one attribute in the record structure of the first file should be compatible with an attribute in the record structure of the second. These are called join attributes. Join produces a new file whose record structure consists of all attributes of the first file, followed by all attributes of the second except the join attribute. It contains concatenations of records in the first file with those coming from the second file for all possible combinations of records satisfying the join condition. The most commonly used join condition requires that the respective join fields in two records be equal.

An example of join is provided in Figure 20b based on the two files of Figure 20a. Both the EMPLOYEE-JOB-DESCRIPTION-FILE and DEPARTMENT-FILE in Figure 20a have a compatible join field in their record structures. They are DEPARTMENT-CODE in the first and DEPT-CODE in the second. Therefore, these two files are joinable over this compatible attribute. The result, called EXTENDED-JOB-DESCR-FILE in Figure 20b, has a record structure that contains the record structure of the first file, followed by that of the second except for the common attribute DEPT-CODE. It includes concatenations of records coming from the first file with those coming from the second, provided they belong to the same department. The resulting file may be more useful within the scope of some applications in that its records include identification number, department code, and salary field values for employees, together with the location of the department and its yearly operating budget.

It should be noted that the join operation produces a new file with an extended record structure. The number of records, however, is limited by the number of records in the larger of the two files that are joined.

REVIEW QUESTIONS

1. Which of the following is not a fundamental operation of files?
   a. Access and retrieval
   b. Maintenance
   c. Printing
   d. Indexing
2. In defining a file, we should associate the file with a mass storage device, or a physical file on a mass storage device. (T or F)
3. In application programming, the definitions for files in a program are compiled and stored in a system catalog. (T or F)
4. Fetching a record consists of _____ and _____ .
5. Adding new records at the end of a file is known as _____ .
6. In the traditional file update strategy, three files are involved: the old master file, the new master file, and the transaction file. (T or F)
7. The main advantage of in situ file update compared to the traditional strategy is that it is possible to avoid _____ records.
8. The operation of copying records in a file for a subset of attributes in its record structure is known as _____ , whereas the operation of copying some records in a file with all of their attribute values is known as _____ .
9. In access-by-content, records are identified by values of some of their attributes. (T or F)
10. In file merging, source files do not have to have identical record structures, whereas in joining files they must have similar record structures. (T or F)

Answers: 1. c; 2. T; 3. F; 4. accessing, retrieving; 5. appending; 6. T; 7. copying; 8. projection, selection; 9. T; 10. F.

Physical Data Organization

In this section we study issues related to the physical organization and storage of data in computer files. We discuss file storage devices and their characteristics, how records are stored in external storage medium, and timing and storage considerations for sequential- and direct-access storage devices.

File Storage Device Characteristics

External storage media that can be used with storage devices linked to computer systems can be classified as mechanical, magnetic tape, rotating magnetic, and new technology data storage media.

Mechanical storage media are older external storage means, principally, punched cards and paper tapes. These were prominent in the first- and second-generation computer systems, but have been replaced by high-efficiency storage media. Today, they are seldom used in data processing. We need not spend any time on mechanical storage.

Magnetic tape storage media are open reel tapes and cassettes. They are mostly used for archival files and file backup purposes. We take a closer look at their hardware characteristics later in this section. Rotating magnetic storage media include fixed disks, floppy disks, exchangeable disk packs, and drum storage. Especially high-capacity disk packs are predominant in data processing applications. New storage media, such as optical disks and semiconductor storage, are still largely in the development phase. In data processing our emphasis is primarily on disk storage and, to a limited extent, magnetic tape storage.

Access to data stored on magnetic tape is sequential (or consecutive) by the nature of the device. This means that to access data somewhere in the middle of a tape reel or cassette, we should consecutively access all data recorded prior to this point. Such a device is commonly known as a **sequential-access storage device**, or SASD. In addition to magnetic tape readers, punch card and paper tape readers are sequential-access devices.

Rotating magnetic storage devices permit the computer system to access a specified segment of the storage directly. In other words, although data are recorded consecutively, accessing a given segment does not require accessing data recorded before it. Furthermore, the time it takes to access random storage segments is approximately the same. Such a device is called a **direct-access storage device**. All rotating magnetic storage devices are DASDs.

Sequential-access storage devices permit only sequential access to records in stored files. Therefore, no matter what type of logical organization is imposed on a file, the only way it can be accessed when stored on a SASD is sequentially. Because such files are treated as if they are sequentially organized, it makes sense to store only sequentially organized files on SASDs.

A direct-access storage device allows both sequential and direct access by an absolute or a relative address to any user-accessible segment of the storage area. Thus, a sequential file can be stored and processed on such devices. A file that requires direct access to its records by its organization can also be kept and used on DASDs. The built-in file organization techniques known as relative and indexed sequential in COBOL are basically direct-access files and thus require compatible direct-access devices. Records in these files can also be accessed sequentially, however.

In summary, there is a strong interdependence among file organization, file access, and the storage device characteristics, as reflected in the table.

File Organization	File Access Mode	Allowable Storage Devices
Sequential	Sequential	SASD or DASD
Direct	Sequential or direct	DASD only

Record Storage and Blocking

A file on a mass storage device is similar to an array. It consists of consecutive memory locations, each of which contains logical records for the file.

> A **logical record** is a record in a file as perceived by the user. The memory locations that store occurrences of logical records are called **physical records** or **blocks**, and are individually addressable in a consecutive fashion.

In other words, the computer system can detect the beginning and end of each physical record, read its contents into the main memory, or write some character string that is in the memory into it. For this, a block separator is used between any two consecutive physical records. This block separator is called **interblock gap** (IBG).

As far as the computer system is concerned, the content of a physical record is a character string, and the individual fields reserved for data values are not distinguishable or addressable in the mass storage. Once the content of a physical record is brought into the main memory, the computer is able to extract individual fields by making use of the record structure specification included in the application program as a template.

Each physical record may be specified to contain one or more logical records at the programmer's discretion during file creation. If blocks in a file contain a single logical record each, the file is said to be **unblocked**. A file is **blocked** if more than one logical record is stored in its blocks. The number of logical records stored in a physical record is defined as the **blocking factor** for the file. Figure 21 shows the organization of logical records in an unblocked file. The organization in Figure 22 is for a blocked file, where two logical records are blocked into each physical record. Therefore, the blocking factor for this file is 2.

Blocking records in a file is useful because, for such a file, the number of IBGs used by the system to separate blocks in mass storage is reduced. An IBG requires space, and limits the amount of storage left for data. The space required depends on the device used. Typical amounts on computer tape devices vary from 600 to about 2000 characters. For disk storage devices, IBG size is anywhere between 60 and 600 characters.

To see the effect of blocking on storage overhead, let us consider an example.

Example   Suppose we have a sequentially organized file containing 50,000 logical records. The records are of fixed size, and each has a length of 300 characters. Let us assume that we store the file on tape storage and that the recording density (i.e., number of characters per inch) of the device is 6250 characters per inch, with an IBG of 0.3 inch. This IBG is equivalent to $0.3 * 6250 = 1875$ characters. The total amount of storage needed for this file if the blocking factor is 1 (i.e., the file is unblocked) is

$$50,000 * 300 + (50,000 - 1) * 1875 = 108,748,125 \text{ characters}$$

If we use a blocking factor of 10, the number of blocks in the file will be reduced to 5000, and the storage requirement will become

$$50,000 * 300 + (5000 - 1) * 1875 = 24,373,125 \text{ characters}$$

This is a saving of 78%.

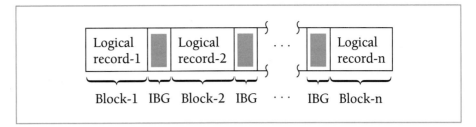

Figure 21 Unblocked Record Storage

Because an input instruction fetches an entire block and brings its contents into the main memory, however, a large block requires more main memory space as the input-output buffer to store its contents. Also, a large block generally slows the overall performance of the file system by causing more characters to be transferred during I-O. Therefore, the blocking factor for a file must be optimized in view of the permissible storage overhead and desirable performance parameters of the file processing system. Similar considerations apply for files stored on direct-access devices.

We mentioned earlier that magnetic tape and rotating magnetic devices are most commonly used for files. In the remainder of this section we study their characteristics, especially those that pertain to arranging data in storage and accessing them, because these parameters greatly influence the performance characteristics of files stored on them.

Sequential-Access Storage Devices

Typical sequential-access magnetic storage devices are open reel tape, cartridge, and cassette tape drives. In principle, they are all similar and can be exemplified by the open reel version.

Open reel tape storage devices are half-inch-wide magnetic tapes (usually of 2400 feet long) loaded on a supply reel. The transport mechanism pulls the tape past the read/write heads onto the take-up reel. At a given time, the tape drive can be in either read or write mode, but not both. While in the write mode the device is capable of recording information on the tape in a consecutive fashion. To record data, tape drives use either eight or nine parallel magnetic tracks on the surface of the tape, which is coated with a magnetizable material. Data are recorded as character strings and formed into blocks. As explained previously, blocks are separated from each other by IBGs.

Important tape drive parameters are recording density, tape transport speed, and full reel rewind time. Typical recording densities are 800, 1600, and 6250 bytes per inch (bpi). Tape transport speed generally varies in the range of 75 to 225 inches per second.

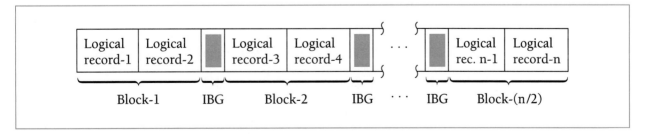

Figure 22 Blocked Record Storage (Blocking Factor = 2)

Most tape drives are capable of the following operations:

1. Reading or writing forward
2. Reading backward
3. Skipping forward to the next IBG
4. Skipping backward to the previous IBG
5. Skipping forward to the end of file
6. Rewinding to the beginning of the tape

With magnetic tape drives it is possible to write in an existing file starting from a point somewhere in the middle. If this is done, however, all data existing beyond the point at which we start writing will be lost. This means that, in general, a tape file can be extended at its end, but cannot be rewritten to update data.

Timing Parameters. As records on magnetic tapes can be accessed only sequentially, the time that the system takes to access and retrieve a random record depends on its location relative to the current record. If the record desired is far away from the current location, the access time can be unacceptably high. On the other hand, accessing and retrieving the next record is generally fast.

Example Let us consider a hypothetical tape drive as an example, with the following device parameters:

- Recording density = 1600 bpi
- Transport speed = 150 inches/second
- Interblock gap = 0.6 inch

Suppose our file contains 100,000 logical records, each 200 bytes long. Let the blocking factor be 10. Therefore, the block length for the file is 2000 bytes, and we have 10,000 blocks in the file. An IBG of 0.6 inch is equivalent to 960 bytes with this recording density.

Assuming that the file has just been opened in input mode, the access time for the first ten logical records in the file is

$$((2000 + 960)/(1600 * 150)) * 1000 = 12.3 \text{ milliseconds}$$

On the other hand, the time it takes to access the last block, or any record in the last block is

$$1000 * ((10,000 * 2000) + ((10,000 - 1) * 960))/(1600 * 150)$$

$$= 123,329 \text{ msec} = 2.06 \text{ minutes}$$

Clearly, this is too slow.

Storage Considerations. Most storage considerations for tape devices have been explained. The effect of the file blocking factor was demonstrated using an example. Tape storage is cheaper than direct-access storage. For example, for the device considered in the example above, the length of tape required to store the given file is

$$((10,000 * 2000) + ((10,000 - 1) * 960))/(1600 * 12) = 1541.6 \text{ ft.}$$

This is less than what is available in a reel of standard computer tape.

Direct-Access Magnetic Storage Devices

The many types of direct access rotating magnetic storage devices range from small-capacity floppy disks to high-capacity exchangeable disk pack drives. It is not our intention to provide a detailed discussion of physical characteristics of these devices. Rather, we concentrate on the issues of data organization, storage, and timing parameters for DASDs. Nevertheless, an understanding of their components and how they work together to store and access data will be useful.

In general, a DASD consists of one or more recording surfaces, a read/write head mechanism, a transport mechanism, and control electronics. On drum storage, data are stored on invisible tracks that are on the outer surface of a rotating cylinder (Figure 23). Each track is assigned an independent read/write head. This is referred to as a **head-per-track device.**

A disk storage device has a number of platters. Depending on the type of device and where the platters are placed in it, each platter has one or two magnetizable surfaces. Figure 24 shows the arrangement of platters on a spindle in exchangeable disk pack storage devices. Each surface contains a fixed number of concentric circular tracks on which data are recorded. The read/write mechanism consists of a boom with a number of read/write heads attached to it. Normally, for exchangeable disk packs, one head is assigned to each magnetizable surface. These heads move in unison in and out of the spaces between the set of platters rotating around a spindle. This way, a head associated with a disk surface can reach any track on the surface through a mechanical movement for data recording or retrieval. These are called **head-per-surface devices.** For fixed disk storage devices, each track on each surface may have its individual read/write head. Hence, fixed disk drives are head-per-track devices.

The magnetizable surfaces in rotating magnetic storage devices are coated with a ferromagnetic oxide. Disks or drums rotate at high speeds, and the tracks fly under the read/write heads. In floppy disk drives, the diskettes rotate only when in use. In other devices, rotation is continuous. Data can be read or written when the designated part of a track is passing under the associated read/write head.

An important storage concept in DASDs is the cylinder.

> A **cylinder** is the amount of storage that is accessible in one position of the read/write head mechanism.

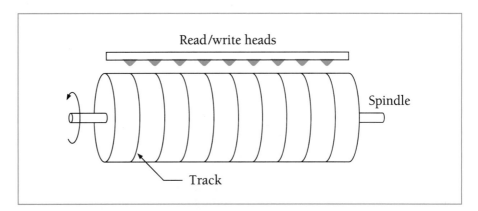

Figure 23 Magnetic Drum Storage

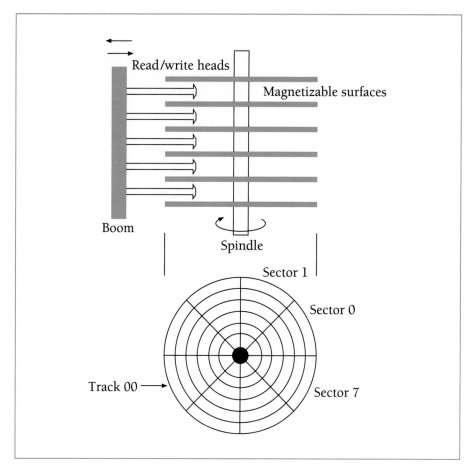

Figure 24 Exchangeable Disk Pack Storage

Head movement is mechanical and therefore contributes substantially and un-favorably to access time for DASDs. The importance of the cylinder stems from the fact that the device does not have to undergo another head movement once a cylinder is located to read or write data in that cylinder.

Let us summarize the device characteristics for rotating magnetic storage devices.

1. A double-sided floppy disk drive has 2 recording surfaces; 2 read/write heads, 1 for each surface; and usually 80 tracks per surface. Therefore, each cylinder consists of two tracks. A single-sided floppy disk drive has one recording surface and one track per cylinder.

2. An exchangeable disk pack typically has up to 11 platters. The top and bot-tom surfaces of the stack of platters are not used for data recording due to their increased vulnerability to external factors. One of the magnetizable surfaces may be reserved for use by the system and is not available to the program. Each head usually serves one surface. Each cylinder contains one track from each recording surface. A cylinder for such devices contains a set of tracks equidistant from the center of rotation. The number of cylinders for disk packs is equal to the number of tracks available on a recording sur-face.

3. As drum storage has one head per track, there is only one cylinder, and its capacity is the total device storage capacity. Thus, it is possible to access any segment of the storage without mechanical movement.

Timing Parameters. Reading or writing data on a DASD consists of two consecutive operations: locating the storage segment for input or output, and actual reading or writing. These operations result in an access delay, also called access time. Access time is the most important timing parameter for DASDs.

> **Access time** is the time it takes for the computer system to access data in the external storage and bring them into the user work area after an I-O instruction has been issued.

The location operation consists of four components: unit selection, seeking, head switching, and rotational delay.

Unit selection is the operation of determining the device containing the data sought. It is electronic, and does not contribute substantially to access time.

Seeking is the operation of positioning the read/write heads over the proper track. It is mechanical, and seek time is of the order of milliseconds. It is one of the major components of access time.

In **head switching** a read/write head can be in either read or write mode at a given time. Depending on the mode of the heads and the I-O instruction, a mode switch may be required. Because this is an electronic operation, its contribution to access time is negligible.

Rotational delay is also called **latency**. After the access mechanism is positioned on the proper track, the system should wait for the block containing the data sought to pass under the read/write head. This wait time is known as latency and is on the order of milliseconds. The best situation we can hope for is that the desired block is immediately underneath the read/write head at the time the system is ready for I-O, and hence, there is no wait. The worst is when the system has to wait a full rotation to continue reading or writing. In general, latency is expressed as one-half the rotation time and is referred to as average latency.

Actual reading/writing time is a function of the data transfer rate of the device. While writing data on a track, a write verification may be performed. This is a reread operation and requires an additional rotation immediately after data have been written.

In summary, average access time for a DASD consists of seek time, rotational delay, data transfer time, and, in case of writing, time for write verification. For head-per-track devices, seek time is zero, as no read/write head movement is required. Generally, for head-per-surface DASDs, manufacturers provide an average value for seek time. Seek time can be optimized by placing data that are related by applications within a single cylinder or in adjacent cylinders. Another strategy to reduce seek time for large files is to fragment the files over several disk units.

Average latency cannot be controlled by the programmer; however, it is easily computable as one-half the full rotation time. Read/write time is dependent on the data transfer rate for the device used. For disk devices, data transfer rate is a function of rotational speed and recording density. Most DASDs have the same data transfer rate for read and write operations.

Typical values for average seek time vary from 140 milliseconds for floppy drives to 15 milliseconds for mainframe exchangeable disk packs. The range for average latency is from approximately 80 milliseconds for floppy drives to 8 milliseconds for fast disk drives. Typical range for data transfer rate is 60 to 3000 characters per millisecond.

Storage Considerations. Here we concentrate on the manner in which data are organized on tracks for DASDs. In general, all data that are stored on one track can be too large to copy into the memory. It may either take too long to do that or the I-O buffer in the main memory may not be sufficiently large to contain them. Consequently, tracks are divided into smaller, more manageable, individually addressable storage segments called **blocks**.

Dividing a track into segments of equal size is handled by either hardware or software. In the hardware-oriented approach, tracks are divided into a fixed number of **sectors**, each of equal capacity. This organization is sometimes called **hard sectoring**.

In some devices, dividing tracks into segments is performed by a formatting software that is provided by the vendor of the operating system. The addressable storage segments are called **blocks**, and this organization is referred to as **soft sectoring**.

Occasionally, the size of a hard sector may be too small for an application. When this is the case, the programmer may define a block in terms of two, four, or more sectors. Such blocks are also known as **buckets**. A DASD may support different bucket capacities for different files; however, a given file usually has a fixed bucket size.

In case soft sectoring is not supported by hardware, programs supplied by vendors may be available to divide data stored on a track into smaller units before they are presented to the user.

> To repeat, a **block**, no matter how it is defined, is a fixed-size storage unit that is individually addressable, and is transferred as a unit between the DASD and the computer's main memory.

It should be understood that not all space available on a track can be used to store data. Some storage will be needed by the operating system to separate consecutive blocks, or consecutive areas within blocks. Also, logical records may have to be blocked in such a way that additional storage may be wasted. In computer systems based on the concept of hard-sectoring, the entire track is divided into a fixed number of sectors. Therefore, no storage is wasted for fitting sectors into the track. However, sectors are separated from each other by interblock gaps, each requiring 50 to 600 bytes, depending on the device. In addition, fitting logical records into blocks of fixed size may result in wasted storage, even when sectors can be combined into buckets. The principle here is that a logical record cannot be spanned over bucket boundaries. In other words, it is not possible to store the first segment of a logical record in one bucket and place the remaining segment in the next.

As an example, let us consider Figure 25. Here we have a bucket size of 1024 bytes. If our application defines a logical record length of 500 bytes, we can store two logical records, one after the other in a bucket. This leaves 24 bytes worth of unused space in each bucket, which accumulates to a substantial amount of storage in a large file.

This problem is nonexistent on systems that allow soft-sectoring. In such systems, a track can be divided into blocks whose size may be fixed for each individual file, or may even vary within a given file. Block size can be an exact multiple of the logical record size, thus causing no wasted storage due to fitting records into blocks. Soft-sectoring also requires interblock and interfield gaps, inserted by the operating system while storing data. Therefore, not all space on a track is available for storing user data. Depending on the capacity of a track and size of the blocks, some additional storage may be wasted at the end of the track. For example, if our block size is 1,024 bytes and the track capacity is 13,030 bytes, we can have 12 blocks stored on the track, but we will waste 742 bytes that are at the end of it.

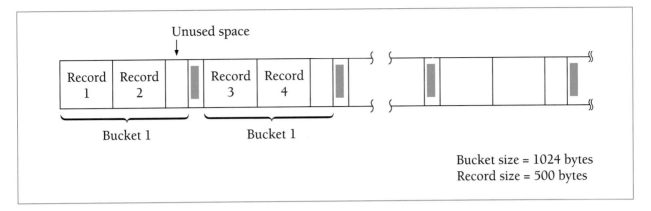

Figure 25 Storing Records in Fixed-Size Buckets

Soft-sectoring offers some other flexibilities regarding track organization and block formatting on tracks. Two different formats can be used for tracks: count-data and count-key-data. Figures 26 and 27 show the arrangement of data on tracks according to these formats. In both, all but one area are common. Let us take a brief look at the functional aspects of different areas on a track.

The first thing that we encounter on a track is the **index point**. It is a special marker that indicates the beginning of the track. Reading/writing data on a track starts there.

After the index point is the area called **home address**, which contains the self-identifying information of a flag, cylinder number, head number, and a cyclic check field. The flag is in a single byte and indicates whether the track is operative or defective. The cylinder number shows within which cylinder the track is to be found. The head number references the R/W head reserved for the track. The cyclic check field is used to check errors.

After home address, the rest of the track is divided into blocks, or physical records. Each block is separated from the next by an IBG. Also, each one begins with a **home marker** that is written by the system and used at read time to locate the beginning. Every block consists of two or three areas depending on the track format used. In the count-data format, these are count area and data area. In the count-key-data track format each block consists of a count area, a key area, and a data area.

Depending on the characteristics of the computer system, the **count area** in a block may contain a flag, an identifier, a key length field, a data length field, and a cyclic check field. The flag indicates whether the track is operative or defective, and whether it is to be used as the primary or alternate track. The identifier consists of cylinder number, head number, and block number. The

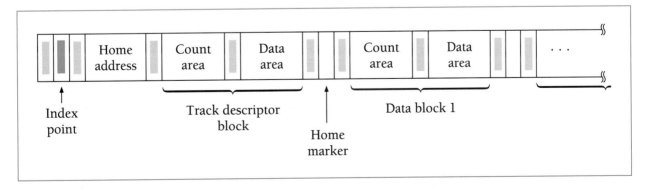

Figure 26 Count-Data Track Organization

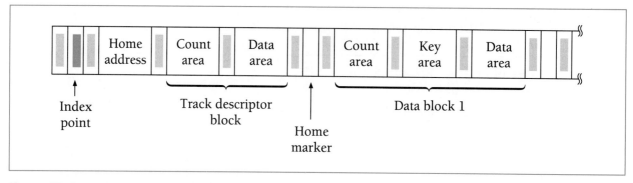

Figure 27 Count-Key-Data Track Organization

key length field shows the length of the key in the count-key-data track format. The data length field contains the length of the data area for the block. The cyclic check field is used to detect errors, as in the home address.

The first block in a track is special and is called the **track descriptor block**, designated block zero or R0. The count area of the track descriptor block contains the same information found in a typical count area. Here, the block number and the key length are zero. Also, the number of unused bytes after the last block on the track may be stored in the count area of R0. The data area of the track descriptor block describes the content of the track in terms of the number and length of blocks on the track.

All other blocks contain user data. The relative block number is indicated in the count area. The key area is optional. If specified, the organizational key for the file is duplicated in this area. This duplication costs storage, but somewhat speeds up processing. This is because the system does not have to go through additional processing to isolate the key in the main memory.

The data area in a block stores logical records. The number of logical records and the logical record length have to be specified by the programmer. Logical records in data blocks may be unblocked or blocked, and may have fixed or variable lengths. In variable-length logical records, for a fixed blocking factor the length of the data area in each block will be different. In variable-length record formatting, in addition to the logical records, the data area of each block contains a block length field, and for each logical record in the block, a record length field.

The programmer has the flexibility to specify a variety of record formats for logical records. The records are structured in each block according to the requested record format. In general, the following record formats may be supported:

1. Unblocked fixed-length (designated F)
2. Blocked fixed-length (FB)
3. Unblocked variable-length (V)
4. Blocked variable-length (VB)
5. Unblocked variable-length spanned (VS)
6. Blocked variable-length spanned (VBS)
7. Undefined (U)

In the **unblocked fixed-length (F)** format, each data block contains a single fixed-length data record (Figure 28). **Blocked fixed-length (FB)** record arrangement is shown in Figure 29. Here, two or more logical data records of the same length are blocked together and stored in the data area. The key of each record is kept as part of the record in the data area, and the logical records are arranged in increasing order by key. If the key area is requested for track formatting, the largest value is duplicated in the key area.

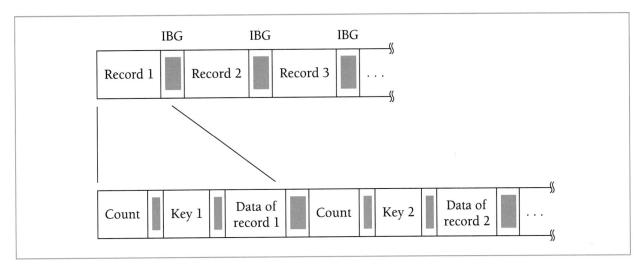

Figure 28 Unblocked Fixed-Length Record Format (F)

Figure 30 shows the **unblocked variable-length (V)** format. There is only one variable-length record in each data block. In the data area of each block, in addition to the actual logical record, block length (BL) and record length (RL) are recorded.

In the **blocked variable-length (VB)** format (Figure 31), the data area of each block contains two or more logical records of varying length. It also contains a block length field and a record length field for each logical record. The computer system uses these fields to separate logical records in a block in the main memory. Again, as in the FB format, the records are arranged in each block in increasing order of their keys, and the largest key is duplicated in the key area.

The **unblocked variable-length spanned (VS)** format is used if a logical record is very long. In such a case, it may be preferable to break it into two or more segments and store each segment in a separate block. When a logical record continues across block boundaries, we call it **spanned**. Usually, spanned formatting requires variable-length records. In the data area of each block are a

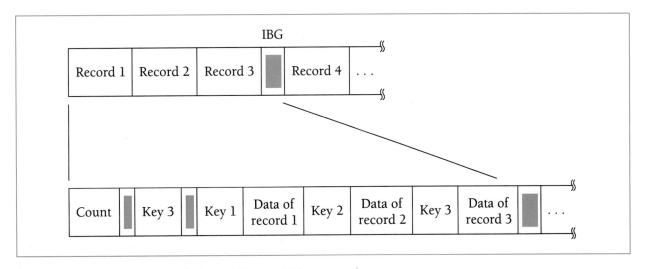

Figure 29 Blocked Fixed-Length Record Format (FB)

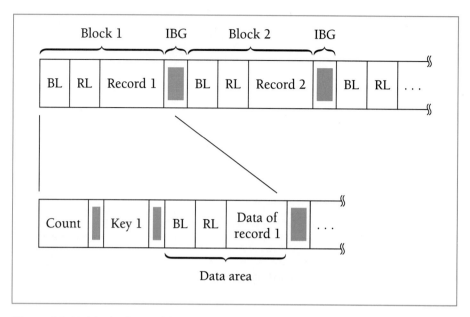

Figure 30 Unblocked Variable-Length Record Format (V)

block length field, a record length field, and a logical record, either in its entirety, or a segment of it (Figure 32).

Blocked variable-length spanned (VBS) format is basically a combination of the arrangements for VB and VS formats, as shown in Figure 33.

In the **undefined (U)** format, the blocks are unstructured. Each block is identified by the preceding and following interblock gaps. The content of a block varies from one to another. A block is treated as a character string, brought into the memory, and its content is analyzed and identified. This record format is rarely used today, but may come in handy if we have an old unstructured file and would like to interpret its contents.

Before we conclude our discussion of rotating magnetic storage devices, let us consider a hypothetical device in terms of its standard specifications, and compute some timing and storage parameters.

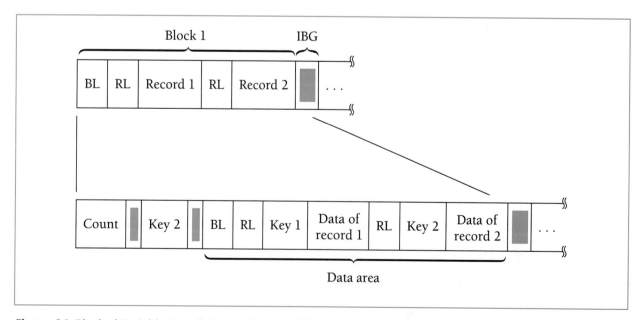

Figure 31 Blocked Variable-Length Record Format (VB)

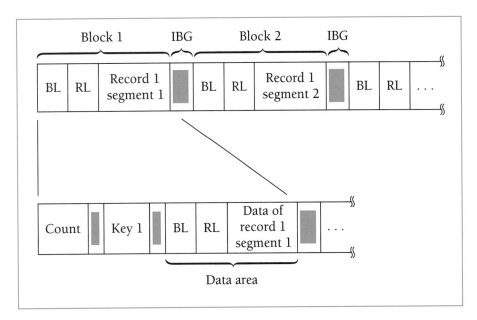

Figure 32 Unblocked Variable-Length Spanned Record Format (VS)

Example The device is an exchangeable disk pack drive with the following characteristics:

- Number of usable surfaces per pack = 19
- Number of tracks per surface = 500
- Net track capacity = 15,000 bytes
- Rotation speed = 3600 rpm

Using these specifications, we can compute the following:

- Rotation time = (1000 * 60/3600) = 16.7 msec
- Average latency = 1/2 * rotation time = 8.3 msec
- Number of cylinders = number of tracks per surface = 500
- Full cylinder capacity = (19 * 15,000) = 285,000 bytes
- Pack capacity = 285,000 * 500 = 142,500,000 bytes = 142.5 megabytes

File Directories and Labels

As many files are created by and maintained for different users in a computing environment, each one must be properly identified. Information that identifies files is kept in file directories. There is a file directory entry for every file on magnetic mass storage. In addition, as magnetic tape drives or disk drives can store many files, they have their own directories, known as **volume directories**.

Information included in volume and file directories and its organization vary from one operating system to another, and are somewhat different for tape and disk storage devices. Both can be tailored to meet the particular needs of a computer installation.

For tape storage, the operating system creates and maintains a volume directory in a special record called **volume label**. A single volume label is generated for a tape reel, written as the first record on the tape immediately after the tape index marker. It is approximately 80 bytes long, and contains information about the contents of a tape reel. This includes volume serial number, name of the tape owner, whether the volume is write-protected or not, and so on.

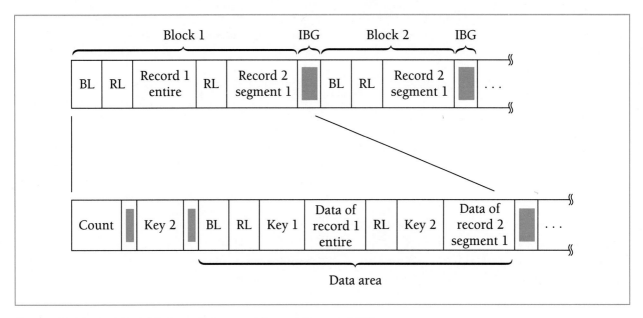

Figure 33 Blocked Variable-Length Spanned Record Format (VBS)

In addition, for each file in a volume the operating system generates a file directory that is kept partly in a **header label record** and partly in a **trailer label record**. The header label record is physically placed before the first data record in a file, and the trailer label record comes after the last data record in it (Figure 34.) The header label record contains the following information describing the contents of the file:

1. Name or identification number
2. Its version number
3. Creation date
4. Retention date (the date prior to which it cannot be overwritten)
5. Access group (users who have access privileges for it)
6. Sequence number, if the file is a multivolume file requiring more than one tape reel, and so on

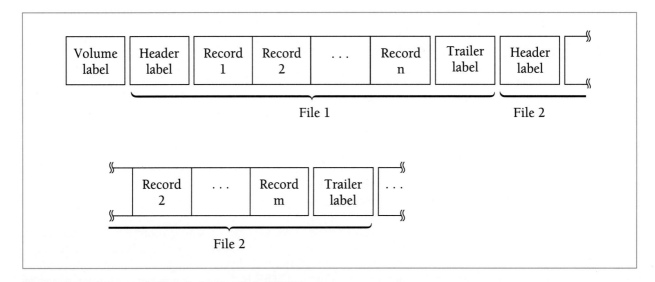

Figure 34 Volume and File Label Records for SASD

This information is usually replicated in the trailer label record. In addition, the number of blocks in the file is stored in the trailer label for control purposes.

File and volume directories for direct-access storage devices are organized differently. The volume label specifies location of a master catalog or directory that defines the entry point into a set of tree-structured file directories. As a DASD allows for direct access using location addresses, the computer system can directly access the next level file directory until it finds a file descriptor entry for the searched file. Each file directory is itself a file and contains records that reference either another lower level directory file or a file descriptor table, also called the **volume table of contents** (VTOC). The VTOC contains entries for each file stored in the DASD volume, consisting of

1. Physical address of the beginning of the file
2. Creation date
3. Date of the most recent change
4. Owner name
5. Authorized access level (either read-only or read-and-write)
6. File organization
7. Maximum size, allocated size, and size used
8. Record format used, and so on

Some of the information included in file directories or labels can be supplied from within the application program by the user. These generally include file name or identification number, retention period, owner name, access group, and so on. The remaining information is generated and recorded automatically by the operating system during file creation or immediately after a file is used.

REVIEW QUESTIONS

1. Punch card readers, paper tape readers, and magnetic tape drives are direct-access storage devices. (T or F)
2. In direct-access storage devices, access time is approximately the same for all stored records. (T or F)
3. Memory locations that are used to store logical records are called _____ .
4. In a file, the number of logical records in a block is called the _____ .
5. Important tape drive parameters are _____ , _____ , and _____ .
6. Which of the following is not a capability of magnetic tape drives?
   a. Reading backward
   b. Skipping forward to the next IBG
   c. Rewinding to the beginning of the tape
   d. Reading a record directly by the content of an attribute
7. In a rotating magnetic storage device, if each track is assigned an independent read/write head, it is called a _____ device.
8. The amount of storage that is accessible in one position of the read/write head mechanism is called a _____ .

9. Which of the following statements concerning timing parameters in direct access storage devices is correct?
   a. Unit selection and head switching are mechanical operations and require substantial amounts of time.
   b. Seeking is an electronic process and is independent of where data are stored.
   c. Average latency is equal to one-half the rotation time.
   d. All of the above are correct.
10. In hard sectoring, each track is divided into a fixed number of equal-size sectors by the hardware. (T or F)
11. The track formats used in soft sectoring are _____ and _____ .
12. Concerning the arrangement of data in soft sectoring,
    a. Index point is a special marker that indicates the beginning of each track.
    b. Home address is the area that contains self-identifying information for each track.
    c. Count area contains key length, data length, and a cyclic check field in addition to track identification information.
    d. All of the above are correct.
13. In soft sectoring, the first block in a track is called the _____ block.
14. In variable-length record formatting, the data area of each block contains a block length field, and for each logical record in the block, a record length field. (T or F)
15. Which of the following is not an acceptable physical record format in soft sectoring?
    a. Blocked fixed-length spanned record format
    b. Unblocked variable-length record format
    c. Blocked variable-length record format
    d. Undefined record format
16. For DASDs, the volume label specifies the location of a master catalog. (T or F)
17. Which of the following items is among those contained in the volume table of contents for each DASD file?
    a. Physical address of the beginning of the file
    b. Date of the most recent change
    c. Authorized access level
    d. Record format used
    e. All of the above

Answers: 1. F; 2. T; 3. blocks; 4. blocking factor; 5. recording density, tape transport speed, rewind time; 6. d; 7. head-per-track; 8. cylinder; 9. c; 10. T; 11. count-data format, count-key-data format; 12. d; 13. track descriptor; 14. T; 15. a; 16. T; 17. e.

Key Terms

access time	index
access-by-address	interblock gap
access-by-content	join
appending records	key
attribute	latency
block	logical data organization
blocking factor	logical file organization technique
bucket	logical record
built-in file organization technique	master file
count-data format	new master file
count-key-data format	old master file
cylinder	physical data organization
data base	physical record
direct access	projection
direct-access storage device	record
entity	record access
entity identifier	record deletion
entity set	record insertion
fetching records	record organization
file	record retrieval
file access	record update
file copying	relationship
file creation	sector
file definition	seeking
file indexing	selection
file maintenance	sequential access
file merging	sequential-access storage device
file organization	soft sectoring
file sorting	spanned record
hard sectoring	track descriptor block
head-per-surface device	traditional file update
head-per-track device	trailer label record
header label record	transaction file
home address	volume directory
home marker	volume label
in situ file update	volume table of contents

Study Guide

Quick Scan

- Files stored on mass storage devices are important in data processing for several reasons. (1) The corporate data resource can be kept permanently in files. (2) Tape and disk files can store large volumes of data inexpensively. (3) Data stored in files can be shared. (4) Files can be structured to reflect relationships among the corporate data.
- The permanence characteristic of files is a function of the storage medium. Therefore, it is a physical characteristic. The way data are structured in files is a matter of design. Hence, this characteristic is logical. Both physical and logical characteristics of files are important, and an application programmer should be well acquainted with them.
- The user's point of view of how data are structured makes up logical data organization. The manner in which data are actually stored in a storage medium defines physical data organization.

- The three phases in logical data organization are record organization, file organization, and data base organization.
- In an information system, we collect, structure, store, and use data about entities and relationships existing among entities in the real world. Entities and relationships are described in terms of their properties, called attributes.
- For a specific entity or relationship set, we collect attributes together, structure them linearly, and come up with a template. This template is called a record structure. When this template is filled with data values for a member of an entity or relationship set, it is called a record.
- Different occurrences of a record structure are brought together and structured in a manner to reflect some relationship among them. Such a structured collection of records is called a file.
- Certain attributes in a record type may uniquely identify records based on that type. These attributes are called entity identifiers, or key attributes.
- Files representing the corporate data resource may be related to one another. It is possible to organize different files such that the existing relationships are also represented. The result of such an organization is known as a data base.
- Records in files can be structured in a variety of ways. The collection of all possible file structures is referred to as logical data organization techniques. Computer languages recognize only a small subset of these, known as the built-in file organization techniques for a given language.
- COBOL is richer than most other computer languages in its built-in file organization techniques, supporting sequential, indexed sequential, and relative organizations.
- File access is closely related to file organization. It is the manner in which records in a file can be accessed and retrieved.
- In addition to file organization, file access depends on the characteristics of the file storage device. Files stored on devices that permit only sequential access can be accessed only sequentially. If the device allows direct access, records may be accessed sequentially and, depending on the organization, directly.
- The fundamental file operations are definition and creation, access and retrieval, maintenance, copying, sorting, and indexing.
- File definition requires defining record structure, specifying file characteristics including organization and access mode, associating the file with a storage device, and specifying additional options for it.
- File creation is the initial loading of a file with records.
- Record access and retrieval are collectively referred to as record fetching. Three kinds of fetch operations are significant in determining the efficiency of a file system: fetching a specified record, fetching the next record, and fetching all records.
- File maintenance includes record update, insertion, and deletion.
- The strategies for file maintenance are traditional file update and in situ file update. Both use a master file and a transaction file.
- File update operations require copying if the file is stored on a SASD. For DASD files, both update through copying and in situ update are possible.
- Other file operations are making full or partial copies, sorting, and indexing files.
- Two or more files may be combined either by merging or by the join operation.
- There are a variety of file storage devices. In data processing, we are interested in magnetic tape storage, rotating magnetic storage, and the associated media.

- Magnetic tape storage devices allow only sequential access to data. They are also known as sequential-access storage devices (SASD). Rotating magnetic storage devices allow both sequential and direct access to data and thus are called direct-access storage devices (DASD).

- Sequential-access storage devices are appropriate only for sequentially organized files. Direct-access storage devices can be used for any file organization technique that is suitable for sequential or direct access.

- A logical record is a record as perceived by the user. A physical record, or a block, on the other hand, is the memory location that stores logical records.

- On mass storage media, blocks are sequences of characters written one after another. A block is separated from the next by an interblock gap.

- It is possible to store one or more logical records in a block. The number of logical records in a block is a file's blocking factor.

- Blocking records in a file is useful in that the storage space necessarily allocated for the interblock gaps is reduced. As an input instruction copies the content of an entire block in the main memory buffers, too large a block size may require more main memory space than can be reserved for an application program. Also, it may slow the overall performance of the system by causing more characters to be transferred during I-O. Therefore, the blocking factor for a file has to be optimized carefully.

- Sequential-access storage devices include open reel tape, cartridge, and cassette tape drives. At any given time they can be in either read or write mode, but not both.

- Most tape drives can read and write forward, read backward, skip a block forward or backward, skip to the end of the file, and rewind to the beginning of the file.

- With magnetic tape drives, it is possible to write in a file starting from any point in it; however, this erases all data beyond the point at which writing begins. This implies that a file stored on a SASD can be extended at its end, but cannot be rewritten to update data.

- Access time for a SASD depends on the device transport speed and recording density. It also depends on the relative location of the record to be accessed. Accessing the next record is fast. Accessing a record far away from the current record may take a long time.

- Direct-access storage devices include floppy disk drives, drums, and large-capacity exchangeable disk pack drives. They consist of one or more recording surfaces, a read/write head mechanism, a transport mechanism, and control electronics.

- Devices in which each recording track is assigned an individual head are known as head-per-track devices. In the majority of DASDs, a recording surface is assigned one read/write head. These are head-per-surface devices.

- Cylinder is an important storage concept in rotating magnetic devices. A cylinder is the amount of storage accessible in one position of the read/write heads. Head movement is mechanical. Therefore, it slows down the average access time. The cylinder is important because it represents the amount of data that can be accessed without moving the read/write heads.

- Access time for DASDs consists of time to locate data, and time to read or write it. The location operation has four components: unit selection, seeking, head switching, and rotational delay. Unit selection and head switching are electronic operations. Therefore, their effects on access time are negligible.

- Seeking is the operation of positioning the read/write heads over the proper track, and is a mechanical process. Seek time can be minimized by storing related data in neighboring cylinders.

- Rotational delay, or latency, is the time delay due to the system's having to wait for the target block to pass under the read/write head. Average latency is expressed as one-half the full rotation time and depends on the rotational speed of the device.
- In DASDs, data are stored on tracks. Tracks are divided into individually addressable storage segments called blocks. If blocks are defined through hardware, they are known as sectors, and this organization is referred to as hard sectoring. If software is used for blocking, the corresponding organization is called soft sectoring.
- In soft sectoring, data stored on tracks are formatted by software. Two formats are available: count-data and count-key-data.
- In both formatting techniques, the beginning of a track is indicated by a special marker called the index point. After the index point is the home address, a field containing information to identify the track. Next is a special block called the track descriptor block, also used to store information about the contents of the track. The rest of the track contains data records, each beginning with a home marker.
- Data records are blocks consisting of a count and a data area in the count-data track format. In the count-key-data track format, blocks also include a key area in which a key value is stored to identify the logical records in the data area.
- The count area in each block stores cylinder, head, block identifiers, status flags, and key length and data length information. The data area is used for storing logical records.
- Logical records can be stored in a variety of manners in most systems. They may be unblocked or blocked, of fixed or variable length, and even spanned.
- To identify files stored on a storage device, the operating system creates and maintains directories for the device, called volume directories, and labels for the files stored on it.
- For tape storage, the volume directory is called the volume label. In addition, for each file, a header and a trailer label record are generated. Label records contain information that describe the file's contents and some additional characteristics.
- For DASDs, the volume label points to the location of the master catalog. The master catalog itself defines the entry point into a set of tree-structured file directories. At the lowest level of the tree structure are some file descriptor tables, also called the volume table of contents. The volume table of contents contains entries for each file stored in the DASD volume. These specify the location of the file together with additional information about it.

Test Your Comprehension

Multiple-Choice Questions

1. Which of the following statements expresses the importance of computer files in data processing?
   a. Files store data permanently.
   b. Files are inexpensive data storage facilities.
   c. Files facilitate sharing of data by several applications.
   d. Files can be used to represent data and data relationships.
   e. All of the above are true.
2. Which of the following statements concerning file access is correct?
   a. In direct-access mode, a READ statement accesses the next physical record in a file.
   b. In sequential-access mode, a READ statement accesses an arbitrary record specified by its address.
   c. Any file, no matter how it is organized, can be accessed sequentially.

d. A sequentially organized file can be accessed directly.

e. All of the above are correct.

3. Which of the following about file update is correct?

   a. In traditional file update, all files involved should be tape files.

   b. In situ file update can be applied to tape files as well as disk files.

   c. In situ file update for sequential files does not readily permit record insertion.

   d. All of the above are correct.

   e. None of a, b, or c is correct.

4. Choose the correct statement concerning record blocking.

   a. An interblock gap is a block separator placed in between two consecutive blocks in external storage.

   b. If blocks in a file are large enough to store two or more logical records, the file is called blocked.

   c. The number of logical records in a file in a block is called the blocking factor.

   d. All of the above are correct.

5. Which of the following is a capability of magnetic tape drives?

   a. Writing forward

   b. Reading backward

   c. Skipping forward to the end of a file

   d. All of the above

6. Which of the following statements about the timing parameters in direct-access storage devices is correct?

   a. In drum storage, seek time is effectively zero.

   b. Average latency in direct-access storage devices is one-half the rotation time.

   c. The operation of writing is followed by a reread operation for write verification.

   d. All of the above are correct.

7. Which of the following statements concerning the physical record formats available in soft sectoring is correct?

   a. In the blocked fixed-length record format, if count-key-data track formatting is used, the smallest key value is duplicated in the key area.

   b. In the unblocked variable-length record format, the data area contains only the logical record.

   c. It is possible to specify a blocked fixed-length spanned record format.

   d. All of the above are correct.

   e. None of a, b, or c is correct.

8. Which of the following items is not among those contained in the volume table of contents for each DASD file?

   a. Owner name

   b. Name of user who made the most recent changes in the file

   c. Maximum size, allocated size, and size used

   d. Record format

Answers: 1. e; 2. c; 3. c; 4. d; 5. d; 6. d; 7. e; 8. b.

Short Essay Questions

1. Explain why files are important in data processing.

2. Briefly define the following concepts:

   a. Entity

   b. Relationship

   c. Attributes

3. Define the concepts of record structure and record occurrence.

4. What are the three levels of data organization?
5. Define the following related concepts:
   a. File
   b. File organization
   c. File access
   d. Data base
6. What are the differences between logical and built-in file organization techniques?
7. How are file organization and file access related to each other?
8. Explain how file organization depends on the characteristics of storage devices.
9. What are the fundamental operations on files?
10. What are the elements required in the complete definition of a file?
11. Briefly explain the difference between file update through copying and in situ file update.
12. Distinguish between logical and physical record deletion.
13. Explain the difference among full copying of a file, the operation of selection, and the operation of projection.
14. Why is indexing a file important? For what types of storage devices is file indexing meaningful? Explain why.
15. Explain the difference between access-by-address and access-by-content.
16. What is meant by record fetching? What type of fetch operations are significant in determining the efficiency of a file system?
17. Briefly explain the file join operation and distinguish it from the file merge operation.
18. How do we classify file storage devices?
19. Explain the difference between sequential- and direct-access storage devices.
20. Explain the interdependence of file organization, file access, and the type of file storage devices.
21. What is the difference between a logical record and a physical record?
22. Why are interblock gaps needed in data storage on file storage devices?
23. Define blocking factor and explain its effect on file performance.
24. What are the basic capabilities of magnetic tape storage devices?
25. Discuss the factors that affect access time for sequential-access storage devices.
26. What are the basic components of rotating magnetic storage devices?
27. What are meant by head-per-track and head-per-surface DASDs? Give an example of each.
28. Define the concept of cylinder for DASDs. Why is it an important storage concept?
29. What are the components of access time for DASDs?
30. What is meant by seeking?
31. What is the value of the seek time for head-per-track storage devices? How can we minimize the seek time for head-per-surface storage devices?
32. Explain the concepts of latency and average latency.
33. What are the differences between hard and soft sectoring for DASDs?
34. Explain the difference between count-data and count-key-data track formats.
35. What are the functions and contents of the home address area on a track?
36. What information is usually stored in the count area on a track?
37. What types of record formats are supported for DASDs?
38. Draw a figure of the track map and explain the arrangement and functions of different fields for each of the following record formats:
    a. FB
    b. VB
    c. VBS

39. Explain the function and contents of
    a. Volume label record
    b. Header label record
    c. Trailer label record
40. What are the information stored in the volume table of contents for a DASD?

Improve Your Problem-Solving Ability

Problems

Given are the following two logical files.

STUDENT–FILE

	STUDENT–IDNO	STUDENT–NAME	YEAR	MAJOR
1	1000	JOHN SMITH	2	MIS
2	2500	KAREN DALY	2	MTH
3	2700	TIMOTHY BLACK	3	MIS
4	3000	JOYCE TALISMAN	2	PHY
5	3500	THOMAS JOHNSON	3	MIS

ENROLLMENT–FILE

	STUDENT–IDNO	COURSE–CODE	ACADEMIC–YEAR	SEMESTER	GRADE
1	1000	BUS210	88	1	A
2	1000	MTH250	88	1	A
3	2500	MTH250	88	1	C
4	2500	MTH275	88	1	B
5	2500	PHY232	88	1	C
6	2700	BUS210	88	1	A
7	3000	MTH250	88	1	A
8	3000	PHY232	88	1	B
9	3500	BUS210	88	1	D

Problems 1 through 5 are based on the instance of schema for these files. In each problem, draw a figure to show the content of the file obtained as a result of the indicated file operation.

1. Copy the STUDENT-IDNO, STUDENT-NAME, and MAJOR attributes in STUDENT-FILE into a file called SUMMARY-STUDENT-FILE.
2. Copy the records in STUDENT-FILE corresponding to sophomores into a file called SOPHOMORES-FILE.
3. Sort STUDENT-FILE records in increasing order of YEAR, and decreasing order of MAJOR into a file called SORTED-FILE.
4. Create an index file with respect to GRADE for ENROLLMENT-FILE.

5. Join STUDENT-FILE and ENROLLMENT-FILE over STUDENT-IDNO into a file called FULL-INFORMATION-FILE.
6. Suppose we have the following transaction file for the STUDENT-FILE above.

STUDENT−TRANSACTION−FILE

	STUDENT−IDNO	TRANS−CODE	STUDENT−NAME	YEAR	MAJOR
1	1000	UPDATE	JOHN SMITH	2	MTH
2	2500	DELETE			
3	2700	UPDATE	TIMOTHY BLACK	4	MIS
4	3000	DELETE			

Draw a trace table similar to that in Figure 11 to show the steps in the traditional file update strategy as applied to STUDENT-FILE and STUDENT-TRANSACTION-FILE.
7. Do problem 6 using in situ file update, and produce a trace table similar to that in Figure 13.
8. Suppose we have a sequential tape file of 100,000 logical records. Logical record length is 100 bytes. The recording density of the tape storage device is 1600 characters per inch and the interblock gap length is 0.3 inch.
   a. What length of tape will be needed to store the entire file if the blocking factor for the file is 1?
   b. What will be the necessary tape length if the blocking factor is 10?
9. Again consider the file and the tape storage device described in problem 8. Assume that the tape transport speed is 150 inches per second and that the file blocking factor is 10. Also assume that the file has just been opened in input mode. Compute
   a. The access time for the first 10 logical records.
   b. The access time for the last block in the file.
10. We have a hypothetical exchangeable disk pack drive with the following characteristics:

   - Number of usable surfaces per track = 10
   - Number of tracks per surface   = 400
   - Net track capacity   = 13,000 bytes
   - Rotation speed   = 3600 rpm

   Compute the following for the device:
   a. Number of cylinders
   b. Cylinder capacity
   c. Full disk pack capacity
   d. Rotation time
   e. Average latency

11

Sequential File Organization

Introduction

This chapter concentrates on the first COBOL built-in file organization technique, that is, sequential organization. Sequential organization is the simplest of all file organization techniques. All COBOL files we defined and used previously have been sequential. We have acquired a substantial background on sequential files. Here, we will review the basics and discuss the more advanced aspects of their processing. These include sequential files with variable-length records and the REWRITE statement for sequential disk files. We will present five application programs in this chapter. Two of them correspond to the traditional and in situ file update strategies for sequential files that were discussed in Chapter 10.

Characteristics of Sequential Files

Certain characteristics distinguish sequential organization from other file organization techniques.

Sequence of Records in Sequential Files

As far as the computer system is concerned, a sequential file does not have a recognizable key. The order of records is determined by an **implicit key**, which is the sequence number of records in the file. In other words, the sequence of records depends on their physical order in the file. The first record that is accessed when we process a sequential file from its beginning is the first record that was written into the file during its creation. If we wish to define a logical order based on a key for a sequential file, we must either create it accordingly, or sort it after creation. Only then does the physical order of records become parallel to the logical order in which they should exist.

File Size

The size of sequential files is determined during creation. The number of records stored in a physical file during creation is fixed and usually cannot be changed. Some file processing systems allow extending a file by adding records at its end, however.

Once created, the content of a sequentially organized tape file cannot be altered. We cannot update fields in a record, or delete or add records. The only way we can change the content of such a file is by copying the updated records into another sequential file. This constitutes the essence of traditional master file update. The logic of this strategy was discussed in Chapter 10. One of the sample programs developed in this chapter is an implementation of this strategy (see Program 4-Source).

Sequentially organized disk files are somewhat more flexible with respect to update. Certain file processing systems, including COBOL, allow rewriting the most recently read record. As a result, we can update records by reading them, changing their content in the main memory, and rewriting them. If we reserve a field in the record structure, we may also logically delete records through the rewrite capability. Also, provided we store some dummy records in a sequential file during creation, it is possible to insert (again logically) new records into the file. This process eliminates the need for copying, and hence, is more efficient than the traditional file update algorithm. This strategy, known as in situ file update, was discussed in Chapter 10. It is implemented in Program 5.

Efficiency of Sequential Files

The performance characteristics of a sequentially organized file depend on two factors: characteristics of the storage device and type of operation to be performed on the file. In general, most operations done on sequential files stored on direct-access storage devices are more efficient than those stored on tapes. That is because of the favorable access time with the DASDs; however, the nature of the operation has a more significant effect on the overall performance.

Fetching a specified record in a sequentially organized file requires consecutive access to records. If the desired record is the first one in the file, access is very fast. All it takes is to open the file and issue a read instruction. If, on the other hand, the last record is to be fetched, processing may take an excessively long time. Fetching an arbitrary record in a sequential file is essentially similar to searching a table sequentially. If the record to be fetched is associated with a search key, ordering the file helps, as in searching an ordered table.

In a sequential file, fetching the next record is extremely efficient. All it takes is a single READ instruction. The successor record may even be available in the I-O buffers if the file is blocked. In this case, no input is required.

Fetching all records is also efficient, provided the desired sequence is the same as the physical sequence of records in the storage. The performance of the file for this operation is dependent on the device characteristics and the blocking factor associated with the file.

| COBOL Statements for Sequential Files | Most of the language elements for sequential file processing were discussed in Chapters 2 and 3. Here, we provide a brief review and concentrate on characteristics that are relatively more advanced. |

Review of COBOL Features for Sequential Files

For each sequential file in the program there must be a SELECT statement in the ENVIRONMENT DIVISION. The SELECT statement associates the internal file name for a file with an external file name (or device name) and specifies the file organization technique and a permissible file access mode.

The definition for a sequential file is completed in the FILE SECTION of the DATA DIVISION. Here, in an FD block, we describe record length, blocking factor, label record parameters, if any, and record structure description for each record in the file. Two issues not covered previously are the specification of label record parameters and definition of variable-length records. We discuss these below.

The PROCEDURE DIVISION of a program may contain five I-O statements that we may need for sequential files: OPEN, CLOSE, READ, WRITE, and REWRITE. We have studied the first four. OPEN readies a file for input, output, or input-output. If a file is nonexistent prior to processing, it should be opened in output mode. If an output mode is specified for a file that exists, subsequent executions of the WRITE statement will destroy the old file and create new records in it. A file that has been opened in input mode can be used only for input purposes with a READ statement. A file whose open mode is output can be processed using WRITE statements only. The open mode of a file can be changed by closing and subsequently reopening it.

The input-output open mode and the REWRITE statement go together. They are explained below.

Label Record Parameters

We have studied the concepts of file identification and label records. We know that for a file, a header and a trailer label record may be created. Contents of label records are determined by individual data processing shops at the time of system installation and vary from one shop to the next.

For magnetic tape and disk files, the user may choose not to specify label records, using the LABEL RECORDS ARE OMITTED clause, as in the following example.

```
FD  MASTER-FILE
    LABEL RECORDS ARE OMITTED
    RECORD CONTAINS 49 CHARACTERS
    DATA RECORD IS MASTER-RECORD.
01  MASTER-RECORD.
. . . . . . . . . . . . . .
```

If the operating system is to generate standard label records, the programmer should specify LABEL RECORDS ARE STANDARD. The values of the label record parameters can be supplied through job control language (JCL) statements outside a COBOL program or by using the VALUE OF clause in an FD block. The VALUE OF clause is exemplified below.

```
FD  MASTER-FILE
    LABEL RECORDS ARE OMITTED
    VALUE OF FILE-ID              IS "PERSMF001"
    VALUE OF ACCESS-GROUP         IS "PERSDEPT"
    VALUE OF WRITE-PROTECT-PERIOD IS 100
    RECORD CONTAINS 49 CHARACTERS
    DATA RECORD IS MASTER-RECORD.
01  MASTER-RECORD.
. . . . . . . . . . . . . . . .
```

It should be noted that the example is system specific. FILE-ID, ACCESS-GROUP, and WRITE-PROTECT-PERIOD are names of label record parameters that are standard for a given installation. If you must provide label record parameter values in your program, you should consult the installation manager about standard names and procedures.

COBOL 85   It is interesting to note that COBOL 85 considers the use of the VALUE OF clause obsolete.

REWRITE Statement

A sequential file stored on a DASD can be opened in input-output mode if the programmer has to update records in the file, as in the in situ update strategy. As discussed earlier, updating a record necessitates access to it, and hence a READ statement is required. After the content of the retrieved record is altered in the main memory, we must write it into the same storage location as the original version. For this we use the REWRITE statement. Because both READ and REWRITE statements should be used for the same file without closing and reopening it, the file open mode should be I-O.

The syntax of the REWRITE statement is similar to that of WRITE. It is given below.

REWRITE record-name [FROM identifier]

An example of the REWRITE for in situ update is shown in the following partial program.

```
. . . . . . . . . . . . . . . . .
ENVIRONMENT DIVISION.
. . . . . . . . . . . . . . . . .
FILE-CONTROL.
    SELECT MASTER-FILE ASSIGN TO  UPFILE.
. . . . . . . . . . . . . . . . .
DATA DIVISION.
FILE SECTION.
FD  MASTER-FILE
    LABEL RECORDS ARE STANDARD
    RECORD CONTAINS 43 CHARACTERS
    DATA RECORD IS MASTER-RECORD.
01  MASTER-RECORD.
    05 STUDENT-MAJOR                PIC X(15).
    05 STUDENT-NAME                 PIC X(25).
    05 STUDENT-CREDITS              PIC 9(3).
. . . . . . . . . . . . . . . . .
PROCEDURE DIVISION.
MAINLINE.
    OPEN I-O  MASTER-FILE.
    READ MASTER-FILE
        AT END MOVE "NO" TO DATA-REMAINS-SWITCH.
    PERFORM CHANGE-THEN-READ
        UNTIL DATA-REMAINS-SWITCH = "NO".
    CLOSE MASTER-FILE.
    STOP RUN.

CHANGE-THEN-READ.
    MOVE 100 TO STUDENT-CREDITS.
    REWRITE MASTER-RECORD.
    READ MASTER-FILE
        AT END MOVE "NO" TO DATA-REMAINS-SWITCH.
```

Files with Variable-Length Records

So far we have dealt exclusively with fixed-length record files. Occasionally in some applications one comes across logical files that contain records of varying length. As discussed in Chapter 10, mass storage devices are generally capable of storing variable-length records. COBOL also has some features that do this. Therefore, files with variable-length records can be defined and used in COBOL application programs.

There are primarily two reasons for using variable-length records in files: to conform to logical design requirements and to minimize storage waste. If a logical design indicates variable-length records, it may be desirable to reflect this characteristic in the physical implementation. In principle, any variable-length record file can be transformed into a fixed-length record counterpart. Such a transformation may result in a storage waste, however, because the record length in the fixed-length record file should be equal to the length of the longest record in its variable-length record counterpart, and shorter records will have to be padded on the right with spaces. For large files, this storage waste may become substantial.

Variable-length record files have some significant disadvantages. Application software based on variable-length record design is substantially more difficult to develop than for fixed-length design, as will become obvious in the following discussion. The execution efficiency of application software based on variable-length record files is somewhat low. This is because the system has to recompute the record length using the record length and block length fields (RL and BL in the block format) whenever the size of the record changes.

Software portability is negatively affected for programs using variable-length record files. In general, the way these records are handled is left to the implementer and it changes from one installation to another.

Finally, the block formats necessitate record length (RL) fields in each logical record and a block length (BL) field in each block. These parameters require extra disk or tape storage, which must be weighed against any possible storage savings when variable-length records are preferred.

A file can contain variable-length records under three circumstances.

1. It is a multiple record file.
2. Its record structure contains a variable number of fields.
3. Fields in its record structure are of variable length.

In some applications, the design of a file may consist of two or more record types of different lengths. Even though each one may be of fixed length, when viewed as a whole, such a multiple-record file will have variable-length records. Some files may have only one record type, but the record length would be variable because some fields in its record structure are of variable length.

Variable-Length Records in Multiple-Record Files

An example of variable-length records in a multiple-record file is shown in Figure 1. The PERSONNEL-FILE in this figure has two record types, PARENT-RECORD and CHILD-RECORD. Records in the file may belong to one or the other record structure and thus their length varies accordingly.

If such a file is an input file, a READ statement will input the record that is currently being pointed to. The current record can be of either type. Therefore, it is essential that the record structures include a special field that enables the programmer to distinguish records. In Figure 1 we used the field RECORD-TYPE-CODE for this purpose. This field is called RECORD-TYPE-CODE-PARENT in the PARENT-RECORD and RECORD-TYPE-CODE-CHILD in the CHILD-RECORD, and the records contain the literals P and C, respectively, to denote the record type.

As the WRITE statement in COBOL references the record name, writing records into such files is straightforward. All we have to do is prepare the record in the appropriate record structure and issue a WRITE statement.

Reading and subsequent processing can be tricky, however, and necessitate a good understanding of what happens upon input and the requirements of the specific application. After a READ statement is executed, the record fetched

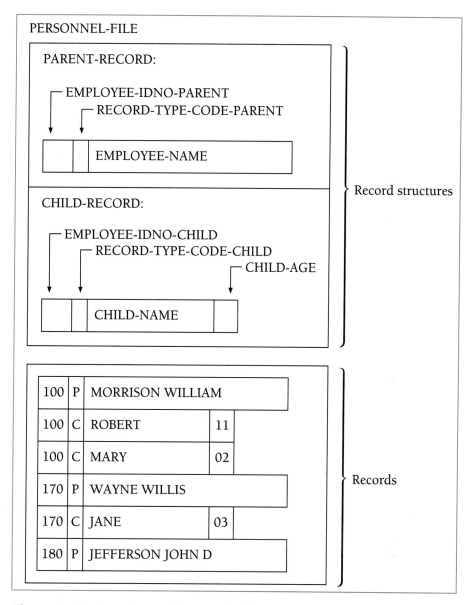

Figure 1 A Multiple-Record File with Variable-Length Records

into the main memory can fit any one of the record structures in the file. We should determine the record type using a type code field, such as RECORD-TYPE-CODE-PARENT in Figure 1, and continue processing. Otherwise, a blind reference to an arbitrary field may cause programming errors.

Again consider Figure 1. Suppose the current record that has just been input is a parent record with P as its type code. A reference to either RECORD-TYPE-CODE-PARENT or RECORD-TYPE-CODE-CHILD will reveal the value P. A blind reference to CHILD-AGE will bring a substring into the EMPLOYEE-NAME field, and a subsequent arithmetic operation on CHILD-AGE will result in an error.

Before we consider and study a COBOL program example for variable-length records, let us emphasize that, to the extent possible, variable-length record files should be avoided in application program development. We can take basically two approaches to transform a variable-length record into its fixed-length counterpart.

1. Replace the file with an equivalent fixed-length record file.
2. Replace the variable-length multiple-record file with two or more single-record files of fixed record length.

Any variable-length record file can be replaced with an equivalent fixed-length record file by right-padding the shorter records to bring the record length to that of the longest record. This is illustrated in Figure 2 for the PERSONNEL-FILE of Figure 1. The CHILD-RECORD, being the shorter of the two, is padded on the right with a FILLER to make its length the same as that of the PARENT-RECORD. This approach has the disadvantage of wasted storage. It should be noted that in this case, processing complexity due to different record types has not been eliminated.

A better approach is to replace the variable-length multiple-record file with two or more single-record files of fixed record length. Figure 3 shows the result of doing this for the PERSONNEL-FILE, which is replaced with the PARENT-

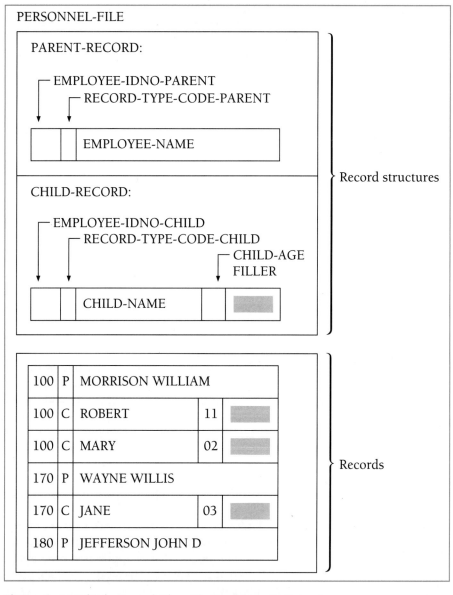

Figure 2 A Multiple-Record File with Fixed-Length Records

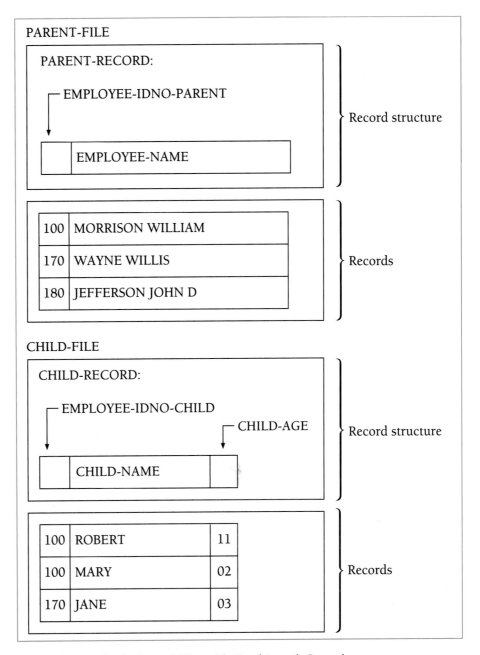

Figure 3 Two Single-Record Files with Fixed-Length Records

FILE and the CHILD-FILE. There is no wasted storage in this design. Also, all shortcomings of variable-length record files have been eliminated.

Variable-Length Records with Variable-Length Field Occurrences

The logical record structure may involve fields of varying lengths. A variable-length field may be a varying repetition of a fixed-size substructure emerging as a repeating group, or it may be a single field whose size may vary from one record to another.

The repeating group case is exemplified in the PERSONNEL-FILE of Figure 4. The substructure consisting of the CHILD-NAME and CHILD-AGE fields is of fixed length; however, the number of times it appears in a record

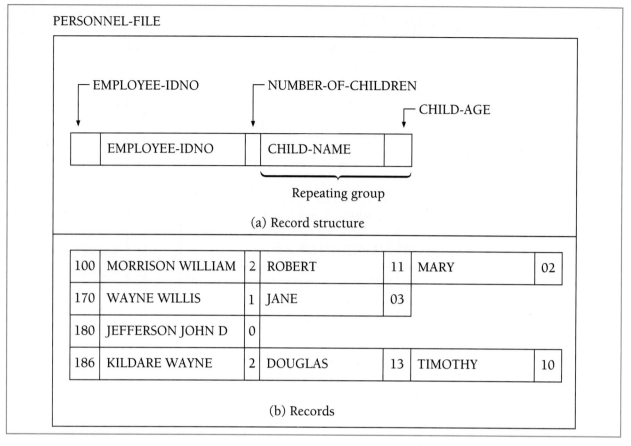

PERSONNEL-FILE

(a) Record structure

100	MORRISON WILLIAM	2	ROBERT	11	MARY	02
170	WAYNE WILLIS	1	JANE	03		
180	JEFFERSON JOHN D	0				
186	KILDARE WAYNE	2	DOUGLAS	13	TIMOTHY	10

(b) Records

Figure 4 A Variable-Length Record File with Multiple Fixed-Length Repeating Groups

depends on the employee represented by it. This can be handled in COBOL by including a field in the record structure that indicates the number of repetitions. In Figure 4, it is the NUMBER-OF-CHILDREN field. In COBOL, to describe the dependency of the repeating groups on such a field and the structure of the variable-length record, we use the OCCURS . . . DEPENDING ON clause in the FD block for the file. The repeating group is treated as an array. An example for the PERSONNEL-FILE of Figure 4 is given below.

```
FD  OUT-PERS-FILE
    LABEL RECORDS ARE STANDARD
    RECORD CONTAINS 29 TO 80 CHARACTERS
    DATA RECORD IS EMPLOYEE-RECORD.
01  EMPLOYEE-RECORD.
    05  EMPLOYEE-IDNO              PIC XXX.
    05  EMPLOYEE-NAME              PIC X(25).
    05  NUMBER-OF-CHILDREN         PIC 9.
    05  CHILD-DATA OCCURS 0 TO 3 TIMES DEPENDING ON
        NUMBER-OF-CHILDREN.
        10  CHILD-NAME             PIC X(15).
        10  CHILD-AGE              PIC 99.
```

In this record description, the fields EMPLOYEE-IDNO, EMPLOYEE-NAME, and NUMBER-OF-CHILDREN require 29 characters. The minimum and maximum values for NUMBER-OF-CHILDREN are 0 and 3. The repeating group of CHILD-NAME and CHILD-AGE occupies 17 characters. Therefore, the minimum record length for EMPLOYEE-RECORD is 29 and the maximum is 80.

In some applications, a variable-length logical record may be necessary due to the fact that one or more atomic fields are of variable length. The PERSONNEL-RECORD in Figure 5 has a variable length depending on the number of characters in the EMPLOYEE-NAME field. If the EMPLOYEE-NAME field is defined as a single data field, we treat it as a fixed-length field. What we should do is similar to what we did in the previous example. We include in the PERSONNEL-RECORD structure another field, called EM-PLOYEE-NAME-FIELD-LENGTH. Then we treat the EMPLOYEE-NAME as an array of single characters. The FD block for such a file would be

```
FD   PERSONNEL-FILE
     LABEL RECORDS ARE STANDARD
     RECORD CONTAINS 15 TO 40 CHARACTERS
     DATA RECORD IS PERSONNEL-RECORD.
01   PERSONNEL-RECORD.
     05   EMPLOYEE-IDNO                PIC XXX.
     05   EMPLOYEE-NAME-FIELD-LENGTH   PIC 99.
     05   EMPLOYEE-NAME.
          10   EMPL-NAME-BYTES         PIC X
               OCCURS 10 TO 35 TIMES
               DEPENDING ON EMPLOYEE-NAME-FIELD-LENGTH.
```

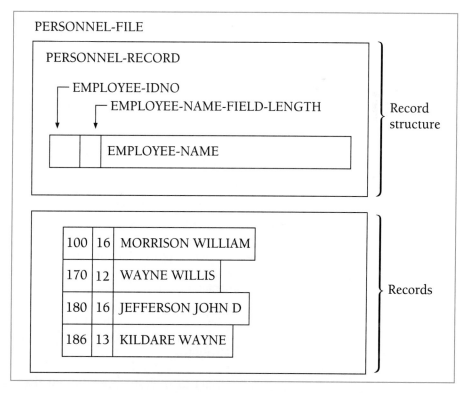

Figure 5 A Variable-Length Record with a Variable-Length Field

1. The logical sequence of records in a sequential file is the same as the physical sequence. (T or F)
2. The sequence number of records in a sequential file is that file's _____ key.
3. The content of a sequential tape file cannot be changed without copying. For sequential disk files, however, it is possible to update records without copying the entire file. (T or F)
4. The overall performance of a sequential file depends on _____ and _____ .
5. Fetching the next record is an efficient operation for sequential files. (T or F)
6. The LABEL RECORDS clause has no meaning for card and printer files in COBOL. (T or F)
7. The values of the label record parameters can be supplied either through _____ outside a COBOL program or by using the _____ in a COBOL program.
8. The REWRITE statement cannot be used for sequential tape files. (T or F)
9. Which of the following is a disadvantage of variable-length record files?
   a. Application software development is difficult.
   b. Execution efficiency of the software is negatively affected.
   c. Software portability is adversely affected.
   d. All of the above.
10. If one or more fields in the record structure of a file is of variable length, it is a variable-length record file. (T or F)

Answers: 1. T; 2. implicit; 3. T; 4. storage device characteristics, type of file operation; 5. T; 6. T; 7. job control language statements, VALUE OF clause; 8. T; 9. d; 10. T.

Example Program 1:   *Creation of a Variable-Length Record File*

To illustrate the programming considerations for variable-length input and output files, we will develop a COBOL program that generates a variable-length output file from a multiple-record file.

Problem   We have a PERSONNEL-FILE consisting of two record types. The first is called PARENT-RECORD and consists of the following fields:

1. A 3-character employee identification number
2. A 1-character code containing P for this record type
3. A 25-character employee name

The second record type in the file is called CHILD-RECORD. It is used to describe children of the employees in the PERSONNEL-FILE in terms of the following attributes:

1. A 3-character identification number for the parent employee
2. A 1-character code with the value C for the record type
3. A 15-character child name field
4. A 2-digit child age field

An instance of the PERSONNEL-FILE is shown in Program 1-Input. As far as the structure of this file is concerned, there are no restrictions on the number of children an employee may have.

We wish to develop a COBOL program that reads such a PERSONNEL-FILE and generates a variable-length record file called OUT-PERS-FILE with a single record type. The record structure of OUT-PERS-FILE consists of

1. A 3-character employee identification number
2. A 25-character employee name
3. A 1-digit field for number of children of an employee
4. From zero to 3 repeating groups of children information consisting of
   a. A 15-character child name
   b. A 2-digit child age

Solution

The source program listing of the COBOL program for this application is given in Program 1-Source. Lines 00050–00061 correspond to the FD block for OUT-PERS-FILE. It is defined as a variable-length record file through the RECORD CONTAINS 29 TO 80 CHARACTERS clause, and the OCCURS DEPENDING ON clause in line 00058.

An important aspect of the program is concerned with reading PERSON-NEL-FILE and processing its records. The nested IF statement in lines 00113–00129 identifies the record type after input, accordingly fills in the output fields, and writes a record into the output file OUT-PERS-FILE.

Program 1-Output shows an instance of the generated OUT-PERS-FILE using the file of Program 1-Input.

Example Program 2:   Creation of a Multiple-Record File with Variable-Length Records

The next sample program reads a multiple-record, fixed-length record file and generates a corresponding file that is a variable-length record file, again with multiple records.

Problem

We have a file called TRANSACTION-FILE with fixed-length records. The record length is 80 characters. Each record consists of

1. A 3-character employee identification number in columns 1–3
2. A 3-character transaction type in columns 6–8
3. Additional data in the rest of the record

The additional data depend on the transaction type, for which the following values are used:

DLT   Delete a record
ADD   Add a record
UEN   Update employee name
UDC   Update department code
UES   Update employee salary
UEY   Update employee years

In the transaction records, if the transaction type is DLT, there are no values in the additional data field. For ADD, a new record in terms of an employee name, department, salary, and number of years employed is stored as additional data. For different types of updates, appropriate new values are written in the additional data field. Program 2-Input shows an instance of the TRANSACTION-FILE.

Using this file, we want to create a new file with variable-length records such that storage waste caused by the fixed-length record design of the TRANSACTION-FILE is eliminated. This new file called OUT-TRANS-FILE will have multiple records, one record type for each value of the transaction type. For example, the transaction record for deleting a record (DLT) will have the record structure

```
01   WS-DLT-RECORD.
     05   EMPLOYEE-IDNO-DLT          PIC XXX.
     05   FILLER                     PIC XX.
     05   TRANSACTION-TYPE-DLT       PIC XXX.
```

whereas the transaction record for adding a record (ADD) will be

```
01 WS-ADD-RECORD.
     05   EMPLOYEE-IDNO-ADD          PIC XXX.
     05   FILLER                     PIC XX.
     05   TRANSACTION-TYPE-ADD       PIC XXX.
     05   FILLER                     PIC XX.
     05   EMPLOYEE-NAME-ADD          PIC X(25).
     05   FILLER                     PIC XX.
     05   DEPARTMENT-CODE-ADD        PIC XXX.
     05   FILLER                     PIC XX.
     05   YEARLY-SALARY-ADD          PIC 9(6)V99.
     05   FILLER                     PIC XX.
     05   YEARS-IN-COMPANY-ADD       PIC 99.
```

Also, the program is expected to identify the incorrect transaction type values and filter them out during the file copy operation.

Solution   The source listing of the program developed to solve the problem described above is shown in Program 2-Source. OUT-TRANS-FILE is defined as a variable-length record file in the FD block of lines 00042–00068. Its record length varies from 8 to 54 characters. An instance of the OUT-TRANS-FILE created by Program 2 is given in Program 2-Output.

Example Program 3: *Interactive Creation of a Sequential File*

In the remainder of this chapter we develop a series of related COBOL application programs that create and process sequential files. The first of the series is a program that enables the user to create a sequential disk file interactively. In on-line computer applications, data are structured and permanently stored in files immediately after they are entered by the data entry operator. The following application is typical of such file creation applications.

Problem   The sequential disk file that we will create is an employee master file. Its record structure consists of

1. A 3-digit employee identification number
2. A 25-character employee name
3. A 3-character code for the department in which the employee works
4. An 8-byte yearly salary field with PICTURE 9(6)V99
5. A 2-digit field representing the years an employee has been with the company

Input is interactive through the terminal keyboard. The user is expected to type natural values for different fields without taking into consideration COBOL language restrictions and requirements. For example, yearly salary should be typed as 34,500.00, not as 03450000. Years in company field value should be typed as 5, not as 05. The proper data conversions will be carried out by the program while creating the master file.

Solution   The compiler listing of the program developed for this application is given in Program 3-Source. The following points are noteworthy.

1. Field values are read using the ACCEPT statement, and adequate prompts are provided to aid the data entry operator.
2. To convert a salary value such as 45,000.00 to 04500000, which is the required form in the disk file, we make use of the string processing statements INSPECT REPLACING, UNSTRING, and STRING, as shown in lines 00140–00152.

Program 3-Output(a) is a sample interactive terminal session for this program. Program 3-Output(b) shows an instance of the created sequential disk file.

Example Program 4:   *Traditional File Update of a Sequential File*

The next program is an implementation of the traditional file update strategy.

Problem   In this application, we have four sequential disk files, but the logic is equally applicable to tape files. The files are as follows:

1. A MASTER-FILE containing personnel data
2. A TRANSACTION-FILE defining update operations on the MASTER-FILE
3. A NEW-MASTER-FILE that will be generated by the program to store the updated MASTER-FILE record
4. A REPORT-FILE that will contain error messages describing the update transactions that have failed

The record structure of the MASTER-FILE file is identical to that of the sequential file created in the previous application. The record structure of the NEW-MASTER-FILE is naturally the same as that of the MASTER-FILE.

The TRANSACTION-FILE has been conceived as a multiple-record sequential file, each record type describing a different transaction type. Each record type has a common field, a three-character transaction type. Six transaction types have been defined for this application. The transaction codes for them are

ADD	Add a new record
DLT	Delete an existing record
UEN	Update employee name field of an existing record
UDC	Update department code field of an existing record
UES	Update salary field of an existing record
UEY	Update years in company field of an existing record

Transaction records consist of the following fields:

1. An employee identification number to point to the record to be updated
2. A transaction code
3. Additional data values that depend on the transaction code:
   a. For ADD, data values for all fields in the MASTER-FILE record
   b. For DLT, none
   c. For UEN, UDC, UES, and UEY, the corresponding new field value

Program 3-Output(b), which shows the file generated by the previous sample application, is our MASTER-FILE. An instance of the TRANSACTION-FILE is given in Program 4-Input. Note that both the MASTER-FILE and the TRANSACTION-FILE are ordered in ascending sequence by employee identification number. In the process, the following are error conditions:

1. Attempt to add a new record for an existing MASTER-FILE record
2. Attempt to delete a nonexisting record
3. Attempt to update a nonexisting record
4. Illegal transaction code

In addition to the sequential order of records by employee identification number, we put the following restrictions on records in the TRANSACTION-FILE.

1. A record that has just been deleted cannot be updated.
2. A new record that has just been added to the NEW-MASTER-FILE cannot be deleted or updated in this batch cycle.
3. The transaction codes UEN, UDC, UES, and UEY for updating different fields of the same record can be mixed in any arbitrary order.

Solution   The logic of the traditional file update through copying process is described in the structured English-action diagram of Figure 6. This logic is implemented in COBOL, as shown in Program 4-Source. A run of this program with the MASTER-FILE of Program 3-Output and the TRANSACTION-FILE of Program 4-Input produces the updated master file of Program 4-Output(a) and the report file of Program 4-Output(b).

MAIN-PROGRAM:

      open MASTER-FILE and TRANSACTION-FILE in input mode;
      open NEW-MASTER-FILE and REPORT-FILE in output mode;
      read MASTER-FILE record;
      IF end of TRANSACTION-FILE is reached THEN
          copy rest of MASTER-FILE to NEW-MASTER-FILE;
      ENDIF;
      read TRANSACTION-FILE record;

      REPEAT UNTIL end of MASTER-FILE is reached
             AND end of TRANSACTION-FILE is reached
        execute UPDATE-MASTER-FILE;
      ENDREPEAT;

      close all files;
END MAIN-PROGRAM;

UPDATE-MASTER-FILE:

    IF EMPLOYEE-IDNO of MASTER-RECORD = EMPLOYEE-IDNO of
                    TRANSACTION-RECORD THEN
      IF transaction is "ADD A RECORD" THEN
          write error message into REPORT-FILE;
          read TRANSACTION-FILE record;
      ELSE
          IF transaction is "DELETE A RECORD" THEN
             read MASTER-FILE record;
             IF end of TRANSACTION-FILE is reached THEN
                copy rest of MASTER-FILE to NEW-MASTER-FILE;
             ENDIF;
             read TRANSACTION-FILE record;
          ELSE
             execute UPDATE-A-RECORD;
          ENDIF;
      ENDIF;
    ELSE
      IF EMPLOYEE-IDNO of MASTER-RECORD < EMPLOYEE-IDNO of
                    TRANSACTION-RECORD THEN
          write MASTER-RECORD into NEW-MASTER-FILE;
          read MASTER-FILE record;
          IF end of TRANSACTION-FILE is reached THEN
             copy rest of MASTER-FILE to NEW-MASTER-FILE;
          ENDIF;
      ELSE
          IF transaction is "ADD A RECORD" THEN
             execute ADD-A-NEW-RECORD;
          ELSE
             write error message into REPORT-FILE;
          ENDIF;
      ENDIF;
    ENDIF;
END UPDATE-MASTER-FILE;

Figure 6 Structured English Description of Traditional File Update Strategy with Action Diagram

```
UPDATE-A-RECORD:

        REPEAT UNTIL EMPLOYEE-IDNO of MASTER-RECORD NOT =
                       EMPLOYEE-IDNO of TRANSACTION-RECORD
                 OR end of TRANSACTION-FILE is reached
            modify MASTER-RECORD in memory according to updates;
              read TRANSACTION-FILE record;
        ENDREPEAT;

        write MASTER-RECORD into NEW-MASTER-FILE;
        read MASTER-FILE record;
        IF end of TRANSACTION-FILE is reached THEN
            copy rest of MASTER-FILE to NEW-MASTER-FILE;
        ENDIF;
END UPDATE-A-RECORD;


ADD-A-NEW-RECORD:

        prepare NEW-MASTER-RECORD in memory using TRANSACTION-RECORD;
        write NEW-MASTER-RECORD;
        read TRANSACTION-FILE record;
        IF EMPLOYEE-IDNO of TRANSACTION-RECORD = EMPLOYEE-IDNO of
              previous TRANSACTION-RECORD THEN


              REPEAT UNTIL EMPLOYEE-IDNO of TRANSACTION-RECORD NOT =
                             EMPLOYEE-IDNO of previous TRANSACTION-RECORD
                       OR end of TRANSACTION-FILE is reached
                  modify MASTER-RECORD in memory according to updates;
                    read TRANSACTION-FILE record;
              ENDREPEAT;

        ENDIF;
END ADD-A-NEW-RECORD;
```

Figure 6 (Continued)

Example Program 5:   *In Situ Update of a Sequential Disk File*

If a sequential file is stored on a direct-access device such as a disk, it can be maintained most efficiently by updating records in the master file. The primary advantage is that this avoids copying the master file, thus resulting in substantial savings in file I-O.

Problem   Here we implement the in situ file update logic for the application of the preceding section. Essentially, we have the same set of files: the MASTER-FILE that contains records to be updated, the TRANSACTION-FILE consisting of transaction descriptions, and the REPORT-FILE that will be generated by the program to store descriptions of invalid transactions. As no copying is necessary, a new master file will not be generated. All updates will be reflected in the source MASTER-FILE.

We propose to allow all kinds of updates as in the preceding application with the same restrictions. In other words, record deletions, additions, and modification of all fields except the employee identification number field are allowed. Both the MASTER-FILE and the TRANSACTION-FILE are ordered by employee identification numbers. Therefore, locating the record to be updated is handled similarly. Field value modification presents no problems. We simply locate the MASTER-FILE record, retrieve it, modify it in memory, and write it back. The only difference is that we use REWRITE instead of WRITE to do the last step.

Deleting an existing record does present a problem. There is no way we can physically do it without copying the master file. Therefore, we resort to logical deletion. We locate a record, mark it as deleted, and rewrite it. This requires that the record structure of the MASTER-FILE be modified to include an additional field called DELETE-FIELD. Our convention is that a record with DELETE-FIELD containing * is logically deleted, whereas one with a blank DELETE-FIELD is still active in the file. After a deleted record is marked, it is possible to copy the file at our convenience and get rid of it physically.

Another problem is adding records. This poses two difficulties. First, in general, an existing file cannot be expanded without destroying its content. Second, for a sequentially organized file, new records cannot be inserted easily into proper locations.

To overcome these problems we propose to include a few dummy records at the end of the MASTER-FILE. A dummy record in our application is identified by an employee identification number field value of 999. Whenever a new record is encountered in the TRANSACTION-FILE, we temporarily transfer it to another sequential file, called the ADDITION-FILE. After all transaction records have been processed, we copy the content of the ADDITION-FILE to the end of the MASTER-FILE onto the dummy records, to the extent permitted by the number of dummy records. Of course, whenever we add records, the order of records in the MASTER-FILE will be destroyed. We accept this and the necessity of occasionally sorting the MASTER-FILE, and proceed with the implementation.

Solution The compiler listing of the COBOL program developed for in situ update is given in Program 5-Source. Note the use of the REWRITE statement in line 00320 for writing records coming from the ADDITION-FILE onto the dummy records at the end of the MASTER-FILE. The REWRITE statement in line 00339 accomplishes record updates.

One weakness of Program 5-Source, as is apparent in line 00244, is the hard-coded value of 5 for the number of dummy records in the MASTER-FILE. In an actual application program, this statement should be replaced with a simple procedure that dynamically determines the number of dummy records. As this is not central to the discussion, we will leave it for the reader to tackle as one of the problems at the end of this chapter.

Program 5-Input(a) is an instance of the MASTER-FILE before update. Program 5-Input(b) shows an instance of the TRANSACTION-FILE. Program 5-Output(a) is the MASTER-FILE after update. Program 5-Output(b) and (c) are the error report file and the ADDITION-FILE, respectively, generated by the developed program.

Key Terms

implicit key
in situ file update
interactive input
label records
LABEL RECORDS clause
OCCURS DEPENDING ON clause

REWRITE statement
sequential organization
traditional file update
VALUE OF clause
variable-length record

Study Guide

Quick Scan

- The sequence of records in a sequential file is determined by their physical order. Logical ordering of records based on a key field can be established only by sorting the file.
- A sequential file does not have a recognizable and explicit organization key; however, the sequence number of records in it may be considered as an implicit key.
- File size for sequential files is determined during creation, but in some systems it can be changed later by adding records at their end. Records cannot be inserted at arbitrary points in sequential files.
- After creation, the content of a sequential tape file cannot be altered. Records can be modified or deleted only by copying the entire file. This is the basis of the traditional file update logic.
- Sequential disk files allow record update and logical record delete without copying. This principle is the essence of the in situ file update logic.
- In situ file update requires rewriting a record after modification.
- Efficiency of sequential files depend on the characteristics of the storage device and the type of the operation to be performed on the file.
- For retrieval of the next record, sequential files provide very fast access. On the other hand, retrieving a record that is far away from the current record may take a long time in a large file. Fetching all records in a sequential file is quite efficient, provided the desired retrieval sequence is the same as the physical sequence of records in the file.
- For magnetic tape and disk files, the user may create label records. The content of the label records are specified using the JCL statements, or the VALUE OF clause in the FD block for the file in a COBOL program.
- In COBOL, the I-O statements for sequential files are OPEN, CLOSE, READ, WRITE, and REWRITE.
- To use the REWRITE statement the file must be a disk file and must be opened in input-output mode. REWRITE is used for in situ update of records.
- For in situ update, a copy of the proper record is brought into the main memory using the READ statement and its content is altered in the record structure. A REWRITE statement is issued to write the modified record into the file.
- It is possible to store variable-length record files on mass storage devices. Also, COBOL has language features for variable-length records.
- Variable-length record files may be preferred if the logical design so dictates, or if transforming them into an equivalent fixed-length design results in a substantial storage waste.
- Using variable-length records in application software has its shortcomings: application software development difficulty, inefficient software execution, and adversely affected software portability.

- A file can contain variable-length records under two circumstances: it may be a multiple-record file with different record lengths, or it may consist of a single record type, but the record length may be variable because some fields in the record structure may have variable length.
- In a multiple-record variable-length file the record structures should include a field that identifies the record type. In a variable-length record with one or more variable-length fields, there must be a field in the record structure to specify the upper and lower bounds for the record length.
- In general, variable-length record files should be avoided in application software development. They can easily be transformed into their fixed-size counterpart.
- To transform a variable-length record file into a fixed-length record file, record structures may be replaced with fixed-length record structures by using a uniform record length that is equal to that of the longest record. This approach may result in storage waste. A better technique is to replace the file with several files of fixed record length.

Test Your Comprehension

Multiple-Choice Questions

1. Concerning file size in sequential files,
   a. Size is determined during file creation.
   b. Some file processing systems allow extending a sequential file by adding records at its end.
   c. The content of a sequential tape file cannot be altered without copying.
   d. All of the above are correct.
2. Concerning label records for COBOL files, which of the following statements is correct?
   a. The LABEL RECORDS clause should be used only for tape or disk files.
   b. The label record parameter values may be supplied either by JCLs outside a COBOL program or by using the VALUE OF clause in it.
   c. The label record parameters and their names change from one installation to the next.
   d. All of the above are correct.
3. Which of the following statements concerning variable-length record files is incorrect?
   a. If a file contains two or more record types of different lengths, it is a variable-length record file.
   b. In a single-record file, if one or more fields have variable size, the file is a variable-length record file.
   c. In general, it is not possible to transform a variable-length record file into an equivalent fixed-length record file.
   d. In multiple-record files with variable-length records, different record types should be identified using a field in the record structures.

Answers: 1. d; 2. d; 3. c.

Short Essay Questions

1. Explain how records are physically organized in a sequential file, and state what is meant by the term implicit key.
2. How can we add new records to an existing sequential file without copying it? Does COBOL allow this operation?
3. Explain the difference between traditional and in situ file update.
4. Discuss the factors that affect the efficiency of sequential files.
5. Explain under what circumstances sequential files are acceptably efficient.

6. Explain the function of the COBOL REWRITE statement.
7. How do we create label records for files? Explain why card files and printer files cannot have label records.
8. Under what circumstances does one have to use variable-length record files in application software development?
9. What are the disadvantages of variable-length record files?
10. Under what circumstances does a file emerge as a variable-length record file?
11. Why does reading a variable-length record file require more attention than writing it?
12. How can we transform variable-length record files to equivalent fixed-length record files? Explain and discuss the pros and cons of the available transformation techniques.

Improve Your Problem-Solving Ability

Programming Exercises

1. Write a complete COBOL FD block for each file described pictorially in Figures 1 through 5.
2. We want to store the following information in a student data base:

STUDENT-IDNO	4-digit, numeric, not to be used for computation
STUDENT-NAME	25-byte, alphabetic
STUDENT-MAJOR	3-byte, alphabetic department code
ACADEMIC-YEAR	2-digit, numeric
SEMESTER	F for fall, S for spring
COURSE-CODE	6-character alphanumeric
COURSE-GRADE	1-character, alphabetic

A student can enroll in a maximum of six courses each semester and should complete degree requirements in a maximum of 10 semesters. Accordingly, write complete FD blocks together with record descriptions for several possible designs, variable- or fixed-length records, and discuss the strengths and weaknesses of each.

3. Write a structured English description of the in situ file update program of Program 5-Source.
4. Rewrite Program 5-Source such that the number of dummy records in the sequential file before in situ update is determined by the program, and not hard-coded as in line 00244 of Program 5-Source.

Programming Problems

1. We have the following table of employee skills for employees of our company.

EMPLOYEE-ID	EMPLOYEE-NAME	SKILL-CODE	YEARS-OF-EXPERIENCE
111-11-1111	JOHN JOHNSON	1101	2
		1102	3
		1103	2
		1110	1
111-22-1111	ELLEN BRONSON	1101	2
		1102	5
		1104	2
111-33-1111	JANE TAILOR	1201	3
		1204	2
111-44-1111	ROBERT RULES	1102	7
		1103	1
111-55-1111	GEENA FRY	1201	1

Develop and run a COBOL program that allows a data entry operator to input data values for EMPLOYEE-ID, EMPLOYEE-NAME, SKILL-CODE, and YEARS-OF-EXPERIENCE for each employee at the terminal, and create a variable-length record sequential disk file called EMPLOYEE-SKILLS with the following record structure.

```
01  EMP-SKILLS-RECORD.
    05   EMPLOYEE-ID                PIC X(9).
    05   EMPLOYEE-NAME              PIC X(25).
    05   NO-OF-SKILLS               PIC 99.
    05   SKILLS-DATA OCCURS 0 TO 7 TIMES
         DEPENDING ON NO-OF-SKILLS.
         10   SKILL-CODE            PIC X(4).
         10   YRS-OF-EXP            PIC 99.
```

The data entry operator is not expected to type in a value for NO-OF-SKILLS. Your program should inquire as to whether there are any more skills data for an employee, and, in case the operator indicates that there are not, the program should compute and store a value for NO-OF-SKILLS.

2. Develop a COBOL program that reads the variable-length record sequential file EMPLOYEE-SKILLS of the previous programming problem and creates two sequential disk files.
   a. A file called EMPLOYEE, whose records consist of EMPLOYEE-ID, EMPLOYEE-NAME, and NO-OF-SKILLS
   b. A file called EMPLOYEE-SKILL-FILE, whose records are based on EMPLOYEE-ID, SKILL-CODE, and YRS-OF-EXP for each employee-skill pair

3. Write a COBOL program that is capable of updating both the EMPLOYEE and EMPLOYEE-SKILLS-FILE of programming problem 3 using a transaction file. The transaction file has a record structure that is based on EMPLOYEE-ID, SKILL-CODE, and YRS-OF-EXP. The transaction file may contain new skill descriptions for an employee or updates of YRS-OF-EXP for an employee-skill pair. It may not contain information about a new employee. This program should use the traditional file update strategy.

4. Write a program for programming problem 3, but this time use the in situ file update strategy for sequential disk files.

```
                              COLUMNS
1   5    10   15   20   25   30   35   40   45   50   55   60   65   70   75
----|----|----|----|----|----|----|----|----|----|----|----|----|----|----|

100   P   MORRISON WILLIAM
100   C   ROBERT              11
100   C   MARY                02
150   P   EASTMAN THOMAS
170   P   WAYNE WILLIS
170   C   JANE                03
170   C   GREGORY             05
180   P   JEFFERSON JOHN D
186   P   KILDARE WAYNE
186   C   DOUGLAS             13
```

Program 1-Input An Instance of PERSONNEL-FILE of Program 1

```
00001    *..............................................................
00002    IDENTIFICATION DIVISION.
00003    PROGRAM-ID. VARIABLE-LENGTH-RECORDS-1.
00004
00005    ***************************************************************
00006    ***   THIS PROGRAM READS RECORD OCCURRENCES FROM A MULTIPLE-   *
00007    ***     RECORD, VARIABLE RECORD LENGTH PERSONNEL FILE, AND      *
00008    ***     CREATES A VARIABLE RECORD LENGTH FILE WITH MULTIPLE     *
00009    ***     GROUP OCCURRENCES.                                      *
00010    ***************************************************************
00011
00012    AUTHOR.   UCKAN.
00013    DATE-WRITTEN. FEB 23, 1991.
00014    DATE-COMPILED. FEB 25,1991.
00015    *..............................................................
00016    ENVIRONMENT DIVISION.
00017    CONFIGURATION SECTION.
00018    SOURCE-COMPUTER. IBM-370.
00019    OBJECT-COMPUTER. IBM-370.
00020    INPUT-OUTPUT SECTION.
00021    FILE-CONTROL.
00022        SELECT PERSONNEL-FILE  ASSIGN TO INFILE.
00023        SELECT OUT-PERS-FILE   ASSIGN TO OUTFILE.
00024
00025    *..............................................................
00026    DATA DIVISION.
00027
00028    FILE SECTION.
00029    FD   PERSONNEL-FILE
00030         LABEL RECORDS ARE STANDARD
00031         RECORD CONTAINS 27 TO 33 CHARACTERS
00032         DATA RECORDS ARE PARENT-RECORD
00033                          CHILD-RECORD.
00034    01   PARENT-RECORD.
00035         05   EMPLOYEE-IDNO-PARENT       PIC XXX.
00036         05   FILLER                     PIC XX.
00037         05   RECORD-TYPE-CODE-PARENT    PIC X.
00038         05   FILLER                     PIC XX.
00039         05   EMPLOYEE-NAME              PIC X(25).
00040
00041    01   CHILD-RECORD.
00042         05   EMPLOYEE-IDNO-CHILD        PIC XXX.
00043         05   FILLER                     PIC XX.
00044         05   RECORD-TYPE-CODE-CHILD     PIC X.
00045         05   FILLER                     PIC XX.
00046         05   CHILD-NAME                 PIC X(15).
00047         05   FILLER                     PIC XX.
00048         05   CHILD-AGE                  PIC 99.
00049
00050    FD   OUT-PERS-FILE
00051         LABEL RECORDS ARE STANDARD
00052         RECORD CONTAINS 29 TO 80 CHARACTERS
00053         DATA RECORD IS OUT-PERS-RECORD.
```

Program 1-Source A Sample Program with Variable-Length Record I-O Files

```
00054     01  OUT-PERS-RECORD.
00055         05  EMPLOYEE-IDNO-OUT          PIC XXX.
00056         05  EMPLOYEE-NAME-OUT          PIC X(25).
00057         05  NUMBER-OF-CHILDREN         PIC 9.
00058         05  CHILD-DATA OCCURS 0 TO 3 TIMES DEPENDING ON
00059             NUMBER-OF-CHILDREN.
00060             10  CHILD-NAME-OUT         PIC X(15).
00061             10  CHILD-AGE-OUT          PIC 99.
00062
00063     WORKING-STORAGE SECTION.
00064
00065     **********> SWITCHES:
00066
00067     01  END-OF-PERSONNEL-FILE-FLAG   PIC XXX       VALUE "NO".
00068         88  PERSONNEL-FILE-ENDS                    VALUE "YES".
00069
00070     **********> VARIABLES:
00071
00072     01  NO-OF-CHILDREN               PIC 99.
00073     01  WS-EMPLOYEE-IDNO             PIC XXX.
00074     01  WS-EMPLOYEE-NAME             PIC X(25).
00075
00076     *..........................................................
00077     PROCEDURE DIVISION.
00078     A-MAINLINE.
00079         OPEN INPUT  PERSONNEL-FILE
00080              OUTPUT OUT-PERS-FILE.
00081
00082         MOVE SPACES TO EMPLOYEE-NAME.
00083         PERFORM B1-READ-NEXT-RECORD.
00084
00085         MOVE EMPLOYEE-IDNO-PARENT TO WS-EMPLOYEE-IDNO.
00086         MOVE EMPLOYEE-NAME        TO WS-EMPLOYEE-NAME.
00087         MOVE 0                    TO NO-OF-CHILDREN.
00088
00089         PERFORM B2-READ-AND-WRITE
00090              UNTIL PERSONNEL-FILE-ENDS.
00091
00092         CLOSE PERSONNEL-FILE
00093               OUT-PERS-FILE.
00094
00095         STOP RUN.
00096
00097     B1-READ-NEXT-RECORD.
00098         READ PERSONNEL-FILE
00099              AT END MOVE "YES" TO END-OF-PERSONNEL-FILE-FLAG.
00100
00101
00102     B2-READ-AND-WRITE.
00103
00104         PERFORM B1-READ-NEXT-RECORD.
00105
```

Program 1-Source (Continued)

```
00106          IF PERSONNEL-FILE-ENDS
00107                  MOVE WS-EMPLOYEE-IDNO TO EMPLOYEE-IDNO-OUT
00108                  MOVE WS-EMPLOYEE-NAME TO EMPLOYEE-NAME-OUT
00109                  MOVE NO-OF-CHILDREN    TO NUMBER-OF-CHILDREN
00110
00111                  WRITE OUT-PERS-RECORD
00112          ELSE
00113             IF RECORD-TYPE-CODE-PARENT = "P"
00114                  MOVE NO-OF-CHILDREN    TO NUMBER-OF-CHILDREN
00115                  MOVE WS-EMPLOYEE-IDNO TO EMPLOYEE-IDNO-OUT
00116                  MOVE WS-EMPLOYEE-NAME TO EMPLOYEE-NAME-OUT
00117
00118                  WRITE OUT-PERS-RECORD
00119
00120                  MOVE EMPLOYEE-IDNO-PARENT TO WS-EMPLOYEE-IDNO
00121                  MOVE EMPLOYEE-NAME        TO WS-EMPLOYEE-NAME
00122                  MOVE O                    TO NO-OF-CHILDREN
00123          ELSE
00124                  ADD 1 TO NO-OF-CHILDREN
00125                  MOVE CHILD-NAME TO
00126                          CHILD-NAME-OUT (NO-OF-CHILDREN)
00127                  MOVE CHILD-AGE TO
00128                          CHILD-AGE-OUT (NO-OF-CHILDREN)
00129                  MOVE SPACES    TO EMPLOYEE-NAME.
```

Program 1-Source (Continued)

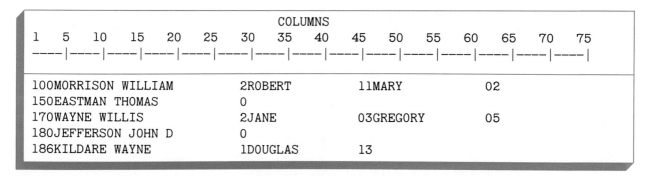

```
                              COLUMNS
 1    5    10   15   20   25   30   35   40   45   50   55   60   65   70   75
----|----|----|----|----|----|----|----|----|----|----|----|----|----|----|

100MORRISON WILLIAM           2ROBERT          11MARY              02
150EASTMAN THOMAS             0
170WAYNE WILLIS               2JANE            03GREGORY           05
180JEFFERSON JOHN D           0
186KILDARE WAYNE              1DOUGLAS         13
```

Program 1-Output An Instance of OUT-PERS-FILE of Program 1

```
                              COLUMNS
 1    5    10   15   20   25   30   35   40   45   50   55   60   65   70   75
----|----|----|----|----|----|----|----|----|----|----|----|----|----|----|

100   UDC   SLS
105   ADD   NELSON KIM              DP    04250000   06
156   DLT
170   UEY   03
170   UES   02950000
189   UDT   09
200   UEN   DONNEL JANE
208   UEV   RONSON MEREDITH         SLS   04260000   07
```

Program 2-Input An Instance of TRANSACTION-FILE of Program 2

```
00001    *..............................................................
00002    IDENTIFICATION DIVISION.
00003    PROGRAM-ID. VARIABLE-LENGTH-RECORDS-2.
00004    ****************************************************************
00005    ***   THIS PROGRAM READS TRANSACTION RECORD OCCURRENCES FROM A   *
00006    ***   FIXED-LENGTH RECORD FILE, AND CREATES A MULTIPLE-RECORD,   *
00007    ***   VARIABLE-LENGTH-RECORD FILE, CALLED OUT-TRANS-FILE.        *
00008    ****************************************************************
00009
00010    AUTHOR.   UCKAN.
00011    DATE-WRITTEN. FEB 22, 1991.
00012    DATE-COMPILED. FEB 26,1991.
00013    *..............................................................
00014    ENVIRONMENT DIVISION.
00015    CONFIGURATION SECTION.
00016    SOURCE-COMPUTER. IBM-370.
00017    OBJECT-COMPUTER. IBM-370.
00018    INPUT-OUTPUT SECTION.
00019    FILE-CONTROL.
00020        SELECT TRANSACTION-FILE  ASSIGN TO INFILE.
00021        SELECT OUT-TRANS-FILE    ASSIGN TO OUTFILE.
00022
00023    *..............................................................
00024    DATA DIVISION.
00025    FILE SECTION.
00026    FD   TRANSACTION-FILE
00027        LABEL RECORDS ARE STANDARD
00028        RECORD CONTAINS 80 CHARACTERS
00029        DATA RECORD IS TRANSACTION-RECORD.
00030    01   TRANSACTION-RECORD.
00031        05   EMPLOYEE-IDNO-IN        PIC XXX.
00032        05   FILLER                  PIC XX.
00033        05   TRANSACTION-TYPE-IN     PIC XXX.
00034            88   DELETE-A-RECORD                 VALUE "DLT".
00035            88   ADD-A-RECORD                    VALUE "ADD".
00036            88   UPDATE-EMPLOYEE-NAME            VALUE "UEN".
00037            88   UPDATE-DEPARTMENT-CODE          VALUE "UDC".
00038            88   UPDATE-EMPLOYEE-SALARY          VALUE "UES".
00039            88   UPDATE-EMPLOYEE-YEARS           VALUE "UEY".
00040        05   FILLER                  PIC X(72).
00041
00042    FD   OUT-TRANS-FILE
00043        LABEL RECORDS ARE STANDARD
00044        RECORD CONTAINS 8 TO 54 CHARACTERS
00045        DATA RECORDS ARE
00046                            ADD-RECORD-OUT
00047                            DELETE-RECORD-OUT
00048                            CHANGE-NAME-RECORD-OUT
00049                            CHANGE-DEPT-CODE-RECORD-OUT
00050                            CHANGE-SALARY-RECORD-OUT
00051                            CHANGE-YEARS-RECORD-OUT.
00052    01   ADD-RECORD-OUT.
00053        05   FILLER                  PIC X(54).
00054
```

Program 2-Source A Sample Program Using a Variable-Length Record Output File

```
00055    01  DELETE-RECORD-OUT.
00056        05  FILLER                    PIC X(8).
00057
00058    01  CHANGE-NAME-RECORD-OUT.
00059        05  FILLER                    PIC X(35).
00060
00061    01  CHANGE-DEPT-CODE-RECORD-OUT.
00062        05  FILLER                    PIC X(13).
00063
00064    01  CHANGE-SALARY-RECORD-OUT.
00065        05  FILLER                    PIC X(18).
00066
00067    01  CHANGE-YEARS-RECORD-OUT.
00068        05  FILLER                    PIC X(12).
00069
00070
00071    WORKING-STORAGE SECTION.
00072
00073    **********> SWITCHES:
00074
00075    01  END-OF-TRANSACTION-FILE-FLAG  PIC XXX      VALUE "NO".
00076        88  TRANSACTION-FILE-ENDS                  VALUE "YES".
00077
00078    **********> STRUCTURES:
00079
00080    01  WS-ADD-RECORD.
00081        05  EMPLOYEE-IDNO-ADD         PIC XXX.
00082        05  FILLER                    PIC XX.
00083        05  TRANSACTION-TYPE-ADD      PIC XXX.
00084        05  FILLER                    PIC XX.
00085        05  EMPLOYEE-NAME-ADD         PIC X(25).
00086        05  FILLER                    PIC XX.
00087        05  DEPARTMENT-CODE-ADD       PIC XXX.
00088        05  FILLER                    PIC XX.
00089        05  YEARLY-SALARY-ADD         PIC 9(6)V99.
00090        05  FILLER                    PIC XX.
00091        05  YEARS-IN-COMPANY-ADD      PIC 99.
00092
00093    01  WS-DLT-RECORD.
00094        05  EMPLOYEE-IDNO-DLT         PIC XXX.
00095        05  FILLER                    PIC XX.
00096        05  TRANSACTION-TYPE-DLT      PIC XXX.
00097
00098    01  WS-UEN-RECORD.
00099        05  EMPLOYEE-IDNO-UEN         PIC XXX.
00100        05  FILLER                    PIC XX.
00101        05  TRANSACTION-TYPE-UEN      PIC XXX.
00102        05  FILLER                    PIC XX.
00103        05  EMPLOYEE-NAME-UEN         PIC X(25).
00104
00105    01  WS-UDC-RECORD.
00106        05  EMPLOYEE-IDNO-UDC         PIC XXX.
00107        05  FILLER                    PIC XX.
00108        05  TRANSACTION-TYPE-UDC      PIC XXX.
```

Program 2-Source (Continued)

```
00109          05   FILLER                 PIC XX.
00110          05   DEPARTMENT-CODE-UDC    PIC XXX.
00111
00112     01   WS-UES-RECORD.
00113          05   EMPLOYEE-IDNO-UES      PIC XXX.
00114          05   FILLER                 PIC XX.
00115          05   TRANSACTION-TYPE-UES   PIC XXX.
00116          05   FILLER                 PIC XX.
00117          05   YEARLY-SALARY-UES      PIC 9(6)V99.
00118
00119     01   WS-UEY-RECORD.
00120          05   EMPLOYEE-IDNO-UEY      PIC XXX.
00121          05   FILLER                 PIC XX.
00122          05   TRANSACTION-TYPE-UEY   PIC XXX.
00123          05   FILLER                 PIC XX.
00124          05   YEARS-IN-COMPANY-UEY   PIC 99.
00125     *..................................................................
00126     PROCEDURE DIVISION.
00127     A-MAINLINE.
00128         OPEN INPUT  TRANSACTION-FILE
00129              OUTPUT OUT-TRANS-FILE.
00130         READ TRANSACTION-FILE
00131              AT END MOVE "YES" TO END-OF-TRANSACTION-FILE-FLAG.
00132
00133         PERFORM B1-WRITE-AND-READ
00134              UNTIL TRANSACTION-FILE-ENDS.
00135
00136         CLOSE TRANSACTION-FILE
00137              OUT-TRANS-FILE.
00138         STOP RUN.
00139
00140     B1-WRITE-AND-READ.
00141        IF DELETE-A-RECORD
00142              MOVE TRANSACTION-RECORD TO WS-DLT-RECORD
00143              WRITE DELETE-RECORD-OUT FROM WS-DLT-RECORD.
00144
00145        IF ADD-A-RECORD
00146              MOVE TRANSACTION-RECORD TO WS-ADD-RECORD
00147              WRITE ADD-RECORD-OUT FROM WS-ADD-RECORD.
00148
00149        IF UPDATE-EMPLOYEE-NAME
00150              MOVE TRANSACTION-RECORD TO WS-UEN-RECORD
00151              WRITE CHANGE-NAME-RECORD-OUT FROM WS-UEN-RECORD.
00152
00153        IF UPDATE-DEPARTMENT-CODE
00154              MOVE TRANSACTION-RECORD TO WS-UDC-RECORD
00155              WRITE CHANGE-DEPT-CODE-RECORD-OUT FROM WS-UDC-RECORD.
00156
00157        IF UPDATE-EMPLOYEE-SALARY
00158              MOVE TRANSACTION-RECORD TO WS-UES-RECORD
00159              WRITE CHANGE-SALARY-RECORD-OUT FROM WS-UES-RECORD.
00160
```

Program 2-Source (Continued)

```
00161          IF UPDATE-EMPLOYEE-YEARS
00162                  MOVE TRANSACTION-RECORD TO WS-UEY-RECORD
00163                  WRITE CHANGE-YEARS-RECORD-OUT FROM WS-UEY-RECORD.
00164
00165          READ TRANSACTION-FILE
00166                  AT END MOVE "YES" TO END-OF-TRANSACTION-FILE-FLAG.
```

Program 2-Source (Continued)

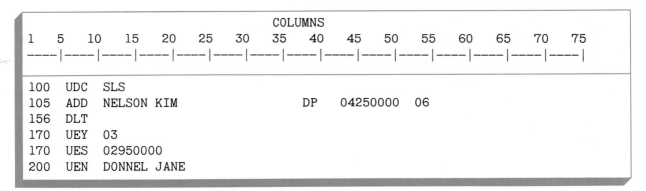

```
                                    COLUMNS
1    5    10   15   20   25   30   35   40   45   50   55   60   65   70   75
----|----|----|----|----|----|----|----|----|----|----|----|----|----|----|

100  UDC  SLS
105  ADD  NELSON KIM                    DP    04250000   06
156  DLT
170  UEY  03
170  UES  02950000
200  UEN  DONNEL JANE
```

Program 2-Output An Instance of OUT-TRANS-FILE of Program 2

```
00001    *...................................................................
00002      IDENTIFICATION DIVISION.
00003      PROGRAM-ID.  INTERACTIVE-INPUT.
00004
00005    *********************************************************************
00006    ***   THIS PROGRAM DEMONSTRATES INTERACTIVE INPUT CAPABILITIES OF *
00007    ***   THE STANDARD COBOL COMPILER.  IT CAN BE USED TO CREATE A    *
00008    ***   SEQUENTIAL DISK FILE, CALLED "MASTER-FILE" IN THE PROGRAM,  *
00009    ***   WITH THE FOLLOWING DATA FIELDS:                             *
00010    ***      1. A 3-DIGIT EMPLOYEE IDENTIFICATION NUMBER,             *
00011    ***      2. A 25-BYTE EMPLOYEE NAME,                              *
00012    ***      3. A 3-CHARACTER DEPARTMENT CODE,                        *
00013    ***      4. AN 8-BYTE NUMERIC YEARLY SALARY, AND                  *
00014    ***      5. A 2-DIGIT YEARS-IN-COMPANY VALUE.                     *
00015    *********************************************************************
00016
00017      AUTHOR.  UCKAN.
00018      DATE-WRITTEN. NOV 3, 1990.
00019      DATE-COMPILED. FEB 16,1991.
00021    *...................................................................
00022      ENVIRONMENT DIVISION.
00023      CONFIGURATION SECTION.
00024      SOURCE-COMPUTER. IBM-370.
00025      OBJECT-COMPUTER. IBM-370.
00026      INPUT-OUTPUT SECTION.
00027      FILE-CONTROL.
00028          SELECT MASTER-FILE ASSIGN TO OUTFILE.
00029
```

Program 3-Source Sample COBOL Program to Create a Sequential File Interactively

```
00030    *.................................................................
00031    DATA DIVISION.
00032    FILE SECTION.
00033
00034    FD  MASTER-FILE
00035        LABEL RECORDS ARE STANDARD
00036        RECORD CONTAINS 49 CHARACTERS
00037        DATA RECORD IS MASTER-RECORD.
00038    01  MASTER-RECORD.
00039        05   EMPLOYEE-IDNO-MS          PIC XXX.
00040        05   FILLER                    PIC XX.
00041        05   EMPLOYEE-NAME-MS          PIC X(25).
00042        05   FILLER                    PIC XX.
00043        05   DEPARTMENT-CODE-MS        PIC XXX.
00044        05   FILLER                    PIC XX.
00045        05   YEARLY-SALARY-MS          PIC 9(6)V99.
00046        05   FILLER                    PIC XX.
00047        05   YEARS-IN-COMPANY-MS       PIC 99.
00048
00049    WORKING-STORAGE SECTION.
00050
00051    **********> SWITCHES:
00052
00053    01   START-OF-INPUT-FLAG          PIC X(3)      VALUE "NO".
00054        88   INPUT-STARTS                           VALUE "YES".
00055
00056    01   END-OF-INPUT-FLAG            PIC X(4)      VALUE "NO".
00057        88   INPUT-ENDS                             VALUE "DONE".
00058
00059    **********> STRUCTURES:
00060
00061    01   NEW-RECORD.
00062        05   EMPLOYEE-IDNO            PIC XXX.
00063        05   FILLER                  PIC XX        VALUE SPACES.
00064        05   EMPLOYEE-NAME            PIC X(25).
00065        05   FILLER                  PIC XX        VALUE SPACES.
00066        05   DEPARTMENT-CODE          PIC XXX.
00067        05   FILLER                  PIC XX        VALUE SPACES.
00068        05   YEARLY-SALARY           PIC 9(6)V99.
00069        05   FILLER                  PIC XX        VALUE SPACES.
00070        05   YEARS-IN-COMPANY         PIC 99.
00071
00072    01   INPUT-FIELDS.
00073        05   YEARLY-SALARY-IN         PIC X(10).
00074        05   YEARS-IN.
00075            10   YEARS-PART-1        PIC X.
00076            10   YEARS-PART-2        PIC X.
00077
00078    01   RECORD-COUNT-LINE.
00079        05   FILLER                  PIC X(7)      VALUE "*****> ".
00080        05   RECORD-COUNT            PIC 99.
00081        05   RECORD-OR-RECORDS        PIC X(8).
00082        05   FILLER                  PIC X(8)      VALUE " STORED.".
00083
```

Program 3-Source (Continued)

```
00084     01  PARTS-OF-YEARLY-SALARY.
00085         05  PART-1                  PIC 999.
00086         05  PART-2                  PIC 999.
00087         05  PART-3                  PIC 99.
00088
00089     *............................................................
00090     PROCEDURE DIVISION.
00091     A-MAINLINE.
00092         OPEN OUTPUT MASTER-FILE.
00093         MOVE ZEROS TO RECORD-COUNT.
00094
00095         DISPLAY "*****************************************************".
00096         DISPLAY "DO YOU WANT TO INPUT RECORDS FOR PERSONNEL FILE?".
00097         DISPLAY "TYPE YES OR NO".
00098         DISPLAY "*****************************************************".
00099         ACCEPT START-OF-INPUT-FLAG FROM CONSOLE.
00100
00101         IF INPUT-STARTS
00102                 PERFORM B1-INPUT-EMPLOYEE-INFORMATION
00103                     UNTIL INPUT-ENDS.
00104
00105         CLOSE MASTER-FILE.
00106         STOP RUN.
00107
00108     B1-INPUT-EMPLOYEE-INFORMATION.
00109         DISPLAY "*****************************************************".
00110         DISPLAY  "ENTER EMPLOYEE ID NUMBER".
00111         ACCEPT EMPLOYEE-IDNO FROM CONSOLE.
00112
00113         DISPLAY  "ENTER EMPLOYEE NAME".
00114         ACCEPT EMPLOYEE-NAME FROM CONSOLE.
00115
00116         DISPLAY  "ENTER DEPARTMENT CODE".
00117         ACCEPT DEPARTMENT-CODE FROM CONSOLE.
00118
00119         DISPLAY  "ENTER YEARLY SALARY".
00120         DISPLAY  "TYPE SALARY WITH DECIMAL POINT AS IN: 15,000.00".
00121         ACCEPT YEARLY-SALARY-IN FROM CONSOLE.
00122
00123         PERFORM  C1-CONVERT-SALARY-TO-NUMERIC.
00124
00125         DISPLAY  "ENTER YEARS IN THE COMPANY".
00126         ACCEPT YEARS-IN FROM CONSOLE.
00127
00128         IF YEARS-PART-2 = SPACE
00129                 MOVE YEARS-PART-1 TO YEARS-PART-2
00130                 MOVE ZERO         TO YEARS-PART-1.
00131
00132         MOVE YEARS-IN TO YEARS-IN-COMPANY.
00133
00134         WRITE MASTER-RECORD FROM NEW-RECORD.
00135         ADD 1 TO RECORD-COUNT.
00136
00137         PERFORM C2-CHECK-FOR-CONTINUATION.
```

Program 3-Source (Continued)

```
00138
00139      Cl-CONVERT-SALARY-TO-NUMERIC.
00140          INSPECT YEARLY-SALARY-IN
00141                  REPLACING LEADING SPACES BY ZERO.
00142
00143          UNSTRING YEARLY-SALARY-IN
00144                  DELIMITED BY "," OR "."
00145            INTO   PART-1
00146                   PART-2
00147                   PART-3.
00148
00149          STRING   PART-1 DELIMITED BY SIZE
00150                   PART-2 DELIMITED BY SIZE
00151                   PART-3 DELIMITED BY SIZE
00152            INTO   YEARLY-SALARY.
00153
00154      C2-CHECK-FOR-CONTINUATION.
00155          IF RECORD-COUNT > 1
00156                  MOVE " RECORDS" TO RECORD-OR-RECORDS
00157          ELSE
00158                  MOVE " RECORD" TO RECORD-OR-RECORDS.
00159
00160          DISPLAY RECORD-COUNT-LINE.
00161
00162          DISPLAY "***********************************************".
00163          DISPLAY "DO YOU WANT TO CONTINUE?".
00164          DISPLAY "TO TERMINATE INPUT TYPE DONE".
00165          DISPLAY "TO CONTINUE PRESS RETURN".
00166          DISPLAY "***********************************************".
00167          ACCEPT END-OF-INPUT-FLAG FROM CONSOLE.
```

Program 3-Source (Continued)

```
***************************************************
DO YOU WANT TO INPUT RECORDS FOR PERSONNEL FILE?
TYPE YES OR NO
***************************************************
IKF990D, AWAITING REPLY.
 YES
***************************************************
 ENTER EMPLOYEE ID NUMBER
IKF990D, AWAITING REPLY.
 100
 ENTER EMPLOYEE NAME
IKF990D, AWAITING REPLY.
 MORRISON WILLIAM F
 ENTER DEPARTMENT CODE
IKF990D, AWAITING REPLY.
 ACC
 ENTER YEARLY SALARY
 TYPE SALARY WITH DECIMAL POINT AS IN: 15,000.00
IKF990D, AWAITING REPLY.
 32,770.00
 ENTER YEARS IN THE COMPANY
```

Program 3-Output(a) An Interactive Terminal Session for Program 3

```
IKF990D, AWAITING REPLY.
 5
*****> 01  RECORD STORED.
*************************************************
DO YOU WANT TO CONTINUE?
TO TERMINATE INPUT TYPE DONE
TO CONTINUE PRESS RETURN
*************************************************
IKF990D, AWAITING REPLY.
 ................
 ................
```

Program 3-Output(a) (Continued)

```
                                COLUMNS
 1    5    10   15   20   25   30   35   40   45   50   55
----|----|----|----|----|----|----|----|----|----|----|--

100   MORRISON WILLIAM F      ACC  03277000  05
150   EASTMAN THOMAS          ACC  04530000  07
170   WAYNE WILLIS            DP   02760000  02
180   JEFFERSON JOHN D        DP   03530000  03
186   KILDARE WAYNE           SLS  03600000  04
189   CROSETTE CARLOS J       SLS  04470000  08
190   DOWSON DAVID            DP   03400000  06
200   PEAR JANE               ACC  03775000  06
205   JASON TERRY             ACC  02344000  01
210   DIONNE WILLIAM          DP   02500000  02
219   PETERS DAVID            SLS  03560000  08
220   TEAL JASON              ACC  02875000  05
225   MASON ELLEN             DP   02356000  01
240   PAULSON TERENCE         DP   02575000  02
```

Program 3-Output(b) An Instance of a Sequential Personnel File Created by Program 3

```
                                COLUMNS
 1    5    10   15   20   25   30   35   40   45   50   55
----|----|----|----|----|----|----|----|----|----|----|--

100   UDC   SLS
120   ADD   SAWYER LESLIE            ACC   03265000  04
170   ADD   THURNTON MARIA           SLS   02500000  02
170   UEY   03
170   UES   02950000
186   DLT
188   DLT
189   UDT   09
189   UDC   DP
189   UEY   09
200   UEN   DONNEL JANE
200   UEY   07
205   UES   02560000
```

Program 4-Input An Instance of a Transaction File for Program 4

```
205   UEN   MC DOUGAL TERRY
208   UEN   RONSON MEREDITH
208   ADD   RONSON MEREDITH              SLS   04260000   07
210   UDC   ACC
210   UEY   03
```

Program 4-Input (Continued)

```
00001      *.................................................................
00002        IDENTIFICATION DIVISION.
00003        PROGRAM-ID.  FILE-MAINTENANCE.
00004        *****************************************************************
00005        ***   THIS PROGRAM MAINTAINS A SEQUENTIAL DISK FILE USING THE    *
00006        ***   TRADITIONAL FILE-UPDATE-THROUGH-COPYING LOGIC.             *
00007        ***      THE FOLLOWING FILES ARE INVOLVED IN THE UPDATE LOGIC:   *
00008        ***      1. MASTER-FILE: CONTAINS RECORDS TO BE UPDATED;         *
00009        ***      2. TRANSACTION-FILE: CONTAINS TRANSACTION RECORDS;      *
00010        ***      3. NEW-MASTER-FILE: IS AN OUTPUT FILE THAT STORES THE   *
00011        ***         UPDATED RECORDS; AND                                 *
00012        ***      4. ERROR-FILE: STORES MESSAGES FOR INAPPROPRIATE UPDATE *
00013        ***         OPERATIONS.                                          *
00014        *****************************************************************
00015
00016        AUTHOR.  UCKAN.
00017        DATE-WRITTEN. NOV 6, 1990.
00018        DATE-COMPILED. FEB 16,1991.
00020      *.................................................................
00021        ENVIRONMENT DIVISION.
00022        CONFIGURATION SECTION.
00023        SOURCE-COMPUTER. IBM-370.
00024        OBJECT-COMPUTER. IBM-370.
00025        INPUT-OUTPUT SECTION.
00026        FILE-CONTROL.
00027            SELECT MASTER-FILE        ASSIGN TO DATAFILE.
00028            SELECT TRANSACTION-FILE   ASSIGN TO  INFILE.
00029            SELECT NEW-MASTER-FILE    ASSIGN TO OUTFILE.
00030            SELECT REPORT-FILE        ASSIGN TO PRTFILE.
00031
00032      *.................................................................
00033        DATA DIVISION.
00034        FILE SECTION.
00035
00036        FD  MASTER-FILE
00037            LABEL RECORDS ARE STANDARD
00038            RECORD CONTAINS 49 CHARACTERS
00039            DATA RECORD IS MASTER-RECORD.
00040        01  MASTER-RECORD.
00041            05   EMPLOYEE-IDNO-MS        PIC XXX.
00042            05   FILLER                  PIC XX.
00043            05   EMPLOYEE-NAME-MS         PIC X(25).
00044            05   FILLER                  PIC XX.
00045            05   DEPARTMENT-CODE-MS       PIC XXX.
```

Program 4-Source Sample COBOL Program to Update a Sequential File Using Traditional File Update Strategy

```
00046          05  FILLER                    PIC XX.
00047          05  YEARLY-SALARY-MS          PIC 9(6)V99.
00048          05  FILLER                    PIC XX.
00049          05  YEARS-IN-COMPANY-MS       PIC 99.
00050
00051      FD  TRANSACTION-FILE
00052          LABEL RECORDS ARE STANDARD
00053          RECORD CONTAINS 80 CHARACTERS
00054          DATA RECORDS ARE    ADD-RECORD
00055                              DELETE-RECORD
00056                              CHANGE-NAME-RECORD
00057                              CHANGE-DEPT-CODE-RECORD
00058                              CHANGE-SALARY-RECORD
00059                              CHANGE-YEARS-RECORD.
00060      01  ADD-RECORD.
00061          05  EMPLOYEE-IDNO-ADD         PIC XXX.
00062          05  FILLER                    PIC XX.
00063          05  TRANSACTION-TYPE-ADD      PIC XXX.
00064          05  FILLER                    PIC XX.
00065          05  EMPLOYEE-NAME-ADD         PIC X(25).
00066          05  FILLER                    PIC XX.
00067          05  DEPARTMENT-CODE-ADD       PIC XXX.
00068          05  FILLER                    PIC XX.
00069          05  YEARLY-SALARY-ADD         PIC 9(6)V99.
00070          05  FILLER                    PIC XX.
00071          05  YEARS-IN-COMPANY-ADD      PIC 99.
00072          05  FILLER                    PIC X(26).
00073
00074      01  DELETE-RECORD.
00075          05  EMPLOYEE-IDNO-DLT         PIC XXX.
00076          05  FILLER                    PIC XX.
00077          05  TRANSACTION-TYPE-DLT      PIC XXX.
00078          05  FILLER                    PIC X(72).
00079
00080      01  CHANGE-NAME-RECORD.
00081          05  EMPLOYEE-IDNO-UEN         PIC XXX.
00082          05  FILLER                    PIC XX.
00083          05  TRANSACTION-TYPE-UEN      PIC XXX.
00084          05  FILLER                    PIC XX.
00085          05  EMPLOYEE-NAME-UEN         PIC X(25).
00086          05  FILLER                    PIC X(45).
00087
00088      01  CHANGE-DEPT-CODE-RECORD.
00089          05  EMPLOYEE-IDNO-UDC         PIC XXX.
00090          05  FILLER                    PIC XX.
00091          05  TRANSACTION-TYPE-UDC      PIC XXX.
00092          05  FILLER                    PIC XX.
00093          05  DEPARTMENT-CODE-UDC       PIC XXX.
00094          05  FILLER                    PIC X(67).
00095
00096      01  CHANGE-SALARY-RECORD.
00097          05  EMPLOYEE-IDNO-UES         PIC XXX.
00098          05  FILLER                    PIC XX.
00099          05  TRANSACTION-TYPE-UES      PIC XXX.
```

Program 4-Source (Continued)

```
00100          05   FILLER                   PIC XX.
00101          05   YEARLY—SALARY—UES        PIC 9(6)V99.
00102          05   FILLER                   PIC X(62).
00103
00104     01   CHANGE—YEARS—RECORD.
00105          05   EMPLOYEE—IDNO—UEY        PIC XXX.
00106          05   FILLER                   PIC XX.
00107          05   TRANSACTION—TYPE—UEY     PIC XXX.
00108          05   FILLER                   PIC XX.
00109          05   YEARS—IN—COMPANY—UEY     PIC 99.
00110          05   FILLER                   PIC X(68).
00111
00112     FD NEW—MASTER—FILE
00113          LABEL RECORDS ARE STANDARD
00114          RECORD CONTAINS 49 CHARACTERS
00115          DATA RECORD IS NEW—MASTER—RECORD.
00116     01   NEW—MASTER—RECORD.
00117          05   EMPLOYEE—IDNO—NEW        PIC XXX.
00118          05   FILLER                   PIC XX.
00119          05   EMPLOYEE—NAME—NEW        PIC X(25).
00120          05   FILLER                   PIC XX.
00121          05   DEPARTMENT—CODE—NEW      PIC XXX.
00122          05   FILLER                   PIC XX.
00123          05   YEARLY—SALARY—NEW        PIC 9(6)V99.
00124          05   FILLER                   PIC XX.
00125          05   YEARS—IN—COMPANY—NEW     PIC 99.
00126
00127     FD  REPORT—FILE
00128          LABEL RECORDS ARE OMITTED
00129          RECORD CONTAINS 131 CHARACTERS
00130          DATA RECORD IS REPORT—LINE.
00131     01  REPORT—LINE                    PIC X(131).
00132
00133     WORKING—STORAGE SECTION.
00134
00135     **********> SWITCHES:
00136
00137     01   END—OF—MASTER—FILE—FLAG       PIC XXX       VALUE "NO".
00138          88   MASTER—FILE—ENDS                       VALUE "YES".
00139
00140     01   END—OF—TRANSACTION—FILE—FLAG  PIC XXX       VALUE "NO".
00141          88   TRANSACTION—FILE—ENDS                  VALUE "YES".
00142
00143     01   ERROR—FLAG                    PIC 9.
00144          88   ADD—FOR—EXISTING—RECORD                VALUE 1.
00145          88   NOT—ADD—FOR—NEW—RECORD                 VALUE 2.
00146          88   WRONG—CODE—FOR—TRANS—TYPE              VALUE 3.
00147
00148     **********> STRUCTURES:
00149
00150     01   TRANSACTION—RECORD.
00151          05   EMPLOYEE—IDNO—TR         PIC XXX.
00152          05   FILLER                   PIC XX.
```

Program 4-Source (Continued)

```
00153         05  TRANSACTION-TYPE-TR        PIC XXX.
00154             88  ADD-A-RECORD                          VALUE "ADD".
00155             88  DELETE-A-RECORD                       VALUE "DLT".
00156             88  UPDATE-EMPLOYEE-NAME                  VALUE "UEN".
00157             88  UPDATE-DEPARTMENT-CODE                VALUE "UDC".
00158             88  UPDATE-EMPLOYEE-SALARY                VALUE "UES".
00159             88  UPDATE-EMPLOYEE-YEARS                 VALUE "UEY".
00160         05  FILLER                     PIC XX.
00161         05  EMPLOYEE-NAME-TR           PIC X(25).
00162         05  FILLER                     PIC XX.
00163         05  DEPARTMENT-CODE-TR         PIC XXX.
00164         05  FILLER                     PIC XX.
00165         05  YEARLY-SALARY-TR           PIC 9(6)V99.
00166         05  FILLER                     PIC XX.
00167         05  YEARS-IN-COMPANY-TR        PIC 99.
00168         05  FILLER                     PIC X(26).
00169
00170     01  TEMPORARY-STORAGE-RECORD.
00171         05  EMPLOYEE-IDNO-TEMP         PIC XXX.
00172         05  FILLER                     PIC XX          VALUE SPACES.
00173         05  EMPLOYEE-NAME-TEMP         PIC X(25).
00174         05  FILLER                     PIC XX          VALUE SPACES.
00175         05  DEPARTMENT-CODE-TEMP       PIC XXX.
00176         05  FILLER                     PIC XX          VALUE SPACES.
00177         05  YEARLY-SALARY-TEMP         PIC 9(6)V99.
00178         05  FILLER                     PIC XX          VALUE SPACES.
00179         05  YEARS-IN-COMPANY-TEMP      PIC 99.
00180
00181     01  ERROR-TITLE-LINE.
00182         05  FILLER                     PIC X(10)    VALUE SPACES.
00183         05  FILLER                     PIC X(46)    VALUE
00184             "ERROR OCCURED WHILE UPDATING THE MASTER FILE. ".
00185
00186     01  ERROR-EXPLANATION-LINE-1.
00187         05  FILLER                     PIC X(20)    VALUE SPACES.
00188         05  FILLER                     PIC X(41)    VALUE
00189             "ERROR: ADD OPERATION FOR EXISTING RECORD.".
00190
00191     01  ERROR-EXPLANATION-LINE-2.
00192         05  FILLER                     PIC X(20)    VALUE SPACES.
00193         05  FILLER                     PIC X(54)    VALUE
00194           "ERROR: DELETE\UPDATE OPERATION FOR NONEXISTING RECORD.".
00195
00196     01  ERROR-EXPLANATION-LINE-3.
00197         05  FILLER                     PIC X(20)    VALUE SPACES.
00198         05  FILLER                     PIC X(41)    VALUE
00199             "ERROR: CODING ERROR FOR TRANSACTION CODE.".
00200
00201     01  ERROR-RECORD-IDNO-LINE.
00202         05  FILLER                     PIC X(20)    VALUE SPACES.
00203         05  FILLER                     PIC X(30)    VALUE
00204                     "TRANSACTION RECORD ID NUMBER: ".
00205         05  ERROR-TRANS-IDNO           PIC XXX.
00206
```

Program 4-Source (Continued)

```
00207      01   ERROR-TRANSACTION-TYPE-LINE.
00208           05   FILLER                      PIC X(20)    VALUE SPACES.
00209           05   FILLER                      PIC X(18)    VALUE
00210                                            "TRANSACTION TYPE: ".
00211           05   ERROR-TRANS-TYPE            PIC XXX.
00212
00213      01   ERROR-ACTION-LINE.
00214           05   FILLER                      PIC X(20)    VALUE SPACES.
00215           05   FILLER                      PIC X(23)    VALUE
00216                                            "TRANSACTION IS IGNORED.".
00217
00218      **********> VARIABLES:
00219
00220      01   LAST-PROCESSED-TRANS-IDNO    PIC XXX.
00221
00222      *..............................................................
00223      PROCEDURE DIVISION.
00224      A-MAINLINE.
00225          OPEN INPUT   MASTER-FILE
00226                       TRANSACTION-FILE
00227               OUTPUT  NEW-MASTER-FILE
00228                       REPORT-FILE.
00229
00230          PERFORM B1-READ-MASTER-FILE.
00231
00232          PERFORM B2-READ-TRANSACTION-FILE.
00233
00234          PERFORM B3-UPDATE-MASTER-FILE
00235              UNTIL MASTER-FILE-ENDS
00236                        AND
00237                  TRANSACTION-FILE-ENDS.
00238
00239          CLOSE   MASTER-FILE
00240                  TRANSACTION-FILE
00241                  NEW-MASTER-FILE
00242                  REPORT-FILE.
00243
00244          STOP RUN.
00245
00246      B1-READ-MASTER-FILE.
00247          READ MASTER-FILE
00248                  AT END MOVE "YES" TO END-OF-MASTER-FILE-FLAG.
00249
00250          IF TRANSACTION-FILE-ENDS
00251                  PERFORM C1-COPY-MASTER-FILE
00252                      UNTIL MASTER-FILE-ENDS.
00253
00254      B2-READ-TRANSACTION-FILE.
00255          READ TRANSACTION-FILE INTO TRANSACTION-RECORD
00256                  AT END MOVE "YES" TO END-OF-TRANSACTION-FILE-FLAG.
00257
00258      B3-UPDATE-MASTER-FILE.
00259          MOVE EMPLOYEE-IDNO-TR TO LAST-PROCESSED-TRANS-IDNO.
00260
```

Program 4-Source (Continued)

```
00261          IF  EMPLOYEE-IDNO-MS = EMPLOYEE-IDNO-TR
00262                   PERFORM C2-CHECK-FOR-ADD-OR-DELETE
00263       ELSE
00264               IF EMPLOYEE-IDNO-MS < EMPLOYEE-IDNO-TR
00265                       WRITE NEW-MASTER-RECORD FROM MASTER-RECORD
00266                       PERFORM B1-READ-MASTER-FILE
00267               ELSE
00268                       PERFORM C3-CHECK-FOR-ADD.
00269
00270   C1-COPY-MASTER-FILE.
00271       WRITE NEW-MASTER-RECORD FROM MASTER-RECORD.
00272
00273       READ MASTER-FILE
00274               AT END MOVE "YES" TO END-OF-MASTER-FILE-FLAG.
00275
00276   C2-CHECK-FOR-ADD-OR-DELETE.
00277       IF ADD-A-RECORD
00278               MOVE 1 TO ERROR-FLAG
00279               PERFORM D1-REPORT-ERROR
00280               PERFORM B2-READ-TRANSACTION-FILE
00281       ELSE
00282               IF DELETE-A-RECORD
00283                       PERFORM B1-READ-MASTER-FILE
00284                       PERFORM B2-READ-TRANSACTION-FILE
00285               ELSE
00286                       PERFORM D2-UPDATE-A-RECORD.
00287
00288   C3-CHECK-FOR-ADD.
00289       IF ADD-A-RECORD
00290               PERFORM D3-ADD-A-NEW-RECORD
00291       ELSE
00292               MOVE 2 TO ERROR-FLAG
00293               PERFORM D1-REPORT-ERROR
00294               PERFORM B2-READ-TRANSACTION-FILE.
00295
00296   D1-REPORT-ERROR.
00297       MOVE EMPLOYEE-IDNO-TR    TO ERROR-TRANS-IDNO.
00298       MOVE TRANSACTION-TYPE-TR TO ERROR-TRANS-TYPE.
00299       PERFORM E2-PRINT-ERROR-MESSAGES.
00300
00301   D2-UPDATE-A-RECORD.
00302       MOVE MASTER-RECORD TO TEMPORARY-STORAGE-RECORD.
00303
00304       PERFORM E1-PROCESS-TRANSACTIONS
00305               UNTIL EMPLOYEE-IDNO-MS NOT = EMPLOYEE-IDNO-TR
00306                              OR
00307                       TRANSACTION-FILE-ENDS.
00308
00309       WRITE NEW-MASTER-RECORD FROM TEMPORARY-STORAGE-RECORD.
00310
00311       PERFORM B1-READ-MASTER-FILE.
00312
00313   D3-ADD-A-NEW-RECORD.
00314       MOVE TRANSACTION-RECORD    TO ADD-RECORD.
00315
```

Program 4-Source (Continued)

```
00316          MOVE EMPLOYEE-IDNO-ADD        TO EMPLOYEE-IDNO-TEMP.
00317          MOVE EMPLOYEE-NAME-ADD        TO EMPLOYEE-NAME-TEMP.
00318          MOVE DEPARTMENT-CODE-ADD      TO DEPARTMENT-CODE-TEMP.
00319          MOVE YEARLY-SALARY-ADD        TO YEARLY-SALARY-TEMP.
00320          MOVE YEARS-IN-COMPANY-ADD     TO YEARS-IN-COMPANY-TEMP.
00321
00322          WRITE NEW-MASTER-RECORD FROM TEMPORARY-STORAGE-RECORD.
00323
00324          PERFORM B2-READ-TRANSACTION-FILE.
00325
00326          IF EMPLOYEE-IDNO-TR = LAST-PROCESSED-TRANS-IDNO
00327                  PERFORM E1-PROCESS-TRANSACTIONS
00328                        UNTIL EMPLOYEE-IDNO-TR NOT =
00329                                           LAST-PROCESSED-TRANS-IDNO
00330                                    OR
00331                              TRANSACTION-FILE-ENDS.
00332
00333      E1-PROCESS-TRANSACTIONS.
00334          IF UPDATE-EMPLOYEE-NAME
00335                  MOVE TRANSACTION-RECORD     TO CHANGE-NAME-RECORD
00336                  MOVE EMPLOYEE-NAME-UEN      TO EMPLOYEE-NAME-TEMP.
00337
00338          IF UPDATE-DEPARTMENT-CODE
00339                  MOVE TRANSACTION-RECORD     TO CHANGE-DEPT-CODE-RECORD
00340                  MOVE DEPARTMENT-CODE-UDC    TO DEPARTMENT-CODE-TEMP.
00341
00342          IF UPDATE-EMPLOYEE-SALARY
00343                  MOVE TRANSACTION-RECORD     TO CHANGE-SALARY-RECORD
00344                  MOVE YEARLY-SALARY-UES      TO YEARLY-SALARY-TEMP.
00345
00346          IF UPDATE-EMPLOYEE-YEARS
00347                  MOVE TRANSACTION-RECORD     TO CHANGE-YEARS-RECORD
00348                  MOVE YEARS-IN-COMPANY-UEY   TO YEARS-IN-COMPANY-TEMP.
00349
00350          IF NOT (UPDATE-EMPLOYEE-NAME
00351                  OR
00352                  UPDATE-DEPARTMENT-CODE
00353                  OR
00354                  UPDATE-EMPLOYEE-SALARY
00355                  OR
00356                  UPDATE-EMPLOYEE-YEARS)
00357                      MOVE 3 TO ERROR-FLAG
00358                      PERFORM D1-REPORT-ERROR.
00359
00360          PERFORM B2-READ-TRANSACTION-FILE.
00361
00362      E2-PRINT-ERROR-MESSAGES.
00363          MOVE SPACES               TO REPORT-LINE.
00364          MOVE ERROR-TITLE-LINE TO REPORT-LINE.
00365          WRITE REPORT-LINE
00366                  AFTER 3 LINES.
00367          MOVE SPACES TO REPORT-LINE.
00368
```

Program 4-Source (Continued)

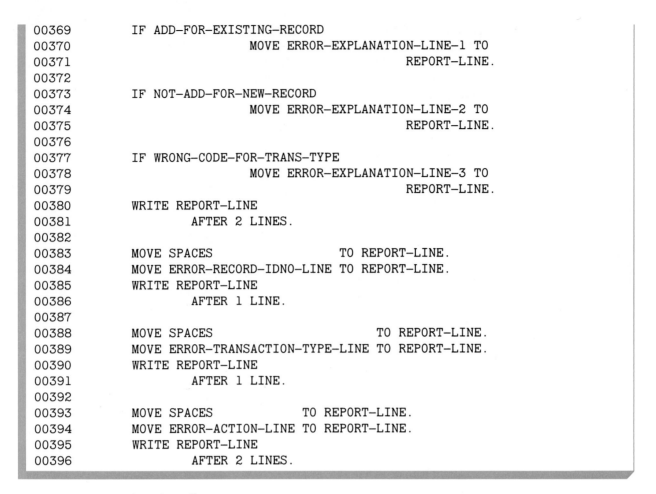

```
00369          IF ADD-FOR-EXISTING-RECORD
00370                      MOVE ERROR-EXPLANATION-LINE-1 TO
00371                                   REPORT-LINE.
00372
00373          IF NOT-ADD-FOR-NEW-RECORD
00374                      MOVE ERROR-EXPLANATION-LINE-2 TO
00375                                   REPORT-LINE.
00376
00377          IF WRONG-CODE-FOR-TRANS-TYPE
00378                      MOVE ERROR-EXPLANATION-LINE-3 TO
00379                                   REPORT-LINE.
00380          WRITE REPORT-LINE
00381              AFTER 2 LINES.
00382
00383          MOVE SPACES             TO REPORT-LINE.
00384          MOVE ERROR-RECORD-IDNO-LINE TO REPORT-LINE.
00385          WRITE REPORT-LINE
00386              AFTER 1 LINE.
00387
00388          MOVE SPACES                TO REPORT-LINE.
00389          MOVE ERROR-TRANSACTION-TYPE-LINE TO REPORT-LINE.
00390          WRITE REPORT-LINE
00391              AFTER 1 LINE.
00392
00393          MOVE SPACES          TO REPORT-LINE.
00394          MOVE ERROR-ACTION-LINE TO REPORT-LINE.
00395          WRITE REPORT-LINE
00396              AFTER 2 LINES.
```

Program 4-Source (Continued)

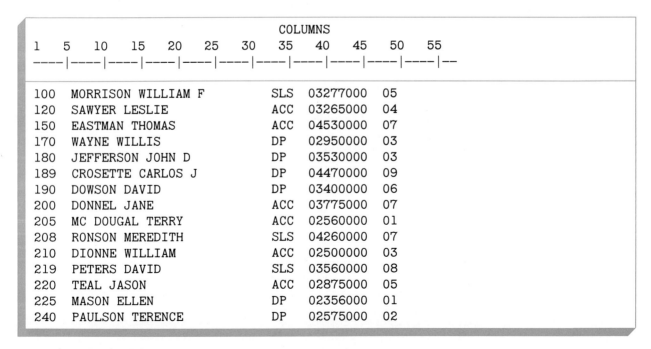

```
                                 COLUMNS
 1    5    10    15    20    25    30    35    40    45    50    55
----|----|----|----|----|----|----|----|----|----|----|--

 100   MORRISON WILLIAM F        SLS   03277000   05
 120   SAWYER LESLIE             ACC   03265000   04
 150   EASTMAN THOMAS            ACC   04530000   07
 170   WAYNE WILLIS              DP    02950000   03
 180   JEFFERSON JOHN D          DP    03530000   03
 189   CROSETTE CARLOS J         DP    04470000   09
 190   DOWSON DAVID              DP    03400000   06
 200   DONNEL JANE               ACC   03775000   07
 205   MC DOUGAL TERRY           ACC   02560000   01
 208   RONSON MEREDITH           SLS   04260000   07
 210   DIONNE WILLIAM            ACC   02500000   03
 219   PETERS DAVID              SLS   03560000   08
 220   TEAL JASON                ACC   02875000   05
 225   MASON ELLEN               DP    02356000   01
 240   PAULSON TERENCE           DP    02575000   02
```

Program 4-Output(a) Master Personnel File After Update for Program 4

```
                                    COLUMNS
    1    5   10   15   20   25   30   35   40   45   50   55   60   65   70
   ----|----|----|----|----|----|----|----|----|----|----|----|----|----|--
```

```
              ERROR OCCURRED WHILE UPDATING THE MASTER FILE.

                      ERROR: ADD OPERATION FOR EXISTING RECORD.
                      TRANSACTION RECORD ID NUMBER: 170
                      TRANSACTION TYPE: ADD

                      TRANSACTION IS IGNORED.


              ERROR OCCURRED WHILE UPDATING THE MASTER FILE.

                      ERROR: DELETE/UPDATE OPERATION FOR NONEXISTING RECORD.
                      TRANSACTION RECORD ID NUMBER: 188
                      TRANSACTION TYPE: DLT

                      TRANSACTION IS IGNORED.


              ERROR OCCURRED WHILE UPDATING THE MASTER FILE.

                      ERROR: CODING ERROR FOR TRANSACTION CODE.
                      TRANSACTION RECORD ID NUMBER: 189
                      TRANSACTION TYPE: UDT

                      TRANSACTION IS IGNORED.


              ERROR OCCURRED WHILE UPDATING THE MASTER FILE.

                      ERROR: DELETE/UPDATE OPERATION FOR NONEXISTING RECORD.
                      TRANSACTION RECORD ID NUMBER: 208
                      TRANSACTION TYPE: UEN

                      TRANSACTION IS IGNORED.
```

Program 4-Output(b) Update Error Report File for Program 4

```
00001    *....................................................................
00002      IDENTIFICATION DIVISION.
00003      PROGRAM-ID. IN-SITU-FILE-MAINTENANCE.
00004      ***********************************************************************
00005    ***   THIS PROGRAM UPDATES A SEQUENTIAL DISK FILE USING THE INSITU*
00006    ***   FILE UPDATE LOGIC.                                          *
00007    ***      THE FOLLOWING FILES ARE DEFINED AND USED IN THE PROGRAM:  *
00008    ***      1. MASTER-FILE: CONTAINS RECORDS TO BE UPDATED.  AFTER    *
00009    ***         PROCESSING, IT WILL CONTAIN THE UPDATED RECORDS.      *
00010    ***      2. TRANSACTION-FILE: CONTAINS TRANSACTION RECORDS.       *
```

Program 5-Source Sample COBOL Program for In Situ Update of a Sequential Disk File

```
00011   ***     3. ADDITION-FILE: STORES TEMPORARILY THE RECORDS MARKED     *
00012   ***        FOR ADDITION IN THE TRANSACTION-FILE, UNTIL THE END      *
00013   ***        OF UPDATES.  THESE RECORDS WILL THEN BE ADDED TO THE     *
00014   ***        END OF THE MASTER-FILE.  IF THERE ARE N NUMBER OF        *
00015   ***        "DUMMY" RECORDS IN THE MASTER-FILE, THE ADDITION-FILE    *
00016   ***        WILL CONTAIN ONLY N RECORDS IN IT.                       *
00017   ***     4. ERROR-FILE: STORES MESSAGES FOR INAPPROPRIATE UPDATE     *
00018   ***        OPERATIONS.                                              *
00019   **********************************************************************
00020
00021   AUTHOR.   UCKAN.
00022   DATE-WRITTEN. DEC 17, 1990.
00023   DATE-COMPILED. FEB 18,1991.
00024   *..................................................................
00025   ENVIRONMENT DIVISION.
00026   CONFIGURATION SECTION.
00027   SOURCE-COMPUTER. IBM-370.
00028   OBJECT-COMPUTER. IBM-370.
00029   INPUT-OUTPUT SECTION.
00030   FILE-CONTROL.
00031       SELECT MASTER-FILE        ASSIGN TO DATAFILE.
00032       SELECT TRANSACTION-FILE   ASSIGN TO INFILE.
00033       SELECT ADDITION-FILE      ASSIGN TO ADDFILE.
00034       SELECT REPORT-FILE        ASSIGN TO PRTFILE.
00035
00036   *..................................................................
00037   DATA DIVISION.
00038   FILE SECTION.
00039
00040   FD  MASTER-FILE
00041       LABEL RECORDS ARE STANDARD
00042       RECORD CONTAINS 52 CHARACTERS
00043       DATA RECORD IS MASTER-RECORD.
00044   01  MASTER-RECORD.
00045       05   DELETE-FIELD-MS           PIC X.
00046       05   FILLER                    PIC XX.
00047       05   EMPLOYEE-IDNO-MS          PIC XXX.
00048       05   FILLER                    PIC XX.
00049       05   EMPLOYEE-NAME-MS          PIC X(25).
00050       05   FILLER                    PIC XX.
00051       05   DEPARTMENT-CODE-MS        PIC XXX.
00052       05   FILLER                    PIC XX.
00053       05   YEARLY-SALARY-MS          PIC 9(6)V99.
00054       05   FILLER                    PIC XX.
00055       05   YEARS-IN-COMPANY-MS       PIC 99.
00056
00057   FD  ADDITION-FILE
00058       LABEL RECORDS ARE STANDARD
00059       RECORD CONTAINS 52 CHARACTERS
00060       DATA RECORD IS ADDITION-RECORD.
00061   01  ADDITION-RECORD.
00062       05   DELETE-FIELD-ADT          PIC X.
00063       05   FILLER                    PIC XX.
00064       05   EMPLOYEE-IDNO-ADT         PIC XXX.
```

Program 5-Source (Continued)

```
00065          05   FILLER                   PIC XX.
00066          05   EMPLOYEE-NAME-ADT        PIC X(25).
00067          05   FILLER                   PIC XX.
00068          05   DEPARTMENT-CODE-ADT      PIC XXX.
00069          05   FILLER                   PIC XX.
00070          05   YEARLY-SALARY-ADT        PIC 9(6)V99.
00071          05   FILLER                   PIC XX.
00072          05   YEARS-IN-COMPANY-ADT     PIC 99.
00073
00074     FD   TRANSACTION-FILE
00075          LABEL RECORDS ARE STANDARD
00076          RECORD CONTAINS 80 CHARACTERS
00077          DATA RECORDS ARE
00078                         ADD-RECORD
00079                         DELETE-RECORD
00080                         CHANGE-NAME-RECORD
00081                         CHANGE-DEPT-CODE-RECORD
00082                         CHANGE-SALARY-RECORD
00083                         CHANGE-YEARS-RECORD.
00084     01   ADD-RECORD.
00085          05   EMPLOYEE-IDNO-ADD        PIC XXX.
00086          05   FILLER                   PIC XX.
00087          05   TRANSACTION-TYPE-ADD     PIC XXX.
00088          05   FILLER                   PIC X(72).
00089
00090     01   DELETE-RECORD.
00091          05   EMPLOYEE-IDNO-DLT        PIC XXX.
00092          05   FILLER                   PIC XX.
00093          05   TRANSACTION-TYPE-DLT     PIC XXX.
00094          05   FILLER                   PIC X(72).
00095
00096     01   CHANGE-NAME-RECORD.
00097          05   EMPLOYEE-IDNO-UEN        PIC XXX.
00098          05   FILLER                   PIC XX.
00099          05   TRANSACTION-TYPE-UEN     PIC XXX.
00100          05   FILLER                   PIC XX.
00101          05   EMPLOYEE-NAME-UEN        PIC X(25).
00102          05   FILLER                   PIC X(45).
00103
00104     01   CHANGE-DEPT-CODE-RECORD.
00105          05   EMPLOYEE-IDNO-UDC        PIC XXX.
00106          05   FILLER                   PIC XX.
00107          05   TRANSACTION-TYPE-UDC     PIC XXX.
00108          05   FILLER                   PIC XX.
00109          05   DEPARTMENT-CODE-UDC      PIC XXX.
00110          05   FILLER                   PIC X(67).
00111
00112     01   CHANGE-SALARY-RECORD.
00113          05   EMPLOYEE-IDNO-UES        PIC XXX.
00114          05   FILLER                   PIC XX.
00115          05   TRANSACTION-TYPE-UES     PIC XXX.
00116          05   FILLER                   PIC XX.
00117          05   YEARLY-SALARY-UES        PIC 9(6)V99.
00118          05   FILLER                   PIC X(62).
```

Program 5-Source (Continued)

```
00119
00120     01   CHANGE-YEARS-RECORD.
00121          05   EMPLOYEE-IDNO-UEY          PIC XXX.
00122          05   FILLER                     PIC XX.
00123          05   TRANSACTION-TYPE-UEY       PIC XXX.
00124          05   FILLER                     PIC XX.
00125          05   YEARS-IN-COMPANY-UEY       PIC 99.
00126          05   FILLER                     PIC X(68).
00127
00128     FD REPORT-FILE
00129          LABEL RECORDS ARE OMITTED
00130          RECORD CONTAINS 131 CHARACTERS
00131          DATA RECORD IS REPORT-LINE.
00132     01   REPORT-LINE                     PIC X(131).
00133
00134     WORKING-STORAGE SECTION.
00135
00136     **********> SWITCHES:
00137
00138     01   END-OF-MASTER-FILE-FLAG        PIC XXX      VALUE "NO".
00139          88   MASTER-FILE-ENDS                       VALUE "YES".
00140
00141     01   END-OF-TRANSACTION-FILE-FLAG   PIC XXX      VALUE "NO".
00142          88   TRANSACTION-FILE-ENDS                  VALUE "YES".
00143
00144     01   END-OF-ADDITION-FILE-FLAG      PIC XXX      VALUE "NO".
00145          88   ADDITION-FILE-ENDS                     VALUE "YES".
00146
00147     01   ERROR-FLAG                     PIC 9.
00148          88   RECORD-NOT-IN-FILE                     VALUE 1.
00149          88   WRONG-CODE-FOR-TRANS-TYPE              VALUE 2.
00150          88   RECORD-CANNOT-BE-ADDED                 VALUE 3.
00151          88   ADD-FOR-EXISTING-RECORD                VALUE 4.
00152
00153     **********> VARIABLES:
00154
00155     01   NUMBER-OF-EMPTY-RECORDS        PIC 99.
00156     01   NUMBER-OF-ADDITIONS            PIC 99.
00157
00158     **********> STRUCTURES:
00159
00160     01   TRANSACTION-RECORD.
00161          05   EMPLOYEE-IDNO-TR           PIC XXX.
00162          05   FILLER                     PIC XX.
00163          05   TRANSACTION-TYPE-TR        PIC XXX.
00164               88   DELETE-A-RECORD                   VALUE "DLT".
00165               88   ADD-A-RECORD                      VALUE "ADD".
00166               88   UPDATE-EMPLOYEE-NAME              VALUE "UEN".
00167               88   UPDATE-DEPARTMENT-CODE            VALUE "UDC".
00168               88   UPDATE-EMPLOYEE-SALARY            VALUE "UES".
00169               88   UPDATE-EMPLOYEE-YEARS             VALUE "UEY".
00170          05   FILLER                     PIC XX.
00171          05   EMPLOYEE-NAME-TR           PIC X(25).
00172          05   FILLER                     PIC XX.
```

Program 5-Source (Continued)

```
00173          05   DEPARTMENT-CODE-TR        PIC XXX.
00174          05   FILLER                    PIC XX.
00175          05   YEARLY-SALARY-TR          PIC 9(6)V99.
00176          05   FILLER                    PIC XX.
00177          05   YEARS-IN-COMPANY-TR       PIC 99.
00178          05   FILLER                    PIC X(26).
00179
00180     01   TEMPORARY-STORAGE-RECORD.
00181          05   DELETE-FIELD-TEMP         PIC X.
00182          05   FILLER                    PIC XX        VALUE SPACES.
00183          05   EMPLOYEE-IDNO-TEMP        PIC XXX.
00184          05   FILLER                    PIC XX        VALUE SPACES.
00185          05   EMPLOYEE-NAME-TEMP        PIC X(25).
00186          05   FILLER                    PIC XX        VALUE SPACES.
00187          05   DEPARTMENT-CODE-TEMP      PIC XXX.
00188          05   FILLER                    PIC XX        VALUE SPACES.
00189          05   YEARLY-SALARY-TEMP        PIC 9(6)V99.
00190          05   FILLER                    PIC XX        VALUE SPACES.
00191          05   YEARS-IN-COMPANY-TEMP     PIC 99.
00192
00193     01   ERROR-TITLE-LINE.
00194          05   FILLER                    PIC X(10)     VALUE SPACES.
00195          05   FILLER                    PIC X(47)     VALUE
00196               "ERROR OCCURRED WHILE UPDATING THE MASTER FILE. ".
00197
00198
00199     01   ERROR-EXPLANATION-LINE-1.
00200          05   FILLER                    PIC X(20)     VALUE SPACES.
00201          05   FILLER                    PIC X(40)     VALUE
00202               "ERROR: RECORD IS NOT IN THE MASTER FILE.".
00203
00204     01   ERROR-EXPLANATION-LINE-2.
00205          05   FILLER                    PIC X(20)     VALUE SPACES.
00206          05   FILLER                    PIC X(41)     VALUE
00207               "ERROR: CODING ERROR FOR TRANSACTION CODE.".
00208
00209     01   ERROR-EXPLANATION-LINE-3.
00210          05   FILLER                    PIC X(20)     VALUE SPACES.
00211          05   FILLER                    PIC X(45)     VALUE
00212               "ERROR: FILE IS FULL. RECORD CANNOT BE ADDED.".
00213
00214     01   ERROR-EXPLANATION-LINE-4.
00215          05   FILLER                    PIC X(20)     VALUE SPACES.
00216          05   FILLER                    PIC X(41)     VALUE
00217               "ERROR: ADD OPERATION FOR EXISTING RECORD.".
00218
00219     01   ERROR-RECORD-IDNO-LINE.
00220          05   FILLER                    PIC X(20)     VALUE SPACES.
00221          05   FILLER                    PIC X(30)     VALUE
00222                                "TRANSACTION RECORD ID NUMBER: ".
00223          05   ERROR-TRANS-IDNO          PIC XXX.
00224
00225     01   ERROR-TRANSACTION-TYPE-LINE.
00226          05   FILLER                    PIC X(20)     VALUE SPACES.
00227          05   FILLER                    PIC X(18)     VALUE
```

Program 5-Source (Continued)

```
00228                                    "TRANSACTION TYPE: ".
00229        05   ERROR-TRANS-TYPE       PIC XXX.
00230
00231   01  ERROR-ACTION-LINE.
00232        05   FILLER                 PIC X(20)    VALUE SPACES.
00233        05   FILLER                 PIC X(23)    VALUE
00234                                    "TRANSACTION IS IGNORED.".
00235
00236   *..............................................................
00237   PROCEDURE DIVISION.
00238   A-MAINLINE.
00239        OPEN I-O    MASTER-FILE
00240             INPUT   TRANSACTION-FILE
00241             OUTPUT  REPORT-FILE
00242                     ADDITION-FILE.
00243
00244        MOVE 5 TO NUMBER-OF-EMPTY-RECORDS.
00245        MOVE 0 TO NUMBER-OF-ADDITIONS.
00246
00247        PERFORM B1-READ-MASTER-FILE.
00248
00249        PERFORM B2-READ-TRANSACTION-FILE.
00250
00251        PERFORM B3-UPDATE-MASTER-FILE
00252             UNTIL TRANSACTION-FILE-ENDS.
00253
00254        CLOSE   MASTER-FILE
00255                TRANSACTION-FILE
00256                ADDITION-FILE
00257                REPORT-FILE.
00258
00259        IF NUMBER-OF-ADDITIONS > 0
00260             OPEN I-O    MASTER-FILE
00261                  INPUT   ADDITION-FILE
00262             PERFORM B4-WRITE-NEW-RECORDS
00263             CLOSE MASTER-FILE
00264                   ADDITION-FILE.
00265
00266        STOP RUN.
00267
00268   B1-READ-MASTER-FILE.
00269        READ MASTER-FILE
00270             AT END MOVE "YES" TO END-OF-MASTER-FILE-FLAG.
00271
00272   B2-READ-TRANSACTION-FILE.
00273        READ TRANSACTION-FILE INTO TRANSACTION-RECORD
00274             AT END MOVE "YES" TO END-OF-TRANSACTION-FILE-FLAG.
00275
00276   B3-UPDATE-MASTER-FILE.
00277        IF   EMPLOYEE-IDNO-MS = EMPLOYEE-IDNO-TR
00278                  PERFORM C1-CHECK-FOR-ADD-ERROR
00279        ELSE
00280             IF EMPLOYEE-IDNO-MS < EMPLOYEE-IDNO-TR
00281                  PERFORM B1-READ-MASTER-FILE
```

Program 5-Source (Continued)

```
00282                       ELSE
00283                            PERFORM C2-CHECK-FOR-ADDITION.
00284
00285      B4-WRITE-NEW-RECORDS.
00286          PERFORM B1-READ-MASTER-FILE
00287                  UNTIL EMPLOYEE-IDNO-MS = 999.
00288
00289          PERFORM C3-READ-ADDITION-FILE.
00290
00291          PERFORM C4-ADD-RECORD-TO-MASTER-FILE
00292                  UNTIL ADDITION-FILE-ENDS.
00293
00294      C1-CHECK-FOR-ADD-ERROR.
00295          IF ADD-A-RECORD
00296                  MOVE 4 TO ERROR-FLAG
00297                  PERFORM D1-REPORT-ERROR
00298                  PERFORM B2-READ-TRANSACTION-FILE
00299          ELSE
00300                  PERFORM D2-UPDATE-A-RECORD.
00301
00302      C2-CHECK-FOR-ADDITION.
00303          IF ADD-A-RECORD
00304                  IF NUMBER-OF-ADDITIONS = NUMBER-OF-EMPTY-RECORDS
00305                          MOVE 3 TO ERROR-FLAG
00306                          PERFORM D1-REPORT-ERROR
00307                  ELSE
00308                          PERFORM D3-WRITE-INTO-ADDITION-FILE
00309          ELSE
00310                  MOVE 1 TO ERROR-FLAG
00311                  PERFORM D1-REPORT-ERROR.
00312
00313          PERFORM B2-READ-TRANSACTION-FILE.
00314
00315      C3-READ-ADDITION-FILE.
00316          READ ADDITION-FILE
00317                  AT END MOVE "YES" TO END-OF-ADDITION-FILE-FLAG.
00318
00319      C4-ADD-RECORD-TO-MASTER-FILE.
00320          REWRITE MASTER-RECORD FROM ADDITION-RECORD.
00321
00322          PERFORM B1-READ-MASTER-FILE.
00323
00324          PERFORM C3-READ-ADDITION-FILE.
00325
00326      D1-REPORT-ERROR.
00327          MOVE EMPLOYEE-IDNO-TR    TO ERROR-TRANS-IDNO.
00328          MOVE TRANSACTION-TYPE-TR TO ERROR-TRANS-TYPE.
00329          PERFORM E1-PRINT-ERROR-MESSAGES.
00330
00331      D2-UPDATE-A-RECORD.
00332          MOVE MASTER-RECORD TO TEMPORARY-STORAGE-RECORD.
00333
```

Program 5-Source (Continued)

```
00334          PERFORM E2-PROCESS-TRANSACTIONS
00335                  UNTIL EMPLOYEE-IDNO-MS NOT = EMPLOYEE-IDNO-TR
00336                                   OR
00337                         TRANSACTION-FILE-ENDS.
00338
00339      REWRITE MASTER-RECORD FROM TEMPORARY-STORAGE-RECORD.
00340
00341      PERFORM B1-READ-MASTER-FILE.
00342
00343  D3-WRITE-INTO-ADDITION-FILE.
00344      MOVE SPACES                TO ADDITION-RECORD.
00345      MOVE EMPLOYEE-IDNO-TR      TO EMPLOYEE-IDNO-ADT.
00346      MOVE EMPLOYEE-NAME-TR      TO EMPLOYEE-NAME-ADT.
00347      MOVE DEPARTMENT-CODE-TR    TO DEPARTMENT-CODE-ADT.
00348      MOVE YEARLY-SALARY-TR      TO YEARLY-SALARY-ADT.
00349      MOVE YEARS-IN-COMPANY-TR TO YEARS-IN-COMPANY-ADT.
00350      WRITE ADDITION-RECORD.
00351      ADD 1 TO NUMBER-OF-ADDITIONS.
00352
00353  E1-PRINT-ERROR-MESSAGES.
00354      MOVE SPACES              TO REPORT-LINE.
00355      MOVE ERROR-TITLE-LINE TO REPORT-LINE.
00356      WRITE REPORT-LINE
00357              AFTER 3 LINES.
00358      MOVE SPACES              TO REPORT-LINE.
00359
00360      IF RECORD-NOT-IN-FILE
00361              MOVE ERROR-EXPLANATION-LINE-1 TO REPORT-LINE.
00362
00363      IF WRONG-CODE-FOR-TRANS-TYPE
00364              MOVE ERROR-EXPLANATION-LINE-2 TO REPORT-LINE.
00365
00366      IF RECORD-CANNOT-BE-ADDED
00367              MOVE ERROR-EXPLANATION-LINE-3 TO REPORT-LINE.
00368
00369      IF ADD-FOR-EXISTING-RECORD
00370              MOVE ERROR-EXPLANATION-LINE-4 TO REPORT-LINE.
00371
00372      WRITE REPORT-LINE
00373              AFTER 2 LINES.
00374      MOVE SPACES                TO REPORT-LINE.
00375      MOVE ERROR-RECORD-IDNO-LINE TO REPORT-LINE.
00376      WRITE REPORT-LINE
00377              AFTER 1 LINE.
00378
00379      MOVE SPACES                   TO REPORT-LINE.
00380      MOVE ERROR-TRANSACTION-TYPE-LINE TO REPORT-LINE.
00381      WRITE REPORT-LINE
00382              AFTER 1 LINE.
00383
00384      MOVE SPACES            TO REPORT-LINE.
00385      MOVE ERROR-ACTION-LINE TO REPORT-LINE.
00386      WRITE REPORT-LINE
00387              AFTER 2 LINES.
```

Program 5-Source (Continued)

```
00388
00389     E2-PROCESS-TRANSACTIONS.
00390         IF DELETE-A-RECORD
00391             MOVE TRANSACTION-RECORD   TO DELETE-RECORD
00392             MOVE "*"                  TO DELETE-FIELD-TEMP.
00393
00394         IF UPDATE-EMPLOYEE-NAME
00395             MOVE TRANSACTION-RECORD   TO CHANGE-NAME-RECORD
00396             MOVE EMPLOYEE-NAME-UEN    TO EMPLOYEE-NAME-TEMP.
00397
00398         IF UPDATE-DEPARTMENT-CODE
00399             MOVE TRANSACTION-RECORD   TO CHANGE-DEPT-CODE-RECORD
00400             MOVE DEPARTMENT-CODE-UDC  TO DEPARTMENT-CODE-TEMP.
00401
00402         IF UPDATE-EMPLOYEE-SALARY
00403             MOVE TRANSACTION-RECORD   TO CHANGE-SALARY-RECORD
00404             MOVE YEARLY-SALARY-UES    TO YEARLY-SALARY-TEMP.
00405
00406         IF UPDATE-EMPLOYEE-YEARS
00407             MOVE TRANSACTION-RECORD   TO CHANGE-YEARS-RECORD
00408             MOVE YEARS-IN-COMPANY-UEY TO YEARS-IN-COMPANY-TEMP.
00409
00410         IF NOT (DELETE-A-RECORD
00411             OR
00412             UPDATE-EMPLOYEE-NAME
00413             OR
00414             UPDATE-DEPARTMENT-CODE
00415             OR
00416             UPDATE-EMPLOYEE-SALARY
00417             OR
00418             UPDATE-EMPLOYEE-YEARS)
00419                 MOVE 2 TO ERROR-FLAG
00420                 PERFORM D1-REPORT-ERROR.
00421
00422         PERFORM B2-READ-TRANSACTION-FILE.
```

Program 5-Source (Continued)

```
                              COLUMNS
1   5   10   15   20   25   30   35   40   45   50   55   60   65   70
----|----|----|----|----|----|----|----|----|----|----|----|----|----|--

    100   MORRISON WILLIAM F        ACC   03277000   05
    150   EASTMAN THOMAS            ACC   04530000   07
    170   WAYNE WILLIS              DP    02760000   02
    180   JEFFERSON JOHN D          DP    03530000   03
    186   KILDARE WAYNE             SLS   03600000   04
    189   CROSETTE CARLOS J         SLS   04470000   08
    190   DOWSON DAVID              DP    03400000   06
    200   PEAR JANE                 ACC   03775000   06
    205   JASON TERRY               ACC   02344000   01
    210   DIONNE WILLIAM            DP    02500000   02
```

Program 5-Input(a) Master Personnel File Before Updates for Program 5

```
219   PETERS DAVID         SLS   03560000   08
220   TEAL JASON           ACC   02875000   05
225   MASON ELLEN          DP    02356000   01
240   PAULSON TERENCE      DP    02575000   02
999
999
999
999
999
```

Program 5-Input(a) (Continued)

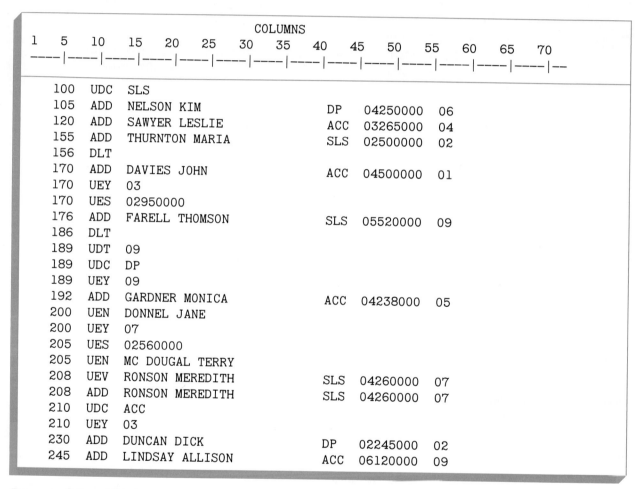

```
                              COLUMNS
1    5    10   15   20   25   30   35   40   45   50   55   60   65   70
----|----|----|----|----|----|----|----|----|----|----|----|----|----|--

100   UDC   SLS
105   ADD   NELSON KIM          DP    04250000   06
120   ADD   SAWYER LESLIE       ACC   03265000   04
155   ADD   THURNTON MARIA      SLS   02500000   02
156   DLT
170   ADD   DAVIES JOHN         ACC   04500000   01
170   UEY   03
170   UES   02950000
176   ADD   FARELL THOMSON      SLS   05520000   09
186   DLT
189   UDT   09
189   UDC   DP
189   UEY   09
192   ADD   GARDNER MONICA      ACC   04238000   05
200   UEN   DONNEL JANE
200   UEY   07
205   UES   02560000
205   UEN   MC DOUGAL TERRY
208   UEV   RONSON MEREDITH     SLS   04260000   07
208   ADD   RONSON MEREDITH     SLS   04260000   07
210   UDC   ACC
210   UEY   03
230   ADD   DUNCAN DICK         DP    02245000   02
245   ADD   LINDSAY ALLISON     ACC   06120000   09
```

Program 5-Input(b) An Instance of Transaction File for Program 5

```
                              COLUMNS
1    5    10   15   20   25   30   35   40   45   50   55   60   65   70
----|----|----|----|----|----|----|----|----|----|----|----|----|----|--

100   MORRISON WILLIAM F     SLS   03277000   05
150   EASTMAN THOMAS         ACC   04530000   07
170   WAYNE WILLIS           DP    02950000   03
180   JEFFERSON JOHN D       DP    03530000   03
```

Program 5-Output(a) Master Personnel File After Updates for Program 5

```
*  186   KILDARE WAYNE          SLS   03600000   04
   189   CROSETTE CARLOS J      DP    04470000   09
   190   DOWSON DAVID           DP    03400000   06
   200   DONNEL JANE            ACC   03775000   07
   205   MC DOUGAL TERRY        ACC   02560000   01
   210   DIONNE WILLIAM         ACC   02500000   03
   219   PETERS DAVID           SLS   03560000   08
   220   TEAL JASON             ACC   02875000   05
   225   MASON ELLEN            DP    02356000   01
   240   PAULSON TERENCE        DP    02575000   02
   105   NELSON KIM             DP    04250000   06
   120   SAWYER LESLIE          ACC   03265000   04
   155   THURNTON MARIA         SLS   02500000   02
   176   FARELL THOMSON         SLS   05520000   09
   192   GARDNER MONICA         ACC   04238000   05
```

Program 5-Output(a) (Continued)

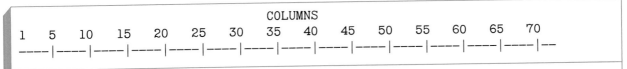

```
                        COLUMNS
1    5   10   15   20   25   30   35   40   45   50   55   60   65   70
————|————|————|————|————|————|————|————|————|————|————|————|————|————|——
```

```
        ERROR OCCURRED WHILE UPDATING THE MASTER FILE.

              ERROR: RECORD IS NOT IN THE MASTER FILE.
              TRANSACTION RECORD ID NUMBER: 156
              TRANSACTION TYPE: DLT

              TRANSACTION IS IGNORED.


        ERROR OCCURRED WHILE UPDATING THE MASTER FILE.

              ERROR: ADD OPERATION FOR EXISTING RECORD.
              TRANSACTION RECORD ID NUMBER: 170
              TRANSACTION TYPE: ADD

              TRANSACTION IS IGNORED.


        ERROR OCCURRED WHILE UPDATING THE MASTER FILE.

              ERROR: CODING ERROR FOR TRANSACTION CODE.
              TRANSACTION RECORD ID NUMBER: 189
              TRANSACTION TYPE: UDT

              TRANSACTION IS IGNORED.
```

Program 5-Output(b) Update Error Report File for Program 5

```
        ERROR OCCURRED WHILE UPDATING THE MASTER FILE.

                ERROR: RECORD IS NOT IN THE MASTER FILE.
                TRANSACTION RECORD ID NUMBER: 208
                TRANSACTION TYPE: UEV

                TRANSACTION IS IGNORED.


        ERROR OCCURRED WHILE UPDATING THE MASTER FILE.

                ERROR: FILE IS FULL.  RECORD CANNOT BE ADDED.
                TRANSACTION RECORD ID NUMBER: 208
                TRANSACTION TYPE: ADD

                TRANSACTION IS IGNORED.


        ERROR OCCURRED WHILE UPDATING THE MASTER FILE.

                ERROR: FILE IS FULL.  RECORD CANNOT BE ADDED.
                TRANSACTION RECORD ID NUMBER: 230
                TRANSACTION TYPE: ADD

                TRANSACTION IS IGNORED.


        ERROR OCCURRED WHILE UPDATING THE MASTER FILE.

                ERROR: FILE IS FULL.  RECORD CANNOT BE ADDED.
                TRANSACTION RECORD ID NUMBER: 245
                TRANSACTION TYPE: ADD

                TRANSACTION IS IGNORED.
```

Program 5-Output(b) (Continued)

```
                          COLUMNS
    5    10   15   20   25   30   35   40   45   50   55   60   65   70
----|----|----|----|----|----|----|----|----|----|----|----|----|----|--

    105    NELSON KIM            DP   04250000   06
    120    SAWYER LESLIE         ACC  03265000   04
    155    THURNTON MARIA        SLS  02500000   02
    176    FARELL THOMSON        SLS  05520000   09
    192    GARDNER MONICA        ACC  04238000   05
```

Program 5-Output(c) Intermediate Addition File for Program 5

12

File Merging and Sorting

CHAPTER CONTENTS

631

IN THIS CHAPTER YOU WILL LEARN ABOUT

- Merging
  - Fundamental concepts
  - Merge strategies
- COBOL merge feature
  - MERGE statement
  - RETURN statement
- File sorting
  - File sorting using internal sort algorithms and merging
  - Merge sort algorithm
  - Balanced merge sort algorithm
  - Polyphase merge algorithm
- COBOL sort feature
  - SORT statement
  - RELEASE statement

Introduction

Earlier we touched on the concepts and techniques of sorting and merging. In Chapter 8, when discussing arrays, we introduced internal sorting. Internal sorting is the process of ordering a list of data elements kept in a main memory structure such as an array or a linked list. In this context, we presented two algorithms, insertion sort and bubble sort. In Chapter 10 we pointed out the importance of file sorting and an associated file operation known as file merging.

Files can be sorted using a variety of algorithms called external sorting algorithms. External sorting algorithms place records in a file in either increasing or decreasing order of one or more attributes, called **sort keys**, in the record structure. While doing that, the sort algorithms access a file that is stored in an external storage medium such as a magnetic tape or disk drive. Hence, the qualification of external in the generic name for this class of algorithms.

File sorting is a ubiquitous process in file and data base processing. For example, we saw in Chapter 11 that sequential file update logic is based on the assumption that the master file and the transaction file involved in the process are sorted. In accessing records in a file, no matter what the underlying file organization technique is, it is quite common to keep the records sorted so that some useful access methods may be defined.

Merging is a central operation in external sorting and is part of the logic of most external sorting algorithms. Merging two files is a relatively simple operation. COBOL supports a file merge feature that makes the process quite easy.

Vendor-supplied programs can be used to sort and merge files without writing elaborate computer programs for them. Such programs are called **sort/merge utilities**. In addition to its merge feature, COBOL incorporates a sort feature that can sort sequential COBOL files with minimal programming. To understand how such programs work, we will briefly discuss a few external sorting techniques in this chapter. Later we will concentrate on the COBOL sort feature.

File Merging

In general, it is possible to merge any number of files into a single file. Several strategies can be used to achieve this, and not all are equally efficient. Before examining these, we should go over the fundamentals of merging.

Fundamental Concepts and Techniques of File Merging

Suppose we have two sequential files with the same record structure that contain different records. One way to combine them into a single file is to merge them with respect to a common attribute. This attribute is called a **merge key**.

> **Merging** is an operation on two or more files of similar record structures containing records that are similarly ordered (i.e., either all ascending or all descending) with respect to a merge key. It produces a new file of all the records in all source files such that the new file is also ordered with respect to the same merge key.

Merging two files is known as **2-way merge**. Clearly, a 3-way merge is a 2-way merge algorithm applied twice. In other words, we can merge two files into an ordered file and then merge the result with the third file, in both cases using the 2-way merge logic. It is possible to generalize the operation to any number of source files, say, P of them. Then the operation is known as **P-way merge**.

The 2-way merge of two similarly ordered sequential files requires two internal buffers, one for each source file. Each buffer is capable of storing a record coming from its respective file. Let us call the two files FILE-1 and FILE-2, and their respective buffers BUFFER-1 and BUFFER-2. Let the file to be created after merging be NEW-FILE. During 2-way merge, FILE-1 and FILE-2 are input files, and NEW-FILE is an output file. Accordingly, the logic of 2-way merge consists of the following steps.

Step 1: Read a record from FILE-1 into BUFFER-1. If the end of file is reached for FILE-1, copy the remaining content of FILE-2 into NEW-FILE and terminate processing.

Step 2: Read a record from FILE-2 into BUFFER-2. If the end of file is reached for FILE-2, simply copy the remaining records in FILE-1 into NEW-FILE and terminate processing.

Step 3: If the merge key field value of BUFFER-1 is less than or equal to that of BUFFER-2, write the content of BUFFER-1 into NEW-FILE, go to step 1, and skip step 2. Otherwise, write the content of BUFFER-2 into NEW-FILE and go to step 2.

In this algorithm, copying the content of one of the files into NEW-FILE in case the other file is fully processed can be regarded as 1-way merge. To accomplish this without writing additional code, we may store a dummy record in the buffer corresponding to the file that has been exhausted. We make the merge key field of this dummy record a value that is larger than any value for the merge key attribute in both files, so that the algorithm never attempts to read from the exhausted file again. This technique ensures copying a file using essentially the same code devised for 2-way merge.

For 3-way merge of three files the same logic can be modified to incorporate three internal buffers, one for each source file. In this case we must select the content of the buffer with the smallest merge key value among three buffers and write it into NEW-FILE. If a source file is fully processed, we store in its corresponding buffer a dummy record with a large merge key value so that it never is picked as the smallest. When this happens, the 3-way merge becomes equivalent to 2-way merge. When the second source file is also exhausted, the process is reduced to 1-way merge. The program is terminated if all three buffers contain dummy records.

Figure 1 shows the steps involved in the 3-way merge of three sequential files. The source files are sorted in increasing order of the merge key, which has two-digit integer values as shown in the figure. In step 1, the first records from FILE-1, FILE-2, and FILE-3 are read into BUFFER-1, BUFFER-2, and BUFFER-3, respectively. The record with the smallest merge key value, that is, 10, is picked and written into the OUTPUT-FILE. In step 2, BUFFER-3 is replaced with the next record from FILE-3. The process continues this way until step 5.

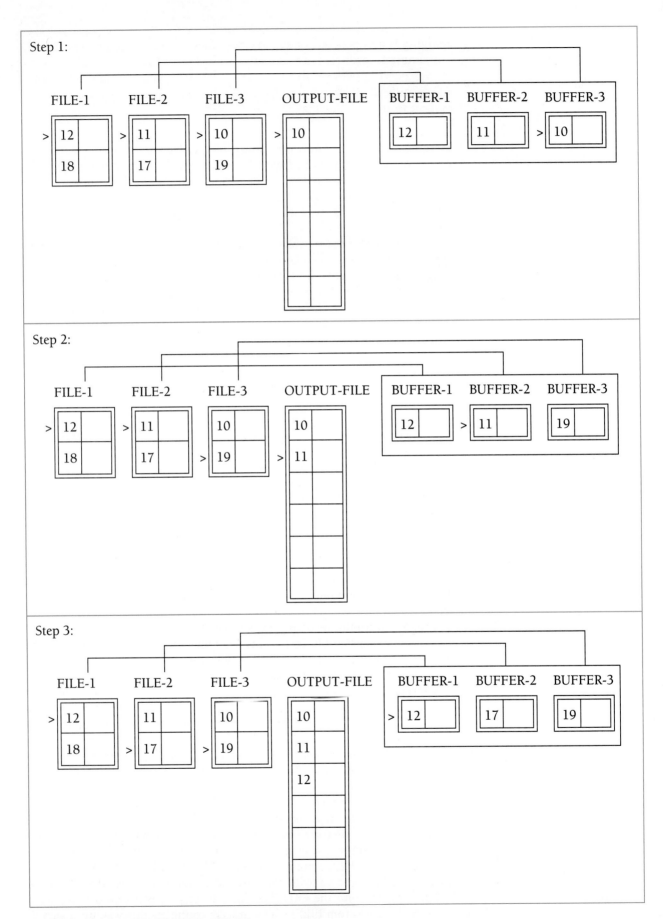

Figure 1 Steps Involved in 3-Way Merge

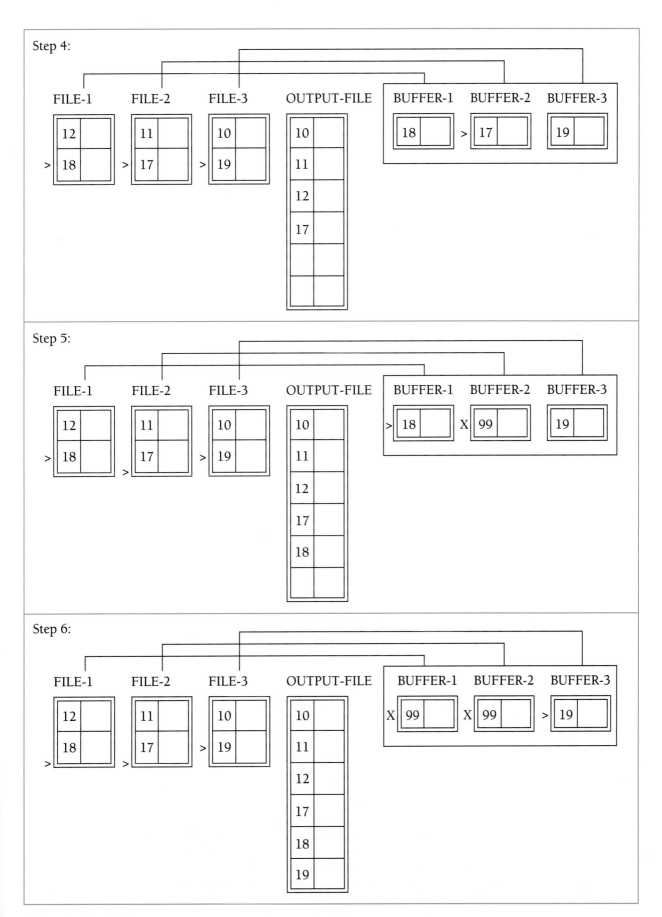

Figure 1 (Continued)

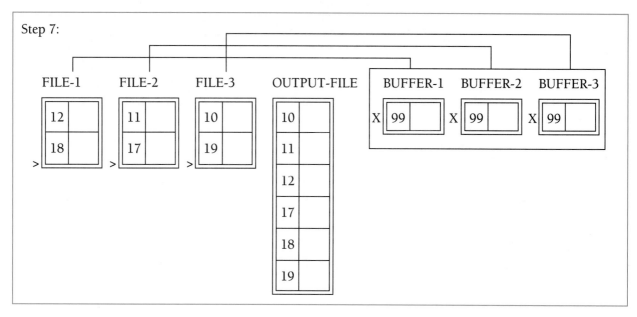

Step 7:

Figure 1 (Continued)

An attempt to read a record in FILE-2 in this step results in an end-of-file condition being raised. In this case, we store a dummy record in BUFFER-2 with a merge key value of 99. As 99 is larger than any merge key value in the source files, the content of BUFFER-2 will never be picked by the algorithm. In step 7, all three buffers will contain 99, and the algorithm terminates. This algorithm creates OUTPUT-FILE that contains a sorted collection of all records existing in the source files.

File Merge Strategies

Many different strategies can be adopted for merging files. In general, they depend on three basic factors: the number of files to be merged, the size of internal memory that is available for use as merge buffers, and the type and number of available external file storage devices.

For tape storage files, the number of input files is restricted by the number of available tape drives in a computer installation. If eight files are to be merged, nine tape drive units are needed for a single-pass 8-way merge operation, eight of them containing the input files and the ninth to store the resulting merged file. This corresponds to the most efficient mode of processing for eight files (Figure 2a).

What if we have only four tape drive units and eight files to merge? This means we will use a 3-way merge algorithm and make more than one pass to complete the merging. A variety of different strategies can be formulated for this task. We consider two of them.

Strategy 1   For this we use the tree of Figure 2b as our basis. We can start by arranging the eight input files as follows.

- Tape drive 1 contains FILE-1, FILE-4, and FILE-7, in that order.
- Tape drive 2 contains FILE-2, FILE-5, and FILE-8.
- Tape drive 3 contains FILE-3 and FILE-6.
- Tape drive 4 contains an empty reel in output mode.

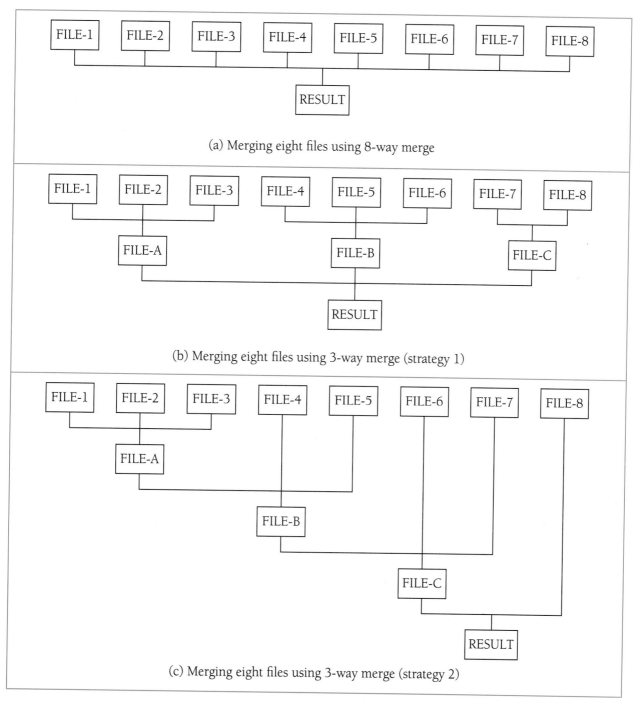

(a) Merging eight files using 8-way merge

(b) Merging eight files using 3-way merge (strategy 1)

(c) Merging eight files using 3-way merge (strategy 2)

Figure 2 File Merge Strategies

In the first pass we merge FILE-1, FILE-2, and FILE-3 into FILE-A, and store it on tape drive 4. Then FILE-4, FILE-5, and FILE-6 are merged into FILE-B and stored on tape drive 4 after FILE-A. Finally, FILE-7 and FILE-8 are merged into FILE-C and recorded on tape drive 4, after FILE-B.

In preparation for the second pass, we rewind tape drive 4, change its mode to input, and copy FILE-A, FILE-B, and FILE-C onto tape drives 1, 2, and 3, respectively. Then, we open FILE-A, FILE-B, and FILE-C in input mode, and tape drive 4 in output mode. Using 3-way merge, we combine FILE-A, FILE-B, and FILE-C into RESULT, the merged file, stored on tape drive 4.

The cost of this particular strategy is a function of the number of records copied during the merge. To simplify our analysis, let us assume that all eight input files contain the same number of records, say, 1000 each. In the first pass we merge 3000 records into FILE-A, 3000 into FILE-B, and 2000 into FILE-C, which totals 8000 records. Before the second pass we distribute these three intermediate files onto drives 1, 2, and 3. This is equivalent to copying the 8000 records. During the second pass we merge 3000 records from FILE-A, with 3000 from FILE-B, and 2000 from FILE-C. This amounts to copying another 8000 records. Hence, the entire process has cost us the time for copying 24,000 records, excluding the time for tape rewind.

It is possible to write a formula for this strategy for the general case when there are different numbers of records in the source files. If NR1 denotes the number of records in FILE-1, NR2 those in FILE-2, and so on, the total number of records copied during the entire process can be expressed as

$$3 (NR1 + NR2 + NR3 + \cdots + NR8)$$

Strategy 2 This time we consider the structure of Figure 2c and accordingly define our passes. We arrange the eight input files on the available tape drives as follows.

- Tape drive 1 contains FILE-1, FILE-4, FILE-6, and FILE-8.
- Tape drive 2 contains FILE-2, FILE-5, and FILE-7.
- Tape drive 3 contains FILE-3.
- Tape drive 4 contains an empty reel in output mode.

In pass 1 we merge FILE-1, FILE-2, and FILE-3 from drives 1, 2, and 3, respectively, into FILE-A, stored on drive 4. In pass 2 we rewind drives 3 and 4 and change their modes to input and output, respectively. Then we merge FILE-4, FILE-5, and FILE-A on drives 1, 2, and 4 to FILE-B, stored on drive 3. In pass 3 we rewind drive 4 and change its mode to output. Drives 1, 2, and 3 are in input mode. We merge FILE-6, FILE-7, and FILE-B into FILE-C on drive 4. Finally, we rewind drive 3, change its mode to output, and merge FILE-8 on drive 1 with FILE-C on drive 4 into RESULT on drive 3. The cost of this strategy can be computed as

$$4 (NR1 + NR2 + NR3) + 3 (NR4 + NR5) + 2 (NR6 + NR7) + NR8$$

Assuming all eight files contain 1000 records each, the total cost of merging them using this strategy is equivalent to copying 23,000 records, excluding rewind times. This is somewhat better than strategy 1, but much worse than directly merging eight files using 8-way merge with a cost of 8000 record copies. It should also be noted that in strategy 2, if the number of records in the eight input files is different, the processing cost can be minimized provided the files are arranged such that their sizes increase from FILE-1 to FILE-8 in a uniform fashion.

In case of merging done using disk storage, and if the storage capacity is sufficient for (P+1) files when merging P files, the best strategy is to apply P-way merge directly. Sometimes, the internal memory space for merge buffers is limited, or the available merge program may be such that fewer than P files may be merged in one pass. Under such circumstances, it is the application programmer's responsibility to find the best possible merge strategy.

Commercially available file merge utilities have been designed to handle tape files as well as disk files, and thus incorporate some specific strategy to expedite merging. Generally, such strategies are closely guarded trade secrets.

Example Program 1: *3-Way Merge of Three Ordered Files*

In this section we develop a COBOL implementation of the 3-way merge algorithm as described.

Problem   We consider three sequential disk files of the same record structure consisting of the following fields:

- A 3-digit personnel identification number
- A 22-character personnel name
- A 5-digit yearly salary field
- A 3-character department code

We assume that FILE-1, FILE-2, and FILE-3 contain records for personnel affiliated with the accounting, sales, and management information systems departments, respectively. Program 1-Input(a) through (c) show simplified instances of the three files we will use to test our program. The merge key for these files is the personnel identification number field, and thus the records are in increasing order of this field in each file.

Solution   The compiler source listing of the 3-way merge program is given in Program 1-Source. The merge key for the three source files, FILE-1, FILE-2, and FILE-3, and the resulting merged file, RESULT, consists of the first three characters in their record structure descriptions. For example, in RECORD-1 we call this field MERGE-KEY-1, which is the merge key field for FILE-1, and refer to the rest of the structure as a FILLER field.

The three WORKING-STORAGE SECTION structures called BUFFER-1, BUFFER-2, and BUFFER-3 correspond to the three source files and will store records coming from them. We open the three source files in input mode, and the file RESULT in output mode. One record each from FILE-1, FILE-2, and FILE-3 is read into BUFFER-1, BUFFER-2, and BUFFER-3. During input, whenever an end-of-file condition is raised for a source file, we place 999 in the buffer key field of the corresponding buffer structure for this file. The central procedure for this program is given in the paragraph B4-MERGE-RECORDS. Here we find the record in the three buffers with the smallest merge key value. Then we write the content of this buffer into RESULT and fill it with another record from the corresponding source file. This procedure is carried out until all three source files are completely exhausted. It should be noted that the paragraph B4-MERGE-RECORDS performs 3-way, 2-way, and 1-way merges depending on how many source files have been exhausted.

Program 1-Output shows an instance of the merged file, RESULT, produced by Program 1-Source.

COBOL File Merge Feature

COBOL has a special language feature for merging files. It uses the MERGE statement to merge any number of source files without requiring the programmer to write a procedure. The MERGE statement describes what we want the computer to do (i.e., the intent of the operation), not how the computer should go about doing it (i.e., the procedural aspect of the operation). Therefore, the MERGE statement is a very high-level, nonprocedural statement. Syntactically, it is defined as follows.

$$\text{MERGE file-name-1} \left\{ \text{ON} \left\{ \begin{matrix} \underline{\text{ASCENDING}} \\ \underline{\text{DESCENDING}} \end{matrix} \right\} \text{KEY \{data-name\}} \cdots \right\} \cdots$$

[COLLATING <u>SEQUENCE</u> IS alphabet-name]
<u>USING</u> file-name-2 {file-name-3} · · ·

$$\left\{ \begin{matrix} \underline{\text{OUTPUT}} \ \underline{\text{PROCEDURE}} \ \text{IS procedure-name-1} \left[\left\{ \begin{matrix} \underline{\text{THROUGH}} \\ \underline{\text{THRU}} \end{matrix} \right\} \text{procedure-name-2} \right] \\ \underline{\text{GIVING}} \ \{\text{file-name-4}\} \cdots \end{matrix} \right\}$$

A MERGE statement may contain one or more ON ASCENDING or DESCENDING KEY clauses. Each is followed by one or more data names that are field names in the record structure of the files to be merged. This clause is used to specify the merge key.

The COLLATING SEQUENCE clause is optional. It references an alphabet. If it is not used, the collating sequence that is intrinsic to the computer will determine the result of the merge operation.

The USING clause references two or more files by their in-program names. These files are the source files to be merged. In all implementations of the COBOL language, there is a limit to the number of files that can be merged in one invocation of the MERGE statement.

A MERGE statement must have either a GIVING clause with the name of the file that contains the result, or an OUTPUT PROCEDURE clause. The OUTPUT PROCEDURE clause specifies the name of the PROCEDURE DIVISION section or a range of sections that will be executed after the merge operation is completed.

Functionally, the MERGE statement merges two or more identically ordered files using one or more merge keys, and makes available the records obtained this way to either an output file or an output procedure. The following are examples of the MERGE statement.

Example 1   For the 3-way merge application that we considered in the previous section, the equivalent MERGE statement will look like:

```
MERGE MERGE-FILE
    ON ASCENDING KEY MERGE-KEY
    USING FILE-1 FILE-2 FILE-3
    GIVING RESULT.
```

Example 2   Consider two files called ART-STUDENTS and SCIENCE-STUDENTS, as in Figure 3. These files have similar record structures consisting of STUDENT-IDNO, COURSE-CODE, DIVISION, and GRADE fields. Suppose both files are sorted in increasing order of STUDENT-IDNO, which is the primary sort key, and also in increasing order of COURSE-CODE, the secondary sort key. This means that for more than one record for the same value of STUDENT-IDNO,

ART-STUDENTS

STUDENT-IDNO	COURSE-CODE	DIV	GRADE
1500	CSC100	ART	A
1500	SOC110	ART	B
1600	MTH151	ART	C
1600	SOC110	ART	A
. . .			
1800	ARC121	ART	A

SCIENCE-STUDENTS

STUDENT-IDNO	COURSE-CODE	DIV	GRADE
1400	CSC100	SCI	A
1400	MTH151	SCI	C
1400	PHY155	SCI	C
1550	CSC100	SCI	A
1550	PHY155	SCI	B
. . .			
1850	SOC110	SCI	A

ALL-STUDENTS

STUDENT-IDNO	COURSE-CODE	DIV	GRADE
1400	CSC100	SCI	A
1400	MTH151	SCI	C
1400	PHY155	SCI	C
1500	CSC100	ART	A
1500	SOC110	ART	B
1550	CSC100	SCI	A
1550	PHY155	SCI	B
1600	MTH151	ART	C
1600	SOC110	ART	A
. . .			
1800	ARC121	ART	A
. . .			
1850	SOC110	SCI	A

COBOL code:

```
MERGE MERGE-FILE
    ON ASCENDING KEY STUDENT-IDNO COURSE-CODE
    USING ART-STUDENTS SCIENCE-STUDENTS
    GIVING ALL-STUDENTS.
```

Or:

```
MERGE MERGE-FILE
    ON ASCENDING KEY STUDENT-IDNO
    ON ASCENDING KEY COURSE-CODE
    USING ART-STUDENTS SCIENCE-STUDENTS
    GIVING ALL-STUDENTS.
```

Figure 3 Merging Files on Multiple Keys (Both Merge Keys Ascending)

the records are arranged in increasing order of COURSE-CODE values. These two source files can be merged into a similarly ordered file called ALL-STUDENTS, as shown in Figure 3, using the MERGE statement:

```
MERGE MERGE-FILE
    ON ASCENDING KEY STUDENT-IDNO COURSE-CODE
    USING ART-STUDENTS SCIENCE-STUDENTS
    GIVING ALL-STUDENTS.
```

The same task can be accomplished by specifying the merge keys separately as follows.

```
MERGE MERGE-FILE
    ON ASCENDING KEY STUDENT-IDNO
    ON ASCENDING KEY COURSE-CODE
    USING ART-STUDENTS SCIENCE-STUDENTS
    GIVING ALL-STUDENTS.
```

Example 3   Figure 4 shows ART-STUDENTS and SCIENCE-STUDENTS files sorted in increasing order of STUDENT-IDNO but in decreasing order of COURSE-CODE. Such a mixed order requires the use of separate ON ASCENDING/ DESCENDING KEY clauses for the sort keys. The following MERGE statement is appropriate here.

```
MERGE MERGE-FILE
    ON ASCENDING KEY STUDENT-IDNO
    ON DESCENDING KEY COURSE-CODE
    USING ART-STUDENTS SCIENCE-STUDENTS
    GIVING ALL-STUDENTS.
```

Example 4   The following MERGE statement references a block of PROCEDURE DIVISION sections to be executed after the merge operation is completed. These sections begin with the one named COMPUTE-GRADE-PT-AVG, and go up to and include the section named PRODUCE-LISTING.

```
MERGE MERGE-FILE
    ON ASCENDING KEY STUDENT-IDNO
    ON DESCENDING KEY COURSE-CODE
    USING ART-STUDENTS SCIENCE-STUDENTS
    OUTPUT PROCEDURE IS COMPUTE-GRADE-PT-AVG
                THRU PRODUCE-LISTING.
```

The merge file is used as a work file for merging. The user has no control over the content of this file during processing. It is processed through a MERGE statement in the PROCEDURE DIVISION. Like any other file, it should be defined in the ENVIRONMENT DIVISION FILE-CONTROL paragraph using a SELECT statement. Unlike the SELECT statements for ordinary

ART-STUDENTS

STUDENT-IDNO	COURSE-CODE	DIV	GRADE
1500	SOC110	ART	B
1500	CSC100	ART	A
1600	SOC110	ART	A
1600	MTH151	ART	C
. . .			
1800	ARC121	ART	A

SCIENCE-STUDENTS

STUDENT-IDNO	COURSE-CODE	DIV	GRADE
1400	PHY155	SCI	C
1400	MTH151	SCI	C
1400	CSC100	SCI	A
1550	PHY155	SCI	B
1550	CSC100	SCI	A
. . .			
1850	SOC110	SCI	A

ALL-STUDENTS

STUDENT-IDNO	COURSE-CODE	DIV	GRADE
1400	PHY155	SCI	C
1400	MTH151	SCI	C
1400	CSC100	SCI	A
1500	SOC110	ART	B
1500	CSC100	ART	A
1550	PHY155	SCI	B
1550	CSC100	SCI	A
1600	SOC110	ART	A
1600	MTH151	ART	C
. . .			
1800	ARC121	ART	A
. . .			
1850	SOC110	SCI	A

COBOL code:

```
MERGE MERGE-FILE
    ON ASCENDING KEY STUDENT-IDNO
    ON DESCENDING KEY COURSE-CODE
    USING ART-STUDENTS SCIENCE-STUDENTS
    GIVING ALL-STUDENTS.
```

Figure 4 Merging Files on Multiple Keys (Major Key Ascending, Minor Key Descending)

files, the SELECT statement for the merge file can contain only the ASSIGN clause. For example:

```
SELECT MERGE-FILE ASSIGN TO EXTMERGE.
```

The merge file and its record structures should also be defined in the DATA DIVISION, FILE SECTION, using an SD block. An SD block is similar to an FD block for ordinary user files, except it can contain only the RECORD CONTAINS and DATA RECORD clauses. Following is an example:

```
SD  MERGE-FILE
    RECORD CONTAINS 80 CHARACTERS
    DATA RECORD IS MERGE-RECORD.
01  MERGE-RECORD.
    05  MERGE-KEY                   PIC XXX.
    05  FILLER                      PIC X(77).
```

In the PROCEDURE DIVISION of the program, no input or output statements may be used for the merge file.

The ON ASCENDING/DESCENDING KEY clause is used to specify the merge keys and the type of ordering for the source files and the merged file. The merge keys are data items in the record structure description of the merge file and are defined in its SD block. Record structure descriptions for all source files and the merged file should contain data items corresponding to the merge keys. These data items must be located in the same positions in all record structures, and must have the same lengths and data types. Their names, however, need not be the same. Merge key data items should be fixed-length fields. The maximum number of merge keys that can be specified depends on the implementation of the COBOL compiler being used.

The key data items may not be subscripted or indexed variables. They should be listed in order of decreasing significance. The first merge key data item is the primary sort key for the files concerned, the second is the secondary sort key, and so on.

The COLLATING SEQUENCE clause is optional and, when missing, it is the collating sequence that is natural to the computer system. Usually, this is either EBCDIC or ASCII. If an alternative is desired, this clause should explicitly specify the alphabet, and the alphabet name should be included in the SPECIAL-NAMES paragraph.

The USING clause indicates the source files to be merged. The files must be defined by SELECT statements in the ENVIRONMENT DIVISION as sequential files. Certain merge utilities also accept other file organizations, provided they permit sequential access. For each source file, there must be an FD block in the FILE SECTION of the DATA DIVISION. Record size for all source files must be the same as that of the merge file.

At the time the MERGE statement is executed, the source files must not be open. These files are first automatically opened by the system while the MERGE statement is being executed, then their contents are accessed, and finally they are closed.

Only one merged file name can be specified in the GIVING clause. This file must also be fully described as a sequential file by a SELECT statement and an FD block. Its record size should be the same as that of the merge file. While the MERGE statement is being executed, this file should not be open. Like source files, the merged file is also fully controlled by the system with respect to opening, accessing, and closing.

The OUTPUT PROCEDURE clause can be used in lieu of the GIVING clause in the MERGE statement. It references one or two PROCEDURE DIVISION sections. If two section names are included with this clause, its scope will contain all sections that are physically consecutive in the PROCEDURE DIVISION. The first section name in the OUTPUT PROCEDURE clause specifies the first or the only section, and the second section name specifies the last section that is in the scope of this clause. The sections that constitute the output procedure for the MERGE statement should logically be written to process the records produced by the merge operation. There must be at least one execution of an input statement in the output procedure to bring a merged record into a memory structure. COBOL has a special input statement for this purpose, the RETURN statement. We discuss this in greater detail below.

When all the records coming from the source files are merged into the merge file, the program control passes to the output procedure. After all the sections of the output procedure are executed, the program control is transferred to the statement that follows the MERGE statement in the PROCEDURE DIVISION. The program control should not be passed to the output procedure except by a related MERGE statement. The output procedure should not contain any MERGE or SORT statements, or statements that transfer control to other program statements that are outside it.

Records in the merge file can be transferred to an internal memory structure using the RETURN statement. The RETURN statement is syntactically similar to the sequential READ statement.

COBOL 85

```
RETURN file-name RECORD [ INTO identifier ]
    [ AT END imperative-statement-1 ]
    [ NOT AT END imperative-statement-2 ]
    [ END-RETURN ]
```

Here is an example:

```
RETURN MERGE-FILE RECORD INTO WS-MERGED-RECORD
    AT END PERFORM START-PROCESSING.
```

The RETURN statement can be used only in conjunction with the merge file, and only in the output procedure of a MERGE statement. Anywhere else in the PROCEDURE DIVISION, it has no effect. Every execution of the RETURN statement causes a record from the merge file to be transferred to its record structure, and if the INTO option is used, also to the indicated memory structure.

REVIEW QUESTIONS

1. Attributes in a record structure of a file that are used by an external sorting technique to order records in that file are called _____ .
2. The majority of external sorting algorithms use file merging as part of their logic. (T or F)
3. The vendor-supplied programs that can be used to sort and merge files are known as _____ .

4. The sort keys used in ordering the source files in file merging are known as _____ .

5. Which of the following statements concerning file merging is incorrect?
   a. A 3-way merge is equivalent to a 2-way merge applied twice.
   b. The 1-way merge is equivalent to copying a file.
   c. In P-way merge, we need P internal buffers.
   d. A 4-way merge algorithm requires a minimum of four files.

6. The efficiency of a file merge strategy depends on the number of files to be merged, the size of available internal memory for use as merge buffers, and the type and number of available external storage devices. (T or F)

7. The COBOL MERGE statement is a procedural specification of a specific merge strategy. (T or F)

8. Which of the following concerning the COBOL MERGE statement is correct?
   a. To merge three files, we must have two MERGE statements in a program.
   b. It can be used to merge both unordered and ordered source files.
   c. The merge keys are specified in the USING clause.
   d. The GIVING clause defines the file in which the merged records are stored.
   e. All of the above are correct.

9. While using the MERGE statement to merge files, the merge file should be defined in an FD block. Also, in the PROCEDURE DIVISION, normal I-O statements can be used for it. (T or F)

10. Records in the merge file can be transferred to an internal memory structure using the _____ statement.

Answers: 1. sort keys; 2. T; 3. sort/merge utilities; 4. merge keys; 5. d; 6. T; 7. F; 8. d; 9. F; 10. RETURN.

Example Program 2: *File Merging Using the COBOL Merge Feature*

Here we develop a program in which the COBOL MERGE statement is used to merge three ordered sequential files. This exercise is an extension of Program 1, which was concerned with 3-way merge of the three files of Program 1-Input. This time, instead of an explicit 3-way merge algorithm, we make use of the MERGE statement.

Problem All files involved in the merge process have the same record structure as previously described, consisting of employee identification number, employee name, yearly salary, and department code. The application program is expected to do the following tasks.

- Check the ordering of records in source files FILE-1, FILE-2, and FILE-3, and make sure that all are sorted in ascending order by the merge key, that is, the employee identification number. If one or more of the files are improperly ordered or unordered, the program should not attempt to merge them. To ensure this, the programmer should include warning messages in the application program and terminate its execution.
- If the files are correctly ordered, they should be merged. For this we use the MERGE statement.

■ After the merge, the records should be validated for correctness based on the following tests before they are stored in the file called RESULT.
The employee identification number should be in the range of 050–250.
Correct salary range is 25,000–45,000.
Department codes are MIS, ACC, and SLS.

Solution The compiler listing of the program developed for this exercise is given in Program 2-Source. Several aspects of the program are noteworthy.

1. The merge file is specified using a SELECT statement in the FILE-CONTROL paragraph, and in an SD block in the FILE SECTION of the DATA DIVISION (lines 00041 and 00049–00057).
2. The record structures of the three source files and the merge file are similar.
3. After the ordering of the three source files is validated, the merge operation is attempted by calling on the paragraph B7-MERGE-FILES.
4. The paragraph B7-MERGE-FILES contains a MERGE statement to merge FILE-1, FILE-2, and FILE-3, using MERGE-EMP-IDNO data field of MERGE-RECORD as the merge key. It should be noted that all files involved in the MERGE statement are closed at this time. After the merge operation, an output procedure is specified.
5. The output procedure is described in the PROCEDURE DIVISION section called C1-POST-MERGE-PROCESSING. It starts with the paragraph D1-LOAD-OUTPUT-FILE, which contains a RETURN statement and a statement that invokes the paragraph E1-VALIDATE-MERGE-RECORD. Other paragraphs in this section are subordinate to the first paragraph.
6. The paragraph E1-VALIDATE-MERGE-RECORD also contains a RETURN statement.
7. After the validated merge records have been written into the file RESULT, the file is closed in the paragraph D1-LOAD-OUTPUT-FILE. Here we would like to terminate the output procedure that was invoked by the MERGE statement. The output procedure is a section, however, and unless we pass control at this point to the end of the section, all the paragraphs in that section will be executed consecutively, resulting in errors. To eliminate this, we have included in this section a final paragraph called D2-TERMINATE-SECTION, and must use, to our chagrin, a GO TO statement at the end of the paragraph D1-LOAD-OUTPUT-FILE.

Program 2-Output shows an instance of the RESULT file produced by Program 2-Source.

File Sorting

In principle, external sorting is quite different from internal sorting. Quite a few external sorting techniques have been discovered and are in use currently. In this section we study three of them, starting with the simplest and the most obvious, which combines an appropriate internal sort technique with file merging. Then we will describe the balanced merge and polyphase merge external sort techniques as algorithms. We will not attempt to program them in COBOL; however, we stress once again that a basic understanding of the concepts involved in external sorting is important for the computer professional. Finally we will describe the COBOL SORT feature that can be used to sort files easily in application programs.

File Sorting Using Internal Sort Algorithms and Merging

We can demonstrate in a simplified example how internal sort algorithms can be used in conjunction with file merging to sort files. Suppose, as in Figure 5, we have a file of 11 records, and the internal memory that we can use to store records (i.e., the buffer capacity for internal sort) is restricted to 4 records. This means that we cannot load all 11 records into the buffer and apply an internal sort technique, such as bubble sort, to solve the problem. Suppose, however, that in addition to FILE-1 that contains the unsorted records, we have three more files, FILE-2, FILE-3, and FILE-4, that we can use to sort our file. In Figure 5, we represent the records by their sort key values, which are two-digit integer numbers. With these resources and constraints, the following operations are done.

Step 1: Read the first four records in FILE-1 into the internal memory, apply some internal sort technique (say, the bubble sort algorithm) to sort them, and write these records into FILE-2. Then do the same for the next four records in FILE-1: read them into the buffer, internally sort them, and copy them into FILE-3 this time. The theme in this step has been "internal sort followed by distribution" of sorted groups of records into two files.

Step 2: Merge the ordered contents of FILE-2 and FILE-3 into an ordered file and store it in FILE-4. This requires the application of a 2-way merge algorithm for which our buffer capacity is more than adequate. Therefore, step 2 is a merge step.

Step 3: Consider the records left in FILE-1. Copy the remaining three records into the sort buffer, apply the internal sort algorithm to order them, and transfer them to FILE-2. For this it is necessary to close FILE-2 and reopen it in output mode, thus destroying its previous content. This, however, is not important, as its content was already duplicated in FILE-4 in step 2.

Step 4: Merge the three ordered records in FILE-2 with FILE-4 and write the merged file into FILE-3.

As we have already processed the entire content of the source file FILE-1, we can terminate the algorithm here. For a larger file, this pattern of "internal sort and distribute, and then merge" will continue until all the records in the unordered file are processed. The number of steps involved in this algorithm is a function of the size of the source file, the buffer capacity, and the number of files we can use for merging.

It should be noted that in every step involving distribution we are copying records. To improve the efficiency of this technique, we should try to eliminate, or at least minimize, this process of copying. One such technique that minimizes copying is the polyphase merge, which is discussed later.

Merge Sort and Balanced Merge Sort

Instead of using an internal sort algorithm, we rely completely on file merging to sort our file. We assume that a general file merge algorithm is available. We observe that n files containing one record each can be merged into a file containing n ordered records, and that this basic operation requires (n + 1) files, n to be in input mode and one in output mode. We will use this observation in developing our technique.

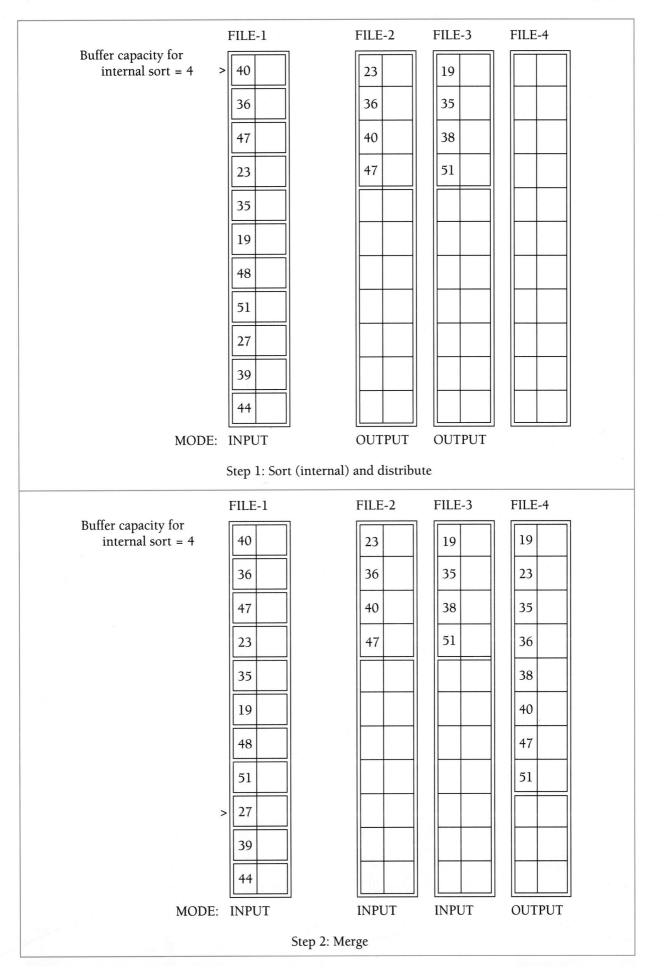

Figure 5 External Sorting by Internal Sort and Merge

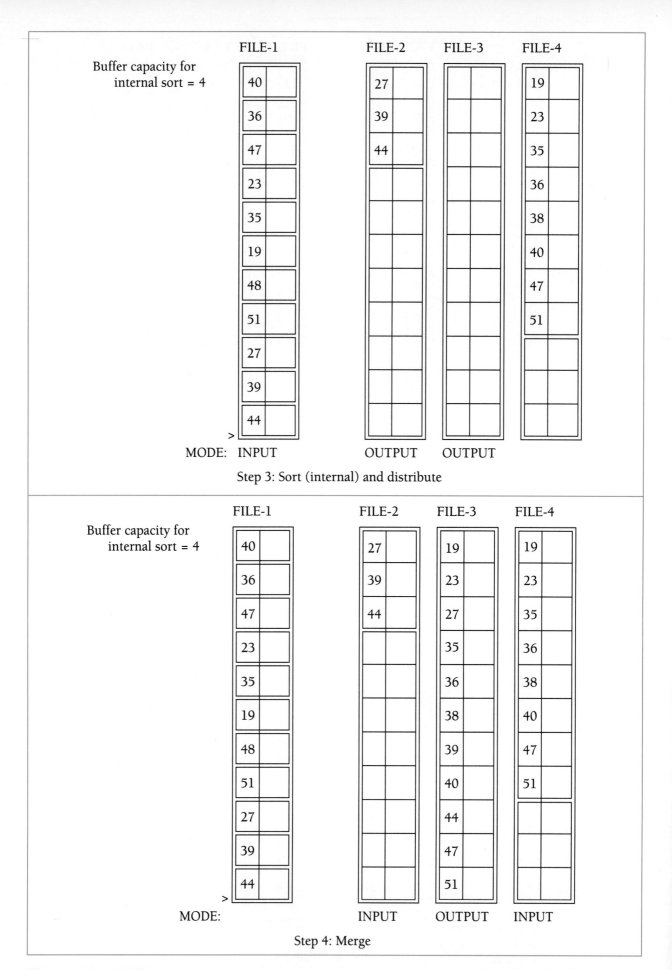

Figure 5 (Continued)

We first consider the simplified example illustrated in Figure 6. Suppose we have an unsorted file of nine records as FILE-1. Three other files, FILE-2, FILE-3, and FILE-4, are also available. We can proceed as follows.

Step 1: Read records from FILE-1 and copy them alternately into FILE-2, FILE-3, and FILE-4. At the end of this step, we end up with the three output files containing three records each. As yet these files are unordered. In this step we have distributed the records from FILE-1 to the other files.

Step 2: Change the modes of FILE-2, FILE-3, and FILE-4 to input, and make FILE-1 an output file. Then merge the first records from the three files into a block of ordered records and write them into FILE-1. This requires a 3-way merge. Do the same thing for the second records from the three input files and write this block after the first block in FILE-1. Continue this way until all records are transferred to FILE-1. At the end of this step FILE-1 contains ordered blocks of three records each. The last block may have fewer than three records.

Step 3: Distribute blocks of three or less records from FILE-1 to FILE-2, FILE-3, and FILE-4 in an alternating fashion, until all records in FILE-1 are distributed.

Step 4: Again using 3-way merge, combine the three ordered files, FILE-2, FILE-3, and FILE-4, into FILE-1. At the end of this step FILE-1 is completely sorted and we can terminate the algorithm.

This algorithm is referred to as **merge sort**, and is characterized by a pattern in which distribute and merge steps (also called passes) alternate. The number of passes necessary to sort a file depends on the file size and the number of files available for use as output files during a distribute pass. This number essentially is the same as P in the associated P-way merge algorithm. Therefore, in merge sort, to use P-way merge we need (P + 1) files, P of them as output files and one as input file during distribution passes. In Figure 6 we had three files that could be used as output files during a distribution pass, and we used a 3-way merge technique and a total of four files.

The main flaw of this algorithm is that a distribution pass is, in fact, equivalent to copying all records that we want to sort. If we can eliminate this copying, or at least minimize it, our algorithm will become more efficient. To do that, we can resort to two techniques.

1. We can use more files in a balanced fashion so that at every pass the records are merged, and no superfluous copying (i.e., without any merge) is required.
2. Initially, we can distribute the right number of records to the available files, and in the subsequent passes avoid copying.

The first technique leads us to a variation of merge sort known as **balanced merge sort**. The second technique is used in a number of algorithms. We discuss one of them, **polyphase merge sort**, in the next section.

Let us illustrate the balanced merge sort using Figure 7. We have nine records in FILE-1 and five additional files, FILE-2 through FILE-6. We are planning to use 3-way merge. Before we describe the steps involved, however, we introduce a term that is convenient in describing this algorithm.

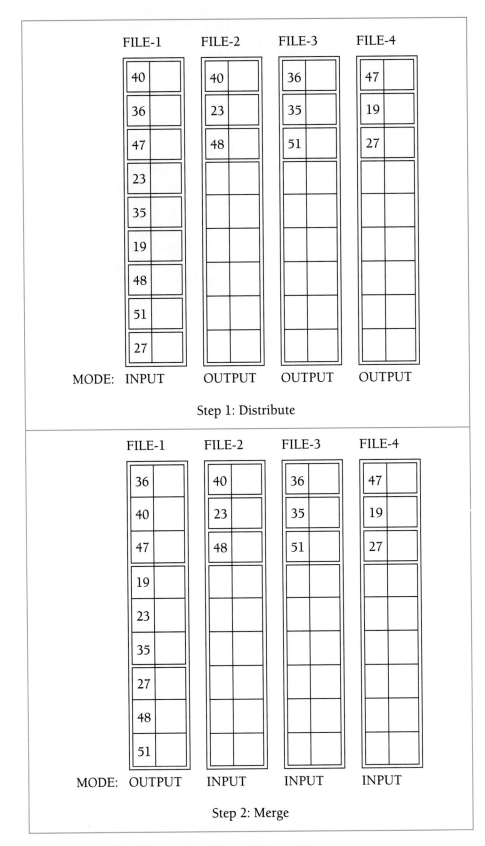

Figure 6 Merge Sort Using Four Files and 3-Way Merge

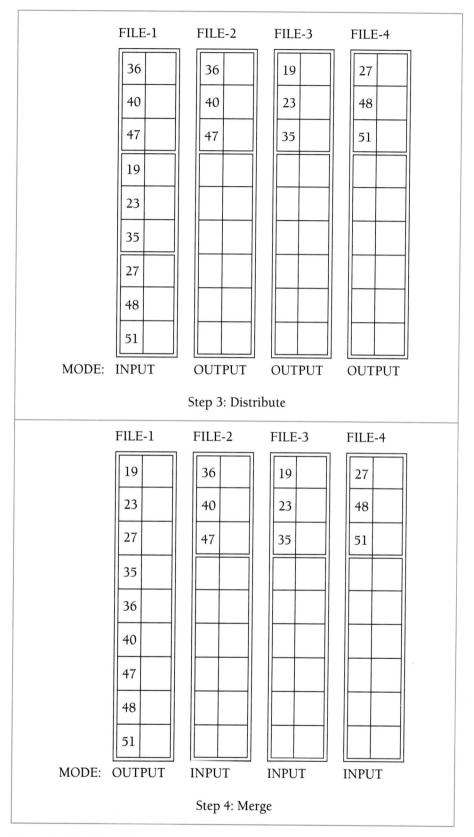

Figure 6 (Continued)

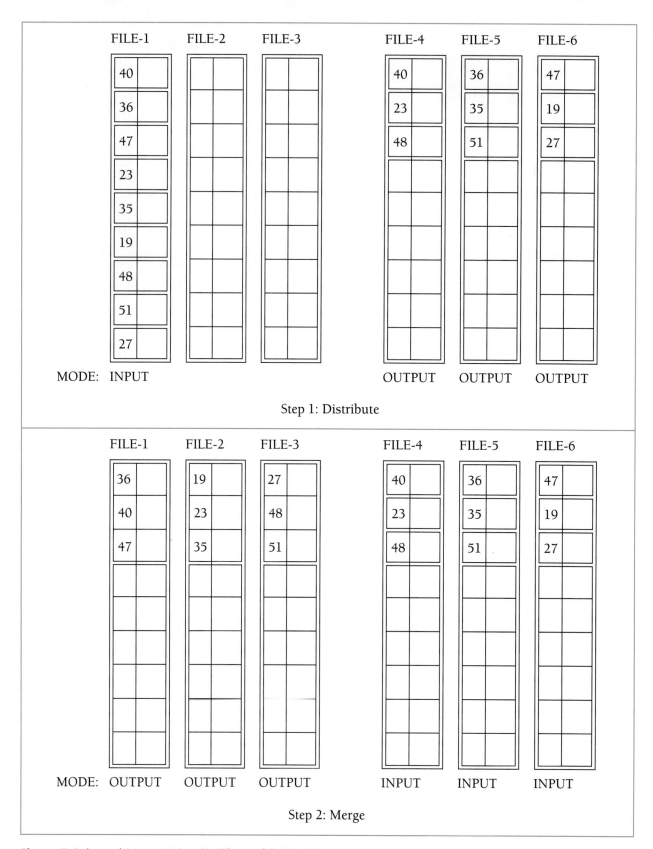

Figure 7 Balanced Merge Using Six Files and 3-Way Merge

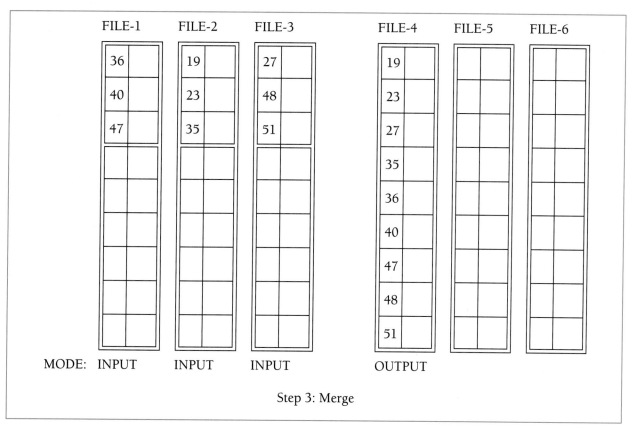

Figure 7 (Continued)

A sequence of n records sorted in increasing (or decreasing) order by some sort key is called a **run of size n**. Trivially, a single record is a **run of size 1**.

Now we turn our attention to Figure 7.

Step 1: First distribute all records in FILE-1 alternately to FILE-4, FILE-5, and FILE-6, opening the last three files in output mode. When the distribution process is completed, close all files.

Step 2: Open FILE-1, FILE-2, and FILE-3 in output mode, and FILE-4, FILE-5, and FILE-6 in input mode. Using 3-way merge, create three runs of size 3 each and write them on FILE-1, FILE-2, and FILE-3, respectively. When done, close all files.

Step 3: Open FILE-1, FILE-2, and FILE-3 in input mode and the remaining three files in output mode. Again using 3-way merge, merge three runs of size 3 each from the input files into a single run of size 9 and write it in FILE-4. As the size of the generated run is the same as the number of records that we had in step 1 in the input file, we terminate the algorithm.

As can be seen, balanced merge sort is superior to merge sort in that after the initial distribution pass, all passes are of merge character, and copying is eliminated. A problem with this technique is that we must use more files than with merge sort. If we decide to use P-way merge, balanced merge sort requires a total of $(2 * P + 1)$ files, whereas merge sort necessitates $(P + 1)$ files.

Polyphase Merge Sort

This external sorting technique can sort files using P-way merge and only (P + 1) files without any distribution except the initial one. Suppose we are given an unordered file of n records (i.e., n runs of size 1 each) and P additional files. How can we sort this file using P-way merge without having to copy records between merge-type passes? The critical point here lies in the initial distribution pattern. It can be shown that if the n initial runs can be distributed to P files according to a specific pattern, copying can be avoided.

This distribution pattern for polyphase merge sort can be formally specified. Suppose we have four files and are planning to use 3-way merge. At the end of the sort process, after the final merge we should have one run of size n in one of the files, say, FILE-1. Here, n is the number of records to be sorted. This last step can be represented as follows.

Step	FILE-1	FILE-2	FILE-3	FILE-4

Ultimately, we wish to have one run in FILE-1. For this we could have had one run each in FILE-2, FILE-3, and FILE-4 in the previous step, and could have merged them into a single run to be stored in FILE-1. To show this, we extend the above table.

Step	FILE-1	FILE-2	FILE-3	FILE-4
m	1	0	0	0
m-1	0	1	1	1

This means that in step m-1, if we have one record each in FILE-2, FILE-3, and FILE-4, we can merge them into a single run of size 3 and store this run in FILE-1. Consider step m-2.

Step	FILE-1	FILE-2	FILE-3	FILE-4
m	1	0	0	0
m-1	0	1	1	1
m-2	1	2	2	0

In step m-2, if we have a single record in FILE-1 and two records each in FILE-2 and FILE-3, using these as input files we can merge three runs of size 1 each into a run of size 3, and write this run to FILE-4. This will leave only one run each in FILE-2 and FILE-3, and will free FILE-1 so that it can be used as an output file in step m-1. The process just described for step m-2 produces the situation for step m-1. An equivalent interpretation of this table is that, if we have a five-record file, we can start with an initial distribution pattern as shown for step m-2; that is, one record in FILE-1, and two each in FILE-2 and FILE-3. In two steps of merging we can end up with a single run of size 5, that is, the sorted file, in FILE-1.

We can continue this way building the table. To see the pattern clearly, let us assume that the three files used as input files in every step are shown in the table only as FILE-1, FILE-2, and FILE-3, since the output file at the beginning of a step is empty. The above table can be accordingly modified to become:

Step	FILE-1	FILE-2	FILE-3	Sum of Records
m	1	0	0	1
m-1	1	1	1	3
m-2	2	2	1	5
m-3	4	3	2	9
m-4	7	6	4	17
m-5	13	11	7	31
	....	....	....	....

The following pattern in this table can be used to generate the distribution at step i-1 given the distribution at step i.

Step	FILE-1	FILE-2	FILE-3
i	a	b	c
i-1	a + b	a + c	a

The rows that can be generated according to this pattern are known as **perfect Fibonacci distributions**. For two input files, the distributions contain integers that are elements of the Fibonacci sequence; hence, the term.

Perfect Fibonacci distributions can be generated up to any number of levels (or steps) for a given number of input files. Figure 8 shows these distributions partially generated for two through six input files. These tables define the perfect distribution patterns necessary for polyphase merge sort. For example, if we wish to sort a file of 65 records, we can use a total of 6 files (5 for input, 1 for output during a 5-way merge) and expect the sort to terminate in five merge passes, provided we start with the perfect distribution of (16, 15, 14, 12, 8).

In practical applications, we may not have the exact number of records as required by perfect Fibonacci distributions. In such cases, we may add some dummy records to the file to be sorted. For example, if we actually have 60 records to be sorted, we can add 5 dummy records to the file, thus bringing the number up to 65 to match a perfect distribution. Then we do the sort, and eliminate the dummy records through one final copy pass.

Let us now consider an example and work it out to show the logic involved in polyphase merge. We assume that there are 25 records to be sorted in FILE-1, and we have a total of 5 files. A 4-way merge is indicated. In Figure 8 the distribution table for four input files reveals that there is a perfect distribution for 25 records, (8, 7, 6, 4). In view of this, we should start the algorithm with eight records distributed to FILE-2, seven to FILE-3, six to FILE-4, and four to FILE-5. This initial distribution is shown in Figure 9. In this table, we use a special notation to facilitate the description of the algorithm: X(Y) denotes X runs of size Y each. Thus, 8(1) stands for 8 runs of size 1 each, or simply, 8 unsorted records. The steps involved in the polyphase algorithm for this example are as follows.

Step 1: Distribute 25 runs of size one on FILE-1 to FILE-2 through FILE-5 according to the pattern (8, 7, 6, 4).

Step 2: Open FILE-2 through FILE-5 as input files and merge the first four runs from each file into four runs of size 4 each, to be written to

Two input files

FILE 1	FILE 2	Sum of Records
1	0	1
1	1	2
2	1	3
3	2	5
5	3	8
8	5	13
...	...	...

Three input files

FILE 1	FILE 2	FILE 3	Sum of Records
1	0	0	1
1	1	1	3
2	2	1	5
4	3	2	9
7	6	4	17
13	11	7	31
...	...	...	...

Four input files

FILE 1	FILE 2	FILE 3	FILE 4	Sum of Records
1	0	0	0	1
1	1	1	1	4
2	2	2	1	7
4	4	3	2	13
8	7	6	4	25
15	14	12	8	49
...	...	...	...	...

Five input files

FILE 1	FILE 2	FILE 3	FILE 4	FILE 5	Sum of Records
1	0	0	0	0	1
1	1	1	1	1	5
2	2	2	2	1	9
4	4	4	3	2	17
8	8	7	6	4	33
16	15	14	12	8	65
...	...	...	...	...	...

Six input files

FILE 1	FILE 2	FILE 3	FILE 4	FILE 5	FILE 6	Sum of Records
1	0	0	0	0	0	1
1	1	1	1	1	1	6
2	2	2	2	2	1	11
4	4	4	4	3	2	21
8	8	8	7	6	4	41
16	16	15	14	12	8	81
...	...	...	...	...	...	...

Figure 8 Perfect Fibonacci Distributions for Two to Six Input Files for Polyphase Merge Algorithm

FILE-1. This will leave 4(1), 3(1), and 2(1) in FILE-2, FILE-3, and FILE-4, respectively, and thus all records in FILE-5 will be processed.

Step 3: FILE-5 is the output file, and the other files are all in input mode. It is possible to merge 2(4) from FILE-1, and 2(1) from FILE-2, FILE-3, and FILE-4 into 2(7), and write them in FILE-7. This merge step leaves 2(4), 2(1), and 1(1) in FILE-1, FILE-2, and FILE-3, respectively. FILE-4 will have no records left in it.

Step 4: FILE-4 is the output file, with others being in input mode. We can merge 1(4), 1(1), 1(1), and 1(7) from FILE-1, FILE-2, FILE-3, and FILE-5, respectively, into 1(13) and store it in FILE-4. We will have 1(4), 1(1), and 1(7) left in FILE-1, FILE-2, and FILE-5.

PHASE	FILE-1	FILE-2	FILE-3	FILE-4	FILE-5
1	INPUT	OUTPUT	OUTPUT	OUTPUT	OUTPUT
Distrib.	25(1)	8(1)	7(1)	6(1)	4(1)
2	OUTPUT	INPUT	INPUT	INPUT	INPUT
Merge	4(4)	4(1)	3(1)	2(1)	----
3	INPUT	INPUT	INPUT	INPUT	OUTPUT
Merge	2(4)	2(1)	1(1)	----	2(7)
4	INPUT	INPUT	INPUT	OUTPUT	INPUT
Merge	1(4)	1(1)	----	1(13)	1(7)
5	INPUT	INPUT	OUTPUT	INPUT	INPUT
Merge	----	----	1(25)	----	----

Figure 9 Pattern for Polyphase Merge for 25 Records Using a Total of 5 Files

Step 5: Merge the contents of FILE-1, FILE-2, FILE-4, and FILE-5, which are 1(4), 1(1), 1(13), and 1(7), respectively. This produces 1(25) on FILE-3. FILE-3 is our sorted file.

Figure 10 illustrates these steps in an explicit fashion, using two-digit integer sort keys to represent records to be sorted. As an exercise, the student should carefully match the steps in Figure 10 with those shown in Figure 9.

Polyphase merge is one of the efficient external sorting techniques. Other file sorting techniques and many possible file sort strategies take into consideration characteristics of the external storage device used and the available internal memory space that can be defined as buffers. They are outside the scope of our discussion.

COBOL File Sort Feature

In addition to a file merge, COBOL supports a built-in file sort utility. This feature is a very high-level statement that triggers a utility program to sort disk or tape files. The specific sort technique in such sort utilities is devised and implemented by the vendor. We do not know how it works, and we do not have to. All we have to do is to specify our intent to sort a file. For this we use the COBOL sort statement in our application programs.

From a syntactical point of view, the SORT statement consists of the following elements.

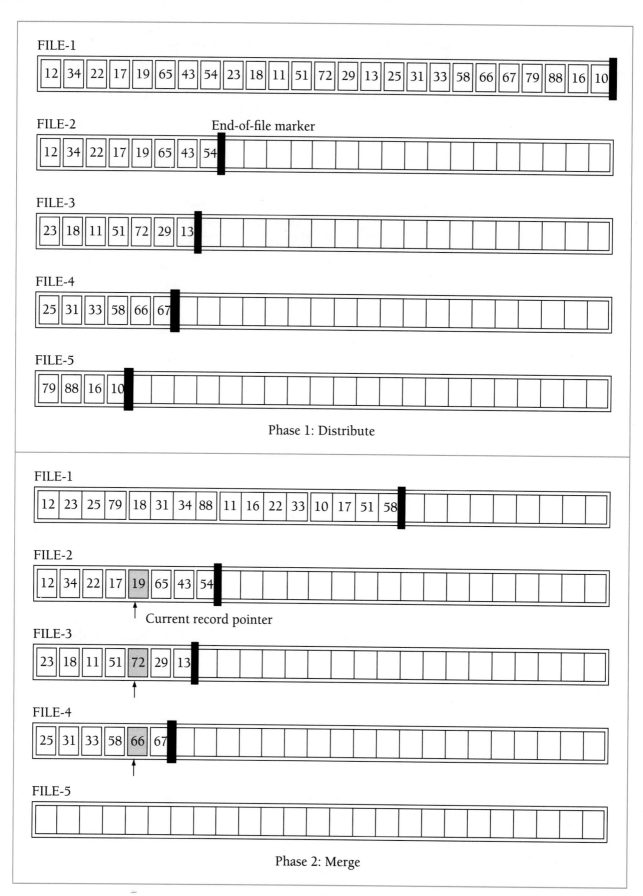

Figure 10 Example of Polyphase Merge Sort Using a Total of Five Files

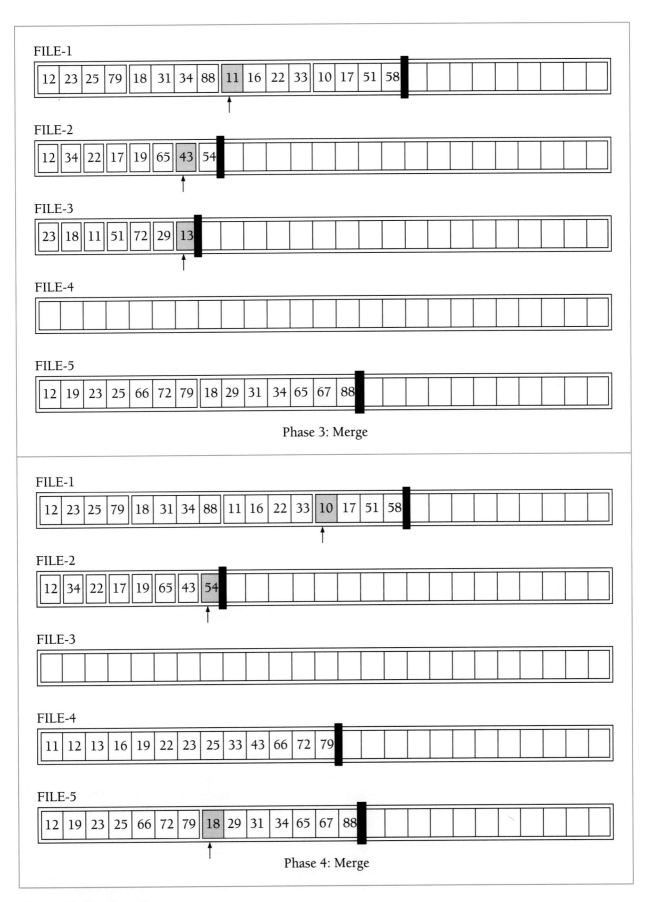

Phase 3: Merge

Phase 4: Merge

Figure 10 (Continued)

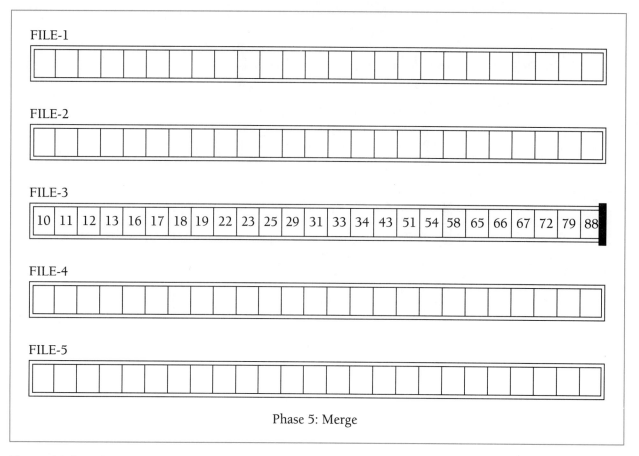

FILE-1

FILE-2

FILE-3

| 10 | 11 | 12 | 13 | 16 | 17 | 18 | 19 | 22 | 23 | 25 | 29 | 31 | 33 | 34 | 43 | 51 | 54 | 58 | 65 | 66 | 67 | 72 | 79 | 88 |

FILE-4

FILE-5

Phase 5: Merge

Figure 10 (Continued)

The SORT statement contains one or more ON ASCENDING or DESCEN-DING KEY clauses. Each of these clauses contains one or more data names that are field names in the record structure of the files to be sorted. The ASCEND-ING/DESCENDING KEY clause specifies the sort key. The COLLATING SE-QUENCE clause is optional and references an alphabet.

There must be either a USING clause referencing one or more files by their in-program names, or an INPUT PROCEDURE clause. If a USING clause is chosen, the files listed by their names are the source files to be combined be-fore sorting. If an INPUT PROCEDURE clause is used, it contains the name of a PROCEDURE DIVISION section, or it specifies a range for sections that are executed before the sorting operation begins.

Either a GIVING clause or an OUTPUT PROCEDURE clause is required in the SORT statement. The GIVING clause references the name of the file that contains the result. The OUTPUT PROCEDURE clause specifies the name of a PROCEDURE DIVISION section or a range of sections. These are sections that will be executed after the sort operation is completed.

The syntax of the SORT statement closely resembles that of the MERGE statement, with the exception of the INPUT PROCEDURE clause. The COLLA-TING SEQUENCE, USING, GIVING, and OUTPUT PROCEDURE clauses have the same syntax and meaning as those in the MERGE statement. The applicable rules are also the same and therefore we will not repeat them here. The differences can be touched on briefly.

First, the semantics of SORT and MERGE are different. The SORT statement considers records in one or more files specified in the USING clause, or those modified in the PROCEDURE DIVISION sections mentioned in the INPUT PROCEDURE clause, and sorts them in some order according to the sort keys. The resulting ordered set of records is made available either to an output file specified in the GIVING clause, or the program section of the OUTPUT PROCEDURE clause.

Second, the file whose name follows the key word SORT is a sort work file. Just like a merge work file, it should be defined in the ENVIRONMENT DIVISION using a SELECT statement, and in the DATA DIVISION, FILE SECTION, using an SD block.

Finally, it is possible to use the INPUT PROCEDURE option instead of the USING clause in the SORT statement. The INPUT PROCEDURE clause refers to the program section or sections that may modify the input records prior to the sort.

The following are examples of the SORT statement.

Example 1 To sort a file called STUDENT-FILE in increasing order of the major sort key STUDENT-IDNO and in decreasing order of the secondary sort key COURSE-CODE, and to store the result in the file ORDERED-STUDENT-FILE, we can use the SORT statement:

```
SORT SORT-FILE
    ON ASCENDING KEY STUDENT-IDNO
    ON DESCENDING KEY COURSE-CODE
    USING STUDENT-FILE
    GIVING ORDERED-STUDENT-FILE.
```

Example 2 This time we are sorting one or more files released in the input procedure called PRESORT-FILTER. The sort keys are STUDENT-IDNO and COURSE-CODE, both ascending, and the sorted file will be ORDERED-STUDENT-FILE.

```
SORT SORT-FILE
    ON ASCENDING KEY STUDENT-IDNO COURSE-CODE
    INPUT PROCEDURE IS PRESORT-FILTER
    GIVING ORDERED-STUDENT-FILE.
```

Example 3   This is similar to example 1, except after sorting we want to pass control to an output procedure called POSTSORT-FILTER in which the sorted records will be processed and collected into a sorted file.

```
SORT SORT-FILE
    ON ASCENDING KEY STUDENT-IDNO
    ON DESCENDING KEY COURSE-CODE
    USING STUDENT-FILE
    OUTPUT PROCEDURE IS POSTSORT-FILTER.
```

Example 4   Again, this is similar to examples 1 and 3, combining and illustrating the use of input and output procedures.

```
SORT SORT-FILE
    ON ASCENDING KEY STUDENT-IDNO
    ON DESCENDING KEY COURSE-CODE
    INPUT PROCEDURE IS  PRESORT-FILTER
    OUTPUT PROCEDURE IS POSTSORT-FILTER.
```

The rules governing the use of the SORT statement are quite similar to those for the MERGE statement, with some differences and additions. The sort file is similar to the merge file. It should be defined using a SELECT statement in the ENVIRONMENT DIVISION and an SD block in the FILE SECTION. Its record structure should contain the sort key fields.

The output procedure considerations are similar to those for the MERGE statement. The output procedure should contain one or more RETURN statements.

If the GIVING clause is used to specify the sorted file, it should not be opened and closed explicitly in the program. These tasks will be handled by the SORT utility.

If the USING clause is chosen, the files referenced in it should have compatible record structures. Records in these files will be released into the sort file, and the sort file will be sorted. The programmer should not open and close the source files in the program. The SORT statement will automatically open these files. Their contents will be transferred to the sort file, after which they will be closed.

The input procedure option can be used instead of the USING clause in the SORT statement. The input procedure is one or more physically consecutive PROCEDURE DIVISION sections. If the SORT statement contains an input procedure specification, the execution starts with the first section in the input procedure and continues until the physical end of the procedure is reached. After this point, program control passes to the sort utility.

The primary purpose of the input procedure is to write records to be sorted into the sort file. In this section, the source files containing the records to be sorted should be opened in input mode, and records should be read. The records may be processed before they are written into the sort file. However, those that are to be sorted should be written into the sort file using one or more executions of the RELEASE statement (see below). The section containing the input procedure should not form a part of any output procedure for a SORT or MERGE statement.

In the PROCEDURE DIVISION, control should not be permitted to pass to an input procedure or a part of an input procedure by any statement except the SORT statement for which the input procedure is written. The input procedure should not contain any SORT or MERGE statements. Also, there should be no transfer of control from a point inside an input procedure to a point outside it.

The RELEASE statement is used for writing records into the sort file. Thus, its syntax is similar to that of the WRITE statement.

RELEASE record-name [FROM identifier]

The record name after the key word RELEASE is the record name for the sort file. Here is an example of the RELEASE statement.

```
RELEASE SORT-RECORD FROM WS-STUDENT-RECORD.
```

REVIEW QUESTIONS

1. Although external sorting is logically different from internal sorting, it is possible to combine internal sorting algorithms and merging to sort files. (T or F)
2. The merge sort algorithm is characterized by a pattern of alternating _____ and _____ steps.
3. The main weakness of the merge sort algorithm is that every alternate step of distribute type is equivalent to copying the entire file to be sorted. (T or F)
4. In balanced merge sort, after the initial distribution pass, all passes are of merge type except the last pass. The last pass is again a distribute type pass. (T or F)
5. In balanced merge sort, if we decide to use P-way merge, a total of _____ files is required.
6. In polyphase merge, the initial distribution of records must conform to a _____.
7. The main advantage of the polyphase merge technique compared to the balanced merge algorithm is that it requires a smaller number of files. (T or F)
8. The COBOL SORT utility can be used to sort _____ or _____ files.
9. Which of the following concerning the COBOL SORT statement is correct?
   a. The sort work file should be defined using an SD block.
   b. The USING clause specifies one or more files to be combined and sorted.
   c. The sort keys are defined in the ON ASCENDING or ON DESCENDING KEY clause.
   d. All of the above are correct.
10. The OUTPUT PROCEDURE clause references one or more PROCEDURE DIVISION sections that are executed after the SORT statement is fully executed. (T or F)

11. The RETURN statement is used in the sections specified by the _____ clause, and the RELEASE statement is used in the sections specified by the _____ clause.

Answers: 1. T; 2. distribute, merge; 3. T; 4. F; 5. (2 * P + 1); 6. perfect Fibonacci distribution; 7. T; 8. disk, tape; 9. d; 10. T; 11. OUTPUT PROCEDURE, INPUT PROCEDURE.

Example Program 3:   *File Sorting Using the COBOL Sort Feature*

In this section we present an application program that sorts a number of files using the SORT statement.

Problem   Suppose in the Registrar's Office three data entry operators regularly type records for student transcripts into separate disk files. The student transcripts file is generated by combining the three input files, FILE-1, FILE-2, and FILE-3. Their record structures consist of

- A 4-digit student identification number
- A 6-character course code (course code values consist of a 3-character department designator followed by a 3-digit course number)
- A letter grade earned by a student in a course, using the values A, B, C, D, and F

We want to develop a program that combines the records in the three input files into a file that is sorted in increasing order by both the primary and the secondary sort keys. The sort keys are STUDENT-IDNO and COURSE-CODE data fields. Before we sort these files, however, we would like to validate the records and eliminate the incorrectly entered ones. Data validation rules to be used for this application are listed below.

- The STUDENT-IDNO field values are in the range of 0100–6500.
- The first three characters of the COURSE-CODE field must be alphabetic and the last three characters must be numeric.
- The letter grade values can be A, B, C, D, and F only.

These data validation operations will be done in an input procedure associated with the SORT statement.

After the correct records are entered into the sort file and sorted, and before we obtain a disk file containing them, we would like to compute the distribution of letter grades, that is, the number of As, Bs, and so on, in the transcript file. These operations will be incorporated into the output procedure of the SORT statement.

Solution   Program 3-Input(a) through (c) shows example instances for the three files to be sorted. The source listing of the application program developed for the problem is given in Program 3-Source. Concerning this program, we note the following.

1. The PROCEDURE DIVISION of the program consists of a monitor paragraph called A-MAINLINE, and two sections called B1-PRESORT-FILTERING and B2-POST-SORT-PROCESSING. The paragraph A-MAINLINE contains a SORT statement and a STOP RUN statement.

2. The SORT statement (lines 00132–00135) references a SORT-FILE, and specifies sort keys as being SORT-STUDENT-IDNO and SORT-COURSE-CODE, two fields in the record structure of SORT-FILE. The sort order is ascending for both keys. An input and an output procedure are also specified.

3. The source files processed in the input procedure (FILE-1, FILE-2, and FILE-3), the SORT-FILE, and the output sorted file RESULT generated by the output procedure have identical record structures.

4. The SORT statement passes control to the input procedure B1-PRESORT-FILTERING. In it, the three files are opened, records are read one at a time and validated, and the correct records are written into the SORT-FILE using the RELEASE statement (lines 00183, 00203, and 00223).

5. At the end of the nameless paragraph under the B1-PRESORT-FILTERING section, the three source files are closed and control is passed to the last paragraph in this section, that is, the paragraph called C7-TERMINATE-INPUT-PROCEDURE, using a GO TO statement. The reason for the GO TO was explained previously in this chapter.

6. The input procedure has been fully executed, and the SORT-FILE now contains the records to be sorted. Next, the program control passes to the SORT statement, which sorts the file and triggers the output procedure.

7. The output procedure section is entitled B2-POST-SORT-PROCESSING and contains three paragraphs. The first paragraph is C8-LOAD-SORTED-FL-AND-PROCESS, which opens the RESULT file in output mode, uses the RE-TURN statement to access sorted records in the SORT-FILE, triggers the subordinate paragraph D4-GENERATE-FILE-AND-DISTR in a loop, closes the RESULT file, and passes control to the last paragraph of the section, C9-TERMINATE-OUTPUT-PROC. In the paragraph D4-GENERATE-FILE-AND-DISTR, the sorted records are written into the RESULT file, and the distributions of letter grades are computed. Finally, in the paragraph called C9-TERMINATE-OUTPUT-PROC, the computed distributions are displayed, and control is returned again to the SORT statement.

Program 3-Output shows the instance of the RESULT file produced by this program.

Key Terms

balanced merge sort
COLLATING SEQUENCE clause
GIVING clause
INPUT PROCEDURE clause
merge key
merge sort
MERGE statement
merge strategies
merge work file
merging
ON ASCENDING KEY clause
ON DESCENDING KEY clause
OUTPUT PROCEDURE clause

P-way merge
perfect Fibonacci distribution
polyphase merge sort
RELEASE statement
RETURN statement
run
SD block
sort key
SORT statement
sort work file
sort/merge utility
2-way merge
USING clause

Study Guide

Quick Scan

- Algorithms that can be used to sort files are referred to as external sorting algorithms. In sorting files, certain data fields in the record structure are used to define the order of records in the file. These data fields are known as sort keys.
- File sorting is a common process in file and data base processing.
- Another common operation is file merging, that is, combining two or more similarly ordered files into a sorted file. The majority of external sorting algorithms rely on file merging. For this reason, external sorting and merging are usually studied together.
- Vendor-supplied software can be used for sorting and merging files. These programs are known as sort/merge utilities. COBOL has built-in merge and sort features that facilitate the use of sort/merge utilities.
- The operation of merging two or more files requires specification of a merge key. A merge key can be one or more data items in the record structure of the files involved. Merging also requires that the records in the source files be similarly structured and sorted, either in increasing or decreasing order of the merge keys. The result of merging is a sorted file that contains all records in the source files.
- If two source files are involved in merging, the merge technique is called 2-way merge. Generalizing, for P source files, the technique becomes known as P-way merge.
- A P-way merge algorithm necessitates P internal buffers to hold one record each from the source files. The contents of these buffers are examined, and the one with the record corresponding to the smallest (or largest, if the order of the files is descending) merge key is selected. This record is copied to the output file, and a new record is brought into the buffer from the corresponding source file. This operation is carried out until all records in the source files are processed.
- Many different strategies can be used for merging files. Their efficiency depends on the number of source files, the internal memory available for use as buffers, and the types and numbers of available external storage devices. In practice, of all possible strategies, the simplest and the most efficient should be chosen.
- Merge utility programs incorporate some strategies to handle merging efficiently. Generally, such strategies are regarded as trade secrets.
- COBOL supports a MERGE statement that can be used to merge two or more files without writing a procedure. The programmer has to specify a merge work file using an SD block in the FILE SECTION, the merge keys, the source files, and either the merged output file or an output procedure. If an output procedure is specified in the MERGE statement, in the corresponding PROCEDURE DIVISION section the records in the merge work file should be accessed and copied into the output file. For accessing the content of a merge work file, the RETURN statement is used.
- External sorting is quite different from internal sorting, and a majority of such algorithms are based on the concept of merging.
- The simplest external sort algorithm is the one that combines an internal sort technique with merging. In this technique, blocks of source file records are read into the internal memory and are sorted using an internal sort algorithm. Sorting is done with respect to one or more data fields in the record structure of the file. These data values are known as sort keys. After an internal sort, the ordered blocks of records are written into files, and these files are eventually merged together to obtain the sorted file.
- Another technique for external sorting is known as merge sort. The records in the source file are distributed to a known number, say, P, of available files

in an alternating fashion. After the initial distribution, the records from each file are merged into a subfile using P-way merge. This pattern of "distribute and merge" is repeated, causing the size of the ordered subfiles to grow. Eventually, a single subfile containing all source records in an ordered fashion will be generated.

- Despite its simplicity, the main weakness of merge sort is the distributions before each merge. A distribution is equivalent to an unnecessary file copy operation. Two techniques are available to eliminate such unwanted distribution passes.

- In the first technique, we use a larger number of files and ensure that, in each pass, we have the same number of input files as output files. This is known as balanced merge sort. It eliminates copying after the initial distribution pass. However, it requires more files for the same P-way merge routine.

- The second technique calls for finding a perfect initial distribution so that after the initial distribution, all copying is eliminated. This is the essence of the algorithm known as polyphase merge sort.

- In polyphase merge, P files are used as input files during a merge phase, and one file is used as an output file. Therefore, the total number of files needed is $(P + 1)$ if we are planning to use P-way merge. A perfect Fibonacci distribution can be found for the initial distribution phase so that the algorithm does sorting without copying. If the number of records in the file to be sorted does not match the number of records indicated by an appropriate perfect distribution, it is possible to add dummy records to the end of the source file so that polyphase merge sort may converge.

- In addition to a MERGE statement, COBOL also supports a SORT statement. Syntactically, the SORT statement resembles MERGE.

- In the SORT statement either the source files must be specified explicitly through the USING clause, or an input procedure must be indicated. The input procedure refers to PROCEDURE DIVISION sections in which the source records may be processed and must be loaded into the sort work file using the RELEASE statement.

- The SORT statement also includes either a GIVING clause that names the output sorted file, or an output procedure. If used, an output procedure references PROCEDURE DIVISION sections in which the sorted records may be processed, but must be read from the sort work file using the RETURN statement.

Test Your Comprehension

Multiple-Choice Questions

1. Which of the following statements concerning file merging is correct?
   a. The source files in merging should have similar record structures.
   b. All source files should be identically ordered.
   c. The sort keys used in ordering the source files in file merging are also known as merge keys.
   d. If there are P source files in file merging, the applicable merge technique is known as P-way merge.
   e. All of the above are correct.

2. Which of the following concerning the COBOL MERGE statement is correct?
   a. It is a procedural specification of a specific merge strategy.
   b. It can be used to merge only two files.
   c. The ON ASCENDING or DESCENDING KEY clause can be used to define the merge keys.
   d. The USING clause is optional, and it defines the output file.

3. Which of the following is not a correct step among the first three steps of the merge sort technique based on a total of five files?
   a. Alternately distribute records stored on the source file onto the five output files one at a time.
   b. Change the modes of all output files to input, and the mode of the input file to output.
   c. Using 6-way merge, merge the first records from five input files into a block of five ordered records stored on the output file. Do this for all records coming from the input files.
   d. All of the above are correct.
4. Which of the following statements concerning balanced merge sort with a P-way merge algorithm is correct?
   a. In the initial distribute type pass, P files are in output and one file is in input mode.
   b. A total of $(2 * P + 1)$ files are required.
   c. In any merge-type pass, one file is in input and P files are in output mode.
   d. Balanced merge sort is less efficient than merge sort.
5. Which of the following statements concerning polyphase merge sort with a P-way merge algorithm is correct?
   a. It is more efficient than any internal sort algorithm.
   b. It requires a total of $(2 * P + 1)$ files.
   c. The initial distribution of records should be made according to an appropriate perfect Fibonacci distribution.
   d. All of the above are correct.
6. Which of the following is correct about the COBOL SORT statement?
   a. It can be used to sort records in one or more source files.
   b. The GIVING clause specifies the source files for the sort.
   c. The OUTPUT PROCEDURE clause can be used instead of the USING clause to specify the file containing sorted records.
   d. Only one attribute may be used as a sort key.
   e. All of the above are correct.

Answers: 1. e; 2. c; 3. c; 4. b; 5. c; 6. a.

Short Essay Questions

1. How do internal sorting techniques differ from external sorting techniques?
2. Explain why merging is central to external sorting algorithms.
3. Define 2-way merge. Generalize your definition to P-way merge.
4. Briefly explain the logic of the 2-way merge algorithm.
5. Briefly outline the logic of the P-way merge algorithm.
6. Explain the syntax and semantics of the COBOL MERGE statement.
7. Explain the following concepts related to the MERGE statement:
   a. Primary merge key
   b. Secondary merge key
   c. The output procedure option
   d. The merge work file
8. What is the purpose of the RETURN statement in COBOL? Where can we use it in a program?
9. Briefly explain the external sort technique that uses internal sort algorithms and merging.
10. Explain the steps involved in the merge sort technique. What is the primary shortcoming of this algorithm?
11. Briefly explain the balanced merge sort technique. Why is it superior to merge sorting?

12. Outline the phases required for polyphase merge sort. Explain why polyphase merge sort is superior to balanced merge sort.
13. Explain the concept of perfect Fibonacci distributions for polyphase merge.
14. Briefly explain the following concepts related to the COBOL SORT statement:
    a. The sort work file
    b. Primary and secondary sort keys
    c. The input procedure option
    d. The output procedure option
15. What is the function of the RELEASE statement in COBOL? Where do we use this statement in a program?

Improve Your Problem-Solving Ability

Exercises

1. Suppose we have four files called FILE-1, FILE-2, FILE-3, and FILE-4. They contain records that are structurally similar, and have four-character strings as key attribute values. The records in the files are sorted in decreasing order of the key, as shown below:

   FILE-1: {WILL, WARD, VERY, BATE, AXES}
   FILE-2: {ROSS, PORT, ABBY}
   FILE-3: {YALE, TORN, CALL, BALL}
   FILE-4: {SORE, MORE, LORE}

   Draw a figure similar to Figure 1, and show in it the steps involved in a 4-way merge for these files.
2. Suppose you have to merge four similarly ordered files using a program that implements 2-way merge. Describe at least two different strategies for this problem, and for each strategy compute the cost in terms of the total number of records to be copied during merge. Assume that the four files contain 5000, 4500, 7000, and 8000 records, respectively.
3. Modify the COBOL program of Program 1-Source such that it can merge four files sorted in decreasing order of the merge key, using 4-way merge.
4. Suppose we have two files called ART-STUDENTS and SCIENCE-STUDENTS, as in Figure 3. The records in both files are sorted in increasing order of GRADE and in decreasing order of DIV. GRADE is the primary sort key and DIV the secondary sort key. Write a COBOL MERGE statement that takes these files as source files and generates a similarly ordered file called ALL-STUDENTS.
5. Draw a figure similar to Figure 5 to illustrate the steps involved in the basic algorithm for external sorting by internal sorting and merging for a total of three files, FILE-1, FILE-2, and FILE-3. Assume that FILE-1 is initially as given in Figure 5, step 1.
6. Draw a figure as in Figure 6 to illustrate the steps involved in the merge sort algorithm for three files and 2-way merge. Assume that the source file FILE-1 is the same as in step 1 of Figure 6.
7. Illustrate the steps involved in balanced merge sort for a total of four files. For this, draw a figure similar to Figure 7, starting with FILE-1 as given in step 1.
8. Suppose we have a total of eight files for polyphase merge sort. Generate a table similar to those in Figure 8 for perfect Fibonacci distributions up to eight levels.
9. Suppose we have a total of eight files to be used for polyphase merge sort. We would like to sort a file containing 95 records. Explain what has to be done for polyphase merge sort to be possible. Then draw a table as in Figure 9 to illustrate the phases in polyphase merge sort for this problem.

10. Write a COBOL SORT statement that takes the two files called ART-STUDENTS and SCIENCE-STUDENTS given in Figure 3, and sorts them in increasing order by GRADE and in decreasing order by DIV, with GRADE and DIV being the primary and secondary sort keys, respectively. The SORT statement should produce an ordered file called ALL-STUDENTS.

11. Modify the COBOL program of Program 3-Source so that the data validation operations on the records of FILE-1, FILE-2, and FILE-3 are done before the program encounters the SORT statement, and the correct records are copied into another file called FILE-4. After this step, the SORT statement should be triggered to sort the file and compute the letter grade distributions.

Programming Problems

1. Consider the sequential disk file EMPLOYEE-SKILLS-FILE of programming problem 2 in Chapter 11. This file has a record structure based on EMPLOYEE-ID, SKILL-CODE, and YRS-OF-EXP. Let us suppose that there are three employee-skills files for the three departments of our company, numbered 1, 2, and 3. Write a program that sorts the three employee-skills files (in three separate runs) in increasing order of EMPLOYEE-ID (primary sort key) and decreasing order of SKILL-CODE (secondary sort key). Use the COBOL SORT feature in your program.

2. Write another program that reads records from three EMPLOYEE-SKILLS-FILEs, verifies that their contents are properly ordered (i.e., in increasing order of EMPLOYEE-ID, and decreasing order of SKILL-CODE), and merges them into a single file using 3-way merge. Do not use the COBOL MERGE feature.

3. Write a program to do the same thing as in programming problem 2, except this time, make use of the COBOL MERGE feature.

```
                              COLUMNS
        5    10   15   20   25   30   35   40   45   50   55   60   65
    ----|----|----|----|----|----|----|----|----|----|----|----|----|--

    100JANEL HARRISON        36700ACC
    175JODEAN ASH            33500ACC
    185MARK WARBER           38600ACC
    195ERIC WALSH            41500ACC
    200JEFFREY GROSS         23800ACC
```

Program 1-Input(a) FILE-1 for Program 1

```
                              COLUMNS
        5    10   15   20   25   30   35   40   45   50   55   60   65
    ----|----|----|----|----|----|----|----|----|----|----|----|----|--

    150RANDALL MITCHINER     43200SLS
    180MICHELLE JOHNSON      33400SLS
    190DARRELL THOMAS        33250SLS
    230SEAN BUCKLEY          26700SLS
    235JAMES FOREMAN         25000SLS
    250ROBERT BURNETT        38900SLS
```

Program 1-Input(b) FILE-2 for Program 1

```
                                    COLUMNS
        5     10    15    20    25    30    35    40    45    50    55    60    65
    ----|----|----|----|----|----|----|----|----|----|----|----|----|--

    080ALICE HALE           34670MIS
    110JENNIFER TAYLOR      23400MIS
    115DANIEL KRICKER       21900MIS
    205JOANNE BALDWIN       45050MIS
    240DEAN KISSINGER       39875MIS
    270SCOTT WILLIAMS       35000MIS
```

Program 1-Input(c) FILE-3 for Program 1

```
00001     *.........................................................
00002       IDENTIFICATION DIVISION.
00003       PROGRAM-ID. MERGING-THREE-FILES.
00004     ***************************************************************
00005     ***   THIS PROGRAM MERGES THREE SEQUENTIAL DISK FILES USING THE   *
00006     ***   3-WAY MERGE LOGIC.  THE RESULT IS A NEW ORDERED DISK FILE.   *
00007     ***                                                               *
00008     ***   ALL THREE SOURCE FILES HAVE RECORD STRUCTURES CONSISTING    *
00009     ***   OF A MERGE KEY FIELD AND A FILLER.  THE SOURCE FILES ARE     *
00010     ***   ASSUMED TO BE SORTED IN INCREASING ORDER OF THE MERGE KEY    *
00011     ***   FIELD.                                                       *
00012     ***************************************************************
00013
00014       AUTHOR.        UCKAN.
00015       DATE-WRITTEN.  OCT 5, 1990.
00016       DATE-COMPILED. OCT  5,1990.
00017     *.........................................................
00018       ENVIRONMENT DIVISION.
00019       CONFIGURATION SECTION.
00020       SOURCE-COMPUTER. UNIVERSITY-MAINFRAME.
00021       OBJECT-COMPUTER. UNIVERSITY-MAINFRAME.
00022       INPUT-OUTPUT SECTION.
00023       FILE-CONTROL.
00024
00025           SELECT FILE-1 ASSIGN TO FILE1.
00026           SELECT FILE-2 ASSIGN TO FILE2.
00027           SELECT FILE-3 ASSIGN TO FILE3.
00028
00029           SELECT RESULT ASSIGN TO OUTFILE.
00030
00031     *.........................................................
00032       DATA DIVISION.
00033       FILE SECTION.
00034
00035       FD  FILE-1
00036           LABEL RECORDS ARE OMITTED
00037           RECORD CONTAINS 80 CHARACTERS
00038           DATA RECORD IS RECORD-1.
```

Program 1-Source Sample Program to Merge Three Files Using 3-Way Merge

```
00039      01   RECORD-1.
00040           05   MERGE-KEY-1               PIC XXX.
00041           05   FILLER                    PIC X(77).
00042
00043      FD   FILE-2
00044           LABEL RECORDS ARE OMITTED
00045           RECORD CONTAINS 80 CHARACTERS
00046           DATA RECORD IS RECORD-2.
00047      01   RECORD-2.
00048           05   MERGE-KEY-2               PIC XXX.
00049           05   FILLER                    PIC X(77).
00050
00051      FD   FILE-3
00052           LABEL RECORDS ARE OMITTED
00053           RECORD CONTAINS 80 CHARACTERS
00054           DATA RECORD IS RECORD-3.
00055      01   RECORD-3.
00056           05   MERGE-KEY-3               PIC XXX.
00057           05   FILLER                    PIC X(77).
00058
00059      FD   RESULT
00060           LABEL RECORDS ARE OMITTED
00061           RECORD CONTAINS 80 CHARACTERS
00062           DATA RECORD IS RESULT-RECORD.
00063      01   RESULT-RECORD.
00064           05   MERGE-KEY                 PIC XXX.
00065           05   FILLER                    PIC X(77).
00066
00067      WORKING-STORAGE SECTION.
00068
00069      **********> VARIABLES:
00070
00071      01   END-OF-FILE-1     PIC XXX.
00072      01   END-OF-FILE-2     PIC XXX.
00073      01   END-OF-FILE-3     PIC XXX.
00074
00075      **********> STRUCTURES:
00076
00077      01   BUFFER-1.
00078           05   BUFFER-1-KEY              PIC XXX.
00079           05   FILLER                    PIC X(77).
00080
00081      01   BUFFER-2.
00082           05   BUFFER-2-KEY              PIC XXX.
00083           05   FILLER                    PIC X(77).
00084
00085      01   BUFFER-3.
00086           05   BUFFER-3-KEY              PIC XXX.
00087           05   FILLER                    PIC X(77).
00088
```

Program 1-Source (Continued)

```
00089    *.........................................................................
00090    PROCEDURE DIVISION.
00091    A-MAINLINE.
00092        OPEN INPUT  FILE-1
00093                    FILE-2
00094                    FILE-3
00095            OUTPUT RESULT.
00096
00097        MOVE "NO"  TO END-OF-FILE-1
00098                      END-OF-FILE-2
00099                      END-OF-FILE-3.
00100
00101        MOVE "000" TO BUFFER-1-KEY
00102                      BUFFER-2-KEY
00103                      BUFFER-3-KEY.
00104
00105        PERFORM B1-READ-FROM-FILE-1.
00106        PERFORM B2-READ-FROM-FILE-2.
00107        PERFORM B3-READ-FROM-FILE-3.
00108
00109        IF END-OF-FILE-1 = "YES"
00110            MOVE "999" TO BUFFER-1-KEY.
00111
00112        IF END-OF-FILE-2 = "YES"
00113            MOVE "999" TO BUFFER-2-KEY.
00114
00115        IF END-OF-FILE-3 = "YES"
00116            MOVE "999" TO BUFFER-3-KEY.
00117
00118        IF END-OF-FILE-1 = "NO"
00119              OR
00120           END-OF-FILE-2 = "NO"
00121              OR
00122           END-OF-FILE-3 = "NO"
00123            PERFORM B4-MERGE-RECORDS
00124                UNTIL BUFFER-1-KEY = "999"
00125                            AND
00126                      BUFFER-2-KEY = "999"
00127                            AND
00128                      BUFFER-3-KEY = "999".
00129
00130        CLOSE FILE-1 FILE-2 FILE-3 RESULT.
00131
00132        STOP RUN.
00133
00134    B1-READ-FROM-FILE-1.
00135        READ FILE-1 INTO BUFFER-1
00136            AT END MOVE "YES" TO END-OF-FILE-1.
00137
00138    B2-READ-FROM-FILE-2.
00139        READ FILE-2 INTO BUFFER-2
00140            AT END MOVE "YES" TO END-OF-FILE-2.
00141
```

Program 1-Source (Continued)

```
00142      B3-READ-FROM-FILE-3.
00143          READ FILE-3 INTO BUFFER-3
00144              AT END MOVE "YES" TO END-OF-FILE-3.
00145
00146      B4-MERGE-RECORDS.
00147
00148          IF BUFFER-1-KEY IS LESS THAN BUFFER-2-KEY
00149                          AND
00150            BUFFER-1-KEY IS LESS THAN BUFFER-3-KEY
00151                  PERFORM C1-WRITE-FROM-BUFFER-1
00152                  PERFORM B1-READ-FROM-FILE-1.
00153
00154          IF BUFFER-2-KEY IS LESS THAN BUFFER-1-KEY
00155                          AND
00156            BUFFER-2-KEY IS LESS THAN BUFFER-3-KEY
00157                  PERFORM C2-WRITE-FROM-BUFFER-2
00158                  PERFORM B2-READ-FROM-FILE-2.
00159
00160          IF BUFFER-3-KEY IS LESS THAN BUFFER-1-KEY
00161                          AND
00162            BUFFER-3-KEY IS LESS THAN BUFFER-2-KEY
00163                  PERFORM C3-WRITE-FROM-BUFFER-3
00164                  PERFORM B3-READ-FROM-FILE-3.
00165
00166          IF END-OF-FILE-1 = "YES"
00167                  MOVE "999" TO BUFFER-1-KEY.
00168
00169          IF END-OF-FILE-2 = "YES"
00170                  MOVE "999" TO BUFFER-2-KEY.
00171
00172          IF END-OF-FILE-3 = "YES"
00173                  MOVE "999" TO BUFFER-3-KEY.
00174
00175      C1-WRITE-FROM-BUFFER-1.
00176          WRITE RESULT-RECORD FROM BUFFER-1.
00177
00178      C2-WRITE-FROM-BUFFER-2.
00179          WRITE RESULT-RECORD FROM BUFFER-2.
00180
00181      C3-WRITE-FROM-BUFFER-3.
00182          WRITE RESULT-RECORD FROM BUFFER-3.
```

Program 1-Source (Continued)

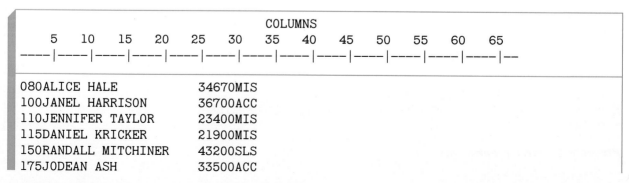

```
                              COLUMNS
     5    10   15   20   25   30   35   40   45   50   55   60   65
----|----|----|----|----|----|----|----|----|----|----|----|----|--

080ALICE HALE           34670MIS
100JANEL HARRISON        36700ACC
110JENNIFER TAYLOR       23400MIS
115DANIEL KRICKER        21900MIS
150RANDALL MITCHINER     43200SLS
175JODEAN ASH            33500ACC
```

Program 1-Output Merged File Produced by Program 1

```
180MICHELLE JOHNSON      33400SLS
185MARK WARBER           38600ACC
190DARRELL THOMAS        33250SLS
195ERIC WALSH            41500ACC
200JEFFREY GROSS         23800ACC
205JOANNE BALDWIN        45050MIS
230SEAN BUCKLEY          26700SLS
235JAMES FOREMAN         25000SLS
240DEAN KISSINGER        39875MIS
250ROBERT BURNETT        38900SLS
270SCOTT WILLIAMS        35000MIS
```

Program 1-Output (Continued)

```
00001    *.....................................................
00002      IDENTIFICATION DIVISION.
00003      PROGRAM-ID. USE-OF-COBOL-MERGE.
00004    ****************************************************************
00005    ***   THIS PROGRAM MERGES THREE SEQUENTIAL DISK FILES USING THE  *
00006    ***   COBOL MERGE FEATURE.  THE RESULT IS STORED IN A DISK FILE  *
00007    ***   AFTER EACH RECORD IS VALIDATED FOR CORRECTNESS ON THE      *
00008    ***   EMPLOYEE IDENTIFICATION NUMBER, SALARY, AND DEPARTMENT     *
00009    ***   FIELDS.                                                    *
00010    ***                                                             *
00011    ***   THE FIELD VALIDATION TESTS ARE BASED ON THE FOLLOWING     *
00012    ***   CONSTRAINTS:                                              *
00013    ***   1. EMPLOYEE NUMBER IS IN THE RANGE 050 THROUGH 250.       *
00014    ***   2. MINIMUM YEARLY SALARY IS 25,000, AND THE MAXIMUM IS    *
00015    ***      45,000.                                                *
00016    ***   3. DEPARTMENT CODE VALUES ARE "MIS", "ACC", AND "SLS".    *
00017    ***                                                             *
00018    ***   ALL THREE SOURCE FILES HAVE RECORD STRUCTURES CONSISTING  *
00019    ***   OF EMPLOYEE IDNO, NAME, SALARY AND DEPARTMENT CODE FIELDS. *
00020    ***   EMPLOYEE IDNO IS THE MERGE KEY.  THE SOURCE FILES ARE     *
00021    ***   ASSUMED TO BE SORTED IN INCREASING ORDER OF THE MERGE KEY  *
00022    ***   FIELD.  BEFORE MERGING IS ATTEMPTED, THE PROGRAM ASCERTAINS *
00023    ***   THAT THE SOURCE FILES ARE PROPERLY ORDERED.               *
00024    ****************************************************************
00025
00026      AUTHOR.        UCKAN.
00027      DATE-WRITTEN.  OCT 12, 1990.
00028      DATE-COMPILED. OCT 12,1990.
00029    *.....................................................
00030      ENVIRONMENT DIVISION.
00031      CONFIGURATION SECTION.
00032      SOURCE-COMPUTER. UNIVERSITY-MAINFRAME.
00033      OBJECT-COMPUTER. UNIVERSITY-MAINFRAME.
00034      INPUT-OUTPUT SECTION.
00035      FILE-CONTROL.
00036
00037          SELECT FILE-1     ASSIGN TO FILE1.
00038          SELECT FILE-2     ASSIGN TO FILE2.
00039          SELECT FILE-3     ASSIGN TO FILE3.
```

Program 2-Source Program to Merge Files Using COBOL Merge Feature

```
00040
00041          SELECT MERGE-FILE ASSIGN TO EXTMERGE.
00042
00043          SELECT RESULT    ASSIGN TO OUTFILE.
00044
00045   *...........................................................
00046   DATA DIVISION.
00047   FILE SECTION.
00048
00049   SD   MERGE-FILE
00050        RECORD CONTAINS 80 CHARACTERS
00051        DATA RECORD IS MERGE-RECORD.
00052   01   MERGE-RECORD.
00053          05   MERGE-EMP-IDNO         PIC XXX.
00054          05   MERGE-EMP-NAME         PIC X(21).
00055          05   MERGE-EMP-SALARY       PIC 9(5).
00056          05   MERGE-EMP-DEPT         PIC XXX.
00057          05   FILLER                 PIC X(48).
00058
00059   FD   FILE-1
00060        LABEL RECORDS ARE OMITTED
00061        RECORD CONTAINS 80 CHARACTERS
00062        DATA RECORD IS RECORD-1.
00063   01   RECORD-1.
00064          05   EMP-IDNO-1             PIC XXX.
00065          05   EMP-NAME-1             PIC X(21).
00066          05   EMP-SALARY-1           PIC 9(5).
00067          05   EMP-DEPT-1             PIC XXX.
00068          05   FILLER                 PIC X(48).
00069
00070   FD   FILE-2
00071        LABEL RECORDS ARE OMITTED
00072        RECORD CONTAINS 80 CHARACTERS
00073        DATA RECORD IS RECORD-2.
00074   01   RECORD-2.
00075          05   EMP-IDNO-2             PIC XXX.
00076          05   EMP-NAME-2             PIC X(21).
00077          05   EMP-SALARY-2           PIC 9(5).
00078          05   EMP-DEPT-2             PIC XXX.
00079          05   FILLER                 PIC X(48).
00080
00081   FD   FILE-3
00082        LABEL RECORDS ARE OMITTED
00083        RECORD CONTAINS 80 CHARACTERS
00084        DATA RECORD IS RECORD-3.
00085   01   RECORD-3.
00086          05   EMP-IDNO-3             PIC XXX.
00087          05   EMP-NAME-3             PIC X(21).
00088          05   EMP-SALARY-3           PIC 9(5).
00089          05   EMP-DEPT-3             PIC XXX.
00090          05   FILLER                 PIC X(48).
00091
```

Program 2-Source (Continued)

```
00092    FD  RESULT
00093        LABEL RECORDS ARE OMITTED
00094        RECORD CONTAINS 80 CHARACTERS
00095        DATA RECORD IS RESULT-RECORD.
00096    01  RESULT-RECORD.
00097        05  EMP-IDNO                    PIC XXX.
00098        05  EMP-NAME                    PIC X(21).
00099        05  EMP-SALARY                  PIC 9(5).
00100        05  EMP-DEPT                    PIC XXX.
00101        05  FILLER                      PIC X(48).
00102
00103    WORKING-STORAGE SECTION.
00104
00105    **********> VARIABLES:
00106
00107    01  END-OF-FILE-1       PIC XXX.
00108    01  END-OF-FILE-2       PIC XXX.
00109    01  END-OF-FILE-3       PIC XXX.
00110    01  END-OF-MERGE-FILE   PIC XXX.
00111    01  SAVE-IDNO           PIC XXX.
00112    01  FILE-NOT-ORDERED    PIC XXX.
00113    01  INVALID-RECORD      PIC XXX.
00114
00115    *...................................................................
00116    PROCEDURE DIVISION.
00117    A-MAINLINE.
00118        OPEN INPUT  FILE-1
00119                    FILE-2
00120                    FILE-3.
00121
00122        MOVE "NO"  TO END-OF-FILE-1
00123                      END-OF-FILE-2
00124                      END-OF-FILE-3.
00125
00126        MOVE "NO"  TO FILE-NOT-ORDERED.
00127        MOVE "000" TO SAVE-IDNO.
00128
00129        PERFORM B1-READ-FROM-FILE-1.
00130
00131        PERFORM B2-CHECK-ORDER-OF-FILE-1
00132            UNTIL END-OF-FILE-1 = "YES"
00133                            OR
00134                FILE-NOT-ORDERED = "YES".
00135
00136        IF FILE-NOT-ORDERED = "NO"
00137            MOVE "000" TO SAVE-IDNO
00138
00139            PERFORM B3-READ-FROM-FILE-2
00140
00141            PERFORM B4-CHECK-ORDER-OF-FILE-2
00142                UNTIL END-OF-FILE-2 = "YES"
00143                                OR
00144                    FILE-NOT-ORDERED = "YES".
00145
```

Program 2-Source (Continued)

```
00146            IF FILE-NOT-ORDERED = "NO"
00147                    MOVE "000" TO SAVE-IDNO
00148
00149                    PERFORM B5-READ-FROM-FILE-3
00150
00151                    PERFORM B6-CHECK-ORDER-OF-FILE-3
00152                            UNTIL END-OF-FILE-3 = "YES"
00153                                        OR
00154                              FILE-NOT-ORDERED = "YES".
00155
00156        CLOSE FILE-1 FILE-2 FILE-3.
00157
00158        IF FILE-NOT-ORDERED = "NO"
00159                    PERFORM B7-MERGE-FILES
00160        ELSE
00161                    DISPLAY "INPUT FILES NOT PROPERLY ORDERED."
00162                    DISPLAY "MERGE OPERATION WILL NOT BE ATTEMPTED."
00163                    DISPLAY "PROGRAM TERMINATING...".
00164
00165        STOP RUN.
00166
00167    B1-READ-FROM-FILE-1.
00168        READ FILE-1
00169                    AT END MOVE "YES" TO END-OF-FILE-1.
00170
00171    B2-CHECK-ORDER-OF-FILE-1.
00172        IF EMP-IDNO-1 NOT < SAVE-IDNO
00173                    MOVE EMP-IDNO-1 TO SAVE-IDNO
00174                    PERFORM B1-READ-FROM-FILE-1
00175        ELSE
00176                    MOVE "YES" TO FILE-NOT-ORDERED.
00177
00178    B3-READ-FROM-FILE-2.
00179        READ FILE-2
00180                    AT END MOVE "YES" TO END-OF-FILE-2.
00181
00182    B4-CHECK-ORDER-OF-FILE-2.
00183        IF EMP-IDNO-2 NOT < SAVE-IDNO
00184                    MOVE EMP-IDNO-2 TO SAVE-IDNO
00185                    PERFORM B3-READ-FROM-FILE-2
00186        ELSE
00187                    MOVE "YES" TO FILE-NOT-ORDERED.
00188
00189    B5-READ-FROM-FILE-3.
00190        READ FILE-3
00191                    AT END MOVE "YES" TO END-OF-FILE-3.
00192
00193    B6-CHECK-ORDER-OF-FILE-3.
00194        IF EMP-IDNO-3 NOT < SAVE-IDNO
00195                    MOVE EMP-IDNO-3 TO SAVE-IDNO
00196                    PERFORM B5-READ-FROM-FILE-3
00197        ELSE
00198                    MOVE "YES" TO FILE-NOT-ORDERED.
00199
```

Program 2-Source (Continued)

```
00200      B7-MERGE-FILES.
00201          MERGE MERGE-FILE
00202                  ON ASCENDING KEY MERGE-EMP-IDNO
00203                  USING FILE-1 FILE-2 FILE-3
00204                  OUTPUT PROCEDURE IS C1-POST-MERGE-PROCESSING.
00205
00206      C1-POST-MERGE-PROCESSING SECTION.
00207
00208      D1-LOAD-OUTPUT-FILE.
00209          OPEN OUTPUT RESULT.
00210          MOVE "NO" TO INVALID-RECORD.
00211          MOVE "NO" TO END-OF-MERGE-FILE.
00212
00213          RETURN MERGE-FILE
00214                  AT END MOVE "YES" TO END-OF-MERGE-FILE.
00215
00216          PERFORM E1-VALIDATE-MERGE-RECORD
00217                  UNTIL END-OF-MERGE-FILE = "YES".
00218
00219          CLOSE RESULT.
00220
00221          GO TO D2-TERMINATE-SECTION.
00222
00223      E1-VALIDATE-MERGE-RECORD.
00224
00225          PERFORM F1-VALIDATE-IDNO.
00226          PERFORM F2-VALIDATE-SALARY.
00227          PERFORM F3-VALIDATE-DEPT-CODE.
00228
00229          IF INVALID-RECORD = "YES"
00230                  MOVE MERGE-RECORD TO RESULT-RECORD
00231                  WRITE RESULT-RECORD.
00232
00233          MOVE "NO" TO INVALID-RECORD.
00234          RETURN MERGE-FILE
00235                  AT END MOVE "YES" TO END-OF-MERGE-FILE.
00236
00237      F1-VALIDATE-IDNO.
00238
00239          IF MERGE-EMP-IDNO < "050"
00240                  OR
00241            MERGE-EMP-IDNO > "250"
00242                  MOVE "YES" TO INVALID-RECORD.
00243
00244      F2-VALIDATE-SALARY.
00245
00246          IF MERGE-EMP-SALARY < 25000
00247                  OR
00248            MERGE-EMP-SALARY > 45000
00249                  MOVE "YES" TO INVALID-RECORD.
00250
```

Program 2-Source (Continued)

```
00251     F3-VALIDATE-DEPT-CODE.
00252
00253         IF MERGE-EMP-DEPT = "MIS"
00254                   OR
00255           MERGE-EMP-DEPT = "ACC"
00256                   OR
00257           MERGE-EMP-DEPT = "SLS"
00258               NEXT SENTENCE
00259         ELSE
00260               MOVE "YES" TO INVALID-RECORD.
00261
00262     D2-TERMINATE-SECTION.
00263         DISPLAY "MERGE COMPLETED...".
```

Program 2-Source (Continued)

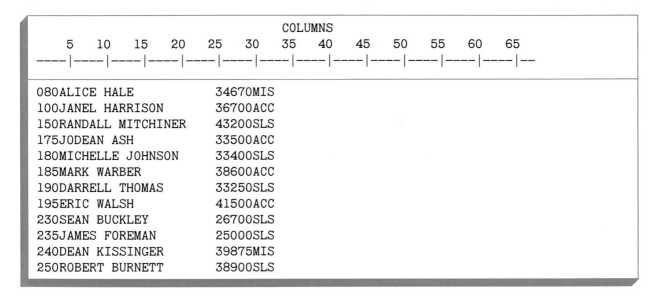

Program 2-Output Merged File Produced by Program 2

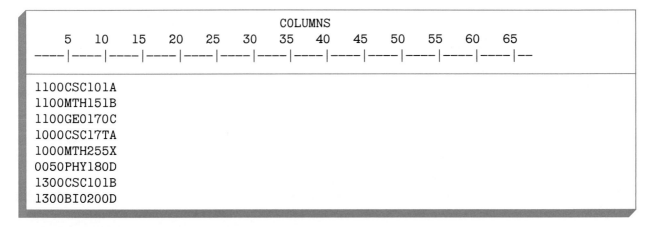

Program 3-Input(a) FILE-1 for Program 3

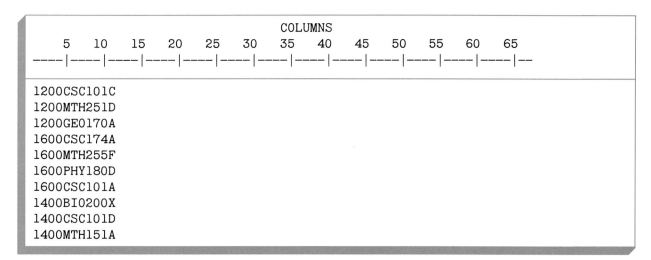

```
                              COLUMNS
      5    10   15   20   25   30   35   40   45   50   55   60   65
----|----|----|----|----|----|----|----|----|----|----|----|----|--

1200CSC101C
1200MTH251D
1200GE0170A
1600CSC174A
1600MTH255F
1600PHY180D
1600CSC101A
1400BI0200X
1400CSC101D
1400MTH151A
```

Program 3-Input(b) FILE-2 for Program 3

```
                              COLUMNS
      5    10   15   20   25   30   35   40   45   50   55   60   65
----|----|----|----|----|----|----|----|----|----|----|----|----|--

0800MTH151A
0800MTH251A
0900GE0170C
0900CSC174B
0700CSC174D
0700PHY180D
```

Program 3-Input(c) FILE-3 for Program 3

```
00001    *.......................................................
00002     IDENTIFICATION DIVISION.
00003     PROGRAM-ID. USE-OF-COBOL-SORT.
00004     ***********************************************************
00005    ***   THIS PROGRAM SORTS THREE SEQUENTIAL DISK FILES USING THE   *
00006    ***   COBOL SORT FEATURE.  BEFORE THE SORT OPERATION, THE RECORD  *
00007    ***   OCCURRENCES IN THE THREE INPUT FILES ARE VALIDATED FOR      *
00008    ***   CORRECTNESS ON THE STUDENT IDENTIFICATION NUMBER, COURSE    *
00009    ***   CODE, AND GRADE FIELDS, AND THE INCORRECT RECORD OCCURRENCES*
00010    ***   ARE REJECTED.                                              *
00011    ***                                                             *
00012    ***   AFTER SORTING IS COMPLETED, WHILE THE SORTED RECORD OCCUR- *
00013    ***   RENCES ARE BEING TRANSFERRED TO THE OUTPUT FILE, THEY  ARE *
00014    ***   PROCESSED TO DETERMINE THE DISTRIBUTION OF LETTER GRADES IN *
00015    ***   THE FINAL FILE.                                            *
00016    ***                                                             *
```

Program 3-Source Program to Sort Files Using COBOL Sort Feature

```
00017   ***   THE FIELD VALIDATION TESTS ARE BASED ON THE FOLLOWING        *
00018   ***   CONSTRAINTS:                                                 *
00019   ***   1. STUDENT ID NUMBER IS IN THE RANGE 0100 THROUGH 6500.      *
00020   ***   2. COURSE CODES ARE ALPHANUMERIC WITH THE FIRST THREE        *
00021   ***      CHARACTERS BEING ALPHABETIC, AND THE REMAINING BEING      *
00022   ***      NUMERIC.                                                  *
00023   ***   3. LETTER GRADE VALUES ARE "A", "B", "C", "D" AND "F".       *
00024   ***                                                                *
00025   ***   ALL THREE SOURCE FILES HAVE RECORD STRUCTURES CONSISTING     *
00026   ***   OF STUDENT IDNO, COURSE CODE AND LETTER GRADE FIELDS.  THE    *
00027   ***   STUDENT IDNO IS THE PRIMARY SORT KEY, AND THE COURSE CODE     *
00028   ***   IS THE SECONDARY SORT KEY.  THE SORT ORDER IS ASCENDING       *
00029   ***   WITH RESPECT TO BOTH SORT KEYS.                              *
00030   *******************************************************************
00031
00032    AUTHOR.         UCKAN.
00033    DATE-WRITTEN.  OCT 16, 1990.
00034    DATE-COMPILED. OCT 17,1990.
00035   *...................................................................
00036    ENVIRONMENT DIVISION.
00037    CONFIGURATION SECTION.
00038    SOURCE-COMPUTER. UNIVERSITY-MAINFRAME.
00039    OBJECT-COMPUTER. UNIVERSITY-MAINFRAME.
00040    INPUT-OUTPUT SECTION.
00041    FILE-CONTROL.
00042
00043        SELECT FILE-1    ASSIGN TO FILE1.
00044        SELECT FILE-2    ASSIGN TO FILE2.
00045        SELECT FILE-3    ASSIGN TO FILE3.
00046
00047        SELECT SORT-FILE ASSIGN TO EXTSORT.
00048
00049        SELECT RESULT    ASSIGN TO OUTFILE.
00050
00051   *...................................................................
00052    DATA DIVISION.
00053    FILE SECTION.
00054
00055    SD  SORT-FILE
00056        RECORD CONTAINS 80 CHARACTERS
00057        DATA RECORD IS SORT-RECORD.
00058    01  SORT-RECORD.
00059        05  SORT-STUDENT-IDNO        PIC XXXX.
00060        05  SORT-COURSE-CODE         PIC X(6).
00061        05  SORT-LETTER-GRADE        PIC X.
00062        05  FILLER                   PIC X(69).
00063
00064    FD  FILE-1
00065        LABEL RECORDS ARE OMITTED
00066        RECORD CONTAINS 80 CHARACTERS
00067        DATA RECORD IS RECORD-1.
```

Program 3-Source (Continued)

```
00068    01   RECORD-1.
00069         05   STUDENT-IDNO-1                PIC XXXX.
00070         05   COURSE-CODE-1                 PIC X(6).
00071         05   LETTER-GRADE-1                PIC X.
00072         05   FILLER                        PIC X(69).
00073
00074    FD   FILE-2
00075         LABEL RECORDS ARE OMITTED
00076         RECORD CONTAINS 80 CHARACTERS
00077         DATA RECORD IS RECORD-2.
00078    01   RECORD-2.
00079         05   STUDENT-IDNO-2                PIC XXXX.
00080         05   COURSE-CODE-2                 PIC X(6).
00081         05   LETTER-GRADE-2                PIC X.
00082         05   FILLER                        PIC X(69).
00083
00084    FD   FILE-3
00085         LABEL RECORDS ARE OMITTED
00086         RECORD CONTAINS 80 CHARACTERS
00087         DATA RECORD IS RECORD-3.
00088    01   RECORD-3.
00089         05   STUDENT-IDNO-3                PIC XXXX.
00090         05   COURSE-CODE-3                 PIC X(6).
00091         05   LETTER-GRADE-3                PIC X.
00092         05   FILLER                        PIC X(69).
00093
00094    FD   RESULT
00095         LABEL RECORDS ARE OMITTED
00096         RECORD CONTAINS 80 CHARACTERS
00097         DATA RECORD IS RESULT-RECORD.
00098    01   RESULT-RECORD.
00099         05   STUDENT-IDNO                  PIC XXXX.
00100         05   COURSE-CODE                   PIC X(6).
00101         05   LETTER-GRADE                  PIC X.
00102         05   FILLER                        PIC X(69).
00103
00104    WORKING-STORAGE SECTION.
00105
00106    **********> VARIABLES:
00107
00108    01   END-OF-FILE-1       PIC XXX.
00109    01   END-OF-FILE-2       PIC XXX.
00110    01   END-OF-FILE-3       PIC XXX.
00111    01   END-OF-SORT-FILE    PIC XXX.
00112    01   SAVE-STUDENT-IDNO   PIC XXXX.
00113    01   SAVE-COURSE-CODE    PIC X(6).
00114    01   SAVE-LETTER-GRADE   PIC X.
00115    01   INVALID-RECORD      PIC XXX.
00116    01   NUMBER-OF-A         PIC 999.
00117    01   NUMBER-OF-B         PIC 999.
00118    01   NUMBER-OF-C         PIC 999.
00119    01   NUMBER-OF-D         PIC 999.
00120    01   NUMBER-OF-F         PIC 999.
00121
```

Program 3-Source (Continued)

```
00122    **********> STRUCTURES:
00123
00124    01  WS-COURSE-CODE.
00125        05  DEPT-CODE        PIC AAA.
00126        05  SEQ-NO          PIC 999.
00127
00128    *..................................................................
00129    PROCEDURE DIVISION.
00130    A-MAINLINE.
00131
00132        SORT SORT-FILE
00133             ON ASCENDING KEY SORT-STUDENT-IDNO SORT-COURSE-CODE
00134             INPUT PROCEDURE  IS B1-PRESORT-FILTERING
00135             OUTPUT PROCEDURE IS B2-POST-SORT-PROCESSING.
00136
00137        STOP RUN.
00138
00139    B1-PRESORT-FILTERING SECTION.
00140        OPEN INPUT  FILE-1
00141                    FILE-2
00142                    FILE-3.
00143
00144        MOVE "NO"  TO END-OF-FILE-1
00145                      END-OF-FILE-2
00146                      END-OF-FILE-3.
00147
00148        PERFORM C1-READ-FROM-FILE-1.
00149
00150        PERFORM C2-VALIDATE-FILE-1
00151             UNTIL END-OF-FILE-1 = "YES".
00152
00153        PERFORM C3-READ-FROM-FILE-2.
00154
00155        PERFORM C4-VALIDATE-FILE-2
00156             UNTIL END-OF-FILE-2 = "YES".
00157
00158        PERFORM C5-READ-FROM-FILE-3.
00159
00160        PERFORM C6-VALIDATE-FILE-3
00161             UNTIL END-OF-FILE-3 = "YES".
00162
00163        CLOSE FILE-1 FILE-2 FILE-3.
00164
00165        GO TO C7-TERMINATE-INPUT-PROCEDURE.
00166
00167    C1-READ-FROM-FILE-1.
00168        READ FILE-1
00169             AT END MOVE "YES" TO END-OF-FILE-1.
00170
00171    C2-VALIDATE-FILE-1.
00172        MOVE STUDENT-IDNO-1 TO SAVE-STUDENT-IDNO.
00173        MOVE COURSE-CODE-1  TO SAVE-COURSE-CODE.
00174        MOVE LETTER-GRADE-1 TO SAVE-LETTER-GRADE.
00175
```

Program 3-Source (Continued)

```
00176              MOVE "NO" TO INVALID-RECORD.
00177
00178              PERFORM D1-VALIDATE-IDNO.
00179              PERFORM D2-VALIDATE-COURSE-CODE.
00180              PERFORM D3-VALIDATE-LETTER-GRADE.
00181
00182              IF INVALID-RECORD = "NO"
00183                    RELEASE SORT-RECORD FROM RECORD-1.
00184
00185              PERFORM C1-READ-FROM-FILE-1.
00186
00187       C3-READ-FROM-FILE-2.
00188              READ FILE-2
00189                    AT END MOVE "YES" TO END-OF-FILE-2.
00190
00191       C4-VALIDATE-FILE-2.
00192              MOVE STUDENT-IDNO-2 TO SAVE-STUDENT-IDNO.
00193              MOVE COURSE-CODE-2  TO SAVE-COURSE-CODE.
00194              MOVE LETTER-GRADE-2 TO SAVE-LETTER-GRADE.
00195
00196              MOVE "NO" TO INVALID-RECORD.
00197
00198              PERFORM D1-VALIDATE-IDNO.
00199              PERFORM D2-VALIDATE-COURSE-CODE.
00200              PERFORM D3-VALIDATE-LETTER-GRADE.
00201
00202              IF INVALID-RECORD = "NO"
00203                    RELEASE SORT-RECORD FROM RECORD-2.
00204
00205              PERFORM C3-READ-FROM-FILE-2.
00206
00207       C5-READ-FROM-FILE-3.
00208              READ FILE-3
00209                    AT END MOVE "YES" TO END-OF-FILE-3.
00210
00211       C6-VALIDATE-FILE-3.
00212              MOVE STUDENT-IDNO-3 TO SAVE-STUDENT-IDNO.
00213              MOVE COURSE-CODE-3  TO SAVE-COURSE-CODE.
00214              MOVE LETTER-GRADE-3 TO SAVE-LETTER-GRADE.
00215
00216              MOVE "NO" TO INVALID-RECORD.
00217
00218              PERFORM D1-VALIDATE-IDNO.
00219              PERFORM D2-VALIDATE-COURSE-CODE.
00220              PERFORM D3-VALIDATE-LETTER-GRADE.
00221
00222              IF INVALID-RECORD = "NO"
00223                    RELEASE SORT-RECORD FROM RECORD-3.
00224
00225              PERFORM C5-READ-FROM-FILE-3.
00226
00227       D1-VALIDATE-IDNO.
00228
```

Program 3-Source (Continued)

```
00229              IF SAVE-STUDENT-IDNO < "0100"
00230                       OR
00231                 SAVE-STUDENT-IDNO > "6500"
00232                    MOVE "YES" TO INVALID-RECORD.
00233
00234      D2-VALIDATE-COURSE-CODE.
00235          MOVE SAVE-COURSE-CODE TO WS-COURSE-CODE.
00236
00237          IF SEQ-NO NOT NUMERIC
00238                    MOVE "YES" TO INVALID-RECORD.
00239
00240          IF DEPT-CODE NOT ALPHABETIC
00241                    MOVE "YES" TO INVALID-RECORD.
00242
00243      D3-VALIDATE-LETTER-GRADE.
00244
00245          IF SAVE-LETTER-GRADE = "A" OR "B" OR "C" OR "D" OR "F"
00246                    NEXT SENTENCE
00247          ELSE
00248                    MOVE "YES" TO INVALID-RECORD.
00249
00250      C7-TERMINATE-INPUT-PROCEDURE.
00251          DISPLAY "DATA VALIDATION COMPLETED...".
00252
00253      B2-POST-SORT-PROCESSING SECTION.
00254
00255      C8-LOAD-SORTED-FL-AND-PROCESS.
00256          OPEN OUTPUT RESULT.
00257          MOVE "NO" TO END-OF-SORT-FILE.
00258
00259          MOVE ZERO TO NUMBER-OF-A NUMBER-OF-B NUMBER-OF-C
00260                    NUMBER-OF-D NUMBER-OF-F.
00261
00262          RETURN SORT-FILE
00263                    AT END MOVE "YES" TO END-OF-SORT-FILE.
00264
00265          PERFORM D4-GENERATE-FILE-AND-DISTR
00266                    UNTIL END-OF-SORT-FILE = "YES".
00267
00268          CLOSE RESULT.
00269
00270          GO TO C9-TERMINATE-OUTPUT-PROC.
00271
00272      D4-GENERATE-FILE-AND-DISTR.
00273          WRITE RESULT-RECORD FROM SORT-RECORD.
00274
00275          IF SORT-LETTER-GRADE = "A"
00276                    ADD 1 TO NUMBER-OF-A.
00277
00278          IF SORT-LETTER-GRADE = "B"
00279                    ADD 1 TO NUMBER-OF-B.
00280
00281          IF SORT-LETTER-GRADE = "C"
00282                    ADD 1 TO NUMBER-OF-C.
```

Program 3-Source (Continued)

```
00283
00284            IF SORT-LETTER-GRADE = "D"
00285                    ADD 1 TO NUMBER-OF-D.
00286
00287            IF SORT-LETTER-GRADE = "F"
00288                    ADD 1 TO NUMBER-OF-F.
00289
00290            RETURN SORT-FILE
00291                    AT END MOVE "YES" TO END-OF-SORT-FILE.
00292
00293        C9-TERMINATE-OUTPUT-PROC.
00294            DISPLAY "NUMBER OF A'S: " NUMBER-OF-A.
00295            DISPLAY "NUMBER OF B'S: " NUMBER-OF-B.
00296            DISPLAY "NUMBER OF C'S: " NUMBER-OF-C.
00297            DISPLAY "NUMBER OF D'S: " NUMBER-OF-D.
00298            DISPLAY "NUMBER OF F'S: " NUMBER-OF-F.
00299            DISPLAY "PROCESSING COMPLETED...".
```

Program 3-Source (Continued)

```
                                    COLUMNS
        5    10   15   20   25   30   35   40   45   50   55   60   65
----|----|----|----|----|----|----|----|----|----|----|----|----|--

0700CSC174D
0700PHY180D
0800MTH151A
0800MTH251A
0900CSC174B
0900GE0170C
1100CSC101A
1100GE0170C
1100MTH151B
1200CSC101C
1200GE0170A
1200MTH251D
1300BI0200D
1300CSC101B
1400CSC101D
1400MTH151A
1600CSC101A
1600CSC174A
1600MTH255F
1600PHY180D
```

Program 3-Output Sorted File Produced by Program 3

13

Indexed Sequential File Organization

Example Program 2: Indexed Sequential File Access

Key Terms

Study Guide
Quick Scan
Test Your Comprehension
Improve Your Problem-Solving Ability

IN THIS CHAPTER YOU WILL LEARN ABOUT

- Indexing and indexed files
   Indexed nonsequential organization
   Indexed sequential organization
   B-tree indexing
- ISAM implementation of indexed files
   Data organization in ISAM
   Record deletion in ISAM files
   Record insertion in ISAM files
   ISAM file reorganization
- VSAM/KSDS implementation of indexed files
   Data organization in VSAM/KSDS
   Primary key indexing
   Alternate indexing
   VSAM catalog
   VSAM command language
   Record deletion in VSAM/KSDS files
   Record insertion in VSAM/KSDS files
- COBOL features for indexed files
   Defining indexed files
   WRITE statement
   READ statement
   REWRITE statement
   DELETE statement
   START statement

Introduction

As discussed earlier, in the classic computer architecture, a memory location can be accessed only by its address. This is the basis for access-by-address. From the user's point of view, it is more desirable to access a memory location by its content. First, access-by-content does not require the user to keep track of what happens in the computer's storage and to have a memory map available at all times. Therefore, it is far easier than what is provided by the current state-of-the-art in computer technology, namely, access-by-address. Second, in practical applications it is more natural to define access paths to data stored in a computer by some attribute of the data, rather than by where they are located.

Memory architectures that permit access-by-content are also called associative memory devices. Research and development efforts on associative memory devices that make genuine access-by-content possible are continuing, but it will be some time before these devices can be used widely in business. In the meantime, we rely on interfaces that simulate access-by-content, at the core of which is indexing.

The concept of indexing was introduced in Chapter 10. The second built-in file organization technique in COBOL, indexed sequential organization, is based on indexing. It is, in fact, a bridge between sequential files and relative files, which are pure direct-access files. Indexed sequential organization not only permits sequential access to records, but also enables the programmer to specify direct access to them by some of their fields. Therefore, where direct access to records by content of a field is indicated, this file organization technique comes in handy.

In this chapter we will discuss techniques of file indexing and study the indexed sequential organization, its implementations in file management systems, and the COBOL language aspects for indexed files.

Indexing and Indexed Files

It is possible to simulate access-by-content by providing a transformative interface between the user and the computer. Such an interface converts a data value for a data field to a memory address. The two principal techniques used in transforming data values to memory location addresses are hashing and indexing.

In **hashing**, an algorithm is executed to transform a data value to a memory address. Hashing and hashed files are the subject of Chapter 14. **Indexing** uses tables that contain entries associating data values with memory locations. These are called **index tables**.

The idea of indexing is quite common. For example, a telephone directory is nothing but an index whose entries associate person names with telephone numbers. In computer applications, an index transforms a data value into a memory address.

Index tables can be constructed and maintained in many different ways. If we build index tables for data values stored in files, we commonly refer to this task as **indexing files**. The file for which an index table is created and maintained is referred to as an **indexed file**. Sometimes, the index table itself for a large file is extensive. In such cases it is stored as a file, called an **index file**. Even when an index file is not too large, generally we wish to keep it in permanent storage, because, as we will see later in this chapter, indexing and index maintenance are costly operations. Thus, ordinarily, index tables are stored as files.

Occasionally, the burden of generating and maintaining index and indexed files falls to the application programmer. This is one of the reasons why we should study and understand indexing. Generally, and quite fortunately, file and data base management systems are available for file indexing. Even then, to make intelligent use of such software systems, the programmer should be familiar with fundamental techniques.

Indexed Nonsequential Organization

Let us consider a file in which the records are identified by a key field called NAME. Naturally, each record also contains additional information, but they are irrelevant to our discussion here. Assume that the records are stored in a DASD at memory locations whose relative addresses are 1 through 16, as shown in Figure 1. The portion of the file reserved for actual records is called the **prime data area**. Note that the prime data area in Figure 1 contains records that are not ordered by their key values. Thus, it is an unordered, or nonsequential, list.

So far, this memory organization permits direct access in that we can retrieve records by their relative addresses. Also, once in the prime data area we can access records consecutively. The direct-access capability is not by content

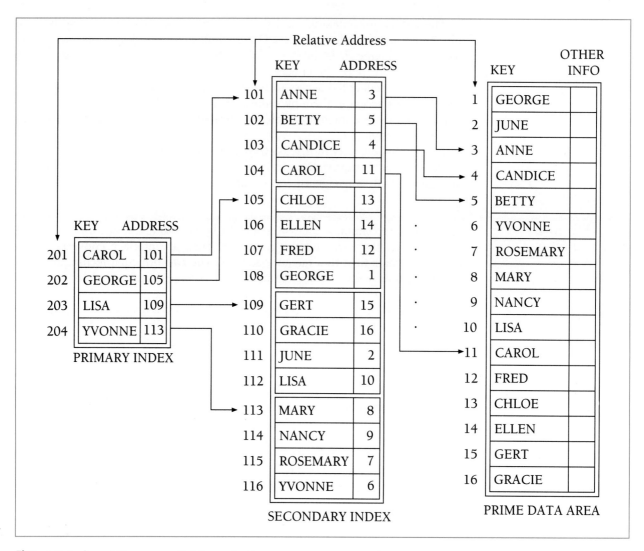

Figure 1 Indexed Nonsequential Organization

of the key field, however. We construct an index and store its entries in another segment of the direct-access storage. In constructing this index, we do the following.

1. For each record in the prime data area, we create an index entry consisting of the record key value and its relative address in the prime data area.
2. We sort the index entries in ascending order by the key values and store them in an index area. In Figure 1, the index area includes memory locations 101 through 116.

To access a record in the prime data area by its key value, we enter the index area at its beginning, execute a sequential search, find the corresponding index entry, and, using the relative address in the index entry, access the prime data area location containing the record. For example, to access and retrieve the record for ELLEN, we access the index entry at 101 and compare its key value with ELLEN. We proceed with the next location in the index area, 102, until we find the index entry for ELLEN in 106. This index entry yields the relative address 14 for the record belonging to ELLEN. We finally access this address directly and retrieve ELLEN's record. If we use a program that incorporates this logic, to the user it will appear as if the access is by content, although in reality, it is by address.

> An index that contains the same number of entries as the number of records in the prime data area is called a **total index** (or **total directory**). Another term for a total index is **sequence set**.

The secondary index table in Figure 1 is a total index.

The reason we sort the index table entries by key value is that the index table is searched sequentially, and sequentially searching an ordered list is more efficient than searching an equivalent unordered list. Although a total index contains the same number of entries as those in the prime data area, index entries consist of only key values and relative addresses, and their length is generally shorter than that of prime area records. Therefore, considering the time required for data transfer, the indexing technique discussed so far would be more efficient compared to sequentially processing the content of the prime data area.

The organization of Figure 1 is characterized by a prime data area containing records that are not ordered, and an index area consisting of a total index. This organization is known as **indexed nonsequential organization**. To facilitate searching the index area, a higher-level index table can be created as follows.

1. Divide the index area into blocks of equal length, for example, four index entries.
2. For each such block, create an index entry consisting of the highest key value in the block, and the relative location of the first index entry in it. In Figure 1, for the first block containing index entries with keys ANNE, BETTY, CANDICE, and CAROL in locations 101, 102, 103, and 104, respectively, the higher-level index entry would be:

CAROL	101

3. Again, order the generated high-level index entries by their key values and store them in another segment of the direct-access storage.

Here, the new index table is the primary index, and the total index table that it controls is the secondary index. In Figure 1 we have multiple index tables hierarchically arranged in the index area. The number of index entries in the higher-level index table is equal to the number of blocks in the secondary index table. This organization is known as a **multiple-level indexed file**.

The primary index in Figure 1 is not a total index. It is a partial index.

> A **partial index** consists of entries controlling more than one entry in another index table or in the prime data area.

Searching the file in Figure 1 has now become more efficient. Let us demonstrate this. Suppose we are searching for the record belonging to ELLEN. We enter the primary index area at the relative location 201. We compare ELLEN with data values in the index entries until we find an index entry whose data value is greater than ELLEN, the search key. In this case, it will be the entry in 202 with key value GEORGE. We conclude that if ELLEN is at all in the file, it must be in the block controlled by GEORGE in the primary index. This is the block beginning with 105 and extending four index entries. Next, we access

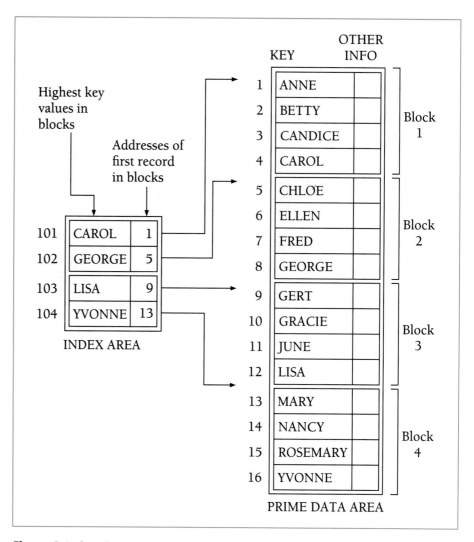

Figure 2 Indexed Sequential Organization with a Single-Level Index

105 and search this block sequentially until we locate the secondary index entry for ELLEN. When we find it, we access the prime area location 14 directly and retrieve the record.

Indexed Sequential Organization

Additional savings on the search time can be realized if we maintain the file in the prime data area as an ordered list. An example is shown in Figure 2. The records in the prime area are in ascending order of the key field NAME. In this case, we do not have to build a total directory. Instead, as we did for the secondary index table of Figure 1, we divide the prime area into blocks of equal length and create an index entry for each block. Such index entries include the highest key value in the block (i.e., the key value of the last record) and the relative address of the first record in it. This way, we end up with a smaller, single-level index.

> Because the prime area records are ordered, and access to them is sequential once an index entry is used to enter it, this organization is called **indexed sequential organization**.

Maintaining an indexed sequential organization is not easy and requires careful considerations with regard to the overall efficiency of the system. If the content of the prime data area changes due to record insertions and deletions, the index entries may also change. To minimize the changes in the index area, certain strategies can be used. These include logically deleting records instead of physically removing them from the prime data area, and using another segment of the direct access storage (usually referred to as **overflow area**) to accommodate insertions. We return to these maintenance considerations later.

Improvements on Indexed Sequential Organization

In its most primitive form as introduced in the previous section, indexed sequential organization has two basic drawbacks. For a high-volume prime data file, the index tables themselves may be large; and searching them sequentially may negatively affect the overall performance of the system. The solution to these problems lies in compacting the index tables. This may be done in two ways.

1. Block more than one index entry into physical records of longer length.
2. Use index entries that can control more than one block in the prime data area or in the lower-level index tables.

The first strategy is useful in that it effectively reduces the number of physical records in index files. The second approach takes us into a modified and highly efficient indexing scheme known as B-tree indexing.

Let us consider Figure 3 where the sequence set is a total index table for a prime data area file. Again, the prime data area contains records with NAME as the organization key. Each entry in the sequence set is a typical index, as shown in the blow-up for CHANEY, consisting of a name and an address to a prime area record. We take a blocking factor of 4 and group four sequence set entries into a physical record. The first sequence set entries for ADAMS, BRADLEY, BREHM, and CHANEY are blocked and stored in location 101, and the rest are handled similarly. We also reorganize the primary index in the same way. Each index entry in the primary index in Figure 3 consists of the highest key value in a block of the sequence set and the address of the memory location containing it. We block four index entries together and store each block in a directly accessible memory location.

It should be noted that this blocking of index entries does not change the file organization, since the contents of the blocks are processed sequentially. In case the primary index table is still too large for sequential processing, we can generate higher-level index tables, as shown in Figure 4, where the indexed sequential organization has a three-level index and a hierarchical structure.

B-Tree Indexing

Another technique that enables us to compact index tables further is to increase the scope of index entries. In the previous indexed organizations, each index entry controlled a single block in the lower level index or the prime data area. For example, in Figure 4, the index entry

FERRIS	11

has the memory location 11 in its scope. This means that if a search key is less than or equal to FERRIS, we use the pointer 11 to access a lower-level index

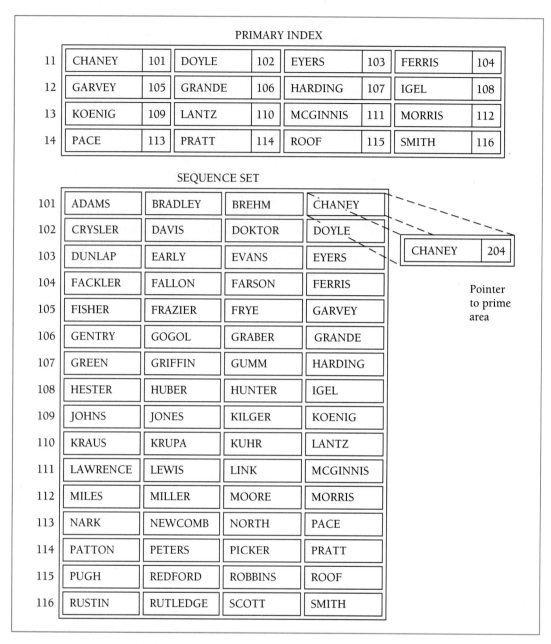

Figure 3 A Single-Level Indexing Scheme

entry directly. Otherwise, we sequentially access the next primary index entry and investigate its content and scope.

We can define index entries with enhanced scopes. An example is provided in Figure 5. The primary index entry

12	FERRIS	13	IGEL	14	MORRIS	15

reflects a four-block scope. These are the blocks beginning at locations 12, 13, 14, and 15. In effect, it says that all entries identified by a key value less than or equal to FERRIS are in location 12; those larger than FERRIS but smaller than or equal to IGEL are in 13; key values larger than IGEL and smaller than or equal to MORRIS are in 14; and, finally, those that are larger than MORRIS are

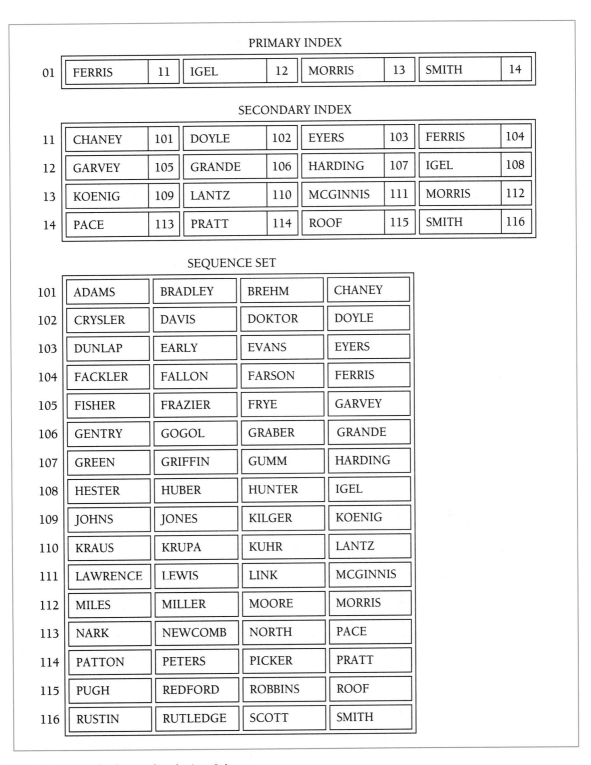

PRIMARY INDEX

| 01 | FERRIS | 11 | IGEL | 12 | MORRIS | 13 | SMITH | 14 |

SECONDARY INDEX

11	CHANEY	101	DOYLE	102	EYERS	103	FERRIS	104
12	GARVEY	105	GRANDE	106	HARDING	107	IGEL	108
13	KOENIG	109	LANTZ	110	MCGINNIS	111	MORRIS	112
14	PACE	113	PRATT	114	ROOF	115	SMITH	116

SEQUENCE SET

101	ADAMS	BRADLEY	BREHM	CHANEY
102	CRYSLER	DAVIS	DOKTOR	DOYLE
103	DUNLAP	EARLY	EVANS	EYERS
104	FACKLER	FALLON	FARSON	FERRIS
105	FISHER	FRAZIER	FRYE	GARVEY
106	GENTRY	GOGOL	GRABER	GRANDE
107	GREEN	GRIFFIN	GUMM	HARDING
108	HESTER	HUBER	HUNTER	IGEL
109	JOHNS	JONES	KILGER	KOENIG
110	KRAUS	KRUPA	KUHR	LANTZ
111	LAWRENCE	LEWIS	LINK	MCGINNIS
112	MILES	MILLER	MOORE	MORRIS
113	NARK	NEWCOMB	NORTH	PACE
114	PATTON	PETERS	PICKER	PRATT
115	PUGH	REDFORD	ROBBINS	ROOF
116	RUSTIN	RUTLEDGE	SCOTT	SMITH

Figure 4 A Multiple-Level Indexing Scheme

found in 15. Such an index entry is better than the previous limited-scope ones in that, on accessing it, we are able to select the right block from a greater number of alternatives.

The indexing scheme exemplified in Figure 5 is called **B-tree indexing**, and is commonly used in data base management systems. There are additional considerations of B-trees that are not immediately obvious in the figure. Because of the widespread use of this technique, it is worth spending some time on it.

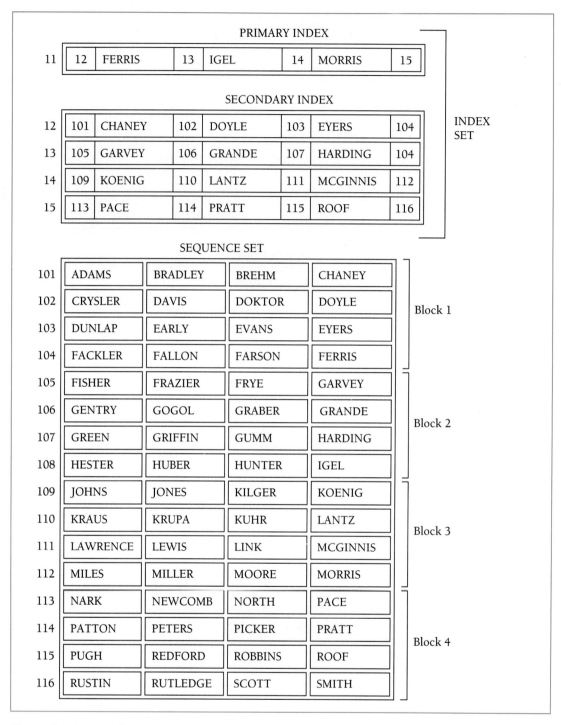

Figure 5 A B-Tree of Order 4

Formally, a B-tree of order n is a data structure satisfying the following properties.

1. Every entry has sufficient room to store (n − 1) data values (i.e., key values) and n pointers (or addresses).
2. The root entry is the highest-level index entry and has at least two pointers. All other entries have at least (n / 2) pointers.
3. The lowest-level entries are in the prime data area. They make up the terminal entries of the tree and are all at the same level.

4. For all nonterminal entries in the tree, data values are arranged in increasing order.
5. In all nonterminal entries, a pointer to the left of a key value leads to entries with data values that are less than or equal to the considered key value. A pointer to the right of a key value, on the other hand, leads to entries with data values that are larger than the data value under consideration.

The indexed organization in Figure 5 is a B-tree of order 4, and it satisfies all the above properties.

Indexing Based on Composite Data Elements

So far in our discussion of indexing techniques and all the examples we have considered, we used one elementary data field as the basis for indexing. An index table based on a single field is good for processing simple queries. For example, the indexing scheme of Figure 3 can be used to access and retrieve information for a record for which NAME = DOYLE. An attribute-value pair such as NAME = DOYLE is called a **simple query**. The pair NAME > DOYLE is called a **range query** because it specifies a range of NAME values. The index table of Figure 3 can be used to process range queries as well. For the query NAME > DOYLE, all we have to do is find the primary index entry for DOYLE, get the associated address (103, in this case), and process the sequence set starting at the location 103 and beyond.

Sometimes we may be interested in defining access paths through an index table such that access to one or more prime area records is based on more than one data field. In the example in Figure 6 the index table specifies the access paths to prime area records by the composite element SEX and AGE. The key values consist of the concatenation of sex and age values for the corresponding record in the prime area. This indexing scheme is good for a query such as, "Retrieve records for which SEX = F and AGE = 19." This is known as a **complex query**, another name for which is Boolean query. Apart from these, all other considerations discussed for indexing apply to composite data element indexing.

REVIEW QUESTIONS

1. In simulating file access-by-content, we can use two techniques to transform data values to memory addresses: _____ and _____ .
2. A file for which an index table is built is called an _____ file. The index table, if stored as a file, is called an _____ file.
3. If the number of entries in an index table for a file is the same as the number of records in that file, such an index table is called a total index. (T or F)
4. In an indexed nonsequential organization, data records in the prime data area are ordered by an attribute in their record structure. (T or F)
5. In a multiple-level indexed file, all index tables are total index tables. (T or F)
6. In indexed sequential organization, index table entries are accessed _____ , an index entry is used to access the prime data area _____ , and the prime data area records are again accessed _____ .
7. One of the advantages of B-tree indexing is that each index entry has an increased scope. (T or F)

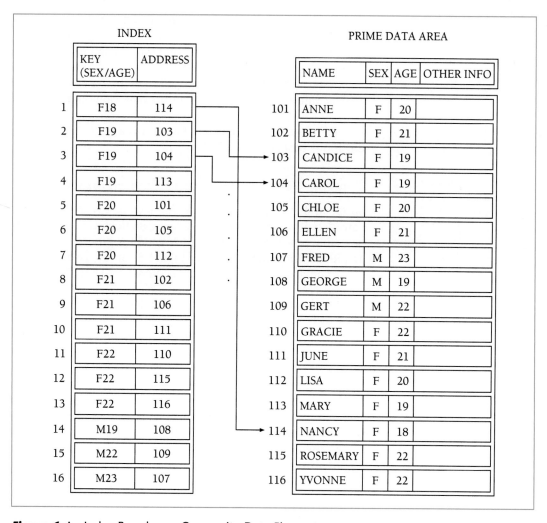

Figure 6 An Index Based on a Composite Data Element

8. An attribute-value pair associated through the equal-comparison operator is called a _____ . Such an attribute-value association through any other comparison operator is called a _____ .

Answers: 1. hashing, indexing; 2. indexed, index; 3. T; 4. F; 5. F; 6. sequentially, directly, sequentially; 7. T; 8. simple query, range query.

Structure of ISAM Implementation

Many file and data base management systems for micro, mini, and mainframe computers are commercially available. A majority make use of one or more indexing techniques to facilitate access-by-content. By its design, the COBOL language is suitable to interface with file management software that supports indexed sequential organization. As we will see, it is possible to specify a file as an indexed sequential file in a COBOL program; however, the manner in which the intricacies of indexing are implemented is left to the underlying file management system, which significantly simplifies our programming efforts. Despite this, it is important that the application programmer have a good understanding of file management systems.

A variety of file management systems developed by different vendors support the indexed sequential file organization. We briefly study two implementations, ISAM (indexed sequential access method) and VSAM (virtual storage access method). ISAM is significant because it was one of the earliest implementations of the technique and incorporates many important concepts of indexing. VSAM, on the other hand, is widely used for file management and is at the core of some modern data base management systems (e.g., DB2 and SQL/DS) for mainframe computers.

ISAM Data Organization

The direct-access storage reserved for an ISAM file is divided into three areas: prime data, overflow, and index areas. The ISAM data organization and its elements are shown in Figure 7. The **prime data area** contains actual records in the file. Each record is identified by a key field. The ISAM organization is based on this key field. This key is also used to access a record directly. In soft-sectored DASDs, so that the system may recognize a record by its key, the count-key-data track format is used. Records in the prime area are stored consecutively in increasing order of their organization keys. They may be blocked or unblocked. The prime data area consists of one or more preferably adjacent cylinders, depending on how large the file is and the cylinder capacity of the device.

The **overflow area** is, in fact, part of the prime data area. It also stores records. There are two overflow areas, and both are optional. There is one cylinder overflow area for each cylinder, and one independent overflow area for the file. In each cylinder of an ISAM file, the user may allocate a number of contiguous tracks to hold overflow records. These tracks make up the **cylinder overflow area** for that cylinder, and are reserved exclusively for the records that overflow from the prime data area of that cylinder during record addition. The overflow area in a cylinder is adjacent to its prime data area.

The user may also specify an **independent overflow area** for an ISAM file, which can be used by all cylinders in the file. During record addition, if the cylinder overflow area becomes full, the independent overflow area stores records that overflow from any cylinder. During initial file loading, all records are placed in the prime data area, and the overflow areas are empty. During the lifetime of an ISAM file, whenever a record is pushed off a prime area track, it goes to the overflow area of the cylinder containing that track. In case the cylinder overflow area is full or has not been specified, the overflow record is accommodated in the independent overflow area. If this too is not possible, the record addition operation is rejected.

The main advantage of cylinder overflow areas is that they can be accessed faster than the independent overflow area. This is because they are in the same cylinder as the prime data, and no seeking is necessary to access them after the prime area records are processed in sequential processing. On the other hand, the independent overflow area makes better use of disk storage.

The ISAM index area consists of three kinds of index tables: track, cylinder, and master. **Track index tables** constitute the lowest level of ISAM indexing. There is one for each cylinder built and maintained by the system. A track index for a cylinder contains index entries, with one for each track. A track index entry consists of a self-identifying address of the track index table, a prime index subentry, and an overflow index subentry. Each **prime index subentry** associates the largest key value in a track with that track's address. Such subentries are constructed during file loading.

Each **overflow index subentry** consists of the key value of the first record that has overflowed from a track and the address of the record in the overflow area that has most recently been pushed off that track. Each overflow record contains a pointer, also called **sequence link indicator** (SLI), that points to the next overflow record coming from the track. Using these pointers, the system

CYLINDER INDEX TABLE

Cylinder Number	Highest Key	Address of Track Index
0	FRED	000
1	YVONNE	100

TRACK INDEX TABLES

Address of Track Index	Prime Index		Overflow Index	
	Key	Address	Key	Address
000	ANNE	000	——	——
000	COLLEEN	001	——	——
000	FRED	002	——	——
100	GERT	100	——	——
100	LISA	101	——	——
100	YVONNE	102	——	——

For cyl. 0 → rows with 000
For cyl. 1 → rows with 100

CYLINDER 0

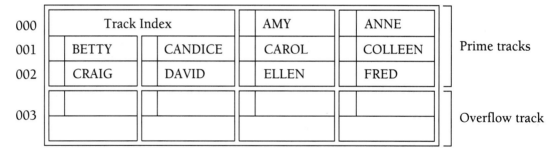

000	Track Index	AMY	ANNE
001	BETTY	CANDICE	CAROL	COLLEEN
002	CRAIG	DAVID	ELLEN	FRED

Prime tracks

003 — Overflow track

CYLINDER 1

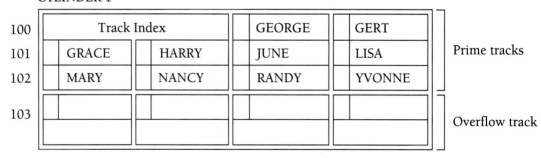

100	Track Index	GEORGE	GERT
101	GRACE	HARRY	JUNE	LISA
102	MARY	NANCY	RANDY	YVONNE

Prime tracks

103 — Overflow track

INDEPENDENT OVERFLOW AREA

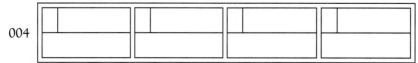

004

Figure 7 ISAM Data Organization

creates and maintains chains of overflow records for each track, thus preserving the sequential order of records in the file. The overflow index subentry for a track is created as soon as the first overflow occurs from the track.

The next index level in an ISAM file is the **cylinder index**. It consists of one entry for each cylinder and contains a cylinder number, the address of the track index for that cylinder, and the largest key value in it. The cylinder index table is created if the file requires more than one cylinder. It is stored in the first track of the first cylinder reserved for an ISAM file. Next to it is the track index of the first cylinder. For all other cylinders, track index tables are stored in their first tracks.

For large indexed files, to speed up searching, and if requested by the user, the system creates up to three levels of master index tables. A **master index table** is similar to a cylinder index table, except its entries correspond to segments of the cylinder index table. As a result of these different index tables, ISAM is a multiple-level indexed sequential organization, with a maximum of five and a minimum of two index levels. The search logic for ISAM files is described below.

Step 1: Given a search key value, first the master index tables are accessed directly and searched sequentially. If there are no master index tables, the cylinder index table is accessed and searched, and the cylinder in which the record being sought may exist is determined.

Step 2: The track index table of the indicated cylinder is directly accessed and again sequentially searched to determine the track in which the record is probably stored.

Step 3: This track is accessed by its address and its content is sequentially searched. If the track index table contains an overflow index subentry for this track, the search is extended to include the overflow areas. To do that, the system makes use of the sequence link indicators in the overflow records and accesses appropriate records in the overflow areas.

Let us illustrate this logic using the ISAM file of Figure 7. Suppose our search key value is NANCY.

1. We enter the cylinder index table, and access its first entry. On comparison, we conclude that, as NANCY > FRED, our target cannot be in cylinder zero.
2. We access the second entry of the cylinder index table. As NANCY < YVONNE, it should be in cylinder 1. The track index address for cylinder 1 is 100.
3. We access location 100 and get the track index table. We sequentially process it and compare the search key with the largest key value in each track. After three accesses, we conclude that the target should be in track 102.
4. Finally, we access track 102 and search its content to locate NANCY as the second record.

ISAM files can also be processed sequentially, in ascending order of the organization key, starting from the beginning of the file or any point in it. For this, first the cylinder index is accessed, and the address of the first track index is found. Then, in view of the overflow index subentries in the track index table, records in the corresponding cylinder are sequentially accessed. All remaining cylinders are similarly processed until the end of file is reached.

Maintenance of ISAM Files

Before an ISAM file can be created, the user must specify the following parameters for the physical file through appropriate job control language statements.

1. Size of prime data area, in number of tracks
2. Size of cylinder overflow areas, in number of tracks
3. Size of independent overflow area, in number of tracks
4. Whether or not master index tables are requested
5. Record length
6. Record format
7. Record key length

These specifications will cause the system to allocate a fixed-size storage segment for the ISAM file. This storage segment is referred to as a **cluster**. That an ISAM cluster is of fixed size means that once created, an ISAM file cannot be extended beyond the storage available in the prime and overflow data areas.

Next, the file is loaded with records, either interactively or in batch mode. Certain implementations require that the records be input in increasing order of the organization key. It should be noted that record key values must be distinct, that is, they should not repeat for more than one record in the file. During file loading, records are placed in prime data areas of the available cylinders, as the overflow areas cannot be used for record storage. After all records have been loaded, track index tables and, if the file requires more than one cylinder, a cylinder index table are generated. The initial configuration of an ISAM file created this way is shown in Figure 7.

The actual size of an ISAM file is defined at the time of its initial loading. If the prime data area is not filled during initial loading, the unused portion cannot be used for overflow records or for records that may be added subsequently after creation. However, it is possible to reserve space for later use in the prime area by writing dummy records at the end of the file during creation. A **dummy record** is identified by a special marker flag in its first byte. In some implementations, this special marker is the bit string 11111111. The application programmer may create dummy records in the program and write them after the last actual record has been written into the file.

The ISAM file management system treats dummy records somewhat differently. As we will see, during file maintenance, if they are pushed off a prime track, dummy records are not allowed to go to an overflow area. Also, during sequential processing of the file, they are identified and ignored.

Record deletion and insertion are two basic file maintenance operations that may alter the index structures in an ISAM file and eventually influence its performance characteristics. For these reasons, we study them briefly.

Record Deletion. The delete operation in an ISAM file is a logical delete. When a record identified by its unique key value is specified for deletion in an application program, the ISAM system accesses it and flags it as deleted by placing a specific bit string, such as 11111111, in its first byte. Thus, the record becomes a dummy record. A dummy record, or a deleted record, will remain in the file until it is pushed off the track because of subsequent record insertions into its home track.

Let us assume that Figure 7 is the initial configuration of an ISAM file consisting of two cylinders, a one-track independent overflow area, a one-track cylinder overflow area, two and one-half tracks of prime data area per cylinder, and a track capacity of four logical records. The figure shows the file after it has been loaded with 20 records. Suppose an application program requests deletion of records for CAROL, ANNE, NANCY, and RANDY, in that order. Each record will be accessed and rendered dummy records, as shown in Figure 8a. So far, none of the index tables are affected.

CYLINDER INDEX TABLE

Cylinder Number	Highest Key	Address of Track Index
0	FRED	000
1	YVONNE	100

TRACK INDEX TABLES

Address of Track Index	Prime Index		Overflow Index	
	Key	Address	Key	Address
000	ANNE	000	—	—
000	COLLEEN	001	—	—
000	FRED	002	—	—
100	GERT	100	—	—
100	LISA	101	—	—
100	YVONNE	102	—	—

For cyl. 0: rows with address 000
For cyl. 1: rows with address 100

CYLINDER 0

000	Track Index		AMY	D	ANNE
001	BETTY	CANDICE	D CAROL		COLLEEN
002	CRAIG	DAVID	ELLEN		FRED
003					

Prime tracks (000–002), Overflow track (003)

CYLINDER 1

100	Track Index		GEORGE		GERT
101	GRACE	HARRY	JUNE		LISA
102	MARY	D NANCY	D RANDY		YVONNE
103					

Prime tracks (100–102), Overflow track (103)

INDEPENDENT OVERFLOW AREA

004				

D : Delete marker

Figure 8a ISAM Maintenance: Delete CAROL, ANNE, NANCY, RANDY

Record Insertion. A record to be inserted must be specified by its key value. The ISAM record insertion logic works as follows.

Step 1:   A search is initiated using the supplied key value. If there is another record with the same identifier, the insertion request will be rejected. Otherwise, ISAM locates the point of insertion for the new record.

Step 2:   If the record to be inserted has a key value that is larger than the key value of the last record in some track but smaller than that of the first record key value in the next track, the new record is stored in the cylinder overflow area, and an overflow chain for this track will be created.

Step 3:   If, however, the point of insertion is within a track, all records to the right of the point of insertion are moved to the right by one record length, and the new record is accommodated in the prime track. This causes the last record in that track to be pushed off the track.

Step 4:   If the record that is pushed off the track is a dummy record, it will not be stored in the overflow area and will vanish. This is the only way of deleting records physically in ISAM. As is seen, ISAM physical record deletion is under neither the user's nor the system's control.

Step 5:   If it is not a dummy record, it will be pushed into the cylinder overflow area, and an overflow chain for the track will be either created or updated. In case the cylinder overflow area is full, the system will try to store it in the independent overflow area. After the record is stored, the index entries will be updated appropriately.

Step 6:   If no overflow areas have been defined, or if both the cylinder and the independent overflow areas are full, even though space may be available in the other cylinder prime or overflow areas, the file will be considered to be full to capacity, and the insertion request will be denied.

Figure 8b exemplifies the above principles. Suppose we insert four records identified by the key values ALAN, BAYES, DALE, and JERRY, in that order, into the file of Figure 8a. The following will happen. First, the point of insertion for ALAN is to the left of AMY in track 000, cylinder zero. This insertion pushes ANNE off the track. But, because ANNE has been previously deleted, its record will vanish. Second, BAYES will be stored as the first record in track 001, cylinder zero. This will cause the last record in that track, that is, COLLEEN, to be pushed off the track and into the overflow track 003. An overflow index subentry for track 001 is generated to include COLLEEN as the key value of the first overflow record, and 003-1 as the location of the last overflow record for that track. The notation 003-1 denotes the first record in track 003.

The remaining insertions are handled similarly. Figure 8c shows the schema of the ISAM file after three additional insertions, EILEEN, EMMA, and ERIN. These insertions will cause the overflow track for cylinder zero to become full. After this, the system will make use of the independent overflow area to accommodate the overflows, including those from any cylinder overflow area.

ISAM File Deterioration and Reorganization

The ISAM implementation of indexed sequential file organization has three major disadvantages. (1) New record insertions into a particular cylinder may not be accommodated if that cylinder's overflow area and the independent overflow area are full, even when space exists in the other cylinders. (2) If there are many insertions into an ISAM file such that they fall into the same prime area track, the overflow chain for such a track may become too long and consequently, the search efficiency may deteriorate. (3) The number of logically

CYLINDER INDEX TABLE

Cylinder Number	Highest Key	Address of Track Index
0	FRED	000
1	YVONNE	100

TRACK INDEX TABLES

Address of Track Index	Prime Index		Overflow Index	
	Key	Address	Key	Address
000	AMY	000	——	——
000	CAROL	001	COLLEEN	003-1
000	ELLEN	002	FRED	003-2
100	GERT	100	——	——
100	JUNE	101	LISA	103-1
100	YVONNE	102	——	——

For cyl. 0 — rows with address 000
For cyl. 1 — rows with address 100

CYLINDER 0

000	Track Index		ALAN	AMY
001	BAYES	BETTY	CANDICE	D CAROL
002	CRAIG	DALE	DAVID	ELLEN

Prime tracks

003	COLLEEN	FRED		
	*	*		

Overflow track

CYLINDER 1

100	Track Index		GEORGE	GERT
101	GRACE	HARRY	JERRY	JUNE
102	MARY	D NANCY	D RANDY	YVONNE

Prime tracks

103	LISA			
	*			

Overflow track

INDEPENDENT OVERFLOW AREA

004

D : Delete marker
* : End-of-chain marker

Figure 8b ISAM Maintenance: Add ALAN, BAYES, DALE, JERRY

CYLINDER INDEX TABLE

Cylinder Number	Highest Key	Address of Track Index
0	FRED	000
1	YVONNE	100

TRACK INDEX TABLES

Address of Track Index	Prime Index		Overflow Index	
	Key	Address	Key	Address
000	AMY	000		
000	CAROL	001	COLLEEN	003-1
000	EILEEN	002	FRED	003-2
100	GERT	100	——	——
100	JUNE	101	LISA	103-1
100	YVONNE	102	——	——

For cyl. 0 — rows with address 000
For cyl. 1 — rows with address 100

CYLINDER 0

000	Track Index		ALAN		AMY	
001	BAYES	BETTY	CANDICE	D	CAROL	
002	CRAIG	DALE	DAVID		EILEEN	
003	COLLEEN	FRED	ELLEN		EMMA	
	*	*	003-4		004-1	

Prime tracks (001, 002)
Overflow track (003)

CYLINDER 1

100	Track Index		GEORGE		GERT	
101	GRACE	HARRY	JERRY		JUNE	
102	MARY	D NANCY	D RANDY		YVONNE	
103	LISA					
	*					

Prime tracks (101, 102)
Overflow track (103)

INDEPENDENT OVERFLOW AREA

004	ERIN			
	003-2			

D : Delete marker
* : End-of-chain marker

Figure 8c ISAM Maintenance: Add EILEEN, EMMA, ERIN

deleted records may become excessive. As the storage occupied by such records cannot be released at will by the programmer, the ability to insert new records will be impeded, and the overall file performance will become sluggish in time.

To overcome these shortcomings temporarily, ISAM files must be reorganized occasionally. This requires copying them onto another tape or disk file and reloading the file. File reloading causes all records to be stored in the prime data area and all index tables to be regenerated.

REVIEW QUESTIONS

1. The direct access storage reserved for an ISAM file consists of _____ , _____ , and _____ areas.
2. Which of the following about the ISAM data organization is correct?
   a. Records are identified by a key field.
   b. Records in the prime data area are stored consecutively, in increasing order of their organization key values.
   c. A cylinder in ISAM consists of prime area tracks, overflow tracks, and a cylinder index.
   d. All of the above are correct.
3. For each cylinder in an ISAM file, an independent overflow area is reserved. (T or F)
4. The ISAM index area consists of _____ , _____ , and _____ index tables.
5. An overflow index subentry consists of the key value of the first record that has overflowed from a track and the address of the overflow record that has most recently been pushed off that track. (T or F)
6. ISAM is a multiple-level indexed sequential organization. (T or F)
7. Before an ISAM file can be created, which of the following parameters should be specified using job control language statements?
   a. Size of prime data, cylinder overflow, and independent overflow areas in number of tracks
   b. Whether or not master index tables are requested
   c. Record length, record format, and key length
   d. All of the above
8. The fixed-size storage segment allocated by the ISAM system for an ISAM file is called a _____ .
9. In inserting a record into an ISAM file, the operation will be rejected if the cylinder overflow area in which the new record belongs is full. (T or F)
10. ISAM files must be reorganized periodically, since they may become sluggish due to an excessive amount of logically deleted records. (T or F)

Answers: 1. prime data, overflow, index; 2. d; 3. F; 4. track, cylinder, master; 5. T; 6. T; 7. d; 8. cluster; 9. F; 10. T.

Structure of VSAM/KSDS Implementation

As discussed above, the main weakness of IBM's ISAM relates to record addition. Also, ISAM relies on the concepts of cylinder and track as it builds cylinder and track index tables. Therefore, it is somewhat device dependent. To alleviate these shortcomings, newer and better file management systems have been developed. One of them is IBM's VSAM.

VSAM is more extensive in its scope than ISAM. It supports three file organization techniques: entry sequence data set (ESDS), keyed sequence data set (KSDS), and relative record data set (RRDS).

The file organization technique known as ESDS is similar to the sequential file organization and access method discussed in Chapter 11. The KSDS is the counterpart of ISAM, or the COBOL indexed file organization technique. The RRDS enables record access by relative record number, and is the basis of the relative file organization and access technique in COBOL. We will study this technique in Chapter 14. Here, our emphasis is on the KSDS component of VSAM.

VSAM/KSDS Data Organization

In all VSAM file organization modes, data records are stored in a segment of the DASD called the **data area**. In addition to it, in KSDS access mode, VSAM creates and maintains an **index area**.

Data and index area for an indexed sequential VSAM file are collectively referred to as a **base cluster**. After a VSAM/KSDS base cluster is created and at least partially loaded, it is possible to generate alternate index clusters for it. Similar to base clusters, each **alternate index cluster** may consist of a data area and an index area.

Base Cluster Data Area. The basic building block of a VSAM file is the **control interval (CI)**. Control intervals are used for data and index areas, but their respective structures are different. As shown in Figure 9a, the CI for the data area consists of a number of logical data records, free space, one record descriptor field for each logical record, and a control interval descriptor field. The **record descriptor field (RDF)** stores pointers to logical records in the control interval.

VSAM supports three record format types: fixed-length, variable-length, and spanned. For fixed-length records and records that span over CI boundaries, each CI has only two record descriptor fields. For variable-length records, a CI contains one record descriptor field for each logical record.

Finally, each CI has one **control interval descriptor field (CIDF)**. This field contains information about available space, in bytes, within the control interval.

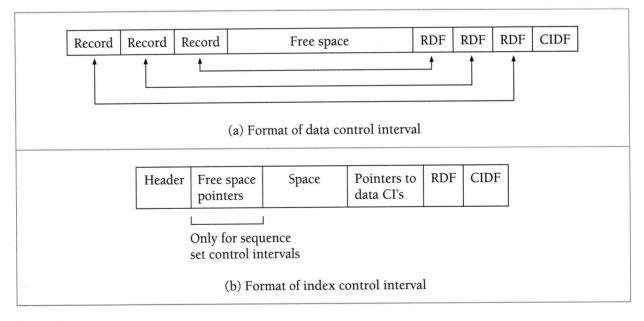

(a) Format of data control interval

(b) Format of index control interval

Figure 9 VSAM Control Interval Structures

Another storage concept that is applicable only in VSAM/KSDS is that of control areas (CA). A **control area** is simply a logical group of control intervals. Its size in terms of control intervals partially depends on the device type, but it never exceeds the capacity of a cylinder. As is seen, control area and control interval concepts in VSAM are somewhat analogous to the ISAM cylinder and track concepts, respectively; however, they are not as hardware oriented. Control areas in VSAM/KSDS are principally used as allocation units for free space during file loading or record insertion. At file creation time, VSAM can be instructed to reserve part of the available storage in a base cluster as the free space. The free space is requested in terms of a certain number of control areas, some control intervals in each control area, and a percentage of storage in each control interval. The purpose of free space is to provide for future file expansion.

Base Cluster Index Area. VSAM creates index entries for both KSDS and ESDS access modes. For entry sequenced data sets, an index area may or may not be created, but for keyed sequence data sets, VSAM always generates one. The index entries for these two modes are different. We are concerned only with the one for keyed sequence data sets.

The VSAM/KSDS index structure is essentially a multiple-level index of B-tree type. The lowest level is known as the **sequence set**, and the other levels as the **index set**. The sequence set makes up an index control interval for each data control area. The highest-level element of the index set consists of a single index record.

The structure of index control intervals is shown in Figure 9b. An index CI consists of the following fields:

1. A header field
2. Free space pointers
3. A free space for this index CI
4. Pointers to control intervals that contain data
5. A record descriptor field
6. A control interval descriptor field

The header field contains information about the length of the index record, length of pointers to free space in the data CIs, a horizontal pointer, index level number, and so on. A horizontal pointer links this index CI to the next CI on the same index level. Horizontal pointers are useful for sequential access and retrieval of records in VSAM/KSDS files.

The free space pointers point to free data control intervals in the control area monitored by this index CI. Free space pointers exist only in the index CIs at the sequence set level. The pointers to control intervals that contain data actually consist of a unique key value that is the largest key value in a data CI within a CA, a pointer to that CI, length of key, and other information.

In summary, index CIs for the sequence set contain vertical pointers to the occupied data CIs, vertical pointers to the empty data CIs, and horizontal pointers. Index CIs for the index set do not include vertical pointers to the empty lower-level index CIs, because VSAM does not create empty index CIs.

Alternate Index Clusters. As we have seen, the VSAM/KSDS index structure is based on a unique key field in the record structure, and permits access-by-content of that key field. In a VSAM file, key field values cannot be duplicated and the key field should be chosen accordingly. For example, in a personnel file, the social security number ensures uniqueness and can be used as the VSAM record key field.

Quite frequently in data processing, accessing records by other field values may be required. For example, it may be necessary to retrieve records in a personnel file by age, as in, "Get all personnel names whose ages are in the range of 25 through 35." This type of retrieval is termed **secondary key retrieval**, and is the most important and challenging retrieval and search problem in the nonassociative computer architecture. In such cases, depending on whether or not the retrieval key satisfies the property of uniqueness, more than one record may be retrieved. To facilitate secondary key retrieval, additional index structures have to be built and maintained.

VSAM offers a facility for secondary key retrieval through alternate indexing. An **alternate index** allows access-by-content based on any field in the record structure. In fact, in VSAM it is a cluster that may consist of a data area and an index area. The data area of an alternate index cluster for a VSAM/KSDS is composed of entries that associate alternate key values with the corresponding primary key values. For example, if in a VSAM/KSDS file the primary key field is employee name, and an alternate index based on age is built, a typical alternate index data area entry would look like:

28	DAVID

When an alternate key value such as 28 for age is specified in an application program, VSAM first enters the index area of the alternate index cluster for age and eventually accesses the above data area entry. Then, using DAVID as the primary key value, it enters the KSDS cluster and retrieves the record. This access path is depicted in Figure 10.

VSAM is capable of building and maintaining any number of alternate index structures for a VSAM/KSDS file. As each alternate index structure is a cluster, however, the number is limited by the available direct-access storage.

VSAM Catalog

In addition to clusters for data files, the VSAM system makes use of a VSAM catalog that is a special-purpose cluster also maintained in direct-access storage. The VSAM catalog stores the metadata for the system. **Metadata** is information about data in all user files and data spaces under VSAM's control.

The VSAM catalog contains the following information about user files:

1. File name
2. Location in direct-access memory
3. VSAM access mode (i.e., ESDS, KSDS, or RRDS)
4. Record length and key length
5. Access password for protected files
6. Physical extents of data sets
7. Statistical information about data sets, (e.g., number of records read, deleted, or inserted, number of records in the file, etc.)
8. Information about data spaces

The VSAM catalog consists of two components: a single **master catalog** for each installation, and any number of **user catalogs**. Master and user catalogs are KSDS type VSAM data sets, and have similar structures and functions, with one difference. The master catalog has access to and control over all user catalogs, whereas a user catalog controls only the clusters and data spaces defined for it. A master catalog is required whenever a VSAM cluster is generated. User catalogs are optional.

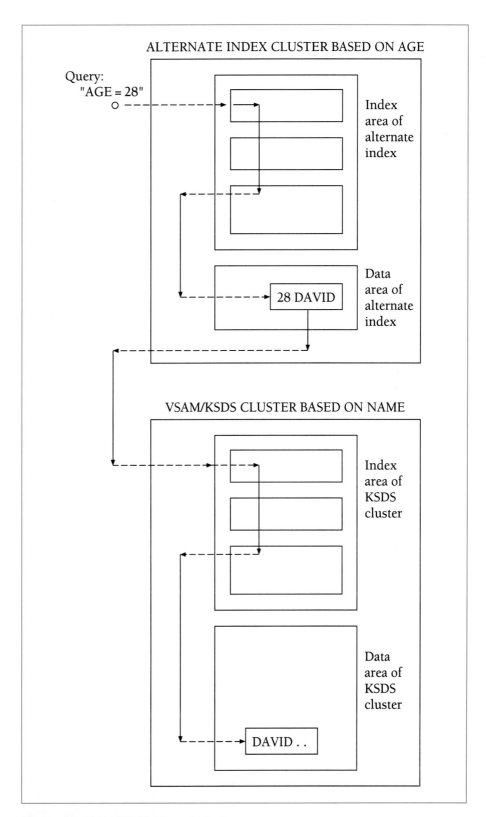

Figure 10 VSAM/KSDS Alternate Index

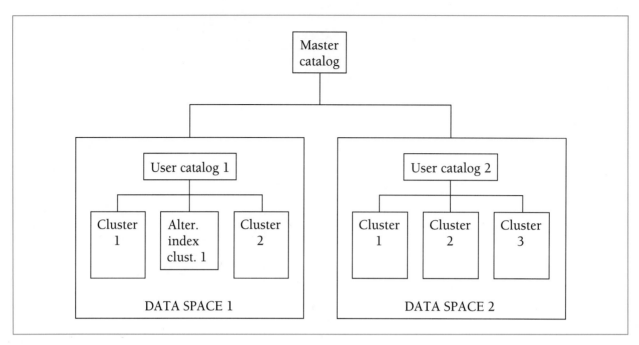

Figure 11 Overall Structure of the VSAM System

The overall structure of a VSAM system is shown in Figure 11 in terms of catalogs, clusters, and data spaces. As shown, the control structure is hierarchical. The master catalog controls all user catalogs and data spaces. A user catalog, on the other hand, enables access only to the clusters and alternate index clusters in its data space.

Although user catalogs are optional, their use is strongly recommended for two reasons. First, if no user catalogs have been defined, all pointers to clusters will be included in the master catalog. This will make the master catalog a large KSDS cluster, and may eventually degrade the overall system performance as the volume of the VSAM system for an installation becomes large. Second, and more significant, if the master catalog is damaged due to a system failure, all VSAM data clusters will be lost. If user catalogs are maintained, after a possible system failure that may result in a damaged master catalog one can still access the user catalogs and recover the data clusters.

VSAM Access Method Services

A set of utility programs are provided as part of the VSAM system to enable users to generate and use its features. These utilities are collectively referred to as **access method services (AMS)**. They are invoked by appropriate job control language statements. Then, AMS control statements are executed to create, maintain, and use VSAM catalogs and data clusters.

Many AMS control statement types can be combined together to form VSAM command language programs. Such programs are compiled and executed by the VSAM system to perform their specific functions. Some of the important AMS control statements are given in the following table, together with their functions. Other AMS statements and their optional or required parameters are outside the scope of our discussion. For these, the reader should consult the technical manuals supplied by the vendor.

AMS Command	Function
DEFINE MASTERCATALOG	Defines the VSAM master catalog
DEFINE USERCATALOG	Defines user catalogs
DEFINE SPACE	Defines space or acquires additional space
DEFINE CLUSTER/DATA/INDEX	Defines user clusters, their data, and index areas
DEFINE ALTERNATEINDEX	Defines alternate index clusters
DEFINE PATH	Defines a VSAM path, which is a relationship between an alternate index and its base cluster (a VSAM path does not occupy data space but is stored in the catalog)
BLDINDEX	Creates an alternate index cluster after it has been properly defined and at least partially loaded
REPRO	Copies VSAM clusters, loads clusters, merges two VSAM files, copies catalogs, reorganizes VSAM data sets
LISTCAT	Lists cluster entries, data entries, index entries, alternate index entries, and so on
DELETE	Deletes clusters, alternate index clusters, master catalog, spaces, user catalogs, and so on
ALTER	Modifies definitions of VSAM objects

Maintenance of VSAM/KSDS Files

Earlier we mentioned that VSAM is an improvement on the older ISAM system because it facilitates maintenance by adding records to existing indexed files. It has other advantages, some of which pertain to file maintenance.

Before a VSAM file can be loaded, it should be created using the AMS DEFINE CLUSTER command. In such a command the programmer should specify, among other parameters, the following:

1. Initial space to be allocated for data and index areas of the cluster
2. Dynamic secondary allocation for the cluster in case initial space becomes insufficient
3. Size of control intervals
4. Amount of free space to be left in control intervals and control areas
5. Length and location of the key within a data record structure

After a cluster is properly defined, we can write a program in a high-level language such as COBOL to load the file with records. VSAM distributes records in the control intervals of the prime data area evenly, without using the free space in CIs. In each CI and CA, records are in increasing order of the record key values. After this, the sequence set and index set components of the index area are created.

Figure 12a is a simplified instance of a VSAM data cluster. In this figure, we assume that the logical records are uniquely identified by employee first names. (In a real application there would definitely be other data fields in addition to

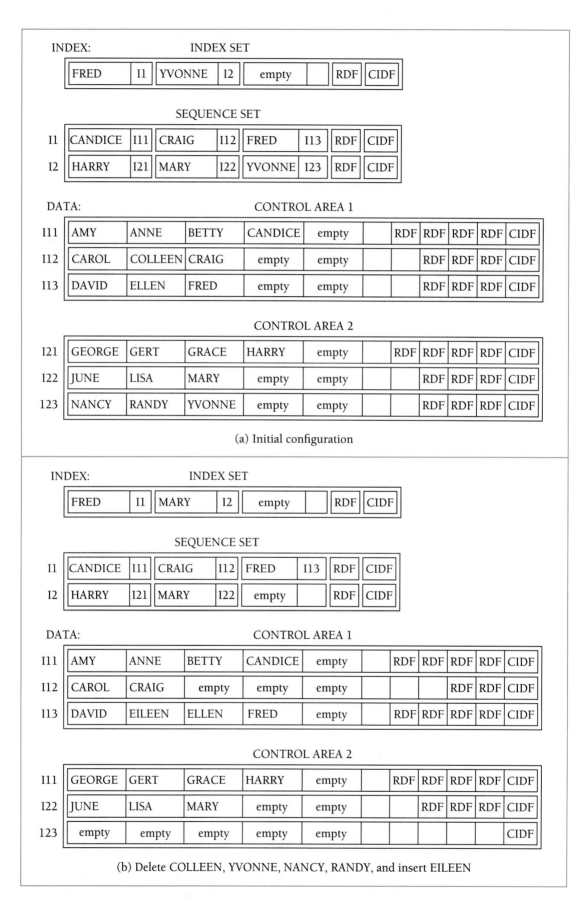

(a) Initial configuration

(b) Delete COLLEEN, YVONNE, NANCY, RANDY, and insert EILEEN

Figure 12 VSAM Data Maintenance

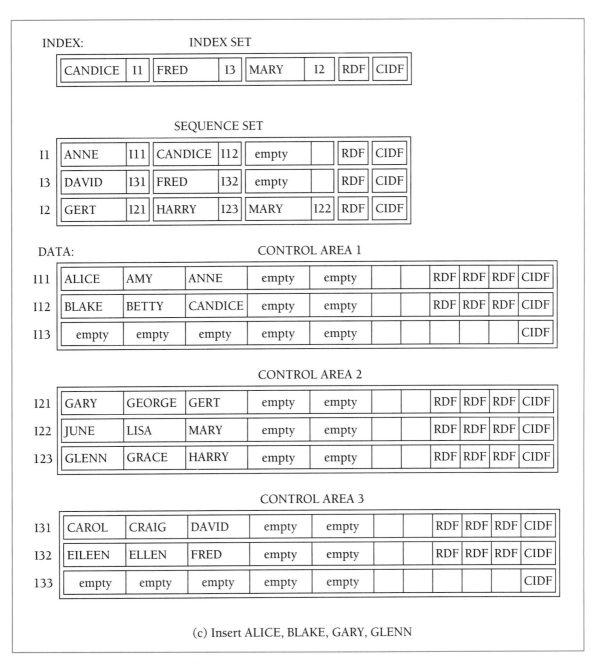

(c) Insert ALICE, BLAKE, GARY, GLENN

Figure 12 (Continued)

first names. Here, for simplification, we are using first names to represent data records.) Also, we assume that initially we have two control areas in the data area, each consisting of three control intervals, and that the maximum capacity of control intervals is five logical records. It should be noted that the instance shown in Figure 12a does not necessarily correspond to the instance of the file immediately after loading.

For each CA in the data area, VSAM creates a set of index entries and stores them in a control interval in the index area. There will be one sequence set CI for each data area CA in the index area. The sequence set index entries combine the largest key value in each data area CI with the address of that CI.

Finally, VSAM creates an index set based on the sequence set. The index set entries are combinations of the largest key values in a data area CA and the address of the corresponding sequence set CI.

Given a search key, the search logic for VSAM is as follows.

Step 1:   Enter the index set CIs and process them sequentially until an index entry is located such that its key value is larger than the search key.
Step 2:   Using the associated control interval address, access directly the appropriate sequence set CI.
Step 3:   Search the sequence set CIs sequentially until an index entry is found such that its key value is larger than the search key.
Step 4:   Using the control interval address thus found, directly access it in the data area.
Step 5:   Search that CI sequentially to retrieve the requested record.

Record Deletion. Records to be deleted are specified by their keys in a proper DELETE statement in an application program. Such records are found and are physically deleted by shifting records to the left in their data area CIs. This releases storage and increases the control interval free space. If the physically last record is deleted in a CI or CA, the corresponding sequence set and index set index entries are updated by the VSAM system.

Figure 12b shows the instance of the example cluster of Figure 12a after the records for COLLEEN, YVONNE, NANCY, and RANDY have been deleted, and a new record for EILEEN has been inserted.

Record Insertion. The record insertion logic for VSAM/KSDS files is somewhat more complicated.

Step 1:   The system accesses the index area and the data area of the KSDS cluster and ensures that there is no record with the same key value as that of the record to be inserted.
Step 2:   It determines the point of insertion for the new record in the data area. If free space is available in the CI into which the record can be inserted, all records after the point of insertion are moved to the right, the new record is accommodated in the CI at the point of insertion, and the RDFs and CIDF in the CI are updated. If the record just inserted is physically the last one in the CI or CA, the corresponding index entries in the index area are also updated.
Step 3:   If there is no free space in the CI into which insertion can be made, one of two phenomena will occur.
   a.   If there is an empty CI in the same control area, a **control interval split** takes place. The content of the full CI is evenly divided between itself and the empty CI.
   b.   If there is no totally empty CI in the control area, VSAM causes a **control area split**. A new and empty control area is claimed for the cluster, and the contents of the overflowing CA are evenly divided among the original and the newly acquired CAs. The index area entries are updated to reflect the new instance of the cluster.

Figure 12c illustrates these concepts. It shows the final configuration of the KSDS cluster after records for ALICE, BLAKE, GARY, and GLENN are inserted into the cluster of Figure 12b. Let us consider the insertions one at a time.

1. ALICE can be accommodated in the control interval I11 of control area 1 because it has free space for one record.
2. After this, however, BLAKE cannot be inserted into the control interval I11. As there is no completely empty CI in the control area 1, a control area split takes place. A new control area, control area 3, is acquired, and the present

contents of CA 1 together with BLAKE are evenly distributed between CA 1 and CA 3.

3. GARY can be inserted into the control interval I21 of CA 2 without causing a split of any kind.
4. GLENN, however, causes a control interval split in CA 2. Before its insertion, the control interval I23 has been empty. As I21, the newcomer's home control interval, is full, the entire content of the control interval I21, together with GLENN, is distributed between I21 and I23.

Advantages of VSAM/KSDS

Both VSAM/KSDS and ISAM files are essentially similar implementations of indexed file organization. VSAM is more versatile than ISAM in that, in addition to indexed organization, it supports other file organization techniques (i.e., ESDS and RRDS). In addition, VSAM has several other advantages over ISAM.

ISAM is a more device-oriented implementation than VSAM. Its organization is in terms of cylinders and tracks that clearly point to disk storage. VSAM is more flexible in that control intervals and control areas are basically direct-access storage segments. A control area in a VSAM cluster can be one or more cylinders, and a control interval can be a portion of a track. Therefore, disk storage is not necessarily the only device type for VSAM files.

File deterioration and reorganization are not as serious problems for VSAM as they are for ISAM. We have seen that VSAM can handle record insertions efficiently and elegantly without creating chains of excessive length. In general, a VSAM file has to be reorganized if it shows an unanticipated growth in size, and the space initially allocated for it becomes insufficient.

VSAM/KSDS clusters permit alternate indexing. This is a significant feature, as secondary key retrieval is a frequent requirement in data processing. In general, it is possible to construct index tables for a direct access file to facilitate secondary key retrieval. Chapter 15 deals with this issue. Without an alternate indexing feature as in VSAM, the burden of constructing and maintaining necessary index tables lies with the application programmer. In this respect, VSAM offers a great deal of convenience. VSAM has many other features that are outside the scope of our discussion.

REVIEW QUESTIONS

1. Compared to ISAM, VSAM is less device dependent because it is not based on cylinders and tracks, but uses control areas and control intervals. (T or F)
2. VSAM supports three file organization techniques: _____, _____, and _____ data sets.
3. In a VSAM/KSDS, data and index areas constitute a _____ .
4. Which of the following concerning the base cluster data area in a VSAM/KSDS is correct?
   a. The basic building block is a control interval.
   b. A control interval consists of logical records, free space, a record descriptor field for each record, and a control interval descriptor field.
   c. The control interval descriptor field contains information about available space within a control interval.
   d. A control area is a logical group of control intervals.
   e. All of the above are correct.
5. The VSAM/KSDS base index area structure is essentially the same as a _____ .
6. Secondary key retrieval in a VSAM/KSDS is possible through alternate index clusters. (T or F)

7. The metadata for a VSAM system is stored in the _____, which consists of a single _____ and any number of _____ .
8. Although VSAM user catalogs are optional, they are recommended because they facilitate data recovery in case the master catalog is damaged. (T or F)
9. In VSAM, record deletion is physical and is accomplished by shifting records to the left in their data area control intervals. (T or F)
10. In a VSAM/KSDS, a control interval split takes place if no free space is available in the control interval into which a record is to be inserted, and if there is an empty control interval in the control area. (T or F)
11. VSAM files deteriorate as rapidly as ISAM files and therefore require frequent reorganization. (T or F)

Answers: 1. T; 2. entry sequence, keyed sequence, relative record; 3. base cluster; 4. e; 5. B-tree; 6. T; 7. VSAM catalog, master catalog, user catalogs; 8. T; 9. T; 10. T; 11. F.

COBOL Language Features for Indexed Sequential Files

Before we begin our discussion of COBOL input and output instructions for indexed sequential files, we should mention that the underlying indexed file implementation technique (ISAM, VSAM, or any other file management system supporting the indexed organization) is essentially transparent to the application programmer. Only a few features of the implementation are reflected in the language instructions, and we stress them as we encounter them.

Defining Indexed Sequential Files

Like any other file, an indexed sequential file in a COBOL program should be defined in the ENVIRONMENT DIVISION and DATA DIVISION, FILE SECTION. The FILE SECTION specifications for indexed files are similar to those for sequential files.

In the ENVIRONMENT DIVISION, compared to sequential files, the differences for indexed files are with respect to

1. File organization specification
2. File access mode specification
3. Primary organization key specification
4. The optional alternate key specifications (for a file management system such as VSAM, supporting alternate index clusters)

The ENVIRONMENT DIVISION of the program must have one SELECT statement for each indexed file. A SELECT statement is syntactically composed of

1. The key word SELECT
2. The internal file name
3. ASSIGN TO, followed by an external file name
4. The ORGANIZATION IS INDEXED clause
5. An optional ACCESS MODE clause
6. The RECORD KEY clause, referencing a data name in the record structure, to serve as the organization key
7. One or more optional ALTERNATE RECORD KEY clauses, each containing a data name in the record structure and an optional WITH DUPLICATES subclause
8. An optional FILE STATUS clause referencing a data name defined in the WORKING-STORAGE SECTION

The following is an example.

```
SELECT PERSONNEL-FILE
    ASSIGN               TO INFILE
    ORGANIZATION         IS INDEXED
    ACCESS MODE          IS RANDOM
    RECORD KEY           IS EMPLOYEE-NUMBER
    ALTERNATE RECORD KEY IS EMPLOYEE-AGE WITH DUPLICATES
    ALTERNATE RECORD KEY IS DEPARTMENT-CODE WITH DUPLICATES
    FILE STATUS          IS PERSONNEL-FILE-STATUS.
```

A COBOL indexed file can be defined to access its records in three modes: sequential, random, and dynamic. If for an indexed file ACCESS MODE IS SEQUENTIAL is specified, this file can be accessed only sequentially in the program in ascending order of the primary key. Sequential access mode is the default mode. If the ACCESS MODE clause is missing from a SELECT statement, the system will assume a sequential access mode.

A direct (or random)-access mode specification is made possible by the clause ACCESS MODE IS RANDOM. This implies that records in the file will be accessed directly by their primary or alternate key values, if specified, and no sequential access will be attempted for this file in the program. For random access, an appropriate record key value should be moved to the record key field, and then an input-output statement should be issued.

In an application program it may be our intention to access an indexed file sometimes in a sequential manner, and other times randomly. The file access mode should be specified as dynamic, as in ACCESS MODE IS DYNAMIC. In this case, we may open the indexed file, process it sequentially, close it, and then in the same program we may reopen it, access it randomly, and so on.

The record key should be an elementary or group item in the record structure of the file, and it should satisfy the property of uniqueness. During the creation of an indexed file, if an incoming record has a record key field value that is equal to that of a record already in the file, an error condition will be raised. If the file is a multiple-record file, the record key field should be common to all record types, albeit with different names. In case different names are used for the record key field, any one of such fields may be specified as the record key.

Alternate keys can be specified only if the underlying file management system supports alternate index clusters, as in the case of VSAM/KSDS. Alternate key fields need not be unique. In this case, the WITH DUPLICATES clause is required. Otherwise, an error condition will be raised during file loading.

The FILE STATUS option causes the system to store two-digit status codes in the file status variable. This variable should be defined in the WORKING-STORAGE SECTION of the program. If the status code value for a file is 00, it implies that processing is progressing normally and without errors. File status code variable values are generally implementation dependent, and the programmer should consult the technical reference manual for them and their meaning.

Input-Output Operations for Indexed Files

In addition to OPEN and CLOSE, COBOL provides five I-O statements for indexed files: READ, WRITE, REWRITE, DELETE, and START. The READ, WRITE, REWRITE, and DELETE statements can be used in sequential, random, or dynamic access mode, with some variations in their syntax. The START statement can be used in sequential or dynamic access mode.

The file OPEN mode depends on the I-O statement used and the file access mode. These dependencies are summarized in the table of Figure 13. The following is a discussion of the input-output statements for indexed sequential COBOL files.

WRITE Statement. There is only one syntax for the WRITE statement for indexed sequential files. It resembles the WRITE statement for sequential files except for the optional INVALID KEY clause.

COBOL 85

WRITE record-name [FROM identifier]
   [INVALID KEY imperative-statement-1]
    [NOT INVALID KEY imperative-statement-2] [END-WRITE]

An example is provided below.

```
WRITE PERSONNEL-RECORD
    FROM WS-PERS-RECORD
    INVALID KEY PERFORM ERROR-IN-OUTPUT.
```

The WRITE statement can be used during file creation to load a file with records. It can also be used to add new records to an indexed file any time after

I-O STATEMENT	FILE ACCESS MODE	PERMISSIBLE FILE OPEN MODES
WRITE	SEQUENTIAL	OUTPUT
	RANDOM	OUTPUT, I-O
	DYNAMIC	OUTPUT, I-O
READ	SEQUENTIAL	INPUT, I-O
	RANDOM	INPUT, I-O
	DYNAMIC	INPUT, I-O
REWRITE	SEQUENTIAL	I-O
	RANDOM	I-O
	DYNAMIC	I-O
DELETE	SEQUENTIAL	I-O
	RANDOM	I-O
	DYNAMIC	1-O
START	SEQUENTIAL	INPUT, I-O
	RANDOM	Not Applicable
	DYNAMIC	INPUT, I-O

Figure 13 Dependencies of I-O Statements and File Open Modes for COBOL Indexed Files

its creation. If for reasons explained below the output operation is unsuccessful, an invalid key condition is raised. In this case, provided the WRITE statement includes an INVALID KEY clause, the content of that clause is executed. Before a WRITE statement can be executed, the programmer should make sure that the primary key field and the alternate key fields contain supplied values in the record structure of the file.

The WRITE statement can be used to load a file with records. In this case, the file open mode should be OUTPUT, and the access mode should be SEQUENTIAL. Some indexed sequential file management systems require that during initial loading the records should be written in increasing order of their primary key values.

The WRITE statement can also be used to add new records to an existing indexed file. For record addition, the file open mode should be I-O and the file access mode should be RANDOM or DYNAMIC. New records will be inserted into the file at their proper logical positions.

Under the following circumstances, an output operation will fail and an invalid key condition will be raised:

1. Key order violation during loading
2. Record key duplication during insertion
3. Alternate key duplication
4. Attempting to write into a full file

Key order violation during loading: During initial file loading, the primary key value of the record that is to be written must be larger than the largest key value of all records already in the file. (This rule is true of some less flexible file management systems. It does not apply to VSAM/KSDS files.)

Record key duplication during insertion: When inserting a new record, the primary key value of the record to be written cannot match that of a record already existing in the file.

Alternate key duplication occurs during initial file loading or new record insertion when the alternate key value of the record to be written is equal to that of another record in the file when this is not allowed (i.e., the alternate key specification does not have the WITH DUPLICATES clause).

Attempting to write into a full file: A WRITE request cannot be accommodated when a file is full.

If the WRITE statement contains an INVALID KEY clause, its content is executed if any one of the above four conditions is met. To determine the cause of the invalid key condition, the system-generated file status code has to be examined.

READ Statement. An indexed file can be read in sequential or random access modes. Sequential input requires the exact same syntax of the READ statement for sequential files, with the exception of the NEXT clause. The syntax of this format is as follows.

COBOL 85

```
READ file-name [ NEXT ] RECORD [ INTO identifier ]
     [ AT END imperative-statement-1 ]
     [ NOT AT END imperative-statement-2 ] [ END-READ ]
```

An example is given below.

```
READ PERSONNEL-FILE RECORD
    INTO WS-PERS-RECORD
    AT END PERFORM INPUT-COMPLETED.
```

For sequential input, an indexed file should be opened in either INPUT or I-O mode. Records will be accessed and read in increasing order of their primary key values. Unless the START statement is used to point to another record in a file, the first record that will be read is the one with the smallest primary key value.

As input is sequential, no primary or alternate key value should be specified before the READ statement. Alternatively, the file access mode may be SEQUENTIAL or DYNAMIC. If the file access mode is DYNAMIC, the sequential READ requires the use of the NEXT phrase.

```
READ PERSONNEL-FILE NEXT RECORD
    INTO WS-PERS-RECORD
    AT END PERFORM INPUT-COMPLETED.
```

Random-access input requires a different syntax for the READ statement.

COBOL 85

```
READ file-name RECORD [ INTO identifier ]
     [ KEY IS data-name ]
     [ INVALID KEY imperative-statement-1 ]
     [ NOT INVALID KEY imperative-statement-2 ]
     [ END-READ ]
```

The random READ statement uses the INVALID KEY clause in lieu of the AT END clause. It also requires that a value be moved into the primary key field or one of the alternate key fields, if any, before the record is randomly accessed. Examples are as follows.

```
. . . . . . . . . . . . . . . . . . . .
ENVIRONMENT DIVISION.
. . . . . . . . . . . . . . . . . . . .
SELECT PERSONNEL-FILE
     ASSIGN              TO INFILE
     ORGANIZATION        IS INDEXED
     ACCESS              IS RANDOM
     RECORD KEY          IS EMPLOYEE-NUMBER
     ALTERNATE RECORD KEY IS EMPLOYEE-AGE WITH DUPLICATES
     ALTERNATE RECORD KEY IS DEPARTMENT-CODE WITH DUPLICATES.
. . . . . . . . . . . . . . . . . . . .
PROCEDURE DIVISION.
. . . . . . . . . . . . . . . . . . . .
```

```
***** RANDOM RETRIEVAL BY PRIMARY KEY, "EMPLOYEE-NUMBER":

    MOVE "1200" TO EMPLOYEE-NUMBER.

    READ PERSONNEL-FILE
        KEY IS EMPLOYEE-NUMBER
        INVALID KEY PERFORM ERROR-IN-INPUT.
.....................
***** RANDOM RETRIEVAL BY ALTERNATE KEY, "EMPLOYEE-AGE":

    MOVE 29 TO EMPLOYEE-AGE.

    READ PERSONNEL-FILE
        KEY IS EMPLOYEE-AGE
        INVALID KEY PERFORM ERROR-IN-INPUT.
...................
```

The first READ statement in this example directly accesses the record whose primary key value, EMPLOYEE-NUMBER, is 1200. The second READ statement accesses the record for which the alternate key value EMPLOYEE-AGE is 29. Note the use of the KEY IS clause in both cases. If during either access attempts no record can be found whose primary or alternate key value matches the supplied value, an INVALID KEY condition is raised and the procedure ERROR-IN-INPUT is executed.

For random input of an indexed file, the file should be opened in either INPUT or I-O mode. The file access mode should be either RANDOM or DYNAMIC. If access by a primary key is requested, an admissible value should be moved to the primary key field before a random READ is executed. In this case, the KEY IS clause may be missing.

If access is by an alternate key, a value should be supplied for that alternate key field. After this, a random READ can be executed. The READ statement should contain the KEY IS clause referencing the alternate key. In case the alternate key field comes with duplicates, the random READ will access the first record that is encountered satisfying the condition. If all such records are to be accessed, repetitive execution of a sequential READ statement is required after the first random record retrieval.

An invalid key condition is raised if the underlying file management system determines that the file contains no records whose primary or alternate key field value matches the supplied value for the primary or alternate key.

REWRITE Statement. The purpose of the REWRITE statement for indexed files is to update a record. Syntactically, it resembles the WRITE statement.

COBOL 85

```
REWRITE  record-name  [ FROM  identifier ]
         [ INVALID KEY  imperative-statement-1 ]
         [ NOT INVALID KEY  imperative-statement-2 ]
         [ END-REWRITE ]
```

The REWRITE statement may contain an optional INVALID KEY clause. To update a record in an indexed file, we must first access it sequentially or directly, then change any of its fields except the primary key field, and finally execute a REWRITE. For example:

```
. . . . . . . . . . . . . . . . . . . . . .
MOVE "1200" TO EMPLOYEE-NUMBER.

READ PERSONNEL-FILE
    INVALID KEY PERFORM ERROR-IN-INPUT.

MOVE "SHEILA GORDON" TO EMPLOYEE-NAME.
ADD 1 TO EMPLOYEE-AGE.
. . . . . . . . . . . . . . . . . . . . . .
REWRITE PERSONNEL-RECORD
    INVALID KEY PERFORM ERROR-IN-REWRITE.
```

In using the REWRITE statement, the file should be opened in I-O mode, as update requires reading and rewriting. The file access mode may be SEQUENTIAL or RANDOM. If it is SEQUENTIAL, a record should be accessed using the sequential READ format. After this, its fields should be modified in the record structure. Care should be exercised not to change the primary key field of the record. Finally, a REWRITE should be executed.

If the file access mode is RANDOM, a random READ should be used to access a record. An invalid key condition will be raised with REWRITE under two circumstances.

1. The primary key value of the record that has been read most recently is changed prior to rewriting.
2. An alternate key value of the record has been changed such that rewriting violates its uniqueness. This happens if the alternate key has been defined without a WITH DUPLICATES clause.

DELETE Statement. This statement is used to access a record either sequentially or directly and delete it from the file. Syntactically, the DELETE statement is defined as follows.

```
DELETE  file-name RECORD
        [ INVALID KEY imperative-statement-1 ]
        [ NOT INVALID KEY imperative-statement-2 ]  [ END-DELETE ]
```

An example is provided below.

```
. . . . . . . . . . . . . . . . . . . . . .
MOVE "1200" TO EMPLOYEE-NUMBER.

DELETE PERSONNEL-FILE
    INVALID KEY PERFORM ERROR-IN-DELETE.
```

Syntactically, DELETE is similar to READ. From a functional point of view, it is also similar to REWRITE, the major difference being that instead of rewriting, it marks the record as deleted, or as in VSAM, gets rid of the record physically. Therefore, it requires the file to be opened in I-O mode. A record can be deleted in sequential-, random-, or dynamic-access mode.

In using the DELETE statement, the file should be opened in I-O mode. If the file access mode is SEQUENTIAL, we must first execute a sequential READ followed by a DELETE. The DELETE statement will then remove the record that was read previously.

If the file access mode is RANDOM, we must first move a primary key value to the key field, and then execute a DELETE statement. The record that will be deleted is the one identified by that key value. An invalid key condition will be raised if the record to be deleted is not found in the file.

START Statement. Sometimes we may want to access an indexed file sequentially, starting not from the beginning but from a record that is elsewhere in the file. The START statement enables the programmer to mark a starting point for sequential retrieval in an indexed file. The syntax of the START statement consists of the following elements.

COBOL 85

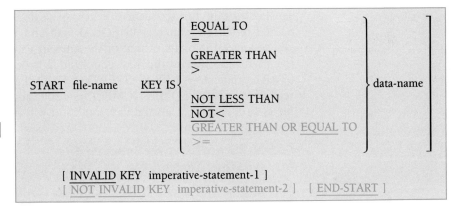

```
. . . . . . . . . . . . . . . . . . . . . . .
MOVE "1200" TO EMPLOYEE-NUMBER.

START PERSONNEL-FILE
    KEY IS GREATER THAN EMPLOYEE-NUMBER
    INVALID KEY PERFORM ERROR-IN-START.

READ PERSONNEL-FILE
    AT END MOVE "YES" TO END-OF-FILE-FLAG.
. . . . . . . . . . . . . . . . . . . . . . .
```

The START statement above locates the first record whose primary key value is larger than "1200", and the READ statement accesses that record.

Here is another example.

```
.....................
MOVE "1200" TO EMPLOYEE-NUMBER.

START PERSONNEL-FILE
   INVALID KEY PERFORM ERROR-IN-START.

READ PERSONNEL-FILE
    AT END MOVE "YES" TO END-OF-FILE-FLAG.
.....................
```

In this case, the START predicate is implicit and is equivalent to KEY IS EQUAL TO EMPLOYEE-NUMBER. Therefore, the READ statement will access the record whose primary key value is equal to "1200".

In using the START statement, the file must be opened in INPUT or I-O mode. The file access mode must be SEQUENTIAL or DYNAMIC. The START statement should be followed by a sequential READ statement.

An invalid key condition will be raised if the START predicate cannot be satisfied within the scope of the key space for the file. For example, if the START predicate contains IS EQUAL TO and there is no record in the file whose key value matches that of the current value stored in the data name in the predicate, the invalid key condition is true. As another example, if the START predicate is KEY IS GREATER THAN EMPLOYEE-NUMBER, the current value of EMPLOYEE-NUMBER is 1200, and the largest key value in the file is 1100, again an invalid key condition will be raised.

COBOL 85 Features for Indexed File Input-Output Statements

COBOL 85

The only two variations COBOL 85 offers for indexed I-O statements are the optional NOT INVALID KEY and NOT AT END clauses, and the optional right bracket key words END-READ, END-WRITE, END-REWRITE, END-DELETE, and END-START. The following examples illustrate their use.

```
READ PERSONNEL-FILE RECORD
    INTO WS-PERS-RECORD
    AT END
        PERFORM INPUT-COMPLETED
    NOT AT END
        PERFORM TRANSACTION-PROCESSING
END-READ.
.....................
.....................
MOVE "1200" TO EMPLOYEE-NUMBER.

READ PERSONNEL-FILE
   INVALID KEY
        PERFORM ERROR-IN-INPUT
   NOT INVALID KEY
        PERFORM TRANSACTION PROCESSING
END-READ.
.....................
```

1. In a SELECT statement for a COBOL indexed file, the ORGANIZATION clause is required, but the ACCESS MODE clause is optional. (T or F)
2. A COBOL indexed file has three access modes: _____, _____ , and _____ .
3. If an alternate key is to be specified for an indexed file, the WITH DUPLI-CATES subclause in the ALTERNATE RECORD KEY clause is required. (T or F)
4. The WRITE statement can be used initially to create an indexed file, but cannot be used to insert records into an indexed file. (T or F)
5. Which of the following will result in an invalid key condition while using a WRITE statement for an indexed file?
   a. Key order violation during loading
   b. Record key duplication during insertion
   c. Alternate key duplication when it is not allowed
   d. Attempting to write into a full file
   e. All of the above
6. In sequential or random input of an indexed file, the file open mode should be _____ .
7. In sequential input of an indexed file, if the file access mode is DYNAMIC, the READ statement should contain the NEXT phrase. (T or F)
8. In random input of an indexed file, the KEY IS clause in the READ state-ment is required if access is based on an alternate key. (T or F)
9. The REWRITE statement for an indexed file is used to _____ a record.
10. Before a REWRITE, we must execute either a sequential or a random READ statement. (T or F)
11. To use DELETE for an indexed file, the file should be opened in _____ mode.
12. The START statement makes it possible to access an indexed file sequen-tially starting from any point in the file. (T or F)
13. To use the START statement, the file must be opened in _____ mode, and its access mode should be _____ .

Answers: 1. T; 2. sequential, random, dynamic; 3. T; 4. F; 5. e; 6. INPUT or I-O; 7. T; 8. T; 9. update; 10. T; 11. I-O; 12. T; 13. INPUT or I-O, SE-QUENTIAL or DYNAMIC.

Example Program 1:   *Indexed Sequential File Creation and Maintenance*

Here we present a COBOL program that can be used to create and maintain an indexed sequential file. As discussed previously, some file maintenance systems require an increasing order of primary record key values during the initial cre-ation of an indexed file. IBM's VSAM system is somewhat more flexible in this respect. Using VSAM keyed sequence data sets, an indexed sequential file can be created by loading records in an arbitrary order of the primary record key values. This makes interactive loading easier on the part of the user in that no attention need be paid to the order of the incoming records. Furthermore, the operations of loading an empty file and inserting a record into a partially full file can be thought of as being identical. That is the approach we take here.

As far as the maintenance of an indexed sequential file is concerned, the ba-sic operations are record insertion, deletion, and update. In update, VSAM pro-hibits modification of the primary record key value. Therefore, we allow modification of nonkey fields only. In practice, if the primary key value has to be updated for a record, it can be achieved by deleting the old record, and subsequently inserting a new record in which the primary field key value is the new value, while all other field values are retained.

In addition to record insertion, deletion, and update we include the following capabilities in our program: direct access to a record by the primary key field value, full file listing, and partial file listing in a specified key range. Direct access to records based on alternate (or secondary) key fields is the theme of the program that is developed and discussed in the next section.

Problem   The file in this application is called PERSONNEL-FILE, and its record structure consists of the following fields:

- A 4-byte personnel identification number, PERS-ID, that will be used as the primary key for the file
- A 25-byte personnel name field, PERS-NAME
- A 3-byte department code field, named PERS-DEPT-CODE, standing for the company department with which a given employee is affiliated

The program is fully interactive as far as input is concerned. It is also menu driven. The main menu is based on a variable called FUNCTION-CODE, which may assume the following legal values.

FUNCTION-CODE	Operation
I	Insert records
D	Delete records
U	Update records
A	Directly access a record specified by primary key field value
L	Produce a full sequential listing of the file
P	Produce a partial sequential listing of the file from a specified primary key value to another primary key value
M	Display operations menu
T	Terminate program execution

Solution   Program 1-Source gives the compiler-generated listing of the COBOL program developed for the creation and maintenance of the indexed sequential PERSONNEL-FILE. Let us discuss the important features of the program relevant to the topics covered in this chapter.

1. The SELECT statement (lines 00036–00040) for PERSONNEL-FILE defines it as an indexed sequential file with a primary record key field of PERS-ID. The file access mode is specified as DYNAMIC. This is because PERSONNEL-FILE will be accessed randomly for record insertion, deletion, update, and individual record retrieval, and also within the same program, sequentially for full or partial file listing.
2. At the beginning of program execution, the program identifies itself and displays the operation menu. Then, the user is prompted to enter a value for FUNCTION-CODE. If the value entered is illegal, the user is warned, the operation menu is again displayed, and the user is advised to enter a

correct value. The operation menu can be displayed any time by supplying the value M for FUNCTION-CODE. This logic is implemented by paragraphs B1-DISPLAY-INSTRUCTIONS and C1-DISPLAY-SELECTION-MENU.

3. Before this program can be run, PERSONNEL-FILE has to be defined as a VSAM/KSDS cluster controlled by a VSAM master catalog or a user catalog. The catalogs and the cluster are created by executing DEFINE MASTERCATALOG, DEFINE USERCATALOG, and DEFINE CLUSTER access method services commands. The generated definitions are linked to our application program by some appropriate job control statements, which vary in syntax and options depending on the operating system. As far as the program is concerned, the cluster allocated for PERSONNEL-FILE may be empty or may have been filled by another application program. If the cluster is empty, our program will reveal this when asked to produce a file listing (paragraph C6-LIST-FULL-FILE, lines 00212–00225). If the cluster is full or eventually becomes full, the WORKING-STORAGE SECTION variable FILE-FULL assumes the value YES (lines 00284–00285). It is possible to modify the program so that the user is warned about this situation.

4. Records are inserted into PERSONNEL-FILE by the paragraph named D1-PROCESS-FOR-INSERTION. First, the user is prompted to enter PERS-ID, PERS-NAME, and PERS-DEPT-CODE values. Then the file is directly accessed to check if the record is already in the file (lines 00278–00279). If the record is found to exist, the user is notified and no insertion is attempted. Otherwise, a random WRITE (lines 00284–00285) is executed to insert the record. If random WRITE fails, the only reason can be that the file is full. After insertion, the user is asked either to continue with this operation or terminate insertion.

5. For record deletion, the proper logic is coded in the paragraph D2-PROCESS-FOR-DELETION. First, the user is prompted to enter the personnel identification number of the record to be deleted. Then a DELETE statement is issued (lines 00302–00303) to delete the record. In case the DELETE statement gives rise to an INVALID KEY condition, the program concludes that the record to be deleted is not in the file and informs the user. Any number of records can be deleted by the controlled loop incorporated into the program, until the user decides to terminate this operation.

6. Record update is handled by the paragraphs D3-PROCESS-FOR-UPDATE and E1-GET-NEW-DATA as follows. First the user is asked to enter the personnel identification number of the record to be updated. Then a random READ statement (lines 00322–00323) is executed to verify the existence of the record. If the record is found, the user is asked to enter new values for PERS-NAME and PERS-DEPT-CODE fields. If any of these fields is to retain its old value, the user should simply hit return when asked for a new value. After the record is formed in the memory, a REWRITE statement (lines 00327–00328) is executed to complete the update.

7. The user may wish to access a record randomly and display it. For this, the user types A for FUNCTION-CODE. Then the program passes control to the paragraph D4-DISPLAY-RECORD, which asks the user to supply the PERS-ID value of the record to be retrieved. After this, a random READ (lines 00343–00344) is executed and, if the record can be found, the field values are displayed.

8. At any time during processing a full file listing may be requested. In this case, the program control passes to the paragraph C6-LIST-FULL-FILE, in which the PERSONNEL-FILE is opened in I-O mode. If the file is opened in INPUT mode, a file listing can be produced only if there are some

records in the file. If the file is empty, the INPUT open mode results in a file-open error; hence, the I-O mode. The file is sequentially accessed using READ/NEXT statements in this paragraph (lines 00216–00217) and in the paragraph D5-PRODUCE-FULL-LISTING (lines 00363–00364), and the records are displayed on the terminal screen.

9. The paragraphs C7-LIST-PARTIAL-FILE and D6-PRODUCE-PARTIAL-LISTING are incorporated into the program to enable the user to access the file sequentially and display the records in a specified range of PERS-ID values. Paragraph C7-LIST-PARTIAL-FILE verifies the correctness of the range. Then the current record pointer is set to the first record in the range by a START statement (lines 00245–00247). After this the records are retrieved by READ/NEXT statements.

10. To terminate the program, the user should type T for FUNCTION-CODE.

Program 1-Output shows a listing of a terminal session for this program, exemplifying all of its features.

Example Program 2: *Indexed Sequential File Access*

In the sample program developed above, we demonstrated direct access for an indexed sequential file by its primary record key. Previously in this chapter we mentioned that an indexed sequential file can also be accessed by its secondary keys, also called alternate keys in the COBOL and VSAM jargon. Here, we present a program that enables the user to access an indexed sequential file by alternate record keys.

Problem The file is the same PERSONNEL-FILE as in Program 1. We assume that it is not empty. We would like to write a COBOL program that can be used to

- Access and display records directly by the primary record key PERS-ID
- Access and display records by the secondary key PERS-NAME, which is assumed to have unique field values for all records in the file
- Access and display records by the secondary key PERS-DEPT-CODE, which is a nonunique field; that is, the same field value may exist in more than one record in the file

This program is also interactive and menu driven.

Solution Program 2-Source contains the compiler-generated listing of the COBOL program written to satisfy the above requirements. We note the following.

1. The PERSONNEL-FILE is defined using a SELECT statement (lines 00037–00044) as an indexed file, with PERS-ID as the primary record key, PERS-NAME as an alternate key, and PERS-DEPT-CODE as another alternate key WITH DUPLICATES. The file access mode is DYNAMIC because access to records by PERS-ID and PERS-NAME will be random, and to records by PERS-DEPT-CODE sequential.

2. Before we can run this program, we must inform the VSAM system of our intentions and request three tasks to be performed.

   a. Two alternate index clusters, one each with respect to PERS-NAME and PERS-DEPT-CODE, should be defined for the base cluster corresponding to PERSONNEL-FILE. These definitions are made through the DEFINE ALTERNATEINDEX control command of the VSAM access method services command language.

b. Each alternate index cluster should be linked to the base cluster by a path so that VSAM can be directed through the alternate index to the base cluster during processing. This requires a DEFINE PATH control command for each alternate index cluster. DEFINE PATH is one of the commands in the AMS command language.

c. Each alternate index cluster should be created using the base cluster. For this the BLDINDEX command of VSAM/AMS is needed. It should be noted that until this point the base cluster may be empty. But before BLDINDEX can be executed, the programmer must make sure that there are some records in the base cluster.

In addition to these AMS commands, specific job control language statements are required to link the PERSONNEL-FILE to the base and alternate index clusters. After these preparations, Program 2-Source can be run. Before running it, however, it is possible to execute another application program, such as the one presented in the previous section, to insert or delete records in the base cluster. Whether or not the alternate index clusters are updated to reflect the changes in the base cluster depends on how they are defined in the DEFINE ALTERNATEINDEX and DEFINE PATH commands. For such command options, the reader is referred to the appropriate technical documentation.

3. This program has an operation menu for the variable FUNCTION-CODE. The legal values for FUNCTION-CODE are ID, NAME, and DEPT, which trigger the procedures that access records by personnel identification number, name, and department code, respectively. Also, M and T are legal values for FUNCTION-CODE, implying display operation menu and terminate program execution, respectively.

4. Record retrieval by the primary record key PERS-ID and the unique alternate key PERS-NAME are handled by paragraphs C2-PREPARE-FOR-RETRIEVAL and D1-DISPLAY-RECORD. For both types of retrieval the PERSONNEL-FILE is opened in INPUT mode, and the user is prompted to type either a PERS-ID or a PERS-NAME field value. After this, appropriate random READ statements are executed to retrieve unique records. Note the use of the KEY IS clause in the READ statements (lines 00192 and 00201). If the record is not in the file, the user is warned accordingly. Otherwise, the retrieved record is displayed.

5. Retrieval based on the alternate record key PERS-DEPT-CODE requires a different logic. Accessing the file directly by PERS-DEPT-CODE retrieves the first record encountered for which the department code is a specified value. However, we know that there may be more than one record in the file for a given department code. To retrieve and display all, we must access the file sequentially. The logic for this program branch is reflected in paragraphs C3-RETRIEVE-FOR-DEPT-CODE, D2-GET-RECORDS, and E1-DISPLAY-AND-RETRIEVE. The user is prompted to type a department code value. The PERSONNEL-FILE is opened in INPUT mode, and a START statement with the predicate KEY IS = PERS-DEPT-CODE is executed (lines 00170–00172). If the START statement fails, there is no record in the file satisfying this predicate. Otherwise, the first record is sequentially accessed (the READ/NEXT statement in lines 00220–00221) and displayed, and the remaining records are iteratively retrieved until the end of the file is encountered.

Program 2-Output shows an interactive terminal session listing for this sample retrieval program.

Key Terms

access method services	KEY IS clause
ACCESS MODE IS DYNAMIC clause	master catalog
	master index
ACCESS MODE IS RANDOM clause	metadata
access-by-address	multiple-level index file
access-by-content	NOT INVALID KEY clause
alternate index cluster	ORGANIZATION IS INDEXED clause
ALTERNATE RECORD KEY clause	
B-tree indexing	overflow area
base cluster	overflow index subentry
Boolean query	partial index
control area	prime data area
control area split	prime index subentry
control interval	range query
control interval split	READ statement
cylinder index	READ/NEXT statement
cylinder overflow area	record descriptor field
DELETE statement	RECORD KEY clause
dummy record	REWRITE statement
file reorganization	secondary key retrieval
FILE STATUS clause	sequence link indicator
independent overflow area	sequence set
index area	simple query
index file	START statement
index set	total index
index table	track index
indexed file	user catalog
indexed nonsequential organization	VSAM
indexed sequential organization	VSAM catalog
indexing	VSAM/ESDS
indexing files	VSAM/KSDS
INVALID KEY clause	VSAM/RRDS
ISAM	WRITE statement

Study Guide

Quick Scan

- In business applications, efficiently accessing records in a file by content of a field in its record structure is of paramount importance. Such access is called associative access, or access-by-content.
- The classic computer architecture is not directly amenable to associative access, as it is based on access-by-address. However, access-by-content can be simulated by defining key-to-address transformations as a layer of human–computer interface.
- The two techniques of key-to-address transformations are index tables and hash functions. This chapter concentrates on concepts and techniques of indexing.
- A direct-access file can be indexed by building and maintaining index tables that associate data field values with record addresses. For large files, index tables themselves are treated as files.
- One of the simplest indexed file organizations is indexed nonsequential. It consists of a direct-access file with the allocated direct-access storage divided into two areas: a prime data area storing records as an unordered list, and an index area containing an index table. The index table consists of index en-

tries that associate data field values of a data item in the record structure with record addresses in the prime data area. This association is one-to-one.

- A one-to-one index table is also known as a total index. A file for which a single index table is constructed is a single-level indexed file. In searching such a file, the index table is processed sequentially until the appropriate index entry is found. Then the prime area is accessed directly using the found address. Finally, the prime area is searched sequentially to retrieve the desired record.

- If the index table is excessively large, it may be feasible to construct a higher-level index table to control the total index table. This can be done by dividing the total index table into blocks of equal size and generating higher-level index tables. Each entry of the higher-level index table controls one block in the lower-level index table by associating the largest key value in the block with the smallest address value in its range. The resulting file organization is a multiple-level indexed file. The higher-level index tables are partial index tables.

- In general, searching a multiple-level indexed file is more efficient than searching its single-level counterpart.

- Another improvement on the indexed nonsequential file organization is achieved if records stored in the prime data area are maintained as an ordered list with respect to the data field on which indexing is based. The resulting organization is referred to as indexed sequential organization, and is widely used in file processing.

- It is possible further to improve the performance of indexed files by compacting index tables. One such method blocks more than one index entry into physical records of longer length in the index area. Another entails constructing index table entries that control more than one block in a subordinate area (prime data area, or a lower-level index table). The latter technique gives rise to a highly efficient indexing scheme known as B-tree indexing, which is widely used in data base applications.

- File indexing may be based on an atomic data field in the file record structure. The resulting indexed file can then be used to simulate access-by-content of that data field, and is good for applications that include simple or range queries containing the index field.

- If access-by-content of another data item in the record structure is desired, an additional index table based on that key item has to be built and maintained. If more complex queries based on multiple data fields are to be processed commonly in a data processing application, we can construct index tables based on composite data fields containing those that are included in the complex query.

- Building and maintaining indexed files are facilitated by file management systems. These are software systems that support a variety of file organization techniques. One that supports the indexed sequential file organization is capable of building and updating index tables, thereby eliminating the need to perform these tasks in application programs.

- Examples of commercially used file management systems are IBM's ISAM and the more recent VSAM.

- In the majority of file management systems, indexing is based on one selected data field. This type of indexing permits primary key retrieval. If direct retrieval based on another key is also desired (known as secondary key retrieval), indexing tasks may become the application programmer's responsibility. Secondary key indexing is supported by some file management systems, such as VSAM.

- Indexing requires substantial storage overhead and a considerable amount of maintenance effort. For these reasons, the application programmer must have a good understanding of the relevant concepts and techniques.

- IBM's ISAM is a file management technique designed to support indexed sequential files. An ISAM data space consists of a prime data area and an index area. In addition, it includes an overflow area that is used to store data records that overflow from the tracks in the prime data area.
- ISAM is based on tracks and cylinders, which are device-oriented concepts. It builds and maintains a track index table for each cylinder in the prime data area, a cylinder index table for the entire file controlling the track index tables, and for very large files, up to three additional levels of master index tables. Therefore, ISAM is a multiple-level indexed organization.
- After the initial loading of an ISAM file, all records are stored in the prime data area within a predetermined number of tracks in a fixed number of cylinders. They are stored in increasing order of key data field values in tracks and cylinders.
- If space is available, new records inserted into an ISAM file are stored in prime area tracks by inserting them at a proper location so that order of records is maintained in the prime area. This may cause a record in a prime area track to overflow. Overflow records are stored in special tracks that make up a cylinder's overflow area and are chained together to facilitate sequential processing. In case the overflow area for a given cylinder becomes full, these records are stored in an independent overflow area shared by all cylinders in the file.
- ISAM deletes records logically by marking them in their first byte that is reserved for this purpose. A logically deleted record is not displayed to the user; however, it still occupies storage. Physical record deletion happens only if a logically deleted record is pushed off a prime track due to a new record insertion. This is because such an overflow record is not accommodated in the overflow area by ISAM.
- Due to these record insertion and deletion strategies, a dynamically changing ISAM file tends to become sluggish eventually and its access time deteriorates. This is the primary shortcoming of the ISAM system. The remedy is to reorganize the file periodically.
- VSAM is a more versatile file management system than ISAM. It supports three file organization techniques: ESDS, KSDS, and RRDS. These are equivalent to sequential, indexed sequential, and relative-access file organization techniques, respectively. VSAM/KSDS is an improved version of ISAM for indexed sequential files.
- Each VSAM file occupies a portion of the available direct-access storage, and is known as a cluster. There are several types of clusters in VSAM: (1) VSAM master or user catalog clusters that control data clusters and store information about data; (2) ESDS, KSDS, and RRDS data clusters; and (3) alternate index clusters.
- A VSAM cluster is made up of control intervals, which are main building blocks in the system. They are storage segments whose size can be defined by the user in terms of tracks, records, blocks, or cylinders. A certain number of control intervals are conceptually grouped into a control area. Control area and control interval are concepts that are somewhat analogous to cylinder and track concepts in ISAM. These building blocks render VSAM less device dependent than ISAM, because the user has more control over their size specifications.
- A KSDS cluster consists of a data area and an index area. Both areas contain control intervals, which are used to store data records, and index tables, respectively.
- During the initial space allocation and definition of VSAM clusters, free space can be provided in the clusters. Free space can be in each control interval, as empty control intervals in control areas, and as empty control areas in a cluster to accommodate future record insertions. When a VSAM cluster is ini-

tially loaded, records are evenly distributed among the available control intervals, leaving some free space for future insertions.

- Whenever a control interval runs out of free space due to record insertions, a control interval split takes place that divides the content of the full control interval between itself and an empty control interval. If no free space is left in a control area, a control area split takes place, during which the VSAM system claims an empty control area and distributes the contents of the full control area among the control intervals of the two control areas. Finally, whenever a data cluster has no more empty space in it, the operating system lets VSAM claim additional control areas. This strategy eliminates the need for overflow areas and renders VSAM more flexible than ISAM.

- In a VSAM/KSDS cluster, record deletion is physical. When a record is deleted, the space it occupies is reclaimed and becomes part of the free space of the control interval. Consequently, unlike ISAM files, the performance of VSAM/KSDS files does not deteriorate in time, and the files do not require reorganization.

- For VSAM/KSDS clusters, the user can also request creation and maintenance of alternate index clusters. These are related to base clusters, and contain index tables that permit secondary key retrieval based on a data field other than the primary key. Any number of alternate index clusters can be defined and built for a VSAM/KSDS cluster.

- VSAM clusters have to be defined before they can be used in an application program. To facilitate space allocation, cluster definitions, and other operations, a set of utility programs is included in the VSAM system.

- VSAM also supports a command language known as access method services. It can be used for catalog, data, and alternate index cluster definitions, and related file utility operations.

- The interface between the user and the actual files is two-layered. One layer is the VSAM file management system, the other is the application programming language. COBOL is one of the application programming languages that can be used with the VSAM system to manage files. In this case, the COBOL counterpart of the VSAM/KSDS clusters is the indexed organization.

- For indexed organization, COBOL supports a variety of language features, including the SELECT statement in the ENVIRONMENT DIVISION, and file I-O statements in the PROCEDURE DIVISION.

- The SELECT statement can be used to specify an indexed file organization, its access mode (as SEQUENTIAL, or RANDOM, or DYNAMIC, which is a combination of both SEQUENTIAL and RANDOM), its primary key, and alternate keys, if any.

- The I-O statements relevant to indexed file organization are WRITE, READ, REWRITE, DELETE, and START.

- The WRITE statement can be used to load an empty indexed file or to insert new records into an indexed file. Writing a record requires moving a unique primary key field value to the primary key data field, and, if specified for the file, alternate key field values to alternate key fields.

- The READ statement has two formats. One is used for sequential access to indexed files and will access records in order of their primary key values. The other is used for random-access. For random-access READ, a primary key field value (or alternate key value, if secondary key retrieval is requested) should be moved to the primary record key field. After this, a random READ statement should be executed.

- The REWRITE statement is used to update nonkey fields in an indexed file.

- The DELETE statement is used to access and delete a record.

- The START statement sets the current record pointer to a record satisfying a START predicate, and thus enables sequential access to records beginning at that record.

Test Your Comprehension

Multiple-Choice Questions

1. Which of the following statements concerning indexing is correct?
   a. A file for which an index table is built and maintained is called an index file.
   b. An index table containing the same number of entries as the number of records in the prime data area of the corresponding file is called a partial index table.
   c. A total index table is also known as a sequence set.
   d. All of the above are correct.

2. Which of the following is not a property of a B-tree of order 4?
   a. Every index entry has sufficient room to store three data values and four pointers.
   b. The root index entry has at least two pointers.
   c. All pointer values in an index entry are arranged in increasing order from left to right.
   d. All data values in an index entry are arranged in increasing order from left to right.

3. Which of the following about the ISAM data organization technique is incorrect?
   a. An ISAM file consists of a prime data area, an overflow area, and an index area.
   b. A cylinder overflow area for a cylinder can be used by all cylinders in the file.
   c. ISAM creates and maintains track index tables, cylinder index tables, and up to three levels of master index tables for each file.
   d. A prime index subentry associates the largest key value in a track with that track's address.

4. Which of the following steps concerning the direct-access logic for ISAM files is incorrect?
   a. First, the master index tables are accessed directly and searched sequentially.
   b. Next, the cylinder index table is accessed directly and searched sequentially.
   c. The cylinder index table contains information about the address of the track that stores the record being searched. Using this track address, the record is accessed directly.
   d. All of the above steps are correct.

5. Which of the following statements concerning the maintenance of ISAM files is correct?
   a. The delete operation in an ISAM file is logical delete.
   b. In inserting a record, the operation is rejected if there is a record in the file with the same key value as that of the inserted record.
   c. If the point of insertion for a new record is in between two consecutive prime area tracks, the new record is accommodated in the overflow area.
   d. While inserting a new record, if the last record in the appropriate track is a dummy record, after it is pushed off that track it is not stored in the overflow area. This is the only way for physical record deletion in ISAM.
   e. All of the above are correct.

6. Which of the following about a VSAM/KSDS is incorrect?
   a. A control area is a logical group of control intervals.
   b. The size of a control area depends on the device type, but never exceeds the capacity of a cylinder.

c. The purpose of a free space reserved in a base cluster is to provide for future file expansion.

d. The lowest-level index in a base cluster index area is called an index set.

7. Which of the following steps concerning the search logic in a VSAM/KSDS is in error?

a. Access the index set control intervals and process them sequentially to find an appropriate index entry.

b. Using the associated control interval address, access directly the appropriate sequence set control interval.

c. Search the sequence set control interval sequentially to find an index entry such that its key value is larger than the search key.

d. Using this index entry, access directly the control area containing the record sought.

8. Which of the following about record insertion in a VSAM/KSDS is correct?

a. In case free space is available, record insertion in a control interval necessitates physical record movement.

b. If there is no free space in the control interval in which the new record belongs, a control area split takes place.

c. If there is no totally empty control area, a control interval split takes place.

d. Each record insertion causes a logically deleted record to be removed from the file.

9. Which of the following clauses is required in a SELECT statement for a COBOL indexed file to be accessed in dynamic access mode?

a. ORGANIZATION
b. ACCESS MODE
c. RECORD KEY
d. All of the above

10. Which of the following concerning the WRITE statement for indexed files is correct?

a. If the WRITE statement is being used for initial file loading, the file-open mode should be I-O.

b. If the WRITE statement is being used for initial file loading, the file access mode should be SEQUENTIAL.

c. For record insertion, the file-open mode should be OUTPUT.

d. For record insertion, the file access mode should be SEQUENTIAL.

11. Which of the following concerning sequential input of an indexed file is correct?

a. If the file access mode is specified as DYNAMIC, the READ statement should contain a NEXT phrase.

b. Records are accessed and read in increasing order of their primary key values.

c. The file should be opened in INPUT or I-O mode.

d. All of the above are correct.

12. Which of the following statements concerning random READ for an indexed file is incorrect?

a. Before a READ statement is executed, a legitimate value should be moved to either the primary or an alternate key.

b. If the file contains no record whose primary or alternate key value matches that in the primary or alternate key field, an invalid key condition is raised.

c. The file access mode may be SEQUENTIAL or RANDOM.

d. The file-open mode should be INPUT or I-O.

Answers: 1. c; 2. c; 3. b; 4. c; 5. e; 6. d; 7. d; 8. a; 9. d; 10. b; 11. d; 12. c.

Short Essay Questions

1. Explain the difference between access-by-address and access-by-content.
2. Explain why access-by-content is preferred in practical applications.
3. Define the following related terms:
   a. Indexing files
   b. Index files
   c. Indexed files
4. Describe the elements of indexed nonsequential file organization.
5. Describe the indexed sequential file organization, and explain why it is more efficient than an equivalent indexed nonsequential file.
6. Explain the following related terms:
   a. Total index
   b. Sequence set
   c. Multiple-level indexed file
7. Explain why a sequence set is not needed in an indexed sequential file.
8. Why is it desirable to reduce the size of index tables? How can we achieve this?
9. Explain the fundamentals of B-tree indexing, and discuss why it is more efficient than indexed sequential files.
10. Define the following related terms and give an example of each:
    a. Simple query
    b. Range query
    c. Complex query
11. Describe how data are organized in an ISAM cluster.
12. What are the functions of track index tables, cylinder index tables, and master index tables in ISAM?
13. Why do we have to allocate overflow areas for an ISAM file? What kinds of overflow areas are available in an ISAM file? Describe their functions.
14. Describe the direct-access search logic for ISAM files.
15. Describe sequential-access search logic for ISAM files.
16. What are the parameters that must be specified to define an ISAM file using job control language statements?
17. Briefly discuss record deletion logic for ISAM files.
18. Give a short description of record insertion logic for ISAM files.
19. Explain why ISAM files deteriorate in time and have to be reorganized.
20. What is meant by ISAM file reorganization?
21. What are the file organization techniques supported by VSAM? To what built-in file organization techniques of COBOL do they correspond?
22. What are the components of a VSAM/KSDS base cluster? What are their functions?
23. Explain and distinguish between control intervals and control areas in VSAM.
24. Briefly explain the elements of VSAM data area control intervals.
25. Explain the elements of VSAM/KSDS index area control intervals.
26. What is the purpose of a VSAM alternate index cluster?
27. Explain the functions and types of VSAM catalogs.
28. What information is contained in the VSAM catalog?
29. What are the functions of the VSAM access method services and the AMS command language?
30. Briefly explain the direct access search logic for VSAM/KSDS files.
31. Explain how record deletion is handled in VSAM/KSDS.
32. Explain the logic of record insertion for VSAM/KSDS. What are meant by control interval split and control area split?
33. What are the principal advantages of VSAM over ISAM?
34. Explain the principal elements of the SELECT statement in COBOL for defining indexed sequential files.

35. Under what circumstances is an invalid key condition raised in connection with a WRITE statement for an indexed COBOL file?
36. When do we use the file open modes OUTPUT and I-O for a WRITE statement applied to an indexed COBOL file?
37. Under what circumstances is the READ/NEXT version of READ statement indicated for indexed files?
38. When is the use of the KEY IS clause mandatory in random reading of indexed files?
39. What causes an invalid key condition for random READ applied to an indexed file?
40. Explain the functional and syntactical similarities and differences of the REWRITE and DELETE statements for indexed files.
41. Under what circumstances is an invalid key condition raised in connection with a REWRITE statement for indexed files?
42. Explain the syntax and the function of the START verb for indexed files in COBOL.
43. What causes an invalid key condition to be raised when using a START statement for indexed files?

Improve Your Problem-Solving Ability

Programming Exercises

We have a STUDENT-FILE with the following record structure:

A 4-byte student identification number
A 25-byte student name
A 1-byte sex code (F for female, M for male)
A 2-digit age
A 1-digit year-at-college (1, 2, 3, or 4)
A 3-byte academic department code (MTH, CS, ACC, etc.)

The following is an instance of STUDENT-FILE.

Relative Address

STU–ID	STUDENT–NAME	SEX–CODE	AGE	YEAR–AT–COLLEGE	DEPT–CODE
1 1000	LAURA BAILEY	F	18	1	MTH
2 1100	HARRY THOMPSON	M	18	2	BUS
3 1200	KIMBERLY JONES	F	19	2	BUS
4 1300	JANICE BLACK	F	21	2	MTH
5 1400	JOHN MCINTOSH	M	22	4	CS
6 1500	DEAN TALLMAN	M	20	3	CS
7 1600	VERA HANSEN	F	20	4	BUS
8 1700	MARGARET COOPER	F	18	1	CS

It is known that only STU-ID data field has the property of unique identification for the file. The records are stored in locations whose relative addresses are in the range 1 through 8, as shown. Programming exercises 1 through 5 are based on STUDENT-FILE.

1. Assume that the file is stored in the prime area of an indexed sequential file for which STU-ID is the primary key. Construct a total index table based on STU-ID and show its content in a table with the following structure:

STU–ID	RELATIVE–ADDRESS
. . .	. . . .

2. Construct a higher-level index table to control the total index table of exercise 1, assuming that each index entry governs a block of two index records in the lower-level index table.

3. Suppose STUDENT-FILE has been created as a VSAM/KSDS cluster and loaded with the above records. We request VSAM to create an alternate index cluster based on SEX-CODE. Draw a table to indicate the logical content of the data area in the alternate index cluster.

4. Solve exercise 3 for an alternate index cluster based on the composite field consisting of SEX-CODE and AGE.

5. Write a complete COBOL SELECT statement to describe STUDENT-FILE as an indexed sequential file whose primary key is STU-ID, with a file access mode of RANDOM, and alternate record keys of STUDENT-NAME and DEPT-CODE.

6. Given is the following sequence set for a B-tree of order 3 stored in a direct-access file.

Relative Address

11	123	126	128
12	130	132	133
13	135	137	138
14	140	142	145
15	147	148	150
16	155	156	157
17	160	166	168
18	169	170	176
19	180	182	183
20	185	188	189
21	190	192	193
22	194	197	198

The three-digit integer numbers are the primary key field values for records stored in the prime data area. Each such key value is assumed to be associated with a relative address to enable direct access to a record. The prime area relative addresses are not shown in the sequence set. Fill in the following tables for the primary and secondary index tables of this B-tree.

PRIMARY INDEX

1 | | | | | |
|---|---|---|---|---|

SECONDARY INDEX

5 | | | | | |
|---|---|---|---|---|
| 6 | | | | | |
| 7 | | | | | |

7. Consider the ISAM file schema of Figure 7 as the initial configuration of an indexed sequential file. Draw a similar figure and show on it the final file schema that emerges after the following sequence of maintenance operations has been executed.

   Delete ANNE, FRED, RANDY.
   Add MAGGIE, BOB, JERRY, LARRY, SALLY, JOHN.

8. Solve problem 7 for a VSAM/KSDS file, as shown in Figure 12a, assuming the figure is the initial configuration of the file.

9. Analyze the sample program given in this chapter (Program 1-Source). It has a flaw (not an error) in paragraph D1-PROCESS-FOR-INSERTION. What is it? Do you see any other flaws in the program? Correct all such flaws and run the new version on your installation's computer system.

Programming Problems

1. Suppose the STUDENT-FILE records of programming exercise 1 are stored in a sequential file. Write a COBOL program to read the sequential file and create an indexed sequential counterpart with a primary key of STU-ID. Test your program thoroughly.

2. Write a maintenance program for the indexed STUDENT-FILE of programming problem 1 that is capable of inserting new records into the file, deleting existing records in it, or updating STUDENT-NAME, SEX-CODE, AGE, YEARS-AT-COLLEGE, and DEPT-CODE field values in its records.

3. Create alternate index clusters for the indexed STUDENT-FILE of programming problem 1 based on SEX-CODE and AGE. Then demonstrate access by SEX-CODE or by AGE.

4. Modify your program of programming problem 3 so that access based on the predicate SEX-CODE = "X" AND AGE = 99 is facilitated and is done as efficiently as possible.

```
00001    *.................................................................
00002    IDENTIFICATION DIVISION.
00003    PROGRAM-ID.        INDEXED-FILE-MAINTENANCE.
00004    AUTHOR.            UCKAN.
00005    ******************************************************************
00006    ***   THIS PROGRAM CAN BE USED TO MAINTAIN THE INDEXED SEQUENTIAL *
00007    ***   FILE, CALLED "PERSONNEL-FILE" IN THE FOLLOWING WAYS:        *
00008    ***                                                               *
00009    ***       1. ADDING NEW RECORD OCCURRENCES;                       *
00010    ***       2. DELETING EXISTING RECORD OCCURRENCES;                *
00011    ***       3. UPDATING RECORD OCCURRENCES (ONLY NONKEY FIELDS CAN  *
00012    ***          BE UPDATED);                                         *
00013    ***       4. ACCESSING RECORD OCCURRENCES DIRECTLY;               *
```

Program 1-Source Program to Maintain an Indexed Sequential File

```
00014   ***        5. GENERATING A FULL FILE LISTING;              *
00015   ***        6. GENERATING PARTIAL FILE LISTINGS WITHIN A SPECIFIED *
00016   ***           RANGE.                                        *
00017   ***                                                         *
00018   ***   THE PERSONNEL FILE RECORD STRUCTURE CONSISTS OF:      *
00019   ***        1. A FOUR-DIGIT PERSONNEL ID NUMBER,             *
00020   ***        2. A 25-BYTE PERSONNEL NAME, AND                 *
00021   ***        3. A 3-BYTE PERSONNEL-DEPARTMENT-CODE.           *
00022   ***   ALL INPUT FOR THE PROGRAM IS PROVIDED INTERACTIVELY.  *
00023   ***************************************************************
00024
00025    DATE-WRITTEN.   JULY 19, 1990.
00026    DATE-COMPILED. JUL 25,1990.
00028   *.................................................................
00029    ENVIRONMENT DIVISION.
00030    CONFIGURATION SECTION.
00031    SOURCE-COMPUTER. IBM-370.
00032    OBJECT-COMPUTER. IBM-370.
00033    INPUT-OUTPUT SECTION.
00034    FILE-CONTROL.
00035
00036       SELECT PERSONNEL-FILE
00037             ASSIGN       TO MASTER
00038             ORGANIZATION IS INDEXED
00039             ACCESS MODE  IS DYNAMIC
00040             RECORD KEY   IS PERS-ID.
00041
00042   *.................................................................
00043    DATA DIVISION.
00044    FILE SECTION.
00045
00046    FD  PERSONNEL-FILE
00047        LABEL RECORDS ARE STANDARD
00048        DATA RECORD IS PERSONNEL-RECORD
00049        RECORD CONTAINS 32 CHARACTERS.
00050    01  PERSONNEL-RECORD.
00051        05  PERS-ID          PIC XXXX.
00052        05  PERS-NAME        PIC X(25).
00053        05  PERS-DEPT-CODE   PIC XXX.
00054
00055    WORKING-STORAGE SECTION.
00056
00057   **********> VARIABLES:
00058
00059    01  START-PERS-ID        PIC XXXX.
00060    01  END-PERS-ID          PIC XXXX.
00061    01  RECORD-READ          PIC XXX.
00062    01  TERMINATE-INPUT      PIC XXX.
00063    01  FILE-FULL            PIC XXX.
00064    01  RECORD-FOUND         PIC XXX.
00065    01  END-OF-FILE-REACHED  PIC XXX.
00066    01  RANGE-EMPTY          PIC XXX.
00067    01  RANGE-INCORRECT      PIC XXX.
00068
```

Program 1-Source (Continued)

```
00069    01   FUNCTION-CODE              PIC X.
00070         88   RECORD-INSERTION      VALUE "I".
00071         88   RECORD-DELETION       VALUE "D".
00072         88   RECORD-UPDATE         VALUE "U".
00073         88   DIRECT-RECORD-ACCESS  VALUE "A".
00074         88   FULL-FILE-LISTING     VALUE "L".
00075         88   PARTIAL-FILE-LISTING  VALUE "P".
00076         88   PROCESS-TERMINATION   VALUE "T".
00077         88   MENU-DISPLAY          VALUE "M".
00078
00079    **********> STRUCTURES:
00080
00081    01   WS-PERSONNEL-RECORD.
00082         05   WS-PERS-ID            PIC XXXX.
00083         05   WS-PERS-NAME          PIC X(25).
00084         05   WS-PERS-DEPT-CODE     PIC XXX.
00085
00086    *.................................................................
00087    PROCEDURE DIVISION.
00088
00089    A-MAIN-PARAGRAPH.
00090        MOVE "#" TO FUNCTION-CODE.
00091
00092        PERFORM B1-DISPLAY-INSTRUCTIONS
00093             UNTIL FUNCTION-CODE = "I" OR "D" OR "U" OR "A" OR "L"
00094                                  OR "P" OR "T" OR "M".
00095
00096        PERFORM B2-PROCESS-REQUEST
00097             UNTIL PROCESS-TERMINATION.
00098
00099        STOP RUN.
00100
00101    B1-DISPLAY-INSTRUCTIONS.
00102
00103        IF FUNCTION-CODE = "#"
00104             DISPLAY " "
00105             DISPLAY "****************************************"
00106             DISPLAY "* THIS PROGRAM CAN BE USED TO MAINTAIN *"
00107             DISPLAY "*         THE INDEXED FILE, CALLED      *"
00108             DISPLAY "*            THE PERSONNEL FILE.        *"
00109             DISPLAY "****************************************"
00110
00111             PERFORM C1-DISPLAY-SELECTION-MENU
00112
00113             DISPLAY " "
00114             DISPLAY "****> PLEASE ENTER FUNCTION CODE: "
00115        ELSE
00116             IF FUNCTION-CODE = "@"
00117                 DISPLAY " "
00118                 DISPLAY "****> PLEASE ENTER FUNCTION CODE: "
00119             ELSE
00120                 DISPLAY FUNCTION-CODE " IS AN ILLEGAL VALUE."
00121                 DISPLAY "LEGAL VALUES ARE SHOWN BELOW:"
```

Program 1-Source (Continued)

```
00122                         PERFORM C1-DISPLAY-SELECTION-MENU
00123                         DISPLAY " "
00124                         DISPLAY "****> PLEASE ENTER A CORRECT FUNCTION CO
00125    -     "DE: ".
00126
00127         ACCEPT FUNCTION-CODE FROM CONSOLE.
00128
00129    B2-PROCESS-REQUEST.
00130
00131         IF MENU-DISPLAY
00132                 PERFORM C1-DISPLAY-SELECTION-MENU.
00133
00134         IF RECORD-INSERTION
00135                 PERFORM C2-INSERT-RECORDS.
00136
00137         IF RECORD-DELETION
00138                 PERFORM C3-DELETE-RECORDS.
00139
00140         IF RECORD-UPDATE
00141                 PERFORM C4-UPDATE-RECORDS.
00142
00143         IF DIRECT-RECORD-ACCESS
00144                 PERFORM C5-ACCESS-RECORDS-DIRECTLY.
00145
00146         IF FULL-FILE-LISTING
00147                 PERFORM C6-LIST-FULL-FILE.
00148
00149         IF PARTIAL-FILE-LISTING
00150                 PERFORM C7-LIST-PARTIAL-FILE.
00151
00152         IF NOT PROCESS-TERMINATION
00153                 MOVE "@" TO FUNCTION-CODE
00154
00155                 PERFORM B1-DISPLAY-INSTRUCTIONS
00156                     UNTIL FUNCTION-CODE = "I" OR "D" OR "U" OR "A"
00157                                        OR "P" OR "L" OR "T" OR "M".
00158
00159
00160    C1-DISPLAY-SELECTION-MENU.
00161         DISPLAY " ".
00162         DISPLAY "****************************************".
00163         DISPLAY "*  FUNCTION                       CODE  *".
00164         DISPLAY "*  --------------------           ----  *".
00165         DISPLAY "*  INSERT RECORDS                  I    *".
00166         DISPLAY "*  DELETE RECORDS                  D    *".
00167         DISPLAY "*  UPDATE RECORDS                  U    *".
00168         DISPLAY "*  ACCESS RECORDS DIRECTLY         A    *".
00169         DISPLAY "*  GENERATE FULL FILE LISTING      L    *".
00170         DISPLAY "*  GENERATE PARTIAL FILE LISTING   P    *".
00171         DISPLAY "*  DISPLAY THIS MENU               M    *".
00172         DISPLAY "*  TERMINATE                       T    *".
00173         DISPLAY "****************************************".
00174         DISPLAY " ".
00175
```

Program 1-Source (Continued)

```
00176     C2-INSERT-RECORDS.
00177         OPEN I-O PERSONNEL-FILE.
00178         MOVE "NO" TO TERMINATE-INPUT.
00179
00180         PERFORM D1-PROCESS-FOR-INSERTION
00181             UNTIL TERMINATE-INPUT = "YES".
00182
00183         CLOSE PERSONNEL-FILE.
00184
00185     C3-DELETE-RECORDS.
00186         OPEN I-O PERSONNEL-FILE.
00187         MOVE "NO" TO TERMINATE-INPUT.
00188
00189         PERFORM D2-PROCESS-FOR-DELETION
00190             UNTIL TERMINATE-INPUT = "YES".
00191
00192         CLOSE PERSONNEL-FILE.
00193
00194     C4-UPDATE-RECORDS.
00195         OPEN I-O PERSONNEL-FILE.
00196         MOVE "NO" TO TERMINATE-INPUT.
00197
00198         PERFORM D3-PROCESS-FOR-UPDATE
00199             UNTIL TERMINATE-INPUT = "YES".
00200
00201         CLOSE PERSONNEL-FILE.
00202
00203     C5-ACCESS-RECORDS-DIRECTLY.
00204         OPEN INPUT PERSONNEL-FILE.
00205         MOVE "NO" TO TERMINATE-INPUT.
00206
00207         PERFORM D4-DISPLAY-RECORD
00208             UNTIL TERMINATE-INPUT = "YES".
00209
00210         CLOSE PERSONNEL-FILE.
00211
00212     C6-LIST-FULL-FILE.
00213         OPEN I-O PERSONNEL-FILE.
00214         MOVE "NO" TO END-OF-FILE-REACHED.
00215
00216         READ PERSONNEL-FILE NEXT
00217             AT END MOVE "YES" TO END-OF-FILE-REACHED.
00218
00219         IF END-OF-FILE-REACHED = "NO"
00220             PERFORM D5-PRODUCE-FULL-LISTING
00221                 UNTIL END-OF-FILE-REACHED = "YES"
00222         ELSE
00223             DISPLAY "FILE IS EMPTY.".
00224
00225         CLOSE PERSONNEL-FILE.
00226
00227     C7-LIST-PARTIAL-FILE.
00228         OPEN I-O PERSONNEL-FILE.
00229         MOVE "NO" TO END-OF-FILE-REACHED.
00230         MOVE "NO" TO RANGE-INCORRECT.
```

Program 1-Source (Continued)

```
00231          MOVE "NO" TO RANGE-EMPTY.
00232
00233          DISPLAY "****> ENTER START PERSONNEL ID NUMBER FOR LISTING:".
00234          ACCEPT START-PERS-ID FROM CONSOLE.
00235
00236          DISPLAY "****> ENTER END PERSONNEL ID NUMBER FOR LISTING:".
00237          ACCEPT END-PERS-ID FROM CONSOLE.
00238
00239          IF START-PERS-ID > END-PERS-ID
00240                  DISPLAY "INCORRECT RANGE SPECIFICATION."
00241                  MOVE "YES" TO RANGE-INCORRECT.
00242
00243          MOVE START-PERS-ID TO PERS-ID.
00244
00245          START PERSONNEL-FILE
00246                  KEY NOT LESS THAN PERS-ID
00247                  INVALID KEY MOVE "YES" TO RANGE-EMPTY.
00248
00249          READ PERSONNEL-FILE NEXT
00250                  AT END MOVE "YES" TO END-OF-FILE-REACHED.
00251
00252          IF RANGE-EMPTY = "YES"
00253                  DISPLAY "THE SPECIFIED RANGE IS EMPTY.".
00254
00255          IF RANGE-INCORRECT = "NO"
00256                  AND
00257             END-OF-FILE-REACHED = "NO"
00258                  IF RANGE-EMPTY = "NO"
00259                          PERFORM D6-PRODUCE-PARTIAL-LISTING
00260                              UNTIL END-OF-FILE-REACHED = "YES".
00261
00262        CLOSE PERSONNEL-FILE.
00263
00264    D1-PROCESS-FOR-INSERTION.
00265        DISPLAY "****> ENTER PERSONNEL ID NUMBER: ".
00266        ACCEPT WS-PERS-ID FROM CONSOLE.
00267
00268        DISPLAY "****> ENTER PERSONNEL NAME: ".
00269        ACCEPT WS-PERS-NAME FROM CONSOLE.
00270
00271        DISPLAY "****> ENTER PERSONNEL DEPARTMENT CODE: ".
00272        ACCEPT WS-PERS-DEPT-CODE FROM CONSOLE.
00273
00274        MOVE "YES" TO RECORD-FOUND.
00275
00276        MOVE WS-PERS-ID TO PERS-ID.
00277
00278        READ PERSONNEL-FILE
00279                INVALID KEY MOVE "NO" TO RECORD-FOUND.
00280
00281        IF RECORD-FOUND = "YES"
00282                DISPLAY "RECORD ALREADY IN THE FILE."
00283        ELSE
00284                WRITE PERSONNEL-RECORD FROM WS-PERSONNEL-RECORD
00285                    INVALID KEY MOVE "YES" TO FILE-FULL.
```

Program 1-Source (Continued)

```
00286
00287          IF FILE-FULL NOT = "YES" AND RECORD-FOUND NOT = "YES"
00288               DISPLAY "RECORD INSERTED.".
00289
00290          DISPLAY "****> DO YOU WANT TO TERMINATE RECORD INSERTION?".
00291          DISPLAY "****> TYPE YES OR NO.".
00292          ACCEPT TERMINATE-INPUT FROM CONSOLE.
00293
00294      D2-PROCESS-FOR-DELETION.
00295          MOVE "YES" TO RECORD-FOUND.
00296          DISPLAY "****> ENTER PERSONNEL ID NUMBER OF RECORD TO BE DELE
00297      -     "TED:".
00298          ACCEPT WS-PERS-ID FROM CONSOLE.
00299
00300          MOVE WS-PERS-ID TO PERS-ID.
00301
00302          DELETE PERSONNEL-FILE
00303               INVALID KEY MOVE "NO" TO RECORD-FOUND.
00304
00305          IF RECORD-FOUND = "YES"
00306              DISPLAY "RECORD WITH KEY " PERS-ID " IS DELETED."
00307          ELSE
00308              DISPLAY "RECORD WITH KEY " PERS-ID " IS NOT FOUND.".
00309
00310          DISPLAY "****> DO YOU WANT TO TERMINATE RECORD DELETION?".
00311          DISPLAY "****> TYPE YES OR NO.".
00312          ACCEPT TERMINATE-INPUT FROM CONSOLE.
00313
00314      D3-PROCESS-FOR-UPDATE.
00315          MOVE "YES" TO RECORD-FOUND.
00316          DISPLAY "****> ENTER PERSONNEL ID NUMBER OF RECORD TO BE UPDA
00317      -     "TED:".
00318          ACCEPT WS-PERS-ID FROM CONSOLE.
00319
00320          MOVE WS-PERS-ID TO PERS-ID.
00321
00322          READ PERSONNEL-FILE
00323               INVALID KEY MOVE "NO" TO RECORD-FOUND.
00324
00325          IF RECORD-FOUND = "YES"
00326              PERFORM E1-GET-NEW-DATA
00327              REWRITE PERSONNEL-RECORD
00328                   INVALID KEY DISPLAY "ERROR IN REWRITE."
00329              DISPLAY "RECORD WITH KEY " WS-PERS-ID " IS UPDATED."
00330          ELSE
00331              DISPLAY "RECORD WITH KEY " WS-PERS-ID " IS NOT FOUND.".
00332
00333          DISPLAY "****> DO YOU WANT TO TERMINATE RECORD UPDATE?".
00334          DISPLAY "****> TYPE YES OR NO.".
00335          ACCEPT TERMINATE-INPUT FROM CONSOLE.
00336
00337      D4-DISPLAY-RECORD.
00338          MOVE "YES" TO RECORD-FOUND.
00339
```

Program 1-Source (Continued)

```
00340          DISPLAY "****> ENTER PERSONNEL ID OF RECORD TO BE RETRIEVED:"
00341          ACCEPT PERS-ID FROM CONSOLE.
00342
00343          READ PERSONNEL-FILE
00344                  INVALID KEY MOVE "NO" TO RECORD-FOUND.
00345
00346          IF RECORD-FOUND = "YES"
00347                  DISPLAY " "
00348                  DISPLAY "PERSONNEL ID IS    : " PERS-ID
00349                  DISPLAY "PERSONNEL NAME IS : " PERS-NAME
00350                  DISPLAY "DEPARTMENT CODE IS: " PERS-DEPT-CODE
00351                  DISPLAY "  "
00352          ELSE
00353                  DISPLAY "RECORD " PERS-ID " IS NOT IN THE FILE."
00354                  DISPLAY " ".
00355
00356          DISPLAY "****> DO YOU WANT TO TERMINATE RECORD RETRIEVAL?".
00357          DISPLAY "****> TYPE YES OR NO.".
00358          ACCEPT TERMINATE-INPUT FROM CONSOLE.
00359
00360      D5-PRODUCE-FULL-LISTING.
00361          DISPLAY PERS-ID "  " PERS-NAME "  " PERS-DEPT-CODE.
00362
00363          READ PERSONNEL-FILE NEXT
00364                  AT END MOVE "YES" TO END-OF-FILE-REACHED.
00365
00366      D6-PRODUCE-PARTIAL-LISTING.
00367          IF PERS-ID > END-PERS-ID
00368                  MOVE "YES" TO END-OF-FILE-REACHED.
00369
00370          IF END-OF-FILE-REACHED = "NO"
00371                  DISPLAY PERS-ID "  " PERS-NAME " " PERS-DEPT-CODE
00372                  READ PERSONNEL-FILE NEXT
00373                          AT END MOVE "YES" TO END-OF-FILE-REACHED.
00374
00375      E1-GET-NEW-DATA.
00376          DISPLAY "PERSONNEL NAME FOR " WS-PERS-ID " IS: " PERS-NAME.
00377          DISPLAY "****> PLEASE ENTER NEW NAME.  IF NO UPDATE IS DESIRE
00378     -    "D, HIT RETURN.".
00379          ACCEPT WS-PERS-NAME FROM CONSOLE.
00380
00381          IF WS-PERS-NAME NOT = SPACES
00382                  MOVE WS-PERS-NAME TO PERS-NAME.
00383
00384          DISPLAY "PERSONNEL DEPARTMENT CODE FOR " WS-PERS-ID " IS: "
00385                  PERS-DEPT-CODE.
00386          DISPLAY "****> PLEASE ENTER NEW DEPARTMENT CODE.  IF NO UPDAT
00387     -    "E IS DESIRED, HIT RETURN.".
00388          ACCEPT WS-PERS-DEPT-CODE FROM CONSOLE.
00389
00390          IF WS-PERS-DEPT-CODE NOT = SPACES
00391                  MOVE WS-PERS-DEPT-CODE TO PERS-DEPT-CODE.
```

Program 1-Source (Continued)

```
******************************************
* THIS PROGRAM CAN BE USED TO MAINTAIN *
*        THE INDEXED FILE, CALLED      *
*           THE PERSONNEL FILE.        *
******************************************


******************************************
*   FUNCTION                    CODE  *
*   _____         ____  *
*   INSERT RECORDS               I    *
*   DELETE RECORDS               D    *
*   UPDATE RECORDS               U    *
*   ACCESS RECORDS DIRECTLY      A    *
*   GENERATE FULL FILE LISTING   L    *
*   GENERATE PARTIAL FILE LISTING P   *
*   DISPLAY THIS MENU            M    *
*   TERMINATE                    T    *
******************************************

****> PLEASE ENTER FUNCTION CODE:
B
B IS AN ILLEGAL VALUE.
LEGAL VALUES ARE SHOWN BELOW:

******************************************
*   FUNCTION                    CODE  *
*   _____         ____  *
*   INSERT RECORDS               I    *
*   DELETE RECORDS               D    *
*   UPDATE RECORDS               U    *
*   ACCESS RECORDS DIRECTLY      A    *
*   GENERATE FULL FILE LISTING   L    *
*   GENERATE PARTIAL FILE LISTING P   *
*   DISPLAY THIS MENU            M    *
*   TERMINATE                    T    *
******************************************

****> PLEASE ENTER A CORRECT FUNCTION CODE:
L
FILE IS EMPTY.

****> PLEASE ENTER FUNCTION CODE:
A
****> ENTER PERSONNEL ID OF RECORD TO BE RETRIEVED:
1111
RECORD 1111 IS NOT IN THE FILE.

****> DO YOU WANT TO TERMINATE RECORD RETRIEVAL?
****> TYPE YES OR NO.
YES
```

Program 1-Output A Terminal Session for Program 1

```
****> PLEASE ENTER FUNCTION CODE:
M


*********************************************
*   FUNCTION                      CODE   *
*   _____             ____   *
*   INSERT RECORDS                 I     *
*   DELETE RECORDS                 D     *
*   UPDATE RECORDS                 U     *
*   ACCESS RECORDS DIRECTLY        A     *
*   GENERATE FULL FILE LISTING     L     *
*   GENERATE PARTIAL FILE LISTING  P     *
*   DISPLAY THIS MENU              M     *
*   TERMINATE                      T     *
*********************************************


****> PLEASE ENTER FUNCTION CODE:
I
****> ENTER PERSONNEL ID NUMBER:
4241
****> ENTER PERSONNEL NAME:
TIMOTHY SANDERS
****> ENTER PERSONNEL DEPARTMENT CODE:
DP
RECORD INSERTED.
****> DO YOU WANT TO TERMINATE RECORD INSERTION?
****> TYPE YES OR NO.
NO
****> ENTER PERSONNEL ID NUMBER:
4146
****> ENTER PERSONNEL NAME:
JOAN HALL
****> ENTER PERSONNEL DEPARTMENT CODE:
SLS
RECORD INSERTED.
****> DO YOU WANT TO TERMINATE RECORD INSERTION?
****> TYPE YES OR NO.
NO
****> ENTER PERSONNEL ID NUMBER:
3812
****> ENTER PERSONNEL NAME:
KAREN WHITE
****> ENTER PERSONNEL DEPARTMENT CODE:
DP
RECORD INSERTED.
****> DO YOU WANT TO TERMINATE RECORD INSERTION?
****> TYPE YES OR NO.
NO
****> ENTER PERSONNEL ID NUMBER:
4031
****> ENTER PERSONNEL NAME:
JUDY SMITH
```

Program 1-Output (Continued)

```
****> ENTER PERSONNEL DEPARTMENT CODE:
DP
RECORD INSERTED.
****> DO YOU WANT TO TERMINATE RECORD INSERTION?
****> TYPE YES OR NO.
NO
****> ENTER PERSONNEL ID NUMBER:
4214
****> ENTER PERSONNEL NAME:
LORRAINE HICKMAN
****> ENTER PERSONNEL DEPARTMENT CODE:
SLS
RECORD INSERTED.
****> DO YOU WANT TO TERMINATE RECORD INSERTION?
****> TYPE YES OR NO.
NO
****> ENTER PERSONNEL ID NUMBER:
3971
****> ENTER PERSONNEL NAME:
DONALD LITTLE
****> ENTER PERSONNEL DEPARTMENT CODE:
DP
RECORD INSERTED.
****> DO YOU WANT TO TERMINATE RECORD INSERTION?
****> TYPE YES OR NO.
NO
****> ENTER PERSONNEL ID NUMBER:
4023
****> ENTER PERSONNEL NAME:
JACK MEYER
****> ENTER PERSONNEL DEPARTMENT CODE:
SLS
RECORD INSERTED.
****> DO YOU WANT TO TERMINATE RECORD INSERTION?
****> TYPE YES OR NO.
NO
****> ENTER PERSONNEL ID NUMBER:
4011
****> ENTER PERSONNEL NAME:
LINDA DAY
****> ENTER PERSONNEL DEPARTMENT CODE:
ACC
RECORD INSERTED.
****> DO YOU WANT TO TERMINATE RECORD INSERTION?
****> TYPE YES OR NO.
YES

****> PLEASE ENTER FUNCTION CODE:
L
3812   KAREN WHITE              DP
3971   DONALD LITTLE            DP
4011   LINDA DAY                ACC
4023   JACK MEYER               SLS
4031   JUDY SMITH               DP
4146   JOAN HALL                SLS
```

Program 1-Output (Continued)

```
4214   LORRAINE HICKMAN             SLS
4241   TIMOTHY SANDERS              DP

****> PLEASE ENTER FUNCTION CODE:
A
****> ENTER PERSONNEL ID OF RECORD TO BE RETRIEVED:
4031

PERSONNEL ID IS   : 4031
PERSONNEL NAME IS : JUDY SMITH
DEPARTMENT CODE IS: DP

****> DO YOU WANT TO TERMINATE RECORD RETRIEVAL?
****> TYPE YES OR NO.
NO
****> ENTER PERSONNEL ID OF RECORD TO BE RETRIEVED:
3812

PERSONNEL ID IS   : 3812
PERSONNEL NAME IS : KAREN WHITE
DEPARTMENT CODE IS: DP

****> DO YOU WANT TO TERMINATE RECORD RETRIEVAL?
****> TYPE YES OR NO.
YES

****> PLEASE ENTER FUNCTION CODE:
P
****> ENTER START PERSONNEL ID NUMBER FOR LISTING:
4000
****> ENTER END PERSONNEL ID NUMBER FOR LISTING:
3999
INCORRECT RANGE SPECIFICATION.

****> PLEASE ENTER FUNCTION CODE:
P
****> ENTER START PERSONNEL ID NUMBER FOR LISTING:
4000
****> ENTER END PERSONNEL ID NUMBER FOR LISTING:
4200
4011   LINDA DAY                    ACC
4023   JACK MEYER                   SLS
4031   JUDY SMITH                   DP
4146   JOAN HALL                    SLS

****> PLEASE ENTER FUNCTION CODE:
D
****> ENTER PERSONNEL ID NUMBER OF RECORD TO BE DELETED:
4214
RECORD WITH KEY 4214 IS DELETED.
****> DO YOU WANT TO TERMINATE RECORD DELETION?
****> TYPE YES OR NO.
NO
```

Program 1-Output (Continued)

```
****> ENTER PERSONNEL ID NUMBER OF RECORD TO BE DELETED:
4214
RECORD WITH KEY 4214 IS NOT FOUND.
****> DO YOU WANT TO TERMINATE RECORD DELETION?
****> TYPE YES OR NO.
YES


****> PLEASE ENTER FUNCTION CODE:
U
****> ENTER PERSONNEL ID NUMBER OF RECORD TO BE UPDATED:
4214
RECORD WITH KEY 4214 IS NOT FOUND.
****> DO YOU WANT TO TERMINATE RECORD UPDATE?
****> TYPE YES OR NO.
NO
****> ENTER PERSONNEL ID NUMBER OF RECORD TO BE UPDATED:
4011
PERSONNEL NAME FOR 4011 IS: LINDA DAY
****> PLEASE ENTER NEW NAME.  IF NO UPDATE IS DESIRED, HIT RETURN.
LINDA SMITH
PERSONNEL DEPARTMENT CODE FOR 4011 IS: ACC
****> PLEASE ENTER NEW DEPARTMENT CODE.  IF NO UPDATE IS DESIRED, HIT RETURN

****> DO YOU WANT TO TERMINATE RECORD UPDATE?
****> TYPE YES OR NO.
YES


****> PLEASE ENTER FUNCTION CODE:
L
3812   KAREN WHITE              DP
3971   DONALD LITTLE            DP
4011   LINDA SMITH              ACC
4023   JACK MEYER               SLS
4031   JUDY SMITH               DP
4146   JOAN HALL                SLS
4241   TIMOTHY SANDERS          DP

****> PLEASE ENTER FUNCTION CODE:
T
```

Program 1-Output (Continued)

```
00001     *...........................................................
00002      IDENTIFICATION DIVISION.
00003      PROGRAM-ID.        ACCESSING-INDEXED-FILES.
00004      ***************************************************************
00005      ***    THIS PROGRAM CAN BE USED TO ACCESS THE INDEXED SEQUENTIAL  *
00006      ***    FILE, CALLED "PERSONNEL-FILE" IN THE FOLLOWING WAYS:       *
00007      ***                                                              *
00008      ***         1. BY THE PRIMARY KEY, PERS-ID;                      *
00009      ***         2. BY THE UNIQUE ALTERNATE KEY, PERS-NAME; OR        *
00010      ***         3. BY THE NONUNIQUE ALTERNATE KEY, PERS-DEPT-CODE.   *
00011      ***                                                              *
```

Program 2-Source Program to Access an Indexed Sequential File

```
00012   ***   IF PERS-DEPT-CODE IS THE ACCESS KEY, ALL RECORD OCCURRENCES *
00013   ***   SATISFYING THE GIVEN DEPARTMENT CODE WILL BE SEQUENTIALLY    *
00014   ***   ACCESSED AND DISPLAYED.                                      *
00015   ***                                                                *
00016   ***   THE PERSONNEL FILE RECORD STRUCTURE CONSISTS OF:             *
00017   ***                                                                *
00018   ***       1. A FOUR-DIGIT PERSONNEL ID NUMBER,                     *
00019   ***       2. A 25-BYTE PERSONNEL NAME, AND                         *
00020   ***       3. A 3-BYTE PERSONNEL-DEPARTMENT-CODE.                   *
00021   ***                                                                *
00022   ***   THE PROGRAM IS FULLY INTERACTIVE.                            *
00023   *********************************************************************
00024
00025    AUTHOR.        UCKAN.
00026    DATE-WRITTEN.  JULY 20, 1990.
00027    DATE-COMPILED. AUG 17,1990.
00029   *.................................................................
00030    ENVIRONMENT DIVISION.
00031    CONFIGURATION SECTION.
00032    SOURCE-COMPUTER. UNIVERSITY-MAINFRAME.
00033    OBJECT-COMPUTER. UNIVERSITY-MAINFRAME.
00034    INPUT-OUTPUT SECTION.
00035    FILE-CONTROL.
00036
00037       SELECT PERSONNEL-FILE
00038              ASSIGN      TO MASTER
00039              ORGANIZATION IS INDEXED
00040              ACCESS MODE  IS DYNAMIC
00041              RECORD KEY   IS PERS-ID
00042              ALTERNATE RECORD KEY IS PERS-NAME
00043              ALTERNATE RECORD KEY IS PERS-DEPT-CODE
00044                                 WITH DUPLICATES.
00045
00046   *.................................................................
00047    DATA DIVISION.
00048    FILE SECTION.
00049
00050    FD  PERSONNEL-FILE
00051        LABEL RECORDS ARE STANDARD
00052        DATA RECORD IS PERSONNEL-RECORD
00053        RECORD CONTAINS 32 CHARACTERS.
00054    01  PERSONNEL-RECORD.
00055        05  PERS-ID         PIC XXXX.
00056        05  PERS-NAME       PIC X(25).
00057        05  PERS-DEPT-CODE  PIC XXX.
00058
00059    WORKING-STORAGE SECTION.
00060
00061   *********> VARIABLES:
00062
00063    01  RETRIEVAL-KEY      PIC X(25).
00064    01  TERMINATE-INPUT    PIC XXX.
00065    01  RECORD-FOUND       PIC XXX.
00066    01  END-OF-FILE        PIC XXX.
```

Program 2-Source (Continued)

```
00067
00068    01  FUNCTION-CODE              PIC XXXX.
00069        88  PERS-ID-ACCESS         VALUE "ID  ".
00070        88  PERS-NAME-ACCESS       VALUE "NAME".
00071        88  DEPT-CODE-ACCESS       VALUE "DEPT".
00072        88  MENU-DISPLAY           VALUE "M   ".
00073        88  PROCESS-TERMINATION    VALUE "T   ".
00074
00075    *................................................................
00076    PROCEDURE DIVISION.
00077
00078    A-MAIN-PARAGRAPH.
00079        MOVE "#" TO FUNCTION-CODE.
00080
00081        PERFORM B1-DISPLAY-INSTRUCTIONS
00082             UNTIL FUNCTION-CODE = "ID" OR "NAME" OR "DEPT" OR "M"
00083                                 OR "T".
00084
00085        PERFORM B2-PROCESS-REQUEST
00086             UNTIL PROCESS-TERMINATION.
00087
00088        STOP RUN.
00089
00090    B1-DISPLAY-INSTRUCTIONS.
00091
00092        IF FUNCTION-CODE = "#"
00093             DISPLAY "  "
00094             DISPLAY "*********************************************"
00095             DISPLAY "* THIS PROGRAM CAN BE USED TO ACCESS THE   *"
00096             DISPLAY "*    INDEXED FILE, CALLED PERSONNEL FILE    *"
00097             DISPLAY "*    EITHER BY PERS-ID, OR PERS-NAME, OR    *"
00098             DISPLAY "*              PERS-DEPT-CODE.              *"
00099             DISPLAY "*********************************************"
00100
00101             PERFORM C1-DISPLAY-SELECTION-MENU
00102
00103             DISPLAY " "
00104             DISPLAY "****> PLEASE ENTER FUNCTION CODE: "
00105        ELSE
00106             IF FUNCTION-CODE = "@"
00107                 DISPLAY " "
00108                 DISPLAY "****> PLEASE ENTER FUNCTION CODE: "
00109             ELSE
00110                 DISPLAY FUNCTION-CODE " IS AN ILLEGAL VALUE."
00111                 DISPLAY "LEGAL VALUES ARE SHOWN BELOW:"
00112                 PERFORM C1-DISPLAY-SELECTION-MENU
00113                 DISPLAY " "
00114                 DISPLAY "****> PLEASE ENTER A CORRECT FUNCTION CO
00115    -        "DE: ".
00116
00117        ACCEPT FUNCTION-CODE FROM CONSOLE.
00118
00119    B2-PROCESS-REQUEST.
00120
```

Program 2-Source (Continued)

```
00121        IF MENU-DISPLAY
00122            PERFORM C1-DISPLAY-SELECTION-MENU.
00123
00124        IF PERS-ID-ACCESS OR PERS-NAME-ACCESS
00125            PERFORM C2-PREPARE-FOR-RETRIEVAL.
00126
00127        IF DEPT-CODE-ACCESS
00128            PERFORM C3-RETRIEVE-FOR-DEPT-CODE.
00129
00130        IF NOT PROCESS-TERMINATION
00131            MOVE "@" TO FUNCTION-CODE
00132
00133            PERFORM B1-DISPLAY-INSTRUCTIONS
00134                UNTIL FUNCTION-CODE = "ID" OR "NAME" OR "DEPT"
00135                                       OR "M" OR "T".
00136
00137    C1-DISPLAY-SELECTION-MENU.
00138        DISPLAY " ".
00139        DISPLAY "*****************************************".
00140        DISPLAY "*   FUNCTION                    CODE   *".
00141        DISPLAY "*   --------------------        ----   *".
00142        DISPLAY "*   ACCESS BY PERS-ID           ID     *".
00143        DISPLAY "*   ACCESS BY NAME              NAME   *".
00144        DISPLAY "*   ACCESS BY DEPT CODE         DEPT   *".
00145        DISPLAY "*   DISPLAY THIS MENU           M      *".
00146        DISPLAY "*   TERMINATE                   T      *".
00147        DISPLAY "*****************************************".
00148        DISPLAY " ".
00149
00150    C2-PREPARE-FOR-RETRIEVAL.
00151        OPEN INPUT PERSONNEL-FILE.
00152
00153        MOVE "NO" TO TERMINATE-INPUT.
00154
00155        PERFORM D1-DISPLAY-RECORD
00156            UNTIL TERMINATE-INPUT = "YES".
00157
00158        CLOSE PERSONNEL-FILE.
00159
00160    C3-RETRIEVE-FOR-DEPT-CODE.
00161        MOVE "YES" TO RECORD-FOUND.
00162        MOVE "NO" TO END-OF-FILE.
00163        DISPLAY "****> ENTER DEPARTMENT CODE OF RECORD TO BE RETRIEVE
00164    -       "D:".
00165        ACCEPT PERS-DEPT-CODE FROM CONSOLE.
00166        MOVE PERS-DEPT-CODE TO RETRIEVAL-KEY.
00167
00168        OPEN INPUT PERSONNEL-FILE.
00169
00170        START PERSONNEL-FILE
00171            KEY IS = PERS-DEPT-CODE
00172            INVALID KEY MOVE "NO" TO RECORD-FOUND.
00173
```

Program 2-Source (Continued)

```
00174          IF RECORD-FOUND = "YES"
00175                  PERFORM D2-GET-RECORDS
00176          ELSE
00177                  DISPLAY "RECORD WITH RETRIEVAL KEY " RETRIEVAL-KEY
00178                      "IS NOT IN THE FILE."
00179                  DISPLAY " ".
00180
00181      CLOSE PERSONNEL-FILE.
00182
00183   D1-DISPLAY-RECORD.
00184      MOVE "YES" TO RECORD-FOUND.
00185
00186      IF PERS-ID-ACCESS
00187          DISPLAY "****> ENTER PERSONNEL ID OF RECORD TO BE RETRIEVE
00188   -     "D:"
00189          ACCEPT PERS-ID FROM CONSOLE
00190          MOVE PERS-ID TO RETRIEVAL-KEY
00191          READ PERSONNEL-FILE
00192              KEY IS PERS-ID
00193              INVALID KEY MOVE "NO" TO RECORD-FOUND.
00194
00195      IF PERS-NAME-ACCESS
00196          DISPLAY "****> ENTER PERSONNEL NAME OF RECORD TO BE RETRIE
00197   -     "VED:"
00198          ACCEPT PERS-NAME FROM CONSOLE
00199          MOVE PERS-NAME TO RETRIEVAL-KEY
00200          READ PERSONNEL-FILE
00201              KEY IS PERS-NAME
00202              INVALID KEY MOVE "NO" TO RECORD-FOUND.
00203
00204      IF RECORD-FOUND = "YES"
00205              DISPLAY " "
00206              DISPLAY "PERSONNEL ID IS   : " PERS-ID
00207              DISPLAY "PERSONNEL NAME IS : " PERS-NAME
00208              DISPLAY "DEPARTMENT CODE IS: " PERS-DEPT-CODE
00209              DISPLAY "  "
00210      ELSE
00211              DISPLAY "RECORD WITH RETRIEVAL KEY " RETRIEVAL-KEY
00212                  " IS NOT IN THE FILE."
00213              DISPLAY " ".
00214
00215      DISPLAY "****> DO YOU WANT TO TERMINATE RECORD RETRIEVAL?".
00216      DISPLAY "****> TYPE YES OR NO.".
00217      ACCEPT TERMINATE-INPUT FROM CONSOLE.
00218
00219   D2-GET-RECORDS.
00220      READ PERSONNEL-FILE NEXT
00221              AT END MOVE "YES" TO END-OF-FILE.
00222
00223      PERFORM E1-DISPLAY-AND-RETRIEVE
00224              UNTIL END-OF-FILE = "YES".
00225
00226   E1-DISPLAY-AND-RETRIEVE.
00227
```

Program 2-Source (Continued)

```
00228              IF PERS-DEPT-CODE = RETRIEVAL-KEY
00229                  DISPLAY " "
00230                  DISPLAY "PERSONNEL ID IS   : " PERS-ID
00231                  DISPLAY "PERSONNEL NAME IS : " PERS-NAME
00232                  DISPLAY "DEPARTMENT CODE IS: " PERS-DEPT-CODE
00233                  DISPLAY "  ".
00234
00235          READ PERSONNEL-FILE NEXT
00236                  AT END MOVE "YES" TO END-OF-FILE.
```

Program 2-Source (Continued)

```
*********************************************
* THIS PROGRAM CAN BE USED TO ACCESS THE  *
*   INDEXED FILE, CALLED PERSONNEL FILE   *
*    EITHER BY PERS-ID, OR PERS-NAME, OR  *
*            PERS-DEPT-CODE.              *
*********************************************


*********************************************
*  FUNCTION                    CODE  *
*  _____         ____  *
*  ACCESS BY PERS-ID           ID    *
*  ACCESS BY NAME              NAME  *
*  ACCESS BY DEPT CODE         DEPT  *
*  DISPLAY THIS MENU           M     *
*  TERMINATE                   T     *
*********************************************

****> PLEASE ENTER FUNCTION CODE:
ID
****> ENTER PERSONNEL ID OF RECORD TO BE RETRIEVED:
4146

PERSONNEL ID IS   :  4146
PERSONNEL NAME IS :  JOAN HALL
DEPARTMENT CODE IS:  SLS

****> DO YOU WANT TO TERMINATE RECORD RETRIEVAL?
****> TYPE YES OR NO.
NO
****> ENTER PERSONNEL ID OF RECORD TO BE RETRIEVED:
4455

RECORD WITH RETRIEVAL KEY 4455                 IS NOT IN THE FILE.

****> DO YOU WANT TO TERMINATE RECORD RETRIEVAL?
****> TYPE YES OR NO.
YES
```

Program 2-Output A Terminal Session for Program 2

```
****> PLEASE ENTER FUNCTION CODE:
NAME
****> ENTER PERSONNEL NAME OF RECORD TO BE RETRIEVED:
JACK MEYER

PERSONNEL ID IS   :  4023
PERSONNEL NAME IS :  JACK MEYER
DEPARTMENT CODE IS:  SLS

****> DO YOU WANT TO TERMINATE RECORD RETRIEVAL?
****> TYPE YES OR NO.
NO
****> ENTER PERSONNEL NAME OF RECORD TO BE RETRIEVED:
JOANNE TAYLOR
RECORD WITH RETRIEVAL KEY JOANNE TAYLOR            IS NOT IN THE FILE.

****> DO YOU WANT TO TERMINATE RECORD RETRIEVAL?
****> TYPE YES OR NO.
YES

****> PLEASE ENTER FUNCTION CODE:
DEPT
****> ENTER DEPARTMENT CODE OF RECORD TO BE RETRIEVED:
DP

PERSONNEL ID IS   :  3812
PERSONNEL NAME IS :  KAREN WHITE
DEPARTMENT CODE IS:  DP


PERSONNEL ID IS   :  3971
PERSONNEL NAME IS :  DONALD LITTLE
DEPARTMENT CODE IS:  DP


PERSONNEL ID IS   :  4031
PERSONNEL NAME IS :  JUDY SMITH
DEPARTMENT CODE IS:  DP


PERSONNEL ID IS   :  4241
PERSONNEL NAME IS :  TIMOTHY SANDERS
DEPARTMENT CODE IS:  DP

****> PLEASE ENTER FUNCTION CODE:
DEPT
****> ENTER DEPARTMENT CODE OF RECORD TO BE RETRIEVED:
ACC

PERSONNEL ID IS   :  4011
PERSONNEL NAME IS :  LINDA DAY
DEPARTMENT CODE IS:  ACC
```

Program 2-Output (Continued)

```
****> PLEASE ENTER FUNCTION CODE:
DPT
DPT  IS AN ILLEGAL VALUE.
LEGAL VALUES ARE SHOWN BELOW:


*****************************************
*   FUNCTION                    CODE   *
*   _____         ____   *
*   ACCESS BY PERS-ID           ID     *
*   ACCESS BY NAME              NAME   *
*   ACCESS BY DEPT CODE         DEPT   *
*   DISPLAY THIS MENU           M      *
*   TERMINATE                   T      *
*****************************************

****> PLEASE ENTER A CORRECT FUNCTION CODE:
T
```

Program 2-Output (Continued)

14

Relative File Organization

Key Terms

Study Guide
Quick Scan
Test Your Comprehension
Improve Your Problem-Solving Ability

IN THIS CHAPTER YOU WILL LEARN ABOUT

- Relative files
    - Storage structures for relative files
    - Efficiency of relative files
- Hashing
    - General algorithm for hashing
    - Division-remainder hash function
    - Midsquare hash function
    - Shift-folding hash function
    - Boundary-folding hash function
    - Digit-analysis hash function
    - Bit-compression hash function
    - Converting nonnumeric keys to integer
- Overflow handling in relative files
    - Open addressing with linear probe
    - Open addressing with quadratic probe
    - Open addressing with random probe
    - Separate chaining
- Structure of VSAM/RRDS for relative files
- COBOL features for relative files
    - Defining relative files
    - WRITE statement
    - READ statement
    - REWRITE statement
    - DELETE statement
    - START statement

Introduction

In Chapter 13 we studied access-by-content through indexing. Indexing is one way of simulating access-by-content in direct-access files. An indexed file is a compromise between pure direct access and pure sequential access in that it permits both methods. Direct access in an indexed file is based on a record identifier field.

We also mentioned that we have an alternative approach to access-by-content. It is called hashing. Hashing makes use of algorithms that take a value for an identifier that is meaningful to the user and converts it to a memory address that is meaningful to the computer. Such algorithms are known as hash functions, or key-to-address transforms.

This chapter concentrates on the concept and applications of hashing for direct-access files. We will investigate a variety of hashing techniques and some commonly used overflow handling methods for hashed files. Also, we will study their COBOL programming implications and implementations of hashed files in COBOL.

Architecture of Relative File Organization

First, we draw a scenario for the relative file organization, as shown in Figure 1. We have a direct-access file, also called a relative file, stored on a direct-access storage device.

> A **relative file** is one that allows direct access to its memory locations by their relative addresses.

Within the context of the present discussion, we will refer to individually addressable memory locations in the relative file as **buckets**. A bucket may contain one or more logical records. In an application program, the number of records that can be stored in a bucket is specified by the programmer. It should be noted that, although similar, a bucket is not exactly the same thing as a block. A block is one or more records organized into a physical record by the computer system using interblock gaps and other information. A bucket is an in-program record structure description that can hold one or more logical records. We will have more to say about buckets, but for the time being this definition should suffice.

Conceptually, the external storage allocated for a relative file is divided into the prime data area and the overflow data area. The **prime data area** consists of a predetermined number of buckets. These buckets need not be consecutive. For example, we may find it appropriate to use buckets 1 through 200 and 250 through 500 as prime data area buckets in a relative file of 450 buckets. **Overflow data area** buckets may be part of the relative file, or may even be another relative file. The fundamental difference between the two is that prime buckets store records that rightfully belong in them, whereas overflow buckets store records that cannot be accommodated in their respective prime buckets, and hence have overflowed. In Figure 1, buckets addressed 1 through N make up the prime data area, and buckets 401 through M are reserved as overflow buckets.

A relative file can be likened to an array in that its buckets can be directly accessed by their relative addresses. So far, the user is provided the capability of accessing contents of any bucket in the data structure. In other words, a query request such as, "Retrieve the records stored in bucket 50," can be easily accommodated. As mentioned previously, however, this is not sufficiently user oriented. We would rather access records by some identifier field value, as in, "Retrieve the record whose key value is K1". To gain this capability, instead of an index table we use an interface in the form of an algorithm. Such an algorithm is known as a hash function.

> A **hash function** (also called a **key-to-address transform**, or **KAT**) is an algorithm that takes a key field value as input and produces as output a relative address value within an admissible range.

To help define a rational and efficient access method, a hash function should exhibit certain desirable characteristics. First, it should be consistent, in the sense that every time the same key value is supplied, the same address value is produced.

Second, a hashing algorithm should be easy to code and extremely efficient to execute. Such efficiency is a strict must, because a hash function is a front-end interface for a relative file, and it is used immediately before any and all input-output operations.

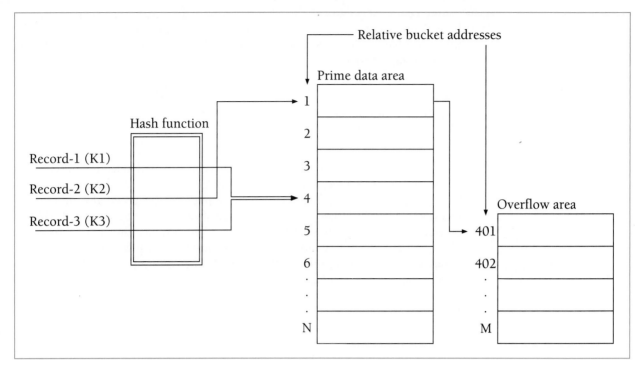

Figure 1 Architecture of a Relative File

Third, for all key values in a key space, the transformation should produce address values that are in the address space for a relative file.

> The **key space** is the set of all key field values for a file. The **address space** is the set of all admissible address values in the prime data area.

Finally, it is desirable to have hash functions that are universally good performers. Defining a hash function that does a good job only for a specific file characterized by its set of key values is probably not a good idea. This is because files are dynamic entities, and the initial set of key values is bound to change in time. We require a hash function to perform satisfactorily at all times, and with different sets of key values.

Certain characteristics of hash functions are due to compromises that have to be made to discover acceptable hash functions. Ordinarily, it appears that we should prefer hash functions that transform a given key value to a particular address, and allow no other key value to hash to that address. Such a function is called **one-to-one**. In practice, however, one-to-one hash functions lead to inefficient memory use in the prime data area. Besides, we may find it convenient to store more than one record in each prime area bucket. Therefore, we compromise and allow the transformation to be **many-to-one**. That is, a hash function may transform more than one key value to the same address.

It may also be desirable to have records stored in the prime data area to form an ordered list after hashing. In other words, given two key values, K1 and K2, such that K1 < K2, K1 hashes to an address that is smaller than the address computed for K2. Such a transform is called an **order-preserving transform**. In practice, it is difficult to come up with hash functions that satisfy this characteristic without any detrimental effects on the other desirable properties. Therefore, in general, we give up our quest for an ordered list in the prime data area and settle for **nonorder-preserving transforms** for hash functions.

As a hash function is many-to-one, a record may hash to a bucket that is fully or partially occupied.

> Given two distinct key values, K1 and K2, if a particular hash function transforms both to the same address, K1 and K2 are called **synonyms** with respect to that hash function. The phenomenon that K1 and K2 hash to the same location is referred to as a **collision**.

As long as space is available in the bucket, the colliding records may be stored in it. Once the bucket is full to capacity, we allow the new record to overflow into a designated overflow area. Although collision and subsequent overflows are permitted, it is desirable to keep their numbers as small as possible. The reason is that overflow records from a bucket form a chain, and such a chain is searched sequentially. Keeping overflows to a minimum means minimizing sequential searches in the direct-access file. Therefore, a hash function should minimize collisions by providing a reasonably uniform distribution of records in the address space. In other words, it should avoid excessive clustering of records around any one bucket in the prime data area. To summarize, the properties of hash functions are as follows:

1. Consistency
2. Ease of coding and efficiency of execution
3. Ability to map a key space to a given address space
4. Universal applicability
5. Many-to-one mapping
6. Nonorder-preserving transformation
7. Ability to minimize collisions and clustering

Efficiency of Relative File Organization

The most significant measure of performance efficiency for the architecture described above is the amount of overflow. Clearly, if overflows can be kept to a minimum, both file maintenance and access operations will be substantially more efficient. Filling this function during the life span of a relative file is one of the requirements expected of a hash function; however, other factors influence amount of overflow and the overall efficiency of this technique, such as hash function, overflow handling technique, bucket capacity, and prime area packing density.

Finding hash functions that satisfy all the stated requirements, including minimizing overflows, is no easy feat. In the next section we will discuss a few of the better known hash functions that are considered to be good performers. The designer of a file system, however, should help the function keep overflows at a minimum by paying attention to other factors.

An important design factor is the technique to handle overflows. We accept collisions and subsequent overflows as inevitable for relative files, and incorporate an appropriate technique into our file management software. These techniques have many variations, each of which exhibits some degree of success in keeping overflow chains short and avoiding clustering in the prime data area. Later in this chapter we will study them separately.

Two simple factors that should be considered for overall file system efficiency are bucket capacity and prime area packing density.

> **Bucket capacity** is the number of records that can be stored in a bucket.

Clearly, if we can store n records in each bucket of a relative file, for a given bucket the first (n − 1) collisions will not cause overflows. Overflows will start with the nth collision. Therefore, the larger the bucket capacity for a relative file, the less is the likelihood of overflow. In practice, however, bucket capacity is restricted by the capacity of input-output buffers and by some hardware parameters such as the capacity of a cylinder track for the DASD.

> **Prime area packing density** is the number of records that are actually stored at a given time in the prime area of a relative file, divided by the total number of records that can be stored in it.

The packing density for a file is 1.0 if the file is full to capacity, and 0.0 if it is empty. It is easy to see that the larger the packing density for a relative file, the higher is the probability of overflow. Also, it is clear that nothing much can be done about packing density except to provide some extra capacity in the prime data area to be used for future file expansion. Commonly in practice, an extra 20% of the prime data area needed to store the initial set of records is specified for a relative file.

The Process of Hashing

Several hash functions discovered in the past satisfy the required properties. A majority of these functions assume that keys to be transformed are integer numbers. If key values for a relative file are alphabetic or alphanumeric, simple transformation techniques can be used to convert them to integer values.

We assume that a hash function transforms all elements of a key space to integer address values in the range zero through n, where n is a positive integer. This means that (n + 1) distinct possible integer values may be generated by our hash function. We also assume that the address space consists of M distinct and consecutive memory addresses starting at address P. If the number of possible integer values that can be generated by the hash function is not equal to the number of available memory locations, the integer value computed by the hash function has to be modified by multiplying it by a **compression factor**, that is, M/(n + 1), and then truncating the result to an integer. Furthermore, if the smallest address value, P, is not equal to zero, a **displacement** of P has to be added to the integer found after applying the compression factor. This way we guarantee that the produced address value is in the correct range.

General Algorithm for Hashing

Given a hash function that generates integers in the range zero through n, a set of M consecutive prime area addresses starting at P, where M and P are integers, and a key value K, the general algorithm for hashing consists of the following steps.

Step 1: If the given key K is not an integer, and if the hash function used requires integer key values as input, use a one-to-one consistent transform to convert the key to an integer.

Step 2: Apply the hash function to the integer key, and generate an integer, A.

Step 3: If the compression factor $M/(n + 1)$ is not equal to 1.0, multiply A by the compression factor and truncate the result to an integer.

Step 4: If the smallest value in the address space, P, is not equal to zero, add P to the result of the previous step. The integer thus generated is in the proper range of the address space and can be used as a relative address.

Some Important Hash Functions

In this section we will discuss five hash functions that are widely used in practical applications. There are many others, but for our purposes, five are sufficient.

Each technique is either theoretically or empirically proved to be capable of providing a reasonably uniform distribution of records in a prime data area. Given a key space for a relative file, however, a specific hash function may indicate a minimum number of collisions and may be better than others. A good strategy for making a choice is to simulate the global hashing process for the file. For example, assume that the keys for a file are all five-digit integers. We can easily write a program that generates random five-digit integer values and triggers different hash functions tailored to fit the file space. The number of collisions defined for different alternatives may help the file designer to make the right choice for a given file.

Division-Remainder Hash Function. Let K be an integer key and M be the number of buckets in the prime data area.

Step 1: Choose an integer divisor, Q, such that Q is as close to the number of buckets, M, as possible, and is either a prime number or an integer with no small factors. An integer that is evenly divisible by small

---

AVAILABLE SPACE : { 21, 22, . . . , 32 }
HASH FUNCTION : DIVISION-REMAINDER (BY 11)

KEY SEQUENCE	KEY	REMAINDER	+ DISPLACEMENT (+21)
1	4023	8	29
2	4031	5	26
3	4011	7	28
4	3971	0	21
5	3812	6	27
6	4214	1	22
7	4241	6	27
8	4146	10	31

Figure 2 Division-Remainder Hash Function

prime numbers such as 2, 3, 5, 7, 11, 13, and so on, tends to result in unfavorable distributions and a high rate of collisions.

Step 2:   Compute the remainder of the division of K by Q. The remainder is an integer in the range of 0 through (Q − 1), and can be used as a raw relative address. In this technique, no compression factor needs to be applied to the result. However, a displacement may have to be added to the remainder to fit the output to the proper address range.

Figure 2 shows an application of the division-remainder hash function for a file of 12 buckets starting at address 21. Here we choose 11 as the divisor, being the closest prime number to the number of available buckets, 12. The keys are four-digit integers. The remainders will be numbers in the range of zero through 10. Then we add a displacement of 21 to the remainder to find the relative address. It should be noted that the last bucket address, 32, will never be used because of our choice of the divisor. This is not a big problem; we can use it as part of the overflow area.

Midsquare Hash Function.   Again, K is an integer key, M is the number of prime area buckets, and P is the start address of the file space.

Step 1:   Compute the square of K.
Step 2:   Truncate the square on the left and on the right to extract a middle portion. The integer that is the middle portion should be of the same order of magnitude as the file size.
Step 3:   Compress this raw address by multiplying it by a compression factor. In this case, the compression factor is $M/10 ** d$, where d is the number of digits in the middle portion. After that, truncate the result to an integer.
Step 4:   Add the displacement amount of P to obtain the relative address.

Examples of the midsquare hashing are shown in Figure 3. Let us consider a four-digit integer key value of 4023. Its square is 16,184,529. The number of prime area buckets for the file is 12. Therefore, the middle portion to be extracted should be a two-digit integer. In this case, it is 84. We multiply this by the compression factor of 0.12, truncate the product, and add to it the displacement of 21. The relative address obtained is 31.

Shift-Folding Hash Function.   Another KAT that works well in practice is shift folding.

Step 1:   Divide the integer key into three segments such that the middle segment is of the same order of magnitude as the file size, and the lengths of the left and right segments are equal. If necessary, pad the key on the left and/or right with a zero.
Step 2:   Shift the left segment to the right until its least significant digit is aligned vertically with that of the middle segment.
Step 3:   Shift the right segment to the left until its least significant digit is aligned with that of the middle segment.
Step 4:   Compute the sum of the three integers. Truncate the most significant digit of the sum, if necessary, so that it is of the same order of magnitude as the file size.
Step 5:   Multiply the result of step 4 with the applicable compression factor and truncate the product to an integer.
Step 6:   Add to this the appropriate displacement. This yields a relative address.

AVAILABLE SPACE : { 21, 22, . . . , 32 }
HASH FUNCTION : MIDSQUARE

KEY SEQUENCE	KEY	KEY SQUARE	MIDDLE PORTION	* COMPRESSION FACTOR (0.12)	+ DISPLACEMENT (+21)
1	4023	16184529	84	10	31
2	4031	16248961	48	5	26
3	4011	16088121	88	10	31
4	3971	15768841	68	8	29
5	3812	14531344	31	3	24
6	4214	17757796	57	6	27
7	4241	17986081	86	10	31
8	4146	17189316	89	10	31

Figure 3 Midsquare Hash Function

Several examples of hashing based on shift-folding are provided in Figure 4. Let us consider one of the key values as an example to demonstrate how this KAT works. Let K be 3812. The file size is 12 buckets. Therefore, the middle segment must be a two-digit integer. First, we pad the key value with a zero on

AVAILABLE SPACE : { 21, 22, . . . , 32 }
HASH FUNCTION : SHIFT-FOLDING

KEY SEQUENCE	KEY	PARTITIONED KEY	SUMMATION	* COMPRESSION FACTOR (0.12)	+ DISPLACEMENT (+21)
1	4023	04.02.30	36	4	25
2	4031	04.03.10	17	2	23
3	4011	04.01.10	15	1	22
4	3971	03.97.10	110	1	22
5	3812	03.81.20	104	0	21
6	4214	04.21.40	65	7	28
7	4241	04.24.10	38	4	25
8	4146	04.14.60	78	9	30

Figure 4 Shift-Folding Hash Function

the left and a zero on the right. Then we split it into three segments, shift the segments, and add them. The process is shown below.

$$03 \wedge 81 \wedge 20$$
$$\hookrightarrow 03$$
$$+ \; 20 \hookleftarrow$$
$$\overline{104}$$

The summation 104 is truncated to 04. This is multiplied by the compression factor of 0.12, and the product is truncated to an integer, yielding zero. Then a displacement of 21 is added to zero to produce 21 as the relative address.

Boundary-Folding Hash Function. This is a variation of the shift-folding hash function.

Step 1: Divide the integer key into three segments such that the middle segment is of the same order of magnitude as the file size, and the lengths of the left and right segments are equal. If necessary, pad the key on the left and/or right with a zero.

Step 2: Take the mirror image of the left segment and shift it to the right so that its least significant digit is aligned with that of the middle segment.

Step 3: Take the mirror image of the right segment and shift it to the left so that its least significant digit is aligned with that of the middle segment.

Step 4: Compute the sum of the three integers and truncate the most significant digit of the sum, if necessary, so that it is of the same order of magnitude as the file size.

Step 5: Multiply the result of the previous step by the applicable compression factor and truncate the product to an integer.

Step 6: Add to this the appropriate displacement. This yields a relative address.

Figure 5 provides examples of this key-to-address transformation technique. Let us consider the key value of 3971. First, we add a leading and a trailing zero to this integer and split it into three segments.

$$03 \wedge 97 \wedge 10$$

Then we reverse the left and right segments and align the three segments as shown below. Finally, we add the three integers, truncate the high-order digit, multiply the result by the compression factor of 0.12, and add the displacement of 21.

$$03 \wedge 97 \wedge 10$$
$$\hookrightarrow 30$$
$$+ \; 01 \hookleftarrow$$
$$\overline{128}$$

Truncating this on the left yields 28. We multiply 28 by the compression factor of 0.12 to get 3.36. We truncate 3.36 to the integer value of 3 and add the displacement of 21. The result, 24, is the relative address.

Digit-Analysis Hash Function. Given a set of integer keys of uniform length, we can obtain relative addresses by selecting and either reversing or shifting digits of the original keys. The algorithm is simple. Given are a set of integer

AVAILABLE SPACE : { 21, 22, . . . , 32 }
HASH FUNCTION   : BOUNDARY-FOLDING

KEY SEQUENCE	KEY	PARTITIONED KEY	SUMMATION	* COMPRESSION FACTOR (0.12)	+ DISPLACEMENT (+21)
1	4023	04.02.30	4<u>5</u>	5	26
2	4031	04.03.10	4<u>4</u>	5	26
3	4011	04.01.10	4<u>2</u>	5	26
4	3971	03.97.10	12<u>8</u>	3	24
5	3812	03.81.20	11<u>3</u>	1	22
6	4214	04.21.40	6<u>5</u>	7	28
7	4241	04.24.10	6<u>5</u>	7	28
8	4146	04.14.60	6<u>0</u>	7	28

Figure 5 Boundary-Folding Hash Function

keys, each of d digits, and a set of prime area addresses of order of magnitude of k, where k and d are integers, and k < d.

Step 1:   Select k digits from specified positions of each key.
Step 2:   Extract the selected k digits to form an integer.
Step 3:   Reverse this integer to obtain a raw address. Instead of a simple reversal, a predetermined pattern can be used to generate an integer from the extracted k digits, such as forming an integer by considering the third, first, and fourth digits of the key.
Step 4:   Multiply the result of step 3 by the applicable compression factor.
Step 5:   Add to this a displacement amount, if necessary, to obtain the relative address.

It is definitely imperative that for a given file the same positions in the keys and the same pattern of integer generation are used consistently. An important issue in this technique is that of selecting the positions in the keys from which digits are extracted. For this, we have to perform a digit analysis on the key space, or at least on a reasonably large subset of the key space. This analysis entails generating the frequency of each digital value for all positions in the keys. Then we select k positions that display the most uniform distributions. For example, given a key space set of 1000 key values, each four digits in length, we could obtain the following frequency distributions.

Digit	Position 1	Position 2	Position 3	Position 4
0	0	100	102	87
1	0	10	104	105
2	0	35	98	95
3	465	345	101	98
4	535	17	95	93
5	0	178	110	113
6	0	66	98	103
7	0	217	107	105
8	0	15	95	89
9	0	17	90	112

Examination of the table reveals that the most uniform distributions are for positions 3 and 4. Thus, we could choose the third and fourth positions in every key, and decide to reverse the extracted two-digit integer and use the outcome as the raw address.

Figure 6 shows several examples of the digit-analysis KAT in which the third and fourth digits are extracted and reversed. For example, for K = 4023, we get 32. We multiply this by the compression factor of 0.12 and add the displacement of 21 to obtain 24 as the relative address.

It should be noted that this method of hashing is appropriate for static files, as very few additions or deletions are expected during their lifetime.

AVAILABLE SPACE : { 21, 22, . . . , 32 }
HASH FUNCTION : DIGIT-ANALYSIS (Select 3rd and 4th digits and reverse)

KEY SEQUENCE	KEY	EXTRACTED ADDRESS	* COMPRESSION FACTOR (0.12)	+ DISPLACEMENT (+21)
1	4023	32	3	24
2	4031	13	1	22
3	4011	11	1	22
4	3971	17	2	23
5	3812	21	2	23
6	4214	41	4	25
7	4241	14	1	22
8	4146	64	7	28

Figure 6 Digit-Analysis Hash Function

Hashing Noninteger Keys

If the key values are noninteger or nonnumeric, two approaches are available: (1) we can use a hash function particularly suited for nonnumeric keys, or (2) before we apply an ordinary hash function for integer key values, we can use a consistent and one-to-one transformation to convert them to integers. Because hashing is arithmetic by nature, both methods transform nonnumeric keys to numeric values. The first approach does it as part of the hashing process, and the second performs this conversion prior to hashing.

Bit-Compression Hash Function. For conversion from nonnumeric to numeric we need an appropriate encoding scheme. It may be the EBCDIC or ASCII data encoding scheme, or another one-to-one transformation. In the following discussion we assume the data encoding scheme given in Figure 7a, where each letter and each decimal digit is represented as a six-bit binary string.

It is possible to devise many different hash functions of the bit-compression type. We discuss one version that enables every character in the key values to participate in the process. The algorithm makes use of the logical operator known as exclusive or.

Simply defined, **exclusive or (XOR)** of two binary digits produces the binary digit zero if both operands are zero, or if both operands are 1. Otherwise, the result is the binary digit 1. In other words, using XOR as the operator;

$$0 \ XOR \ 0 = 0, \ 1 \ XOR \ 1 = 0$$
$$1 \ XOR \ 0 = 1, \ 0 \ XOR \ 1 = 1.$$

The truth table for XOR is given below.

	1	0
1	0	1
0	1	0

This definition can be extended to two binary strings of equal length. In this case, we consider the corresponding positions in the operands and apply the above truth table to compute XOR. For example, $101101 \ XOR \ 011011 = 110110$.

The steps of the bit compression hashing algorithm for nonnumeric keys are as follows. Let us assume that K is an alphanumeric key value, M is the number of prime area buckets in the relative file, P is the first relative address in the address space, and d is the length of the binary strings in the data encoding scheme.

Step 1: Compute the XOR of the binary strings for all characters in K.
Step 2: Convert the binary string thus obtained to its equivalent decimal integer.
Step 3: Multiply the result of the previous step by the compression factor of $(M/(2 ** d))$ and truncate the product to an integer.
Step 4: Add to this the displacement amount of P to get the relative address.

This hashing technique is exemplified in Figure 7b for three-character alphabetic key values, based on the encoding scheme of Figure 7a. Let us consider the key value TOM. The binary strings for T, O, and M are

T = 010100
O = 001111
M = 001101

CHARACTER	BIT STRING	CHARACTER	BIT STRING	CHARACTER	BIT STRING
A	000001	M	001101	Y	011001
B	000010	N	001110	Z	011010
C	000011	O	001111	0	011011
D	000100	P	010000	1	011100
E	000101	Q	010001	2	011101
F	000110	R	010010	3	011110
G	000111	S	010011	4	011111
H	001000	T	010100	5	100000
I	001001	U	010101	6	100001
J	001010	V	010110	7	100010
K	001011	W	010111	8	100011
L	001100	X	011000	9	100100

(a) A binary string encoding of alphanumeric characters

AVAILABLE SPACE : { 21, 22, . . . , 32 }
HASH FUNCTION : COMPRESSION

KEY SEQUENCE	KEY	BIT STRINGS FOR CHARACTERS			EXCLUSIVE OR (Binary String)	RAW ADDRESS (Deci-mal)	RELATIVE ADDRESS
		CHARACTER 1	CHARACTER 2	CHARACTER 3			
1	TOM	010100	001111	001101	010110	22	25
2	JAN	001010	000001	001110	000101	5	21
3	BOB	000010	001111	000010	001111	15	23
4	TIM	010100	001001	001101	010000	16	24
5	ALI	000001	001100	001001	000100	4	21
6	JIM	001010	001001	001101	001110	14	23
7	AMY	000001	001101	011001	010101	21	24
8	RON	010010	001111	001110	010011	19	24

(b) Compression hash function using exclusive OR

Figure 7 Hashing Nonnumeric Keys

AVAILABLE SPACE : { 21, 22, . . . , 32 }
HASH FUNCTION   : DIVISION-REMAINDER (BY 11)

KEY SEQUENCE	KEY	CONCATENATED BINARY STRING	INTEGER KEY	REMAINDER	+ DISPLACE-MENT (+21)
1	TOM	010100001111001101	82,893	8	29
2	JAN	00101000001001110	41,038	8	29
3	BOB	00001000111100010	9,154	2	23
4	TIM	010100001001001101	82,509	9	30
5	ALI	00000100110000100	4,873	0	21
6	JIM	00101000100100110	41,549	2	23
7	AMY	00000100110101100	4,953	3	24
8	RON	010010001111001110	74,702	1	22

(c) Conversion to integer keys followed by division hashing

Figure 7 (Continued)

The XOR of these binary strings yields 010100 XOR 001111 XOR 001101 = 010110. Interpreted as a binary number, this is equivalent to decimal 22. Remembering that there are 64 different binary strings of length 6 and that we have 12 available prime data area buckets, we have to multiply 22 by the compression factor:

$$12/64 = 0.1875$$

After truncating the result to an integer, this multiplication yields 4. We add the displacement 21 to this and get the relative address of 25.

Converting Nonnumeric Keys to Integer. Nonnumeric keys can be transformed to equivalent integer values in many ways. We describe one technique here.

Let us assume that each character is represented by a d bit binary string in our data encoding scheme, and that each key consists of c characters.

Step 1:   Consider the binary strings for each character of the given key value, and concatenate them into a single binary string of length c * d.
Step 2:   Treat this binary string as an integer representation and convert it to the equivalent decimal integer.
Step 3:   Apply a hash function to the transformed key.

Examples of this conversion process are given in Figure 7c. Here, the data encoding scheme of Figure 7a is used as the basis of conversion. After the keys are transformed to integer values, the division-remainder hashing (by 11) is applied.

1. In a relative file, memory locations are accessed by their _____ .
2. The external storage reserved for a relative file is divided into a prime data area and an overflow area. (T or F)
3. The set of all key values for a file is called _____ , and the set of all admissible address values in the prime data area is called _____ .
4. Which of the following is a desirable property of hash functions?
   a. Consistency
   b. Execution efficiency
   c. Universal applicability.
   d. Ability to minimize collisions and clustering
   e. All of the above
5. Packing density is the number of records that can be stored in a bucket. (T or F)
6. In the division-remainder hash function, the divisor should be either a _____ or an integer with _____ .
7. The division-remainder hash function does not require the remainder to be multiplied by a compression factor. (T or F)
8. In a hashing process, the integer key is split into three segments such that the middle segment is of the same order of magnitude as the file size, and the lengths of the left and right segments are equal. Then the three segments are added, the high-order digit in the result is truncated if necessary, and the number thus found is modified to fit in the acceptable range of addresses. This process corresponds to _____ .
9. In bit-compression hashing, the first step is to compute the XOR of the binary strings for all characters in a given alphanumeric key. (T or F)

Answers: 1. relative addresses; 2. T; 3. key space, address space; 4. e; 5. F; 6. prime number, no small factors; 7. T; 8. shift-folding hash function; 9. T.

Example Program 1:   ***COBOL Implementation of Selected Hash Functions***

Before we conclude our discussion of hashing, we present a simple interactive COBOL program in Program 1-Source that includes implementations of the three functions discussed.

As expected, the program code is simple and extremely efficient for all hash functions. A single COMPUTE statement in line 00108 corresponds to the division-remainder hash function. The three COMPUTE statements in lines 00121 through 00125 transform a key value stored in the variable KEY-VALUE to a relative address using the midsquare hash function. Finally, the five COMPUTE statements in lines 00136 through 00145 correspond to the shift-folding hash function. Some of these implementations are used later in Program 2.

Overflow Handling

As the number of available buckets in a relative file is generally small compared to the number of records we would like to store in it, no matter how carefully we choose a hash function, we are bound to have collisions and overflows. We know that a good hash function may be of some help in keeping the collisions uniformly distributed over the prime data area. Also, having a large bucket capacity will result in fewer overflows. However, it is inevitable that overflows occur, and we must take precautions to accommodate them.

Quite a few overflow handling techniques are available for this. They depend on three factors: the number of hash functions used, whether or not the prime data area and overflow area are separate, and whether or not the overflow records are chained.

In any overflow handling technique, our main purpose is to store overflow records somewhere in the file such that they can be accessed rapidly when sought. Also, an overflow handling technique should be capable of trying every overflow bucket in the file to accommodate records. Only if none is empty should it signal that the file is full.

Some common overflow handling techniques are open addressing with linear probe, open addressing with quadratic probe, open addressing with random probe, and overflow record chaining. Many others exist but these are the most basic and illustrate the fundamental ideas. These cover overflow record chaining and use of separate prime and overflow areas. In some overflow handling techniques, more than one hash function can be relied upon to facilitate overflow handling (e.g., double hashing). These, however, are outside the scope of our discussion.

Before we present the details of these techniques, let us clarify the associated terminology. In one approach we may want to store overflow records in the prime data area. In other words, there is no separate overflow area, and both prime and the overflow records are stored in the prime area. This is referred to as open addressing.

> In **open addressing**, if a record is hashed to a bucket and that bucket is full, other buckets in the prime data area are systematically accessed until an empty bucket is found to store the overflow record.

The main issue here is with regard to systematic access. How do we do that? Other buckets can be probed and examined in several ways if a particular bucket is full during the record insertion process. Three probe techniques are linear, quadratic, and random.

Open Addressing with Linear Probe

In **linear probe** we access buckets that are located after the bucket at which a collision has occurred, until an empty bucket or one that has enough space to store the incoming record can be found. If the end of the file is encountered during probing, we go back to the beginning and continue. If no bucket to store the record can be found before the origin address is encountered, the file is full. In other words, if the address space for the relative file is the sequence

$$\{p, p+1, p+2, \ldots, i, i+1, \ldots, m \}$$

and if an overflow is due to a collision at bucket i, then in linear probe the following sequence of locations is used:

$$\{i+1, i+2, \ldots, m, p, p+1, \ldots, i-1\}$$

Open addressing with linear probe is illustrated in Figure 8. Here we have a relative file of 12 buckets, starting with a relative address of 21. The bucket capacity for the file is one record. No separate overflow area is defined. Therefore, to handle overflow the technique of open addressing in the prime data area is indicated. The hash function used is the midsquare KAT for eight record key values, as shown in Figure 3. Figure 8 indicates the instances of the prime data area after each record insertion. We modify the bucket structure by including a one-byte status indicator field. In our example, the status indicator field may have three values:

- E = the bucket is empty
- F = the bucket is full
- D = the bucket contains a logically deleted record and can be used to store new records

Initially, all buckets are empty and therefore their status indicator fields contain E. The first record has a key value of 4023 and hashes to bucket 31. As bucket 31 is empty, the record is stored there, and the status indicator field is changed to F. The third record insertion results in a collision at 31 and is treated as an overflow record. Using linear probe, we access bucket 32 and store the record in it. Notice that after all eight records are inserted we will have a cluster formed after bucket 31 extending to bucket 22. This cluster is due to three overflows from bucket 31.

The logic of the search process is similar to that of insertion. Suppose we are searching for a record with the key value of 4146. The hash function generates the relative address of 31. We access bucket 31 and compare the key value of its content with the search key, but with no success. Remembering that the file has been loaded using linear probe, we access the next bucket with address 32, again with no success. As 32 is the file boundary, we cyclically proceed to the beginning of the file, bucket 21, and then to bucket 22 where we find the record.

Consider a search key value, say, 4323, that also hashes to 31. Applying the above algorithm, we probe buckets 31, 32, 21, and 22 with no success. We terminate our search after probing bucket 23 and finding that it is empty. It is conceivable that the entire file is full. In that case, the search terminates when the address of the bucket being probed becomes the same as the address generated by the hash function. Therefore, the search termination condition for searching a relative file based on linear probe can be formulated as follows.

(search is successful)
OR
(an empty bucket is being probed)
OR
(address of current bucket = address computed by the hash function)

Suppose we delete the record with key 4241 in Figure 8. We search for 4241, find it in bucket 21, and logically delete it by changing the status indicator field value to D. A physical delete in this file organization is highly unfeasible and boils down to complete rehashing. Clearly, a record that has previously overflowed from bucket 31 may exist beyond bucket 21. Therefore, we do not terminate the search process when we encounter a bucket in a cluster with status indicator value of D.

Open addressing with linear probe is the simplest of all overflow handling techniques; however, it does have some shortcomings. One is its inherent tendency to have overflow records clustering immediately after the bucket of collision. Clearly, the first overflow record due to a collision at bucket i is stored at bucket (i+1), if that bucket is available, and the second overflow from i is stored at bucket (i+2), and so on. Thus, long sequences of occupied buckets are formed after the points of collision while other bucket sequences in the file may be empty. This is known as **primary clustering**. A primary cluster may

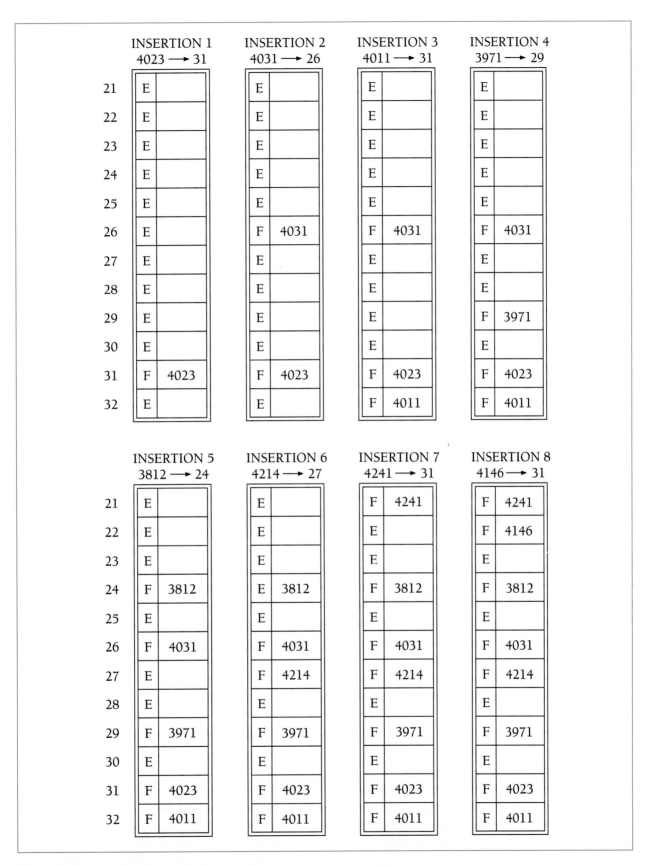

Figure 8 Open Addressing with Linear Probe

also contain buckets that store prime records, that is, records that rightfully belong where they are stored. As a result, insertion and search processes in linear probe are somewhat inefficient. To ensure a more uniform distribution of records in the prime data area, other probing techniques can be used.

Open Addressing with Quadratic Probe

In quadratic probe, if we have an overflow coming from bucket i, the sequence of addresses that we probe is

$$\{i+1, i+4, i+9, i+16, i+25, \ldots \}$$

The pattern here is based on the sequence $\{1, 4, 9, 16, 25, \ldots \}$, which are squares of integers $\{1, 2, 3, 4, 5, \ldots \}$, and hence the name quadratic probe.

The example given in Figure 9 is based on the same relative file environment, key space, and hash function as in Figure 8. The sequence used in quadratic probe for insertion or search operations starting at bucket 31 is

$$\{32, 23, 28, 23, 32, 31, 30, \ldots \}$$

In other words, to store an overflow record from bucket 31, we first try bucket 32, then 23, 28, and so on, until an empty bucket can be found. Figure 9 shows the final schema for the relative file based on quadratic probe. It should be noted that quadratic probe eliminates primary clustering around the point of collision.

Open Addressing with Random Probe

Another way to eliminate primary clustering in open addressing is to generate a sequence of random addresses in the range of the address space and use them for probing. The random numbers need not be ordered, and the process terminates after all possible bucket addresses have been generated once. For each bucket address we should be able to generate a different sequence of random addresses. Then we use these elements corresponding to a given bucket for probing whenever an overflow occurs at that bucket. This method is called random probe.

Different random number-generation techniques can be used to create such sequences of random addresses. The following algorithm is easy to implement, and guarantees a random sequence of distinct integers that cover the entire range of a given address space in the range zero through M.

Let X be the address of the bucket for which we want to generate a random sequence, and C be an integer such that C and M are relatively prime to each other (i.e., the greatest common divisor of C and M is 1).

Step 1:   Store X in Y.
Step 2:   Add Y and C.
Step 3:   Compute the remainder of the division of (Y + C) by M.
Step 4:   Include the remainder in the random sequence of addresses.
Step 5:   If the remainder is equal to X, terminate.
Step 6:   Otherwise, store remainder in Y and go to step 2.

If the actual address space starts with a bucket address of P, all elements of the random sequence will have to be transformed by the displacement of P.

Let us apply this algorithm to the example of Figure 3 and the relative file of the examples in Figures 8 and 9. Suppose we want to generate a random sequence of addresses for bucket 31. Our actual address space is in the range of 21 through 32, with 12 buckets. When this address space is mapped to 12 buckets in the range of zero through 11, bucket 31 becomes bucket 10.

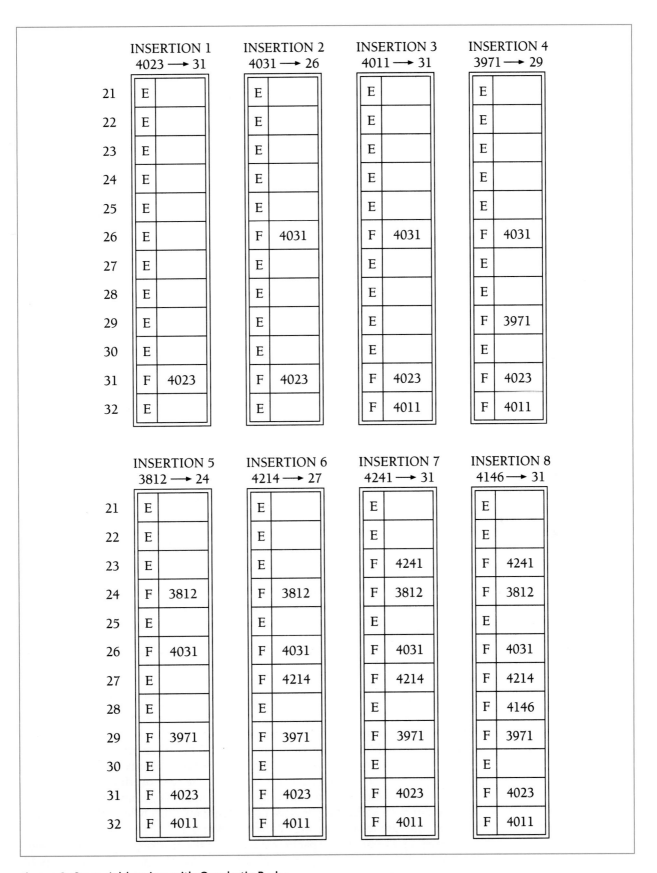

Figure 9 Open Addressing with Quadratic Probe

Therefore, in the algorithm, X = 10 and M = 12. We choose C = 5. The integers 5 and 12 are relatively prime to each other. The algorithm produces the sequence

$$\{3, 8, 1, 6, 11, 4, 9, 2, 7, 0, 5, 10\}$$

Adding the displacement of 21 to each member of the sequence, we get

$$\{24, 29, 22, 27, 32, 25, 30, 23, 28, 21, 26, 31\}$$

Note that this random sequence of addresses covers the entire range of the address space, and every address in it is distinct. Now we can use this sequence to accommodate overflows from bucket 31. For the first overflow we try bucket 24, for the second, bucket 29, and so on.

Figure 10 shows a step-by-step loading of a relative file for which the overflow handling technique is random probe. The third insertion into the file causes a collision at bucket 31. We store this record in bucket 24, which is the first element of the random sequence generated for bucket 31. The fifth insertion also causes a collision at bucket 24, which already contains an overflow record coming from 31. Using the same algorithm, we generate a random sequence of addresses for bucket 24, as

$$\{29, 22, 27, 32, 25, 30, 23, 28, 21, 26, 31, 24\}$$

For the fifth insertion (record key 3812 hashing to 24) we probe the bucket 29 and fail. Our next attempt is successful, and thus we store the record in bucket 22. The seventh and eighth insertions also cause overflows from 31, for which we use the first random sequence.

Separate Chaining

Despite its simplicity, open addressing has some disadvantages. First, we have no way of telling whether a given bucket contains a prime record, that is, a record that initially hashed to that bucket, or an overflow record coming from another bucket. As a result, even when primary clustering is minimized through the use of random probe, searching the file is somewhat inefficient. We occasionally have to examine buckets containing records that do not belong in the set of colliding records determined by a particular relative address.

Second, as different chains of colliding records are not explicitly separated from each other, it is generally difficult to extract all synonym records in the file that have hashed to a given address. Finally, we have seen that physical deletion of records in the file is quite difficult.

These problems can be resolved by constructing overflow chains, that is, linked lists that contain all synonyms at a given address. By linking synonyms together, we can create and maintain separate chains.

Separate chaining is commonly used to manage overflows and requires the use of pointer fields in record structures. The available direct-access storage is divided into a prime area and a separate overflow area. In both areas the record structure is modified to include pointer fields. The prime area is used to store records that do not result in collision. All overflow records are stored in the overflow area. Each prime record is linked to the first overflow record in the overflow area, and all other overflows are chained together in the overflow area. As in open addressing, it is useful to maintain a flag field in the prime area record structure to indicate that a given bucket is full (F) or empty (E).

Figure 11 exemplifies separate chaining for the key sequence and the mid-square hash function of Figure 3. We assume that the prime area consists of buckets 21 through 32, and the overflow area buckets 33 through 41. We further assume that an auxiliary data structure (e.g., stack or queue) will be used systematically to yield an available overflow bucket address whenever needed. The symbol * denotes the end-of-list marker.

INSERTION 1
4023 → 31

21	E	
22	E	
23	E	
24	E	
25	E	
26	E	
27	E	
28	E	
29	E	
30	E	
31	F	4023
32	E	

INSERTION 2
4031 → 26

21	E	
22	E	
23	E	
24	E	
25	E	
26	F	4031
27	E	
28	E	
29	E	
30	E	
31	F	4023
32	E	

INSERTION 3
4011 → 31

21	E	
22	E	
23	E	
24	F	4011
25	E	
26	F	4031
27	E	
28	E	
29	E	
30	E	
31	F	4023
32	E	

INSERTION 4
3971 → 29

21	E	
22	E	
23	E	
24	F	4011
25	E	
26	F	4031
27	E	
28	E	
29	F	3971
30	E	
31	F	4023
32	E	

INSERTION 5
3812 → 24

21	E	
22	F	3812
23	E	
24	F	4011
25	E	
26	F	4031
27	E	
28	E	
29	F	3971
30	E	
31	F	4023
32	E	

INSERTION 6
4214 → 27

21	E	
22	F	3812
23	E	
24	F	4011
25	E	
26	F	4031
27	F	4214
28	E	
29	F	3971
30	E	
31	F	4023
32	E	

INSERTION 7
4241 → 31

21	E	
22	F	3812
23	E	
24	F	4011
25	E	
26	F	4031
27	F	4214
28	E	
29	F	3971
30	E	
31	F	4023
32	F	4241

INSERTION 8
4146 → 31

21	E	
22	F	3812
23	E	
24	F	4011
25	F	4146
26	F	4031
27	F	4214
28	E	
29	F	3971
30	E	
31	F	4023
32	F	4241

Figure 10 Open Addressing with Random Probe

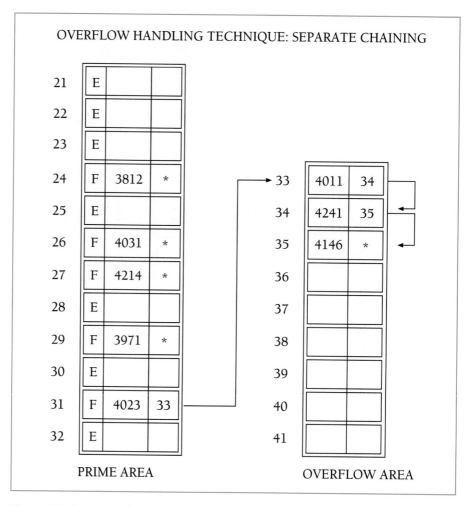

Figure 11 Separate Chaining

In loading this relative file using separate chaining, whenever a record hashes to a prime area bucket we access that bucket and check to see if the flag indicator is E. If so, we store it in that bucket with * in the pointer field of the record and change the flag indicator to F. If the bucket is full, we use its pointer field value to access overflow buckets until we reach a record whose pointer field is *. At this instant we pop a stack (if the auxiliary data structure being used is a stack) to obtain an empty overflow bucket address. This bucket can be used to accommodate the new record as the last element of the linked list.

In Figure 11 the first record that hashes to bucket 31 (4023) is stored in the prime area. The remaining overflow records due to collisions at 31 (i.e., 4011, 4241, and 4146) are formed into a separate linked list in the overflow area. With this data structure it is possible to access a given prime area address and collect all synonyms belonging in that location by traversing the appropriate linked list. Also, a linked-list deletion algorithm can be easily implemented to delete physically any record in the file.

A variation of separate chaining is shown in Figure 12. All records are stored in the overflow area and the prime area is reserved for linked list heads. Each bucket in the prime area is structured to store only a pointer value, leading us to the beginning of the synonyms chain for that bucket in the overflow area. If no record has hashed to a given bucket address, the corresponding prime area bucket contains an * as the end-of-list marker. The prime area in this structure resembles an index table in that it associates relative addresses in the prime area to those in the overflow area in a one-to-one fashion. This table is called a **hash table**. Because a hash table consists of a set of pointer values only, even

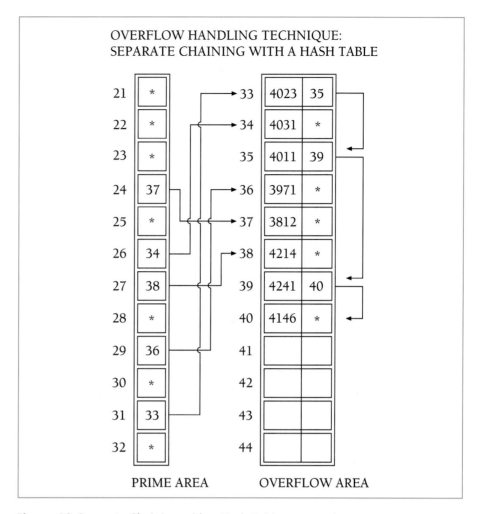

Figure 12 Separate Chaining with a Hash Table

for a large file it does not require excessive storage, and it can even be kept as an internal data structure, thereby improving the overall file system efficiency.

REVIEW QUESTIONS

1. In a relative file, the larger the bucket capacity, the less likely it is to have overflows in the prime data area. (T or F)
2. In open addressing, overflow records are stored in a specially allocated and separate overflow area. (T or F)
3. Open addressing has three commonly used probe techniques: _____ , _____ , and _____ .
4. In open addressing with linear probe, when searching for a record the search is terminated only if the bucket being probed is empty. (T or F)
5. Open addressing with linear probe has a tendency to form long sequences of occupied buckets after the points of collision. This is called _____ .
6. In open addressing with quadratic probe, suppose an overflow has occurred at relative address 25. The first three buckets that will be probed have the addresses _____ , _____ , and _____ .
7. The main advantage of open addressing with random probe is its tendency to minimize primary clustering. (T or F)
8. In open addressing without chaining it is easy to delete records physically and to extract all synonym records that have hashed to the same address in a relative file. (T or F)

Answers: 1. T; 2. F; 3. linear, quadratic, random; 4. F; 5. primary clustering; 6. 26, 30, 34; 7. T; 8. F.

Implementation of Relative Files: Structure of VSAM/RRDS

To create, maintain, and use relative files in an application program, we should have several elements at our disposal:

1. A set of language features that can be used to define a given file logically as a relative file in the program, and specify the necessary input and output operations
2. A file management system that provides proper interaction between the application program and the physical files the program uses
3. Specifically for relative files, a hashing technique as the user-computer interface, making possible meaningful access to data in the files
4. Again for relative files, an appropriate overflow handling technique to process files efficiently

The last two elements are the application programmer's responsibility. Using COBOL as the programming vehicle, we can easily incorporate appropriate hashing algorithms into our application programs. They generate relative addresses that are required by the COBOL input-output instructions to access records. We can also devise data structures and algorithms to implement an overflow handling technique for our file. In addition, COBOL offers basic language constructs through which we can define relative files and prescribe the needed I-O operations for record access or storage. These features are addressed in the next section.

There remains the second element, that is, a file management system that is capable of the following functions:

1. Identifying an in-program relative file and associating it with the correct physical direct-access file stored with other files in direct-access storage
2. Opening and closing a physical file for input or output
3. Accessing storage locations directly by a relative address that is provided by the program

Different file management systems can satisfactorily perform these functions. From a commercial point of view, one of the more significant systems for relative file processing is VSAM/RRDS (virtual storage access method/relative record data set). It is an extension of IBM's VSAM system discussed in Chapter 13.

From a structural point of view, VSAM/RRDS closely resembles the keyed sequence data set component of VSAM. In both, a file is viewed as a cluster consisting of control areas and control intervals. Also, each file is controlled by VSAM master and user catalogs.

Important differences exist between VSAM/KSDS and VSAM/RRDS, however. In contrast to VSAM/KSDS, a RRDS cluster consists of only a data area, with no base index area or alternate index area. An RRDS cluster is made up of control intervals that have buckets in which records are stored. Each record is identified and accessed by a **relative record number (RRN)**. The RRN of the first logical record in a VSAM/RRDS cluster is 1, that of the second record is 2, and so on. To store a record or access a stored record, the relative number of the bucket containing the record is used. The number of buckets in a control interval depends on the CI size and the logical record length. A bucket may be occupied or empty.

VSAM/RRDS permits random access to records by RRN. It also permits sequential access, in which case records are retrieved in increasing order of relative record numbers.

VSAM/RRDS supports only fixed-length record format. Variable-length and spanned record formats are not permitted. Also, it is not possible to allocate free space for control intervals and control areas in an RRDS cluster.

Records in buckets can be deleted physically, thus rendering such buckets reusable. The control information in CIDF (control interval descriptor field) and RDF (record descriptor field) in each control interval indicate whether a given bucket is occupied or available for use.

When adding a record to a bucket in a VSAM/RRDS cluster, the system accesses the bucket by its RRN and stores the record if the bucket is vacant. If not, VSAM specifies a status condition to the application program, indicating that record addition is unsuccessful.

Because no index of any kind is built for and used by a VSAM/RRDS cluster, this file organization and access method is more efficient and faster than VSAM/KSDS. Unless a key-to-address transform is incorporated into the application program, however, it does not permit access-by-content.

COBOL Language Features for Relative Files

For relative files, COBOL provides language features for file definition and input-output operations. They are quite similar to those discussed for indexed files.

Defining Relative Files

A relative file in a COBOL program should be defined in the ENVIRONMENT DIVISION through a SELECT statement, and the definition should be completed in the form of an FD block in the FILE SECTION of the DATA DIVISION. The requirements of the FD block for a relative file are similar to those for sequential or indexed sequential files, so we need not spend any time on them.

The SELECT statement for relative files consists of the following syntactical elements:

1. The key word SELECT
2. An internal file name
3. ASSIGN TO, followed by an external file name
4. The ORGANIZATION IS RELATIVE clause
5. An optional ACCESS MODE clause, consisting of either
   a. The key word SEQUENTIAL, which may be followed by a RELATIVE KEY clause, or
   b. The key word RANDOM or DYNAMIC, which should be followed by a required RELATIVE KEY clause
6. An optional FILE STATUS clause referencing a data name that should be defined in the WORKING-STORAGE SECTION of the program

The RELATIVE KEY clause includes another WORKING-STORAGE data name, which must be an unsigned integer field. If the ACCESS MODE clause is missing, the file access mode will be taken as SEQUENTIAL. An example follows.

```
SELECT PERSONNEL-FILE
    ASSIGN       TO INFILE
    ORGANIZATION IS RELATIVE
    ACCESS MODE  IS RANDOM
    RELATIVE KEY IS RELATIVE-ADDRESS
    FILE STATUS  IS PERS-FILE-STATUS-CODE.
```

As is seen, similar to indexed files, a relative file can be accessed in three different manners: sequential, random, and dynamic. Dynamic access connotes the ability to access records either sequentially or randomly at the programmer's discretion within the same program. It should be stressed that COBOL considers a relative file as a collection of physically adjacent buckets with relative addresses ranging from 1 through n, where n is the number of buckets allocated for the file and specified by the programmer through job control statements. After we open a relative file we may either specify a relative location and access its content directly, or sequentially access the next available logical record in the file.

Random-access mode is more significant in that it allows direct access to any bucket within the file range. For this, the programmer should store an integer value in the RELATIVE KEY data field. For example, given the above PERSONNEL-FILE, the following statements will result in accessing the content of the fifth bucket in the file.

```
MOVE 5 TO RELATIVE-ADDRESS.
READ PERSONNEL-FILE
    INVALID KEY PERFORM ERROR-IN-ACCESS.
```

The RELATIVE KEY for relative files is a data element defined in the WORKING-STORAGE SECTION, and is not part of the record structure for the file. Special care should be taken not to confuse RELATIVE KEY with record key or alternate key of indexed sequential files.

Rather than accessing the fifth bucket of a relative file, we may want to access the record for which the EMPLOYEE-NUMBER is, for example, 1200. This requires that a hash function be included in the program. The hash function processes the supplied value for EMPLOYEE-NUMBER and transforms it to an admissible relative address value. Then we move this relative address value to the RELATIVE KEY data item and subsequently execute a READ statement.

Finally, the FILE STATUS option is similar to that for indexed files. It enables the system to store two-digit status codes in the file status variable that is defined in the WORKING-STORAGE SECTION. The reader should refer to appropriate technical manuals for different values of the file status code variable and their meaning.

Input-Output Operations for Relative Files

For relative files, the relevant COBOL instructions are exactly the same as those for indexed files in type and syntax. They are OPEN and CLOSE statements, and the five I-O statements READ, WRITE, REWRITE, DELETE, and START. Important differences and operational principles exist for relative file processing, however.

WRITE Statement. The WRITE statement can be used to create a relative file either sequentially or randomly. It can also be used to add new records to an existing relative file.

Before we can load a relative file we must allocate space for it on a direct-access storage device. This is done using job control statements that help the programmer to communicate with the VSAM file management system. After space is allocated, we have a prescribed number of buckets reserved for our file on DASD. The buckets are identified by their relative addresses and initially are empty. By "empty" we mean that no data have yet been written into them. Once a data record is written into a bucket, the bucket will become write-protected by the VSAM system until its content is deleted through the execution of a

DELETE statement. Therefore, in the lifetime of a file, data can be written into a bucket provided it is empty or it contains a deleted record.

Whether it is used for sequential or random file loading or for record insertion, there is only one syntax for the WRITE statement. The relevant rules for WRITE are summarized below.

Rules for Sequential Loading of a Relative File

1. The file must be opened in OUTPUT mode.
2. The file access mode must be SEQUENTIAL.
3. In the SELECT statement for the file the RELATIVE KEY clause is not required. However, if this option is used in the SELECT statement and an integer data item is defined in the WORKING-STORAGE SECTION as the relative key, after the execution of a WRITE statement the relative address of the bucket into which a record has just been written will be stored in the RELATIVE KEY data item.
4. No value need be specified for the RELATIVE KEY data item.

The first WRITE statement execution after the file is opened stores a record in the first bucket, and the subsequent WRITE executions make use of the other buckets in increasing order of relative bucket addresses. An INVALID KEY condition is raised if the file is full, and no more records can be written into it.

The underlying principles for sequential loading of relative files are depicted in Figure 13. Figure 13a shows a schema for a relative file of eight buckets after space allocation. In the figure, a bucket containing the string " " " " " " " " " " represents an unused bucket suitable for storing data records. The file access mode is sequential, and the file open mode should be OUTPUT for initial sequential loading. At this point a WRITE statement stores the content of the record structure as the first logical record (record-1) in bucket 1 (Figure 13b). The second WRITE makes use of the next bucket, and so on (Figure 13c). After the file is full, an attempt to write another record will result in an INVALID KEY condition (Figure 13d).

Rules for Random Loading of a Relative File

1. The file open mode must be OUTPUT.
2. The file access mode must be RANDOM or DYNAMIC.
3. An appropriate value must be stored in the RELATIVE KEY data item prior to the execution of the WRITE statement. This RELATIVE KEY value enables the system to locate a bucket directly, and provided that the bucket is unused, a WRITE statement stores a record in it.

If the accessed bucket contains an existing record, or if an attempt is made to write into a location that is beyond the file boundaries, an INVALID KEY condition is raised.

Figure 14a is the schema for an empty relative file. Suppose we specify dynamic access and a file open mode of OUTPUT. Figure 14b shows the file after a record has been written into bucket 2. If we store 6 in the RELATIVE KEY data item and issue a WRITE statement, a second logical record will be stored in bucket 6 (Figure 14c). These WRITE operations are typical of random loading. As shown in Figure 14d, attempting to write into a bucket that contains a record (e.g., bucket 2 or 6) or one that is beyond the file boundaries (e.g., bucket 9) causes an INVALID KEY condition.

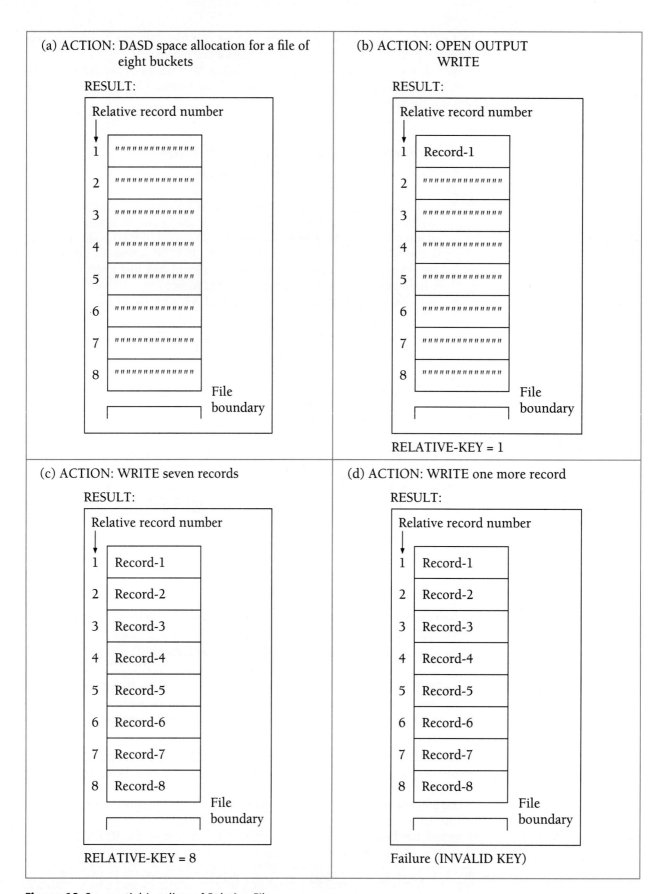

Figure 13 Sequential Loading of Relative Files

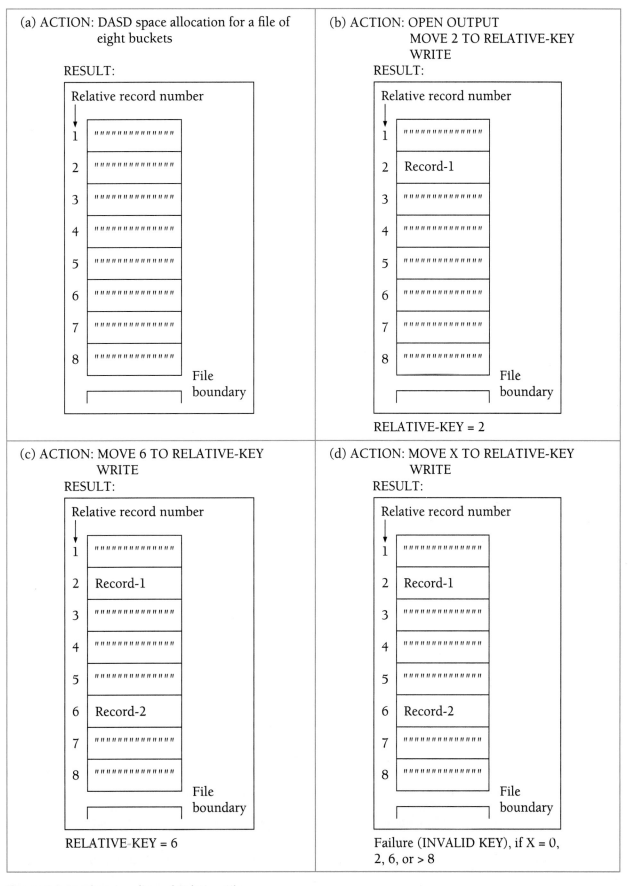

Figure 14 Random Loading of Relative Files

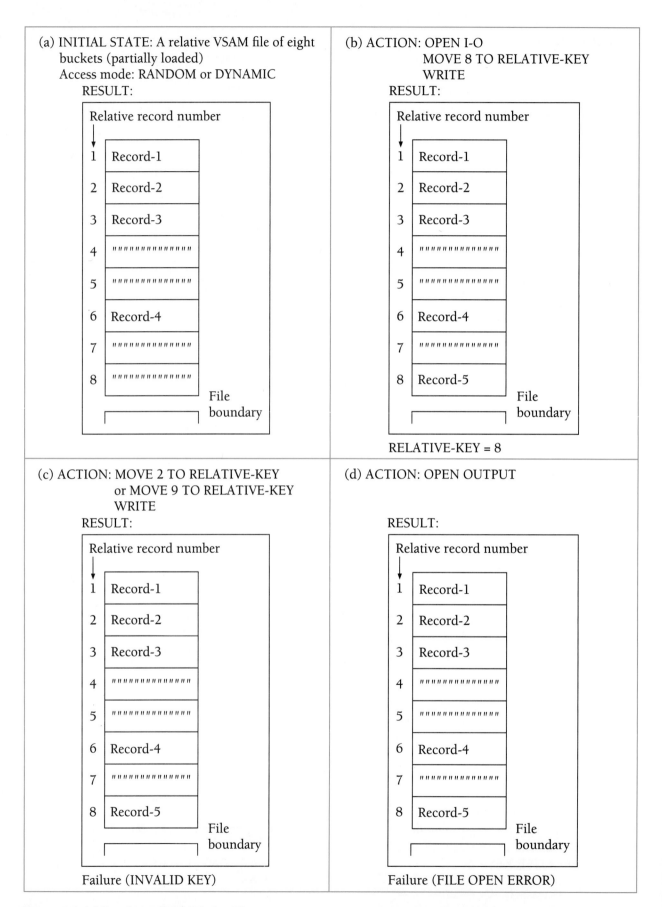

Figure 15 Adding Records to Relative Files

> ## Rules for Adding New Records into an Existing Relative File
>
> 1. The file access mode must be RANDOM or DYNAMIC.
> 2. The file should be opened in I-O mode.
> 3. To insert a new record, the record structure in the program should first be filled with appropriate values. Then an integer value must be moved to the RELATIVE KEY data item. Finally, a WRITE statement should be executed.

If the bucket addressed by a WRITE statement is full or is beyond the file boundaries, an INVALID KEY condition will be raised.

In Figure 15a we have a partially loaded dynamic-access relative file of eight buckets. If we open this file in I-O mode, store 8 in the RELATIVE KEY data item, and execute a WRITE statement, a new record (record-5) will be recorded into bucket 8. This is because bucket 8 is available at that point. An attempt to write a record into, say, bucket 2 or bucket 9 will fail (Figure 15c).

It should be noted that a file that has been previously loaded with records cannot be opened in OUTPUT mode (Figure 15d). Such an attempt will result in a file open error. Let us consider some COBOL examples.

Example 1

The following partial COBOL program loads a relative file sequentially from a sequentially organized source file.

```
 . . . . . . . . . . . . . . . . . . . . .
ENVIRONMENT DIVISION.
FILE-CONTROL.
    SELECT CARD-FILE ASSIGN TO INFILE.
    SELECT RELFILE   ASSIGN TO MASTER
            ORGANIZATION IS RELATIVE
            ACCESS MODE  IS SEQUENTIAL
            RELATIVE KEY IS BUCKET-NUMBER.
 . . . . . . . . . . . . . . . . . . . .
DATA DIVISION.
FILE SECTION.
FD  CARD-FILE
    LABEL RECORDS ARE OMITTED
    DATA RECORD IS CARD-RECORD
    RECORD CONTAINS 80 CHARACTERS.
01  CARD-RECORD.
    05  CARD-ID          PIC XXXX.
    05  CARD-NAME        PIC X(25).
    05  FILLER           PIC X(51).

FD  RELFILE
    LABEL RECORDS ARE STANDARD
    DATA RECORD IS REL-RECORD
    RECORD CONTAINS 29 CHARACTERS.
01  REL-RECORD.
    05  REL-ID           PIC XXXX.
    05  REL-NAME         PIC X(25).
```

```
WORKING-STORAGE SECTION.
01   END-OF-INPUT              PIC 9 VALUE ZERO.
01   BUCKET-NUMBER            PIC 999.


PROCEDURE DIVISION.
.......................
     OPEN INPUT  CARD-FILE.
     OPEN OUTPUT RELFILE.
     READ CARD-FILE
            AT END MOVE 1 TO END-OF-INPUT.

     PERFORM LOAD-RELATIVE-FILE
            UNTIL END-OF-INPUT = 1.

     CLOSE CARD-FILE, RELFILE.
     DISPLAY "FILE CREATED".
     STOP RUN.
.......................
LOAD-RELATIVE-FILE.
     MOVE CARD-ID   TO REL-ID.
     MOVE CARD-NAME TO REL-NAME.
     WRITE REL-RECORD.
     READ CARD-FILE
            AT END MOVE 1 TO END-OF-INPUT.
.......................
```

The relative file RELFILE is in sequential-access mode and is opened as an OUTPUT file. The records coming from the source file, called CARD-FILE, are duplicated in the record structure of RELFILE before writing. The records will be written sequentially into RELFILE beginning at bucket 1.

Example 2   Random loading of a relative file.

```
.......................
ENVIRONMENT DIVISION.
INPUT-OUTPUT SECTION.
FILE-CONTROL.
     SELECT CARD-FILE ASSIGN TO INFILE.
     SELECT RELFILE    ASSIGN TO MASTER
            ORGANIZATION IS RELATIVE
            ACCESS MODE   IS RANDOM
            RELATIVE KEY IS BUCKET-NUMBER.
.......................
DATA DIVISION.
FILE SECTION.
FD   CARD-FILE
     LABEL RECORDS ARE OMITTED
     DATA RECORD IS CARD-RECORD
     RECORD CONTAINS 80 CHARACTERS.
01   CARD-RECORD.
     05   CARD-ID            PIC XXXX.
     05   CARD-NAME          PIC X(25).
     05   FILLER             PIC X(51).
```

```
      FD  RELFILE
          LABEL RECORDS ARE STANDARD
          DATA RECORD IS REL-RECORD
          RECORD CONTAINS 29 CHARACTERS.
      01  REL-RECORD.
          05  REL-ID            PIC XXXX.
          05  REL-NAME          PIC X(25).


      WORKING-STORAGE SECTION.
      01  END-OF-INPUT          PIC 9 VALUE ZERO.
      01  BUCKET-NUMBER         PIC 999.


      PROCEDURE DIVISION.
      . . . . . . . . . . . . . . . . . . . . . .
          OPEN INPUT  CARD-FILE.
          OPEN OUTPUT RELFILE.
          READ CARD-FILE
                  AT END MOVE 1 TO END-OF-INPUT.
          MOVE 1 TO BUCKET-NUMBER.
          PERFORM LOAD-RELATIVE-FILE
                  UNTIL END-OF-INPUT = 1.

          CLOSE CARD-FILE, RELFILE.
          DISPLAY "FILE CREATED".

          STOP RUN.
      . . . . . . . . . . . . . . . . . . . . . .
      LOAD-RELATIVE-FILE.
          MOVE CARD-ID   TO REL-ID.
          MOVE CARD-NAME TO REL-NAME.
          WRITE REL-RECORD
                  INVALID KEY DISPLAY "CANT WRITE".
          ADD 2 TO BUCKET-NUMBER.
          READ CARD-FILE
                  AT END MOVE 1 TO END-OF-INPUT.
      . . . . . . . . . . . . . . . . . . . . . .
```

Again the relative file is opened in OUTPUT mode, but this time its access mode is RANDOM. The first record will be written into bucket 1 as the value of the RELATIVE KEY data item, BUCKET-NUMBER, is initially set to 1. The second record will be stored in bucket 3, the third in bucket 5, and so on.

Example 3   The following partial COBOL program inserts new records into a relative file.

```
      . . . . . . . . . . . . . . . . . . . . . .
      ENVIRONMENT DIVISION.
      INPUT-OUTPUT SECTION.
      FILE-CONTROL.
          SELECT RELFILE ASSIGN TO MASTER
                  ORGANIZATION IS RELATIVE
                  ACCESS MODE  IS RANDOM
                  RELATIVE KEY IS BUCKET-NUMBER.
```

```
. . . . . . . . . . . . . . . . . . . .
DATA DIVISION.
FILE SECTION.
FD  RELFILE
    LABEL RECORDS ARE STANDARD
    DATA RECORD IS REL-RECORD
    RECORD CONTAINS 29 CHARACTERS.
01  REL-RECORD.
    05  REL-ID          PIC XXXX.
    05  REL-NAME        PIC X(25).

WORKING-STORAGE SECTION.
01  BUCKET-NUMBER       PIC 9999.
01  BUCKET-AVAILABLE    PIC XXX.
01  RECORD-READ         PIC XXX.
01  TERMINATE-INPUT     PIC XXX.

PROCEDURE DIVISION.
. . . . . . . . . . . . . . . . . . . .
    OPEN I-O RELFILE.
    MOVE "NO" TO TERMINATE-INPUT.

    PERFORM RECORD-INSERTION
            UNTIL TERMINATE-INPUT = "YES".

    CLOSE RELFILE.
    STOP RUN.
. . . . . . . . . . . . . . . . . . . .
RECORD-INSERTION.
    MOVE "NO" TO BUCKET-AVAILABLE.
    PERFORM WHAT-BUCKET-NUMBER
            UNTIL BUCKET-AVAILABLE = "YES".
    PERFORM INSERT-RECORD.
    DISPLAY "RECORD INSERTED.".
    DISPLAY "DO YOU WANT TO TERMINATE INPUT?  TYPE YES OR NO.".
    ACCEPT TERMINATE-INPUT FROM CONSOLE.

WHAT-BUCKET-NUMBER.
    DISPLAY "ENTER BUCKET NUMBER FOR THE NEW RECORD:"
    ACCEPT BUCKET-NUMBER FROM CONSOLE.
    MOVE "YES" TO RECORD-READ.
    READ RELFILE
            INVALID KEY MOVE "NO" TO RECORD-READ.

    IF RECORD-READ = "YES" OR ( BUCKET-NUMBER < 1 OR > 999 )
            DISPLAY "BUCKET " BUCKET-NUMBER " IS UNAVAILABLE"
    ELSE
            MOVE "YES" TO BUCKET-AVAILABLE.

INSERT-RECORD.
    DISPLAY "ENTER ID NUMBER:".
    ACCEPT REL-ID FROM CONSOLE.
    DISPLAY "ENTER NAME:".
```

```
ACCEPT REL-NAME FROM CONSOLE.
WRITE REL-RECORD
          INVALID KEY DISPLAY "CANT WRITE".
. . . . . . . . . . . . . . . . . . . . .
```

The file access mode is RANDOM, and the file is opened as an I-O file. The program is designed so that a record can be stored in a bucket that is inside the file boundaries provided the bucket is empty. The file boundaries are defined by the bucket address range of 1 through 999.

READ Statement. A relative file can be read either sequentially or randomly. For sequential access, the file must be opened in either INPUT or I-O mode. The file access mode may be SEQUENTIAL or DYNAMIC. In the DYNAMIC mode the READ statement requires the use of the NEXT clause.

For sequential access, it is not necessary to include the optional RELATIVE KEY clause in the file SELECT statement. However, if the RELATIVE KEY clause is part of the SELECT statement and a RELATIVE KEY data item has been defined in the WORKING-STORAGE SECTION, a sequential READ statement execution causes this data item to be updated such that it contains the relative address of the bucket that has just been accessed.

When the file is first opened, the system establishes a current record pointer and sets it to the relative address of the first bucket in the file containing a logical record. In doing that, all buckets that are empty and those containing deleted records are ignored.

A sequential READ statement execution causes retrieval of the logical record in the bucket whose address is in the current record pointer. Also, in preparation for the next sequential READ, a READ statement updates the current record pointer such that it points to the next bucket containing another logical record. This update operation is carried out in increasing order of the relative bucket addresses. During update of the current record pointer the empty buckets and those containing deleted records are ignored. When the file boundary is reached during sequential READ, an end-of-file condition is raised.

Figure 16 summarizes these principles. Figure 16a shows a partially loaded relative file of eight buckets. Its access mode may be SEQUENTIAL or DYNAMIC, and it may be opened in INPUT or I-O mode. Due to the OPEN statement execution, the conceptual current record pointer is set to 2, which is the address of the first logical record in the file. In Figure 16b a sequential READ statement is executed. This causes the logical record in bucket 2 (record-1) to be brought into the memory. Now the RELATIVE KEY data item stores the value of 2, which is the address of the bucket that has just been accessed. The current record pointer is also updated to point to bucket 3, which contains a logical record. Figure 16c shows the effect of another sequential READ. This time record-2 in bucket 3 is accessed, the RELATIVE KEY data item becomes 3, and as bucket 8 is the next bucket that contains a logical record, the current record pointer is updated to 8. Note that bucket 4 is ignored because it contains a deleted record. As shown in Figure 16d, two more sequential READs result in an end-of-file condition for this file schema. The following are examples of sequential READ for relative files.

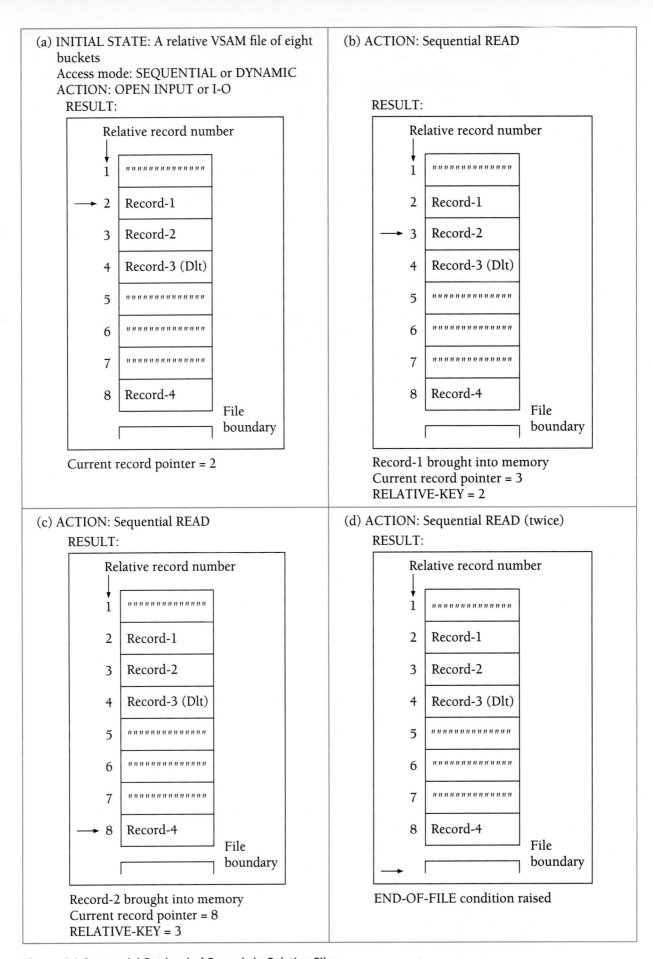

Figure 16 Sequential Retrieval of Records in Relative Files

```
        . . . . . . . . . . . . . . . . . . . . . .
***** SEQUENTIAL READ FOR SEQUENTIAL ACCESS MODE:

      READ PERSONNEL-FILE RECORD
          INTO WS-PERS-RECORD
          AT END PERFORM INPUT-COMPLETED.
        . . . . . . . . . . . . . . . . . . . . .
***** SEQUENTIAL READ FOR DYNAMIC ACCESS MODE:

      READ PERSONNEL-FILE NEXT RECORD
          INTO WS-PERS-RECORD
          AT END PERFORM INPUT-COMPLETED.
```

For random access to records in a relative file, the file must be opened in either INPUT or I-O mode. The file access mode should be RANDOM or DYNAMIC.

Before a READ statement is executed, an admissible relative address value should be stored in the RELATIVE KEY data item of the file. Then the READ statement will retrieve the content of the bucket with that address. The value of the RELATIVE KEY data item is also stored in the current record pointer; however, the current record pointer is not used or updated by random READ executions. An INVALID KEY condition is raised if the RELATIVE KEY data item contains a value that is outside the boundaries of the file, or if the indicated bucket contains a deleted record.

Figure 17a shows a relative file of eight buckets containing some records. To access records randomly, we specify the file access mode as DYNAMIC, and open the file as INPUT or I-O. In Figure 17b we store 2 in the RELATIVE KEY data item and issue a random READ. This retrieves record-1 in bucket 2 and sets the current record pointer to 2. Suppose after that, as in Figure 17c, we execute a sequential READ/NEXT statement. The next logical record in the file is in bucket 3, which is retrieved. As a result of the READ statement, the RELATIVE KEY data item becomes 3 and the current record pointer is updated to 8. Finally, Figure 17d reiterates the principle that only existing records within file boundaries can be randomly accessed. An example of random READ is given below.

```
        . . . . . . . . . . . . . . . . . . . . .
***** RANDOM RETRIEVAL OF RECORD IN BUCKET 10:

      MOVE 10 TO RELATIVE-ADDRESS.

      READ PERSONNEL-FILE
          INVALID KEY PERFORM ERROR-IN-INPUT.
```

It should be noted that provided the file access mode is DYNAMIC, it is possible to mix sequential and random retrieval in a relative file. If a random READ is followed by a sequential READ, however, the READ statement will retrieve the content of the next bucket that is not empty or does not contain a deleted record. The following example illustrates this.

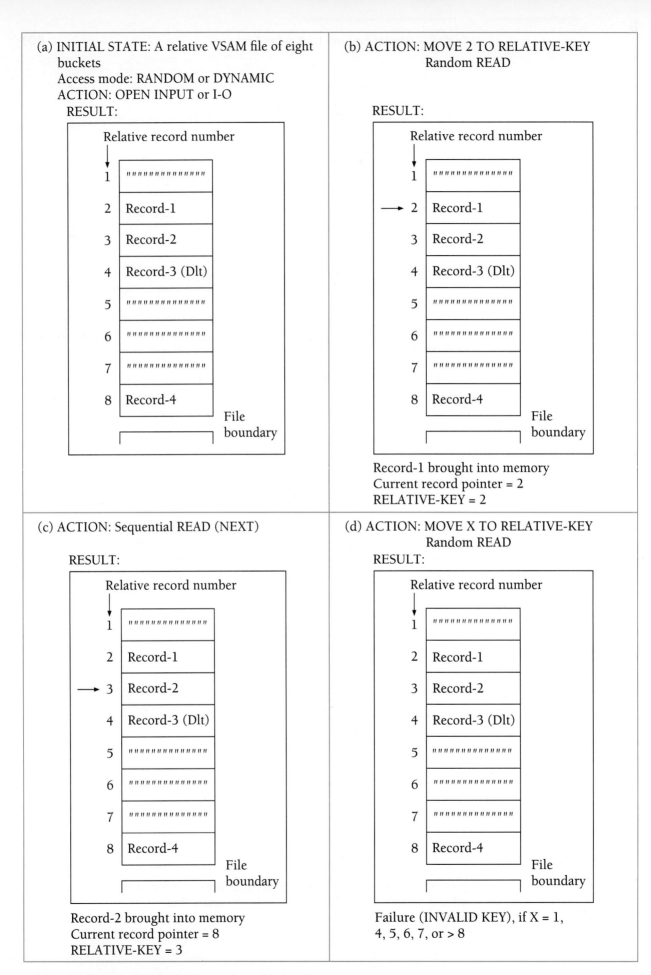

Figure 17 Random Retrieval of Records in Relative Files

```
         . . . . . . . . . . . . . . . . . . . .
***** RANDOM RETRIEVAL OF RECORD IN BUCKET 10:

      MOVE 10 TO RELATIVE-ADDRESS.

      READ PERSONNEL-FILE
         INVALID KEY PERFORM ERROR-IN-INPUT.

***** THE FOLLOWING READ STATEMENT RETRIEVES THE RECORD
***** IN BUCKET 11:

      READ PERSONNEL-FILE NEXT RECORD
         AT END PERFORM INPUT-COMPLETED.
```

REWRITE Statement. This statement is used for updating an existing record in a relative file. All general principles of record update are applicable for relative files.

Rules Relevant to the Use of the REWRITE Statement

1. The file should be opened in I-O mode.
2. The file access mode should be SEQUENTIAL, RANDOM, or DYNAMIC. DYNAMIC encompasses both SEQUENTIAL and RANDOM.
3. For sequential update, first a record should be retrieved using sequential READ. Next, its fields should be modified in the record structure. Finally, a REWRITE statement should be executed.
4. For random update, before a random READ is executed the relative address of the bucket should be stored in the RELATIVE KEY data item. After this the proper logical sequence consists of a random READ, a record structure content update, and a REWRITE.

An invalid key condition will be raised with REWRITE if the RELATIVE KEY data item value is altered between READ and REWRITE statement executions. The following example demonstrates these rules.

```
         . . . . . . . . . . . . . . . . . . . .
   FILE-CONTROL.
       SELECT PERSONNEL-FILE
           ASSIGN      TO INFILE
           ORGANIZATION IS RELATIVE
           ACCESS MODE  IS DYNAMIC
           RELATIVE KEY IS RELATIVE-ADDRESS.
         . . . . . . . . . . . . . . . . . . . .
   PROCEDURE DIVISION.
         . . . . . . . . . . . . . . . . . . . .
       OPEN I-O PERSONNEL-FILE.
 * SEQUENTIAL EXHAUSTIVE UPDATE:

       READ PERSONNEL-FILE NEXT RECORD
           AT END MOVE "YES" TO END-OF-FILE.
```

```
            PERFORM INCREMENT-AGE
                UNTIL END-OF-FILE = "YES".
     ........................
 * RANDOM UPDATE:

            PERFORM MODIFY-EMPLOYEE-NAME.

     ........................

  INCREMENT-AGE.
            ADD 1 TO EMPLOYEE-AGE.

            REWRITE PERSONNEL-RECORD
                INVALID KEY PERFORM ERROR-IN-REWRITE.

            READ PERSONNEL-FILE NEXT RECORD
                AT END MOVE "YES" TO END-OF-FILE.
     ........................

  MODIFY-EMPLOYEE-NAME.
            MOVE 10 TO RELATIVE-ADDRESS.

            READ PERSONNEL-FILE
                INVALID KEY PERFORM ERROR-IN-INPUT.

            MOVE "SHEILA GORDON" TO EMPLOYEE-NAME.

            REWRITE PERSONNEL-RECORD
                INVALID KEY PERFORM ERROR-IN-REWRITE.
     ........................
```

DELETE Statement. This statement is used to access a bucket that contains a logical record, either sequentially or randomly, and delete its content.

Rules for a Proper Delete Operation

1. The file should be opened in I-O mode.
2. The access mode should be SEQUENTIAL or RANDOM.
3. In sequential delete, first a sequential READ must be executed. After this a DELETE statement should be issued, causing the record that has just been read to be deleted.
4. In random delete, before the execution of the DELETE statement the RELATIVE KEY data item should be assigned the address of the bucket to be deleted.

An invalid key condition is raised if the relative address is outside the boundaries of the file. Some examples of DELETE are given below.

```
     ........................
 * EXAMPLE OF SEQUENTIAL DELETE TO DELETE THE CONTENT OF FIRST BUCKET:
        READ PERSONNEL-FILE NEXT RECORD
            AT END MOVE "YES" TO END-OF-FILE.

        DELETE PERSONNEL-FILE
            INVALID KEY PERFORM ERROR-IN-DELETE.
```

```
. . . . . . . . . . . . . . . . . . . . . . . .
* EXAMPLE OF RANDOM DELETE TO DELETE THE CONTENT OF 10TH BUCKET:
    MOVE 10 TO RELATIVE-ADDRESS.

    DELETE PERSONNEL-FILE
        INVALID KEY PERFORM ERROR-IN-DELETE.
. . . . . . . . . . . . . . . . . . . . . . .
```

START Statement. As in indexed file processing, the START statement makes it possible to process a relative file sequentially starting from a point other than the beginning of the file. The syntax and usage are the same as before. The only difference for relative files is that the beginning of sequential processing is based on the RELATIVE KEY data item value.

Rules for the Use of the START Statement

1. The file open mode should be INPUT or I-O.
2. The file access mode should be SEQUENTIAL or DYNAMIC.
3. RELATIVE KEY data item should be fully specified and an admissible value should be stored in it.
4. The START statement should be followed by a sequential READ instruction.

The START statement positions the current record pointer at the first bucket in the file that satisfies the START predicate. An invalid key condition will be raised if the RELATIVE KEY data item contains an incorrect relative address value, or the START predicate cannot be satisfied within the scope of the address space for the relative file. The following example initiates sequential processing at a bucket that contains a logical record and comes after bucket 2.

```
. . . . . . . . . . . . . . . . . . . . . . .
    MOVE 2 TO RELATIVE-ADDRESS.

    START PERSONNEL-FILE
        KEY IS GREATER THAN RELATIVE-ADDRESS
        INVALID KEY PERFORM ERROR-IN-START.

    READ PERSONNEL-FILE
        AT END MOVE "YES" TO END-OF-FILE-FLAG.
. . . . . . . . . . . . . . . . . . . . . . .
```

In Figure 18a we again have a relative file of eight buckets. The effect of a START statement such as the one in the above example sets the current record pointer to 3, the first relative address that is full and is also satisfying the START predicate (Figure 18b). Then a subsequent sequential READ will access record-2 in bucket 3. Also, it will update the current record pointer to 8 for the file schema of Figure 18b.

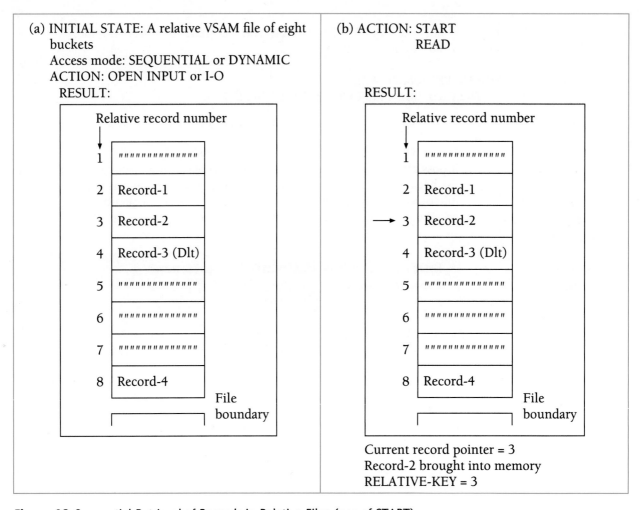

Figure 18 Sequential Retrieval of Records in Relative Files (use of START)

COBOL 85 Features for Relative File Input-Output Statements

COBOL 85   As was previously pointed out for indexed I-O statements, the only changes brought by COBOL 85 to relative file I-O statements are with respect to

1. The optional NOT INVALID KEY and NOT AT END clauses
2. The optional right bracket key words END-READ, END-WRITE, END-REWRITE, END-DELETE, and END-START

REVIEW QUESTIONS

1. The VSAM component for relative files is called _____ .
2. In VSAM/RRDS, each record is identified by its _____ .
3. In VSAM/RRDS files, sequential access as well as random access by relative record number is permitted. (T or F)
4. For a COBOL relative file, the file organization technique is indicated in the _____ clause of the _____ statement.
5. A COBOL relative file can be accessed in sequential, random, or dynamic mode. (T or F)
6. The WRITE statement can be used to create a COBOL relative file sequentially or randomly. It can also be used to add new records to an existing file. (T or F)

7. For random loading of a relative COBOL file, the RELATIVE KEY clause in the SELECT statement is required. (T or F)
8. A sequential READ statement for a relative file causes retrieval of the logical record in the bucket whose address is in the current record pointer. (T or F)
9. In executing a random READ for a relative file, if the RELATIVE KEY data item contains a value that is outside the boundaries of the file, or if the indicated bucket contains a deleted record, an INVALID KEY condition is raised. (T or F)
10. To use the REWRITE statement for a relative COBOL file it should be opened in _____ mode.
11. The DELETE statement can be used for relative files in either sequential or random access modes. (T or F)
12. The START statement for a relative file positions the current record pointer at the first bucket that satisfies the START predicate. (T or F)

Answers: 1. relative record data set; 2. relative record number; 3. T;
        4. ORGANIZATION IS RELATIVE, SELECT; 5. T; 6. T; 7. T;
        8. T; 9. T; 10. I-O; 11. T; 12. T.

Example Program 2:   *Relative File Creation and Maintenance*

In this section we present and discuss a COBOL application program that can be used to create and maintain a relative file. The maintenance operations include adding new records, deleting or updating existing ones, and generating a full or partial listing of records in the file. The program is written to process a specific file, and can be revised easily to perform similar functions on other files. It somewhat resembles the indexed file maintenance program developed and discussed in Chapter 13. In the program, access-by-content is made possible using a key-to-address transform (midsquare hashing) and an overflow handling technique (open addressing with linear probe).

Problem   The file for this application is called PERSONNEL-FILE and its record structure consists of the following fields:

- A 1-byte DELETE-FLAG field indicating whether a record has been logically deleted or not (if this field contains *, the record is considered to be deleted)
- A 4-digit personnel identification number that uniquely defines each record in the file and is used as the primary access key for the file
- A 25-byte personnel name field
- A 3-byte department code field indicating the department in which a given employee works

The personnel identification number will be used as our basis for accessing records. As the file is a relative COBOL file, to permit access-by-content using the personnel identification number field, a hash function is needed. We choose the midsquare hash function as our KAT.

In this application, the address space consists of 12 buckets in the range 21 through 32. Therefore, we have to implement the midsquare KAT such that it transforms any given four-digit personnel identification number to a two-digit relative address in this range. As record collisions are expected, we also need an overflow handling technique. For this application, we choose open addressing with linear probe.

A relative file can be created sequentially or randomly. As we intend to hash the personnel identification number field to determine relative addresses, the sequential file creation logic cannot be used. Therefore, the file will be created by inserting records into it after hashing and random access. This means that our initial file loading and record insertion routines are identical.

As for record deletion, we could have decided to let VSAM do the dirty work, that is, delete a record specified by a personnel identification number field value. This way, the program would be somewhat simpler compared to the logical delete technique that we will use. As was discussed previously, however, open addressing with linear probe has to differentiate between a vacant bucket and one that contains a deleted record. For this reason, the delete operation in the sample program is logical. Any record with * in the DELETE-FLAG field will be considered deleted.

The program is interactive and menu driven. The user can specify different operations by supplying admissible values for the variable FUNCTION-CODE. Legal values for FUNCTION-CODE and their meaning are shown below.

Function-Code	Operation
I	Insert records
D	Delete records
U	Update records
L	Produce a full sequential listing of the file
P	Produce a partial sequential listing of the file from a specified bucket to another bucket address
M	Display operations menu
T	Terminate program execution

Solution The compiler-generated listing of the COBOL program developed for the problem is given in Program 2-Source. The following items should be noted.

1. The PERSONNEL-FILE is defined as a RELATIVE file with DYNAMIC file access mode (lines 00042–00046). The reason for DYNAMIC access mode is that we intend to access this file randomly for record insertion, deletion, and update. We also plan to access it sequentially to produce file listings. The relative key has been defined as the WORKING-STORAGE SECTION variable, BUCKET-NUMBER.

2. Initially, the program displays the operation menu and prompts the user for a FUNCTION-CODE value. If an incorrect FUNCTION-CODE value is supplied, the program warns the user and again displays the operation menu, followed by another prompt for input. The user can always recall the menu by typing M for FUNCTION-CODE. These operations are handled by the code in paragraphs B1-DISPLAY-INSTRUCTIONS and C1-DISPLAY-SE-LECTION-MENU.

3. The relative file PERSONNEL-FILE must be defined as a VSAM/RRDS and have a disk space allocated for it. These can be done by executing appropriate access method services commands and job control statements before this application program is run. PERSONNEL-FILE may be initially empty, or it may be loaded by executing another application program. If the file has been loaded before this program is run, care must be taken to use the same hash function and overflow handling technique as those used in the present program.

4. In case PERSONNEL-FILE is empty, it can be loaded using the insert routine (paragraphs C2-INSERT-RECORDS and D1-PROCESS-FOR-INSERTION, and its subprocedures). New record insertions are handled by the same program elements. To insert a record, the user should type I when asked for a value for FUNCTION-CODE. Then the program control passes to the paragraph C2-INSERT-RECORD, in which the file is opened in I-O mode (line 00189). This is because we intend to search the file for the record to be inserted, and prohibit insertion if that record is found in it.

   In D1-PROCESS-FOR-INSERTION, the user is prompted to enter personnel identification number, name, and department code values so that the record can be constructed in the memory (lines 00274–00281). Next, the paragraph E1-COMPUTE-BUCKET-NUMBER is called on to hash the personnel identification number to a relative address in the correct range of 21 through 32. Then the procedure E2-SEARCH-FILE is triggered to search the file for the record. The search procedure makes use of the logic inherent in open addressing with linear probe. If the record is found, record insertion is blocked and the user is informed of the situation. Otherwise, to insert the record paragraph E3-STORE-RECORD is executed. For this the program calls on the paragraph F2-FIND-AVAILABLE-BUCKET, which either concludes that the file is full or finds an empty bucket using open addressing with linear probe (paragraph G1-TRY-NEXT-BUCKET). If the file is full the user is so informed. Otherwise, the record is inserted using a random WRITE statement (line 00409).

5. To delete a record the user should type D for FUNCTION-CODE. This triggers the paragraph C3-DELETE-RECORDS, in which the PERSONNEL-FILE is opened in I-O mode in preparation for delete. As was explained before, this is logical delete, which requires retrieving the record, changing the DELETE-FLAG to *, and rewriting it. Paragraph D2-PROCESS-FOR-DELETION, invoked by C3-DELETE-RECORDS, first prompts the user to enter the personnel identification number for the record to be deleted. Next, it accesses the record in the file by transforming the key to an address (line 00306) and searching the file (line 00308). If the record is not found, the user is informed and the operation is terminated. Otherwise, the DELETE-FLAG field is changed (line 00314) and a REWRITE statement is executed (line 00315).

6. To update a record the user should type U for FUNCTION-CODE. The update logic is reflected in paragraphs C4-UPDATE-RECORDS, D3-PROCESS-FOR-UPDATE, and their subprocedures. The program permits updates of the personnel name and/or department code fields. For obvious reasons, the personnel identification number field cannot be updated using this set of subprocedures; however, this is not a serious shortcoming. If the need arises for personnel identification number update, the user can delete the record with the old value as the record key and insert a new record in which the personnel identification number is the new value.

   The logic and program elements for record update are quite similar to those for logical record delete. Before update, the record is searched and retrieved. If such a record can be found, line 00339 invokes the paragraph E4-GET-NEW-DATA, which prompts the user to enter new values for personnel name and/or department code, and line 00340 rewrites the modified record.

7. At any time during processing the user may request a full sequential file listing by typing L for FUNCTION-CODE. This results in a reference to paragraph C5-LIST-FULL-FILE, in which the PERSONNEL-FILE is opened in I-O mode. Next, control passes to the paragraph D4-PRODUCE-FULL-LISTING, in which buckets are accessed randomly using a READ statement (line 00354). If a bucket is full, its content is displayed. If empty, the message BUCKET XX IS EMPTY is displayed.

8. A partial sequential file listing can also be displayed if the FUNCTION-CODE value is entered as P. In this case, the program control passes to paragraph C6-LIST-PARTIAL-FILE. This time the file is opened in INPUT mode, and the user is asked for start and end bucket numbers to specify the file range to be listed. The file range is verified and, if correct, the START statement is used to set the current record pointer to the first record to be retrieved (line 00246). Then a sequential READ statement with NEXT is repetitively executed (line 00250 and line 00369 in paragraph D5-PRODUCE-PARTIAL-LISTING) to access and display the buckets that are full in the specified range.

9. Finally, to terminate the program the user should enter T for FUNCTION-CODE.

Program 2-Output is the printout of an interactive terminal session for Program 2. It exemplifies all features of the relative file maintenance program.

'Key Terms

address space
bit-compression hash function
boundary-folding hash function
bucket
collision
DELETE statement
digit-analysis hash function
division-remainder hash function
hash function
hashing
key space
key-to-address transform
linear probe
midsquare hash function
open addressing
ORGANIZATION IS RELATIVE
  clause
overflow area

overflow handling
packing density
primary clustering
prime data area
quadratic probe
random probe
READ statement
relative file
RELATIVE KEY clause
relative record number
REWRITE statement
separate chaining
shift-folding hash function
START statement
synonym
VSAM/RRDS
WRITE statement

Study Guide

Quick Scan

- A relative file is one that permits direct access to its memory locations by their relative addresses. In principle, it can also be accessed sequentially.
- For direct access, a relative file is the most efficient file organization.
- Individually accessible memory locations in a relative file are called buckets. A bucket may contain one or more logical records.
- Direct-access storage allocated for a relative file can be partitioned into two areas: prime data area and overflow data area. Prime data area buckets are used to store records that rightfully belong there, whereas overflow buckets store records that cannot be accommodated in their respective buckets.
- A relative file can be accessed by relative bucket addresses. In a majority of practical applications we have to access records by some key data value. To reconcile the computer's and the user's viewpoints, we can define algorithms that transform a record key value to a relative address before writing or reading a record. Such algorithms are called hash functions, or key-to-address transforms.

- A hash function may transform more than one key value to the same address in the file. Also, it need not be an order-preserving transformation. This means that more than one record may transform to the same bucket for storage. The phenomenon of having more than one record hashing to the same bucket is called a collision. If two or more colliding records cannot be accommodated in the same bucket, the late-comers are allowed to overflow into the overflow area buckets.

- A hash function should consistently transform a key value to the same bucket address. It should be easy to code. Its code should execute efficiently. It should be able to map all record key values to some addresses in the key space. It should be universally applicable to all direct-access files. It should be able to minimize collisions, overflows, and clustering.

- The efficiency of a hashed relative file is determined by the hash function, overflow handling technique, bucket capacity, and prime area packing density.

- Several hash functions are used in practice for hashed relative files. A majority of them require numeric integer keys. For alphabetic or alphanumeric keys, the programmer should incorporate into the application program a module that transforms nonnumeric keys into numeric integers before hashing. This chapter discussed several popular hashing algorithms: division-remainder, midsquare, shift-folding, boundary-folding, digit-analysis, and bit-compression hash functions.

- Another important consideration for hashed relative files is the overflow handling technique incorporated into an application program. Four commonly used techniques are open addressing with linear probe, quadratic probe, random probe, and overflow record chaining.

- In open addressing, no distinction is made between prime data and overflow data buckets. To accommodate an overflow record we systematically look for an available bucket. In linear probe we search for an empty bucket immediately after the point of collision until one is found. Despite its simplicity, this method has one shortcoming: it tends to create long sequences of occupied buckets below the point of collision. This type of clustering is known as primary clustering.

- To minimize primary clustering, open addressing with quadratic probe or random probe may be used. In quadratic probe, to find an available bucket we examine the first bucket, then the fourth bucket, then the ninth bucket, and so on, after the point of collision. In random probe, for each bucket in the file we generate a sequence of random bucket addresses and try them one at a time until we find an available one.

- The above three overflow handling techniques do not use linked lists to separate overflow records due to collisions at a given bucket from those overflowing from other buckets. As a result, the search time may be negatively affected. To alleviate this problem, records hashing to the same address may be linked together into chains. This technique is known as separate chaining.

- Creation, maintenance, and use of hashed relative files require an application programming language with direct-access file I-O capability, a hashing technique incorporated into the application program, an overflow handling technique also built into the application program, and a file management system that provides an interface between the application program and the physical files the program uses.

- Different file management systems enable application programs to interface with direct access files. One such system is IBM's VSAM relative record data set (VSAM/RRDS).

- VSAM/RRDS closely resembles VSAM/KSDS. A VSAM/RRDS cluster consists of control areas and control intervals, and is controlled by VSAM master or user catalogs. However, there are some important differences.

- A VSAM/RRDS cluster does not have a base index or alternate index area. It consists of control intervals that contain buckets in which logical records are stored. Buckets are identified by relative record numbers (RRNs). A bucket may be accessed directly by its RRN. Also, the entire cluster may be accessed sequentially. Records in buckets may be deleted physically. VSAM/RRDS supports only fixed-length logical record format. Variable-length records and spanned records are not supported.

- COBOL supports relative files, and contains language features and I-O statements to define and use them. To define a relative file in a COBOL program, a SELECT statement in the ENVIRONMENT DIVISION is used.

- The SELECT statement for a relative file should specify organization as RELATIVE; file access mode as SEQUENTIAL, RANDOM, or DYNAMIC; and a relative key as a data item to be defined in the WORKING-STORAGE SECTION. The relative key data item has nothing to do with the record structure of the file, and is an integer data item used to specify the relative bucket number.

- A COBOL relative file can be created sequentially or randomly. After such a file is initially created, provided empty buckets can be found, it is possible to insert new records into it. All of these operations require the WRITE statement.

- A relative file can be accessed sequentially or randomly using either the sequential format or the random format for the READ statement.

- The REWRITE statement can be used to update records in a relative file.

- To delete a record physically from a relative file, the DELETE statement is needed.

- The START statement makes it possible to process a relative file sequentially beginning at any bucket in the file.

Test Your Comprehension

Multiple-Choice Questions

1. Which of the following is not a property of hash functions?
   a. Execution efficiency
   b. One-to-one mapping of records to buckets
   c. Universal applicability
   d. Nonorder-preserving transformation

2. Given is a physical file of 500 cells whose relative addresses are in the range 201–700. For hashing, we are using the division-remainder KAT with a divisor that will result in a minimum number of unusable buckets. Accordingly, a key value of 34,558 will hash to the cell whose address is
   a. 264
   b. 265
   c. 127
   d. 328
   e. None of the above

3. In a hashed file, keys are 6-digit integers and addresses are obtained using the expression

$$mod\ ((mod\ (x, 100) + floor\ (x\ /\ 10{,}000) + mod\ (\ (floor\ (x\ /\ 100)), 100)), 100)$$

   where x is a key value, mod (x, y) is a function that returns the integer remainder of dividing x by y, and floor is a single-argument function that returns the largest integer that is equal to or smaller than its argument. The hash function used in this file is
   a. Division-remainder
   b. Midsquare
   c. Shift-folding

d. Boundary-folding
e. None of the above

4. Given is a physical file of 10 cells whose relative addresses are in the range 21–30. For hashing we are using the midsquare KAT. A key value of 345 will hash to the cell whose address is
   a. 21
   b. 30
   c. 25
   d. Outside the range of available cells
   e. None of the above

5. In open addressing with linear probe,
   a. Overflow records are stored in a separate overflow area.
   b. An overflow record is accommodated in a cell that is as far from the point of collision as possible.
   c. There is a tendency for record clustering.
   d. All of the above are correct.

6. In open addressing with quadratic probe, suppose an overflow has occurred at relative address 30. The sequence of buckets that will be probed to accommodate the overflow record is
   a. Determined by a random number generator
   b. 31, 32, 33, 34, and so on
   c. 31, 41, 51, 61, and so on
   d. 31, 34, 39, 46, and so on

7. Which of the following is a shortcoming of open addressing without chaining as an overflow handling technique?
   a. It is relatively difficult to implement.
   b. Physical deletion of records is difficult.
   c. Buckets containing prime records can be distinguished from those containing overflow records.
   d. All of the above.

8. Which of the following statements concerning VSAM/RRDS files is incorrect?
   a. Records in buckets can be deleted physically.
   b. Records are accessed by their relative record numbers.
   c. Fixed, variable, and spanned record formats are supported.
   d. VSAM/RRDS files are more efficient and faster than VSAM/KSDS files.

9. Which of the following statements concerning sequential loading of a relative file is correct?
   a. The file should be opened in I-O mode.
   b. The file access mode should be sequential.
   c. The RELATIVE KEY clause in the SELECT statement for such a file is required.
   d. All of the above are correct.

10. In adding new records to an existing COBOL relative file,
    a. The file should be opened in I-O mode.
    b. The file access mode should be SEQUENTIAL.
    c. A RELATIVE KEY data item need not be defined.
    d. All of the above are correct.

11. In using a REWRITE statement for a relative COBOL file,
    a. The file should be opened in I-O mode.
    b. The file access mode may be sequential, random, or dynamic.
    c. For sequential update, the REWRITE statement should be preceded by a sequential READ statement.
    d. All of the above are correct.

Answers: 1. b; 2. d; 3. c; 4. b; 5. c; 6. d; 7. b; 8. c; 9. b; 10. a; 11. d.

Short Essay Questions

1. Define a relative file.
2. Briefly explain the differences between access-by-content for indexed sequential files and for relative files.
3. What is the difference between the prime data area and the overflow data area in a relative file?
4. Give a definition for hash function.
5. What are the properties of hash functions?
6. Define the related words synonyms, collision, and overflow in a hashed relative file.
7. What are the factors that influence overall efficiency of relative files?
8. What are the effects of bucket capacity and prime area packing density on the efficiency of a relative file?
9. Describe the general algorithm for hashing.
10. Give a brief description of the division-remainder hash function. Explain why it does not require a compression factor to be applied to the generated bucket address.
11. Describe the steps in midsquare hashing.
12. Distinguish between shift-folding and boundary-folding hash functions.
13. Give a description of the digit-analysis hash function.
14. Discuss the steps involved in the bit-compression hash function. Define exclusive or.
15. Why do we need to implement a suitable overflow handling technique for hashed relative files?
16. Give a description of open addressing with linear probe as an overflow handling technique in a hashed relative file.
17. Explain why open addressing with linear probe results in primary clustering in a relative file.
18. What is the termination condition for searching a hashed relative file based on open addressing with linear probe? Explain your answer.
19. Briefly explain the logic of open addressing with quadratic probe.
20. Give an explanation of the steps involved in open addressing with random probe.
21. What are the disadvantages of open addressing as an overflow handling technique?
22. Briefly describe separate chaining.
23. What are the similarities and differences between VSAM/KSDS and VSAM/RRDS?
24. Explain the special features of the COBOL SELECT statement applicable to relative files.
25. Discuss the rules for sequential loading of COBOL relative files.
26. Discuss the rules for random loading of COBOL relative files.
27. Discuss the rules for record insertion into COBOL relative files.
28. Under what circumstances is an INVALID KEY condition raised when a WRITE statement is executed for a relative file?
29. What are the rules for reading a COBOL relative file sequentially?
30. What are the rules for reading a COBOL relative file randomly?
31. Under what circumstances is an INVALID KEY condition raised when a READ statement is executed for a relative file?
32. Explain what is meant by current record pointer. Which COBOL statements make use of the current record pointer? For each, explain how.
33. When do we have to use the READ/NEXT format of the READ statement for COBOL relative files?
34. Briefly explain the rules applicable to the REWRITE statement for COBOL relative files.

35. Explain how a record is physically deleted in a relative file, and discuss the applicable COBOL language rules.
36. What causes an INVALID KEY condition associated with the DELETE statement for a relative file?
37. Discuss the function and use of the START statement for relative files.
38. What are the relevant rules regarding the use of the START statement for relative files?

Improve Your Problem-Solving Ability

Exercises

Given is a relative file of 20 buckets with relative bucket addresses in the range of 145–164. We also have 15 logical records whose key values are 4-digit integer numbers making up the following key space: {7661, 7888, 8767, 8775, 6755, 6700, 8180, 8081, 7886, 6577, 7700, 6688, 8522, 9002, 6444}. These records will be loaded into the file in the same order as their key values appear. That is, the first record to be loaded is the one with key 7661, the second has the key 7888, and so on. Exercises 1–11 are based on this setup.

For each file bucket capacity, hash function, and the overflow handling technique indicated, draw a table such as the one in Figure 2 showing the relative address produced by hashing, and a final file schema such as the one in Figure 11 showing the file content after loading of all 15 records.

1. Bucket capacity =   1
   Hash function =   division-remainder
   Overflow handling technique = open addressing with linear probe
2. Bucket capacity =   1
   Hash function =   division-remainder
   Overflow handling technique = open addressing with quadratic probe
3. Bucket capacity =   1
   Hash function =   division-remainder
   Overflow handling technique = open addressing with random probe
4. Bucket capacity =   1
   Hash function =   midsquare
   Overflow handling technique = open addressing with linear probe
5. Bucket capacity =   2
   Hash function =   midsquare
   Overflow handling technique = open addressing with linear probe
6. Bucket capacity =   1
   Hash function =   shift-folding
   Overflow handling technique = open addressing with linear probe
7. Bucket capacity =   1
   Hash function =   boundary-folding
   Overflow handling technique = open addressing with linear probe
8. Bucket capacity =   1
   Hash function =   digit-analysis
   Overflow handling technique = open addressing with linear probe
   In this case, you may assume that an extensive digit analysis has been performed on the key space for a much larger file with the same characteristics for the key values, and this analysis has revealed that selecting the second and the fourth digits in the keys and reversing them would define a good distribution.

9. Bucket capacity =   1
   Hash function =   bit-compression
   Overflow handling technique = open addressing with linear probe
   For this problem, use the binary string encoding of characters as given in
   Figure 7a.

10. Modify and run Program 1 to verify your key-to-address transformation tables for problems 1, 4, and 6.

11. Now assume that for the above file buckets 145–164 are used as the prime data area, and overflow records are stored in a separate overflow area consisting of buckets 170–179. The bucket capacity is one record. Suppose we use the midsquare hash function, and separate chaining as the overflow handling technique. Draw a figure depicting the file content after loading all the records.

Programming Problems

1. Extend Program 1 to include a subprocedure for the boundary folding hash function as it can be applied to exercise 7, and run it to verify your key-to-address transformation table for exercise 7.

2. Modify and run Program 2 such that the hash function is the division-remainder KAT, and the overflow handling technique is open addressing with random probe.

3. Although the hash functions discussed in this chapter are generally good performers in the sense that they tend to minimize collisions, for a given file, they exhibit different performance characteristics. To determine which hash function is the best for a given file, it is a good idea to do a preliminary analysis and simulate actual hashing for that file. The theme of this programming problem is preimplementation simulation to determine the best hash function for a file.

   Assume that the key values for our file are random 5-digit integers. We know that 500 buckets are available in the prime data area, whose relative addresses are in the range 1–500. Develop a COBOL program that reads 200 distinct random 5-digit integers stored in a sequential file, and applies division-remainder, midsquare, shift-folding, and boundary-folding hash functions to determine the best one for our file. The best hash function is the one that produces the minimum number of collisions. Discuss the reliability of your results.

```
00001    *............................................................
00002     IDENTIFICATION DIVISION.
00003     PROGRAM-ID.   HASH-FUNCTIONS.
00004     ***************************************************************
00005     ***   THIS PROGRAM SHOWS IMPLEMENTATIONS OF SOME OF THE HASH    *
00006     ***   FUNCTIONS DISCUSSED IN THIS CHAPTER AS COBOL INTERNAL     *
00007     ***   PROCEDURES.                                               *
00008     ***************************************************************
00009
00010     AUTHOR.        UCKAN.
00011     DATE-WRITTEN.  MAY 11, 1991.
00012     DATE-COMPILED. MAY 11,1991.
00014    *............................................................
00015     ENVIRONMENT DIVISION.
00016     CONFIGURATION SECTION.
00017     SOURCE-COMPUTER. IBM-370.
00018     OBJECT-COMPUTER. IBM-370.
```

Program 1-Source A Program with Hash Function Implementations

```
00019
00020      *...........................................................
00021      DATA DIVISION.
00022      WORKING-STORAGE SECTION.
00023
00024      **********> SWITCHES:
00025
00026      01   MORE-KEYS             VALUE "YES"    PIC X(3).
00027           88   NO-MORE-KEYS  VALUE "NO".
00028
00029      01   CHOICE-CODE        PIC 9.
00030           88   DIVISION-REMAINDER     VALUE 1.
00031           88   MID-SQUARE             VALUE 2.
00032           88   SHIFT-FOLDING          VALUE 3.
00033           88   ILLEGAL-CHOICE         VALUES 0, 4 THRU 9.
00034
00035      **********> VARIABLES:
00036
00037      01   ADDRESS-OF-FIRST-BUCKET      PIC 9(4).
00038      01   NO-OF-BUCKETS                PIC 9(4).
00039      01   DIVISOR                      PIC 9(4).
00040      01   KEY-VALUE                    PIC 9(4).
00041      01   RELATIVE-ADDRESS             PIC 9(4).
00042      01   KEY-SQUARE                   PIC 9(8).
00043      01   MID-VALUE              PIC 99.
00044      01   TOTAL-OF-SEGMENTS      PIC 99.
00045      01   MIDDLE-SEGMENT        PIC 99.
00046      01   LEFT-SEGMENT          PIC 99.
00047      01   RIGHT-SEGMENT         PIC 99.
00048
00049      *...........................................................
00050      PROCEDURE DIVISION.
00051
00052      A-DRIVER.
00053
00054          DISPLAY "YOU HAVE THE FOLLOWING HASH FUNCTION CHOICES: ".
00055          DISPLAY "    1    DIVISION REMAINDER ".
00056          DISPLAY "    2    MID-SQUARE".
00057          DISPLAY "    3    SHIFT-FOLDING".
00058          DISPLAY " ".
00059          DISPLAY "****> ENTER YOUR CHOICE AS A DIGIT FROM 1 TO 3: ".
00060          ACCEPT CHOICE-CODE FROM CONSOLE.
00061
00062          IF DIVISION-REMAINDER
00063              PERFORM B1-DIVISION-REMAINDER-HASHING.
00064
00065          IF MID-SQUARE
00066              PERFORM B2-MID-SQUARE-HASHING.
00067
00068          IF SHIFT-FOLDING
00069              PERFORM B3-SHIFT-FOLDING-HASHING.
00070
00071          IF ILLEGAL-CHOICE
00072              DISPLAY "ILLEGAL CHOICE.  TERMINATING.... ".
```

Program 1-Source (Continued)

```
00073
00074          STOP RUN.
00075
00076    B1-DIVISION-REMAINDER-HASHING.
00077          PERFORM C1-PREPARATIONS.
00078
00079          DISPLAY "****> ENTER DIVISOR: ".
00080          ACCEPT DIVISOR FROM CONSOLE.
00081
00082          PERFORM C2-COMPUTE-ADDRESS-BY-DIVISION
00083                  UNTIL NO-MORE-KEYS.
00084
00085    B2-MID-SQUARE-HASHING.
00086          PERFORM C1-PREPARATIONS.
00087
00088          PERFORM C3-COMPUTE-ADDRESS-BY-MID-SQR
00089                  UNTIL NO-MORE-KEYS.
00090
00091    B3-SHIFT-FOLDING-HASHING.
00092          PERFORM C1-PREPARATIONS.
00093
00094          PERFORM C4-COMPUTE-ADDRESS-BY-SFOLDING
00095                  UNTIL NO-MORE-KEYS.
00096
00097    C1-PREPARATIONS.
00098          DISPLAY "****> ENTER ADDRESS-OF-FIRST-BUCKET: ".
00099          ACCEPT ADDRESS-OF-FIRST-BUCKET FROM CONSOLE.
00100
00101          DISPLAY "****> ENTER NUMBER OF BUCKETS AVAILABLE: ".
00102          ACCEPT NO-OF-BUCKETS FROM CONSOLE.
00103
00104    C2-COMPUTE-ADDRESS-BY-DIVISION.
00105          DISPLAY "****> ENTER KEY VALUE: ".
00106          ACCEPT KEY-VALUE FROM CONSOLE.
00107
00108          COMPUTE RELATIVE-ADDRESS = ADDRESS-OF-FIRST-BUCKET
00109                  + (KEY-VALUE - (KEY-VALUE / DIVISOR) * DIVISOR).
00110
00111
00112          DISPLAY "RELATIVE ADDRESS IS: " RELATIVE-ADDRESS.
00113
00114          DISPLAY "DO YOU WANT TO CONTINUE? TYPE YES OR NO: ".
00115          ACCEPT MORE-KEYS FROM CONSOLE.
00116
00117    C3-COMPUTE-ADDRESS-BY-MID-SQR.
00118          DISPLAY "****> ENTER KEY VALUE: ".
00119          ACCEPT KEY-VALUE FROM CONSOLE.
00120
00121          COMPUTE KEY-SQUARE = KEY-VALUE * KEY-VALUE.
00122          COMPUTE MID-VALUE = (KEY-SQUARE / 1000) -
00123                  (KEY-SQUARE / 100000) * 100.
00124          COMPUTE RELATIVE-ADDRESS = MID-VALUE * NO-OF-BUCKETS / 100 +
00125                  ADDRESS-OF-FIRST-BUCKET.
00126
```

Program 1-Source (Continued)

```
00127            DISPLAY "RELATIVE ADDRESS IS: " RELATIVE-ADDRESS.
00128
00129            DISPLAY "DO YOU WANT TO CONTINUE? TYPE YES OR NO: ".
00130            ACCEPT MORE-KEYS FROM CONSOLE.
00131
00132     C4-COMPUTE-ADDRESS-BY-SFOLDING.
00133            DISPLAY "****> ENTER KEY VALUE: ".
00134            ACCEPT KEY-VALUE FROM CONSOLE.
00135
00136            COMPUTE MIDDLE-SEGMENT = KEY-VALUE / 10 - (KEY-VALUE / 1000)
00137                         * 100.
00138            COMPUTE LEFT-SEGMENT = KEY-VALUE / 1000.
00139            COMPUTE RIGHT-SEGMENT = 10 * ( KEY-VALUE - (KEY-VALUE / 10 )
00140                         * 10 ).
00141            COMPUTE TOTAL-OF-SEGMENTS = MIDDLE-SEGMENT + LEFT-SEGMENT +
00142                           RIGHT-SEGMENT.
00143
00144            COMPUTE RELATIVE-ADDRESS = TOTAL-OF-SEGMENTS * NO-OF-BUCKETS
00145                         / 100 + ADDRESS-OF-FIRST-BUCKET.
00146
00147            DISPLAY "RELATIVE ADDRESS IS: " RELATIVE-ADDRESS.
00148
00149            DISPLAY "DO YOU WANT TO CONTINUE? TYPE YES OR NO: ".
00150            ACCEPT MORE-KEYS FROM CONSOLE.
```

Program 1-Source (Continued)

```
00001     *.............................................................
00002        IDENTIFICATION DIVISION.
00003        PROGRAM-ID.          RELATIVE-FILE-MAINTENANCE.
00004        AUTHOR.              UCKAN.
00005     *************************************************************
00006     ***   THIS PROGRAM CAN BE USED TO MAINTAIN THE RELATIVE FILE    *
00007     ***   CALLED "PERSONNEL-FILE" IN THE FOLLOWING WAYS:            *
00008     ***                                                            *
00009     ***      1. ADDING NEW RECORD OCCURRENCES;                     *
00010     ***      2. DELETING EXISTING RECORD OCCURRENCES;              *
00011     ***      3. UPDATING RECORD OCCURRENCES (ONLY NONKEY FIELDS CAN *
00012     ***         BE UPDATED);                                       *
00013     ***      4. GENERATING A FULL FILE LISTING;                    *
00014     ***      5. GENERATING PARTIAL FILE LISTINGS WITHIN A SPECIFIED *
00015     ***         RANGE.                                             *
00016     ***                                                            *
00017     ***   THE RELATIVE FILE RANGE IS RESTRICTED TO BUCKETS 21 THROUGH *
00018     ***   32.  THE HASH FUNCTION USED IS MID-SQUARE KAT.  THE OVERFLOW*
00019     ***   HANDLING TECHNIQUE IS OPEN ADDRESSING WITH LINEAR PROBE.  *
00020     ***   THE HASH FUNCTION TRANSFORMS THE PERSONNEL ID NUMBER TO A *
00021     ***   BUCKET ADDRESS.                                          *
00022     ***                                                            *
00023     ***   THE PERSONNEL FILE RECORD STRUCTURE CONSISTS OF:         *
00024     ***      1. A ONE-BYTE DELETE FLAG,                            *
00025     ***      2. A FOUR-DIGIT PERSONNEL ID NUMBER,                  *
00026     ***      3. A 25-BYTE PERSONNEL NAME, AND                      *
```

Program 2-Source A Program to Maintain a Relative File

```
00027    ***          4. A 3-BYTE PERSONNEL-DEPARTMENT-CODE.              *
00028    ***    ALL INPUT FOR THE PROGRAM IS PROVIDED INTERACTIVELY.      *
00029    *******************************************************************
00030
00031    DATE-WRITTEN.    JULY 14, 1991.
00032    DATE-COMPILED. JUL 25,1991.
00034    *................................................................
00035    ENVIRONMENT DIVISION.
00036    CONFIGURATION SECTION.
00037    SOURCE-COMPUTER. IBM-370.
00038    OBJECT-COMPUTER. IBM-370.
00039    INPUT-OUTPUT SECTION.
00040    FILE-CONTROL.
00041
00042        SELECT PERSONNEL-FILE
00043              ASSIGN        TO MASTER
00044              ORGANIZATION IS RELATIVE
00045              ACCESS MODE  IS DYNAMIC
00046              RELATIVE KEY IS BUCKET-NUMBER.
00047
00048    *................................................................
00049    DATA DIVISION.
00050    FILE SECTION.
00051
00052    FD   PERSONNEL-FILE
00053         LABEL RECORDS ARE STANDARD
00054         DATA RECORD IS PERSONNEL-RECORD
00055         RECORD CONTAINS 33 CHARACTERS.
00056    01   PERSONNEL-RECORD.
00057         05   DELETE-FLAG       PIC X.
00058         05   PERS-ID           PIC 9999.
00059         05   PERS-NAME         PIC X(25).
00060         05   PERS-DEPT-CODE    PIC XXX.
00061
00062    WORKING-STORAGE SECTION.
00063
00064    **********> VARIABLES:
00065
00066    01   BUCKET-NUMBER       PIC 99.
00067    01   MID-VALUE           PIC 99.
00068    01   ORIGINAL-ADDRESS    PIC 99.
00069    01   KEY-SQUARE          PIC 9(8).
00070    01   COUNTER             PIC 99.
00071    01   START-BUCKET        PIC 99.
00072    01   END-BUCKET          PIC 99.
00073    01   CURRENT-BUCKET      PIC 99.
00074    01   BUCKET-AVAILABLE    PIC XXX.
00075    01   RECORD-READ         PIC XXX.
00076    01   TERMINATE-INPUT     PIC XXX.
00077    01   FILE-FULL           PIC XXX.
00078    01   EMPTY-BUCKET        PIC XXX.
00079    01   RECORD-FOUND        PIC XXX.
00080    01   EMPTY-BUCKET-FOUND  PIC XXX.
00081    01   END-OF-FILE-REACHED PIC XXX.
```

Program 2-Source (Continued)

```
00082      01   RANGE-EMPTY              PIC XXX.
00083      01   RANGE-INCORRECT          PIC XXX.
00084      01   SOME-RECORD-ACCESSED     PIC XXX.
00085
00086      01   FUNCTION-CODE            PIC X.
00087           88   RECORD-INSERTION       VALUE "I".
00088           88   RECORD-DELETION        VALUE "D".
00089           88   RECORD-UPDATE          VALUE "U".
00090           88   FULL-FILE-LISTING      VALUE "L".
00091           88   PARTIAL-FILE-LISTING   VALUE "P".
00092           88   PROCESS-TERMINATION    VALUE "T".
00093           88   MENU-DISPLAY           VALUE "M".
00094
00095      **********> STRUCTURES:
00096
00097      01   WS-PERSONNEL-RECORD.
00098           05   WS-DELETE-FLAG      PIC X.
00099           05   WS-PERS-ID          PIC 9999.
00100           05   WS-PERS-NAME        PIC X(25).
00101           05   WS-PERS-DEPT-CODE   PIC XXX.
00102
00103      *...........................................................
00104      PROCEDURE DIVISION.
00105
00106      A-MAIN-PARAGRAPH.
00107          MOVE "#" TO FUNCTION-CODE.
00108
00109          PERFORM B1-DISPLAY-INSTRUCTIONS
00110              UNTIL FUNCTION-CODE = "I" OR "D" OR "U" OR "L" OR "P"
00111                                     OR "T" OR "M".
00112
00113          PERFORM B2-PROCESS-REQUEST
00114              UNTIL PROCESS-TERMINATION.
00115
00116          STOP RUN.
00117
00118      B1-DISPLAY-INSTRUCTIONS.
00119
00120          IF FUNCTION-CODE = "#"
00121              DISPLAY "  "
00122              DISPLAY "*****************************************"
00123              DISPLAY "* THIS PROGRAM CAN BE USED TO MAINTAIN *"
00124              DISPLAY "*        THE RELATIVE FILE, CALLED      *"
00125              DISPLAY "*            THE PERSONNEL FILE.        *"
00126              DISPLAY "*****************************************"
00127
00128              PERFORM C1-DISPLAY-SELECTION-MENU
00129
00130              DISPLAY " "
00131              DISPLAY "****> PLEASE ENTER FUNCTION CODE: "
00132          ELSE
00133              IF FUNCTION-CODE = "@"
00134                  DISPLAY " "
00135                  DISPLAY "****> PLEASE ENTER FUNCTION CODE: "
```

Program 2-Source (Continued)

```
00136                     ELSE
00137                         DISPLAY FUNCTION-CODE " IS AN ILLEGAL VALUE."
00138                         DISPLAY "LEGAL VALUES ARE SHOWN BELOW:"
00139                         PERFORM C1-DISPLAY-SELECTION-MENU
00140                         DISPLAY " "
00141                         DISPLAY "****> PLEASE ENTER A CORRECT FUNCTION CO
00142     -      "DE.".
00143
00144         ACCEPT FUNCTION-CODE FROM CONSOLE.
00145
00146     B2-PROCESS-REQUEST.
00147
00148         IF MENU-DISPLAY
00149             PERFORM C1-DISPLAY-SELECTION-MENU.
00150
00151         IF RECORD-INSERTION
00152             PERFORM C2-INSERT-RECORDS.
00153
00154         IF RECORD-DELETION
00155             PERFORM C3-DELETE-RECORDS.
00156
00157         IF RECORD-UPDATE
00158             PERFORM C4-UPDATE-RECORDS.
00159
00160         IF FULL-FILE-LISTING
00161             PERFORM C5-LIST-FULL-FILE.
00162
00163         IF PARTIAL-FILE-LISTING
00164             PERFORM C6-LIST-PARTIAL-FILE.
00165
00166         IF NOT PROCESS-TERMINATION
00167             MOVE "@" TO FUNCTION-CODE
00168
00169             PERFORM B1-DISPLAY-INSTRUCTIONS
00170                 UNTIL FUNCTION-CODE = "I" OR "D" OR "U" OR
00171                                       "P" OR "L" OR "T" OR "M".
00172
00173
00174     C1-DISPLAY-SELECTION-MENU.
00175         DISPLAY " ".
00176         DISPLAY "*****************************************".
00177         DISPLAY "*    FUNCTION                      CODE  *".
00178         DISPLAY "*    --------------------          ----  *".
00179         DISPLAY "*    INSERT RECORDS                 I    *".
00180         DISPLAY "*    DELETE RECORDS                 D    *".
00181         DISPLAY "*    UPDATE RECORDS                 U    *".
00182         DISPLAY "*    GENERATE FULL FILE LISTING     L    *".
00183         DISPLAY "*    GENERATE PARTIAL FILE LISTING  P    *".
00184         DISPLAY "*    DISPLAY THIS MENU              M    *".
00185         DISPLAY "*    TERMINATE                      T    *".
00186         DISPLAY "*****************************************".
00187         DISPLAY " ".
00188
00189     C2-INSERT-RECORDS.
00190         OPEN I-O PERSONNEL-FILE.
```

Program 2-Source (Continued)

```
00191              MOVE "NO" TO TERMINATE-INPUT.
00192
00193              PERFORM D1-PROCESS-FOR-INSERTION
00194                     UNTIL TERMINATE-INPUT = "YES".
00195
00196              CLOSE PERSONNEL-FILE.
00197
00198         C3-DELETE-RECORDS.
00199              OPEN I-O PERSONNEL-FILE.
00200              MOVE "NO" TO TERMINATE-INPUT.
00201
00202              PERFORM D2-PROCESS-FOR-DELETION
00203                     UNTIL TERMINATE-INPUT = "YES".
00204
00205              CLOSE PERSONNEL-FILE.
00206
00207         C4-UPDATE-RECORDS.
00208              OPEN I-O PERSONNEL-FILE.
00209              MOVE "NO" TO TERMINATE-INPUT.
00210
00211              PERFORM D3-PROCESS-FOR-UPDATE
00212                     UNTIL TERMINATE-INPUT = "YES".
00213
00214              CLOSE PERSONNEL-FILE.
00215
00216         C5-LIST-FULL-FILE.
00217              OPEN I-O PERSONNEL-FILE.
00218
00219              PERFORM D4-PRODUCE-FULL-LISTING
00220                     VARYING BUCKET-NUMBER FROM 21 BY 1
00221                         UNTIL BUCKET-NUMBER > 32.
00222
00223              CLOSE PERSONNEL-FILE.
00224
00225         C6-LIST-PARTIAL-FILE.
00226              OPEN INPUT PERSONNEL-FILE.
00227              MOVE "NO" TO END-OF-FILE-REACHED.
00228              MOVE "NO" TO RANGE-EMPTY.
00229              MOVE "NO" TO RANGE-INCORRECT.
00230              MOVE "NO" TO SOME-RECORD-ACCESSED.
00231
00232              DISPLAY "****> ENTER START BUCKET ADDRESS FOR LISTING.  CORRE
00233          -   "CT RANGE IS 21 - 32.".
00234              ACCEPT START-BUCKET FROM CONSOLE.
00235
00236              DISPLAY "****> ENTER END BUCKET ADDRESS FOR LISTING.  CORRECT
00237          -   " RANGE IS 21 - 32.".
00238              ACCEPT END-BUCKET FROM CONSOLE.
00239
00240              IF START-BUCKET < 21 OR END-BUCKET > 32
00241                 OR START-BUCKET > END-BUCKET
00242                     DISPLAY "INCORRECT RANGE SPECIFICATION."
00243                     MOVE "YES" TO RANGE-INCORRECT.
00244
```

Program 2-Source (Continued)

```
00245          MOVE START-BUCKET TO BUCKET-NUMBER.
00246
00247          START PERSONNEL-FILE
00248                  KEY NOT LESS THAN BUCKET-NUMBER
00249                  INVALID KEY MOVE "YES" TO RANGE-EMPTY.
00250
00251          READ PERSONNEL-FILE NEXT
00252                  AT END MOVE "YES" TO END-OF-FILE-REACHED.
00253
00254          MOVE BUCKET-NUMBER TO CURRENT-BUCKET.
00255
00256          IF RANGE-INCORRECT = "NO"
00257                  AND
00258             END-OF-FILE-REACHED = "NO"
00259                  IF RANGE-EMPTY = "NO"
00260                          PERFORM D5-PRODUCE-PARTIAL-LISTING
00261                                  UNTIL CURRENT-BUCKET > END-BUCKET
00262                                              OR
00263                                  END-OF-FILE-REACHED = "YES".
00264
00265          IF RANGE-INCORRECT = "NO"
00266                    AND
00267            ( SOME-RECORD-ACCESSED = "NO"
00268                    OR
00269              RANGE-EMPTY = "YES" )
00270                  DISPLAY "SPECIFIED FILE RANGE IS EMPTY.".
00271
00272          CLOSE PERSONNEL-FILE.
00273
00274      D1-PROCESS-FOR-INSERTION.
00275          DISPLAY "****> ENTER PERSONNEL ID NUMBER: ".
00276          ACCEPT WS-PERS-ID FROM CONSOLE.
00277
00278          DISPLAY "****> ENTER PERSONNEL NAME: ".
00279          ACCEPT WS-PERS-NAME FROM CONSOLE.
00280
00281          DISPLAY "****> ENTER PERSONNEL DEPARTMENT CODE: ".
00282          ACCEPT WS-PERS-DEPT-CODE FROM CONSOLE.
00283
00284          MOVE SPACE TO WS-DELETE-FLAG.
00285
00286          PERFORM E1-COMPUTE-BUCKET-NUMBER.
00287
00288          PERFORM E2-SEARCH-FILE.
00289
00290          IF RECORD-FOUND = "YES"
00291                  DISPLAY "RECORD ALREADY IN THE FILE."
00292          ELSE
00293                  MOVE ORIGINAL-ADDRESS TO BUCKET-NUMBER
00294                  PERFORM E3-STORE-RECORD.
00295
00296          IF FILE-FULL NOT = "YES" AND RECORD-FOUND NOT = "YES"
00297                  DISPLAY "RECORD INSERTED.".
00298
```

Program 2-Source (Continued)

```
00299          DISPLAY "****> DO YOU WANT TO TERMINATE RECORD INSERTION?".
00300          DISPLAY "****> TYPE YES OR NO.".
00301          ACCEPT TERMINATE-INPUT FROM CONSOLE.
00302
00303      D2-PROCESS-FOR-DELETION.
00304          DISPLAY "****> ENTER PERSONNEL ID NUMBER OF RECORD TO BE DELE
00305      -   "TED:".
00306          ACCEPT WS-PERS-ID FROM CONSOLE.
00307
00308          PERFORM E1-COMPUTE-BUCKET-NUMBER.
00309
00310          PERFORM E2-SEARCH-FILE.
00311
00312          IF RECORD-FOUND = "YES"
00313              IF DELETE-FLAG = "*"
00314                      MOVE "NO" TO RECORD-FOUND
00315              ELSE
00316                      MOVE "*" TO DELETE-FLAG
00317                      REWRITE PERSONNEL-RECORD
00318                          INVALID KEY DISPLAY "ERROR IN REWRITE.".
00319
00320          IF RECORD-FOUND = "YES"
00321              DISPLAY "RECORD WITH KEY " WS-PERS-ID " IS DELETED."
00322          ELSE
00323              DISPLAY "RECORD WITH KEY " WS-PERS-ID " IS NOT FOUND.".
00324
00325          DISPLAY "****> DO YOU WANT TO TERMINATE RECORD DELETION?".
00326          DISPLAY "****> TYPE YES OR NO.".
00327          ACCEPT TERMINATE-INPUT FROM CONSOLE.
00328
00329      D3-PROCESS-FOR-UPDATE.
00330          DISPLAY "****> ENTER PERSONNEL ID NUMBER OF RECORD TO BE UPDA
00331      -   "TED:".
00332          ACCEPT WS-PERS-ID FROM CONSOLE.
00333
00334          PERFORM E1-COMPUTE-BUCKET-NUMBER.
00335
00336          PERFORM E2-SEARCH-FILE.
00337
00338          IF RECORD-FOUND = "YES"
00339              IF DELETE-FLAG = "*"
00340                      MOVE "NO" TO RECORD-FOUND
00341              ELSE
00342                      PERFORM E4-GET-NEW-DATA
00343                      REWRITE PERSONNEL-RECORD
00344                          INVALID KEY DISPLAY "ERROR IN REWRITE.".
00345
00346          IF RECORD-FOUND = "YES"
00347              DISPLAY "RECORD WITH KEY " WS-PERS-ID " IS UPDATED."
00348          ELSE
00349              DISPLAY "RECORD WITH KEY " WS-PERS-ID " IS NOT FOUND.".
00350
00351          DISPLAY "****> DO YOU WANT TO TERMINATE RECORD UPDATE?".
00352          DISPLAY "****> TYPE YES OR NO.".
00353          ACCEPT TERMINATE-INPUT FROM CONSOLE.
```

Program 2-Source (Continued)

```
00354
00355     D4-PRODUCE-FULL-LISTING.
00356         MOVE "NO" TO BUCKET-AVAILABLE.
00357         READ PERSONNEL-FILE
00358                 INVALID KEY MOVE "YES" TO BUCKET-AVAILABLE.
00359
00360         IF BUCKET-AVAILABLE = "NO"
00361                 DISPLAY "BUCKET " BUCKET-NUMBER " CONTAINS: "
00362                         DELETE-FLAG "  " PERS-ID "  " PERS-NAME "   "
00363                         PERS-DEPT-CODE
00364         ELSE
00365                 DISPLAY "BUCKET " BUCKET-NUMBER " IS EMPTY.".
00366
00367     D5-PRODUCE-PARTIAL-LISTING.
00368         MOVE "YES" TO SOME-RECORD-ACCESSED.
00369         DISPLAY "BUCKET " CURRENT-BUCKET " CONTAINS: " DELETE-FLAG
00370                 "  " PERS-ID "  " PERS-NAME " " PERS-DEPT-CODE.
00371
00372         READ PERSONNEL-FILE NEXT
00373                 AT END MOVE "YES" TO END-OF-FILE-REACHED.
00374
00375         MOVE BUCKET-NUMBER TO CURRENT-BUCKET.
00376
00377     E1-COMPUTE-BUCKET-NUMBER.
00378
00379     ***** THIS PARAGRAPH IS THE IMPLEMENTATION OF THE MID-SQUARE
00380     ***** HASH FUNCTION FOR THE GIVEN FILE.
00381
00382         COMPUTE KEY-SQUARE = WS-PERS-ID * WS-PERS-ID.
00383         COMPUTE MID-VALUE = (KEY-SQUARE / 1000) -
00384                             (KEY-SQUARE / 100000) * 100.
00385         COMPUTE BUCKET-NUMBER = MID-VALUE * 12 / 100 + 21.
00386
00387     E2-SEARCH-FILE.
00388         MOVE "NO" TO RECORD-FOUND.
00389         MOVE "NO" TO EMPTY-BUCKET-FOUND.
00390         MOVE "NO" TO FILE-FULL.
00391         MOVE BUCKET-NUMBER TO ORIGINAL-ADDRESS.
00392
00393         PERFORM F1-ACCESS-BUCKETS
00394                 UNTIL RECORD-FOUND = "YES"
00395                         OR
00396                     FILE-FULL = "YES"
00397                         OR
00398                     EMPTY-BUCKET-FOUND = "YES".
00399
00400     E3-STORE-RECORD.
00401         MOVE BUCKET-NUMBER TO ORIGINAL-ADDRESS.
00402         MOVE "NO" TO BUCKET-AVAILABLE.
00403
00404         PERFORM F2-FIND-AVAILABLE-BUCKET
00405                 UNTIL BUCKET-AVAILABLE = "YES"
00406                         OR
00407                     FILE-FULL = "YES".
```

Program 2-Source (Continued)

```
00408
00409          IF FILE-FULL = "YES"
00410                  DISPLAY "FILE FULL, RECORD CANNOT BE INSERTED."
00411          ELSE
00412                  WRITE PERSONNEL-RECORD FROM WS-PERSONNEL-RECORD
00413                      INVALID KEY DISPLAY "ERROR IN WRITING.".
00414
00415   E4-GET-NEW-DATA.
00416          DISPLAY "PERSONNEL NAME FOR " WS-PERS-ID " IS: " PERS-NAME.
00417          DISPLAY "****> PLEASE ENTER NEW NAME.  IF NO UPDATE IS DESIRE
00418   -      "D, HIT RETURN.".
00419          ACCEPT WS-PERS-NAME FROM CONSOLE.
00420
00421          IF WS-PERS-NAME NOT = SPACES
00422                  MOVE WS-PERS-NAME TO PERS-NAME.
00423
00424          DISPLAY "PERSONNEL DEPARTMENT CODE FOR " WS-PERS-ID " IS: "
00425                  PERS-DEPT-CODE.
00426          DISPLAY "****> PLEASE ENTER NEW DEPARTMENT CODE.  IF NO UPDAT
00427   -      "E IS DESIRED, HIT RETURN.".
00428          ACCEPT WS-PERS-DEPT-CODE FROM CONSOLE.
00429
00430          IF WS-PERS-DEPT-CODE NOT = SPACES
00431                  MOVE WS-PERS-DEPT-CODE TO PERS-DEPT-CODE.
00432
00433   F1-ACCESS-BUCKETS.
00434          READ PERSONNEL-FILE
00435                  INVALID KEY MOVE "YES" TO EMPTY-BUCKET-FOUND.
00436
00437          IF EMPTY-BUCKET-FOUND = "NO"
00438                  IF PERS-ID = WS-PERS-ID
00439                      MOVE "YES" TO RECORD-FOUND.
00440
00441          IF RECORD-FOUND = "NO" AND EMPTY-BUCKET-FOUND = "NO" AND
00442                      FILE-FULL = "NO"
00443                  PERFORM G1-TRY-NEXT-BUCKET.
00444
00445   F2-FIND-AVAILABLE-BUCKET.
00446
00447   ***** THIS PARAGRAPH IS THE IMPLEMENTATION OF OPEN ADDRESSING
00448   ***** WITH LINEAR PROBE FOR THE GIVEN FILE.
00449
00450          MOVE "YES" TO RECORD-READ.
00451          READ PERSONNEL-FILE
00452                  INVALID KEY MOVE "NO" TO RECORD-READ.
00453
00454          IF RECORD-READ = "YES"
00455                  PERFORM G1-TRY-NEXT-BUCKET
00456          ELSE
00457                  MOVE "YES" TO BUCKET-AVAILABLE.
00458
00459   G1-TRY-NEXT-BUCKET.
```

Program 2-Source (Continued)

```
00460
00461          IF BUCKET-NUMBER = 32
00462                  MOVE 21 TO BUCKET-NUMBER
00463          ELSE
00464                  ADD 1 TO BUCKET-NUMBER.
00465
00466          IF BUCKET-NUMBER = ORIGINAL-ADDRESS
00467                  MOVE "YES" TO FILE-FULL.
```

Program 2-Source (Continued)

```
*****************************************
* THIS PROGRAM CAN BE USED TO MAINTAIN *
*      THE RELATIVE FILE, CALLED        *
*          THE PERSONNEL FILE.          *
*****************************************


*****************************************
*  FUNCTION                    CODE    *
*  _____            ____    *
*  INSERT RECORDS               I      *
*  DELETE RECORDS               D      *
*  UPDATE RECORDS               U      *
*  GENERATE FULL FILE LISTING   L      *
*  GENERATE PARTIAL FILE LISTING P     *
*  DISPLAY THIS MENU            M      *
*  TERMINATE                    T      *
*****************************************

****> PLEASE ENTER FUNCTION CODE:
A
A IS AN ILLEGAL VALUE.
LEGAL VALUES ARE SHOWN BELOW:


*****************************************
*  FUNCTION                    CODE    *
*  _____            ____    *
*  INSERT RECORDS               I      *
*  DELETE RECORDS               D      *
*  UPDATE RECORDS               U      *
*  GENERATE FULL FILE LISTING   L      *
*  GENERATE PARTIAL FILE LISTING P     *
*  DISPLAY THIS MENU            M      *
*  TERMINATE                    T      *
*****************************************

****> PLEASE ENTER A CORRECT FUNCTION CODE:
I
****> ENTER PERSONNEL ID NUMBER:
4023
****> ENTER PERSONNEL NAME:
JACK MEYER
****> ENTER PERSONNEL DEPARTMENT CODE:
SLS
```

Program 2-Output A Terminal Session for Program 2

```
RECORD INSERTED.
****> DO YOU WANT TO TERMINATE RECORD INSERTION?
****> TYPE YES OR NO.
NO
****> ENTER PERSONNEL ID NUMBER:
4031
****> ENTER PERSONNEL NAME:
JUDY SMITH
****> ENTER PERSONNEL DEPARTMENT CODE:
DP
RECORD INSERTED.
****> DO YOU WANT TO TERMINATE RECORD INSERTION?
****> TYPE YES OR NO.
NO
****> ENTER PERSONNEL ID NUMBER:
4011
****> ENTER PERSONNEL NAME:
LINDA DAY
****> ENTER PERSONNEL DEPARTMENT CODE:
ACC
RECORD INSERTED.
****> DO YOU WANT TO TERMINATE RECORD INSERTION?
****> TYPE YES OR NO.
NO
****> ENTER PERSONNEL ID NUMBER:
3971
****> ENTER PERSONNEL NAME:
DONALD LITTLE
****> ENTER PERSONNEL DEPARTMENT CODE:
DP
RECORD INSERTED.
****> DO YOU WANT TO TERMINATE RECORD INSERTION?
****> TYPE YES OR NO.
NO
****> ENTER PERSONNEL ID NUMBER:
3812
****> ENTER PERSONNEL NAME:
KAREN WHITE
****> ENTER PERSONNEL DEPARTMENT CODE:
DP
RECORD INSERTED.
****> DO YOU WANT TO TERMINATE RECORD INSERTION?
****> TYPE YES OR NO.
NO
****> ENTER PERSONNEL ID NUMBER:
4214
****> ENTER PERSONNEL NAME:
LORRAINE HICKMAN
****> ENTER PERSONNEL DEPARTMENT CODE:
SLS
RECORD INSERTED.
****> DO YOU WANT TO TERMINATE RECORD INSERTION?
****> TYPE YES OR NO.
NO
```

Program 2-Output (Continued)

```
****> ENTER PERSONNEL ID NUMBER:
4241
****> ENTER PERSONNEL NAME:
TIMOTHY SANDERS
****> ENTER PERSONNEL DEPARTMENT CODE:
DP
RECORD INSERTED.
****> DO YOU WANT TO TERMINATE RECORD INSERTION?
****> TYPE YES OR NO.
NO
****> ENTER PERSONNEL ID NUMBER:
4146
****> ENTER PERSONNEL NAME:
JOAN HALL
****> ENTER PERSONNEL DEPARTMENT CODE:

RECORD INSERTED.
****> DO YOU WANT TO TERMINATE RECORD INSERTION?
****> TYPE YES OR NO.
NO
****> ENTER PERSONNEL ID NUMBER:
4146
****> ENTER PERSONNEL NAME:
JOAN HALL
****> ENTER PERSONNEL DEPARTMENT CODE:
DP
RECORD ALREADY IN THE FILE.
****> DO YOU WANT TO TERMINATE RECORD INSERTION?
****> TYPE YES OR NO.
YES

****> PLEASE ENTER FUNCTION CODE:
L
BUCKET 21 CONTAINS:     4241   TIMOTHY SANDERS          DP
BUCKET 22 CONTAINS:     4146   JOAN HALL
BUCKET 23 IS EMPTY.
BUCKET 24 CONTAINS:     3812   KAREN WHITE              DP
BUCKET 25 IS EMPTY.
BUCKET 26 CONTAINS:     4031   JUDY SMITH               DP
BUCKET 27 CONTAINS:     4214   LORRAINE HICKMAN         SLS
BUCKET 28 IS EMPTY.
BUCKET 29 CONTAINS:     3971   DONALD LITTLE            DP
BUCKET 30 IS EMPTY.
BUCKET 31 CONTAINS:     4023   JACK MEYER               SLS
BUCKET 32 CONTAINS:     4011   LINDA DAY                ACC

****> PLEASE ENTER FUNCTION CODE:
P
****> ENTER START BUCKET ADDRESS FOR LISTING.  CORRECT RANGE IS 21 - 32.
21
****> ENTER END BUCKET ADDRESS FOR LISTING.  CORRECT RANGE IS 21 - 32.
32
BUCKET 21 CONTAINS:     4241   TIMOTHY SANDERS          DP
BUCKET 22 CONTAINS:     4146   JOAN HALL
```

Program 2-Output (Continued)

```
BUCKET 24 CONTAINS:      3812   KAREN WHITE            DP
BUCKET 26 CONTAINS:      4031   JUDY SMITH             DP
BUCKET 27 CONTAINS:      4214   LORRAINE HICKMAN       SLS
BUCKET 29 CONTAINS:      3971   DONALD LITTLE          DP
BUCKET 31 CONTAINS:      4023   JACK MEYER             SLS
BUCKET 32 CONTAINS:      4011   LINDA DAY              ACC


****> PLEASE ENTER FUNCTION CODE:
P
****> ENTER START BUCKET ADDRESS FOR LISTING.   CORRECT RANGE IS 21 - 32.
20
****> ENTER END BUCKET ADDRESS FOR LISTING.   CORRECT RANGE IS 21 - 32.
32
INCORRECT RANGE SPECIFICATION.


****> PLEASE ENTER FUNCTION CODE:
P
****> ENTER START BUCKET ADDRESS FOR LISTING.   CORRECT RANGE IS 21 - 32.
21
****> ENTER END BUCKET ADDRESS FOR LISTING.   CORRECT RANGE IS 21 - 32.
33
INCORRECT RANGE SPECIFICATION.


****> PLEASE ENTER FUNCTION CODE:
P
****> ENTER START BUCKET ADDRESS FOR LISTING.   CORRECT RANGE IS 21 - 32.
21
****> ENTER END BUCKET ADDRESS FOR LISTING.   CORRECT RANGE IS 21 - 32.
27
BUCKET 21 CONTAINS:      4241   TIMOTHY SANDERS        DP
BUCKET 22 CONTAINS:      4146   JOAN HALL
BUCKET 24 CONTAINS:      3812   KAREN WHITE            DP
BUCKET 26 CONTAINS:      4031   JUDY SMITH             DP
BUCKET 27 CONTAINS:      4214   LORRAINE HICKMAN       SLS


****> PLEASE ENTER FUNCTION CODE:
U
****> ENTER PERSONNEL ID NUMBER OF RECORD TO BE UPDATED:
4146
PERSONNEL NAME FOR 4146 IS: JOAN HALL
****> PLEASE ENTER NEW NAME.   IF NO UPDATE IS DESIRED, HIT RETURN.

PERSONNEL DEPARTMENT CODE FOR 4146 IS:
****> PLEASE ENTER NEW DEPARTMENT CODE.   IF NO UPDATE IS DESIRED, HIT RETURN
SLS
RECORD WITH KEY 4146 IS UPDATED.
****> DO YOU WANT TO TERMINATE RECORD UPDATE?
****> TYPE YES OR NO.
YES


****> PLEASE ENTER FUNCTION CODE:
L
BUCKET 21 CONTAINS:      4241   TIMOTHY SANDERS        DP
BUCKET 22 CONTAINS:      4146   JOAN HALL              SLS
BUCKET 23 IS EMPTY.
```

Program 2-Output (Continued)

```
BUCKET 24 CONTAINS:      3812   KAREN WHITE              DP
BUCKET 25 IS EMPTY.
BUCKET 26 CONTAINS:      4031   JUDY SMITH               DP
BUCKET 27 CONTAINS:      4214   LORRAINE HICKMAN         SLS
BUCKET 28 IS EMPTY.
BUCKET 29 CONTAINS:      3971   DONALD LITTLE            DP
BUCKET 30 IS EMPTY.
BUCKET 31 CONTAINS:      4023   JACK MEYER               SLS
BUCKET 32 CONTAINS:      4011   LINDA DAY                ACC


****> PLEASE ENTER FUNCTION CODE:
D
****> ENTER PERSONNEL ID NUMBER OF RECORD TO BE DELETED:
3812
RECORD WITH KEY 3812 IS DELETED.
****> DO YOU WANT TO TERMINATE RECORD DELETION?
****> TYPE YES OR NO.
YES


****> PLEASE ENTER FUNCTION CODE:
L
BUCKET 21 CONTAINS:      4241   TIMOTHY SANDERS         DP
BUCKET 22 CONTAINS:      4146   JOAN HALL               SLS
BUCKET 23 IS EMPTY.
BUCKET 24 CONTAINS:  *   3812   KAREN WHITE             DP
BUCKET 25 IS EMPTY.
BUCKET 26 CONTAINS:      4031   JUDY SMITH              DP
BUCKET 27 CONTAINS:      4214   LORRAINE HICKMAN        SLS
BUCKET 28 IS EMPTY.
BUCKET 29 CONTAINS:      3971   DONALD LITTLE           DP
BUCKET 30 IS EMPTY.
BUCKET 31 CONTAINS:      4023   JACK MEYER              SLS
BUCKET 32 CONTAINS:      4011   LINDA DAY               ACC


****> PLEASE ENTER FUNCTION CODE:
U
****> ENTER PERSONNEL ID NUMBER OF RECORD TO BE UPDATED:
3812
RECORD WITH KEY 3812 IS NOT FOUND.
****> DO YOU WANT TO TERMINATE RECORD UPDATE?
****> TYPE YES OR NO.
YES


****> PLEASE ENTER FUNCTION CODE:
T
```

Program 2-Output (Continued)

15

Logical File Organization Techniques: Linear Files

IN THIS CHAPTER YOU WILL LEARN ABOUT

- Linked-list files
- Operations on linked lists
  - Searching
  - Adding new elements
  - Deleting existing elements
- Types of linked lists
  - Forward linked lists
  - Backward linked lists
  - Circular linked lists
  - Doubly linked lists
  - Multiple lists
- List inversion
  - Partially inverted lists
  - Fully inverted lists and inverted files
- File management
  - Data structures for file management: stacks and queues
  - Garbage collection
- COBOL implementation of linked-list files

Introduction

In Chapter 10 we identified three phases of data organization: record structure, file structure, and data base organization. File structure organization is concerned with structuring different occurrences of a given record structure in a file. We stressed that a file structure is a data structure, and its purpose is to enable the users of the information system to process easily and efficiently the applications based on that file.

Many file organization techniques exist. We refer to them as **logical file organization techniques**, because each can be perceived independently of a computer system. Programming languages support a small subset of file organization techniques, called **built-in**, or **language-supported, file organization techniques**. We have seen that COBOL has three built-in file organization techniques: sequential, indexed sequential, and relative. All remaining techniques, although not directly supported by COBOL, can be simulated using an appropriate built-in file organization as the basis for simulation. Thus, we can design and implement file systems in COBOL that respond quite efficiently to special classes of applications. We should note that no single file organization can optimally handle all conceivable user queries on a file system. For this reason we will study a variety of them.

All logical file structures are data structures. They represent data elements (i.e., records) and one or more relationships among them. Depending on the nature of a relationship, a corresponding data structure may be linear or nonlinear. Lists, including linked lists, are examples of linear data structures. Trees and networks represent more complex relationships and are nonlinear data structures.

Linear Files: Linked Lists

Essentially, linear data structures are those based on sequential and linked allocation. We studied sequential allocation in connection with arrays and sequential and relative files. We briefly touched on linked allocation in Chapter 9 and introduced its use in conjunction with string processing. Also, in Chapter 13, while learning about indexed organization, we came across linked allocation in the form of pointers. Linked allocation and linked lists are frequently used in data management and are the bases of many interesting and flexible file organization techniques.

Linked-List Concepts

> A **linked list** is a data structure that consists of a dynamically varying number of elements. Each element is explicitly linked to its logical successor by a pointer. This linkage is based on a data element in the data structure. In addition, a linked list includes a **list head**, which points to the first element in the list.

Links in a linked list represent a relationship. It is the "logical precedes" relationship as defined by values of a common data field in the list elements. A linked list is based on this common data element. For full specification, a linked list requires the following components:

1. A modified cell structure for list elements
2. A data element with respect to which the linked list is constructed
3. An index entry to specify the starting point in the linked list
4. An end-of-list marker to indicate the last list element.

In addition to data fields, the modified cell structure for list elements includes a link (or pointer) field. A **cell** is a structured combination of data fields in the computer's memory. When dealing with files, cell structure is conceptually equivalent to record structure. For each list element, the link field contains the address of its logical successor. The cell structure for linked lists is shown in Figure 1a.

The index entry that defines the starting point in a linked list is called **list head**. It consists of a list identifier (i.e., a unique name to identify the list from among others) and a list head pointer that points to the first list element. The cell structure for index entries is shown in Figure 1b.

The end-of-list marker is contained in the link field of the last list element. In our discussions we denote the end-of-list marker by an asterisk, *. In actual implementations it may be a data value that is compatible with, but not included in, the value set of the link field. For example, if pointers are relative cell addresses in the range 1 through M, the end-of-list marker may be chosen as either zero or a value that is larger than M.

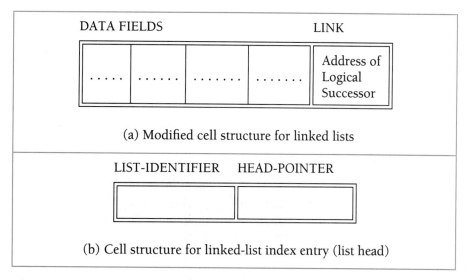

(a) Modified cell structure for linked lists

(b) Cell structure for linked-list index entry (list head)

Figure 1 Storage Structures for Linked-List Elements

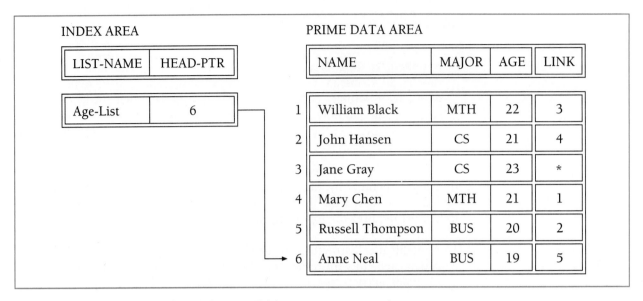

INDEX AREA   PRIME DATA AREA

LIST-NAME	HEAD-PTR
Age-List	6

	NAME	MAJOR	AGE	LINK
1	William Black	MTH	22	3
2	John Hansen	CS	21	4
3	Jane Gray	CS	23	*
4	Mary Chen	MTH	21	1
5	Russell Thompson	BUS	20	2
6	Anne Neal	BUS	19	5

Figure 2 A Linked List Based on AGE Data Field

Figure 2 shows an example of a linked list. The list elements are records of a file stored in buckets 1 through 6 in a prime data area. The record structure for this file consists of three data items: NAME, MAJOR, and AGE for college students. The linked list is based on the data item AGE. Also, each record includes a LINK field containing the relative address of the bucket that stores its successor record. The index area consists of one entry for the list head.

This linked list ties records together in increasing order of AGE. As the record for Anne Neal in bucket 6 is the one with the smallest AGE value, it is the beginning of the list, and the index area list head entry points to bucket 6. The record has as its successor the one for Russell Thompson in bucket 5, whose age is the next smallest age in the file. Thus, the LINK field in bucket 6 has the value 5 pointing to that bucket. The rest of the linked list is constructed similarly. The end of the list is bucket 3, containing the record for Jane Gray, the list element with the largest AGE value. Its LINK field stores the end-of-list marker *.

Clearly, the linked list has to be stored in a direct-access environment so that we can jump from a list element to its logical successor using the pointer value associated with it. Otherwise, such a data structure would be meaningless. Traversing a linked list entails accessing its index area list head entry, entering the first element in the list using the list head pointer, and continuing element access in this fashion until the end of the list is reached. Such a traversal produces an ordered list of records by the AGE field. Therefore, constructing a linked list based on a data field is equivalent to sorting its elements with respect to that data field. It constitutes a logical sort technique.

A linked list can also be pictured as a graph structure (Figure 3). Boxes representing the cells are **nodes** and the interconnecting directional lines are **arcs**. Such a graph is called a directional graph, or **digraph**. A digraph is useful in visually depicting relationships. In Chapter 4 we used graphs and digraphs to represent program structures and data structures. As our interest here lies in data and relationships among them, we will occasionally resort to this representation when studying data and file structures. The arcs in Figure 3 are, in fact, pointers. Each corresponds to one element of the relationship set (i.e., the set of pointers in the linked list). One can easily rearrange Figure 3 such that the entire structure can be mapped onto a straight line without losing any in-

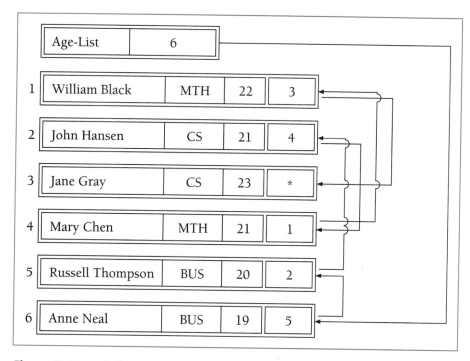

Figure 3 Digraph Representation of Linked List of Figure 2

formation from the data structure (Figure 4). Whenever such a transformation is possible, the data structure under consideration is **linear**; otherwise, it is **nonlinear**. Tree structures cannot be mapped onto a straight line and therefore are nonlinear.

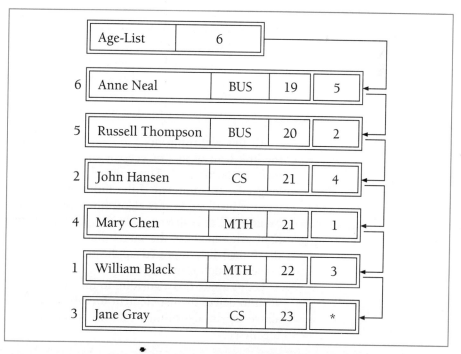

Figure 4 Transformed Digraph for Linked List of Figure 2

Operations on Linked Lists

As for any data structure, we consider three operations for linked lists: searching, adding a new element while maintaining list order, and deleting an existing element while maintaining list order. Searching accesses a list element to process its content. As we have stressed previously several times, this operation is also essential for data structure update (i.e., addition, deletion, or element content modification). A linked list is an ordered linear structure, and to search it, a search key value has to be specified. This search key value should be compatible with the value domain of the data element with respect to which the linked list has been constructed. Therefore, searching a linked list is tantamount to sequentially searching an ordered table. We should remember that for searching, as well as for any proper processing of a linked list, the list should be entered at its head.

Addition and deletion can be handled more efficiently for linked lists than for lists based on sequential allocation because these operations do not require physical data movement. They basically entail modifying appropriate pointers in it. Let us consider the algorithm for record deletion in a linked list.

Let D represent the data item with respect to which the given linked list is constructed, and let K be the search argument that identifies the list element to be deleted. K must be compatible with the value domain of D.

Step 1:   Using its list head, enter the linked list.

Step 2:   Traverse the linked list sequentially with respect to the data item D. Preserve in two main memory structures (buffers A and B) two list elements at a time: a list element in buffer A and its logical successor in buffer B. New list elements are read and copied into buffer B immediately after moving the content of buffer B to buffer A. At the start of the algorithm buffer A should contain the list head entry, and buffer B should store the first list element.

Step 3:   If K matches the D field value of the list element in buffer B, store the LINK field value of the element in buffer B in the LINK field of the list element in buffer A. This takes the logical successor of the list element in buffer B and makes it the logical successor of the list element in buffer A. It also severs the connection between the elements in buffers A and B, thus excluding the element in buffer B from the list. Finally, rewrite the modified content of buffer A into the list.

All this algorithm does is locate the list element to be deleted, and modify the link field of its predecessor such that it points to the successor of the element to be deleted. Thus, the element will be logically deleted and will no longer be encountered if the linked list is traversed properly. No data movement is involved in this algorithm. Consequently, it is quite efficient. It should be noted that it deletes only the first occurrence of the list element whose D field value matches the search key value K. In case D is not a unique field in the linked list, repeated applications of this algorithm can delete all occurrences of such elements.

Let us apply this algorithm to the linked list of Figure 2 and suppose that we wish to delete the list element for which AGE is 22. A step-by-step trace of the above delete algorithm is shown in Figure 5. Let us go through these steps together.

1. Access the list head and store it in buffer A. Next, access the first list element using the relative address 6 picked from the list head and store this record in buffer B. The record in buffer B belonging to Anne Neal has an AGE value of 19, which does not match the search argument value 22.
2. Move the content of buffer B to buffer A, and using its pointer value of 5, access the next record in the list and store it in buffer B. This record is the

Step	Operation	Buffers				Comparison (AGE-B = 22)
1	Access two list elements and store in buffers A and B, and compare	A	Age-List			6	No match
		B	Anne Neal	BUS	19	5	
2	Move buffer B to buffer A, read an element to B, and compare	A	Anne Neal	BUS	19	5	No match
		B	Russell Thompson	BUS	20	2	
3	Move buffer B to buffer A, read an element to B, and compare	A	Russell Thompson	BUS	20	2	No match
		B	John Hansen	CS	21	4	
4	Move buffer B to buffer A, read an element to B, and compare	A	John Hansen	CS	21	4	No match
		B	Mary Chen	MTH	21	1	
5	Move buffer B to buffer A, read an element to B, and compare	A	Mary Chen	MTH	21	1	Match
		B	William Black	MTH	22	3	
6	Change LINK in buffer A to LINK value in buffer B.	A	Mary Chen	MTH	21	3	
		B	William Black	MTH	22	3	
7	Rewrite buffer A.	A	Mary Chen	MTH	21	3	

Figure 5 Trace of Linked-List Delete Algorithm for Linked List of Figure 2

one that belongs to Russell Thompson, whose age is 20. As yet, we do not have a match.

3. Do the same thing as in the previous step. Russell Thompson is now in buffer A. Its pointer value of 2 is used to read and store in buffer B a new record. This one belongs to John Hansen, whose age is 21. Still no match.

4. Repeat the process once again, and find that the search is still unsuccessful.

5. Finally, in this step we get a record stored in buffer B for William Black whose age is 22. This is the record to be deleted.

6. Move the LINK value of the record in buffer B to the LINK field of buffer A. This takes the successor record for William Black in bucket 3 and makes it the successor of Mary Chen. Also, it breaks the linkage between Mary Chen and William Black, effectively expelling the record for William Black from the list.

7. Finally, rewrite the record in buffer A into the file.

The resulting list schema is shown in Figure 6. The deleted list element is still in the list, but no other list element points to it any more.

Now let us consider the record insertion logic for a linked list. Again, D represents the data item on which the given linked list is based, and K is the search argument that identifies the list element to be added. K is the value of attribute D for the record to be inserted, and it is compatible with the value domain of D.

Step 1:   Construct the record to be inserted into the linked list in a memory location, called buffer C.

Step 2:   Get an empty bucket or one that contains a deleted list element in the file.

Step 3:   Traverse the linked list keeping two list elements in two memory structures, buffers A and B, respectively, such that buffer B contains the logical successor of the element in buffer A at any time.

Step 4:   Continue list traversal until the D field value of the list element in buffer A is smaller than K, and the D field value of the list element in buffer B is larger than K. This means that the new element to be inserted must be between the elements in buffers A and B.

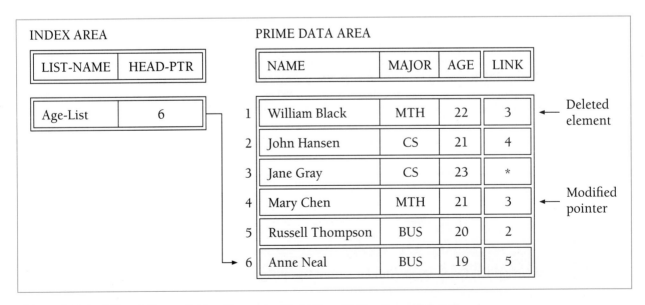

Figure 6 Linked List of Figure 2 After Element with AGE = 22 Has Been Deleted

Step 5: At this point, do the following two link field updates.

   a. Copy the link field value of buffer A into the link field of buffer C. This makes the element in buffer B the logical successor of the element in buffer C.

   b. Copy the relative address of the bucket into which the new element will be inserted into the link field of buffer A. This renders the element in buffer C the logical successor of the element in buffer A.

Step 6: Write the new list element in buffer C into the available bucket, and rewrite the content of bucket A into its original bucket in the list.

It should be noted that step 5 is somewhat different if the new element to be inserted becomes either the first or the last element in the list. These variations are left as exercises for the reader.

Unlike the algorithm for inserting a record into a sequential list, this one does not require data movement. It locates the point of insertion, thus identifying the predecessor and successor list elements for the newcomer. Then it modifies the pointer of the predecessor element and links the new element to its proper successor.

An application of the algorithm to the linked list of Figure 6 to insert a new record George Brentano/BUS/21 is shown in the trace table of Figure 7. To clarify the algorithm, we explain it as follows.

1. First, we reserve a bucket for the new record. For this we pick bucket 1, as it contains a deleted element and can be reclaimed for use.

2. Then we construct the record to be inserted in an internal memory location, buffer C, by moving George Brentano, BUS, and 21 to NAME, MAJOR, and AGE fields, respectively. The LINK field in buffer C is still empty.

3. Now we are ready to start list traversal. The logic here is the same as in the previous algorithm; however, the search condition is different. We want to find a configuration such that AGE of record in buffer A is less than 21, and AGE of record in buffer B is greater than or equal to 21. This is the point of insertion. We fail to find it in this step.

4. This is another configuration encountered during traversal, and it also proves to be unsuccessful.

5. In this step the search condition is satisfied. The new record should have the record in buffer A as its predecessor, and the record in buffer B as its successor.

6. To make John Hansen the successor for George Brentano, we duplicate the LINK value of buffer A (which points to John Hansen) in the LINK field of buffer C.

7. The new record is ready for insertion, and we write it into bucket 1 in the file.

8. To make George Brentano the successor for Russell Thompson, we change the LINK field value in buffer A to 1, the relative address of the bucket containing the new record.

9. In the final step we rewrite the content of buffer A into the file.

The linked list after insertion is shown in Figure 8.

The problem remains of securing an available bucket for the new list element. Before inserting a new list element, how do we know which buckets are available? This is the main theme of the garbage collection in data management, and we return to this subject shortly.

Step	Operation	Buffers				Comparison (AGE-A < 21 and AGE-B > = 21)
1	Get a free bucket, say bucket 1.					
2	Construct record in buffer c.	C	George Brentano	BUS	21		
3	Access two list elements and store in buffers A and B, and compare	A	Age-List			6	Not satisfied
		B	Anne Neal	BUS	19	5	
4	Move buffer B to buffer A, read an element into B, and compare	A	Anne Neal	BUS	19	5	Not satisfied
		B	Russell Thompson	BUS	20	2	
5	Move buffer B to buffer A, read an element into B, and compare	A	Russell Thompson	BUS	20	2	Satisfied
		B	John Hansen	CS	21	4	
6	Copy LINK of buffer A into LINK of buffer C.	C	George Brentano	BUS	21	2	
		A	Russell Thompson	BUS	20	2	
		B	John Hansen	CS	21	4	
7	Write buffer C into the file.	C	George Brentano	BUS	21	2	
8	Change LINK in buffer A to address of bucket containing the new record.	A	Russell Thompson	BUS	20	1	
		B	John Hansen	CS	21	4	
9	Rewrite buffer A into the file.	A	Russell Thompson	BUS	20	1	

Figure 7 Trace of Linked-List Insert Algorithm for Linked List of Figure 6

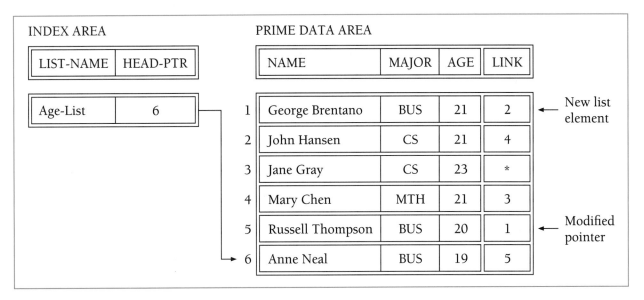

Figure 8 Linked List of Figure 6 After Record George Brentano/BUS/21 Has Been Inserted

Linked-List Variations

Linked lists have many variations, each useful for some application categories in practice. The basic types are forward linked lists, backward linked lists, circular linked lists or rings (forward and backward rings), doubly linked lists, and multiple lists. In addition, one can dream of many other types. Such "hybrid" lists are combinations of basic types and may be suitable for certain applications because of flexibility and ease of processing they might offer. There are endless numbers of such combinations, and we provide one example toward the end of this section.

Forward and Backward Linked Lists. We have seen that a linked list defines an order based on a data element. This order may be increasing or decreasing. Accordingly, the linked list is called forward or backward.

> A **forward linked list** is one that defines an ascending ordering among the list elements based on a specified data item.

All of the linked lists we used as examples in the previous section are forward lists. Figure 9 provides another example, in which the forward linked list called FMajor is based on the data field MAJOR for the file we considered in our previous discussion.

> If the data item on which the linked list is based decreases in value along the list, it is a **backward linked list**.

Figure 10 is an example of a backward linked list. Again, it is based on MAJOR. Traversal of this linked list enables access to records in decreasing order of MAJOR field values in the records.

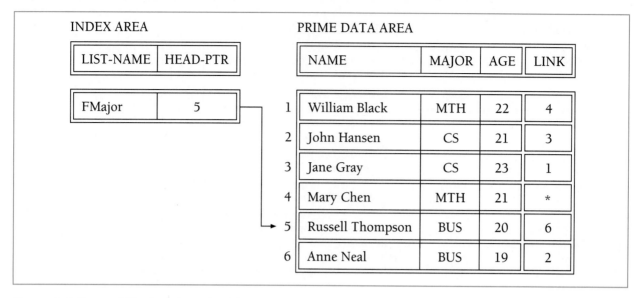

Figure 9 A Forward List Based on MAJOR

Circularly Linked Lists. Forward and backward lists enable us to navigate in the list in only one direction. When we come across the list element with an end-of-list marker in its pointer field, we should exit the prime data area. If we wish to get back to a list element, we have to reenter the list through its head. Writing procedures to process a linked list may be somewhat facilitated if a circular navigational path is introduced into the data structure. Such a variation is called a ring.

> In a **ring,** or **circularly linked list,** the last element has the first element as its logical successor.

A circularly linked list has no predefined exit point and can be traversed circularly any number of times without leaving the prime area. It still requires a point of entry, though, again in the form of an index entry list head. Depending

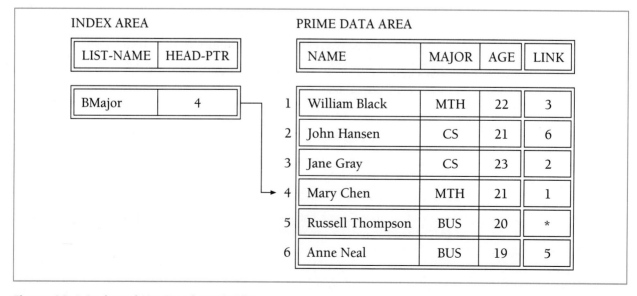

Figure 10 A Backward List Based on MAJOR

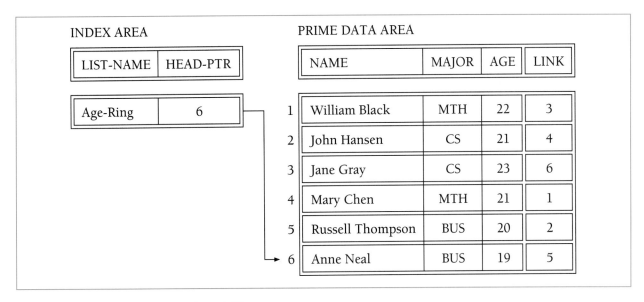

Figure 11 A Forward Ring Based on AGE

on the logical order defined by the linked list, a ring may be forward or backward. Figure 11 is an example of a forward ring based on the data field AGE.

Doubly Linked Lists. The linked lists we have discussed so far contain a single pointer field in each list element. For this reason, they are also called **singly linked lists**.

> It is possible to define **doubly linked lists** that enable us to navigate either forward or backward at will. This is achieved by adding one more link field to the cell structure. In a doubly linked list, each list element includes data plus two links, one to point to the logical successor, the other to the logical predecessor. The index area entry, list head, is also modified by adding one more pointer field to it. Now there are two pointers in the list head, one to the beginning of the forward list and the other to the beginning of the backward list.

The modified cell structures for doubly linked lists are shown in Figure 12.

The main advantage gained in structuring data into a doubly linked list is the ability to traverse the structure in either direction. Put somewhat differently, we have data sorted in ascending and also descending order. Figure 13 is an example of a doubly linked list based on the attribute AGE. The reader is encouraged to draw a digraph for this list and note the parallelism between the two paths in the list structure.

Multiple Lists. A list such as the one given in Figure 13 is useful in that it facilitates processing certain queries if the list elements are to be accessed in a specific order. For example, the data structure in Figure 13 can be used to process student records efficiently in ascending or descending age order. What if we would like to process the records with equal convenience and efficiency in ascending order of MAJOR? All we have to do—of course, at the expense of additional memory space—is to construct a similar linked list and superimpose it on the first one. This necessitates an additional index entry and inclusion of one more pointer field in each cell.

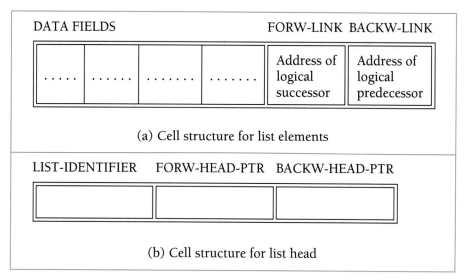

Figure 12 Modified Cell Structures for Doubly Linked Lists

A data structure that incorporates two or more linked lists, each based on a different data field and each with its own list head, is called a **multiple list**.

An example of a multiple list file is given in Figure 14. It consists of a forward list based on NAME and another forward list based on AGE. Each has its corresponding list head entry in the index area. Notice that adding linked lists to a file results in longer records and a larger index area for the file.

Clearly, the possibilities are numerous, but we should exercise caution and prudence in designing complex data structures. Not only are we limited by storage, but we may end up with structures that are excessively difficult to maintain. Think about the steps involved in adding new elements to the multiple list of Figure 14.

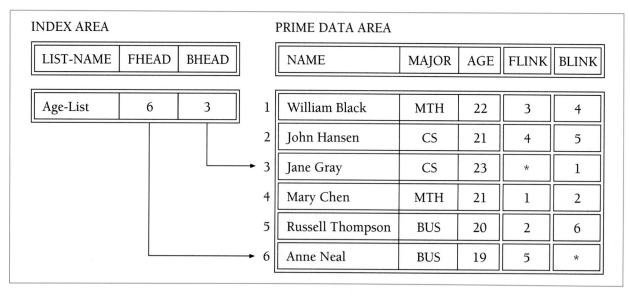

Figure 13 A Doubly Linked List Based on AGE

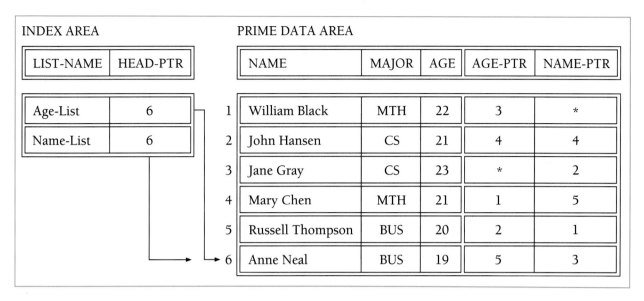

Figure 14 A Multiple List: A Forward List Based on NAME and a Forward List Based on AGE

An Example of Complex Linked Lists: CORAL Ring. Let us examine a hybrid list structure, called CORAL ring. This structure is basically a forward ring with respect to a specific data field, plus a backward ring complemented by pointers that enable us to jump back to the list head without having to traverse the ring fully. Instead of using three pointer fields for each cell, we use only two. The first defines the forward ring, the second is a dual-purpose pointer. It points back to the predecessor of the previous list element at every other cell and provides linkage to the list head at every cell in between.

Figure 15a is an instance of an example CORAL ring. The list elements are assumed to consist of any number of data elements, only one of which, IDNO, is shown. IDNO is the basis of the CORAL ring constructed. The digraph for this CORAL ring is given in Figure 15b.

In our discussion of linked lists so far, we assumed that we have a direct-access environment making access by relative address possible. Some linked lists have an environment that permits access to records directly by content of a data field, as in indexed files. If the list resides in an indexed sequential file, we have to use primary record key values to access cells containing list elements. An example is provided in Figure 16. Here, we assume that NAME is the primary record key. The linked list is a forward list based on AGE. Because the file is an indexed sequential file, records are in increasing order of the primary key filed, NAME. Link fields in each record and the pointer in the list head contain primary key field values, that is, names instead of bucket addresses. Otherwise, the structure in Figure 16 is essentially the same as that in Figure 2.

REVIEW QUESTIONS

1. Of all possible logical file organization techniques, those that are supported by a computer language are called _____ .
2. A linked list consists of a dynamically varying number of _____ that are linked to each other, and a single _____ .
3. A linked list defines a logical order with respect to a data field. (T or F)
4. In searching a linked list, we can begin at an arbitrary list element. (T or F)

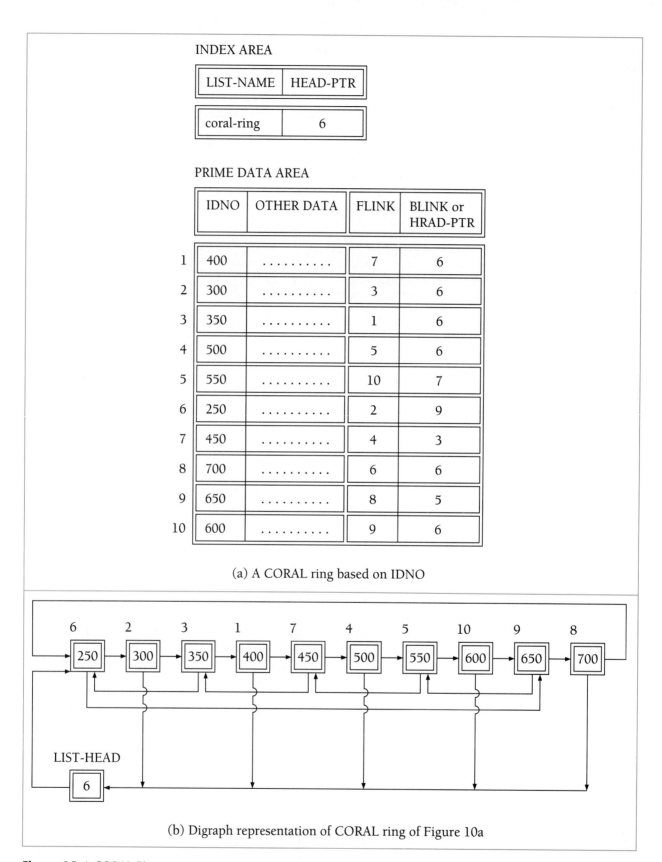

(a) A CORAL ring based on IDNO

(b) Digraph representation of CORAL ring of Figure 10a

Figure 15 A CORAL Ring

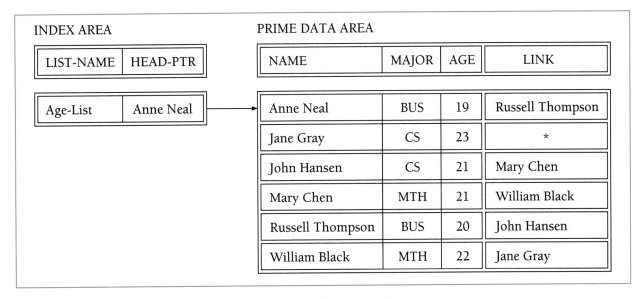

Figure 16 A Forward Linked List Based on AGE Using Content for Linkages

5. The linked list delete algorithm results in deleting a list element physically from the list. (T or F)
6. In inserting a new element into a linked list, we update only the pointer from the predecessor of the new element, and the pointer associated with the new element. (T or F)
7. A linked list that defines an ascending ordering among the list elements based on a specified data item is a _____ linked list. If that ordering is descending, it is called a _____ linked list.
8. In a circular linked list the last element points to the list head. (T or F)
9. A multiple list consists of two or more linked lists, each based on a different data field and each with its own list head. (T or F)

Answers: 1. built-in file organization techniques; 2. list elements, list head; 3. T; 4. F; 5. F; 6. T; 7. forward, backward; 8. F; 9. T.

Linear Files: Inverted Lists

The linked-list variations discussed have one major drawback. In all cases they include every list element. For example, the forward list of Figure 9, which is based on MAJOR, is size 6. It is an efficient data structure only if our application requires access to all list elements in ascending order of MAJOR. In that case, we will have to access seven records (or list elements)—the index entry and six prime area records. Since all record accesses are relevant, the structure is optimal for such an application.

Partially Inverted Lists

Suppose we are not interested in all student records, but only those for mathematics majors (MAJOR = MTH). The linked list of Figure 9 can still be used but rather inefficiently. As we have to enter the list through the list head and proceed sequentially in it, we must access four list elements before we come to the block of relevant elements. In a practical application, the number of irrelevant list elements may be excessive.

To remedy this problem, we propose to split the original linked list into partial lists such that each one has an index entry of its own specifying its list head, and each list contains list elements satisfying a simple condition based on MAJOR.

> The process of splitting a linked list into partial linked lists of smaller size, each corresponding to a specific value of the base data element, is called **inversion**. The resulting set of lists is referred to as a **partially inverted list**.

An example of partial inversion is given in Figure 17. Here the list of Figure 9 has been expanded to include a new record, Amy Sheldon/CS/20. In this partially inverted list we have three partial lists: one for MAJOR = BUS of size 2, one for MAJOR = CS of size 3, and another for MAJOR = MTH of size 2. The sum of sizes of the partial lists is the same as the size of the original list before inversion. The number of index area entries has been tripled. We would need one index area entry for each discrete value of the base data item, MAJOR. Therefore, the index entries have now become a table, or another list.

It should be noted that unless the block of records satisfying a certain attribute-value pair is at the beginning of the list, an inverted list is much more efficient than its uninverted version. Let us demonstrate this by considering a real-life example.

Assume that in a college we have a direct-access student file of 15,000 records. Let MAJOR be one of the attributes in its record structure. Let us suppose that there are 30 different majors and each one has some students. We are interested in processing zoology students, all 300 of them. We further assume that zoology is the last major among all majors in alphabetical order.

First, suppose that the student file is organized in a forward linked list with respect to MAJOR. Such a file will have one index area entry defining the list head, and the number of record accesses necessary to process zoology students will be 15,001. This is because we have to access the list head and traverse the list of 15,000 records. Out of 15,001 record accesses, only 301 will be relevant.

Next, suppose that the same file is organized as a partially inverted file based on MAJOR. In this case we have 30 index area entries in the index table in

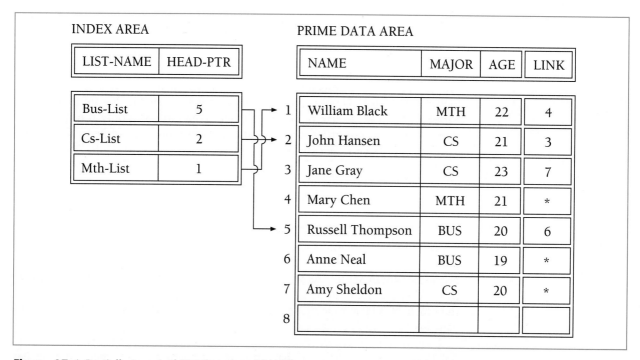

Figure 17 A Partially Inverted List Based on MAJOR

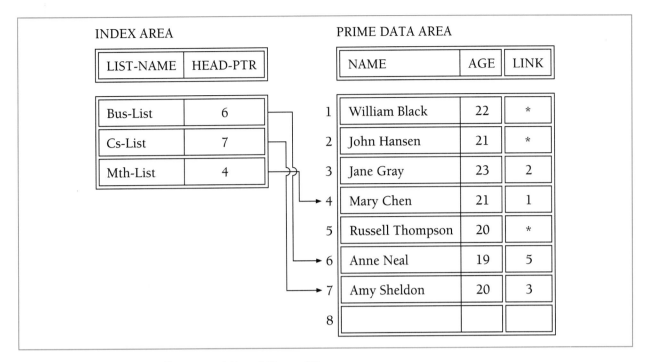

Figure 18 Modified Partially Inverted List of Figure 17

which the last one corresponds to the zoology list. The number of record accesses will be 330 (30 index area records, assuming we perform sequential search in the index table, plus 300 prime area records for zoology students). Only 29 record accesses are irrelevant. This is clearly a more efficient data structure than the previous one, with the savings in the number of accesses amounting to 14,671, or about 98%.

There are two additional advantages of inversion. As each partial list consists of list elements for the same value of base attribute, within each list we can prescribe an order based on another attribute. For example, for the list of Figure 17 we may have students of a given major arranged in alphabetical sequence by their names. We may also eliminate the MAJOR field from each record, thus compensating for the storage overhead due to link fields. The list of Figure 17 changes as shown in Figure 18.

Fully Inverted Lists

We can carry the process of inversion to its limit and split the original linked list (of size n) into n lists, each of size 1.

A list structure that consists of several lists all based on the same base data field, each corresponding to a base attribute value, and containing a single prime area record, is known as a **fully inverted list**, or simply an **inverted list**. An inverted list consists of a prime data area cell structure with no linkages, and an expanded index table. Each index table entry corresponds to a base attribute-value pair and associates it with list elements satisfying the pair.

An example of a fully inverted list is given in Figure 19. The inversion is again with respect to the data field MAJOR. Notice that the prime cells no longer contain pointers. In fact, they need not contain the data field MAJOR either. Therefore, we have a simpler prime area cell structure and less storage

INDEX AREA

LIST-NAME	HEAD-POINTERS		
Bus-List	5	6	
Cs-List	2	3	7
Mth-List	1	4	

PRIME DATA AREA

	NAME	MAJOR	AGE
1	William Black	MTH	22
2	John Hansen	CS	21
3	Jane Gray	CS	23
4	Mary Chen	MTH	21
5	Russell Thompson	BUS	20
6	Anne Neal	BUS	19
7	Amy Sheldon	CS	20
8			

Figure 19 A Fully Inverted List Based on MAJOR (variable-length index area records)

overhead in the prime area. Since the list has three MAJOR values, the index table has three index entries, each one for an attribute-value pair. The first index entry, for example, belongs to the list called Bus-list and corresponds to the pair MAJOR = BUS. In addition to the index entry identifier, it contains relative addresses of all prime area cells hosting student records for students who are majoring in business.

As in partially inverted lists, the primary advantage of inverted list structures is their processing efficiency. Also, without having to access any prime area data, we can extract some information about list elements from index entries. For instance, the index entry called Bus-list in the example enables us to determine the number of business students in the file as 2, and the addresses of prime area cells for them as 5 and 7. In case the inverted list is simulated using the COBOL indexed sequential organization, we would even know who those students are, provided NAME were used as the primary file organization key.

On the other hand, some problems exist with inverted lists, in that index table entries are of variable length and for actual files they are excessively long. To resolve this issue of intolerably high storage overhead, some data-compaction techniques can be used. One good approach is to associate a fixed-length bit string, also called **bit maps**, with each index entry such that its

INDEX AREA

LIST-NAME	BIT-STRING

Bus-List	00001100
Cs-List	01100010
Mth-List	10010000

PRIME DATA AREA

	NAME	MAJOR	AGE
1	William Black	MTH	22
2	John Hansen	CS	21
3	Jane Gray	CS	23
4	Mary Chen	MTH	21
5	Russell Thompson	BUS	20
6	Anne Neal	BUS	19
7	Amy Sheldon	CS	20
8			

Figure 20 A Fully Inverted List Based on MAJOR (use of bit maps in index records)

length is equal to the size of the list, and an existence of 1 in the jth position of the bit string denotes that the jth cell contains a qualifying list element for this index entry. The inverted list of Figure 19 is modified to reflect this method and is shown in Figure 20. We can use the bit string manipulation capabilities of a programming language to translate the bit map to relative address strings prior to accessing relevant list elements.

Another way to simplify index area structure for fully inverted files is to use an equivalent total index for it. For example, the index area table of Figure 19 consists of variable-length records, which makes processing such a file difficult and inefficient. Instead, we can represent this variable-length record structure as a fixed-length record structure by including an index entry for each record in prime data area. The modified inverted file is shown in Figure 21. Here, the index table is a total index, a topic that was discussed in Chapter 13 in connection with indexing and indexed files. We have come a full circle and, in the process, demonstrated the close connection between inverted lists and indexing.

INDEX AREA

	DATA-VALUE	ADDRESS
21	BUS	6
22	BUS	5
23	CS	7
24	CS	3
25	CS	2
26	MTH	4
27	MTH	1
28		

PRIME DATA AREA

	NAME	MAJOR	AGE
1	William Black	MTH	22
2	John Hansen	CS	21
3	Jane Gray	CS	23
4	Mary Chen	MTH	21
5	Russell Thompson	BUS	20
6	Anne Neal	BUS	19
7	Amy Sheldon	CS	20
8			

Figure 21 A Fully Inverted List Based on MAJOR (use of total index)

REVIEW QUESTIONS

1. In a partially inverted list we have one or more lists, each corresponding to a specific value of the base data element, and each with its own list head. (T or F)
2. A partially inverted list based on AGE is a data structure that is more efficient than its uninverted counterpart for processing a simple query such as AGE = 25. (T or F)
3. In a partially inverted list, the number of linked lists is the same as the number of different _____ of the base data element.

4. In a partially inverted list, the number of index entries is the same as the number of different linked lists. (T or F)
5. In a fully inverted list, corresponding to each list element there is one index entry in the index area. (T or F)
6. In a fully inverted list the prime area list elements do not contain pointer fields. (T or F)
7. In a fully inverted file it is not possible to determine how many prime area records satisfy a simple condition, such as AGE = 25, without accessing them. (T or F)

Answers: 1. T; 2. T; 3. data values; 4. T; 5. T; 6. T; 7. F.

File Management

Only in rare cases in practice is a file created and used for a single task. Generally, a systems designer faces a number of different tasks or users wanting to use the same file, each with its own requirements. The number of access methods built into a file greatly influences its design and organization.

Language-supported file organization techniques are quite easy to use, and they impose less of a burden on designers and programmers. However, they provide only a few access methods that are optimally satisfactory in a multiple-user, multiple-task computing environment. Even VSAM/KSDS files, although quite versatile, are limited to four access patterns: sequential access and direct access based on primary and alternate record keys. Every data field in a record structure can be specified as an alternate key, and VSAM will build several alternate index clusters and permit direct access by alternate keys. We pay dearly for this flexibility in terms of direct-access storage needed for large numbers of alternate clusters, however. Despite its power and flexibility, VSAM cannot come to our rescue for all file access requirements. For example, if the record structure of a VSAM/KSDS file does not contain a composite data field made up of, say, two atomic data fields, and if an application requires indexing based on that composite field, we cannot create a corresponding alternate index without changing and recompiling the source code. What do we do under such circumstances? Or if our installation does not have VSAM? Or when our file is simply a relative access file?

Clearly, it becomes the responsibility of designers and programmers to design properly and implement a file system satisfying a variety of possible conflicting access requirements. This is no small task. We have to choose a proper logical file organization technique. We have to decide which built-in file organization technique will carry the final organization to be imposed upon the file. We have to ensure that the design is effective and optimally efficient to satisfy all requirements. Then we have to design and create the software to load and structure the file, to maintain it in its lifetime, and to use it for applications.

Fortunately, the processes of file creation, maintenance, and use have a few common central themes. A procedure to create a linked structure is concerned with defining a prescribed order among list elements, that is, sorting. An element delete algorithm, or an element update logic, has to access a specified element. An insertion routine should first determine the point of insertion. In other words, any file processing application inevitably incorporates element access, and hence, searching is omnipresent. The remaining programming tasks are correct input-output and relatively simple in-memory processing.

Sorting and searching are familiar techniques by now. Several fundamental algorithms explored or suggested in this chapter incorporate searching, sorting, or both. There remains the issue of properly managing data and storage available in our file environment.

Data Structures for File Management

All linear list variations we have discussed so far, linked or otherwise, can be manipulated freely. In other words, list elements can be accessed regardless of where they are located in the list, any arbitrary list element can be accessed and, if need be, deleted, and a new element can be inserted into the list at any point in it.

A special class of linear lists has accessibility limitations. Usually known as **fixed-format lists**, they are not suitable data structures for file systems in that in a list file we must be able to navigate freely without restrictions and without losing list elements. They are highly convenient as internal or external auxiliary data structures for file management purposes, however. Also, they find many other applications in computer science and information systems.

We are interested in two types of fixed-format lists: stacks and queues. They are basically linear lists. Both possess the following properties.

1. Accessing an element results in deleting it from the structure.
2. Only elements at one specific end of the structure can be deleted or accessed.
3. Elements can be inserted only at a specific end of the linear structure.

Stacks.

> A **stack** is a limited-access list to which all additions and deletions are made only at one end. The open end of the stack is called the **top**.

As the name implies, a stack is analogous to a stack of trays or plates. The last element left on top of the stack will be the first to be taken out. Hence, an alternate name for stacks is **last-in-first-out (LIFO) lists**.

Adding an element to a stack is known as **pushing** an element into the stack. Deleting an element is called **popping the stack**, and is equivalent to accessing the stack element at its top. Conversely, accessing the stack element at the top results in deleting this element from the stack.

Figure 22 shows a conceptual stack and effects of stack operations on its content. Popping the stack configuration of Figure 22a releases the first element A, and leaves the stack as shown in Figure 22b. For example, if we wish to access the element N in location 5, we pop the stack four more times, thus emptying it out. A new element may be inserted to the stack and becomes the first element in it. Figure 22c shows the stack after the element E is inserted into the stack of Figure 22b.

To implement a stack in the computer's memory, we may use an array to host the list and a pointer variable to identify its changing top. The array may contain stack elements as a linear list or as a linked list. Figure 23 depicts a linear list implementation for stacks. In popping this stack containing city names we do not move up the list elements. Also, in pushing new elements we do not push down all stack elements. Instead, we update the top pointer, as shown in Figures 23a and 23b.

Figure 24 is the same stack of Figure 23, implemented as a linked list. The initial content of the stack is as shown in the "before" section of Figure 24a. Popping it releases the element pointed to by the stack top, that is Nice. Then the stack top is updated to point to the logical successor of Nice, which is the content of the memory location 3 before deletion. Figure 24b shows the effect of element push into the stack.

Pop and push algorithms for stacks depend on the way they are implemented in the memory, and are quite simple. We can illustrate their implemen-

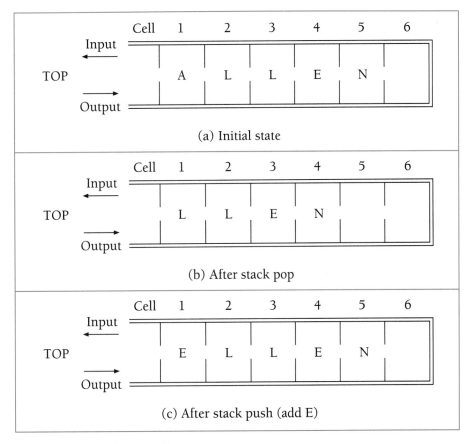

Figure 22 Operations on Stacks

tation by providing a partial COBOL procedure for popping a stack stored in a COBOL array. We assume that an empty array element contains a special marker, * in this application.

```
. . . . . . . . . . . . . .
WORKING-STORAGE SECTION.
01   STACK.
     05   STACK-ELEMENT   OCCURS 50 TIMES    PIC X(10).

01   TOP-PTR                                 PIC 99.
01   ACCESSED-ELEMENT                        PIC X(10).

01   EMPTY-CELL                              PIC X(10).
     88   EMPTY             VALUE "*".
. . . . . . . . . . . . . .
PROCEDURE DIVISION.
. . . . . . . . . . . . . . .
     PERFORM STACK-POP.
. . . . . . . . . . . . . . .
STACK-POP.
     IF STACK-ELEMENT (TOP-PTR) IS EMPTY
          DISPLAY "EMPTY STACK: NO ACTION."
     ELSE
          MOVE STACK-ELEMENT (TOP-PTR) TO ACCESSED-ELEMENT
          ADD 1 TO TOP-PTR.
. . . . . . . . . . . . . . .
```

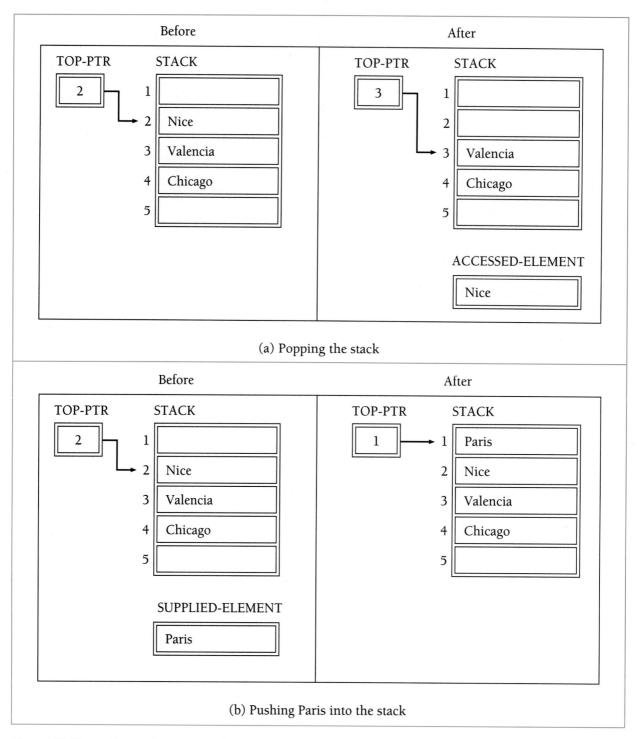

Figure 23 Linear List Implementation for Stacks

Queues.

A **queue** is a list in which all additions are made at one end and all deletions at the other. The input end of a queue is called the **tail** (or rear) and the output end is referred to as the **head** (or front).

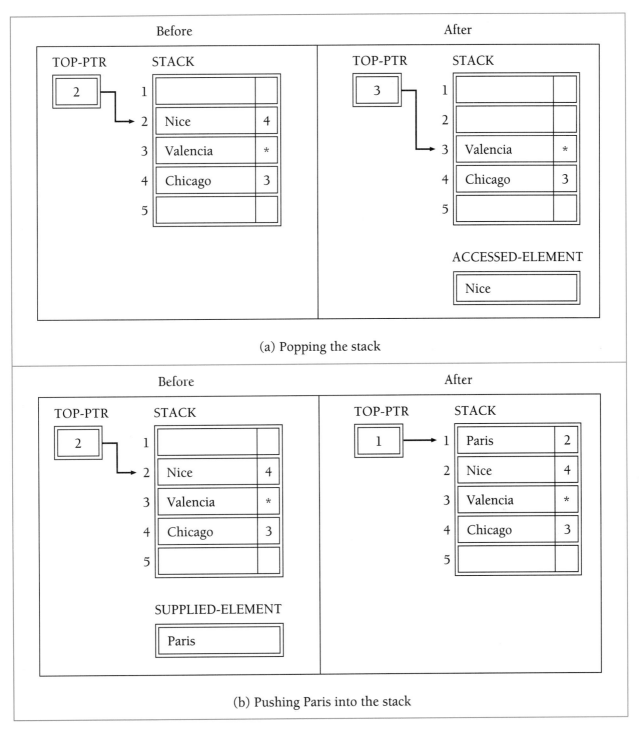

Figure 24 Linked-List Implementation for Stacks

Queues have many real-world counterparts. One example is a line of people waiting to purchase tickets in front of a theater box office.

In computer applications, a queue is regarded as a fixed-format structure. In other words, only the element at the front end may leave the queue, and the motion in the queue is unidirectional, from the tail to the head. A queue is also known as a **first-in-first-out (FIFO) list**.

Adding an element to a queue is known as **enqueueing**. Deleting an element from a queue is sometimes referred to as **dequeueing**. In this book we use the simpler terms, addition and deletion.

Figure 25 illustrates a conceptual queue and how it behaves when elements are added and deleted. The queue initially contains the string TIRE in four consecutive cells. It will lose E on element delete (or access), and will gain the prefix S if the element S is added at the tail. Again, notice that, given the initial state of Figure 25a, the queue will empty out after four successive deletes.

Like stacks, queues can be implemented as linear or linked lists. Figures 26 and 27 are examples of the two approaches. As queues are double-ended lists, in addition to a host array, we need two end pointers for them: one for the tail and one for the head.

To understand the behavior of a linked queue, let us take a closer look at Figure 27. In the "before" section of the queue in Figure 27a the tail pointer has a value of 2, indicating that the element in bucket 2 (i.e., Nice) is the first element in the linked list. It is followed by its successor in bucket 3 (Valencia) and ends with the element in bucket 4 (Chicago). The queue head is bucket 4. Therefore, a queue delete operation will release the content of bucket 4 and change the head pointer to the previous element in the queue, that is, bucket 3. Also, to indicate the end of the list, the link field of the record in bucket 3 is changed to *. The final configuration is shown in the "after" section of Figure 27a.

Insertion and its effects are shown in Figure 27b. The "before" part is the same as in Figure 27a. We want to insert a new element, Paris. It is accommodated in bucket 1, the tail pointer is changed to point to bucket 1, and the link field of the new element in bucket 1 is made to point to bucket 2, the previous queue tail.

We should realize that queues implemented as linear lists are substantially more difficult to handle than stacks. This is because queues exhibit circular

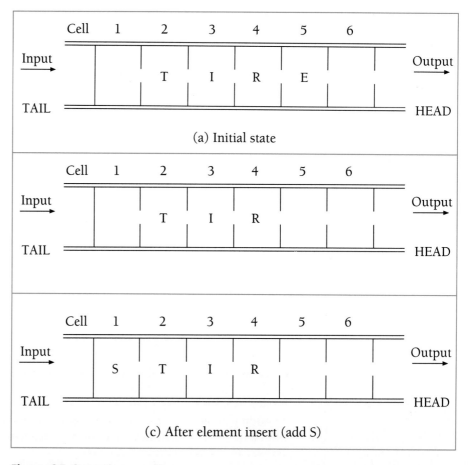

(a) Initial state

(c) After element insert (add S)

Figure 25 Operations on Queues

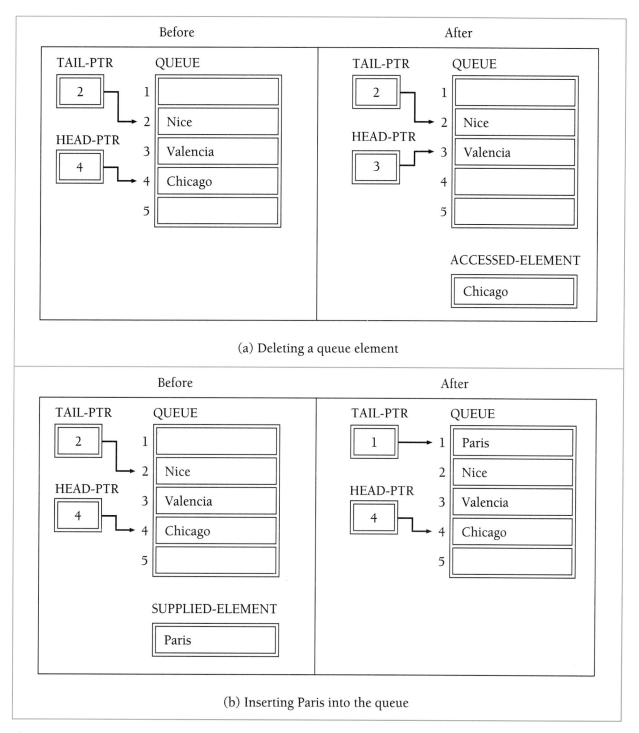

Figure 26 Linear List Implementation for Queues

characteristics, whereas the computer storage structures hosting them (i.e., arrays with beginnings and ends) are linear. Consequently, extreme cases of full and empty queues can cause problems and require caution on the part of the programmer. Linked-list queue implementations are definitely more flexible and quite suitable for this kind of data structure.

The fundamental algorithms for queue operations (queue-delete and queue-insert) naturally depend on whether the queue is conceived as a linear list or linked list. They are not given here, and are suggested as exercises for the reader.

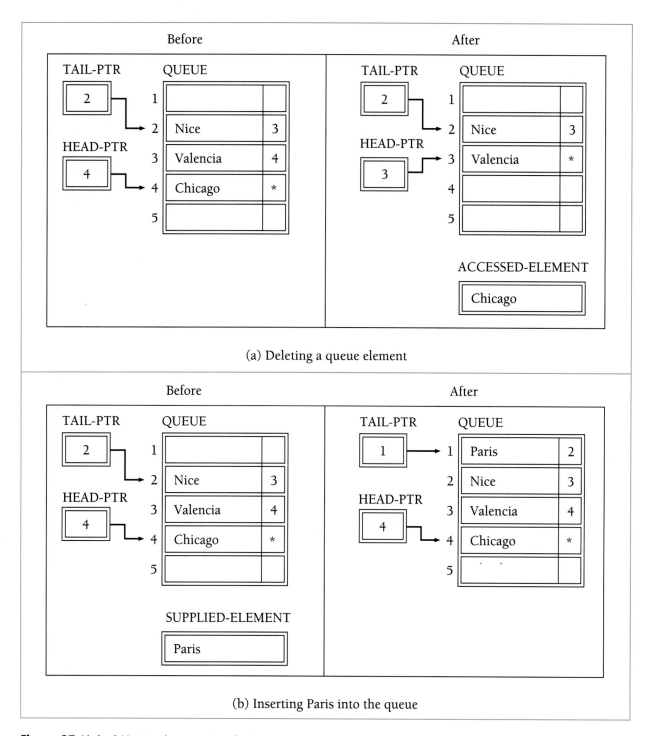

(a) Deleting a queue element

(b) Inserting Paris into the queue

Figure 27 Linked-List Implementation for Queues

Garbage Collection

The last technique we discuss before we conclude our treatment of linear files has to do with methodically handling storage resources during file creation and maintenance phases. This problem first arose in conjunction with logical deletes in linked lists. After we exclude a list element from a linked list by properly adjusting pointers, the element is said to contain **garbage**. For effective storage management, such memory locations should be recovered and used for new list elements.

Techniques that aim to recover the memory locations that contain garbage or those that have not been used previously so that they can be reallocated are called **garbage collection techniques**.

At the foundation of garbage collection lies a list structure, called the available space list, or simply space list. A **space list** is a structured collection of memory locations that do not contain relevant data, but can be used to store data as necessary. It can be made to recover systematically memory locations that are no longer required in a data structure, and release them for use in the same or another data structure in case a memory cell is needed to accommodate a new data element. To avoid ambiguity in identifying the memory location to be released from the space list, we conceive the space list either as a stack or as a queue.

Let us exemplify the use of space lists in an application that includes garbage collection. At the same time, we will be giving an example of stack application. Consider the linked list of Figure 2, restructured as shown in Figure 28.

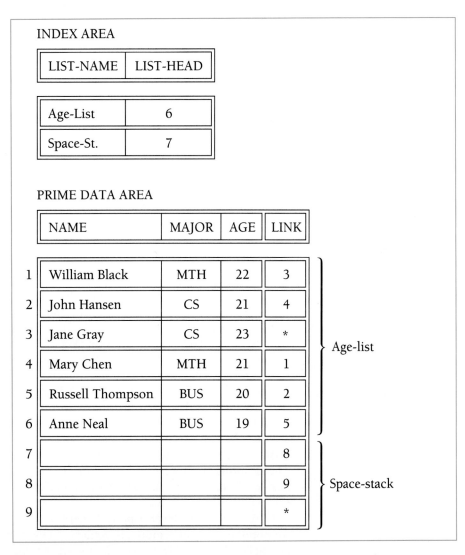

Figure 28 A Linked-List File Based on AGE with a Space Stack

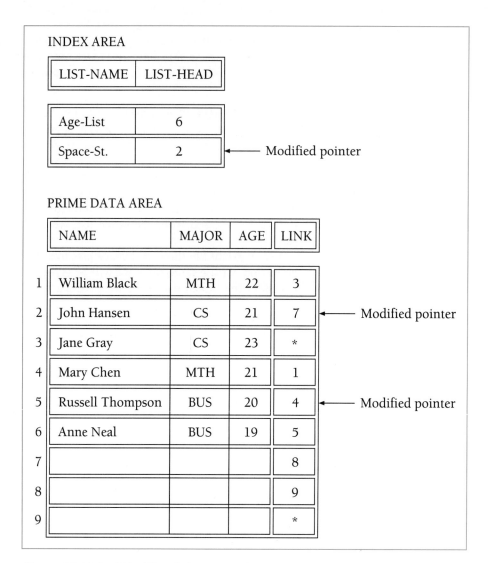

Figure 29 Linked-List File of Figure 28 After Element Delete (garbage collection)

Figure 28 shows a storage structure consisting of six direct-access buckets that host a linked list based on AGE, and another linked list of three empty cells. The latter is our space list, which is regarded as a stack in this application. It is a linked stack of size 3 (buckets 7, 8, and 9) together with a stack top pointer, the second entry in the index area. Note that the two lists that make up the prime data area are disjoint, and that no buckets are unaccounted for.

Let us delete the list element John Hansen/CS/21. We use the linked-list delete algorithm described previously in this chapter. This algorithm modifies the LINK field of the bucket containing the logical predecessor of John's record. The Age-List excludes bucket 2. To recover this bucket, we use a stack-push algorithm and include the bucket as the first element in the space stack. The resulting instance of the structure is shown in Figure 29. The space stack size has increased by one, and again all buckets in both lists are fully accounted for.

Conversely, whenever a new element is to be inserted in the data list, first we pop the stack to acquire an available bucket. For the above example, it will be bucket 2, as it is closest to the top of the space stack. Then we use the released bucket to store the record that will subsequently be inserted into the data list by an insertion algorithm. This fundamental algorithm was described earlier in this chapter. A similar technique constitutes the basis for the routine that initially creates and loads a list file. It should be noted that it is also possible to use a space queue instead of a space stack in garbage collection.

Finally, we should mention other variations of garbage collection such as the so-called buddy system, which are outside the scope of this book. Interested readers are referred to many available standard textbooks on data structures.

REVIEW QUESTIONS

1. A linear list in which only some specific elements can be accessed is called a _____ list.
2. All additions to and deletions from a stack are made only at one end, which is called the _____ of the stack.
3. Adding an element into a stack is called _____ an element into it. Deleting an element from a stack is referred to as _____ it.
4. In a queue, the input end is called _____ and the output end is called _____ .
5. A garbage collection technique aims to recover only the memory locations that have not been used previously to store data. (T or F)
6. A space list is a structured collection of memory locations that do not contain relevant data, but can be used for data storage when needed. (T or F)

Answers: 1. fixed-format; 2. top; 3. pushing, popping; 4. tail, head; 5. F; 6. T.

Example Programs: Creating, Accessing, and Maintaining a Linked-List File

In this section we develop and discuss a COBOL application software system consisting of three programs. The programs are based on a relative file storing a variety of linear data structures: a linked list, a set of partially inverted lists, and a fully inverted list.

Suppose we have a student file with the following record structure:

- A 25-character student name field that is assumed to identify uniquely all records in the student file
- A 3-character student major field indicating the academic discipline in which a given student is majoring
- A 2-digit student age

The student file is structured as a relative-access file. It is known that the following types of access patterns are required for this file:

- Access to records in increasing order of student names
- Access to all student records satisfying a given major value
- Access to all records for a given age value

The first access requirement indicates a forward linked list based on student name. The second calls for a set of partially inverted linked lists based on the student major field. The third is handled by constructing a fully inverted list with respect to student age.

In our application we assume that the file will reside in a direct-access cluster consisting of 233 buckets. The first 100 buckets will be used to store data records. Buckets 101 through 233 will be reserved for index entries needed for the three linked lists.

The index entries for these linked lists fall into three categories, one for each type. In other words, we will create and maintain in the index area a list head for the name list, a number of list heads for the major lists, and index entries for the inverted list based on age. In addition, as the basis for a garbage collection scheme, we will keep two stacks as linked lists, a data stack and an index stack. As the names imply, they are free space stacks for the data and the index areas. Each requires one list head entry in the index area. Consequently, the index area entries are identified by the following list names.

1. DATASTACK for the data area free space list.
2. INDEXSTACK for the index area stack, implemented as a linked list.
3. NAME for the name linked list.
4. MAJORXXX for a partially inverted list corresponding to the major value of XXX. For example, MAJORBUS is the name of the list for all records in which the student major is business administration. There will be one such list identifier for each different major value in the file.
5. AGEXX for each record in the data area for which the age value is XX. For example, AGE19 will be used as the index entry identifier for a student record with AGE field value of 19. There will be as many index entries of this type as the number of records in the data area.

We assume that the first bucket in the index area, bucket 101, will be used to store the DATASTACK index entry, and bucket 102 will store the IN-DEXSTACK list head. The other buckets are reserved for the remaining index entries. The order in which these entries are stored depends on two factors: (1) the logic of the programs to be developed to build and maintain the list structures, and (2) the order of data records in the data area as far as the major and age values are concerned.

We reserved 133 buckets in the index area because we are limiting our file to a maximum of 100 student data records. Also, we are assuming 30 different academic disciplines in the college. As one age index entry will be needed for each student record, one major index entry for each major list, and one index entry for the name, DATASTACK, and INDEXSTACK lists, we must have 133 buckets to store the index table for this file.

Naturally, each index entry in the index area will have a list name and a start address. The start address is the address of the bucket in which the first data or index record for the list is stored. For example, the index area for this application will be as follows.

Bucket Number	List Identifier	Start Address
101	DATASTACK	011
102	INDEXSTACK	121
103	NAME	007
104	MAJORBUS	005
105	MAJORCS	002
. . . .
110	MAJORMTH	001
111	AGE22	001
112	AGE19	002
. . . .
120	AGE19	010

The index area can be implemented as a separate file. In this case, we choose to include the index area in the same cluster as the data area. As the index area record structure is different from that for the data area, our student file becomes a multiple-record file. Clearly, the index area record structure will include two fields for list names and start addresses. We also incorporate two one-character fields into both the index and the data record structures: a record type field with values of D for data records and I for index records to help differentiate between different record types, and a record status field. The record status field is used to indicate whether the bucket is full, empty, or contains a deleted record, with values F, E, and D, respectively. Hence, the data record structure, expressed in COBOL, is

```
01  PRIME-RECORD.
    05  DATA-RECORD-TYPE      PIC X.
    05  DATA-RECORD-STATUS    PIC X.
    05  STUDENT-NAME          PIC X(25).
    05  STUDENT-MAJOR         PIC X(3).
    05  STUDENT-AGE           PIC XX.
    05  NAME-LINK             PIC X(3).
    05  MAJOR-LINK            PIC X(3).
```

and the index record structure becomes:

```
01  INDEX-RECORD.
    05  INDEX-RECORD-TYPE     PIC X.
    05  INDEX-RECORD-STATUS   PIC X.
    05  LIST-NAME             PIC X(20).
    05  START-ADDRESS         PIC X(3).
    05  FILLER                PIC X(13).
```

NAME-LINK and MAJOR-LINK in the data record structure are pointer fields for the name and major lists, respectively, and contain relative addresses to buckets in which successor records are stored.

Example Program 1: Linked-List File Creation

The first component of the application software system we develop is a program that creates the linked lists described above. Base data for student records come from a sequential file, so the input for the creation module is in batch mode. An instance of the sequential student file consisting of 10 records is shown in Program 1-Input. It should be noted that student records in the sequential file are not in any particular order.

Program 1-Source is the compiler listing of the linked-list creation program. Here, REL-STUDENT-FILE is the direct-access student file with linked lists. As explained before, it is a multiple-record file.

The first task of this program is to build the data and index space stacks. This is done by the paragraph B1-BUILD-SPACE-STACKS. The relative student file is opened in output mode. The index records

IFDATASTACK	001

and

IFINDEXSTACK	103

are written into buckets 101 and 102, respectively. After this, an empty data stack is built in the prime data area by storing empty data records in the rest of the data area. An empty record has D in DATA-RECORD-TYPE, E in DATA-RECORD-STATUS, blanks in STUDENT-NAME, STUDENT-MAJOR, and STUDENT-AGE, zero in MAJOR-LINK, and the address of the next available bucket in the data area stored in NAME-LINK. Finally, an empty index stack is also built using the available buckets in the index area. The principles used in constructing both the data and the index stacks are similar. An empty index stack record is characterized by I in INDEX-RECORD-TYPE, E in INDEX-RECORD-STATUS, blanks in LIST-NAME, and the address of the next available bucket in the index area in START-ADDRESS. Therefore, we use NAME-LINK as the pointer field for the data stack, and START-ADDRESS for the index stack. The last elements of both stacks contain 999 in their respective pointer fields. The value 999 is selected as the end-of-list marker in our application.

Figure 30a shows the structures built into the empty file in this first step, namely, the data and index space stacks. As is seen, the data stack consists of buckets 1 through 100, and the index stack includes buckets 103 through 233.

The second task performed in the program is to load the relative student file. In paragraph B2-BUILD-RAW-FILE, we open the sequential student file in input and the relative student file in output mode. After reading a data record from the sequential input file, we first pop the data stack (paragraph D1-POP-DATA-STACK). This gives us the address of an available bucket in the prime data area stored in SAVE-BUCKET-NUMBER. Using this as the bucket number, which is our relative key for the file, we access the empty bucket thus provided and fill it with data.

The stack pop algorithm of the paragraph D1-POP-DATA-STACK also modifies the stack head pointer by changing the top pointer, the value of the variable START-ADDRESS in bucket 101, to point to the next available bucket in the data stack.

```
00533      D1-POP-DATA-STACK.
00534          MOVE 101 TO BUCKET-NUMBER.
00535          PERFORM D2-READ-REL-FILE-DIRECTLY.
00536          MOVE INDEX-RECORD TO WS-INDEX-RECORD.
00537
00538          MOVE WS-START-ADDRESS TO BUCKET-NUMBER SAVE-BUCKET-NUMBER.
00539          PERFORM D2-READ-REL-FILE-DIRECTLY.
00540          MOVE PRIME-RECORD TO WS-PRIME-RECORD.
00541
00542          MOVE WS-NAME-LINK TO STACK-HEAD-POINTER.
00543
00544          MOVE 101 TO BUCKET-NUMBER.
00545          PERFORM D2-READ-REL-FILE-DIRECTLY.
00546          MOVE INDEX-RECORD TO WS-INDEX-RECORD.
00547          MOVE STACK-HEAD-POINTER TO WS-START-ADDRESS.
00548          PERFORM D4-REWRITE-INDEX-RECORD.
```

Lines 00534 and 00535 enable direct access to the data stack head in bucket 101. Line 00536 makes a copy of the accessed index entry in WS-INDEX-RECORD. Statement 00538 saves the pointer to the first stack element (i.e., WS-START-ADDRESS) in the variable SAVE-BUCKET-NUMBER. It also copies the content of WS-START-ADDRESS into BUCKET-NUMBER. After this, lines 00539 and 00540 access the first stack element in the prime area and

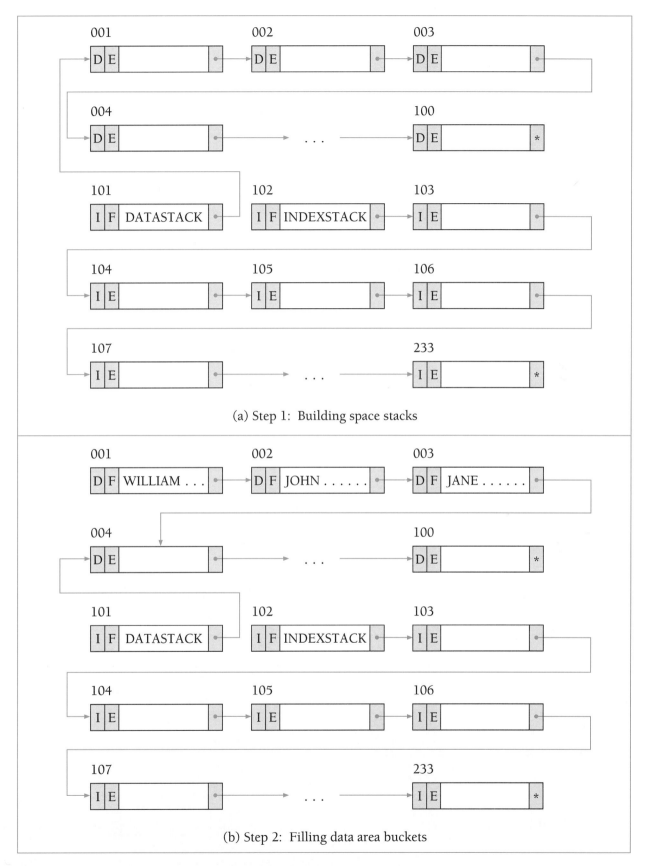

(a) Step 1: Building space stacks

(b) Step 2: Filling data area buckets

Figure 30 Steps in Constructing Data Structures in Program 1

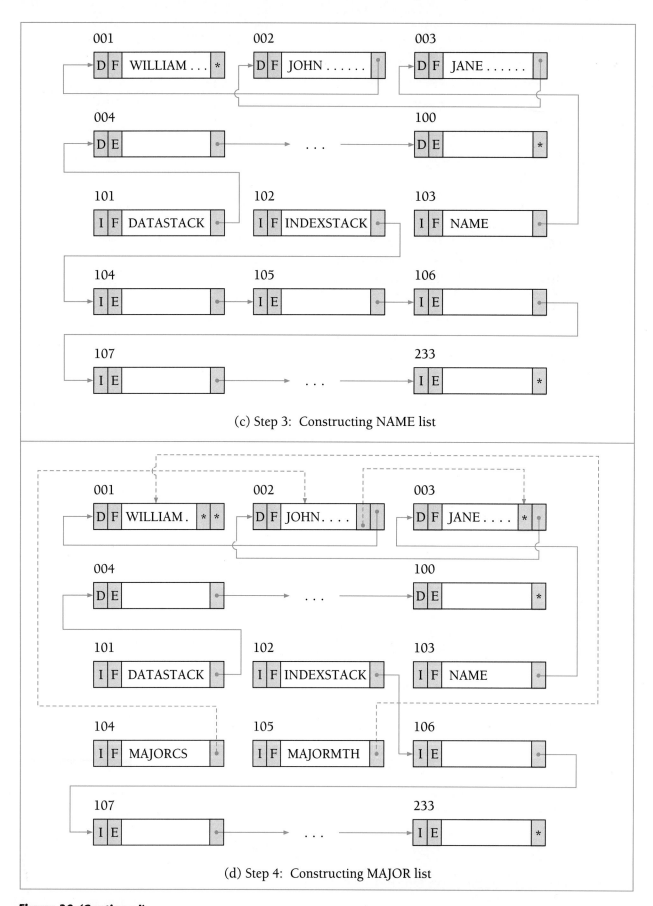

(c) Step 3: Constructing NAME list

(d) Step 4: Constructing MAJOR list

Figure 30 (Continued)

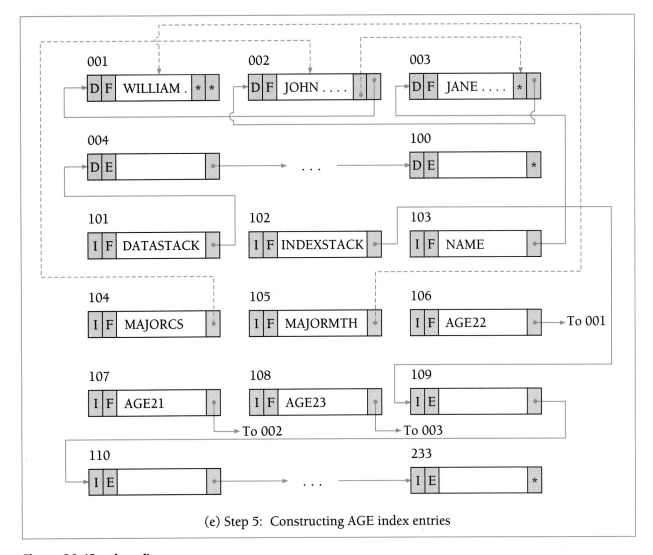

(e) Step 5: Constructing AGE index entries

Figure 30 (Continued)

store it in WS-PRIME-RECORD. At this point we have a copy of the data stack head entry and the first stack element in the main memory in WS-INDEX-RECORD and WS-PRIME-RECORD, respectively.

Next we copy the WS-NAME-LINK field value of the first stack element into STACK-HEAD-POINTER. In lines 00544 through 00548 we access bucket 101, modify its content by changing WS-START-ADDRESS to assume the value preserved in STACK-HEAD-POINTER, and rewrite the stack. This completes the stack pop operation. The variable SAVE-BUCKET-NUMBER contains the relative address of a bucket in the prime data area, which we can use to accommodate a data record.

Figure 30b shows the changes in the data area and data stack after three records have been written into the relative file. Now the data stack top is bucket 004, pointed to by the stack head pointer in bucket 101. It should be noted that the first three buckets in the prime area are still linked together, although there is no pointer in the index area that can take us to them. We are planning to access the full prime buckets sequentially in the next step, however, and therefore no harm is done.

The next step entails constructing the forward linked list based on NAME. The method we have chosen in the program is to load the prime area records into three parallel arrays collected under the structure name ATTRIBUTE-ORDER-ARRAY (lines 00136–00139). The three one-dimensional arrays are ATTRIBUTE-VALUE, REL-ADDRESS, and SUCCESSOR-ADDRESS. The elements of the first two contain STUDENT-NAME values and their bucket addresses, respectively. We load array elements by reading the relative student file sequentially, having opened it in input mode. We continue reading data records from the file until we encounter one in which DATA-RECORD-STATUS is E (indicating that we have come to the end of the full portion in the prime area) or until the relative address of the bucket to be read has become larger than 100.

When the first two parallel arrays are loaded, we close the relative student file and reopen it as I-O. Then we sort the array ATTRIBUTE-VALUE in increasing order, maintaining its parallelism with the array REL-ADDRESS. The internal sorting technique that we use is reflected in the paragraphs C5-SORT-ARRAY and its subordinate D5-COMPARE-AND-EXCHANGE. It is the bubble sort algorithm that we studied previously.

To see what actually happens, let us assume that we have only the first three records in Program 1-Input in the prime data area. Immediately after loading name values into the array, and before sorting we have:

	ATTRIBUTE–VALUE	REL–ADDRESS	SUCCESSOR–ADDRESS
1	WILLIAM BLACK	001	
2	JOHN HANSEN	002	
3	JANE GRAY	003	

After the sort process the arrays become:

	ATTRIBUTE–VALUE	REL–ADDRESS	SUCCESSOR–ADDRESS
1	JANE GRAY	003	
2	JOHN HANSEN	002	
3	WILLIAM BLACK	001	

To determine the logical successors of the records represented in the array ATTRIBUTE-VALUE by student name values, all we have to do is to store the next subscript value in the corresponding SUCCESSOR-ADDRESS element. For the very last array element we make an exception and store 999 to indicate that it is the end of the list. The parallel arrays become:

	ATTRIBUTE–VALUE	REL–ADDRESS	SUCCESSOR–ADDRESS
1	JANE GRAY	003	002
2	JOHN HANSEN	002	003
3	WILLIAM BLACK	001	999

We are ready to generate the NAME list head. Its START-ADDRESS value is the value of the first array element of the array REL-ADDRESS (see paragraph C7-FORM-NAME-INDEX). Our final tasks in this step consist of accessing the bucket whose relative address is the value of an element of the array REL-ADDRESS, storing in the NAME-LINK field of the record the value of SUCCESSOR-ADDRESS, and rewriting the record. We do this for all full elements in the ATTRIBUTE-VALUE array by repetitively executing the paragraph C8-BUILD-NAME-LINKS. Now that the NAME forward linked list has been constructed and the file structure is as depicted in Figure 30c, we have three linked lists in the file: NAME list, DATASTACK, and INDEXSTACK.

The next step is to construct the MAJOR lists. This is done in paragraph B4-BUILD-MAJOR-LIST. The logic we have adopted here is similar to the previous step that dealt with the NAME linked list. The main difference is that after loading the array ATTRIBUTE-VALUE, we have STUDENT-MAJOR field values in it. We sort this array, grouping together the student records with the same major. After sorting, we link the major list elements in the parallel arrays (paragraph C10-LINK-MAJOR-ARRAY-ELEMENTS) and form the major index entries for each value of the STUDENT-MAJOR attribute in paragraph C11-FORM-MAJOR-INDEX. This operation involves popping the index stack (paragraph D6-POP-INDEX-STACK) using a logic that is quite similar to that in popping the data stack. This way, we get available index area buckets, detach them from the index stack, and store in them MAJOR list heads. Finally, in paragraph C12-BUILD-MAJOR-LINKS, we form MAJOR linked lists and write them into the file. Figure 30d shows the data structures built into the file after the fourth step in the process.

There remains building the AGE inverted list, and it is done by the paragraph B5-BUILD-AGE-LIST. This is a relatively easy task in that no changes are required in the prime data area. We load the ATTRIBUTE-VALUE array with STUDENT-AGE values from data records. We do not even have to sort the parallel arrays. Then, using the parallel arrays as guides, we build AGE index entries in the paragraph C14-FORM-AGE-INDEX. Again, this involves popping the index stack to obtain the address of an empty index bucket, and storing in that bucket the list identifier and the relative address of the prime area bucket for a considered AGE value. This way, we build one index area entry for each data record. Figure 30e shows the final configuration of the data structures in the relative file.

Example Program 2:   Linked-List File Access

Next we develop a program module that enables access to REL-STUDENT-FILE on which we have superimposed a variety of linked lists. The compiler listing of this program is shown in Program 2-Source. The program is menu driven. It permits the following types of access:

1. Sequential access to all records in the prime data area and the index data area
2. Access to data records in ascending order of STUDENT-NAME field values using the NAME forward linked list
3. Access to data records for all students majoring in a specified academic discipline using the MAJOR linked lists
4. Access to data records for all students whose STUDENT-AGE field value matches a specified age value using the AGE inverted list

The program menu is based on a variable called FUNCTION-CODE. The defined FUNCTION-CODE values and the corresponding operations are shown below.

Function-Code	Operation
S	Sequential listing of data and index area records
N	Ordered listing of data records by NAME
M	Listing of all data records for the query MAJOR = XXX
A	Listing of all data records for the query AGE = XX
X	Display of program menu
T	Termination of program

Getting a sequential listing of REL-STUDENT-FILE is easy and is done by paragraph C2-LIST-FILE-SEQUENTIALLY. In this paragraph, we open the file in input mode and directly access and display the contents of the prime data area provided the RECORD-STATUS is F for records. The prime area buckets are addressed 1 through 100, so we vary the relative key BUCKET-NUMBER in this range to access all data records. Then we do the same thing for index records, varying the relative key BUCKET-NUMBER from 101 to 233.

To get an ordered name listing we execute the paragraph C3-LIST-BY-NAME. In this paragraph, we open the file in input mode and first access the beginning of the index area at bucket 101. Then we search the index area sequentially until we find the NAME list head (lines 00222–00227). When we find the NAME list head we bring it into the memory and, using the START-ADDRESS value, directly access and display the first data record in the ordered list. We use the NAME-LINK of the previously accessed record to access its logical successor until the NAME-LINK field is found to contain 999, the end-of-list marker. This is the typical linked-list traversal algorithm and is coded in paragraph D3-DISPLAY-LIST-BY-NAME.

The third access pattern is based on a STUDENT-MAJOR value. The user is prompted to enter a STUDENT-MAJOR value (lines 00242–00243). Using this value, the string MAJORXXX is formed, where XXX is the supplied STUDENT-MAJOR value. This string is used as the search key for a sequential search of the index area starting at bucket 101 (lines 00251–00257). If the index entry for the MAJOR list head is found, a linked-list traversal is undertaken for that particular list, as reflected in the paragraph D5-DISPLAY-LIST-BY-MAJOR.

The final access pattern is by STUDENT-AGE, handled in the paragraph C5-LIST-BY-AGE. The program again prompts the user to enter a STUDENT-AGE value, and forms the search key string AGEXX, where XX is the AGE value. The index area is sequentially searched starting at bucket 101, and every time a match is found the corresponding data record is directly accessed using the START-ADDRESS field value in the index area AGE entry. This process is carried out until all buckets in the index area are exhausted. Program 2-Output shows the printout for a comprehensive terminal session corresponding to the current program module.

Example Program 3:   Linked-List File Maintenance

The third program is a linked-list maintenance program. Maintaining a multiple linked-list file is an involved process. As mentioned several times previously, there are three maintenance tasks: record deletion, record insertion, and record update.

Record deletion requires locating and either physically or logically deleting a specified data record in the file. It also requires updating all linked lists in which the record to be deleted exists. In our application we must modify the NAME and MAJOR linked lists so that the deleted record is excluded from them. Also, we must delete the corresponding AGE index entry in the index area.

For record insertion we must first check the data area to ensure that the new record is not already in the file. Then we store the record to be inserted in the prime area. After this, we traverse the NAME list and the appropriate MAJOR list, and by updating pointers, we include the new record in these lists. Finally, we create a new AGE index entry and store it in the index area.

Record update calls for accessing the data record to be updated and changing its content. Then we determine the list corresponding to the field being updated. If STUDENT-NAME is the update field, we traverse the NAME list and locate the data record, detach it from the list, and insert the modified record into the list at the correct place. If the STUDENT-MAJOR field is being updated, we traverse the MAJOR list corresponding to the old MAJOR field value and detach the record from that list. After this we get into the MAJOR list corresponding to the new MAJOR field value and insert the record into that list. Finally, if the change is in the AGE field value, we search the index area, find the corresponding AGE index entry, and modify its LIST-NAME field to reflect the change.

In this section we offer a limited-scope linked-list file maintenance program that can delete records from the file. Record insertion and update are left as exercises for the reader. The compiler-generated source listing of the COBOL program developed for this purpose is given in Program 3-Source.

The program first prompts the user to enter a STUDENT-NAME value to identify the record to be deleted (lines 00168 and 00169). More than one record can be deleted in one run of this program, but only one is considered at a time. Program control then passes to the module B1-DELETE-RECORD.

In this module, an index area search is initiated to find the NAME list head (paragraph C1-FIND-NAME-LIST-HEAD). After finding the NAME list head, we get into the NAME list and traverse it until we locate the record to be deleted. It is the record whose STUDENT-NAME field value matches the supplied DELETE-NAME. This traversal is reflected in the paragraph C2-FIND-RECORD-TO-BE-DELETED and its subordinate module D2-TRAVERSE-NAME-LIST.

We have defined two buffers for data records in the program: the WORKING-STORAGE SECTION structures called BUFFER-A and BUFFER-B, respectively (lines 00132–00148). The traversal logic is such that, if the record to be deleted is found, it will be stored in BUFFER-B with its logical predecessor in BUFFER-A. If the record is found, we are ready to proceed with the record deletion. At this point, program control passes to the paragraph C3-COMPLETE-DELETION where the following operations are performed.

1. The data record that has been located is detached from the NAME list (paragraph D3-DELETE-FROM-NAME-LIST). For this, the NAME-LINK field value of the record in BUFFER-B is duplicated in the NAME-LINK field value of BUFFER-A, and the content of BUFFER-A is rewritten into the file.
2. The data record is deleted from the AGE list (paragraph DELETE-FROM-AGE-LIST). This requires searching the index area to locate the corresponding AGE index entry, changing its INDEX-RECORD-STATUS to D, and pushing the released bucket into the index stack as part of the garbage collection routine devised for the current application. The push stack logic is coded in the paragraph E4-PUSH-INTO-INDEX-STACK.

3. We trigger the paragraph D5-DELETE-FROM-MAJOR-LIST. In that paragraph we form a search string MAJORXXX, where XXX is the STUDENT-MAJOR field value of the record to be deleted. Using this as the search key, we search and find the index area MAJOR list head and initiate a MAJOR list traversal in the paragraph E6-FIND-RECORD-IN-MAJOR-LIST. The logic of this paragraph and the ensuing pointer adjustments to drop the record from the MAJOR list are quite similar to that discussed for NAME list deletion above.

4. We change the DATA-RECORD-STATUS field value of BUFFER-B containing the record to be deleted to D, thus logically marking it as a deleted bucket. We do these in paragraph D6-MARK-RECORD-AS-DELETED and then rewrite the modified record into the file.

5. We complete garbage collection by executing the paragraph D7-PUSH-INTO-DATA-STACK, which takes the released bucket currently duplicated in BUFFER-B and includes it in the DATASTACK.

Program 3-Output(a) shows the listing of an interactive terminal session for the deletion program. During this session three records have been deleted. The data and index area structures are modified as shown in Program 3-Output(b). This figure depicts the linked list file after the three record deletions of Program 3-Output(a).

Finally, Program 3-Output(c) is an interactive terminal session obtained by using the second program module developed for accessing the student file after the above record deletions. It is a useful exercise for the reader to study Program 3-Output(b) and (c) and verify the correctness of the data structures after deletions.

Key Terms

backward linked list	inversion
built-in file organization	inverted list
circular linked list	linked list
CORAL ring	list head
doubly linked list	logical file organization
end-of-list marker	multiple list
file management	partially inverted list
fixed-format list	queue
forward linked list	space list
garbage collection technique	stack

Study Guide

Quick Scan

- There are many different file organization techniques. To distinguish them from built-in techniques, we refer to them as logical file organization techniques. Built-in file organization techniques are those that are supported directly by language processors.
- All file organization techniques that are not directly supported by a language processor can be simulated using an appropriate built-in technique. In this chapter we emphasize linear file organization techniques.
- A linear file is based on a linear data structure. A linear data structure incorporates a set of relationships that can be mapped onto a straight line without losing any information from data stored in it. Sequential and linked lists are linear structures.

- A linked list consists of a list head that points to the first element in the list, and a set of linearly connected data elements. Each data element has associated with it a pointer that defines the logical successor of the element.
- A linked list necessitates a modified cell structure that contains data fields and a link (or pointer) field. The link field stores the address of the logical successor of the node under consideration. The last element in the list has no successor; this is indicated by storing an end-of-list marker * in its pointer field.
- A linked list has to be stored in a direct-access storage environment so that it is possible to jump from a list element to its logical successor, which may be stored at a distance from the node. As a matter of convention, a linked list is entered at its list head. The list head is an index entry that assigns a name to the linked list and associates the name with the address of the first element in it.
- The fundamental operations on linked lists are maintenance (adding a new element, deleting an element, and updating an element) and searching.
- Searching is essential for maintenance operations, as well. To search a linked list we enter it at its head and traverse it using pointers and accessing data nodes directly.
- Element insertion and deletion in a linked list require locating the point of insertion or the node to be deleted, followed by an update of appropriate pointer fields. These algorithms are efficient because they do not necessitate physical data movement in the list.
- There are many different variations of linked lists. A linked list that defines an increasing order of data field values associated with its nodes is called a forward linked list. If this order is decreasing, it is a backward linked list.
- If the last element in a linked list points to the first element, the linked list is called a ring (or a circularly linked list). A ring may be forward or backward.
- A doubly linked list permits traversal in both forward and backward directions because it associates with each node a forward and a backward pointer.
- It is possible to have two or more linked lists embedded in a data structure, such that each one is based on a different data element and each has its own list head. Such a structure is called a multiple list.
- Linked lists can be used to define order with respect to a data element in a data structure. Especially in cases of data elements with nonunique values, however, searching a linked list may take a long time as the process is basically sequential. To shorten the list, it is possible to split it into sublists, each corresponding to a value of the data element on which the list is based. This process is called list inversion.
- A linked list may be inverted in two ways: by splitting it into sublists such that each one corresponds to a value of the base data element, or by splitting the list into sublists of length 1 each. The first is called partial inversion. The second approach produces a fully inverted list.
- In a partially inverted list each sublist has an index element that serves as the list head. In a fully inverted list each list element has an index element associating the base data element name to a data value that identifies a list element. Fully inverted lists and files are commonly used in file and data base management. They define highly efficient access techniques.
- Occasionally, it becomes necessary to build and maintain direct-access files that carry certain data structures based on data elements. These data structures (e.g., linked lists) are not directly supported by built-in file organization techniques. In such cases, the application programmer may have to develop software to build, maintain, and use such files.
- In creating and maintaining files, it is essential that the available storage be used optimally and without any waste. This requires certain file management techniques (called garbage collection techniques) and some useful data structures that can be employed in implementing them.

- Two list structures, called fixed-format lists, are especially useful in file management. They are stacks and queues. Elements in stacks and queues can be accessed only at one prescribed end.
- A stack is a list structure to which all additions and deletions are made at the open end, the top. A stack may be implemented as a simple list or a linked list.
- A queue is a list in which all additions are made at one end (tail) and all deletions are performed at the other end (head). Queues can also be implemented either as simple or linked lists.
- A technique that aims to recover memory locations that contain data that are no longer needed, or locations that have not been previously used, is called garbage collection. Stacks and queues may be used in garbage collection.
- A simple garbage collection technique is based on an available space list. An available space list can be a stack or a queue. Initially, it contains all memory locations that have not yet been used. Whenever a new element (or a record) is to be added to the file, the address of an available memory location is obtained from the space list. Whenever a record is deleted from the file, its address is pushed into the available space list. This provides a foundation for a controlled file management environment.

Test Your Comprehension

Multiple-Choice Questions

1. Which of the following statements concerning operations on linked lists is correct?
   a. In searching a linked list, we enter it using the list head pointer.
   b. The linked list delete algorithm modifies pointers such that the predecessor of the element to be deleted points to its successor.
   c. The linked list delete algorithm is a logical delete operation.
   d. All of the above are correct.
2. In the linked-list insertion algorithm, the pointers to be updated are
   a. The ones associated with the new element's predecessor and with the new element
   b. The ones associated with the new element's successor and with the new element
   c. The ones associated with the new element's predecessor and successor
   d. None of the above
3. For which of the following queries is a partially inverted list based on AGE most efficient?
   a. A listing of list elements in increasing order by AGE
   b. A listing of list elements in decreasing order by AGE
   c. A listing of list elements with respect to an arbitrary data field
   d. A query such as AGE = 25
4. In a fully inverted linked list,
   a. The length of each linked list is equal to 1.
   b. The number of index entries in the index area is the same as the number of elements in the list.
   c. The list elements in the data area are not linked by pointers.
   d. All of the above are correct.
5. Which of the following is a property of a stack or a queue?
   a. Accessing an element results in deleting it from a stack or a queue.
   b. Only elements at one specific end of a stack or a queue can be accessed.
   c. Elements can be inserted only at a specific end of a stack or a queue.
   d. All of the above are correct.

Answers: 1. d; 2. a; 3. d; 4. d; 5. d.

Short Essay Questions

1. Distinguish between logical and built-in file organization techniques.
2. What is the difference between linear and nonlinear data structures?
3. What is a linked list? What components should be included in a complete specification of a linked list?
4. What are the three basic operations on linked lists?
5. Describe the record deletion algorithm for linked lists.
6. Describe the record insertion algorithm for linked lists.
7. What is the difference between a forward linked list and a backward linked list?
8. Explain why the linked list construction algorithm is equivalent to a sort algorithm.
9. What is the difference between a linked list and a circularly linked list?
10. Define a doubly linked list.
11. What are the differences between a doubly linked list and a multiple list?
12. Describe the structure of the CORAL ring, and explain why it is a flexible data structure.
13. What is meant by list inversion? Why is it desirable to construct inverted lists?
14. Explain the differences between a partially inverted linked list and a fully inverted list.
15. Describe your understanding of the term file management.
16. What is a stack? What are its properties?
17. How do we distinguish a queue from a stack?
18. What is meant by garbage collection?
19. Describe how we can use an available space list as the basis for a garbage collection technique.

Improve Your Problem-Solving Ability

Exercises

Given is an instance of the STUDENT-ENROLLMENT file, as shown in Figure 31. Ten records are stored in buckets 1 through 10 in the file. The file is assumed to be a relative file. Exercises 1 through 8 are based on this file instance. For each, draw a complete figure, with the necessary cell structures, to show the implementation of the following linear data structures:

1. A forward linked list based on STUDENT-IDNO
2. A backward linked list based on COURSE-CODE
3. A forward ring based on the combined field SEMESTER/YEAR
4. A doubly linked list based on GRADE
5. A CORAL ring with respect to the combined field STUDENT-IDNO/ COURSE-CODE
6. A partially inverted set of lists based on GRADE
7. A fully inverted file based on STUDENT-IDNO
8. For the STUDENT-ENROLLMENT file, draw a figure depicting a forward linked list based on GRADE. Then show what happens to the pointers
   a. After the record stored in bucket 4 has been deleted
   b. After a new record (1000, CS255, 2, 88, A) has been inserted into the file at bucket 11
9. Suppose a stack has been defined as a linked list to store character strings in its nodes. Initially the stack is empty. Draw digraphs to show the content of this stack after each of the following operations.
   a. Add COMPUTER.
   b. Add AND.

REL-ADDRESS	STUDENT-IDNO	COURSE-CODE	SEMESTER	YEAR	GRADE
1	1000	ENG101	1	87	A
2	1000	MTH102	1	87	A
3	1000	CS101	1	87	B
4	1000	ENG102	2	87	A
5	1000	MTH151	2	87	C
6	1200	ENG101	1	88	A
7	1200	CS101	1	88	A
8	1400	ENG101	1	87	C
9	1400	MTH102	2	87	B
10	1400	CS101	1	88	B

Figure 31 An Instance of STUDENT-ENROLLMENT File

    c. Add INFORMATION.

    d. Add SCIENCE.

    e. Delete an element.

    f. Delete another element.

10. Solve exercise 9 assuming we have a queue instead of a stack.

Programming Problems

1. The linked list maintenance program of Program 3-Source is capable of deleting records in the relative student file. Modify and enhance it such that it can also be used to update any field of student records. Test the final program thoroughly.

2. Expand the maintenance program of Program 3-Source such that interactive record insertion can be handled. Test your program thoroughly.

```
                                             COLUMN
          5    10    15    20    25    30    35    40
       ----|----|----|----|----|----|----|----|----

       WILLIAM BLACK            MTH22
       JOHN HANSEN              CS 21
       JANE GRAY                CS 23
       MARY CHEN                MTH21
       RUSSELL THOMPSON         BUS20
       ANNE NEAL                BUS19
       ALICE KROGER             BUS21
       DAVID HILLMAN            CS 26
       KELLY TOWERS             MTH22
       LAUREN THOMAS            BUS19
```

Program 1-Input Instance of Sequential Student File for Program 1

```
00001      *.................................................................
00002      IDENTIFICATION DIVISION.
00003      PROGRAM-ID.   LINKED-LIST-FILE-CONSTRUCTION.
00004      ********************************************************************
00005      ***   THIS PROGRAM CREATES A VARIETY OF LINKED LISTS BASED ON       *
00006      ***   DIFFERENT DATA FIELDS IN A RELATIVE STUDENT FILE.             *
00007      ***                                                                 *
00008      ***   THE STUDENT FILE HAS A RECORD STRUCTURE THAT CONSISTS OF      *
00009      ***   THE FOLLOWING BASE FIELDS:                                    *
00010      ***       1. A 25-BYTE STUDENT-NAME,                                *
00011      ***       2. A THREE-BYTE STUDENT-MAJOR, AND                        *
00012      ***       3. A TWO-BYTE STUDENT-AGE.                                *
00013      ***                                                                 *
00014      ***   THE SUPERIMPOSED LINEAR STRUCTURES ARE:                       *
00015      ***       1. A FORWARD LINKED LIST BASED ON STUDENT-NAME,           *
00016      ***       2. A PARTIALLY INVERTED LIST BASED ON STUDENT-MAJOR, AND  *
00017      ***       3. A FULLY INVERTED LIST BASED ON STUDENT-AGE.            *
00018      ***                                                                 *
00019      ***   THE STUDENT FILE IS A RELATIVE FILE OF 233 BUCKETS.  BUCKETS*
00020      ***   1 THROUGH 100 ARE USED FOR DATA RECORDS, AND BUCKETS 101      *
00021      ***   THROUGH 233 ARE RESERVED FOR INDEX RECORDS.                   *
00022      ***                                                                 *
00023      ***   THE STUDENT FILE IS A MULTIPLE-RECORD FILE, WITH TWO RECORD *
00024      ***   TYPES:                                                        *
00025      ***       1. DATA RECORD, AND                                       *
00026      ***       2. INDEX RECORD.                                          *
00027      ***                                                                 *
00028      ***   ACCORDINGLY, THE MODIFIED DATA RECORD STRUCTURE FOR THE       *
00029      ***   RELATIVE STUDENT FILE INCLUDES THE FOLLOWING FIELDS:          *
00030      ***       1. A ONE-BYTE RECORD-TYPE ("D" FOR DATA RECORDS.)         *
00031      ***       2. A ONE-BYTE RECORD-STATUS ("E" FOR EMPTY, "D" FOR       *
00032      ***                                 DELETED, "F" FOR FULL.)         *
00033      ***       3. A 25-BYTE STUDENT-NAME,                                *
00034      ***       4. A THREE-BYTE STUDENT-MAJOR,                            *
00035      ***       5. A TWO-BYTE STUDENT-AGE,                                *
00036      ***       6. A THREE-BYTE NAME-LINK FIELD, AND                      *
00037      ***       7. A THREE-BYTE MAJOR-LINK FIELD.                         *
00038      ***                                                                 *
00039      ***   THE INDEX RECORD STRUCTURE IS:                                *
00040      ***       1. A ONE-BYTE RECORD-TYPE ("I" FOR INDEX RECORDS.)        *
00041      ***       2. A ONE-BYTE RECORD-STATUS ("E" FOR EMPTY, "D" FOR       *
00042      ***                                 DELETED, "F" FOR FULL.)         *
00043      ***       3. A 20-BYTE LIST-NAME FIELD, AND                         *
00044      ***       4. A THREE-BYTE START-ADDRESS FIELD.                      *
00045      ***                                                                 *
00046      ***   THE PROGRAM DOES THE FOLLOWING TASKS:                         *
00047      ***       1. READ A SEQUENTIAL STUDENT FILE, AND CREATE A RAW       *
00048      ***          RELATIVE STUDENT FILE.                                 *
00049      ***       2. BUILD A FORWARD LINKED LIST BASED ON STUDENT-NAME,     *
00050      ***       3. BUILD A PARTIALLY INVERTED LIST BASED ON MAJOR,        *
00051      ***       4. BUILD A FULLY INVERTED LIST BASED ON AGE,              *
```

Program 1-Source Program to Build Linked Lists in a Relative File

```
00052   ***                                                              *
00053   ***  A GARBAGE COLLECTION LOGIC IS INCORPORATED INTO THIS PRO-   *
00054   ***  RAM.  IT IS BASED ON A DATA AREA SPACE STACK, AND AN INDEX  *
00055   ***  AREA SPACE STACK.  FIRST THESE SPACE STACKS ARE CREATED.    *
00056   ***  DATA STACK POP AND INDEX STACK POP PROCEDURES ARE CALLED    *
00057   ***  UPON WHENEVER DATA OR INDEX RECORD OCCURRENCES ARE          *
00058   ***  CREATED.                                                    *
00059   *****************************************************************
00060
00061    AUTHOR.      UCKAN.
00062    DATE-WRITTEN.  AUGUST 5, 1991.
00063    DATE-COMPILED. AUG 16,1991.
00065   *...........................................................
00066    ENVIRONMENT DIVISION.
00067    CONFIGURATION SECTION.
00068    SOURCE-COMPUTER. UNIVERSITY-MAINFRAME.
00069    OBJECT-COMPUTER. UNIVERSITY-MAINFRAME.
00070    INPUT-OUTPUT SECTION.
00071
00072    FILE-CONTROL.
00073
00074        SELECT SEQ-STUDENT-FILE ASSIGN TO SEQDATA.
00075        SELECT REL-STUDENT-FILE ASSIGN TO MASTER
00076                ORGANIZATION IS RELATIVE
00077                ACCESS MODE IS DYNAMIC
00078                RELATIVE KEY IS BUCKET-NUMBER.
00079
00080   *...........................................................
00081    DATA DIVISION.
00082    FILE SECTION.
00083    FD  SEQ-STUDENT-FILE
00084        LABEL RECORDS ARE OMITTED
00085        DATA RECORD IS SEQ-STUDENT-RECORD
00086        RECORD CONTAINS 30 CHARACTERS.
00087
00088    01  SEQ-STUDENT-RECORD.
00089        05   SEQ-STUDENT-NAME      PIC X(25).
00090        05   SEQ-STUDENT-MAJOR     PIC X(3).
00091        05   SEQ-STUDENT-AGE       PIC X(2).
00092
00093    FD  REL-STUDENT-FILE
00094        LABEL RECORDS ARE STANDARD
00095        DATA RECORDS ARE PRIME-RECORD INDEX-RECORD
00096        RECORD CONTAINS 38 CHARACTERS.
00097
00098    01  PRIME-RECORD.
00099        05   DATA-RECORD-TYPE      PIC X.
00100        05   DATA-RECORD-STATUS    PIC X.
00101        05   STUDENT-NAME          PIC X(25).
00102        05   STUDENT-MAJOR         PIC X(3).
00103        05   STUDENT-AGE           PIC XX.
00104        05   NAME-LINK             PIC X(3).
00105        05   MAJOR-LINK            PIC X(3).
00106
```

Program 1-Source (Continued)

```
00107    01   INDEX-RECORD.
00108         05   INDEX-RECORD-TYPE        PIC X.
00109         05   INDEX-RECORD-STATUS      PIC X.
00110         05   LIST-NAME                PIC X(20).
00111         05   START-ADDRESS            PIC X(3).
00112         05   FILLER                   PIC X(13).
00113
00114    WORKING-STORAGE SECTION.
00115
00116    **********> VARIABLES:
00117
00118    01   END-OF-INPUT          PIC 9.
00119    01   BUCKET-NUMBER         PIC 999.
00120    01   PASS-NUMBER           PIC 999.
00121    01   FIRST-ELEMENT         PIC 999.
00122    01   SECOND-ELEMENT        PIC 999.
00123    01   NUMBER-OF-PASSES      PIC 999.
00124    01   TEMP-VALUE            PIC X(25).
00125    01   TEMP-ADDRESS          PIC 999.
00126    01   ARRAY-SIZE            PIC 999.
00127    01   ARRAY-LIMIT           PIC 999.
00128    01   MAJOR-VALUE           PIC X(25).
00129    01   NEW-LIST              PIC XXX.
00130    01   LINK-VALUE            PIC 999.
00131    01   SAVE-BUCKET-NUMBER    PIC 999.
00132    01   STACK-HEAD-POINTER    PIC 999.
00133
00134    **********> ARRAYS:
00135
00136    01   ATTRIBUTE-ORDER-ARRAY.
00137         05   ATTRIBUTE-VALUE     PIC X(25)  OCCURS 100 TIMES.
00138         05   REL-ADDRESS         PIC 999    OCCURS 100 TIMES.
00139         05   SUCCESSOR-ADDRESS   PIC 999    OCCURS 100 TIMES.
00140
00141    **********> STRUCTURES:
00142
00143    01   WS-PRIME-RECORD.
00144         05   WS-DATA-RECORD-TYPE      PIC X.
00145         05   WS-DATA-RECORD-STATUS    PIC X.
00146         05   WS-STUDENT-NAME          PIC X(25).
00147         05   WS-STUDENT-MAJOR         PIC X(3).
00148         05   WS-STUDENT-AGE           PIC XX.
00149         05   WS-NAME-LINK             PIC 9(3).
00150         05   WS-MAJOR-LINK            PIC 9(3).
00151
00152    01   WS-INDEX-RECORD.
00153         05   WS-INDEX-RECORD-TYPE     PIC X.
00154         05   WS-INDEX-RECORD-STATUS   PIC X.
00155         05   WS-LIST-NAME             PIC X(20).
00156         05   WS-START-ADDRESS         PIC 9(3).
00157         05   FILLER                   PIC X(13).
00158
00159    *.................................................................
00160    PROCEDURE DIVISION.
```

Program 1-Source (Continued)

```
00161
00162     A-MONITOR-PROCEDURE.
00163
00164         DISPLAY "BUILDING EMPTY SPACE STACKS... ".
00165
00166         PERFORM B1-BUILD-SPACE-STACKS.
00167
00168         DISPLAY "BUILDING RAW STUDENT FILE...".
00169
00170         PERFORM B2-BUILD-RAW-FILE.
00171
00172         DISPLAY "BUILDING LINKED LISTS...".
00173
00174         PERFORM B3-BUILD-NAME-LIST.
00175
00176         PERFORM B4-BUILD-MAJOR-LIST.
00177
00178         PERFORM B5-BUILD-AGE-LIST.
00179
00180         DISPLAY "ALL LINKED LISTS SUCCESSFULLY BUILT...".
00181
00182         DISPLAY "PROGRAM TERMINATING...".
00183
00184         STOP RUN.
00185
00186     B1-BUILD-SPACE-STACKS.
00187         OPEN OUTPUT REL-STUDENT-FILE.
00188
00189         MOVE 101       TO BUCKET-NUMBER.
00190         MOVE "I"        TO WS-INDEX-RECORD-TYPE.
00191         MOVE "F"        TO WS-INDEX-RECORD-STATUS.
00192         MOVE "DATASTACK" TO WS-LIST-NAME.
00193         MOVE 1         TO WS-START-ADDRESS.
00194
00195         WRITE INDEX-RECORD FROM WS-INDEX-RECORD
00196             INVALID KEY DISPLAY "ERROR IN WRITING.".
00197
00198         MOVE 102        TO BUCKET-NUMBER.
00199         MOVE "INDEXSTACK" TO WS-LIST-NAME.
00200         MOVE 103        TO WS-START-ADDRESS.
00201
00202         WRITE INDEX-RECORD FROM WS-INDEX-RECORD
00203             INVALID KEY DISPLAY "ERROR IN WRITING.".
00204
00205         PERFORM C1-BUILD-EMPTY-DATA-STACK
00206             VARYING BUCKET-NUMBER FROM 1 BY 1
00207                 UNTIL BUCKET-NUMBER > 99.
00208
00209         MOVE 100    TO BUCKET-NUMBER.
00210
00211         MOVE "D"    TO WS-DATA-RECORD-TYPE.
00212         MOVE "E"    TO WS-DATA-RECORD-STATUS.
00213         MOVE SPACES TO WS-STUDENT-NAME WS-STUDENT-MAJOR
00214                 WS-STUDENT-AGE.
```

Program 1-Source (Continued)

```
00215            MOVE ZERO    TO WS-MAJOR-LINK.
00216            MOVE 999     TO WS-NAME-LINK.
00217
00218            WRITE PRIME-RECORD FROM WS-PRIME-RECORD
00219                    INVALID KEY DISPLAY "ERROR IN WRITING.".
00220
00221            MOVE ZERO TO WS-NAME-LINK.
00222
00223            PERFORM C2-BUILD-EMPTY-INDEX-STACK
00224                    VARYING BUCKET-NUMBER FROM 103 BY 1
00225                            UNTIL BUCKET-NUMBER > 232.
00226
00227            MOVE 233     TO BUCKET-NUMBER.
00228
00229            MOVE "I"     TO WS-INDEX-RECORD-TYPE.
00230            MOVE "E"     TO WS-INDEX-RECORD-STATUS.
00231            MOVE SPACES TO WS-LIST-NAME.
00232            MOVE 999     TO WS-START-ADDRESS.
00233
00234            WRITE INDEX-RECORD FROM WS-INDEX-RECORD
00235                    INVALID KEY DISPLAY "ERROR IN WRITING.".
00236
00237            CLOSE REL-STUDENT-FILE.
00238
00239        B2-BUILD-RAW-FILE.
00240            OPEN INPUT SEQ-STUDENT-FILE.
00241            OPEN I-O   REL-STUDENT-FILE.
00242
00243            MOVE ZERO TO END-OF-INPUT.
00244
00245            READ SEQ-STUDENT-FILE
00246                    AT END MOVE 1 TO END-OF-INPUT.
00247
00248            PERFORM C3-LOAD-RELATIVE-FILE
00249                    UNTIL END-OF-INPUT = 1.
00250
00251            CLOSE SEQ-STUDENT-FILE  REL-STUDENT-FILE.
00252
00253        B3-BUILD-NAME-LIST.
00254            OPEN INPUT REL-STUDENT-FILE.
00255            MOVE 1 TO BUCKET-NUMBER.
00256
00257            PERFORM D2-READ-REL-FILE-DIRECTLY.
00258
00259            PERFORM C4-LOAD-NAME-ARRAY
00260                    UNTIL DATA-RECORD-STATUS = "E"
00261                                OR
00262                        BUCKET-NUMBER > 100.
00263
00264            CLOSE REL-STUDENT-FILE.
00265
00266            OPEN I-O REL-STUDENT-FILE.
00267
00268            COMPUTE ARRAY-SIZE       = BUCKET-NUMBER - 1.
00269            COMPUTE NUMBER-OF-PASSES = BUCKET-NUMBER - 2.
```

Program 1-Source (Continued)

```
00270
00271          MOVE 1 TO PASS-NUMBER.
00272
00273          PERFORM C5-SORT-ARRAY
00274                  UNTIL PASS-NUMBER > NUMBER-OF-PASSES.
00275
00276          COMPUTE ARRAY-LIMIT = ARRAY-SIZE - 1.
00277
00278          PERFORM C6-LINK-NAME-ARRAY-ELEMENTS
00279                  VARYING FIRST-ELEMENT FROM 1 BY 1
00280                          UNTIL FIRST-ELEMENT > ARRAY-LIMIT.
00281
00282          MOVE 999 TO SUCCESSOR-ADDRESS (ARRAY-SIZE)
00283
00284          PERFORM C7-FORM-NAME-INDEX.
00285
00286          PERFORM C8-BUILD-NAME-LINKS
00287                  VARYING FIRST-ELEMENT FROM 1 BY 1
00288                          UNTIL FIRST-ELEMENT > ARRAY-SIZE.
00289
00290          CLOSE REL-STUDENT-FILE.
00291
00292      B4-BUILD-MAJOR-LIST.
00293          OPEN INPUT REL-STUDENT-FILE.
00294          MOVE 1 TO BUCKET-NUMBER.
00295
00296          PERFORM D2-READ-REL-FILE-DIRECTLY.
00297
00298          PERFORM C9-LOAD-MAJOR-ARRAY
00299                  UNTIL DATA-RECORD-STATUS = "E"
00300                              OR
00301                     BUCKET-NUMBER > 100.
00302
00303          CLOSE REL-STUDENT-FILE.
00304
00305          OPEN I-O REL-STUDENT-FILE.
00306
00307          COMPUTE ARRAY-SIZE      = BUCKET-NUMBER - 1.
00308          COMPUTE NUMBER-OF-PASSES = BUCKET-NUMBER - 2.
00309
00310          MOVE 1 TO PASS-NUMBER.
00311
00312          PERFORM C5-SORT-ARRAY
00313                  UNTIL PASS-NUMBER > NUMBER-OF-PASSES.
00314
00315          COMPUTE ARRAY-LIMIT = ARRAY-SIZE - 1.
00316
00317          MOVE ATTRIBUTE-VALUE (1) TO MAJOR-VALUE.
00318
00319          PERFORM C10-LINK-MAJOR-ARRAY-ELEMENTS
00320                  VARYING FIRST-ELEMENT FROM 1 BY 1
00321                          UNTIL FIRST-ELEMENT > ARRAY-LIMIT.
00322
00323          MOVE 999                   TO SUCCESSOR-ADDRESS (ARRAY-SIZE).
00324
```

Program 1-Source (Continued)

```
00325              MOVE ATTRIBUTE-VALUE (1) TO MAJOR-VALUE.
00326              MOVE "YES"              TO NEW-LIST.
00327              MOVE 1                  TO FIRST-ELEMENT.
00328
00329              PERFORM C11-FORM-MAJOR-INDEX
00330                  UNTIL FIRST-ELEMENT > ARRAY-LIMIT.
00331
00332              PERFORM C12-BUILD-MAJOR-LINKS
00333                  VARYING FIRST-ELEMENT FROM 1 BY 1
00334                       UNTIL FIRST-ELEMENT > ARRAY-SIZE.
00335
00336              CLOSE REL-STUDENT-FILE.
00337
00338          B5-BUILD-AGE-LIST.
00339              OPEN INPUT REL-STUDENT-FILE.
00340              MOVE 1 TO BUCKET-NUMBER.
00341
00342              PERFORM D2-READ-REL-FILE-DIRECTLY.
00343
00344              PERFORM C13-LOAD-AGE-ARRAY
00345                  UNTIL DATA-RECORD-STATUS = "E"
00346                                 OR
00347                       BUCKET-NUMBER > 100.
00348
00349              CLOSE REL-STUDENT-FILE.
00350
00351              OPEN I-O REL-STUDENT-FILE.
00352              COMPUTE ARRAY-SIZE = BUCKET-NUMBER - 1.
00353              MOVE 1                  TO FIRST-ELEMENT.
00354
00355              PERFORM C14-FORM-AGE-INDEX
00356                  UNTIL FIRST-ELEMENT > ARRAY-SIZE.
00357
00358              CLOSE REL-STUDENT-FILE.
00359
00360          C1-BUILD-EMPTY-DATA-STACK.
00361              COMPUTE LINK-VALUE = BUCKET-NUMBER + 1.
00362
00363              MOVE "D"       TO WS-DATA-RECORD-TYPE.
00364              MOVE "E"       TO WS-DATA-RECORD-STATUS.
00365              MOVE SPACES    TO WS-STUDENT-NAME WS-STUDENT-MAJOR
00366                                WS-STUDENT-AGE.
00367              MOVE ZERO      TO WS-MAJOR-LINK.
00368              MOVE LINK-VALUE TO WS-NAME-LINK.
00369
00370              WRITE PRIME-RECORD FROM WS-PRIME-RECORD
00371                  INVALID KEY DISPLAY "ERROR IN WRITING.".
00372
00373          C2-BUILD-EMPTY-INDEX-STACK.
00374              COMPUTE LINK-VALUE = BUCKET-NUMBER + 1.
00375
00376              MOVE "I"       TO WS-INDEX-RECORD-TYPE.
00377              MOVE "E"       TO WS-INDEX-RECORD-STATUS.
00378              MOVE SPACES    TO WS-LIST-NAME.
00379              MOVE LINK-VALUE TO WS-START-ADDRESS.
```

Program 1-Source (Continued)

```
00380
00381          WRITE INDEX-RECORD FROM WS-INDEX-RECORD
00382                INVALID KEY DISPLAY "ERROR IN WRITING.".
00383
00384     C3-LOAD-RELATIVE-FILE.
00385          PERFORM D1-POP-DATA-STACK.
00386
00387          MOVE SAVE-BUCKET-NUMBER TO BUCKET-NUMBER.
00388
00389          PERFORM D2-READ-REL-FILE-DIRECTLY.
00390
00391          MOVE SEQ-STUDENT-NAME  TO WS-STUDENT-NAME.
00392          MOVE SEQ-STUDENT-MAJOR TO WS-STUDENT-MAJOR.
00393          MOVE SEQ-STUDENT-AGE   TO WS-STUDENT-AGE.
00394          MOVE "F"               TO WS-DATA-RECORD-STATUS.
00395          MOVE ZERO              TO WS-NAME-LINK.
00396
00397          PERFORM D3-REWRITE-PRIME-RECORD.
00398
00399          READ SEQ-STUDENT-FILE
00400                AT END MOVE 1 TO END-OF-INPUT.
00401
00402     C4-LOAD-NAME-ARRAY.
00403          MOVE BUCKET-NUMBER TO REL-ADDRESS (BUCKET-NUMBER).
00404          MOVE STUDENT-NAME  TO ATTRIBUTE-VALUE (BUCKET-NUMBER).
00405          ADD 1 TO BUCKET-NUMBER.
00406
00407          PERFORM D2-READ-REL-FILE-DIRECTLY.
00408
00409     C5-SORT-ARRAY.
00410          MOVE 1 TO FIRST-ELEMENT.
00411          COMPUTE SECOND-ELEMENT = FIRST-ELEMENT + 1.
00412
00413          PERFORM D5-COMPARE-AND-EXCHANGE
00414                UNTIL SECOND-ELEMENT > ARRAY-SIZE.
00415
00416          ADD 1 TO PASS-NUMBER.
00417
00418     C6-LINK-NAME-ARRAY-ELEMENTS.
00419          COMPUTE SECOND-ELEMENT = FIRST-ELEMENT + 1.
00420          MOVE REL-ADDRESS (SECOND-ELEMENT) TO
00421                SUCCESSOR-ADDRESS (FIRST-ELEMENT).
00422
00423     C7-FORM-NAME-INDEX.
00424          PERFORM D6-POP-INDEX-STACK.
00425
00426          MOVE SAVE-BUCKET-NUMBER TO BUCKET-NUMBER.
00427          PERFORM D2-READ-REL-FILE-DIRECTLY.
00428
00429          MOVE INDEX-RECORD TO WS-INDEX-RECORD.
00430          MOVE "I"                TO WS-INDEX-RECORD-TYPE.
00431          MOVE "F"                TO WS-INDEX-RECORD-STATUS.
00432          MOVE "NAME"             TO WS-LIST-NAME.
00433          MOVE REL-ADDRESS (1) TO WS-START-ADDRESS.
```

Program 1-Source (Continued)

```
00434
00435              PERFORM D4-REWRITE-INDEX-RECORD.
00436
00437     C8-BUILD-NAME-LINKS.
00438         MOVE REL-ADDRESS (FIRST-ELEMENT) TO BUCKET-NUMBER.
00439
00440         PERFORM D2-READ-REL-FILE-DIRECTLY.
00441         MOVE PRIME-RECORD                        TO WS-PRIME-RECORD.
00442         MOVE SUCCESSOR-ADDRESS (FIRST-ELEMENT) TO WS-NAME-LINK.
00443
00444         PERFORM D3-REWRITE-PRIME-RECORD.
00445
00446     C9-LOAD-MAJOR-ARRAY.
00447         MOVE BUCKET-NUMBER TO REL-ADDRESS (BUCKET-NUMBER).
00448         MOVE STUDENT-MAJOR TO ATTRIBUTE-VALUE (BUCKET-NUMBER).
00449         ADD 1 TO BUCKET-NUMBER.
00450
00451         PERFORM D2-READ-REL-FILE-DIRECTLY.
00452
00453     C10-LINK-MAJOR-ARRAY-ELEMENTS.
00454         COMPUTE SECOND-ELEMENT = FIRST-ELEMENT + 1.
00455
00456         IF ATTRIBUTE-VALUE (SECOND-ELEMENT) = MAJOR-VALUE
00457                 MOVE REL-ADDRESS (SECOND-ELEMENT) TO
00458                      SUCCESSOR-ADDRESS (FIRST-ELEMENT)
00459         ELSE
00460                 MOVE 999 TO SUCCESSOR-ADDRESS (FIRST-ELEMENT)
00461                 MOVE ATTRIBUTE-VALUE (SECOND-ELEMENT) TO MAJOR-VALUE.
00462
00463     C11-FORM-MAJOR-INDEX.
00464
00465         IF NEW-LIST = "YES"
00466
00467                 PERFORM D6-POP-INDEX-STACK
00468
00469                 MOVE SAVE-BUCKET-NUMBER TO BUCKET-NUMBER
00470
00471                 PERFORM D2-READ-REL-FILE-DIRECTLY
00472
00473                 MOVE INDEX-RECORD TO WS-INDEX-RECORD
00474                 MOVE "I"          TO WS-INDEX-RECORD-TYPE
00475                 MOVE "F"          TO WS-INDEX-RECORD-STATUS
00476
00477                 STRING "MAJOR" DELIMITED BY SIZE
00478                        MAJOR-VALUE DELIMITED BY SIZE
00479                    INTO WS-LIST-NAME
00480
00481                 MOVE REL-ADDRESS (FIRST-ELEMENT) TO WS-START-ADDRESS
00482
00483                 PERFORM D4-REWRITE-INDEX-RECORD.
00484
00485         COMPUTE SECOND-ELEMENT = FIRST-ELEMENT + 1.
00486
```

Program 1-Source (Continued)

```
00487          IF ATTRIBUTE-VALUE (FIRST-ELEMENT) =
00488             ATTRIBUTE-VALUE (SECOND-ELEMENT)
00489                MOVE "NO" TO NEW-LIST
00490          ELSE
00491                MOVE "YES" TO NEW-LIST
00492                MOVE ATTRIBUTE-VALUE (SECOND-ELEMENT) TO MAJOR-VALUE.
00493
00494          ADD 1 TO FIRST-ELEMENT.
00495
00496     C12-BUILD-MAJOR-LINKS.
00497          MOVE REL-ADDRESS (FIRST-ELEMENT) TO BUCKET-NUMBER.
00498
00499          PERFORM D2-READ-REL-FILE-DIRECTLY.
00500
00501          MOVE PRIME-RECORD                        TO WS-PRIME-RECORD.
00502          MOVE SUCCESSOR-ADDRESS (FIRST-ELEMENT) TO WS-MAJOR-LINK.
00503
00504          PERFORM D3-REWRITE-PRIME-RECORD.
00505
00506     C13-LOAD-AGE-ARRAY.
00507          MOVE BUCKET-NUMBER TO REL-ADDRESS (BUCKET-NUMBER).
00508          MOVE STUDENT-AGE   TO ATTRIBUTE-VALUE (BUCKET-NUMBER).
00509          ADD 1 TO BUCKET-NUMBER.
00510
00511          PERFORM D2-READ-REL-FILE-DIRECTLY.
00512
00513     C14-FORM-AGE-INDEX.
00514          PERFORM D6-POP-INDEX-STACK.
00515
00516          MOVE SAVE-BUCKET-NUMBER TO BUCKET-NUMBER.
00517
00518          PERFORM D2-READ-REL-FILE-DIRECTLY.
00519
00520          MOVE INDEX-RECORD TO WS-INDEX-RECORD.
00521
00522          STRING "AGE" DELIMITED BY SIZE
00523                 ATTRIBUTE-VALUE (FIRST-ELEMENT) DELIMITED BY SIZE
00524            INTO WS-LIST-NAME.
00525
00526          MOVE REL-ADDRESS (FIRST-ELEMENT) TO WS-START-ADDRESS.
00527          MOVE "F"                         TO WS-INDEX-RECORD-STATUS.
00528
00529          PERFORM D4-REWRITE-INDEX-RECORD.
00530
00531          ADD 1 TO FIRST-ELEMENT.
00532
00533      D1-POP-DATA-STACK.
00534          MOVE 101 TO BUCKET-NUMBER.
00535          PERFORM D2-READ-REL-FILE-DIRECTLY.
00536          MOVE INDEX-RECORD TO WS-INDEX-RECORD.
00537
00538          MOVE WS-START-ADDRESS TO BUCKET-NUMBER SAVE-BUCKET-NUMBER.
00539          PERFORM D2-READ-REL-FILE-DIRECTLY.
00540          MOVE PRIME-RECORD TO WS-PRIME-RECORD.
```

Program 1-Source (Continued)

```
00541
00542            MOVE WS-NAME-LINK TO STACK-HEAD-POINTER.
00543
00544            MOVE 101 TO BUCKET-NUMBER.
00545            PERFORM D2-READ-REL-FILE-DIRECTLY.
00546            MOVE INDEX-RECORD TO WS-INDEX-RECORD.
00547            MOVE STACK-HEAD-POINTER TO WS-START-ADDRESS.
00548            PERFORM D4-REWRITE-INDEX-RECORD.
00549
00550     D2-READ-REL-FILE-DIRECTLY.
00551         READ REL-STUDENT-FILE
00552            INVALID KEY DISPLAY "ERROR IN READING STUDENT FILE.".
00553
00554     D3-REWRITE-PRIME-RECORD.
00555         REWRITE PRIME-RECORD FROM WS-PRIME-RECORD
00556             INVALID KEY DISPLAY "ERROR IN UPDATING PRIME RECORD.".
00557
00558     D4-REWRITE-INDEX-RECORD.
00559         REWRITE INDEX-RECORD FROM WS-INDEX-RECORD
00560             INVALID KEY DISPLAY "ERROR IN UPDATING INDEX RECORD.".
00561
00562     D5-COMPARE-AND-EXCHANGE.
00563
00564         IF ATTRIBUTE-VALUE (FIRST-ELEMENT) >
00565             ATTRIBUTE-VALUE (SECOND-ELEMENT)
00566                 MOVE ATTRIBUTE-VALUE (FIRST-ELEMENT) TO TEMP-VALUE
00567                 MOVE REL-ADDRESS (FIRST-ELEMENT)     TO TEMP-ADDRESS
00568
00569                 MOVE ATTRIBUTE-VALUE (SECOND-ELEMENT) TO
00570                         ATTRIBUTE-VALUE (FIRST-ELEMENT)
00571                 MOVE REL-ADDRESS (SECOND-ELEMENT) TO
00572                         REL-ADDRESS (FIRST-ELEMENT)
00573
00574                 MOVE TEMP-VALUE   TO ATTRIBUTE-VALUE (SECOND-ELEMENT)
00575                 MOVE TEMP-ADDRESS TO REL-ADDRESS (SECOND-ELEMENT).
00576
00577         ADD 1 TO FIRST-ELEMENT SECOND-ELEMENT.
00578
00579     D6-POP-INDEX-STACK.
00580         MOVE 102 TO BUCKET-NUMBER.
00581         PERFORM D2-READ-REL-FILE-DIRECTLY.
00582         MOVE INDEX-RECORD TO WS-INDEX-RECORD.
00583
00584         MOVE WS-START-ADDRESS TO BUCKET-NUMBER SAVE-BUCKET-NUMBER.
00585         PERFORM D2-READ-REL-FILE-DIRECTLY.
00586         MOVE INDEX-RECORD TO WS-INDEX-RECORD.
00587
00588         MOVE WS-START-ADDRESS TO STACK-HEAD-POINTER.
00589
00590         MOVE 102 TO BUCKET-NUMBER.
00591         PERFORM D2-READ-REL-FILE-DIRECTLY.
00592         MOVE INDEX-RECORD         TO WS-INDEX-RECORD.
00593         MOVE STACK-HEAD-POINTER TO WS-START-ADDRESS.
00594         PERFORM D4-REWRITE-INDEX-RECORD.
```

Program 1-Source (Continued)

```
00001    *.............................................................
00002    IDENTIFICATION DIVISION.
00003    PROGRAM-ID.  ACCESSING-LINKED-LIST-FILES.
00004    *********************************************************************
00005    ***   THIS PROGRAM ACCESSES A RELATIVE ACCESS STUDENT FILE WITH    *
00006    ***   A VARIETY OF LINKED LIST STRUCTURES.                         *
00007    ***                                                                *
00008    ***   THE STUDENT FILE HAS A RECORD STRUCTURE THAT CONSISTS OF     *
00009    ***   THE FOLLOWING BASE FIELDS:                                   *
00010    ***       1. A 25-BYTE STUDENT-NAME,                               *
00011    ***       2. A THREE-BYTE STUDENT-MAJOR, AND                       *
00012    ***       3. A TWO-BYTE STUDENT-AGE.                               *
00013    ***                                                                *
00014    ***   THE SUPERIMPOSED LINEAR STRUCTURES ARE:                      *
00015    ***       1. A FORWARD LINKED LIST BASED ON STUDENT-NAME,          *
00016    ***       2. A PARTIALLY INVERTED LIST BASED ON STUDENT-MAJOR, AND *
00017    ***       3. A FULLY INVERTED LIST BASED ON STUDENT-AGE.           *
00018    ***                                                                *
00019    ***   THE STUDENT FILE IS A RELATIVE FILE OF 233 BUCKETS.  BUCKETS *
00020    ***   1 THROUGH 100 ARE USED FOR DATA RECORDS, AND BUCKETS 101     *
00021    ***   THROUGH 233 ARE RESERVED FOR INDEX RECORDS.                  *
00022    ***                                                                *
00023    ***   THE STUDENT FILE IS A MULTIPLE-RECORD FILE, WITH TWO RECORD  *
00024    ***   TYPES:                                                       *
00025    ***       1. DATA RECORD, AND                                      *
00026    ***       2. INDEX RECORD.                                         *
00027    ***                                                                *
00028    ***   ACCORDINGLY, THE MODIFIED DATA RECORD STRUCTURE FOR THE      *
00029    ***   RELATIVE STUDENT FILE INCLUDES THE FOLLOWING FIELDS:         *
00030    ***       1. A ONE-BYTE RECORD-TYPE ("D" FOR DATA RECORDS.)        *
00031    ***       2. A ONE-BYTE RECORD-STATUS ("E" FOR EMPTY, "D" FOR      *
00032    ***                                   DELETED, "F" FOR FULL.)      *
00033    ***       3. A 25-BYTE STUDENT-NAME,                               *
00034    ***       4. A THREE-BYTE STUDENT-MAJOR,                           *
00035    ***       5. A TWO-BYTE STUDENT-AGE,                               *
00036    ***       6. A THREE-BYTE NAME-LINK FIELD, AND                     *
00037    ***       7. A THREE-BYTE MAJOR-LINK FIELD.                        *
00038    ***                                                                *
00039    ***   THE INDEX RECORD STRUCTURE IS:                               *
00040    ***       1. A ONE-BYTE RECORD-TYPE ("I" FOR INDEX RECORDS.)       *
00041    ***       2. A ONE-BYTE RECORD-STATUS ("E" FOR EMPTY, "D" FOR      *
00042    ***                                   DELETED, "F" FOR FULL.)      *
00043    ***       3. A 20-BYTE LIST-NAME FIELD, AND                        *
00044    ***       4. A THREE-BYTE START-ADDRESS FIELD.                     *
00045    ***                                                                *
00046    ***   THE PROGRAM DOES THE FOLLOWING TASKS:                        *
00047    ***       1. PRINT A SEQUENTIAL LISTING OF THE RELATIVE FILE       *
00048    ***          (ONLY FULL BUCKETS ARE PRINTED,)                      *
00049    ***       2. PRINT A LISTING IN ASCENDING ORDER OF NAME,           *
00050    ***       3. PRINT A LISTING FOR THE QUERY "STUDENT-MAJOR = XXX",  *
00051    ***       4. PRINT A LISTING FOR THE QUERY "STUDENT-AGE = XX", AND *
00052    ***       5. TERMINATE PROGRAM EXECUTION.                          *
00053    ***                                                                *
00054    ***   THE PROGRAM IS DESIGNED AS AN INTERACTIVE PROGRAM.           *
00055    *********************************************************************
```

Program 2-Source Program to Access a Relative File Using Linked Lists

```
00056
00057      AUTHOR.        UCKAN.
00058     DATE-WRITTEN.   AUGUST 11,1991.
00059     DATE-COMPILED.  AUG 16,1991.
00061      *.......................................................
00062      ENVIRONMENT DIVISION.
00063      CONFIGURATION SECTION.
00064     SOURCE-COMPUTER.  UNIVERSITY-MAINFRAME.
00065     OBJECT-COMPUTER.  UNIVERSITY-MAINFRAME.
00066     INPUT-OUTPUT SECTION.
00067
00068     FILE-CONTROL.
00069
00070         SELECT REL-STUDENT-FILE ASSIGN TO MASTER
00071                 ORGANIZATION IS RELATIVE
00072                 ACCESS MODE IS DYNAMIC
00073                 RELATIVE KEY IS BUCKET-NUMBER.
00074
00075      *.......................................................
00076      DATA DIVISION.
00077      FILE SECTION.
00078     FD  REL-STUDENT-FILE
00079         LABEL RECORDS ARE STANDARD
00080         DATA RECORDS ARE PRIME-RECORD INDEX-RECORD
00081         RECORD CONTAINS 38 CHARACTERS.
00082
00083     01  PRIME-RECORD.
00084         05  DATA-RECORD-TYPE       PIC X.
00085         05  DATA-RECORD-STATUS     PIC X.
00086         05  STUDENT-NAME           PIC X(25).
00087         05  STUDENT-MAJOR          PIC X(3).
00088         05  STUDENT-AGE            PIC XX.
00089         05  NAME-LINK              PIC X(3).
00090         05  MAJOR-LINK             PIC X(3).
00091
00092     01  INDEX-RECORD.
00093         05  INDEX-RECORD-TYPE      PIC X.
00094         05  INDEX-RECORD-STATUS    PIC X.
00095         05  LIST-NAME              PIC X(20).
00096         05  START-ADDRESS          PIC X(3).
00097         05  FILLER                 PIC X(13).
00098
00099     WORKING-STORAGE SECTION.
00100
00101     *********> VARIABLES:
00102
00103     01  BUCKET-NUMBER         PIC 999.
00104     01  INDEX-BUCKET-NUMBER   PIC 999.
00105     01  NAME-LIST-HEAD-FOUND  PIC XXX.
00106     01  MAJOR-VALUE           PIC XXX.
00107     01  MAJOR-LIST-NAME       PIC X(20).
00108     01  MAJOR-LIST-HEAD-FOUND PIC XXX.
00109     01  AGE-VALUE             PIC 99.
00110     01  AGE-LIST-NAME         PIC X(20).
```

Program 2-Source (Continued)

```
00111     01  AGE-LIST-EMPTY        PIC XXX.
00112     01  AGE-INDEX-ENTRY-FOUND  PIC XXX.
00113
00114     01  FUNCTION-CODE         PIC X.
00115         88  SEQUENTIAL-LISTING    VALUE "S".
00116         88  NAME-LISTING          VALUE "N".
00117         88  MAJOR-LISTING         VALUE "M".
00118         88  AGE-LISTING           VALUE "A".
00119         88  MENU-DISPLAY          VALUE "X".
00120         88  PROCESS-TERMINATION   VALUE "T".
00121
00122  *..................................................................
00123    PROCEDURE DIVISION.
00124
00125    A-MONITOR-PROCEDURE.
00126         MOVE "#" TO FUNCTION-CODE.
00127
00128         PERFORM B1-PROMPT-FOR-FUNCTION-CODE
00129             UNTIL FUNCTION-CODE = "S" OR "N" OR "M" OR "A"
00130                                 OR "X" OR "T".
00131
00132         PERFORM B2-PROCESS-REQUEST
00133             UNTIL PROCESS-TERMINATION.
00134
00135         STOP RUN.
00136
00137    B1-PROMPT-FOR-FUNCTION-CODE.
00138
00139         IF FUNCTION-CODE = "#"
00140
00141             PERFORM C1-DISPLAY-MENU
00142
00143             DISPLAY "****> WHAT DO YOU WANT TO DO NEXT?"
00144             DISPLAY "****> PLEASE ENTER A FUNCTION CODE VALUE: "
00145         ELSE
00146             IF FUNCTION-CODE = "@"
00147                 DISPLAY "  "
00148                 DISPLAY "*****> PLEASE ENTER FUNCTION CODE:"
00149             ELSE
00150                 DISPLAY FUNCTION-CODE " IS AN ILLEGAL VALUE."
00151                 DISPLAY "LEGAL VALUES ARE SHOWN BELOW:"
00152
00153                 PERFORM C1-DISPLAY-MENU
00154
00155                 DISPLAY "****> PLEASE ENTER A CORRECT VALUE:".
00156
00157         ACCEPT FUNCTION-CODE FROM CONSOLE.
00158
00159    B2-PROCESS-REQUEST.
00160
00161         IF MENU-DISPLAY
00162             PERFORM C1-DISPLAY-MENU.
00163
00164         IF SEQUENTIAL-LISTING
00165             PERFORM C2-LIST-FILE-SEQUENTIALLY.
```

Program 2-Source (Continued)

```
00166
00167        IF NAME-LISTING
00168             PERFORM C3-LIST-BY-NAME.
00169
00170        IF MAJOR-LISTING
00171             PERFORM C4-LIST-BY-MAJOR.
00172
00173        IF AGE-LISTING
00174             PERFORM C5-LIST-BY-AGE.
00175
00176        IF NOT PROCESS-TERMINATION
00177             MOVE "@" TO FUNCTION-CODE
00178
00179             PERFORM B1-PROMPT-FOR-FUNCTION-CODE
00180                UNTIL FUNCTION-CODE = "S" OR "N" OR "M" OR "A"
00181                                          OR "X" OR "T".
00182
00183    C1-DISPLAY-MENU.
00184        DISPLAY " ".
00185        DISPLAY "*********************************************".
00186        DISPLAY "* FUNCTION                          CODE *".
00187        DISPLAY "* ------------------------------    ------ *".
00188        DISPLAY "* PRODUCE SEQUENTIAL FILE LISTING    S   *".
00189        DISPLAY "* PRODUCE ORDERED LISTING BY NAME    N   *".
00190        DISPLAY "* PRODUCE LISTING FOR A MAJOR VALUE  M   *".
00191        DISPLAY "* PRODUCE LISTING FOR AN AGE VALUE   A   *".
00192        DISPLAY "* DISPLAY THIS MENU AGAIN            X   *".
00193        DISPLAY "* TERMINATE PROCESSING              T   *".
00194        DISPLAY "*********************************************".
00195        DISPLAY " ".
00196
00197    C2-LIST-FILE-SEQUENTIALLY.
00198        OPEN INPUT REL-STUDENT-FILE.
00199        MOVE 1 TO BUCKET-NUMBER.
00200        DISPLAY "SEQUENTIAL LISTING OF DATA AREA:".
00201        DISPLAY " ".
00202
00203        PERFORM  D1-READ-AND-DISPLAY-FILE
00204             UNTIL BUCKET-NUMBER > 100.
00205
00206        MOVE 101 TO BUCKET-NUMBER.
00207        DISPLAY " ".
00208        DISPLAY "SEQUENTIAL LISTING OF INDEX AREA:".
00209        DISPLAY " ".
00210
00211        PERFORM  D1-READ-AND-DISPLAY-FILE
00212             UNTIL BUCKET-NUMBER > 233.
00213
00214        CLOSE REL-STUDENT-FILE.
00215
00216    C3-LIST-BY-NAME.
00217        OPEN INPUT REL-STUDENT-FILE.
00218
00219        MOVE 101  TO BUCKET-NUMBER.
00220        MOVE "NO" TO NAME-LIST-HEAD-FOUND.
```

Program 2-Source (Continued)

```
00221
00222          PERFORM E1-READ-RECORD-DIRECTLY.
00223
00224          PERFORM D2-FIND-NAME-LIST-HEAD
00225                  UNTIL BUCKET-NUMBER > 150
00226                              OR
00227                      NAME-LIST-HEAD-FOUND = "YES"
00228
00229          IF NAME-LIST-HEAD-FOUND = "YES"
00230                  MOVE START-ADDRESS TO BUCKET-NUMBER
00231
00232                  PERFORM E1-READ-RECORD-DIRECTLY
00233
00234                  PERFORM D3-DISPLAY-LIST-BY-NAME
00235                      UNTIL BUCKET-NUMBER = 999.
00236
00237          CLOSE REL-STUDENT-FILE.
00238
00239      C4-LIST-BY-MAJOR.
00240          OPEN INPUT REL-STUDENT-FILE.
00241
00242          DISPLAY "****> ENTER STUDENT MAJOR VALUE FOR WHICH LISTING IS
00243       -   " REQUESTED: ".
00244          ACCEPT MAJOR-VALUE FROM CONSOLE.
00245          MOVE SPACES TO MAJOR-LIST-NAME.
00246
00247          STRING "MAJOR" DELIMITED BY SIZE
00248                  MAJOR-VALUE DELIMITED BY SIZE
00249             INTO MAJOR-LIST-NAME.
00250
00251          MOVE 101  TO BUCKET-NUMBER.
00252          MOVE "NO" TO MAJOR-LIST-HEAD-FOUND.
00253
00254          PERFORM D4-FIND-MAJOR-LIST-HEAD
00255                  UNTIL BUCKET-NUMBER > 233
00256                              OR
00257                      MAJOR-LIST-HEAD-FOUND = "YES".
00258
00259          IF MAJOR-LIST-HEAD-FOUND = "YES"
00260                  MOVE START-ADDRESS TO BUCKET-NUMBER
00261
00262                  IF BUCKET-NUMBER = 999
00263                          DISPLAY "MAJOR LIST FOR MAJOR = "
00264                                  MAJOR-VALUE " IS EMPTY."
00265                  ELSE
00266
00267                          PERFORM D5-DISPLAY-LIST-BY-MAJOR
00268                                  UNTIL BUCKET-NUMBER = 999
00269
00270          ELSE
00271                  DISPLAY "NO RECORD OCCURRENCE WITH MAJOR = "
00272                          MAJOR-VALUE " EXISTS IN THE FILE.".
00273
00274          CLOSE REL-STUDENT-FILE.
```

Program 2-Source (Continued)

```
00275
00276     C5-LIST-BY-AGE.
00277         OPEN INPUT REL-STUDENT-FILE.
00278
00279         DISPLAY "****> ENTER STUDENT AGE VALUE FOR WHICH LISTING IS R
00280         "EQUESTED:".
00281         ACCEPT AGE-VALUE FROM CONSOLE.
00282         MOVE SPACES TO AGE-LIST-NAME.
00283
00284         STRING "AGE" DELIMITED BY SIZE
00285                 AGE-VALUE DELIMITED BY SIZE
00286           INTO AGE-LIST-NAME.
00287
00288         MOVE 101  TO INDEX-BUCKET-NUMBER.
00289         MOVE "YES" TO AGE-LIST-EMPTY.
00290         MOVE "NO"  TO AGE-INDEX-ENTRY-FOUND.
00291
00292         PERFORM D6-FIND-ALL-AGE-ENTRIES
00293                 UNTIL INDEX-BUCKET-NUMBER > 233.
00294
00295         IF AGE-LIST-EMPTY = "YES"
00296                 DISPLAY "NO RECORD OCCURRENCE WITH AGE = "
00297                         AGE-VALUE " EXISTS IN THE FILE.".
00298
00299         CLOSE REL-STUDENT-FILE.
00300
00301     D1-READ-AND-DISPLAY-FILE.
00302         PERFORM E1-READ-RECORD-DIRECTLY.
00303
00304         IF DATA-RECORD-STATUS = "F"
00305
00306                 IF DATA-RECORD-TYPE = "D"
00307                         DISPLAY BUCKET-NUMBER PRIME-RECORD
00308                 ELSE
00309                         DISPLAY BUCKET-NUMBER INDEX-RECORD.
00310
00311         ADD 1 TO BUCKET-NUMBER.
00312
00313     D2-FIND-NAME-LIST-HEAD.
00314
00315         IF LIST-NAME = "NAME"
00316                 MOVE "YES" TO NAME-LIST-HEAD-FOUND
00317         ELSE
00318                 PERFORM E1-READ-RECORD-DIRECTLY
00319                 ADD 1 TO BUCKET-NUMBER.
00320
00321     D3-DISPLAY-LIST-BY-NAME.
00322         DISPLAY STUDENT-NAME STUDENT-MAJOR STUDENT-AGE.
00323         MOVE NAME-LINK TO BUCKET-NUMBER.
00324         IF BUCKET-NUMBER NOT = 999
00325                 PERFORM E1-READ-RECORD-DIRECTLY.
00326
00327     D4-FIND-MAJOR-LIST-HEAD.
00328         PERFORM E1-READ-RECORD-DIRECTLY.
```

Program 2-Source (Continued)

```
00329
00330          IF LIST-NAME = MAJOR-LIST-NAME
00331                  MOVE "YES" TO MAJOR-LIST-HEAD-FOUND
00332          ELSE
00333                  ADD 1 TO BUCKET-NUMBER.
00334
00335      D5-DISPLAY-LIST-BY-MAJOR.
00336
00337          IF BUCKET-NUMBER NOT = 999
00338                  PERFORM E1-READ-RECORD-DIRECTLY
00339                  DISPLAY STUDENT-NAME STUDENT-MAJOR STUDENT-AGE
00340                  MOVE MAJOR-LINK TO BUCKET-NUMBER.
00341
00342      D6-FIND-ALL-AGE-ENTRIES.
00343          PERFORM E2-ACCESS-AGE-INDEX-ENTRY.
00344
00345          IF AGE-INDEX-ENTRY-FOUND = "YES"
00346                  MOVE START-ADDRESS TO BUCKET-NUMBER
00347
00348                  PERFORM E1-READ-RECORD-DIRECTLY
00349
00350                  DISPLAY STUDENT-NAME STUDENT-MAJOR STUDENT-AGE
00351                  ADD 1 TO INDEX-BUCKET-NUMBER
00352                  MOVE "NO" TO AGE-INDEX-ENTRY-FOUND.
00353
00354      E1-READ-RECORD-DIRECTLY.
00355          READ REL-STUDENT-FILE
00356                  INVALID KEY DISPLAY "READ ERROR.".
00357
00358      E2-ACCESS-AGE-INDEX-ENTRY.
00359          MOVE INDEX-BUCKET-NUMBER TO BUCKET-NUMBER.
00360
00361          IF BUCKET-NUMBER NOT > 233
00362                  PERFORM E1-READ-RECORD-DIRECTLY
00363
00364                  PERFORM F1-FIND-INDEX-RECORD
00365                      UNTIL AGE-INDEX-ENTRY-FOUND = "YES"
00366                                      OR
00367                          BUCKET-NUMBER > 233.
00368
00369      F1-FIND-INDEX-RECORD.
00370
00371          IF LIST-NAME = AGE-LIST-NAME
00372                      AND
00373            INDEX-RECORD-STATUS = "F"
00374                  MOVE "NO"  TO AGE-LIST-EMPTY
00375                  MOVE "YES" TO AGE-INDEX-ENTRY-FOUND
00376          ELSE
00377                  ADD 1 TO BUCKET-NUMBER INDEX-BUCKET-NUMBER
00378
00379                  IF BUCKET-NUMBER NOT > 233
00380                      PERFORM E1-READ-RECORD-DIRECTLY.
```

Program 2-Source (Continued)

```
*************************************************
* FUNCTION                          CODE  *
* _____   ____  *
* PRODUCE SEQUENTIAL FILE LISTING    S    *
* PRODUCE ORDERED LISTING BY NAME    N    *
* PRODUCE LISTING FOR A MAJOR VALUE  M    *
* PRODUCE LISTING FOR AN AGE VALUE   A    *
* DISPLAY THIS MENU AGAIN            X    *
* TERMINATE PROCESSING               T    *
*************************************************


****> WHAT DO YOU WANT TO DO NEXT?
****> PLEASE ENTER A FUNCTION CODE VALUE:
S
SEQUENTIAL LISTING OF DATA AREA:


001DFWILLIAM BLACK             MTH22999004
002DFJOHN HANSEN               CS 21009003
003DFJANE GRAY                 CS 23002008
004DFMARY CHEN                 MTH21005009
005DFRUSSELL THOMPSON          BUS20001006
006DFANNE NEAL                 BUS19008007
007DFALICE KROGER              BUS21006010
008DFDAVID HILLMAN             CS 26003999
009DFKELLY TOWERS              MTH22010999
010DFLAUREN THOMAS             BUS19004999


SEQUENTIAL LISTING OF INDEX AREA:


101IFDATASTACK          011
102IFINDEXSTACK         117
103IFNAME               007
104IFMAJORBUS           005
105IFMAJORCS            002
106IFMAJORMTH           001
107IFAGE22              001
108IFAGE21              002
109IFAGE23              003
110IFAGE21              004
111IFAGE20              005
112IFAGE19              006
113IFAGE21              007
114IFAGE26              008
115IFAGE22              009
116IFAGE19              010


****> PLEASE ENTER FUNCTION CODE:
N
ALICE KROGER            BUS21
ANNE NEAL               BUS19
DAVID HILLMAN           CS 26
JANE GRAY               CS 23
JOHN HANSEN             CS 21
KELLY TOWERS            MTH22
```

Program 2-Output An Interactive Terminal Session for Program 2

```
LAUREN THOMAS               BUS19
MARY CHEN                   MTH21
RUSSELL THOMPSON            BUS20
WILLIAM BLACK               MTH22


****> PLEASE ENTER FUNCTION CODE:
M
****> ENTER STUDENT MAJOR VALUE FOR WHICH LISTING IS REQUESTED:
BUS
RUSSELL THOMPSON            BUS20
ANNE NEAL                   BUS19
ALICE KROGER                BUS21
LAUREN THOMAS               BUS19


****> PLEASE ENTER FUNCTION CODE:
M
****> ENTER STUDENT MAJOR VALUE FOR WHICH LISTING IS REQUESTED:
CS
JOHN HANSEN                 CS 21
JANE GRAY                   CS 23
DAVID HILLMAN               CS 26


****> PLEASE ENTER FUNCTION CODE:
M
****> ENTER STUDENT MAJOR VALUE FOR WHICH LISTING IS REQUESTED:
MTH
WILLIAM BLACK               MTH22
MARY CHEN                   MTH21
KELLY TOWERS                MTH22


****> PLEASE ENTER FUNCTION CODE:
M
****> ENTER STUDENT MAJOR VALUE FOR WHICH LISTING IS REQUESTED:
PHY
NO RECORD OCCURRENCE WITH MAJOR = PHY EXISTS IN THE FILE.


****> PLEASE ENTER FUNCTION CODE:
A
****> ENTER STUDENT AGE VALUE FOR WHICH LISTING IS REQUESTED:
21
JOHN HANSEN                 CS 21
MARY CHEN                   MTH21
ALICE KROGER                BUS21


****> PLEASE ENTER FUNCTION CODE:
A
****> ENTER STUDENT AGE VALUE FOR WHICH LISTING IS REQUESTED:
19
ANNE NEAL                   BUS19
LAUREN THOMAS               BUS19


****> PLEASE ENTER FUNCTION CODE:
A
```

Program 2-Output (Continued)

```
****> ENTER STUDENT AGE VALUE FOR WHICH LISTING IS REQUESTED:
27
NO RECORD OCCURRENCE WITH AGE = 27 EXISTS IN THE FILE.

****> PLEASE ENTER FUNCTION CODE:
A
****> ENTER STUDENT AGE VALUE FOR WHICH LISTING IS REQUESTED:
26
DAVID HILLMAN            CS 26

****> PLEASE ENTER FUNCTION CODE:
X


*********************************************
* FUNCTION                        CODE  *
* _____    ____  *
* PRODUCE SEQUENTIAL FILE LISTING   S   *
* PRODUCE ORDERED LISTING BY NAME   N   *
* PRODUCE LISTING FOR A MAJOR VALUE M   *
* PRODUCE LISTING FOR AN AGE VALUE  A   *
* DISPLAY THIS MENU AGAIN           X   *
* TERMINATE PROCESSING              T   *
*********************************************

****> PLEASE ENTER FUNCTION CODE:
T
```

Program 2-Output (Continued)

```
00001    *...............................................................
00002      IDENTIFICATION DIVISION.
00003      PROGRAM-ID.  LINKED-LIST-FILE-MAINTENANCE.
00004    *****************************************************************
00005    ***   THIS PROGRAM MAINTAINS A RELATIVE ACCESS STUDENT FILE WITH  *
00006    ***   A VARIETY OF LINKED LIST STRUCTURES.                        *
00007    ***                                                              *
00008    ***   THE STUDENT FILE HAS A RECORD STRUCTURE THAT CONSISTS OF    *
00009    ***   THE FOLLOWING BASE FIELDS:                                  *
00010    ***      1. A 25-BYTE STUDENT-NAME,                              *
00011    ***      2. A THREE-BYTE STUDENT-MAJOR, AND                      *
00012    ***      3. A TWO-BYTE STUDENT-AGE.                              *
00013    ***                                                              *
00014    ***   THE SUPERIMPOSED LINEAR STRUCTURES ARE:                    *
00015    ***      1. A FORWARD LINKED LIST BASED ON STUDENT-NAME,         *
00016    ***      2. A PARTIALLY INVERTED LIST BASED ON STUDENT-MAJOR, AND *
00017    ***      3. A FULLY INVERTED LIST BASED ON STUDENT-AGE.          *
00018    ***                                                              *
00019    ***   THE STUDENT FILE IS A RELATIVE FILE OF 233 BUCKETS.  BUCKETS*
00020    ***   1 THROUGH 100 ARE USED FOR DATA RECORDS, AND BUCKETS 101    *
00021    ***   THROUGH 233 ARE RESERVED FOR INDEX RECORDS.                 *
00022    ***                                                              *
```

Program 3-Source Program to Maintain a Linked-List Relative File

```
00023    ***    THE STUDENT FILE IS A MULTIPLE-RECORD FILE, WITH TWO RECORD *
00024    ***    TYPES:                                                      *
00025    ***       1. DATA RECORD, AND                                      *
00026    ***       2. INDEX RECORD.                                         *
00027    ***                                                                *
00028    ***    ACCORDINGLY, THE MODIFIED DATA RECORD STRUCTURE FOR THE     *
00029    ***    RELATIVE STUDENT FILE INCLUDES THE FOLLOWING FIELDS:        *
00030    ***       1. A ONE-BYTE RECORD-TYPE ("D" FOR DATA RECORDS.)        *
00031    ***       2. A ONE-BYTE RECORD-STATUS ("E" FOR EMPTY, "D" FOR      *
00032    ***                                  DELETED, "F" FOR FULL.)       *
00033    ***       3. A 25-BYTE STUDENT-NAME,                               *
00034    ***       4. A THREE-BYTE STUDENT-MAJOR,                           *
00035    ***       5. A TWO-BYTE STUDENT-AGE,                               *
00036    ***       6. A THREE-BYTE NAME-LINK FIELD, AND                     *
00037    ***       7. A THREE-BYTE MAJOR-LINK FIELD.                        *
00038    ***                                                                *
00039    ***    THE INDEX RECORD STRUCTURE IS:                              *
00040    ***       1. A ONE-BYTE RECORD-TYPE ("I" FOR INDEX RECORDS.)       *
00041    ***       2. A ONE-BYTE RECORD-STATUS ("E" FOR EMPTY, "D" FOR      *
00042    ***                                  DELETED, "F" FOR FULL.)       *
00043    ***       3. A 20-BYTE LIST-NAME FIELD, AND                        *
00044    ***       4. A THREE-BYTE START-ADDRESS FIELD.                     *
00045    ***                                                                *
00046    ***    THE PROGRAM CAN BE USED TO DELETE A DATA RECORD OCCURRENCE  *
00047    ***    SPECIFIED BY STUDENT-NAME, AND MODIFY ALL LINKED LISTS AND  *
00048    ***    CORRESPONDING INDEX AREA RECORD OCCURRENCES.                *
00049    ***                                                                *
00050    ***    A GARBAGE COLLECTION LOGIC IS INCORPORATED INTO THIS PRO-   *
00051    ***    GRAM.  IT IS BASED ON A DATA AREA SPACE STACK, AND AN INDEX *
00052    ***    AREA SPACE STACK.  IF A DELETE OPERATION AFFECTS THE INDEX  *
00053    ***    AREA RECORD OCCURRENCES, THE INDEX AREA SPACE STACK WILL    *
00054    ***    BE USED TO RECOVER THE DELETED BUCKET.  THE DELETED RECORD  *
00055    ***    OCCURRENCE WILL BE PUSHED INTO THE DATA AREA SPACE STACK.   *
00056    ***                                                                *
00057    ***    THE PROGRAM IS DESIGNED AS AN INTERACTIVE PROGRAM.          *
00058    *****************************************************************************
00059
00060    AUTHOR.        UCKAN.
00061    DATE-WRITTEN.  AUGUST 8, 1991.
00062    DATE-COMPILED. AUG 16,1991.
00064    *..........................................................................
00065    ENVIRONMENT DIVISION.
00066    CONFIGURATION SECTION.
00067    SOURCE-COMPUTER. UNIVERSITY-MAINFRAME.
00068    OBJECT-COMPUTER. UNIVERSITY-MAINFRAME.
00069    INPUT-OUTPUT SECTION.
00070
00071    FILE-CONTROL.
00072
00073        SELECT REL-STUDENT-FILE ASSIGN TO MASTER
00074             ORGANIZATION IS RELATIVE
00075             ACCESS MODE IS DYNAMIC
00076             RELATIVE KEY IS BUCKET-NUMBER.
00077
```

Program 3-Source (Continued)

```
00078    *.................................................................
00079    DATA DIVISION.
00080    FILE SECTION.
00081    FD   REL-STUDENT-FILE
00082         LABEL RECORDS ARE STANDARD
00083         DATA RECORDS ARE PRIME-RECORD INDEX-RECORD
00084         RECORD CONTAINS 38 CHARACTERS.
00085
00086    01   PRIME-RECORD.
00087         05   DATA-RECORD-TYPE        PIC X.
00088         05   DATA-RECORD-STATUS      PIC X.
00089         05   STUDENT-NAME            PIC X(25).
00090         05   STUDENT-MAJOR           PIC X(3).
00091         05   STUDENT-AGE             PIC XX.
00092         05   NAME-LINK               PIC X(3).
00093         05   MAJOR-LINK              PIC X(3).
00094
00095    01   INDEX-RECORD.
00096         05   INDEX-RECORD-TYPE       PIC X.
00097         05   INDEX-RECORD-STATUS     PIC X.
00098         05   LIST-NAME               PIC X(20).
00099         05   START-ADDRESS           PIC X(3).
00100         05   FILLER                  PIC X(13).
00101
00102    WORKING-STORAGE SECTION.
00103
00104    **********> VARIABLES:
00105
00106    01   CONTINUE-PROCESSING          PIC XXX.
00107    01   NUMBER-OF-DELETED-RECORDS PIC 999.
00108    01   OUT-NO-OF-DELETED-RECORDS PIC ZZZ.
00109
00110    01   BUCKET-NUMBER                PIC 999.
00111    01   INDEX-BUCKET-NUMBER          PIC 999.
00112    01   BUFFER-A-BUCKET-NUMBER       PIC 999.
00113    01   BUFFER-B-BUCKET-NUMBER       PIC 999.
00114
00115    01   NAME-LIST-EMPTY              PIC XXX.
00116    01   NAME-LIST-HEAD-FOUND         PIC XXX.
00117
00118    01   MAJOR-LIST-NAME              PIC X(20).
00119    01   MAJOR-LIST-EMPTY             PIC XXX.
00120    01   MAJOR-LIST-HEAD-FOUND        PIC XXX.
00121
00122    01   AGE-INDEX-NAME               PIC X(20).
00123    01   AGE-INDEX-ENTRY-FOUND        PIC XXX.
00124
00125    01   DELETE-NAME                  PIC X(25).
00126    01   RECORD-FOUND                 PIC XXX.
00127    01   DELETE-FIRST-RECORD          PIC XXX.
00128    01   SAVE-START-ADDRESS           PIC 999.
00129
00130    **********> STRUCTURES:
00131
```

Program 3-Source (Continued)

```
00132        01   BUFFER-A.
00133             05   BUFFER-A-RECORD-TYPE      PIC X.
00134             05   BUFFER-A-RECORD-STATUS    PIC X.
00135             05   BUFFER-A-STUDENT-NAME     PIC X(25).
00136             05   BUFFER-A-STUDENT-MAJOR    PIC X(3).
00137             05   BUFFER-A-STUDENT-AGE      PIC XX.
00138             05   BUFFER-A-NAME-LINK        PIC 9(3).
00139             05   BUFFER-A-MAJOR-LINK       PIC 9(3).
00140
00141        01   BUFFER-B.
00142             05   BUFFER-B-RECORD-TYPE      PIC X.
00143             05   BUFFER-B-RECORD-STATUS    PIC X.
00144             05   BUFFER-B-STUDENT-NAME     PIC X(25).
00145             05   BUFFER-B-STUDENT-MAJOR    PIC X(3).
00146             05   BUFFER-B-STUDENT-AGE      PIC XX.
00147             05   BUFFER-B-NAME-LINK        PIC 9(3).
00148             05   BUFFER-B-MAJOR-LINK       PIC 9(3).
00149
00150        *.................................................................
00151        PROCEDURE DIVISION.
00152
00153        A-MONITOR-PROCEDURE.
00154             OPEN I-O REL-STUDENT-FILE.
00155
00156             MOVE "YES" TO CONTINUE-PROCESSING.
00157             MOVE ZERO  TO NUMBER-OF-DELETED-RECORDS.
00158
00159             DISPLAY "  ".
00160             DISPLAY "*******************************************".
00161             DISPLAY "*** THIS PROGRAM CAN BE USED TO DELETE ***".
00162             DISPLAY "*** RECORD OCCURRENCES FROM THE STUDENT***".
00163             DISPLAY "*** FILE.  RECORDS TO BE DELETED SHOULD***".
00164             DISPLAY "*** BE SPECIFIED BY STUDENT-NAME.      ***".
00165             DISPLAY "*******************************************".
00166             DISPLAY "  ".
00167
00168             DISPLAY "****> ENTER STUDENT-NAME OF RECORD OCCURRENCE TO BE
00169        -    "DELETED: ".
00170             ACCEPT DELETE-NAME FROM CONSOLE.
00171
00172             PERFORM B1-DELETE-RECORD
00173                  UNTIL CONTINUE-PROCESSING = "NO".
00174
00175             MOVE NUMBER-OF-DELETED-RECORDS TO OUT-NO-OF-DELETED-RECORDS.
00176
00177             DISPLAY "NUMBER OF RECORD OCCURRENCES DELETED DURING THIS SES
00178        -    "SION: " OUT-NO-OF-DELETED-RECORDS.
00179
00180             CLOSE REL-STUDENT-FILE.
00181             STOP RUN.
00182
00183        B1-DELETE-RECORD.
00184             MOVE "NO" TO RECORD-FOUND.
00185             MOVE "NO" TO NAME-LIST-HEAD-FOUND.
```

Program 3-Source (Continued)

```
00186              MOVE "NO" TO NAME-LIST-EMPTY.
00187              MOVE "NO" TO DELETE-FIRST-RECORD.
00188              MOVE 103  TO BUCKET-NUMBER.
00189
00190              PERFORM C1-FIND-NAME-LIST-HEAD
00191                     UNTIL BUCKET-NUMBER > 233
00192                                  OR
00193                          NAME-LIST-HEAD-FOUND = "YES".
00194
00195              IF NAME-LIST-HEAD-FOUND = "YES"
00196                     IF START-ADDRESS = 999
00197                             DISPLAY "NAME LIST IS EMPTY."
00198                             MOVE "YES" TO NAME-LIST-EMPTY
00199                     ELSE
00200                             NEXT SENTENCE
00201              ELSE
00202                     DISPLAY "NAME LIST HEAD DOES NOT EXIST.".
00203
00204              IF NAME-LIST-HEAD-FOUND = "YES"
00205                     AND
00206                 NAME-LIST-EMPTY = "NO"
00207                 MOVE BUCKET-NUMBER TO INDEX-BUCKET-NUMBER
00208                 MOVE START-ADDRESS TO BUCKET-NUMBER
00209
00210                 PERFORM C2-FIND-RECORD-TO-BE-DELETED
00211
00212                 IF RECORD-FOUND = "YES"
00213                     PERFORM C3-COMPLETE-DELETION
00214                     DISPLAY "RECORD OCCURRENCE DELETED."
00215                     ADD 1 TO NUMBER-OF-DELETED-RECORDS
00216                 ELSE
00217                     DISPLAY "RECORD TO BE DELETED IS NOT IN THE FILE.".
00218
00219              DISPLAY "****> DO YOU WANT TO CONTINUE?  TYPE YES OR NO.".
00220              ACCEPT CONTINUE-PROCESSING FROM CONSOLE.
00221
00222              IF CONTINUE-PROCESSING = "YES"
00223                     DISPLAY "****> ENTER STUDENT-NAME OF RECORD OCCURRENC
00224          -    "E TO BE DELETED: "
00225                     ACCEPT DELETE-NAME FROM CONSOLE.
00226
00227      C1-FIND-NAME-LIST-HEAD.
00228          PERFORM D1-READ-FILE-DIRECTLY.
00229
00230          IF LIST-NAME = "NAME"
00231                  MOVE "YES" TO NAME-LIST-HEAD-FOUND
00232          ELSE
00233                  ADD 1 TO BUCKET-NUMBER.
00234
00235      C2-FIND-RECORD-TO-BE-DELETED.
00236          PERFORM D1-READ-FILE-DIRECTLY.
00237
00238          MOVE PRIME-RECORD  TO BUFFER-A.
00239          MOVE BUCKET-NUMBER TO BUFFER-A-BUCKET-NUMBER.
```

Program 3-Source (Continued)

```
00240
00241            IF DELETE-NAME = BUFFER-A-STUDENT-NAME
00242                   MOVE "YES"            TO DELETE-FIRST-RECORD
00243                   MOVE "YES"            TO RECORD-FOUND
00244                   MOVE PRIME-RECORD     TO BUFFER-B
00245                   MOVE BUCKET-NUMBER TO BUFFER-B-BUCKET-NUMBER.
00246
00247            IF RECORD-FOUND = "NO" AND NAME-LINK NOT = 999
00248                   MOVE NAME-LINK TO BUCKET-NUMBER
00249                   PERFORM D1-READ-FILE-DIRECTLY
00250
00251                   MOVE PRIME-RECORD     TO BUFFER-B
00252                   MOVE BUCKET-NUMBER TO BUFFER-B-BUCKET-NUMBER
00253
00254                   PERFORM D2-TRAVERSE-NAME-LIST
00255                        UNTIL RECORD-FOUND = "YES"
00256                                          OR
00257                            BUFFER-B-NAME-LINK = 999.
00258
00259            IF RECORD-FOUND = "NO"
00260                   IF DELETE-NAME = BUFFER-B-STUDENT-NAME
00261                        MOVE "YES" TO RECORD-FOUND.
00262
00263      C3-COMPLETE-DELETION.
00264           PERFORM D3-DELETE-FROM-NAME-LIST.
00265
00266           PERFORM D4-DELETE-FROM-AGE-LIST.
00267
00268           PERFORM D5-DELETE-FROM-MAJOR-LIST.
00269
00270           PERFORM D6-MARK-RECORD-AS-DELETED.
00271
00272           PERFORM D7-PUSH-INTO-DATA-STACK.
00273
00274      D1-READ-FILE-DIRECTLY.
00275           READ REL-STUDENT-FILE
00276                   INVALID KEY DISPLAY "READ ERROR.".
00277
00278      D2-TRAVERSE-NAME-LIST.
00279
00280           IF DELETE-NAME = BUFFER-B-STUDENT-NAME
00281                   MOVE "YES" TO RECORD-FOUND
00282           ELSE
00283                   MOVE BUFFER-B               TO BUFFER-A
00284                   MOVE BUFFER-B-BUCKET-NUMBER TO BUFFER-A-BUCKET-NUMBER
00285                   MOVE NAME-LINK              TO BUCKET-NUMBER
00286
00287                   PERFORM D1-READ-FILE-DIRECTLY
00288
00289                   MOVE PRIME-RECORD     TO BUFFER-B
00290                   MOVE BUCKET-NUMBER TO BUFFER-B-BUCKET-NUMBER.
00291
00292      D3-DELETE-FROM-NAME-LIST.
00293
```

Program 3-Source (Continued)

```
00294            IF DELETE-FIRST-RECORD = "YES"
00295                 MOVE INDEX-BUCKET-NUMBER TO BUCKET-NUMBER
00296
00297                 PERFORM D1-READ-FILE-DIRECTLY
00298
00299                 MOVE BUFFER-B-NAME-LINK TO START-ADDRESS
00300
00301                 PERFORM E1-REWRITE-INDEX-RECORD
00302        ELSE
00303                 MOVE BUFFER-A-BUCKET-NUMBER TO BUCKET-NUMBER
00304
00305                 PERFORM D1-READ-FILE-DIRECTLY
00306
00307                 MOVE BUFFER-B-NAME-LINK TO NAME-LINK
00308
00309                 PERFORM E2-REWRITE-PRIME-RECORD.
00310
00311    D4-DELETE-FROM-AGE-LIST.
00312        MOVE "NO"    TO AGE-INDEX-ENTRY-FOUND.
00313        MOVE 103     TO BUCKET-NUMBER.
00314
00315        MOVE SPACES TO AGE-INDEX-NAME.
00316
00317        STRING "AGE" DELIMITED BY SIZE
00318              BUFFER-B-STUDENT-AGE DELIMITED BY SIZE
00319           INTO AGE-INDEX-NAME.
00320
00321        PERFORM E3-FIND-AGE-INDEX-ENTRY
00322              UNTIL BUCKET-NUMBER > 233
00323                         OR
00324                  AGE-INDEX-ENTRY-FOUND = "YES".
00325
00326        IF AGE-INDEX-ENTRY-FOUND = "YES"
00327              MOVE "D" TO INDEX-RECORD-STATUS
00328              PERFORM E1-REWRITE-INDEX-RECORD
00329              MOVE BUCKET-NUMBER TO INDEX-BUCKET-NUMBER.
00330              PERFORM E4-PUSH-INTO-INDEX-STACK.
00331
00332    D5-DELETE-FROM-MAJOR-LIST.
00333        MOVE "NO"    TO MAJOR-LIST-EMPTY.
00334        MOVE "NO"    TO MAJOR-LIST-HEAD-FOUND.
00335        MOVE "NO"    TO RECORD-FOUND.
00336        MOVE "NO"    TO DELETE-FIRST-RECORD.
00337        MOVE 103     TO BUCKET-NUMBER.
00338        MOVE SPACES TO MAJOR-LIST-NAME.
00339
00340        STRING "MAJOR" DELIMITED BY SIZE
00341              BUFFER-B-STUDENT-MAJOR DELIMITED BY SIZE
00342           INTO MAJOR-LIST-NAME.
00343
00344        PERFORM E5-FIND-MAJOR-LIST-HEAD
00345              UNTIL BUCKET-NUMBER > 233
00346                         OR
00347                  MAJOR-LIST-HEAD-FOUND = "YES".
```

Program 3-Source (Continued)

```
00348
00349          IF MAJOR-LIST-HEAD-FOUND = "YES"
00350              IF START-ADDRESS = 999
00351                      DISPLAY "MAJOR LIST FOR MAJOR = "
00352                          MAJOR-LIST-NAME " IS EMPTY."
00353                      MOVE "YES" TO MAJOR-LIST-EMPTY
00354          ELSE
00355                      NEXT SENTENCE
00356      ELSE
00357              DISPLAY "MAJOR LIST HEAD FOR MAJOR = "
00358                      MAJOR-LIST-NAME " DOES NOT EXIST.".
00359
00360      IF MAJOR-LIST-HEAD-FOUND = "YES"
00361                  AND
00362        MAJOR-LIST-EMPTY = "NO"
00363              MOVE BUCKET-NUMBER TO INDEX-BUCKET-NUMBER
00364              MOVE START-ADDRESS TO BUCKET-NUMBER
00365
00366              PERFORM E6-FIND-RECORD-IN-MAJOR-LIST
00367
00368              IF RECORD-FOUND = "YES"
00369                      PERFORM E7-COMPLETE-MAJOR-DELETE
00370              ELSE
00371                      DISPLAY "RECORD TO BE DELETED IS NOT IN THE F
00372  -      "ILE.".
00373
00374  D6-MARK-RECORD-AS-DELETED.
00375      MOVE BUFFER-B-BUCKET-NUMBER TO BUCKET-NUMBER.
00376
00377      PERFORM D1-READ-FILE-DIRECTLY.
00378
00379      MOVE "D" TO DATA-RECORD-STATUS.
00380
00381      PERFORM E2-REWRITE-PRIME-RECORD.
00382
00383  D7-PUSH-INTO-DATA-STACK.
00384      MOVE 101 TO BUCKET-NUMBER.
00385
00386      PERFORM D1-READ-FILE-DIRECTLY.
00387
00388      MOVE START-ADDRESS          TO SAVE-START-ADDRESS.
00389      MOVE BUFFER-B-BUCKET-NUMBER TO START-ADDRESS.
00390
00391      PERFORM E1-REWRITE-INDEX-RECORD.
00392
00393      MOVE BUFFER-B-BUCKET-NUMBER TO BUCKET-NUMBER.
00394
00395      PERFORM D1-READ-FILE-DIRECTLY.
00396
00397      MOVE SPACES             TO MAJOR-LINK.
00398      MOVE SAVE-START-ADDRESS TO NAME-LINK.
00399
00400      PERFORM E2-REWRITE-PRIME-RECORD.
00401
```

Program 3-Source (Continued)

```
00402        E1-REWRITE-INDEX-RECORD.
00403            REWRITE INDEX-RECORD
00404                INVALID KEY DISPLAY "ERROR IN REWRITING INDEX RECORD.".
00405

00406        E2-REWRITE-PRIME-RECORD.
00407            REWRITE PRIME-RECORD
00408                INVALID KEY DISPLAY "ERROR IN REWRITING INDEX RECORD.".
00409

00410        E3-FIND-AGE-INDEX-ENTRY.
00411            PERFORM D1-READ-FILE-DIRECTLY.
00412

00413            IF LIST-NAME = AGE-INDEX-NAME
00414                        AND
00415              START-ADDRESS = BUFFER-B-BUCKET-NUMBER
00416                    MOVE "YES" TO AGE-INDEX-ENTRY-FOUND
00417            ELSE
00418                    ADD 1 TO BUCKET-NUMBER.
00419

00420        E4-PUSH-INTO-INDEX-STACK.
00421            MOVE 102 TO BUCKET-NUMBER.
00422

00423            PERFORM D1-READ-FILE-DIRECTLY.
00424

00425            MOVE START-ADDRESS          TO SAVE-START-ADDRESS.
00426            MOVE INDEX-BUCKET-NUMBER TO START-ADDRESS.
00427

00428            PERFORM E1-REWRITE-INDEX-RECORD.
00429

00430            MOVE INDEX-BUCKET-NUMBER TO BUCKET-NUMBER.
00431

00432            PERFORM D1-READ-FILE-DIRECTLY.
00433

00434            MOVE SAVE-START-ADDRESS TO START-ADDRESS.
00435

00436            PERFORM E1-REWRITE-INDEX-RECORD.
00437

00438        E5-FIND-MAJOR-LIST-HEAD.
00439            PERFORM D1-READ-FILE-DIRECTLY.
00440

00441            IF LIST-NAME = MAJOR-LIST-NAME
00442                    MOVE "YES" TO MAJOR-LIST-HEAD-FOUND
00443            ELSE
00444                    ADD 1 TO BUCKET-NUMBER.
00445

00446        E6-FIND-RECORD-IN-MAJOR-LIST.
00447            PERFORM D1-READ-FILE-DIRECTLY.
00448

00449            MOVE PRIME-RECORD  TO BUFFER-A.
00450            MOVE BUCKET-NUMBER TO BUFFER-A-BUCKET-NUMBER.
00451

00452            IF DELETE-NAME = BUFFER-A-STUDENT-NAME
00453                    MOVE "YES"          TO DELETE-FIRST-RECORD
00454                    MOVE "YES"          TO RECORD-FOUND
00455                    MOVE PRIME-RECORD  TO BUFFER-B
00456                    MOVE BUCKET-NUMBER TO BUFFER-B-BUCKET-NUMBER.
```

Program 3-Source (Continued)

```
00457
00458            IF RECORD-FOUND = "NO" AND MAJOR-LINK NOT = 999
00459                    MOVE MAJOR-LINK TO BUCKET-NUMBER
00460
00461                    PERFORM D1-READ-FILE-DIRECTLY
00462
00463                    MOVE PRIME-RECORD   TO BUFFER-B
00464                    MOVE BUCKET-NUMBER TO BUFFER-B-BUCKET-NUMBER
00465
00466                    PERFORM F1-TRAVERSE-MAJOR-LIST
00467                        UNTIL RECORD-FOUND = "YES"
00468                                        OR
00469                              BUFFER-B-NAME-LINK = 999.
00470
00471         IF RECORD-FOUND = "NO"
00472                 IF DELETE-NAME = BUFFER-B-STUDENT-NAME
00473                        MOVE "YES" TO RECORD-FOUND.
00474
00475     E7-COMPLETE-MAJOR-DELETE.
00476         IF DELETE-FIRST-RECORD = "YES"
00477                    MOVE INDEX-BUCKET-NUMBER TO BUCKET-NUMBER
00478
00479                    PERFORM D1-READ-FILE-DIRECTLY
00480
00481                    MOVE BUFFER-B-MAJOR-LINK TO START-ADDRESS
00482
00483                    PERFORM E1-REWRITE-INDEX-RECORD
00484         ELSE
00485                    MOVE BUFFER-A-BUCKET-NUMBER TO BUCKET-NUMBER
00486
00487                    PERFORM D1-READ-FILE-DIRECTLY
00488
00489                    MOVE BUFFER-B-MAJOR-LINK TO MAJOR-LINK
00490
00491                    PERFORM E2-REWRITE-PRIME-RECORD.
00492
00493     F1-TRAVERSE-MAJOR-LIST.
00494
00495         IF DELETE-NAME = BUFFER-B-STUDENT-NAME
00496                    MOVE "YES" TO RECORD-FOUND
00497         ELSE
00498                    MOVE BUFFER-B                 TO BUFFER-A
00499                    MOVE BUFFER-B-BUCKET-NUMBER TO BUFFER-A-BUCKET-NUMBER
00500                    MOVE MAJOR-LINK             TO BUCKET-NUMBER
00501
00502                    PERFORM D1-READ-FILE-DIRECTLY
00503
00504                    MOVE PRIME-RECORD   TO BUFFER-B
00505                    MOVE BUCKET-NUMBER TO BUFFER-B-BUCKET-NUMBER.
```

Program 3-Source (Continued)

```
*********************************************
*** THIS PROGRAM CAN BE USED TO DELETE ***
*** RECORD OCCURRENCES FROM THE STUDENT***
*** FILE.   RECORDS TO BE DELETED SHOULD***
*** BE SPECIFIED BY STUDENT-NAME.       ***
*********************************************


****> ENTER STUDENT-NAME OF RECORD OCCURRENCE TO BE DELETED:
MARY CHEN
RECORD OCCURRENCE DELETED.
****> DO YOU WANT TO CONTINUE? TYPE YES OR NO.
YES
****> ENTER STUDENT-NAME OF RECORD OCCURRENCE TO BE DELETED:
WILLIAM BLACK
RECORD OCCURRENCE DELETED.
****> DO YOU WANT TO CONTINUE? TYPE YES OR NO.
YES
****> ENTER STUDENT-NAME OF RECORD OCCURRENCE TO BE DELETED:
KELLY TOWERS
RECORD OCCURRENCE DELETED.
****> DO YOU WANT TO CONTINUE? TYPE YES OR NO.
YES
****> ENTER STUDENT-NAME OF RECORD OCCURRENCE TO BE DELETED:
MARY CHEN
RECORD TO BE DELETED IS NOT IN THE FILE.
****> DO YOU WANT TO CONTINUE? TYPE YES OR NO.
YES
****> ENTER STUDENT-NAME OF RECORD OCCURRENCE TO BE DELETED:
JANICE HILL
RECORD TO BE DELETED IS NOT IN THE FILE.
****> DO YOU WANT TO CONTINUE? TYPE YES OR NO.
NO
NUMBER OF RECORD OCCURRENCES DELETED DURING THIS SESSION:    3
```

Program 3-Output(a) An Interactive Terminal Session for Program 3

```
............
S
SEQUENTIAL LISTING OF DATA AREA:

001DDWILLIAM BLACK          MTH22004
002DFJOHN HANSEN            CS 21010003
003DFJANE GRAY             CS 23002008
004DDMARY CHEN              MTH21011
005DFRUSSELL THOMPSON       BUS20999006
006DFANNE NEAL              BUS19008007
007DFALICE KROGER           BUS21006010
008DFDAVID HILLMAN          CS 26003999
009DDKELLY TOWERS           MTH22001
010DFLAUREN THOMAS          BUS19005999
011DE                            012000
012DE                            013000
............
```

Program 3-Output(b) An Instance of the Linked-List Student File After Record
Deletions as Shown in Program 3-Output(a)

```
  . . . . . . . . . . . .
  100DE                                        999000

  SEQUENTIAL LISTING OF INDEX AREA:

  101IFDATASTACK            009
  102IFINDEXSTACK           115
  103IFNAME                 007
  104IFMAJORBUS             005
  105IFMAJORCS              002
  106IFMAJORMTH             999
  107IDAGE22                110
  108IFAGE21                002
  109IFAGE23                003
  110IDAGE21                117
  111IFAGE20                005
  112IFAGE19                006
  113IFAGE21                007
  114IFAGE26                008
  115IDAGE22                107
  116IFAGE19                010
  117IE                     118
  118IE                     119
  . . . . . . . . . . . .
  . . . . . . . . . . . .
  233IE                                        999
  . . . . . . . . . . . .
```

Program 3-Output(b) (Continued)

```
  . . . . . . . . . . . .

****> PLEASE ENTER FUNCTION CODE:
N
ALICE KROGER              BUS21
ANNE NEAL                 BUS19
DAVID HILLMAN             CS 26
JANE GRAY                 CS 23
JOHN HANSEN               CS 21
LAUREN THOMAS             BUS19
RUSSELL THOMPSON          BUS20

****> PLEASE ENTER FUNCTION CODE:
M
****> ENTER STUDENT MAJOR VALUE FOR WHICH LISTING IS REQUESTED:
BUS
RUSSELL THOMPSON          BUS20
ANNE NEAL                 BUS19
ALICE KROGER              BUS21
LAUREN THOMAS             BUS19
```

Program 3-Output(c) An Interactive Terminal Session for Program 3 After Record Deletions as Shown in Program 3-Output(a)

```
****> PLEASE ENTER FUNCTION CODE:
M
****> ENTER STUDENT MAJOR VALUE FOR WHICH LISTING IS REQUESTED:
MTH
MAJOR LIST FOR MAJOR = MTH IS EMPTY.

****> PLEASE ENTER FUNCTION CODE:
A
****> ENTER STUDENT AGE VALUE FOR WHICH LISTING IS REQUESTED:
22
NO RECORD OCCURRENCE WITH AGE = 22 EXISTS IN THE FILE.

****> PLEASE ENTER FUNCTION CODE:
A
****> ENTER STUDENT AGE VALUE FOR WHICH LISTING IS REQUESTED:
21
JOHN HANSEN               CS 21
ALICE KROGER              BUS21

****> PLEASE ENTER FUNCTION CODE:
S
SEQUENTIAL LISTING OF DATA AREA:

002DFJOHN HANSEN              CS 21010003
003DFJANE GRAY               CS 23002008
005DFRUSSELL THOMPSON        BUS20999006
006DFANNE NEAL               BUS19008007
007DFALICE KROGER            BUS21006010
008DFDAVID HILLMAN           CS 26003999
010DFLAUREN THOMAS           BUS19005999

SEQUENTIAL LISTING OF INDEX AREA:

101IFDATASTACK       009
102IFINDEXSTACK      115
103IFNAME            007
104IFMAJORBUS        005
105IFMAJORCS         002
106IFMAJORMTH        999
108IFAGE21           002
109IFAGE23           003
111IFAGE20           005
112IFAGE19           006
113IFAGE21           007
114IFAGE26           008
116IFAGE19           010

****> PLEASE ENTER FUNCTION CODE:
T
```

Program 3-Output(c) (Continued)

Logical File Organization Techniques: Nonlinear Files

IN THIS CHAPTER YOU WILL LEARN ABOUT

- Nonlinear data structures: trees and networks
- Importance of trees as data structures
- Fundamental concepts and terminology for trees
  - Root node, leaf nodes, intermediate nodes
  - Parent node and child node
  - Levels of nodes
  - Height of a tree
- Binary trees
  - Skewed and zigzag trees
  - Full binary trees
  - Complete binary trees
  - Height-balanced binary trees
- Storage representation of trees
- Transforming a general tree into binary trees
- Searching binary trees
  - Preorder traversal
  - In-order traversal
  - Postorder traversal
  - Binary search trees
- Binary tree files
  - Creating binary tree files
  - Maintaining binary tree files
  - Access to binary tree files
- COBOL implementation of binary tree files

Introduction

The data structures we have studied so far have been linear. This is because the relationships inherent in them could be mapped onto a straight line without loss of data or change in structure. In some applications we come across data structures that reflect nonlinear relationships. Nonlinear structures are further characterized by the fact that each node may have one or more logical successors and predecessors, whereas in a linear structure, such as a linked list, every node can have at most one logical successor and one predecessor.

Nonlinear data structures are classified as two types: networks and trees. We briefly touched on them in Chapter 4, while discussing concepts and techniques pertinent to program structure. The program structure depicted in Figure 13 of Chapter 4, for example, is a network. In Chapter 5 we introduced tree structures in connection with decision trees and decision tables. The decision tree of Figure 9a in Chapter 5 is an example.

Compared to trees, networks are more complex and more difficult to process. Tree structures have been investigated extensively, and many techniques and algorithms have been developed for them. For this reason, quite often in computer applications, if the nature of the problem permits, we tend to reduce network structures to equivalent tree structures and then attempt to resolve them. This reduction process is possible for most problems in file and data base management. Consequently, in this chapter we will concentrate on tree structures rather than networks.

Importance of Trees as Data Structures

We have encountered tree structures on two occasions, once as a desirable program structure, as in Figures 10 and 11 in Chapter 4, and once as decision trees. They emerge as natural representation techniques in many applications. Before we begin a detailed study of this useful structure, let us give some examples.

Figure 1a is a lineal genealogical chart showing the descendants of James Johnson up to the third generation in the family. The inherent relationship is

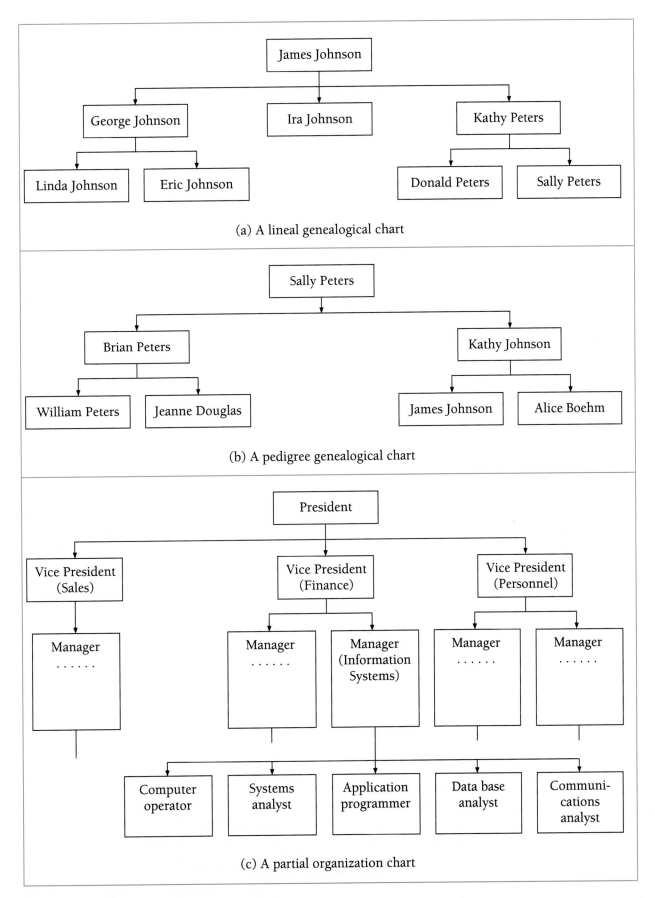

(a) A lineal genealogical chart

(b) A pedigree genealogical chart

(c) A partial organization chart

Figure 1 Examples of Tree Structures

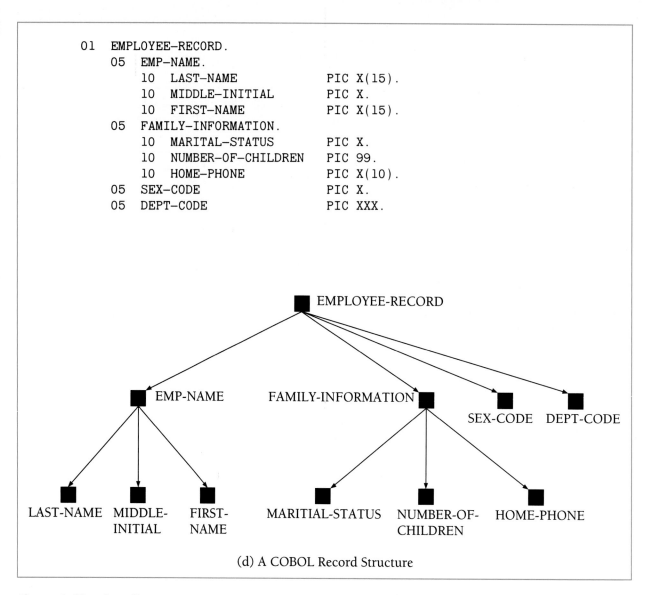

```
01   EMPLOYEE-RECORD.
     05  EMP-NAME.
         10  LAST-NAME          PIC X(15).
         10  MIDDLE-INITIAL     PIC X.
         10  FIRST-NAME         PIC X(15).
     05  FAMILY-INFORMATION.
         10  MARITAL-STATUS     PIC X.
         10  NUMBER-OF-CHILDREN PIC 99.
         10  HOME-PHONE         PIC X(10).
     05  SEX-CODE               PIC X.
     05  DEPT-CODE              PIC XXX.
```

(d) A COBOL Record Structure

Figure 1 (Continued)

the "a descendant of." That George Johnson is below James Johnson in the chart means that George Johnson is a descendant of James Johnson, and so on.

Figure 1b is a pedigree genealogical chart, also a tree structure. In this representation we see two generations of Sally Peters's ancestors in which the relationship is "a parent of." Brian Peters is a parent of Sally Peters, James Johnson is a parent of Kathy Johnson, and so on. As a person can have only two parents, this tree structure is special in that each person included has two parents. Parents of some nodes, such as William Peters, are not shown in the pedigree tree. The tree in Figure 1b is a binary tree.

Figure 1c is a partial organization chart. It shows several job positions and the relationships between them. The relationship is "subordinate to."

The familiar COBOL structure is basically a tree structure. Figure 1d shows a COBOL record structure, called EMPLOYEE-RECORD, and the corresponding tree structure. It consists of two group structures, EMP-NAME and FAMILY-INFORMATION, and two data items, SEX-CODE and DEPT-CODE. In turn, EMP-NAME and FAMILY-INFORMATION each consists of three data items. The relationships of data items, group structures, and EMPLOYEE-RECORD constitute a tree. The relationship here is "subordinate to" or "an ele-

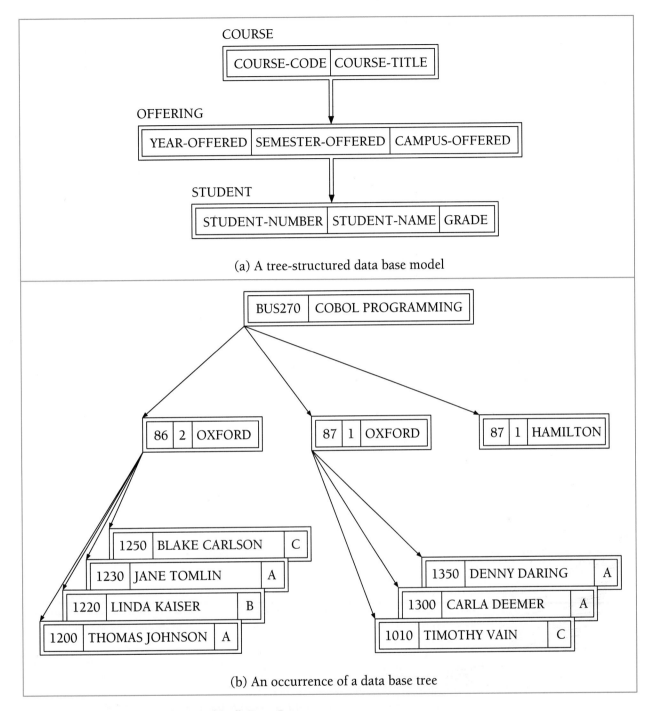

Figure 2 A Tree-Structure (Hierarchical) Data Base

ment of." For example, HOME-PHONE is an element of the substructure FAMILY-INFORMATION.

Tree structures also arise in data base modeling. A simple example is shown in Figure 2a. This data base consists of three files, COURSE, OFFERING, and STUDENT. Record structures for each file are also shown. The file COURSE has a record structure consisting of the fields COURSE-CODE and COURSE-TITLE. Two relationships are of interest in this data base. The first one is shown in the figure as the arc connecting COURSE to OFFERING. In fact, this relationship is "an offering of," associating one or more occurrences of OFFER-ING with an occurrence of COURSE. The second relationship is graphically shown as the arc connecting STUDENT to OFFERING. It associates one or more occurrences of STUDENT to one occurrence of OFFERING. Clearly, the data model is a tree structure.

An occurrence of this tree model is shown in Figure 2b in terms of a related set of records. It is also a tree structure. The data base would contain many other similar tree structures, one for each record in the file named COURSE. Therefore, the actual data base occurrence for the data base model of Figure 2a is a collection of trees, also called a **forest**. This data base model is in confor-mity with the data modeling principles of IMS, a hierarchical data base system that is discussed briefly in Chapter 18.

It is conceivable that in an application, the three files of Figure 2a could be structured as a single file of multiple-record type. In other words, we could have a single direct-access file called ENROLLMENT consisting of three record structures similar to COURSE, OFFERING, and STUDENT. Such a file would be a tree structure. Many other practical occasions necessitate design and im-plementation of tree structured files. This is one of the main reasons why tree structures should be well understood by application programmers and analysts.

Finally, we would like to note that almost all of the indexing techniques we studied in Chapter 13 are basically tree structures. Any multiple-level index structure, including indexed sequential organization and B-trees, or even a sin-gle-level index table, together with prime data area records, is a tree. Figure 2 in Chapter 13 shows an indexed sequential organization. That it is a tree is ob-vious.

Fundamental Tree Concepts and Terminology

We have been exposed to tree structures and their associated terminology. Here we briefly review some concepts and introduce other significant ones. Some of these are shown in Figure 3.

We can define a tree as follows.

A **tree** is a connected digraph with no cycles.

In other words, every node of a tree structure is connected by some path to ev-ery other node, thus ensuring connectedness. Also, no path in a tree originates at a given node and terminates at the same node, which ensures acyclicity.

The arcs connecting any pair of nodes in a tree are elements of the rela-tionship represented by it. Given one such arc, the node at the higher level of hierarchy is the **parent node** and the other is the **child node**.

In Figure 3, the node whose label is 5 is a child of the parent node 2.

In a tree, there is only one node with no parents; it is called the **root**. All nodes with no child nodes are known as **leaf nodes**, or **terminal nodes**. The remaining nodes are called **intermediate nodes**, or simply **nodes**.

For example, in the tree of Figure 3, node 1 is the root and nodes 4 through 11 are leaf nodes. Nodes 2 and 3 have child nodes and hence are intermediate

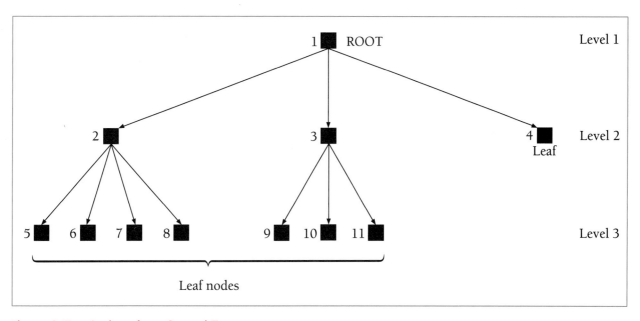

Figure 3 Terminology for a General Tree

nodes. Customarily, we enter a tree structure through its root. In this respect, root node is equivalent to list head for linked lists.

A tree is a hierarchical structure in that its nodes define several levels.

> As a matter of convention, the tree root is at **level 1**. All child nodes of the root node constitute **level 2**, their children are at **level 3**, and so on.

> The **height** or **depth** of a tree is the maximum level of any node in it.

Accordingly, the tree of Figure 3 is a tree of height 3.

> If no restriction is imposed on the number of child nodes the root and the intermediate nodes can have, such a tree is known as a **general tree**.

In Figure 3, the root, node 1, has three child nodes, node 2 has four child nodes, and node 3 has three child nodes. This is a general tree.

Binary Trees

> A **binary tree** is a tree in which every node can have zero, 1, or 2 child nodes.

Figure 4 shows a binary tree in which nodes 1, 3, and 4 have two child nodes. Nodes 2, 5, and 6 all have a single descendant. The remaining nodes are leaf nodes, with no child nodes.

Binary trees are predominant in many computer applications. There are mainly two reasons for this. As we will see shortly, binary trees are easy and

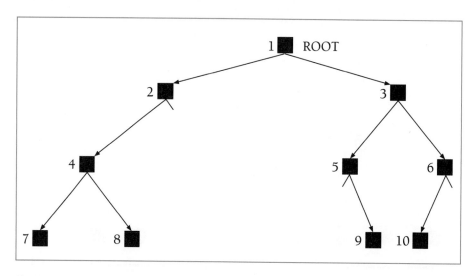

Figure 4 A Binary Tree

economical to represent in computer storage. Also, they have been investigated thoroughly, and we know a lot about them. Consequently, even when our application calls for a general tree, it may be feasible and advisable to transform that representation to an equivalent binary tree. More about this later.

> In a binary tree each node has a **left child node** and a **right child node**. The left child node together with its descendants define the **left subtree** for the node under consideration. The right child and and all of its descendants make up the **right subtree** of the node. The left or right subtree of a node may be empty. Each terminal node in a binary tree has empty left and right subtrees.

In the binary tree of Figure 4, the left child of node 2 is node 4. The left subtree of node 2 is the tree structure made up of nodes 4, 7, and 8. The right subtree of node 2 is empty.

Several varieties of binary trees are noteworthy for practical reasons (Figure 5). Here we consider skewed and zigzag, full, complete, and height-balanced binary trees.

Skewed and Zigzag Binary Trees

Figure 5a shows two skewed and one zigzag binary tree. The one on the left is left-skewed, the one next to it is right-skewed. The rightmost is a zigzag tree.

> A **skewed** or a **zigzag** binary tree has only one node at each level and a single terminal node. If all nodes except the terminal node have nonempty left subtrees, the tree is **left-skewed**. If right subtrees for all nodes except the terminal node are nonempty, it is a **right-skewed** tree. If the left and right subtrees of nodes at consecutive levels are alternately not empty, the tree is a **zigzag** binary tree.

Skewed and zigzag trees are deep structures. Searching them is inefficient compared to trees containing the same number of nodes within a smaller depth. This is because searching a skewed or zigzag tree is equivalent to making an exhaustive sequential search of a list consisting of all the nodes. There-

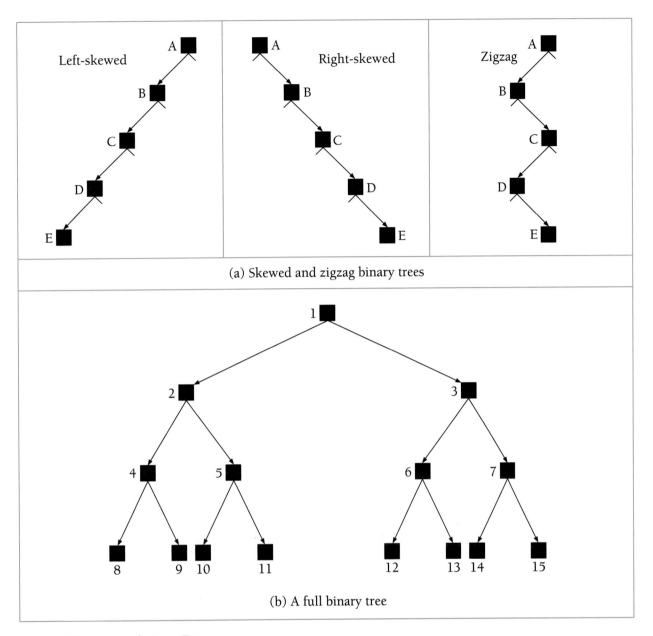

(a) Skewed and zigzag binary trees

(b) A full binary tree

Figure 5 Variations of Binary Trees

fore, in practical applications, whenever possible, skewed and zigzag trees should be avoided.

Full Binary Trees

The opposite is found in a full binary tree, which accommodates a maximum number of nodes in a minimum depth.

> A **full binary tree** of depth d is a binary tree containing $(2^d - 1)$ nodes.

Figure 5b shows a full binary tree of depth 4. It contains

$$(2^4 - 1) = 15$$

nodes. The length of all branches in a full binary tree is the same and is equal

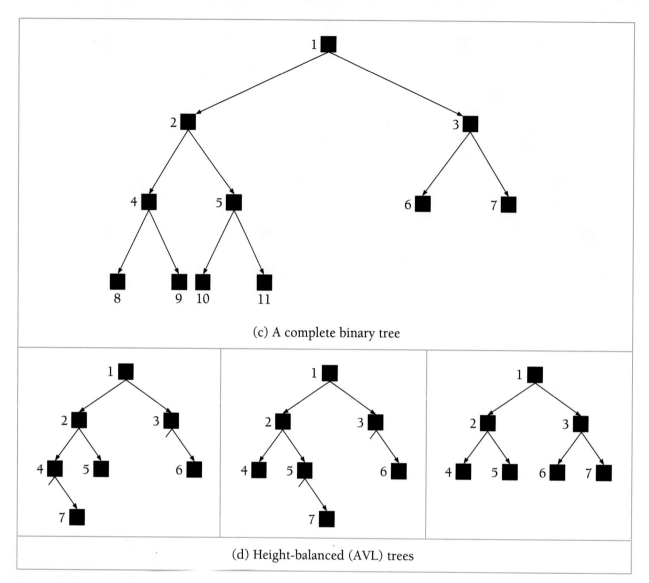

(c) A complete binary tree

(d) Height-balanced (AVL) trees

Figure 5 (Continued)

to its depth, d. Therefore, a search process progressing on a tree branch requires access to a maximum of d nodes. Full binary trees are the most efficient trees for searching, provided there is some order among values associated with the nodes. A full binary tree is also known as a **fully balanced binary tree.**

Complete Binary Trees

From the above discussion it should be clear that full binary trees of depth 2, 3, 4, 5, 6, and so on, can have 3, 7, 15, 31, 63, and so on, nodes. What if we have, say, 11 nodes, and still would like to have a reasonably balanced tree structure so that searching it is as efficient as possible? This consideration gives way to two additional binary tree types, complete and height-balanced.

Suppose we use the numbering scheme to assign labels to nodes of a full binary tree, as in Figure 5b. The root is labeled 1. Then we assign consecutive integer labels to the nodes at each level from left to right. This way, the rightmost node at the last level for a full tree of depth 4 will have a label of 15. Based on this label assignment scheme, we define a complete binary tree as follows.

> A **complete binary tree** of depth d with n nodes is a binary tree whose nodes correspond to the nodes numbered 1 to n in the full binary tree of the same depth.

Figure 5c shows a complete binary tree of 11 nodes that has a depth of 4. Every branch is either of depth 4 or 3. Generalizing, all branches of a complete binary tree of depth d are of depth d or (d − 1). Therefore, a complete binary tree is reasonably balanced and is the next best thing to a full binary tree as far as searching is concerned.

Height-Balanced Binary Trees

One problem is that, given a certain number of nodes, the corresponding complete binary tree conforms to a fixed template, as in Figure 5c, which is necessarily left-heavy. A reasonably balanced binary tree with no such limitation is a height-balanced binary tree (also called an AVL tree after its inventors, Adelson-Velskii and Landis).

> A **height-balanced binary tree** is one in which, for every node, the difference in height of the left and right subtrees does not exceed 1.

Figure 5d shows three different height-balanced trees, all of 7 nodes. In each tree, for each node the difference between left and right subtree heights is either zero or 1. The rightmost AVL tree is also a full binary tree of depth 3.

REVIEW QUESTIONS

1. In a nonlinear data structure, each node may have one or more logical predecessors and successors. (T or F)
2. A chart showing the descendants of people is called a _____ genealogical chart, whereas one showing the ancestors of people is a _____ genealogical chart.
3. By definition a tree is a _____ and _____ digraph.
4. In a binary tree every node can have _____, _____, or _____ child nodes.
5. The height of a left-skewed binary tree of six nodes is 6. (T or F)
6. A binary tree of depth d with n nodes that correspond to the nodes numbered 1 to n in the full binary tree of the same depth is called _____.
7. A binary tree in which, for every node, the difference in height of the left and right subtrees does not exceed 1 is called _____.

Answers: 1. T; 2. lineal, pedigree; 3. acyclic, connected; 4. zero, one, two; 5. T; 6. complete; 7. height-balanced.

Storage Representation of Tree Structures

Nodes of a tree used as a data structure have labels, data, and pointers associated with them. Labels are identifiers that distinguish one node from the others. They may be a name, a digit, a letter, or address of memory location that stores data belonging to the node in the computer's memory.

Data stored in a node may be a single data item value or a composite field value, such as a record. The tree structure in Figure 2b has records associated with its nodes.

Finally, each node has some pointers that identify its child nodes. The number of pointers associated with a given node depends on the number of its descendants.

A storage structure for trees should be capable of representing node labels, data values associated with each node, and parent-child relationships between each pair of nodes. Trees can be represented in the memory in a variety of different ways, including simple lists and, for special tree structures, even arrays. In general, however, linked lists are best suited for trees, general or binary.

Figure 6 shows a memory structure suitable for a general tree such as the one in Figure 3. It is based on a cell structure consisting of an explicit or implicit field for node label, fields to store data carried by a node, and a sufficient number of pointer fields linking the node to its descendants. For a general tree, the number of pointer fields varies for each node. For the general tree of Figure 3, the maximum number of descendants is four for node 2. Therefore, in Figure 6 we provide four pointer fields in each cell.

The pointer fields contain some linkage information connecting each cell to cells that store information about its child nodes. The nature of the pointer

TREE-ROOT

TREE-NAME	POINTER-TO-ROOT
TREE-A	1

NODE-LABEL
(Relative address)

	DATA	1ST-CHILD-PTR	2ND-CHILD-PTR	3RD-CHILD-PTR	4TH-CHILD-PTR
1	Data ..	2	3	4	*
2	Data ..	5	6	7	8
3	Data ..	9	10	11	*
4	Data ..	*	*	*	*
5	Data ..	*	*	*	*
6	Data ..	*	*	*	*
7	Data ..	*	*	*	*
8	Data ..	*	*	*	*
9	Data ..	*	*	*	*
10	Data ..	*	*	*	*
11	Data ..	*	*	*	*

Figure 6 Memory Representation of the General Tree of Figure 3

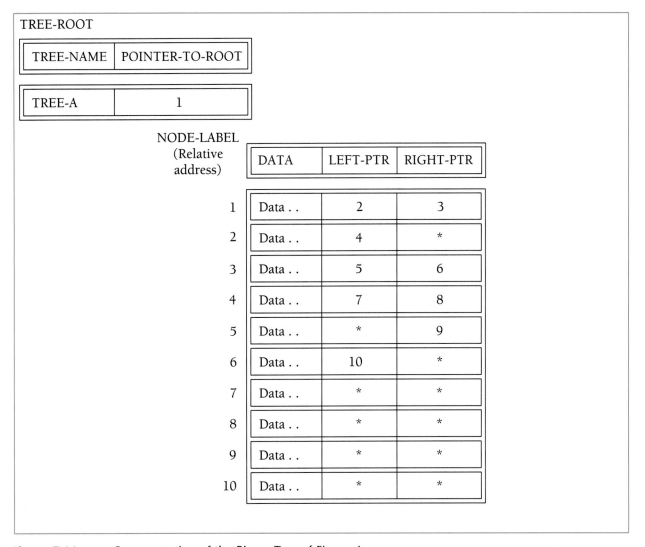

Figure 7 Memory Representation of the Binary Tree of Figure 4

field contents depends on the built-in data structure for the storage structure used for the tree. In a relative file, the data field and pointer fields of the cell structure of Figure 6 can be incorporated into the record structure of the file, and the node label field values can be relative bucket addresses. In this case, pointer fields also contain relative bucket addresses of child nodes.

Such a storage structure for a general tree is wasteful of memory in that many nodes in Figure 6 have fewer than four descendants. This is shown by including the end-of-list marker, *, in pointer fields. For a binary tree, the storage waste is minimized because, as shown in Figure 7, number of pointer fields per node is two, one for the left child and one for the right child. Figure 7 is the storage structure for the binary tree of Figure 4. Note that both in Figures 6 and 7, the tree root is pointed to in a separate cell. To access nodes in the tree we first access the root cell, and using the pointer in it, we enter the tree structure. We use this storage structure in the application program for this chapter.

Transforming General Trees into Binary Trees

As mentioned, it is desirable to transform a general tree into an equivalent binary tree before processing it in application programs. This stems from the difficulty of representing general trees in memory. Different techniques exist to make the transformation, but they should preserve basic structural properties of the general tree with respect to data stored in it and relationships represented by it.

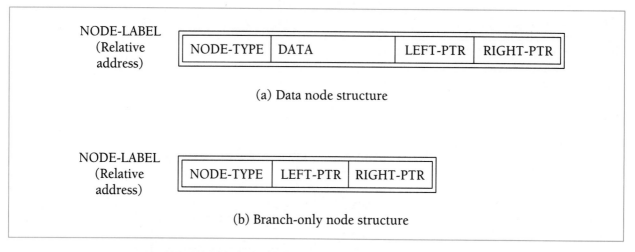

NODE-LABEL
(Relative
address)

| NODE-TYPE | DATA | LEFT-PTR | RIGHT-PTR |

(a) Data node structure

NODE-LABEL
(Relative
address)

| NODE-TYPE | LEFT-PTR | RIGHT-PTR |

(b) Branch-only node structure

Figure 8 Data and Branch-Only Node Structures

One transformation technique makes use of branch-only cells in the tree in addition to data cells.

> A **branch-only cell** represents a node with no data and a left and a right pointer.

The structures of data and branch-only cells are shown in Figure 8. In a data cell used to represent a tree node with two descendants, we have a NODE-TYPE field, fields to store data, a left pointer, and a right pointer. NODE-TYPE is used to distinguish it as a data cell. In contrast, the cell structure for a branch-only node has a NODE-TYPE field, and two pointer fields, LEFT-PTR and RIGHT-PTR. Branch-only nodes do not store data. If a binary tree with branch-only nodes is implemented within a file, we should define a multiple-record file with two record structures. The transformation process is easily done.

Step 1: If a node in the general tree has zero, one, or two descendants, maintain it in the binary tree without any change.

Step 2: If, however, a node in the general tree has more than two descendants, keep the first descendant as the left subtree of that node, and insert a branch-only node as the root of its right subtree, attaching the remaining descendants to the branch-only node.

Step 3: Continue this process until all nodes in the transformed tree have no more than two descendants, thus rendering it a binary tree.

Figure 9 shows an example of this transformation process. The tree shown at the top is a general tree. Root node 1 has three descendants, so we keep the child node 2 as the left subtree, introduce a branch-only node labeled B1 as the root of the right subtree, and attach the child nodes 3 and 4 to B1. A complete application of this transformation produces the binary tree shown at the bottom of the figure.

It should be noted that the two trees are not exactly the same; however, the fundamental parent-child relationships have been maintained. For example, in the transformed tree, the parent node for node 7 is found by moving up three levels until a data node, node 2, is encountered. The child nodes for any given node can be reached by moving down along some branch, ignoring branch-only nodes during traversal until a data node is encountered. A branch-only

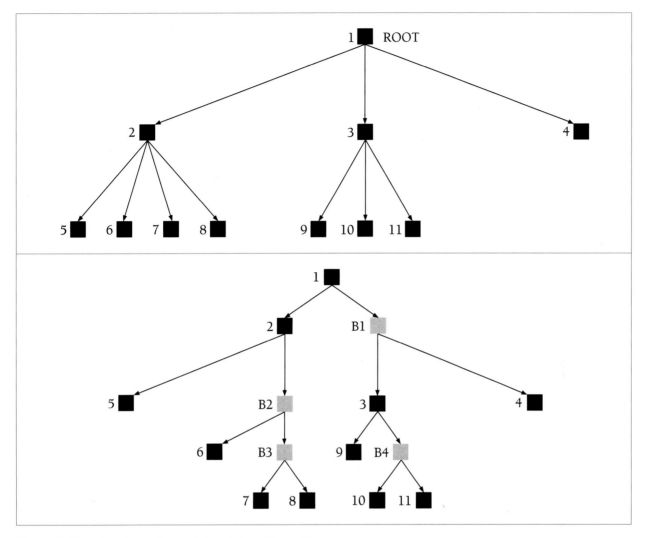

Figure 9 Transforming a General Tree into a Binary Tree

node is obviously never a terminal node in the transformed binary tree. One disadvantage of this process is the extra storage needed for branch-only nodes, but that is a small price to pay for its benefits that become apparent during tree processing.

Figure 10 shows a memory structure for the transformed binary tree of Figure 9. NODE-TYPE for data nodes has the value D, and for the branch-only nodes its value is B. The tree is stored in a relative file. The data nodes are in buckets 1 through 11. Buckets 21 through 24 are reserved for branch-only nodes.

Searching Binary Trees

As in any data structure, one of the most important operations on a binary tree is searching it for a data element. Searching a tree calls for traversing it methodically. If a certain traversal pattern tends to produce an ordered sequence of data values stored in nodes with respect to some data field, such a tree is called an **ordered binary tree** (more specifically, a binary search tree, as discussed below). Efficient search techniques can be developed for ordered binary trees. Trees that are not ordered can be searched only exhaustively.

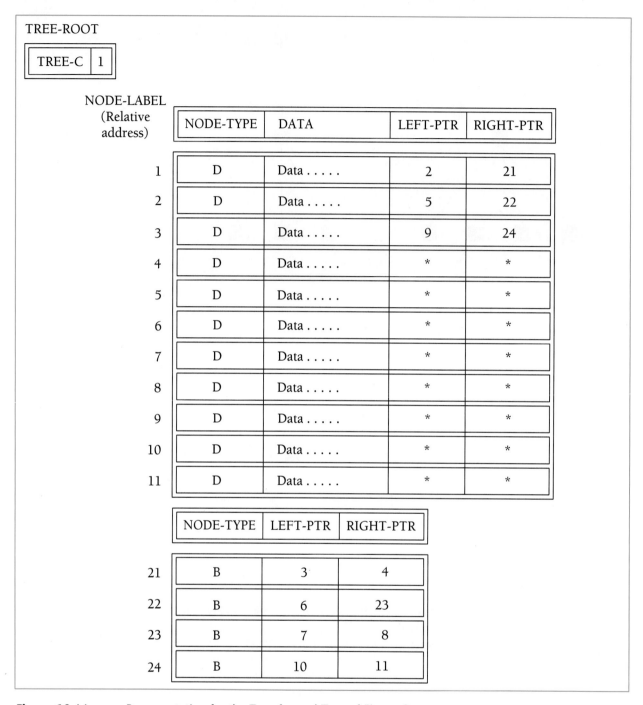

Figure 10 Memory Representation for the Transformed Tree of Figure 9

Exhaustive Search: Binary Tree Traversal Techniques

In an exhaustive search of a binary tree we have to visit and examine every node exactly once without bypassing any. For this, some methodical traversal procedures are needed. The three most commonly used are preorder, in-order, and postorder traversals.

In all of these procedures we enter the tree at its root, take the leftmost branch and go down until we encounter a leaf, and move up and to the right until all nodes have been visited. We note that a binary tree has three components: a root node, a left subtree, and a right subtree. These can be used to define three distinct combinations.

1. Node, left subtree, right subtree: the basis for preorder traversal
2. Left subtree, node, right subtree: the pattern for in-order traversal
3. Left subtree, right subtree, node: the pattern for postorder traversal

Preorder Traversal. In preorder traversal we first consider a node, then its left subtree, and finally its right subtree. A nonrecursive procedure has the following steps.

Step 1: Enter the tree at its root, mark the root, and take the leftmost branch to go down.

Step 2: Mark each node encountered along the leftmost branch until the first leaf is found.

Step 3: Mark the first leaf, which is the left subtree of the last node that was marked in step 2.

Step 4: Move up to the parent node of the first leaf and go down the rightmost untraversed branch in the remainder of the tree, doing the tasks described in steps 2 through 4, until the tree is fully traversed.

Figure 11a shows an example binary tree and the direction of traversal. Figure 11b illustrates the order in which the nodes are visited for preorder traversal. The first node encountered after we enter the tree is node 1. Along the leftmost branch we visit nodes 2 and 4. Node 7 is the first leaf; we mark it, also. Then we move up to 4, and come down to 8, including it in the node sequence. So far we have the node sequence (1, 2, 4, 7, 8) in which (4, 7, 8) is according to the pattern node, left subtree, right subtree for the subtree consisting of the nodes 4, 7, and 8. The string in Figure 11b shows the nested subtrees in the binary tree represented in accordance with the pattern for preorder traversal. The notation ( ) stands for an empty subtree. When parentheses are omitted, we get the node sequence (1, 2, 4, 7, 8, 3, 5, 9, 6, 10). This is the order in which the nodes are visited for exhaustive processing.

Figure 12 illustrates the steps in a computer implementation of the preorder traversal technique for the binary tree of Figure 11a. It can easily be generalized and coded as a COBOL procedure. In Figure 12 we make use of a stack to remember the right subtrees that have not been processed yet, and a queue to store the node sequence produced by preorder traversal. Otherwise, the logic of the figure is essentially similar to the algorithm described for preorder traversal. Let us examine closely some of the steps involved.

We enter the tree at its root, node 1. We push node 1 into the node sequence queue and take the left pointer to access the next node. Whenever the left pointer of an accessed node is not empty (i.e., it does not contain the symbol *) we push it into the queue. Also, while processing a node, whenever we find that the right pointer is not empty we push the right pointer value into the stack. This way, at the end of step 3 in Figure 12 we have the sequence (8, 3, *) in the stack of right subtrees, and the node sequence (4, 2, 1) in the queue.

If the left pointer of an accessed node is empty, we can no longer proceed using the left pointer. In this case, we push the node label into the queue, and pop the stack of right subtrees to get a new label to determine which node we should access next. We pursue this logic until the left pointer of the last node accessed is empty, and at the same time the stack is empty. Then we will have traversed the entire tree. Finally, we empty out the queue, remembering that the first element out is the first element that has been put into it. This will be the node sequence according to preorder traversal, and it can be used later to search the tree exhaustively.

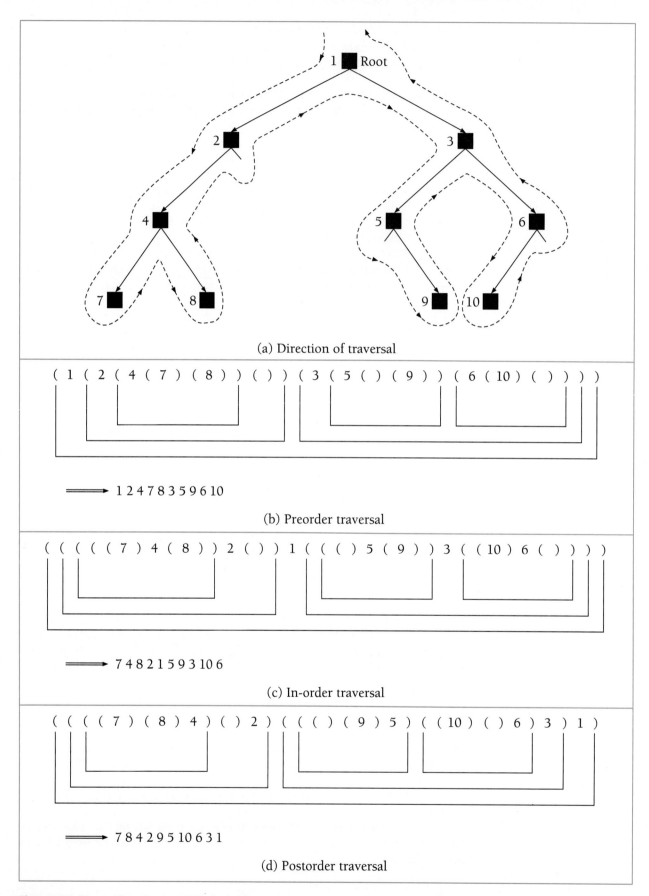

(a) Direction of traversal

(1 (2 (4 (7) (8)) ( )) (3 (5 ( ) (9)) (6 (10) ( ))))

⟹ 1 2 4 7 8 3 5 9 6 10

(b) Preorder traversal

(((((7) 4 (8)) 2 ( )) 1 ((( ) 5 (9)) 3 ((10) 6 ( ))))

⟹ 7 4 8 2 1 5 9 3 10 6

(c) In-order traversal

((((7) (8) 4) ( ) 2) ((( ) (9) 5) ((10) ( ) 6) 3) 1)

⟹ 7 8 4 2 9 5 10 6 3 1

(d) Postorder traversal

Figure 11 Binary Tree Traversal Techniques

S T E P	N O D E	LEFT PTR	RIGHT PTR	STACK CONTENT		NEXT NODE OBTAINED FROM	NODE SEQUENCE QUEUE
				BEFORE ⟷	AFTER ⟷		⟹ ⟹
1	1	2	3	*	3 *	LEFT-PTR	1
2	2	4	*	3 *	3 *	LEFT-PTR	2 1
3	4	7	8	3 *	8 3 *	LEFT-PTR	4 2 1
4	7	*	*	8 3 *	3 *	STACK	7 4 2 1
5	8	*	*	3 *	*	STACK	8 7 4 2 1
6	3	5	6	*	6 *	LEFT-PTR	3 8 7 4 2 1
7	5	*	9	6 *	9 6 *	STACK	5 3 8 7 4 2 1
8	9	*	*	6 *	*	STACK	9 5 3 8 7 4 2 1
9	6	10	*	*	*	LEFT-PTR	6 9 5 3 8 7 4 2 1
10	10	*	*	*	*	—	10 6 9 5 3 8 7 4 2 1

Figure 12 Steps in Preorder Traversal of the Binary Tree of Figure 4

In-Order Traversal. In-order traversal is based on the pattern left subtree, node, right subtree. The following is a nonrecursive procedure description.

Step 1: Enter the tree at its root and, using the left pointers at each root, go down the leftmost branch until a leaf node is encountered.

Step 2: Mark that leaf, which is the left subtree of the previous node encountered during traversal, and move up to its parent node.

Step 3: Mark the parent node.

Step 4: Using the right pointer of the current node, go down one level, and traverse the leftmost branch of the subtree of the current node according to steps 1 through 4 until the entire tree is traversed.

Figure 11c illustrates in-order traversal applied to the binary tree of Figure 11a, and gives the node sequence according to which the tree is exhaustively processed. Figure 13 describes the steps involved in a nonrecursive algorithm for in-order traversal on the basis of the same example tree. In this algorithm we again use a stack to remember the right subtrees that have not yet been processed, and a queue to store the node sequence as the result of the tree traversal procedure. An explanation of Figure 13 is left as an exercise for the reader.

Postorder Traversal. Postorder traversal uses the pattern left subtree, right subtree, node. Figure 11d shows its application to the binary tree of Figure 11a. The logic of the procedure reflected in Figure 13 can be easily modified into an algorithm for postorder traversal.

Binary Search Trees

In some applications we can identify nodes in a binary tree structure by some data value stored in them. Then a special class of binary trees can be constructed such that an increasing or decreasing order becomes inherent in the set of data values identifying nodes. These are called binary search trees.

S T E P	N O D E	LEFT PTR	RIGHT PTR	STACK CONTENT BEFORE ⟷	STACK CONTENT AFTER ⟷	NEXT NODE OBTAINED FROM	NODE SEQUENCE QUEUE ⟹ ⟹
1	1	2	3	*	1 3 *	LEFT-PTR	−
2	2	4	*	1 3 *	2 1 3 *	LEFT-PTR	−
3	4	7	8	2 1 3 *	4 8 2 1 3 *	LEFT-PTR	−
4	7	*	*	4 8 2 1 3 *	4 8 2 1 3 *	STACK	−
5	7	*	*	4 8 2 1 3 *	8 2 1 3 *	STACK	7
6	4	−	−	8 2 1 3 *	2 1 3 *	STACK	4 7
7	8	*	*	2 1 3 *	1 3 *	STACK	8 4 7
8	2	−	−	1 3 *	3 *	STACK	2 8 4 7
9	1	−	−	3 *	*	STACK	1 2 8 4 7
10	3	5	6	*	3 6 *	LEFT-PTR	1 2 8 4 7
11	5	*	9	3 6 *	5 9 3 6 *	STACK	1 2 8 4 7
12	5	−	−	9 3 6 *	3 6 *	STACK	5 1 2 8 4 7
13	9	*	*	3 6 *	6 *	STACK	9 5 1 2 8 4 7
14	3	−	−	6 *	*	STACK	3 9 5 1 2 8 4 7
15	6	10	*	*	6 *	LEFT-PTR	3 9 5 1 2 8 4 7
16	10	*	*	6 *	10 6 *	STACK	3 9 5 1 2 8 4 7
17	10	−	−	6 *	6 *	STACK	10 3 9 5 1 2 8 4 7
18	6	−	−	*	*	−	6 10 3 9 5 1 2 8 4 7

Figure 13 Steps in In-Order Traversal of the Binary Tree of Figure 4

In a **binary search tree** each node contains an identifier. For all nodes in the tree except the leaves, the identifiers in the left subtree are all less than the identifier in the node, and the identifiers in the right subtree are all greater than that in the node.

Figure 14 shows an example binary search tree in which node identifiers are first names. In node 1 the identifier is CAROL, which is alphabetically larger than all node identifiers in the left subtree, and smaller than all node identifiers in the right subtree. Similarly, the identifier value JOHN in node 3 is larger than all node values in the left subtree of node 3 (GREG, DAVID, and HARRY) and smaller than all node values in the right subtree (ROGER and LINDA). This property is satisfied by all nodes in Figure 14 except the leaf nodes.

Three issues pertain to binary search trees: how to construct them, how to use them in searching a tree file, and the fact that their construction algorithm is also a sort algorithm. To construct a binary search tree we should be given a set of data values that will be stored in its nodes and also will be used as node

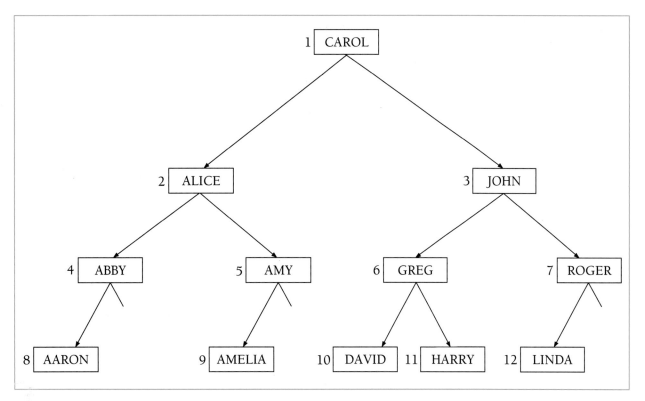

Figure 14 Example of a Binary Search Tree

identifiers. The node identifier data values may be accompanied by other data field values, as in a record occurrence.

The binary search tree construction algorithm can be described as follows.

Step 1: Access an available memory structure consisting of fields for the identifier data attribute, other accompanying data attributes, a left pointer field, and a right pointer field. This may be a cell structure as in Figure 8a. Store the data values corresponding to the first node identifier data value in their respective fields, and the end-of-list marker * in the left and right pointer fields. This node will be the root of the tree.

Step 2: Consider the second node identifier data value and the accompanying data values. Enter the tree at its root. Compare the new node identifier with that of the root node identifier. If the new node identifier is less than the root node identifier, and the left pointer field is not empty, take the left branch to go down to the root of the left subtree. Otherwise, take the right branch and go down to the root of the right subtree.

Step 3: Continue the process of step 2 until either the left or the right subtree of the node under consideration is empty. In this case, access an empty cell, fill it with data values and pointer values as in step 1, and update either the left or the right pointer of the tree node under consideration to point to the new cell. Store the new cell in the file.

An example of binary search tree construction is given in Figure 15. Consider the search tree of step 3 in the figure. Suppose AMY is to be inserted. We enter the binary search tree at its root and compare AMY with the root node identifier CAROL. As the comparison yields less than, we take the left branch

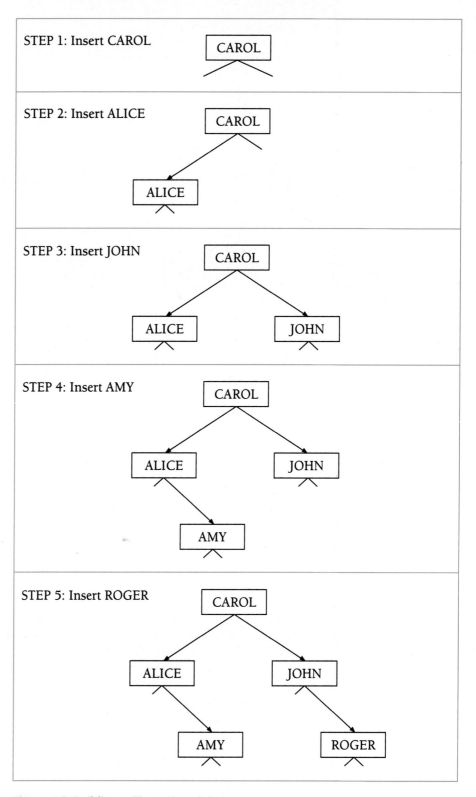

Figure 15 Building a Binary Search Tree

and access ALICE in the tree. Again, we compare and find that AMY is larger than ALICE. Also, the right subtree of the node ALICE is empty. Therefore, we attach AMY as the right child node of ALICE, as shown in step 4.

The shape of a binary search tree constructed for a given sequence of node identifier values depends on the order of entry of node identifiers. The first node identifier value is always associated with the root node, and the others are placed in the tree accordingly. It is interesting to note that an ordered sequence of node identifier values used in constructing a binary search tree yields a skewed tree, an unfortunate data structure.

Let us now consider the problem of searching a binary search tree. The search key is a data value that is compatible with the node identifier data values in the tree.

The binary tree search algorithm is a variation of the binary tree construction algorithm.

Step 1: Enter the binary search tree at its root.
Step 2: For every tree node accessed, compare the value of the search key with the node identifier. If they match, the search is successful and should be terminated. If the comparison yields less than, take the left branch to a lower-level node. Otherwise, take the right branch and access the right child node.
Step 3: Repeat step 2 until a match is found or the indicated left or right child pointer for the node under consideration is empty, in which case the search is unsuccessful.

This procedure is more efficient than an exhaustive search of a binary tree in that only nodes on a single branch have to be accessed and examined instead of all nodes in it. Therefore, the maximum number of node accesses is limited by the length of the longest branch.

Finally, we observe an interesting property of binary search trees; that is, in-order traversal produces an ordered sequence of node identifier values in increasing order. Because of this, binary search trees are also called ordered binary trees. For example, if we apply in-order traversal to the binary search tree of Figure 14, we get the sequence (AARON, ABBY, ALICE, AMELIA, AMY, CAROL, DAVID, GREG, HARRY, JOHN, LINDA, ROGER), which is in alphabetical order. Because of this property, binary search trees can be used as an internal or external sort technique, depending on whether the tree structure is internal to the main memory or a tree file.

Binary Tree File Creation, Maintenance, and Access Considerations

For binary tree files, as for any other data structure, the basic operations are file creation; file maintenance, which includes node insertion, deletion, and update; and node access, or search. A binary tree can either be ordered with respect to some node identifier data field, or it may be unordered. Accordingly, in our discussion of creation, maintenance, and access we will pay attention to both ordered and unordered binary trees.

Binary Tree File Creation

To create a binary tree file we must first select a built-in file organization technique that permits direct access to records. In COBOL we may decide to use an indexed sequential or a relative file.

If the binary tree file is unordered, an application program developed for the purpose of creating it has to be supplied the following information for each node:

1. The record to be stored in the node
2. The memory location (or node identifier data value) of its left child, if any
3. The memory location (or node identifier data value) of its right child, if any

If a binary tree file is intended to become a binary search tree (i.e., an ordered tree), we must supply only the records to be stored in its nodes. The routine is identical to the binary search tree creation algorithm.

Binary Tree File Maintenance: Record Update

For record update we must identify the node to be updated. This can be done either by supplying a memory location address or by a node identifier value. After this, a search is initiated to find and modify the record. If the tree is unordered, a tree traversal routine (preorder, in-order, or postorder) becomes necessary. For ordered trees, we can use the binary search tree search algorithm.

Binary Tree File Maintenance: Record Deletion

To delete a record we first specify it either by its memory location or by its node identifier. If the node to be deleted happens to be a leaf node in the tree, the operation is relatively simple. We have to locate the node to be deleted and its parent node. Then we sever the linkage between them by storing an end-of-list marker in the left or right pointer of the parent node, depending on which pointer links the parent node to the node to be deleted.

For example, to delete DAVID in the tree structure of Figure 14, we execute a search procedure and locate DAVID and its parent GREG. DAVID is stored in a leaf node, and its deletion will not have any direct bearing on any other node in the tree. Then we store an end-of-list marker in the left pointer field of the node for GREG. Here, a garbage collection routine may be useful to recover the bucket containing the deleted record.

If the node to be deleted is not a leaf node, simply cutting it from the tree structure may lead to undesirable results. We must decide what to do with its descendants. There are three possibilities.

1. We may decide to delete a node together with all of its descendants. This is illustrated in Figure 16a, which shows the tree structure of Figure 14 after GREG and all its descendants have been deleted.
2. It may be necessary to delete a record but maintain its descendants at their previous levels in the tree structure. This is illustrated in Figure 16b. Here, we wish to delete the record for GREG without deleting its descendants DAVID and HARRY. The correct procedural logic for this operation consists of searching the tree to locate the record for GREG and its parent node JOHN, accessing and defining a branch-only node at, say, location 13, changing the left pointer field for JOHN to point to the branch-only node, and copying the left and right pointer field values of GREG into left and right pointer fields of the branch-only node at location 13.
3. If the binary tree file is a binary search tree, and if after the delete operation it is important to maintain the order in the tree, we can proceed as follows. We access JOHN and GREG and break the linkage between them, which is the record we want to delete. Then we traverse the subtree whose root is GREG and store all the descendants of GREG into a temporary storage structure. This may be a stack or a queue. Next, we take the records thus saved and, using the binary search tree construction algorithm, insert the descendants of GREG back into the tree, ending with the binary search tree in Figure 16c.

Binary Tree File Maintenance: Record Insertion

To insert a new record into a binary tree we have to know where the new node is to be attached. If the tree is not ordered, we must specify the location explicitly. Figure 17a shows the configuration of a binary tree file after the record for BOB has been inserted as the left child of ABBY into the tree of Figure 14. It should be noted that this operation may be quite complicated, especially if the new record must have some already existing records as its descendants. Also, it

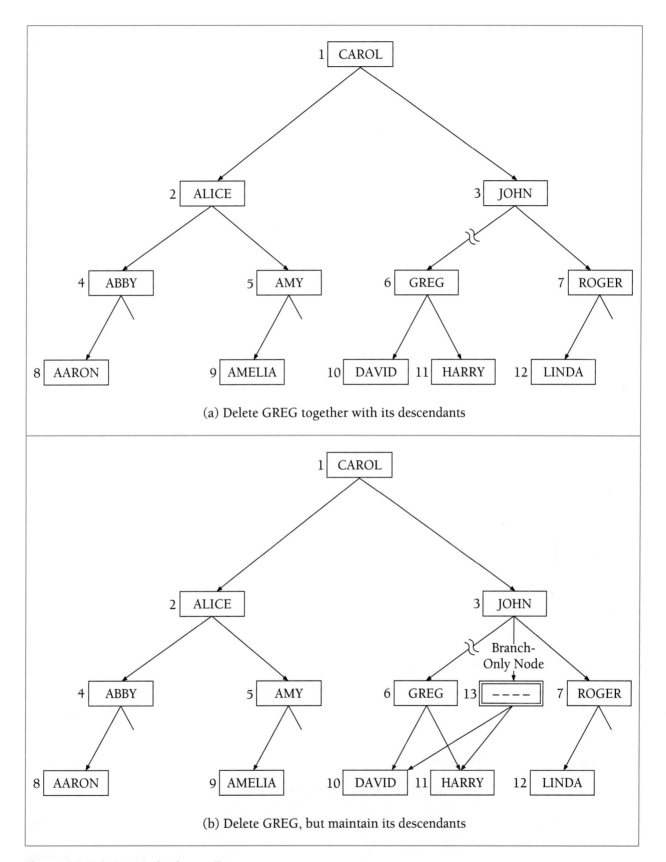

(a) Delete GREG together with its descendants

(b) Delete GREG, but maintain its descendants

Figure 16 Deleting Nodes from a Tree

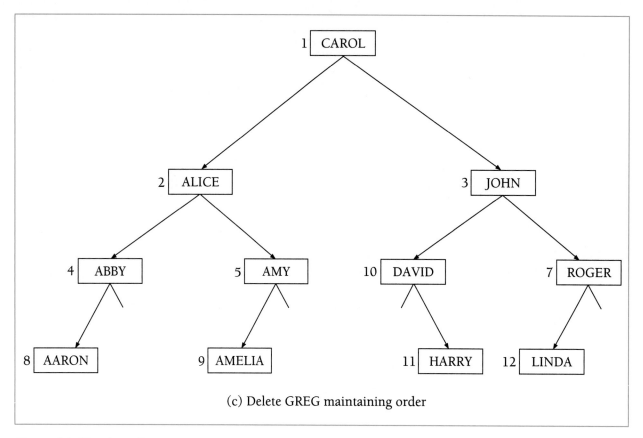

(c) Delete GREG maintaining order

Figure 16 (Continued)

should be noted that after such an insertion the initial binary search tree file may no longer remain as an ordered tree. This is the case in Figure 17a.

If the tree file is a binary search tree and should remain so after insertion, the binary search tree construction algorithm can be used to insert a new node. Figure 17b shows the binary search tree of Figure 14 after a new record for BOB has been inserted.

Binary Tree File Access

To access and retrieve a record in a binary tree file we must first identify it either by its location or by a node identifier. Then we can use an appropriate search algorithm. It can be an exhaustive search for an unordered tree, or the binary search tree search algorithm for an ordered tree.

The creation, maintenance, and access considerations for binary tree files are illustrated in the program example presented in the next section.

REVIEW QUESTIONS

1. The memory structure that can be used to represent nodes in a binary tree consists of node label, data, and _____ pointer fields.
2. A cell representing a tree node with no data and two pointers is called _____.
3. To search an unordered binary tree we have to use exhaustive tree traversal techniques. (T or F)
4. A binary tree can be exhaustively searched using _____, _____, or _____ traversal technique.

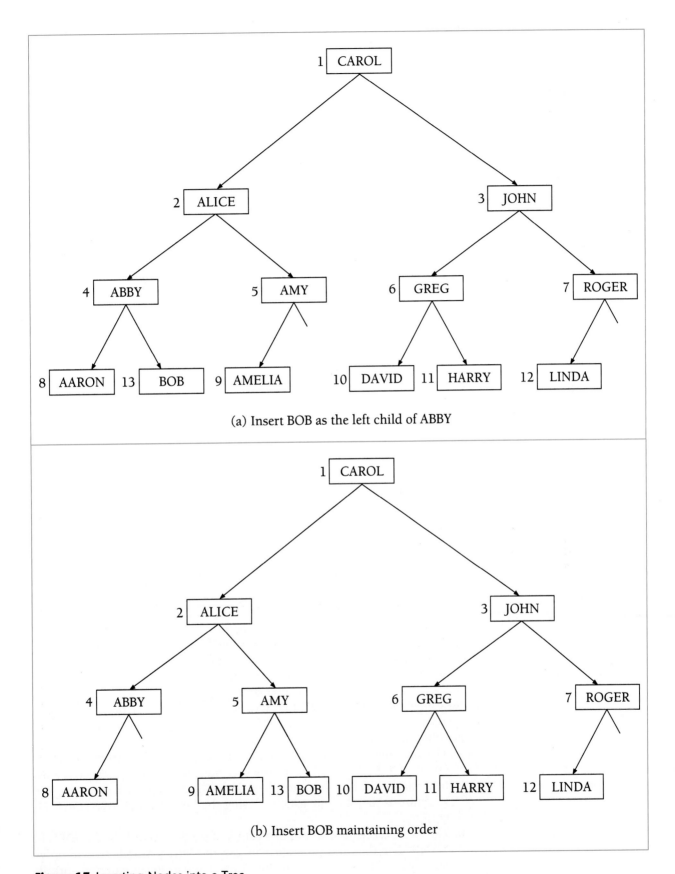

(a) Insert BOB as the left child of ABBY

(b) Insert BOB maintaining order

Figure 17 Inserting Nodes into a Tree

5. If in a binary tree the identifiers for all nodes in the left subtree of any given node are all less than the node identifier of the considered node, and identifiers of nodes in the right subtree are all greater than that of the node, the tree is called a _____ .

6. In a binary search tree, _____ traversal produces an ordered sequence of node identifiers.

Answers: 1. two; 2. branch-only cell; 3. T; 4. preorder, in-order, postorder; 5. binary search tree; 6. in-order.

Example Program 1:   Creating, Maintaining, and Searching a Binary Tree File

Here we develop a COBOL application program to process a binary tree file embedded in a relative file. We use it to illustrate some of the basic techniques discussed in this chapter.

Problem
As we have many new concepts and techniques to master in this chapter, we will not base the current application on a new problem. We are already familiar with the problem that was the essence of the application programs developed in Chapter 15. Here we take the same problem, but implement its underlying data structure as a binary search tree. To refresh our memory, we have a sequential student file, the same one as that of Program 1-Input in Chapter 15, whose record structure includes STUDENT-NAME, STUDENT-MAJOR, and STUDENT-AGE data fields. This sequential file will be stored within a relative file, called REL-STUDENT-FILE, as a binary search tree based on the STUDENT-NAME field. The relative file is assumed to consist of 200 buckets. The program is expected to do the following tasks.

1. First, it will build an empty space stack in the form of a linked list. The list head for the space stack will be stored in bucket 2. Initially, when the file is empty, buckets 3 through 200 will be incorporated into the space stack. This structure is the basis of a garbage collection routine. Whenever a data record is to be transferred from the sequential file to the relative file, the space stack will be popped to provide us with an empty bucket. The stack pop procedure is similar to that in Program 1 in Chapter 15.

2. After the space stack has been built, the program will read one record at a time from the sequential student file, and will include it in the relative file as a node of a binary search tree. For this purpose we will use the insertion algorithm to build the binary search tree. The tree root pointer will be stored in bucket 1 of the available relative-access cluster.

3. Now that the binary search tree has been structured on the basis of the available records in the sequential student file and the space stack is modified accordingly, the program will give the user two choices.
   a. The user may request that a record in the binary tree structure be accessed and displayed. For this, the user must supply a STUDENT-NAME field value, which is the search key. Then the program will enter the tree structure at its root and search it using the binary search tree search algorithm.
   b. The user may request an ordered listing of student records by STUDENT-NAME. For this, the program will use the binary search tree in-order traversal technique, which in this context serves as an external sort algorithm.

Again, the relative student file is a multiple-record file, with PRIME-RECORD used for data records, and INDEX-RECORD for the tree root pointer and data stack list head entries. The record structures are similar to those in the programs developed for Chapter 15, except for the DATA-RECORD-STATUS and INDEX-RECORD-STATUS flag fields.

Solution   The COBOL program developed for this problem is presented in Program 1-Source, which contains implementations of several techniques discussed in this chapter. It also contains a variety of data structures; therefore, it may be instructive if we take a closer look at it.

The main program paragraph, A-MONITOR-PROCEDURE, first invokes a subprocedure B1-BUILD-SPACE-STACK. This subprocedure constructs a linked list of buckets 3 through 200, and is quite similar to the implementation of the data space stack in the sample programs of Chapter 15. In addition to the space stack, it builds and stores the TREE-ROOT index entry in bucket 1 (lines 00184–00190). For the time being, the tree is nonexistent, and hence, the pointer field, START-ADDRESS, associated with this index entry has the value 999 (999 is used as the end-of-list indicator in this application program).

Next, the main procedure calls on B2-BUILD-BINARY-SEARCH-TREE, in which the sequential student file and its relative counterpart, SEQ-STUDENT-FILE and REL-STUDENT-FILE, are opened in input and I-O modes, respectively. Then, for every record coming from SEQ-STUDENT-FILE, the module C2-LOAD-RELATIVE-FILE is executed. In this module, an available data bucket is obtained by popping the space stack through an execution of the procedure D1-POP-DATA-STACK. The student record is then built into the WORKING-STORAGE-SECTION structure WS-PRIME-RECORD, with the value 999 stored in the LEFT-PTR and RIGHT-PTR fields (lines 00270–00273). After this the tree root index entry is accessed to allow entry into the tree. If the data record is the first into the tree, it is stored as its root. That it is the tree root is indicated in the updated index entry (lines 00282–00287). Otherwise, a search algorithm for the binary search tree is triggered to find the point of insertion for the new record. This search algorithm is represented by the procedures D3-FIND-INSERTION-POINT and D4-COMPLETE-CONSTRUCTION. The proper point of insertion is found by searching the tree using STUDENT-NAME as the search key.

After the binary search tree is built completely for all records in the sequential file, the user is given choices in the paragraph B3-DO-NEXT-OPERATION based on the value supplied for the variable OPERATION-CODE. The value A for OPERATION-CODE initiates a search for the student record, provided the user enters a student name value. This search algorithm is somewhat similar to the insertion algorithm used previously. It is reflected in paragraph C3-ACCESS-A-RECORD and its subordinates D5-FIND-RECORD and E3-SEARCH-BINARY-TREE. If the supplied student name value is not found in the binary search tree, the user is informed of its nonexistence.

Another choice the user is given in B3-DO-NEXT-OPERATION is to get a complete listing of records in the binary tree by STUDENT-NAME. The value L for OPERATION-CODE indicates this choice. The paragraph C4-GET-LISTING triggers an in-order traversal algorithm in the form of the paragraph D6-TRAVERSE-INORDER and its subprocedure E4-CONTINUE-TRAVERSAL. The in-order traversal logic inherent in these paragraphs is the implementation of the logic described in Figure 13. For this purpose, we use two auxiliary structures as one-dimensional arrays called BRANCH-STACK and NODE-QUEUE. BRANCH-STACK is a stack into which right child nodes and current node labels are pushed during traversal. Whenever we cannot use the left pointer for a node, this stack is popped to continue traversal. NODE-QUEUE is used to store the relative addresses for the nodes that are processed fully during the traversal. The in-order traversal is terminated if we come across a terminal

```
                  COLUMNS
          5    10   15   20   25   30   35   40   45
     ----|----|----|----|----|----|----|----|----|--

     001ITREE-ROOT              003
     002IDATASTACK              013
     003DWILLIAM BLACK               MTH22004999
     004DJOHN HANSEN                 CS 21005006
     005DJANE GRAY                   CS 23008999
     006DMARY CHEN                   MTH21011007
     007DRUSSELL THOMPSON            BUS20999999
     008DANNE NEAL                   BUS19009010
     009DALICE KROGER                BUS21999999
     010DDAVID HILLMAN               CS 26999999
     011DKELLY TOWERS                MTH22999012
     012DLAUREN THOMAS               BUS19999999
     013D                              014999

     . . . . . . . . . . . . . . . . . . . . . . . . . .

     . . . . . . . . . . . . . . . . . . . . . . . . . .
     198D                              199999
     199D                              200999
     200D                              999999
```

Figure 18 An Instance of Data Structures Built by Program 1

node in the tree and if, at the same time, the BRANCH-STACK is empty (lines 00409–00416). The program execution is terminated by typing the value T for OPERATION-CODE.

Figure 18 gives an instance of the data structures generated by this application program. Figure 19 depicts graphically the tree structure and the space stack after the sequential student file has been completely transferred to the relative student file. Program 1-Output is a listing of an interactive terminal session for Program 1.

It should be noted that this application program can be expanded further by adding to it routines for accessing and updating data records, and for deleting them. As we have already laid a foundation for garbage collection in this program, record deletion should make use of it. To delete a record, first a student name should be supplied. Using this name value as the search key, the record should be located and its descendants temporarily stored in an appropriate storage structure. Such a structure may be a stack or a queue. Both the bucket storing the record to be deleted and all of its descendants should be severed from the tree and should be recovered by pushing them into the space stack. After this, all descendant records should be inserted one at a time into the binary search tree, thereby maintaining the order inherent in it. This is left as an exercise for the reader.

Key Terms

binary search tree
binary tree
branch-only cell
child node
complete binary tree
forest
full binary tree
height
height-balanced binary tree
in-order traversal
intermediate node
leaf node

level
network structure
nonlinear data structure
ordered binary tree
parent node
postorder traversal
preorder traversal
root
skewed tree
tree
zigzag tree

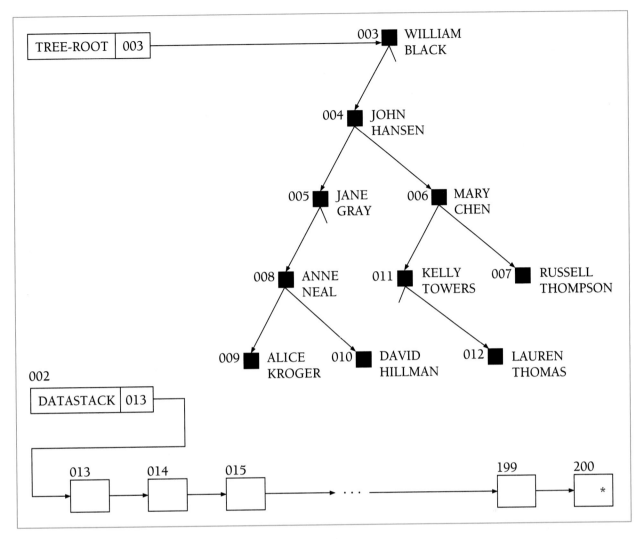

Figure 19 Binary Search Tree and Space Stack of Figure 18

Study Guide   **Quick Scan**

- In certain business-oriented applications, the application programs make use of nonlinear data structures. These represent complex relationships among data elements in which each data node has one or more logical successors and predecessors.

- Networks and trees are two important nonlinear data structures. Networks are more complex and difficult to process than trees. In some computer applications network structures can be decomposed into equivalent tree structures. Tree structures have been investigated extensively, and many techniques have been devised to resolve problems involving them. For these reasons, they are emphasized in this chapter.

- Tree structures are encountered as natural representation techniques in a variety of applications. Some examples are program structures in structured programming, lineal and pedigree genealogical charts, organization charts, data base models, and data structuring in indexing techniques.

- A tree is a connected graph structure containing no cycles. It consists of nodes representing data elements, and arcs representing relationships. It is a hierarchical structure that defines different levels.

- Each arc in a tree essentially stands for a relationship between a parent node and a child node. A parent node is at a higher level of hierarchy than its child node. A node may have only one parent but any number of child nodes, including none.

- A tree contains only one node with no parent. This node is called the root. As a matter of convention, entry into a tree structure is always at the root node. Some nodes have no child nodes. They are called leaf nodes.

- The root node in a tree constitutes level 1. Its child nodes are said to be at level 2, and so on. The height or depth of a tree is the maximum level of any node in it. The depth of a tree is also the number of nodes on its longest branch. A branch is a path from the root to a leaf node.

- A tree structure with no restrictions on the number of child nodes for any of its nodes is called a general tree. If the number of child nodes is restricted to a maximum of 2, it is called a binary tree.

- Binary trees are predominant in a variety of computer applications. They can be easily represented in the computer storage, and we know a lot about them. Consequently, it is common practice to transform a general tree into an equivalent binary tree prior to processing.

- Each node in a binary tree may have a left child and a right child node. The left child node of a node with all of its descendants defines a subtree, which is the left subtree of that node. A node also has a right subtree, empty or otherwise.

- There are several types of binary trees, including skewed and zigzag, full and complete, and height-balanced binary trees. As balanced height for each node tends to optimize search processes confined to its branches, this is an important consideration.

- A tree can be represented in computer storage using a special cell structure. Each occurrence of this cell structure corresponds to a node in the tree. The cell structure for a general tree consists of a node identifier, a field for storing data, and an arbitrary number of pointer fields, each specifying the location storing a child node. For a binary tree the cell structure is simpler. It involves a node identifier, a data field, and two pointer fields, one for the node's left child and one for its right child. If for a node either the left child or right child or both are nonexistent, the corresponding pointer fields contain the end-of-list marker, *.

- A general tree can be transformed into an equivalent binary tree in a variety of ways. One method that preserves the original parent-descendants relationships uses an additional node structure for branch-only nodes. A branch-only node contains a node identifier, a left child pointer, and a right child pointer. It does not provide for data storage. In transforming a general tree into a binary tree, one or more branch-only nodes are introduced whenever we encounter a node with more than two child nodes. This process is carried out until all nodes in the tree have no more than two child nodes.

- As for all data structures, searching is an important process for binary trees. The search algorithm to be used depends on whether the binary tree reflects some order based on a set of values stored in its nodes. If it is unordered, the only applicable search technique is a systematic exhaustive search.

- For an exhaustive search of a binary tree, every one of its nodes must be accessed and examined exactly once. This requires tree traversal. The three commonly used binary tree traversal techniques are preorder, in-order, and postorder.

- In all techniques the tree is entered at its root node. Traversal continues down the leftmost branch, upward, and to the right until all nodes are visited.

- Noting that a binary tree has a root, a left subtree, and a right subtree, preorder traversal is based on the pattern node, left subtree, right subtree. In other words, we first visit the root node, then process its left subtree using the basic pattern, and finally process the right subtree similarly. The pattern for in-order traversal is left subtree, node, right subtree. Postorder traversal visits all nodes using the pattern left subtree, right subtree, node. All these strategies ensure an exhaustive search for binary trees.

- In certain applications a binary tree may be ordered with respect to some data value associated with its nodes. This is called a binary search tree. The identifier data value associated with each node is larger than all node identifiers for nodes in its left subtree, and smaller than all node identifiers for nodes in its right subtree.

- A binary search tree for a sequence of node identifiers can be constructed easily using the basic insertion algorithm. A new node is attached to the tree as a leaf node by going down a specific branch. In defining this branch, for each node visited we use the left child pointer if the new node identifier is less than that of the node. Otherwise, we use the right child pointer.

- A binary search tree can be searched efficiently using an algorithm that is a variation of the binary search tree insertion algorithm. In this technique, the maximum number of nodes that must be accessed is limited by the height of the longest tree branch.

- In-order traversal of a binary search tree produces an ordered sequence of node identifiers. Consequently, it is equivalent to a sort technique.

- Direct-access files may be used as storage structures for building and processing tree structured files. The record structure of such files has to be modified to contain a left and a right child pointer in addition to data values. Algorithms for building, maintaining (node insertion, deletion, or update), and accessing binary tree files depend on whether the binary tree is ordered or not.

Test Your Comprehension

Multiple-Choice Questions

1. Which of the following about a tree structure is correct?
   a. A tree may contain one or more cycles.
   b. A tree has only one root node with no parents.
   c. A leaf node in a tree may have no parents.
   d. The height of a tree is the total number of nodes in it.
2. Which of the following about binary trees is correct?
   a. All nodes in a binary tree have zero, one, or two child nodes.
   b. A skewed or zigzag binary tree has only one node at each level.
   c. In a full binary tree of depth 5, there are 31 nodes.
   d. All of the above are correct.
3. In exhaustively searching a binary tree, if the pattern that is followed conforms to left subtree, right subtree, node, this traversal technique is
   a. Preorder.
   b. In-order.
   c. Postorder.
   d. Searching an ordered binary tree
4. Which of the following statements concerning binary search trees is incorrect?
   a. A binary search tree is also called an ordered binary tree.
   b. A preorder traversal of a binary search tree produces an ordered sequence of node identifiers.
   c. In searching a binary search tree we enter the tree at its root, and take the left branch if the search argument is less than the root identifier.
   d. Searching a binary search tree is more efficient than preorder traversal.

Answers: 1. b; 2. d; 3. c; 4. b.

Short Essay Questions

1. Explain why tree structures are preferred to network structures.
2. Why are tree structures important in data processing?
3. Give brief definitions of the related concepts of tree, general tree, and binary tree.
4. What are the properties of the root node and leaf nodes in a tree?
5. Define the concept of level and the height (or depth) of trees.
6. Why are binary trees preferable to general trees in computer applications?
7. Briefly describe skewed and zigzag binary trees. Why should they be avoided as data structures?
8. Explain the differences between a full binary tree and a complete binary tree.
9. What is a height-balanced binary tree? Why is height balancing an important consideration for tree structures?
10. Explain how a general tree can be represented in internal and external storage. Then briefly describe the corresponding structures for a binary tree.
11. What is a branch-only node? How can we transform a general tree into a binary tree using branch-only nodes?
12. Briefly explain the preorder traversal algorithm for binary trees.
13. Give a description of the in-order traversal algorithm for binary trees.
14. How does postorder traversal differ from in-order traversal?
15. What is a binary search tree?
16. Describe the binary search tree construction algorithm.
17. Briefly describe the binary search tree search algorithm. Why is it more efficient than an exhaustive search?
18. How can we use a binary search tree as the basis for a sort algorithm?
19. Briefly discuss the important considerations for binary tree file creation.
20. Discuss the important considerations for binary tree file maintenance.

Improve Your Problem-Solving Ability

Exercises

1. Given is the general tree of 14 nodes in Figure 20.
   a. Draw a table as in Figure 6 to show the instance of the memory structure for this general tree.
   b. Using branch-only nodes, transform this general tree into an equivalent binary tree and represent the result as a graph.
   c. For the transformed binary tree, construct a table as in Figure 10 to show the instance of the memory structure for it.
2. Figure 21 shows a binary tree of 15 nodes.
   a. Is it an AVL tree? Explain why or why not.
   b. Write list expressions for this tree corresponding to preorder, in-order, and postorder traversals, as in Figure 11b–d.
   c. Show the steps involved in the preorder traversal of this tree in a tabular form that is similar to that in Figure 12.
   d. Show the steps involved in the in-order traversal of this tree in a table similar to that in Figure 13.
   e. Do the postorder traversal version of Figure 13 for the given tree.
3. Consider the binary tree of Figure 21 with the indicated node identifier values, which are shown in parentheses next to each node in the figure as two-digit integers. With these node identifiers, is this a binary search tree? Explain why or why not.
4. Given are the following four sequences of two-digit integers.
   a. {78, 66, 45, 23, 15}
   b. {15, 23, 45, 66, 78}

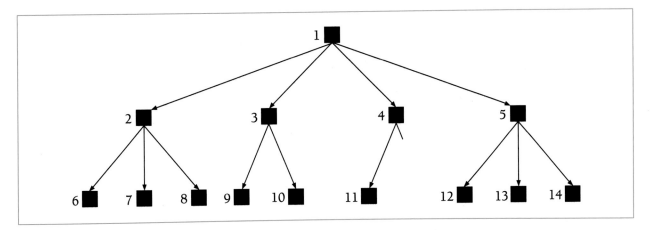

Figure 20 A General Tree of 14 Nodes

c. {78, 15, 66, 23, 45}
d. {66, 78, 45, 15, 23}
For each sequence, the first element is the first entry into a binary search, the second is the second entry, and so on. Accordingly, for each sequence, draw graphs showing the binary search trees that are constructed, and identify the type of each tree as one of the types we have covered in this chapter. What conclusions can you draw about binary search trees on the basis of your solution?

Programming Problem

1. Enhance Program 1 by including among its capabilities record update (of the STUDENT-MAJOR and STUDENT-AGE fields only) and record delete. Remember that after delete the tree should remain a binary search tree.

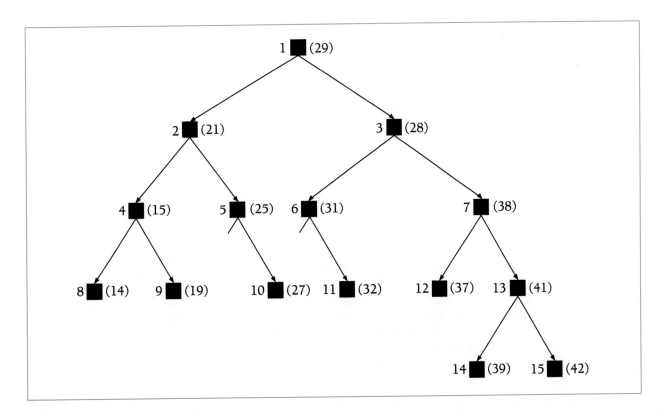

Figure 21 A Binary Tree

```
00001    *....................................................................
00002       IDENTIFICATION DIVISION.
00003       PROGRAM-ID.   BINARY-TREE-FILE-PROCESSING.
00004    **********************************************************************
00005    ***   THIS PROGRAM CREATES A BINARY SEARCH TREE FILE BASED ON      *
00006    ***   THE STUDENT-NAME DATA FIELD IN A RELATIVE STUDENT FILE.       *
00007    ***                                                                 *
00008    ***   THE STUDENT FILE HAS A RECORD STRUCTURE THAT CONSISTS OF      *
00009    ***   THE FOLLOWING BASE FIELDS:                                    *
00010    ***       1. A 25-BYTE STUDENT-NAME,                                *
00011    ***       2. A THREE-BYTE STUDENT-MAJOR, AND                        *
00012    ***       3. A TWO-BYTE STUDENT-AGE.                                *
00013    ***                                                                 *
00014    ***   THE STUDENT FILE IS A RELATIVE FILE OF 200 BUCKETS.  BUCKET   *
00015    ***   1 IS USED FOR THE TREE ROOT POINTER.  BUCKET 2 CONTAINS THE   *
00016    ***   DATA SPACE STACK LIST HEAD, USED FOR GARBAGE COLLECTION.      *
00017    ***   THE REMAINING BUCKETS, 3 THROUGH 200 ARE RESERVED FOR DATA    *
00018    ***   RECORD OCCURRENCES.                                           *
00019    ***                                                                 *
00020    ***   THE STUDENT FILE IS A MULTIPLE-RECORD FILE, WITH TWO RECORD   *
00021    ***   TYPES:                                                        *
00022    ***       1. INDEX RECORD, FOR TREE ROOT POINTER, AND STACK HEAD,   *
00023    ***       2. DATA RECORD.                                           *
00024    ***                                                                 *
00025    ***   ACCORDINGLY, THE MODIFIED DATA RECORD STRUCTURE FOR THE       *
00026    ***   RELATIVE STUDENT FILE INCLUDES THE FOLLOWING FIELDS:          *
00027    ***       1. A ONE-BYTE RECORD-TYPE ("D" FOR DATA RECORDS.)         *
00028    ***       2. A 25-BYTE STUDENT-NAME,                                *
00029    ***       3. A THREE-BYTE STUDENT-MAJOR,                            *
00030    ***       4. A TWO-BYTE STUDENT-AGE,                                *
00031    ***       5. A THREE-BYTE LEFT-POINTER FIELD, AND                   *
00032    ***       6. A THREE-BYTE RIGHT-POINTER FIELD.                      *
00033    ***                                                                 *
00034    ***   THE INDEX RECORD STRUCTURE IS:                                *
00035    ***       1. A ONE-BYTE RECORD-TYPE ("I" FOR INDEX RECORDS.)        *
00036    ***       3. A 20-BYTE INDEX-NAME FIELD, AND                        *
00037    ***       4. A THREE-BYTE START-ADDRESS FIELD.                      *
00038    ***                                                                 *
00039    ***   THE PROGRAM CAN DO THE FOLLOWING:                             *
00040    ***       1. READ SEQUENTIAL STUDENT FILE RECORD OCCURRENCES, ONE   *
00041    ***          AT A TIME, AND INSERT THEM INTO A BINARY SEARCH TREE   *
00042    ***          FILE,                                                  *
00043    ***       2. ACCESS A STUDENT RECORD OCCURRENCE IN THE TREE FILE    *
00044    ***          THAT IS SPECIFIED BY STUDENT-NAME, AND                 *
00045    ***       3. PRODUCE A COMPLETE LISTING OF RECORD OCCURRENCES IN    *
00046    ***          THE RELATIVE FILE ORDERED BY STUDENT-NAME.             *
00047    ***                                                                 *
00048    ***   A GARBAGE COLLECTION LOGIC IS INCORPORATED INTO THIS PRO-     *
00049    ***   RAM.  IT IS BASED ON A DATA AREA SPACE STACK.  FIRST THIS     *
00050    ***   SPACE STACK IS CREATED.  A DATA STACK POP PROCEDURE IS        *
00051    ***   CALLED UPON WHENEVER A DATA RECORD OCCURRENCE IS INSERTED.    *
00052    **********************************************************************
00053
```

Program 1-Source Program to Process a Binary Tree File

```
00054      AUTHOR.         UCKAN.
00055      DATE-WRITTEN.   SEPTEMBER 2, 1990.
00056      DATE-COMPILED.  SEP  7,1990.
00058      *.................................................................
00059      ENVIRONMENT DIVISION.
00060      CONFIGURATION SECTION.
00061      SOURCE-COMPUTER. UNIVERSITY-MAINFRAME.
00062      OBJECT-COMPUTER. UNIVERSITY-MAINFRAME.
00063      INPUT-OUTPUT SECTION.
00064
00065      FILE-CONTROL.
00066
00067          SELECT SEQ-STUDENT-FILE ASSIGN TO SEQDATA.
00068
00069          SELECT REL-STUDENT-FILE ASSIGN TO MASTER
00070                  ORGANIZATION IS RELATIVE
00071                  ACCESS MODE IS DYNAMIC
00072                  RELATIVE KEY IS BUCKET-NUMBER.
00073
00074      *.................................................................
00075      DATA DIVISION.
00076      FILE SECTION.
00077      FD   SEQ-STUDENT-FILE
00078           LABEL RECORDS ARE OMITTED
00079           DATA RECORD IS SEQ-STUDENT-RECORD
00080           RECORD CONTAINS 30 CHARACTERS.
00081
00082      01   SEQ-STUDENT-RECORD.
00083           05   SEQ-STUDENT-NAME      PIC X(25).
00084           05   SEQ-STUDENT-MAJOR     PIC X(3).
00085           05   SEQ-STUDENT-AGE       PIC X(2).
00086
00087      FD   REL-STUDENT-FILE
00088           LABEL RECORDS ARE STANDARD
00089           DATA RECORDS ARE PRIME-RECORD INDEX-RECORD
00090           RECORD CONTAINS 37 CHARACTERS.
00091
00092      01   PRIME-RECORD.
00093           05   DATA-RECORD-TYPE      PIC X.
00094           05   STUDENT-NAME          PIC X(25).
00095           05   STUDENT-MAJOR         PIC X(3).
00096           05   STUDENT-AGE           PIC XX.
00097           05   LEFT-PTR              PIC X(3).
00098           05   RIGHT-PTR             PIC X(3).
00099
00100      01   INDEX-RECORD.
00101           05   INDEX-RECORD-TYPE     PIC X.
00102           05   INDEX-NAME            PIC X(20).
00103           05   START-ADDRESS         PIC X(3).
00104           05   FILLER                PIC X(13).
00105
00106      WORKING-STORAGE SECTION.
00107
00108      **********> VARIABLES:
00109
```

Program 1-Source (Continued)

```
00110      01   OPERATION-CODE           PIC X.
00111      01   END-OF-INPUT             PIC 9.
00112      01   RECORD-FOUND             PIC XXX.
00113      01   RECORD-NOT-IN-TREE       PIC XXX.
00114      01   LEFT-CHILD               PIC XXX.
00115      01   RIGHT-CHILD              PIC XXX.
00116      01   TRAVERSAL-COMPLETED      PIC XXX.
00117      01   FROM-STACK               PIC XXX.
00118      01   FROM-LEFT-PTR            PIC XXX.
00119      01   SEARCH-NAME              PIC X(25).
00120      01   LINK-VALUE               PIC 999.
00121      01   BUCKET-NUMBER            PIC 999.
00122      01   SAVE-BUCKET-NUMBER       PIC 999.
00123      01   STACK-HEAD-POINTER       PIC 999.
00124      01   ARRAY-INDEX              PIC 999.
00125      01   QUEUE-INDEX              PIC 999.
00126      01   STACK-INDEX              PIC 999.
00127
00128   **********> STRUCTURES:
00129
00130      01   WS-PRIME-RECORD.
00131         05   WS-DATA-RECORD-TYPE      PIC X.
00132         05   WS-STUDENT-NAME          PIC X(25).
00133         05   WS-STUDENT-MAJOR         PIC X(3).
00134         05   WS-STUDENT-AGE           PIC XX.
00135         05   WS-LEFT-PTR              PIC 9(3).
00136         05   WS-RIGHT-PTR             PIC 9(3).
00137
00138      01   WS-INDEX-RECORD.
00139         05   WS-INDEX-RECORD-TYPE     PIC X.
00140         05   WS-INDEX-NAME            PIC X(20).
00141         05   WS-START-ADDRESS         PIC 9(3).
00142         05   FILLER                   PIC X(13).
00143
00144   **********> ARRAYS:
00145
00146      01   AUXILIARY-ARRAYS.
00147         05   BRANCH-STACK      PIC 999 OCCURS 200 TIMES.
00148         05   NODE-QUEUE        PIC 999 OCCURS 200 TIMES.
00149         05   NODE-VISITED      PIC 999 OCCURS 200 TIMES.
00150
00151   *........................................................................
00152   PROCEDURE DIVISION.
00153
00154   A-MONITOR-PROCEDURE.
00155      MOVE ZERO TO END-OF-INPUT.
00156
00157      DISPLAY "BUILDING EMPTY SPACE STACK... ".
00158
00159      PERFORM B1-BUILD-SPACE-STACK.
00160
00161      DISPLAY "INSERTING RECORD OCCURRENCES INTO THE TREE...".
00162
00163      PERFORM B2-BUILD-BINARY-SEARCH-TREE.
00164
```

Program 1-Source (Continued)

```
00165        DISPLAY "BINARY TREE FILE SUCCESSFULLY BUILT...".
00166
00167        DISPLAY "****> NOW YOU CAN ACCESS THE FILE.".
00168        DISPLAY " ".
00169
00170        OPEN INPUT REL-STUDENT-FILE.
00171
00172        MOVE "@" TO OPERATION-CODE.
00173
00174        PERFORM B3-DO-NEXT-OPERATION
00175             UNTIL OPERATION-CODE = "T"
00176
00177        CLOSE REL-STUDENT-FILE.
00178
00179        STOP RUN.
00180
00181    B1-BUILD-SPACE-STACK.
00182        OPEN OUTPUT REL-STUDENT-FILE.
00183
00184        MOVE 1          TO BUCKET-NUMBER.
00185        MOVE "I"          TO WS-INDEX-RECORD-TYPE.
00186        MOVE "TREE-ROOT" TO WS-INDEX-NAME.
00187        MOVE 999          TO WS-START-ADDRESS.
00188
00189        WRITE INDEX-RECORD FROM WS-INDEX-RECORD
00190             INVALID KEY DISPLAY "ERROR IN WRITING.".
00191
00192        MOVE 2          TO BUCKET-NUMBER.
00193        MOVE "I"          TO WS-INDEX-RECORD-TYPE.
00194        MOVE "DATASTACK" TO WS-INDEX-NAME.
00195        MOVE 3          TO WS-START-ADDRESS.
00196
00197        WRITE INDEX-RECORD FROM WS-INDEX-RECORD
00198             INVALID KEY DISPLAY "ERROR IN WRITING.".
00199
00200        PERFORM C1-BUILD-EMPTY-DATA-STACK
00201             VARYING BUCKET-NUMBER FROM 3 BY 1
00202                 UNTIL BUCKET-NUMBER > 199.
00203
00204        MOVE 200    TO BUCKET-NUMBER.
00205
00206        MOVE "D"    TO WS-DATA-RECORD-TYPE.
00207        MOVE SPACES TO WS-STUDENT-NAME WS-STUDENT-MAJOR
00208                 WS-STUDENT-AGE.
00209        MOVE 999    TO WS-LEFT-PTR WS-RIGHT-PTR.
00210
00211        WRITE PRIME-RECORD FROM WS-PRIME-RECORD
00212             INVALID KEY DISPLAY "ERROR IN WRITING.".
00213
00214        CLOSE REL-STUDENT-FILE.
00215
00216    B2-BUILD-BINARY-SEARCH-TREE.
00217        OPEN INPUT SEQ-STUDENT-FILE.
00218        OPEN I-O   REL-STUDENT-FILE.
```

Program 1-Source (Continued)

```
00219
00220          MOVE ZERO TO END-OF-INPUT.
00221
00222          READ SEQ-STUDENT-FILE
00223               AT END MOVE 1 TO END-OF-INPUT.
00224
00225          PERFORM C2-LOAD-RELATIVE-FILE
00226               UNTIL END-OF-INPUT = 1.
00227
00228          CLOSE SEQ-STUDENT-FILE  REL-STUDENT-FILE.
00229
00230      B3-DO-NEXT-OPERATION.
00231          DISPLAY " ".
00232          DISPLAY "****> CHOOSE ONE OF THE FOLLOWING OPERATIONS:".
00233          DISPLAY " ".
00234          DISPLAY "****> TO ACCESS A RECORD OCCURRENCE....... TYPE A".
00235          DISPLAY "****> TO GET A COMPLETE ORDERED LISTING.... TYPE L".
00236          DISPLAY "****> TO TERMINATE PROGRAM................. TYPE T".
00237          DISPLAY " ".
00238
00239          DISPLAY "****> ENTER AN OPERATION CODE:".
00240          ACCEPT OPERATION-CODE FROM CONSOLE.
00241
00242          IF OPERATION-CODE = "A"
00243                  PERFORM C3-ACCESS-A-RECORD
00244          ELSE
00245                  IF OPERATION-CODE = "L"
00246                          PERFORM C4-GET-LISTING
00247                  ELSE
00248                          IF OPERATION-CODE = "T"
00249                              NEXT SENTENCE
00250                          ELSE
00251                              DISPLAY "****> YOU HAVE ENTERED AN INCOR
00252      -    "RECT OPERATION CODE.  TRY AGAIN.".
00253
00254      C1-BUILD-EMPTY-DATA-STACK.
00255
00256          COMPUTE LINK-VALUE = BUCKET-NUMBER + 1.
00257
00258          MOVE "D"        TO WS-DATA-RECORD-TYPE.
00259          MOVE SPACES     TO WS-STUDENT-NAME WS-STUDENT-MAJOR
00260                             WS-STUDENT-AGE.
00261          MOVE 999        TO WS-RIGHT-PTR.
00262          MOVE LINK-VALUE TO WS-LEFT-PTR.
00263
00264          WRITE PRIME-RECORD FROM WS-PRIME-RECORD
00265               INVALID KEY DISPLAY "ERROR IN WRITING.".
00266
00267      C2-LOAD-RELATIVE-FILE.
00268          PERFORM D1-POP-DATA-STACK.
00269
00270          MOVE SEQ-STUDENT-NAME  TO WS-STUDENT-NAME.
00271          MOVE SEQ-STUDENT-MAJOR TO WS-STUDENT-MAJOR.
00272          MOVE SEQ-STUDENT-AGE   TO WS-STUDENT-AGE.
00273          MOVE 999               TO WS-LEFT-PTR WS-RIGHT-PTR.
```

Program 1-Source (Continued)

```
00274
00275          MOVE "NO"                    TO RECORD-FOUND LEFT-CHILD
00276                                          RIGHT-CHILD.
00277
00278          MOVE 1                       TO BUCKET-NUMBER.
00279          PERFORM E1-READ-REL-FILE-DIRECTLY.
00280
00281          IF START-ADDRESS = 999
00282                  MOVE SAVE-BUCKET-NUMBER TO START-ADDRESS
00283                  PERFORM E2-REWRITE-INDEX-RECORD
00284                  MOVE SAVE-BUCKET-NUMBER TO BUCKET-NUMBER
00285                  PERFORM E1-READ-REL-FILE-DIRECTLY
00286                  MOVE WS-PRIME-RECORD TO PRIME-RECORD
00287                  PERFORM D2-REWRITE-PRIME-RECORD
00288          ELSE
00289                  MOVE START-ADDRESS TO BUCKET-NUMBER
00290
00291                  PERFORM D3-FIND-INSERTION-POINT
00292                      UNTIL RECORD-FOUND = "YES"
00293                                      OR
00294                              LEFT-CHILD = "YES"
00295                                      OR
00296                              RIGHT-CHILD = "YES"
00297
00298                  PERFORM D4-COMPLETE-CONSTRUCTION.
00299
00300          READ SEQ-STUDENT-FILE
00301                  AT END MOVE 1 TO END-OF-INPUT.
00302
00303      C3-ACCESS-A-RECORD.
00304          DISPLAY "****> ENTER STUDENT NAME OF THE RECORD OCCURRENCE TO
00305      -    " BE RETRIEVED:".
00306          ACCEPT SEARCH-NAME FROM CONSOLE.
00307
00308          MOVE "NO" TO RECORD-FOUND RECORD-NOT-IN-TREE.
00309
00310          PERFORM D5-FIND-RECORD.
00311
00312          IF RECORD-FOUND = "YES"
00313                  DISPLAY " "
00314                  DISPLAY "STUDENT NAME : " STUDENT-NAME
00315                  DISPLAY "STUDENT MAJOR: " STUDENT-MAJOR
00316                  DISPLAY "STUDENT AGE  : " STUDENT-AGE
00317                  DISPLAY " ".
00318
00319          IF RECORD-NOT-IN-TREE = "YES"
00320                  DISPLAY "RECORD OCCURRENCE WITH NAME = " SEARCH-NAME
00321                          " IS NOT IN THE FILE.".
00322
00323      C4-GET-LISTING.
00324          MOVE ALL ZEROS TO AUXILIARY-ARRAYS.
00325          MOVE ZERO       TO STACK-INDEX QUEUE-INDEX.
00326
00327          MOVE "NO"       TO TRAVERSAL-COMPLETED.
00328          MOVE 1          TO BUCKET-NUMBER.
```

Program 1-Source (Continued)

```
00329
00330          PERFORM E1-READ-REL-FILE-DIRECTLY.
00331
00332          MOVE START-ADDRESS TO BUCKET-NUMBER.
00333
00334          PERFORM D6-TRAVERSE-INORDER
00335                  UNTIL TRAVERSAL-COMPLETED = "YES".
00336
00337          MOVE 1 TO ARRAY-INDEX.
00338
00339          PERFORM D7-ACCESS-AND-LIST
00340                  UNTIL NODE-QUEUE (ARRAY-INDEX) = 0.
00341
00342      D1-POP-DATA-STACK.
00343          MOVE 2 TO BUCKET-NUMBER.
00344          PERFORM E1-READ-REL-FILE-DIRECTLY.
00345
00346          MOVE START-ADDRESS TO BUCKET-NUMBER SAVE-BUCKET-NUMBER.
00347          PERFORM E1-READ-REL-FILE-DIRECTLY.
00348
00349          MOVE LEFT-PTR TO STACK-HEAD-POINTER.
00350
00351          MOVE 2        TO BUCKET-NUMBER.
00352          PERFORM E1-READ-REL-FILE-DIRECTLY.
00353          MOVE STACK-HEAD-POINTER TO START-ADDRESS.
00354          PERFORM E2-REWRITE-INDEX-RECORD.
00355
00356      D2-REWRITE-PRIME-RECORD.
00357          REWRITE PRIME-RECORD
00358              INVALID KEY DISPLAY "ERROR IN UPDATING PRIME RECORD.".
00359
00360      D3-FIND-INSERTION-POINT.
00361          PERFORM E1-READ-REL-FILE-DIRECTLY.
00362
00363          IF WS-STUDENT-NAME = STUDENT-NAME
00364                  MOVE "YES" TO RECORD-FOUND
00365          ELSE
00366                  IF WS-STUDENT-NAME < STUDENT-NAME
00367
00368                          IF LEFT-PTR = 999
00369                                  MOVE "YES" TO LEFT-CHILD
00370                          ELSE
00371                                  MOVE LEFT-PTR TO BUCKET-NUMBER
00372                  ELSE
00373                          IF RIGHT-PTR = 999
00374                                  MOVE "YES" TO RIGHT-CHILD
00375                          ELSE
00376                                  MOVE RIGHT-PTR TO BUCKET-NUMBER.
00377
00378      D4-COMPLETE-CONSTRUCTION.
00379
00380          IF LEFT-CHILD = "YES"
00381                  MOVE SAVE-BUCKET-NUMBER TO LEFT-PTR
```

Program 1-Source (Continued)

```
00382            ELSE
00383                    IF RIGHT-CHILD = "YES"
00384                        MOVE SAVE-BUCKET-NUMBER TO RIGHT-PTR.
00385
00386        IF RECORD-FOUND = "NO"
00387                PERFORM D2-REWRITE-PRIME-RECORD
00388                MOVE SAVE-BUCKET-NUMBER TO BUCKET-NUMBER
00389                PERFORM E1-READ-REL-FILE-DIRECTLY
00390                MOVE WS-PRIME-RECORD TO PRIME-RECORD
00391                PERFORM D2-REWRITE-PRIME-RECORD.
00392
00393    D5-FIND-RECORD.
00394        MOVE 1 TO BUCKET-NUMBER.
00395        PERFORM E1-READ-REL-FILE-DIRECTLY.
00396
00397        IF START-ADDRESS = 999
00398                MOVE "YES" TO RECORD-NOT-IN-TREE
00399        ELSE
00400                MOVE START-ADDRESS TO BUCKET-NUMBER
00401                PERFORM E3-SEARCH-BINARY-TREE
00402                    UNTIL RECORD-FOUND = "YES"
00403                               OR
00404                    RECORD-NOT-IN-TREE = "YES".
00405
00406    D6-TRAVERSE-INORDER.
00407        MOVE "NO" TO FROM-STACK FROM-LEFT-PTR.
00408
00409        IF LEFT-PTR = 999
00410                AND
00411          RIGHT-PTR = 999
00412                AND
00413          STACK-INDEX = 0
00414                MOVE "YES" TO TRAVERSAL-COMPLETED
00415        ELSE
00416                PERFORM E4-CONTINUE-TRAVERSAL.
00417
00418    D7-ACCESS-AND-LIST.
00419        MOVE NODE-QUEUE (ARRAY-INDEX) TO BUCKET-NUMBER.
00420
00421        PERFORM E1-READ-REL-FILE-DIRECTLY.
00422
00423        DISPLAY ARRAY-INDEX " " STUDENT-NAME " " STUDENT-MAJOR
00424                    " " STUDENT-AGE.
00425        ADD 1 TO ARRAY-INDEX.
00426
00427    E1-READ-REL-FILE-DIRECTLY.
00428        READ REL-STUDENT-FILE
00429            INVALID KEY DISPLAY "ERROR IN READING STUDENT FILE.".
00430
00431    E2-REWRITE-INDEX-RECORD.
00432        REWRITE INDEX-RECORD
00433            INVALID KEY DISPLAY "ERROR IN UPDATING INDEX RECORD.".
00434
00435    E3-SEARCH-BINARY-TREE.
00436        PERFORM E1-READ-REL-FILE-DIRECTLY.
```

Program 1-Source (Continued)

```
00437
00438          IF SEARCH-NAME = STUDENT-NAME
00439               MOVE "YES" TO RECORD-FOUND
00440          ELSE
00441               IF SEARCH-NAME < STUDENT-NAME
00442
00443                    IF LEFT-PTR = 999
00444                         MOVE "YES" TO RECORD-NOT-IN-TREE
00445                    ELSE
00446                         MOVE LEFT-PTR TO BUCKET-NUMBER
00447               ELSE
00448                    IF RIGHT-PTR = 999
00449                         MOVE "YES" TO RECORD-NOT-IN-TREE
00450                    ELSE
00451                         MOVE RIGHT-PTR TO BUCKET-NUMBER.
00452
00453     E4-CONTINUE-TRAVERSAL.
00454
00455          IF BUCKET-NUMBER NOT = 999
00456               PERFORM E1-READ-REL-FILE-DIRECTLY.
00457
00458          IF LEFT-PTR = 999
00459               AND
00460            NODE-VISITED (BUCKET-NUMBER) = 0
00461               MOVE "YES" TO FROM-STACK
00462               PERFORM F1-PUSH-RPTR-INTO-BRANCH-STACK
00463               PERFORM F2-PUSH-NODE-INTO-BRANCH-STACK
00464          ELSE
00465               IF NODE-VISITED (BUCKET-NUMBER) = 1
00466                    MOVE "YES" TO FROM-STACK
00467               ELSE
00468                    MOVE "YES" TO FROM-LEFT-PTR.
00469
00470          IF TRAVERSAL-COMPLETED = "NO"
00471               IF FROM-LEFT-PTR = "YES"
00472                    PERFORM F3-DO-FOR-FROM-LEFT-PTR
00473               ELSE
00474                    IF FROM-STACK = "YES"
00475                         PERFORM F4-DO-FOR-FROM-STACK.
00476
00477     F1-PUSH-RPTR-INTO-BRANCH-STACK.
00478
00479          IF RIGHT-PTR NOT = 999
00480               ADD 1 TO STACK-INDEX
00481               MOVE RIGHT-PTR TO BRANCH-STACK (STACK-INDEX).
00482
00483     F2-PUSH-NODE-INTO-BRANCH-STACK.
00484          ADD 1 TO STACK-INDEX
00485          MOVE BUCKET-NUMBER TO BRANCH-STACK (STACK INDEX).
00486
00487     F3-DO-FOR-FROM-LEFT-PTR.
00488          PERFORM F1-PUSH-RPTR-INTO-BRANCH-STACK.
00489          PERFORM F2-PUSH-NODE-INTO-BRANCH-STACK.
00490
```

Program 1-Source (Continued)

```
00491          MOVE 1 TO NODE-VISITED (BUCKET-NUMBER).
00492          MOVE LEFT-PTR TO BUCKET-NUMBER.
00493
00494      F4-DO-FOR-FROM-STACK.
00495          MOVE 1 TO NODE-VISITED (BUCKET-NUMBER).
00496          MOVE BRANCH-STACK (STACK-INDEX) TO BUCKET-NUMBER.
00497          SUBTRACT 1 FROM STACK-INDEX.
00498
00499          IF NODE-VISITED (BUCKET-NUMBER) = 1
00500                  PERFORM G1-PUSH-INTO-NODE-QUEUE.
00501
00502      G1-PUSH-INTO-NODE-QUEUE.
00503          ADD 1 TO QUEUE-INDEX.
00504          MOVE BUCKET-NUMBER TO NODE-QUEUE (QUEUE-INDEX).
```

Program 1-Source (Continued)

```
BUILDING EMPTY SPACE STACK...
INSERTING RECORD OCCURRENCES INTO THE TREE...
BINARY TREE FILE SUCESSFULLY BUILT...
****> NOW YOU CAN ACCESS THE FILE


****> CHOOSE ONE OF THE FOLLOWING OPERATIONS:


****> TO ACCESS A RECORD OCCURRENCE....... TYPE A
****> TO GET A COMPLETE ORDERED LISTING.... TYPE L
****> TO TERMINATE PROGRAM................ TYPE T


****> ENTER AN OPERATION CODE:
A
****> ENTER STUDENT NAME OF THE RECORD OCCURRENCE TO BE RETRIEVED:
MARY CHEN

STUDENT NAME : MARY CHEN
STUDENT MAJOR: MTH
STUDENT AGE  : 21



****> CHOOSE ONE OF THE FOLLOWING OPERATIONS:


****> TO ACCESS A RECORD OCCURRENCE....... TYPE A
****> TO GET A COMPLETE ORDERED LISTING.... TYPE L
****> TO TERMINATE PROGRAM................ TYPE T


****> ENTER AN OPERATION CODE:
A
****> ENTER STUDENT NAME OF THE RECORD OCCURRENCE TO BE RETRIEVED:
WILLIAM BLACK

STUDENT NAME : WILLIAM BLACK
STUDENT MAJOR: MTH
STUDENT AGE  : 22
```

Program 1-Output An Interactive Terminal Session for Program 1

```
****> CHOOSE ONE OF THE FOLLOWING OPERATIONS:

****> TO ACCESS A RECORD OCCURRENCE........ TYPE A
****> TO GET A COMPLETE ORDERED LISTING.... TYPE L
****> TO TERMINATE PROGRAM................. TYPE T

****> ENTER AN OPERATION CODE:
A
****> ENTER STUDENT NAME OF THE RECORD OCCURRENCE TO BE RETRIEVED:
ROGER JONES
RECORD OCCURRENCE WITH NAME = ROGER JONES          IS NOT IN THE FILE.


****> CHOOSE ONE OF THE FOLLOWING OPERATIONS:

****> TO ACCESS A RECORD OCCURRENCE........ TYPE A
****> TO GET A COMPLETE ORDERED LISTING.... TYPE L
****> TO TERMINATE PROGRAM................. TYPE T

****> ENTER AN OPERATION CODE:
L
001 ALICE KROGER            BUS 21
002 ANNE NEAL               BUS 19
003 DAVID HILLMAN           CS  26
004 JANE GRAY               CS  23
005 JOHN HANSEN             CS  21
006 KELLY TOWERS            MTH 22
007 LAUREN THOMAS           BUS 19
008 MARY CHEN               MTH 21
009 RUSSELL THOMPSON        BUS 20
010 WILLIAM BLACK           MTH 22

****> CHOOSE ONE OF THE FOLLOWING OPERATIONS:

****> TO ACCESS A RECORD OCCURRENCE........ TYPE A
****> TO GET A COMPLETE ORDERED LISTING.... TYPE L
****> TO TERMINATE PROGRAM................. TYPE T

****> ENTER AN OPERATION CODE:
T
```

Program 1-Output (Continued)

Data Design and Data Semantics for Computer Files

Summary of Data Design Rules

A Data Design Methodology

A Data Design Example

Key Terms

Study Guide
Quick Scan
Test Your Comprehension
Improve Your Problem-Solving Ability

IN THIS CHAPTER YOU WILL LEARN ABOUT

- Properties of data in computer files
   Data relevance
   Data currency, accuracy, and validity
   Data usability, time dependency, and storage requirements
- Record structures and data semantics
   Data dependencies
   Representation of entities and relationships
   Logical modeling of entities and relationships
   Record identification
   Data duplications and redundancies
- Data integrity
   Entity integrity
   Referential integrity
   Potential inconsistencies, and deletion and insertion anomalies
- Normalizing record structures
   First normal form
   Second normal form
   Third normal form
   Boyce/Codd normal form

Introduction   Computer files contain valuable data that are used as information resources. Data are collected and stored at considerable effort and expense. The files are generally used for a long time, and during their lifetime they are kept up to date to reflect the most current situation in that portion of the real world that they represent. File maintenance is an expensive task. So as not to waste resources spent on creating and maintaining data files, and to keep the files optimally usable, they should be designed with utmost care.

Earlier in the book we pointed out that data organization is a three-phase process encompassing record structure, file, and data base organization. We studied principles and techniques of file structure design extensively in Chapters 10 through 16. We will take a brief look at concepts and principles of data base design in the next chapter. Here, we will reconsider the first phase, that is, data and record structure design.

On one hand, record structure design is quite simple in that it entails grouping together attributes of interest in a linear structure. On the other hand, that kind of simplistic approach, without paying attention to its impact on file maintenance and storage requirements, has been one of the major sources of headache in file and data base processing. Until the early 1970s, although designers of file and data base systems were quite aware of the problems stemming from careless or sloppy approaches, they did not clearly understand the reasons and the cures for the anomalous characteristics exhibited by some data files. With the advent of the theory of relational data bases during the 1970s (a data base management approach that we will explore briefly in Chapter 18) it became clear that such anomalies were due to a lack of understanding of data semantics on the part of designers. A concept known as the theory of normalization gradually emerged, with the objectives of exploring and explaining the reasons for bad record structure design, and finding remedies for it. It is concerned with different types of dependencies that exist among data in the real world, and that constitute part of data semantics in data management.

Properties of Data Stored in Computer Files

Some necessary and desirable properties are associated with data stored in computer files. These properties have to do with data considered in isolation, and are independent of structuring or semantics.

Data Versus Information

In general, we store data in computer files and process them to derive information. The words data and information are quite frequently used synonymously. Let us clarify the difference between them.

> The word **data** pertains to values of properties associated with entities, relationships, or events in the real world that can be obtained through observations or measurements. **Information** is some value obtained through computations or manipulations of data values.

For example, letter grades earned by a student during a semester are data. The semester grade point average computed from the grades is information. If data are collected and entered on a daily basis in a department store, the number of a particular item of merchandise sold on a given day is a datum. The total number of that item of merchandise sold in a week can be computed if we know the daily sales figures, and hence, it is information.

We collect, keep, and use data to derive information. In general, however, information should not be stored in data files unless such files are transient and intended to be used as terminal products of information systems. There are good reasons for this.

First, if we discover an error in a data value we can correct it easily by updating the data field in a file. If some information has been derived using incorrect data values and stored in a file, however, on discovering that error not only should we correct the data values in the file, we should also regenerate the information and update all of its previous and incorrect occurrences. This is a costly and tedious process. It is also highly error prone. Failure to update the dependent information in a file may lead to inconsistencies in the stored date and information.

Second, if we use data and information stored in files indiscriminately to produce and store additional information, errors that may exist in original data or in computed information may propagate uncontrollably. It may be quite difficult to backtrack, locate, and correct the sources of errors.

> **Design Rule**
>
> A data file should store only data, not information.

Data Relevance

A data item is **relevant** if there is an application that requires it, or if we can envision some application in the foreseeable future that will need it. Unless a data item is relevant, it should not be included in data files. For example, in an inventory-control information system it is likely that descriptions of the chemical composition of inventory items are irrelevant.

In a corporate environment, data are shared resources. A data file may and should be used by more than one person for many different applications. This requirement dictates that files be designed and maintained as components of integrated data base systems. We will introduce data base concepts in Chapter 18. For the time being, it should be emphasized that if a corporate data base system exists, files that are already part of it should be used in applications, and new files should not be built independently of the data base. If an existing data base does not include data required for an application, new files should be designed and should be integrated with it.

> **Design Rule**
>
> Data files should contain data that are relevant to applications of more than one user in a multiple-user computing environment.

Data Currency, Accuracy, and Validity

> Data stored in files should be **current** in that they should reflect the present situation in an enterprise.

If ITEM-UNIT-COST for an inventory item goes up from, say, $25 to $26, the corresponding data field value should be updated promptly to reflect this new value. Whether the old value should be stored elsewhere in the file depends on the requirements of applications that use the file as their data source.

> By data **accuracy** we mean that the values stored for a data field are correct and precise representations of that part of the reality. We distinguish accuracy from validity. A data field value is **valid** if it conforms to the specifications for the data field and for the range of values that may be associated with it.

For example, if ITEM-UNIT-COST has been defined as a numeric field of length 3, and if the stored value is 655 for an item whose unit cost is, in fact 625, the stored data value is inaccurate. If, however, we know that the unit cost for an inventory item cannot exceed the upper limit of 650, 655 is not only inaccurate but also invalid. Accuracy and validity of data stored in data files can be verified by manual control and automated validity checks during data entry or input.

> **Design Rule**
>
> Files should store only current, accurate, valid data.

Data Usability

Usability of a data field depends on the manner in which its values are intended for use in pertinent applications. If a data field is FULL-EMPLOYEE-NAME storing a value such as JOHN SMITH or JOAN LESLIE GRANT, this data item is suitable for use in applications in which no distinction need be made among first, middle, and last names. Extracting the last name from values of this data item requires extra processing. If during data entry, the proper order for names has not been maintained for all personnel, it may even lead to inaccuracies.

> **Design Rule**
> Data files should contain data in usable form.

Time Dependency of Data

It makes sense to avoid using time-dependent versions of data in order to minimize data field updates. For example, it is better to use DATE-OF-BIRTH than AGE in an employee file, as the former does not change in value whereas the latter has to be updated once a year. In this regard, DATE-OF-BIRTH is a datum, and AGE is information that can be computed given a value for DATE-OF-BIRTH.

> **Design Rule**
> If for a data field more than one equivalent version exists, the one that is least likely to change in time should be used.

Storage Requirements for Data

> **Design Rule**
> Data in a file should require a minimum amount of storage.

We can do two things to store data in a minimum amount of storage. We can transform external data values to compact representations using data encoding schemes that are maintained in the corporate data dictionary, and we can use data compression techniques to further save on storage. Whether or not to compress data is basically a matter of trade-off between cost of processing time and degree of compression. Elaborate techniques can be used to compress data; however, compressed data eventually have to be reconstructed either for processing or for reporting. Therefore, time needed to compress and reconstruct data has to be carefully weighed against savings in storage. Certainly, there are cases in practice that justify data compression, but the techniques are outside the scope of our discussion.

Data encoding schemes are commonly used in data files for several reasons. They help standardize data, they facilitate avoiding errors that may occur during data entry, they facilitate data processing, and they provide compact representations for external data values, thereby saving storage. Consider the following data encoding scheme for the attribute ACADEMIC-DEPARTMENT.

External Data Value	Code
DEPARTMENT OF COMPUTER SCIENCE	CSC
DEPARTMENT OF ACCOUNTING	ACC
DEPARTMENT OF ZOOLOGY	ZOO

Instead of entering a full department name into a file, we type the corresponding abbreviation. This way we reduce the probability of committing errors during input, save a substantial amount of storage, and expedite processing since the file has become more compact. As we are using more or less standard and mnemonic codes for the attribute, the data values retain a certain degree of legibility.

REVIEW QUESTIONS

1. The difference between data and information is that data are generated by processing information. (T or F)
2. If data values for a field in a computer file are correct and precise representations of that part of the reality, they are _____ . If a data field value conforms to the specifications for the data field and the range of values associated with it, it is _____ .
3. If for a data field more than one equivalent version exists, the form that is least likely to change in time should be preferred. (T or F)
4. To minimize storage requirements for data, we may use _____ and/ or _____ .
5. Data encoding schemes help standardize data, minimize errors during data entry, facilitate data processing, and result in storage savings. (T or F)

Answers: 1. F; 2. accurate, valid; 3. T; 4. data encoding schemes, data compression techniques; 5. T.

Record Structures and Data Semantics

Data structuring cannot be done while disregarding the meaning of data in the real world, that is, data semantics. The two should be considered together for a good design. At every point in the design process, the meanings of data should be kept in view and be related to their structure.

Structuring Related Data

In a computer data file we structure and store only data that are semantically related, in the sense that they all describe either an entity, relationship, or an event in the real world.

> Two data fields are **related** if, given a value for one, a value for the other can be found.

For example, in an inventory control system, ITEM-UNIT-COST is related to ITEM-CODE that describes an inventory item, since a value for ITEM-UNIT-COST is dependent on a value for ITEM-CODE. Therefore, these data fields can be brought together in a record structure. On the other hand, ACADEMIC-RANK describing academic rank of a faculty member in a university is a data field that is unrelated to ITEM-CODE within the context of an inventory control system, and has no place in its files.

> **Design Rule**
>
> Only data that are semantically related to each other should be structured and stored in a computer data file.

Data Dependencies

If two data items are semantically related to each other, one is dependent on the other, or both are interdependent. Data dependencies constitute a significant aspect of data semantics and should be well understood before an attempt is made to structure data. There are different types of data dependencies. Some of them are natural and desirable. Some, on the other hand, lead to problems with data structures and are to be avoided.

> A **dependency** among two sets of attributes is an association from one attribute set to the other, in the sense that an occurrence of the first determines one or more occurrences of the second.

An association is another term for a relationship. Thus, like relationships, there are three types of associations: one-to-one, one-to-many, and many-to-many.

A **one-to-one** association ties a single occurrence of an attribute set to a given occurrence of another related attribute set. A **one-to-many** association links a single occurrence of an attribute set to multiple occurrences of another attribute set. In a **many-to-many** association, more than one occurrence of an attribute set is associated with multiple occurrences of another attribute set.

A many-to-many dependency can be equivalently expressed as two one-to-many dependencies. For example, if more than one value of an attribute A can be mapped to more than one value of attribute B, we can represent such a dependency as a one-to-many mapping from A to B, and another one-to-many mapping from B to A. Therefore, in data semantics analysis from the point of view of dependencies, it is sufficient to consider only one-to-one and one-to-many dependencies.

> If an instance of an attribute set A defines a single instance of another attribute set B, and also for an instance of B there is only one instance of A, the dependency between A and B is one-to-one. A one-to-one dependency is represented in terms of two dependencies, as A → B and B → A. If, on the other hand, for an instance of attribute A there is only one instance of attribute B, but for an instance of attribute B there exist many instances of A, the dependency is many-to-one from A to B, and is denoted as A → B.

> In a dependency such as A → B, we say that the attribute set B is **dependent** on A, or equivalently, A **determines** B. In A → B, A is called the **determinant**.

Consider the following record structure for a file called STUDENT-COURSE-FILE.

STU-IDNO	STU-NAME	YEAR	MAJOR	COURSE-NUMBER	COURSE-NAME	CREDIT	GRADE

Assuming that for the student population described in the file STU-NAME values are distinct, the dependency between the attributes STU-IDNO and STU-NAME is one-to-one. In other words, for each valid value of the STU-IDNO attribute, there is only one distinct value of STU-NAME, and conversely, a distinct value of STU-NAME defines a single value of STU-IDNO. Rules such as these that help clarify data semantics are sometimes known as **enterprise rules**. They can be represented as two pair dependencies: STU-IDNO → STU-NAME, STU-NAME → STU-IDNO.

Another enterprise rule is that for a given value of STU-IDNO there is only one value of MAJOR, as we have assumed that a student can have only one major. For a distinct value of MAJOR, however, there is more than one value of STU-IDNO because many students would choose an academic discipline as their major. Hence, the dependency from STU-IDNO to MAJOR is many-to-one, denoted as STU-IDNO → MAJOR.

Semantically, in the record structure of STUDENT-COURSE-FILE, the attributes STU-IDNO and COURSE-NUMBER together determine the attribute GRADE. This is equivalent to the pair dependencies STU-IDNO → GRADE and COURSE-NUMBER → GRADE. Combining them, we can write {STU-IDNO, COURSE-NUMBER} → GRADE.

After having studied the concept of data dependency, we now can take a look at different types of data dependencies.

Full and Partial Dependencies. It may be that every attribute in a determinant involved in a pair dependency is necessary for that dependency to hold true. It may also be that certain attributes in a determinant are superfluous and the dependency still holds even if they are removed from the determinant. Accordingly, we have two types of dependencies, full and partial.

> If in a pair dependency A → B, where A and B are sets of attributes, all attributes in the set A are needed to determine B, this dependency is called a **full functional dependency**, or simply, a **full dependency**. If, on the other hand, only a proper subset of attributes in the set A is needed to determine an instance of B, B is said to be **partially dependent** on A.

In the record structure of STUDENT-COURSE-FILE, the attribute GRADE is fully dependent on the set of attributes {STU-IDNO, COURSE-NUMBER}. However, the attribute CREDIT is partially dependent on the set {STU-IDNO, COURSE-NUMBER}, yet fully dependent on the attribute COURSE-NUMBER.

Let us now specify all relevant pair dependencies for the attributes of the record structure of STUDENT-COURSE-FILE.

1. STU-IDNO → STU-NAME
2. STU-NAME → STU-IDNO
3. STU-IDNO → YEAR
4. STU-IDNO → MAJOR
5. COURSE-NUMBER → COURSE-NAME
6. COURSE-NAME → COURSE-NUMBER
7. COURSE-NUMBER → CREDIT
8. COURSE-NAME → CREDIT
9. STU-NAME → YEAR
10. STU-NAME → MAJOR
11. STU-IDNO, COURSE-NUMBER → GRADE

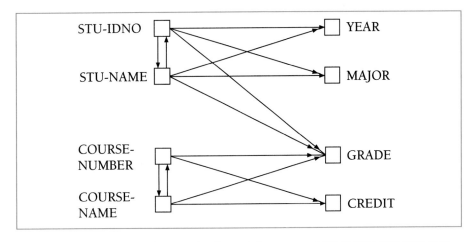

Figure 1 Dependency Diagram for Record Structure of STUDENT-COURSE-FILE

12. STU-IDNO, COURSE-NAME → GRADE
13. STU-NAME, COURSE-NUMBER → GRADE
14. STU-NAME, COURSE-NAME → GRADE

These pair dependencies can be combined into a graph structure such as the one shown in Figure 1. In this graph, attributes are represented as nodes. Each pair dependency is shown with a directional line from one node to the other. Such a graph is called a **dependency diagram**. Dependency diagrams are useful tools in representing data semantics and in identifying different types of dependencies.

In some cases it may be useful to simplify a dependency diagram by combining interdependent key attributes into a set and showing them contained in a box. Here, we are mostly concerned with dependencies of nonkey attributes on keys, and interdependencies among nonkey attributes. As key attribute dependencies matter only in rare circumstances, such a simplification is justified. Figure 2 shows a simplified dependency diagram for the STUDENT-COURSE-FILE record structure.

Transitive Dependencies. Another type of data dependency emerges when we consider pair dependencies among three sets of attributes.

> Let A, B, and C be three sets of attributes belonging to a record structure. Let us assume that the pair dependencies for A, B, and C are A → B, B → C, and A → C. We say that C is **transitively dependent** on A under the host record structure.

In other words, if two paths exist from A to C, one direct, the other by way of B, A transitively determines C.

As an example, let us consider the record structure for a file called STUDENT-DESCRIPTION-FILE.

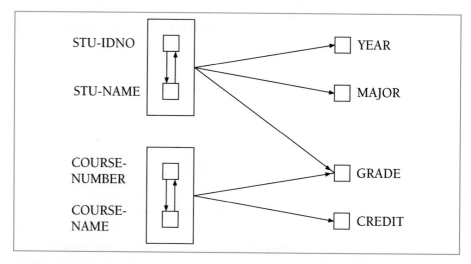

Figure 2 Simplified Dependency Diagram for Record Structure of STUDENT-COURSE-FILE

STU–IDNO	STU–NAME	YEAR	MAJOR	SCHOOL

The following is a list of pair dependencies for this record structure.

1. STU-IDNO → STU-NAME
2. STU-NAME → STU-IDNO
3. STU-IDNO → YEAR
4. STU-IDNO → MAJOR
5. STU-IDNO → SCHOOL
6. STU-NAME → YEAR
7. STU-NAME → MAJOR
8. STU-NAME → SCHOOL
9. MAJOR → SCHOOL

Figure 3 shows these pair dependencies combined into a dependency diagram for the record structure of STUDENT-DESCRIPTION-FILE. This diagram reveals that the attribute SCHOOL is transitively dependent on each of the attributes STU-IDNO and STU-NAME. The transitive dependency is due to the pair dependency MAJOR → SCHOOL.

Of the three dependency types discussed so far, full dependencies are natural and desirable in a record structure. For reasons that will become clear in our discussion of the process of normalization later in this chapter, partial and transitive dependencies are harmful and must be eliminated from record structures.

Representation of Entities

Computer files store data about properties of entities that are of interest to us in an information system. They may also be made to store properties associated with relationships between entities. Therefore, a file is an informational counterpart of an entity set or a relationship set in a problem domain.

In Chapter 10 we defined an entity set as a collection of similar but distinguishable beings, objects, or things. All employees working for a company form an entity set. The inventory items in stock make up another. All human emotions constitute an abstract entity set.

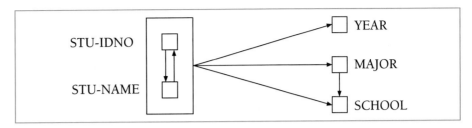

Figure 3 Dependency Diagram for STUDENT-DESCRIPTION-FILE Record

Representation of Relationships

In addition to entities, we are interested in relationships that exist among and between entity sets. We defined a relationship as a set of specifications that associate two or more entity sets. Doctors and patients in a hospital are two distinct entity sets. The fact that the doctors provide care for the patients helps to associate them. Therefore, ATTENDING-PHYSICIAN is a reference to a relationship. In fact, such a relationship is a set because it contains several relevant associations among all doctors and all patients.

Types of Relationships. A relationship between two related files is an association. So is a relationship between two related data elements, which we previously called dependency. Similar to a dependency, a relationship between two files may be one-to-one, one-to-many, or many-to-many.

A **one-to-one** relationship is a set of associations between records of one file and those of the other such that, for each record in one file, there is only one corresponding record in the other. Figure 4a shows an instance of a one-to-one relationship between FILE-1 and FILE-2.

In a **one-to-many** relationship between two files, for each record in one file there exists any number of records in the other. Figure 4b is an example of a one-to-many relationship from FILE-1 to FILE-2. The reverse relationship, that is, the relationship from FILE-2 to FILE-1, is many-to-one.

A relationship between two files is **many-to-many** if there are no restrictions on the number of records in a file that correspond to a record in the other file, and if this is true for both files. Figure 4c depicts a many-to-many relationship between FILE-1 and FILE-2.

Decomposition of Many-to-Many Relationships. In practical applications, many-to-many relationships are difficult to implement and process. In addition, some commercially available data base management systems do not allow many-to-many relationships between files. To represent in file systems a many-to-many relationship that exists in the real world, we decompose it into two one-to-many relationships by introducing a third file, known as an intersection file. An **intersection file** contains records based on the combination of identifiers in the record structures of two files involved. These properties may be either primary keys of the records or their memory addresses.

Let us consider a student file and a course file, and the following two records.

101	1000	JANE SMITH	2	CSC

301	MTH251	CALCULUS	4

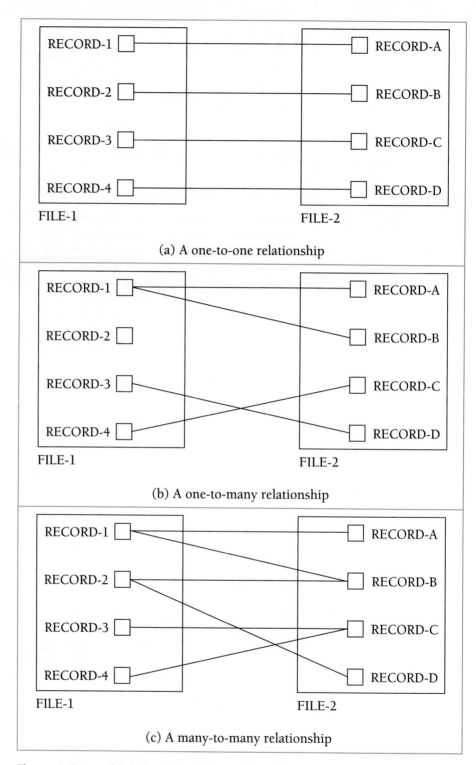

Figure 4 Types of Relationships Between Two Files

In this case we may be interested in a relationship set that represents, among others, the fact that this student is enrolled in MTH251. This enrollment relationship is many-to-many. We can create an intersection record such as

1000	MTH251

which combines the primary keys of the two records. Alternatively, the intersection record can be in terms of memory addresses as in

101	301

which combines the memory addresses of the student and course records. An intersection file effectively breaks down the many-to-many relationship between the student and course files into two one-to-many relationships: one from the student file to the intersection file, and another from the course file to the intersection file. It should be noted that after this decomposition, the data semantics are intact. The only problem is with respect to the intersection file. We should create it and maintain it.

Figure 5 graphically illustrates this decomposition process for the STUDENT-FILE and COURSE-FILE. The intersection file is named ENROLLMENT-FILE because it represents student enrollment in courses.

Storage Representation of Relationships. A relationship between entities can be established in various ways in a file system. Conceivably, we can do one of the following to represent attributes that describe relationships and those that belong to the relevant entity sets.

1. We can collapse all relevant attributes into a single file.
2. We can keep two files, one to correspond to an entity set, and the other to include attributes of the second entity set together with the attributes that belong to the relationship. Then we can link the related records in these files using pointers.
3. We can define three files, two for the entity sets and one for the relationship, and use pointers to reflect the relationships.
4. We can define three physically independent files, keeping in mind during processing that two are for entity sets and the third corresponds to the relationship set between them.

The STUDENT-COURSE-FILE shown in Figure 6 is an example of the first design approach. It consists of three groups of data.

1. The attributes STU-IDNO, STU-NAME, YEAR, and MAJOR that belong to the entity set STUDENT.
2. COURSE-NUMBER, COURSE-NAME, and CREDIT that can be used to describe members of another entity set COURSE.
3. GRADE, which is an attribute that is associated with the relationship ENROLLMENT that exists between STUDENT and COURSE.

This approach has several disadvantages. In designing record structures we should try to bring together attributes that are directly relevant to an entity set, or a relationship between attribute sets, or an event. Mixing attributes that belong to one or more entity sets with those that describe relationships results in record structures that are difficult for the user to understand. It also leads to structures with poor semantic properties, a high degree of data redundancies, or maintenance difficulties. Another example of this poor design approach is in the following record structure.

EMPLOYEE-IDNO	EMPLOYEE-NAME	EDUCATION-LEVEL	DEPARTMENT-CODE	JOB-TITLE

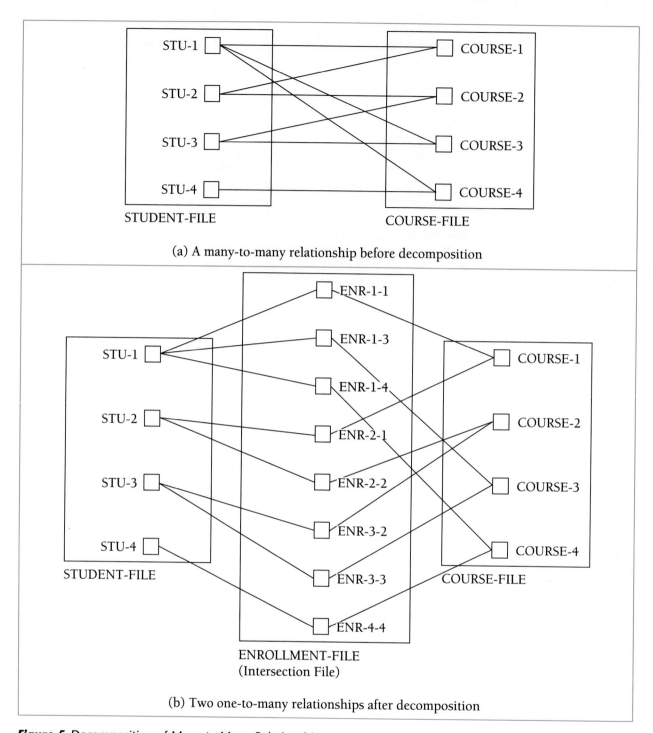

(a) A many-to-many relationship before decomposition

(b) Two one-to-many relationships after decomposition

Figure 5 Decomposition of Many-to-Many Relationships

The attributes EMPLOYEE-IDNO, EMPLOYEE-NAME, and EDUCATION-LEVEL are data that directly describe an employee. DEPARTMENT-CODE relates the employee to a department in the organization, and JOB-TITLE is an attribute of this relationship. Therefore, this structure partially belongs to an entity set of employees in an organization, and partially to a relationship set that associates employees with departments in the organization. Semantically, it is better and more descriptive to split the record structure in two.

STUDENT-COURSE-FILE

STU-IDNO	STU-NAME	YEAR	MAJOR	COURSE-NUMBER	COURSE-NAME	CREDIT	GRADE
1000	JANE SMITH	2	CSC	MTH251	CALCULUS	4	B
1000	JANE SMITH	2	CSC	CSC217	DATA STRUCTURES	3	A
1000	JANE SMITH	2	CSC	ENG211	TECHNICAL WRITING	3	B
1000	JANE SMITH	2	CSC	CSC221	DISCRETE MATH	3	B
2000	THOMAS COLLINS	2	MGT	CSC200	COBOL PROGRAMMING	3	A
2000	THOMAS COLLINS	2	MGT	MTH217	STATISTICS I	3	A
2000	THOMAS COLLINS	2	MGT	ENG211	TECHNICAL WRITING	3	C
2000	THOMAS COLLINS	2	MGT	ACC220	INTR. ACCOUNTING	4	A
2000	THOMAS COLLINS	2	MGT	MGT213	PRIN. OF MANAG.	3	A
....	....	....	......	....	....	......	......

Figure 6 A Data File Representing Two Entity Sets and a Relationship Set

EMPLOYEE—IDNO	EMPLOYEE—NAME	EDUCATION—LEVEL

EMPLOYEE—IDNO	DEPARTMENT—CODE	JOB—TITLE

The first record structure represents an entity set and the second is equivalent to a relationship. They are simpler and easier to understand than the earlier version.

> **Design Rule**
>
> Data in a record structure should accurately reflect real-world entites, relationships, and events. This significantly expedites users' perception of data and the development of application programs that make use of the data.

Figure 7 shows a variation of the same design approach in which the original STUDENT-COURSE-FILE is split into a STUDENT-FILE corresponding to the entity set STUDENT, and a COURSE-ENROLLMENT-FILE representing both the entity set COURSE and the relationship set ENROLLMENT. The two files are linked together by pointers to preserve the relationship. For this, the record structures are expanded to include a LINK field in each file. During processing we first access one of the files and then, using the LINK field value in the retrieved record, access the associated record in the related file. It should be

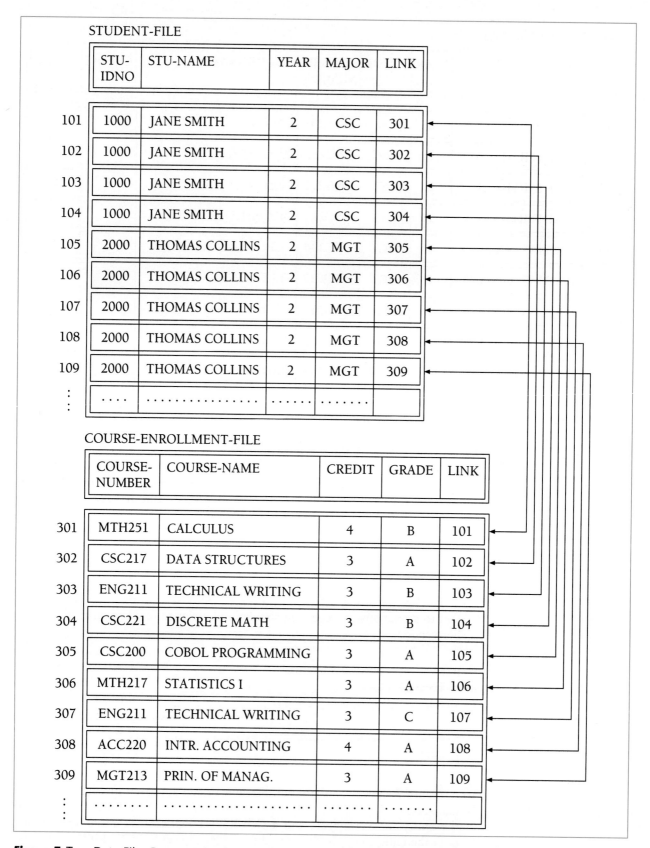

Figure 7 Two Data Files Representing Two Entity Sets and a Relationship Set

noted that the relationship between the two files is one-to-one: for each record in STUDENT-FILE there is only one record in the COURSE-ENROLLMENT-FILE. As far as COURSE-ENROLLMENT-FILE is concerned, this design suffers from the same problems as the one in Figure 6, that is, data redundancies and maintenance difficulties. In addition, because of the physical linkages, it has become more difficult to maintain the relationships between the files, and processing this file system will certainly be inefficient.

The third design approach is exemplified in Figure 8. The two entity sets STUDENT and COURSE are represented by STUDENT-FILE and COURSE-FILE. The only attribute of the ENROLLMENT relationship is stored in a separate file, ENROLLMENT-FILE. We use pointers in all three files to associate appropriate records in order to retain the data semantics. This design is somewhat better than the previous two versions in that the entity and relationship sets are separated. Using files that are connected together by pointer fields again leads to maintenance difficulties and processing inefficiencies, however.

STUDENT-FILE

	STU-IDNO	STU-NAME	YEAR	MAJOR	LINK-1	LINK-2	LINK-3	LINK-4	LINK-5
101	1000	JANE SMITH	2	CSC	301	302	303	304	
102	2000	THOMAS COLLINS	2	MGT	305	306	307	308	309
⋮	. . . .	. . . .	. . . .	. . . . .	. . . . .	. . . . .	. . . . .	. . . . .	. . . . .

COURSE-FILE

	COURSE-NUMBER	COURSE-NAME	CREDIT	LINK-1	LINK-2
201	MTH251	CALCULUS	4	301	
202	CSC217	DATA STRUCTURES	3	302	
203	ENG211	TECHNICAL WRITING	3	303	307
204	CSC221	DISCRETE MATH	3	304	
205	CSC200	COBOL PROGRAMMING	3	305	
206	MTH217	STATISTICS I	3	306	
207	ACC220	INTR. ACCOUNTING	4	308	
208	MGT213	PRIN. OF MANAG.	3	309	
⋮	. . . . . .	. . . .	. . . . .	. . . . .	. . . . .

ENROLLMENT-FILE

	LINK	GRADE	LINK
301	101	B	201
302	101	A	202
303	101	B	203
304	101	B	204
305	102	A	205
306	102	A	206
307	102	C	203
308	102	A	207
309	102	A	208
⋮	. . . . .	. . . .	. . . .

Figure 8 Three Linked Data Files Representing Two Entity Sets and a Relationship Set

STUDENT-FILE

STU-IDNO	STU-NAME	YEAR	MAJOR
1000	JANE SMITH	2	CSC
2000	THOMAS COLLINS	2	MGT
. . . .	. . . .	. . . . . .	. . . . . .

COURSE-FILE

COURSE-NUMBER	COURSE-NAME	CREDIT
MTH251	CALCULUS	4
CSC217	DATA STRUCTURES	3
ENG211	TECHNICAL WRITING	3
CSC221	DISCRETE MATH	3
CSC200	COBOL PROGRAMMING	3
MTH217	STATISTICS I	3
ACC220	INTR. ACCOUNTING	4
MGT213	PRIN. OF MANAG.	3
. . . .	. . . .	. . . .

ENROLLMENT-FILE

STU-IDNO	COURSE-NUMBER	GRADE
1000	MTH251	B
1000	CSC217	A
1000	ENG211	B
1000	CSC221	B
2000	CSC200	A
2000	MTH217	A
2000	ENG211	C
2000	ACC220	A
2000	MGT213	A
. . . . .	. . . .	. . . .

Figure 9 Three Independent Data Files Representing Two Entity Sets and a Relationship Set

The fourth approach is the best and is consistent with the current data base practice. As shown in Figure 9, we represent the entity sets as STUDENT-FILE and COURSE-FILE. The relationship between them is depicted by ENROLLMENT-FILE. In addition to the attribute GRADE, the record structure of the ENROLLMENT-FILE involves STU-IDNO and COURSE-NUMBER, two identifying attributes for the entity sets STUDENT and COURSE. In this file system we have no complications that are due to linkages, and the real-world semantics are perfectly preserved. This file system is in agreement with the principles of relational design. We will get into this in Chapter 18 when studying data base systems.

Logical Modeling of Entities and Relationships

To ensure a semantically sound and trouble-free file system design, we need a logical model of that part of the real world that is within the domain of interest of an information system. Such a model will be concerned with entities, relationships, their types, attributes that help define entities and relationships, and domain sets that are associated with attribute. We know the meanings of entity and relationship sets. The concept of domain set is new.

> A **domain set** for an attribute is a finite or infinite set of admissible values for that attribute from which it is assigned a value.

Different logical modeling techniques aim to describe data semantics without considering the characteristics of a computer system on which an information system is built. One such logical modeling technique is the entity-relationship model.

Entity-Relationship Data Modeling. In the entity-relationship modeling technique, a limited part of the real world is represented using an **entity-relationship diagram**. Such a diagram is shown in Figure 10.

Conventions Used to Construct Entity-Relationship Diagrams

1. Entity sets are represented by rectangular boxes.
2. Relationship sets are denoted by diamond-shaped boxes.
3. Domain sets for attributes are shown using oval symbols.
4. A box representing a relationship is connected to boxes representing entity sets to which that relationship applies.
5. The type of a relationship is indicated by writing on the connecting lines, next to the boxes for entity sets, an appropriate type indicator. Type indicators are 1 and 1 for relationships that are one-to-one, 1 and N for those that are one-to-many, and M and N for those that are many-to-many.
6. Attributes are indicated as labels of arcs that connect symbols for entity or relationship sets with symbols that denote domain sets.
7. Names of entity, relationship, and domain sets are written in capital letters. Names of attributes are written in lower-case letters.

Figure 10a is an overall entity-relationship (E-R) diagram for the file system of Figure 9. This diagram is a pictorial depiction of two requirements.

1. STUDENT and COURSE are two entity sets.
2. These entity sets are related by the relationship set ENROLLMENT. As any number of students can enroll in a given course, and as a course can have any number of students in it, this relationship is many-to-many.

Figure 10b shows a detailed E-R diagram for the same file system. This time, in addition to all the information contained in Figure 10a, the attributes and the domain sets for them are shown.

Additional examples of E-R diagrams can be found in Figure 11. Let us examine closely the file system of Figure 11b. According to this E-R diagram, we have identified the following.

1. The entity sets EMPLOYEE, DEPARTMENT, BUILDING, and SPOUSE are recognized as being of interest to the information system design.
2. For the relationship WORKS-FOR, which is between EMPLOYEE and DEPARTMENT, the enterprise rule is that an employee can work for only

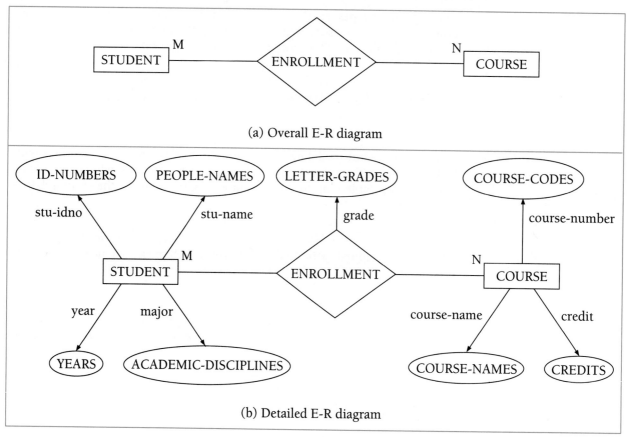

Figure 10 An Entity-Relationship Diagram

one department; that is, joint appointments are not permitted. More than one employee may work for a given department, however, so the relationship WORKS-FOR is one-to-many from DEPARTMENT to EMPLOYEE.

3. The relationship MARRIED-TO links EMPLOYEE and SPOUSE and is one-to-one, implying that we are interested only in the current spouses of our employees.

4. A company building may accommodate more than one department; however, the current placement is such that a department occupies either all or part of a single company building. Hence, the relationship LOCATED-IN from BUILDING to DEPARTMENT is one-to-many.

5. Some of the employees are maintenance staff who work in teams in the company buildings. Their assignments vary in the sense that a team may have the responsibility of maintaining more than one building. This enterprise rule defines the relationship MAINTAINED-BY as a many-to-many relationship.

As can be seen, an E-R diagram is an abbreviated and effective way of reflecting a large number of requirements and enterprise rules. It also contains some of the data semantics. For these reasons, E-R diagrams are used as the primary tool to describe logical design of file systems or data bases. They are one of the outputs of the logical design phase and a significant input for the physical design phase.

Entity-relationship modeling plays a prominent role in data base design and involves additional considerations that are outside the scope of our discussion.

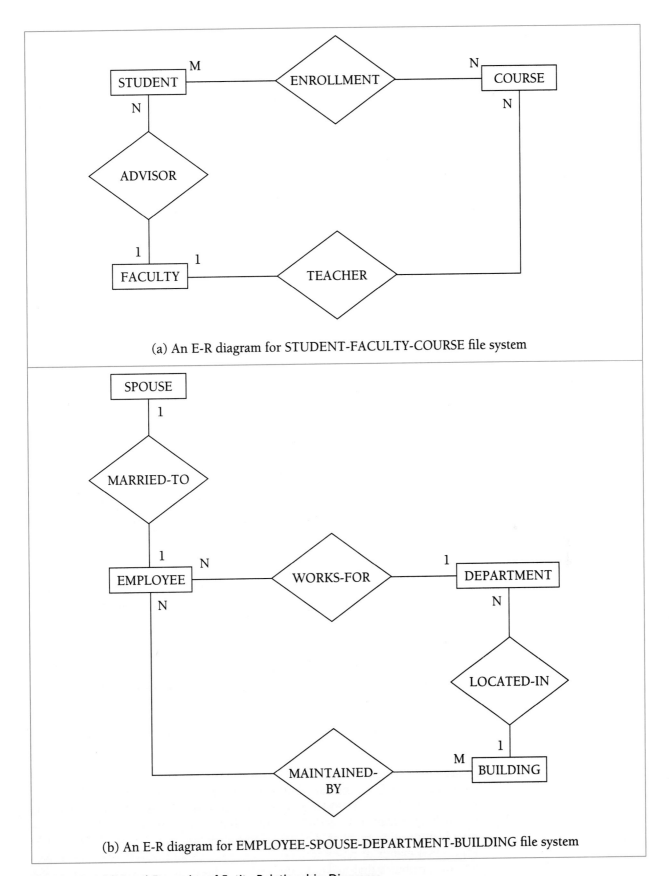

(a) An E-R diagram for STUDENT-FACULTY-COURSE file system

(b) An E-R diagram for EMPLOYEE-SPOUSE-DEPARTMENT-BUILDING file system

Figure 11 Additional Examples of Entity-Relationship Diagrams

Identification of Records

The first problem in describing an entity or a relationship set is concerned with description. We describe the members using attributes. The second problem is the need to identify distinct occurrences in an entity or a relationship set. This is equivalent to specifying distinct records in a file. For this purpose, we make use of the concept of key.

Design Rule

All records in a data file should be distinct. To ensure this, appropriate attributes should be formed into keys for the file's record structure.

In reality, every entity set consists of distinct entities that can be identified uniquely by some of their properties. This is also true of relationships. Each element of a relationship associates a distinct member of an entity set with a distinct member of another entity set. For example, in the relationship exhibited by the record structure

EMPLOYEE—IDNO	DEPARTMENT—CODE	JOB—TITLE

we are describing an association between an employee identified by an EMPLOYEE-IDNO field value and a department identified by a DEPARTMENT-CODE field value. Consequently, EMPLOYEE-IDNO and DEPARTMENT-CODE attributes are key attributes, and together they form the key for this record structure.

Earlier in this book a key was defined as a set of one or more attributes that uniquely identify a member of an entity set, a member of a relationship set, or a record in a file. In this discussion we expound on this concept to form a basis for record structure design principles.

A key for a file is a set of one or more attributes in its record structure that satisfies the following three properties at all times and for any file instance.

1. **Unique identification:** key values for all records are unique, and key attributes uniquely identify each record.
2. **Nonredundancy:** if an attribute is removed from the set of attributes making up a key, the remaining attributes do not satisfy the property of unique identification.
3. **Validity:** all values that can be assumed by key attributes are valid in the sense that none of them can be empty.

Let us consider the files in Figure 12. The EMPLOYEE-FILE record structure consists of the attributes EMPLOYEE-IDNO, EMPLOYEE-NAME, DEPARTMENT, and YEARLY-SALARY. Of these attributes, EMPLOYEE-IDNO uniquely identifies each record, provided that each employee is assigned a distinct identification number. Therefore, this attribute is the key for EMPLOYEE-FILE. As a matter of representational convenience and convention, we underline the attributes that make up the key for a file.

On the other hand, INVENTORY-DELIVERIES-FILE of Figure 12 has a key consisting of INVENTORY-CODE, SUPPLIER, and DATE-DELIVERED

EMPLOYEE-FILE

EMPLOYEE-IDNO	EMPLOYEE-NAME	DEPARTMENT	YEARLY-SALARY
1000	JOHN SMITH	MIS	32,000
2000	JANE EYERS	ACC	45,000
3000	JILL THOMAS	ACC	32,000
....	....	....	....

INVENTORY-DELIVERIES-FILE

INVENTORY-CODE	SUPPLIER	DATE DELIVERED	QUANTITY
J500	ACME	870123	54
J500	ACME	870330	54
J500	ACE	870505	22
J500	ACME	870410	36
J550	ACE	870505	22
J550	QUICK	870620	45
M200	QUICK	870620	10
....	....	....	....

Figure 12 Key Attributes in Record Structure Design

attributes. This is because in the real world of inventory control a particular inventory item may be delivered by more than one manufacturing company, and a given item can be delivered more than once. We are assuming, however, that an inventory item is never delivered more than once on a given date by a manufacturing company, which probably is a reasonable assumption. This is another example of data base semantics. In the case of INVENTORY-DELIVERIES-FILE, unique identification of each record requires a distinct combination of attribute values in the key set, that is, {INVENTORY-CODE, SUPPLIER, DATE-DELIVERED}. We could have specified {INVENTORY-CODE, SUPPLIER, DATE-DELIVERED, QUANTITY} as the key set. However, the removal of QUANTITY from this set does not destroy the property of unique identification. Therefore, the attribute QUANTITY in the key set is redundant. It should be noted that EMPLOYEE-FILE corresponds to an entity set, and INVENTORY-DELIVERIES-FILE is a relationship set, associating inventory items with suppliers.

> It is possible that more than one set of attributes in a file may satisfy all the requirements for keys. Such sets of attributes are called **candidate keys**.

In the EMPLOYEE-FILE of Figure 12 the attribute EMPLOYEE-NAME may also define each record distinctly, provided every employee described in the file has a unique name. In this case both EMPLOYEE-IDNO and EMPLOYEE-NAME are candidate keys. For purposes of physical implementation, one of the candidate keys may be selected to serve as the principal identifer. It is called **primary key**.

> All attributes in a record structure design that do not participate in a candidate key are called **nonkey attributes**. Attributes that make up candidate keys are known as **key attributes**.

In the INVENTORY-DELIVERIES-FILE of Figure 12, the attributes INVENTORY-CODE, SUPPLIER, and DATE-DELIVERED are key attributes, and QUANTITY is a nonkey attribute.

Updating primary key values in a file is an expensive operation. In most files, records are maintained in order by the primary key. Updating the primary key generally destroys the order and requires that the file be sorted afterward. Instead, we usually delete the record whose primary key is to be updated, and insert a new record with new attribute values in its proper place in the file so that record order is maintained. If possible, to minimize updates it is best to choose for primary keys those attributes that are least likely to change in time.

> **Design Rule**
>
> If for a record structure more than one candidate key exists, the one that is least likely to change in time should be selected as the primary key.

In an employee file it may be that both EMPLOYEE-IDNO and EMPLOYEE-NAME may possess the property of unique identification. EMPLOYEE-IDNO values are assigned by the personnel department, and once correctly assigned, are not expected to change. EMPLOYEE-NAME, however, may change due to marriages and divorces. Although both attributes are candidate keys, it is better to use EMPLOYEE-IDNO as primary key for such a file.

Data Duplications and Redundancies

In data files certain data values may be duplicated in different records, or even at different points within the same record. For some data, duplications are necessary and acceptable. For others, however, they are not needed and waste storage. Such duplications are considered redundancies.

As an example, let us consider the STUDENT-COURSE-FILE of Figure 13, which is an extended version of the file of Figure 6. The set of attributes {STU-IDNO, COURSE-NUMBER} is a key set for this file, because together their values uniquely identify each record. We notice three different instances of data duplications.

STUDENT-COURSE-FILE

STU-IDNO	STU-NAME	YEAR	MAJOR	COURSE-NUMBER	COURSE-NAME	CREDIT	GRADE
1000	JANE SMITH	2	CSC	MTH251	CALCULUS	4	B
1000	JANE SMITH	2	CSC	CSC217	DATA STRUCTURES	3	A
1000	JANE SMITH	2	CSC	ENG211	TECHNICAL WRITING	3	B
1000	JANE SMITH	2	CSC	CSC221	DISCRETE MATH	3	B
2000	THOMAS COLLINS	2	MGT	CSC200	COBOL PROGRAMMING	3	A
2000	THOMAS COLLINS	2	MGT	MTH217	STATISTICS I	3	A
2000	THOMAS COLLINS	2	MGT	ENG211	TECHNICAL WRITING	3	C
2000	THOMAS COLLINS	2	MGT	ACC220	INTR. ACCOUNTING	4	A
2000	THOMAS COLLINS	2	MGT	MGT213	PRIN. OF MANAG.	3	A
2500	JAMES KIRKLAND	3	ACC	ACC220	INTR. ACCOUNTING	4	B
2500	JAMES KIRKLAND	3	ACC	MTH217	STATISTICS I	3	D
2500	JAMES KIRKLAND	3	ACC	MTH251	CALCULUS	4	C
2500	JAMES KIRKLAND	3	ACC	MGT378	INTERNATIONAL BUS.	3	B
....	....	....	....	....	....	....	......

Figure 13 A Data File with Redundancies

1. The YEAR attribute value is the same for both JANE SMITH and THOMAS COLLINS. This is obviously not an instance of data redundancy. It so happens that both students are sophomores. Sharing the same value in the domain of a nonkey attribute by more than one entity does not constitute redundancy.

2. The STU-IDNO field value 1000 for JANE SMITH is given four times. Similarly, the COURSE-NUMBER field value, MTH251, for CALCULUS is given twice. However, in the record structure of the STUDENT-COURSE-FILE, STU-IDNO and COURSE-NUMBER are key attributes. Since this file represents a relationship in addition to two entity sets, duplications of these attribute values in the file are expected and normal. The relationship, that of a student enrolling in courses, is many-to-many. That means a student may take more than one course per semester, and a course would have more than one student enrolled in it, hence, duplication of key data values.

3. The nonkey attributes STU-NAME, YEAR, and MAJOR are shown more than once for each student because a student may enroll in more than one course in a given semester. Similarly, the nonkey attributes COURSE-NAME and CREDIT are repeated within the file because a course may have more than one student enrolled in it. These repetitions are not necessary, as the involved attributes belong to entity sets and not to a relationship set.

Duplicating the same data value for nonkey attributes in a file or in related files is wasteful of storage. Storage, although not as expensive now as it used to be, is still a valuable commodity in computer information systems. In addition, as we will see in our discussion of normalization below, data redundancies cause problems during file maintenance.

> **Design Rule**
>
> Data field duplications should be allowed only for key attributes that participate in the primary key for the file, and for nonkey attributes that map more than one member of an entity or relationship set to the same value of the attribute domain. For all other attributes, data duplications are redundancies and should be eliminated.

REVIEW QUESTIONS

1. If for a given value of a data field a value for another data field can be found, the two data fields are _____ .
2. A dependency between two sets of attributes is an association from one attribute set to the other. (T or F)
3. If in a pair dependency all attributes of the determinant set are needed for the dependent set of attributes, such a dependency is called _____ . Otherwise, it is called _____ .
4. A transitive dependency requires three sets of attributes A, B, and C, and three pairs of dependencies _____ , _____ , and _____ .
5. It is possible to decompose a many-to-many relationship between two files into two one-to-many relationships by introducing a new file called a _____ .
6. In a logical model for a file system, entities, relationships, types of relationships, attributes, and their domain sets should be represented. (T or F)
7. A set of admissible values for an attribute is called the _____ for that attribute.
8. In an entity-relationship diagram, all relevent data dependencies among attributes are shown. (T or F)
9. A key for a file should satisfy three conditions: _____ , _____ , and _____ .
10. A candidate key is one of the primary keys that is selected for record identification in the physical implementation for a file. (T or F)

Answers: 1. related; 2. T; 3. full functional dependency, partial dependency; 4. A → B, B → C, A → C; 5. intersection file; 6. T; 7. domain set; 8. F; 9. unique identification, nonredundancy, validity; 10. F.

Data Integrity

Not only should data in computer files be accurate, they should be consistently accurate. In other words, if for some reason a data field belonging to the same entity or relationship element is duplicated in a file or file system, we expect the duplicated values to be the same at all times. Also, if a data field value is the logical consequence of other data field values, we expect this dependency to be maintained. These requirements point to another desirable property of data known as integrity.

> **Data integrity** is concerned with the issue of representing and maintaining data without any conflicts and inconsistencies within a file or a file system.

Data integrity can easily be violated if we store in a file data values that are somehow related to one another. Consider the EMPLOYEE-DEPENDENTS-FILE of Figure 14a. The first record for JOHN SMITH has the value of 3 for the field NO-OF-CHILDREN, which says that he has three children. This is inconsistent with the four child names listed in the rest of the record.

Figure 14b shows two related files, EMPLOYEE-FILE and DEPENDENTS-FILE, in which we observe another instance of data inconsistency. Again, NO-OF-CHILDREN field in EMPLOYEE-FILE record has a value of 3 for the employee with identification number 1000. The DEPENDENTS-FILE, on the other hand, contains four records for the employee 1000 and his children, implying that he has four children.

> **Design Rule**
>
> Related data values in a data file or system of related files should be consistent and should not violate the integrity of data.

Entity Integrity

The values of key attributes that make up the primary key together distinguish records from one another. If a value for a key attribute is not available, a record should not be inserted into the file, since it would be impossible to identify it uniquely. In fact, violation of this integrity rule causes some file management systems such as the VSAM keyed sequence data sets to prohibit record insertion, because they require that a primary key value be supplied for record access. This is known as the **entity integrity rule**.

> **Entity Integrity Rule**
>
> In data file records, no attribute of the primary key should be left empty.

As an example of this type of integrity violation, we again consider the DEPENDENTS-FILE of Figure 14b. Employee 2000 seems to have a newborn who is currently without a name, and a record has already been inserted for this event with CHILD-NAME left empty. It should be noted that an empty value does not mean blank. It means that no value is available for that field.

Referential Integrity

In Figure 14b and c we detect two other violations of data integrity.

1. The second record in the EMPLOYEE-FILE of Figure 14b indicates that the employee whose identification number is 2000 has two children. Given the picture drawn by the instance of EMPLOYEE-DEPENDENTS-FILE of Figure 14a, and assuming that the situation is identical to that depicted in the files of Figure 14b, for employee 2000, SALLY appears to be one of the children. The DEPENDENTS-FILE of Figure 14b associates SALLY with the employee with identification number 3000. It is likely that 3000 is an error

EMPLOYEE-DEPENDENTS-FILE

EMPL-IDNO	EMP-NAME	NO-OF-CHILDREN	CHILD-1-NAME	CHILD-2-NAME	CHILD-3-NAME	CHILD-4-NAME
1000	JOHN SMITH	3	KAREN	JAMES	THOMAS	EDWARD
2000	JANE DOLE	2	WILLIAM	SALLY		
....	....	....	....	....	....	....

(a) Integrity violation within a file

EMPLOYEE-FILE

EMPL-IDNO	EMP-NAME	NO-OF-CHILDREN
1000	JOHN SMITH	3
2000	JANE DOLE	2
....	....	....

DEPENDENTS-FILE

EMPL-IDNO	CHILD-NAME	CHILD-B-YEAR
1000	KAREN	76
1000	JAMES	78
1000	THOMAS	80
1000	EDWARD	85
2000	WILLIAM	68
3000	SALLY	70
2000		88
....	....	....

(b) Integrity violations between two files

FACULTY-FILE

FACULTY-IDNO	FACULTY-NAME	DEPARTMENT	RANK
1000	WILSON	ACC	PROF
2000	BLACK	CSC	ASSO
3000	SMITH	ACC	PROF
....	....	....	.....
3500	JOHNSON	CSC	ASST

ACADEMIC-DEPTS-FILE

DEPT-NAME	CHAIR	SCHOOL	ENROLLMENT
ACC	1000	BUS	530
CSC	4000	A&S	198
.....	.....	.....	....

(c) Integrity violations between two files

Figure 14 Files with Data Integrity Violations

and should have been 2000. This is also a violation of data integrity, and a serious one at that.

2. In Figure 14c we have a FACULTY-FILE and an ACADEMIC-DEPTS-FILE. The FACULTY-IDNO attribute is the key of the FACULTY-FILE record structure. The attribute CHAIR in the ACADEMIC-DEPTS-FILE record structure contains faculty identification number values to indicate the faculty member who also is the department chair. The second record reveals that department chair for the department of computer science (CSC) is the person whose identification number is 4000. No such faculty record exists in the FACULTY-FILE. Thus, data integrity has been violated.

This type of violation is based on the concept of foreign key.

> An attribute in a record structure is a **foreign key** for that record structure if it is a candidate key for another related record structure.

In Figure 14c the attribute CHAIR of the record structure of ACADEMIC-DEPTS-FILE is a foreign key, as FACULTY-IDNO, which basically is the same attribute as CHAIR, is the primary key for the FACULTY-FILE. The **referential integrity rule** applies to this type of integrity violations.

> ## Referential Integrity Rule
>
> If an attribute in a record structure A is a candidate key in another related record structure B, every value of that attribute in different occurrences of A should either be empty or be equal to the value of the corresponding candidate key attribute in some occurrence of B.

Potential Inconsistencies

Sometimes a file may contain no integrity violations. Due to its structural properties, however, it may be susceptible to potential violations if data are carelessly updated during maintenance. Again consider the STUDENT-COURSE-FILE of Figure 13.

Suppose the student with identification number 1000 named JANE SMITH gets married and changes her name to JANE SMITH-MYERS. This change should be reflected in the file and requires update of appropriate records. As is seen in Figure 13, the name JANE SMITH appears in four records. In this case, proper field update calls for accessing all four records and changing the value of the STU-NAME attribute. In other words, updating an attribute indicates multiple record access and modifications. This is known as **multiple-point update**. It not only complicates the file update logic, it also has a tendency to cause erroneous processing during file maintenance. Conceivably, not all relevant records may be updated, resulting in an inconsistent data set. This problem is known as an update anomaly.

> **Update anomaly** (also known as **potential inconsistency**) is a record structure's tendency to result in inconsistent data in a file because the structure necessitates update of several records whenever update of an attribute value is logically required.

STUDENT-COURSE-FILE

STU-IDNO	STU-NAME	YEAR	MAJOR	COURSE-NUMBER	COURSE-NAME	CREDIT	GRADE
1000	JANE SMITH-MYERS	2	CSC	MTH251	CALCULUS	4	B
1000	JANE SMITH-MYERS	2	CSC	CSC217	DATA STRUCTURES	3	A
1000	JANE SMITH-MYERS	2	CSC	ENG211	TECHNICAL WRITING	3	B
1000	JANE SMITH-MYERS	2	CSC	CSC221	DISCRETE MATH	3	B
2000	THOMAS COLLINS	2	MGT	CSC200	COBOL PROGRAMMING	3	A
2000	THOMAS COLLINS	2	MGT	MTH217	STATISTICS I	3	A
2000	THOMAS COLLINS	2	MGT	ENG211	TECHNICAL WRITING	3	C
2000	THOMAS COLLINS	2	MGT	ACC220	INTR. ACCOUNTING	4	A
2000	THOMAS COLLINS	2	MGT	MGT213	PRIN. OF MANAG.	3	A
2500	JAMES KIRKLAND	3	ACC	ACC220	INTR. ACCOUNTING	4	B
2500	JAMES KIRKLAND	3	ACC	MTH217	STATISTICS I	3	D
2500	JAMES KIRKLAND	3	ACC	MTH251	CALCULUS	4	C
2500	JAMES KIRKLAND	3	ACC	MGT378	INTERNATIONAL BUS	3	B
....	....	....	....	....	....	....	......

Figure 15 Example of Update Anomaly (updating STU-NAME attribute for STU-IDNO = 1000; modified values underlined)

It is obvious that the update anomaly in STUDENT-COURSE-FILE of Figure 15 is a result of the data redundancies existing in it. That is, data redundancies and potential inconsistencies are interrelated characteristics.

> **Design Rule**
>
> Updating a data element in a file should require no more than one access and modification, and should not result in inconsistencies and violations of data integrity.

Unintentional Loss of Data

There is another problem with the STUDENT-COURSE-FILE of Figure 13. Consider Figure 16. Suppose the student whose identification number is 2500 decides to drop the course MGT378. At the time the student drop request is processed, a grade may not be available for this student, and the GRADE attribute field may be null. As GRADE is a nonkey attribute, this is acceptable. How do we reflect this course drop phenomenon in the file? Obviously, by deleting the corresponding record. If we do so, however, not only will we lose,

STUDENT-COURSE-FILE

STU-IDNO	STU-NAME	YEAR	MAJOR	COURSE-NUMBER	COURSE-NAME	CREDIT	GRADE
1000	JANE SMITH	2	CSC	MTH251	CALCULUS	4	B
1000	JANE SMITH	2	CSC	CSC217	DATA STRUCTURES	3	A
1000	JANE SMITH	2	CSC	ENG211	TECHNICAL WRITING	3	B
1000	JANE SMITH	2	CSC	CSC221	DISCRETE MATH	3	B
2000	THOMAS COLLINS	2	MGT	CSC200	COBOL PROGRAMMING	3	A
2000	THOMAS COLLINS	2	MGT	MTH217	STATISTICS I	3	A
2000	THOMAS COLLINS	2	MGT	ENG211	TECHNICAL WRITING	3	C
2000	THOMAS COLLINS	2	MGT	ACC220	INTR. ACCOUNTING	4	A
2000	THOMAS COLLINS	2	MGT	MGT213	PRIN. OF MANAG.	3	A
2500	JAMES KIRKLAND	3	ACC	ACC220	INTR. ACCOUNTING	4	B
2500	JAMES KIRKLAND	3	ACC	MTH217	STATISTICS I	3	D
2500	JAMES KIRKLAND	3	ACC	MTH251	CALCULUS	4	C
....	....	....	......	....	....	......	......

Deleted record:

2500	JAMES KIRKLAND	3	ACC	MGT378	INTERNATIONAL BUS	3	B

Information lost

Figure 16 Example of Deletion Anomaly (James Kirkland drops MGT378)

as intended, the information to the effect that student 2500 was enrolled in MGT378, we also will lose the description of the course MGT378, that is, its name and credit hours. This was not intended at all. However, it happened because at the time of drop no student other than 2500 was enrolled in MGT378. This problem is known as deletion anomaly.

> **Deletion anomaly** is a record structure's tendency to cause unintended loss of data from a file as a consequence of deleting a record.

Inability to Represent Data

The opposite of deletion anomaly is insertion anomaly. To illustrate this type of behavior in a record structure, let us consider the STUDENT-COURSE-FILE in Figure 17. Suppose we wish to insert some data concerning a new student into

STUDENT-COURSE-FILE

STU-IDNO	STU-NAME	YEAR	MAJOR	COURSE-NUMBER	COURSE-NAME	CREDIT	GRADE
1000	JANE SMITH	2	CSC	MTH251	CALCULUS	4	B
1000	JANE SMITH	2	CSC	CSC217	DATA STRUCTURES	3	A
1000	JANE SMITH	2	CSC	ENG211	TECHNICAL WRITING	3	B
1000	JANE SMITH	2	CSC	CSC221	DISCRETE MATH	3	B
2000	THOMAS COLLINS	2	MGT	CSC200	COBOL PROGRAMMING	3	A
2000	THOMAS COLLINS	2	MGT	MTH217	STATISTICS I	3	A
2000	THOMAS COLLINS	2	MGT	ENG211	TECHNICAL WRITING	3	C
2000	THOMAS COLLINS	2	MGT	ACC220	INTR. ACCOUNTING	4	A
2000	THOMAS COLLINS	2	MGT	MGT213	PRIN. OF MANAG.	3	A
2500	JAMES KIRKLAND	3	ACC	ACC220	INTR. ACCOUNTING	4	B
2500	JAMES KIRKLAND	3	ACC	MTH217	STATISTICS I	3	D
2500	JAMES KIRKLAND	3	ACC	MTH251	CALCULUS	4	C
2500	JAMES KIRKLAND	3	ACC	MGT378	INTERNATIONAL BUS	3	B
. . . .	. . . .	. . . .	. . . . . .	. . . .	. . . .	. . . . . .	. . . . . .

Record that cannot be stored in the file:

STU-IDNO	STU-NAME	YEAR	MAJOR	COURSE-NUMBER	COURSE-NAME	CREDIT	GRADE
2200	SALLY TURNER	4	CSC				

Figure 17 Example of Insertion Anomaly (Sally Turner is not taking any courses this semester)

the STUDENT-COURSE-FILE. The record for the student is 2200/SALLY TURNER/4/CSC. She has not enrolled in any course yet, and therefore, we have no course information (i.e., COURSE-NUMBER, COURSE-NAME, and CREDIT). As COURSE-NUMBER is a key attribute for STUDENT-COURSE-FILE, we cannot make it empty in forming a record for that student. As a result, until she enrolls in at least one course, we have no way of inserting the partial record for SALLY TURNER. This problem is due to an insertion anomaly in the record structure.

> **Insertion anomaly** is a record structure's tendency not to allow insertion of partial information about some entity into a file unless some pertinent condition is satisfied.

Both deletion and insertion anomalies are results of undesirable properties of record structures. Later in the chapter we will see that they are due to certain types of data dependencies and can be eliminated through a process of normalization.

> **Design Rule**
>
> File maintenance operations should not have undesirable side effects, such as loss of data, or should not hinder storage of new data values in a file.

REVIEW QUESTIONS

1. Data integrity is concerned only with the issue of representing and maintaining correct and accurate data in a file. (T or F)
2. The rule stating that in data file records no attribute of the primary key should be left empty is called the _____ .
3. A foreign key in a record structure is an attribute that appears as a candidate key in another related record structure. (T or F)
4. The referential integrity rule requires that a foreign key be either empty or have the same value as that associated with a corresponding candidate key in a file system. (T or F)
5. A record structure's tendency to result in inconsistent data in a file because the structure necessitates update of multiple records whenever update of an attribute is required is called _____ .
6. A record structure's tendency to cause unintended loss of data from a file as a consequence of deleting a record is called insertion anomaly. (T or F)
7. If a record structure does not allow insertion of partial information about some entity into a file unless some pertinent condition is satisfied, this property is called _____ .

Answers: 1. F; 2. entity integrity rule; 3. T; 4. T; 5. update anomaly; 6. F; 7. insertion anomaly.

Normalizing Record Structures

Normalization is a step-by-step process of transforming a record structure without losing data so that the resulting structure has no undesirable properties such as redundancies, and update, insertion, and deletion anomalies. As these properties are due to data dependencies, normalization eliminates unwanted data dependencies and, while doing that, produces simpler and more regular record structures.

First Normal Form Record Structures

The starting point for the theory of normalization is a form known as the first normal form.

> A record structure (or a file) is in **first normal form** if every attribute in it is atomic (or cannot be decomposed into subordinate data fields).

The EMPLOYEE-FILE of Figure 12 has a record structure that is in first normal form, as it consists of four atomic attributes. The record structure description for this file in COBOL could be:

```
01   EMPLOYEE-RECORD.
     05   EMPLOYEE-IDNO         PIC X(4).
     05   EMPLOYEE-NAME         PIC X(25).
     05   DEPARTMENT            PIC X(3).
     05   YEARLY-SALARY         PIC 9(5).
```

The following slightly different but equivalent record structure is not in first normal form since it contains the composite attribute EMPLOYEE-NAME consisting of the attributes FIRST-NAME and LAST-NAME.

```
01   EMPLOYEE-RECORD-1.
     05   EMPLOYEE-IDNO         PIC X(4).
     05   EMPLOYEE-NAME.
          10   FIRST-NAME       PIC X(10).
          10   LAST-NAME        PIC X(15).
     05   DEPARTMENT            PIC X(3).
     05   YEARLY-SALARY         PIC 9(5).
```

As another example, we consider the EMPLOYEE-DEPENDENTS-FILE of Figure 14a. The record structure of this file appears as follows in COBOL.

```
01   EMPLOYEE-DEPENDENTS-RECORD.
     05   EMPL-IDNO             PIC X(4).
     05   EMP-NAME              PIC X(25).
     05   NO-OF-CHILDREN        PIC 9.
     05   CHILDREN-DATA OCCURS 0 TO 9 TIMES
          DEPENDING ON NO-OF-CHILDREN.
          10   CHILD-NAME       PIC X(15).
```

CHILDREN-DATA is a repeating group and repeats a variable number of times. Also, it is not an atomic data field. Thus, this record structure is not in first normal form.

In general, a record structure that encompasses group items or repeating groups is not in first normal form. It can be transformed into first normal form by replacing composite attributes with their respective constituents. This simple process flattens the record structure. For this reason, files whose record structures are in first normal form are also called **flat files**.

Being in first normal form is important for a record structure for a variety of reasons. First, it simplifies the record structure, and simplicity in design is an important consideration in implementation and use. Second, if the structure is in first normal form, it becomes easier to formalize data semantics that include specification of dependencies among its attributes. Third, avoiding repeating groups eliminates the necessity of having variable-length records in a file. Finally, as repeating groups are not used in a first normal form record structure, any field can be considered as a sort key, depending on the purpose. In the above EMPLOYEE-DEPENDENTS-FILE record structure it is difficult to keep child names sorted in a record.

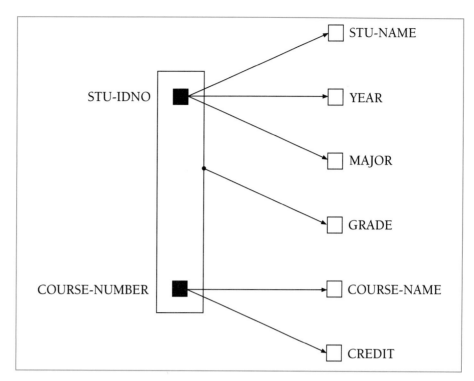

Figure 18 Dependency Diagram of STUDENT-COURSE-FILE Record Structure of Figure 13

Despite these advantages, the first normal form record structure is not free of problems. As we saw earlier, it may cause data redundancies in a file. Also, it may result in maintenance problems due to update, insertion, and deletion anomalies. The STUDENT-COURSE-FILE of Figure 13 is in first normal form; however, it contains redundant data (Figure 13), update anomalies (Figure 15), deletion anomalies (Figure 16), and insertion anomalies (Figure 17).

Assuming that for students, only the attribute STU-IDNO, and for courses, only the attribute COURSE-NUMBER, possess the property of unique identification, we can draw the dependency diagram for STUDENT-COURSE-FILE record structure as shown in Figure 18. As a matter of convention, we represent key attributes by solid boxes and nonkey attributes by empty boxes. It can be seen that only GRADE is fully functionally dependent on the candidate key {STU-IDNO, COURSE-NUMBER}. The problems mentioned in the record structure are due to the existence of partial dependencies of nonkey attributes on candidate keys. These partial dependencies can be eliminated, giving rise to another normal form, called the second normal form.

Second Normal Form

A record structure is said to be in **second normal form** if it is in first normal form, and if all nonkey attributes in it are fully dependent on all candidate keys.

We can take a record structure design that is in first normal form and decompose it into two or more record structures that do not contain any partial dependencies on candidate keys; hence, they are all in second normal form. This decomposition process generally yields record structures that are simpler and more regular in the sense that they may be free of data redundancies and anomalies. However, care must be exercised while decomposing a record

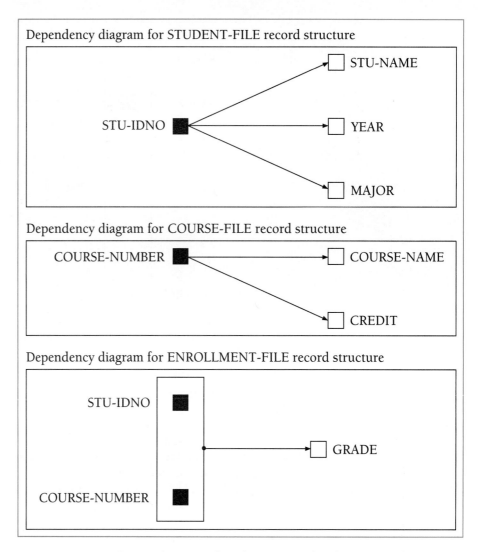

Figure 19 Dependency Diagrams After Elimination of Redundancies and Anomalies in STUDENT-COURSE-FILE Record Structure of Figure 13

structure into second normal form so that no data are lost. For the record structure of STUDENT-COURSE-FILE, the decomposition process yields three record structures for three files.

1. STUDENT-FILE, consisting of STU-IDNO, STU-NAME, YEAR, and MAJOR
2. COURSE-FILE, made up of COURSE-NUMBER, COURSE-NAME, and CREDIT
3. ENROLLMENT-FILE, which includes the attributes STU-IDNO, COURSE-NUMBER, and GRADE

Figure 19 shows the dependency diagrams for the three record structures obtained by decomposing the original file. All three record structures are in second normal form. Not only are the irregularities and redundancies eliminated and the record structures simplified, the three record structures have become more descriptive of the real world. This is because the corresponding files now represent two entity sets, one containing students and the other courses, and a third relationship set that links the two together. Also, the decomposition process is reversible, because the three record structures can be combined by joining them over common attributes, yielding the original structure. Therefore, no data are lost during decomposition.

STUDENT-FILE

STU-IDNO	STU-NAME	YEAR	MAJOR
1000	JANE SMITH	2	CSC
2000	THOMAS COLLINS	2	MGT
2500	JAMES KIRKLAND	3	ACC
....	....	.....	......

COURSE-FILE

COURSE-NUMBER	COURSE-NAME	CREDIT
MTH251	CALCULUS	4
CSC200	COBOL PROGRAMMING	3
ACC220	INTR. ACCOUNTING	4
CSC217	DATA STRUCTURES	3
ENG211	TECHNICAL WRITING	3
CSC221	DESCRETE MATH	3
MTH217	STATISTICS I	3
MGT213	PRIN. OF MANAG.	3
MGT378	INTERNATIONAL BUS	3
....	....	......

ENROLLMENT-FILE

STU-IDNO	COURSE-NUMBER	GRADE
1000	MTH251	B
1000	CSC217	A
1000	ENG211	B
1000	CSC221	B
2000	CSC200	A
2000	MTH217	A
2000	ENG211	C
2000	ACC220	A
2000	MGT213	A
2500	ACC220	B
2500	MTH217	D
2500	MTH251	C
2500	MGT378	B
.....	....	....

Figure 20 Eliminating Redundancies by Normalizing Record Structure Design

Figure 20 shows the instances of the three files obtained by transforming the first normal form STUDENT-COURSE-FILE into the three second normal form files, STUDENT-FILE, COURSE-FILE, and ENROLLMENT-FILE. The record structures of these files now are fully normalized in the sense that they no longer contain data redundancies and exhibit anomalies.

As another example of a record structure that is in the first normal form, we take the STUDENT-DESCRIPTION-FILE of Figure 21a. Its dependency diagram is shown in Figure 21b. It has only one candidate key, STU-IDNO. All other attributes are nonkey and fully depend on STU-IDNO. Therefore, this record structure contains no partial dependencies on candidate keys and is in first normal form. Despite this, it has some problems.

1. The fact that a department is affiliated with a school is unnecessarily repeated many times in the file. For example, the records for the students with identification numbers 2800 and 3500 indicate that the MAJOR value MGT is the code for a department that is one of the departments of the same SCHOOL, that is, SBA.
2. In the event the code for this department changes (say, from MGT to MAN), more than one data field will have to be updated. This is an indication of an update anomaly.

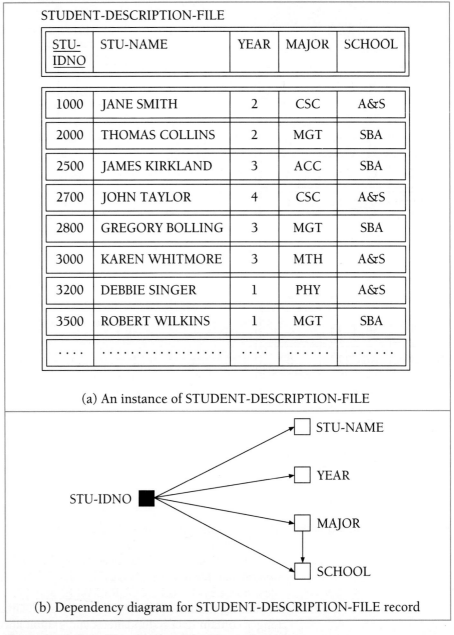

STUDENT-DESCRIPTION-FILE

STU-IDNO	STU-NAME	YEAR	MAJOR	SCHOOL
1000	JANE SMITH	2	CSC	A&S
2000	THOMAS COLLINS	2	MGT	SBA
2500	JAMES KIRKLAND	3	ACC	SBA
2700	JOHN TAYLOR	4	CSC	A&S
2800	GREGORY BOLLING	3	MGT	SBA
3000	KAREN WHITMORE	3	MTH	A&S
3200	DEBBIE SINGER	1	PHY	A&S
3500	ROBERT WILKINS	1	MGT	SBA
....	....	....	......	......

(a) An instance of STUDENT-DESCRIPTION-FILE

(b) Dependency diagram for STUDENT-DESCRIPTION-FILE record

Figure 21 A Data File with Transitive Dependencies

3. It is easy to recognize the deletion and insertion anomalies as consequences of the dependency of the attribute SCHOOL on MAJOR.

These problems are due to the transitive dependency of SCHOOL on STU-IDNO by way of MAJOR in the record structure, and imply another normal form.

Third Normal Form

> A record structure is in **third normal form** if it is in second normal form, and no nonkey attribute in it is transitively dependent on any candidate key.

The transitive dependency in the record structure of STUDENT-DESCRIPTION-FILE is due to the pair dependency MAJOR → SCHOOL, and can easily be removed by decomposing the structure into two structures shown in Figure 22. Thus, two files with simpler and more normal record structures are created. They are STUDENT-FILE of STU-IDNO, STU-NAME, YEAR, and MAJOR attributes, and MAJORS-FILE of MAJOR and SCHOOL attributes, as shown in Figure 22a. Their dependency diagrams are given in Figure 22b. It should be noted that this decomposition process is also reversible and does not result in any data loss.

Eliminating transitive dependencies through decomposition from a record structure that is in second normal form produces two or more structures that are all in third normal form. The record structures of STUDENT-FILE and MAJORS-FILE in Figure 22 are both in third normal form.

To summarize what we have studied so far, let us consider the dependency diagram given in Figure 23. We assume that the nodes labeled A through G represent simple, atomic attributes in a record structure. Hence, the structure is in first normal form. The dependency diagram indicates the existence of full, partial, and transitive dependencies. Clearly, attributes D and G are fully dependent on key attributes A, B, and C. Attribute E is dependent on A only, and thus its dependency on the key consisting of A, B, and C is partial. F is also partially dependent on the set of key attributes, as its determinants are B and C only.

Therefore, we conclude that the structure is not in second normal form. We decompose it into three structures whose dependency diagrams are shown in Figure 24. Two partial dependencies have been eliminated and the resulting structures are now in second normal form.

There is, however, a transitive dependency of G on the key attributes. We can eliminate this by extracting D and G from the original structure and turning them into an independent structure, as shown in Figure 25. Now all structures are in third normal form.

It should be observed that a record structure consisting of only two attributes is in all normal forms, as no partial or transitive dependencies can possibly exist in such a structure. Also, a record structure consisting of any number of attributes such that all of them are key attributes is necessarily in third normal form, since a transitive dependency of a nonkey attribute on key attributes is possible only if a dependency exists between two nonkey attributes.

Boyce/Codd Normal Form

Some record structures are already in third normal form, or can be normalized into third normal form record structures such that they contain no undesirable properties. Certain third normal form record structures may still exhibit

STUDENT-FILE

STU-IDNO	STU-NAME	YEAR	MAJOR
1000	JANE SMITH	2	CSC
2000	THOMAS COLLINS	2	MGT
2500	JAMES KIRKLAND	3	ACC
2700	JOHN TAYLOR	4	CSC
2800	GREGORY BOLLING	3	MGT
3000	KAREN WHITMORE	3	MTH
3200	DEBBIE SINGER	1	PHY
3500	ROBERT WILKINS	1	MGT
....	....	....	......

MAJORS-FILE

MAJOR	SCHOOL
CSC	A&S
MGT	SBA
ACC	SBA
MTH	A&S
PHY	A&S
....	....

(a) Instances of STUDENT-FILE and MAJORS-FILE

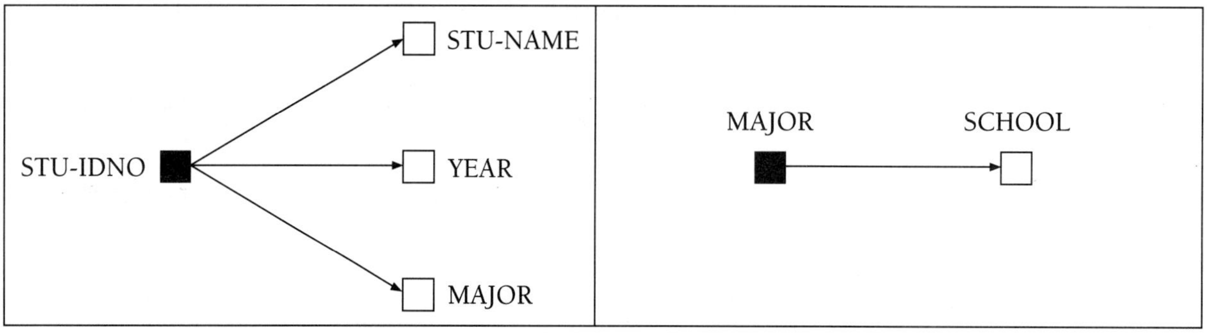

(b) Dependency diagrams for STUDENT-FILE record and MAJORS-FILE record

Figure 22 STUDENT-DESCRIPTION-FILE of Figure 21 After Transitive Dependencies Have Been Eliminated

anomalous behavior, however. An example is the ENROLLMENT-FILE in Figure 26a.

The ENROLLMENT-FILE record structure includes the attributes STU-IDNO, STU-NAME, COURSE-NUMBER, and GRADE. The key attributes are underlined. The candidate keys for this file are {STU-IDNO, COURSE-NUMBER} and {STU-NAME, COURSE-NUMBER}. As the dependency diagram for its record structure in Figure 26b shows, the nonkey attribute GRADE is fully dependent on the two candidate keys. Therefore, the record structure is in third normal form. However, the STU-NAME field values are redundant for students who enroll in more than one course. As a result of this redundancy, we have update, deletion, and insertion anomalies in this file.

These problems are due to the interdependency of the two key attributes STU-IDNO and STU-NAME. Removing this interdependency suggests another normal form known as Boyce/Codd normal form.

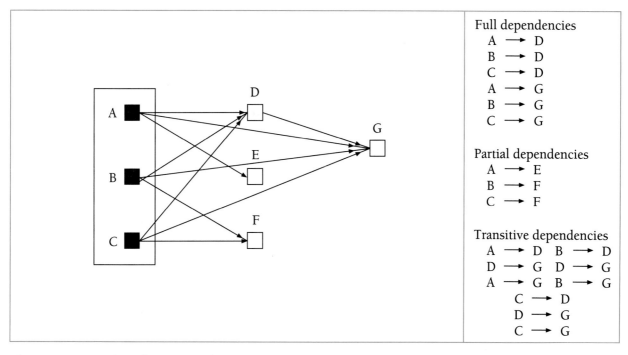

Figure 23 Types of Attribute Dependencies

> A record structure is in **Boyce/Codd normal form** if every determinant in its dependency diagram is a candidate key.

In the dependency diagram of Figure 26b, the determinants are {STU-IDNO, COURSE-NUMBER}, {STU-NAME, COURSE-NUMBER}, {STU-IDNO}, and {STU-NAME}. The first two are candidate keys; the last two, however, are not. Therefore, this record structure is not in Boyce/Codd normal form, and suffers from redundancies and anomalies.

A record structure that is not in Boyce/Codd normal form can be decomposed into two or more record structures that are all in that normal form. For the record structure of ENROLLMENT-FILE of Figure 26, decomposition

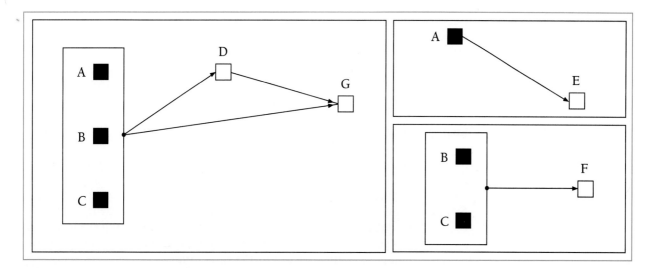

Figure 24 Eliminating Partial Dependencies in Figure 23

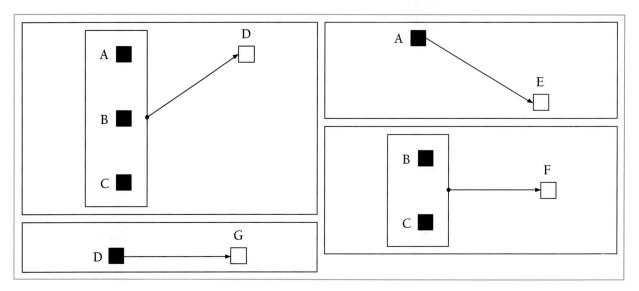

Figure 25 Eliminating Transitive Dependencies in Figure 23

yields two record structures, as shown in Figure 27a. The record structure of NEW-ENROLLMENT-FILE contains STU-IDNO, COURSE-NUMBER, and GRADE. The interdependent attributes STU-IDNO and STU-NAME have been removed from the original structure and combined into that of the IDNO-NAME-FILE. Now both of the record structures are in Boyce/Codd normal form and are completely normalized. Their dependency diagrams are shown in Figure 27b.

The Goal of Normalization

So far we have studied four normal forms. In addition to these, other normal forms apply only in rare situations and therefore are outside the scope of our discussion. However, all normal forms have the same objective: to define record structures that are completely free of any data redundancies and anomalies. In general, a record structure that exhibits no data redundancies or anomalies is said to be in **domain-key normal form**. Therefore, the goal of the process of normalization is to arrive at record structures that are equivalent to the original structure and are all in the domain-key normal form.

Given the current state of the theory of normalization, there is no simple one-step way of transforming a record structure into structures that are in domain-key normal form. Therefore, as outlined above, we apply the following steps for normalizing structures.

Step 1:   If a structure is not in first normal form, replace each group item and repeating group by their constituents so that the resulting structure is based on atomic fields only, and hence is in first normal form.

Step 2:   If the structure has data redundancies and anomalies, identify partial dependencies of nonkey attributes on candidate keys, and decompose the structure into two or more structures such that none contains such partial dependencies. Now the structures are in second normal form.

Step 3:   If any one of the structures contains transitive dependencies of nonkey attributes on keys, eliminate them by decomposing the structure into structures that no longer contain transitive dependencies. The resulting structures are in third normal form.

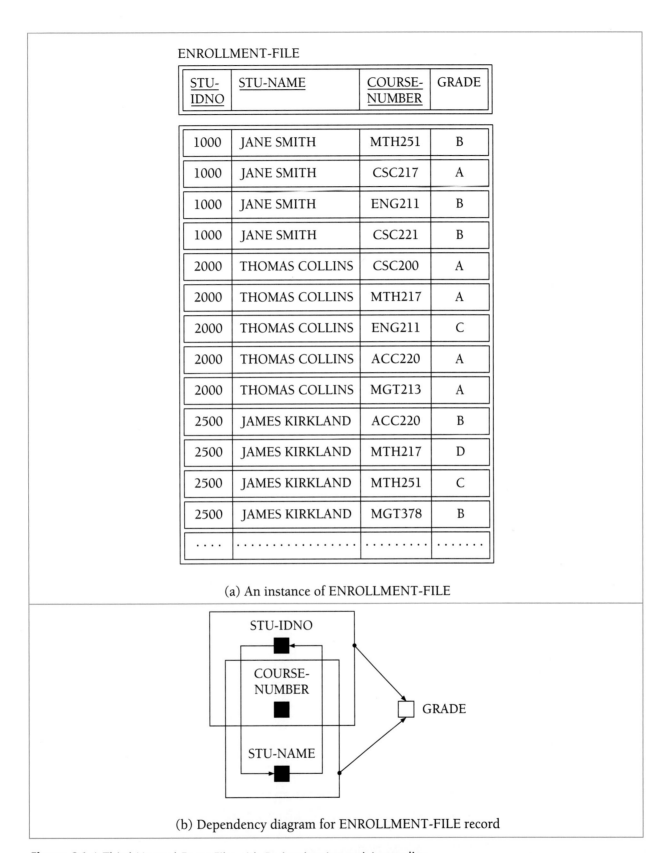

(a) An instance of ENROLLMENT-FILE

(b) Dependency diagram for ENROLLMENT-FILE record

Figure 26 A Third Normal Form File with Redundancies and Anomalies

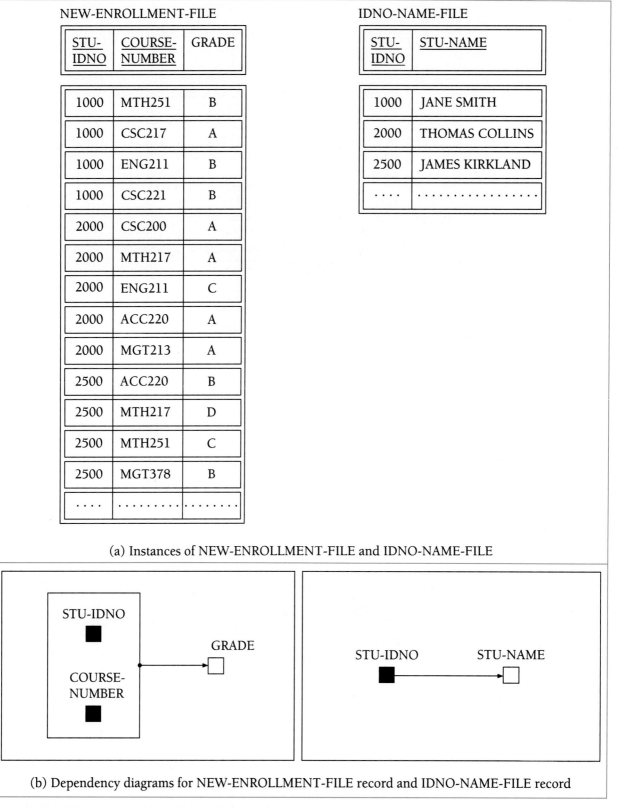

(a) Instances of NEW-ENROLLMENT-FILE and IDNO-NAME-FILE

(b) Dependency diagrams for NEW-ENROLLMENT-FILE record and IDNO-NAME-FILE record

Figure 27 ENROLLMENT-FILE of Figure 26 After Normalization

Step 4: If data redundancies and anomalies persist in any one of the structures, identify Boyce/Codd dependencies, that is, determinants that are not candidate keys, and eliminate them by taking appropriate projections.

This procedure will normalize the majority of record structures that we meet in practical applications.

REVIEW QUESTIONS

1. A record structure containing no repeating groups is in first normal form even if it contains some group items. (T or F)
2. A flat file is one with a first normal form record structure. (T or F)
3. A first normal form record structure in which no nonkey attribute is partially dependent on any candidate key is in _____ .
4. If all transitive dependencies of nonkey attributes on key attributes are removed from a second normal form record structure, it becomes a Boyce/Codd normal form relation. (T or F)
5. If every determinant is a candidate key in a record structure, this record structure is in _____ .

Answers: 1. F; 2. T; 3. second normal form; 4. F; 5. Boyce/Codd normal form.

Summary of Data Design Rules

Up to this point we have stated and justified a number of important design rules to be used in record structure design. For easy reference, we collect them together and repeat them.

Record Structure Design Rules

1. A data file should store only data, not information.
2. Data files should contain data that are relevant to applications of more than one user in a multiple-user computing environment.
3. Files should store only current, accurate, valid data.
4. Data files should contain data in usable form.
5. If more than one equivalent version exists for a data field, the form that is least likely to change in time should be preferred.
6. Data in a file should require a minimum amount of storage.
7. In a computer data file, only data that are semantically related to each other should be structured and stored.
8. Data in a record structure should accurately reflect real-world entities, relationships, and events. This significantly expedites users' perception of data, and the development of application programs that make use of the data.
9. All records in a data file should be distinct. To ensure this, appropriate attributes should be formed into keys for the record structure.
10. If more than one candidate key exists for a record structure, the one that is least likely to change in time should be selected as the primary key.
11. In data files, data field duplications should be allowed only for key attributes that participate in the primary key for the file, and for nonkey attributes that map more than one member of an entity or relationship set to the same value of the attribute domain. For all other attributes data duplications are redundancies and should be eliminated.

> 12. Related data values in a data file or a system of related files should be consistent and should not violate the integrity of data.
> 13. In data file records, no attribute of the primary key should be left empty.
> 14. If an attribute in a record structure A is a candidate key in another related record structure B, every value of that attribute in different occurrences of A should either be empty, or be equal to the value of the corresponding candidate key attribute in some occurrence of B.
> 15. Updating a data element in a file should require no more than one access and modification, and should not result in inconsistencies and violations of data integrity.
> 16. File maintenance operations should not have undesirable side effects, such as loss of data, and should not hinder storage of new data values.

A Data Design Methodology

In view of the data design rules discussed in this chapter, we formulate the following steps to make a design methodology. We assume that an initial analysis phase has been undertaken and, in view of the system requirements, data elements that are to be included in a file system have been identified.

Step 1: Data element analysis. Consider each data element in isolation.
  a. Verify that the data element is a datum and not information. If not, offer alternatives.
  b. Verify that the data element is usable. If not, enhance usability by offering alternatives, or by simply defining additional data elements.
  c. Verify that the data element is not time dependent. If so, offer alternatives.
  d. Determine the nature of the data element in terms of its type (e.g., numeric integer, alphabetic, etc.), length, and whether it requires a fixed-length or variable-length field.
  e. Verify the data encoding scheme suggested for the data element. If none exists, suggest an optimal scheme.

Step 2: Data semantics analysis. At this step we are interested in data semantics, which are generally expressed as enterprise rules.
  a. Identify relevant enterprise rules and verify them.
  b. Using each enterprise rule, determine dependencies.
  c. Represent all data dependencies in a dependency diagram.
  d. Using the dependency diagram and its properties (i.e., connectedness of the diagram, whether a given data element is a determinant or not in the diagram, etc.), tentatively identify entities, relationships, and candidate keys for entities and relationships. (It should be noted that if a dependency diagram is connected, data elements included in it are related.)
  e. Specify one or more record structures, each corresponding to a connected component of the dependency diagram.
  f. Verify that each record structure is in first normal form. If not, transform it into first normal form by replacing composite data fields with their ingredients.

Step 3: Normalization to second normal form.
  a. Consider each record structure and if necessary, normalize it to second normal form structures by eliminating partial dependencies of nonkey attributes on candidate keys.
  b. Again verify that each structure corresponds to either an entity or a relationship set, and that the identified candidate keys are appropriate. If not, suggest modifications.

Step 4: Normalization to third normal form.
   a. If any of the record structures identified so far contain transitive dependencies, eliminate such dependencies by decomposing the structure into third normal form structures.
   b. Again verify entities and relationships involved and the candidate keys for each relation. Suggest modifications if necessary.

Step 5: Normalization to Boyce/Codd normal form.
   a. If any of the record structures contains Boyce/Codd dependencies, eliminate them through decomposition to Boyce/Codd normal form structures.
   b. Verify the correspondence of record structures to entities and relationships. Ascertain correctness of candidate keys.

Step 6: Finalizing design.
   a. If a record structure lacks certain characteristics to evolve into a computer data file, specify how it should be incorporated into the systems design.
   b. Considering the remaining record structures, draw an entity-relationship diagram for the file system.

A Data Design Example

In this section we consider a logical data and record structure design example for a file system. In the design process we make use of the concepts and design rules discussed in this chapter, and follow the design methodology given in the previous section.

Problem

The file system we are to design is for the ACE Video Rental Outlet, a small, family-operated business that rents out movie feature cassettes in a small town. To control its expanding business, the outlet wants to design and implement an information system that will use some computer data files.

A preliminary feasibility study was undertaken, and the system was analyzed. It was decided that the computer files should include the following data items.

VIDEO-TITLE	DISTRIBUTOR-NAME
VIDEO-NUMBER	DISTRIBUTOR-ADDRESS
PRINCIPAL-ACTOR	CUSTOMER-ACCOUNT-NO
PRINCIPAL-ACTRESS	CUSTOMER-NAME
LENGTH (in minutes)	CUSTOMER-ADDRESS
PURCHASE-PRICE	RENTAL-DATE
COPIES-AVAILABLE	DUE-DATE
COPIES-DISPOSED	RENTAL-TYPE (weekday or weekend)

These data names are reasonably descriptive and should reflect their meaning in most cases. Early in the design process, we will clarify their semantics further.

Solution

We carry out the logical design according to the methodology outlined in the previous section, in six steps.

Step 1: Data element analysis. We consider each data item separately, and describe them in terms of their meaning, type, length, format, and associated data encoding schemes. The data field definitions are given in Figure 28.

We analyze each data item to determine whether it is purely data or information. We also study them from relevance, usability, time dependency, and compactness points of view. We notice the following deficiencies.

a. RENTAL-DATE field has the format YY/MM/DD (year/month/ day). We can save two characters by eliminating the / separators in storage. The proposed new format is YYMMDD.

Attribute name:	VIDEO-TITLE	
Description	:	Name of movie feature
Attribute type	:	ALPHABETIC
Field length	:	30
Data encoding	:	None

Attribute name: VIDEO-NUMBER
Description   : Distinct code, in-house assigned to each video feature upon purchase
Attribute type : ALPHANUMERIC
Field length : 7
Data encoding : XYYYYZZ
　　　　　　　　X:　　FEATURE CATEGORY CODE
　　　　　　　　YYYY:　Serial sequence number, in-house assigned.
　　　　　　　　ZZ :　Copy number.

FEATURE CATEGORY CODE	Meaning
C	Comedy
D	Drama
F	Family
H	Horror
I	Instructional
S	Science fiction

Attribute name: PRINCIPAL-ACTOR, PRINCIPAL-ACTRESS
Description   : Names of the principal actor and actress
Attribute type : ALPHABETIC
Field length : 25
Data encoding : None

Attribute name: LENGTH
Description   : Length of movie feature in minutes
Attribute type : INTEGER
Field length : 3
Data encoding : None

Attribute name: PURCHASE-PRICE
Description   : Cost of video cassette to the outlet
Attribute type : DECIMAL
Field length : 5
Data encoding : 99.99 in dollars and cents.

Attribute name: COPIES AVAILABLE
Description   : Number of copies in use of movie feature
Attribute type : INTEGER
Field length : 2
Data encoding : None

Figure 28 Data Design Example: Preliminary Data Field Definitions

Attribute name:	COPIES-DISPOSED	
Description	:	Number of copies discarded due to defects or nonreturns
Attribute type	:	INTEGER
Field length	:	2
Data encoding	:	None
Attribute name:	DISTRIBUTOR-NAME	
Description	:	Name of distribution company supplying video cassettes
Attribute type	:	ALPHABETIC
Field length	:	25
Data encoding	:	None
Attribute name:	DISTRIBUTOR-ADDRESS	
Description	:	Correspondence address of distribution company
Attribute type	:	ALPHANUMERIC
Field length	:	30
Data encoding	:	None
Attribute name:	CUSTOMER-ACCOUNT-NO	
Description	:	Distinct account numbers assigned to customers
Attribute type	:	INTEGER
Field length	:	4
Data encoding	:	None
Attribute name:	CUSTOMER-NAME	
Description	:	Full name of customer
Attribute type	:	ALPHABETIC
Field length	:	25
Data encoding	:	None
Attribute name:	CUSTOMER-ADDRESS	
Description	:	Residence address of customer
Attribute type	:	ALPHANUMERIC
Field length	:	30
Data encoding	:	None
Attribute name:	RENTAL-DATE	
Description	:	Date cassette rented
Attribute type	:	ALPHANUMERIC
Field length	:	8
Data encoding	:	YY/MM/DD, year/month/day

Attribute name:	RENTAL-TYPE		
Description	:	Weekday or weekend rental indicator	
Attribute type	:	ALPHABETIC	
Field length	:	1	
Data encoding	:	RENTAL-TYPE	Meaning
		R	Weekday rental
		W	Weekend rental

Attribute name:	DUE-DATE	
Description	:	Date cassette to be returned by customer
Attribute type	:	ALPHANUMERIC
Field length	:	8
Data encoding	:	YY/MM/DD, year/month/day

Figure 28 (Continued)

b. DUE-DATE has the same format as RENTAL-DATE, that is, YY/MM/DD. Not only can we eliminate the / separators, we can also discard the year part, YY, since DUE-DATE is dependent on RENTAL-DATE, and the year part for DUE-DATE can easily be obtained from its determinant RENTAL-DATE value. Thus, we reduce the field size to four characters.

c. Each video acquisition is to be assigned a distinct VIDEO-NUMBER value by the outlet according to the format XYYYYZZ. Here, X is a one-letter feature category code, YYYY is a sequence number to be assigned to a title, and ZZ is the copy number associated with a copy of a movie feature. This formatting technique ensures distinctness for each movie feature and each of its copies in stock. It is intended to keep descriptions of every cassette in stock in a computer file in terms of its VIDEO-NUMBER and other associated attributes. Furthermore, if in the future a copy becomes unusable and is discarded or lost, the corresponding record in the computer file will be deleted. Therefore, at any given time we can process the files on the VIDEO-NUMBER field values to determine the total number of copies of a video title currently in stock, and the number of copies that have been discarded. This consideration indicates that the data elements COPIES-AVAILABLE and COPIES-DISPOSED are in fact information that can be derived through processing. In view of the first design rule, we eliminate them from the set of data elements. The data field definitions in Figure 28 are modified accordingly and are finalized as shown in Figure 29. Data descriptions such as those in Figure 29 are usually stored in a data dictionary.

We observe no further problems with the data elements, and are ready for the next step.

Step 2: Data semantics analysis. We determine the enterprise rules applicable to the data elements and formulate them. Then we formalize these rules in the form of pair dependencies, as shown in Figure 30.

Six enterprise rules govern the data semantics in this system. As an example, let us consider one of them, enterprise rule 3. It implies that VIDEO-TITLE values are distinct, and thus VIDEO-TITLE may be used as a candidate key in some record structures. We also know from the semantics of the VIDEO-NUMBER data item that corresponding to a distinct title, we may have more than one copy, in other words, more than one value of VIDEO-NUMBER. Therefore, the following data dependency can be written: VIDEO-NUMBER → VIDEO-TITLE.

The other data dependencies together with the corresponding enterprise rules are given in Figure 30. In view of these dependencies, the attributes VIDEO-NUMBER, CUSTOMER-NAME, CUSTOMER-ACCOUNT-NO, RENTAL-DATE, and RENTAL-TYPE appear to be key attributes, and together they constitute the candidate key for the record structure of VIDEO-FILE-1. VIDEO-FILE-1 is a tentative file that includes all attributes. We represent these data dependencies in a dependency diagram for the record structure of VIDEO-FILE-1, as shown in Figure 31. As this dependency diagram is a connected graph, we conclude that all data attributes are related to each other.

Because every attribute in the record structure of VIDEO-FILE-1 is atomic, this record structure is in first normal form. As far as dependencies of nonkey attributes on the candidate key are concerned,

Attribute name:	VIDEO-TITLE
Description :	Name of movie feature
Attribute type :	ALPHABETIC
Field length :	30
Data encoding :	None

Attribute name:	VIDEO-NUMBER
Description :	Distinct code, in-house assigned to each video feature upon purchase
Attribute type :	ALPHANUMERIC
Field length :	7
Data encoding :	XYYYYZZ

X: FEATURE CATEGORY CODE
YYYY: Serial sequence number, in-house assigned.
ZZ :   Copy number.

FEATURE CATEGORY CODE	Meaning
C	Comedy
D	Drama
F	Family
H	Horror
I	Instructional
S	Science fiction

Attribute name:	PRINCIPAL-ACTOR, PRINCIPAL-ACTRESS
Description :	Names of the principal actor and actress
Attribute type :	ALPHABETIC
Field length :	25
Data encoding :	None

Attribute name:	LENGTH
Description :	Length of movie feature in minutes
Attribute type :	INTEGER
Field length :	3
Data encoding :	None

Attribute name:	PURCHASE-PRICE
Description :	Cost of video cassette to the outlet
Attribute type :	DECIMAL
Field length :	5
Data encoding :	99.99 in dollars in cents

Attribute name:	DISTRIBUTOR-NAME
Description :	Name of distribution company supplying video cassettes
Attribute type :	ALPHABETIC
Field length :	25
Data encoding :	None

Attribute name:	DISTRIBUTOR-ADDRESS
Description :	Correspondence address of distribution company
Attribute type :	ALPHANUMERIC
Field length :	30
Data encoding :	None

Figure 29 Data Design Example: Final Data Field Definitions

Attribute name:	CUSTOMER-ACCOUNT-NO
Description :	Distinct account numbers assigned to customers
Attribute type :	INTEGER
Field length :	4
Data encoding :	None

Attribute name:	CUSTOMER-NAME
Description :	Full name of customer
Attribute type :	ALPHABETIC
Field length :	25
Data encoding :	None

Attribute name:	CUSTOMER-ADDRESS
Description :	Residence address of customer
Attribute type :	ALPHANUMERIC
Field length :	30
Data encoding :	None

Attribute name:	RENTAL-DATE
Description :	Date cassette rented
Attribute type :	INTEGER
Field length :	6
Data encoding :	YY/MM/DD, year/month/day

Attribute name: RENTAL-TYPE
Description : Weekday or weekend rental indicator
Attribute type : ALPHABETIC
Field length : 1
Data encoding :

RENTAL-TYPE	Meaning
R	Weekday rental
W	Weekend rental

Attribute name:	DUE-DATE
Description :	Date cassette to be returned by customer
Attribute type :	INTEGER
Field length :	4
Data encoding :	MMDD, month-day

Figure 29 (Continued)

however, we notice some partial dependencies, implying that this record structure is not in second normal form.

Step 3: Normalization to second normal form. To get rid of data redundancies and update, insertion, and deletion anomalies that are due to the partial dependencies, we decompose the record structure of VIDEO-FILE-1 into the record structures of VIDEO-FILE-2, CUSTOMER-FILE-2, and RENTALS-FILE-2. These record structures together with their corresponding dependency diagrams are shown in Figure 32. As can be seen, in all of these record structures the nonkey attributes are fully dependent on the candidate keys. In other words, these record structures are all in second normal form, and the decomposition process did not result in any loss of data. Also, we realize that the record structure of CUSTOMER-FILE-2 is fully normalized and is in all normal forms. Its design is therefore final at this step.

The record structure of VIDEO-FILE-2, however, although in second normal form, is not in third normal form, as all the nonkey attributes in it are transitively dependent on the candidate key VIDEO-NUMBER.

Enterprise rule 1. PRINCIPAL-ACTOR, PRINCIPAL-ACTRESS, LENGTH, and PURCHASE-PRICE are properties that are directly related to a video cassette, which can be identified either by its VIDEO-TITLE or distinct VIDEO-NUMBER.

VIDEO NUMBER → PRINCIPAL-ACTOR	VIDEO-TITLE → PRINCIPAL-ACTOR
VIDEO-NUMBER → PRINCIPAL-ACTRESS	VIDEO-TITLE → PRINCIPAL-ACTRESS
VIDEO-NUMBER → LENGTH	VIDEO-TITLE → LENGTH
VIDEO-NUMBER → PURCHASE-PRICE	VIDEO-TITLE → PURCHASE-PRICE

Enterprise rule 2. A movie video is licensed to only one distribution company, and every distribution company supplies the outlet by many titles.

VIDEO-NUMBER → DISTRIBUTOR NAME	VIDEO-TITLE → DISTRIBUTOR-NAME
VIDEO-NUMBER → DISTRIBUTOR-ADDRESS	VIDEO-TITLE → DISTRIBUTOR-ADDRESS

Enterprise rule 3. Due to copyright laws, all movie cassettes have distinct titles. They are also assigned distinct identification numbers as soon as they are acquired by the outlet.

VIDEO-NUMBER → VIDEO-TITLE

Enterprise rule 4. All distribution companies with which the outlet does business have distinct company names; however, their correspondence addresses occasionally change.

DISTRIBUTOR-NAME → DISTRIBUTOR-ADDRESS

Enterprise rule 5. Customers are identified by their full names. Also, the outlet opens accounts for each customer and assigns distinct account numbers to each.

CUSTOMER-NAME → CUSTOMER-ADDRESS
CUSTOMER-ACCOUNT-NO → CUSTOMER-ADDRESS
CUSTOMER-ACCOUNT-NO → CUSTOMER-NAME
CUSTOMER-NAME → CUSTOMER-ACCOUNT-NO

Enterprise rule 6. When a customer rents a video on a weekday, the due date is the next day before 9:00 p.m. For Saturday rentals, the due date is the next Monday before 9:00 p.m.

{VIDEO-NUMBER, CUSTOMER-NAME, RENTAL-DATE, RENTAL-TYPE} → DUE-DATE
{VIDEO-NUMBER, CUSTOMER-ACCOUNT-NO, RENTAL-DATE, RENTAL-TYPE} → DUE-DATE
{RENTAL-DATE, RENTAL-TYPE} → DUE DATE
RENTAL-DATE → RENTAL-TYPE

Figure 30 Data Design Example: Enterprise Rules and Data Dependencies

Step 4: Normalization to third normal form. We can eliminate the transitive dependencies of nonkey attributes on the candidate key by taking appropriate projections. This decomposition process yields the record structures for VIDEO-FILE-3, DISTRIBUTED-BY-FILE-3, VIDEO-NUMBER-TITLE-FILE-3, and DISTRIBUTOR-FILE-3, as shown in Figure 33. The remaining record structures for CUSTOMER-FILE-3 and RENTALS-FILE-3 are simply carried over from the previous design phase. All the record structures in Figure 33 are in third normal form. In fact, all except RENTALS-FILE-3 are fully normalized.

Step 5: Normalization to Boyce/Codd normal form. The record structure of RENTALS-FILE-3 is not in Boyce/Codd normal form. This is because the attribute set {RENTAL-DATE, RENTAL-TYPE}, although not the candidate key, is a determinant. We convert this record structure to two record structures for DATES-FILE-4 and RENTALS-FILE-4 by taking appropriate projections. The results are shown in Figure 34.

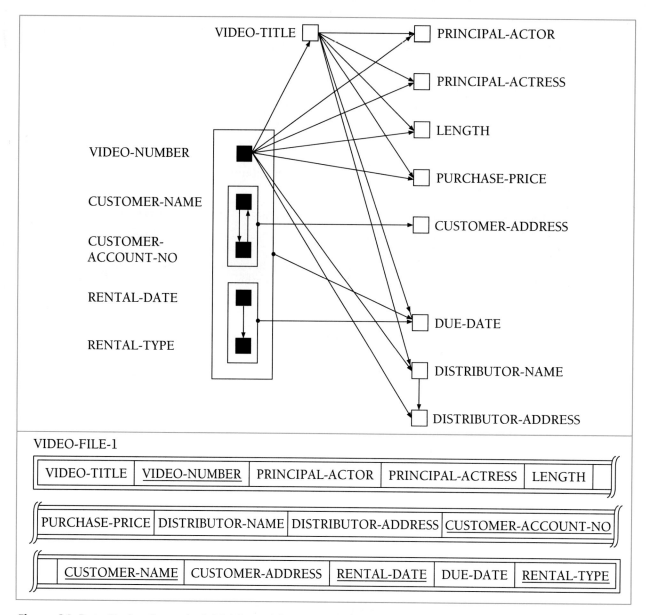

Figure 31 Data Design Example: Initial Record Structure Design

We note that the record structure of DATES-FILE-4 is still not in Boyce/Codd normal form because RENTAL-DATE, which is not a candidate key, is still a determinant. We do not bother to normalize this any further for reasons explained below.

Step 6: Finalizing design. Except for DATES-FILE-4, all the record structures in our design are now fully normalized. We realize that DATES-FILE-4 is, in fact, a determinate process description, as DUE-DATE is either the next day or Monday, depending on the RENTAL-DATE. Hence, we eliminate this file from the file system and include it in the system as a procedure.

The final design for the record structures is presented in Figure 35. Figure 36 is the entity-relationship diagram for the file system. It is obvious that the files VIDEO-FILE, CUSTOMER-FILE, and DISTRIBUTOR-FILE correspond to entity sets, and the files RENTALS-FILE and DISTRIBUTED-BY-FILE represent the relationships RENTED-BY and DISTRIBUTED-BY between the entity sets.

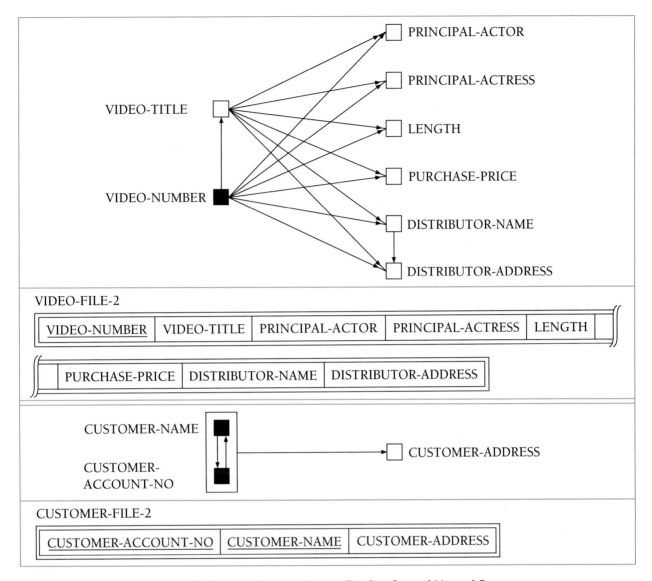

Figure 32 Data Design Example: Record Structures Normalized to Second Normal Form

Key Terms

Boyce/Codd normal form
candidate key
data
data accuracy
data dependency
data integrity
data relevance
data semantics
data usability
data validity
deletion anomaly
determinant
domain set
entity integrity
entity-relationship diagram
entity-relationship model
first normal form
foreign key

full dependency
information
insertion anomaly
intersection file
key
key attributes
multiple-point update
nonkey attributes
normalization
pair dependency
partial dependency
potential inconsistency
primary key
referential integrity
second normal form
third normal form
transitive dependency
update anomaly

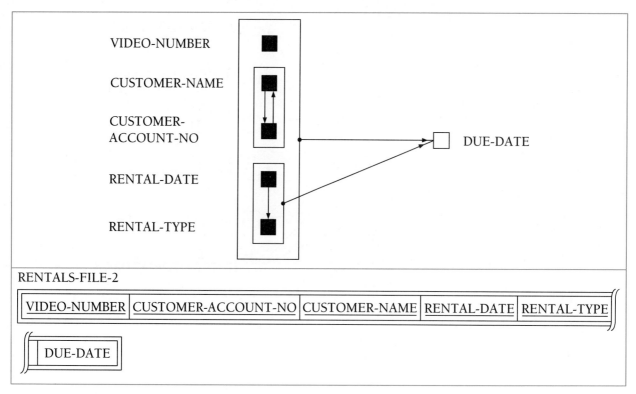

Figure 32 (Continued)

Study Guide

Quick Scan

- The first level of data design is concerned with record structures. In designing record structures we concentrate on the characteristics of data in isolation, as well as data in a record structure.
- In a computer file we generally store data, not information. Data have something to do with measurable or observable properties of entities, relationships, or events in the real world. Information, on the other hand, refers to values obtained through computations or manipulations of data values.
- In computer data files we store data that are relevant to applications of several users. Data should be current in that they should reflect the present situation in an enterprise. They should be accurate to represent correctly and precisely that part of the reality that they aim to represent. Data should also be valid, that is, in conformity with the specifications for their fields and the range of admissible values that can be assigned to them.
- Data in isolation should be usable, should not be time dependent, if possible, and should require a minimum amount of storage.
- In computer data files, data that are semantically related are structured together. Two data fields are related if, corresponding to a value for one, a value for the other can be found.
- Relationships between and among data items are also known as data dependencies. Data dependencies constitute a significant aspect of data semantics.
- The three types of data dependencies are one-to-one, one-to-many, and many-to-many. Many-to-many dependencies can be equivalently expressed as two one-to-many dependencies. Therefore, it is sufficient to consider only one-to-one and one-to-many dependencies.
- Dependencies among and between data elements are reflected by enterprise rules. An enterprise rule describes some constraints that data elements should satisfy in the real world with respect to one another.

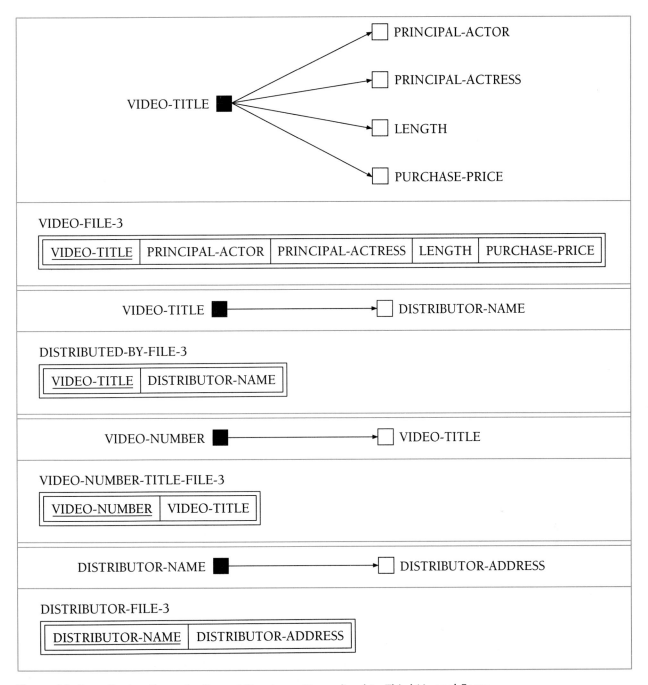

Figure 33 Data Design Example: Record Structures Normalized to Third Normal Form

- There are several types of data dependencies, some desirable and natural, and others quite detrimental to record structure design. If a set of attributes determines another set of attributes, such a dependency is known as full functional dependency. If, however, only a subset of a set of attributes is required to determine a second set of attributes, the dependency between the two sets of attributes is partial.
- Another type of data dependency is transitive. Given three sets of attributes, if the first determines the second, the second determines the third, and the first also determines the third, we say the third set of attributes is transitively dependent on the first set.
- Data dependencies in a record structure can be represented graphically using a dependency diagram, in which pair dependencies are shown by directional lines from one attribute to another.

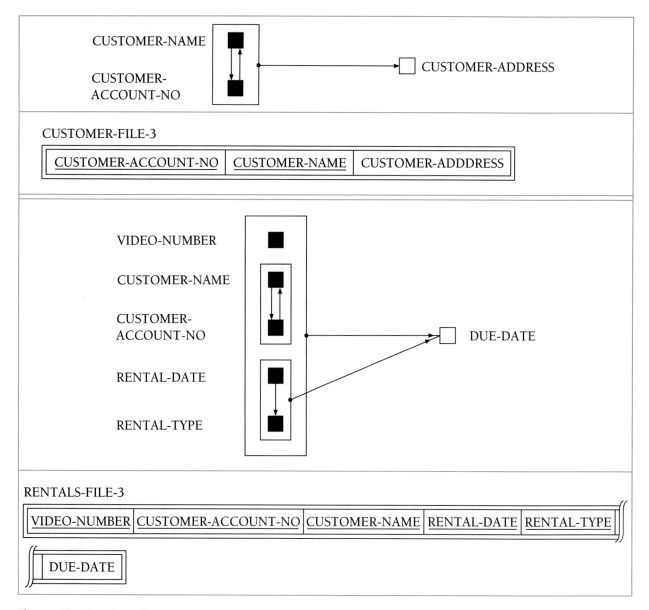

CUSTOMER-NAME

CUSTOMER-ACCOUNT-NO

CUSTOMER-ADDRESS

CUSTOMER-FILE-3

CUSTOMER-ACCOUNT-NO	CUSTOMER-NAME	CUSTOMER-ADDDRESS

VIDEO-NUMBER

CUSTOMER-NAME

CUSTOMER-ACCOUNT-NO

RENTAL-DATE

RENTAL-TYPE

DUE-DATE

RENTALS-FILE-3

VIDEO-NUMBER	CUSTOMER-ACCOUNT-NO	CUSTOMER-NAME	RENTAL-DATE	RENTAL-TYPE

DUE-DATE

Figure 33 (Continued)

- A computer file stores data about properties of entities or relationships in the real world. A relationship is a set of specifications that associate two or more distinct entity sets.
- A relationship between two entity sets, or equivalently, between two computer files, may be one-to-one, one-to-many, or many-to-many.
- In practical applications, many-to-many relationships are difficult to implement and process. In general, they are decomposed into two one-to-many relationships by introducing a third file, known as an intersection file. Records in an intersection file are based on some identifying properties of records in the two files involved.
- Different methods can be used to represent a relationship in computer storage. Some entail collapsing attributes associated with relationships onto the files tied by the relationships. Others use pointers. A preferred approach is to use independent files for relationships.
- In file system design, a good design rule is to have record structures that represent either an entity or a relationship, but not both.

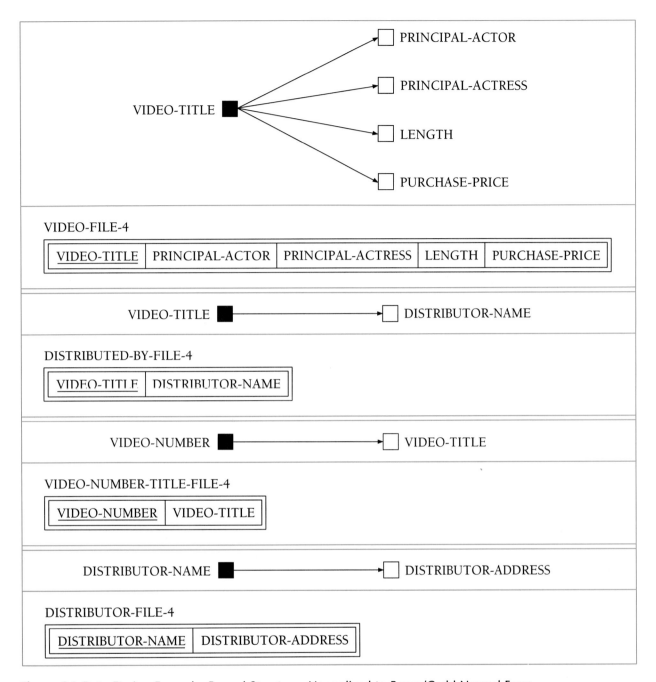

Figure 34 Data Design Example: Record Structures Normalized to Boyce/Codd Normal Form

- A model that describes data semantics for data represented in a file system without considering the characteristics of a computer system is a logical model. One of the more commonly used logical data modeling techniques is the entity-relationship model.
- The entity-relationship technique uses an entity-relationship diagram to represent data semantics. In the diagram, entity sets are represented by rectangles and relationship sets by diamond-shaped boxes. The type of each relationship is explicitly indicated. The corresponding domain set for each attribute is also shown.
- Entity-relationship diagrams constitute one of the outputs of the logical system design phase, and a significant input for the physical design.

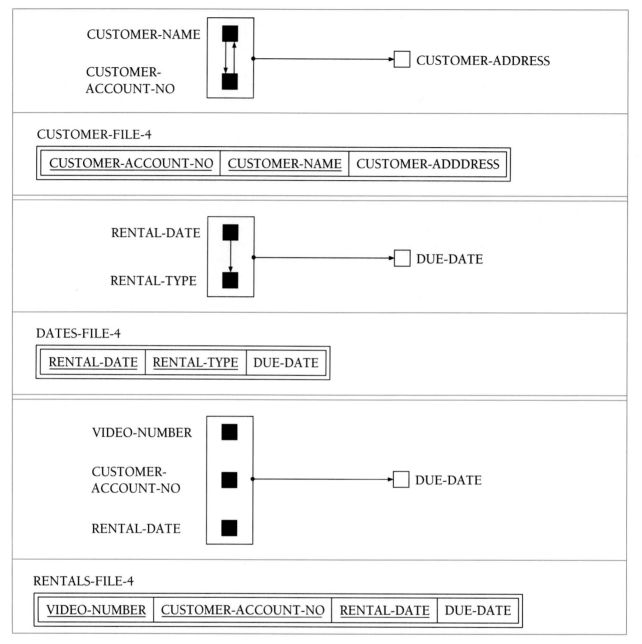

Figure 34 (Continued)

- In a data file all records should be distinct. Distinctness is achieved by using a set of attributes as a key. A key set of attributes satisfies the properties of unique identification, nonredundancy, and validity.
- More than one set of attributes may satisfy all requirements for keys. Such attribute sets are called candidate keys. For physical implementation purposes, one of the candidate keys may be chosen to serve as the principal identifier. This candidate key is called the primary key.
- As much as possible, we should avoid updating primary key attributes. Therefore, during design, if, for a record structure we have more than one candidate key, we should choose as a primary key the one that is least likely to change in time.
- Certain data values may be duplicated in computer files. Unnecessary duplications are wasteful of storage. In general, they should be allowed only for key attributes that participate in the primary key for the file, and nonkey at-

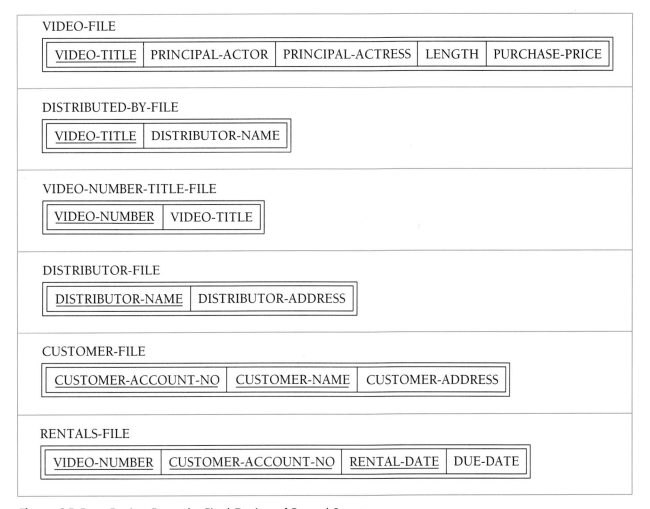

Figure 35 Data Design Example: Final Design of Record Structures

tributes that map more than one member of an entity or relationship set to the same value of the attribute domain.

- Data in computer files should not violate integrity rules. Data integrity is concerned with the issue of representing and maintaining data without conflicts and inconsistencies within a file or file system.

- In data file records, no attribute of the primary key should be left empty. This is known as the entity integrity rule.

- An attribute in a record structure is called a foreign key if it is a candidate key for another related record structure. For foreign keys, the referential integrity rule states that every value assigned to a foreign key should either be empty, or should match a value of a compatible attribute in some occurrence of the record structure in which the latter attribute is a candidate key.

- In a file containing no integrity violations, potential inconsistencies may exist. Such inconsistencies are due to a record structure's tendency to result in inconsistent data in a file because the structure necessitates update of several records whenever update of an attribute value is logically required. Another term for potential inconsistency is update anomaly. Update anomalies are due to data redundancies.

- Another problem with record structure design is deletion anomaly. It is a record structure's tendency to cause unintended loss of data from a file as a consequence of deleting a record.

- Insertion anomaly is a record structure's tendency not to allow insertion of partial information about some entity into a file unless some pertinent

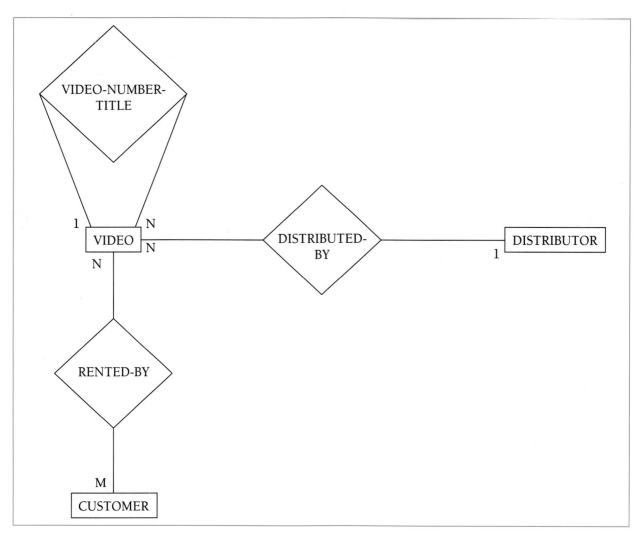

Figure 36 Data Design Example: Entity-Relationship Diagram

relationship is satisfied. Both insertion and deletion anomalies are results of undesirable properties of record structures and can be eliminated through normalization.

- Normalization is a step-by-step process of transforming a record structure without losing data, so that the transformed structure has no undesirable properties such as redundancies, and update, insertion, and deletion anomalies.

- A record structure is in first normal form if no attribute in it can be decomposed into subordinate fields.

- A record structure containing group items or repeating groups is not in first normal form. It can be transformed into first normal form by replacing composite attributes with their respective constituents. A first normal form record structure has advantages over one that is not in that form.

- A first normal form record structure may exhibit data redundancies and certain structural anomalies. This may be due to the fact that it is not in second normal form.

- A record structure that is in first normal form is in second normal form if all nonkey attributes in it are fully dependent on all candidate keys.

- A record structure that is not in second normal form can be decomposed into two or more equivalent record structures that are in second normal form by considering appropriate projections such that all partial dependencies on key attributes are eliminated. The resulting record structures are generally better than the original in that they may be free of redundancies and anomalies.

- Certain problems may persist in a second normal form record structure. They may be due to the existence of transitive dependencies.
- A record structure that is in second normal form is said to be in third normal form if no nonkey attribute in it is transitively dependent on any candidate key.
- Again, a second normal form record structure can be decomposed into two or more third normal form structures by considering projections that eliminate transitive dependencies. If the resulting collection of structures still is not problem free, it may be due to the fact that it is not in Boyce/Codd normal form.
- A record structure is in Boyce/Codd normal form if every determinant in its dependency diagram is a candidate key.
- In practice, a majority of record structures that are in Boyce/Codd normal form are free of anomalies and redundancies.
- In record structure design, all record structures should be in the ultimate normal form, known as domain-key normal form, so that no future maintenance difficulties may arise.

Test Your Comprehension

Multiple-Choice Questions

1. Which of the following statements concerning data in computer files is correct?
   a. Information is processed data.
   b. Computer data files should store data, not information.
   c. Data in computer files should be relevant to the needs of many applications.
   d. All of the above are correct.

2. Which of the following statements concerning properties of data in computer files is incorrect?
   a. A data field value is valid if it is a correct and precise representation of that part of the reality.
   b. Files should contain only current, accurate, valid data.
   c. If several versions exist for a data field, the form that is least likely to change in time is preferred.
   d. Data compression techniques can be used to minimize storage requirements for data.

3. Which of the following statements concerning data dependencies is correct?
   a. Data dependencies constitute a significant aspect of data semantics.
   b. A dependency can be one-to-one, one-to-many, or many-to-many.
   c. In a pair dependency, if for a single value of the determinant, multiple values of the dependent attribute set exist, such a pair dependency is one-to-many.
   d. All of the above are correct.

4. Suppose the following pair dependencies are known to exist in a record structure: $A \rightarrow B$, $\{A, C\} \rightarrow B$, $B \rightarrow D$, $A \rightarrow D$. Which of the following statements is correct?
   a. D is transitively dependent on A.
   b. D is fully functionally dependent on $\{A, C\}$
   c. A is partially dependent on $\{A, C\}$.
   d. All of the above are correct.

5. In an entity-relationship diagram,
   a. Domain sets are represented by rectangular boxes.
   b. Relationship sets are represented by diamond-shaped boxes.
   c. Entity sets are represented by oval boxes.
   d. Types of relationships are not shown.

6. Which of the following statements concerning data integrity is incorrect?
    a. Data integrity is concerned with representing and maintaining data without any conflicts or inconsistencies within a file or a file system.
    b. The entity integrity rule requires that foreign key attributes be compatible with their corresponding candidate keys in a related file.
    c. A foreign key in a record structure is an attribute that appears as a candidate key in another related record structure.
    d. No attribute participating in the primary key of a record structure may be empty.
7. Insertion anomaly is a record structure's tendency
    a. Not to allow insertion of partial information about some entity into a file unless some pertinent condition is satisfied
    b. To cause unintended loss of data from a file as a result of a record insertion
    c. To cause unintended loss of data from a file as a result of a record deletion
    d. To do none of the above.
8. Which of the following statements concerning normalization and normal forms is correct?
    a. A record structure containing no nonkey attributes is in Boyce/Codd normal form.
    b. A record structure based on only two attributes is in Boyce/Codd normal form.
    c. In a third normal form relation, no nonkey attribute is partially dependent on any candidate key.
    d. All of the above are correct.

Answers: 1. d; 2. a; 3. d; 4. a; 5. b; 6. b; 7. a; 8. d.

Short Essay Questions

1. What is the difference between data and information?
2. Why should we be careful to store data rather than information in computer files?
3. Explain the meaning of the terms data currency, data accuracy, and data validity.
4. What is meant by data usability? Give an example of data that is not in usable form.
5. Explain the meaning of time dependency of data.
6. What is meant by two data items being related? Give an example of two data items that are unrelated.
7. Define data dependency.
8. What is meant by one-to-one data dependency? One-to-many data dependency?
9. Briefly define the following types of data dependencies, and for each give an example:
    a. Full functional dependency
    b. Partial dependency
    c. Transitive dependency
10. Discuss different approaches available for representing relationships between entity sets in computer storage.
11. What is meant by an intersection file? Devise an example and discuss it.
12. Explain the significance of the entity-relationship data modeling technique in file design.
13. Briefly explain the convention used in constructing entity-relationship diagrams.

14. Define the related concepts of key, property of nonredundancy, property of validity, candidate key, and primary key.
15. What is meant by data redundancy? Under what circumstances is data duplication not considered redundancy?
16. Define data integrity.
17. What is meant by entity integrity? Can entity integrity for a keyed sequence VSAM data set be violated? Why?
18. What is meant by referential integrity?
19. Define the related concepts of update anomaly, deletion anomaly, and insertion anomaly.
20. Define normalization.
21. What is meant by first normal form? Why is it desirable to transform record structures into first normal form in file design?
22. Define the related concepts of second normal form, third normal form, and Boyce/Codd normal form.
23. Explain the steps in the process of normalization for record structures.

Improve Your Problem-Solving Ability

Problem

1. We have the following preliminary design for a record structure.

```
EMPLOYEE-RECORD (SOCIAL-SECURITY-NUMBER, EMPLOYEE-NAME, DATE-OF-BIRTH,
            EMPLOYEE-SEX, SPOUSE-NAME, CITY-OF-RESIDENCE, MANAGER-SSNO,
            CURRENT-JOB-TITLE, CURRENT-SALARY, CURRENT-JOB-START-DATE,
   repeating-group-of-JOB-HISTORY (COMPANY-NAME, COMPANY-LOCATED-AT, COMPANY-
            BUSINESS-TYPE, EMPLOYEE-JOB-TITLE-IN-COMPANY, START-DATE,
            END-DATE, SALARY),
   repeating-group-of-CHILDREN-INFORMATION (CHILD-NAME, CHILD-AGE),
   repeating-group-of-COLLEGE-EDUCATION (COLLEGE-NAME, COLLEGE-TYPE,
            ACCREDITED-OR-NOT, COLLEGE-LOCATED-AT, DEGREE-EARNED,
            MAJOR-OF-DEGREE, YEAR-CONFERRED-FOR-DEGREE) )
```

The applicable enterprise rules for this set of data elements are as follows.

An employee works full-time in the company for which this file system is being designed, and cannot hold a part-time job elsewhere.

There is no limit on the number of children an employee may have.

There is no limit on the number of previous jobs for employees.

There is no limit on the number of degrees an employee may have earned.

A given company is identified by a single business type (e.g., manufacturing, transportation, utilities, service, etc.).

As is seen, the given record structure is not in first normal form.

Carry out the record structure design process according to the design methodology given in this chapter and finalize it.

Normalize all record structures to Boyce/Codd normal form.

For each record structure, clearly indicate all candidate keys and your choice of the primary key, with your reasons for the choice.

Draw an entity-relationship diagram for the design of the file system.

If you feel that you must make certain assumptions to clarify the data semantics further, state them and the reasons behind them.

V

COBOL and Data Base Systems

18. An Introduction to Data Base Management

An Introduction to Data Base Management

Introduction

In our study of file systems we have seen that in many applications files are semantically and structurally related. A great variety of applications require more than one file to be available as their input. To make optimal use of the data resource, we allow many users to access components of the same file system. Furthermore, we allow the users to access and process computer files concurrently.

So far we have used the term "file system" to connote a set of related files each containing integrated data to be used in many applications by many users. So as not to distract the reader, we have intentionally refrained from using the more precise term "data base." In fact, a file system consisting of interrelated files is known as a data base. Since the 1970s, theories, techniques, and implementations have been developed for data base systems. Data base management is now a well-defined and established area of computer information systems and computer science, and is usually studied after a course on file management.

In this concluding chapter we will give a brief introduction to data base management, emphasizing its strong correlation with file management and COBOL programming. Also, we will establish a bridge to data base management with the hope that the reader will find the area sufficiently interesting for further study.

Fundamental Concepts of Data Base Systems

In Chapter 17 we came across some data bases; in fact, we designed a data base—the ACE Video Outlet file system of Figure 35. As is seen in the entity-relationship model drawn for it in Figure 36 of Chapter 17, it consists of six interrelated files, some representing entity sets, and others representing relationship sets. In all of these files, data redundancies are eliminated, maintenance difficulties are minimized, and the logical real-world relationships are properly reflected. Obviously, these files can be used for a variety of applications. They are not a random collection, but a set of related files satisfying certain constraints.

A data base is a component of a data base system, just as a file is a component of a file system. To process a file system, we need a general-purpose software system known as a file management system. An example of a file management system is VSAM. Similarly, to process a data base we use a data base management system (DBMS). A DBMS is one of the most complex software systems ever designed for computers.

Data Bases Versus File Systems

> A **data base** is a named and structured collection of related files satisfying the following requirements.
> 1. Data redundancies are fully eliminated or minimized.
> 2. Real-world entities and relationships are appropriately represented.
> 3. A large number of applications can be supported.
> 4. More than one user can concurrently access and process the files.
> 5. Access to data is handled by general-purpose systems software. In application programs, the user need not be concerned with issues related to data access.
> 6. Security is provided in the sense that access to data is controlled, and users can access all or part of the stored data.
> 7. Data are protected against computer system failures, and in case of failure, the data base can be restored to its original state.
> 8. Integrity of data can be maintained at all times.

These requirements stress the differences between a collection of files designed and implemented for an application, and a data base. A collection of files for an application considers only the data required by that application, and probably is not suitable for another application requiring the same data in addition to others. Therefore, a different collection of files may be required for another application. This may cause a high degree of data duplication in a business data processing environment. Also, there is the issue of extra hours wasted on designing, structuring, collecting, and maintaining data that are already available in another file system.

Even in designing individual files we stressed the importance of providing one-to-one correspondence between files, and the entity and relationship sets in the problem domain. We have seen that this design rule can occasionally be violated, and computer files may emerge as counterparts to mixtures of entity and relationship sets. In a data base environment, this principle is all the more important.

In file processing, an application program declares a lock on the files specified in it and thus prohibits other application systems from concurrently accessing their data. On the other hand, a data base allows simultaneous access to data by more than one application program.

While processing files in an application program, all data elements in the files' record structures are explicitly defined and thus are readily available to anybody who has access to the program. In a data base environment, only data elements that are needed by an application program may be made available to a user, and the remaining classified data may be suppressed. This allows some degree of data security, which is more difficult to achieve in applications that use a collection of files.

In this book we have developed many programs in COBOL that access data in computer files. In all of them, it was our responsibility to specify file organization techniques and access methods, and use proper I-O statements. In a data base environment, physical access to data in files is done by a vendor-supplied software system that intervenes between the user and the file management system. This substantially facilitates application program development.

In file processing, system crashes may cause loss of valuable data in computer files, and loss of information that is produced by an application program until the time of crash. In a data base environment, certain recovery precautions are incorporated into the system that manages the data base.

It is because of these considerable advantages that data bases are generally preferred to individually designed files for application programming in corporate data centers. These advantages are gained by incorporating data bases into data base systems.

Data Base System Components

In file processing, files constitute only one component of a human-computer system. In addition to data that are structured and stored in files, we have

1. Application programs written in a computer language
2. Compilers that translate application programs to executable object codes
3. File management systems that interact with computer data files and application programs to permit access to data
4. Other systems software such as utility programs that are used for file maintenance purposes
5. Procedures that specify operational aspects in a data processing environment
6. People who are involved as application programmers, system programmers, operations personnel, and customers

A **data base system** is also a human-computer system that is similar to, but somewhat more complex and involved than, a file system. It consists of people, data resources, hardware, software, and procedures. In addition to application programmers, system programmers, operations personnel, and customers, there is a special group of technical people known as data base administrators. A **data base administrator** is a person who is knowledgeable about the functions of a corporation, and is responsible for defining, structuring, maintaining, and administering the corporate data base.

The data resource consists of one or more data bases permanently storing data required for periodic and ad hoc information processing. Hardware includes one or more computer systems and appropriate direct-access data storage devices. Software consists of systems software (operating systems, language compilers and processors, file management systems, utility programs, etc.), application programs, and general-purpose DBMS software.

Procedures define steps to be followed and precautions to be taken for normal operations, data base management and maintenance, data base access, failure, and data base recovery. In such a system, the principal component that is new for us is the data base management system.

Data Definition in Data Base Processing

Before we get into a discussion of data base management systems, we should introduce the three separate but related views of data in a data base. One of them focuses on the data from a logical point of view, without any considerations as to how they are actually stored.

The complete and machine-independent (logical) description of data in a data base is known as **data base schema.**

The record structure designs for ACE Video Outlet as shown in Figure 35 of Chapter 17, together with the overall view of files in the E-R diagram of Figure 36 in Chapter 17, make up the schema for the ACE Video data base. Describing such a schema to the supporting computer system is one of the responsibilities of the data base administrator, who does this by writing and executing a program. A data base schema may be made available fully or partially to application programmers depending on their requirements and their data access privileges.

The second view has to do with the way data are actually stored in a computer storage medium.

> The form of the data in a data base as they would appear to a computer system is called the **physical view**.

The physical view is concerned with physical data clusters, indexes, pointers, memory locations storing encoded data, and internal representation techniques used by a specific computer system. This view is also described and maintained by the data base administrator.

Finally, there are the data requirements of application programmers or users.

> A subset of the data base schema consisting of data needed for an application program or a user of the data base is known as a **subschema**.

Figure 1 shows different subschemas that can be derived from the data base schema of Figure 35 in Chapter 17. Subschema 1 is appropriate for an application in which we would like to get names of movie features for a specified actor. In this application, we do not have to include complete record structure descriptions of all files in our application program. We need only the first two fields of the VIDEO-FILE record structure of Figure 35 in Chapter 17. Subschema 2 contains the data fields required to get a listing of movie names, their suppliers, and purchase prices. Subschema 3 is for the same application, except here we collect all necessary attributes into a single record structure. Finally, subschema 4 is suitable if we want to produce a listing of all cassettes rented out including their titles, customer names, and due dates.

Corresponding to a data base schema, several subschemas can be defined, each suitable for a specific application. In defining a subschema, we may change file and data field names. In subschema 1 of Figure 1, MOVIE-NAME is the same field as VIDEO-TITLE of Figure 35 in Chapter 17. Different subschemas that can be derived from a given data base may be disjoint or they may overlap.

Clearly, from the point of view of application program development, defining only subschemas and having them related to appropriate data base schemas by a DBMS form a more efficient approach than including full data definitions of all files in an application program. Also, it gives a user the flexibility of assigning different names to data elements.

As in the case of a file, the three fundamental types of operations on a data base are definition, maintenance, and retrieval. Definition entails schema, subschema, and physical view definitions. Maintenance includes updates, record insertions into, and record deletions from a data base file.

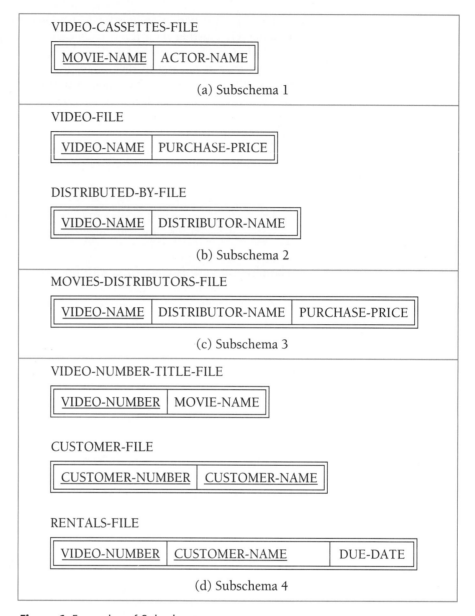

Figure 1 Examples of Subschemas

   All three operations are facilitated in a data base environment through the use of a special, very high-level language. This is known as **data base language** and is supported by a data base management system. A data base language depends on the data base model on which the DBMS is built. For a given model, the language also depends on the approach taken to design the system, and the software vendor's particular implementation characteristics. We will take a closer look at data base languages later in this chapter. For now we should realize that each DBMS comes with a special language that we can use to define data base schemas, maintain data bases, and access data.

Data Base Processing Modes

A data base may be processed in two different modes: interactive and application programming. In **interactive mode** the user can interact directly with a data base through a terminal to access, or update the stored data. We may use a data base language to create the data base schema and to load files with records. We also may make use of retrieval instructions of the data base language to retrieve data. In interactive mode, retrieved data are simply reported to the user, and in general, additional processing on them is not possible.

In **application programming mode** a data base is accessed by an application program that is written using an appropriate programming language. To facilitate data base operations, we include instructions of the data base language in the program. The language in which the application program is coded is referred to as the **host language** with respect to the data base language. COBOL is an acceptable host language for many existing data base management systems. The version of the data base language that allows embedding of its instructions in an application program is referred to as its **embedded** version. Embedded instructions of a language may create a data base schema, or may aim to update or access data base files.

Compared to writing an application program in which all data base operations are explicitly defined by the programmer, using embedded data language instructions in a host language program has several advantages. First, developing the application program is faster, easier, and more efficient. Second, the resulting application program is more concise. Third, the application programmer need not be concerned with the intricacies of the underlying file management system, and file organization and access techniques.

Data Base System Architecture

To explain the functions of a DBMS, we have to develop a clear view of a data base processing environment and the architecture of the system. In such a picture, we understand that data are stored permanently and kept current in a data base. The data base administrator is the person or persons responsible for this, and the one who defines the structure of data.

Figure 2 shows the architecture of a typical data base system. Obviously, it is quite complex. Its central component is the data base management system, which, together with the operating system, interacts with and monitors almost every element in the system. Let us examine closely the components of this architecture.

In interactive mode of processing a user of a data base directly interacts with the system through a terminal by typing instructions in the data language supported by the DBMS. These instructions may aim to define data base schema or access an already existing data base. A schema definition instruction is processed by the DBMS, converted into machine language, and stored in one or more special system files known as **system catalog files.** After a schema definition is created and stored, every data language instruction referencing a data base component causes the system first to access the system catalog files and verify the correctness of the data base component. If the user issues a data base access instruction, the DBMS maps the implied subschema against the stored schema, verifies its correctness, and accesses the physical data base. An access instruction may be for the purpose of loading a data base file, inserting, deleting, or updating records, or retrieving and displaying records in a file.

In application programming mode the program should contain embedded subschema definition instructions and some appropriate data base access instructions. Before any processing can be done, the program is precompiled by a special software element known as precompiler. A **precompiler** takes as input an application program that is written, say, in COBOL and produces a pure COBOL program in which the embedded data language instructions are replaced by some subroutine calls to program modules existing as parts of the DBMS.

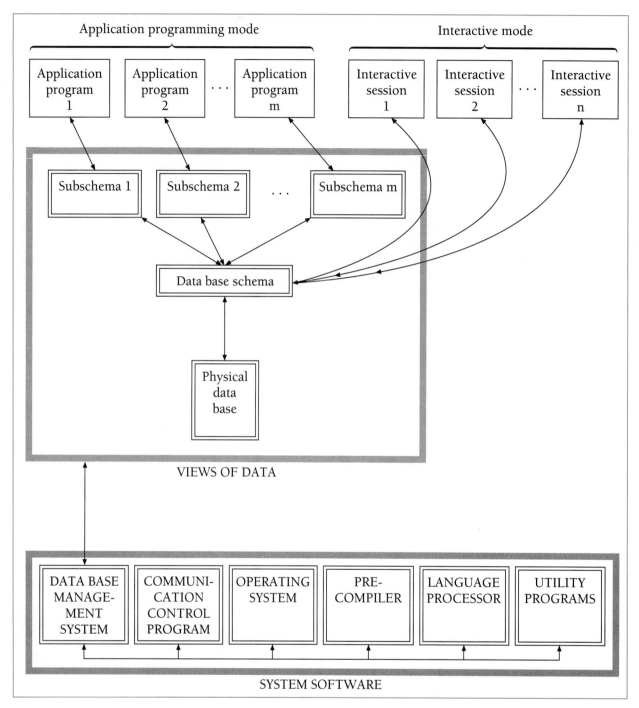

Figure 2 Architecture of a Data Base System

The output from the precompiler is routinely compiled by the language compiler and the DBMS. The DBMS verifies the subschema in the application program against the data base schema stored in system catalog files. If no errors are found, in cooperation with the host language compiler, the DBMS generates an object program and an application plan. An **application plan** is the machine language description of the data base access strategy required for an application program.

Finally, the object program and the application plan are executed together. During execution, the DBMS accesses appropriate data base elements and makes them available to the application program for further processing.

Functions of a Data Base Management System

In the architecture described above, the special software system called data base management system plays a prominent part. It monitors almost every component and process in a data base system. The following are its major functions.

1. Provide user–data base interface in interactive mode, and application program–data base interface in application programming mode.
2. Support a data base language through which it is possible to
   a. Define and store data base schema.
   b. Define subschemas for application programs.
   c. Define and store physical data base definition.
   d. Load data base data.
   e. Store and maintain data.
   f. Access and retrieve data using a variety of access techniques.
3. Create and maintain a system catalog of files concerning information about the data base itself, including authorized data base users, data base structure, and so on.
4. Provide for subschema-to-schema mapping, and schema-to-physical view mapping.
5. Provide for enforcement of data base integrity rules.
6. Provide security features to protect data against unauthorized access and processing.
7. Provide control over concurrent data base operations.
8. Facilitate data base backup and recovery.
9. Provide file utility services by interacting with utility programs.
10. Interface with other software in performing its tasks, including
    a. The operating system
    b. Language compilers
    c. Precompiler
    d. Communication control program (which controls the flow of data base transactions to application programs)

The special-purpose data base language supported by a DBMS consists of three components: data definition language, data manipulation language, and query formulation language. **Data definition language (DDL)** consists of instructions that can be used to define a data base schema, subschemas necessary for application programs, and physical data base view. **Data manipulation language (DML)** includes instructions to load a data base and to maintain it (update, insert, delete, etc.). **Query formulation language (QFL)** consists of instructions for accessing and retrieving data from data base files.

Advantages and Disadvantages of Data Base Systems

The following considerations can be cited as primary advantages of data base systems.

1. Because the corporate data are integrated into a data base, data redundancies are greatly reduced.
2. The use of good file design principles helps eliminate anomalies in data base structures.
3. All corporate data resources are available to an application programmer at any time. This significantly facilitates data processing.
4. In a data base environment, stored data are independent of an individual application program. Thus, a certain degree of program/data independence is immediately achieved.

5. Data base languages are generally easy to learn and easy to use, which expedites application program development.

6. Because a data base is a shared resource, its maintenance and management are centralized and left to a particular department in the corporate environment. This department can specify standards for data resource, and can effectively serve the information needs of other departments. Such a strategy leads to better data management.

7. In a data base, compared to a collection of disjoint file systems, real-world entities and relationships can be represented more easily and conveniently. Hence, stored data is more meaningful from an application programmer's point of view.

However, there are certain disadvantages to a data base system.

1. Because it requires a more powerful computer system, a DBMS, and additional system software, it is more expensive than a file system. Also, its operating cost is higher.

2. It is considerably more complex than a file system and requires more technically specialized personnel.

Whether a business should shift its data processing operations to a data base environment is a decision that largely depends on data processing requirements. Such a decision should not be made without a careful feasibility study.

REVIEW QUESTIONS

1. A data base is an arbitrary collection of files that may or may not be related to each other. (T or F)

2. In a data base
   a. Data redundancies are fully eliminated or minimized.
   b. Real-world entities and relationships are appropriately represented.
   c. Concurrent access to data base files is permitted.
   d. Access to data is controlled by a central software element.
   e. All of the above are correct.

3. In a data base, data integrity is maintained at all times. (T or F)

4. The components of a data base system are _____ , _____ , _____ , _____ , and _____ .

5. The complete and machine-independent description of data in a data base is called _____ .

6. A subschema is a subset of a data base schema needed for an application program. (T or F)

7. A data base may be processed in _____ or _____ mode.

8. In interactive data base processing, in addition to a data base language, a host language is needed. (T or F)

9. The software element that converts an application program containing embedded data base language instructions to a program that can be compiled by a language compiler is called a _____ .

10. Which of the following is not a function of a data base management system?
    a. Providing user–data base interface
    b. Precompiling application programs
    c. Defining data base schema
    d. Providing for enforcement of integrity rules.
    e. Providing control over concurrent data base operations.

11. The main disadvantages of data base systems are their high cost and complexity compared to file systems. (T or F)

Answers: 1. F; 2. e; 3. T; 4. people, data resource, hardware, software, procedures; 5. data base schema; 6. T; 7. interactive, application programming; 8. F; 9. precompiler; 10. b; 11. T.

Data Base Modeling

By now we realize that data structures are omnipresent in file processing and application programming. A record structure in a file is a data structure. The way records are logically organized in a file defines a data structure for it. In all such data structures, we emphasize data elements and relationships among them.

In a data base we are concerned with files and some logical relationships between them. Therefore, a data base is also a data structure in which files are data elements. It can be depicted as a model, or an abstraction that provides us with an overall view of the entire data base. Many different abstractions can be used; we refer to them as data base models.

Data Modeling for Data Base Systems

> A **data base model** is an abstraction that can be used to describe the structure and semantics of a data base.

In Chapter 17 we studied such a data model, called the entity-relationship data model. In entity-relationship modeling for a data base, we use an entity-relationship diagram to represent

1. Entities, which evolve into files during the physical design phase
2. Relationships between entities
3. Type of each relationship
4. Attributes associated with entities and relationships
5. Domain sets from which attributes derive their values.

Such a model provides us with structural as well as semantic information about a data base. An example of an entity-relationship diagram for a STUDENT-COURSE data base is shown in Figure 3.

Another logical technique that is equivalent to the entity-relationship model uses networks to represent the structure of a data base. In a network diagram, relationships are represented as labeled arcs. One-to-one relationships are shown as ⟵⟶, one-to-many as ⟵⟶⟶, and many-to-many as ⟷⟶⟶. The rest of the conventions are similar to those for E-R diagrams. Figure 4 is an example of a network diagram for the STUDENT-COURSE data base.

Data base modeling is important in data base management for several reasons. First, it is this model that provides the user with valuable information about data base structure and access patterns. Second, every commercially available data base management system is based on a specific data model, which forces the user to specify data base elements accordingly. Finally, the data base language a DBMS supports is directly influenced by the underlying data base model.

Many different data base models have been proposed. Some of them have limited significance in that, although useful for particular applications or purposes, no data base management system is patterned after them. An example is the entity-relationship data model. It is significant as a design tool, but is not

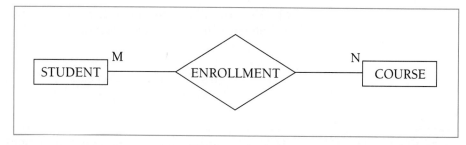

Figure 3 Logical Modeling for STUDENT-COURSE Data Base: Entity-Relationship Diagram

supported by a DBMS. Many other data models are theoretical, and for one reason or another have not enjoyed commercial success and longevity. Three techniques, however, have become prominent in practice. They are the relational, hierarchical, and network models.

Relational Data Model

The relational model is the newest of the three major data base modeling techniques. It was proposed in 1970 and its first implementation as DBMSs became available in the early 1980s. It is currently in widespread use in business and industry. One of the major reasons for its success is its simplicity with respect to its underlying data structures.

In the relational model of data, the basic data structure is a relation, also called a table.

> A **relation** is a two-dimensional data structure consisting of a fixed number of columns and a variable number of rows. Each column in a relation corresponds to an **attribute**, and each row corresponds to a record in a flat file.

In the previous chapter we came across the concept of flat file, in which every attribute is atomic. In other words, the record structure of a relation is in first normal form.

The relational model has its own terminology. A record is known as a **tuple**. The number of columns in a relation is called the **degree of relation**. A relation with one column is a **unary relation**, one with two columns is a **binary relation**, or a relation of degree 2, and so on. The number of rows in a relation is called its **cardinality**.

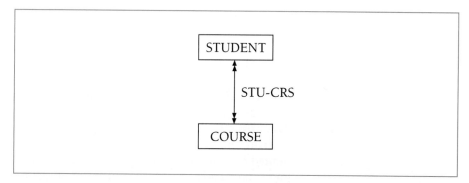

Figure 4 Logical Modeling for STUDENT-COURSE Data Base: Network Diagram

As a matter of convention, the structure of a relation is represented using the notation R (*A*, *B*, C, ...). Here, R is the name of the relation, A, B, C, and so on, are its attributes, and the underlined attributes are those that form its primary key.

A relation satisfies the following properties.

1. Column order is significant; that is, the relations R(A, B) and S(B, A) are not identically structured.
2. Row order is insignificant. For example, the following two relations are equivalent.

        EMP1 (NUMBER, NAME)   EMP2 (NUMBER, NAME)
              100   John   200   Mary
              200   Mary   100   John

3. Each row is distinct; that is, a primary key is used to identify rows of a relation uniquely.
4. No attribute participating in the primary key of a relation may be null (or empty).
5. All attributes (columns) are atomic, implying no group items and no repeating groups. Consequently, tuple length is fixed.
6. Each relation has only one structure (i.e., one record type).

In the relational model of data, a data base is represented using relations as the fundamental data structure. All entity and relationship sets are represented as relations. This model is suitable for representing all types of relationships; however, the types are not explicitly stated. Despite this, an instance of a relation corresponding to a relationship together with the knowledge of its primary key may give us a clue as to the type of the relationship (i.e., one-to-one, one-to-many, or many-to-many).

Figure 5 is an example of a data base represented in the relational model. The relations STUDENT-FILE and COURSE-FILE correspond to entity sets, and ENROLLMENT-FILE corresponds to a many-to-many relationship. It should be noted that the relationships in this model are implied by data values. For example, ENROLLMENT-FILE represents a relationship between STUDENT-FILE and COURSE-FILE, because the attribute STU-IDNO is common to STUDENT-FILE and ENROLLMENT-FILE, and the attribute COURSE-NUMBER is common to COURSE-FILE and ENROLLMENT-FILE.

The relational representation of a data base is logical. In other words, the picture of a data base as a set of tables is the user's view, and not necessarily the computer's view. Each relation is implemented as a file, and the file organization and access techniques are hidden from the user. The user is concerned with the logical schema. Depending on the processing requirements, the physical storage structures and access paths are optimally determined by the DBMS.

Now that we have a common logical data structure for data base elements, that is, a relation, our next concern is to find a mechanism that will enable us to process queries. We note that, given a relational data base, the answer to any user query is also a relation. For example, if we want to determine the courses taken by Jane Smith and the grades she earned in them, we can use the data base of Figure 5 and obtain the result as shown in Figure 6. The answer to this query is a relation. This is true of any query. Therefore, what is needed is some consistent approach that processes relations to produce another relation. This is the essence of data base and file processing.

The four principal approaches developed for processing relations are relational algebra, relational calculus, set-oriented approaches, and graphic approaches. Each has its own strengths and weaknesses and is implemented by different vendors as relational data base management systems. A given approach defines a data language with its own syntax. Figure 7 shows some of the commercially available relational implementations.

STUDENT-FILE

STU-IDNO	STU-NAME	YEAR	MAJOR

STU-IDNO	STU-NAME	YEAR	MAJOR
1000	JANE SMITH	2	CSC
2000	THOMAS COLLINS	2	MGT
. . . .	. . . .	. . . . . .	. . . .

COURSE-FILE

COURSE-NUMBER	COURSE-NAME	CREDIT

COURSE-NUMBER	COURSE-NAME	CREDIT
MTH251	CALCULUS	4
CSC217	DATA STRUCTURES	3
ENG211	TECHNICAL WRITING	3
CSC221	DISCRETE MATH	3
CSC200	COBOL PROGRAMMING	3
MTH217	STATISTICS I	3
ACC220	INTR. ACCOUNTING	4
MGT213	PRIN. OF MANAG.	3
. . . .	. . . .	. . . .

ENROLLMENT-FILE

STU-IDNO	COURSE-NUMBER	GRADE

STU-IDNO	COURSE-NUMBER	GRADE
1000	MTH251	B
1000	CSC217	A
1000	ENG211	B
1000	CSC221	B
2000	CSC200	A
2000	MTH217	A
2000	ENG211	C
2000	ACC220	A
2000	MGT213	A
. . . .	. . . .	. . . .

Figure 5 Relational Representation for STUDENT-COURSE Data Base

Hierarchical Data Model

In contrast to the relational model, which is quite recent, the hierarchical data base model has been around the longest. The most well-known implementation of the hierarchical model is IBM's IMS (Information Management System). It was released in 1968 and is still in widespread use. The following brief discussion is in terms of the IMS DBMS.

A **hierarchical data base** consists of numerous ordered occurrences of a single type of tree structure. The tree structure, also known as a **physical data base record (PDBR)**, contains record structures called **segments** as its nodes. These are connected by arcs representing one-to-one or one-to-many relationships between segments. Segment occurrences have fixed lengths and contain data field values. Given two connected segments, the one at the higher level of hierarchy is called **parent segment** and the other is called **dependent segment**.

As an example of hierarchical data base modeling, again we consider the STUDENT-COURSE data base of Figure 4. The relationship ENROLLMENT between STUDENT and COURSE is many-to-many. Because IMS cannot support many-to-many relationships, the network diagram of Figure 4 is not suitable as an IMS data base.

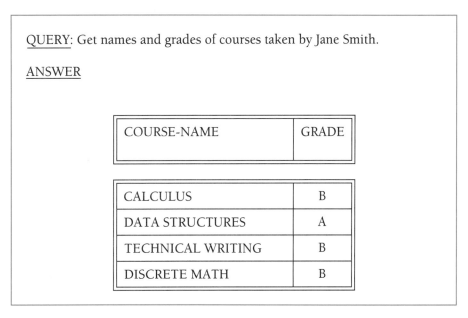

QUERY: Get names and grades of courses taken by Jane Smith.

ANSWER

COURSE-NAME	GRADE

COURSE-NAME	GRADE
CALCULUS	B
DATA STRUCTURES	A
TECHNICAL WRITING	B
DISCRETE MATH	B

Figure 6 An Example Query and Its Answer in a Relational Data Base

We decompose this many-to-many relationship into two one-to-many relationships and obtain two tree structures as shown in Figure 8a. Each of the two tree structures is a physical data base record. The first has STUDENT as its root segment and COURSE as a dependent segment. The relationship from STUDENT to COURSE is one-to-many. The second PDBR has COURSE as its root segment and STUDENT as a dependent segment, with a one-to-many relationship from COURSE to STUDENT.

Figure 8b shows the detailed segment structures for the two PDBRs. The attribute GRADE, which belongs to the relationship ENROLLMENT, has been collapsed onto the COURSE segment and has become an attribute of the COURSE-FILE segment structure. Segments in a PDBR evolve into files in

	DBMS	APPROACH	DEVELOPER/VENDOR	DATA LANGUAGE
*	PRTV	Relational algebra	IBM United Kingdom	ISBL
	INGRES	Relational calculus	Relational Technology	QUEL
	DB2	Set-oriented	IBM	SQL
	SQL/DS	Set-oriented	IBM	SQL
**	QMF	Graphic	IBM	Query-by-Example (QBE)

* PRTV is an experimental DBMS developed by the IBM United Kingdom Scientific Center in Peterlee, England.

** QMF is a frontend product for DB2 and SQL/DS, supporting both SQL and Query-by-Example.

Figure 7 Examples of Relational DBMSs

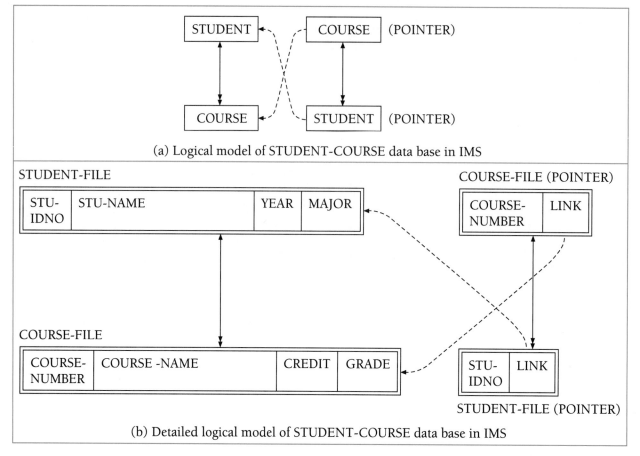

Figure 8 Hierarchical IMS Representation and Implementation of STUDENT-COURSE Data Base

the physical data base. Furthermore, as COURSE and STUDENT segments in the second PDBR are already in the first tree, we need not duplicate the corresponding files here. Instead, we can specify them as **pointer segments**. A pointer segment contains some segment occurrence identifiers and pointers to the segment occurrence in the base segments.

Figure 8c shows two occurrences of the STUDENT-COURSE PDBR of the logical model of Figure 8b. In each, one occurrence of the root segment STU-DENT-FILE is linked to several occurrences of the COURSE-FILE by **vertical linkages**. This way they form a tree structure. Also, occurrences of the dependent segment COURSE-FILE are linked to each other by some **horizontal linkages**. Next to the tree structure for Jane Smith is the PDBR occurrence for Thomas Collins. This means that the PDBR occurrences are ordered by the STU-IDNO field. The linkages are created and maintained by the IMS DBMS. This set of linkages allows both vertical and horizontal navigation in the data base.

The following is a summary of important properties in the IMS hierarchical data modeling.

1. Each PDBR is a tree with a single root segment; thus, a segment can have no more than one parent segment.
2. A parent segment may have any number of dependent segments attached to it.
3. Segments consist of data fields, and segment occurrences are of fixed length.

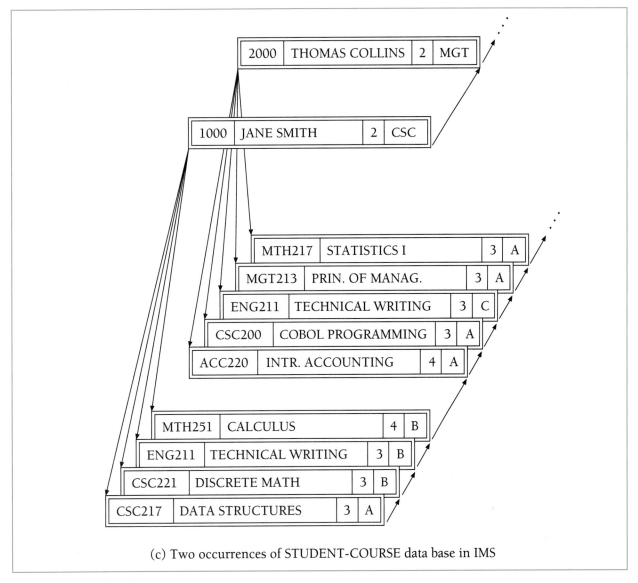

(c) Two occurrences of STUDENT-COURSE data base in IMS

Figure 8 (Continued)

4. Vertical linkages from a parent segment occurrence to dependent segment occurrences correspond to the elements of a one-to-one or one-to-many relationship set from parent to dependent segments.
5. Relationships in a PDBR may not be many-to-many.
6. Relationships in a PDBR do not require labels for identification.

Network Data Model

Almost all implementations of the network data base model are based on the recommendations of the Data Base Task Group (DBTG) of CODASYL (Conference on Data Systems Languages), published in 1971. CODASYL is the group that developed the standards for COBOL. Several implementations of the DBTG became available in the 1970s, one of which is IDMS (Integrated Database Management System) by Cullinet Software, Inc.

The fundamental building block in a DBTG data base is a set, which has absolutely no relation to the set concept of the traditional set theory. A **DBTG set** consists of a single **owner record type**, one or more **member record types**, and a named one-to-many relationship from the owner to the member record types.

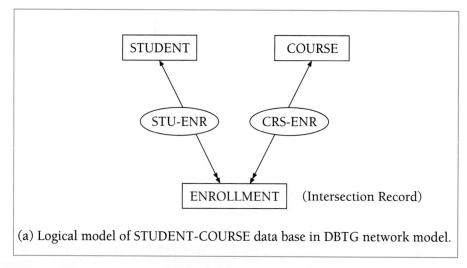

(a) Logical model of STUDENT-COURSE data base in DBTG network model.

Figure 9 DBTG Network Representation and Implementation of STUDENT-COURSE Data Base

A **record type** is a fixed-length collection of data items. The name of the relationship is used to identify the entire DBTG set.

Let us again consider the STUDENT-COURSE data base of Figure 3. The relationship ENROLLMENT between STUDENT and COURSE is many-to-many, but DBTG data bases cannot accommodate many-to-many relationships. To render this data base acceptable to a DBTG implementation, we consider ENROLLMENT as a record type. Each record type evolves into a file during the physical implementation. The modified data model is shown in Figure 9a. In fact, ENROLLMENT is an intersection file, as discussed in the previous chapter. Now, we have two relationships, STU-ENR from STUDENT to ENROLLMENT, and CRS-ENR from COURSE to ENROLLMENT, both one-to-many. The network of Figure 9a is composed of two sets: the set STU-ENR based on STUDENT and ENROLLMENT, and the set CRS-ENR based on COURSE and ENROLLMENT.

Some occurrences of these two sets are schematically shown in Figure 9b. Note that each occurrence of an owner record type is included in a ring structure using pointers together with its related member record type occurrences. These pointers are created and maintained by the DBMS. As each grade value is associated with a student within the STU-ENR set and with a course in the CRS-ENR set, the record type ENROLLMENT should store only the attribute GRADE.

The following are the important properties of DBTG data modeling.

1. A DBTG data base is a network formed by a number of DBTG sets.
2. In a DBTG set, the owner record type can have one or more dependent record types.
3. A dependent record type in a set may have only one owner record type.
4. A dependent record type may have more than one owner record type, provided they are in different sets.
5. A record type in a set may be both owner and dependent.

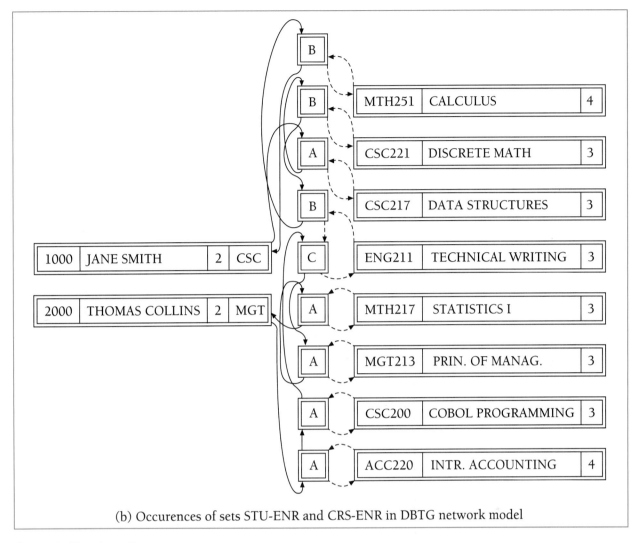

(b) Occurences of sets STU-ENR and CRS-ENR in DBTG network model

Figure 9 (Continued)

REVIEW QUESTIONS

1. A data base model can be used to describe only the structure of a data base. (T or F)
2. The entity-relationship data modeling is a logical data base modeling technique. (T or F)
3. In the relational model of data, the basic data structure is a _____ .
4. The number of columns in a relation is called the _____ and the number of rows is called the _____ .
5. Which of the following is a property of a relation?
   a. Row order is immaterial.
   b. Each row is distinct.
   c. No attribute participating in the primary key may be null.
   d. All attributes are atomic.
   e. All of the above.
6. A hierarchical data base consists of numerous ordered occurrences of a single type of tree structure. (T or F)

7. A hierarchical IMS data base can represent all kinds of relationships between segments, including many-to-many. (T or F)

8. The basic data structure in the DBTG network data model is called a _____ .

9. In a DBTG data base, a member record type may have more than one owner record type, provided they are in different sets. (T or F)

Answers: 1. F; 2. T; 3. relation; 4. degree of relation, cardinality of relation; 5. e; 6. T; 7. F; 8. set; 9. T.

Data Base Languages

Earlier we mentioned that one of the features that makes data base processing efficient is an easy to use, very high-level language supported by a data base management system. In general, data base languages have three components: a data definition language to define schemas, a data manipulation language to maintain the data base, and a query formulation language to access and retrieve data from the data base.

The nature of a data base language depends on the underlying data model, the approach used to extract answers to user queries, and, of course, the vendor responsible for the implementation. Recent languages tend to be easier than older ones for the novice data base user to learn. They also are **nonprocedural**, that is, they produce code consisting of a single statement that does not specify a procedure. Such a statement tells the system what is to be done to process a query, and not how it should be done. For example, SQL is a nonprocedural language, whereas data base languages accompanying hierarchical and DBTG systems produce mutiple-statement procedural codes that necessarily reflect the physical structure of the data base.

Data Definition Languages

A data definition language can be used to create a data base schema, a subschema in an application program, or a physical data base structure. It can also be used to change data base schema and to delete data base files. Usually, a separate component of the DDL can be used to define schema and subschema, and another component is suitable to specify physical data base structure.

In SQL the schema for the data base file STUDENT of the relational data base of Figure 5 can be defined using the CREATE TABLE statement.

```
CREATE TABLE STUDENT_FILE
    (STU_IDNO SMALLINT NOT NULL,
     STU_NAME CHAR(25),
     YEAR SMALLINT,
     MAJOR CHAR(3))
```

This statement will insert appropriate definitions into system catalog files concerning the table STUDENT_FILE. SMALLINT (for small integer) and CHAR (for character) are two SQL data types. STU-IDNO is an attribute that is specified not to accept null values by the clause NOT NULL. This is because STU_IDNO is the primary key for this table.

An authorized user may delete a data base table's definition and content by using a DROP TABLE statement.

```
DROP TABLE STUDENT_FILE
```

Before a data base file can be loaded and processed, its schema definition should be executed either in interactive mode or in an application program.

Data Manipulation Languages

After the schema for a data base file has been defined, compiled, and stored in the data base system catalog, the user may load it with data and may change the content of the corresponding file. These operations require a set of instructions that make up a DML.

In interactive SQL, a table may be loaded with records using the INPUT statement.

```
INPUT STUDENT_FILE
```

After this, the system prompts the user to type records.

```
1000, 'JANE SMITH', 2, 'CSC'
2000, 'THOMAS COLLINS', 2, 'MGT'
.............
END
```

Data input is terminated by the END statement.

A record in a data base file can be deleted using the DELETE statement.

```
DELETE
FROM STUDENT_FILE
WHERE STU_IDNO = 1000
```

This statement will delete the record satisfying the condition STU_IDNO = 1000 in STUDENT_FILE.

The SQL UPDATE statement can be used to update an attribute value in a record.

```
UPDATE STUDENT_FILE
    SET YEAR = 3
    WHERE STU_IDNO = 2000
```

This statement will change the YEAR attribute value for the record in STUDENT_FILE in which STU_IDNO = 2000 from its current value of 2 to a new value of 3.

New records can be inserted into a data base file.

```
INSERT INTO STUDENT_FILE
    VALUES (3000, 'KAREN WHITE', 3, 'CSC')
```

As shown, these operations, which ordinarily require rather elaborate procedures in COBOL or any other programming language, can be easily specified using single statements in a nonprocedural fashion in SQL.

Query Languages

A query language consists of instructions that enable the user to access and retrieve data from data base files. SQL has only one data retrieval statement, the SELECT statement.

Syntactically, the SQL SELECT statement is quite simple. It consists of the key word SELECT followed by a list of attribute names for which values are to be retrieved, a FROM clause that specifies the data base files by their names, and a WHERE clause in which a predicate is included. The predicate defines the records that should be accessed. No matter what attribute values are accessed, the query formulation in SQL requires a single SELECT statement. Despite its syntactical simplicity, depending on the data base structure and the query under consideration, an SQL SELECT statement can be quite involved. The following example corresponds to the query, "Get a complete listing of records in the STUDENT_FILE."

```
SELECT *
FROM STUDENT_FILE
```

This statement produces the following report.

```
STU   STU
IDNO  NAME                       YEAR  MAJOR
----  ------------------------   ----  -----
1000  JANE SMITH                   2   CSC
2000  THOMAS COLLINS               2   MGT
3000  KAREN WHITE                  3   CSC
```

In the SELECT statement, * is a shorthand notation meaning all attributes in the data base file.

The SELECT statement corresponding to the query, "Get names and years of students majoring in computer science" is:

```
SELECT STU_NAME, YEAR
FROM STUDENT_FILE
WHERE MAJOR = 'CSC'
```

On execution, this statement produces the following report.

```
STU
NAME                        YEAR
-------------------------   ----
JANE SMITH                    2
KAREN WHITE                   3
```

In the interactive mode of data base processing, an SQL SELECT retrieves and displays the result of a user query. In the application programming mode, it makes the retrieved table available to the program for further processing.

The capabilities of the SQL language are extensive. A SELECT statement can access and retrieve data from any number of related data base files. SQL also supports a set of library functions that can be used to retrieve computational values from a data base, such as the number of records satisfying a certain condition, the sum of a numeric field for a subset of records, and so on.

COBOL as a Host Language for Data Base Processing

In the application programming mode, a data base can be processed by developing a program in a host language and inserting into it appropriate instructions in a particular data base language. Such versions of data base languages are known as **embedded**. Every data base management system supports an embedded data base language; however, only the more recent ones have both interactive and embedded data languages. SQL is one language that has both versions. The IMS and IDMS data base management systems have no interactive data languages.

One of the most commonly used host languages in data base application programming is COBOL. This is not surprising, since both COBOL and data base systems are fundamental elements of business data processing. In addition to COBOL, most DBMSs also accept other host languages (Fortran, PL/I, C, asembler, etc.) for application programming. Here, we restrict our discussion to COBOL as the host language and SQL as the data base language.

The language considerations in embedded SQL are somewhat different than those for interactive SQL. Using a simple application program as a background, we can briefly explain the language features.

Figure 10 shows a COBOL program listing with embedded SQL statements. The data base for this application is the STUDENT-COURSE relational data base of Figure 5. We would like to develop a program to do the following.

1. Access STUDENT-FILE and retrieve and display the name of a student whose identification number is supplied by the user.
2. Access COURSE-FILE and retrieve and display the name of a course whose number is also interactively input by the user.
3. Access ENROLLMENT-FILE and retrieve and display the letter grade for that student and course pair.

The following features are noteworthy about this simple application program.

1. In the WORKING-STORAGE SECTION of the program lines 00039 through 00050 define a block of host variables. Host variables are counterparts of data base variables in the application program. In other words, any variable that appears in an embedded SQL instruction in the application program and also is accessed by the application program itself is a host variable. Host variables include the data base subschema for the application program. In this example the subschema consists of the variables STUDENT-NUMBER and STUDENT-NAME of the STUDENT-FILE, COURSE-CODE and COURSE-TITLE of the COURSE-FILE, and STUDENT-NUMBER, COURSE-TITLE, and LETTER-GRADE of the ENROLLMENT-FILE. It should be noted that names assigned to host variables need not be the same as those used in the data base schema.
2. Any embedded SQL instruction in the application program begins with EXEC SQL and ends with END-EXEC, so the precompiler can identify such statements during precompilation.

```
00001     *............................................................
00002       IDENTIFICATION DIVISION.
00003       PROGRAM-ID.  EMBEDDED-SQL-WITH-COBOL.
00004       ****************************************************************
00005       ***    THIS PROGRAM IS A SAMPLE COBOL PROGRAM WITH EMBEDDED SQL
00006       ***    STATEMENTS.
00007       ***
00008       ***    THE PROGRAM IS DESIGNED TO RETRIEVE THE FOLLOWING THREE DATA
00009       ***    VALUES FROM A STUDENT-COURSE RELATIONAL DATA BASE:
00010       ***        1. STUDENT NAME.
00011       ***        2. COURSE NAME, AND
00012       ***        3. LETTER GRADE EARNED BY THAT STUDENT IN THE COURSE.
00013       ***
00014       ***    THE USER SHOULD INTERACTIVELY INPUT:
00015       ***        1. A 3-DIGIT STUDENT IDENTIFICATION NUMBER, AND
00016       ***        2. A 6-CHARACTER COURSE CODE
00017       ***    USING THE KEYBOARD. THE PROGRAM ACCESSES THE DATA BASE
00018       ***    FILES, RETRIEVES THE DATA, AND DISPLAYS THEM ON THE SCREEN.
00019       ****************************************************************
00020
00021       AUTHOR.       UCKAN.
00022       DATE-WRITTEN.  JANUARY 2, 1991.
00023       DATE-COMPILED. JAN 2, 1991.
00024       *............................................................
00025       ENVIRONMENT DIVISION.
00026       CONFIGURATION SECTION.
00027       SOURCE-COMPUTER. UNIVERSITY-MAINFRAME.
00028       OBJECT-COMPUTER. UNIVERSITY-MAINFRAME.
00029       INPUT-OUTPUT SECTION.
00030
00031       *............................................................
00032       DATA DIVISION.
00033       FILE SECTION.
00034
00035       WORKING-STORAGE SECTION.
00036
00037      *********> HOST VARIABLES:
00038
00039           EXEC SQL BEGIN DECLARE SECTION END-EXEC.
00040
00041       01  STUDENT-NUMBER        PIC 999.
00042       01  STUDENT-NAME          PIC X(25).
00043       01  COURSE-CODE           PIC X(6).
00044       01  COURSE-TITLE          PIC X(15).
00045       01  LETTER-GRADE          PIC X.
00046
00047       01  USERID                PIC X(8).
00048       01  USER-PASSW            PIC X(4).
00049
00050           EXEC SQL END DECLARE SECTION END-EXEC.
00051
00052           EXEC SQL INCLUDE SQLCA END-EXEC.
00053
```

Figure 10 A Sample Application Program in Embedded SQL Using COBOL as Host Language

```
00054    **********> PROGRAM VARIABLES:
00055
00056    01  TERMINATE-PROCESSING    PIC XXX.
00057
00058    *..........................................................................
00059    PROCEDURE DIVISION.
00060
00061    A-MAIN-PROCEDURE.
00062        MOVE "NO" TO TERMINATE-PROCESSING.
00063
00064        DISPLAY "ENTER YOUR OWN SQL USERID:".
00065        ACCEPT USERID FROM CONSOLE.
00066
00067        DISPLAY "ENTER SQL PASSWORD: ".
00068        ACCEPT USER-PASSW FROM CONSOLE.
00069
00070        EXEC SQL CONNECT :USERID IDENTIFIED BY :USER-PASSW END-EXEC.
00071
00072        PERFORM B1-RETRIEVE-AND-DISPLAY
00073            UNTIL TERMINATE-PROCESSING = "YES".
00074
00075        STOP RUN.
00076
00077    B1-RETRIEVE-AND-DISPLAY.
00078
00079        DISPLAY "ENTER STUDENT IDENTIFICATION NUMBER:".
00080        ACCEPT STUDENT-NUMBER FROM CONSOLE.
00081
00082        DISPLAY "ENTER COURSE CODE: ".
00083        ACCEPT COURSE-CODE FROM CONSOLE.
00084
00085        EXEC SQL SELECT STU-NAME
00086                INTO :STUDENT-NAME
00087                FROM STUDENT-FILE
00088                WHERE STUD-IDNO = :STUDENT-NUMBER
00089        END-EXEC.
00090
00091        EXEC SQL SELECT COURSE-NAME
00092                INTO :COURSE-TITLE
00093                FROM COURSE-FILE
00094                WHERE COURSE-NUMBER = :COURSE-CODE
00095        END-EXEC.
00096
00097        EXEC SQL SELECT GRADE
00098                INTO :LETTER-GRADE
00099                FROM ENROLLMENT-FILE
00100                WHERE STU-IDNO = :STUDENT-NUMBER
00101                AND   COURSE-NUMBER = :COURSE-CODE
00102        END-EXEC.
00103
00104        DISPLAY " ".
00105        DISPLAY "STUDENT NAME: " STUDENT-NAME.
00106        DISPLAY "COURSE NAME: " COURSE-TITLE.
00107        DISPLAY "LETTER GRADE: " LETTER-GRADE.
```

Figure 10 (Continued)

```
00108
00109          DISPLAY " ".
00110          DISPLAY "DO YOU WISH TO TERMINATE PROCESSING?".
00111          DISPLAY "ENTER YES OR NO: ".
00112          ACCEPT TERMINATE-PROCESSING FROM CONSOLE.
00113
```

Figure 10 (Continued)

3. Line 00039 is the BEGIN DECLARE SECTION embedded SQL statement, marking the beginning of the host variable declaration section in the WORKING-STORAGE SECTION. Line 00050 is the END DECLARE SECTION statement, which terminates the host variable declaration section.

4. Line 00052 is the INCLUDE SQLCA statement. This statement enables the precompiler to include in the application program the SQLCA (SQL communication area) declarations. The SQLCA consists of some system-maintained variables through which the application program may communicate with the SQL system. These variables are fundamentally for the purpose of informing the application program of error and of warning conditions generated after the execution of embedded SQL statements.

5. Line 00070 is the CONNECT statement that links the user identified by user idenfication number and password to the SQL data base.

6. One of the SQL SELECT statements used for data base access and retrieval comprises lines 00085 through 00089. The SELECT statement was discussed previously. The embedded version of SELECT is slightly different. It contains an additional INTO clause that references the host variables in which the retrieved data base variables will be stored. The meaning of the SELECT statement in line 00085 is equivalent to the following: retrieve the STU-NAME value from the STUDENT-FILE corresponding to the record in which the STU-IDNO value is the same as the current value of STUDENT-NUMBER, and save the result in the host variable STUDENT-NAME.

7. The SQL SELECT statements in lines 00091 and 00097 of the program can be interpreted similarly.

As is seen, using embedded data base language instructions in a COBOL program facilitates substantially the application program development process.

REVIEW QUESTIONS

1. A language that can produce code consisting of a single statement that does not specify a procedure is called _____ .

2. The data definition component of a data base language can be used to create data base schema, subschemas in application programs, and a physical data base structure. (T or F)

3. Before a data base file can be processed, its schema definition should be executed either in interactive mode or in an application program. (T or F)

4. The data manipulation component of a data base language can be used to load the data base with data and to _____ the data base.

5. In the interactive mode of data base processing, a query language can be used to retrieve and display results of a user query; however, the retrieved result cannot be processed. (T or F)

Answers: 1. nonprocedural; 2. T; 3. T; 4. update; 5. T.

Key Terms

application plan	host language
application programming mode	interactive mode
attribute	member record
cardinality of relation	network data model
data base	owner record
data base language	parent segment
data base management system	physical data base record
data base model	physical view
data base schema	precompiler
data base system	query language
data definition language	relation
data manipulation language	relational model
DBTG set	segment
degree of relation	SQL
dependent segment	subschema
embedded data language	system catalog files
hierarchical data model	tuple

Study Guide

Quick Scan

- A file system consisting of interrelated files is called a data base.
- A data base is an extension of a file system. In a data base, (1) redundancies are fully eliminated or minimized. (2) real-world entities and relationships are appropriately represented, (3) multiple applications can be supported concurrently, (4) access to data is handled by systems software, and (5) data security, integrity, protection against system failure, and recovery features are provided.
- Because of these advantages, in business data processing, data bases are preferred to individually designed, program dependent file systems.
- A data base system is a human-computer system. Its components include people, data resource, hardware, software, and procedures.
- People involved in a data base system are application programmers, system programmers, operations personnel, customers, and data base administrators.
- The data resource consists of one or more permanently stored data bases.
- Hardware includes computer systems and fast direct-access storage devices.
- Software consists of systems software (operating systems, language processors, file management systems, utility programs, etc.), applications programs, and a general-purpose data base management system software.
- Procedures describe the steps to be followed and precautions to be taken for normal operations, data base failure, and recovery.
- In a data base environment, there are three views of data. The first is the complete and logical view of data base data, known as schema. The second is the data requirements of an application program, and is called subschema. Finally, there is the physical view, the form of the data as it would appear to a computer system.
- Many different subschemas can be derived from a data base schema. They may be disjointed, or they may overlap.
- The three fundamental operations on a data base are data definition, data base maintenance, and data base retrieval.
- In a data base environment these operations are facilitated through the use of some special high-level languages known as data base languages.
- Procedures written in data base languages are compiled and executed by a DBMS.

- A data base may be processed in two different modes, interactively or within an application program. In interactive mode, a data base language is used to process the data base. In application programming mode, an application program is developed using a procedural high-level language, and appropriate data base language instructions are embedded in the program.
- A procedural language that is used to develop an application program is called host language. COBOL is a host language for many DBMSs. The version of a data base language that can be embedded in an application program is called its embedded version.
- Use of embedded data base languages in application programming facilitates program development, tends to produce more concise programs, and relieves the programmer from the intricacies of file management systems.
- In a data base system, data are stored permanently and kept current in a data base. A data base administrator is the person responsible for maintaining a data base.
- The central component of a data base system is a data base management system. It is the DBMS that provides user–data base or application program–data base interface, supports a data base language, creates and maintains a system catalog that contains data about the data base, and provides mappings among different types of data views. The DBMS also provides for enforcement of data base integrity rules, data base security, backup and recovery, and control over concurrent operations.
- In interactive data base processing, the user enters queries expressed in the data base language through a terminal. The DBMS verifies the validity of data base components implied in the user query, and accesses the data base to retrieve data corresponding to the query.
- In application programming mode, the program contains subschema definitions, and data base access instructions expressed in a data base language and embedded in a host language. First, a precompiler processes the source program and replaces the embedded instructions with some subroutine calls in the host language. After this, the source program is compiled, and an object program and an application plan are generated. An application plan is the machine language description of the data base access strategy required for the application program. Finally, the object code and the application program are executed.
- A data language consists of a data definition, a data base manipulation, and a query formulation component.
- Data base systems have many advantages over file systems, including reduced data redundancy, data base structures with no anomalies, availability of all data resources for application programming, a certain degree of program/data independence, better data management, more meaningful data, and more efficient application program development.
- The principal disadvantages of a data base system are its relatively high cost and its complexity.
- A data base model is an abstraction for describing structure and semantics of a data base.
- The major data base models are entity-relationship, relational, hierarchical, and network. The entity-relationship data model is essentially a logical design tool and has no implementation as a DBMS.
- The relational data model uses a relation as its basic data structure. A relation is a two-dimensional tabular structure with a fixed number of atomic columns and a variable number of rows. Columns in a relation correspond to attributes, and rows correspond to records.

- Both entity sets and relationships in a data base are represented as relations in a relational data base. The relational model permits all types of relationships, including many-to-many.
- The relational model is logical in that a relation is the user's view of data, and not necessarily the system's view. Each relation becomes a file, and file organization and access techniques are hidden from the user.
- In general, the answer to any user query is another relation derivable from those existing in a data base. The four fundamental approaches to manipulating relations are algebra, calculus, set-oriented approaches, and graphic approaches. All of them have been implemented as either experimental or commercial DBMSs.
- The most well-known implementation of the hierarchical model is IBM's IMS.
- A hierarchical data base consists of many ordered occurrences of a single type of tree structure. The tree structure contains record structures called segments as its nodes. Segments in a PDBR evolve into files in the physical data base. They are connected by arcs representing one-to-one or one-to-many relationships between segments. IMS does not support many-to-many relationships. In physical implementation, the arcs become pointers.
- Almost all implementations of the network data base model are based on the recommendations of the Data Base Task Group (DBTG) of CODASYL. One of the prominent implementations is IDMS.
- The fundamental building block in a DBTG data base is a set. A DBTG set consists of a single owner record type, one or more member record types, and a named one-to-many relationship from owner to member record types. A record type is a fixed-length collection of data items. The name of the relationship is used to identify the entire DBTG set. In the physical data base, record types become files.
- Each occurrence of an owner record type is included in a ring structure together with its related member record type occurrences by pointers. These pointers are created and maintained by the DBMS.
- The nature of a data base language depends on the underlying data model, the approach used to extract answers to user queries, and the approach used by the vendor responsible for the implementation. More recent data base languages tend to be easier to use. They also are nonprocedural. A nonprocedural data language produces code consisting of a single statement that specifies what is to be done to process a query, and not how it should be done.
- A data definition language can be used to create a data base schema, a subschema in an application program, and a physical data base structure. It can also be used to change the data base schema and delete data base files.
- After the schema for a data base file has been defined, compiled, and stored in the data base system catalog, the user may load the data base and change the content of any file in it. These operations require a set of instructions, which together make up a data base manipulation language.
- A query language consists of instructions that enable the user to access and retrieve data from data base files.
- In application programming mode, a data base can be processed by developing a program in a host language and inserting into it appropriate instructions in a particular data base language; however, only more recent DBMSs have both interactive and embedded data languages.

Test Your Comprehension

Multiple-Choice Questions

1. Which of the following is not a requirement satisfied by a data base?
    a. Data redundancies are minimized or fully eliminated.
    b. Real-world entities and relationships are appropriately represented.
    c. Concurrent access to data base files by many users is permitted.
    d. Control of access to data bases is left to application programs.

2. Which of the following is a component of a data base system?
    a. Data resource
    b. Hardware
    c. Software
    d. People
    e. All of the above

3. Which of the following is not a function of a data base management system?
    a. Providing enforcement of data base integrity rules
    b. Facilitating data base backup and recovery
    c. Defining data base schema
    d. Compiling application programs written in a host language and an embedded data language
    e. Providing for subschema-to-schema mapping

4. Which of the following statements about data base modeling is incorrect?
    a. A data base model is an abstraction that is used to describe structure and semantics of a data base.
    b. The entity-relationship data model is a logical data base model.
    c. In the relational model of data the basic data structure is a network.
    d. In the hierarchical data model the basic data structure is a tree.

5. Which of the following is not a property of a relation?
    a. Row order is significant.
    b. Column order is significant.
    c. All tuples are distinct.
    d. A relation is in first normal form.

6. Which of the following is not a correct property of the IMS data model?
    a. Each physical data base record is a tree with a single root segment.
    b. A segment may have any number of dependent segments.
    c. A segment may have any number of parent segments.
    d. Segment occurrences are of fixed length.

7. Which of the following is a property of DBTG network data bases?
    a. A DBTG data base is a network formed by a number of DBTG sets.
    b. In a DBTG set, the owner record type can have one or more member record types.
    c. A member record type in a set may have only one owner record type.
    d. A member record type may have more than one owner record type, provided they are in different sets.
    e. All of the above are correct.

8. Which of the following statements about data base languages is correct?
    a. Defining a data base schema is a function of the data definition sublanguage.
    b. A delete instruction is part of a data base manipulation sublanguage.
    c. Data definition and data base manipulation commands may be embedded in application programs.
    d. A data base access request is a function of a query language.
    e. All of the above are correct.

Answers: 1. d; 2. e; 3. d; 4. c; 5. a; 6. c; 7. e; 8. e.

Short Essay Questions

1. Give a detailed definition of a data base.
2. Explain the fundamental differences between a file system and a data base.
3. What is a data base system?
4. What are the components of a data base system?
5. Who are the people involved in a data base system?
6. What is the function of a data base administrator?
7. What software is involved in a data base system?
8. Define the related concepts of schema, subschema, and physical view of data.
9. What are the fundamental operations on a data base?
10. What is the purpose of a data base language?
11. Explain the differences between interactive and application programming modes of data base processing.
12. What are the elements of an application program written for data base processing?
13. What are the advantages of using embedded data base languages in application programming compared to writing application programs for file systems?
14. What is the purpose of a data base system catalog?
15. Explain the function of a precompiler.
16. What is an application plan?
17. Discuss in detail the functions of a data base management system.
18. What are the components of a data base language?
19. Explain the fundamental advantages and disadvantages of data base systems compared to file systems.
20. What is a data base model? Why is data base modeling important?
21. Explain the reason why the entity-relationship data base model is a logical modeling technique.
22. What is a relation in the relational model of data?
23. What are the conditions that should be satisfied by a relation in the relational data model?
24. Explain how many-to-many relationships are represented in the relational model.
25. What are the principal approaches for processing relations in relational data base management?
26. Briefly explain the logical and physical aspects of the hierarchical data base model.
27. What are the limitations of the hierarchical data base model compared to the relational data base model?
28. Explain the logical and physical aspects of the network data models.
29. How do we handle many-to-many relationships in IDMS?
30. What are the functions of a data base definition language?
31. Explain the functions of data base manipulation languages and query formulation languages.

COBOL Reserved Words

** A **	COMPUTATIONAL	**** E ****	IF
	COMPUTE		IN
ACCEPT	CONFIGURATION	EGI	
ACCESS		ELSE	INDEX
ADD	CONTAINS	EMI	INDEXED
ADVANCING	CONTROL	ENABLE	INDICATE
AFTER	CONTROLS	END	INITIAL
	COPY		INITIATE
ALL	CORR	END-OF-PAGE	
ALPHABETIC		+ENTER	INPUT
ALSO	CORRESPONDING	ENVIRONMENT	INPUT-OUTPUT
ALTER	COUNT	EOP	INSPECT
ALTERNATE	CURRENCY	EQUAL	INSTALLATION
			INTO
AND	**** D ****	ERROR	
ARE		ESI	INVALID
AREA	DATA	+EVERY	IS
AREAS	DATE	EXCEPTION	
ASCENDING	DATE-COMPILED	EXIT	**** J ****
	DATE-WRITTEN		
ASSIGN	DAY	EXTEND	JUST
AT			JUSTIFIED
AUTHOR	DE	**** F ****	
	DEBUG-CONTENTS		**** K ****
** B **	DEBUG-ITEM	FD	
	DEBUG-LINE	FILE	KEY
BEFORE	DEBUG-NAME	FILE-CONTROL	
BLANK		FILLER	**** L ****
BLOCK	DEBUG-SUB-1	FINAL	
BOTTOM	DEBUG-SUB-2		LABEL
BY	DEBUG-SUB-3	FIRST	LAST
	DEBUGGING	FOOTING	LEADING
** C **	DECIMAL-POINT	FOR	LEFT
		FROM	LENGTH
CALL	DECLARATIVES		
CANCEL	DELETE	**** G ****	LESS
CD	DELIMITED		LIMIT
CF	DELIMITER	GENERATE	LIMITS
CH	DEPENDING	GIVING	LINAGE
		GO	LINAGE-COUNTER
CHARACTER	DESCENDING	GREATER	
CHARACTERS	DESTINATION	GROUP	LINE
+CLOCK-UNITS	DETAIL		LINE-COUNTER
CLOSE	DISABLE	**** H ****	LINES
+COBOL	DISPLAY		LINKAGE
		HEADING	LOCK
CODE	DIVIDE	HIGH-VALUE	
CODE-SET	DIVISION	HIGH-VALUES	LOW-VALUE
COLLATING	DOWN		LOW-VALUES
COLUMN	DUPLICATES	**** I ****	
COMMA	DYNAMIC		**** M ****
		I-O	
COMMUNICATION		I-O-CONTROL	+MEMORY
COMP		IDENTIFICATION	MERGE

(+) denotes reserved words that are not reserved in COBOL 85.

MESSAGE	PRINTING	** S **	** T **
MODE	PROCEDURE		
+MODULES	PROCEDURES	SAME	TABLE
	PROCEED	SD	TALLYING
MOVE		SEARCH	TAPE
MULTIPLE	PROGRAM	SECTION	TERMINAL
MULTIPLY	PROGRAM-ID	SECURITY	TERMINATE
** N **	** Q **	SEGMENT	TEXT
		SEGMENT-LIMIT	THAN
NATIVE	QUEUE	SELECT	THROUGH
NEGATIVE	QUOTE	SEND	THRU
NEXT	QUOTES	SENTENCE	TIME
NO			
NOT	** R **	SEPARATE	TIMES
		SEQUENCE	TO
NUMBER	RANDOM	SEQUENTIAL	TOP
NUMERIC	RD	SET	TRAILING
	READ	SIGN	TYPE
** O **	RECEIVE		
	RECORD	SIZE	** U **
OBJECT-COMPUTER		SORT	
OCCURS	RECORDS	SORT-MERGE	UNIT
OF	REDEFINES	SOURCE	UNSTRING
OFF	REEL	SOURCE-COMPUTER	UNTIL
OMITTED	REFERENCES		UP
	RELATIVE	SPACE	UPON
ON		SPACES	
OPEN	RELEASE	SPECIAL-NAMES	USAGE
OPTIONAL	REMAINDER	STANDARD	USE
OR	REMOVAL	STANDARD-1	USING
ORGANIZATION	RENAMES		
	REPLACING	START	** V **
OUTPUT		STATUS	
OVERFLOW	REPORT	STOP	VALUE
	REPORTING	STRING	VALUES
** P **	REPORTS	SUB-QUEUE-1	VARYING
	+RERUN		
PAGE	RESERVE	SUB-QUEUE-2	** W **
PAGE-COUNTER		SUB-QUEUE-3	
PERFORM	RESET	SUBTRACT	WHEN
PF	RETURN	SUM	WITH
PH	REVERSED	SUPPRESS	+WORDS
	REWIND		WORKING-STORAGE
PIC	REWRITE	SYMBOLIC	WRITE
PICTURE		SYNC	
PLUS	RF	SYNCHRONIZED	** Z **
POINTER	RH		
POSITION	RIGHT		ZERO
	ROUNDED		ZEROES
POSITIVE	RUN		ZEROS

COBOL 85 Reserved Words

** A **	** E **	EXTERNAL	** P **
ALPHABET ALPHABETIC-LOWER ALPHABETIC-UPPER ALPHANUMERIC ALPHANUMERIC-EDITED	END-ADD END-CALL END-COMPUTE END-DELETE END-DIVIDE	** F ** FALSE	PACKED-DECIMAL PADDING PURGE
** B **	END-EVALUATE END-IF	** G ** GLOBAL	** R ** REFERENCES REPLACE
BINARY	END-MULTIPLY END-PERFORM	** I **	
** C **	END-READ	INITIALIZE	** S ** STANDARD-2
CLASS CONTENT CONTINUE CONVERTING	END-RECEIVE END-RETURN END-REWRITE END-SEARCH END-START	** N ** NUMERIC-EDITED	** T ** TEST THEN TRUE
** D **	END-STRING END-SUBTRACT END-UNSTRING END-WRITE EVALUATE	** O ** ORDER OTHER	
DAY-OF-WEEK			

COBOL Language Syntax

In this appendix the complete COBOL language syntax is described using the CBL syntax (COBOL-like syntax). The CBL syntax notation uses the following conventions:

1. Upper-case words are COBOL reserved words.
    a. Underlined upper-case words indicate required words.
    b. Upper-case words that are not underlined are optional, and may be included in the language element to improve readability.
2. Lower-case words are programmer-supplied identifiers or constants.
3. Braces { } enclose one or more items of which one must be used in obtaining a syntactically valid generation.
4. Brackets [ ] enclose one or more items that are optional. None or one of them may be used.
5. Braces { } or brackets [ ] followed by three points . . . indicate that the last syntactical unit can be used any number of times in generation.

The syntactical elements introduced by COBOL 85 are printed in color.

General Format for IDENTIFICATION DIVISION

IDENTIFICATION DIVISION.

    PROGRAM-ID. program-name $\left[\text{ IS } \left\{ \begin{array}{l} \underline{\text{COMMON}} \\ \underline{\text{INITIAL}} \end{array} \right\} \text{ PROGRAM} \right]$.

    [AUTHOR. [comment-entry] . . .]   [INSTALLATION. [comment-entry] . . .]
    [DATE-WRITTEN. [comment-entry] . . .]   [DATE-COMPILED. [comment-entry] . . .]
    [SECURITY. [comment-entry] . . .]

General Format for ENVIRONMENT DIVISION

[ENVIRONMENT DIVISION.
    [CONFIGURATION SECTION.
    [SOURCE-COMPUTER. [computer-name [WITH DEBUGGING MODE]].]

    [OBJECT-COMPUTER. [computer-name $\left[\underline{\text{MEMORY}} \text{ SIZE integer} \left\{ \begin{array}{l} \underline{\text{WORDS}} \\ \underline{\text{CHARACTERS}} \\ \underline{\text{MODULES}} \end{array} \right\} \right]$].]

    [PROGRAM COLLATING SEQUENCE IS alphabet-name-1.]   [SEGMENT-LIMIT IS segment-number .]]
    [SPECIAL-NAMES.

$$\left[\begin{array}{l} \left[\text{ implementor-name-1} \left\{ \begin{array}{l} \underline{\text{IS}} \text{ mnemonic-name-1} \left[\underline{\text{ON}} \text{ STATUS } \underline{\text{IS}} \text{ condition-name-1} \right. \\ \qquad\qquad\qquad\qquad \left[\underline{\text{ OFF}} \text{ STATUS } \underline{\text{IS}} \text{ condition-name-2 } \right] \right] \\ \underline{\text{IS}} \text{ mnemonic-name-2} \left[\underline{\text{ OFF}} \text{ STATUS } \underline{\text{IS}} \text{ condition-name-2} \right. \\ \qquad\qquad\qquad\qquad \left[\underline{\text{ ON}} \text{ STATUS } \underline{\text{IS}} \text{ condition-name-1 } \right] \right] \\ \underline{\text{ON}} \text{ STATUS } \underline{\text{IS}} \text{ condition-name-1} \left[\underline{\text{ OFF}} \text{ STATUS } \underline{\text{IS}} \text{ condition-name-2 } \right] \\ \underline{\text{OFF}} \text{ STATUS } \underline{\text{IS}} \text{ condition-name-2} \left[\underline{\text{ON}} \text{ STATUS } \underline{\text{IS}} \text{ condition-name-1 } \right] \end{array} \right\} \right] \end{array} \right] \dots$$

$$\left[\text{ALPHABET alphabet-name-2 IS} \left\{ \begin{array}{l} \underline{\text{STANDARD-1}} \\ \underline{\text{STANDARD-2}} \\ \underline{\text{NATIVE}} \\ \text{implementor-name-2} \\ \left\{ \text{literal-1} \left[\left\{ \begin{array}{l} \underline{\text{THROUGH}} \\ \underline{\text{THRU}} \end{array} \right\} \text{literal-2} \\ \underline{\text{ALSO}} \text{ literal-3} \right\} \ldots \right] \right\} \ldots \end{array} \right\} \ldots \right]$$

$$\left[\underline{\text{SYMBOLIC}} \text{ CHARACTERS} \left\{ \left\{ \left\{ \text{symbolic-character-1} \right\} \ldots \left\{ \begin{array}{l} \text{IS} \\ \text{ARE} \end{array} \right\} \left\{ \text{integer-1} \right\} \ldots \right\} \ldots \right. \right.$$
$$\left. \left. [\underline{\text{IN}} \text{ alphabet-name-3}] \right\} \right] \ldots$$

$$\left[\underline{\text{CLASS}} \text{ class-name IS} \left\{ \text{literal-4} \left[\left\{ \begin{array}{l} \underline{\text{THROUGH}} \\ \underline{\text{THRU}} \end{array} \right\} \text{literal-5} \right] \right\} \ldots \right] \ldots$$

$$\left[\underline{\text{CURRENCY}} \text{ SIGN IS literal-6} \right] \left[\underline{\text{DECIMAL-POINT}} \text{ IS } \underline{\text{COMMA}} \right] . \,] \,] \,]$$
$$[\underline{\text{INPUT-OUTPUT}} \underline{\text{SECTION}}.$$
$$\underline{\text{FILE-CONTROL}}.$$
$$\{ \text{file-control entry} \} \ldots$$

$$[\underline{\text{I-O-CONTROL}}.$$

$$\left[\underline{\text{RERUN}} \left[\underline{\text{ON}} \left\{ \begin{array}{l} \text{file-name-1} \\ \text{implementor-name-3} \end{array} \right\} \right] \text{EVERY} \left\{ \begin{array}{l} \left\{ [\underline{\text{END}} \text{ OF}] \left\{ \begin{array}{l} \underline{\text{REEL}} \\ \underline{\text{UNIT}} \end{array} \right\} \\ \text{integer-1} \underline{\text{RECORDS}} \end{array} \right\} \text{OF file-name-2} \\ \text{integer-2} \underline{\text{CLOCK-UNITS}} \\ \text{condition-name} \end{array} \right\} \right] \ldots$$

$$\left[\left[\underline{\text{SAME}} \left[\begin{array}{l} \underline{\text{RECORD}} \\ \underline{\text{SORT}} \\ \underline{\text{SORT-MERGE}} \end{array} \right] \text{AREA FOR file-name-3} \{ \text{file-name-4} \} \ldots \right] \ldots$$

$$\left[\underline{\text{MULTIPLE}} \underline{\text{FILE}} \text{ TAPE CONTAINS} \left\{ \text{file-name-3} [\underline{\text{POSITION}} \text{ IS integer-1}] \right\} \ldots \right] \ldots] \,] \,] \,]$$

File-Control Entry for Sequential and Report Files

$$\underline{\text{SELECT}} \, [\underline{\text{OPTIONAL}}] \text{ file-name } \underline{\text{ASSIGN}} \text{ TO} \left\{ \begin{array}{l} \text{implementor-name-1} \\ \text{literal-1} \end{array} \right\} \ldots$$

$$\left[\underline{\text{RESERVE}} \text{ integer-1} \left[\begin{array}{l} \text{AREA} \\ \text{AREAS} \end{array} \right] \right] \quad \left[\, [\underline{\text{ORGANIZATION}} \text{ IS}] \underline{\text{SEQUENTIAL}} \, \right]$$

$$\left[\underline{\text{PADDING}} \text{ CHARACTER IS} \left\{ \begin{array}{l} \text{data-name-1} \\ \text{literal-2} \end{array} \right\} \right] \left[\underline{\text{RECORD}} \underline{\text{DELIMITER}} \text{ IS} \left\{ \begin{array}{l} \underline{\text{STANDARD-1}} \\ \text{implementor-name-2} \end{array} \right\} \right]$$

$$[\underline{\text{ACCESS}} \text{ MODE IS } \underline{\text{SEQUENTIAL}}] \quad [\text{FILE } \underline{\text{STATUS}} \text{ IS data-name-2}].$$

File-Control Entry for Relative Files

$$\underline{\text{SELECT}} \, [\underline{\text{OPTIONAL}}] \text{ file-name } \underline{\text{ASSIGN}} \text{ TO} \left\{ \begin{array}{l} \text{implementor-name-1} \\ \text{literal-1} \end{array} \right\} \ldots$$

$$\left[\underline{\text{RESERVE}} \text{ integer-1} \left[\begin{array}{l} \text{AREA} \\ \text{AREAS} \end{array} \right] \right] \quad [\underline{\text{ORGANIZATION}} \text{ IS}] \underline{\text{RELATIVE}}$$

$$\left[\underline{ACCESS} \text{ MODE IS } \begin{array}{l} \underline{SEQUENTIAL} \ [\ \underline{RELATIVE} \text{ KEY IS data-name-1}] \\ \left\{ \begin{array}{l} \underline{RANDOM} \\ \underline{DYNAMIC} \end{array} \right\} \underline{RELATIVE} \text{ KEY IS data-name-1} \end{array} \right] \quad [\text{ FILE } \underline{STATUS} \text{ IS data-name-2 }] \ .$$

File-Control Entry for Sort/Merge Files

$$\underline{SELECT} \text{ file-name-1 } \underline{ASSIGN} \text{ TO } \left\{ \begin{array}{l} \text{implementor-name-1} \\ \text{literal-1} \end{array} \right\} \ . \ . \ . \ .$$

File-Control Entry for Indexed Files

$$\underline{SELECT} \ [\ \underline{OPTIONAL} \ ] \text{ file-name } \underline{ASSIGN} \text{ TO } \left\{ \begin{array}{l} \text{implementor-name-1} \\ \text{literal-1} \end{array} \right\} \ . \ . \ .$$

$$\left[\ \underline{RESERVE} \text{ integer-1} \left[\begin{array}{l} \text{AREA} \\ \text{AREAS} \end{array} \right] \ \right] \quad [\ \underline{ORGANIZATION} \text{ IS }] \ \underline{INDEXED}$$

$$\left[\ \underline{ACCESS} \text{ MODE IS} \left\{ \begin{array}{l} \underline{SEQUENTIAL} \\ \underline{RANDOM} \\ \underline{DYNAMIC} \end{array} \right\} \ \right] \ \underline{RECORD} \text{ KEY IS data-name-1}$$

$$[\ \underline{ALTERNATE} \ \underline{RECORD} \text{ KEY IS data-name-2 } [\text{ WITH } \underline{DUPLICATES} \ ] \ ] \ . \ . \ . \ [\text{FILE } \underline{STATUS} \text{ IS data-name-3 }].$$

General Format for DATA DIVISION

[<u>DATA DIVISION</u>.

    [<u>FILE SECTION</u>.

$$\left\{ \begin{array}{l} \{ \text{ file-description-entry } \{ \text{ record-description-entry } \} \ . \ . \ . \} \ . \ . \ . \\ \{ \text{ sort-merge-file-description-entry } \{ \text{ record-description-entry } \} \ . \ . \ . \} \ . \ . \ . \\ \{ \text{ report-file-description-entry } \} \ . \ . \ . \end{array} \right\}$$

    [<u>WORKING-STORAGE SECTION</u>.   [<u>LINKAGE SECTION</u>.

$$\left[\begin{array}{l} \text{01-level-description-entry} \\ \text{77-level-description-entry} \\ \text{record-description-entry} \end{array} \right] \ . \ . \ . \ ] \qquad \left[\begin{array}{l} \text{01-level-description-entry} \\ \text{77-level-description-entry} \\ \text{record-description-entry} \end{array} \right] \ . \ . \ . \ ]$$

    [<u>COMMUNICATION SECTION</u>.

        [communication-description-entry [record-description-entry] . . .] . . .]

    [<u>REPORT SECTION</u>.

        [report-description-entry { report-group-description-entry } . . .] . . .]]

File Description Entry for Sequential Files

FD file-name
  [IS EXTERNAL] [IS GLOBAL]

  $$\left[\text{BLOCK CONTAINS [integer-1 } \underline{\text{TO}} \text{] integer-2} \left\{ \begin{array}{l} \underline{\text{RECORDS}} \\ \text{CHARACTERS} \end{array} \right\} \right]$$

  $$\left[\underline{\text{RECORD}} \left\{ \begin{array}{l} \text{CONTAINS integer-3 CHARACTERS} \\ \text{IS } \underline{\text{VARYING}} \text{ IN SIZE [[} \underline{\text{FROM}} \text{ integer-4] [} \underline{\text{TO}} \text{ integer-5] CHARACTERS]} \\ \quad\quad [\underline{\text{DEPENDING}} \text{ ON data-name-1]} \\ \text{CONTAINS integer-6 } \underline{\text{TO}} \text{ integer-7 CHARACTERS} \end{array} \right\} \right]$$

  $$\left[\underline{\text{LABEL}} \left\{ \begin{array}{l} \underline{\text{RECORD}} \text{ IS} \\ \underline{\text{RECORDS}} \text{ ARE} \end{array} \right\} \left\{ \begin{array}{l} \underline{\text{STANDARD}} \\ \underline{\text{OMITTED}} \end{array} \right\} \right] \left[\underline{\text{VALUE OF}} \left\{ \text{implementor-name IS} \left\{ \begin{array}{l} \text{data-name-2} \\ \text{literal-1} \end{array} \right\} \right\} \dots \right]$$

  $$\left[\underline{\text{DATA}} \left\{ \begin{array}{l} \underline{\text{RECORD}} \text{ IS} \\ \underline{\text{RECORDS}} \text{ ARE} \end{array} \right\} \left\{ \text{data-name-3} \right\} \dots \right]$$

  $$\left[\underline{\text{LINAGE}} \text{ IS} \left\{ \begin{array}{l} \text{data-name-4} \\ \text{integer-8} \end{array} \right\} \text{ LINES } \left[\text{WITH } \underline{\text{FOOTING}} \text{ AT} \left\{ \begin{array}{l} \text{data-name-5} \\ \text{integer-9} \end{array} \right\} \right] \right.$$

  $$\left. \left[\text{LINES AT } \underline{\text{TOP}} \left\{ \begin{array}{l} \text{data-name-6} \\ \text{integer-10} \end{array} \right\} \right] \left[\text{LINES AT } \underline{\text{BOTTOM}} \left\{ \begin{array}{l} \text{data-name-7} \\ \text{integer-11} \end{array} \right\} \right] \right]$$

  [CODE-SET IS alphabet-name-1].

File Description Entry for Relative and Indexed Files

FD file-name
  [IS EXTERNAL] [IS GLOBAL]

  $$\left[\text{BLOCK CONTAINS [integer-1 } \underline{\text{TO}} \text{] integer-2} \left\{ \begin{array}{l} \underline{\text{RECORDS}} \\ \text{CHARACTERS} \end{array} \right\} \right]$$

  $$\left[\underline{\text{RECORD}} \left\{ \begin{array}{l} \text{CONTAINS integer-3 CHARACTERS} \\ \text{IS } \underline{\text{VARYING}} \text{ IN SIZE [[} \underline{\text{FROM}} \text{ integer-4] [} \underline{\text{TO}} \text{ integer-5] CHARACTERS]} \\ \quad\quad [\underline{\text{DEPENDING}} \text{ ON data-name-1]} \\ \text{CONTAINS integer-6 } \underline{\text{TO}} \text{ integer-7 CHARACTERS} \end{array} \right\} \right]$$

  $$\left[\underline{\text{LABEL}} \left\{ \begin{array}{l} \underline{\text{RECORD}} \text{ IS} \\ \underline{\text{RECORDS}} \text{ ARE} \end{array} \right\} \left\{ \begin{array}{l} \underline{\text{STANDARD}} \\ \underline{\text{OMITTED}} \end{array} \right\} \right] \left[\underline{\text{VALUE OF}} \left\{ \text{implementor-name IS} \left\{ \begin{array}{l} \text{data-name-2} \\ \text{literal-1} \end{array} \right\} \right\} \dots \right]$$

  $$\left[\underline{\text{DATA}} \left\{ \begin{array}{l} \underline{\text{RECORD}} \text{ IS} \\ \underline{\text{RECORDS}} \text{ ARE} \end{array} \right\} \left\{ \text{data-name-3} \right\} \dots \right] .$$

File Description Entry for Sort/Merge Files

SD file-name

$$\left[\underline{\text{RECORD}} \left\{ \begin{array}{l} \text{CONTAINS integer-3 CHARACTERS} \\ \text{IS } \underline{\text{VARYING}} \text{ IN SIZE } [\ [\ \underline{\text{FROM}} \text{ integer-4 }]\ [\ \underline{\text{TO}} \text{ integer-5 }] \text{ CHARACTERS }] \\ \qquad [\ \underline{\text{DEPENDING}} \text{ ON data-name-1 }] \\ \text{CONTAINS integer-6 } \underline{\text{TO}} \text{ integer-7 CHARACTERS} \end{array} \right\} \right]$$

$$\left[\underline{\text{DATA}} \quad \left\{ \begin{array}{l} \underline{\text{RECORD}} \text{ IS} \\ \underline{\text{RECORDS}} \text{ ARE} \end{array} \right\} \left\{ \text{data-name-3} \right\} \ldots \right].$$

File Description Entry for Report Files

FD file-name

[IS EXTERNAL] [IS GLOBAL]

$$\left[\underline{\text{BLOCK}} \text{ CONTAINS } [\ \text{integer-1 } \underline{\text{TO}} \ ] \text{ integer-2} \left\{ \begin{array}{l} \underline{\text{RECORDS}} \\ \underline{\text{CHARACTERS}} \end{array} \right\} \right]$$

$$\left[\underline{\text{RECORD}} \left\{ \begin{array}{l} \text{CONTAINS integer-3 CHARACTERS} \\ \text{CONTAINS integer-6 } \underline{\text{TO}} \text{ integer-7 CHARACTERS} \end{array} \right\} \right]$$

$$\left[\underline{\text{LABEL}} \quad \left\{ \begin{array}{l} \underline{\text{RECORD}} \text{ IS} \\ \underline{\text{RECORDS}} \text{ ARE} \end{array} \right\} \left\{ \begin{array}{l} \underline{\text{STANDARD}} \\ \underline{\text{OMITTED}} \end{array} \right\} \right] \left[\underline{\text{VALUE}} \ \underline{\text{OF}} \left\{ \text{implementor-name IS} \left\{ \begin{array}{l} \text{data-name-2} \\ \text{literal-1} \end{array} \right\} \right\} \ldots \right]$$

$$\left\{ \begin{array}{l} \underline{\text{REPORT}} \text{ IS} \\ \underline{\text{REPORTS}} \text{ ARE} \end{array} \right\} \left\{ \text{report-name-1} \right\} \ldots [\ \underline{\text{CODE-SET}} \text{ IS alphabet-name-1 }].$$

Data Description Entry

FORMAT 1:

$$\text{level-number} \left[\begin{array}{l} \text{data-name-1} \\ \underline{\text{FILLER}} \end{array} \right] [\ \underline{\text{REDEFINES}} \text{ data-name-2 }] [\ \text{IS EXTERNAL }] [\ \text{IS GLOBAL }]$$

$$\left[\left\{ \begin{array}{l} \underline{\text{PICTURE}} \\ \underline{\text{PIC}} \end{array} \right\} \text{IS character-string} \right]$$

$$\left[[\ \underline{\text{USAGE}} \text{ IS }] \left\{ \begin{array}{l} \text{BINARY} \\ \underline{\text{COMPUTATIONAL}} \\ \underline{\text{COMP}} \\ \underline{\text{DISPLAY}} \\ \underline{\text{INDEX}} \\ \text{PACKED-DECIMAL} \end{array} \right\} \right] \left[[\ \underline{\text{SIGN}} \text{ IS }] \left\{ \begin{array}{l} \underline{\text{LEADING}} \\ \underline{\text{TRAILING}} \end{array} \right\} [\ \underline{\text{SEPARATE}} \text{ CHARACTER }] \right]$$

$$\left\{ \begin{array}{l} \underline{\text{OCCURS}} \text{ integer-1 TIMES} \\ \underline{\text{OCCURS}} \text{ integer-1 } [\ \underline{\text{TO}} \text{ integer-2 TIMES } \underline{\text{DEPENDING}} \text{ ON data-name-3 }] \end{array} \right\}$$

$$\left[\left\{ \begin{array}{l} \underline{\text{ASCENDING}} \\ \underline{\text{DESCENDING}} \end{array} \right\} \text{KEY IS } \left\{ \text{data-name-4} \right\} \ldots \right] \ldots [\ \underline{\text{INDEXED}} \text{ BY } \left\{ \text{index-name-1} \right\} \ldots] \right]$$

$$\left[\left\{ \begin{array}{l} \underline{\text{SYNCHRONIZED}} \\ \underline{\text{SYNC}} \end{array} \right\} \left[\begin{array}{l} \underline{\text{LEFT}} \\ \underline{\text{RIGHT}} \end{array} \right] \right] \left[\left\{ \begin{array}{l} \underline{\text{JUSTIFIED}} \\ \underline{\text{JUST}} \end{array} \right\} \text{RIGHT} \right] [\ \underline{\text{BLANK}} \text{ WHEN } \underline{\text{ZERO}} \ ] [\ \underline{\text{VALUE}} \text{ IS literal }].$$

FORMAT 2:

66   data-name-1 <u>RENAMES</u> data-name-2 $\left[\left\{ \begin{array}{l} \underline{THROUGH} \\ \underline{THRU} \end{array} \right\} \text{data-name-3} \right]$.

FORMAT 3:

88   condition-name-1 $\left\{ \begin{array}{l} \underline{VALUE} \text{ IS} \\ \underline{VALUES} \text{ ARE} \end{array} \right\}$ $\left\{ \text{literal-1} \left[\left\{ \begin{array}{l} \underline{THROUGH} \\ \underline{THRU} \end{array} \right\} \text{literal-2} \right] \right\}$ . . . .

Communication Description Entry

FORMAT 1:

<u>CD</u> cd-name

FOR [<u>INITIAL</u>] INPUT $\left[\begin{array}{l} [\ [\ \underline{SYMBOLIC}\ \underline{QUEUE}\ \text{IS data-name-1}\ ]\ [\ \underline{SYMBOLIC}\ \underline{SUB\text{-}QUEUE\text{-}1}\ \text{IS data-name-2}\ ] \\ \quad [\ \underline{SYMBOLIC}\ \underline{SUB\text{-}QUEUE\text{-}2}\ \text{IS data-name-3}\ ] \\ \quad [\ \underline{SYMBOLIC}\ \underline{SUB\text{-}QUEUE\text{-}3}\ \text{IS data-name-4}\ ]\ [\ \underline{MESSAGE}\ \underline{DATE}\ \text{IS data-name-5}\ ] \\ \quad [\ \underline{MESSAGE}\ \underline{TIME}\ \text{IS data-name-6}\ ]\ [\ \underline{SYMBOLIC}\ \underline{SOURCE}\ \text{IS data-name-7}\ ] \\ \quad [\ \underline{TEXT}\ \underline{LENGTH}\ \text{IS data-name-8}\ ]\ [\ \underline{END}\ \underline{KEY}\ \text{IS data-name-9}\ ] \\ \quad [\ \underline{STATUS}\ \underline{KEY}\ \text{IS data-name-10}\ ]\ [\ \underline{MESSAGE}\ \underline{COUNT}\ \text{IS data-name-11}\ ]\ ] \\ [\ \text{data-name-1, data-name-2, data-name-3, data-name-4, data-name-5,} \\ \quad \text{data-name-6, data-name-7, data-name-8, data-name-9, data-name-10,} \\ \quad \text{data-name-11}] \end{array} \right]$

FORMAT 2:

<u>CD</u> cd-name FOR <u>OUTPUT</u> [<u>DESTINATION</u> <u>COUNT</u> IS data-name-1] [<u>TEXT</u> <u>LENGTH</u> IS data-name-2]
[<u>STATUS</u> <u>KEY</u> IS data-name-3] [<u>DESTINATION</u> <u>TABLE</u> <u>OCCURS</u> integer-1 TIMES

[<u>INDEXED</u> BY {index-name-1} . . .]]

[<u>ERROR</u> <u>KEY</u> IS data-name-4] [<u>SYMBOLIC</u> <u>DESTINATION</u> IS data-name-5] .

FORMAT 3:

<u>CD</u> cd-name

FOR [<u>INITIAL</u>] I-O $\left[\begin{array}{l} [\ [\ \underline{MESSAGE}\ \underline{DATE}\ \text{IS data-name-1}\ ]\ [\ \underline{MESSAGE}\ \underline{TIME}\ \text{IS data-name-2}\ ] \\ \quad [\ \underline{SYMBOLIC}\ \underline{TERMINAL}\ \text{IS data-name-3}\ ]\ [\ \underline{TEXT}\ \underline{LENGTH}\ \text{IS data-name-4}\ ] \\ \quad [\ \underline{END}\ \underline{KEY}\ \text{IS data-name-5}\ ]\ [\ \underline{STATUS}\ \underline{KEY}\ \text{IS data-name-6}\ ]\ ] \\ [\ \text{data-name-1, data-name-2, data-name-3, data-name-4, data-name-5, data-name-6}\ ] \end{array} \right]$

Report Description Entry

RD report-name [IS GLOBAL] [CODE literal]

$$
\left[
\left\{
\begin{array}{l}
\underline{\text{CONTROL}}\ \text{IS} \\
\underline{\text{CONTROLS}}\ \text{ARE}
\end{array}
\right\}
\left\{
\begin{array}{l}
\{\text{data-name-1}\}\ \dots \\
\underline{\text{FINAL}}\ [\text{data-name-2}]\ \dots
\end{array}
\right\}
\right]
$$

$$
\left[
\underline{\text{PAGE}}
\left[
\begin{array}{l}
\underline{\text{LIMIT}}\ \text{IS} \\
\underline{\text{LIMITS}}\ \text{ARE}
\end{array}
\right]
\text{integer-1}
\left\{
\begin{array}{l}
\underline{\text{LINE}} \\
\underline{\text{LINES}}
\end{array}
\right\}
[\underline{\text{HEADING}}\ \text{integer-2}]\ [\underline{\text{FIRST}}\ \underline{\text{DETAIL}}\ \text{integer-3}]
\right.
$$

$$
\left. [\underline{\text{LAST}}\ \underline{\text{DETAIL}}\ \text{integer-4}]\ [\underline{\text{FOOTING}}\ \text{integer-5}]\right].
$$

Report Group Description Entry

FORMAT 1:

$$
\text{level-number}\ [\text{data-name-1}]
\left\{
\begin{array}{l}
\underline{\text{PICTURE}} \\
\underline{\text{PIC}}
\end{array}
\right\}
\text{IS character-string}\quad [[\underline{\text{USAGE}}\ \text{IS}]\ \underline{\text{DISPLAY}}]
$$

$$
\left[
[\underline{\text{SIGN}}\ \text{IS}]
\left\{
\begin{array}{l}
\underline{\text{LEADING}} \\
\underline{\text{TRAILING}}
\end{array}
\right\}
\underline{\text{SEPARATE}}\ \text{CHARACTER}
\right]
\left[
\left\{
\begin{array}{l}
\underline{\text{JUSTIFIED}} \\
\underline{\text{JUST}}
\end{array}
\right\}
\text{RIGHT}
\right]
[\underline{\text{BLANK}}\ \text{WHEN}\ \underline{\text{ZERO}}]
$$

$$
\left[
\underline{\text{LINE}}\ \text{NUMBER IS}
\left\{
\begin{array}{l}
\text{integer-1}\ [\text{ON}\ \underline{\text{NEXT}}\ \underline{\text{PAGE}}] \\
\underline{\text{PLUS}}\ \text{integer-2}
\end{array}
\right\}
\right]
[\underline{\text{COLUMN}}\ \text{NUMBER IS integer-3}]
$$

$$
\left\{
\begin{array}{l}
\underline{\text{SOURCE}}\ \text{IS identifier-1} \\
\underline{\text{VALUE}}\ \text{IS literal-1} \\
\{\underline{\text{SUM}}\{\text{identifier-2}\}\ \dots\ [\underline{\text{UPON}}\{\text{data-name-2}\}\ \dots\ ]\ \}\ \dots \\
\quad\left[\underline{\text{RESET}}\ \text{ON}\left\{\begin{array}{l}\text{data-name-3}\\ \underline{\text{FINAL}}\end{array}\right\}\right]
\end{array}
\right\}
\quad [\underline{\text{GROUP}}\ \text{INDICATE}].
$$

FORMAT 2:

01 [data-name]

$$
\left[
\underline{\text{LINE}}\ \text{NUMBER IS}
\left\{
\begin{array}{l}
\text{integer-1}\ [\text{ON}\ \underline{\text{NEXT}}\ \underline{\text{PAGE}}] \\
\underline{\text{PLUS}}\ \text{integer-2}
\end{array}
\right\}
\right]
\quad
\underline{\text{NEXT}}\ \underline{\text{GROUP}}\ \text{IS}
\left\{
\begin{array}{l}
\text{integer-3} \\
\underline{\text{PLUS}}\ \text{integer-4} \\
\underline{\text{NEXT}}\ \underline{\text{PAGE}}
\end{array}
\right\}
$$

$$TYPE\ IS \begin{cases} \begin{Bmatrix} \underline{REPORT}\ \underline{HEADING} \\ \underline{RH} \end{Bmatrix} \\ \begin{Bmatrix} \underline{PAGE}\ \underline{HEADING} \\ \underline{PH} \end{Bmatrix} \\ \begin{Bmatrix} \underline{CONTROL}\ \underline{HEADING} \\ \underline{CH} \end{Bmatrix} \begin{Bmatrix} data\text{-}name\text{-}2 \\ \underline{FINAL} \end{Bmatrix} \\ \begin{Bmatrix} \underline{DETAIL} \\ \underline{DE} \end{Bmatrix} \\ \begin{Bmatrix} \underline{CONTROL}\ \underline{FOOTING} \\ \underline{CF} \end{Bmatrix} \begin{Bmatrix} data\text{-}name\text{-}3 \\ \underline{FINAL} \end{Bmatrix} \\ \begin{Bmatrix} \underline{PAGE}\ \underline{FOOTING} \\ \underline{PF} \end{Bmatrix} \\ \begin{Bmatrix} \underline{REPORT}\ \underline{FOOTING} \\ \underline{RF} \end{Bmatrix} \end{cases} \quad [[\underline{USAGE}\ IS]\ \underline{DISPLAY}].$$

FORMAT 3:

$$\text{level-number}\ [\text{data-name}]\ \left[\underline{LINE}\ NUMBER\ IS \begin{Bmatrix} \text{integer-1}\ [\text{ON}\ \underline{NEXT}\ \underline{PAGE}] \\ \underline{PLUS}\ \text{integer-2} \end{Bmatrix} \right] [[\underline{USAGE}\ IS]\underline{DISPLAY}].$$

General Format for Procedure Division

FORMAT 1:

[<u>PROCEDURE</u> <u>DIVISION</u> [<u>USING</u> { data-name } . . .].

  [<u>DECLARATIVES</u> .

    { section-name <u>SECTION</u> [segment-number].

      USE-statement.

    [paragraph-name.

      [sentence] . . .] . . . } . . . .

<u>END-DECLARATIVES</u>.]

{ section-name <u>SECTION</u> [segment-number].

  [paragraph name.

    [sentence] . . .] . . . } . . . .]

FORMAT 2:

[<u>PROCEDURE</u> <u>DIVISION</u> [<u>USING</u> { data-name } . . .].

  { paragraph-name.

    [sentence] . . . } . . .]

Procedure Division Statements

FORMAT 1:

$$ACCEPT\ identifier\ \underline{FROM} \begin{cases} \underline{DATE} \\ \underline{DAY} \\ \underline{DAY\text{-}OF\text{-}WEEK} \\ \underline{TIME} \end{cases}$$

FORMAT 2:

<u>ACCEPT</u> identifier [<u>FROM</u> mnemonic-name]

FORMAT 3:

<u>ACCEPT</u> cd-name MESSAGE <u>COUNT</u>

FORMAT 1:

ADD $\begin{Bmatrix} \text{identifier-1} \\ \text{literal-1} \end{Bmatrix}$ $\begin{bmatrix} \text{identifier-2} \\ \text{literal-2} \end{bmatrix}$ . . . TO identifier-m [ROUNDED] [identifier-n [ROUNDED]] . . .

[ON SIZE ERROR imperative-statement-1]   [NOT ON SIZE ERROR imperative-statement-2]   [END-ADD]

FORMAT 2:

ADD $\begin{Bmatrix} \text{identifier-1} \\ \text{literal-1} \end{Bmatrix}$ $\begin{Bmatrix} \text{identifier-2} \\ \text{literal-2} \end{Bmatrix}$ $\begin{bmatrix} \text{identifier-3} \\ \text{literal-3} \end{bmatrix}$ . . . GIVING { identifier-n [ROUNDED] } . . .

[ON SIZE ERROR imperative-statement-1]   [NOT ON SIZE ERROR imperative-statement-2]   [END-ADD]

FORMAT 3:

ADD $\begin{Bmatrix} \text{CORRESPONDING} \\ \text{CORR} \end{Bmatrix}$ identifier-1 TO identifier-2 [ROUNDED]

[ON SIZE ERROR imperative-statement-1]   [NOT ON SIZE ERROR imperative-statement-2]   [END-ADD]

ALTER { procedure-name-1 TO [PROCEED TO] procedure-name-2 } . . .

FORMAT 1:

CALL $\begin{Bmatrix} \text{identifier-1} \\ \text{literal-1} \end{Bmatrix}$ $\begin{bmatrix} \text{USING} \begin{Bmatrix} [\text{BY REFERENCE}] \ \{ \text{identifier-2} \} . . . \\ \text{BY CONTENT} \ \{ \text{identifier-3} \} . . . \end{Bmatrix} . . . \end{bmatrix}$

[ON OVERFLOW imperative-statement-1]   [END-CALL]

FORMAT 2:

CALL $\begin{Bmatrix} \text{identifier-1} \\ \text{literal-1} \end{Bmatrix}$ $\begin{bmatrix} \text{USING} \begin{Bmatrix} [\text{BY REFERENCE}] \ \{ \text{identifier-2} \} . . . \\ \text{BY CONTENT} \ \{ \text{identifier-3} \} . . . \end{Bmatrix} . . . \end{bmatrix}$

[ON EXCEPTION imperative-statement-1]   [NOT ON EXCEPTION imperative-statement-2]   [END-CALL]

CANCEL $\begin{Bmatrix} \text{identifier-1} \\ \text{literal-1} \end{Bmatrix}$ . . .

FORMAT 1:

CLOSE $\left\{ \text{file-name} \begin{bmatrix} \begin{Bmatrix} \text{REEL} \\ \text{UNIT} \end{Bmatrix} \begin{bmatrix} \text{WITH NO REWIND} \\ \text{FOR REMOVAL} \end{bmatrix} \\ \text{WITH} \begin{Bmatrix} \text{NO REWIND} \\ \text{LOCK} \end{Bmatrix} \end{bmatrix} \right\}$ . . .

FORMAT 2:

CLOSE {file-name [WITH LOCK]} . . .

COMPUTE { identifier [ROUNDED] } . . . = arithmetic-expression
[ON SIZE ERROR imperative-statement-1]   [NOT ON SIZE ERROR imperative-statement-2]   [END-COMPUTE]

CONTINUE

DELETE file-name RECORD

[INVALID KEY imperative-statement-1]   [NOT INVALID KEY imperative-statement-2]   [END-DELETE]

DISABLE $\begin{Bmatrix} \text{INPUT [TERMINAL]} \\ \text{I-O TERMINAL} \\ \text{OUTPUT} \end{Bmatrix}$ cd-name WITH KEY $\begin{Bmatrix} \text{identifier} \\ \text{literal} \end{Bmatrix}$

DISPLAY $\begin{Bmatrix} \text{identifier} \\ \text{literal} \end{Bmatrix}$ . . . [UPON mnemonic-name]   [WITH NO ADVANCING]

FORMAT 1:

DIVIDE $\begin{Bmatrix} \text{identifier-1} \\ \text{literal} \end{Bmatrix}$ INTO $\begin{Bmatrix} \text{identifier-2 [ROUNDED]} \end{Bmatrix}$ . . .
[ON SIZE ERROR imperative-statement-1]
[NOT ON SIZE ERROR imperative-statement-2]
[END-DIVIDE]

FORMAT 2:

DIVIDE $\begin{Bmatrix} \text{identifier-1} \\ \text{literal-1} \end{Bmatrix}$ INTO $\begin{Bmatrix} \text{identifier-2} \\ \text{literal-2} \end{Bmatrix}$

GIVING $\begin{Bmatrix} \text{identifier-3   [ROUNDED]} \end{Bmatrix}$ . . .
[ON SIZE ERROR imperative-statement-1]
[NOT ON SIZE ERROR imperative-statement-2]
[END-DIVIDE]

FORMAT 3:

DIVIDE $\begin{Bmatrix} \text{identifier-1} \\ \text{literal-1} \end{Bmatrix}$ BY $\begin{Bmatrix} \text{identifier-2} \\ \text{literal-2} \end{Bmatrix}$

GIVING $\begin{Bmatrix} \text{identifier-3   [ROUNDED]} \end{Bmatrix}$ . . .
[ON SIZE ERROR imperative-statement-1]
[NOT ON SIZE ERROR imperative-statement-2]
[END-DIVIDE]

FORMAT 4:

DIVIDE $\begin{Bmatrix} \text{identifier-1} \\ \text{literal-1} \end{Bmatrix}$ INTO $\begin{Bmatrix} \text{identifier-2} \\ \text{literal-2} \end{Bmatrix}$

GIVING identifier-3   [ROUNDED]
REMAINDER identifier-4
[ON SIZE ERROR imperative-statement-1]
[NOT ON SIZE ERROR imperative-statement-2]
[END-DIVIDE]

FORMAT 5:

DIVIDE $\begin{Bmatrix} \text{identifier-1} \\ \text{literal-1} \end{Bmatrix}$ BY $\begin{Bmatrix} \text{identifier-2} \\ \text{literal-2} \end{Bmatrix}$

GIVING identifier-3   [ROUNDED]
REMAINDER identifier-4
[ON SIZE ERROR imperative-statement-1]
[NOT ON SIZE ERROR imperative-statement-2]
[END-DIVIDE]

ENABLE $\begin{Bmatrix} \text{INPUT [TERMINAL]} \\ \text{I-O TERMINAL} \\ \text{OUTPUT} \end{Bmatrix}$ cd-name WITH KEY $\begin{Bmatrix} \text{identifier} \\ \text{literal} \end{Bmatrix}$

$$
\underline{\text{EVALUATE}} \left\{ \begin{array}{l} \text{identifier-1} \\ \text{literal-1} \\ \text{expression-1} \\ \underline{\text{TRUE}} \\ \underline{\text{FALSE}} \end{array} \right\} \left[\underline{\text{ALSO}} \left\{ \begin{array}{l} \text{identifier-2} \\ \text{literal-2} \\ \text{expression-2} \\ \underline{\text{TRUE}} \\ \underline{\text{FALSE}} \end{array} \right\} \right] \ldots
$$

$$
\left\{ \left\{ \underline{\text{WHEN}} \left\{ \begin{array}{l} \underline{\text{ANY}} \\ \text{condition-1} \\ \underline{\text{TRUE}} \\ \underline{\text{FALSE}} \\ [\ \underline{\text{NOT}}\ ] \left\{ \begin{array}{l} \text{identifier-3} \\ \text{literal-3} \\ \text{arithmetic-expression-1} \end{array} \right\} \left[\left\{ \begin{array}{l} \underline{\text{THROUGH}} \\ \underline{\text{THRU}} \end{array} \right\} \left\{ \begin{array}{l} \text{identifier-4} \\ \text{literal-4} \\ \text{arithmetic-expression-2} \end{array} \right\} \right] \end{array} \right. \right. \right.
$$

$$
\left[\underline{\text{ALSO}} \left\{ \begin{array}{l} \underline{\text{ANY}} \\ \text{condition-2} \\ \underline{\text{TRUE}} \\ \underline{\text{FALSE}} \\ [\text{NOT}] \left\{ \begin{array}{l} \text{identifier-5} \\ \text{literal-5} \\ \text{arithmetic-expression-3} \end{array} \right\} \left[\left\{ \begin{array}{l} \underline{\text{THROUGH}} \\ \underline{\text{THRU}} \end{array} \right\} \left\{ \begin{array}{l} \text{identifier-6} \\ \text{literal-6} \\ \text{arithmetic-expression-4} \end{array} \right\} \right] \end{array} \right. \right] \ldots \ldots
$$

imperative-statement-1} . . .   [<u>WHEN</u> <u>OTHER</u> imperative-statement-2] [<u>END-EVALUATE</u>]

<u>EXIT</u> [<u>PROGRAM</u>]

$$
\underline{\text{GENERATE}} \left\{ \begin{array}{l} \text{data-name} \\ \text{report-name} \end{array} \right\}
$$

<u>GO</u> <u>TO</u> [procedure-name]

<u>GO</u> <u>TO</u> { procedure-name } . . . <u>DEPENDING</u> ON identifier

---

$$
\underline{\text{IF}}\ \text{condition THEN} \left\{ \begin{array}{l} \{ \text{statement-1} \} \ldots \\ \underline{\text{NEXT}}\ \underline{\text{SENTENCE}} \end{array} \right\} \left\{ \begin{array}{l} \underline{\text{ELSE}}\ \{ \text{statement-2} \} \ldots \underline{\text{END-IF}} \\ \underline{\text{ELSE}}\ \underline{\text{NEXT}}\ \underline{\text{SENTENCE}} \\ \underline{\text{END-IF}} \end{array} \right\}
$$

$$
\underline{\text{INITIALIZE}}\ \{ \text{identifier-1} \} \ldots \left[\underline{\text{REPLACING}} \left\{ \begin{array}{l} \underline{\text{ALPHABETIC}} \\ \underline{\text{ALPHANUMERIC}} \\ \underline{\text{NUMERIC}} \\ \text{ALPHANUMERIC-EDITED} \\ \text{NUMERIC-EDITED} \end{array} \right\} \underline{\text{DATA}}\ \underline{\text{BY}} \left\{ \begin{array}{l} \text{identifier-2} \\ \text{literal} \end{array} \right\} \ldots \right]
$$

<u>INITIATE</u> { report-name } . . .

INSPECT identifier-1 TALLYING

$$\left\{ \text{identifier-2 } \underline{\text{FOR}} \left\{ \begin{array}{l} \underline{\text{CHARACTERS}} \quad \left[\left\{ \begin{array}{l} \underline{\text{BEFORE}} \\ \underline{\text{AFTER}} \end{array} \right\} \text{INITIAL} \left\{ \begin{array}{l} \text{identifier-3} \\ \text{literal-1} \end{array} \right\} \right] \dots \\ \left\{ \begin{array}{l} \underline{\text{ALL}} \\ \underline{\text{LEADING}} \end{array} \right\} \left\{ \left\{ \begin{array}{l} \text{identifier-4} \\ \text{literal-2} \end{array} \right\} \left[\left\{ \begin{array}{l} \underline{\text{BEFORE}} \\ \underline{\text{AFTER}} \end{array} \right\} \text{INITIAL} \left\{ \begin{array}{l} \text{identifier-5} \\ \text{literal-3} \end{array} \right\} \right] \dots \right\} \dots \end{array} \right\} \dots \right\} \dots$$

INSPECT identifier-1 REPLACING

$$\left\{ \begin{array}{l} \underline{\text{CHARACTERS}} \ \underline{\text{BY}} \left\{ \begin{array}{l} \text{identifier-2} \\ \text{literal-1} \end{array} \right\} \left[\left\{ \begin{array}{l} \underline{\text{BEFORE}} \\ \underline{\text{AFTER}} \end{array} \right\} \text{INITIAL} \left\{ \begin{array}{l} \text{identifier-3} \\ \text{literal-2} \end{array} \right\} \right] \dots \\ \left\{ \begin{array}{l} \underline{\text{ALL}} \\ \underline{\text{LEADING}} \\ \underline{\text{FIRST}} \end{array} \right\} \left\{ \begin{array}{l} \text{identifier-4} \\ \text{literal-3} \end{array} \right\} \underline{\text{BY}} \left\{ \begin{array}{l} \text{identifier-5} \\ \text{literal-4} \end{array} \right\} \left[\left\{ \begin{array}{l} \underline{\text{BEFORE}} \\ \underline{\text{AFTER}} \end{array} \right\} \text{INITIAL} \left\{ \begin{array}{l} \text{identifier-6} \\ \text{literal-5} \end{array} \right\} \right] \dots \end{array} \right\} \dots$$

INSPECT identifier-1 TALLYING

$$\left\{ \text{identifier-2 } \underline{\text{FOR}} \left\{ \begin{array}{l} \underline{\text{CHARACTERS}} \left[\left\{ \begin{array}{l} \underline{\text{BEFORE}} \\ \underline{\text{AFTER}} \end{array} \right\} \text{INITIAL} \left\{ \begin{array}{l} \text{identifier-3} \\ \text{literal-1} \end{array} \right\} \right] \dots \\ \left\{ \begin{array}{l} \underline{\text{ALL}} \\ \underline{\text{LEADING}} \end{array} \right\} \left\{ \left\{ \begin{array}{l} \text{identifier-4} \\ \text{literal-2} \end{array} \right\} \left[\left\{ \begin{array}{l} \underline{\text{BEFORE}} \\ \underline{\text{AFTER}} \end{array} \right\} \text{INITIAL} \left\{ \begin{array}{l} \text{identifier-5} \\ \text{literal-3} \end{array} \right\} \right] \dots \right\} \dots \end{array} \right\} \dots \right\} \dots$$

REPLACING

$$\left\{ \begin{array}{l} \underline{\text{CHARACTERS}} \ \underline{\text{BY}} \left\{ \begin{array}{l} \text{identifier-6} \\ \text{literal-4} \end{array} \right\} \left[\left\{ \begin{array}{l} \underline{\text{BEFORE}} \\ \underline{\text{AFTER}} \end{array} \right\} \text{INITIAL} \left\{ \begin{array}{l} \text{identifier-7} \\ \text{literal-5} \end{array} \right\} \right] \dots \\ \left\{ \begin{array}{l} \underline{\text{ALL}} \\ \underline{\text{LEADING}} \\ \underline{\text{FIRST}} \end{array} \right\} \left\{ \begin{array}{l} \text{identifier-8} \\ \text{literal-6} \end{array} \right\} \underline{\text{BY}} \left\{ \begin{array}{l} \text{identifier-9} \\ \text{literal-7} \end{array} \right\} \left[\left\{ \begin{array}{l} \underline{\text{BEFORE}} \\ \underline{\text{AFTER}} \end{array} \right\} \text{INITIAL} \left\{ \begin{array}{l} \text{identifier-10} \\ \text{literal-8} \end{array} \right\} \right] \dots \end{array} \right\} \dots$$

INSPECT identifier-1 CONVERTING $\left\{ \begin{array}{l} \text{identifier-2} \\ \text{literal-1} \end{array} \right\}$ TO $\left\{ \begin{array}{l} \text{identifier-3} \\ \text{literal-2} \end{array} \right\}$

$$\left[\left\{ \begin{array}{l} \underline{\text{BEFORE}} \\ \underline{\text{AFTER}} \end{array} \right\} \text{INITIAL} \left\{ \begin{array}{l} \text{identifier-4} \\ \text{literal-3} \end{array} \right\} \right] \dots$$

MERGE file-name-1 $\left\{ \text{ON} \left\{ \begin{array}{l} \underline{\text{ASCENDING}} \\ \underline{\text{DESCENDING}} \end{array} \right\} \text{KEY} \{ \text{data-name} \} \dots \right\} \dots$

   [COLLATING SEQUENCE IS alphabet-name]

   USING file-name-2 { file-name-3 } . . .

   $$\left\{ \begin{array}{l} \underline{\text{OUTPUT}} \ \underline{\text{PROCEDURE}} \text{ IS procedure-name-1} \left[\left\{ \begin{array}{l} \underline{\text{THROUGH}} \\ \underline{\text{THRU}} \end{array} \right\} \text{procedure-name-2} \right] \\ \underline{\text{GIVING}} \ \{ \text{file-name-4} \} \dots \end{array} \right\}$$

FORMAT 1:

$$\text{\underline{MOVE}} \begin{Bmatrix} \text{identifier-1} \\ \text{literal} \end{Bmatrix} \text{\underline{TO}} \begin{Bmatrix} \text{identifier-2} \end{Bmatrix} \dots$$

FORMAT 2:

$$\text{\underline{MOVE}} \begin{Bmatrix} \text{\underline{CORRESPONDING}} \\ \text{\underline{CORR}} \end{Bmatrix} \text{identifier-1 \underline{TO} identifier-2}$$

FORMAT 1:

$$\text{\underline{MULTIPLY}} \begin{Bmatrix} \text{identifier-1} \\ \text{literal} \end{Bmatrix} \text{\underline{BY}} \{ \text{identifier-2 [\underline{ROUNDED}]} \} \dots$$

[ON SIZE ERROR imperative-statement-1] [NOT ON SIZE ERROR imperative-statement-2] [END-MULTIPLY]

FORMAT 2:

$$\text{\underline{MULTIPLY}} \begin{Bmatrix} \text{identifier-1} \\ \text{literal} \end{Bmatrix} \text{\underline{BY}} \{ \text{identifier-2 [\underline{ROUNDED}]} \} \dots$$

GIVING { identifier-3 [ROUNDED]} ...

[ON SIZE ERROR imperative-statement-1] [NOT ON SIZE ERROR imperative-statement-2] [END-MULTIPLY]

$$\text{\underline{OPEN}} \begin{Bmatrix} \text{\underline{INPUT}} \left\{ \text{file-name-1} \begin{bmatrix} \text{\underline{REVERSED}} \\ \text{WITH \underline{NO} REWIND} \end{bmatrix} \right\} \dots \\ \text{\underline{OUTPUT}} \{ \text{file-name-2 [WITH \underline{NO} REWIND]} \} \dots \\ \text{I-O} \{ \text{file-name-3} \} \dots \\ \text{\underline{EXTEND}} \{ \text{file-name-4} \} \dots \end{Bmatrix} \dots$$

FORMAT 1:

$$\text{\underline{PERFORM}} \left[\text{procedure-name-1} \left[\begin{Bmatrix} \text{\underline{THROUGH}} \\ \text{\underline{THRU}} \end{Bmatrix} \text{procedure-name-2} \right] \right] \text{[imperative-statement \underline{END-PERFORM}]}$$

FORMAT 2:

$$\text{\underline{PERFORM}} \left[\text{procedure-name-1} \left[\begin{Bmatrix} \text{\underline{THROUGH}} \\ \text{\underline{THRU}} \end{Bmatrix} \text{procedure-name-2} \right] \right] \left[\text{WITH \underline{TEST}} \begin{Bmatrix} \text{\underline{BEFORE}} \\ \text{\underline{AFTER}} \end{Bmatrix} \right] \text{\underline{UNTIL} condition}$$

[imperative-statement END-PERFORM]

FORMAT 3:

$$\text{\underline{PERFORM}} \left[\text{procedure-name-1} \left[\begin{Bmatrix} \text{\underline{THROUGH}} \\ \text{\underline{THRU}} \end{Bmatrix} \text{procedure-name-2} \right] \right] \begin{Bmatrix} \text{identifier} \\ \text{integer} \end{Bmatrix} \text{\underline{TIMES}}$$

[imperative-statement END-PERFORM]

FORMAT 4:

PERFORM $\left[\text{procedure-name-1}\left[\left\{\dfrac{\text{THROUGH}}{\text{THRU}}\right\}\text{procedure-name-2}\right]\right]\left[\text{WITH TEST}\left\{\dfrac{\text{BEFORE}}{\text{AFTER}}\right\}\right]$

VARYING $\left\{\begin{array}{l}\text{identifier-1}\\\text{index-name-1}\end{array}\right\}$ FROM $\left\{\begin{array}{l}\text{identifier-2}\\\text{index-name-2}\\\text{literal-1}\end{array}\right\}$ BY $\left\{\begin{array}{l}\text{identifier-3}\\\text{literal-2}\end{array}\right\}$ UNTIL condition-1

$\left[\text{AFTER}\left\{\begin{array}{l}\text{identifier-4}\\\text{index-name-3}\end{array}\right\}\text{FROM}\left\{\begin{array}{l}\text{identifier-5}\\\text{index-name-4}\\\text{literal-3}\end{array}\right\}\text{BY}\left\{\begin{array}{l}\text{identifier-6}\\\text{literal-4}\end{array}\right\}\text{UNTIL condition-2}\right]$ . . .

[imperative-statement END-PERFORM]

PURGE cd-name-1

FORMAT 1:

READ file-name [NEXT] RECORD [INTO identifier]

[AT END imperative-statement-1]   [NOT AT END imperative-statement-2]   [END-READ]

FORMAT 2:

READ file-name RECORD [INTO identifier]

[INVALID KEY imperative-statement-1]   [NOT INVALID KEY imperative-statement-2]   [END-READ]

FORMAT 3:

READ file-name RECORD [INTO identifier]

[KEY IS data-name]

[INVALID KEY imperative-statement-1]

[NOT INVALID KEY imperative-statement-2]

[END-READ]

RECEIVE cd-name $\left\{\dfrac{\text{MESSAGE}}{\text{SEGMENT}}\right\}$ INTO identifier

[NO DATA imperative-statement-1]

[WITH DATA imperative-statement-2]

[END-RECEIVE]

RELEASE record-name [FROM identifier]

RETURN file-name RECORD [INTO identifier]

[AT END imperative-statement-1]

[NOT AT END imperative-statement-2]

[END-RETURN]

FORMAT 1:

REWRITE record-name [FROM identifier]

FORMAT 2:

REWRITE record-name [FROM identifier]

[INVALID KEY imperative-statement-1]

[NOT INVALID KEY imperative-statement-2]

[END-REWRITE]

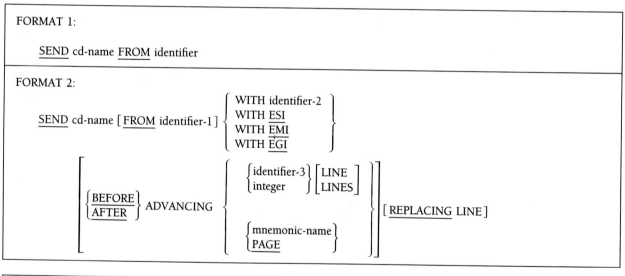

FORMAT 1:

SEARCH identifier-1 $\left[\underline{\text{VARYING}} \left\{ \begin{array}{l} \text{identifier-2} \\ \text{index-name} \end{array} \right\} \right]$ [AT <u>END</u> imperative-statement-1]

$\left\{ \underline{\text{WHEN}} \text{ condition} \left\{ \begin{array}{l} \text{imperative-statement-2} \\ \underline{\text{NEXT}} \ \underline{\text{SENTENCE}} \end{array} \right\} \right\} \dots$ [END-SEARCH]

FORMAT 2:

<u>SEARCH</u> <u>ALL</u> identifier-1   [AT <u>END</u> imperative-statement-1]

$\underline{\text{WHEN}} \left\{ \begin{array}{l} \text{data-name-1} \left\{ \begin{array}{l} \text{IS } \underline{\text{EQUAL}} \text{ TO} \\ \text{IS } = \end{array} \right\} \left\{ \begin{array}{l} \text{identifier-2} \\ \text{literal-1} \\ \text{arithmetic-expression-1} \end{array} \right\} \\ \text{condition-name-1} \end{array} \right\}$

$\left[\underline{\text{AND}} \left\{ \begin{array}{l} \text{data-name-2} \left\{ \begin{array}{l} \text{IS } \underline{\text{EQUAL}} \text{ TO} \\ \text{IS } = \end{array} \right\} \left\{ \begin{array}{l} \text{identifier-3} \\ \text{literal-2} \\ \text{arithmetic-expression-2} \end{array} \right\} \\ \text{condition-name-2} \end{array} \right\} \right] \dots$

$\left\{ \begin{array}{l} \text{imperative-statement-2} \\ \underline{\text{NEXT}} \ \underline{\text{SENTENCE}} \end{array} \right\}$ [END-SEARCH]

FORMAT 1:

<u>SEND</u> cd-name <u>FROM</u> identifier

FORMAT 2:

<u>SEND</u> cd-name [<u>FROM</u> identifier-1] $\left\{ \begin{array}{l} \text{WITH identifier-2} \\ \text{WITH } \underline{\text{ESI}} \\ \text{WITH } \underline{\text{EMI}} \\ \text{WITH } \underline{\text{EGI}} \end{array} \right\}$

$\left[\left\{ \begin{array}{l} \underline{\text{BEFORE}} \\ \underline{\text{AFTER}} \end{array} \right\} \text{ADVANCING} \left\{ \begin{array}{l} \left\{ \begin{array}{l} \text{identifier-3} \\ \text{integer} \end{array} \right\} \left[\begin{array}{l} \text{LINE} \\ \text{LINES} \end{array} \right] \\ \left\{ \begin{array}{l} \text{mnemonic-name} \\ \underline{\text{PAGE}} \end{array} \right\} \end{array} \right\} \right]$ [<u>REPLACING</u> LINE]

FORMAT 1:

<u>SET</u> $\left\{ \begin{array}{l} \text{index-name-1} \\ \text{identifier-1} \end{array} \right\} \dots \underline{\text{TO}} \left\{ \begin{array}{l} \text{index-name-2} \\ \text{identifier-2} \\ \text{integer} \end{array} \right\}$

FORMAT 2:

<u>SET</u> { index-name } $\dots \left\{ \begin{array}{l} \underline{\text{UP}} \ \underline{\text{BY}} \\ \underline{\text{DOWN}} \ \underline{\text{BY}} \end{array} \right\} \left\{ \begin{array}{l} \text{identifier} \\ \text{integer} \end{array} \right\}$

FORMAT 3:

$$\underline{SET} \left\{ \{ \text{mnemonic-name} \} \ldots \underline{TO} \left\{ \begin{array}{c} \underline{ON} \\ \underline{OFF} \end{array} \right\} \right\} \ldots$$

FORMAT 4:

$$\underline{SET} \{ \text{condition-name} \} \ldots \underline{TO} \ \underline{TRUE}$$

$$\underline{SORT} \ \text{file-name-1} \left\{ \underline{ON} \left\{ \begin{array}{c} \underline{ASCENDING} \\ \underline{DESCENDING} \end{array} \right\} \underline{KEY} \left\{ \text{data-name} \right\} \ldots \right\} \ldots$$

[WITH <u>DUPLICATES</u> IN ORDER]   [COLLATING <u>SEQUENCE</u> IS alphabet-name]

$$\left\{ \begin{array}{l} \underline{INPUT} \ \underline{PROCEDURE} \ IS \ \text{procedure-name-1} \left[\left\{ \begin{array}{c} \underline{THROUGH} \\ \underline{THRU} \end{array} \right\} \text{procedure-name-2} \right] \\ \underline{USING} \ \{ \text{file-name-2} \} \ldots \end{array} \right\}$$

$$\left\{ \begin{array}{l} \underline{OUTPUT} \ \underline{PROCEDURE} \ IS \ \text{procedure-name-3} \left[\left\{ \begin{array}{c} \underline{THROUGH} \\ \underline{THRU} \end{array} \right\} \text{procedure-name-4} \right] \\ \underline{GIVING} \ \{ \text{file-name-3} \} \ldots \end{array} \right\}$$

$$\underline{START} \ \text{file-name} \left[\underline{KEY} \ IS \left\{ \begin{array}{l} \underline{EQUAL} \ TO \\ = \\ \underline{GREATER} \ THAN \\ > \\ \underline{NOT} \ \underline{LESS} \ THAN \\ \underline{NOT} \ < \\ \underline{GREATER} \ THAN \ OR \ \underline{EQUAL} \ TO \\ >= \end{array} \right\} \text{data-name} \right]$$

[<u>INVALID</u> KEY imperative-statement-1]   [<u>NOT</u> <u>INVALID</u> KEY imperative-statement-2]   [<u>END-START</u>]

$$\underline{STOP} \left\{ \begin{array}{c} \underline{RUN} \\ \text{literal} \end{array} \right\}$$

$$\underline{STRING} \left\{ \left\{ \begin{array}{c} \text{identifier-1} \\ \text{literal-1} \end{array} \right\} \ldots \underline{DELIMITED} \ BY \left\{ \begin{array}{c} \text{identifier-2} \\ \text{literal-2} \\ \underline{SIZE} \end{array} \right\} \right\} \ldots$$

<u>INTO</u> identifier-3   [WITH <u>POINTER</u> identifier-4]

[ON <u>OVERFLOW</u> imperative-statement-1] [<u>NOT</u> ON <u>OVERFLOW</u> imperative-statement-2] [<u>END-STRING</u>]

FORMAT 1:

$$\underline{SUBTRACT} \left\{ \begin{array}{c} \text{identifier-1} \\ \text{literal} \end{array} \right\} \ldots \underline{FROM} \ \{ \text{identifier-2} \ [\underline{ROUNDED}] \} \ldots$$

[ON <u>SIZE</u> <u>ERROR</u> imperative-statement-1] [<u>NOT</u> ON <u>SIZE</u> <u>ERROR</u> imperative-statement-2] [<u>END-SUBTRACT</u>]

FORMAT 2:

SUBTRACT $\left\{\begin{array}{l}\text{identifier-1} \\ \text{literal-1}\end{array}\right\}$ . . . FROM $\left\{\begin{array}{l}\text{identifier-2} \\ \text{literal-2}\end{array}\right\}$

GIVING { identifier-3 [ROUNDED] } . . .

[ON SIZE ERROR imperative-statement-1] [NOT ON SIZE ERROR imperative-statement-2] [END-SUBRACT]

FORMAT 3:

SUBTRACT $\left\{\begin{array}{l}\text{CORRESPONDING} \\ \text{CORR}\end{array}\right\}$ identifier-1 FROM identifier-2 [ROUNDED]

[ON SIZE ERROR imperative-statement-1] [NOT ON SIZE ERROR imperative-statement-2] [END-SUBTRACT]

SUPPRESS PRINTING

TERMINATE { report-name } . . .

UNSTRING identifier-1

$\left[\text{DELIMITED BY [ALL]} \left\{\begin{array}{l}\text{identifier-2} \\ \text{literal-1}\end{array}\right\} \left[\text{OR} \quad \text{[ALL]} \left\{\begin{array}{l}\text{identifier-3} \\ \text{literal-2}\end{array}\right\}\right] \ldots \right]$

INTO { identifier-4   [DELIMITER IN identifier-5]   [COUNT IN identifier-6] } . . .

[WITH POINTER identifier-7]   [TALLYING IN identifier-8]

[ON OVERFLOW imperative-statement-1] [NOT ON OVERFLOW imperative-statement-2] [END-UNSTRING]

FORMAT 1:

USE [GLOBAL] AFTER STANDARD $\left\{\begin{array}{l}\text{EXCEPTION} \\ \text{ERROR}\end{array}\right\}$ PROCEDURE ON $\left\{\begin{array}{l}\text{\{file-name\} . . .} \\ \text{INPUT} \\ \text{OUTPUT} \\ \text{I-O} \\ \text{EXTEND}\end{array}\right\}$

FORMAT 2:

USE [GLOBAL] BEFORE REPORTING identifier

FORMAT 3:

USE FOR DEBUGGING ON $\left\{\begin{array}{l}\text{cd-name} \\ \text{[ALL REFERENCES OF] identifier} \\ \text{file-name} \\ \text{procedure-name} \\ \text{ALL PROCEDURES}\end{array}\right\}$ . . .

FORMAT 1:

WRITE record-name [FROM identifier-1]

$$\left[\left\{ \begin{matrix} \underline{BEFORE} \\ \underline{AFTER} \end{matrix} \right\} ADVANCING \left\{ \begin{matrix} \left\{ \begin{matrix} identifier\text{-}2 \\ integer \end{matrix} \right\} \left[\begin{matrix} LINE \\ LINES \end{matrix} \right] \\ \left\{ \begin{matrix} mnemonic\text{-}name \\ \underline{PAGE} \end{matrix} \right\} \end{matrix} \right\} \left[AT \left\{ \begin{matrix} \underline{END\text{-}OF\text{-}PAGE} \\ \underline{EOP} \end{matrix} \right\} imperative\text{-}statement\text{-}1 \right] \right]$$

$$\left[\underline{NOT} \ AT \left\{ \begin{matrix} \underline{END\text{-}OF\text{-}PAGE} \\ \underline{EOP} \end{matrix} \right\} imperative\text{-}statement\text{-}2 \right] \quad [\underline{END\text{-}WRITE}]$$

FORMAT 2:

WRITE record-name [FROM identifier]

[INVALID KEY imperative-statement-1]   [NOT INVALID KEY imperative-statement-2]   [END-WRITE]

General Formats for Copy and Replace Statements

COPY text-name $\left[\left\{ \begin{matrix} \underline{OF} \\ \underline{IN} \end{matrix} \right\} library\text{-}name \right]$

$$\left[\underline{REPLACING} \left\{ \left\{ \begin{matrix} ==pseudo\text{-}text\text{-}1== \\ identifier\text{-}1 \\ literal\text{-}1 \\ word\text{-}1 \end{matrix} \right\} \underline{BY} \left\{ \begin{matrix} ==pseudo\text{-}text\text{-}2== \\ identifier\text{-}2 \\ literal\text{-}2 \\ word\text{-}2 \end{matrix} \right\} \right\} \ldots \right]$$

REPLACE { ==pseudo-text-1== BY ==pseudo-text-2== } . . .

REPLACE OFF

General Formats for Conditions

RELATION CONDITION:

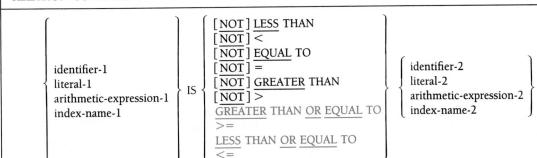

CLASS CONDITION:

identifier IS [NOT] $\begin{Bmatrix} \underline{\text{NUMERIC}} \\ \underline{\text{ALPHABETIC}} \\ \underline{\text{ALPHABETIC-LOWER}} \\ \underline{\text{ALPHABETIC-UPPER}} \\ \text{class-name} \end{Bmatrix}$

SIGN CONDITION:

arithmetic-expression IS [NOT] $\begin{Bmatrix} \underline{\text{POSITIVE}} \\ \underline{\text{NEGATIVE}} \\ \underline{\text{ZERO}} \end{Bmatrix}$

NEGATED CONDITION:

NOT condition

COMBINED CONDITION:

condition-1 $\left\{ \begin{Bmatrix} \underline{\text{AND}} \\ \underline{\text{OR}} \end{Bmatrix} \text{condition-2} \right\}$ ...

ABBREVIATED COMBINED CONDITION:

relation-condition $\left\{ \begin{Bmatrix} \underline{\text{AND}} \\ \underline{\text{OR}} \end{Bmatrix} [\underline{\text{NOT}}] \; [\text{relational-operator}] \quad \text{object} \right\}$ ...

Miscellaneous Formats

QUALIFICATION:

FORMAT 1:

$\begin{Bmatrix} \text{data-name-1} \\ \text{condition-name} \end{Bmatrix} \left\{ \begin{array}{l} \left\{ \begin{Bmatrix} \underline{\text{IN}} \\ \underline{\text{OF}} \end{Bmatrix} \text{data-name-2} \right\} \dots \left[\begin{Bmatrix} \underline{\text{IN}} \\ \underline{\text{OF}} \end{Bmatrix} \begin{Bmatrix} \text{file-name-1} \\ \text{cd-name-1} \end{Bmatrix} \right] \\ \\ \begin{Bmatrix} \underline{\text{IN}} \\ \underline{\text{OF}} \end{Bmatrix} \begin{Bmatrix} \text{file-name-2} \\ \text{cd-name-2} \end{Bmatrix} \end{array} \right\}$

FORMAT 2:

paragraph-name $\begin{Bmatrix} \underline{\text{IN}} \\ \underline{\text{OF}} \end{Bmatrix}$ section-name

FORMAT 3:

text-name $\begin{Bmatrix} \underline{\text{IN}} \\ \underline{\text{OF}} \end{Bmatrix}$ library-name

FORMAT 4:

LINAGE-COUNTER $\begin{Bmatrix} \underline{\text{IN}} \\ \underline{\text{OF}} \end{Bmatrix}$ report-name

FORMAT 5:

$\begin{Bmatrix} \underline{\text{PAGE-COUNTER}} \\ \underline{\text{LINE-COUNTER}} \end{Bmatrix} \begin{Bmatrix} \underline{\text{IN}} \\ \underline{\text{OF}} \end{Bmatrix}$ report-name

QUALIFICATION:

FORMAT 6:

$$
\text{data-name-1}
\begin{Bmatrix}
\begin{Bmatrix} \underline{\text{IN}} \\ \underline{\text{OF}} \end{Bmatrix} \text{data-name-2} \left[\begin{Bmatrix} \underline{\text{IN}} \\ \underline{\text{OF}} \end{Bmatrix} \text{report-name-1} \right] \\
\begin{Bmatrix} \underline{\text{IN}} \\ \underline{\text{OF}} \end{Bmatrix} \text{report-name-2}
\end{Bmatrix}
$$

SUBSCRIPTING:

$$
\begin{Bmatrix} \text{condition-name} \\ \text{data-name-1} \end{Bmatrix}
\left(
\begin{Bmatrix}
\text{integer-1} \\
\text{data-name-2} \left[\begin{Bmatrix} + \\ - \end{Bmatrix} \text{integer-2} \right] \\
\text{index-name} \left[\begin{Bmatrix} + \\ - \end{Bmatrix} \text{integer-3} \right]
\end{Bmatrix}
\dots
\right)
$$

General Format for Program Nesting

```
    IDENTIFICATION DIVISION.
    PROGRAM-ID. program-name [ IS INITIAL PROGRAM ].
[ ENVIRONMENT DIVISION. environment-division-content ]
[ DATA DIVISION. data-division-content ]
[ PROCEDURE DIVISION. procedure-division-content ]
[ [ nested-source-program ] . . .
    END PROGRAM program-name. ]
```

General Format for Nested Source Programs

```
    IDENTIFICATION DIVISION.
    PROGRAM-ID. program-name [ IS { COMMON / INITIAL } PROGRAM ] .
[ ENVIRONMENT DIVISION. environment-division-content ]
[ DATA DIVISION. data-division-content ]
[ PROCEDURE DIVISION. procedure-division-content ]
[ nested-source-program ] . . .
    END PROGRAM program-name.
```

General Format for a Sequence of Source Programs
IDENTIFICATION DIVISION. PROGRAM-ID. program-name-1 [IS INITIAL PROGRAM] . [ENVIRONMENT DIVISION. environment-division-content] [DATA DIVISION. data-division-content] [PROCEDURE DIVISION. procedure-division-content] [[nested-source-program] . . . END PROGRAM program-name-1.] IDENTIFICATION DIVISION. PROGRAM-ID. program-name-2 [IS INITIAL PROGRAM]. [ENVIRONMENT DIVISION. environment-division-content] [DATA DIVISION. data-division-content] [PROCEDURE DIVISION. procedure-division-content] [[nested-source-program] . . . END PROGRAM program-name-2.]

Flow Charting

Graphic Symbol	Name and Meaning
	Terminal Symbol indicates the beginning point and end point(s) of an algorithm.
	Input-Output shows the input data to and output generated by an algorithm.
	Process shows one or more instructions to be processed in sequence (i.e., a sequence structure).
	Predefined Process indicates an external or internal subalgorithm (or a program module) with a name whose logic is detailed elsewhere.
	Decision shows a decision process for two-way decision making.
	Flow Lines indicate the logical sequence of execution of algorithm steps in the algorithm.
	Off-Page Connector provides continuation of a logical path on another page.
	On-Page Connector provides continuation of a logical path at another point in the same page.

Figure C1 Conventional Flow Charting Symbols

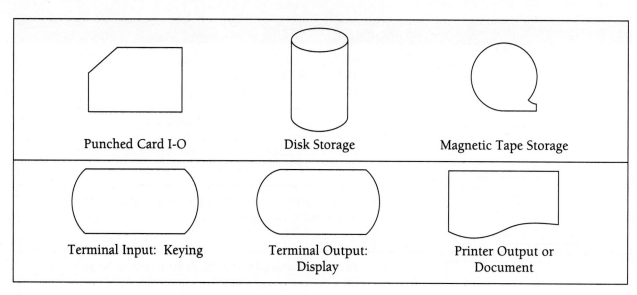

Figure C2 Additional Flow Charting Symbols for Input and Output

Algorithm for Binary Search of an Array: Let ARRAY be a one-dimensional array of size SIZE. Let SEARCH-KEY be a value that is compatible with elements of ARRAY. The following algorithm applies binary search to ARRAY. If SEARCH-KEY is in the ARRAY, the algorithm returns its INDEX. If not, the returned value for INDEX will be zero. FLOOR is a function with a floating-point argument, and it returns the largest integer that is smaller than its argument.

```
BINARY-SEARCH:
    read SIZE;
    initialize POINTER to 1;

    REPEAT UNTIL POINTER > SIZE
        read ARRAY (POINTER);
        add 1 to POINTER;
    ENDREPEAT;

    read SEARCH-KEY;

    set LEFT to 1;
    set RIGHT to SIZE;

    set MIDPOINT = FLOOR ( (LEFT + RIGHT) / 2);

    REPEAT UNTIL (SEARCH-KEY = ARRAY (MIDPOINT)) OR (LEFT > RIGHT)
        IF SEARCH-KEY < ARRAY (MIDPOINT) THEN
            set RIGHT = MIDPOINT − 1;
        ELSE
            set LEFT = MIDPOINT + 1;
        ENDIF;

        set MIDPOINT = FLOOR ( (LEFT + RIGHT) / 2);

    ENDREPEAT;

    IF SEARCH-KEY = ARRAY (MIDPOINT) THEN
        set INDEX = MIDPOINT;
    ELSE
        set INDEX = 0;
    ENDIF;

    write INDEX;

END BINARY-SEARCH.
```

Figure C3 An Example Algorithm Expressed in Structured English

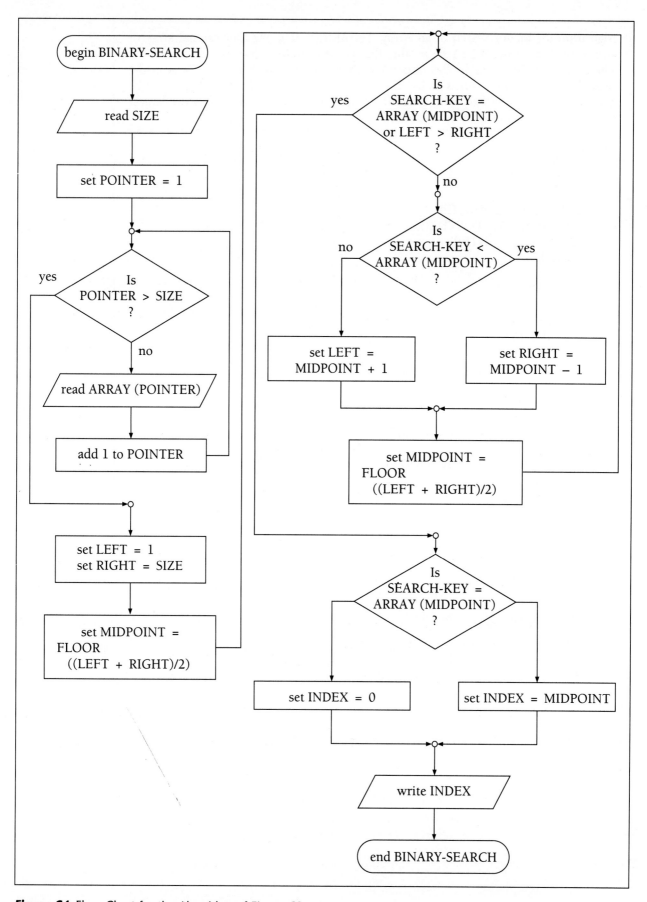

Figure C4 Flow Chart for the Algorithm of Figure C3

COBOL Report Writer

Introduction

Through many examples we have seen that data stored in computer files can be processed and printed in the form of a business report. A business report is an appropriately organized collection of a report heading, page headings, data extracted from files, summations, counts, page footings, and a report footing. They can be generated either through conventional programming or by using the COBOL report writer. The report writer is one of COBOL's nonstandard features and can be used in the automatic generation of reports in business applications.

A COBOL program designed to produce a business report uses READ statements to access data stored in files; WRITE statements to print headings, footings, and data lines; IF statements to determine when to break pages and for control breaks; arithmetic statements to compute summations and counts; and MOVE statements to transfer values from input area to program variables and output area. If the report is complex, the program to generate it may also be quite complicated. Under such circumstances, instead of programming a procedural description of the report generation process, we may prefer to use an automated report generator. The COBOL report writer feature allows us to generate business reports with minimal PROCEDURE DIVISION programming.

Structure of Business Reports

If we examine several typical printed business reports, we see that they generally conform to a common structure, and consist of similar elements.

1. A report heading at the top of the first page
2. One or more report pages, each consisting of
   a. A page heading
   b. A report body
   c. A page footing
3. A report footing, usually at the bottom of the last page

The report body consists of one or more blocks of information, each containing a control heading, one or more lines of detail, and a control footing.

Figure D1 shows the elements and structure of a business report using a sample report as an example. The ACE Company Personnel Salary Report is five pages long. It lists the company employees grouped by LOCATION and, for each location, by DEPARTMENT. It prints the salary totals for each group and subgroup. The detail lines consist of EMP IDNO, EMPLOYEE NAME, LOCATION, and yearly SALARY field values. Each page is concluded with a summary line specifying the range of departments reported on that page, and the final page ends with a line that reports the total of all personnel salaries.

The first line on page 1 is produced only once at the beginning of the report. A few lines on top of the first page of a report are used to identify it. They are called the **report heading**. Depending on the design, it may consist of more than one line. The report heading lines usually are not duplicated at the beginning of other pages. The corresponding lines in the other pages are left blank.

The report heading is followed by three lines in Figure D1. These are lines 2, 3, and 4 on each page, and they form the **page heading**. A page heading may consist of the name of the report, the date on which the report was printed, a page number, and the column headings for the information in the rest of the

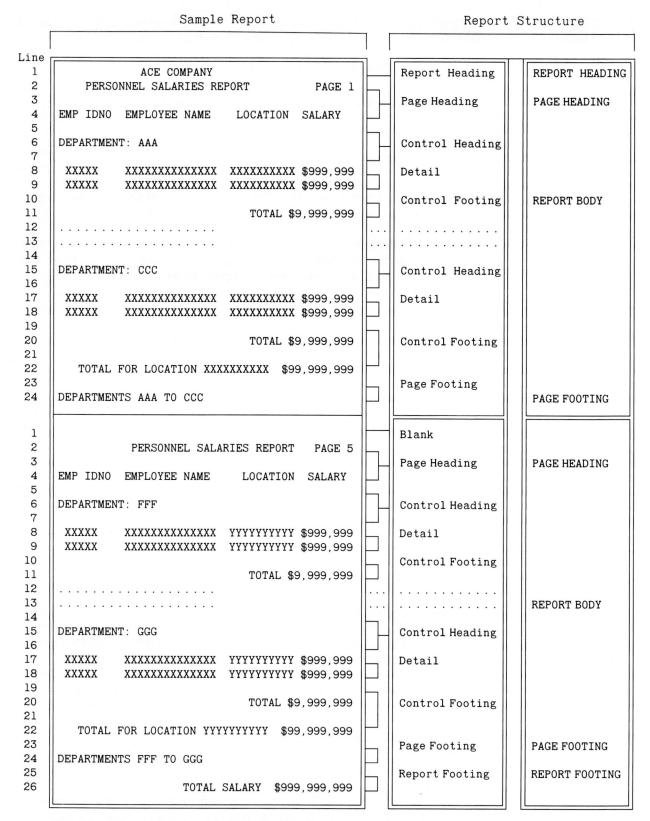

Figure D1 An Example Report and Its Structure

page. In some cases the report heading and page heading may be compressed together and appear as page heading on each page.

After the page heading comes the **report body**. This consists of a set of printed lines composed of data field values that are derived using the data records from one or more data files. These lines are known as **detail lines**. Lines 8 and 9 are examples of detail lines in Figure D1.

In a majority of business reports the detail lines are grouped together according to some data item values. In our report, we group them according to a LOCATION value. Furthermore, for each LOCATION value they are subgrouped with respect to a DEPARTMENT value. The grouping of detail lines is known as a **control break** in report generation. Each control break is reflected by three elements: a control heading, the detail lines belonging to the control break, and a control footing.

The **control heading** for a control break appropriately identifies that control break. In the report of Figure D1, a control break based on DEPARTMENT is identified by line 6. A control heading is followed by the detail lines that belong to that control break. Immediately after detail lines is the control footing for the control break. It usually includes summary information, such as totals, derived from its corresponding detail lines. Lines 9 and 10 are control footing lines in our report. Some control breaks may not generate control headings at all, and may combine the control heading information with the control footing content. Lines 21 and 22 constitute such a control footing.

Information that should be included at the bottom of each page depends on the report design. They may be a page number, totals for the page, or an indication of the page content. Lines 23 and 24 in Figure D1 are examples of such lines, called **page footing**.

Finally, at the bottom of the last page of a report we may want to produce lines that reflect summaries of the information presented. This block of lines is referred to as a **report footing**. Lines 25 and 26 on page 5 of the example report constitute the report footing.

COBOL Program Features for Report Writer

We discuss the COBOL report writer in view of an example program. In Figure D2 we have a template for a business report. It is a variation of the report of Figure D1. It has no report heading, and each page begins with a page heading. We have a control break based on DEPARTMENT and another control break with respect to LOCATION. The control breaks generate detail lines followed by control footings. At the end of the last page we have a report footing.

The COBOL program that uses the report writer to generate the report of Figure D2 is given in Figure D3. As can be seen, the following program divisions are affected by the report writer:

1. The FILE-CONTROL paragraph of the INPUT-OUTPUT SECTION of the ENVIRONMENT DIVISION. Here, using a SELECT statement we have to define a report file that will be generated by the report writer as its only output.
2. The FILE SECTION and REPORT SECTION of the DATA DIVISION
3. The PROCEDURE DIVISION

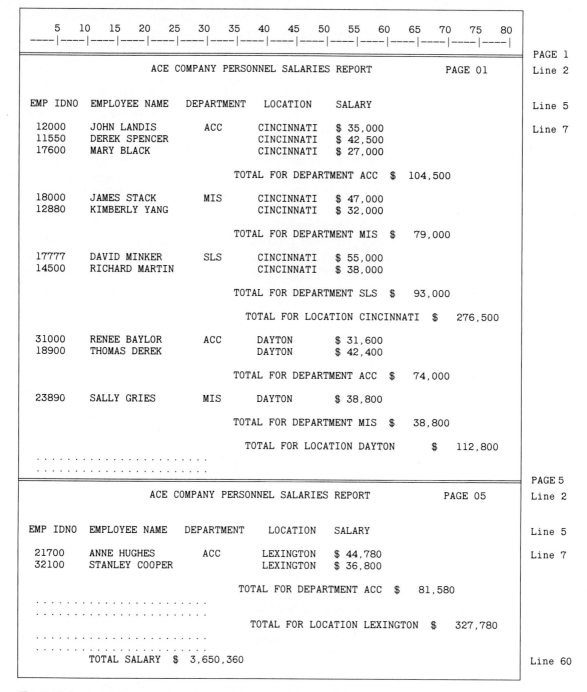

Figure D2 Template for a Report to Be Generated by the Program of Figure D3

```
00001    *...................................................
00002    IDENTIFICATION DIVISION.
00003    PROGRAM-ID. PERS-SALARIES-REPORT-GENERATOR.
00004    ********************************************************************
00005    ***   THIS PROGRAM USES THE COBOL REPORT WRITER TO GENERATE A      *
00006    ***   PERSONNEL SALARIES REPORT FOR THE ABC COMPANY.               *
00007    ********************************************************************
00008
00009    AUTHOR.         UCKAN.
00010    DATE-WRITTEN.  MARCH 22, 1991.
00011    DATE-COMPILED. MAR 22, 1991.
00012    *...................................................
00013    ENVIRONMENT DIVISION.
00014    CONFIGURATION SECTION.
00015    SOURCE-COMPUTER. UNIVERSITY-MAINFRAME.
00016    OBJECT-COMPUTER. UNIVERSITY-MAINFRAME.
00017    INPUT-OUTPUT SECTION.
00018    FILE-CONTROL.
00019
00020        SELECT PERSONNEL-FILE   ASSIGN TO FILE1.
00021        SELECT PERS-REPORT-FILE ASSIGN TO FILE2.
00022
00023    *...................................................
00024    DATA DIVISION.
00025    FILE SECTION.
00026
00027    FD  PERSONNEL-FILE
00028        LABEL RECORDS ARE OMITTED
00029        RECORD CONTAINS 80 CHARACTERS
00030        DATA RECORD IS PERSONNEL-RECORD.
00031    01  PERSONNEL-RECORD.
00032        05   PERSONNEL-IDNO        PIC X(5).
00033        05   PERSONNEL-NAME        PIC X(14).
00034        05   DEPARTMENT            PIC X(3).
00035        05   LOCATION              PIC X(10).
00036        05   SALARY                PIC 9(6).
00037        05   FILLER                PIC X(42).
00038
00039    FD  PERS-REPORT-FILE
00040        LABEL RECORDS ARE OMITTED
00041        REPORT IS PERS-REPORT.
00042
00043    WORKING-STORAGE SECTION.
00044
00045    *********> VARIABLES:
00046
00047    01  END-OF-PERS-FILE    PIC XXX.
00048
```

Figure D3 Sample COBOL Program with Report Writer Feature

```
00049    REPORT SECTION.
00050    RD   PERS-REPORT
00051         CONTROLS ARE FINAL, LOCATION, DEPARTMENT
00052         PAGE LIMIT IS 60 LINES
00053         HEADING 2
00054         FIRST DETAIL 7.
00055
00056    01   TYPE IS REPORT HEADING.
00057         05   LINE NUMBER IS 2.
00058              10   COLUMN NUMBER IS 21      PIC X(37)
00059                   VALUE IS "ACE COMPANY PERSONNEL SALARIES REPORT".
00060              10   COLUMN NUMBER IS 70      PIC X(4)
00061                   VALUE IS "PAGE".
00062              10   COLUMN NUMBER IS 75      PIC 99
00063                   SOURCE IS PAGE-COUNTER.
00064
00065    01   TYPE IS PAGE HEADING.
00066         05   LINE NUMBER IS 5
00067              10   COLUMN NUMBER IS 1       PIC X(8)
00068                   VALUE IS "EMP IDNO".
00069              10   COLUMN NUMBER IS 11      PIC X(13)
00070                   VALUE IS "EMPLOYEE NAME".
00071              10   COLUMN NUMBER IS 27      PIC X(10)
00072                   VALUE IS "DEPARTMENT".
00073              10   COLUMN NUMBER IS 40      PIC X(8)
00074                   VALUE IS "LOCATION".
00075              10   COLUMN NUMBER IS 51      PIC X(6)
00076                   VALUE IS "SALARY".
00077
00078    01   PERS-REPORT-LINE TYPE IS DETAIL
00079              LINE NUMBER IS PLUS 1.
00080         05   COLUMN NUMBER IS 2           PIC X(5)
00081              SOURCE IS PERSONNEL-IDNO.
00082         05   COLUMN NUMBER IS 11          PIC X(14)
00083              SOURCE IS PERSONNEL-NAME.
00084         05   COLUMN NUMBER IS 30          PIC X(3)
00085              SOURCE IS DEPARTMENT   GROUP INDICATE.
00086         05   COLUMN NUMBER IS 39          PIC X(10)
00087              SOURCE IS LOCATION.
00088         05   COLUMN NUMBER IS 51              PIC $ZZZ,Z
00089              SOURCE IS SALARY.
00090
00091    01   TYPE IS CONTROL FOOTING DEPARTMENT
00092              LINE NUMBER IS PLUS 2.
00093         05   COLUMN NUMBER IS 35          PIC X(20)
00094              VALUE IS "TOTAL FOR DEPARTMENT".
00095         05   COLUMN NUMBER IS 56          PIC X(3)
00096              SOURCE IS DEPARTMENT.
00097         05   DEPT-TOTAL
00098              COLUMN NUMBER IS 61              PIC $Z,ZZZ,ZZ9
00099              SUM UPON SALARY.
00100
00101    01   TYPE IS CONTROL FOOTING LOCATION
00102              LINE NUMBER IS PLUS 2.
00103         05   COLUMN NUMBER IS 37          PIC X(18)
00104              VALUE IS "TOTAL FOR LOCATION".
```

Figure D3 (Continued)

```
00105           05   COLUMN NUMBER IS 56          PIC X(10)
00106                   SOURCE IS LOCATION.
00107           05   LOC-TOTAL
00108                COLUMN NUMBER IS 68          PIC $ZZ,ZZZ,ZZ9
00109                   SUM UPON DEPT-TOTAL.
00110
00111     01   TYPE IS CONTROL FOOTING FINAL.
00112           05   LINE NUMBER IS 60.
00113                10   COLUMN NUMBER IS 10     PIC X(12)
00114                       VALUE IS "TOTAL SALARY".
00115                10   COLUMN NUMBER IS 24     PIC $ZZZ,ZZZ,ZZ9
00116                       SUM UPON LOC-TOTAL.
00117
00118     *.........................................................................
00119     PROCEDURE DIVISION.
00120     A-MAINLINE.
00121        OPEN INPUT  PERSONNEL-FILE
00122             OUTPUT PERS-REPORT-FILE.
00123
00124        MOVE "NO"  TO END-OF-PERS-FILE.
00125
00126        INITIATE PERS-REPORT.
00127
00128        READ PERSONNEL-FILE
00129             AT END MOVE "YES" TO END-OF-PERS-FILE.
00130
00131        PERFORM GENERATE-PERS-REPORT
00132             UNTIL END-OF-PERS-FILE = "YES".
00133
00134        TERMINATE PERS-REPORT.
00135
00136        CLOSE PERSONNEL-FILE PERS-REPORT-FILE
00137
00138        STOP RUN.
00139
00140     GENERATE-PERS-REPORT.
00141
00142        GENERATE PERS-REPORT-LINE.
00143
00144        READ PERSONNEL-FILE
00145             AT END MOVE "YES" TO END-OF-PERS-FILE.
```

Figure D3 (Continued)

FILE SECTION Entries for Report Writer

The only element of concern in the FILE SECTION of the DATA DIVISION is
the FD block specification for the report file, called PERS-REPORT-FILE in the
program of Figure D3. The FD block here is a simplified version of FD blocks
for regular data files. The elements specified in the FD block for a report file are

1. The clause LABEL RECORDS ARE OMITTED
2. The REPORT clause, which references by their names one or more reports to be generated within this file
3. An optional 01 record description entry

The 01 record description entry is not necessary, since the report writer automatically generates the output records using the information provided in the REPORT SECTION of the DATA DIVISION. If this 01 record description is included, the WRITE statements based on the report file will insert additional lines into the report file. The insertion of such lines cannot be controlled by the report writer, and hence may produce a confusing report. Resolving this problem is the programmer's responsibility.

The FD block for PERS-REPORT-FILE of Figure D3 is coded in lines 00039 through 00041.

REPORT SECTION for Report Writer

The report to be generated by the report writer is fully described in the REPORT SECTION of the DATA DIVISION. The REPORT SECTION should follow the WORKING-STORAGE SECTION. It is somewhat similar to the FILE SECTION. It consists of a report description (RD) block and several 01 level entries.

RD Block for Report Specification.   The RD block partially defines the layout of a report. It is used to specify

1. The name of the report
2. A PAGE LIMIT clause that defines the maximum number of printed lines per page of the report
3. A HEADING CLAUSE that determines the beginning line of each page
4. A FIRST DETAIL clause, which specifies the beginning location of the first detail line
5. A LAST DETAIL clause, which specifies the last line on a page that may be used for a detail line
6. A FOOTING clause that specifies the line number of the first line of the page footing
7. A CONTROL clause, which defines the control breaks for the report

The report of Figure D3, called PERS-REPORT, is described as follows.

```
          . . . . . . . . . . . . . . . . .
          . . . . . . . . . . . . . . . . .
00049     REPORT SECTION.
00050     RD PERS-REPORT
00051        CONTROLS ARE FINAL, LOCATION, DEPARTMENT
00052        PAGE LIMIT IS 60 LINES
00053        HEADING 2
00054        FIRST DETAIL 7.
          . . . . . . . . . . . . . . . . .
          . . . . . . . . . . . . . . . . .
```

This RD block specifies a report with a page limit of 60 lines in which the report heading or the page heading starts at line 2, the first detail line is located at line 7, and there are three control breaks. The control breaks are with respect to the fields DEPARTMENT and LOCATION, and a global control break identified by the reserved word FINAL. This report apparently has no page footings.

The report writer automatically creates two special registers, LINE-COUNTER and PAGE-COUNTER. LINE-COUNTER and PAGE-COUNTER are reserved words, and if the program is using the report writer, they should not be defined by the programmer in the program. They are used by the report writer to keep track of the lines per page and the pages in the report.

Record Descriptions Within REPORT SECTION. Several different lines in the report are described using level 01 entries after the RD block. These entries can be used to describe report heading, page heading, control heading, detail lines, control footing, page footing, and report footing. Examples of level 01 entries for report heading, page heading, detail lines, and control footings are shown in lines 00056 through 00116 of Figure D3. The following elements of the level 01 entries are significant:

1. The TYPE clause identifies the type of the record to be described.
2. Detail lines are identified by a detail line name, such as PERS-REPORT-LINE, since there may be more than one type of detail lines in a report.
3. The LINE clause is used to control vertical line spacing before a report line is printed in a manner that is similar to the AFTER ADVANCING clause of the WRITE statement. For example, line 00057 has a LINE clause for the report heading LINE NUMBER IS 2. This causes the special register LINE-COUNTER to be set to 2, and instructs the report writer to print the report heading on the second line of each page. On the other hand, the LINE NUMBER IS PLUS 1 clause on line 00079 for the detail lines specifies a line position of 1 relative to the most recently printed line. It also increments the register LINE-COUNTER by 1.
4. The COLUMN clause is used to define the horizontal position of a value on a report line. The PICTURE and VALUE clauses have the same function as the corresponding clauses for data definition (see Chapter 2). Therefore, in the following example extracted from Figure D3,

```
00067              10 COLUMN NUMBER IS 1      PIC X(8)
00068                  VALUE IS "EMP IDNO".
```

the 8-character literal EMP IDNO is specified to be printed with its leftmost character starting at column 1 of the current report line.

5. The SOURCE clause simulates the behavior of a MOVE statement. It transfers the value contained in a specified data field to the field associated with the SOURCE clause.

Here is an example:

```
00082        05  COLUMN NUMBER IS 11        PIC X(14)
00083              SOURCE IS PERSONNEL-NAME.
```

Here, the value of the identifier PESONNEL-NAME is transferred from an input file record to an alphanumeric field of length 14 before it is printed starting at column 11 of the current report line.

6. The SUM clause causes automatic accumulation of the values of a numeric identifier in the input records before printing. As shown in line 00099, this

clause can be used only in a control footing line description. Here, the SUM UPON SALARY clause causes a summation of SALARY field values of all input records processed prior to printing. This accumulated value will be moved to the identifier DEPT-TOTAL (line 00097) and will be printed beginning at column 61 of the current report line according to PIC $Z,ZZZ,ZZ9.

7. The GROUP INDICATE clause can be used to suppress the printing of redundant values. It is used in line 00085 in conjunction with the field DEPARTMENT. As a result, the DEPARTMENT field values will be printed only in the first detail line of a group and will be suppressed in the remaining detail lines.

8. Other clauses can be used in the level 01 entries of the REPORT SECTION. Among them are the USAGE, BLANK WHEN ZERO, and JUSTIFIED clauses, whose functions are the same as those described in Chapter 2.

PROCEDURE DIVISION Statements for Report Writer

As far as the COBOL report writer is concerned, most of the procedural aspects of report generation are handled in a declarative fashion in the REPORT SECTION. In the PROCEDURE DIVISION of a program, the programmer's responsibilities are limited to three operations:

1. Initializing the special registers and accumulators associated with the report writer through the use of the INITIATE statement
2. Generating the report
3. Concluding the report generation through the use of a TERMINATE statement

The INITIATE statement has a simple syntax, and includes the report name to be generated after the INITIATE key word. Report generation requires repeated executions of the GENERATE statement within a controlled loop, as shown in Figure D3, line 00142. Syntactically, the word GENERATE should be followed by the name of the detail line.

In addition we can include in the PROCEDURE DIVISION of a report generation program a USE BEFORE REPORTING declarative to specify a particular procedure that should be executed before the report writer commences report generation.

Advantages and Disadvantages of COBOL Report Writer

The main advantage of the COBOL report writer is its ability to generate business reports easily with several levels of control break implementations without writing lengthy procedures in the PROCEDURE DIVISION.

It has some important disadvantages, however. First, it is not a standard COBOL feature, and therefore, even when available may show variations from one vendor's implementation to another. Second, it produces COBOL object modules that are relatively inefficient in processing. Finally, the report writer effectively builds a barrier between the programmer and the printed report, and programming around it may become quite difficult.

A margin   the zone defined by columns 8 through 11 on the COBOL coding form (Ch. 1)

abend   see **abnormal end** (Ch. 6)

abnormal end   termination of execution of a program without completing its function (Ch. 6)

acceptance testing   functional testing of an entire software system using live data (Ch. 6)

access technique   the manner in which records are accessed in a file (Ch. 2)

access time   the time it takes for the computer system to access data in external storage and bring them into the user work area after I-O instruction has been issued (Ch. 10)

access-by-address   ability to access a memory location by its address (Chs. 10, 13)

access-by-content   ability to access a memory location by its content (Chs. 10, 13)

actual parameter list   a list of parameters in a statement that calls on a subprogram (Ch. 7)

acyclic graph   a graph that contains no cycles (Ch. 5)

address space   the set of all admissible address values in the prime data area of a file (Ch. 14)

algorithm   a finite collection of logically related steps that can be used to solve a problem correctly and efficiently in a finite amount of time (Ch. 4)

alternate index   a VSAM index table that allows access-by-content based on any field in the record structure other than the primary key (Ch. 13)

alternate index cluster   the prime data and alternate index tables in a VSAM indexed file (Ch. 13)

appending records   the operation of inserting records after the last record in a file (Ch. 10)

application plan   a machine-language description of data base access strategy required for an application program (Ch. 18)

application programming mode   a processing mode for a data base in which the data base is accessed by an application program (Ch. 18)

arc   a directional line connecting two nodes in a digraph (Chs. 5, 15)

arithmetic expression   a valid combination of numeric variables, constants, and arithmetic operators (Ch. 3)

array   an ordered set of a fixed number of consecutive memory locations, each accessed by its relative address (Ch. 8)

artificial system   a system that is conceived and developed by humans (Ch. 4)

assignment operator   the equality operator in the COBOL COMPUTE statement that causes a value to be assigned to a variable (Ch. 3)

attribute   a measurable or observable property of an entity or a relationship that can be used to describe it or distinguish it from similar elements (Chs. 10, 18)

automated debugging   a type of debugging technique that is based on the use of special computer software to detect programming errors (Ch. 6)

automated testing   testing programs by using computer software that is developed to increase testing efficiency (Ch. 6)

AVL tree   see **height-balanced binary tree** (Ch. 16)

B margin   the zone from columns 12 through 72 on the COBOL coding form (Ch. 1)

backward linked list   a linked list that defines a decreasing order among its elements based on a specified data item (Ch. 15)

base cluster   the data and index area for an indexed sequential VSAM file (Ch. 13)

basis set   a minimal set of test cases that can be used with reasonable assurance in software testing (Ch. 6)

binary search tree   a binary tree in which each node contains an identifier, and for all nodes in the tree except the leaves, the identifiers in the left subtree are all less than the identifier in the node, and the identifiers in the right subtree are all greater than that in the node (Ch. 16)

binary tree   a tree in which all nodes have outdegrees of zero, one, or two (Chs. 5, 16)

block   see **physical record** (Chs. 2, 10)

blocked file   a file in which physical record size is a multiple of logical record size (Chs. 2, 10)

blocking factor   the number of logical records stored in a physical record in a file (Ch. 10)

Boolean operator   any of the operators NOT, AND, and OR that can be used to combine conditions into more complex conditions (Ch. 3)

Boolean quantity   a quantity that may assume only a logical value of true or false (Ch. 2)

Boolean query   see **complex query** (Ch. 13)

bottom-up design   a software design strategy in which the designing, coding, and testing of modules proceed from bottom to top (Ch. 4)

branch   a path in a tree that originates at the tree root and terminates at a leaf (Ch. 5)

branch-only cell a memory structure containing no data and two pointers, used to represent a node in a binary tree (Ch. 16)

bucket a block of two, four, or more sectors on a rotating magnetic storage device (Chs. 10, 14)

buffer a segment of the main memory reserved for a record (Ch. 10)

built-in data structure a data structure type that is supported by a high-level programming language (Ch. 4)

built-in file organization a file organization that is built into a computer language, and is readily recognized by it (Chs. 10, 15)

candidate key any set of attributes in a file which satisfies the requirements for keys (Ch. 17)

cardinality of a relation the number of rows in a relation (Ch. 18)

case structure a program structure that can be used for multiway decision making (Ch. 4)

cell an individually addressable memory location that can store a word of information (Chs. 4, 15)

child node a node in a tree that is at a lower level of hierarchy relative to a parent node (Chs. 5, 16)

circularly linked list see **ring** (Ch. 15)

clause a subset of a statement that complements it or specifies certain program entries (Ch. 1)

cluster a segment of a VSAM indexed file that contains data and index records (Ch. 13)

COBOL data structure a COBOL representation for data elements, substructures, and some relationships among them (Ch. 2)

cohesion a measure of a module's capacity to represent a single function (Ch. 4)

coincidental cohesion a form of cohesion in which a module performs a set of unrelated or loosely related tasks (Ch. 4)

collating sequence the ordering of characters in a character coding system (Ch. 9)

collision the phenomenon of two or more key values being transformed to the same memory location by a hash function (Ch. 14)

combined condition a COBOL condition type that combines other conditions using the operators AND and OR (Ch. 3)

command-driven system a software system with a user interface that permits the user to communicate with the system through a set of commands (Ch. 9)

comment line a COBOL line with an asterisk in column 7, ignored by the compiler but included in the source program listing as part of in-program documentation (Ch. 1)

common coupling a form of coupling in which two or more modules reference a global data area such as a file (Ch. 4)

communicational cohesion a form of cohesion in which all statements in a module make use of the same data structure or the same portion of a data structure (Ch. 4)

compilation error a type of error caused by violations of syntax and certain semantic rules of a programming language (Ch. 6)

complete binary tree a binary tree of depth d with n nodes such that its nodes correspond to the nodes numbered 1 to n in the full binary tree of the same depth (Ch. 16)

complex query a logical expression formed by using Boolean operators on simple, range, and other complex queries (Ch. 13)

composite data structure a data structure that is made up of primitive data structures (Ch. 4)

computer program a series of instructions expressed in a computer language that can be interpreted and executed by a computer system to produce the solution for a problem (Ch. 4)

computer-based system a system that uses computers to achieve its goals (Ch. 4)

concatenation an operation on two strings that produces a new string by attaching the second string after the first (Ch. 9)

condition name a COBOL name for simple comparison conditions that use the equality operator (Ch. 2)

conditionals COBOL statements used for decision making (Ch. 3)

constant a computational value that appears in a source program code (Ch. 1)

content coupling a form of coupling in which a module of a program contains a one-way reference to another module (Ch. 4)

control area a logical group of control intervals in a VSAM-indexed file (Ch. 13)

control break a manner in which a report-generating program is designed to produce output for an entity before the next entity is considered (Ch. 3, App. D)

control coupling a form of coupling in which some information that may affect the execution of a subordinate module is passed from one module to another (Ch. 4)

control interval the basic building block for VSAM files that consists of a number of logical data records, free space, and some descriptor fields (Ch. 13)

coupling a measure of module interface complexity in modular programming (Ch. 4)

cylinder the amount of storage that is accessible in one positioning of the read-write head mechanism in a rotating magnetic storage device (Ch. 10)

cylinder index an index table built for an ISAM file that contains one index entry for each cylinder of the file (Ch. 13)

cylinder overflow area a number of tracks in each cylinder of an ISAM file reserved for records overflowing from the prime data area of that cylinder (Ch. 13)

data values of properties associated with entities, relationships, or events in the real world that can be obtained through observations or measurements (Ch. 17)

data base a named and structured collection of files that represents all files pertinent to one or more applications and all relationships that exist among them (Chs. 5, 10, 18)

data base language a special, very high-level language that can be used for data base definition, maintenance, and retrieval (Ch. 18)

data base management system a vendor-supplied software system that monitors almost every component and process in a data base system (Ch. 18)

data base model an abstraction that can be used to describe the structure and semantics of a data base (Ch. 18)

data base schema a complete and machine-independent description of data in a data base (Ch. 18)

data base system a human-computer system that consists of hardware, software, data resource, procedures, and people (Ch. 18)

data coupling a form of coupling in which a module transfers simple data items to a subordinate module through an argument list (Ch. 4)

data definition language a subset of a data base language consisting of instructions that can be used to define a data base schema, subschemas necessary for application programs, and physical data base view (Ch. 18)

data integrity a set of considerations that permits representation and maintenance of data without any conflicts and inconsistencies in a file or a file system (Ch. 17)

data item a symbolic name for which a single nondecomposable value is stored in the computer's memory (Chs. 2, 4)

data manipulation language a subset of a data base language consisting of instructions that can be used to load and maintain a data base (Ch. 18)

data structure a model that represents data elements and relationships among them (Chs. 2, 4)

data type see **built-in data structure** (Ch. 4)

debugging see **program debugging** (Ch. 6)

decision table a table that represents a decision process in terms of conditions or variables, and actions to be taken depending on the outcome of condition or variable values (Ch. 5)

decision tree a tree structure in which intermediate nodes represent conditions or variables, and terminal nodes represent actions to be performed depending on the outcome of conditions or variable values (Ch. 5)

degree of a relation the number of columns in a relation (Ch. 18)

deletion anomaly a record structure's tendency to cause unintended loss of data from a file as a consequence of deleting a record (Ch. 17)

design error a type of error that occurs during the analysis and design phases (Ch. 6)

determinant an attribute or attribute set on which another attribute set depends (Ch. 17)

digraph a graph that consists of a set of nodes and a set of directional arcs connecting pairs of nodes (Ch. 15)

direct access an access mode that permits records in a file to be accessed by the addresses of memory locations in which they are stored (Ch. 10)

direct-access storage device a secondary storage device that permits direct access to its storage segments (Ch. 10)

displacement of an array element the relative address of the first byte of an array element within the segment of storage allocated to the array (Ch. 8)

division a COBOL program block that consists of sections and/or paragraphs (Ch. 1)

domain set a set of admissible values for an attribute from which it is assigned a value (Ch. 17)

dummy record a record in an ISAM file identified by a special marker flag in its first byte, generally used for reserving memory space for future records (Ch. 13)

embedded data language a version of a data base language that allows embedding of its instructions in an application program coded in a host language (Ch. 18)

entity an element of a set of similar but distinct beings, objects, or things (Ch. 10)

entity identifier see **key** (Ch. 10)

entity set a set whose elements are entities of the same type (Ch. 10)

error diagnostic a type of diagnostic message generated by a compiler indicating an error for which the compiler can make default adjustments (Ch. 6)

exclusive OR a binary Boolean operator that produces the binary digit 0 if both operands are 0 or if both operands are 1; otherwise, it produces the binary digit 1 (Ch. 14)

execution error a type of error that surfaces during program execution (Ch. 6)

external coupling a form of coupling in which a module is tied to an external storage device (Ch. 4)

external data structure a data structure that resides in external storage during and after processing (Ch. 4)

external error a type of error that is due to hardware or an interfacing software (Ch. 6)

external file name a name by which a file is referenced from outside a program (Ch. 2)

external search a search technique in which the list to be searched is kept in a file, and only parts of it are brought into the main memory for processing (Ch. 8)

external sorting a technique that requires list elements to be stored in external storage during and after the sorting process (Ch. 8)

external subprogram a subprogram that is coded and compiled independently of its calling programs, but is executed together with them (Ch. 7)

external variable a type of program variable that is stored in a segment of the main memory, which permits access to it by all modules in which such a variable is declared (Ch. 7)

fan-in the number of modules that invoke a given module (Ch. 4)

fan-out the number of modules that are invoked by a given module (Ch. 4)

fetching records the operation of accessing and subsequently retrieving records (Ch. 10)

FIFO list see **queue** (Ch. 15)

figurative constant a constant whose value is implied by its name (Ch. 1)

file a named and structured collection of similar records (Chs. 1, 2, 10)

file access the manner in which records in a file can be accessed and retrieved (Ch. 10)

file organization the manner in which records in a file are organized to describe relationships among records (Chs. 2, 10)

file update operations operations that change data values stored in records, add new records, or delete existing records in files (Ch. 10)

file-oriented I-O a mode of data input-output in which the source or target is a data file (Ch. 3)

fixed-format list a list with accessibility limitations (Ch. 15)

flow chart a graph structure consisting of nodes that represent types and functions of program steps in a program, and flow lines that represent the order in which the program steps are executed (Ch. 5)

flow graph a form of flow chart in which the details of operations are disregarded, and the program flow of control is emphasized (Chs. 4, 6)

foreign key an attribute in a record structure which is a candidate key for another related record structure (Ch. 17)

forest a collection of trees representing similar data and relationships (Ch. 16)

formal parameter list a list of variables that provide input-output for a subprogram (Ch. 7)

forward linked list a linked list that defines an increasing order among its elements based on a specified data item (Ch. 15)

full binary tree a binary tree of depth d containing $(2 ** d - 1)$ nodes (Ch. 16)

full dependency a type of data dependency in which all attributes in the determinant are needed to determine a set of attributes (Ch. 17)

function subprogram a subprogram that computes and returns a single value under its name when it transfers control to a calling program (Ch. 7)

functional cohesion a form of cohesion in which each element of a module is essential to perform only one well-defined function (Ch. 4)

functional specification the output of the systems analysis phase during which the needs of future users, the system constraints, and the requirements are determined, and a solution is proposed (Ch. 4)

functional testing a form of program testing whose purpose is to ensure that the program does what it is expected to do from a functional point of view (Ch. 6)

garbage the content of a memory location that has been excluded from a data structure, and hence is no longer needed (Ch. 15)

garbage collection technique a technique that aims to recover the memory locations containing garbage so that they can be reallocated (Ch. 15)

global variable a type of program variable that is specified in the calling program in a modular program system where subprograms are internal to the calling program (Ch. 7)

graph a set of nodes that usually represents data, and a set of lines connecting nodes that usually represents relationships (Chs. 4, 5)

group item a data structure that consists of elementary data items and the adjacency relationship among them (Chs. 2, 4)

hard sectoring an organization in which tracks on a rotating magnetic storage device are divided by the hardware into a fixed number of sectors (Ch. 10)

hash function an algorithm that transforms a key field value to a relative address within an admissible range (Ch. 14)

hashing the operation of transforming a key field value to a relative address (Chs. 13, 14)

head of a queue the output end of a queue (Ch. 15)

header label record a label record created for a file by the operating system and placed physically before the first data record (Ch. 10)

head-per-surface device a rotating magnetic storage device in which each magnetizable surface has one read-write head allocated to it (Ch. 10)

head-per-track device a rotating magnetic storage device in which each track on every magnetizable surface has one read-write head allocated to it (Ch. 10)

height of a tree the maximum level of nodes in a tree (Ch. 16)

height-balanced binary tree a binary search tree in which, for every node, the difference in height of the left and right subtrees does not exceed 1 (Ch. 16)

hierarchical structure a structure that reflects some hierarchical relationship among its components (Ch. 4)

home address an area on each track in rotating magnetic storage devices that contains self-identifying information (Ch. 10)

home marker a marker written by the computer system that is used at read time to locate the beginning of a physical record on a track in rotating magnetic storage devices (Ch. 10)

host language a procedural programming language used to write application programs that access a data base and contain embedded data base language commands (Ch. 18)

identifier a word that represents and references certain program entities (Ch. 1)

imperative statements all COBOL statement types except those used for decision making (Ch. 3)

implicit key the sequence number of records that determines record order in a sequential file (Ch. 11)

in situ file update a file update strategy in which records in the master file are updated without making a copy of the master records (Chs. 10, 11)

in-degree the number of arcs in a digraph that terminate at a given node. See also **fan-in** (Chs. 4, 5)

independent overflow area a segment of an ISAM file that is used to store records overflowing from any cylinder in the file (Ch. 13)

index a table whose entries associate data values with memory addresses (Chs. 8, 10)

index file a large index table that is stored as a file (Ch. 13)

index set the index entries other than those in the sequence set of a VSAM indexed file (Ch. 13)

index table see **index** (Ch. 13)

indexed file a file for which index tables are created and maintained (Ch. 13)

indexed sequential organization a file organization technique in which the data records are ordered in the prime data area, and index tables that associate data records with memory locations are kept in the index area (Ch. 13)

indexing a technique that simulates access-by-content by using tables that contain entries associating data values with addresses of memory locations (Ch. 13)

indexing files the process of building index tables for data stored in files (Ch. 13)

informal testing a form of program testing which relies on rules of thumb and the programmer's instinct (Ch. 6)

information a value obtained through computation or manipulation of data values (Ch. 17)

information retrieval an area of computer and library sciences that deals with the search and retrieval of data, information, or documents stored in direct-access mass storage devices (Ch. 9)

information system a system whose main goal is processing information to facilitate corporate functions (Ch. 4)

in-order traversal an exhaustive binary tree traversal technique based on the pattern of left subtree, node, right subtree (Ch. 16)

insertion anomaly a record structure's tendency not to allow insertion of partial information about some entity into a file unless some pertinent condition is satisfied (Ch. 17)

instance of file the current content of a file (Ch. 1)

integration testing a form of structural testing performed on groups of program modules that make up software subsystems (Ch. 6)

interactive input a mode of input in which values for input variables are supplied by the programmer through a terminal while the program is being executed (Ch. 11)

interactive mode a processing mode for a data base in which the user of a data base can interact directly with it through a terminal to update or access data stored in the data base (Ch. 18)

interactive processing a processing mode for computer programs in which the user participates in the execution of the program by providing input values for program variables at a terminal (Ch. 3)

inter-block gap a block separator inserted between any two consecutive physical records in secondary magnetic storage (Ch. 10)

internal data structure a data structure that is stored in the computer's main memory during processing (Ch. 4)

internal file name a name by which a file is referenced in a program (Ch. 2)

internal procedure a procedure that is designed, compiled, and executed as an integral part of a program (Chs. 3, 7)

internal search a technique in which the data structure to be searched is kept in the main memory during the entire search process (Ch. 8)

internal sorting a technique that requires list elements to be kept in the computer's main memory throughout the sorting process (Ch. 8)

internal subprogram see **internal procedure** (Ch. 7)

inversion the process of splitting a linked list into partial linked lists of smaller size, each corresponding to a specific value of the base data element (Ch. 15)

inverted list a list structure that consists of several lists, all based on the same data field, each corresponding to a base data value, and each containing a single prime area record (Ch. 15)

iteration structure a program structure that executes a block of statements a finite number of times (Ch. 4)

join an operation that combines two files to produce a new file, whose record structure consists of all attributes of the first file followed by all attributes of the second, provided the two record structures have at least one compatible attribute each (Ch. 10)

key a set of one or more attributes that uniquely identifies records in a file (Chs. 10, 17)

key attributes an attribute in a file that participates in a candidate key (Ch. 17)

key space the set of all key field values for a file (Ch. 14)

key-to-address transform see **hash function** (Ch. 14)

key-word-in-context indexing an indexing scheme commonly used in library systems to facilitate retrieval of documents by making use of index tables based on key words that are indicative of the context of documents (Ch. 9)

label record a special record generated by the operating system so that a file can identify it (Chs. 2, 11)

latency the time it takes for the system to wait for a block containing the data sought to pass under the read-write head after the access mechanism is positioned on the proper track in rotating magnetic storage devices (Ch. 10)

leaf a node in a tree for which out-degree is zero (Chs. 5, 16)

level a collection of nodes in a tree that are at the same level of hierarchy (Ch. 16)

level number an unsigned, two-digit integer that is used to define the type and relative position of data in the DATA DIVISION of a COBOL program (Ch. 1)

LIFO list see **stack** (Ch. 15)

linear list see **list** (Ch. 8)

linear probe an overflow-handling technique based on open probe of the prime data area in which buckets after the point of collision are accessed consecutively until an empty bucket is found (Ch. 14)

linked allocation a manner of memory allocation for lists in which each element of a list is related to its logical successor by an associated address pointer (Chs. 4, 8)

linked list a data structure based on linked allocation in which each list element has a pointer to its logical successor, and a list head points to the first list element (Chs. 4, 9, 15)

list a set of data and the preceded-by relationship among the data (Chs. 4, 8)

list head a pointer external to a linked list that points to the first element in the list (Ch. 15)

load library a collection of subroutine object modules saved in secondary storage for future use (Ch. 7)

load module an executable form of object programs generated by the link-editor (Ch. 7)

local variable a type of program variable that is defined in a module exclusively for its use (Ch. 7)

logical cohesion a form of cohesion in which all statements in a module perform a certain class of tasks (Ch. 4)

logical data organization data organization from a user's point of view in which organization and management of data are abstractions (Chs. 5, 10)

logical design a system design phase in which general design specifications are developed (Ch. 4)

logical file organization a form of file organization that does not depend on a programming language or a file management system (Chs. 10, 15)

logical record a record in a file as perceived by the user (Ch. 10)

logical sorting a sorting technique that establishes an order of elements of a list without actually moving the list elements (Chs. 4, 8)

loop control variable a variable associated with an iteration structure that is used to control repetitive execution of a set of statements (Ch. 3)

master catalog a VSAM cluster maintained in direct-access storage that contains information about all other clusters and has control over all user catalogs (Ch. 13)

master index an index table for an ISAM file whose entries correspond to segments of the cylinder index table (Ch. 13)

matrix see **two-dimensional array** (Ch. 8)

menu-driven system a software system with a user interface that permits the user to communicate with the system through menus (Ch. 9)

merge key an attribute or attribute combination in the record structure of two or more ordered files that is used in merging them into an ordered file (Ch. 12)

merging the operation of combining two or more ordered lists (or files) into a single ordered list (or file) (Chs. 10, 12)

meta-data information about data stored in a file or a data base (Ch. 13)

modular programming a form of program design in which a program is organized into small and independent modules that are separately named and addressable program elements, and are integrated by a controlling module (Ch. 4)

module size the number of statements in a program module (Ch. 4)

multiple list a data structure that incorporates two or more linked lists, each based on a different data field (Ch. 15)

multiple record file a file that contains records conforming to two or more record structures (Ch. 2)

nested IF an IF statement that includes one or more IF statements in its then-part or else-part (Ch. 4)

nested program a type of COBOL program that contains other functionally related, full COBOL programs (Ch. 7)

network structure a structure that exhibits an arbitrary and complex relationship among its components (Chs. 4, 16)

new master file a file that is created as the output of the traditional sequential file update strategy (Ch. 10)

nonkey attribute an attribute in a file that does not participate in any candidate key (Ch. 17)

nonlinear data structure a data structure in which each element may have one or more logical successors and predecessors (Ch. 16)

nonnumeric literal any string enclosed between quotes (Ch. 1)

normalization a step-by-step process of transforming a record structure without losing data so that the transformed structure has no undesirable properties such as redundancies and anomalies (Ch. 17)

numeric literal any computational numeric value with or without decimal digits (Ch. 1)

old master file the file to be updated before updates take place in the traditional sequential file update strategy (Ch. 10)

one-dimensional array an array that requires a single subscript to specify relative locations of its elements (Ch. 8)

open addressing an overflow-handling technique in which, if a bucket is full, other buckets in the prime data area are systematically accessed until an empty bucket is found (Ch. 14)

open mode a mode in which a file is readied for processing as an input, output, or I-O file (Chs. 2, 3)

ordered binary tree see **binary search tree** (Ch. 16)

order-preserving transform a transform that preserves the order of key values by mapping them to memory addresses that define an order similar to that of the key values (Ch. 14)

out-degree the number of arcs in a graph that originate from a given node. See also **fan-out** (Chs. 4, 5)

overflow area a separate segment of the direct-access storage in which records that cannot be accommodated in the prime data area are stored (Chs. 13, 14)

overflow handling a strategy of storing records that cannot be accommodated in the prime data area of a file because of lack of space (Ch. 14)

packing density the ratio of the number of records stored in a file to the total number of records that can be stored in it (Ch. 14)

paragraph a named COBOL program block that is made up of statements and/or sentences (Ch. 1)

paragraph-oriented design a design strategy for COBOL programs in which the PROCEDURE DIVISION is made up of paragraphs only (Chs. 1, 7)

parameter association by content a manner of parameter association in modular program systems that write-protects the formal parameters in a subroutine (Ch. 7)

parameter association by reference a manner of parameter association in modular program systems that allows a subroutine to change the values of its formal parameters (Ch. 7)

parent node a node in a tree that is at a higher level of hierarchy relative to its child node (Chs. 5, 16)

partial dependency a type of data dependency in which a proper subset of attributes in the determinant are needed to determine another set of attributes (Ch. 17)

partial index an index that consists of entries controlling more than one entry in another index table or in the prime data area (Ch. 13)

partially inverted list a set of linked lists, each corresponding to one value of the base data element with respect to which the list is inverted (Ch. 15)

pattern matching a technique of searching a string for a substring in which the substring is specified explicitly by its value (Ch. 9)

phantom paragraph an unnamed sequence of statements that is neither a paragraph nor a section in a COBOL program PROCEDURE DIVISION (Ch. 7)

physical data base record a tree structure in IMS that contains record structures (segments) connected by arcs that represent one-to-many relationships among segments (Ch. 18)

physical data organization data organization from a computer's point of view, which is concerned with issues related to the actual storage of data (Chs. 5, 10)

physical design a system design phase in which logical design specifications are tailored to the characteristics of the computer system used for implementation (Ch. 4)

physical record the amount of storage enclosed by two consecutive inter-block markers in a file (Chs. 2, 10)

physical sorting a sorting technique that moves list elements within an array to establish an order of elements (Chs. 4, 8)

physical view of a data base the form of data in a data base as it would appear to a computer system (Ch. 18)

point of entry the first statement that is executed in a called subprogram when the program control passes to it (Ch. 7)

point of exit the statement in a called subprogram that returns control to the calling program (Ch. 7)

point of invocation the statement in a calling program that calls on a subprogram to pass control to it (Ch. 7)

point of return the statement in a calling program after which program execution continues once control is passed back to it by a called subprogram (Ch. 7)

post-order traversal an exhaustive binary tree traversal technique based on the pattern of left subtree, right subtree, node (Ch. 16)

post-test iteration structure a repetitive program structure in which a test is done after the loop body is executed (Ch. 4)

potential inconsistency see **update anomaly** (Ch. 17)

precompiler a vendor-supplied software that translates an application program written in a host language and containing embedded data base language instructions into a program that consists of only the commands of the host language (Ch. 18)

pre-order traversal an exhaustive binary tree traversal technique based on the pattern of node, left subtree, right subtree (Ch. 16)

pretest iteration structure a repetitive program structure in which a test is done before the loop body is executed (Chs. 3, 4)

primary clustering the phenomenon of long sequences of occupied buckets forming after a point of collision in a relative file (Ch. 14)

primary key the candidate key in a file that is selected to serve as the principal identifier in its physical implementation (Ch. 17)

prime data area a segment of a file in which actual data records are stored (Chs. 13, 14)

primitive data structure a list, a tree, or a network data structure (Ch. 4)

printer file a file that contains only records to be printed (Ch. 3)

procedural cohesion a form of cohesion in which a module defines a decision or iteration process as the sole basis for procedure (Ch. 4)

procedure a general type of subprogram that does not transfer any value under its name when it returns control to the calling program (Ch. 7)

program debugging the activity of identifying the source of errors in a program, and modifying the program in order to eliminate them (Ch. 6)

program scope the set of procedures that can be called by a program (Ch. 7)

program structure a collection of logical program modules and the invoked-by relationship among them (Ch. 4)

program testing the process of executing a program to demonstrate its correctness or find errors in it (Ch. 6)

program validation the process of ascertaining correctness of the finished program and its ability to meet user requirements (Ch. 6)

program verification the process of ascertaining program correctness at different phases of program life cycle—during and after analysis, design, and coding (Ch. 6)

programming error a type of error that surfaces during program compilation and execution (Ch. 6)

projection the operation of extracting a vertical subset of the content of a file (Ch. 10)

pseudocode a formal, rather cryptic, program logic representation in terms of statements that resemble instructions of computer languages (Ch. 5)

P-way merge the process of merging P files (Chs. 10, 12)

qualifier an entity name of a higher hierarchical level than the name of the entity it qualifies (Ch. 2)

query language a subset of a data base language consisting of instructions that can be used to access and retrieve data from the data base (Ch. 18)

queue a limited accessibility list in which all additions are made at one end, and all deletions are made at the other (Ch. 15)

random access see **direct access** (Ch. 10)

range query an attribute-value pair that associates an attribute by its name with a range of admissible values, using a comparison operator other than "equal to" (Ch. 13)

record a named and structured collection of related data elements (Chs. 2, 10)

record access the operation of locating the storage segment in which a record resides (Ch. 10)

record retrieval the operation of bringing a copy of the located record to the main memory for processing (Ch. 10)

record structure composition of a record in terms of data elements (Ch. 2)

recursive procedure a type of procedure that calls on itself (Ch. 7)

relation a two-dimensional data structure used as a data base structure, which consists of a fixed number of columns and a variable number of rows (Ch. 18)

relation condition a COBOL condition type that compares two arithmetic quantities using comparison operators (Ch. 3)

relationship a specification that associates two or more entity sets (Ch. 10)

relative file a file that allows direct access to its memory locations by their relative addresses (Ch. 14)

relative record number a number that is used to identify and access records in VSAM relative record data set clusters (Ch. 14)

reserved word a key word that identifies a language entity such as a statement, paragraph, section, etc. (Ch. 1)

ring a linked list in which the last element points to the first element (Ch. 15)

root the only node in a tree with zero in-degree (Chs. 5, 16)

rotational delay see **latency** (Ch. 10)

run a sequence of records that are ordered according to a sort key (Ch. 12)

run unit a memory partition that is allocated to external variables in a modular program system (Ch. 7)

scope of effect the set consisting of all modules that are affected by a decision in a given module (Ch. 4)

search key a data element which is compatible with the data elements stored in a list, and for which a match is sought in the list (Ch. 8)

searching the process of matching a search key to an element of a data structure or a list (Ch. 8)

secondary key retrieval retrieval of records using values for attributes other than the primary key attribute (Ch. 13)

section a COBOL program block that consists of paragraphs (Ch. 1)

section-oriented design a design strategy for COBOL programs in which the PROCEDURE DIVISION is made up of sections only (Chs. 1, 7)

sector a fixed-size portion of a track on a rotating magnetic storage device (Ch. 10)

seeking the operation of positioning the read-write heads over the proper track in a rotating magnetic storage device (Ch. 10)

segment an IMS term for record structure (Ch. 18)

selection the operation of extracting a horizontal subset of the content of a file using a condition (Ch. 10)

selection structure a program structure that executes different blocks of statements depending on the outcome of a test (Ch. 4)

semantics a set of rules that describes the meaning and function of language elements in a program (Ch. 1)

sentence a COBOL program block that is made up of one or more statements, the last of which ends with a period (Ch. 1)

sequence set the lowest-level index table in a VSAM indexed file. See also **total index** (Ch. 13)

sequence structure a program structure that consists of a set of statements executed one after another (Ch. 4)

sequential access an access mode in which records in a file are accessed one after another, according to the physical order in which they are stored (Ch. 10)

sequential allocation a manner of memory allocation in which all elements of a list are stored in consecutive memory locations (Chs. 4, 8)

sequential cohesion a form of cohesion in which the elements of a module perform a series of tasks for which the output of one is the input for the next task (Ch. 4)

sequential organization a manner of organization for files in which records are stored and accessed one after another (Chs. 2, 11)

sequential-access storage device a secondary storage device that permits only sequential access to consecutive storage segments (Ch. 10)

severe error diagnostics a type of system-generated message that indicates that there are errors for which no automatic correction can be made, and therefore the compilation process cannot continue (Ch. 6)

simple query an attribute-value pair that associates an attribute by its name with an admissible value for it (Ch. 13)

skewed tree a binary tree with one node at each level such that all nodes except the leaf have only nonempty left subtrees or nonempty right subtrees (Ch. 16)

soft sectoring an organization in which tracks on a rotating magnetic storage device are divided into segments by a formatting software (Ch. 10)

software a set of related programs that interact with each other to produce the solution for a relatively complex problem (Ch. 4)

software engineering a formal discipline that uses methods, tools, and procedures to develop high-quality software in a productive and efficient manner (Ch. 4)

software system a system of related computer programs (Ch. 4)

sort key an attribute or a set of attributes in a record structure with respect to which the records in a file are ordered (Ch. 12)

sorting the process of establishing an order of elements in a list (Chs. 4, 8)

sort/merge utility a vendor-supplied program that can be used to sort and merge files (Ch. 12)

space list a structured collection of memory locations that does not contain relevant data, but can be used for data storage when needed (Ch. 15)

stack a limited accessibility list to which all additions and deletions are made only at one end (Ch. 15)

stamp coupling a form of coupling in which a module passes a data structure, or a portion of a data structure, to another module (Ch. 4)

statement a combination of words, symbols, and constants that instructs the computer what to do (Ch. 1)

string a finite sequence of characters of an alphabet (Ch. 9)

structural testing verification of structure of the procedural design of a program (Ch. 6)

structured programming the discipline of making a program's logic easy to follow by using only sequence, selection, and iteration structures (Ch. 4)

structured technique a formal technique that can be used to simplify program development, make team work easy, and render the program development process feasible (Ch. 5)

structured walk-through a debugging technique in which the programmer examines the source code of a program in view of a carefully selected sample data set to ensure that it does what it is supposed to do correctly (Ch. 6)

subprogram a procedure that can be invoked by another program (Ch. 7)

subroutine see **external subprogram** (Ch. 7)

subschema a subset of a data base schema consisting of the data needed by an application program or a user of the data base (Ch. 18)

subscript a quantity that indicates relative locations of elements in an array (Ch. 8)

subscripted variable an identifier followed by one or more subscripts (Ch. 8)

subsystem a component of a system that is itself a system (Ch. 4)

synonyms two or more key values that are transformed to the same relative address by a hash function (Ch. 14)

syntax a set of rules that specifies the language elements that may be used and the way they can be combined to form other language elements (Ch. 1)

system a collection of interrelated components that performs some function to satisfy a set of goals (Ch. 4)

system testing a form of testing a software system to demonstrate that the entire system performs according to its requirements specification (Ch. 6)

table see **array** (Ch. 8)

tail of a queue the input end of a queue (Ch. 15)

temporal cohesion a form of cohesion in which all statements in a module define tasks that take place within the same time span (Ch. 4)

terminal node see **leaf** (Chs. 5, 16)

terminating error diagnostics a type of system-generated message that indicates major errors that may cause the compilation to fail to start or to cease immediately (Ch. 6)

testing error a type of error that occurs during program testing due to invalid test procedures and test data or misinterpretation of test results (Ch. 6)

text editing the process of creating and restructuring a text (Ch. 9)

text formatting the process of producing output in a desired layout in a text-processing system (Ch. 9)

three-dimensional array an array of two-dimensional arrays (Ch. 8)

top of a stack the open end of a stack at which additions and deletions can be made (Ch. 15)

top-down design a software design strategy in which the designing, coding, and testing of modules proceed from top to bottom (Ch. 4)

total directory see **total index** (Ch. 13)

total index an index that contains the same number of entries as the number of records in the prime data area (Ch. 13)

track descriptor block the first block in a track in rotating magnetic storage devices, which is used by the system to identify the rest of the track (Ch. 10)

track index an index table built for each cylinder of an ISAM file which contains one index entry for each track in the cylinder (Ch. 13)

traditional file update a file update strategy in which records in a master file are updated by using a transaction file and by copying the updated records into a new master file (Ch. 11)

trailer label record a label record created by the operating system for a file and placed physically after the last data record (Ch. 10)

transaction file the file that contains the new records to be inserted and updated, and identifies the records to be deleted in traditional sequential file update (Ch. 10)

transitive dependency a type of data dependency among three sets of attributes in which only the first set is a determinant for the second and the third, and the second set is a determinant for the third (Ch. 17)

tree a connected digraph with no cycles (Chs. 4, 5, 16)

tuple a record in the relational model of data (Ch. 18)

two-dimensional array an array of one-dimensional arrays (Ch. 8)

2-way merge a process of merging two files (Ch. 10)

unblocked file a file in which physical and logical record sizes are the same (Chs. 2, 10)

unit testing a form of testing program modules before integration with other modules in a software system (Ch. 6)

update anomaly a record structure's tendency to result in inconsistent data in a file because the structure necessitates update of more than one record whenever update of an attribute value is logically required (Ch. 17)

user catalog a special-purpose VSAM cluster maintained in direct-access storage which contains information about the clusters built by a user, and has access to and control over such clusters (Ch. 13)

user-defined word a word that is made up by the user to represent and reference certain program entities (Ch. 1)

volume directory   a directory built and maintained by the computer system for magnetic tape or disk drives that store many files (Ch. 10)

volume label   a special record that contains a volume directory created and maintained by the operating system for tape storage (Ch. 10)

volume table of contents   a file descriptor table that contains information about each file stored in a direct-access volume (Ch. 10)

warning diagnostics   a type of system-generated message that pinpoints minor errors which may cause problems during program execution (Ch. 6)

zigzag tree   a binary tree that has only one node at each level such that the left and right subtrees of nodes at consecutive levels are alternately nonempty (Ch. 16)